The
Ultimate Flight Simulator
Pilot's Guidebook

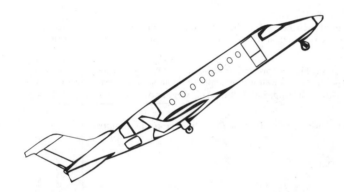

Nick Dargahi

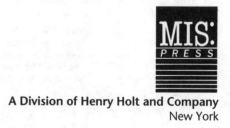

MIS:
PRESS

A Division of Henry Holt and Company
New York

NOTE: *The Instructions and data in this book/CD-ROM package are not intended for use in any real-world flight application. Because navigation data is updated periodically, none of the data in this book is valid for real navigational purposes.*

MIS:Press
A Division of Henry Holt and Company, Inc.
115 West 18th Street
New York, New York 10011
http://www.mispress.com

Printed in the United States of America

Limits of Liability and Disclaimer of Warranty

The Author and Publisher of this book have used their best efforts in preparing the book and the programs contained in it. These efforts include the development, research, and testing of the theories and programs to determine their effectiveness.

The Author and Publisher make no warranty of any kind, expressed or implied, with regard to these programs or the documentation contained in this book. The Author and Publisher shall not be liable in any event for incidental or consequential damages in connection with, or arising out of, the furnishing, performance, or use of these programs.

All products, names and services are trademarks or registered trademarks of their respective companies.

First Edition—1998

Library of Congress Cataloging-in-Publication Data

Dargahi, Nick
    The ultimate flight simulator pilot's guidebook / Nick Dargahi.
      p.   cm.
    ISBN 1-55828-574-1
      1. Microsoft flight simulator (Computer file). 2. Airplanes—
Piloting—Computer simulation. 3. Computer flight games. I. Title.
TL712.8D3723   1997
794.8'763—dc21   97-38726
                                                  CIP

MIS:Press and M&T Books are available at special discounts for bulk purchases for sales promotions, premiums, and fundraising.

For details contact: Special Sales Director
                        MIS:Press and M&T Books
                        Divisions of Henry Holt and Company, Inc.
                        115 West 18th Street
                        New York, New York 10011

10 9 8 7 6 5 4 3 2 1

Associate Publisher: *Paul Farrell*

Editor: *Andy Neusner*
Technical Editor: *Mark Rice*
Managing Editor: *Shari Chappell*

Production Editor: *Kitty May*
Copy Edit Manager: *Karen Tongish*
Copy Editor: *Betsy Hardinger*

ACKNOWLEDGMENTS

In writing this book, I was fortunate to receive the help of many Flight Simulator experts around the world. Without their contributions and assistance, this book would not have been possible. I was also ably assisted by my Editor Andy Neusner at MIS Press, and the many other "behind the scenes" production staff at MIS:Press, particularly including Shari Chappell, Kitty May, and Karen Tongish.

I am indebted to Michael Mott, Mike Schroeter, Jose Pinero, and the entire Flight Simulator development team at Microsoft. I appreciated their unflagging cooperation in answering innumerable questions, and providing me with betas of the program during the writing of this book.

I would like to express my deep appreciation to my co-authors Captain Sean Trestrail (for his IFR chapter on flying the Boeing 737 and for his pilot's advice), Ed Williams (for his Great Circle Navigation chapter), and Ray Proudfoot (for his Scenery Management chapter). The expertise they brought to the book was incalculable. My thanks go to David Wishnia, for his insightful comments and review of the mathematical portions of the text. Mark Rice's enthusiastic comments were a big boost as well.

I would also like to pay tribute to the dozens of other contributors to this book's CD. This includes: Terry Hill (KC-135 Tanker, Cessna 210), Col. Dennis Archer , USAF (Ret.) & Major Joe Worsley, USAF (Ret.) & Steve Kruze (Inflight Refueling Software and Concept), Math Maessen (Flight Planner 4.0), Kenneth Kerr of VIP (VIP Shorts 360 aircraft), Bernt Stolle of Stolle Systems (Hi-Fi DC-8, Hi-Fi DC-10, Hi-Fi MD-80 aircraft),, Jim Tester & Dick Roberts & Bob Langendorfer of AeroAirlines (for the Amelia Earhart "Great Adventure" Concept), Hans vanWyhe, Herve Devred, Lars Kornstaedt (A300, A319, Beechcraft 76, F-16,Focke Wulf Fw190), Rod Conklin (Cessna Citation X), Kerry Gipe (Gulfstream IV), Jim Wolf (King Air B200), Goetz Scheuermann (Lockheed Electra, Lockheed C-5A Galaxy), Herve Devred (Messerschmitt M2.262), Christian Noetzli (DC-3 "Queen of the Night"), Michael L. Cunningham (Avanti Piaggio), George Lorsche (Final Approach), Ted Denison (ILS-Fix), Martin Smith (APLC32 Adventure Compiler), Robert MacKay (see the Acrobat version of MicroWINGS Magazine on the CD), Robert L. Ferraro of Computer Pilot Magazine (Flight videos), Chuck Dome (F-15, AirMod, and PanMan), Floris Wouterlood & Johan Cranenburgh (India Airports), Allan Wheeler (GPS waypoints), Pete Dowson (SCU-TILS), Wilco van Deijl (GPWS6), Dean Salmon (Alaska Scenery), Shigeru Tanaka (SST & Lear 60), Siggy Schwartz (Landing Lights), David C. Maschino (ACEdit), Matthias Weidemann. (AirDec), Javier Gallego (AllWorld), Tony Z Pluta (Lon Nav Fix), David Cole (PanWav95), John Waller (Egcc.ZIP contains a bgl from John Waller's England and Wales scenery with an exclude file). If I have left anyone out, the fault is entirely mine.

The incredible array of software, utilities, aircraft, and scenery on this book's CD was only made possible by the talent and inspiration of the above authors. I salute them all.

Just Planes Videos, makers of the "Flight in the Cockpit" VHS tape series (see the advertisement in the back of the book), provided many photographs of the Boeing 737 cockpit that were used to illustrate the real cockpit instrumentation in the book.

Jesse Lund of Resolution Mapping (see the advertisement in the back of the book) gets a special note of recognition for his personally shepherding the AeroView Moving Map Software to successful fruition. This is an amazing piece of software that I'm convinced will dazzle all who see it. However, without Adam Szoufran's software driver, we would not have been able to link the map program to Flight Simulator, so thank you Adam!

I also want to thank David Drouin for developing a unique version of his GPS 2.0 navigation software for us that comes complete with all the world's navaids built in. This special version of the program also contains all the Amelia Earhart airports, and without it, the Amelia Earhart around the world flight would have been much harder for people to fly.

Johan Cranenburgh and Manfred Moldenhauer deserve acknowledgement for having compiled all the world's navaids into Flight Simulator scenery files that we have included on the CD. This was no small task, and I am grateful to them both for their hard effort.

The Airport 2.0 Scenery Design program on the book's CD is the brainchild of Pascal Meziat and Manfred Moldenhauer, and it was my good fortune that they both agreed to provide their excellent software to accompany the book.

The scenery notes on the CD are the work of Konstantin Kukushkin and Maurizio M. Gavioli. This seminal work on the Flight Simulator scenery file format has benefited all Flight Simulator pilots around the world, for it has allowed third party scenery and software tools to proliferate, and it has expanded awareness of the inner workings of the Flight Simulator program. We all owe them a great deal for this intellectual achievement.

The Great Circle Navigation spreadsheet utility on the CD was created by Alan Parkinson, and with this superbly crafted tool, you will be able to easily calculate any great circle course around the world.

Alfred Grech, the noted scenery designer, lent his expert hand in creating all the Amelia Earhart scenery on the CD. This scenery together with Goetz Scheuermann's marvelous recreation of the Lockheed L-10e Electra that was used by Earhart, will give you many hours of enjoyment as you re-experience Earhart's "Great Adventure."

Melvin Lee and David Pierce at the National Imaging and Mapping Agency (NIMA), along with Margaret Pittman at the Defense Mapping Agency and Congressman Ronald Dellums, were most helpful in providing me with the Digital Aeronautical Flight Information File (DAFIF) that is used extensively in this book.

Lastly, I would like to thank my family, including Xenia, Kira, Milou, and Ali, without whose support I would not have undertaken such a large project. To Adriene goes my deep appreciation for all her personal assistance, encouragement and love.

Nick Dargahi

CONTENTS

Introduction

Flight Simulator is back, and it is better than ever. With the new Microsoft Windows 95 operating system, and Windows 98, Flight Simulator for Windows has leapfrogged from the world of MS-DOS to the Windows graphical user interface (GUI) without so much as a hiccup. Legions of Flight Simulator pilots who were wedded to the DOS version of Flight Simulator 5.1 have now made the jump to the Windows version with no regrets. There were well-grounded fears that porting this program to Windows would have a disastrous effect on frame rates—especially with the experience of Windows 3.1, which showed that Windows was no match for DOS when it came to speedy graphics. However, the wizards at Microsoft, which purchased Flight Simulator from the Bruce Artwick Organization (BAO) in 1996, have overcome the Windows graphics bottleneck—they not only equaled the old DOS frame rates but surpassed them.

This is even more impressive when one considers that when it first came out, Flight Simulator for Windows 95 (hereafter referred to as FSW95) ran at a higher resolution (640 horizontal pixels by 480 vertical pixels) than the DOS version of Flight Simulator (640 × 400) (hereafter referred to as FS5.1). The newly released Flight Simulator 98 (hereafter referred to as FS98) runs at resolutions as high as 1280 × 1024 with 8- or 16-bit color (some 3-D cards will only do 102 × 4768, or 1152 × 864 with 16-bit color), and takes advantage of the new generation of 3-D–capable DirectDraw video cards and Pentiums equipped with MMX. (FS98 will also run on the AMD-K6 MMX from

Advanced Micro Devices and the Cyrix 686MX.) Unfortunately, FS98 does not directly benefit from AGP (accelerated graphics port) motherboards, but the video cards that support this standard may be able to take advantage of AGP using software drivers.

Why are people raving about FS98? After all, there are many more capable but more expensive professional flight simulator programs out on the market. There are two reasons. First, the new Flight Simulator allows you to add new aircraft, which you could not do before without purchasing Flight Shop separately. Second, although you could add scenery to FS5.1, the wide availability of scenery building tools makes it easier than ever before for people to create scenery of their own hometowns.

Third, with FS98 Microsoft has significantly upgraded the visual capabilities of the program, and it has included all the airports in the United States, including their instrument landing systems (close to 3,000). In addition, the program has been beefed up with a whole raft of new features, including multiplayer Internet play capabilities and the first-ever realistic modeling of a helicopter simulator for the PC. Many people are saying that the jump from FSW95 to FS98 is as great as the jump from FS4.0 to FS5.1.

In the last year, a huge array of worldwide scenery and aircraft has been posted on the World Wide Web. The number of commercial and free add-ons is also growing at a staggering rate, so much so that one could truthfully say that Flight Simulator has started a cottage industry of its own. So, although you can buy other more detailed-flight simulators, Flight Simulator beats out all the other programs in terms of versatility, affordability, and degree of customization. Some fans have even gone so far as to build their own cockpits using Flight Simulator. For example, Robert MacKay, president of the 5,000-member MicroWINGS Association (see his magazine on the book's CD-ROM), has built a $7,000 mock-up of a single-engine Cessna in his home. Another enthusiast bought the shell of a Boeing 727 cockpit and converted it into his own private computerized flight deck. In short, the Flight Simulator phenomenon has attracted a huge following. Microsoft says it has shipped more than 10 million copies of Flight Simulator, including 1 million copies of FSW95 in 1996, making it the top-selling computer game ever (Tibbits 1997).

IS THIS BOOK FOR YOU?

If you are intimidated by the scope of this book, don't be! There's plenty of material that is designed for beginner-to-intermediate Flight Simulator pilots, as well as more advanced topics for the more experienced. You won't find a more comprehensive book with as much detailed technical information. Flight Simulator is a complex program with many features that require some technical understanding before you can take full advantage of them. You'll appreciate having a handy reference that you can pick up time and again to answer those nagging questions.

This book is intended for anyone who wants to increase his or her mastery of Flight Simulator. Whether you want to learn how to fly or navigate, or you just want to try out new aircraft and scenery, you'll find a treasure trove of information in this book that will help you reach your own personal goals.

WHY BUY THIS BOOK?

Many people have barely scratched the surface of what Flight Simulator contains. If you would like to know what you're missing, you won't go wrong by purchasing this book. The knowledge and skills you will gain this book will show you what you might have overlooked or not understood in the program. Even better, you'll also learn how to tinker with the program in new ways. The many goodies on the CD-ROM that accompanies the book will enhance your enjoyment of the program.

Aside from teaching you about the program itself, this book will open your eyes to the tremendous burst of activity and creativity that is going on in the Flight Simulator community. When people discovered that it was possible to hack the scenery files and create custom scenery for any part of the world, the Pandora's box of Microsoft's Flight Simulator was opened. Multitudes of hobbyists discovered how aircraft models were stored, and soon hardy souls cracked the secrets of the instrument panels. Others were busy reverse engineering the Adventure Programming Language Compiler so that anybody could craft a custom module for Flight Simulator (yes, Flight Simulator *is* programmable!). Recently, interest has shifted into high gear in anticipation of the release of the Flight Simulator software development kit (SDK) as well as the release of the new aircraft and adventure converter which allows people to freely add new aircraft (which they couldn't do before without separately purchasing Flight Shop). There is now so much interest in Flight Simulator that there are whole magazines, annual conventions, Web sites, and Internet forums that are solely devoted to the subject.

With the advent of cheap CD-ROMs, low-cost distribution of massive scenery databases become suddenly possible. Microsoft and BAO were slow to provide scenery, and as a result many individuals took it upon themselves to create their own home brewed scenery. Soon the motto *Let's cover the whole Flight Simulator world* was being heard as people organized into teams that would focus on specific scenery areas of the world. Pioneers such as Alfred Grech, Konstantin Kukushkin, Charlie Gulick, Robert MacKay, John Trindle, Johan Cranenburgh, Pascal Meziat, Manfred Moldenhauer, Adam Szoufran, David Drouin, Hans van Wijhe, Juan Cabeza, Andras Kozma, Enrico Schiratti, Chuck Dome, Joerg Dolgner, Jorge Alsina, Maurizio M. Gavioli, and Enno Borgsteede paved the way by publishing add-on software, new scenery and tutorials on how to crack Flight Simulator wide open. You'll appreciate the insight and knowledge that these founding fathers have given us, which this book distills into an easy-to-understand format.

This book also offers you a great deal of software and maps on the accompanying CD-ROM that are simply not available from any one source. Yes, you can go out and buy dozens of maps and books that would cover some of the subject matter in this book, but you wouldn't necessarily benefit: what you get in this book is aviation knowledge, expertise, and skills that are uniquely applied to Microsoft Flight Simulator. The addition of the CD-ROM's aviation maps and moving map display, along with the GPS Navigation System, make this book a real value; no other book offers you the specialized resources that will allow you to fully enjoy Flight Simulator.

The following sections highlight the practical benefits of owning this book.

Configuration and Customization FAQ

Have you ever wondered if you were getting the best possible performance out of your computer? Have you wondered whether your frame rate is up to par with other people's computers? Or have you had an installation or setup question that you needed to have answered, but couldn't find out yourself? Appendix A constitutes an invaluable resource which answers these and many other questions that well help you to get the most out of Flight Simulator. Joysticks, video cards, drivers; you name it and it's covered.

New GPS Navigation Computer and Ground Proximity Warning System for Your Aircraft

The CD-ROM that accompanies this book includes two powerful add-on programs called GPS 2.02 and GPWS 6.0 that give Flight Simulator extraordinary new navigation capabilities. However, the GPS 2.0 software works well with FS98, so you can enjoy the full benefits of waypoint navigation in either FSW95 or FS98.

GPS 2.02 for Both FSW95 and FS98

The GPS 2.0 program provides a very powerful and easy-to-use inertial navigation system. This program mimics the capabilities of modern aircraft navigational equipment and uses the DAFIF navaid database to allow you to fly around the world at the touch of a button. Note that the GPS 2.0 version found on this book is the only one you will find that contains the entire DAFIF navaid database. You can't purchase GPS 2.0 elsewhere with the DAFIF; other versions that are being distributed do not come with all the world's navaids built in.

GPS 2.0 has an easy-to-use Windows 95 interface, and it docks conveniently inside your Flight Simulator main window. The version of GPS on the CD-ROM is an evaluation copy, so access to certain features of the program will be disabled until you register it. However, all the main navigational features of the program work, and you can fly anywhere in the world that has a navaid. The complete DAFIF navaid listings for the world are found in a searchable database on the CD-ROM.

GPWS 6.0

Built into GPWS 6.0 are an inertial guidance system (INS) for navigating great circle routes of your choice around the world, a ground proximity warning system (GPWS), a voice alert for calling out altitudes and airspeeds, new autopilot commands, and new radio keyboard shortcuts that greatly simplify navigation. Created by Wilco van Deijl, GPWS is an astounding program that provides a number of tools in one package that will help you tame the 737-400 and the Learjet. Although GPWS 6.0 works best with FSW95, I have created a separate version of the program that works in a more limited way with FS98. For more information, consult the CD-ROM.

Navaids Plotted on Global Charts Based on the Digital Chart of the World

In the back of the book, you'll find 52 charts of air routes across the Pacific and Atlantic Oceans, as well as highly detailed charts of Hawaii, Japan, and the Caribbean Ocean regions to cover the new FS98 default scenery. These charts, which have navaids plotted with frequencies and names listed, allow you to navigate your aircraft from the United States to Europe as well as to Asia and around the world. Of course, you must install the missing worldwide navaids from this book's CD-ROM before doing so.

Over 6,124 Missing VOR/NDB/ILS Navaids

The Microsoft FSW95 and FS98 CD-ROMs do not include all the world's navaids. Thus navigating around the world can be troublesome if you are just limited to the VOR and NDB stations that are found in the default FSW95 scenery. Happily, through the efforts of Johan Cranenburgh and Manfred Moldenhauer, we are able to provide you with all the missing navaids for the Pacific, Latin America, South America, Africa, Europe, the Middle East, Asia, and Oceania/Australia regions of the Earth. After following the instructions and installing these specially created BGL files into Flight Simulator, you will be able to use the global maps in this book to fly almost anywhere in the world. We have even added many missing African airports, courtesy of Terblanche Jordaan, which enables you to fly across Africa with relative ease knowing that you can land and refuel the aircraft.

NOTE

BGL files are the scenery files that Flight Simulator uses to store scenery data. They include airports, navaids, static scenery, dynamic scenery, and instructions for using texture maps.

With these new BGL files, the total navaid count (instrument landing system (ILS), VOR, and nondirectional beacon (NDB)) swells to 11,108 worldwide. For comparison purposes, FSW95 has only 4,984 built-in navaids (ILS, VOR, and NDB); thus by purchasing this book you can add 6,124 new navaids. After installing these files, every single navaid that is found in the real world is then found in Flight Simulator, and the world will truly be your oyster!

Learn How to Plot Great Circle Paths Around the World

Great circle paths are the means by which navigators plot the shortest distances between any two points on the spherical surface of the Earth. They are the most fuel-efficient routes for aircraft traveling long distances, and are used over most oceans and as well as over land where approved (principally at altitudes greater than 45,000 feet in the United States). You'll learn the derivation of great circle navigation formulas from spherical trigonometry and how to apply these formulas to real world situations. Even if math isn't your forte, you can always use the accompanying software on the CD-ROM to automatically perform the calculations for you.

For example, by using Alan Parkinson's Great Circle Calculator, you can automatically calculate the intermediate great circle waypoints between any two points on Earth. Then, if you plug these latitude/longitude coordinates into the registered version of GPS 2.0, your autopilot can fly the entire trip with great precision.

Whether you like to plan and do everything yourself, or whether you prefer to sit back and enjoy flights, you can have fun flying great circle trips around the world. At the very least, you'll come away with an impressive understanding of how real aircraft are navigated across oceans.

Fly Amelia Earhart's 1937 Around the World Flight

This mission is preplanned and ready to go. All you need to do is load the Amelia Earhart scenery from the CD-ROM and convert the Lockheed Electra by running the new FS98 Aircraft Converter. Once you have installed GPS 2.0, you are ready to fly the entire flight, landing at all the same airports that Earhart used. At any time, you can stop the flight and resume it later at any of the airports along Earhart's route via the **World/Go To Airports** menu.

Bonus Software, Maps, Aircraft, Scenery, and Utilities

We don't list all the contents of the CD-ROM here (see Chapter 12 for complete coverage); some of the most interesting features are as follows:

- Thanks to Resolution Mapping Inc. and Adam Szofran, our CD-ROM is crammed full of hundreds of megabytes of real aviation maps that you can view and print out, including full-color world aviation charts (with topography and navaids shown for the United States) and high-altitude airway charts for the United States. The maps are linked with FS98 or FSW95 so that the map moves as your airplane changes position. As you fly, the map continuously updates its position in a real "moving map display." An airplane symbol at the center of the display shows the direction your aircraft's nose is pointing.

- New sample aircraft, including an Airbus A-300-600ST Beluga, Beechcraft 76 Duchess UA, DC-3, DC-10, DC-8, an MD-80, SST, Focke Wulf Fw190A-6/R-11, Messerschmitt Me 262, C5-A Galaxy, C-17, F-15, F-16, Gulfstream IV, Piaggio P.180 Avanti, Amelia Earhart's Lockheed L-10e Electra, DC-3, Cessna 210 Centurian, Piper Navajo Chieftain, along with some other aircraft. These aircraft will work with FSW95, but they must be converted using the new FS98 Aircraft Converter before you can use them with FS98.

- The CD-ROM also contains all the navaids (e.g., radio navigation beacons) for the entire world, so that you can fly around the world on realistic missions. These include all the missing navaids that Flight Simulator omits from its own database. These navaids were compiled from the Department of Defense's Digital Aeronautical Flight Information File (DAFIF) and are included in a comprehensive listing that allows you to easily find any navaid by region, country, or state.

- All 9,406 worldwide airports from the DAFIF are listed on the CD-ROM. The listing includes airport names, country, state (only for the United States), International Civil Aviation Organization (ICAO) identifiers, airport elevations, magnetic variation, latitude/longitude coordinates, runway orientations, runway lengths and widths, runway surface types, and lighting systems for both ends of the runways. Using this information in combination with the airport scenery designer also on the CD-ROM, you can re-create virtually any airport on earth. Of course, this database is derived from the Defense Department's DAFIF, so many small airports are not included, but most civil airports used in commercial air transport are listed. Also, at the time of this book's publication, we were not able to include the ILS frequencies for each runway.

- Many African and Indian airports are included on the CD-ROM so you can install them and fly across both Africa and the Indian subcontinent.

- A complete listing of all 10,552 worldwide VOR/NDB navigational radio beacons is included in the book and on the CD-ROM. These listings provide include the latitude and longitude of each station, navaid identifier and name, navaid type, elevation, and magnetic variation where given. Unfortunately, Microsoft omitted the important magnetic variation data, which you need if you are to calculate your own headings using great circle or rhumb line navigation techniques. Using the Excel spreadsheet on the book's CD-ROM, you can sort, filter, and find any navaids using your own criteria. Print out all the navaids for Turkey, or examine just the NDBs for Greece. Name what you want, and you can extract any information you like.

- Other scenery includes Alaska, by Dean Salmon, and Sri Lanka by Andreas Kozma, and India's airports by Johan Cranenburgh and Floris Wouterlood.
- Navigational utilities, allow you to calculate great circle flight paths for transoceanic flights and print maps and flight plans. This includes Great Circle Navigator by Alan Parkinson (an Excel spreadsheet that allows you to calculate the waypoints of any great circle path around the world), and Flight Planner 4.0 by Math Maessen.
- Airport 2 Scenery designer by Pascal Meziat and Manfred Moldenhauer. Allows you to create BGL scenery files for any part of the world. Design your own airports, runways, ILS, runway lighting systems, terrain, navaids, many kinds of buildings with an easy to use Windows 95 graphical interface.
- A comprehensive listing of worldwide shareware scenery is available for download from the Internet, as compiled by Javier Gallego.
- Final Approach Instrument Approach Plate Software by Goerge Lorsche includes 3,000 worldwide airport approachesIf you purchase and register the program, you can print any of the 3,000 included plates. In the demo version included on the CD-ROM, only viewing is allowed.
- GPS2.0 by David Drouin is a Windows 95 program that piggybacks onto Flight Simulator and allows you to easily fly around the world using the built in navigational database of DAFIF navaids, airports, and waypoints.
- Ground Proximity Warning System (GPWS) 6.0 by Wilco van Deigl is an adventure file that can be added to FSW95. It gives you a fully operational GPWS with realistic warning sounds and systems of modern jet aircraft. It also makes your autopilot and radios easier to use and includes a waypoint editor for adding latitude and longitude coordinates for great circle flight paths. The navigation system will fly your aircraft from waypoint to waypoint and will calculate the great circle heading that your aircraft needs to take for between waypoints.
- We've also included several utilities that allow you to easily manage your panels, aircraft, and sounds with FSW95 (but not FS98). On the CD-ROM, you'll find Dr. D.A. Cole's PanWav95 sound manager, Chuck Dome's PanMan 2.2 and AirMod4 (for changing panels and aircraft aerodynamic parameters), Dave Maschino's ACEdit aircraft modifier, and Sigfried Schwarz's landing lights program (so you can add landing lights to your favorite shareware aircraft).
- Adventure Compiler APLC32 by Martin Smith is used to create and compile your own adventures or miniprograms in FSW95 or FS98. You may not have realized it, but Flight Simulator is programmable! As such, you'll appreciate the con-

venient Adventure Programming Language reference in the appendices, along with the program examples that you can try out yourself from the CD-ROM.

- The Adobe Acrobat Reader will let you browse through the complete Acrobat version of *MicroWings* magazine, which is the Official Magazine of the International Association for Aerospace Simulations.

Detailed Information on How to Fly the Cessna, Learjet Boeing 737-400, and the Bell JetRanger III Helicopter

You'll find tables and charts with performance characteristics and other vital information on flying each of the included aircraft. After reading the chapters on each of these aircraft, you'll be better equipped to take full advantage of each aircraft's capabilities, and you will also better understand each aircraft's limitations.

Understand Aviation Weather

Discover how weather affects your aircraft. Learn the basic principles of the atmosphere and how to experiment with different atmospheric conditions in Flight Simulator.

Learn How to Install User-Created Scenery and Aircraft from the Web

With the explosive worldwide growth of user created scenery and aircraft, you'll want to learn how you can install this scenery and not have it conflict with your existing scenery. With hundreds of freeware, shareware, and commercial aircraft now available, you will learn how to install new aircraft for use with FS98.

Have Fun Creating Your Own Custom Scenery

If you aren't satisfied with the scenery that's available, create your own! Inside, you'll get the detailed information needed to create your own scenery BGL files, exclusion files (to prevent scenery conflicts), and navaids. You can create terrain, navaids, airports, and some dynamic scenery.

Learn How to Really Fly Your Airplane

Learn the art of flying, including what your wings really do, basic aerodynamics, the physics of flight, the wind, your flight controls, basic maneuvers, working speeds, and how to land.

Learn How to Fly Real Instrument Approach Procedures

Captain Sean Trestrail, a Boeing 767 pilot, prepared a chapter that delves into the topic of landing your airplane using IFR Instrument Approach Procedures (IAP). You'll learn how to handle a flight in the 737 using actual IAP charts in a real-world flight from San Francisco to Los Angeles. Captain Trestrail's vast experience flying Boeing jet aircraft will give you special insights into how to land the 737 in conditions of limited visibility or poor weather.

Learn Great Circle Navigation Techniques

Because it is indispensable to air navigation, we present a chapter devoted to the subject of great circle navigation. Ed Williams, a physicist and licensed pilot, has written an excellent overview of great circle formulary, and from the examples he provides, you'll learn how to plot your own great circle paths around the world using the equations that navigators have used for more than a century. This tutorial will answer any questions you may have about how real navigation is performed, whether it is done manually or with the assistance of computers.

FLIGHT SIMULATOR HISTORY

Flight Simulator was first created created for the PC in 1978 by Bruce Artwick, an electrical engineer, programmer, and pilot. At first, Artwick created two version of Flight Simulator: Flight Simulator 1.0 for the Apple II, and Flight Simulator II for the Commodore 64, both of which were produced by SubLOGIC, Artwick's company at the time.

It is easy to forget that the personal computer was in its infancy in the late 1970s, and many people were astonished that they could peck in words onto a screen. Working within the limited hardware constraints of the time, Artwick was nonetheless able to create a virtual world with his Flight Simulator program, and it soon became the first mass market hit for entertainment software.

After the release of Flight Simulator II, Artwick left SubLOGIC and founded the Bruce Artwick Organization (BAO). At BAO, Artwick completed work on a new version of Flight Simulator at Microsoft's bequest for the newly created IBM PC. This version was known as Flight Simulator 1.05, which became extremely successful because of its ground breaking use of 3-D graphics routines on a microprocessor. This software pushed the envelope of the original IBM PC to its limits, and so for many clone computers that were being sold at the time, Flight Simulator became a litmus test of compatibility.

In June 1988, Artwick released Flight Simulator 3.0, which offered new aircraft, multiple-window support, and dual-player mode. Then in September 1989, Flight Simulator 4.0 was released with 16-color graphics, customizable weather, and support for the Intel 80386 microprocessor. This version also included dynamic scenery, runway approach lighting systems for night flying, and air traffic control.

A completely rewritten Flight Simulator 5.0 was released in 1993, and this version included better flight models, a 256-color graphics display engine with texture-mapped ground scenery, cyber-graphic synthetic scenery for buildings, expanding scenery that got larger as you approached, creation of local weather areas, city lights at night, vanishing horizons with gradient textures, shadowing effects that change with season and time of day (and latitude—e.g., at the north pole during the winter there is no sunlight), international metric support, digitized aircraft sounds, jump to any airport, new latitude-longitude coordinate system, set exact aircraft position, photo-realistic scenery and flight instrumentation, and program code to take advantage of local bus SVGA graphics cards on Intel 80486 microprocessors. Two years later, in 1995, BAO/Microsoft released Flight Simulator 5.1 (FS 5.1) which included CD-ROM scenery for the first time. With the addition of the worldwide airport refueling facilities and navaids, it became possible for the Flight Simulator pilot to fly around the world.

The performance mode manager was a particularly useful improvement to FS 5.1. Even with the great strides made in computer graphics algorithms, FS 5.1 and FSW95 quickly outpaced the power of many microprocessors on the market. Bruce Artwick, in his book *Applied Microcomputer Graphics* (Prentice Hall 1984), found that routines for graphics accounted for more then 50% of the simulation's execution time. He also discovered that typically 90% of a simulator's time was spent on 10% of a program. By allowing users to shut down that 10% of the program that so profoundly effected frame rates, the original Flight Simulator became one of the most versatile programs on the market because it could be made to run satisfactorily on all kinds of computers, from 386s to Pentiums. Users who were getting poor frame rates could simply shut down the offending module in the program. In FS 5.1 and FSW95, these matters are largely handled by having the user select his or her Performance Mode. This mode, selected from the Preferences dialog box, automatically configured Flight Simulator with the most appropriate modules for the computer that it was being run on.

Flight Simulator 98 followed closely on the heels of FSW95, debuting in the fall of 1997. FS98's core technology was revamped with new support for multiple players (DirectPlay) and new display technology called DirectDraw 5.0, which allowed Direct3D-capable 3-D video cards to enhance visual realism.

Figure I.1 *New virtual cockpit view. Image wraps around the side of the window (if you press the – key to zoom out) for a greater field of view. You can pan the view throughout the interior of the cockpit and see what the real airplane looks like inside.*

As this book went to press, Microsoft had scheduled the release of the Flight Simulator Software Development Kit (SDK) for the fall of 1997. According to Microsoft, the SDK will contain documentation files, help files, header instructions for file formats, and instructions for making new gauges (which are DLLs). The data that will be documented also includes the scenery file format (including the new facilities info) and the multiplayer data packet formats. Microsoft may also release a new **APLC.EXE** for generating adventures in the 32-bit format required for FS98 and FSW95.

The Benefits of Moving to the Windows 95/NT Platform

There are those who cynically accuse Microsoft of trying to "upgrade" everybody into a new operating system every year or two, forcing vast expenditures of money that line the pockets of the company. There are even some camps in the Flight Simulator community that have holed up in DOS, refusing to budge out of their foxholes, even though day by day Windows 95 seems to be asserting worldwide hegemony. What possible advantages could entice these holdouts to move to Windows 95, especially when Windows 3.1 had proved so conclusively that fast graphics weren't possible?

Bruce Artwick, who had deep-seated reservations himself about porting the program into a Windows environment, also was skeptical when Microsoft asked him to consult on the development of FSW95. After working on the project, Artwick became a true believer when he realized that not only was it possible, but there were some truly good reasons for people to leap from the tried but true world of DOS to the uncertain world of Windows 95.

The most immediate benefit was to eliminate the memory problems that have plagued DOS users and dogged Windows 3.1 users from day one. By switching to a 32-bit flat memory model implementation using C and C++, Microsoft could jettison the albatross of DOS memory management. Thus all the old DOS memory thorns that users had grown accustomed to, and which profoundly affected frame rates, could be eliminated in one fell swoop. In effect, the Gordian knot of DOS was severed with one slash of the Windows 95 sword. No longer were memory problems with Extended Memory under DOS (XMS) or Expanded Memory under DOS (EMS) to afflict the user again. And the bane of all DOS users, the 640 KB memory barrier, was banished once and for all.

An added benefit by the switch to 32-bit C and C++ was that FSW95 could take full advantage of Microsoft Foundation Class dialog boxes, virtual memory, and the preemptive multitasking and multithreading capabilities of Windows 95.

The big question was: could frame rates be maintained as high as they were in FS 5.1, given the tremendous software overhead burden that Windows 95 had to bear? The answer, which at first was not known, posed a big risk for Microsoft because if the product barked like a dog, acted like a dog, and performed like a dog, people would rightly assume that Windows 95 was a dog and stick with DOS. This, after all, was not a word processor or spreadsheet where you could fudge a little on performance. In Flight Simulator performance was everything. If Flight Simulator could not run well in Windows 95, then Microsoft was going to have a tough time convincing people that this was the operating system of choice for the new millenium.

So, though Flight Simulator ran reasonably well under DOS, Microsoft had a point to prove by porting it over to Windows 95. The port of FS 5.1 to the Windows 95 platform was no easy task either. FS 5.1 consisted of 750,000 lines of code and 650 MB of source code, yet in a year a dedicated team of Microsoft programmers not only completed the port, but boosted frame rates over FS 5.1 by as much as 50%.

What other changes were made to the internal workings of the program? One big difference in FSW95 is that images are rendered differently than they were in FS 5.1. In FS 5.1, images were generated directly in the graphics card's memory (screen memory), one frame at a time. The display adapter was instructed to have two video pages reserved. While one page (or frame) was visible, FS 5.1 would draw the next frame on the second page. When the second frame was finished, FS 5.1 would switch pages and have the video card send the second page to the monitor. This technique is called double buffering, and although it works well with simple 3-D primitives, it is not robust enough to handle complex bitmapped textures being wrapped around 3-D surfaces. Using the double buffering technique, FS 5.1 draws a new frame on the first video page, which is no longer visible. By repeating this process again and again, Flight Simulator is able to hide the overdrawing of objects (in computer graphics this process is known as *hidden line* or *hidden surface removal*).

FSW95, however, does things a little differently. Rather than address the video card directly, FSW95 creates images in system memory and then calls Windows 95 system routines to copy it to screen memory. Herein lies the rub: everyone had assumed that frame rates would drop precipitously as they did in Windows 3.1 because memory to screen blits (copies) are not very fast. What the programmers were hoping for was that the Windows 95 development team would be able to drastically increase the speed of the blits. They had reason to be hopeful, because the Apple Macintosh's blits had always been lightning quick, and they reasoned that Windows 95 should be able to attain the same level of performance.

Fortunately for the Flight Simulator pilot, that goal was attained and the Windows 95 blits were found to be surprisingly quick. The development team had other tricks up their sleeve that they used to good effect, but near the end they were burning out. Optimizations that they had planned for didn't happen or were overlooked. In the last month of the project, at the last possible moment, a new engineer with some optimizing expertise was brought in. Descending as if from Mount Sinai, he brought with him fresh new views of the graphics system, and this galvanized the team into looking at some overlooked issues that, in the end, considerably boosted frame rates.

Of this experience, Bruce Artwick wrote (as quoted in *MicroWings* magazine):

> Three things saved us. The Win 95 blits [were] surprisingly quick. We also made up much of the time we lost in the blit by generating into the much faster system memory. System memory has no wait states as screen memory does. In generating an image, much screen overwriting occurs as objects in front of other objects are drawn. In these cases, we avoid all the wait states of writing to screen memory over and over again. In FS 5.1 we optimized for wait states by generating scan lines in memory buffers, then copying them to screen memory when all processing was done. In FSW95 we threw out all these in-between steps and generated right to system memory, thus saving a lot of time. FS 5.1's 16-bit 2D drivers must also do all kinds of page flipping and conditional testing to display large screens because even a 640×400 display has 256,000 pixels—much more than 16-bit's 65,535 maximum number. FSW95's 32-bit 2D drivers avoid all this page flipping...

> Did we come close to FS 5.1's display rates? No. We surpassed them by a wide margin. Everything from knocking a few clock cycles off a critical loop here and there to Pentium pipeline stall avoidance produce frame rates nearly 50% higher than FS 5.1 with EMS. Most users (those who run XMS memory only) will see 100% frame rate improvements.

FLIGHT SIMULATOR 98: NEW FEATURES

Flight Simulator 98 has many new features. The principal highlights include:

- **Helicopter.** FS98 includes, for the first time in a PC-based simulator, a true helicopter simulation based on rotary wing dynamics. In the past, helicopter simulations used unrealistic fixed-wing flight dynamics. FS98 now features a Bell 206b JetRanger III turboshaft helicopter with true helicopter controls. Using the collective and cyclic controls, you can maneuver the helicopter to tricky landings atop of skyscrapers with heliport pads (marked with an *H*).

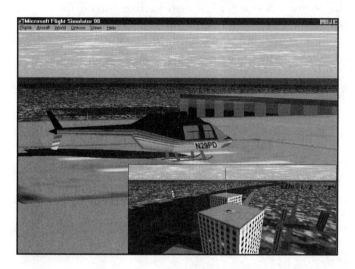

Figure I.2 *The Bell 206B JetRanger III Helicopter waiting to take off at the heliport atop the World Trade Center in FS98. This helicopter landing pad is one of the 3,000 new airports in FS98 that you can easily access from the new Go To Airport dialog box.*

- **DirectX 5.0 and Direct3D support for 3-D video cards.** DirectX 5.0, the driver interface between the FS98 program and your computer's graphics hardware, now supports the MMX instruction set on new Pentium MMX, AMD (Advanced Micro Devices) K6 MMX processors, and Cyrix 686 microprocessors. Direct3D, the software module responsible for accessing 3-D graphics hardware, is supported in 16-bit color screen modes in a window or automatically when in Full Screen mode (**Alt+Enter**) on 3-D–capable video cards with at least 4 MB of RAM. Note that video cards with the 3Dfx chip set are supported -in full screen mode. When suitable 3-D–capable video cards are installed, you'll see bilinear filtering on textures and some transparency in clouds. The new 3-D drivers place textures better on objects, clouds look fluffy and real from below or above, and bodies of water look smooth.
- **Frame rates at least as good as FSW95.** If you are using a 2-D video board, your frame rate should be as good as it was under FSW95. If you have a suitable 3-D video card accelerator, you can double your frame rate even while running the

program at a much higher pixel and color resolution.

- **New high-resolution support.** You can now run the program as high as 1280(1024 resolution with 8-bit color (256 colors), or 1024(768 with 16-bit color (65,536 colors) in Direct 3D mode with a compatible 3-D card. Some 3-D cards, such as for example the ATI 3D RAGE Pro and the Diamond Viper V330, which run FS98 at 1152(864(16-bit color) support higher resolutions. Choose the advanced through the new Hardware Acceleration tab under the **Options/Preferences/Display/Display Options** menu.

- **Advanced MIP mapping and alpha blending.** Alpha blending provides new transparent propeller effects (look through the Cessna's propeller blade while it is spinning slowly, and watch the helicopter rotor speed up and slow down in spot view) and some cloud transparency effects through thinner layers. For example, set visibility to 1 mile and fly low enough to keep the ground in sight. As you do so, you will see streaks of sunlight breaking through the fog. Both effects exact some frame rate performance penalties, but they are really fun to watch. Note that the image smoothing and MIP-mapping effects do not require 3-D video cards, but others, such as the beautiful sunsets with red skies suffusing the horizon available in the Western scenery, and cloud and fog transparency effects do require 3-D cards.

Figure I.3 Undock your 3-D view windows in FS98 and run them separately on different monitors with Windows 98's virtual desktop multiple monitor support. Run up to eight monitors on the same system and create your own panoramic virtual cockpit.

- **New Searchable World/Go To Airport menu.** All airports are now searchable by name, ID, country, region, city, state/province, and FSW95/FS 5.1 scenery type (this is called "Scenery from 6.0 and before"). Also new to FS98 is the ability to place your airplane on any runway.
- **Enhanced Go To Airport Facility database**. At startup, FS98 automatically builds an Airport facility database for your custom FSW95/FS5.1 scenery as well as new scenery written to take advantage of the FS98 format. When you use the **World/Go To Airport** menu, you can easily find the custom scenery you want. For example, if you acquire future FS98 scenery software, it should automatically file itself into the correct region, country, state, and city in your Airport database. Finding the airport becomes much easier, especially when you are dealing with more than 3,000 airports. For older FSW95/FS5.1 scenery that does not take advantage of the new file format, FS98 separates them from the new cities and scenery and lists them all under "Scenery from 6.0 and before.
- **Intellisense AutoComplete technology**. In the Go To Airport dialog box, when you start to type in the name of an airport, the program guesses the city, and before you finish typing, it displays the nearest possible match. This vastly simplifies the task of finding an airport in the database.
- **Set aircraft airspeed under the World/Go To Exact Location menu.**It is now possible to position an airplane at any altitude with an airspeed of your choosing. This is very handy, because in previous versions of Flight Simulator, when you repositioned your airplane to a higher elevation you could not specify the speed, and the airplane would stall.
- **New airport facility and navaid database**. Click on a map that expands and zooms in with greater detail to view a particular state or country's navaids and airport facilities. The database includes name, ICAO identifier, elevation, latitude/longitude, runway names, runway lengths, runway surface type, ILS Identifier, ILS/Localizer frequency, and ATIS frequency.
- **New scenery.** The Microsoft Hawaiian, Caribbean, and Japanese scenery are now included as defaults in FS98. Part of the Southern California Scenery Expansion Pack 1 scenery is in FS98 (e.g., Catalina Island) but most of the Expansion Pack is not in FS98.
- **Dynamic scenery**: In FS98, the dynamic scenery airplanes will try to avoid you. For example, if you park on an access tarmac to an active runway, you will block access to the runway for the airplanes behind you and they will cue up waiting to take off. What's more, if you are occupying the runway and another plane is making an approach, it will abort the landing and execute a go-around.
- **Road, river, lake, coastline, and mountain data in scenery database.**Microsoft Atlas data on roads, rivers, lakes, coastlines and mountains have been extended to both Europe and the United States.

- **Fully textured topographical terrain**. See beautifully rendered mountains that look three-dimensional with textured topographical surfaces. For example, if you go to Las Vegas, Lake Chelan, or the mountain ranges around Denver, Cleveland, or elsewhere you will see the mountain ranges fully texture-mapped with surface details. The new default scenery replaces FSW95's ugly green and brown mountains with Lake Chelan–quality 3-D terrain in many areas of the United States and Europe.
- **3,000 airports and heliports.** This is 10 times what was available in FSW95. According to Microsoft, virtually every public-access field in the United States now has taxiway and apron detail that's based on Jeppeson data. You won't find airports with bare runways in the middle of a field anymore. Also, you'll find many heliports, such as the one atop the World Trade Center in New York City (see Figure I.2). You can jump directly to any of the heliports and airports in FS98 by using the **Go To Airports** dialog box, where you can search the listings by region, country, state, and city.
- **40 new worldwide metropolitan areas, including 20 new U.S. cities**. There are now 45 detailed 3-D scenery cities in FS98, including new photorealistic scenery of Hong Kong.
- **New 3-D scenery objects.** Almost 10,000 towers, buildings, antennas, and other real-world obstacles are included in the scenery database. Watch out if you fly low in low-visibility conditions!
- **New Custom Controls dialog box.** FS98 allows you to customize keyboard commands and joystick buttons through this easy-to-use dialog box. If you don't like the default keyboard commands or joystick button functions, change them. This is a feature for people who use programmable joysticks or EPIC devices.
- **Undockable windows.** If you right-click on any window and choose the **Undock** menu command, you can separate the window from the main FS window.
- **Multiple windows.** You can now open up two or more 3-D view windows and more than one map window. With the new Windows 98 support for multiple video cards and multiple monitors, it will soon be possible to have right, left , and forward views on separate monitors hooked up to the same PC or network.
- **On-screen checklist**. Easy-to-use on-screen aircraft checklists are now only a key press away (press **Shift+C** to cycle through checklists). These checklists include step-by-step instructions for the takeoff, cruise, descent, approach, and landing for each aircraft.
- **VOR and NDB navaids updated.** All navaids for Europe and the United States have been updated.
- **Navaids now have accurate line-of-sight reception ranges.** The higher you are, the farther off you can receive radio navaid signals. No longer does the artificial

FSW95 limit of 80 nm apply. Also, the closer you are to the ground, the more limited the radio reception range, just as in the real world.

- **Morse code identifiers for navaids**. Now when you tune in a navaid, you can hear the Morse code identifiers for the VOR station. Press **Ctrl+1** for NAV1, **Ctrl+2**, for NAV2, **Ctrl+3** for DME1, **Ctrl+4** for DME2, and **Ctrl+5** for the ADF. Alternatively, you can open the radio panel (press **Shift+1**) and with the mouse pull out the IDENT button. This will turn on the Morse code identification for the radio you have selected.

- **New virtual cockpit view mode**. Press **S** to see a virtual cockpit view of your airplane's interior. If you pan your view around with your joystick's hat switch, you can actually see texture-mapped images of the real aircraft interiors. Virtual cockpit is also great for getting a "wrap around" perspective view through the side windows. That can give you extra visual cues about where the horizon is located (to get the full benefit, you'll have to zoom out a little by pressing the – key). This will give you a better sense of your position with respect to the surrounding terrain or airport, but it slows down your machine because you are, in effect, displaying three view windows simultaneously (i.e., left, right, and forward). It's especially fun to look through the glass floor of the Bell JetRanger helicopter as you land. Also, there are new interior and exterior perspectives

- **Preview view.** In the **Views/View Options** dialog box, you can now preview how the various options will affect your currently selected view. For example, if you click **Spot View**, you can drag the pointer in the preview box and the view will shift in three dimensions. You can thus view the airplane from above, or you can view it from any side. You can also change the zoom magnification, view distance, view altitude, and then preview how it will look before committing to the view. This is especially useful when you select **Map View** in the dialog box and zoom out from 200 ft all the way up to 160,000 miles in space.

- **Panning spot view above and below the airplane**: You can pan the view up or down via the keyboard using **Shift+Enter** or **Shift+Backspace** or via the joystick, as described next.

- **Joystick hat switch pans view window.** You can pan your view with your joystick's hat switch in any view. Note that on many joysticks, the landing gear button now returns your view to straight and level with no pan.

- **Force feedback joystick control**. Using DirectX 5.0, FS98 supports force feedback joysticks, such as the new Microsoft SideWinder 3-D Force Feedback Pro. You'll feel your wheels rolling down the runway and the stick shake when the "stick shaker" on the Learjet or 737 activates to warn you of an impending stall. You'll also feel the airplane pull Gs as it turns and performs aerobatic maneuvers, and you'll feel the aerodynamic control surface forces as they are fed back to your hand through the joystick.

- **Up to 16 Joysticks with 512 Different Controls Possible.**FS98 supports up to 16 joysticks in its configuration file (**FLTSIM98.CFG**), each with up to 32 buttons for a total of 512. If you are interested in designing your own cockpit, you can use the EPIC controller to allow all 512 buttons to be implemented.

- **New aircraft.** In addition to the new Bell JetRanger helicopter, there is a new Cessna 182S (fixed landing gear) Skylane. Both come equipped with much-improved cockpit instrumentation. The horizontal situation indicator (HSI) on the helicopter is the best representation I have ever seen; it is even better than the Glass HSI in the 737. The ADF compass card on the Cessna now rotates, which is a big departure from the its FSW95 incarnation. The Cessna panels are excellent and work really well. The existing FSW95 Cessna 182RG (retractable landing gear) remains, but it got a face lift with a brand new photorealistic instrument panel. The Learjet 45 replaces the Learjet 35A. Another nice touch is the automatic gear warning that sounds when you have forgotten to lower your landing gear and throttle the engines down on the Cessna RG, Learjet 45, and 737. Both the Boeing 737 and Learjet come with redesigned instrument panels to accommodate the new autopilot autothrottle, and Mach/IAS speed controls. In addition, the TAT readout now shows correct temperature rise due to surface friction on the 737 and Learjet when traveling at high airspeeds.

- **New autopilot controls (autothrottle).** New Autothrottle for the 737, and IAS/Mach autopilot speed and vertical speed hold for all FS98 airplanes. With a complete autoland using the 737's autothrottle, it is possible to automatically deploy the thrust reversers and spoilers as soon as the wheels are on the ground. If a go around is necessary, a touch of a button will increase the throttle to take-off thrust, and the 737 will be put into the takeoff configuration. In addition, there are moveable autopilot bug markers on the airspeed and heading indicator, HSI (horizontal situation indicator), and OBI (omnibearing indicator).

- **New RMI and HSI for the Learjet and 737.** The radio magnetic compass (RMI) and HSI have been upgraded and improved. The RMI now has a rotating compass card in FS98, and the airspeed tape on the 737-400 now moves downward as speed increases (it moved backward in FSW95).

- **New sounds.** You can hear sounds for both the exterior and interior of the airplane. When you pan your view, the sound levels change accordingly, and you can hear the prop and engine noise change in intensity as you move away or around the aircraft in Spot view or when you change thrust settings. Also, you can hear wind noise (for example try turning off the magnetos in the Cessna and listen to the rushing air, or try listening to the howl of the wind in the sailplane). For the 737 and Learjet, you can hear turbine whine with pitch that varies with thrust setting and a stall warning stick shaker clicking noise. Wind noise is slaved to aircraft speed, so the faster you go, the greater the sound of rushing air. FS98 uses stereo sound, unlike FSW95, although many of the wave files in the program, they are still recorded in mono. If you rock the plane on landing, you'll get separate tire squeals (with corresponding rattles) from the appropriate right or left stereo speaker that corresponds to the right or left tire (note that for this effect to work with the Sound Blaster 64AWE, you'll need to use the Windows 95 or 98 sound control panel and select **Use Creative 3D Stereo Enhancement**—this will give you better spatial resolution). Also, the Cessna now sounds like a Cessna, and the Learjet sounds different than the 737. The chop-chop beating sound of the helicopter blade outside the Jet Ranger is incredible, and just wait till you hear what happens when the blade hits the ground. or when the undercarriage scrapes the tarmac. Using the **Options/Preferences/Sound** dialog box, you can set the volume of the engine, cockpit, environment, adventures, and navigation instruments, or customize the duration or panning effects to the millisecond, via editing of the SOUND.CFG file for each aircraft.

- **Propeller Blade** visual motion is modeled.
- **Completely rewritten high-resolution photorealistic instrument panel system.** The instrument panels are now clear, crisp, and well-defined. All dials and indicators rotate smoothly and realistically. Up to nine instrument panels can be added to new aircraft, which will be a boon for third-party aircraft developers once the new software development kit (SDK) for Flight Simulator is released. Instrument panels and view windows can be displayed at resolutions as high as 1280 pixels wide by 1024 pixels. Contrast this with FSW95's maximum 640(480 pixel resolution with 256 colors (8-bit color), and you can see what an extraordinary jump in graphics capability the program has made. Developed from photographs of actual aircraft cockpits, the new photorealistic instrument panels feature better-looking avionics, autopilots, and other systems. There are a few other nice, realistic touches added to the panels: when you stop the Cessna's engine by turning the Magnetos off, the artificial horizon will slowly sink and drop to one side because the gyroscopes are no longer powered. As in the real airplane, the throttle, prop control, and mixture settings are all moved with knobs that are pushed in or pulled out. Also, when you drop the landing gear, the indicator lights don't change from red to green all at once (in the real airplane, the nose wheel often extends first). Finally, the panels automatically scale to match your screen resolution, and you can have floating secondary instrument panels (for example, a Bendix radio stack on the Cessna or a throttle quadrant on the Learjet) that you can remove with a click of the mouse to clear on-screen clutter. For those who like to tinker, a new **PANEL.CFG** text file is used to store all the panel information for each aircraft. You can thus easily add new third-party panels and gauges to any aircraft by editing the panel configuration file found in each airplane's **Panel** sub-directory.

- **Internet multiplayer capability.** Up to eight players can join an Internet "flyin" over your TCP/IP Internet connection. You can also connect via IPX on an Ethernet network, Windows 95 or Windows NT network (LAN), connect via serial cable, or connect via modem. Fly as a pilot or as an observer if you don't want to fly. You can chat with each player through a special text communication window, and you can download each airplane's exterior model so you can see the custom-built airplanes that other people may be flying. If you don't know anybody to fly with, the Internet Gaming Zone (www.zone.com) will connect you with other pilots on the Internet.

- **Upgraded flight models.** New flight models and instrument panels for the 737, Learjet 45, and other aircraft are available. Unfortunately, the new flight models require a change in the file formats, so Flight Shop–created aircraft for FS5.1 and FSW95-converted aircraft will not work with FS98 unless they have been converted with the new FS98 Aircraft Converter. Also, third-party instrument panels created for FSW95 will not work with FS98. FS98 aircraft files now carry a lot of information in addition to the flight and visual model. Aircraft designers can peg the plane to specific sound and panel configuration files, thus avoiding the problem of having to use a panel manager. In addition, it will be possible to map four analog axis thrust controls for a realistic depiction of a four-engine 747 with asymmetric thrust conditions.

- **Temporary situation restart.** Each time you change aircraft or location, a temporary situation is saved. If you crash or need to reset the situation, you will be reset to the last location with the last selected aircraft, without having to save the situation to disk, and reload it manually. This is a very handy feature if you are trying to practice a landing with a custom setup that you don't want to have to manually fix each time you restart.

- **Adventure programming compatibility.** Adventure Programming Language Adventure files that were converted for FSW95 will run in FS98 because the binary formats are identical to FSW95. Some new autopilot commands and other statements have been added. These will be fully documented in the upcoming release of the Microsoft Flight Simulator SDK. The FS98 CD-ROM has 33 MB of sound wave files that can be used in adventures. To conserve hard disk space, Microsoft has wisely chosen to access these sounds off of the CD-ROM, rather than install it to your hard disk (although you can install them at setup).

- **New adventures.** Many more adventures and lessons are included, with instructor voices to guide you. These sound files are stored on the FS98 CD, and so you must run these adventures with the CD-ROM in your drive to hear them, otherwise you will only see text messages. At setup, you have the option of installing these sound files to your hard drive, but you can always just copy them to the **ADV\WAV** subdirectory where you have installed FS98.

- **Airfoil surfaces** now move on the Cessna and Learjet (but not the other aircraft). You can see your flaps, ailerons, rudder, and elevators move in spot view.
- **Scenery backward compatible with FSW95 and FS5.1.** Although scenery is compatible with FS98, there have been changes to the BGL scenery file format that will allow the facility directory in FS98 to access specialized airport and radio navigational beacon data from each scenery file.
- **Moon texture mapped, star motion modeled.** The moon is now texture mapped and occupies its correct position in the sky for the day, date, and time. Star motion for the principal stars is also modeled, so if you know something about celestial navigation, you could theoretically navigate by the stars.
- **The Map window and NumLock ke y.** No longer does the **NumLock** key activate the Map window. Instead, you must press **Shift+]** to open the Map view.

FLIGHT SIMULATOR FOR WINDOWS 95 FEATURE SET

Flight Simulator for Windows 95 introduced many new features that made it well worth the upgrade from the DOS based FS 5.1:

- **Flight Shop–created aircraft and adventures converter**. With FSW95, it became possible to import new user-created shareware aircraft and commercially created aircraft into the program installing BAO's Flight Shop. This powerful new feature gave Flight Simulator pilots immediate access to hundreds of existing aircraft as well as new aircraft with more polished flight models and livery (these are available from professional designers such as those included on the book's CD-ROM). Before aircraft and adventures created with Flight Shop for Flight Simulator can be transferred into the program, FSW95 requires the use of a converter program called **FSCONV.EXE** (available on the CD-ROM) to translate the aircraft and adventure files into the file format used by FSW95. Note that instrument panels created for Flight Simulator 5.x aircraft will not work in FSW95, but must be rewritten in 32-bit code. Also, because the flight model was revamped in FSW95, many aircraft created for the FS5.1 had to have their aerodynamic model tweaked to fly correctly in FSW95.
- **Multimedia help**. The Flight Simulator CD-ROM includes 136 MB of multimedia help, including 22 video/animation examples, 83 high-resolution pictures (87 pictures in FS98), and hypertext-linked definitions of aviation terminology. Short biographies of famous aviators and aviatrix were also included. In addition, the help files provided detailed explanations of all the flight instruments as well as tutorials, animations, pictures, and airplane-specification handbooks. An

on-line aviation library and listing of FAR (Federal Aviation Regulations), with more than 200,000 words of text, help round out the on-line help.

- **Context-sensitive help**. Right-click on an instrument or object in a dialog box to access instant instant help.

- **Windows 95 interface.** FSW95 took advantage of Windows' easy-to-use interface, with revamped dialog boxes and true compatibility with Windows 95 and Windows NT's 32-bit operating system. Flight Simulator's 32-bit source code also took advantage of Windows' preemptive multitasking 32-bit operating system. With Windows 3.1's 16-bit operating system, applications ran concurrently but had to relinquish control or stop tasks when other programs were running in a process called *cooperative multitasking.* Applications running could run amuck and hog CPU time to the exclusion of all other tasks, including the user wishing to switch to another application. With Windows 95 and Windows NT, the 32-bit operating system uses preemptive multitasking for Win32-based applications (meaning the program is compiled with 32-bit code to run on 32-bit processors). Win32-based applications, such as Flight Simulator, do not need to yield to other tasks to multitask properly, and furthermore can use multithreading to enhance the program's efficiency.

- **Greater screen resolution in FSW95.** FSW95 offers 640(480 at 256 colors versus 640(400 at 256 colors for FS5.1. Although FSW95 could run at any resolution that your monitor supports (such as 1600(1200 for high-end Pentium Pro systems with 21" monitors), the effective resolution remained 640(480. At higher resolutions, the program simply interpolated single pixels to span multiple pixels, so the effect got blockier, or "pixilated," at the higher resolution. Also FSW95 performed best with a 256-color setting rather than the thousands or millions of colors that you may be accustomed to seeing.

- **Better performance and higher frame rates.** Portions of the graphics engine were optimized for the Pentium, and sound card usage and texture mapping performance were substantially improved. Many people report a frame rate improvement of 20% to 50% over FS 5.1.

- **New challenges and adventures**. Using the converter program, it became possible to import Flight Shop–style FS5.1 adventures that you created yourself. Some adventures created in Flight Shop (which was really designed for FS 5.1) could not be converted due to incompatibilities with the new program.

- **New and improved interactive flying lessons.**

Figure I.4 *New on-line Airport Facilities Directory with airports and navaids organized by region, country, and state. Map zooms in as you click on a region, country, or state (FS98).*

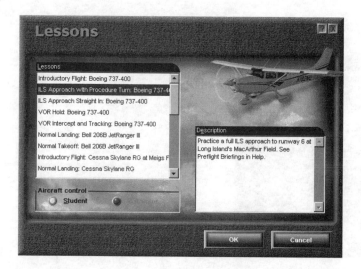

Figure I.5 *New and improved interactive flight lessons teach you all about flying. An instructor will guide you through basic maneuvers such as landings, landings with crosswinds, climbs, turns and descents.*

- **More airports and cities**. The City Pack on the FSW95 CD-ROM added detailed scenery for London, Tokyo, Toronto, Rome, Atlanta, Moscow, St. Louis, Berlin, Athens, Rio de Janeiro, Washington D.C., Mexico City, Jerusalem, and Miami. The same navigational beacons (VORs, NDBs and ILSs) that existed in FS 5.1 also existed in FSW95, although there were problems with missing VORs in Florida and England, as well as misplaced ILS glidepaths due to an unfortunate mismatch between an obsolete magnetic variation database and a new ILS database. As a result of this unhappy marriage, when you followed a glidepath down to a runway, the glidepath would bring you down off to the side of the runway, instead of right on the runway.
- **Enhanced 3-D scenery in FSW95.** Chicago, Boston, Cairo, Los Angeles, Sydney, San Francisco and London had much more scenery added.
- **New Spot View Feature.** In addition to Roll, and Loop in the transition type for the View Options under Spot view, a new Fixed view option allows you to keep your spot view pointed in a particular heading, even while the aircraft rotates.
- **New photorealistic scenery in FSW95**. Areas created from satellite imagery included Las Vegas, Nevada; Chelan, Washington; and Martha's Vineyard, Massachusetts.

Figure I.6 *Photo-realistic outside spot view of the 737 flying over Hong Kong in FS98. To see this view yourself, select the **737 over Hong Kong** flight situation under **Options/Select Flight**. Note that this screen shot was taken with Direct3D video drivers turned off, and the frame rate was poor: only 5.5 frames second (fps) in full screen spot view and 8.5 fps in cockpit view. The display resolution was 1024 ◊ 768 256 colors (8-bit color).*

FRAMES/SEC = 12.3

Figure I.7 *Same spot view as previous figure, except now the Direct3D video drivers are turned on to take advantage of 3-D video card hardware acceleration. Direct3D effects such as MIP mapping, filtered texture maps are on. The frame rate doubles over the previous non-Direct3D picture, and in many other cases it will triple your frame rate. For example, in this image, the frame rate increased to 12 fps in full screen spot view, and 13.5 fps in cockpit view. The display resolution was 1024 ◊x768 (16-bit color). This screenshot was taken with the Canopus Total 3-D with the Rendition VÈritÈ chipset). Keep in mind that the Hong Kong scenery slows down your frame rate because of the complex scenery. With the Canopus video card and a 200 MMX Pentium, you can easily achieve 21 fps with the **Meigs Field-Normal Scenery** flight situation.*

- **Integrated scenery add-ons.** Scenery packages of the Washington D.C., New York, Paris, and Las Vegas (BAO) areas were included with the FSW95 CD and were installed at setup. Formerly, these packages were sold separately.
- **New autopilot keyboard commands**. New autopilot functionality, including a yaw damper for the 737-400, as well as the ability to switch on individual autopilot features directly from the instrument panel.
- **Higher level of scenery detail**. Microsoft imported most roads, rivers, lakes, and bodies of water in the United States from its atlas product. Many people commented favorably on the immense increase in fidelity that this provided for outlying areas, which don't have many 3-D buildings or other scenery.
- **On-line airport/facility directory**. You could now view all the default navaids and airports by region, country, and state on the CD-ROM.
- **Continuing improvements to the flight model**. Many flight simulator pilots feared that Microsoft's acquisition of BAO's Flight Simulator in 1996 would

cause a shift in the program's realism to cater more to the needs of the gaming market. These fears were laid to rest when Microsoft announced agreements with Flight Safety International to help test and validate the flight models in Flight Simulator. Due to the higher accuracy and fidelity of the FSW95 flight model, aircraft created with Flight Shop often exhibited poor flight characteristics and had to be retuned.

N O T E   Flight Safety also has provided content for the CD-ROM's multimedia tutorials and has an agreement with Microsoft to be the exclusive provider of yet-to-be announced add-on products. Flight Safety International operates a network of 38 learning centers in the United States, Canada, and Europe that includes 150 full-motion simulators of more than 23 commercial aircraft types, including such popular aircraft as the Bae Jetstream 31/32, Beech 1900/D, Boeing 737, 757, 767, 747-200, 777, Airbus A310-300, DH Dash, Embraaer EMB-120, Fokker 100, DC-9, MD-80, MD-88/87, Saab 340, Saab 2000, and the Shorts 360.

Figure 11.8 *Flight Safety International, which has created more than 150 full-motion aircraft simulators used for professional airline training, is working with Microsoft to validate the flight models and provide training content for Flight Simulator (courtesy of Flight Safety International).*

- **New aircraft.** The Boeing 737-400 and the Aerobatic Extra 300 were added to the existing stable of aircraft consisting of the Cessna 182RG, LearJet 35A, and the Schweizer 2-32 Sailplane. The flight model for the Extra was validated by Patty Wagstaff, three-time U.S. National Aerobatic Champion, and the flight model for the Boeing 737-400 was validated by Flight Safety International. (Note that there are problems with the 737-400's range and some other flight characteristics in FSW95).

- **New cockpit instruments.** The Boeing 737-400 and the Extra 300 were equipped with new instrumentation. The 737 included an RMI, an HSI, engine instrumentation to monitor N1 and N2 fan speeds, and an engine vibration gauge. The Extra 300 was equipped with a G-meter and other new engine instruments.

- **Support for DirectX.** Support DirectSound, and DirectInput. Direct Draw was not used, though users could enable it through the FSW95 INI file.

- **Digitized sound.** The digitized sound effects included the landing gear retraction and extension sequence, the tires squealing on the pavement, and better engine/cockpit sounds. Unfortunately, FSW95 used monophonic recorded sound files instead of stereo. See the Configuration FAQ in Appendix A for instructions on how to install and run stereo sound.

- **No more memory problems.** Windows 95 and Windows NT use a demand-paged virtual memory system that is based on a flat linear addressing model. The term *demand-paged virtual memory* refers to the method by which code and data are moved in pages from RAM to a temporary swap file on your hard disk. As information is needed, it is "swapped" or paged back into your physical memory, or RAM. With Windows 95 and Windows NT, up to 2 GB (that's 231, or 2,147,483,648 bytes) was directly addressable by Flight Simulator, although only a small fraction of this is used.

- **No more DOS!** Gone were the routine setup hassles, and configuration problems. No **config.sys** and **autoexec.bat** files were necessary for Windows 95, thereby obviating one of the biggest headaches of properly booting the optimum computer configuration.

- **Fewer video card problems and sound card problems.** Plug and Play hardware delivered users from the "plug and pray" days of Windows 3.1 and MS-DOS. Windows 95 was able to handle all the IRQs and ports, so you no longer had to mind your *p*s and *q*s (i.e., port and IRQ conflicts).

- **AutoInstall and AutoPlay.** Flight Simulator would start automatically when you inserted the FSW95 CD into the CD-ROM player. Installation was a snap, and you could select various setup options to optimize the program or conserve hard disk space. Memory and peripheral configuration woes were a thing of the past.

- **True 32-bit compiled code.** As a 32-bit Windows application, Flight Simulator ran on Windows NT, although with NT you had more potential installation problems with sound cards, video cards, and joysticks.

- **New Easter Eggs.**

Hardware Requirements

Although Flight Simulator 98 will run on a 486 with Windows 95, Windows 98, or Windows NT installed, best performance is obtained with Pentium class MMX processors running at 200 Mhz or above. In addition, motherboards equipped with AGP support, such as the Intel 440LX (code named "Atlanta"), allow the new generation of AGP PCI video cards to take full advantage of the new Direct Draw 5.0 3-D video drivers. Note that FS98 does not directly benefit from AGP, but must obtain any benefit through the video card's software drivers.

The optimum system requirements are as follows:

- Multimedia PC with Pentium 200MHz or higher with MMX and AGP equipped motherboard (such as Intel's 440LX).
- Microsoft Windows 95, Windows 98, or Windows NT.
- 16 MB of RAM (Random Access Memory), with 32 MB recommended
- Direct3D-capable video card with at least 4 MB on board memory and compatible with the new AGP motherboards. Recommended non-AGP cards include the Diamond Viper V330 (with the NVIDIA chipset), the Canopus Total 3-D with the Rendition VÈritÈ chipset. The S-3 Virge chipset, such as is found on the Diamond Stealth is not recommended because it performs poorly with FS98.
- 105 to 313 MB of free hard disk space depending on whether you want to cache and use the scenery off your CD-ROM on an as-needed basis (105 MB), or install all the scenery to your hard disk for faster access (313 MB).
- 12x ,16x, or higher CD-ROM player recommended for faster loading of scenery.
- Super VGA or Multisync color monitor.
- Mouse or other compatible pointing device.
- Analog or digital joystick with 4 axis capability (needed for separate rudder action, throttle, and for helicopter tail rotor control). If you want to experience force feedback in your joystick, you'll need the Microsoft SideWinder Force Feedback 3-D Pro (at this time CH-Products joystick will not work with FS98).
- 16-bit stereo sound card with speakers. The new Creative Labs Sound Blaster 64AWE has a special stereo enhancement feature that allows you to hear the squeal of the right or left gear, depending on which wheel strikes the runway first during landing.

You can vastly improve your computer's performance by increasing RAM and installing the CD-ROM scenery directly to your hard drive, instead of running it off your CD. However, installing all the worldwide scenery will gobble 313 MB of your precious hard disk's real estate. Doubling your RAM from 16 to 32 MB is a worthwhile investment, however, since it will almost certainly improve the performance of your machine. For example, if you are likely to run a web browser during multiplayer internet connections in FS98, you may experience more reliable performance with 32 MB as opposed to 16 MB.

If you must run your scenery off your CD-ROM, a 12x or higher CD-ROM player will do wonders in eliminating those annoying pauses when flying from one scenery area to another.

No unbiased look at Flight Simulator should omit the weaknesses in the program. Some criticisms that have been leveled at FS98 include:

- The shapes of the mountains are exaggerated. The depiction of the large hills in many areas of the country are almost cartoonish in appearance. For example, many smooth mountain tops in the real world are replaced with jagged peaks that look like the Matterhorn.
- A complete worldwide navaid databaseis not included with the program (although this book's CD-ROM corrects this problem)
- Although the FS98 737-400 flight model is an improvement over FSW95, there are still glaring problems with incorrect stall speeds when compared to the real Boeing 737-400. The FSW95 737 flight model was flawed: the airplane burned too much fuel (and its range was more limited), and its single engine performance was incorrect. Other serious problems included an incorrect total air temperature (TAT) gauge that skewed atmospheric performance characteristics and handling problems. Many 737 pilots reported that the plane just didn't "feel right." The newly revamped FS98 737 flight model has a much better one engine inoperative performance, handles much better, and fuel burn is much improved. Unfortunately, other problems remain.
- The coordinate system, although expressed in latitude/longitude units of degrees, minutes, and seconds, is based on a bent cylindrical model of the world, not a spherical model. The poles do not exist and so you can never get higher than N89∞ 30' or S89∞ 30' latitude. This rules out some polar flights, and means that you can never reach the south or north poles.
- Clouds and thunderstorms need improvement. When flying close to clouds, they still look like big white cubes.
- There is no lightning.
- You cannot model vertical wind shear.
- There is no rain. There should be visual impairment of the windshield when rain is present.
- The flight instruments don't work or move in Virtual Cockpit view.
- The pitch scale on the 737 attitude indicator is more accurate regarding pitch attitudes than it was in FSW95, but the scale lines are still too thick.

- The reverse thrusters on the 737 are too aggressive and bring the airplane to a stop much more quickly than is the case for the real 737.
- The red cross on the HSI, which signifies that no valid VOR beacon is being received, is less obtrusive than in FSW95, but it is still unrealistic. It would be better to have an OFF FLAG indicator, as the real aircraft displays do.
- Flight Shop–created aircraft don't fly right because their moments and other flying parameters do not translate properly into FS98. Designers must devise new flight models for FSW95 aircraft that take into account the greater accuracy of the FS98 flight dynamics model.
- There is no integrated scenery builder.
- There is no turboprop aircraft model. Users are stuck with jets or piston-powered aircraft. When Flight Shop–created turboprops are brought into FSW95, you hear jet engines instead of turboprop engines.
- There is no accurately modeled supersonic aircraft.
- There is no radio altimeter. Currently, there is no instrument that tells your altitude above ground. This is standard equipment in all commercial jet aircraft
- There is no flight management computer (FMC) with inertial navigation system (INS). FMCs allow you to enter in waypoints for great circle navigation and fly RNAV routes.
- There is no flight director to show you which direction to fly the airplane when using the HSI and autopilot. This is a must for real jet aircraft.
- There is no Global Positioning System (GPS) equipment on the included aircraft, so you can't fly GPS-approved instrument landing approaches. You can simulate a GPS by displaying your latitude/longitude coordinates on screen (press **Shift+Z**), but you cannot figure out which way you need to fly from waypoint to waypoint.
- Many of the airports don't have refueling facilities as they should.
- In FSW95, at least 151 ILS glideslopes were misaligned with their runways, such as the ILS runways around Seattle. (There is a patch file on the C-ROM called **ILS_FIX.zip** to fix some of these ILS runways; it was contributed courtesy of Ted Denison). This problem is fixed in FS98.
- In FSW95, there were annoying pauses in mid flight where the screen freezes as scenery was loaded from the CD or hard drive (see Appendix A for work-arounds for this problem).

ORGANIZATION OF THIS BOOK

The book is organized into four parts along with nine appendices:

Part I: Advanced Flight Simulator Pilot's Guide
Part II: Customizing Flight Simulator
Part III: Compass and Chart
Part IV: Around the World with Flight Simulator

In Part I, you'll explore basic flight maneuvers such as taking off, climbs, turns, descents, and landings. Then you'll be introduced to the aerodynamics of flight, and aircraft engines, both turbine and piston. Next, you'll tour the atmosphere and discover how to manipulate the weather before proceeding to the subject of cockpit instrumentation and what each instrument does. Finally, you'll be introduced to the Cessna, the Learjet, the Boeing 737, and the Bell JetRanger III helicopter. Each of these aircraft have performance characteristics that will be of interest to you when planning flights.

In Part II, you will learn how to modify the program's many features to better suit your needs, and you'll swiftly become adept at managing custom scenery that you add to the program. In addition, you'll enjoy flying new aircraft and adding new scenery as you learn how to manipulate Flight Simulator at a lower level. You'll be guided step-by-step as you install new aircraft, and you'll be shown how to install all the missing world-wide navaids from the book's CD-ROM. Chapter 11, on scenery creation, should prove invaluable if you are planning to write your own scenery for your own local city. Chapter 12 concludes this part of the book with a listing of aviation or Microsoft Flight Simulator–related Web sites and a listing of the CD-ROM's contents.

In Part III, navigation will be the principal topic.

This part of the book discusses navigational instruments, great circle navigation, chart types, spherical trigonometry, and the application of spherical trigonometry to the solution of great circle paths around the world. You'll also learn how to fly real instrument approach procedures (IAP) using VOR approaches, VOR/DME appoaches, NDB (nondirectional beacon) approaches, and the ILS approach.

In addition, you'll be taught how to fly real IAPs using VOR approaches, VOR/DME appoaches, NDB approaches, and the ILS approach.

In Part IV, you'll retrace Ameilia Earhart's steps on her ill-fated 1937 attempt to fly around the world.

Lastly, the appendices provide you with global navigation maps, instrument approach plates, the standard atmosphere table, keyboard shortcuts for the program, configuration help, and a reference guide to the Adventure Programming Language.

The configuration frequently asked questions (FAQ) found in Appendix A is designed so you needn't wade through the whole text trying to find the answer to a single question. This appendix also discusses performance improvements you can make to boost your frame rate, and gives you typical frame rates for various computer setups. By comparing your frame rate to the typical values, you can determine whether your system is performing on par with other equivalent PCs, or whether you need to tweak the FSW95 software to maximize performance.

Do not feel compelled to read this book in linear fashion from cover to cover. If a topic interests you, skip ahead and read just that portion of the book that captures your attention. When you are ready, return and read the parts you skipped. Now that we have finished with this introduction, bring your seat back to an upright position and fasten your seatbelt as we prepare for pushback. Get ready to spread your wings and soar as you explore in-depth the best features of Microsoft's Flight Simulator 98.

REFERENCES

Tibbits, George, "Off into the wild, simulated yonder." The Houston Chronicle, August 22, 1997.

1

The Art of Flying

The aeroplane has unveiled for us the true face
of the earth.

Antoine de Saint-Exupéry (1900–1944),
French aviator, author, *Wind, Sand, and Stars.*

One of the most interesting aspects of Microsoft Flight Simulator is that you can try out flight maneuvers that apply theoretical concepts and see them occur in real time. For example, you can make a turn and watch as your airplane experiences higher g forces on its wings according to basic Newtonian mechanics. To make things more realistic, you can turn on airframe stress so that if you exceed the performance capabilities of your aircraft, the plane will fall apart. Even the atmospheric effects on lift are modeled; attempting to take off from high-altitude airports with the temperature at 100°, you'll discover that it is impossible for the aircraft to leave the ground. A multitude of facts and principles will take on new meaning as you discover how they work in Flight Simulator.

This chapter assumes that you have some basic knowledge of how Flight Simulator works. From time to time, you will see notes and tips that remind you of a facet of the program that you may already know about. These tips are placed so that newcomers to Flight Simulator can discover features of the program that they may not have been aware of. If you are new to Flight Simulator and are not familiar with the keyboard lay-

1

out, it might be advisable to first read Appendix G, "Keyboard Shortcuts and Basic Simulator Functions." You'll also benefit a lot if you first familiarize yourself with the program's basic capabilities by running the demo video, which demonstrates many of the key features. To run the video, start Flight Simulator and select **Options/Flight Video.** In the dialog box that opens, highlight **FS98 Demonstration Video** and click the **Play** button. Let the video run its course, and you'll get an overview of Flight Simulator that will get you up to speed quickly. Learning how to fly, however, is a different matter, and that is what this chapter focuses on.

Before proceeding to advanced topics, let's cover some basic tips for using Flight Simulator. You can skip these sections if you already know how to use it.

MENUS AND COMMANDS

Whenever you see a menu command such as **Options/Preferences/General** listed in this book, it means that you should go to the Options menu, select **Preferences**, and, in the dialog box that opens, select **General**. Sometimes the level of hierarchy is greater than three items, as for example **Options/Preferences/Display/Display Options**. Just follow the menu tree until you find the last command, tab button, check box, button, or other control. To exit any dialog box or menu without activating a command, press the **Esc** key. Also, when you see the text *right-click* or *left-click the mouse*, you should click the right mouse button or the left mouse button, respectively.

Also, you will discover that when you run Flight Simulator 98 at full screen resolution (**Press Alt+Enter**, or choose **Views/Full Screen**), your menu bar will disappear. To make it reappear, press the **Alt** key.

Some of the menu commands have keyboard equivalents displayed next to the menu item (see Figure 1.1). For example, you can select **Views/Full Screen** or press **Alt+Enter**.

Using Your Mouse as a Yoke

FSW95/98 allows you to use your mouse as a yoke in addition to selecting controls and menus. To do this, press the right mouse button and, in the pop-up menu that appears, select **Mouse as Yoke**. Then when you move the mouse the ailerons and elevators move. See Appendix G for a description of the directions and controls affected.

Right-Clicking the Mouse for On-line Help and Other Commands

In addition to using the mouse as a yoke, you can right-click to switch between the cockpit, tower, and spot views. You can also hide a window as well as maximize and close windows, as shown in Figure 1.2.

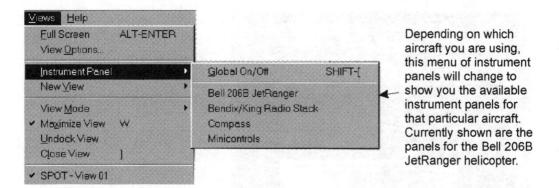

Depending on which aircraft you are using, this menu of instrument panels will change to show you the available instrument panels for that particular aircraft. Currently shown are the panels for the Bell 206B JetRanger helicopter.

Figure 1.1 *The View menu. Some menu commands have keyboard equivalents, as shown to the right of the menu item.*

One of the best new features of FS98 is the built-in on-line help. Whenever you move your mouse over a control, a note describing the control's name pops up. If you want more information about the control, right-click the mouse and the program will respond with a **What's this?** prompt. If you then left-click on the **What's this?** prompt, a description of the control's function pops up (see Figure 1.3). These descriptions are called Quicktips.

To turn Quicktips off, select **Options/Preferences/Show Quicktips**.

T I P

Figure 1.2 *Click the right mouse button to access these features.*

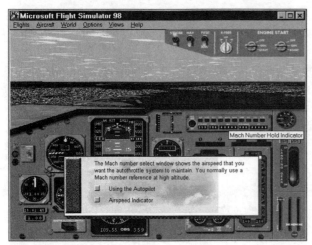

Figure 1.3 *Using Quicktips.*

BASIC TIPS FOR USING YOUR 3-D VIEW WINDOWS

Flight Simulator 98 has changed some of the keyboard viewing commands that previous version users may have become accustomed to. For example, the Map window is no longer viewable by pressing the **NumLock** key; instead to open the Map window in FS98, you need to press **Shift]**. The **NumLock** key is now used in the same way as it is in other programs: it toggles the numeric keypad between numbers and cursor control (such as **Home, End, PgDn, PgUp, Ins, Del,** ←↑→↓). When the **NumLock** key is on, the keyboard controls your views. When it is off, and you have disabled your joystick (or you don't have a joystick), the numeric keypad controls your flight and engine controls (see Appendix G's keyboard shortcuts), but you can still control your view directions by holding down the **Shift** key and pressing a number on the numeric keypad.

In FS98, the numeric keypad controls for the elevator trim, throttle, rudder and steering are normally disabled while the **NumLock** key is on. To re-enable these flight controls, press **NumLock** so that it is off.

T I P

Thus, if you are flying with only a keyboard and no joystick, you should first toggle the **NumLock** key off. Then, to shift your view around your airplane, press **Shift** followed by the keys on the numeric keypad (i.e., **keypad 9, 6, 3, 2, 1, 4, 7, 8**). If you have installed a joystick, you can leave the **NumLock** key on, and directly press **keypad 9, 6, 3, 2, 1, 4, 7, 8** to switch the view. There are nine possible views, including straight down, but you can also pan the view to intermediate positions using the panning feature on your joystick's hat switch, or through the keyboard.

You can also view your aircraft internally from regular Cockpit View, or from FS98's new Virtual Cockpit View. To do this, you can either cycle through the views by pressing the **S** key, or you can right click on the mouse and from the popup menu select the view you want. The new Virtual Cockpit View is especially nice if you zoom back (press the – key several times) to take advantage of the new "wrap around" view out the side windows. If you pan the view inside the Virtual Cockpit View, you'll get real texture mapped images of the real aircraft interiors.

To view your aircraft externally, you have the choice of Tower View (press **S** two times from Cockpit view, or right click and select from the menu), or Spot View (press **S** twice or right click and select). At any time, you can switch a view window to full screen or partial screen with cockpit instruments visible by pressing **W**. Pressing **W** once again will return you to the former view. Also, you might want to run FS98 in Full Screen mode (**Views/Full Screen** menu command, or press **Alt Enter**) because it is easier to read the instruments on a large screen monitor.

If you are using a joystick with a hat switch, such as the Microsoft SideWinder 3-D Force Feedback Pro, Microsoft SideWinder 3-D Pro, or the CH Products Virtual Pilot Pro, you can get a 360 view of your airplane in flight. To do this, enter Spot View, then press the hat switch with your thumb and move it in a circle. Your outside the aircraft spot view will shift you around your airplane so that you can see the whole airplane from any vantage point. The hat switch will also pan your view inside the cockpit as well.

Note that that the joystick's hat positions do not give you the overhead spot view of your airplane which is possible by pressing **Shift 5**. While using cockpit view, **Shift 5** will let you look straight down at the ground, as if your airplane had a looking glass bottom.

To get a really neat overhead view of your airplane, press **S** three times or right click to select **Spot View**. Then press **Shift Keypad 5**. You can transition the view from the front of your airplane over the top and towards the back by holding down the **Shift** key, then pressing **Keypad 8** followed by **Keypad 5** and **Keypad 2**.

T I P

Zooming and Selecting Windows

To zoom a window, first click on the window, then press the + or – key on the main keyboard. To fine zoom, press **Shift +** or **Shift –** (note that FSW95 users will have a problem with fine zoom; see Appendix A's FAQ for instructions on how to use fine zoom).

Opening New View Windows in FS98

FS98 opens a new chapter in simulator technology by giving you the capability of opening as many view windows as you like. In previous versions, you could only have two 3-D view windows open at a time. When Windows 98's new multiple monitor support becomes available, you will be able to drive as many as 8 separate monitors with 8 video cards installed in your PC. The monitors can be arrayed as a virtual desktop, so that you can click and drag the mouse across monitors. Of course, to get an acceptable frame rate with such a setup, much more powerful microprocessors will be required.

Opening a new 3-D View window in FS98 is handled differently than it was in previous versions of Flight Simulator. To open a new view, press [. To close a view select the window and then press]. Once you have selected a particular 3-D View window, you can then decide what view it will display by right clicking in it, and then choosing one of the view options from the popup menu. Thus, for example, you could have multiple Spot Views of your airplane from the front, rear, left, and right of your aircraft by opening four view windows.

Opening and Resizing Multiple 3-D View Windows in FS98

Let's try opening four different spot views of your airplane in FS98. The procedure outlined below will serve as an example of how you can manipulate and customize your viewing system in other ways.

1. Press [four times and you will see four view windows open up. They will overlap each other, so you will need to click and drag on them to move them as necessary.
2. Click and select the first window, and then right click in it. From the popup menu select **Spot View**, then press **Shift Keypad 8** to get a forward view of your airplane. Click and drag this window off to the side so that you can see the remaining windows underneath.
3. Now click and select a second window, and right click on it to select **Spot View**. This time select a right view of your airplane by pressing **Shift Keypad 6**.
4. Follow step 3 above for the third window, but this time press **Shift Keypad 2** for a rear view of your airplane.
5. Follow step 3 above for the fourth window, but this time press **Shift Keypad 5** for a left view of your airplane.
6. All view windows are resizable by clicking and dragging the edge of the window.

Now when you fly, you will have bird's eye view of your airplane from four different directions, in addition to your normal cockpit view!

Undocking the 3-D View Windows in FS98

Another great new feature of FS98 is the ability to undock your windows from the main program window. This allows you to slide the window off to the side of the main window to unclutter your display. In the future, with Windows 98, if you undock your 3-D View windows, you will be able to drag them on a virtual desktop to other monitors that you may have set up with your computer. This will allow you to surround yourself with monitors and immerse yourself in virtual reality like panoramic 3-D setting.

Let's try undocking the spot view windows we just created in the previous example:

1. Click on any one of the spot view windows to select the view window and make it active.
2. Right click on the window, and in the popup menu, select **Undock Window**.
3. Repeat steps 1 and 2 above for the remaining three spot view windows.

After completing step 3 above, you will see that there are now four independent, resizable view windows that are no longer attached to the main Flight Simulator Program. Feel free to move them where you wish, change the viewing angle, change the zoom or right click and change the view mode.

Opening a Second 3-D View Window in FSW95

In FSW95, if you want to open up the second 3-D View window, press]. This window can have a separate view of your aircraft from any vantage point you choose. To switch between active view windows, press [for your 3-D view window #1 and] for your 3-D view window #2. All view windows are resizable and can be moved by dragging the mouse along the window borders. To expand a window to full size, press **W**.

The Map Window

The map window in FS98 can be opened by pressing **Shift]** (in FSW95, press **NumLock**), and you can zoom the map in or out by pressing + or - (in FSW95, press **NumLock** + or -). Sometimes the Map window will not appear when you press **Shift]** . What has happened is that the Map Window is being displayed underneath the 3-D view window(s) and you will need to bring it to the forefront by pressing the **"** key.

The Map window can also be displayed so that it doesn't turn with the aircraft but remains fixed with a north orientation. This arrangement can be useful when you're flying long distances at high altitude in jet aircraft and you want to keep an eye on your heading through graphical means. To change the Map display to a high-altitude north orientation, select **Options/Preferences/Display/Display Options/Map**. In the **Map Display** list box, choose **North at High Altitude**. The Map window is movable (drag it by the top border), and it can be expanded to full window size by pressing **W**. To resize it, drag the edges of the window. Also, if you would like the map display to show ground textures, be sure to enable the Map Ground Texture checkbox.

Panning Windows

To pan the window, press **Shift+Enter** to pan down and **Shift+Backspace** to pan up. To pan left, press **Ctrl+Shift+Backspace**, and to pan right, press **Ctrl+Shift+Enter**. To restore the view to straight and level with no pan, press **Ctrl+Spacebar** (in FSW95 press the **Scroll Lock** key). The panning feature is crucial for landing big jets; without it, you would not be able to see the runway while landing the airplane with a nose-high attitude.

TIPS FOR USING FLIGHT CONTROLS

In FS98, to control your airplane from the keyboard you must first turn off the joystick by pressing **K**. Your basic flight controls, the ailerons, elevators, elevator trim, rudder and throttle can then all be controlled via the numeric keypad, as is shown in Figure 1.4.

NOTE

You can quickly center your ailerons and rudder by pressing **keypad 5** on the numeric keypad. Elevators must be centered manually.

Auto-Coordination

If you are using the keyboard to control your aircraft, the ailerons and rudder are automatically moved together when you press the left aileron (**keypad 4**) or right aileron (**keypad 5**). This is known as *Auto-coordination mode*, and it is useful for beginner pilots or those without rudder pedals to execute balanced turns with just the right amount of rudder applied with the ailerons. With Auto-Coordination turned off, you are flying your aircraft with the rudder controls separated from the ailerons. This mode is more realistic, because you can land the aircraft in crosswinds and fly with engines out in multiengine aircraft. The rudders, which yaw the aircraft left or right, are needed to counteract forces that would otherwise render the aircraft uncontrollable during engine failures, high-performance aerobatic maneuvers, crosswinds, and adverse weather conditions. To turn Auto-coordination on or off, select **Aircraft/Aircraft Settings/Realism**. In the Aircraft Settings dialog box, click the **Auto-coordination** box.

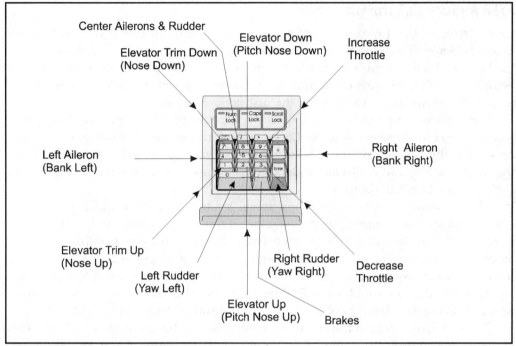

Figure 1.4 *Flight controls on the numeric keypad.*

Although you can use the keyboard to fly with separate rudder controls (left rudder is **keypad 0** and right rudder is **keypad Enter**), it is highly recommended that you obtain a joystick with separate rudder pedals for better control. Even though high-performance joysticks such as the Microsoft SideWinder 3-D Pro let you separate rudder capabilities by twisting the handle left or right, it is awkward to apply left rudder and right ailerons because of the contrary motions that must be applied. For example, on the SideWinder 3-D Pro, to apply left rudder and right ailerons you must tilt the joystick handle right to apply right ailerons and then twist it (i.e., rotate it) left. This is, at best, an awkward way to execute this command. It does not help that the range of motion for rotating the handle left and right to control your rudders is very limited.

Calibrating Joysticks

Joysticks need to be calibrated because Flight Simulator has no way of knowing beforehand where your joystick is centered. If you didn't do this, your joystick would sendthe wrong signals to the program and your airplane would careen off the runway, or fly in an unstable manner.

FS98 Joystick Calibration

Calibration of the joystick in FS98 is accomplished via the **Options/Custom Controls/Sensitivities/Calibrate** command. This will open the Game Controllers dialog box in which you must then select your joystick and click the **Properties** button before proceeding with the calibration testing process. If your joystick is not listed, you must click the **Add** button and follow the instructions as given.

Joystick sensitivity can be adjusted via the Customize Controls dialog box, which you access via the **Options/Custom Controls/Sensitivities** menu command. Here you must select the joystick, and then choose which axis you want to adjust before then sliding the **Sensitivity** and **Null Zone** sliders to a new position. To restore default values, click the **Reset Defaults** button.

The sensitivity settings control how much joystick movement will affect the aircraft's controls. For example, if you have selected Auto-Coordination to be off, and you want to fly with the rudders separated from the ailerons, you may find that the SideWinder 3-D Pro's range of rudder motion is not satisfactory. To heighten the sensitivity so that the rudder moves more quickly in response to your twisting motion of the joystick's handle, you would select **Rudder Axis** from the **Axis** list box in the Custom Controls dialog box, and then slide the Rudder Sensitivity lever to the right.

The null zone refers to the centered position in which your joystick's handle does not move the controls. You can make it wider or narrower as your preferences dictate. By adjusting the null zone to a wider setting, you give your joystick a looser feel, while a narrower zone gives your joystick a tighter feel. Setting the null zone too narrow can be annoying since every joystick jitter will be reflected in the airplane's controls.

If your joystick isn't working, first press **K** to see if this cures your problem. If it still doesn't work, next check that the **Joystick On** is lit in the Customize Controls dialog box under the **Options/Customize Controls** menu. Calibrate as necessary.

T I P

Before your joystick can be used, be sure to check that the **Joystick On** button is lit in the Customize Controls dialog box.

FSW95 Joystick Calibration

Analog joysticks must be calibrated by using the Windows 95 Joystick Control Panel, while digital joysticks, such as the Microsoft SideWinder 3-D Pro need no calibration whatsoever. You can enter the calibration control panel directly through Flight Simulator by using the **Options/Preferences/Controls** menu command, and in the

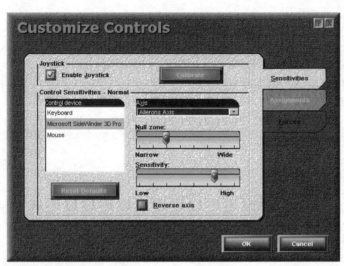

Figure 1.5 *Joystick sensitivity.*

dialog box that opens, click the **Calibrate** button. In the same dialog box, you can adjust the range of motion for your joystick, as well as its sensitivity. Before you can use your joystick, however, you must make sure that the **Joystick On** button is clicked so that it is lit.

SELECTING YOUR AIRPLANE

Flight Simulator 98 comes equipped with eight default aircraft, each with its own instrument panels. To select a particular aircraft, select **Aircraft/Select Aircraft** and make your selection from the dialog box choices.

THE SIX PRIMARY FLIGHT INSTRUMENTS

By law, every airplane must be equipped with an airspeed indicator, altimeter, vertical speed indicator, attitude indicator, turn indicator, heading indicator, and compass. The first six of these instruments are known as the six primary flight instruments (see Figure 1.6). More-advanced aircraft have even more instrumentation, as you will learn in later chapters. For now, let's familiarize ourselves with the primary instruments.

The six primary flight instruments can be divided into two groups: the pitot-static instruments, which measure differences in air pressure, and the gyroscopic instruments, so called because they take measurements from a spinning gyroscope.

The Pitot–Static Instruments

The pressure altimeter, the airspeed indicator, and the vertical speed indicator all derive their readings from the pitot-static system. As the plane flies, dynamic air pressure is rammed into the pitot tube, a hollow cylindrical pipe mounted externally on the leading edge of the wing, nose, or tail of the aircraft. Each instrument then compares this pressure with a static source of air pressure, in which there is no air moving, and then calculates pressure differences between the dynamic and static sources to arrive at a reading.

The Airspeed Indicator

The airspeed indicator for the Cessna, as shown in Figure 1.6, registers airspeed in knots, or nautical miles per hour. A nautical mile is equivalent to 1.15 statute miles, so when you are traveling at 120 knots true airspeed, your true airspeed in statute miles per hour (mph) would be 1.15×120 knots = 138 mph. Thus, airspeed measured in knots represents a speed that is 15% higher than the reading of a standard automobile speedometer. The unit of nautical miles is used in air navigation because it is easy to convert latitude and longitude differences in position to nautical miles; 1°, or 60 minutes, of latitude is equal to 60 nautical miles. For longitude, this relationship between degrees and minutes does not hold. The lines of longitude converge at the poles, and the distance between two longitude points is not constant as you move closer to the poles. At the equator, however, 1° of longitude = 60 minutes = 60 nautical miles.

Note that the Cessna's airspeed indicator has special colored markings that denote special airspeeds. The following standard color code markings on airspeed indicators used are found on single-engine light airplanes:

- White arc: Flap operating range.

- Lower limit of white arc: Power-off stalling speed with the wing flaps and landing gear in the landing position.

- Upper limit of white arc: Maximum flaps extended speed.

- Green arc: Normal operating range.

- Lower limit of green arc: Power-off stalling speed with the wing flaps and landing gear retracted.

- Upper limit of green arc: Maximum structural cruising speed. This is the maximum speed for normal operation.

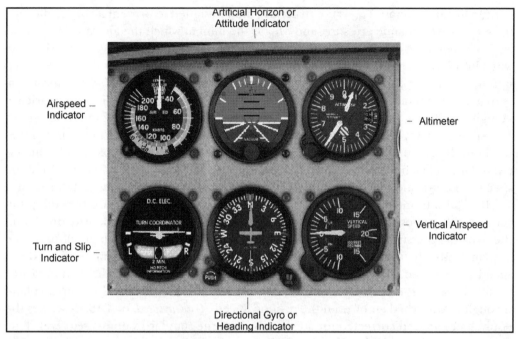

Figure 1.6 The six primary flight instruments

- Yellow arc: Caution range. The pilot should avoid this area unless in smooth air.

- Red line: Never-exceed speed. This is the maximum speed at which the airplane can be operated in smooth air. This speed should never be exceeded intentionally.

The FS98 Cessna airspeed indicator includes a new true airspeed calibration ring, which is adjustable by the knob on the lower left of the airspeed indicator. This ring can tell you what your true airspeed is for non-standard atmospheric conditions, but it must be adjusted properly or else it will give improper results.

The airspeed indicator for a light twin-engine airplane has, in addition to the preceding markings, a red radial line at the minimum controllable airspeed with the critical engine inoperative, and a blue radial line at the best rate of climb airspeed with one engine inoperative. Turbine-engine aircraft, such as the Learjet and 737 have limiting speeds which are similar to those of their piston-engine counterparts. At the high end of the speed range, however, there is no red line on the airspeed indicator but rather a red and white needle (called the barber pole) that indicates the maximum operating limit speed V_{MO} and M_{MO}.

On turbine aircraft, V_{MO} is the structural limit designed to prevent airframe damage from excessive dynamic pressure, and M_{MO} is the limit at which the aircraft is protected against shock wave damage as it approaches the speed of sound. Both V_{MO} and M_{MO} vary with altitude; as a result, the barber pole moves automatically to display the correct maximum operating speed on the turbine aircraft for different altitudes. V_{MO} is of most concern at lower altitudes, where the atmosphere is denser, whereas M_{MO} is most restrictive at higher altitudes, where the atmosphere is colder and the speed of sound is lower.

At cruise, jet speeds are referred to by Mach number rather than in knots or miles per hour. Mach number describes the airspeed relative to the speed of sound, which is equivalent to Mach 1. At 0.81 Mach, for example, an airplane is traveling at 81% of the speed of sound, and this is displayed in the Machmeter inside the airspeed indicator.

Real aircraft measure airspeeds by the amount of dynamic pressure that the pitot-static system senses. As the airplane flies at higher altitudes, the air density drops and the dynamic pressure entering the pitot-static system will drop. At a high altitude, the airplane must fly faster than it would at low altitude to show the same indicated airspeed as measured by the pitot-static system. Thus, the speed on the airspeed indicator is called *indicated airspeed,* or IAS. This speed is not the true speed of the airplane through undisturbed air or even the ground speed. *True airspeed,* or TAS, describes the equivalent airspeed corrected for air density from the standard value at sea level. True airspeed increases with altitude when indicated airspeed remains the same.

By default, Flight Simulator displays true airspeed rather than indicated airspeed, although you can easily swap between TAS and IAS by using the **Options/Preferences/ Instrument/Display Indicated Airspeed** toggle. Note that real airplanes always display indicated airspeed. The **Airspeed.ADV** adventure file on the accompanying CD-ROM will also let you instantly display IAS or TAS at the press of a button, an option that can be convenient when you don't want to interrupt your flight. Once you copy the Airspeed adventure into your Flight Simulator /ADV subdirectory, you run the adventure by selecting **Airspeed** from the **Flights/Flight Adventures** menu and dialog box. To display indicated airspeed at the top of the screen, press **Ctrl+I**. To display true airspeed, press **Ctrl+T**.

The Altimeter

The altimeter measures air pressure to determine the aircraft's current altitude. Every pilot needs to be aware that the altimeter assumes that the atmosphere is following the standard relationship between air pressure and altitude for a given temperature. This standard is known as the StAt (standard atmosphere), and you can see the variation of pressure and air density with altitude and temperature, as shown in Appendix F. If the air pressure or temperature deviates from the StAt, the altimeter will show a wrong altitude, and it must be corrected or calibrated. To quickly calibrate your altimeter to the current referenced sea level air pressure, press **B**. Your altimeter will show the proper airport elevation for nonstandard pressure (when the pressure deviates from 29.92 in. of Hg).

N O T E

Hg is the element name for mercury, which is the liquid used in barometers to measure pressure. In such barometers, a column of mercury rises to a height of 29.92 in. because of the pressure exerted on it by the atmosphere when the temperature is at StAt. At StAt, the temperature is 59° F (15° C), the sea level air pressure is 2116.2 lb/ft^2, or equivalently 29.92 in. Hg (or 14.69 PSI—pounds per square inch), and the air density is 0.0023770 lb/ft^3. When the air pressure drops, the mercury rises to a lower height. For example, at 28.00 in. Hg the air pressure would be 1,980 lb/ft^2 (or 13.75 PSI). Note that StAt exists for other elevations, but the values of air density, pressure, and temperature will change, as shown in Appendix F.

The face of the altimeter resembles a clock, with ten divisions instead of 12. The large hand measures altitude in 100 ft increments, although the smaller divisions on the dial show 20 ft increments in FSW95 and earlier it showed 50 ft increments). The small hand shows thousands of feet, but because it has not yet reached 1, the altimeter shows the plane is below 1,000 ft. At present, if you are using the Default Meigs Situation, the altimeter's large hand will be just below the 6, meaning that the altitude is 590 ft above sea level (not ground level). There is a third much smaller pointer in the FS98 altimeter that shows 10,000 ft increments, with each small division marker indicating 2,000 ft.

At altitudes above 18,000 ft, most planes operate under instrument flight rules (IFR), which means that you must hold an instrument rating on your pilot's license to fly at this altitude or greater. Altitudes at and above 18,000 ft are known as *flight levels*; for example, "FL 370" is pronounced "flight level three seven zero" and represents an altitude of 37,000 ft. All flights in the United States operating at FL 180 to FL 450 are normally flown on *jet routes*, or J routes, and those flights below FL 18 are flown using the Victor airway system. Operation above FL 450 may be conducted on a point-to-point basis using area navigation, or RNAV, waypoints, which are predetermined geographical coordinate locations used for route or progress reporting purposes. These way points are defined relative to a VORTAC radio navigation beacon. With the advent of global positioning system (GPS) navigation and inertial navigation systems (INS), many airlines are finding it more fuel-efficient to fly RNAV routes, which can be more direct, than the jet routes, which must pass over VOR stations. To avoid the possibility of collision, air traffic control approval and radar monitoring are required on these types of routings.

Jet routes are printed in En Route High Altitude Aeronautical Charts and are identified by a *J* (Jet) followed by the airway number (e.g., J 12). The Victor airway routes are printed in En Route Low Altitude Aeronautical Charts, and they consist of airways from 1,200 ft above the surface up to but not including 18,000 ft. Except for Alaska, both Jet routes and Victor airways that use only VOR or VORTAC navigation facilities are drawn with blue lines on the aeronautical charts.

It is important to remember that all aircraft operating at or above FL 180 in the United States—the *transition altitude*—must have their altimeters set to 29.92 in. Hg, or QNE. (QNE means the altimeter is set to 29.92 in. Hg or 1013 millibars regardless of outside air pressure.) Below the transition altitude (i.e., below 18,000 ft in the United States), all aircraft must have the altimeter pressure setting adjusted so that the airport field elevation is correctly shown when the airplane is on the ground, or QNH. (QNH means the altimeter pressure setting is calibrated so that it reads the field elevation at touchdown.) Other countries have different transition altitudes. In Australia, for example, the transition altitude is 10,000 ft, and in the United Kingdom it is, 6000 ft. Over Paris, it is 4,000 ft, over the North Atlantic it is 6,000 ft, and in China it varies for each airfield!

At the transition altitude or greater, all altimeters must be set to QNE regardless of outside air pressure or atmospheric conditions. In this way, all aircraft flying through a given area use the same altimeter reading. Otherwise, an ascending aircraft whose altimeter was set to a nonstandard pressure might collide with an aircraft using standard atmospheric pressure on its altimeter. Both pilots would assume that there was enough altitude separation, as shown on their respective altimeters, when in fact they could be on a collision course at the same altitude. Suppose, for example, that a pilot is taking off from an airport at sea level, where QNH is 28.92 in. Hg. To show the correct runway elevation of 0 ft at takeoff, the altimeter must be adjusted to 28.92 in Hg, which is a nonstandard atmospheric pressure (standard pressure at sea level would be 29.92 in. Hg). Air traffic control tells this pilot to maintain altitude at 17,000 ft, because there is an arriving plane at FL 180; its altimeter is set to 29.92 in. Hg, or QNE. The problem is that the arriving plane's altimeter shows 18,000 ft, but the plane is really at 17,000 ft. The nonstandard pressure difference is giving a false reading of its true altitude.

With the altimeters on both aircraft set to a standard 29.92 in. Hg, a collision due to an altitude misunderstanding cannot occur. In any event, both pilots must realize that even with their altimeters set to QNE, or 29.92 in. Hg, the altimeters may not show the airplane's true altitude above ground. This means that in mountainous terrain when nonstandard atmospheric conditions prevail, a plane may be much lower than is safe to clear a mountain peak. For example, if the temperature at sea level were a nonstandard 0° F (standard is 59°), you would have to climb to an indicated altitude of 32,724 ft to clear Mt. Everest's 29,002 ft peak. Fortunately for Flight Simulator pilots, it is a simple matter to set QNH on the altimeter; simply press **B** to have the altimeter calibrated to the current referenced sea level air pressure. To set QNE on the altimeter, use the **Aircraft/Aircraft Settings/Realism** menu. In the **Altimeter Setting** box, type **29.92**.

Student pilots are often warned to watch out below when flying from high-pressure areas to low-pressure areas or from warm areas to cold areas, because the altimeter will show them to be higher than they really are. The Mt. Everest example demonstrates the problem of flying when the temperature is colder than standard, and the previous example of the arriving airplane at the transition altitude illustrates the problem of flying into a low pressure area. Both rules are summarized in the oft-repeated phrase:

"From high to low, or from warm to cold, watch out below!"

The Vertical Speed Indicator

The vertical speed indicator tells you whether you are descending or ascending in hundreds of feet per minute (ft/min). When the needle moves up (or clockwise) from 0, the airplane is ascending; when the needle moves down from 0, the airplane is descending. On the Cessna, the vertical speed indicator can show vertical speeds between 0 and ±2,000 ft/min. But the scale reads from 0 to ±20, so you must mentally multiply by 100 to arrive at the correct vertical velocity. On the Learjet and 737, the vertical speed indicator shows speeds between 0 and ±6,000 ft/min, but this time you must multiply by 1,000 because the dial indicators are marked from 0 to ±6.

The Gyroscopic Instruments

There are three gyroscopic instruments: the attitude/artificial horizon indicator, the turn indicator, and the heading indicator. All three instruments use a spinning gyroscope that maintains an inertial frame of reference. As the aircraft rotates or moves through space, the gyroscope maintains a stable platform that does not rotate with the aircraft. From the determination of the aircraft's present attitude versus the inertial gyroscope platform, the gyroscopic instruments can measure the aircraft's orientation with regard to the horizon.

The Attitude Indicator or Artificial Horizon Indicator

This instrument shows the aircraft's attitude by showing the pitch and roll of the aircraft in relation to the ground. The brown part of the attitude indicator represents the horizon, and the blue portion represents the sky. The two white horizontal lines in the center of the dial represent the aircraft's wings. Using these reference points, you can determine the plane's distance above or below the horizon for a given pitch angle. Similarly, if you are in a turn, the angle of these white bars to the horizon tells you how much the aircraft is banked. For example, if you bank the airplane right, the colored half of the horizon will rotate to the left. If you lower the nose, the colored half of the horizon will rise above the level of the wings. At the top of the dial, there are markings for bank angles of 0°, 10°, 30°, 60°, and 90°. In the middle of the dial are pitch ladder markings of 5°, 10°, 15°, and 20° that show the upward angle of the nose, and –5°, -10°, -15°, and –20° that show the downward angle of the nose. Unfortunately, because of the small size and poor resolution of this instrument on-screen, these bank and pitch angle markings are hard to read, for example when the Learjet is turning or the 737 is climbing. To remedy this defect, I have created an adventure program, **AutoAlt.ADV**, which is included on the accompanying CD-ROM. This game displays and audibly announces bank and pitch angles at the press of a button.

Note that the artificial horizon does not, at any time, tell you whether you are climbing or descending. It tells you only the airplane's pitch and roll angle with regard to the horizon. For example, your airplane can be in a descending glide with the nose pitched sharply up, as shown on the artificial horizon.

The Heading Indicator (Directional Gyro)

The heading indicator, or directional gyro, shows you the airplane's current compass heading. It needs to be calibrated periodically with the magnetic compass, because it drifts due to gyroscopic precession. To calibrate this device, press **B**. During turns and other maneuvers when there are accelerative forces at work, the heading indicator is the only reliable indicator of the airplane's current heading. The magnetic compass, which also shows direction, is not a reliable indicator of heading except during level flight, because it relies on a mechanism that is sensitive to motion and cannot instantaneously change when the aircraft's heading is altered.

Note that both the heading indicator and the magnetic compass display magnetic headings and not true headings. The magnetic north pole is not located at the geographical north pole. This means that in most areas of the world, if you were to fly due east on your compass, you would not in fact be flying due east but in some other slightly different heading. The same principle applies to all other compass headings. This phenomenon, called magnetic variation, will be further addressed in later chapters.

The Turn and Slip Indicator

The turn and slip indicator tells the pilot whether the plane is in a coordinated turn and whether the turn is a standard two-minute turn. During a turn, if the aircraft's wings are centered on either of the two lower bank markers and if the aircraft is banking at the correct angle, the airplane will make a complete 360° turn in two minutes. If the aircraft is not turning in a coordinated fashion, the aircraft will be skidding or slipping through the air, and the rolling ball in the indicator will roll out of the center marker. FSW95 has a small bug that causes the airplane's wings not to be centered over the bank markers when the airplane banks in a standard turn. This defect has been remedied in FS98.

THE ART OF FLYING

By this time, you must be eager to take off. Were it so simple in the real world, you could take off and get a good feel for flying. You would be getting "As Real as it Gets," as Microsoft proudly trumpets about Flight Simulator. But things are not so simple. Flight Simulator conceals many effects of flying that you experience in the cockpit of a real aircraft. You don't feel the real aerodynamic forces. What's more, you are not being cued by your peripheral vision, and you don't get proper perspective effects. Much information is lost this way, and although you may think you know how to fly, you are missing most of the flight experience that gives you the skills you need to master flying. In short, Flight Simulator may be a great tool for introducing yourself to flying, but it will never replace actual flying because it is a vicarious experience. When we all can afford to install our own full-motion simulators in our garages, we will be at the point where simulators can replace actual flying, but we are not there yet.

Flight Simulator can lead you to a false sense of security, for as Alexander Pope said, "A little learning is a dangerous thing." This chapter attempts to guide you through the elementary principles of flight. In later chapters you will learn how to test each principle so that you come to understand flight. It is not enough to think you know flight; instead, you should prove your knowledge through examples. And this is the beauty of Flight Simulator, because the flight model incorporates all the principles of aerodynamics, from the standard model of the atmosphere to Bernoulli's theorem to the equations of motion. You don't need to be a calculus professor to understand these principles, but if you have a chance to play with them in action, you will, in your own way, be the Flight Simulator wizard on your block.

First, let's look at a few basic terms. In real airplanes, we use the *stick* term to refer to the yoke, or wheel. In state of the art fly-by-wire aircraft, such as the Airbus A-320, the stick is the joystick-like handle installed on the side of the pilot's and copilot's chair. In Flight Simulator, pushing the stick forward lowers the nose by applying down elevator. You can accomplish this by pushing your joystick forward (or by pushing in your Virtual Pilot Pro yoke) or by pressing **keypad 8** (with numlock off in FS98). Pulling the stick back raises the nose by applying up elevator; to do this, pull your joystick back or press **keypad 2**.

NOTE   In FS98, you can access elevator trim from the keyboard only if the numlock key is off. The elevator trim (**keypad 7** and **keypad 1**) is used to relieve pressure on the yoke when you are trying to maintain a stable attitude while flying. If you are using the keyboard, you don't need to use the elevator trim; instead, use the elevators (**keypad 8** and **keypad 2**). But if you are using a joystick, you will need to use elevator trim to stabilize your flight. Otherwise, you must apply constant pressure on the joystick to maintain level flight.

Engineering Units

Most science students learn the metric system of measuring quantities of distance, speed, acceleration, force, temperature, pressure, density, and so on. Despite the prevalence of the universally adopted metric Systèm Internationale (SI), which uses mks, or meter-kilogram-second, units of measurement, aeronautical engineers by convention use English units of measurement. In this book, we will use English units of length, mass, time, temperature, acceleration, speed, pressure, density, and force.

You must be consistent in applying physical units of measurement. You cannot use length units of nautical miles and feet, or speed units of ft/s and knots, in the same context inside an equation and expect to get meaningful results. To be consistent, you must stick with the standard units of measurement, converting any nonstandard units. For example, if the equation uses ft/s units for velocity, you must use ft/s (not knots) for the aircraft's speed. If you see that an equation uses knots as the unit of velocity (which we shall abbreviate in the text as kt), you should use the airplane's speed in knots. Table 1.1 shows the symbolic physical unit notation for both the SI and English systems.

Table 1.1 *Physical Units of Measurement*

	LENGTH	AREA	VOLUME	TIME	VELOCITY	ACCELERATION	MASS	FORCE	PRESSURE	DENSITY	TEMPERATURE
SI unit	M	m^2	m^3	S	m/s	m/s^2	kg (kilogram)	N=kg•m/s^2	Pa (pascal)= 1 N/m^2	kg/m^3	K (kelvin)
English engineering unit	Ft	ft^2	ft^3	S	ft/s	ft/s^2	sl (slug)	lb	lb/ft^2	sl/m^3	R (Rankine)

A point of confusion arises when we talk about mass and weight, which are entirely different quantities. In SI units, mass is measured in kilograms, but in the English system, mass is measured in slugs. When we talk about weight, we refer to the fact that weight = mass × acceleration of gravity. One slug is equivalent to 32.17 lb, or 14.59 kg metric mass. Weight is always measured in Newtons in SI units, whereas in the English system weight is measured in lb. However, the unit lb is used in some cases to refer to mass! If you are confused, you have every right to be. To avoid errors in your calculations, pay attention to the units that are used in the examples that accompany the text:

$$1 \text{ lb} = (\text{mass}) \times (\text{acceleration of gravity}) = (1/32.17 \text{ slug}) \times (32.17 \text{ ft/s}^2)$$

If the computed result of a calculation is in ft/s, you can convert from ft/s to knots by using this equation:

$$\text{Speed in knots} = \left(V_{velocity} \, \frac{ft}{s} \right) \left(\frac{kt}{1.6878 \, \frac{ft}{s}} \right) \qquad (1.1)$$

$$\text{Speed in } ft/s = \left(V_{velocity} \, kt \right) \left(\frac{1.6878 \, \frac{ft}{s}}{kt} \right)$$

Trigonometry

Some of the equations in this book assume that you understand basic trigonometry and angular measurements. If you are unclear on the concepts, it might prove helpful to consult a trigonometry textbook. At any rate, you can perform any of the calculated examples in this book without understanding trigonometry by plugging in values as you see them on a scientific calculator. Remember that angles can be measured in radians or in degree form, but you need to set your calculator to input the correct value. For example, if your calculator is in radian mode and you try to find the value of sin 50°, you will get a wrong result, because the calculator is expecting an angle in radian form. Similarly, if you input a radian angle and your calculator is in degree mode, you will get a wrong result.

Use this formula for conversion:.

$$\theta_{Degrees} = \theta_{Radians} \left(\frac{180°}{\pi} \right) \qquad (1.2)$$

To convert from degrees to radians:

$$\theta_{Radians} = \theta_{Degrees} \left(\frac{\pi}{180°} \right)$$

where

$$\pi = 3.14159265$$

Example 1.1
What is 55°in radian form, and what is 5π/6 radians in degree form?

To convert 55° to radians: (1.3)

$$\theta_{\text{Radians}} = 55° \left(\frac{\pi}{180°} \right) = 0.9599 \text{ radians}$$

To convert $5\pi/6$ to Degrees

$$\theta_{\text{Degrees}} = \frac{5\pi}{6} \left(\frac{180°}{\pi} \right) = 150°$$

Solution

When you see the terms $\cos^{-1}$, $\sin^{-1}$, or $\tan^{-1}$, these are the inverse cosine, inverse sine, and inverse tangent functions. Therefore, on your calculator you must use the arccos (acos), arcsin (asin), or arctan (atan) function. Your result will be in degrees or radians depending on whether you have set the calculator to degree or radian mode.

THE BASIC MANEUVERS OF FLIGHT

There are only four maneuvers that a pilot can perform in an airplane:

- The climb
- Straight and level flight
- The turn
- The glide (or descent)

The takeoff is a part of the climb maneuver, and the landing is a part of the glide. Although similar principles apply to both sets of maneuvers, in this book we shall discuss the landing and takeoff separately.

The Takeoff

Taking off in a Cessna doesn't present much of a challenge. It is so simple that even if you didn't touch the controls except to advance the throttle to maximum, the aircraft would lift off the runway of its own accord. This isn't necessarily the way you would want to do it in a real Cessna, so let's review what needs to be done by the book. Before beginning takeoff preparations, start Flight Simulator so that you have the Cessna ready to roll down the runway at Chicago's Meigs Field.

Check out the *MicroWINGS* magazine article "Short Field Takeoffs and Landings in the Cessna" on the book's CD-ROM. To view the magazine, you'll need to install Acrobat Reader 3.0 or higher (also available on the CD-ROM).

Proper takeoff procedures require that you perform a pretakeoff checklist as well as a takeoff checklist. Because Flight Simulator makes some compromises with realism to simplify the experience for non-pilots, some of the controls don't work as they do on real airplanes. For maximum realism in accomplishing the checklists, first go to the Aircraft Settings Realism dialog box using the **Aircraft/Aircraft Settings/Realism** menu, and under **Prop engines** switch on **Magnetos** and **Mixture Control**, and in the **Prop Advance List box**, select **Manual**.

Perform these steps for the pretakeoff checklist for the Cessna:

1. Fully retract the flaps (press **F6** until the flaps are at the 0° setting).
2. Engage parking brakes (press **Ctrl+period** key).
3. Check the operation of the ailerons, rudder, elevator, and elevator trim. When you move the controls, the control indicator on the instrument panel should move in concert with each motion you make.
4. Enrich the mixture by sliding the mixture control (red knob) all the way up. Note that for the mixture control to work in FS98, you must have first turned on mixture control in the Aircraft Setting Realism dialog box.
5. Check fuel quantity.
6. If the engine hasn't been started, click the **Start** control on the magneto. The engines should start.
7. Perform a magneto check. Set the engine to 1700 RPM (revolutions per minute) with the parking brake engaged. Move the ignition switch to the R position (right magneto) and note the RPM. It should not drop more than 175 RPM. Move the switch to the L position and again note the RPM. The RPM drop on both magnetos should not exceed 175 RPM or show a differential greater than 50 RPM between magnetos. If it does, something is wrong with the ignition system, and if you were in a real airplane you would have a mechanic check it out.
8. Make sure the carburetor heat is off (press **H** to toggle on or off).
9. Cycle the propeller blade angle from high to low and from low to high to ensure correct operation. Increase the propeller pitch from a high angle (when the blue control knob is all the way out) to a low blade angle (slide the blue propeller control all the way in). A low pitch propeller angle means higher RPM and this is what you want for takeoff. Higher pitch angles (when the control is out) are better for cruising at altitude, where you want the propeller to "bite" more thinner air per rotation.

10. Decrease throttle to 800 RPM.
11. Check that oil pressure is not low and that temperature is not too hot.
12. Turn on the strobe lights by pressing the **O** key.
13. Tune in the COM radio to the local automatic terminal information service (ATIS) frequency for the latest weather conditions. You'll want to know the wind direction, current pressure, and temperature.
14. Calibrate the directional gyro (press **D**). This will align the gyro with the magnetic compass.
15. Calibrate the altimeter to show the correct airport elevation (press **B**).
16. Check to see that the autopilot is off.
17. Release parking brakes (press the **period** key).

Now that you have prepared the airplane, it is time to take off. Follow these procedures for the normal takeoff checklist in the Cessna:

1. Wing flaps to 0° or 20°.
2. Carburetor heat: cold.
3. Power: Full throttle and 2,400 RPM. The airplane will begin to accelerate down the runway.
4. Mixture: Full rich (mixture may be leaned above 3,000 ft).
5. Elevator control: Lift nose wheel at 50 knots IAS by pulling back gently on the stick. You should raise the nose about 10° above the horizon, as shown on the artificial horizon.
6. Climb speed: 70 knots IAS (flaps 20°)
                          80 knots IAS (flaps up)
7. Brakes: Apply momentarily when airborne to stop them from rotating before retracting.
8. Landing gear: Retract (press **G**).
9. Wing flaps: Retract.

The normal takeoff ground roll distance is 925 ft for the Cessna when it is at 1,000 ft elevation and the temperature is 20° C (68° F). But to clear a 50 ft obstacle at the end of the runway, the Cessna needs 1,785 ft. You should always plan a takeoff to clear 50 ft above ground level before crossing the runway's end.

    At sea level, a fully loaded Learjet normally requires 5,150 ft for the takeoff when the temperature is 70° F (with 20° flaps). For the same conditions, the 737-400 requires 6,000 ft (with 15° flaps). On both the 737 and the Learjet, you should perform the takeoff roll by pitching the aircraft's nose up by 10°.

Multiengine Aircraft Takeoffs

Multiengine airplanes present a different set of problems. With a dual-engine, three-engine, or even four-engine aircraft, there is always a small possibility that an engine will fail on takeoff. As a pilot, you must always be prepared for this contingency, including the possibility that it will occur at the worst possible moment: just as you are about to rotate the nose up for takeoff. Not only do you lose thrust, but you also must contend with asymmetric thrust from the remaining engine, which causes the airplane to veer left or right in the direction of the failed engine. If there is a crosswind, the yawing problem is compounded. The airplane will want to weathervane nose first into the wind, and the rudder will have to compensate for the yawing thrust of the engine as well as the yawing force of the crosswind.

Pilots must also think about the amount of remaining runway length. The danger of an engine failure on takeoff from a short runway, or one that meets the legal minimum for the type of aircraft being flown, is that the plane may have already passed the *accelerate stop distance*: the total distance required to accelerate a multiengine aircraft to V_1 and, assuming engine failure at that instant, bring the airplane to a safe stop on the remaining runway. The *accelerate go* distance is the total distance required to accelerate the airplane to V_1 and, assuming failure of an engine at that instant, continue takeoff on the remaining engine to a height of 50 ft. Accelerate go distance is always greater than accelerate stop distance. Legally, a pilot cannot take off from a runway if the accelerate go distance is more than the runway length, and this distance will differ according to aircraft type, temperature, and altitude. At higher temperatures or higher elevations, the accelerate go distance will always be greater than at lower temperatures or lower elevations. Thus, at higher elevations or higher temperatures, an airplane must take off from a longer runway or must take off with a lighter payload. Note that approximately 60% the accelerate stop distance is actually used up during the acceleration phase of the takeoff, with only 40% remaining for stopping the aircraft if engine failure occurs at V_1.

An engine failure at takeoff is a scary moment that every pilot dreads. However, if you understand the procedures that have been developed to protect you and your airplane, you will discover that there is no possibility of crashing—as long as you follow the rules.

All multiengine airplanes have the following important speeds:

- V_1 is the takeoff decision speed. After the airplane has passed V_1, the pilot is committed to take off regardless of engine failure. Below V_1, if the engine fails, the pilot must abort the takeoff. On a runway that is approved for the aircraft, there should be enough room to safely stop the airplane if the takeoff is aborted below this speed. For the maximum weight 737-400, V_1 is 150 knots. For the Learjet, V_1 is 136 knots.

- V_R is the rotation speed at which you raise the nose to $10°$ to lift off the runway. For the 737, V_R is 151 knots; for the MTOW (maximum takeoff weight) Learjet, V_R is 137 knots with $20°$ flaps, or 143 knots with $8°$ flaps.

- V_2 is the takeoff safety speed; it is the actual speed of the aircraft at 35 ft above the runway surface as demonstrated in flight during single-engine takeoff. This speed is the minimum safe flying speed with only one engine operative, and, at this speed or higher, the airplane should be able to maintain an FAA-required climb gradient in the climbout flight path. V_2 must not be less than 1.1 times V_{MC} (see next item), nor less than 1.2 times the stalling speed in the takeoff configuration, nor less than V_R. For the MTOW Learjet, V_2 is 139 knots with $20°$ flaps; with $8°$ flaps, V_2 is 146 knots. For the MTOW 737-400, V_2 is 160 knots. V_2 is normally maintained until 400 to 600 ft above ground level; then the airspeed is allowed to increases to engine-inoperative best rate of climb speed up to about 1500 ft above ground level. Once the plane is above that altitude, airspeed can be increased to normal climb speed and the after-takeoff checklist performed.

- V_{MC} is the minimum control speed with the critical engine inoperative. With one engine out, at a speed lower than this, you will lose control of the airplane. The remaining engine is considered to be operating at takeoff thrust. The airplane should never leave the ground at V_{MC} or less.

- V_{REF} is the landing reference speed, which is usually $1.3 \times V_{S0}$ (the stall speed in the landing configuration). V_{REF} must be calculated for every landing, because the stall speed V_{S0} increases with aircraft weight. For example, a Boeing 737 that weighs 88,000 lb would have a V_{REF} of 119 knots with $30°$ flaps, whereas a 122,000 lb 737 would have a V_{REF} of 140 knots (also with $30°$ flaps). V_{REF} on a 14,500 lb Learjet in the landing configuration is 125 knots.

If after starting the takeoff an engine fails before V_1, abort the takeoff and apply maximum braking (with spoilers and reverse thrust to follow). For there to be enough room to land, you must take off from an approved runway for the type of aircraft. For example, it would be ludicrous to take off in the Learjet or the 737 from Meigs Field with its 3,947 ft runway, because the accelerate go distance at this elevation with a standard temperature of $59°$ is 5,020 ft for the 18,000 lb Learjet (with $20°$ flaps), and 6,000 ft for the 138,000 lb 737-400 (with $15°$ flaps).

If an engine fails after V_1, you are committed to the takeoff and must accelerate to at least V_2 on the remaining engine (or remaining engines on a three-engine or four-engine aircraft such as the MD-11 or 747). Because the airplane will yaw toward the failed engine, you will need to apply rudder pressure to maintain directional control and use the ailerons to maintain a wings-level attitude. If the left engine has failed, for example, the airplane will yaw to the left, and you must apply *right* rudder to compensate. After takeoff, you will have to add *right* aileron to keep the wings level. Needless to say, Auto-coordination must be off.

Immediately after takeoff with an engine failure, check to see whether the airplane has a positive rate of climb as shown on the vertical speed indicator or the cockpit view outside; then raise the landing gear. During the climb with the engine out, maintain V_2 until the airplane is at least 400 ft above the ground. (Some airlines want their pilots to climb to 600 ft depending on the type of aircraft being flown.) At 400 ft above ground level (AGL), the pilot must accelerate to $V_2 + 10$ knots and then continue to accelerate to $V_2 + 30$ knots, being sure to retract the flaps according to the flap retraction schedule (which varies with airspeed for each aircraft). After reaching 1,500 ft AGL, the airplane is "cleaned up." This means that the airplane flaps, leading-edge devices, slats, and other lift-enhancing devices are retracted, and the pilots conduct the after-takeoff and climb checklist as well as the engine failure checklist. Once this checklist has been completed, the airplane can continue accelerating to as much as 250 knots IAS below 10,000 ft and can level off to return to the airport or continue the climb. Don't make the mistake of banking into a steep turn in a frantic effort to return to the airport. This would undoubtedly end in disaster, as we shall see later in this chapter. Figure 1.7 and Figure 1.8 illustrate the correct procedures for handling normal takeoff and engine-out takeoff in a multiengine aircraft.

A competent multiengine-rated pilot knows that the airplane must be flown with precision during takeoff; otherwise, disaster may follow. Pilots must rigidly follow the takeoff speed guidelines for V_1, V_R, V_2, and V_{MC} for the type of aircraft being flown. For example, at liftoff the airplane must climb at V_2 and *no faster*, because only at this airspeed will the pilot be able to obtain maximum performance from the airplane. Improperly trained pilots may try to accelerate to a higher speed, thinking that they will climb faster in the event of an engine failure. Also, such pilots might assume that the airplane should accelerate to the maximum cruise speed during the takeoff roll on the ground. These pilots might mistakenly assume that the extra speed will translate into additional altitude and excess energy for the airplane in the event of an engine emergency. Both assumptions are wrong for the following reasons:

- When the airplane is climbing faster than V_2 after takeoff, drag increases as the square of speed. For any increase in speed over and above V_2, the airplane will have greater drag and less climb performance in the event of engine failure. For example, at 123 knots the drag is approximately 1.5 times greater than the drag at 100 knots. At 141 knots, the drag is doubled from 100 knots, and at 200 knots it is four times as great than at 100 knots. With much of the remaining engine's power going to correcting the asymmetric yawing tendency, there isn't enough excess power to overcome the increased drag when the airspeed is much higher than V_2.

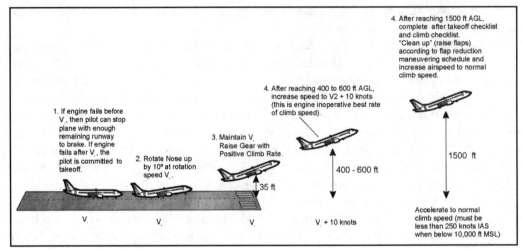

Figure 1.7 *The Normal takeoff for multiengine aircraft.*

- During a high-speed takeoff roll, by the time the pilot is able to react to the surprise of a sudden engine failure, the excess speed has dissipated and the airplane is barely off the ground. From this low altitude, the pilot would still have to climb with an engine inoperative to a safe height to clear obstacles at the end of the runway. Excess speed cannot be converted readily to altitude, nor can it be used to try to reach a far-away landing strip safely.

Altitude is always more essential to safety than is excess airspeed, because extra height can always be traded for velocity or gliding distance when needed. Also, an airplane suffering from an engine failure will find it much easier to fly in level flight than to climb. This is why it is important to gain some altitude early after the takeoff, not only to clear ground obstacles but also so that you can fly level with the engine out.

Before landing the airplane after an engine has failed at takeoff, an important question to ask yourself is, "Do I need to dump fuel to lighten the aircraft for landing?" Remember that the maximum landing weight is always less than the maximum takeoff weight. So if you have loaded the airplane to its MTOW, you must proceed to an authorized fuel dumping area and shed some weight before landing.

Until recently, the FAA has forbidden air carriers to operate single-engine aircraft to carry fare-paying passengers. The reasoning was that twin-engine aircraft offered a degree of safety that single-engine aircraft did not in the event of engine malfunction. With the advent of highly reliable turbine engines and new designs that allow airplanes to take off at lower speeds, manufacturers and airline companies have been petitioning for a change in the rules to allow new single-engine aircraft to carry commercial airline

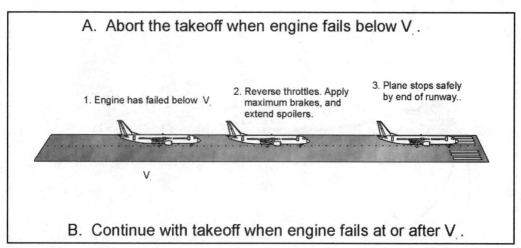

A. Abort the takeoff when engine fails below V.

1. Engine has failed below V.

2. Reverse throttles. Apply maximum brakes, and extend spoilers.

3. Plane stops safely by end of runway..

V.

B. Continue with takeoff when engine fails at or after V.

Figure 1.8 Procedures when one engine has failed on the airplane.

passengers. One disadvantage of twins is that they must take off and land at higher speeds; if one engine quits suddenly, the extra speed is needed to provide rudder authority to overcome asymmetric thrust. If an engine quits on the single-engine plane, directional control is not a question, so takeoff and approach speeds can approach the much slower stalling speed. Also, twins burn more fuel than the single-engine plane, and the added drag of two-engine nacelles versus the single's aerodynamic mounting of the engine in the nose makes for a convincing economic argument in favor of singles. The jury is still out on this issue. The FAA has misgivings about trusting many lives to a single-engine aircraft.

Coping with Engine Failure on a Multiengine Aircraft

The correct way to deal with the loss of an engine is to bank your wings *down* 5° onto the good engine side, which is also to say that you must bank the wings *up* by 5° on the side of the inoperable engine. You do this by applying aileron *into* the operating engine side. Thus, if your left engine has failed but your right engine is still working, you apply *right* aileron to bank the wings *down* 5° on the right side. You will also need to apply enough *right* rudder to keep the airplane from yawing left. The amount of aileron and rudder pressure needed will vary according to the degree of yawing (see Figures 1.9 and 1.10).

If you are unsure about how to handle an engine failure, it is helpful to have the autopilot take over so that you can watch how to do it. Here's how to do this when flying a twin-engine jet such as the Learjet:

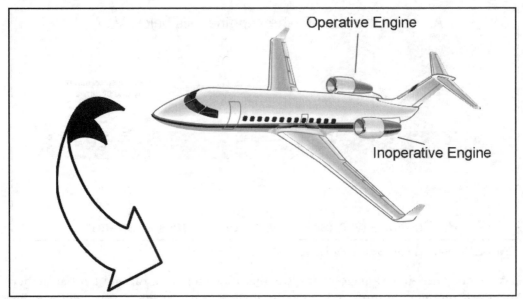

Figure 1.9 *When one engine fails, unbalanced engine thrust on the remaining engine causes a torque force that yaws the aircraft in the direction of the inoperative engine.*

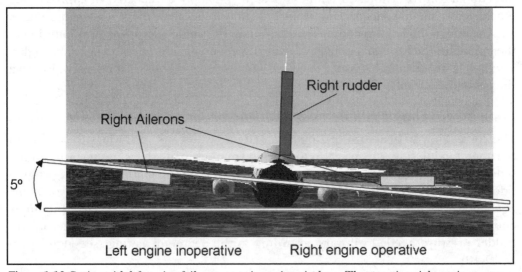

Figure 1.10 *Coping with left engine failure on a twin-engine airplane. The operating right engine causes the airplane to veer left. To stabilize the plane, bank the right wing down on the side of the operable engine side using the ailerons, and keep the airplane flying straight using the right rudder. Auto-coordination must be off.*

1. From the **Aircraft/Select Aircraft** menu command, select the **Learjet** and click **OK**.
2. After taking off, turn on the autopilot (press **Z**), or click the autopilot master switch on the instrument panel. The autopilot light should now be lit green.
3. Click the Autopilot **HDG** control on the instrument panel. The **HDG** heading lamp should be lit green, and the aircraft may bank as the autopilot turns it towards a new heading. You can change the heading to any compass direction you like by clicking to the right or left of the HDG readout to increase or decrease the number shown. Alternatively, you can enter the heading from the Autopilot dialog box. To do this, select the **Aircraft/Autopilot** menu, and in the Autopilot dialog box, type in the heading into the **Deg. mag** numeric entry box.
4. After the airplane is on the proper heading, it should be flying straight; you may want to level the airplane so that it does not climb or descend by using the Altitude Hold. Click a desired altitude into the ALT readout, then click the **ALT** control to engage the Autopilot Altitude Hold.
5. panel. To bring this panel up onscreen, press **Shift 2**.
6. To simulate an engine failure, from the keyboard press **E1** for the left engine or **E2** for the right engine followed by reducing the throttle (press **keypad 3**). With the mouse, just drag one throttle lever down on the secondary instrument panel.
7. To compensate for the failed engine, the autopilot will now bank the wing slightly higher on the side with the engine out. Note too, that the control position indicators will show that the ailerons have moved toward the direction of the still operating engine, while the rudder will move slightly in the opposite direction towards the failed engine.

Because the display isn't sharp enough to show a crisp display of a real artificial horizon, it is difficult to see the exact bank angle. To solve this problem, try using my adventure **AutoAlt.ADV** which allows you to see the exact bank angle displayed at the top of the screen. Once you have installed **AutoAlt.ADV** from the book's CD into the Flight Simulator \ADV directory, you can run it via the **Flights/Adventures** menu. Just choose the **Autopilot Attitude and Heading Control** adventure, and then once the program has loaded, you can activate the bank display by pressing **Ctrl B**. The bank angle will be displayed at the top and if you have installed the AAFWAV.ZIP sound files into the ADV\WAV directory, a voice will annunciate the exact angle.

 To practice an engine failure, simply reduce the throttle on one engine to idle. Make sure Auto-coordination is off.

T I P

Contrary to what you might expect, the loss of a single engine on a two-engine aircraft does not result in the airplane operating half as well. In any twin-engine aircraft, the loss of an engine results in an 80 percent reduction in the airplane's performance! Why this is so is not apparent. It has to do with the increased drag that the operable engine must contend with as well as the asymmetrical yawing forces that occur with thrust being applied on only one side of the airplane. For example, the Learjet's maximum climb with both engines operating is 4,340 ft/min. With only one engine functioning, the rate of climb plummets to 1,290 ft/min, a performance loss of more than 70 percent!

Crosswind Takeoffs

On occasion, it may be necessary to take off with a crosswind. Although it is always preferable to take off with a headwind (but not a tailwind!), you often have no other choice. Crosswinds are winds that cross the runway at a nearly-perpendicular angle, and they cause your airplane to weathercock nose first in their direction. For example, if a wind is blowing from due east to due west at Meigs Field (i.e., a wind direction of 90°), the Cessna will want to yaw rightward into the wind like a weather vane. This yawing tendency must be counteracted by the judicious and independent use of rudders and ailerons. Note: you cannot take off with a crosswind with Auto-coordination on. Because Auto-coordination ties your ailerons and rudder together, you cannot move one without the other. Furthermore, you can't move the ailerons and rudder in different directions, something that is necessary when taking off with a crosswind.

You should not take off with a crosswind in excess of 15 knots.

The correct technique to deal with a crosswind takeoff is to bank the aircraft into the approaching wind while at the same time using the rudders to prevent the aircraft from yawing left or right.

Probably the best way to learn how to cope with a crosswind is to follow Example 1.2 for a crosswind approaching from the aircraft's right side.

EXAMPLE **1.2**

Follow these steps:

1. Turn off Auto-coordination under **Aircraft/Aircraft Settings/Realism**.
2. Set up a crosswind at Meigs that will blow from east to west with a speed of 15 knots (i.e., blowing from the airplane's right side). To create this wind, open the **World/Weather** dialog box. (If you don't see the advanced weather dialog box, you'll first need to go to **Options/Preferences/General** and turn on **Use Advanced Weather Dialog**.) Then click the **Wind** tab. If no surface wind layer

appears in the dialog box, add one by clicking the **Add Layer** button. If a surface layer already appears, select it. Highlight the surface layer and then type **15** for the speed in knots and **90** for the wind direction (magnetic compass direction in degrees).

N O T E Wind direction blows *from* a particular compass direction; it does not blow toward a compass direction. If a wind direction is stated to be 90 at 10 in an ATIS (automatic terminal information service) radio report, it means the wind is blowing *from* 90° due east *toward* 270° due west at 10 knots. Also, surface winds in Flight Simulator are measured with regard to the magnetic compass heading, whereas winds aloft are measured with regard to true north.

3. Before starting the takeoff, apply **FULL** ailerons into the direction of the wind. Because you are facing due north, or 0°, and the wind is blowing from your right, you apply **FULL** right ailerons. Notice that with Auto-coordination turned off, the aileron control now moves to the right independently of the rudder control. You should keep the ailerons at their maximum deflection until the airplane's speed picks up to the point where the ailerons start to affect its direction. At that point, reverse them in the left direction as much as necessary to maintain a straight takeoff.

4. Advance the throttle. As the airplane accelerates down the runway, keep it centered by applying left rudder (you always turn the rudder *away from* the wind). Your airplane acts like a gigantic weathervane that wants to weathercock nose first into the wind; to counteract this tendency, apply opposite rudder.

5. Continue steering the airplane with the rudders only (left **keypad 0** and right **keypad Enter**).

6. At 55 knots, lift off the runway and immediately start applying ailerons opposite the wind direction (i.e., left aileron in this instance) so that the wings remain level. As both main wheels leave the runway and ground friction no longer resists drifting, the airplane will want to weathercock into the wind (i.e., yaw nose right). You can correct this tendency with proper application of the rudder and ailerons. Because the airplane is now moving with the wind, it will also be carried sideways to the left of the runway by the crosswind. If necessary, crab the aircraft (yaw the aircraft slightly right) into the wind.

Just as your wheels leave the ground, your plane may soar awkwardly. However, you should be able to stabilize the airplane into a level climb. Figure 1.11 illustrates the steps to follow for a crosswind takeoff.

The crosswind landing uses similar techniques, as described later in this chapter.

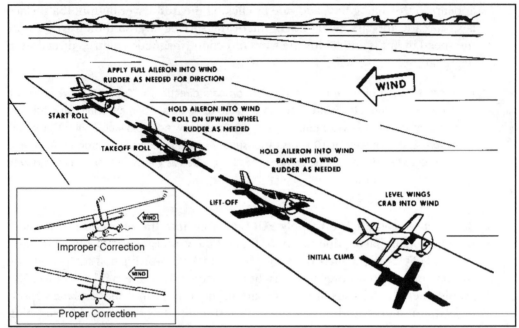

Figure 1.11 Crosswind takeoff. Apply rudders away from wind direction and apply ailerons into the wind direction. Just before liftoff, center the controls.

The Climb

After takeoff, if you have done everything correctly, the Cessna will be climbing at about 1,000 ft/min. Each airplane has its own optimum climb rate; for example, the Learjet can climb at up to 4,340 ft/min on two engines or 1,290 ft/min on a single engine. The 737 likes to climb at about 1,800 ft/min with the autopilot engaged, as does the Learjet. At no point below 10,000 ft should you fly faster than 250 knots IAS, however, because of the worry of bird strikes on the windshield. Also, FAA regulations require compliance with this rule for safe operations.

The normal climb gradient range for most aircraft is 3° to 5° (don't confuse this angle with nose pitch).

Most likely, if you are having trouble maintaining a 1,000 ft/min climb in the Cessna (as shown on your vertical speed indicator), it is because your nose is pitched too high (i.e., your angle of attack is too great). Paradoxically, if you want to increase your rate of climb, you need to pitch the nose down, which will decrease your angle of attack but increase your airspeed. For the Cessna, the maximum rate of climb speed occurs at 88 knots at sea level to 75 knots at 10,000 ft. The vertical airspeed during the maximum rate of climb ranges from 1,140 ft/min at sea level to 415 ft/min at 10,000 ft.

How do you determine how much to pitch your nose up or down as shown on the artificial horizon during the climb? The best predictor is your airspeed indicator. If your nose is too high, the airspeed indicator will show too slow a speed; if the nose is too low, the airspeed indicator will show too fast a speed. If your airspeed is right on the mark, the airplane's nose will be pitched at the proper angle. To make it easier, use the following rules for the nose pitch during the climb:

- The 737-400 can be pitched up 9°, or as much as 18° during the climb.
- The Learjet should be pitched up 7° to as much as 15°.
- The Cessna can be pitched up about 5° to as much as 10°.

When climbing with the 737 and Learjet below 10,000 ft, it is easy to exceed the 250 knot speed limit, so you will have to throttle back the engines to maintain the climb. During a climb with the 737, you normally use 91% N_1 as shown on the fan speed engine indicator. With the Learjet, reduce throttle until the fuel flow is about 1,000 lb/hr and the airspeed indicator is at 250 knots IAS below 10,000 ft, and 0.7 Mach IAS above 10,000 ft.

Normal enroute climbs in the Cessna are performed at 90 to 100 knots, with flaps up, 23 in. HG or full throttle (whichever is less), and 2,400 RPM. The vertical airspeed during a normal climb ranges from 680 ft/min at sea level to 330 ft/min at 10,000 ft. But the best angle of climb (the steepest angle), which is not the same as the maximum climb rate or the normal climb, occurs at 65 knots IAS. During a climb in the Cessna, the mixture should be full rich at altitudes up to 3,000 ft. Above 3,000 ft, the mixture may be leaned as required for smooth engine operation.

Here is the normal enroute climb checklist for the Cessna:

1. Airspeed: 90 to 100 knots IAS.
2. Vertical Airspeed: 680 ft/min at sea level to 330 ft/min at 10,000 ft.
3. Power: 23 in. Hg or full throttle (whichever is less) and 2,400 RPM.
4. Fuel selector valve: Both.
5. Mixture: Full rich (mixture may be leaned above 3,000 ft.).

Here is the maximum performance climb checklist for the Cessna:

1. Airspeed: 88 knots IAS at sea level to 75 knots IAS at 10,000 ft.
2. Vertical Airspeed: 1,140 ft/min at sea level to 415 ft/min at 10,000 ft.
3. Power: Full throttle and 2,400 RPM.
4. Fuel selector valve: Both.
5. Mixture: Full rich (mixture may be leaned above 3,000 ft).

Straight and Level Flight

To level off from the climb and enter into the cruise phase, you need to reduce the throttle. Reducing the throttle will lower the nose; but to trim the airplane, you may use the elevator trim to make any last-minute changes to nose pitch (**keypad 7** and **keypad 1**). A good rule of thumb for determining when to start leveling off is to subtract 50 ft from the desired altitude for each 500 ft/min rate of climb. For example, if you are climbing at 1,000 ft/min and you want to level off at 5,000 ft, begin to level off at 4,900 ft.

Normal cruising is performed at 55% and 75% of the Cessna's rated engine power. The Learjet and 737, being turbine-powered aircraft, have different power settings, which are discussed in later chapters. Special tables found in Chapter tabulate various cruise performance settings for different altitudes and airspeeds. The relationship between power, airspeed, weight, temperature, and altitude is complicated; the easiest way to determine the correct throttle settings is to consult the cruise performance charts for each airplane that are published in its AOM (aircraft operations manual). If you want to cruise the 3,100 lb Cessna at 4,000 ft with 74% power, for example, you would consult the charts and find that for an RPM (engine rotations per minute) of 2,200, you could do so at 148 knots TAS with 23 in. Hg of manifold pressure. Manifold pressure measures the pressure inside a piston engine's induction system and is expressed in inches of mercury. A higher manifold pressure means that the engine is developing more power. As a piston-engine airplane climbs to higher elevations, performance falls off and manifold pressure decreases because of the thinner air.

Normal cruise speed for the Cessna at an altitude of 8,000 ft at 2,100 RPM is 137 knots TAS with 19 in. Hg manifold pressure. Normal cruise speed for the Learjet at 39,000 ft is 0.77 indicated Mach (fuel flow is 571 lb/hr per engine), whereas normal cruise speed for the 737 at 37,000 ft is 0.744 indicated Mach (fuel flow is 2740 lb/hr per engine). Usually, at this altitude with a 127,000 lb 737, the throttle is set to 90% to 92% N_1. Be sure to display indicated airspeed when you attempt to cruise the airplane at these Mach numbers.

NOTE The Learjet's fuel flow meter in FSW95 was misleading, in that it did not show a needle for the second engine. Therefore, fuel flow should be double what you see on the FSW95 Learjet fuel flow dial. This problem was fixed in FS98 and the left and right fuel flow displays now accurately show fuel flow for each engine separately.

To cruise the 737 or Learjet, simply level the plane as shown by the vertical speed indicator and then advance or retard the throttle until you see the airspeed reach the desired Mach number. The fuel flow should be close to what the performance charts predict. Note that outside wind does not have any effect at all on your cruise speed as shown on your airspeed indicator, although temperature does.

Here is the cruise checklist for the Cessna:

1. Power: 15 to 23 in. Hg, 2,100–2,400 RPM (no more than 75% power). Use cruise performance charts to set desired power and airspeed.
2. Elevator and rudder trim: Adjust as needed.
3. Mixture: Lean to hottest EGT temperature; then enrich by 50° (pull out the blue knob down to lean, push in to enrich).
4. Vertical speed indicator: 0 ft/min.

The artificial horizon/attitude indicator does not tell you whether the plane is flying straight and level. All it tells you is whether the nose is pitched higher or lower than the horizon. The airplane may need a small positive angle of attack, in which case the nose should be pitched up slightly to maintain level cruise. Note that the angle of attack is not the same as the aircraft's nose pitch, as will be discussed in Chapter 2. During level flight both the 737-400 and the Learjet, for example, fly with their noses pitched up about 2° from the horizontal (the Learjet sometimes flies with 1°). The Cessna, on the other hand, flies level with its nose at a 0° pitch angle. (Try this with the autopilot flying the airplane in level flight and the **Autopilot Attitude and Heading Control** adventure to see the exact pitch angle displayed on-screen.)

It is often useful to visually observe where the aircraft's nose is pointing with regard to the horizon, so Flight Simulator provides the useful Axis Indicator which you can display on screen as a V marker. Select the **View/View Options** menu. In the dialog box that opens, choose **Large V** or **Small V** in the **Axis Indicator** list box. You also have the option of loading the **Autopilot Attitude and Heading Control** adventure, which lets you display your airplane's pitch angle on screen when you press **Ctrl+P**.

The Turn

One of the biggest fallacies that many Flight Simulator pilots assume is that the rudder turns the airplane. Nothing could be farther from the truth. The rudder can never produce a turn by itself; rather, it yaws the aircraft, and that is all. *Yaw*, in this sense, means to swing the nose from left to right while the airplane's flight path continues unchanged. What happens when you turn the rudder? At first, when you apply rudder by itself without ailerons, the airplane's nose turns, as you might hope it would. But this is not really a turn; instead, the airplane is skidding sideways through the air. If you continue to hold the rudder in the same position, the airplane will begin to bank because one wing, which is ahead of the other wing, is generating more lift. The airplane may be turning at this point, but it is not a controlled turn. Soon, with continued application of the rudder, the airplane will nosedive.

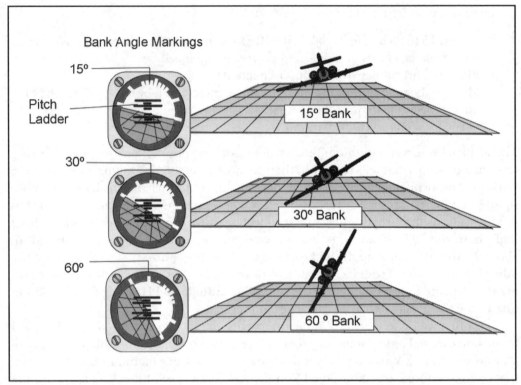

Figure 1.12 *Attitude/artificial horizon instrument references during turns.*

If the rudders don't turn the airplane, then do the ailerons turn the airplane? No, the ailerons only roll the airplane along its longitudinal axis, and by themselves they do not produce turns. When you apply ailerons, one wing produces more lift than the other wing. One wing rises while the other is lowered because of reduced lift on its side. As a consequence, the lift force, which always acts almost perpendicular to the wing, is now banked sideways, producing a sideways force on the airplane. (Actually, the lift force acts perpendicular to the relative wind along the aircraft's flight path. This means that lift can be offset from a perpendicular line with the wing. For the sake of this argument, however, just assume that lift is acting perpendicular to the wings.) With this force, the airplane will want to slip sideways in the direction of the bank; as it does so, the tail acts as a weather vane and wants to weathercock into the direction of the sideways lift force. If the pilot applies just a smidgen of rudder to help the tail weathercock, the airplane will turn.

The airplane turns because a sideways force is imposed on the wings as a result of its wing bank, but the airplane turns only when the tail yaws the airplane's nose into the direction of this force.

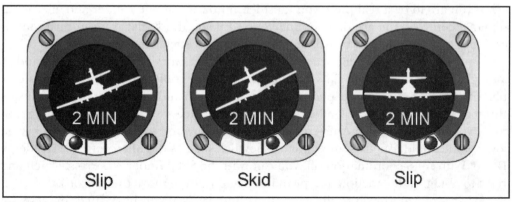

Figure 1.13 *Indications of a slip and skid*

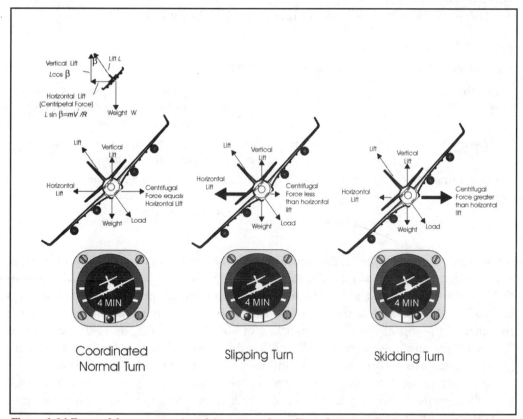

Figure 1.14 *External forces on an aircraft in a normal coordinated turn, a slipping turn, and a skidding turn.*

If you are to be a real pilot, you must learn how to use the rudder and ailerons as separate controls. You are only fooling yourself if you think that you can turn the aircraft by tapping on the keyboard, or swinging your joystick left and right.

Auto-coordinated mode, which takes all the guesswork out of using the rudders and ailerons, has its good points and bad points. One good point is that it allows people with no previous flying experience to jump right in and fly. The drawback of using this mode, however, is that you learn bad habits. If you are serious about learning how to fly, you must fly without Auto-coordination enabled, and to do this you need a good joystick with rudder pedals, or a four-axis joystick such as the Microsoft SideWinder 3-D Pro. With Auto-coordination off, you can twist the SideWinder 3-D Pro stick left and right to obtain rudder action and pivot it left and right to move the ailerons.

What forces are involved during a turn? Both vertical and horizontal forces are at work, as you will see later.

There are three classifications of turns, as shown in Table 1.2.

Table 1.2 *Three Kinds of Turns*

ANGLE OF TURN	CLASS	DESCRIPTION
Less than 20°	Shallow	After initiating the turn, the plane's wings will level themselves unless additional pressure is sustained on the ailerons.
Between 20° and 45°	Medium	The plane will continue to turn with no additional application of ailerons.
Greater than 45°	Steep	The plane will continue its bank, getting steeper unless countered by using the ailerons to reverse the bank.

An airplane likes to stay in a medium turn without any further application of aileron. You can try this in the Cessna: while the airplane is flying at 100 knots, bank the aircraft to 17° using ailerons and rudder. Once the aircraft is turning, quickly center the ailerons and rudder (**keypad 5**). Use the attitude/artificial horizon to determine the bank angle: the lines at the top of the dial are marked in 10°, 20°, 30°, 60°, and 90° increments. Eventually the airplane will trim itself out, but for a short while you can see that the airplane maintains its bank without the continued application of ailerons or rudder.

In general, when climbing or flying at very slow speeds, you should restrict yourself to shallow turns. Otherwise, the plane can stall when you enter the turn because of increased lift requirements.

Turns are not to be taken lightly. Except for landing, turns are the most dangerous maneuver, because many pilots don't realize the capabilities of the invisible forces at work. One acute danger is the high g load imposed on the wings during steep turns. The steeper a turn, the more load a wing must carry. Load is measured in terms of g's, or units of gravity, where 1 g is normal force and 2 g's would be twice the normal force on a wing. When there is a 2 g load on the wings, you will feel twice as heavy as you normally do. With a light airplane such as the Cessna, you shouldn't bank the airplane more than 60°, because it imposes too great a load on the wings. Most commercial jetliners also have stringent guidelines for bank angles, and generally they are not allowed to bank more than 45°, although for passenger comfort most jetliners don't exceed 30°. If you exceed the wing loading, structural failure can occur.

Another danger is that of stalling during a turn. At greater bank angles, stall speed rises dramatically. For example, if you fly a banked turn of 45° in the Cessna, the stall speed rises to 64 knots TAS from its normal level flight stall speed of 54 knots. If you were flying the airplane at 60 knots and banked it in a 45° turn, the airplane would stall and fall from the sky. Try this and see for yourself. The effect becomes even more pronounced for fast-flying jet aircraft; for example, the stall speed of the 737 is around 140 knots in the landing configuration. Suppose you muff the landing and perform a missed-approach procedure, turning the airplane to perform a go-around. Thinking

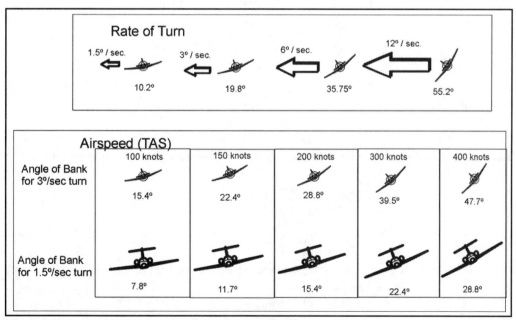

Figure 1.15 *Angle of bank, airspeed, and constant rate turns.*

it's safe, you decide to bank the airplane 45° at 160 knots TAS. Wrong! In a banked turn of 45°, the 737 will stall at any speed less than 168 knots. If you made the mistake of turning at too low an altitude, you and your passengers are doomed, because the plane is too low to perform a stall recovery. If you don't believe this, try it!

The danger of higher stalling speeds leads to this general rule about takeoffs: In the event of engine failure after takeoff, don't turn the plane! In a single-engine plane, if you have to crash-land, crash-land straight ahead, but do not turn back toward the field. You probably won't make it anyway, and if you enter a turn, the airplane will soon pancake onto whatever is under it. If you must crash-land, it is far better to crash-land traveling horizontally than to hit the ground vertically. Chances are you'll even survive such a crash, because a survivable deceleration of 12 g's at 100 knots would mean the aircraft would come to a complete halt in 440 ft.

Table 1.3 shows the optimum glide-turn performance for the Cessna.

Table 1.3 *Optimum Glide-Turn Performance for the Cessna*

BANK ANGLE	VSTALL TAS (KNOTS)	ALTITUDE LOST (FT) (FOR A 180° TURN NEAR STALL SPEED)	RADIUS OF TURN (FT)	OPTIMUM GLIDE ANGLE
5°	55	1,073	3,113	6.3°
15°	56	372	1,049	6.5°
25°	58	243	643	7.0°
30°	59	215	544	7.3°
45°	66	185	386	8.9°
60°	78	210	319	12.4°
70°	94	273	301	17.1°

The exact altitude lost in a banked gliding turn can be calculated by this equation:

$$h = \frac{V^2_{\text{Airspeed in ft/s}} \sin \gamma}{57.3g \tan \beta} (\theta) \tag{1.4}$$

where

h = Altitude lost in ft

$V_{\text{Airspeed in ft/s}}$ = Airplane's true airspeed in ft/s

$g = 32\,\text{ft}/\text{s}^2$

β = Airplane's bank angle

γ = Airplane's glide angle

θ = Angle turned in degrees

The optimum glide angle for an unpowered bank is found by this equation:

$$\tan \gamma = \frac{1}{\left(\dfrac{L}{D}\right)\cos \beta} \tag{1.5}$$

where

λ = Airplane's glide angle

$\dfrac{L}{D} = \dfrac{C_{\text{Lift}}}{C_{\text{Drag}}}$

We shall learn how to calculate the coefficient of lift C_{Lift}, and coefficient of drag C_{Drag} in Chapter 2.

EXAMPLE 1.3

Suppose you were flying the 737 to a gliding landing at 180 knots with engines at idle and you banked the airplane 45° and made a 180° turn to the runway. How much altitude would be lost? Assume that the optimum glide angle is 10° during a banked power-off turn of 45°.

Solution

Using Equation 1.4:

$$h = \frac{V^2_{\text{Airspeed in ft/s}}\,\sin \gamma}{57.3g \tan \beta}\left(\theta\right) \tag{1.6}$$

$$= \frac{\left(180\text{ kt} \times 1.687\,\dfrac{\text{ft/s}}{\text{kt}}\right)^2 (\sin 10°)}{(57.3)\,(32\,\text{ft/s}^2)\tan 45°}\left(180\right)$$

$$= 1{,}572\text{ ft}$$

This result tells you that your altitude must be at least 1,600 ft or more before you attempt such a turn! Even then, it would not be safe without a healthy margin of error because this particular calculation is only accurate to two significant figures.

If you are flying multiengine aircraft and suffer an engine failure, for safety reasons you shouldn't bank the airplane more than 15° because of increased stall speeds and greater induced drag. We will cover this topic in Chapter 3, where you will learn how to precisely calculate the stall speed for any bank angle or wing load factor.

If we calculate the forces in the vertical direction during the turn so that there is no change in the aircraft's altitude, we have the following:

$$\sum F_{\text{Vertical}} = L \cos \beta - W = 0 \qquad (1.7)$$

$$L = \frac{W}{\cos \beta}$$

where

β = Angle of bank
L = Lift lb
W = Weight of airplane lb

We can also obtain the horizontal centripetal force that causes the airplane to turn as follows:

$$\sum F_{\text{Horizontal}} = L \sin \beta = ma_{\text{centripetal}} = \frac{mV^2}{R} \qquad (1.8)$$

where

V = Airplane's speed in ft/s
m = Airplane's mass in slugs
β = Angle of bank
L = Lift lb
R = Radius of turn ft

A standard rate turn is one that is accomplished when the airplane turns through 360° in just 2 min, or 3°/s, which in radians is 0.0524 r/s. Large or fast jets use a slower standard turn rate of 4 min, or 1.5°/s. The radius of the turn R can be determined for any airplane by solving for L in the preceding two equations and then dividing through:

$$L = \frac{mV^2}{R \sin \beta} = \frac{W}{\cos \beta} \qquad (1.9)$$

$$R = \frac{mV^2 \cos \beta}{W \sin \beta} = \frac{V^2 \cos \beta}{g \sin \beta} = \frac{V^2}{g \tan \beta}$$

where

R = Radius of turn ft
g = 32.17 ft/s^2

From the preceding equation, the bank angle β for a standard 2 min rate turn is as follows:

$$\tan\beta = 0.0524\,\frac{V}{g} \tag{1.10}$$

where

$$V = \text{ft}/\text{s}$$
$$g = 32.2\,\text{ft}/\text{s}^2$$

EXAMPLE 1.4

Determine the bank angle and radius of turn for the Cessna traveling at 110 knots in a standard turn.

Solution

Using the previous equation we can determine the bank angle:

$$\tan\beta = 0.0524\,\frac{V}{g} = (0.0524)\,\frac{(110\ \text{kt}\ \times 1.6878\ \text{ft}/\text{s}/\text{kt})}{(32.2\,\text{ft}/\text{s}^2)} = 0.3021$$

$$\beta = \arctan(0.3021) = 17° \tag{1.11}$$

Using Equation 1.9, we can calculate the radius of the turn:

$$R = \frac{V^2}{g\tan\beta} = \frac{(110\ \text{kt}\ \times 1.6878\ \text{ft}/\text{s}/\text{kt})^2}{(32.17\ \text{ft}/\text{s}^2)(0.3021)} = 3543\ \text{ft} \tag{1.12}$$

Thus, we to fly a standard turn at 110 knots, the Cessna must bank 17° in a circle with radius 3,543 ft.

Although you now know how to calculate the bank angle, it is instructive to glance at Figure 1.15 to quickly ascertain the differences between bank angles. Two bank rates—the 2 min turn and the 4 min turn—are displayed so that you will see how different the bank angles are between small propeller planes, such as the Cessna 182, and jets such as the Learjet and 737.

There are two convenient rules of thumb for calculating the constant rate turn bank angle:

- For 3°/s turn rates (2 min turn): Divide your airspeed by 10 and then add 7.
- For 1.5°/s turn rates (4 min turn): Divide your airspeed by 10 and then multiply this number by 0.75.

As mentioned earlier, turbine-powered aircraft such as the Learjet and 737 use a 1.5 °/s turn rate (4 min turns).

Let's try some examples using these rules of thumb.

EXAMPLE 1.5

What is the constant rate turn bank angle for the 737 flying at 400 knots true airspeed? What is the proper bank angle for the Cessna when it is flying at 150 knots?

Solution

Using the second rule, divide 400 by 10, which equals 40. Then multiply 40 by 0.75, giving 30°, which is close enough to the true bank angle of 28.8°.

For the Cessna, use the first rule. Divide 150 by 10, which gives 15. Then add 7. The result, 22°, is close to the true bank angle of 22.4°.

The clock on your instrument panel isn't there just for decoration. It serves a vital purpose in helping determine how many degrees of a turn your plane has completed. This comes in handy when visibility is poor and you need to make a turn without the use of outside visual references. But even with perfect visibility, you can execute a perfect turn with the aid of the clock.

How are you able to use the clock to measure your turn? In a constant rate turn, your airplane turns with a constant angular velocity regardless of airspeed. You already know the rule that the Cessna turns 360° in 2 min, and the Learjet and 737 turn 360° in 4 min. This means that for the Cessna, its angular velocity is 3° per second, and for the Learjet or 737, it is 1.5° per second. Thus, for example, if you wanted to make a complete 180° turn and you were traveling at 100 knots in the Cessna, your bank angle for the constant rate turn is $100/10 +7 = 17°$ (from the bank angle rule of thumb), and you would need to turn for 60 seconds (because $60 \times 3°/s = 180°$). So watching your clock and taking note of your heading indicator (directional gyro), you note the second that is currently displayed and then bank the aircraft 17° until 60 seconds have elapsed. Your airplane should have turned 180° in that time. Note that during turns, the magnetic compass does not give you accurate results as to what your heading is. Instead, you should use the directional gyro during turns.

When do you end a turn to come to a desired heading? Rolling out of a bank, use this convenient formula:

$$\text{Rollout Angle} \ = \ \frac{\text{Bank Angle}}{2} \tag{1.13}$$

EXAMPLE 1.6

Suppose you are turning left to a heading of 270° magnetic. You are turning at a bank angle of 17°. When should you roll out of the turn?

Solution

Using Equation 1.13:

$$\text{Rollout Angle} = \frac{17°}{2} = 8.5° \tag{1.14}$$

Therefore, as you turn left you should start leveling the airplane at least 8.5° before a compass heading of 270°.

Practicing the Turn

Rather than go through a complicated tutorial on how to conduct a turn, it might be better to watch the autopilot perform your first turn so that you can imitate it. Using the **Autopilot Attitude and Heading Control** adventure on the accompanying CD-ROM (the file name is **AutoAlt.ADV**), you can control the airplane's altitude and heading directly from the keyboard. By changing the heading via the keyboard, you can watch as the autopilot takes control and initiates a controlled medium bank turn of about 30° (depending on the airplane's speed, this bank angle may be less or more). To use this adventure, follow these steps:

1. FSW95 only: Install **FSCONVT.EXE**, the Microsoft-approved Adventure and Aircraft Converter, from the CD-ROM. FSCONVT is a self-installing, self-extracting file. Don't install this program if you are using FS98.
2. Unzip **AAFWAV.ZIP** using Winzip (also on the CD-ROM), which contains the sound files needed to play digitized voices. Copy all its files into the **ADV\WAV** subdirectory where you have installed Flight Simulator.
3. Copy **AutoAlt.ADV** from the **Adventures\Misc** directory on the CD-ROM into your **\ADV** directory where you installed Flight Simulator.

Restart Flight Simulator, and you should be ready to roll. After taking off, start the **AutoAlt.ADV** adventure by selecting the **Flights/Adventures** menu command. From the adventures listed, choose **Autopilot Attitude and Heading Control**. Once the adventure has started, you'll see a help message that tells you what the keyboard commands do:

- Press **Shift+A** followed by the flight level altitude you want (don't use the number keys on the numeric keypad). This will force the autopilot to fly your airplane at a particular flight level you desire. Flight level is the altitude divided by 100 (so FL 180 means 18,000 ft altitude, and FL 350 means 35,000 ft). Even though it is technically incorrect to do so, regardless of altitude you must enter all altitudes as a flight level in the **Autopilot Attitude and Heading Control** adventure. Normally, any altitude below 18,000 ft in the United States is referenced by its altitude in ft. Anything at or above 18,000 ft is called a flight level and is referenced to the standard altimeter setting of 1013.2 millibars or 29.92 in. of mercury (QNE).
- Press **Ctrl+A** to audibly announce the altitude.
- Press **Shift+H** and enter the new heading (don't use the number keys on the numeric keypad).
- Press **Ctrl+B** to have the bank angle displayed and spoken back to you.
- Press **Ctrl+P** to have the pitch angle displayed and spoken back to you.
- Press **Ctrl-X** to exit.

If you experiment with these keyboard autopilot controls, you will find that pressing **Shift+A** followed by **1** and **2** (i.e., **12**), will force the autopilot to fly your airplane at 1,200 ft (and your command will be audibly acknowledged.). Note that "flight level" in this context is incorrect, because flight levels are used only to describe altitudes above 18,000 ft in the United States (the transition altitude). For the purpose of this adventure, though, we will refer to all altitudes as a flight level. Pressing **Ctrl+A** will provoke a voice announcement of the airplane's current altitude. Pressing **Shift+H** followed by **1** and **0** will force the autopilot to fly on a compass heading of 10°.

We are now in a position to have the autopilot demonstrate the proper way to perform the turn (Figure 1.16). Let's fly the Cessna north at 0° magnetic heading at 1,200 ft altitude, gear up, flaps up, at about 110 knots (reduce throttle as necessary to about 2,100 RPM). We'll have the autopilot turn the plane 180° around so that we are flying the opposite direction from our initial heading of 0°. Follow these steps:

1. Assuming your airplane is already airborne and that you are running the Autopilot Attitude and Heading Control adventure,, it would be a good idea to make sure that it is facing magnetic north, or 0°, before the turn. Press **Shift+H**

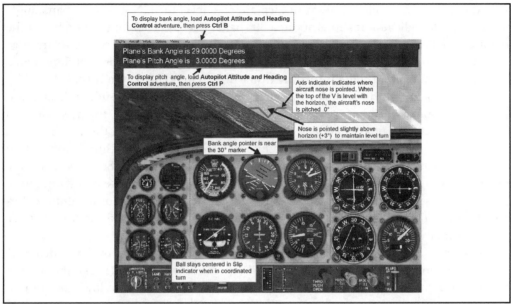

Figure 1.16 Use the **Autopilot Attitude and Heading Control** adventure (**AutoAlt.ADV**) to practice the turn. If you press **Shift+B**, you can see the bank angle displayed and hear it announced. Other commands allow you to precisely turn the airplane, choose an altitude, and display the aircraft's pitch angle.

followed by the zero key **0**. This will cause the autopilot **Heading Hold** to kick in and take charge, banking the airplane until it faces due north.

2. Reduce the throttle to about 2,100 RPM to bring the airspeed down to 110 knots. Make sure the landing gear is up and flaps are up.

3. Turn on the axis indicator (**View/View Options/Axis Indicator** and choose **Small V**). A V should appear on your cockpit windshield. This tells you where the aircraft nose is pointing with regard to the horizon.

4. Press **Ctrl+A** to have your altitude audibly announced.

5. Press **Shift+A** followed by **12** to force the autopilot to maintain level flight at 1,200 ft. A flight level of 12 is equivalent to 1,200 ft (just multiply flight level by 100 to obtain altitude in feet).

6. After the airplane is flying straight and level (from step 5), press **Shift+H** followed by **180**. The heading will be repeated for your confirmation, and the airplane will begin to bank into a turn.

7. To see the exact bank angle displayed as well as hear it being announced, press **Ctrl+B**.

Now watch as the autopilot banks your airplane in a level turn. Notice your bank angle on the attitude indicator. It shows about a 30° bank, because each of the notches at the top of the dial represents 10° of bank. You should realize that this is not a standard turn (which by the rule of thumb for this speed would be 17°) but rather is a medium bank. This means that your airplane is turning faster than a standard 2 min turn.

As the airplane continues its turn, watch your turn indicator, attitude indicator, airspeed, and compass heading change. Shortly before reaching 180°, the autopilot will anticipate the rollout phase needed to align the airplane's nose with the 180° mark on the heading indicator and magnetic compass. Using the rule of thumb for rollout angles, the rollout should start at $30° \div 2 = 15°$ before reaching the 180° compass heading. Notice too that during the turn, the autopilot must pull the nose a little up above the horizon (as shown by the V indicator) to keep the airplane from losing altitude during the turn. This requirement stems from the increased lift requirements that are imposed on all aircraft when they execute turns.

Try turning the airplane at other speeds using **Shift+H** followed by a new heading. Also, try turning when climbing or descending via the autopilot. (Press **Shift+A** followed by a higher altitude to force a climb, or **Shift+A** followed by a lower altitude to force a descent.)

Sometimes you may notice a jitter on-screen as the wings rock when you first turn on the **Autopilot Heading Hold** with this adventure. Do not be alarmed. It will last only a few seconds.

N O T E

Stall Recovery

The term *stall* is used to describe a wing's loss of lift when the angle of attack becomes excessive. This is the primary defining criterion by which a stall occurs; many people erroneously think that you can stall only when an airplane travels too slowly. This is not so. As we shall see in Chapter 2, it is possible to stall an airplane at high speeds during turns and other seemingly routine maneuvers.

In a stall, the airplane is in a semicontrolled state in which, if you don't act soon, the airplane will cease to fly. At angles of attack of 2° to 4°, the airplane's wing produces lift as air flows over and below the wings. As you increase the angle of attack to 8°, the wing produces more and more lift. Upon reaching 18° (on some airplanes it is 16°, and on others it is 20°), the airflow can no longer stick to the wing's surface and becomes disruptive and turbulent. At this point, the wing has entered a stall.

Stall recovery is simple; because stalls are caused by too large an angle of attack, the angle of attack must be reduced for stall recovery. To reduce this angle of attack, push the stick forward. You can test this in the Cessna by flying level and then pulling up the nose so that your angle of attack becomes excessive—greater than 18°. (The maximum angle of attack differs depending on airfoil design. Some airfoils stall at 16°, and others stall at 18°.) When the stall warning light comes on, push the stick forward to lower the nose, and you will reduce the angle of attack. This action will bring you out of the stall.

Just before a stall occurs on a real airplane, you feel the turbulence envelop the airplane as a vibration of the ailerons, which is transmitted through the controls to the yoke. The new FS98 supports force feedback joysticks, and you can feel the stick shaker warn you of impending stalls in the Learjet and 737.

Just as a stall is about to happen, the stall warning appears above the panel. When you enter a stall, the airplane's nose pitches forward involuntarily, and the aircraft's rate of descent begins to increase alarmingly.

What should you do once you have entered a stall? Follow these steps:

1. Release back pressure on the stick. Push it forward.
2. When the airplane's attitude has returned to normal (i.e., the angle of attack is less than 18°), apply full power by increasing throttle to maximum.
3. After recovering from the stall (the stall light will go out), arrest the airplane's rapid rate of descent. Raise the airplane's nose slightly at each opportunity you have, but be careful that your airspeed doesn't fall below the airplane's stall speed. On the Cessna, this occurs at about 54 knots with no flaps or landing gear extended.

When the airplane enters a stall, it may begin to spin out of control. For this reason, FAA rules require that all single-engine airplanes demonstrate recovery from a one-turn spin under all conditions of weight, center of gravity, and control movements. With multiengine air transport airplanes and most types of jets, the FAA requires the installation of a stall barrier system to prevent stalls from occurring. Because jets are harder to control, full stalls are generally not practiced or demonstrated during jet training except in ground simulators. A typical stall barrier system consists of a stick shaker, which shakes the yoke when angle-of-attack sensors built into the wing detect an impending stall. If the pilot ignores the shaking yoke or continues to pull back, a servo is tripped. It pushes the stick forward, thereby reducing the angle of attack before the wing has a chance to stall. The pilot is taken out of the control loop when this happens and probably for good reason, because there is not a moment to lose to prevent the stall from worsening. As described previously, the only acceptable way to recover from a stall is to push the stick forward and apply engine thrust.

The FAA has long had a standing requirement that single engine planes must not have a stall speed greater than 61 knots. However, with the advent of a new generation of micro-turbofan engines small and light enough to carry under your arm, a new age of single engine light jets is upon us. Last year Williams International, a manufacturer of small turbofan engines, was appointed by NASA to develop a new small turbofan engine in the 800 lb thrust class. This engine, called the FJX-2, would provide the take-off and low altitude performance comparable of a 350-hp reciprocating engine. Since jets traditionally take off at much higher speeds than reciprocating engine airplanes, new designs will have to be engineered to meet this FAA mandated 61 knot requirement.

If the FJX-2 works as planned, early in the next century many of us will be able to fly our own affordable single engine jets that can fly high above the hazardous weather conditions that today ground most general aviation singles.

The Descent or Glide

Most glides are performed at about a 3° flight path angle with respect to the local horizon. This means that for a 3° glide, for every 100 ft you travel forward you must drop 5.2 ft vertically, regardless of airspeed. You can also determine what the horizontal or vertical airspeed should be for a given glide angle. For example, if your vertical airspeed is 500 ft/min (8.3 ft/s), your horizontal airspeed should be 8,100 ft/min or 94 knots (158 ft/s) to maintain a 3° glide. The exact relationship is governed by the following equation:

$$\tan \gamma = \frac{\text{Height}}{\text{Horizontal Distance}} \tag{1.15}$$

or

$$\tan \gamma = \frac{\text{Vertical Airspeed}}{\text{Horizontal Airspeed}}$$

Thus

$$\gamma = \arctan\left(\frac{\text{Vertical Airspeed}}{\text{Horizontal Airspeed}}\right)$$

or

$$\gamma = \arctan\left(\frac{\text{Vertical Airspeed}}{\text{Horizontal Airspeed}}\right)$$

where

γ = Glide path angle

As long as the units are consistent, you can use nonstandard English engineering units of ft/min, or knots. Thus, if you plug in 500 ft/min as your vertical airspeed, you must also use ft/min as your horizontal airspeed. The same principle applies to distance. You can use nautical miles (nm) in place of ft as long as you use nm units in both the numerator and the denominator.

NOTE You cannot determine the airplane's descent rate and glide angle by how far up or down the aircraft's nose is pitched.

Note that for a 3° glide, this doesn't mean that you must pitch the airplane's nose down by 3° to enter a glide! You cannot determine the glide angle from the angle of the aircraft's nose with the horizon (see Figure 1.17). The only reliable predictor is to use the airspeed indicator in combination with the vertical airspeed indicator. For example, both the Learjet and the 737 descend from altitude with a pitch angle of 0° when the throttle is reduced to idle. If you don't believe this, try it yourself with the autopilot and the **Autopilot Attitude and Heading Control** adventure so that you can display the pitch angles on-screen. The Cessna descends with a pitch angle of –2°.

Table 1.4 shows the vertical and horizontal airspeeds you must maintain to descend in a 3° glide. At 150 knots, for example, whether you are flying the Cessna or the 737, you must maintain a vertical velocity of 796 ft/min. From the table, it is also clear that vertical velocity will increase as your horizontal speed increases for a 3° glide slope.

Table 1.4 *Glide Angle of 3° for Various Horizontal and Vertical Airspeeds*

3° GLIDE	VERTICAL AIRSPEED
AIRSPEED KNOTS (TAS)*	(FT/MIN)
60	318
70	372
80	425
90	478
100	531
110	584
120	637
130	690
140	743
150	796

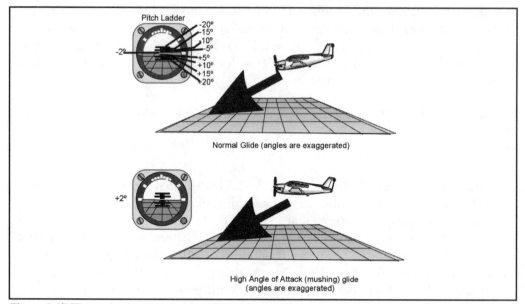

Normal Glide (angles are exaggerated)

High Angle of Attack (mushing) glide
(angles are exaggerated)

Figure 1.17 The angle of attack may vary during a glide. Your aircraft's nose pitch angle doesn't tell you whether you are in a glide.

Table 1.4 *continued*

3° GLIDE	VERTICAL AIRSPEED
AIRSPEED KNOTS (TAS)*	(FT/MIN)
160	849
170	902
180	955
190	1008
200	1061
250	1327
300	1592
350	1858
400	2123
450	2388
500	2654

* The glide speed differs only negligibly from it horizontal component.

Instrument landing systems (ILS) generally impose a glide slope of 3°, so when you're flying blind during an ILS approach, it is helpful to consult Table 1.4 to determine the correct vertical velocity.

To obtain the rate of required descent, a good rule of thumb is to multiply the airplane's true airspeed by 5. For example, if the Cessna is flying at 80 knots, the required rate of descent for a 3° glide is $5 \times 80 = 400$ ft/min. When the 737 or Learjet is flying at 400 knots TAS, the required rate of descent for a 3° glide is $5 \times 400 = 2,000$ ft/min.

The distance to the runway versus the vertical distance above ground is also governed by the glide slope angle, as shown in Table 1.5.

Table 1.5 *Distance to Runway vs. Vertical Distance above Ground (Glide Scope 3°)*

DISTANCE TO LANDING POINT 1,000 FT DOWN RUNWAY (PAST RUNWAY END)	VERTICAL DISTANCE ABOVE GROUND LEVEL (FT)
250 ft	13
500 ft	26
1,000 ft (begin runway threshold)	52
1,500 ft	79
0.5 nm	159
1 nm	318
2 nm	637
3 nm	955
4 nm	1,274
5 nm	1,592
6 nm	1,911
7 nm	2,229
8 nm	2,547
9 nm	2,866
10 nm	3,184
11 nm	3,503
12 nm	3,821
13 nm	4,140
14 nm	4,458
15 nm	4,777

Table 1.5 *continued*

DISTANCE TO LANDING POINT 1,000 FT DOWN RUNWAY (PAST RUNWAY END)	VERTICAL DISTANCE ABOVE GROUND LEVEL (FT)
20 nm	6,369
30 nm	9,553
40 nm	12,737
50 nm	15,922
60 nm	19,106
70 nm	22,290
80 nm	25,475
90 nm	28,659
100 nm	31,843
110 nm	35,028
120 nm	38,212
130 nm	41,397

Whether you are flying a jumbo jet or a single-seat ultralight, Table 1.5 lists the proper relationship between altitude and runway distance for a normal glide. Notice that if you were flying the Learjet or 737 at an altitude of 38,212 ft above ground level, you would need to begin your descent 120 nm from your destination! This is why, on some short-haul trips—such as the 300 nm SF to LA route—no sooner does the airplane climb to altitude than it begins the descent. Also, you should plan to land a jet at least 1,000 ft from the beginning of the runway and land small propeller planes at least 750 ft from the beginning of the runway. In both jets and propeller planes, you must cross the runway threshold at 50 ft in a 3° descent (see Figure 1.18). This principle is very important. Many pilots falsely assume that they should land as close to the runway edge as they can. Because of the additional 1,000 ft that is needed for a jet landing, Meigs Field, with its 3,947 ft runway, is not suitable for the Learjet or 737. The Learjet, for example, requires a 3,050 ft minimum runway for landing, and the 737-400 requires 5,250 ft (with 30° flaps).

During the landing approach, rather than use a cumbersome table such as Table 1.5, it is far easier to remember this rule: Allow 300 ft above-ground altitude for each nautical mile of distance to the landing point on the runway.

This rule is based on the assumption that 1° of glide slope equals 100 ft of vertical distance traveled per horizontal nautical mile. Under this assumption, a 2° glide slope would equal 200 ft/nm, and a 3° glide slope would equal 300 ft/nm.

Let's try an example. If you are 3 nm from the runway, what should the airplane's above-ground altitude be for a 3° glide slope? The answer is 900 ft altitude above ground, because 3 (nm) × 300 ft = 900 ft. If you are 10 nm out, you should be at 3,000 ft above ground, because 10 (nm) × 300 ft = 3,000 ft.

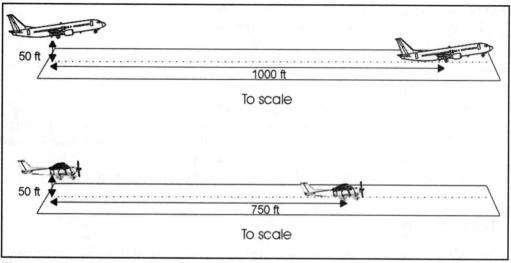

Figure 1.18 *Cross the runway threshold at 50 ft height. Touchdown occurs 1,000 ft past the threshold for jets and 750 ft for single-engine propeller planes.*

Suppose you were to choose a steeper glide of 9°. What should the airplane's altitude above ground be 10 nm out? The answer is 10 (nm) × 900 ft = 9,000 ft.

For your convenience, a rate of climb/rate of descent table for various airspeeds is provided in Table 1.6. The table can be used for both climbs and descents, as you may have guessed.

Table 1.6 *Climb/Rate of Descent for Various Airspeeds*

GROUND SPEED (KNOTS)

CLIMB / DESCENT ANGLE (DEGREES)	CLIMB / DESCENT GRADIENT FT/NM (FT PER NAUT MI.)	60 KT (FT/MIN)	90 KT (FT/MIN)	120 KT (FT/MIN)	150 KT (FT/MIN)	180 KT (FT/MIN)	210 KT (FT/MIN)	240 KT (FT/MIN)	270 KT (FT/MIN)	300 KT (FT/MIN)	330 KT (FT/MIN)	360 KT (FT/MIN)
				VERTICAL SPEED (FEET PER MINUTE)								
2.0°	200	200	300	400	500	600	700	800	900	1000	1100	1200
2.5°	250	250	375	500	625	750	875	1000	1125	1250	1375	1500
3.0°	300	300	450	600	750	900	1050	1200	1350	1500	1650	1800
3.5°	350	350	525	700	875	1050	1225	1400	1575	1750	1925	2100
4.0°	400	400	600	800	1000	1200	1400	1600	1800	2000	2200	2400
4.5°	450	450	675	900	1125	1350	1575	1800	2025	2250	2475	2700
5.0°	500	500	750	1000	1250	1500	1750	2000	2250	2500	2750	3000
5.5°	550	550	825	1100	1375	1650	1925	2200	2475	2750	3025	3300
6.0°	600	600	900	1200	1500	1800	2100	2400	2700	3000	3300	3600
6.5°	650	650	975	1300	1625	1950	2275	2600	2925	3250	3575	3900
7.0°	700	700	1050	1400	1750	2100	2450	2800	3150	3500	3850	4200
7.5°	750	750	1125	1500	1875	2250	2625	3000	3375	3750	4125	4500
8.0°	800	800	1200	1600	2000	2400	2800	3200	3600	4000	4400	4800
8.5°	850	850	1275	1700	2125	2550	2975	3400	3825	4250	4675	5100
9.0°	900	900	1350	1800	2250	2700	3150	3600	4050	4500	4950	5400
9.5°	950	950	1425	1900	2375	2850	3325	3800	4275	4750	5225	5700
10.0°	1000	1000	1500	2000	2500	3000	3500	4000	4500	5000	5500	6000

Figure 1.19 shows the relationship we have discussed.

Following is the descent checklist for the Cessna:

1. Fuel selector valve: both.
2. Power: As desired.
3. Mixture: Enrich as required.
4. Carburetor heat: As required to prevent carburetor icing.
5. Wing flaps: As desired (0° to 10° below 140 knots IAS, 10° to 20° below 120 knots IAS, 20° to full below 95 knots IAS). Note that the landing gear may be used below 140 knots to increase the rate of descent.
6. See Table 1.6 for proper vertical airspeed for a given horizontal airspeed.

The Landing

The landing phase of a flight consists of the base leg, the final approach, the roundout, the touchdown, and the after-landing roll:

- **Base leg:** The portion of the airport traffic pattern in which the airplane proceeds from the downwind leg to the final approach leg and begins the descent to a landing.
- **Final approach:** The last part of the traffic pattern during which the airplane is aligned with the landing runway and a straight line descent is made to the point of touchdown.
- **Roundout:** Also called the *flare*, the roundout occurs when the airplane makes a transition from the approach attitude to the touchdown or landing attitude.
- **Touchdown**: The wheels contact the runway surface as the full weight of the airplane is transferred from wings to landing gear.
- **After-landing roll:** Also called the rollout, this occurs when the airplane is rolling along the runway after touchdown and is decelerating.

There are different kinds of landings: normal landings, flapless landings, and short field landings. We will discuss normal landings in this chapter. *Flapless* landings are performed when mechanical failure causes your flaps to stop working. In the Cessna, a flapless landing means that your approach speeds should be 10 knots faster than in a normal landing, and your rate of descent will be higher. You will also touch down at a faster speed and use much more runway distance for the landing roll.

Short field landings are used for landing on extremely short runways or for emergency landings. With the short field landing, your approach and landing speed are maintained at the slowest speed possible before stall occurs. Usually, this speed is about

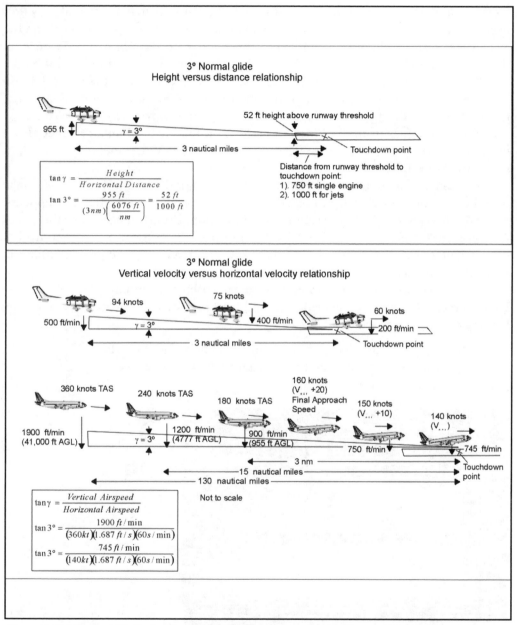

Figure 1.19 *Glide rate 3°. Notice that the proportional relationship between vertical and horizontal distance in the upper diagram remains the same. The same proportional relationship applies between vertical and horizontal velocity as illustrated in the lower diagram.*

65 knots, and, when you land, you must retract the flaps for maximum braking effectiveness (retracting the flaps gets rid of lift and puts the airplane's wheels firmly on the ground). For an excellent introduction to this topic, read the *MicroWINGS* article on short field takeoffs and landings in the Acrobat version of the magazine on this book's CD-ROM. Courtesy of *Computer Pilot Magazine* and Robert Ferraro, the CD-ROM also includes some excellent flight videos that show you how to execute normal landings, flapless landings, short field landings, and an ILS landing in bad weather. To run these videos, copy the files from the **Video** directory into the **Flight Simulator Video** directory; then start any of them by using the **Options/Flight Video** menu command, as shown in Figure 1.20.

Note that if you are using FSW95, at any time during the video, if you want to take over the controls yourself simply press the **Esc** key. In the dialog box that next appears, click **OK**, then press the **P** key to resume the simulation. Unfortunately, since the videos were originally created for FSW95, FS98 has trouble with restoring smooth control of the airplane to you when you press the **ESC** key. This is a bug in the program that will hopefully be fixed in an update of the program.

Figure 1.21 illustrates the segments of the approach and landing.
Each type of airplane has a checklist for the landing. For most propeller planes, the landing checklist consists of the following:

1. Landing gear extended and checked (green light should be lit).
2. Fuel selector set to both tanks or the tank with the most gas.
3. Mixture is set to full rich.

Figure 1.20 *Be sure to try the landing videos on this book's CD-ROM using Flight Simulator's video playback feature. You can interrupt the video and take over the controls by pressing the Esc key.*

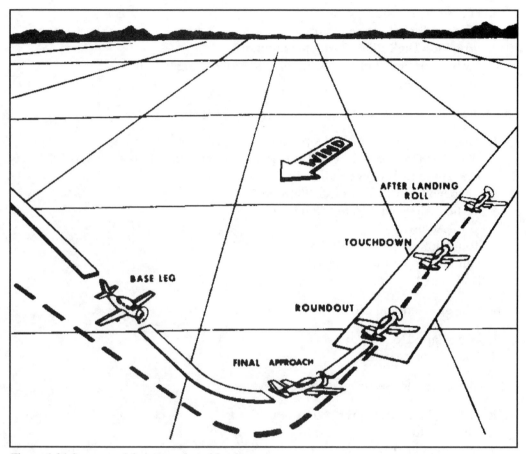

Figure 1.21 *Segments of the approach and landing.*

4. Propeller is set to high RPM.
5. Carburetor heat is on.
6. GUMP check (gas, undercarriage, mixture, and propeller) performed.

As a final check, pilots use the easy-to-remember GUMP check to make sure that the gas is selected for both tanks, the undercarriage (landing gear) is down, the mixture is set to full rich, and the propeller is set to its maximum RPM blade angle.

Here is the before-landing checklist for the Cessna:

1. Landing gear: Down (below 140 knots). Press **G.**
2. Landing gear: Check (observe gear down and green indicator light illuminated).

3. Fuel selector: Both.
4. Mixture: Rich. Push red knob in.
5. Propeller: High RPM. Push blue knob in.
6. Carburetor heat: On (apply full heat before closing throttle).
7. Autopilot: Off.

Following is the normal landing checklist for the Cessna:

1. Airspeed: 70 to 80 knots IAS (flaps up).
2. Wing flaps: As desired (0° to 10° below 140 knots IAS, 10° to 20° below 120 knots IAS, 20° to full below 95 knots IAS).
3. Airspeed 65 to 75 knots IAS (flaps down).
4. Vertical Airspeed: 318 to 372 ft/min.
5. Trim: Adjust.
6. Touchdown: Main wheels first.
7. Landing Roll: Lower nose wheel gently.
8. Braking: Minimum required (press **B**).

Here is the after-landing Checklist:

1. Wing flaps: Up.
2. Carburetor heat: Cold.

Follow these steps for securing the airplane:

1. Parking brake: Set (press **Ctrl+period**).
2. Throttle: Idle.
3. Ignition: Off.
4. Fuel selector valve: Right or left to prevent cross-feeding.

Each aircraft has a maximum landing weight, which is usually less than its takeoff weight. The Boeing 737-400 for example, can take off at 138,500 lb, but it is not allowed to land at this weight. In normal flight operations, so much fuel is burned by the time the aircraft reaches its destination that the aircraft's weight is far below its landing limit threshold, which for the 737-400 is 124,000 lb. In some emergencies, such as engine failure after takeoff, it becomes necessary to dump fuel so that the airplane falls within its landing limit guidelines. Special fuel dump exhaust valves are installed on each wing for this purpose.

Base Leg

During the base leg, the pilot should start the descent with reduced power and an airspeed of approximately $1.4 \times$ stall speed in the landing configuration. For the Cessna, this means that you should reduce speed to 1.4×52 kt = 70 knots. For the Learjet, it would mean 134 knots and for the 737, 196 knots. Landing flaps should be partially lowered at this time, but full flaps are not recommended until the final approach is established. Because landings should be performed into the wind (i.e., with a headwind), during the base leg there may be crosswind that will blow you slightly off course. In this case, you must angle (crab) the airplane sufficiently into the wind to prevent drifting off course.

Just before the runway intersects the airplane's path along the base leg, the pilot should turn the airplane in a shallow to medium banked turn so that the aircraft will be aligned with the runway along the final approach path. Because the airplane is flying so slowly, you should not execute a steep bank. The stall speed for a steep banked turn may exceed the airspeed, and the plane will crash.

Final Approach

After the final turn has been completed, the longitudinal axis of the airplane should be aligned with the centerline of the runway. If there is any drift, you should notice it immediately and take corrective action via the wing-low method or crab method for crosswind landings. After the airplane is on the proper flight path, you should complete the final flap settings and adjust the pitch attitude to maintain the descent rate. As noted before, the descent rate should be $5 \times$ the airspeed, and the airplane's altitude should be 300 ft $\times$ distance (nm), where distance is measured in nautical miles from the touchdown point. For a glide angle of $3°$ in the Cessna, your airspeed should be about 80 knots with a vertical airspeed of 400 ft/min, because $5 \times 80 = 400$ ft/min. If the plane were 3 nm from the touchdown point, the altitude above ground should be 900 ft, because $300 \times 3 = 900$ ft. Because your altimeter is measuring sea level altitude and *not* ground level, which is 593 ft for Meigs Field, this means that your altimeter should show 593 ft + 900 ft = 1,493 ft.

Although we said that during the final approach the Cessna should be flying at $1.4 \times V_{SO}$ (the stall speed in the landing configuration), turbine aircraft such as the Learjet and 737 should be flying at $V_{REF} + 20$ knots, or $1.3 \times V_{SO} + 20$ knots. Note that V_{SO} is not fixed but increases with aircraft weight; thus, V_{REF} must be calculated for each landing because it too will increase with higher aircraft weight. As mentioned earlier, a Boeing 737 that weighs 88,000 lb would have a V_{REF} of 119 knots with $30°$ flaps, whereas a 122,000 lb 737 would have a V_{REF} of 140 knots (also with $30°$ flaps). V_{REF} on a 14,500 lb Learjet in the landing configuration is 125 knots.

Using the preceding figures for V_{REF}, during the final approach a 122,000 lb 737 with 30° flaps should fly at 160 knots (i.e., 140 knots + 20 knots = 160 knots). When the 737 nears the runway threshold, the pilot should reduce speed to V_{REF} + 10 knots, or 150 knots; over the runway, speed should be reduced to V_{REF}, or 140 knots, at touchdown. A lighter 88,000 lb 737 would have lower landing speeds, with V_{REF} + 20 equaling 139 knots during the final approach; when nearing the runway, threshold V_{REF} + 10 equals 129 knots, and at touchdown V_{REF} equals 119 knots.

For the Learjet landing, use the same procedure that was used for the determining the 737's landing speed, except substitute the Learjet's V_{REF} of 125 knots when the aircraft weighs 14,500 lb. The bottom diagram in Figure 1.19 illustrates the speeds that are needed for a turbine engine final approach and landing.

As a practical matter, whenever you land an airplane in Flight Simulator you should turn on the axis indicator, the V-shaped marker located in the middle of the windshield. Select **Views/View Options**. In the dialog box that opens, select **Axis Indicator** and choose **Small V** or **Large V**. Having this marker on-screen is helpful, because it tells you exactly where the nose of the airplane is pointing in relation to the horizon. Also, if you want to see what your glide path looks like after the landing, you should turn on the Landing Analysis Graph (**Options/Flight Analysis/Landing Analysis**). Landing analysis is activated only when the airplane comes within 100 ft above the runway, as illustrated in Figure 1.22 for a landing with a too steep glide path of 9.5°. The glide path angle can be calculated from the information displayed in this dialog box by using Equation 1.15.

Unfortunately, the glide path angle is not correctly displayed in Flight Simulator's Landing Analysis Graph because of a bug that displays an incorrect vertical distance versus horizontal distance. Microsoft has been alerted to this problem, and it is hoped it will be fixed in a future revision. As an example of this problem, Figure 1.22 shows a 9.5° glide slope for a landing in the Cessna that was accomplished using a normal glide path of 3°. You can confirm this by running the **normal.vid** Flight Simulator video file on the accompanying CD-ROM and turn on **Landing Analysis**. This video was recorded for a normal approach glide path of 3°, as can be proved by taking the arctanof $(V_{Vertical}/V_{Horizontal})$, where both airplane speeds are measured in ft/s.

The power setting for the Cessna during the initial part of the landing approach should be about 2,000 RPM. But when you begin the descent, lower the throttle to 1,500 RPM. Be sure to lower the gear and lower the flaps to 20°. In the landing configuration (gear down, flaps extended), the Learjet throttle should be set to about 75% N_1 as shown on the Turbine Speed Dial of your instrument subpanel. (If it is not displayed, press the **Tab** key.) The engine throttle on the 737 should be set to 55% to 60% N_1 with the landing gear down and the flaps extended.

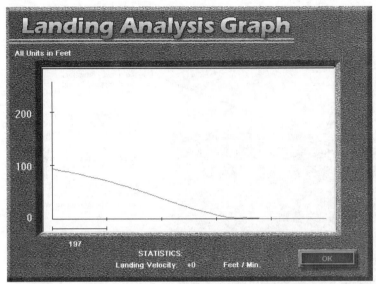

Landing Analysis Graph

All Units in Feet

200

100

0

197

STATISTICS:
Landing Velocity: +0   Feet / Min.

OK

Figure 1.22 Landing Analysis Graph: Use this graph to see how close your glide path was to a 3° normal glide path. In this illustration, the airplane descended at a much too steep 9.5°, because the arctan [(100 ft)/(600 ft)] = 9.5°.

Here's a useful tip that will help you to estimate your height and movement during the landing: Pick an aiming point on the runway in your window, and keep it in a fixed position during the entire descent. This means that you should pick a point on the runway and, as you near it, don't let it move up or down (Figure 1.23). The rest of the runway above and below the aiming point can move, but the aiming point should remain in a fixed spot on the windshield. You will fly right towards that point using the axis indicator V on your windshield. If you are on the right glide path, the aiming point should remain fixed. If it moves up the windshield, you are descending too fast; if it moves down, you need to increase the rate of descent.

The ability to recognize the correct glide path comes only with experience and practice. Many runways are equipped not only with ILS, which allows you to electronically "see" the glide path on your OBI/CDI indicator, but also with VASI (visual approach slope indicators) lighting. At Meigs, there is a VASI lighting system with two colored bars on the left side of the runway threshold when facing north. If the plane is too high, you'll see two white lights; if it is too low, you'll see two red lights. If you are right on the glide path, you'll see a red and white light. Pilots often use this convenient mnemonic rhyme to remember which lights should be lit on the VASI:

Red over white, you're all right
Red over red, you're dead

VASI: Visual Approach Slope Indicator
White over White: Too High
Red Over White: On Glideslope
Red Over Red: Too Low

Use the runway threshold as the aiming point during the approach.

If the threshold moves up the windshield, you are too low and are undershooting the runway.

Keep the aiming point fixed in one position on the windscreen and you'll fly right towards the point.

If the threshold moves down the windshield, you are too high and are overshooting the runway.

Figure 1.23 Pick an aiming point on the runway and keep that position fixed on the windshield.

Use the throttle to help maintain the correct glide path. If you are above the glide path, reduce power. If you are below the glide path, increase power. Use the nose pitch to control airspeed. If the airspeed is too high, raise the nose a little to slow the aircraft. If the airspeed is too low, lower the nose to increase airspeed. You may need to apply a little rudder and aileron to correct the airplane's path so that it remains aligned with the runway. Be sure not to overcorrect; only very small movements are required.

At 500 ft above ground level, apply 30° flaps.

The runway threshold should be crossed at 50 ft. For jets, the landing point is actually 1,000 ft down the runway, and for single-engine aircraft it is around 750 ft. If the plane is too high crossing the end of the runway, you will need additional runway to bring the aircraft to a stop. For example, if the plane is 100 ft above the threshold rather than 50 ft with a normal 3° glide path, you will use an additional 900 ft of runway before touchdown.

Landing the 737 presents an unusual problem of visibility to the Flight Simulator pilot. Because the cockpit is so far forward from the center of the airplane, when the 737 is pitched up slightly during the landing it is almost impossible to see the runway. To remedy this problem, you must pan the view window down by pressing **Shift+Enter**. To pan up, press **Shift+Backspace**, and to restore the view to straight and level with no pan, press the **Scroll Lock** key. Some people liken this action as equivalent to raising or lowering your seat in the cockpit.

The Roundout (Flare)

After crossing the threshold, you should reduce power to idle. The Learjet won't land otherwise. After landing, the usual procedure for jets is to apply reverse thrusters (press **F2** until the throttle moves into the red zone), extend speed brakes/spoilers (press /), and use maximum wheel braking (repeatedly press the **period** key). Be careful on the 737 to remove the thrust reversers when the airspeed drops below 60 knots. For small jet aircraft with tail-mounted engines, such as the Learjet, make sure that the nose wheel of the airplane is firmly planted on the pavement before using thrust reversers. If you don't do this, the thrusting action of the reversers can cause the nose to pitch up and lift the nosewheel off the ground.

When the airplane is 10 to 20 ft above the runway, the airplane is ready for the roundout, or flare (Figure 1.24). This smooth transition from flying to landing is accomplished by applying back elevator pressure to increase the nose pitch and the angle of attack. When the angle of attack is increased, the lift is increased and the airplane may tend to float because of ground effect (to be discussed in Chapter 2). The slower the airplane travels, the more you should pull back on the stick until finally the airplane settles onto the runway with the main wheels first.

Pilots use a different technique for landing taildraggers such as the Extra 300, Sopwith Camel, and DC-3. The steering wheels of these airplanes are mounted in the tail, and at rest the airplane is pivoted nose up in the air. At higher speeds, while taking off or landing, the tail wheel is high off the runway and is useless for steering. To land a taildragger, reduce power as you cross the runway but keep the airplane level to the surface (don't let the tail wheel drop) by pushing the stick forward gently. Don't push the stick too far forward, though, or you'll tip the nose down. Touchdown should be made on the main wheels first and, as soon as the wheels touch, immediately retard the throttle. You may have to push even more forward on the stick to hold the main wheels on the ground. This action will keep the tail wheel off the ground so that the main gear lands first. The opportunity for bouncing is much greater for taildraggers than it is for aircraft equipped with tricycle gears, so you'll want to plant the main wheels firmly on the ground the first time. Also, if you come down too fast, when the main wheels hit the runway the tail will be forced down and the wing's angle of attack will suddenly increase. This will cause the airplane to lift up so that it becomes airborne again; this effect is called *porpoising*. As the airplane's speed decreases, it will settle down again, but more bouncing may occur unless you can get the main wheels to stay down. Keep the stick pushed forward as the airspeed decreases; eventually, the tail will lower itself to the runway as airspeed drops. Remember not to apply brakes until after the tail has settled down, or else the plane will tip onto its nose.

When you are first learning to land a taildragger, it might be helpful to try the DC-3 on this book's CD-ROM. This plane, created by Christian Noetzli (based on John Kelley's airframe and Mike Hill's flight dynamics model), is much gentler and more forgiving to land than the supercharged Extra 300.

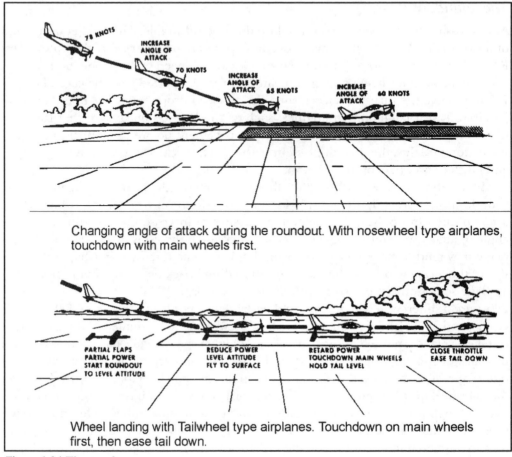

Changing angle of attack during the roundout. With nosewheel type airplanes, touchdown with main wheels first.

Wheel landing with Tailwheel type airplanes. Touchdown on main wheels first, then ease tail down.

Figure 1.24 *The roundout.*

The pitch attitude of the airplane using flaps is considerably lower than with no flaps. Therefore, before touching down, an airplane using flaps must lower the nose much more than the airplane without flaps.

Touchdown

When landing, you must not veer too far right or left while steering, or else the airplane will enter what is known as a *ground loop*: the airplane turns on the ground in an uncontrolled circular motion because of centrifugal forces acting on its wheels (Figure 1.25). You've probably experienced this on occasion when attempting to land with a crosswind, when the side slip motion of the airplane can cause the wheels to move sideways in relation to the runway.

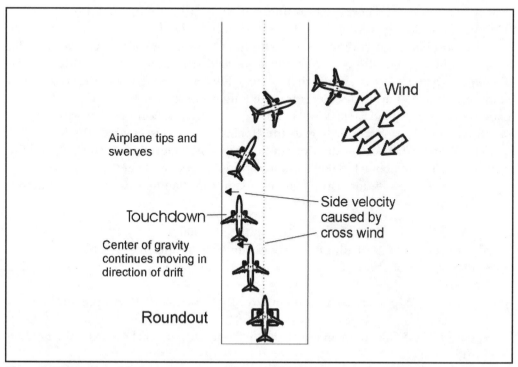

Figure 1.25 The ground loop.

Rules for Estimating Landing Distance

Airplane runway landing length charts usually state the ground roll separately from the distance to clear a 50 ft obstacle. The latter is the distance that is required from the spot where the aircraft crosses the 50 ft above-the-threshold point to the point where the aircraft is stopped on the runway. This also assumes StAt and dry, level runways with the aircraft approaching at the proper speed and glide path. Because the target aiming point for jets is 1,000 ft down the runway, the actual ground roll is the landing distance to clear a 50 ft obstacle minus 1,000 ft. For example, the Learjet manual states that the Learjet requires a landing distance of 3,090 ft at 70° F to clear a 50 ft obstacle. This means that its actual ground roll is 2,090 ft. Because Meigs Field has a 3,947 ft runway, you can legally land the Learjet on this runway. You have to be careful on takeoff, though, because the Meigs runway is too short for a MTOW Learjet, and you will therefore need to shed some fuel before attempting the takeoff.

The Cessna's target aiming point for touchdown is about 750 ft past the runway threshold when crossing it at 50 ft. This point can be determined from the Cessna manual, which states that if the temperature is 30° at sea level, the Cessna needs 1,335 ft to clear a 50 ft obstacle. The actual ground roll is given in the manual as 610 ft. This means that the aiming point is 1,335 ft minus 610 ft, or 725 ft.

At sea level the Learjet requires 3,090 ft minimum runway for landing, but this distance includes the total distance over a 50 ft obstacle at the runway threshold. The 737-400 requires 5,250 ft at sea level (with 30° flaps). For any aircraft, the higher the airport elevation or the higher the temperature, the longer the runway length needed. A fully loaded 737 cannot land at Jackson Hole, Wyoming, elevation 6,445 ft with runway length 6,299 ft, because according to the Boeing operations manual, the 737 needs 6,500 ft of runway because of the thinner air at this high elevation. If you reduced the airplane's weight to about 110,000 lb, landing would be possible at this airport.

Here are some additional rules for estimating the landing distance (Pendleton, 1996):

- For each 100 ft height over the threshold, add 900 ft.
- For each 10 knots headwind, decrease landing distance by 15%.
- For each knot above the recommended landing speed, add 2% to the landing distance.
- For each 15° F increase in temperature from StAt, add 4% to the landing roll distance.
- For each 15° F decrease in temperature from StAt, subtract 4% from the landing roll distance.
- For a 1° uphill runway slope, subtract 4% from the landing roll distance.
- For a 1° downhill runway slope, add 6% to the landing roll distance.
- When the runway is wet, add 25% to the ground roll.
- When the runway is wet and slippery, add 60% the ground roll.
- When the runway is icy, add 125% to the ground roll.

If you use only normal braking rather than maximum, expect to use 60% more runway; if the antiskid system is inoperative, add 75%. Forgetting to deploy the spoilers/speed brakes will cost you an additional 25%, and landing without thrust reversers in a jet... well, one hates to think what would happen if you did that.

Slips

Slips are descents with one wing lowered and the airplane's longitudinal axis at an angle to the flight path. Slips are used to steepen the approach path without increasing the airspeed, and they can also be used to make the airplane move sideways through the air to counteract the force that results from a crosswind.

In earlier days, slips were used as a normal means of controlling landing descents to short runways, but today they are used primarily in crosswind landings and emergency landings.

There are two kinds of slips—the forward slip and the side slip—as illustrated in Figure 1.26. The forward slip is used to rapidly dissipate altitude without increasing the airplane's airspeed, a technique that is especially useful for those airplanes not equipped with flaps. Circumstances that would require the use of a forward slip might include a forced landing in which you realize that the plane is too high on an approach and you need to descend rapidly without gaining forward airspeed. Jets normally don't perform slips as a means of losing altitude; instead, the pilot should execute a missed approach and go around for another landing attempt.

A slip was used to land a gliding Air Canada Boeing 767 that had inadvertently run out of fuel in 1983 because of a mixup by a ground crew that had confused lb with kg of fuel. The pilot came in too high, with the engines out, and needed to lose altitude rapidly to make the runway threshold without overshooting. The forward slip is not a normal maneuver for a jet, but in this emergency it worked; the pilot landed the 132 ton jet safely, although it was damaged during the landing. The story was chronicled in *Freefall* (Hoffer and Hoffer, 1989).

During a forward slip, the airplane continues in the same direction it was traveling before the slip was begun. If there is any crosswind, the slip will be more effective if it is made toward the wind. Slipping should normally be done with the engine idling; it makes little sense to have engines thrusting while you are trying to lose altitude. While the airplane is traveling in a straight path for the runway, begin the slip by lowering the wing on the side toward which the slip is to be made with the ailerons (Auto-coordination must be off). At the same time, yaw the airplane's nose in the opposite direction of the slip by applying opposite rudder so that the airplane's longitudinal axis is at an angle with its original straight flight path. Apply only the amount of yaw necessary to maintain the original straight ground track (even though your nose is no longer pointed along the straight ground track). Also, the nose should be raised as necessary to prevent airspeed from rising.

EXAMPLE 1.7

To perform a forward slip in Flight Simulator, follow these steps:

1. Turn off Auto-coordination. You must have independent use of rudders and ailerons.
2. Lower the wing on the side the slip is to be made. As shown in Figure 1.26, this means that you lower the left wing by applying left aileron.
3. Simultaneously with step 2, yaw the airplane's nose in the opposite direction of the slip. As shown in Figure 1.26, you need to apply right rudder to counteract the airplane's turn to the left and thus maintain a straight flight path.

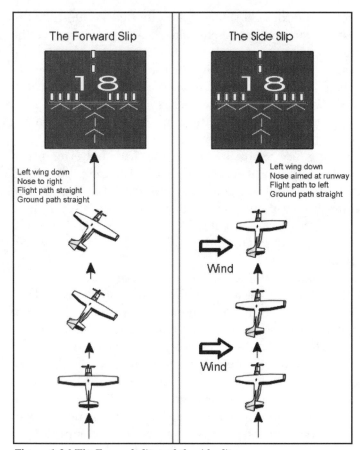

Figure 1.26 *The Forward slip and the side slip.*

4. Raise the nose as necessary to prevent the airspeed from increasing.
5. During the last portion of the approach, just before touchdown, you need to align the airplane with the runway. This requires a timely discontinuation of the slip and a straightening out of the airplane. If you don't do this, when the airplane touches down it will be thrown violently to the side and will ground loop. To discontinue the slip, level the wings and simultaneously move the rudders until the airplane is centered on the runway path. Adjust the nose pitch to maintain the proper glide attitude.

In side slips, as opposed to forward slips, the airplane's longitudinal axis remains parallel to the original flight path. Side slips are particularly useful for landings when a crosswind is present. To perform a side slip with a crosswind blowing, the airplane must bank into the wind while applying opposite rudder. This means that if the wind is blowing from east to west and you are flying north, the wind is blowing from the airplane's left and you must apply left ailerons and right rudder to maintain a side slip.

Crosswind Landings

Crosswind landings are more difficult to perform than are crosswind takeoffs, because it is harder to control the airplane in the air than while it is on the ground. There are two methods of performing a crosswind landing: the crab method and the wing-low method. Most pilots use the wing-low method.

You perform the crab method by heading (i.e., "crabbing") the aircraft toward the wind with the wings level so that the airplane's ground track is aligned with the runway. The crab angle is maintained until just before touchdown, when the airplane's longitudinal axis must be quickly aligned with the runway to avoid sideward velocity and consequent ground loop. This last-minute maneuver of aligning the aircraft with the runway is tricky.

For that reason, the wing-low method is preferred because it allows the pilot to fly the approach and landing with the nose of the airplane pointed in the runway's direction. This technique is far safer, because the airplane's landing gear wheels will strike the pavement in the direction of the airplane's flight path and not sideways, which can damage the landing gear and cause the airplane to go into a ground loop.

The wing-low method is similar to the side slip method. As you can see in Figure 1.27, you perform the wing-low landing by lowering the upwind wing with the ailerons and applying opposite rudder to keep the aircraft flying straight so that it is aligned with the runway. Drift is controlled with the aileron, and heading is controlled with the rudder. During touchdown, the airplane should land first on the upwind main wheel. The airplane should still be banked into the wind with the upwind wing lower than the downwind wing. As the airplane slows, it will lower itself gradually to the other main wheel. It is not advisable to take off in any of the Flight Simulator aircraft when the crosswinds are greater than 15 knots. This operational limitation also applies to real aircraft. For example, Boeing doesn't recommend landing or taking off in the 737 with a crosswind of greater than 15 knots and a tailwind of 10 knots.

TAXIING AND STEERING

In real jet transport airplanes, such as the 737 and 747, pilots use a special *tiller wheel* to steer the airplane while taxiing. This wheel is a separate control from the yoke and rudder pedals. Only when the aircraft picks up enough speed during the takeoff run do pilots use the rudder pedals to steer the airplane. In Flight Simulator, however, steering is performed via the rudder controls.

Steering while taxiing always presents challenges, especially with taildragger airplanes such as the Extra 300 and the DC-3. Taildraggers do not have tricycle landing gear, and they normally steer from a wheel mounted in the bottom of the tail. When you're using separate rudder and ailerons (uncoordinated mode), remember that it is your rudder controls—and not the ailerons—that steer the plane. This means that if you are using the keyboard, use **keypad 0** to turn left and **keypad Enter** to turn right. Press **keypad 5** to quickly center the steering.

How do you steer a taildragger that has a single-engine, such as the Extra? This plane stubbornly refuses to turn when you apply the rudder steering. The only solution is to use differential braking for each of the front two wheels; apply differential braking for the wheel that is on the same side as the direction of turn. For example, to turn left, press the left differential braking key (press **F11**). To turn right, press the right differential brake (press **F12**).

At rest, the nose of a taildragger is pitched sharply up into the air. This position is inconvenient at best when you're trying to steer, because you don't have any way of seeing the runway ahead. You can best deal with this problem by panning the view down (press **Shift+Enter**). This action will allow you to peer over the dash and see the runway. When you gain speed on the takeoff, however, you'll end up viewing the runway pavement, so you'll need to pan the view to its normal position (press **Ctrl+Spacebar**).

Many Flight Simulator pilots have been dissatisfied with the way steering is performed for taildraggers. Some pilots have implemented kluges that trick the simulator into thinking you have a nose wheel. This technique is clever: a taildragger is modified so that it has an "invisible" nose wheel that is normally not touching the ground. As soon as the aircraft gains a little speed, the center of gravity shifts forward, pivoting the nose down, and the "invisible" nose landing gear touches the pavement and can be used for steering. Implementing this workaround is cumbersome, however, because you must have a good understanding of aircraft center of gravity and moment. Still, it is an option for those who lose sleep over such problems.

The steering problems of multi-engine aircraft are different. Turning is usually performed with the nose wheel, which has a special steering mechanism for turning the nose. During the takeoff, after the aircraft has accelerated past a certain speed, called V_{MCG}, steering is handled via the rudders. Unfortunately, turning and steering a large multiengine airplane in Flight Simulator are not easy. Even though you are not supposed to use differential braking while taxiing a real airplane, in Flight Simulator it is helpful to "cheat" and use opposite engine thrust in combination with differential braking to corner a sharp curve. For example, if you want to turn right, you apply *left* engine thrust and engage the right differential brake (press **F12**). To turn left, apply *right* engine thrust and engage the left differential brake (press **F11**). Although you are not supposed to pivot the airplane in place, it can be done if you apply constant differential

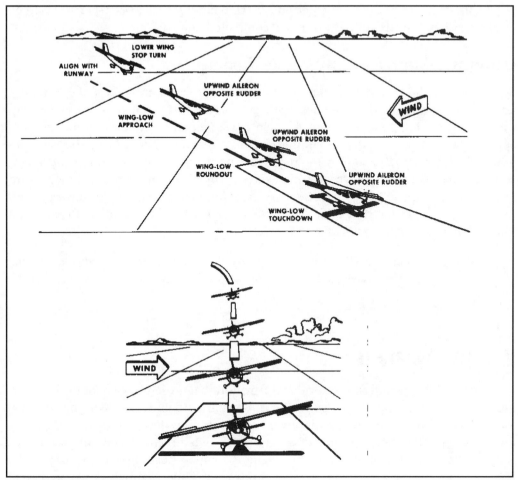

Figure 1.27 *Crosswind landing (wing-low method).*

brake pressure on one wheel while applying opposite thrust. You shouldn't do this in a real airplane, because you'll lock up the nonrotating tire and cause it to skid. It is an option, though, when you are stuck at the end of a runway and you can't turn around any other way. Note that multiengine piston-powered airplanes, such as the DC-3, have a single throttle control for both engines. If you need to apply thrust on only the right engine, press **E1** followed by the thrust control (**keypad +** or **keypad -**). For the left engine, press **E2** followed by the thrust control. To have both engines react to the throttle, press **E12** followed by the thrust control.

To apply the brakes, press the **period** key. The parking brake (**Ctrl+period**) is to be used only when the aircraft has come to a complete halt.

Using the Map Window While Taxiing

Sometimes it is difficult to determine your position in relation to the rest of the runway, taxiway, or airport environs. The best way to overcome this problem is to use the Map window (press **Shift]** once to open,] to close). Sometimes, the Map window doesn't appear when you press **Shift]**; when this happens, press the " key to bring the Map window to the forefront. By zooming out the Map window (press the – key on the main keyboard), you can get a bird's eye view of the airport runway system and see where you are in relation to other buildings and runways. Flight Simulator has painted runway guides that help you align your wheels while turning. If you run off the pavement, the airplane will vibrate, but no harm will come to it.

NOTE

You can zoom the Map window all the way out into space by repeatedly pressing the – key on the main keyboard. To zoom the Map window back down, press the + key.

RUNWAY MARKERS

Airport marking aids and signs provide information that is useful to a pilot during landing, takeoff, and taxiing. Markings on the runways are usually white. Markings for taxiways, closed areas, and holding positions are yellow. Runway designators, such as runway numbers and letters, are determined from the approach direction. The runway number is the whole number nearest $1/10^{th}$ the magnetic compass heading of the runway's centerline, measured clockwise from the magnetic north. Thus, a runway designated as 20 is oriented with a magnetic compass heading of 200° plus or minus 5°. A letter, or letters, differentiates between left (L), right (R), and center (C) parallel runways:

- For two parallel runways, L and R.
- For three parallel runways L, C, and R.

Runways that have precision approach aids such as ILS have the following markings:

1. Centerline marking.
2. Designation marking.
3. Threshold marking.
4. Fixed distance marking (on runways 4000 ft or longer used by jet aircraft).

5. Touchdown zone marking.
6. Side stripes.
7. Holding position markings at runway intersections when runways are normally used for "land, hold short" operations or taxiing.

A *displaced* threshold is an area designated as a nonlanding portion of a runway. Although it is permissible to taxi and takeoff from within a displaced threshold, landing aircraft are not permitted to touch down before the displaced threshold markings.

Some runways have paved areas beyond the runway end that are not intended to be used for takeoffs, landings, or taxiing. Yellow chevrons mark these areas as off-limits to aircraft, as shown in Figure 1.28.

Airport lighting systems will be discussed in later chapters.

THE TRAFFIC PATTERN

Unless directed otherwise by air traffic control, all pilots intending to land should enter the airport environs by means of the traffic pattern. The *traffic pattern* is a rectangular flight path around the airport that extends from 600 ft to as high as 1,500 ft above ground level (AGL), usually to the left of the runway (counterclockwise) with the longer legs flown parallel to the runway. At some point in their training, all pilots perform takeoffs and landings followed in succession by more touch-and-go takeoffs and landings by using the traffic pattern. A complete traffic pattern can be flown in six to ten minutes, but it is challenging to fly a pattern accurately and with precision. Because the traffic pattern is flown close to the airport, you generally use medium bank turns to stay within the confines of the airspace surrounding the airport.

In addition to its usefulness for training purposes, traffic patterns maintain an orderly flow of air traffic into and out of an airport. You can see how the traffic pattern works at Meigs field by examining Figure 1.31, below. If you would like to practice this traffic pattern at Meigs, you should try out the **Introductory Flight Cessna Skylane RG at Meigs Field** lesson under the **Flights/Lessons** menu, where an instructor will verbally walk you through the entire procedure. If you prefer, the instructor can fly the entire traffic pattern for you (just select **Instructor** control in the Flight Lessons dialog box). Before beginning the lesson, however, you should turn on **Options/Flight Analysis/Maneuver Analysis**, as shown in Figure 1.29 so that you when you finish the traffic pattern you can see how well you conformed to the established path. Also, unless you have installed all the sound files from the Microsoft Flight Simulator CD-ROM into your ADV\WAV directory, you will need to insert the CD into your CD-ROM drive in order to hear the instructor's voice. If you don't have the CD available, the instructor will continue the lesson with text messages only.

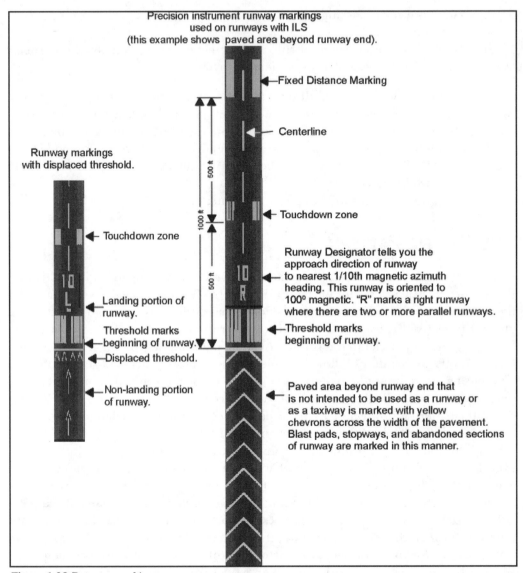

Precision instrument runway markings
used on runways with ILS
(this example shows paved area beyond runway end).

←—Fixed Distance Marking

←— Centerline

Runway markings
with displaced threshold.

500 ft

1000 ft

←— Touchdown zone

←— Touchdown zone

500 ft

Landing portion of
runway.

Runway Designator tells you the
approach direction of runway
←— to nearest 1/10th magnetic azimuth
heading. This runway is oriented to
100° magnetic. "R" marks a right runway
where there are two or more parallel runways.

Threshold marks
—beginning of runway.

←—Threshold marks
beginning of runway.

←—Displaced threshold.

←— Non-landing portion
of runway.

Paved area beyond runway end that
is not intended to be used as a runway or
←— as a taxiway is marked with yellow
chevrons across the width of the pavement.
Blast pads, stopways, and abandoned sections
of runway are marked in this manner.

Figure 1.28 Runway markings.

The Maneuver Analysis feature displays a two-dimensional path of your airplane's flight maneuvers and records everything you do from the moment you turn it on until you turn it off. To stop recording a session, press the \ key. A graph window appear, as illustrated in Figure 1.30.

The traffic pattern has five legs:

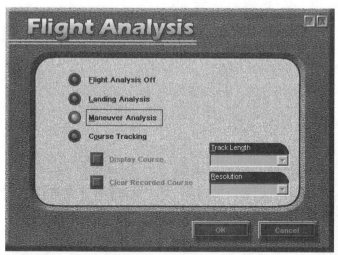

Figure 1.29 *The traffic pattern at Meigs Field.*

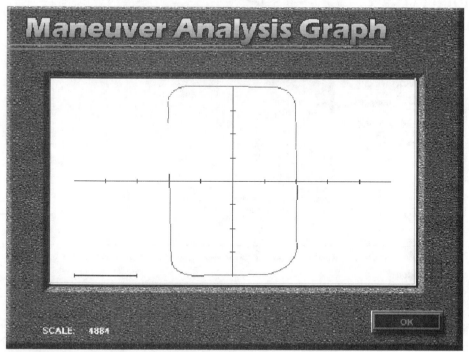

Figure 1.30 *Maneuver Analysis: Select the **Options/Flight Analysis** menu command to open this dialog box. Then click on the **Maneuver Analysis** button to activate the tracking feature for your flights.*

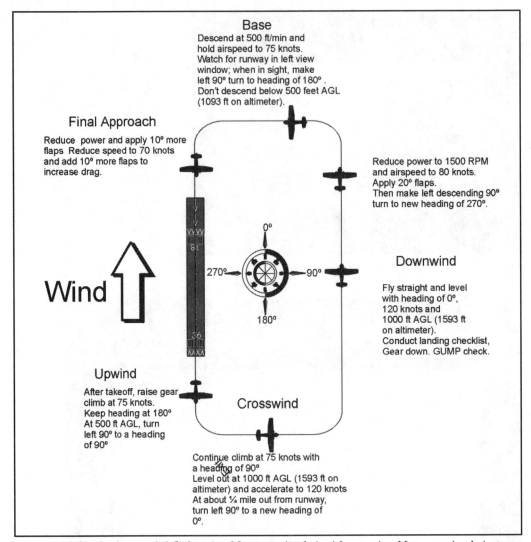

Base
Descend at 500 ft/min and hold airspeed to 75 knots. Watch for runway in left view window; when in sight, make left 90° turn to heading of 180°. Don't descend below 500 feet AGL (1093 ft on altimeter).

Final Approach
Reduce power and apply 10° more flaps Reduce speed to 70 knots and add 10° more flaps to increase drag.

Reduce power to 1500 RPM and airspeed to 80 knots. Apply 20° flaps. Then make left descending 90° turn to new heading of 270°.

Downwind

Fly straight and level with heading of 0°, 120 knots and 1000 ft AGL (1593 ft on altimeter). Conduct landing checklist, Gear down. GUMP check.

Wind

0°
270° — 90°
180°

Upwind
After takeoff, raise gear climb at 75 knots. Keep heading at 180° At 500 ft AGL, turn left 90° to a heading of 90°

Crosswind

Continue climb at 75 knots with a heading of 90° Level out at 1000 ft AGL (1593 ft on altimeter) and accelerate to 120 knots At about ¼ mile out from runway, turn left 90° to a new heading of 0°.

Figure 1.31 Graph of a recorded flight using Maneuver Analysis. After starting Maneuver Analysis, press \ to bring up this window.

- **Upwind**: This leg is flown right after takeoff. The pilot must retract the gear, climb to 500 ft AGL, and then make a 90° left turn onto the crosswind leg. At all airports, the direction of the traffic pattern is always left, unless right turns are indicated by approved light signals or visual markings or the control tower specifically directs otherwise.

- **Crosswind**: During this segment, the pilot climbs to 1,000 ft AGL. This leg is flown with the wind perpendicular to the airplane's flight path. As a result, the airplane must be crabbed, or headed slightly into the wind, while on the crosswind leg to maintain a ground track that is perpendicular to the runway. When the airplane is in the proper position, a medium bank turn of 90° should be made onto the downwind leg.
- **Downwind**: So called because the airplane is now flying with a tailwind. At this point, the pilot is flying straight and parallel to the runway about _ to 1 mile out and at 1,000 ft AGL. The prelanding checks are commenced and the pilot asks the air traffic controllers for permission to land. The landing gear is then lowered, and airspeed is reduced. After passing the end of the runway, the pilot makes a descending turn 90° left onto the base leg.
- **Base**: The pilot prepares for the landing, keeping the proper descent rate but not allowing the airplane to fall below 500 ft AGL. Just before the runway end is reached on the pilot's left side window, a 90° turn left is made.
- **Final Approach**: While on the final approach leg, the airplane has the right-of-way over other aircraft in flight or operating on the surface. When two or more aircraft are approaching an airport for the purpose of landing, the aircraft at the lower altitude has the right-of-way, but the pilot should not take advantage of this rule to cut in front of another plane that is on final approach or to overtake that aircraft. During the final approach, the pilot adjusts power to maintain the 3° glide slope and reduces speed with the flaps lowered. Once in position, the pilot crosses the threshold at 50 ft AGL and proceeds with the landing flare.

If you are entering the airspace around an airport, you should observe the proper way to approach the airport's traffic pattern, as shown in Figure 1.32. At many airports that lack control towers, the pilot is expected to observe other aircraft already in the pattern and to conform to the traffic pattern in use. If no other aircraft are in the pattern, the pilot should look for a segmented circle adjacent to the runway that has L-shaped markers. The short member of the L shows the direction of the traffic pattern turns for airplanes using the runway parallel to the long member. The accepted practice is for arriving airplanes to enter the traffic pattern at a 45° angle to the downwind leg, and for departing airplanes to exit the traffic pattern on the upwind leg by continuing straight or exiting with a 45° left turn beyond the departure runway after reaching 1,000 ft AGL. Arriving aircraft should avoid descending into the traffic pattern; rather, they should enter the traffic pattern at the altitude at which the pattern is being flown. Also, when two aircraft are headed for each other, each airplane should turn right to avoid the other.

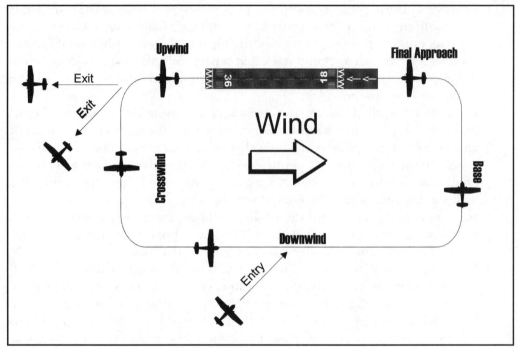

Figure 1.32 *Approaching the airport and joining the traffic pattern.*

REFERENCES

Linda D. Pendleton, *Flying Jets* (New York: McGraw-Hill, 1996), p. 258.
William and Marilyn Mona Hoffer, *Freefall* (New York: St.Martin's Paperbacks, 1989).

2

The Aerodynamics of Flight

"Nobody will fly for a thousand years!"

Wilbur Wright, 1901, in a fit of despair
over a failed experiment in flying.

In ground school, all pilots are taught the four fundamental forces—lift, weight, thrust, and drag—that act on the airplane in flight. These four forces form the foundation of the science of aerodynamics. If you have a solid grasp of how these principles are applied to the airplane, you'll enjoy your flights much more, because you'll be able to understand why things happen the way they do. Many armchair pilots are satisfied to sit back and fly their airplanes without care or worry during their simulated flights. But they are only cheating themselves by not scratching the surface of the program more deeply. There are many things to discover about Flight Simulator that will surprise and delight you as you delve into the mechanics of flight.

Before turning to the topic of aerodynamics, let's first describe the components of the wing.

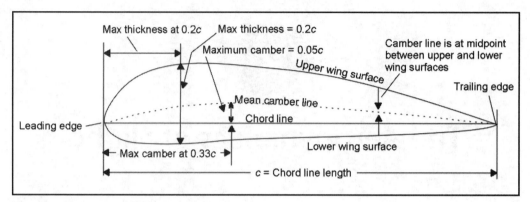

Figure 2.1 *Cambered airfoil terminology.*

THE CAMBERED AIRFOIL

An *airfoil* is any surface, such as an airplane wing, designed to obtain lift from the air through which it moves. Typically, airfoils are pictured so that you see a side view of a sectional slice of a wing. When discussing airfoils, the *planform* (the shape as seen from above), sweep back, dihedral angle, wingtip effects, taper, and other design elements are not taken into consideration. As shown in Figure 2.1, the *chord* is the distance from the leading edge of the airfoil to the trailing edge. The symbol used to define chord length is *c*. The chord *line* is a line that connects the leading and trailing edges. Along the length of the chord, various locations are defined in terms of percentage of chord length. For example, maximum *camber* (curvature), maximum thickness, and other wing components can be defined by how far back they are along the chord line in units of chord length. Another dividing line that is used to describe the wing is the *mean camber* line. This line traces points that lie exactly halfway between the upper and lower surfaces of the wing. The camber of an airfoil is the maximum separation distance of the chord line and the mean line and is measured in units of chord length. Camber measurements are used to describe how much curvature a wing has. A camber of 0.02 means that the maximum distance between the chord line and the mean line is 2% of the chord length of the wing. Cambered airfoils have advantages over symmetrical airfoils in that they produce minimum drag at cruise speeds and they generate positive lift even at a zero degree angle of attack. Symmetrical airfoils, on the other hand, have no camber, because the chord line is exactly halfway between the upper and lower surfaces of the wing.

The maximum thickness of the airfoil and its location are related to airplane type. For example, low-speed aircraft use airfoils with a thickness of $0.12c$ to $0.17c$ (i.e., 12% to 17% of chord length c), whereas supersonic aircraft may have much thinner wings of as little as $0.05c$. The maximum thickness of typical airfoils occurs at about $0.3c$ from the leading edge of the wing.

Many types of airfoil shapes exist. In the 1930s, the National Advisory Committee for Aeronautics (NACA) tested a series of airfoil designs that became known as the NACA four-digit series. Many single-engine aircraft flying today are using these wing designs, including Cessna singles, some of which use the NACA 2412. In the years that followed, other NACA series airfoils were tested and numbered. The numbering system given to the four-digit series wings describes the wing geometry. For example, in the four-digit series, a 2412 airfoil was so called because it was a 12% thick airfoil having a 2% camber that was located 4/10 back from the leading edge.

Aerodynamic Center

Cambered airfoils have an associated aerodynamic center and pitching moment (see Figure 2.2). The location of the associated aerodynamic center varies depending on airfoil shape and speed, but at subsonic speeds it is usually located between 23% and 27% of the chord length behind the leading edge. The aerodynamic center, unlike the center of pressure (described later), does not change with the wing's angle of attack, which is the angle of the wings in the face of the relative wind. The aerodynamic center changes with speed. When an airplane goes supersonic, for example, the aerodynamic center shifts aft to about the middle point of the chord. Note that the center of gravity, the center of pressure, and the aerodynamic center are all in different locations. We will discuss the center of pressure and the center of gravity shortly.

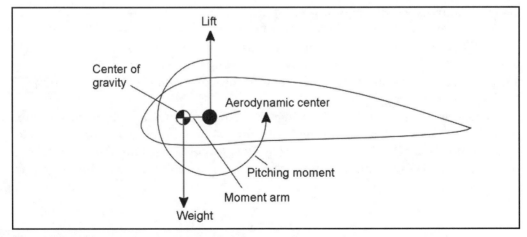

Figure 2.2 *Airfoil's aerodynamic center and pitching moment.*

Increasing Aspect Ratio of the Wing Lowers Induced Drag

The span of the wing, which is the length of the wing from tip to tip, is usually given the symbol b. The area of the wing, which is the surface area in ft^2, is given the symbol S. If you increase the span of a wing, holding the chord length constant, you increase the lift force because there is more wing surface area producing lift.

When you're calculating the amount of lift that nonrectangular wings develop, it is convenient to use the aspect ratio to determine certain uniform characteristics of a wing. Regardless of the shape of a wing, the aspect ratio can be calculated by the following two relations.

$$AR = \frac{b_{span}}{c_{average}} \tag{2.1}$$

or

$$AR = \frac{b^2_{span}}{S}$$

where

b_{span} = Wingspan length ft
$c_{average}$ = Wing chord length ft
S = Wing surface area ft^2

As you can see from the second equation, when calculating AR you don't need to know the wing's chord length if you know the wing's surface area. This is convenient, especially for nonrectangular wings or wings that are tapered at the tips.

Wings with high aspect ratios have small chords and long wingspans. There are certain advantages to designing such wings, the principal one being lower induced drag at low speeds. With lower drag, a high-aspect-ratio wing can generate more lift at a given speed than can a low-aspect-ratio wing. This is why many jetliners have long wingspans and narrow chord lengths.

Let's look at an example of two wings that have the same amount of surface area but different aspect ratios, as illustrated in Figure 2.3. You can see that wing A generates more lift then wing B at low airspeeds even though both wings have the same amount of surface area, because wing A has a higher aspect ratio and thus lower induced drag.

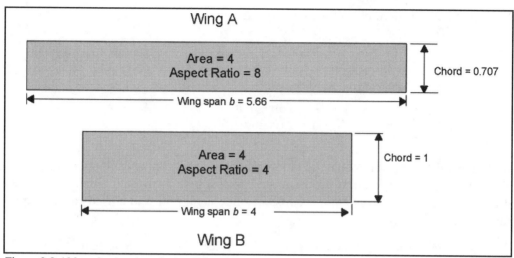

Figure 2.3 *Although wing A and wing B have the same surface area, wing A generates more lift at low air-speeds because of its higher aspect ratio. A higher aspect ratio means less induced drag.*

THE BERNOULLI PRINCIPLE

No discussion of aerodynamics would be complete without mention of Bernoulli's principle and its importance in explaining lift. Daniel Bernoulli (1700–1782) was a Swiss physicist and mathematician who made important discoveries in hydrodynamics. In *Hydrodynamica* (1738), Bernoulli proved that as the velocity of a fluid flow increases, its pressure decreases. This discovery was afterward referred to as Bernoulli's principle.

Every physics student at some point is introduced to the subject of fluid mechanics, a branch of engineering devoted to describing the behavior of fluids in motion. Because air is considered to be a fluid, we can apply the same properties that work with liquids to the motion of air over an airfoil. The Bernoulli principle, as applied to fluid mechanics, is a rephrasing of conservation of energy laws.

First, let's define some terms. The *density* of a substance is defined as its mass per unit volume. A substance of mass m and volume V has a density ρ given by the following:

$$\rho = \frac{m}{V} \qquad (2.2)$$

where

m = Mass in slugs (sl)
V = Volume in ft^3
ρ = Density in sl/ft^3

Next, pressure P is defined as follows:

$$P = \frac{F}{A} \tag{2.3}$$

where

F = Force in lb
A = Area in ft^2
P = Pressure in lb/ft^2

Bernoulli's Equation states that assuming that fluid is incompressible and nonviscous and flows in an irrotational, steady manner, it is possible to prove that the pressure of a fluid plus its kinetic energy equal a constant value at all points in a fluid (assuming no variation in height):

Pressure Potential Energy + Kinetic Energy Density = constant   (2.4)

Static Pressure   + Dynamic Pressure   = constant

$$P \qquad + \qquad \frac{1}{2}\rho v^2 \qquad\qquad = \text{constant}$$

where P is the pressure, ρ is the density, and v is the velocity of the fluid.

Simply put, Bernoulli's equation says that the sum of the pressure P plus the kinetic energy per unit volume ($\frac{1}{2}\rho\, v^2$) has the same value at all points along a streamline. This doesn't mean, however, that P or v cannot vary in a fluid; quite the contrary, they can and do vary, but they must adhere to the preceding relationship and they must equal a constant value when added together.

The middle row of the three rows in the definition of Bernoulli's equation uses the terms *static pressure* and *dynamic pressure*. The static pressure is the pressure that air in a container would have on the walls of the container if the air molecules were relatively stationary. The dynamic pressure, or $\frac{1}{2}\rho\, v^2$, is the pressure that would be exerted if all the air in motion were brought to rest by a barrier. Dynamic pressure is often referred to by the symbol q_∞ and is the quantity that is responsible for the lift force on a wing. Notice that dynamic pressure is proportional to the square of velocity (v^2); when you double an airplane's velocity, you quadruple its lift. Later we shall also see that doubling the velocity also quadruples drag.

Let's look at one result of Bernoulli's equation as it applies to a Venturi tube. As you can see in Figure 2.4, air is flowing through the misshapen tube. At the junction of the narrow portion of the tube and the wide portion, the velocity of the fluid must increase in order for the same amount of mass to enter the narrow portion of the tube as enters the mouth of the wider portion of the tube. For Bernoulli's constant to remain in

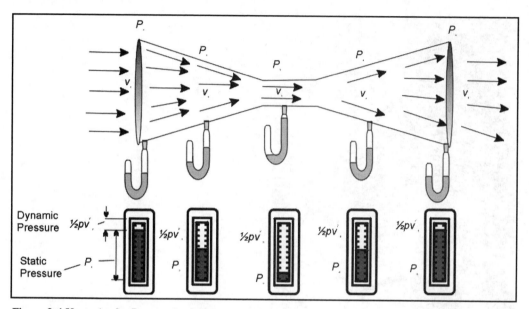

Figure 2.4 *Venturi tube. Pressure in the narrow portion of the tube is lower, because the velocity is higher. Pressure in the wide portion of the tube is higher because the velocity is lower. Thus, when pressure P is higher, velocity v is lower, and vice versa. The Venturi tube is used in automobile carburetors to generate vacuum and is also the basis for some vacuum pumps.*

effect, when the velocity in the narrow portion of the Venturi tube increases, there must be a subsequent decline in pressure. When the fluid stream exits the narrow portion of the Venturi tube, its velocity slows and the pressure rebounds to take up the slack.

How is Bernoulli's principle applied to airplanes? If you think about it, the cambered airfoil causes the relative wind over the wing to travel a greater distance than is traveled by the wind underneath the flatter portion of the airfoil. This means that the wind over the top of the wing must travel faster than the wind underneath the wing. Because the velocity is higher above the wing, the pressure above the wing must be lower than the pressure underneath the wing. With this pressure differential in place, the wing receives lift because the high-pressure area below the wing pushes the wing up into the low-pressure area. If you have trouble visualizing this, try this experiment: hold the edge of a piece of paper close to your mouth, as shown in Figure 2.5. Next, blow over the upper portion of the paper. The paper will rise of its own accord because of the lift force you are creating via pressure differentials.

Believe it or not, very little dynamic pressure is needed to lift a wing. You can calculate how slight the pressure differential is between the pressure over the wing and the pressure under the wing. You need only calculate the wing loading, and from that you

Figure 2.5 *Bernoulli's principle in action. In the top photo, there is no pressure differential above or below the paper, so it sags down from the force of gravity. In the bottom photo, when you blow over the top surface of the paper, the airstream velocity above the paper is greater than below. According to the Bernoulli principle, this means that the pressure above the paper must be less than the pressure below, and the paper lifts in response to the pressure differential. This is exactly the same lift principle that allows a 700,000 lb Boeing 747 to fly.*

have the dynamic pressure that is needed (because dynamic pressure ρ = Force/Area). *Wing loading* is defined as the aircraft's gross (or maximum) weight divided by its wing area. Note that in this case, the wing area refers not only to the wing itself but also to the extension of the wing through the fuselage. The total area would be equivalent to the area of the shadow that would be cast on the ground by a light that is directly overhead. Typical values of wing loading are 4 lb/ft^2 for ultralights, 10 lb/ft^2 for seat trainers, 20 lb/ft^2 for high-performance single-engine aircraft, 40 lb/ft^2 for high-performance twin-engine aircraft, 80 lb/ft^2 for jet fighters, and 120 lb/ft^2 for jet transports.

EXAMPLE 2.1

What is the pressure differential between the upper and lower wing of a 138,500 lb Boeing 737 with a wing area of 1,135 ft^2? What is the speed of the air flowing over the wing versus the speed of the air flowing under the wing if the airplane is traveling at 200 knots at sea level air density?

Solution

The wing loading is 122 lb/ft^2, because 138,500 lb ÷ 1,135 ft^2 = 122 lb/ft^2. To convert from lb/ft^2 into lb/in^2 (or PSI, pounds per square inch), divide by 144. Therefore, converting 120 lb/ft^2 into lb/in^2, we see that the pressure differential between the top and bottom wing is 122 ÷ 144 = 0.85 lb/in^2 (0.85 PSI). This is not very much pressure at all. To put this number into perspective, consider that the pressure differential between the cabin pressure inside the airplane and the atmospheric pressure outside the airplane cruising at 37,000 feet is 8.65 PSI.

For the second question, it is given that the 737 is flying at 200 knots; therefore, you know that the airspeed underneath the wing is 200 knots, or 338 ft/s. Using Bernoulli's principle we can create an equilibrium state on both sides of the equation:

$$P_{\text{Pressure above wing}} + \frac{1}{2}\rho_{\text{Air density}} v^2_{\text{Velocity above wing}} = P_{\text{Pressure below wing}} \qquad (2.5)$$
$$+ \frac{1}{2}\rho_{\text{Air density}} v^2_{\text{Velocity below wing}}$$

Solving for $v_{\text{Velocity above wing}}$:

$$v_{\text{Velocity above wing}} = \sqrt{\frac{2}{\rho_{\text{Air density}}}\left(P_{\text{Pressure below wing}} - P_{\text{Pressure above wing}}\right) + v^2_{\text{Velocity below wing}}}$$

$$= \sqrt{\frac{2}{\rho_{\text{Air density}}}\left(P_{\text{Pressure differential between upper \& lower ring}}\right) + v^2_{\text{Velocity below wing}}}$$

$$= \sqrt{\frac{2}{0.002377 \ \text{sl/ft}^3}\left(122 \ \text{lb}/\text{ft}^2\right) + \left(338 \ \text{ft}/\text{s}\right)^2}$$

$$= 466 \ \text{ft}/\text{s} \quad \text{or} \quad 276 \ \text{knots}$$

Thus, from the preceding calculation, you can see that the airspeed above the wing must be 76 knots greater than the airspeed below the wing if the 737 is to generate enough lift to sustain flight at sea level.

Extrapolating from Example 2.1, if given similar wing loading, you can see how easy it is for a 700,000 lb 747 to generate the lifting force that it needs for takeoff.

THE FOUR FORCES ACTING ON THE AIRPLANE

For the airplane to maintain level flight, the forces of lift, weight, thrust, and drag must balance each other out. Even during a climb, if the airplane is not increasing its vertical velocity or horizontal velocity these four forces must be in equilibrium, as shown in Figure 2.6.

Lift and Aerodynamic Force

Lift is the vector force that pushes up on a wing during flight and it is always perpendicular to the relative wind. This point is very confusing for many people. If the aircraft is pitched up while climbing or pitched down while descending, the lift force is no longer perpendicular to the ground and is no longer directly opposed to the weight force. The weight force of an airplane, on the other hand, is always perpendicular to the ground. How do you reconcile the requirement for lift to cancel out weight if they are no longer acting in opposite directions?

The answer is to apply a vector diagram to separate the vector components, as shown in Figure 2.6. The illustration of the climb shows that the weight force can be broken into vector components along the airplane's x and z axes. Suppose the aircraft were climbing at a 3° angle with respect to the horizon at a constant speed of 2,000 ft/min. According to Newton's laws, if the aircraft is not changing speed, there can be no acceleration and hence no net force. Thus, the z lift force L must cancel out the $W \cos g$ weight force component along the z axis. We can compute the z axis forces by using the following equation (which also includes engine thrust when it is offset slightly from the aircraft's flight path):

$$\sum F_z = L + T \sin \alpha_T - W \cos \gamma = 0 \qquad (2.6)$$

where

W = Aircraft weight lb
L = Lift lb
γ = Angle of the airplane's flight path
    with the horizon
T = Airplane's engine thrust lb
α_T = Engine angle of attack with respect to flight path

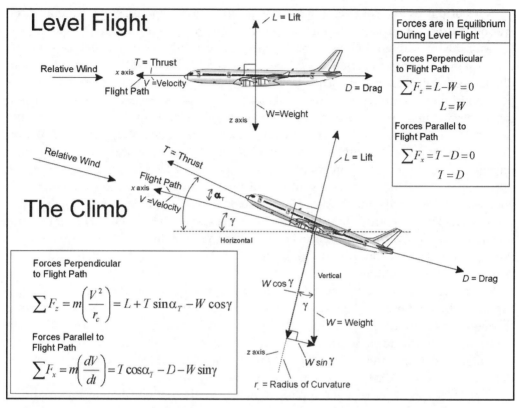

Figure 2.6 *The Four Forces of Lift, Weight, Thrust, and Drag in Level Flight and During a Climb*

Note that the sum of the forces in the z axis direction in Equation 2.6 differs from the equation shown in Figure 2.6. Equation 2.6 assumes that there is no net force acting in the z axis direction, hence $\Sigma F_z = 0$. If the airplane were to suddenly increase or decrease its rate of climb (or descent), $\Sigma F_z \neq 0$; instead, $\Sigma F_z = mV^2/r_c$, where r_c would be the radius of curvature of the acceleration and mV^2/r_c would be the centripetal acceleration of the climb (or descent) arc.

If you make the simplifying assumption that the engine thrust vector α_t is zero—so that the engine thrust is aligned with the airplane's flight path—you can simplify Equation 2.6:

$$L = W \cos \gamma \tag{2.7}$$

From Equation 2.7, you can see that lift L is now less than or equal to weight W and decreases for a steeper glide or climb. Note that the airplane's coordinate axes, the x and z axes, are rotated from the horizontal and vertical axes by γ.

This brings us to a confusing but subtle point. In a banked turn, centripetal acceleration causes the airplane's wing lift to increase with increasing bank angle (this is known as flying with an increased load factor). However, in a steady climb or descent, the airplane does not experience any acceleration and the needed lift force (perpendicular to the airplane's flight path) decreases with increasing glide or climb angle γ—the opposite of what happens during a banked turn! Thus, in a banked turn you will feel somewhat heavier as the wing's lift force pushes up against the bottom of the plane; in a steady descent or climb, you will weigh exactly the same, although the direction that you feel your weight coming from will change. For example, if the plane were in a terminal dive, the lift force needed by the wings would be zero but the drag force opposing the airplane's descent would push up against the airplane; you would feel your seatbelt holding you back with a force equal to your weight. In a terminal dive, you wouldn't feel your weight from the bottom of your seat or the airplane's floor, because it would have shifted to a different direction. On the other hand, if the airplane were falling through a vacuum with no air drag to resist the motion of the airplane, the occupants would feel weightless.

Note that lift never decreases to zero for a vertical dive or vertical climb, although Equation 2.7 implies this (i.e., when $\gamma = 90°$, $\cos 90° = 0$). An airplane's wings moving through air will always generate lift because of the dynamic pressure (Bernoulli's principle). So when the airplane dives vertically, the wing's motion through the air is vertical and the relative wind is now vertical. This relative wind underneath the wing creates dynamic pressure and the airplane will be pushed sideways.

The forces parallel to the flight path along the x axis are described by the following equation:

$$\sum F_x = T \cos \alpha_T - D - W \sin \gamma = 0 \qquad (2.8)$$

where

D = Drag lb

EXAMPLE 2.2

How much total lift does a 138,500 lb Boeing 737 require on its wings during a steady climb of 3° with respect to the horizon (assume a zero angle of attack)? How much thrust is required if we assume a total drag force of 12,000 lb?

Solution

The weight W of the 737 is 138,500 lb and the flight path angle γ is 3°. From Equation 2.7, we find the following:

$$\sum F_z = L - W \cos \gamma = 0 \qquad (2.9)$$
$$L = W \cos \gamma$$
$$L = (138{,}500 \text{ lb})(\cos 3°) = 138{,}310 \text{ lb}$$

This 138,310 lb force is the force that the wings must generate to maintain a steady climb. With this slightly reduced wing lift, the 737's airspeed during a level climb can be less than when flying straight and level, in part because some of the engine thrust is devoted to maintaining vertical airspeed. Note that if you were a passenger in the plane, you would feel not feel lighter, because your weight would be partially shifted from the bottom of your seat to the back of your seat as the engines take over some of the lift that the wings formerly provided.

To find the amount of engine thrust required, we use Equation 2.8:

$$\sum F_x = T \cos \alpha_T - D - W \sin \gamma = 0 \qquad (2.10)$$
$$T = D + W \sin \gamma$$
$$= 12{,}000 \text{ lb} + (138{,}500 \text{ lb}) \sin(3°) = 19{,}249 \text{ lb}$$

It is interesting to observe that the 19,249 lb of thrust needed to maintain the climb is less than the thrust produced by one CFMC-56C engine, which is rated at 23,500 lb thrust. This means that should one engine fail, the 737 should be able to climb on one engine alone.

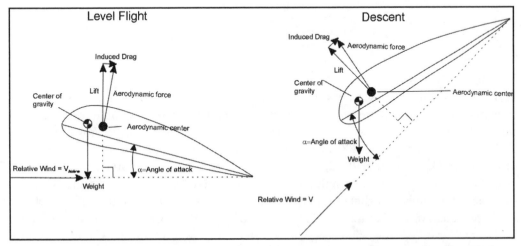

Figure 2.7 *The lift force on a wing is a vector that can be separated into components acting through the aerodynamic center. Lift always acts perpendicular to the relative wind, regardless of the wing's orientation. Note that the aerodynamic center is not in the same location as the center of gravity.*

NOTE These hypothetical numbers should be not be taken as fact for the 737. I have made several simplifying assumptions that would render the results invalid for the actual 737.

Later in this chapter, we will show that when the lift force is greater than the weight, the airplane will experience what is known as a *load factor*. Load factors must not exceed certain values when the plane is executing banked turns, traveling through turbulent air, or performing aerobatic maneuvers, or else the airframe may suffer structural damage. Lift can be calculated by the following equation:

$$L = C_L q_\infty S = C_L \left(\frac{1}{2} \rho V^2_{\text{Airplane's velocity ft/s}} \right) S \qquad (2.11)$$

where

L = Lift force in lb
C_L = Coefficient of aerodynamic lift
q_∞ = Dynamic pressure $\mathrm{lb/ft^2}$

$\qquad = \frac{1}{2} \rho V^2_{\text{Airplane's velocity ft/s}}$

ρ = Density of air at altitude $\mathrm{sl/ft^3}$
S = Surface area of wing $\mathrm{ft^2}$

You can also calculate the lift coefficient if you know the other values:

$$C_L = \frac{L}{\frac{1}{2} \rho V^2 S} \qquad (2.12)$$

The lift coefficient varies for each airplane and depends on the wing shape, wing area, and angle of attack. If we examine a graph of C_L versus the wing's angle of attack, as illustrated in Figure 2.8, we see that it starts at a small value for low angles of attack and peaks at around 14° for the Learjet, 15° for the Cessna 182RG, and 16° for the Boeing 737-400. (The Boeing 737-400's wing has an angle of incidence of +2°. Thus, for any angle of attack, you must add 2° to obtain the effective angle of attack.) At the peak point for each airplane, the graph has a cusp that curves down for an increasing angle of attack. This tells you that the maximum lift occurs at the cusp; if you exceed this angle of attack, you will enter a stall regardless of weight, bank angle, dynamic pressure, and so on. Note that the stall speed will be affected by weight and bank angle, because the lift force must counteract the aircraft's weight in order to keep the aircraft aloft and lift is dependent on speed (dynamic pressure q). Both indicated airspeeds and true airspeeds are depicted for several bank angles for each aircraft. The true airspeed will be

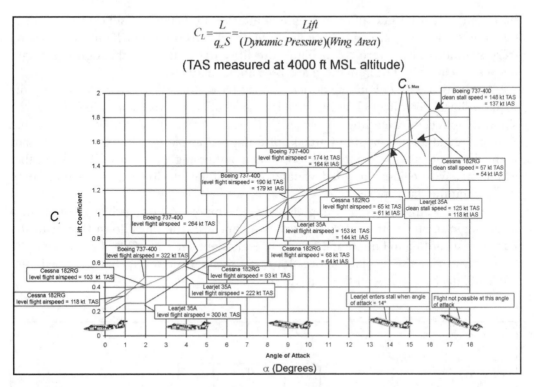

$$C_L = \frac{L}{q_\infty S} = \frac{Lift}{(Dynamic\ Pressure)(Wing\ Area)}$$

Figure 2.8 *Typical lift characteristics for different angles of attack. Graphs of C_L versus angle of attack for the Cessna 182RG, Learjet 35A, and Boeing 737-400 were compiled from the aerodynamic models for each aircraft in Flight Simulator 95. No attempt was made to corroborate these results with the real aircraft. Note that the Boeing 737-400 has a built-in angle of incidence for the wing of +2°. This means that the actual angle of attack will be 2° greater than is shown on the graph or in Flight Simulator; thus, a maximum angle of attack of 16° would, when combined with the +2° wing angle of incidence, translate to 18°.*

applicable only when the airplane is flying at 4,000 ft MSL, but the indicated airspeed will be applicable for all altitudes.

Because the stall speed is the minimum flying speed necessary to maintain flight, the stall speed for any airplane can be calculated if you know the maximum coefficient of lift (C_{Lmax}). C_{Lmax} is plotted as a single point at the top of the graph in Figure 2.8 for the 737, Learjet, and Cessna. (I used actual Flight Simulator 95 aircraft data to compile the results used in Figure 2.8. Actual results of the real aircraft will differ.) We will address the topic of calculating stall speeds in Chapter 3.

You can also deduce the amount of camber of an airfoil by examining its lift curve. If the wing is cambered, the lift curve will not pass through the origin at zero but will have some positive value at a zero angle of attack. This is because all cambered wings generate some lift at a zero degree angle of attack. On the other hand, if the airfoil were symmetrical or were a flat plate, the lift curve would go through the origin because no lift would be generated at a zero angle of attack.

Airplanes use lift-enhancing devices such as flaps, slots, slats, and vortex generators to allow slower takeoff and landing speeds than would otherwise be possible. Figure 2.6 shows the effect of extending an airplane's flaps on the coefficient of lift C_L. Note that C_{Lmax} occurs at a lower angle of attack for a flapped airplane, whereas, when the airplane does not have flaps extended, C_{Lmax} is at a higher angle of attack. This means that when you have the flaps extended, your airplane will stall at a lower angle of attack than it will when the flaps are retracted.

Figure 2.9 illustrates something else of great import. All things being equal, for a given angle of attack, the lift coefficient is higher with the flaps down than with the flaps up. According to Equation 2.11, for an equivalent amount of lift, if you extend the flaps you can fly the airplane more slowly. Remember, however, that the maximum angle of attack is lower with the flaps down.

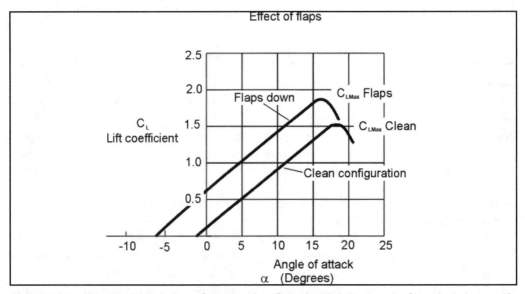

Figure 2.9 *Coefficient of lift curve for a flapped and unflapped airfoil. Because the flapped airplane coefficient of lift curve is higher than that of the unflapped airplane, the aircraft can fly slower for a given angle of attack (i.e., slower stall speed). Notice that the maximum lift coefficient occurs at a lower angle of attack when the airplane has its flaps extended. This means that the aircraft will stall at a lower angle of attack with the flaps extended than when they are retracted.*

Ground Effect

Ground effect refers to the floating effect that airplanes exhibit as they fly close to the ground. As an airplane descends close to the ground during landing, for example, it tends to float over the ground rather than touch down. Some people liken it to a cushion of air that builds up under the wings as the airplane bears down toward the ground. Essentially, ground effect occurs because induced drag at the wingtips is reduced.

For ground effect to occur, an airplane must be within one wingspan of the ground. At this height, induced drag is reduced by about 1.4%. As the airplane nears to within 1/10 of the wingspan distance to the ground, induced drag is reduced to 51%. When the wing is within 1/20 of a span, induced drag is reduced to 75% and the aspect ratio triples, as can be seen in Table 2.1 (Hubin, 1992).

Table 2.1 Ground Effect Results in Decreased Induced Drag

HEIGHT OF WING (h) DIVIDED BY WINGSPAN (b) (m/b)	EFFECTIVE INCREASE IN ASPECT RATIO	DECREASE IN INDUCED DRAG
1.00	1%	1.4%
0.50	10%	9%
0.40	14%	12%
0.30	22%	18%
0.20	40%	29%
0.10	104%	51%
0.05	308%	75%

You can calculate the exact reduction of induced drag by the following relation:

$$\frac{\text{Induced drag in ground effect}}{\text{Induced drag out of ground effect}} = 1 - \frac{2e}{\pi^2} \ln\left[1 + \left(\frac{\pi b}{8h}\right)^2\right] \qquad (2.13)$$

where

b = Wingspan ft
h = Height above ground ft
ln = Natural logarithm (use ln function on your scientific calculator)
e = Wing efficiency factor (usually about 0.9)

The principal effects of ground effect are as follows:

- The airflow over the wings and especially the wingtips is altered so that induced drag at the wingtips is reduced.

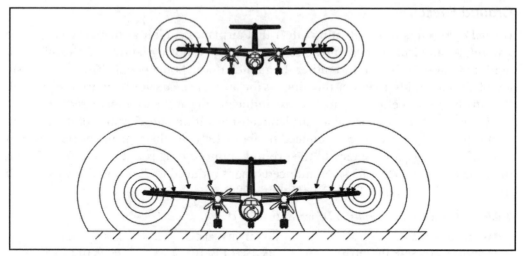

Figure 2.10 *The Airplane in ground effect. The breakup of wingtip vortices by the ground reduces induced drag and increases lift.*

- The upwash and downwash angles of airflow over the wings are reduced, resulting in an effective increase in aspect ratio and a reduction in drag.

These effects are shown in Figure 2.10.

There have been many attempts to create ground effect aircraft over the years, none of which has been realized in a practical way. You can see from Table 2.1. that an airplane must fly very close to the ground for any significant benefit, and that means the only suitable location would be flat areas such as oceans. For example, a Boeing 747-400 with a wingspan *b* of 208 ft would have to fly within 20 ft of the ground to get a 51% decrease in drag. Notice that the effective increase in aspect ratio is 104%. From the equation for total drag, it is clear that doubling the aspect ratio will halve the drag. This means that the 747 could fly with one-half the thrust it ordinarily needs, for a huge cost savings in fuel.

Microsoft has stated that ground effect *is* modeled in Flight Simulator.

Weight

The *weight* of the airplane is a vector force of gravity acting downward on the airplane's center of gravity. The center of gravity is the same location as the airplane's center of mass. *Lift*, on the other hand, is measured upward through the aircraft's aerodynamic center, which is usually rear of the center of gravity some tens of inches. During level flight, lift cancels the force of weight when you total all the components of force in the vertical direction. However, because lift is applied through the wing's aerodynamic center and not the airplane's center of gravity (cg), there is always a rotational force, or *moment*, that is being applied around the cg. This moment force acts as a rotational force that makes the wing tend to pitch the aircraft's nose down. This is where the tail, or horizontal stabilizer, comes in. The tail counteracts the lift force's moment by imposing a smaller negative lift force downward. You can calculate the exact relationships if you understand how torque, or moment force, is calculated.

Moment and Center of Gravity

Moment is a rotational force that causes airplane wings to rotate about a central point. There can be moment forces acting on any axis of the airplane, but the moment we are concerned about here is the torque force that causes the wings to pitch the airplane's nose down. All airplanes have this pitching tendency, which is caused by the lift force not acting at the airplane's center of gravity but acting instead at the aerodynamic center of the wing farther back along the wing's chord length.

In mathematical terms, moment is the product of the distance about a chosen axis of revolution (i.e., the *moment arm*) times the component of force that is perpendicular to the distance. You can see this illustrated in Figure 2.2.

$$M = r \times F \tag{2.14}$$

where

M = Moment or torque force lb-ft
F = Force vector lb
$\times$ = Cross product symbol of two vectors ($r \times F$ is a cross product that produces another vector. $r \times F$ is not a scalar value)
r = Distance vector from center of rotation

The magnitude of the force can be determined from the force component perpendicular to the moment arm as follows:

$$M = |F| \sin \theta \, d \tag{2.15}$$

where

M = Moment lb-ft
$|F| = \sqrt{F_x^2 + F_y^2}$ lb
$|F| \sin \theta$ = Force component perpendicular to moment arm d
d = Moment arm distance ft

Notice that the farther the force is applied from the axis of revolution, the greater the moment force, or torque, being applied.

EXAMPLE 2.3

Suppose that the 3,100 lb Cessna's aerodynamic center on the wing is 6 in. from the center of gravity (cg) and that the moment arm distance of the elevator on the tail from the cg is 15 ft (180 in.). If level flight is to be maintained, how much downward lift force must the elevator exert to counteract the wing's moment?

Solution

We need to figure out the total moment force so that it will exactly equal zero. If we multiply the arm distance d between the cg and the aerodynamic center by the 3,100 lb weight of the Cessna, we find that the sum of the moment arms around the cg must be zero:

$$\sum M = (L)\left(d_{\text{distance between cg and aerod. center}}\right) - \left(F_{\text{Elevator}}\right)\left(b_{\text{distance between elevator and cg}}\right) = 0$$

$$= \left(W_{\text{Airplane Weight}} + F_{\text{Elevator}}\right)\left(d_{\text{distance between cg and aerod. center}}\right) \qquad (2.16)$$

$$- \left(F_{\text{Elevator}}\right)\left(b_{\text{distance between elevator and cg}}\right) = 0$$

Solving for F_{Elevator}:

$$F_{\text{Elevator}} = \frac{\left(W_{\text{Airplane Weight}} + F_{\text{Elevator}}\right)\left(d_{\text{distance between cg and aerod. center}}\right)}{b_{\text{distance between elevator and cg}}}$$

$$F_{\text{Elevator}} = \frac{(W)\left(d_{\text{distance between cg and aerod. center}}\right)}{\left(b_{\text{distance between elevator and cg}} - d_{\text{distance between cg and aerod. center}}\right)}$$

$$= \frac{(3100 \text{ lb})(0.5 \text{ ft})}{(15 \text{ ft} - 0.5 \text{ ft})} = 107 \text{ lb}$$

In the above equation, lift L must include not only the weight of the aircraft $W_{\text{Airplane Weight}}$, but also the downward force F_{Elevator}, because the sum of the forces in the vertical direction must equal zero for level flight:

$$\sum F_{\text{Vertical}} = 0 = L - \left(W_{\text{Airplane Weight}} + F_{\text{Elevator}}\right) = 0 \qquad (2.17)$$

$$\text{therefore } L = W_{\text{Airplane Weight}} + F_{\text{Elevator}}\Big)$$

Ordinarily, the horizontal stabilizer is designed so that it generates negative lift during level flight. Thus, the pilot doesn't need to pull back on the stick with 107 lb of force. However, to maintain a certain angle of attack, such as during a climb, it is often necessary to apply constant pressure while pulling back the stick. This effort can get tiring after a while, and it is the main reason for using the elevator trim tabs. With the trim tabs, the pilot can exert a counterforce on the elevator that will keep it in position without applying any continued force on the stick.

Center of Gravity Limitations

Every airplane must be flown with a carefully balanced center of gravity that does not deviate too far forward or too far back from the aerodynamic center of the wing. This means that the airplane must not be loaded tail heavy or nose heavy so that the center of gravity moves beyond a certain percentage of the mean aerodynamic chord length of the wing. Some aircraft operating manuals describe the center of gravity limits as a percentage of the mean aerodynamic chord (MAC) rather than in inches. In most aircraft, the center of gravity at maximum weight is around 25% MAC. For example, you can see in Figure 2.12 that in an 18,000 lb Learjet, the center of gravity must fall between 19% and 30% of MAC. Because the mean chord length on the Learjet is 6.41 ft, this means that for the aircraft to be balanced the cg must fall between 1.21 ft and

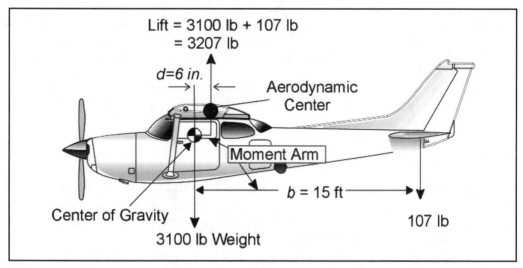

Figure 2.11 *The downward lift of the tail wing, or horizontal stabilizer (elevator), balances the counterclockwise pitching moment of the main wing. Note that the aerodynamic center is in a different location from the center of gravity. The center of gravity is a single point in the aircraft where all the weight of the aircraft is considered to be acting downward.*

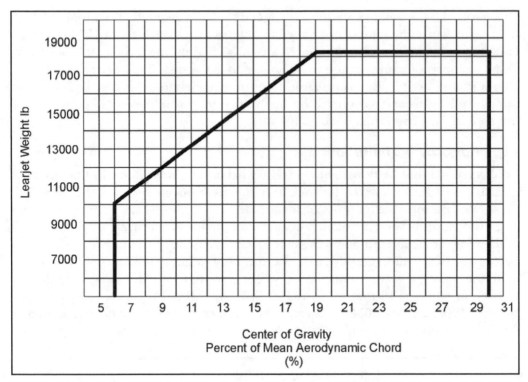

Figure 2.12 *Center of gravity limitation envelope as a percentage of MAC for the Learjet 36A. As the Learjet's weight increases, the forward limit of the center of gravity moves back on the wing.*

1.92 ft from the leading edge of the wing. At 713,000 lb, the 747 is much heavier than the Learjet, but its center of gravity similarly ranges between 15% and 33% of MAC when the gear and flaps are down.

Drag

Drag is the term used to describe resistance to airflow. All airplanes move through air with some drag, in part caused by friction but also because the process of creating lift unavoidably creates drag. Drag is a vector force that is always parallel to and in the opposite direction of the airplane's flight path.

Two kinds of drag describe the airflow over airplanes: parasite drag and induced drag.

Parasite Drag

Parasite drag is the drag associated with the motion of air over the airplane's surface and is independent of lift. It consists of profile drag, interference drag, pressure drag, and friction drag.

- *Profile drag* is the wing's parasite drag, the magnitude of which varies with the wing's angle of attack.
- *Interference drag* is the drag resulting from the intersection of two different parts of the aircraft's body, such as the wing and fuselage.
- *Pressure drag* is the drag caused by the difference in pressure between the fore and aft sides of an airplane as it moves through the air.
- *Friction drag* is the drag caused by the viscosity, or stickiness, of air flowing over a surface such as the wing and fuselage. The smoother a surface, the less friction drag for a given air viscosity. Laminar air flowing over an airfoil has a boundary layer that has zero velocity regardless of the airplane's speed. This surface layer is about 0.05 in. thick at the wing's leading edge and less 0.5 in at the trailing edge. As you progress away from the surface layer, you move into the boundary layer, where the velocity of the air transitions from zero velocity to the free airstream velocity.

Figure 2.13 illustrates pressure drag and friction drag.

Aircraft designers strive to create airplanes that are as "slippery," or drag-free, as possible. Smooth laminar air flowing over the fuselage and wing is a desirable quality and is affected by the viscosity of air and the smoothness of the frontal surfaces exposed to the airflow. Surfaces that are not streamlined cause turbulent air layers, and this in turn creates more friction drag.

Parasite drag, like lift, is proportional to the dynamic pressure of the airstream and the surface area on which it acts. Parasite drag is also proportional to the square of

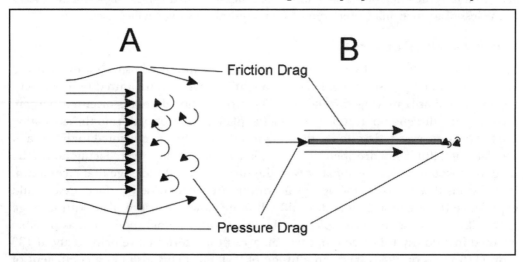

Figure 2.13 *A flat plate aligned perpendicular to the airstream (A), and parallel to the airstream (B) generates differing amounts of pressure drag and friction drag.*

velocity; if you double your speed, you quadruple the drag and quadruple the amount of thrust needed to propel the aircraft forward.

To account for irregularities in the fuselage's surface and shape, the drag coefficient $C_{Parasite}$ is used to define the amount of parasite drag as follows:

$$D_{\text{Parasite Drag Force}} = C_{\text{Parasite}} q_\infty S = C_{\text{Parasite}} \frac{1}{2} \rho V^2_{\text{Airplane's velocity in ft/s}} S \quad (2.18)$$

where

C_{Parasite} = Parasite drag coefficient

q_∞ = Dynamic air pressure = $\dfrac{1}{2} \rho V^2_{\text{Airplane's velocity in ft/s}}$

V = Aircraft velocity ft/s

ρ = Air density sl/ft^3

S = Wing surface area ft^2

The parasite drag coefficient can be determined empirically if you know the surface area of the fuselage and you know the magnitude of the drag force:

$$C_{\text{Parasite}} = \frac{D_{\text{Parasite Drag Force}}}{q_\infty S} \quad (2.19)$$

Comparing the parasite drag coefficients of airplanes of similar size is a measure of the aerodynamic efficiency, or aerodynamic "cleanness," of an airplane. The smaller $C_{Parasite}$ is, the less drag an airplane generates for an equivalent wing surface area.

Equivalent Flat Plate Area

Those who have studied physics may be puzzled by the notion of using a wing's surface area to determine parasite drag. Drag, as taught in physics, is measured by an object's cross-sectional area moving through air. The cross-sectional area is oriented perpendicular to the direction of travel. Thus, if a flat plate were dropped from the sky so that the flat portion were facing down, the drag force would be proportional to the area of the flat plate. But if you dropped the same plate so that its edge were facing down, the drag force would be proportional only to the surface area of the edge that faces down. It is obvious that the plate facing down, with its greater exposed surface area, would experience the greatest drag and would fall more slowly than the plate with its edge down. Sky divers use this principle, too: by flying with as much body area as possible exposed in a downward direction, they can arrest their terminal velocity to about 133 mph (116 knots or 196 ft/s) at an altitude of 2,500 ft. (This assumes a coefficient of drag $C_{Parasite}$ of 0.5, a body area of 7.53 ft ^{2}, a weight of 165 lb, and air density of 0.002280 sl/ft ^{3} at 2,500 ft altitude.) On the other hand, if they plunge foot-first or head-first, their terminal velocity jumps to 254 mph (221 knots or 372 ft/s) (assuming a reduced area of 2.56 ft ^{2} and the same parameters as previously noted). Terminal velocity is the maximum speed an object can reach, because the force of drag precisely matches the force of gravity ($W = D$).

You can calculate the terminal velocity of any object by using the following formula:

$$V_{\text{Terminal Velocity ft/s}} = \sqrt{\frac{2W_{\text{Weight in lb}}}{C_{\text{Parasite}}\,\rho_{\text{Air density}}\,S_{\text{Surface area in ft}^2}}} \qquad (2.20)$$

To see why this is so, you must realize that when an object reaches terminal velocity or constant speed, there are no net forces acting on it. This means that the force of gravity (weight) must precisely equal the drag force. Thus,

$$W_{\text{Weight in lb}} = D_{\text{Parasite Drag Force}} \qquad (2.21)$$

and

$$W_{\text{Weight in lb}} = C_{\text{Parasite}}\,q_\infty S$$

$$W_{\text{Weight in lb}} = C_{\text{Parasite}}\left(\frac{1}{2}\rho V^2_{\text{Terminal Velocity ft/s}}\right)S$$

Solving for $V_{\text{Terminal Velocity ft/s}}$:

$$V_{\text{Terminal Velocity ft/s}} = \sqrt{\frac{2W_{\text{Weight in lb}}}{C_{\text{Parasite}}\,\rho_{\text{Air density}}\,S_{\text{Surface area in ft}^2}}}$$

$C_{Parasite}$ depends on the shape of an object, and, in the case of a sky diver, the shape was assumed to be spherical with a value of 0.5 (in other words, *not* a flat plate area). Note that if you were considering a flat plate area, the coefficient of drag would be 1.28. As can be experimentally proven, any flat plate that is oriented perpendicular to the airstream will have a drag coefficient of 1.28. Thus, the shape of an object can make a huge difference in the value of the coefficient of drag. For example, a sphere that has the same area as a hollow cup will have a different value for $C_{Parasite}$. Irregularly shaped objects can have a drag coefficient as high as 2.

When considering an airplane that is falling nose down toward the ground in a steep dive, it is important to realize that the wings are still generating lift, which acts horizontally, as shown in Figure 2.14.

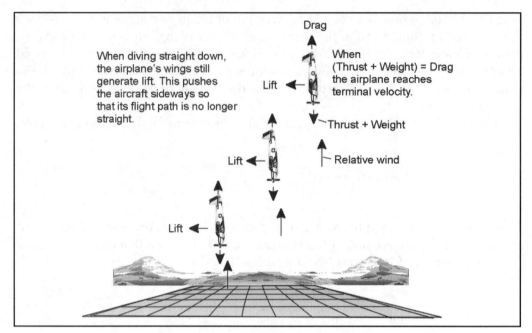

Figure 2.14 Airplane in steep dive generates horizontal lift.

The *equivalent flat plate area* of an airplane is a term used by aerodynamic engineers as a measure of drag efficiency. This method of measuring drag has the airplane's drag being represented by the drag of a flat plate with a specified area that is oriented perpendicular to the relative wind. For this measuring purpose, this "idealized" plate has a parasitic drag coefficient $C_{Parasite}$ of exactly 1.0, although in reality a flat plate has a drag coefficient $C_{Parasite}$ closer to 1.28.

Equivalent flat plate area f is equivalent to drag divided by dynamic pressure, and can be calculated from the following equation:

$$f_{\text{Flat Plate Area}} = \frac{D_{\text{Parasite Drag Force}}}{q_\infty} \tag{2.22}$$

If you rearrange Equation 2.19, the flat plate area is also equivalent to the following:

$$f_{\text{Flat Plate Area}} = \frac{D_{\text{Parasite Drag Force}}}{q_\infty} = C_{\text{Parasite}} S \tag{2.23}$$

It is important to realize that the flat plate area from Equation 2.23 is not the same as the total cross-sectional area of the real airplane.

Knowing the value of $C_{Parasite}$ for the wing (which is not the same as $C_{Parasite}$ for the flate plate), it is possible to figure out the equivalent flat plate area for any airplane. Table 2.2 shows typical values that were calculated from published performance data. Because this information is not from official engineering data, the figures shown are only approximations and should not be used in real performance calculations. In most cases, the data I used for $C_{Parasite}$ was extracted from the AIR model files in Flight Simulator. This means that the flat plate area results that I calculated in the table are by no means precise, because the data upon which it is based is estimated by the designers of these flight simulator aircraft and not taken from real world engineering data. For example, I have noticed that Hubin (*The Science of Flight*) has calculated that the flat plate f for the Cessna 182Q is really 5 ft ^{2} based on actual performance and not the 5.4 ft ^{2} that I have calculated here.

Table 2.2 *Parasite Drag Coefficients, Flat Plate Areas, and Wing Surface Areas of Several Airplanes*

AIRCRAFT	$C_{Parasite}$	WING AREA (FT^2) S	FLAT PLATE AREA (FT^2) f
Boeing 737	0.03613	1,135	41.0
Boeing 757	0.02295	1,994	45.8
Cessna 152	0.03800	160	6.1
Cessna 182	0.03100	174	5.4
Cessna 182RG (retractable landing gear)	0.02246	174	3.9
Cessna Citation Business Jet	0.01953	301	5.9
Douglas DC-3	0.01855	987	18.3
Extra 300 Aerobatic Plane	0.02344	112.38	2.6
General Dynamics F-16A Falcon	0.03174	341	10.8
Learjet 45	0.02295	253.3	5.8
McDonnell Douglas DC 10	0.02881	3,509	101.0
McDonnell Douglas MD-82	0.02490	1,209	30.1
Piper Warrior	0.03400	170	5.8
Schweizer 2-32 Sailplane	0.00977	180	1.8
Sopwith Camel	0.03174	174	5.5

We are now in a position to rewrite the terminal velocity of Equation 2.20 in terms of flat plate area. Because flat plate area equals $C_{Parasite} \times S$, where S is the wing area, we have the following:

$$V_{\text{Terminal Velocity ft/s}} = \sqrt{\frac{2W_{\text{Weight in lb}}}{f_{\text{Flat Plate Area}}\,\rho_{\text{Air density}}}} \qquad (2.24)$$

EXAMPLE 2.4

What is the terminal dive velocity for the Cessna 182RG with the engines off, gear up, flaps up?

Solution

We can use either Equation 2.20 or Equation 2.24, because we know that the equivalent flat plate area of the Cessna 182RG (from Table 2.2) is 3.9 ft^2.

$$\begin{aligned} V_{\text{Terminal Velocity ft/s}} &= \sqrt{\frac{2W_{\text{Weight in lb}}}{f_{\text{Flat Plate Area}}\,\rho_{\text{Air density}}}} \\[2mm] &= \sqrt{\frac{(2)\,(3100\ \text{lb})}{\left(3.9\ \text{ft}^2\right)\left(0.002377\ \text{sl/f}^3\right)}} \\[2mm] &= 818\,\text{ft s} = 485\ \text{kt} \end{aligned} \qquad (2.25)$$

Try this in the Cessna, and you'll see that its true velocity won't exceed about 500 knots, which is close to the predicted 485 knots.

Using Example 2.4 as your guide, you'll find that the terminal dive velocity for the Learjet is about 970 knots. For the 737-400 it should be about 1,000 knots TAS, but it is slightly less because of errors in the Microsoft 737-400 aerodynamic model. For my test, I started the aircraft at an elevation of 70,000 ft (an unrealistic number that is much higher than the aircraft's altitude ceiling) and I removed all temperature layers (to have StAt in effect) and then switched off the engines and put the plane into a steep dive. To keep the plane's nose aimed vertically at the ground, I used the spot view to get an outside view of the airplane as it descended. I also made sure that the airspeed indicator was showing true airspeed and switched on the latitude/longitude/airspeed display (**Shift+Z**) so that I could better monitor the airspeed. At the point of impact with the ground, I then noted the airplane's final airspeed, which was its terminal velocity. You can also switch on **Aircraft/Aircraft Settings/Crash & Damage/Detect Crash and Show Graph** to see what your descent profile and vertical velocity were just before the crash.

Table 2.3 shows typical values of parasite drag coefficients for various parts of the airplane. Notice that the biggest component of parasite drag is found from the fuselage and not the wing. Up till now, we have been discussing drag in terms of wing surface area and have ignored the other components of parasite drag that result from the fuselage, empennage, engine nacelles, landing gear, flaps, and spoilers. In the overall calculation of total parasite drag, however, all these components are summed to arrive at one coefficient of parasite drag. In other words:

$$C_{\text{Parasite Total}} = C_{\text{Parasite Fuselage}} + C_{\text{Parasite Wing}} + C_{\text{Parasite Empennage}} + C_{\text{Parasite Nacelle}}$$
$$+ C_{\text{Parasite Fuselage}} + C_{\text{Parasite Flaps}} + C_{\text{Parasite Landing Gear}} + C_{\text{Parasite Spoilers}} \quad (2.26)$$

Table 2.3 Parasite Drag of Airplane Components (Perkins and Hage, 1949)

PART	DESCRIPTION	$C_{Parasite}$
Wing	Main Wing	0.005 to 0.009
Empennage	Tail Section	0.006 to 0.008
Fuselage	Streamlined body, no external appendages	0.05
Fuselage	Small plane with nose engine	0.01 to 0.13
Fuselage	Large transport plane	0.03 to 0.10
Nacelle	Propeller engine mount above wing on small airplane	0.25
Nacelle	Wing leading edge propeller engine mount on large airplane	0.05 to 0.07
Nacelle	Turbojet/fanjet engine mounted on wing	0.05 to 0.07
Wing Tanks	Suspended below wing tip	0.10
Wing Tanks	Centrally located at wing tip	0.06
Wing Tanks	Below wing, inboard	0.19 to 0.21
Bomb	Suspended below wing (incl. support)	0.22 to 0.25
Flaps	60% span flaps deflected 30°	0.02 to 0.03

Modifying the Parasite Drag Coefficient in FSW95 Aircraft

Inside the aerodynamic models for Flight Shop–created aircraft, you'll find many of the aerodynamic terms used in this chapter. For example, the coefficient of parasite drag $C_{Parasite}$, is described as the zero lift drag coefficient in the **SIM.AIR** files found under the FSW95 **Sim** directory. You can edit and view the **.AIR** files using the software tools found on this book's CD-ROM. ACEdit, created by David Maschino, is an easy-to-use

Windows 95 program, and **AIRDEC.ZIP**, created by Matthias Weidemann, contains DOS programs that extract and annotate the aerodynamic data into text files that you can edit and convert back to data. Both programs should not be used with FS98 aircraft files, because of the different file format used for FS98 aircraft.

The zero lift drag coefficient used in the **.AIR** files is the equivalent of $C_{Parasite}$, and refers to airframe drag. Decreasing this value allows you to increase your cruise speed, and increasing it lowers your maximum speed. When you increase $C_{Parasite}$, you are increasing the equivalent flat plate area; lowering it decreases the airplane's equivalent flat plate area. For example, the 737's zero lift drag coefficient is 0.03613. If you increase this value, the 737's maximum cruise speed will decrease. To make the 737 a supersonic jet, for example, you would drastically reduce the zero lift drag coefficient and increase the maximum Mach value in the **.AIR** file from 0.81001 to 2.2000.

Other parasitic drag coefficients used in the **.AIR** files include the flaps drag coefficient, the gear drag coefficient, and the spoiler drag coefficient. When extended, each of these devices increases the flat plate area and increases drag. Thus, when you activate any of these controls, the appropriate drag coefficient is added to your zero lift drag coefficient to arrive at a total parasite drag coefficient.

Induced Drag

Induced drag is the undesirable but unavoidable consequence of developing lift from wings. Whereas parasite drag predominates at high speed, induced drag predominates at low speed and diminishes with greater speed. The induced drag can be found from the following equation:

$$D_{Induced\,Drag\,Force} = C_{Induced\,Drag} q_\infty S \tag{2.27}$$

where

$C_{Induced\,Drag}$ = Induced drag coefficient

q_∞ = Dynamic pressure = $\dfrac{1}{2}\rho V^2$

ρ = Air density sl/ft^3

V = Aircraft velocity ft/s

S = Surface area of wing ft^2

Note that the coefficient of induced drag $C_{Induced\,Drag}$ is not a fixed quantity, whereas $C_{Parasite\,Drag}$ has a constant value. Because induced drag is a result of the production of lift, it is reasonable to assume that induced drag is proportional to lift; it can be shown (although we do not prove it here) that $C_{Induced\,Drag}$ is proportional to the square of the coefficient of lift C_L. This relationship is illustrated in the following equation:

$$C_{\text{Induced Drag}} = \frac{C_L^2}{\pi e AR} \qquad\qquad (2.28)$$

where

AR = Aspect ratio
C_L = Coefficient of lift
e = Span efficiency factor (usually 0.85 to 0.95)

What causes induced drag? All wings create pressure differential zones between the upper and lower wing. When lift is created, pressure on top of the wing is negative, or less than the pressure underneath the wing. At the wingtips, air tends to flow from the high-pressure zone below the wing to the low-pressure zone above the wing, and this results in air washing up and over the wing. This twisting airflow is called a *wingtip vortice*, and it is quite strong when the airplane is flying at slow speeds (see Figure 2.15). At high speeds the turbulent airflow eases, but at low speeds the turbulence is large and creates induced drag, which is responsible for wake turbulence.

The only way to eliminate the vortices is to have an infinite wing with no edges. This is impossible, so airplane designers instead engineer wings that are long and tapered at the ends to minimize the vortex effect. A new development in recent years is the addition of winglets on the wingtips, which effectively increase the wingspan and thereby reduce induced drag.

NOTE Recent studies have shown that when wild geese fly in a close V formation, they minimize their wingtip vortices. In one such study, it has been suggested that 25 birds could have a range increase of about 70% compared with a lone bird (Lissaman and Shollenberger, 1970).

If you like to tinker with aircraft aerodynamic models, you can adjust the induced drag coefficient found in the FSW95 or Flight Shop **.AIR** files. Once you have done this, you can then use the FS98 Aircraft Converter to import the aircraft and its newly modified **.AIR** file into FS98. If you increase $C_{\text{Induced Drag}}$, at low speeds total drag will increase for a given angle of attack. For example, if you look at the **SIM2.AIR** file, which contains the aerodynamic model for the Learjet 35A in FSW95, you'll find that the induced drag coefficient is 1, whereas for the 737 in **SIM6.AIR**, the induced drag coefficient is 0.40002. If you increase these values, you'll discover that the airplane needs more thrust to maintain flight at slow speeds and that it feels heavier. Note that even though the 737 has a lower $C_{\text{Induced Drag}}$ than the Learjet, this does not mean that the 737 has less induced drag. Other factors come into play, such as the value of C_L, wing efficiency e, and the wing's aspect ratio.

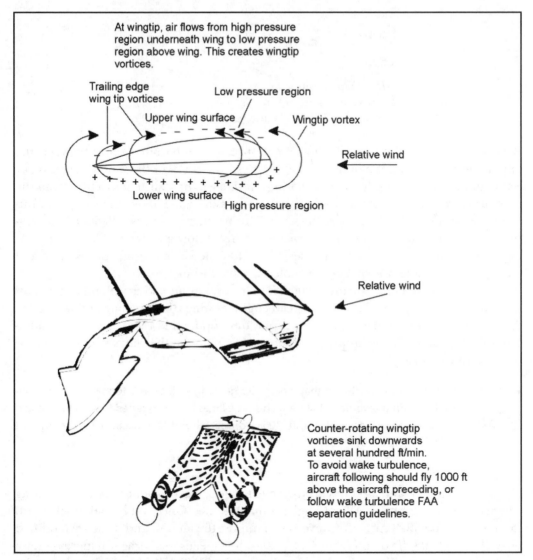

At wingtip, air flows from high pressure region underneath wing to low pressure region above wing. This creates wingtip vortices.

Trailing edge wing tip vortices

Low pressure region

Upper wing surface

Wingtip vortex

Relative wind

Lower wing surface

High pressure region

Relative wind

Counter-rotating wingtip vortices sink downwards at several hundred ft/min. To avoid wake turbulence, aircraft following should fly 1000 ft above the aircraft preceding, or follow wake turbulence FAA separation guidelines.

Figure 2.15 *Wingtip Vortices cause induced drag. The high-pressure zone underneath the wing tends to flow up and over the wingtip into the low-pressure zone on top of the wing. The swirling motion creates a downwash effect that is turbulent and causes drag at low speeds.*

How does this information help you? If you want your plane to sink quickly on final approach, increase the induced drag. On the other hand, if you want more ground effect so that you can "float" over the runway, decrease induced drag. Similarly, if the airplane suffers too much altitude loss in a turn, decrease the induced drag. Increasing the aspect ratio has the same effect as decreasing induced drag.

Wake Turbulence

Although all aircraft produce wingtip vortices, those produced by Cessnas and Learjets are not as feared as those produced by 757s and DC-10s. These huge, lumbering aircraft produce what is known as *wake turbulence*. Aircraft following in their paths can be flipped upside down by the corkscrew-like air vortices, which can reach peak tangential speeds of 300 ft/s (177 knots). Light aircraft are not the only planes affected; in 1972 at Fort Worth, a DC-9 followed too close to a DC-10 (two miles), rolled, caught a wingtip, and cartwheeled, coming to rest in an inverted position on the runway. All those aboard were killed. Because of this danger, air traffic controllers are required to separate small aircraft (12,500 lb or less) departing from an intersection behind a large or heavy aircraft (see following definitions) on the same runway by ensuring at least a 3 minute interval between the time the preceding large aircraft takes off and the succeeding small aircraft begins the takeoff roll. To inform the pilot of the required 3 minute hold, the controller will state, "Hold for wake turbulence."

For the purposes of wake turbulence separation minimums, air traffic control classifies aircraft according to the following definitions:

- Heavy: Aircraft capable of takeoff weights of 300,000 lb or more whether or not they are operating at this weight during a particular phase of flight. A 747, 777, or MD-11 would qualify as a heavy aircraft.
- Large: Aircraft of more than 12,500 lb up to 300,000 lb maximum certified takeoff weight. A 737 or Learjet would qualify as a large aircraft.
- Small: Aircraft of 12,500 lb or less maximum certified takeoff weight. A Cessna 182 would qualify as a small aircraft.

During the landing approach, different air traffic wake turbulence separation distances apply. The following separation distances apply to aircraft operating directly behind a heavy jet at the same altitude or less than 1,000 ft below:

- Heavy jet behind heavy jet: four miles.
- Small or large aircraft behind heavy jet: five miles.

When the separation distance is measured at the time the preceding aircraft is over the landing threshold, different minimums apply to small aircraft:

- Small aircraft landing behind heavy jet: 6 miles.
- Small aircraft landing behind large jet: 4 miles.

Because the counterrotating wingtip vortices trailing from large transport aircraft sink at a rate of several hundred feet per minute, pilots should fly at or above the preceding aircraft's flight path, altering course as necessary to avoid the area behind and below the generating aircraft. A vertical separation of 1,000 ft is considered safe.

Total Drag

Knowing the coefficient of parasite drag and the coefficient of induced drag, we can now calculate the total drag acting on the airplane:

$$D_{\text{Total Drag}} = D_{\text{Parasite Drag}} + D_{\text{Induced Drag}} \tag{2.29}$$

$$= C_{\text{Parasite Drag}} q_\infty S + C_{\text{Induced Drag}} q_\infty S$$

$$= C_{\text{Parasite Drag}} q_\infty S + \frac{C_L^2}{\pi e AR} q_\infty S$$

where

AR = Aspect ratio

C_L = Coefficient of lift

q_∞ = Dynamic pressure $\text{lb}/\text{ft}^2 = \frac{1}{2}\rho V^2_{\text{Aircraft speed in ft/s}}$

ρ = Air density in sl/ft^3

e = Span efficiency factor (usually 0.85 to 0.95)

S = Surface area of wing ft^2

If you consider that C_L is dependent on weight and that weight must exactly equal lift, we have the following:

$$C_L = \frac{L}{q_\infty S} = \frac{L}{\frac{1}{2}\rho V^2 S} \tag{2.30}$$

because

Lift = Weight or $L = W$

$$C_L = \frac{W}{\frac{1}{2}\rho V^2 S}$$

Plugging the coefficient of lift C_L relationship of Equation 2.30 into Equation 2.29, you get the equation for total drag in terms of aircraft weight W, velocity V (ft/s), air density ρ (sl/ft^3), wingspan b, and surface area S of the wing. Wing area is commonly used as the representative area for parasite and induced drag.

$$D_{\text{Total Drag}} = D_{\text{Parasite Drag}} + D_{\text{Induced Drag}} \qquad (2.31)$$

$$= C_{\text{Parasite Drag}} q_{\infty} S + \frac{W^2}{\pi e q_{\infty} b^2}$$

where

W = Aircraft weight in lb

q_{∞} = Dynamic pressure = $\frac{1}{2} \rho V^2$ in lb/ft^2

S = Wing surface area ft^2

b = Wingspan ft

e = Span efficiency factor (usually 0.85 to 0.95)

This is an interesting equation for the pilot, because it tells you a lot about your airplane's performance. Knowing your airplane's weight, wingspan, velocity, and coefficient of parasitic drag, for example, you can determine the exact amount of thrust needed to keep the airplane aloft (because thrust must equal drag for level flight). Even more interesting, if you need to know the velocity your airplane must maintain at a particular altitude with a specific aircraft weight, by a simple rearrangement of variables you can calculate the needed airspeed.

But the item that most captivates the attention of the aircraft designer and pilot is the last term for induced drag. Although we already have a relationship for induced drag from Equation 2.27, we haven't seen induced drag as a function of aircraft weight, wingspan, and airspeed.

$$D_{\text{Induced Drag}} = \frac{W^2}{\pi e q_{\infty} b^2} \qquad (2.32)$$

$$= \frac{W^2}{\pi e \frac{1}{2} \rho V^2 b^2}$$

From Equation 2.32, you can see that induced drag is inversely proportional to velocity squared and wing span. This means that the lower the aircraft's speed, such as when it is landing or taking off, the greater the induced drag. For example, if at sea level the induced drag for a 130,000 lb 737 flying at 450 knots is 970 lb, then at 300 knots the induced drag would be 2,182 lb, and at 150 knots (landing approach speed) induced drag jumps to 8,730 lb! However, the parasite drag follows an opposite pattern; at 450 knots the parasite drag might be 28,000 lb, at 300 knots parasite drag would be 12,500 lb, and at 150 knots parasite drag would be 3,100 lb.

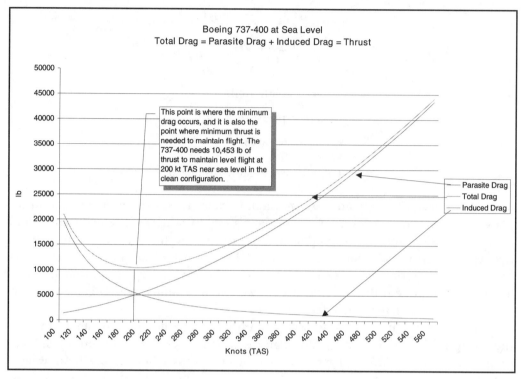

Figure 2.16 *Total drag is the sum of induced drag and parasite drag. Maximum efficiency during cruise is found at the intersection of the two drag curves, where there is a minimum of total drag. This graph is based on published data for a 130,000 lb 737-400 at sea level as it applies to Microsoft's Flight Simulator. Use this graph only as a guideline of general airplane performance; the real 737 will have different performance characteristics.*

Table 2.4 *Relationship between Airspeed, Induced Drag, Parasite Drag, and Total Drag.*

AIRSPEED	INDUCED DRAG	PARASITE DRAG	TOTAL DRAG
450 kt	970 lb	28,000 lb	28,970 lb
300 kt	2,182 lb	12,500 lb	14,462 lb
150 kt	8,730 lb	3,100 lb	11,830 lb

The total drag coefficient, or C_D, can be easily derived from Equation 2.29 by factoring out q_∞ and S as follows:

$$C_D = C_{\text{Parasite Drag}} + C_{\text{Induced Drag}} \tag{2.33}$$

$$= C_{\text{Parasite Drag}} + \frac{C_L^2}{\pi e AR}$$

where the variables are defined as in Equation 2.29.

Figure 2.16 illustrates the total drag in the 737-4000.

Lift to Drag Ratio

An important factor in airplane performance characteristics is the lift to drag ratio, or L/D. The ratio of L/D is also the same as C_L/C_D. Looking at the graph of L/D in Figure 2.17, we see that the L/D increases to some maximum and then decreases at the higher lift and drag coefficients. Note that maximum L/D occurs at only one angle of attack. If an airplane is operated at this angle of attack, the total drag is at a minimum and the most economical flight can be realized. Any angle of attack lower or higher than the maximum L/D point will result in an increase in drag and a consequent increase in thrust and fuel consumption.

In the graph of Figure 2.17, the maximum L/D occurs at a ratio of 12 when the airplane's angle of attack is 6°. Suppose that this airplane weighs 12,000 lb when flying level at a 6° angle of attack. This means that the drag would be 1,000 lb, because $L=W$ and $L/D=12/1$, and 12,000 lb/1,000 lb = 12/1. Table 2.1 shows some typical L/D values for several different airplane types.

Table 2.5 Lift to Drag Ratios for Various Airplane Types (Hurt, 1965)

AIRPLANE TYPE	MAXIMUM L/D
High performance sailplane	25–40
Propeller powered single engine airplane	10–15
Large transport airplane	12–20
Jet trainer	14–16
Supersonic fighter (while in subsonic flight)	4–9

A number of important airplane performance characteristics are found when the L/D ratio is maximum:

- Maximum range and endurance of airplanes
- Maximum climb angle for jet-powered airplanes
- Maximum power-off glide range

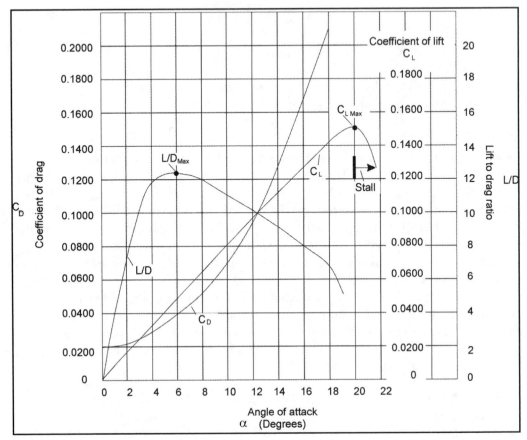

Figure 2.17 *Lift to drag characteristics for changing angle of attack.*

The most interesting of these characteristics is the power-off glide range. We won't prove it here, but it can be shown that the glide ratio is numerically equal to the L/D ratio. For example, if the airplane in a glide has an L/D of 12, each mile of altitude is traded for 12 miles of horizontal distance. Thus, if your engine suddenly decides to go on holiday, and you want to maximize your glide range, you should fly the airplane at a speed and angle of attack in which L/D is at a maximum.

Unbelievably, glide performance does not depend on the airplane's weight. Whether an airplane is a 3,100 lb Cessna or a 135,000 lb Boeing 737-400, if it has a glide ratio of 12 it could coast for a maximum of 12 miles horizontal for each mile of altitude. (These aircraft do not in fact have the same glide ratio.) Note that the angle of attack and the airspeed necessary to maintain the glide would be different for the two aircraft.

Aircraft operating manuals state the maximum glide in case of engine failure. For example, the Cessna 182RG manual states that when the airplane weighs 3,100 lb and the engine has quit with the propeller windmilling, the flaps and gear up, and zero wind assumed, the maximum glide occurs at 80 knots IAS. A graph shows that the glide range is 18.8 nm per 12,000 ft of altitude above the ground. Using these figures, it is easy to see that the glide ratio is as follows:

$$\text{Glide Ratio} = \frac{L}{D} = \frac{(18.8 \text{ nm})(6{,}076 \text{ ft}/\text{nm})}{12{,}000 \text{ ft}} = 9.5 \tag{2.34}$$

because

$$\cot \gamma = \frac{L}{D} = \frac{\text{Glide Range}}{\text{Aircraft Height}} \tag{2.35}$$

where

γ = Glide angle

The glide angle γ is the angle of the airplane's glide path with the ground. Using the preceding definition for the Cessna 182, you can calculate the inverse cotangent of 9.5, which is 6°. To get this result on a scientific calculator that doesn't have inverse cotangent, invert 9.5 by pressing the **1/x** key and then take the arctan of this number. The result will be 6°, which is the angle of your flight path to the ground but not the angle of attack.

Note that in the event of total engine failure during takeoff, it is seldom a good idea to make a 180° gliding turn to try to return to the runway. You lose far too much altitude during the turn to make it back to the airport. If you experiment with this technique with the Cessna 182 in Flight Simulator, you'll discover that this is so.

The maximum *L/D* ratios of gliders, such as the Schweizer 2-32 sailplane, are quoted in feet. Thus, for a quoted *L/D* of 34 for the Schweizer 2-32, this means that for every foot of vertical altitude lost, the pilot will be able to travel a maximum of 34 ft forward. This distance can be translated to miles or nautical miles as the case may be, so that an *L/D* of 34 would mean that the sailplane could fly 34 nm if it were at an altitude of 1 nm above ground (i.e., 6,076 ft).

Thrust

Thrust is the force that the engines apply to counteract drag. Whether it is a propeller or a jet, an engine is designed to push a large mass of air to the rear.

Because thrust must equal drag in level flight and because drag tells us how much lift is required for a given wing, it is possible to calculate the amount of thrust needed to keep an aircraft aloft. Later in the book we shall discover how to do this.

The amount of thrust needed to start taxiing the airplane can be calculated by this simple relation:

$$T_{\text{Thrust for Rolling Resistance}} = uN = uW \tag{2.36}$$

where

$N = m_{\text{Airplane Mass}}\, g$ = Normal force acting upwards on airplane through its landing gear. If you know the airplane's weight in lb, then $N = W$.

$g = 32\,\text{ft}/\text{s}^2$

u = Coefficient of Rolling resistance = 0.02 for rubber tires on concrete

W = Aircraft weight in lb

The coefficient of rolling resistance varies between 0.02 for properly inflated tires on smooth, hard surfaces to 0.2 on grass and up to 0.3 on dirt.

EXAMPLE 2.5

As a practical application of Equation 2.36, let's figure out how much thrust is required to get the 737 to start rolling:

$$
\begin{aligned}
T_{\text{Thrust for Rolling Resistance}} &= uN \\
&= (0.02)\,(138{,}500\,\text{lb}) \\
&= 2{,}770\,\text{lb}
\end{aligned}
\tag{2.37}
$$

The 2,770 lb of thrust needed to begin taxiing is a little more than 10% of the 737's total engine thrust available.

Thrust Required for Level, Unaccelerated Flight

Consider an airplane in level flight at a given altitude and steady velocity. We have already claimed that thrust must equal total drag in level flight. But how much thrust is required for a given airspeed, altitude, and weight? It is possible to use a spreadsheet program such as Excel to generate a graph, such as Figure 2.16 for the 737-400, that plots total drag, induced drag, and parasite drag at a given altitude. Looking at this graph, you can see that the minimum thrust needed to sustain flight near sea level is 10,453 lb and that the airspeed would be 200 knots TAS. This information is useful because it tells you that with one engine out, you can fly the 737 on its remaining 23,500 lb thrust engine and that the most efficient speed to do so is 200 knots.

To generate a graph such as Figure 2.16, you must use Equation 2.31 and plot separate data series for induced drag, parasite drag, and total drag for many different airspeeds. The graph is appropriate only for the given altitude that you choose for the air density, so you must generate a different graph for each desired altitude (use the StAt air density for the altitude from Appendix F). Once you know total drag, you also know thrust. After you have graphed all three curves for speeds up to Mach 1, find where the parasite and induced drag curves intersect, and that point is the most efficient cruise speed. It is also the maximum L/D for the airplane at this altitude and is the speed at which maximum glide range occurs.

Note that the figures and charts calculated here are not from Boeing engineering data but were estimated from Flight Simulator 737-400. Boeing chooses not to release such data to the public, presumably because this information would be useful to competing firms, especially those companies that create mathematical flight models for commercial simulators. Flight Safety International has stated that the cost of a high-fidelity model validated by the FAA for a level D simulator can run well into six figures.

Engine power is related to an aircraft's speed by the relationship $T \times V$, where T is the thrust force required to overcome drag and V is the airplane's velocity. Reciprocating engines and jet engines have slightly different power definitions which are described in the next two sections.

Reciprocating Engines (Propeller)

By definition, the propulsive horsepower required for a piston-powered airplane to fly at a given airspeed is as follows:

$$P_{\text{Horsepower}} = \frac{T_{\text{Thrust}} V}{325} = \frac{D_{\text{Total Drag}} V}{325} \qquad (2.38)$$

where

$P_{\text{Horsepower}}$ = Power required in horsepower
T_{Thrust} = Thrust (equivalent to drag) lbs
$D_{\text{Total Drag}}$ = Total Drag
V = Airspeed in knots
1 Horsepower = (325 knots) $\times$ (1 lb) or (1 knot) $\times$ (325 lb)

Note that horsepower is a nonstandard unit in equations. You must convert horsepower to units of ft-lb/s before employing it in equations using English engineering units:

$$1 \text{ horsepower} = 550 \text{ ft} \cdot \text{lb}/\text{s} \qquad (2.39)$$
$$= 746 \text{ Watts}$$

Two definitions of engine power are commonly used: *power available*, which is the power the engine is capable of producing, and *power required*, which is the power needed to keep the airplane flying. The power available from a piston-powered propeller engine differs from the power required. The power available is a characteristic of the engine's capabilities, whereas power required is a function of the aerodynamic design and weight of the airplane. The graphs of the two curves are plotted in Figure 2.18, where you can see that the excess power is the vertical distance between the two curves. The amount of excess power determines a plane's rate of climb.

The power delivered to the propeller by the crankshaft is defined as shaft brake power. Not all the power is available to drive the airplane; some of it is dissipated by inefficiencies of the propeller. For this reason, a new term, *power available*, is defined:

$$P_A = \eta P \qquad (2.40)$$

or

$$\text{hp}_A = \eta bhp$$

where

P_A = Power available to propel the airplane in ft lb/s

P = Shaft brake horsepower in ft lb/s
η = Propeller efficiency ($\eta < 1$)
hp_A = Horsepower available
bhp = Shaft brake horsepower

For the Cessna 182, the propeller efficiency has been calculated to be around 0.8 (Hubin, 1992).

Jet Engines

Whereas piston engines are rated in terms of horsepower, jet engines are usually rated in terms of pounds of thrust. As before, the power required is given by the following:

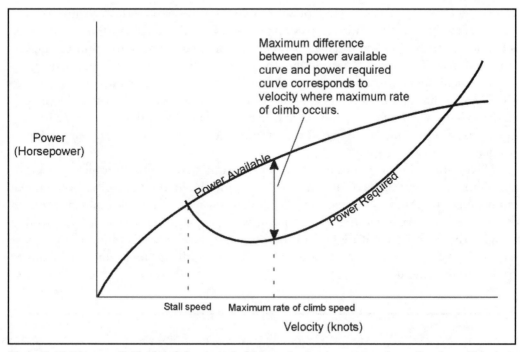

Figure 2.18 *Power available versus power required curves for the piston-powered propeller plane. Note that the excess power allows a plane to climb.*

$$P_R = T \times V = D \times V \qquad (2.41)$$

where

T = Thrust in lb required to overcome drag
D = Total drag
P_R = Power in lb-ft/s
V = Velocity in ft/s

The power available from a jet engine is obtained from the following:

$$P_A = T_{\text{Thrust}} V_\infty \qquad (2.42)$$

where

P_A = Power available ft lb/s
T_{Thrust} = Thrust in lb
V_∞ = Airplane's velocity ft/s

The curves of power available versus power required for the jet-powered airplane are plotted below in Figure 2.19. As with the piston-powered propeller airplane, the excess power is defined to be the vertical distance between the power-available curve and the power-required curve. This excess power defines the maximum rate of climb for the airplane.

The maximum endurance, or time aloft, of a jet airplane occurs when the airplane is flying at minimum thrust required. Endurance is defined as range divided by velocity (E=R/V) This occurs when the airplane is flying at a velocity so that the *L/D* ratio (i.e., C_L/C_D) is at its maximum value. If you examine Figure 2.16, you can see that total drag is at a minimum at this speed.

Maximum endurance does not occur at the same speed as that required for maximum range, therefore, maximum endurance is not obtained by plugging in the maximum range and best L/D speed in the E=R/V formula above. Actually, maximum endurance is governed by fuel consumption, and keeping fuel flow as low as possible will give the most hours of flight. Low fuel flow rates occur when minimum power is required, so for maximum endurance you must fly with the least amount of power applied to the engines.

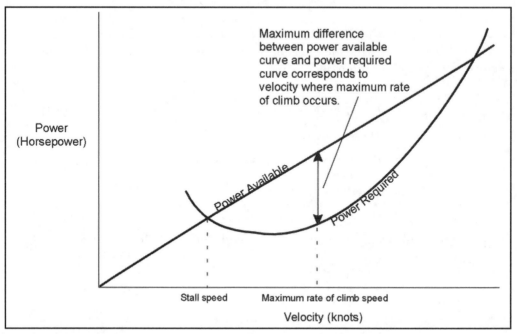

Figure 2.19 *Power-available versus power-required curves for the jet-powered propeller plane. Note that the excess power allows a plane to climb.*

Interestingly, the maximum range for a jet airplane occurs when the airplane is flying at a velocity in which $(C_L)^{1/2}/C_D$ is at a maximum.

THE WING AND THE ANGLE OF ATTACK

Many people falsely assume that the wing generates lift simply by moving through the air. This is partly true, but it is the shape of the wing and the angle of attack that the wing makes with the air it meets that determine how much lift is generated (see Figure 2.20). A flat plate flying through the air at a zero degree angle of attack generates the same lift above itself as it generates below itself. In short, it generates no lift and will come crashing to earth. If you angle that same flat plate slightly upward, creating a positive angle of attack, and fly it again, you will generate lift. Why? The wing's angle of attack creates lift. Note that this same principle would apply to a symmetrical wing but not to a cambered airfoil, whose curved shape on top of the wing creates dynamic pressure differences even at a zero angle of attack.

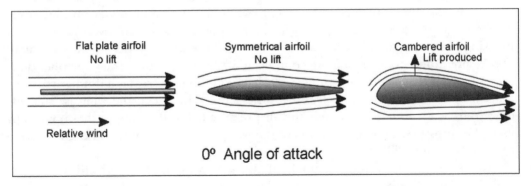

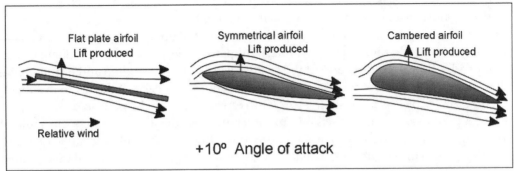

Figure 2.20 *The flat plate and symmetrical plate generate no lift at a zero angle of attack, whereas the cambered airfoil generates lift at a zero angle of attack.*

What is the angle of attack, and why is it so important? First, let's talk about what the angle of attack is *not*. The angle of attack is not the angle that the plane's nose makes with the horizon, nor is it the angle at which the aircraft flies with reference to the horizon. An aircraft can be pointing straight up and have a low angle of attack—for example, when an F-16 flies straight upward. An aircraft can be flying perfectly level with the horizon and have a negative angle of attack as it descends slowly in a power glide. Nor is the angle of attack the angle that your wings make with the aircraft's longitudinal axis.

The angle of attack is the angle at which the wing meets the air. Or put another way, *the angle of attack is the difference between where the airplane points and where the airplane goes.*

In the first definition, what does it mean when we say "the angle at which the wing meets the air"? If you look at Figure 2.21, you'll see that the angle of attack can be different for any attitude that the airplane has. The airplane generates lift in two ways: by pushing air down with a positive angle of attack; and by the principles of Bernoulli's theorem of pressure differentials, with the air pressure being greater under the wing than over the wing. In fact, the angle of attack and Bernoulli's theorem are traits of the same principle: lift is created by the wing pushing down air and the air pushing back. As Newton pointed out, there is an equal and opposite reaction for every action. So if the wing pushes down on the air, the air must push the wing up. Bernoulli's principles of pressure differentials are a more complicated way of explaining the same phenomenon: it is the wing's cambered, or curved, shape on top that creates a downward acceleration of air mass caused by pressure differentials. In effect, the wing is "sucked" upward by a "vacuum" above, while the air pressure below the wing pushes upward by its higher pressure. Both are artifacts of the wing's angle of attack, and both describe the same action for lift.

Now that you know what the angle of attack is, you'll understand why we call aircraft "airplanes." It is because a wing is nothing more than an inclined plane that pushes against air to generate the opposite reaction force of lift.

The Greek letter α is used to symbolize the angle of attack, which is not to be confused with the glide flight path or climb flight path angle γ. Notice that in Figure 2.22, α depends only on the direction of the relative wind to the chord line and is not dependent on whether the aircraft is climbing or descending. In each of the three instances, the angle of attack is a constant +10° with regard to the flight path and the relative wind. A pilot peering out of the side window cannot use the wings to judge the angle of attack unless the plane is flying level in horizontal flight. In a climb, the angle of attack is always less than the angle relative to the horizon, and in a descent it is always greater.

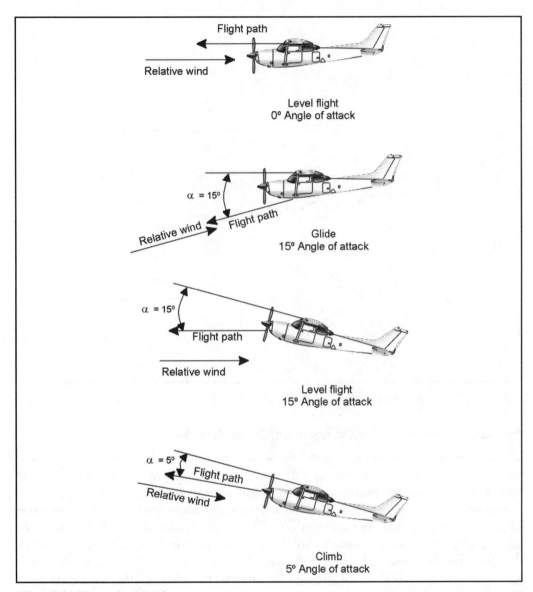

Figure 2.21 The angle of attack.

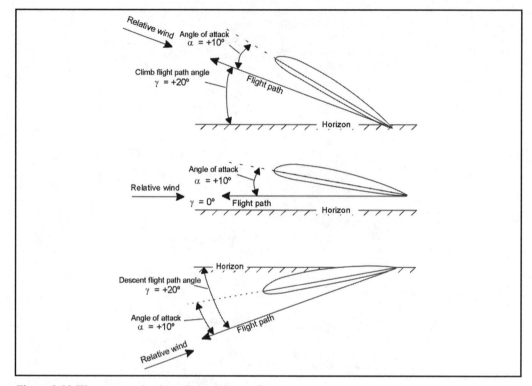

Figure 2.22 The same angle of attack for different flight orientations.

Pressure Distribution for Different Angles of Attack

The air pressure distribution around an airfoil changes for different wing angles of attack. As you can see from Figure 2.23, positive and negative zones of pressure surround the wing. Arrows pointing away from the wing show areas of negative pressure that are pulling the wing in that direction. Arrows pointing toward the wing show areas of positive pressure that are pushing the wing. As you increase the angle of attack, the sizes of the pressure areas change as do their location. At some negative angles of attack, the airfoil produces zero lift, whereas at a slightly positive angle of +3°, the negative pressure above the wing is so much stronger that it pulls the wing up, thereby creating lift. (Cambered airfoils will produce positive lift at small negative angles of attack. Generally speaking, if the angle of attack is less than –2° to –4°, a cambered airfoil will start producing negative lift.) At an angle of attack of 14° to 18° (the angle depends on the airplane and airfoil being used), the wing produces the maximum possible lift. Notice that in this configuration, the negative lift is at a maximum above the wing and there is also positive pressure pushing the wing up from below. Increasing the angle of attack beyond 14° to 18° will cause a stall, as the coefficient of lift falls to zero.

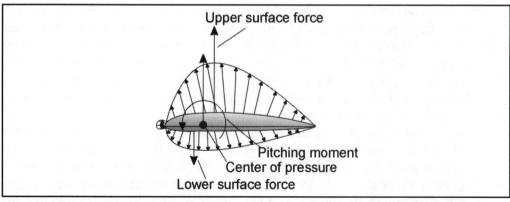

Figure 2.23 *Center of pressure for both upper and lower surfaces on a cambered airfoil. When all the pressure forces are combined into a single vector force, this point is called the center of pressure. The center of pressure moves forward with increasing angles of attack. Note that the resultant force on both upper and lower surfaces causes a nose-down pitching moment.*

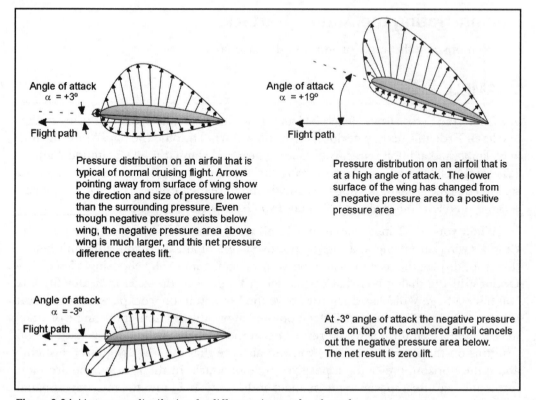

Figure 2.24 *Air pressure distribution for different wing angles of attack.*

Not all aircraft stall at 14° to 18°; the FA-18 Hornet can fly level at a 55° angle of attack! In general, swept-wing aircraft stall at a significantly higher angle of attack than straight-wing aircraft do. However, the 14° to 18° angle of attack figure is typical for light aircraft. Angle of attack is the essence of flight for many pilots, who use it in everyday flying. In the military, for example, one doesn't fly airspeed on the approach; instead, it's the AOA (angle of attack). The same principle can be applied to any other aircraft. All speeds for almost everything are based on AOA.

Typical airliners have a wing incidence of +2°, so you must add another 2° to the displayed pitch attitude to arrive at an approximate AOA. In most current Boeing aircraft, AOA is not directly displayed to the pilot, so the only way you can determine it is by using performance computers. Stall AOA will also dramatically change as a function of flap extension, especially the leading edge devices, which in all Boeing aircraft is the first "notch" of flap selection.

If all the pressure forces on a wing are mathematically combined into one force vector acting at a single point, this point is called the *center of pressure*. As the angle of attack increases, the center of pressure on the upper surface of the wing moves forward.

Demonstrating the Angle of Attack

Let's demonstrate the angle of attack in the Cessna.

EXAMPLE 2.6

Take off in the Cessna from Meigs Field and try to fly the aircraft so that it is flying straight and level. To do this, accelerate down the runway with full throttle (no flaps), raise the nose at 60 knots, and at liftoff retract your landing gear and climb to 1,500 ft altitude. Between 1,500 and 2,000 ft, trim the airplane using the elevator (or elevator if you are using a joystick) so that the airplane is flying level and then reduce the throttle to 2,100 RPM. Your airspeed should level out at about 100 knots if you have done everything correctly.

When you are flying straight and level, you can see in your spot view that your Cessna's wings are flying at a slightly positive angle of attack. If you still don't believe this is so, display the axis indicator on your cockpit window by choosing **Views/View Options**; in the dialog box that opens, select **Large V** in the **Axis Indicator** list box. You'll see a large V displayed slightly above the horizon in the cockpit window, indicating that the aircraft's wings are indeed pointed above the horizon. If the angle of attack were 0°, the axis indicator would rest right on the horizon. Although it is hard to confirm this on the artificial horizon, you can also see that the wing symbols are slightly above the horizon, indicating a positive angle of attack. In the Learjet, you are more fortunate, because a special angle of attack indicator is built into the instrument panel.

When you approach the stall speed for the FS98 Learjet, you'll notice that the angle of attack indicator passes 0.6, which corresponds with 1.3 times the stalling speed in the existing wing configuration (this speed is called VREF). The angle of attack indicator is indexed so that 1.0 corresponds to the stalling angle of attack. If the indicator moves past 0.6 and increases to 0.8, you are in danger of stalling and the stall indicator and stick shaker will activate telling you that that your wings are at too high an angle of attack to generate lift. Generally, in almost every airplane, the way out of a stall is to push the stick forwards and add thrust to lower the angle of attack. If you don't do this swiftly, you'll pancake into the ground.

Now that you are in the right position to experiment, let's play with the Cessna's angle of attack. Reduce the throttle to about 1,660 RPM. Immediately, the nose will start to drop and the plane will start to lose altitude. To correct this, pull the stick back as far back as need be—without entering a stall—and try to maintain level flight. Your airspeed must not drop below 54 knots if you are to avert a stall.

Example 2.6. describes a flight technique known as *mushing* the airplane. Mushing is defined as flying the aircraft in a partly stalled condition with controls ineffective; not being able to gain altitude. When we mush the aircraft, we are flying at a high angle of attack and therefore lift is at a minimum, just barely enough to support the weight of the airplane. In principle, most airplanes fly with their nose high, thereby pointing higher than it actually goes. Otherwise, the wing would have no angle of attack and little or no lift would be generated. When the plane is cruising at high speed, the angle of attack is very small or even zero for some airfoils. In slow flight, the angle of attack must be greater than at high speed, because otherwise the aircraft would not push enough air downward to maintain lift.

If you have trouble setting up a high angle of attack, try the "Mushing the Cessna" situation found in the **Flight Situations** directory on the CD-ROM that accompanies this book. Simply copy this file into your **Pilots** directory where you have installed Flight Simulator and then load the situation using the **Flights\Select Flight** menu command. You can see the extreme angle of attack that the mushing Cessna is flying in Figure 2.25 along with the pitch angle displayed at the top of the window. Although the airplane is pointed up, nose high as if it wanted to climb, its actual flight path is level. Note that even though the airplane appears to be climbing, the lift vector *L* would be perpendicular to the horizontal relative wind; therefore, *L* is oriented vertically straight up and not at an angle as you might otherwise misunderstand from the lower climb diagram of Figure 2.6.

Cockpit View

Spot View

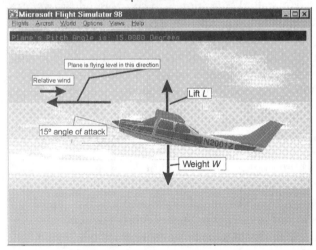

Figure 2.25 Mushing the Cessna in level flight in a high angle of attack.

EXAMPLE 2. 7: HOW TO MUSH ANY AIRPLANE USING THE AUTOPILOT

Using the autopilot, you can mush any airplane at any speed. As an example, let's try mushing the Learjet for various speeds.

1. While flying the Learjet, load the **Autopilot Attitude and Heading Control** adventure using the **Flights/Adventures** menu. This assumes that you have copied **AutoAlt.ADV** from the book's CD-ROM into the **Flight Simulator/ADV** directory and that you have installed **AAFWAV.ZIP**. If you have FSW95, you must also install the Aircraft Converter for FSW95 (File name is FSCONVT.EXE).

2. Press **Shift+A** followed by the plane's current flight level. Be sure to press the number keys on the main keyboard and not the numeric keypad. The flight level is expressed in hundreds of feet; if you wanted to fly at 18,000 ft altitude, you would press **Shift+A+180**, where the 180 represents flight level 180 ($180 \times 100 =$ 18,000). You should hear your altitude repeated, and the autopilot will then kick in to lock in the altitude you selected.

3. Slowly reduce the throttle. As you do so, press **Ctrl+P** to display the airplane's pitch angle on-screen. As the airplane slows, the autopilot will pitch the airplane's nose up in a desperate attempt to maintain the altitude lock.

Eventually, as you reduce thrust to a certain level, the autopilot will mush the airplane's angle of attack past its ultimate C_L for that speed (see Figure 2.8), and the airplane will stall. Remember that C_L changes for each angle of attack, and when the airplane's speed falls below the minimum C_L needed to counteract the airplane's weight, it will stall.

If you jot down the pitch angle for various airspeeds and then use Equation 2.12 (substitute the airplane's weight W for L in the equation, because L is oriented in the same direction as W), you can figure out C_L for each angle of attack. Then you can draw a graph of C_L versus the angle of attack for any airplane (as shown in Figure 2.8 for the Cessna, Learjet, and 737-400). Be sure to conduct your speed tests near sea level at StAt and be sure to display indicated airspeed.

If a positive angle of attack is required for level flight, how then do aircraft fly upside down in aerobatic flying? After all, a wing flying upside down should theoretically generate negative lift downward toward the ground. The answer is that the wing must be flown at a positive angle of attack upside down, as shown in Figure 2.26. You can try this in the Extra, but I wouldn't advise it in the Cessna!

EXAMPLE 2.8

If you want to try flying the Extra 300 upside down with a high angle of attack, you'll need to disable Auto-coordination so that the rudders are disabled from the ailerons. When you reach a safe altitude, roll the aircraft upside down (**keypad 4** or **keypad 6**). When the plane is upside down, you must immediately press push forward on the stick (yes—I mean push the stick *forward* or, from the keyboard, press **keypad 8**) to raise the wing's angle of attack. If you don't do this, you'll crash.

Figure 2.26 Flying upside down with a high angle of attack in the Extra 300 aerobatic plane.

Because flying is a balancing act that involves neutralizing the forces of lift, weight, thrust, and drag, you will find that each airplane has its own angle of attack for level flight that changes with speed and weight. The more speed an aircraft has and the lighter it is, the less angle of attack it will need to sustain flight. Conversely, the less speed and more weight an aircraft has, the greater is the angle of attack for level flight.

EXAMPLE 2.9

You can experiment with the relationship between the angle of attack and airplane weight in the Cessna by ridding your airplane of fuel to make it lighter. First, fly the airplane with almost empty fuel tanks. Then, when you are flying level, fill your tanks and notice how much you must raise the nose to compensate for the additional lift you need through the greater angle of attack.

To empty the fuel tanks, follow these steps:

1. Select **Aircraft/Aircraft Settings/Engines & Fuel/Fuel**.
2. In the dialog box that opens, type **5** in the left and right fuel percentage indicators. This action will reduce your fuel to 5% of capacity and rid you of about 500 lb of fuel.

To fill the tanks, reverse this procedure, this time entering 100% of capacity.

Airplanes get the most miles per gallon of fuel when flown slowly with nose high at a high angle of attack.

T I P

Why Stalls Occur

A stall occurs when there is a breakdown of airflow over the wings, but the reason for this interruption is less obvious. Some people think that stalls occur because the airplane lacks speed, and others think that stalls occur because the aircraft's nose is too high. Both explanations are wrong. An airplane can stall at any speed or in any attitude, as we shall soon see with surprising results.

The main reason stalls occur is that the wing has an excessive angle of attack (see Figure 2.27). Usually, an angle of attack greater than 14° to 18° will cause a stall. Note that at small or negative angles of attack, the wing may not generate enough lift to maintain the airplane in flight, but the airplane is not stalled. In such cases, the airplane will simply descend in a glide. A stall is quite a different matter. When a stall occurs, the wing is at too great an angle of attack to be able to push enough air down to maintain lift. The airflow over the top of the wing is disrupted and burbles and

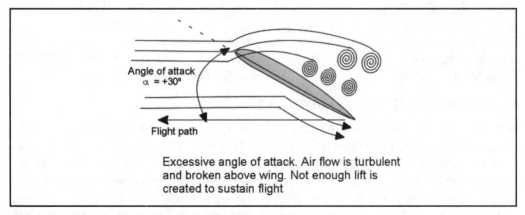

Figure 2.27 Excessive angle of attack is the culprit for stalls.

breaks away, creating turbulent eddies. All this commotion creates much drag but no lift, and the airplane falls from the sky. Furthermore, because airflow is disrupted over the control surfaces, such as the elevators, rudders, and ailerons, these controls become ineffective and you can lose control of the airplane. In some cases, the loss of control is so severe that no matter what you do, you cannot recover. That is why a stall is dangerous and why it must be avoided.

EXAMPLE 2.10

To prove that a stall can occur at any speed, try this demonstration. You can stall the aircraft at slightly less than 112 knots even though the Cessna has a normal stall speed of 54 knots for level flight. Follow these steps:

1. Fly the aircraft at 112 knots or less and then bank the aircraft more than 60° and execute a fast turn by pulling back on the stick. Try not to lose or gain altitude as you make the turn.
2. If you activate the g meter on-screen (press **Shift+Z** twice), you can see that as you pull back on the stick, the g-meter rises. Eventually, you'll reach a point where the stall indicator on the windshield will light. This tells you that rather than exceed the airplane's load limit, your wings stalled at the speed of 112 knots, which is much greater than the 54 knots stall speed of the Cessna for level flight.

Knowing that the Cessna's maximum maneuvering speed V_A is equal to 112 knots when it weighs 3,100 pounds, we know that at this speed or less, the Cessna's wings will stall under the maximum load that is put on them before they will break. In other words, no matter how far you deflect the controls, there is no way you can tear the wings off the airplane by imposing undue aerodynamic stresses on them. This is the definition of maneuvering speed, and each aircraft has its own V_A associated with its design. Generally speaking V_A is arbitrarily set at around twice the airplane's normal straight flight stalling speed, and at this speed the wings never exceed more than 4 g's of force for light aircraft. We shall address this subject in further detail in Chapter 3.

Load and Limit Accelerated Stalls

For light aircraft, such as the Cessna 182, the FAA requires that airplane wings be designed so that they can withstand at least 3.8 g's of force (i.e., a load factor of 3.8) plus a safety margin of 1.5 times the prescribed load limits (i.e., 5.7 g's of force would be the ultimate failsafe load). A single g is the acceleration that any object would undergo if it were dropped close to the Earth's surface, and it is equivalent to 32 feet per second per second, or 32 ft/s^2. Four g's of acceleration would mean that an aircraft would be accelerating at 128 ft/s^2, and at six g's, the aircraft would accelerate at 192 ft/s^2. Heavier aircraft, such as 747s and DC-10s, have different design limitations. Because of their higher wing loading (around 122 lb/ft ^{2} as opposed to 72 lb/ft ^{2} for the Learjet and 17.8 lb/ft ^{2} for the Cessna), large airplanes are not as affected by air turbulence and are seldom faced with load factors greater than 2.5 g's. Thus, the FAA has different load limit requirements for aircraft based on weight and wing size, as shown in Table 2.6.

Table 2.6 Load Limit and Ultimate Load Factors for Aircraft

FACTOR	NORMAL AND COMMUTER AIRPLANES	UTILITY AIRCRAFT	ACROBATIC	AIR TRANSPORT
Load limit factor	+2.1 to +3.8 (depends on aircraft weight)	+4.4g's	+6.0g's	+2.5 to +3.8g's
Ultimate positive load factor	1.5 × limit load factor = +3.15 to 5.7g's (depends on aircraft weight)	+6.6g's	+9g's	3.75g's
Negative load limit factor	−1.52g's	-1.76g's	-3.0g's	-1.0g's
Ultimate neg. load factor	1.5 × negative limit load factor = −2.28g's (depends on aircraft weight)	-2.64g's	-4.5g's	-1.5g's

In Table 2.6, the load factor is defined as the ratio of lift force to the weight of the airplane and is a value that should never be exceeded in flight. If you exceed this limit, the airplane's structure may be permanently deformed. The ultimate load factor includes a safety factor of 150%, or 1.5 times the load limit factor that the FAA uses to certify aircraft. All aircraft must be able to withstand the ultimate load factor for at least 3 before failure occurs. Positive load factors refer to loads that are exerted upward on the wings, and negative load factors refer to loads that are exerted downward.

In level flight, the load factor is 1, because lift equals weight. In turns and any other maneuver in which the airplane experiences accelerations and the lift forces do not equal the airplane's weight, the load factor follows this relationship:

$$n = \frac{L}{W} \tag{2.43}$$

where the components of L and W are generally chosen to be in the same direction as the maximum load being imposed on the airplane (usually in a direction perpendicular to the wings). The value of n is simpy the ratio of the magnitudes of the two vectors L and W.

The FAA calculates the preceding load factors by using this formula:

$$n = 2.1 + \frac{24,000}{W_{\text{Weight of Airplane}} + 10,000}$$ (2.44)

For air transport category aircraft:

where

n may not be less than 2.5 and need not be greater than 3.8
W is the design maximum takeoff weight
For general aviation:
where
n need not be more than 3.8
W is the design maximum takeoff weight

EXAMPLE 2.11

Let's try an example of using a load factor to determine the safe operating characteristics of the Cessna. We know from Table 2.6 and Equation 2.44 that the 3,100 lb Cessna has a load limit of 3.93. This means that you must never exceed this force on your wings, or the airplane will be overstressed. We also know that the ultimate load limit is 1.5× the load limit of 3.93, or 5.89. Thus, if you exceed 5.89 g's for more than 3 on the Cessna's airframe, the aircraft will fall apart.

How do we overstress the Cessna to test this? Here's one way: during level flight, we suddenly change the angle of attack by abruptly pulling back on the stick, generating very large load factors on the wings. This maneuver is known as an *accelerated stall*, and the load factor can be calculated by the following:

$$n = \frac{L}{W} = \left(\frac{V}{V_{\text{Stall}}} \right)^2$$ (2.45)

Thus, if we slightly exceed the V_A maneuvering speed of 112 knots by 1 knot (e.g., 113 knots) and plug in the Cessna's value of 54 knots stall speed, we find that $n = 4.37$. This amount is over the load limit, but it is not enough to cause structural failure, which we know occurs at the ultimate load limit of 5.89. So to exceed the ultimate load limit, we must try a higher airspeed before executing the accelerated stall maneuver. We will try 140 knots, which, if you plug into Equation 2.45, will give you a load factor of 6.72. This exceeds the Cessna's ultimate load factor of 5.89 by a considerable margin.

Follow these steps to overstress the Cessna:

1. To turn on aircraft stress (it is off by default) select **Aircraft/Aircraft Settints/Crash & Damage**. In the dialog box that opens, click on **Aircraft Receives Damage from Stress** and, if needed, click on **Show Aircraft Damage** so that both boxes are lit.
2. Fly the Cessna at maximum throttle, with the flaps raised and the gear up.
3. Display the g-meter on-screen by pressing **Shift+Z** two times (in FSW95 press four times).
4. From **Options/Preferences/Instrument**, turn on **Show Indicated Airspeed**. We need to display indicated airspeed on the airspeed indicator to accurately assess the velocity of the air flowing over the wings. By default, Flight Simulator displays true airspeed and not indicated airspeed.
5. Increase the airspeed to 132 knots. If you have trouble with this, lower the nose slightly until the airspeed starts increasing.
6. At 132 knots, pull back on the stick as quickly as you can. (You must use your mouse, joystick, or yoke to accomplish this step; **keypad 2** will not work quickly enough to raise the elevators.) The g-meter will show an increasing load on the wings. When it exceeds 5.97 g's for 3, the aircraft will fall apart.

Note that Flight Simulator's g-meter will show a load of 6.1 g's when the airplane breaks apart. Although you have exceeded this load in the air, the airplane is designed to break apart at 6.1 g's, and the meter will stay frozen at this level.

Those of you with sharp eyes will notice that Cessna's 6.1 g ultimate load limit differs slightly from the calculated ultimate load limit of 5.89 g's. I can only assume that the program makes other assumptions that I am not accounting for. Perhaps someday Microsoft will publish details of the aerodynamic model that it is using. Until then, however, expect small discrepancies between calculated values and actual values in the simulation.

Load Factor in a Turn

In Chapter 1, we learned that the total lift force in a turn is calculated this way:

$$L = \frac{W}{\cos \beta} \tag{2.46}$$

where

L = lift in lb
W = the aircraft's weight in lb
β = the bank angle

Using the definition of load factor from Equation 2.43 and Equation 2.46, we can calculate the load factor in a turn:

$$n = \frac{1}{\cos \beta} \qquad (2.47)$$

Example 2.12

What is the load factor for any airplane that is flying a 45°, a 66°, and a 88° turn?

Solution

Plugging in the values from Equation 2.47, we have the following:

For the 45° turn: $\qquad\qquad$ (2.48)

$$n = \frac{1}{\cos 45°} = \frac{1}{0.7071} = 1.41\mathrm{g}$$

For the 66° turn:

$$n = \frac{1}{\cos 66°} = \frac{1}{0.4067} = 2.45\mathrm{g}$$

For the 88° turn:

$$n = \frac{1}{\cos 88°} = \frac{1}{0.0349} = 28.7\mathrm{g}$$

In Figure 2.28, you can see the extraordinary jump in load factor as an airplane banks from 45° to almost 90°. Even a 45° bank imposes a 1.5 g load on the airplane's wings. At 60°, the load increases to twice the weight of the aircraft, and at 88°, the airplane would break up. To put this in concrete terms, during a 60° bank, a 150 lb person will feel as if he or she weighs 300 lb. For passenger comfort, airliners usually bank at no more than 30°; small business jets may do as much as 45° in what is called a steep turn. The Cessna operator's manual prohibits turns greater than 60°. Some fly-by-wire aircraft, such as the Airbus A320, have guidance computers that override any attempt to fly at bank angles greater than 66°. An airplane is said to be *fly-by-wire* when there are no mechanical or hydraulic links between the pilot's stick and the airfoil control surfaces. The connection is made instead through electrical wires, which send digital signals to actuators that move the controls. To ensure reliability in the event of component failure, there are usually three or more computers that "vote" to determine whether the pilot's action makes sense. If this committee comes to a consensus, then and only then do the controls move. If one computer is malfunctioning and sending conflicting signals, the other two computers overrule it.

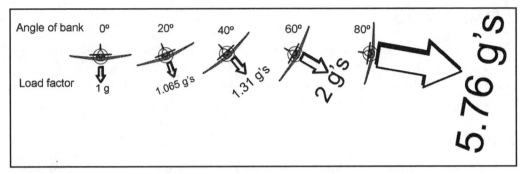

Figure 2.28 *Load factors for the airplane in a banked turn.*

Load Factor in an Encounter with a Wind Gust

Looking at the FAA's definition of the load limit in Equation 2.44, you can see that heavier airplanes have smaller load limits than lighter airplanes have. Although we won't prove it here, the load factor that a given airplane experiences when it is faced with air turbulence is inversely proportional to wing loading, which is the weight of the airplane divided by its wing area. The higher the wing loading, the less load factor an airplane experiences when subjected to wind gusts (Hubin, 1992). As a result, it is much more comfortable and safer to fly in a 737-400 with a wing loading of 122 lb/ft² than it is to fly in a Cessna 182 with a wing loading of 17.8 lb/ft². This is also why the FAA has lower load limits for heavy jet transports than for general aviation.

$$n = 1 + \frac{a \rho_0 U_E V_{TAS}}{2\left(\dfrac{W}{S}\right)} \tag{2.49}$$

n = Load factor in g
a = Slope of the lift curve for C_L
ρ_0 = Density of air

$$U_E = U \sqrt{\frac{\rho}{\rho_0}}$$

where

U_E = Equivalent airspeed of wind corrected
      for density altitude
U = Velocity of wind gust in ft s
ρ = Air density at altitude
ρ_0 = Air density at sea level
V_{TAS} = True airspeed of Airplane in ft/s
$\dfrac{W}{S}$ = Wing loading lb/ft²

EXAMPLE 2.13

Suppose we know that an upward wind gust of 25 ft/s (11.8 knots) causes a wind load factor of 3 g's on a 3,100 lb Cessna when it is traveling at 135 knots. What would the load factor be if the Cessna were flying at 150 knots and it weighed only 2,000 lb when it was hit with an upward gust of 35 ft/s (20.7 knots)?

Solution

Rather than plug in all the values to Equation 2.49, it is easier to use ratios. We know that the incremental load factor due to the gust was 2 (because 1+ 2 in the above equation equals 3 g's). Because all the changes are proportional, we can multiply the original values for the second term of the equation, without worrying about those terms that haven't changed.

$$n = 1 + (2.0)\left(\frac{150 \text{ kt}}{135 \text{ kt}}\right)\left(\frac{20.7 \text{ kt}}{11.8 \text{ kt}}\right)\left(\frac{1}{\dfrac{2000 \text{ lb}}{3100 \text{ lb}}}\right) = 1 + 6.0 = 7 \text{ g} \qquad (2.50)$$

With a 7 g load, the Cessna would break apart. From this you can see that wind gusts are a worry for pilots of light airplanes.

Using the data for the 737 in Equation 2.49, it is possible to calculate that even with abrupt and severe vertical wind gusts up to 33 knots (56 ft/s) there is no danger of structural failure. There is also a safety margin of 1.5 built into the load limit, so this estimate is conservative.

Airspeeds

The seemingly innocuous airspeed indicator conceals a great deal of information about your airplane's performance capabilities. Unlocking those secrets is the focus of this chapter, where you'll learn the difference between indicated airspeed and true airspeed, what critical Mach number represents, and how the stall speed is affected by weight, load factor, and turns.

VELOCITY AND IMPORTANT AIRSPEEDS OF THE AIRPLANE

Both the altimeter and the airspeed indicator are profoundly affected by changes in the atmosphere. At higher altitudes, the atmosphere thins, and the air pressure and air density drop. Airspeed indicators measure air pressure and cannot tell whether the atmosphere is thinner, nor can they tell when the speed of the airplane is high enough to compress air to the point that dynamic pressure is affected. This error is due to the compressibility of air pressure especially shows up when the airplane is traveling faster than 200 knots. At speeds greater than this, the airspeed indicator shows an indicated speed that is much less than the plane's true airspeed. This is the reason for calling it "indicated airspeed." Because air pressure and air density change with altitude and temperature, the dynamic pressure measured inside the pitot tube will never be the same for an aircraft traveling at high altitude as it is for an aircraft traveling at low altitude even if the aircraft moves with the same ground speed.

In real airplanes, the airspeed indicator shows indicated airspeed, or IAS, because it offers an accurate measure of airflow over the wings, with the effects of altitude already taken into account. An airplane that stalls at 54 knots IAS at sea level will stall at 54 knots IAS at 10,000 ft. On the other hand, if we were to use TAS, the airplane stalling at 54 knots TAS at sea level would not stall at 54 knots at 10,000 ft but instead would stall at a much higher speed. The same is true for other flight conditions such as a glide. If a plane's best glide speed at sea level is 80 knots IAS, then at any altitude its best glide will still be 80 knots IAS. At 35,000 ft, its best glide would actually be 136 knots TAS, a far cry from the 80 knots IAS that is shown on the airspeed indicator. This is why IAS is so useful and why TAS is not used to measure airspeed in the cockpit.

TAS is used to measure the airspeed of the aircraft relative to undisturbed air. If you know the velocity and direction of the surrounding air (or "wind"), you can calculate the ground velocity. Therefore, TAS is useful for navigation. As you fly higher and higher, the airplane's true airspeed increases even if the IAS does not. Airflow over the wings must remain constant if the airplane is to generate the same amount of lift at sea level as it generates at 30,000 ft. IAS is thus more useful to the pilot than TAS, because IAS reveals how fast the air is flowing over the wings and, indirectly, how much lift is being generated.

This brings up another curious fact. If the airspeed indicator displays IAS, because of thinner air at higher elevations it can never display airspeeds greater than 350 knots. This may be a great disappointment to speed demons who expect to see their airplanes fly at 450 knots at 37,000 ft. The reality is that you are flying at 450 knots, but the airspeed indicator shows the airspeed to be 350 knots IAS. In most cases, depending on altitude and temperature your maximum IAS will be even lower than 350 knots.

Flight Simulator's airspeed indicator is set to display TAS by default. You can change the display to IAS by choosing **Show Indicated Airspeed** under **Options/Preferences/Instrument**. IAS is more useful than TAS when you are learning how to fly, but if you need to know how much ground you are covering it is convenient to be able to switch back and forth.

A rule of thumb for calculating true airspeed from indicated airspeed is to add 2% to the indicator reading for every 1000 ft of altitude. For example, if your airspeed indicator shows 100 knots and your altitude is 10,000 ft, your true airspeed is 100 knots plus 2% of 100 knots for each 1000 ft of altitude; this adds up to 120 knots true airspeed, because 2 knots (2% of 100 knots) × 10 (thousand feet) = 10 knots, and 100 knots IAS + 20 knots TAS correction factor equals 120 knots TAS.

$$\text{True airspeed} = (\text{Indicated airspeed}) \times (2\% \text{ of Indicated airspeed} \quad (3.1)$$
$$\text{for each 1,000 of altitude)}$$

Each airplane has its own set of restrictions for flying at certain speeds. For example, the Cessna has a maximum landing-gear-extended speed that is different from the Learjet's. Exceeding these published speed restrictions can result in damage to the aircraft. Table 3.1 shows most of the airspeed definitions and symbol labels you are likely to encounter.

Table 3.1 *Working Airspeed Definitions*

SYMBOL	DESCRIPTION	DEFINITION
V_{TAS} (also TAS or KTAS)	(Knots) True Airspeed	True airspeed is equivalent airspeed (V_{EAS}) corrected for air density error and is the speed of the airplane expressed in knots in relation to the air mass in which it is flying. This is not the same as ground speed. Flight Simulator normally displays V_{TAS} unless you change the airspeed indicator to display V_{IAS}. True airspeed increases with altitude when the indicated airspeed remains constant. When the true airspeed remains constant, the indicated airspeed decreases with altitude.
V_{IAS} (also IAS or KIAS)	(Knots) Indicated Airspeed	The speed of the airplane in knots as observed on the airspeed indicator. It is the airspeed without correction for indicator, position, or compressibility errors. At high altitudes, V_{IAS} is always less than V_{TAS}. When airspeed is less than 200 knots at sea level under StAt, V_{IAS} is very close, if not the same as, V_{TAS}.
V_{CAS} (also CAS or KCAS)	(Knots) Calibrated Airspeed	Calibrated airspeed is the indicated airspeed (V_{IAS}) corrected for pitot-static error and instrument position error in the aircraft. When airspeed is less than 200 knots, CAS is approximately equal to TAS at sea level under StAt.
V_{EAS} ($V_{Equivalent}$)	Equivalent Airspeed	Equivalent airspeed is calibrated airspeed (V_{CAS}) corrected for compressibility. Compressibility becomes noticeable when the airspeed is great

Table 3.1 *continued*

Symbol	Description	Definition
		enough to create impact pressure that causes the air molecules to be compressed within the impact chamber of the pitot tube. As the air is compressed at greater speeds, it causes the dynamic pressure to be greater than it should be. Therefore, a negative correction value must be added to calibrated airspeed to show correct equivalent airspeed. At speeds below 200 knots IAS, $V_{EAS} \approx V_{IAS}$ (indicated airspeed). At sea level at 59°F, $V_{EAS} \equiv V_{TAS} \equiv V_{IAS}$ (when airspeed is less than 200 knots and compressibility is not a factor).
V_A	Maneuvering Speed	Maximum speed at which the load limit can be imposed, either by gusts or full deflection control surfaces. Beyond this airspeed, abrupt movements of the controls can cause structural damage.
V_{APP}	Approach speed	Approach speed is defined as $1.3 \times$ the stalling speed of the aircraft with the flaps in the approach configuration and the gear up.
V_B	Design Speed for Maximum Gust Intensity	Maximum speed for maximum gust intensity.
V_C	Design Speed for Cruising Speed	Cruise speed.
V_D	Design Dive Speed	Maximum speed when diving, as measured by $V_D = N_{NE}/0.9$
V_E	Equivalent Airspeed	The airspeed that produces the same dynamic pressure at altitude as does a true airspeed of the same value at sea level under StAt.
V_{FE}	Maximum Flap Extended Speed	Highest speed permissible with the wing flaps extended.
V_{LE}	Maximum Landing Gear Extended Speed	Maximum speed at which the airplane can be flown with the landing gear extended.
V_{LO}	Maximum Landing Gear Operating Speed	Maximum speed at which the landing gear can be safely extended or retracted.

Table 3.1 *continued*

SYMBOL	DESCRIPTION	DEFINITION
V_{MC} or V_{MCA}	Minimum Control Speed with the Critical Engine Inoperative	Minimum speed in the air at which the airplane is still controllable when one engine suddenly becomes inoperative and the remaining engine is operating at full thrust.
V_{MCG}	Minimum Control Speed on the Ground with the Critical Engine Inoperative	Minimum control speed on the ground that allows the airplane to be under control using the aerodynamic controls alone when one engine suddenly becomes inoperative and the remaining engine is operating at takeoff thrust.
V_{MO}/M_{MO}	Maximum Operating Limit Speed	On turbine aircraft, V_{MO} is the structural limit designed to prevent airframe damage from excessive dynamic pressure, and M_{MO} is the limit at which the aircraft is protected against shock wave damage as it approaches the speed of sound. Both V_{MO} and M_{MO} vary with altitude; as a result, the barber pole, which is a red and white striped needle on the airspeed indicator, moves automatically to display the correct maximum operating speed on the turbine aircraft for different altitudes. V_{MO} is of most concern at lower altitudes, where the atmosphere is denser, and M_{MO} is most restrictive at higher altitudes, where the atmosphere is colder and the speed of sound is lower.
V_{NO}	Maximum Structural Cruising Speed	The maximum structural cruising speed. Exceeding this limit may cause permanent deformation of the airplane structure.
V_{NE}	Never Exceed Speed	The airspeed that should never be exceeded. If flight is attempted above this speed, structural damage or structural failure may result.
V_R	Rotation Speed	The speed during takeoff at which the aircraft is rotated (pitched up) $10°$ during the takeoff roll so that the nose gear is off the runway. V_R always occurs after V_1.
V_{REF}	Landing Reference Speed	The speed during the final approach. V_{REF} is usually used with reference to multiengine aircraft. For most turbine-powered aircraft, V_{REF} is calculated at $1.3 V_{SO}$ (i.e., $1.3 \times$ stall speed in the landing configuration).

Table 3.1 *continued*

SYMBOL	DESCRIPTION	DEFINITION
		Because V_{SO} changes with landing weight, V_{REF} must be calculated for every landing.
V_S	Stalling Speed	Minimum steady flight speed at which the aircraft is controllable.
V_{SO}	Stalling Speed	Minimum steady flight speed at which the aircraft is controllable in the landing configuration.
V_{S1}	Stalling Speed	Minimum steady flight speed at which the aircraft is controllable in a particular gear/flap configuration.
V_X	Best Angle of Climb Speed	Airspeed at which the airplane will obtain the maximum altitude per unit of time. Normally this speed decreases with altitude.
V_Y	Best Rate of Climb Speed	The speed that results when the aircraft obtains the highest altitude in a given horizontal distance. Normally this speed increases with altitude.
V_1	Takeoff Decision Speed	The calibrated airspeed at which the critical engine in a multiengine aircraft is assumed to fail. If engine failure occurs at V_1, the distance to continue the takeoff to 35 feet will not exceed the usable takeoff distance. If the engine failure occurs before V_1, the accelerate-stop distance will be less than the remaining runway length.
V_2	Takeoff Safety Speed	The actual speed of the aircraft when it is 35 feet above the runway as demonstrated during single-engine takeoff. V_2 must be at least 1.1 times greater than V_{MCA} and at least 1.2 times greater than V_{SO}. V_2 is always greater than V_R. V_2 must be computed for every takeoff, because it depends on the stall speed of the airplane in the landing configuration (V_{S0}), which is dependent on aircraft weight. Also, V_2 must be calculated for every landing in case a go-around is necessitated by an engine failure during the landing.

In the event of an engine failure, jet aircraft also use similar speed terminology. V_{MCA} specifies the worst-case minimum control speed with the critical engine out while in the air in the takeoff configuration. V_{MCG} defines the minimum speed with the critical engine out while on the ground, and V_{MCL} defines the minimum speed during the landing or final approach with the critical engine out when the airplane is in the landing configuration. The *critical engine* is the engine that, when it fails, causes the most difficulty for the pilot in maintaining directional control. At any airspeed less than V_{MC}, the air flowing past the rudder doesn't provide enough force to overcome the asymmetrical yawing forces caused by takeoff power on the one engine. For both V_{MC} and V_{MCA} the FAA requires the following:

1. Maximum rudder deflection and 5° aileron bank must stop the airplane's turn within 20° of its original heading with the critical engine out.

2. After recovery, the pilot should be able to maintain the airplane in straight flight with not more than a 5° bank (wing lowered toward the operating engine). This does not mean that the airplane must be able to climb or even hold altitude. It means only that a heading can be maintained.

During cruise, a jet's speed is expressed by Mach number rather than by knots, although both units are displayed on the airspeed indicator. Mach numbers and the relationship to the speed of sound are discussed at the end of this chapter.

Dynamic Pressure and Equivalent Airspeed

Dynamic pressure, or q_∞, is the force that is responsible for lift on a wing and is equivalent to $\frac{1}{2}\rho v^2$, where v is the airspeed in ft/s. You may be wondering whether to use true airspeed or indicated airspeed in equations that involve dynamic pressure. The answer is that you can use both, with certain limitations. (Because of the compressibility of air at high speed, indicated airspeed must be less than 200 knots when used in the equations.) But how can this be, if V_{TAS} is always greater than V_{IAS} at high altitude? After all, you should not be able to get similar results for dynamic pressure if you have two different values of velocity. The solution to this seeming paradox lies in the role air density plays; if you vary the air density in the dynamic pressure equation, you can establish a link between velocity at sea level and velocity at altitude. Assuming incompressible airflow (a condition that exists at speeds less than 200 knots IAS), it is possible to show that an equivalent airspeed exists at sea level that generates the same dynamic pressure as a given true airspeed at altitude.

To see why this is so, let's first define some terms. Equivalent airspeed, or $V_{Equivalent}$, has been defined as the airplane's calibrated airspeed corrected for compressibility of air errors in the pitot-static system at high speeds. It is also defined as the airspeed at sea-level air density that would correspond to some true airspeed at some altitude for the same dynamic pressure q_∞. The important thing is that the dynamic pressure (lift on the wings divided by wing area times the coefficient of lift, or L/SC_L) at sea level must be the same as the dynamic pressure at a higher altitude. For example, an airplane flying at 150 knots EAS generates the same amount of dynamic pressure as an airplane flying at 269 knots TAS at 35,000 ft MSL. This means that both airplanes, if they are of the same type, generate exactly the same amount of lift both at sea level and at 35,000 ft! That is why it is called equivalent airspeed.

Equivalent airspeed is related to true airspeed by the following relationship:

$$V_{\text{Equivalent}} \equiv V_{\text{TAS}} \sqrt{\frac{\rho_{\text{Air density at altitude}}}{\rho_{\text{Air density at sea level}}}} \qquad (3.2)$$

Equation 3.2, which is limited to cases in which airspeed is less than 200 knots IAS, can be proved by rearranging terms in Equation 3.3 and solving for $V_{\text{Equivalent}}$.

$$q_{\infty} = \frac{1}{2} \rho_{\text{Air density at sea level}} V_{\text{TAS}}^2 = \frac{1}{2} \rho_{\text{Air density at sea level}} V_{\text{Equivalent}}^2 \qquad (3.3)$$

Be careful not to equate wing loading—weight divided by wing area (W/S)—with dynamic pressure q_{∞}, for they are not equal. This point may be potentially confusing, because both wing loading and dynamic pressure are measured in lb/ft^2 and it is easy to mistakenly think that dynamic pressure in lb/ft^2 must equal wing loading in lb/ft^2 for the airplane to remain aloft. From the lift Equation 2.11 in Chapter 2, we know that dynamic pressure is related to wing loading only by including the coefficient of lift C_L:

$$q_{\infty} = \frac{L}{C_L S} \qquad (3.4)$$

for level flight:

$$q_{\infty} = \frac{W}{C_L S}$$

As seen in Figure 2.8 (Chapter 2), C_L is different for each airplane type and depends on wing shape, angle of attack, and other airplane characteristics.

Using Equation 3.3, you can plug in true airspeed or equivalent airspeed (which is the same as indicated airspeed when the plane is flying at less than 200 knots) to calculate dynamic pressure. Thus, you don't even need to know air density for a given altitude to calculate dynamic pressure; you need only plug in the airspeed shown on your indicated airspeed display and plug in the known value of $\rho_{\text{Air density at sea level}}$. For example, to obtain the dynamic pressure at 10,000 ft, use Equation 3.3 to square the indicated airspeed; then divide by 2 and multiply by the sea level air density of 0.002377 sl/ft^3. Note that you must use always use air density at sea level, or 0.002377 sl/ft^3, in equations involving q_{∞} when using equivalent or indicated airspeed. The relationship between $V_{\text{Equivalent}}$ and sea level air density is important, because it establishes how equivalent airspeed—and by extension indicated airspeed—are the most important speeds aerodynamically that a pilot needs to know. This fact should not be lost on the reader who realizes now that equivalent airspeed tells the pilot the stall speed regardless of altitude as well as the amount of dynamic lift being generated.

Another important point gleaned from the two previous equations is that an airplane's true airspeed at sea level is the same as $V_{\text{Equivalent}}$, assuming speeds less than 200 knots ($V_{\text{Equivalent}} \equiv V_{\text{TAS}}$ at sea level). At a high altitude, to generate the same amount of lift as it does at sea level V_{TAS} must be greater than $V_{\text{Equivalent}}$ because the air density is less. Although we won't prove it here, it is possible to show that at subsonic speeds less than about 200 knots, $V_{\text{Equivalent}}$ is equivalent to V_{IAS}, the indicated airspeed. At 30,000 ft, the maximum compressibility error is only 5 knots when V_{TAS} is less than or equal to 200 knots. At lower altitudes and lower V_{TAS} airspeeds, this difference is much less, becoming zero at sea level.) At airspeeds higher than 200 knots, the compressible form of the Bernoulli equation must be used and an additional correction factor must be subtracted from V_{IAS}. (In other words, $V_{\text{Equivalant}}$ is greater than V_{IAS} at speeds greater than 200 knots.) The reason for this additional correction factor is that at high airspeeds, the air molecules are compressed into the pitot-static system and the airspeed indicator shows a higher value than is actually occurring. We shall learn later in this chapter how to convert V_{TAS} from V_{IAS} accounting for the compressibility error at high speeds.

Let's try an example of converting equivalent airspeed into true airspeed.

EXAMPLE 3.1

Suppose the 737 is flying at 10,000 ft at 190 knots IAS. What is the true airspeed and the equivalent airspeed?

Solution

Because the airspeed is less than 200 knots, we don't need to worry about compressibility error and can use Equation 3.2 with $V_{\text{IAS}} = V_{\text{equivalent}} = 190$ knots. Now we must find the true airspeed corrected for air density variation at 10,000 ft. Consulting Appendix F, we find that air density ρ equals 0.001756 sl/ft^3 at 10,000 ft and equals 0.002377 sl/ft^3 at sea level. Using Equation 3.3, and rearranging terms, we have the following:

$$V_{\text{TAS}} = V_{\text{Equivalent}} \sqrt{\frac{\rho_{\text{Air density at sea level}}}{\rho_{\text{Air density at altitude}}}} = (190 \text{ kt IAS}) \sqrt{\frac{\left(0.002377 \text{ sl}/\text{ft}^3\right)}{\left(0.001756 \text{ sl}/\text{ft}^3\right)}} \quad (3.5)$$

$$= 221 \text{ knots TAS}$$

STALL SPEED IN LEVEL FLIGHT

The clean stall speed of an airplane in level flight is related by this equation:

$$V_S = \sqrt{\frac{2W}{C_{L_{MAX}}\rho S}}$$

(3.6)

where

V_S = Stall speed of aircraft in ft s
W = Weight lb
$C_{L_{MAX}}$ = Maximum coefficient of lift
ρ = Density of air at altitude sl/ft^3
S = Surface area of wing ft^2

Equation 3.6 can be easily derived from the lift equation $L = W$, because lift force L must precisely cancel out weight force W at the point of stall. The stall speed V_S can be expressed as a true airspeed (use the correct value of air density ρ at altitude), or it can be expressed as $V_{\text{Equivalent}}$ (use $\rho = 0.002377$ sl/ft^3).

Clean stall configuration refers to an aircraft that is flying with flaps fully retracted, no leading edge devices deployed, and the landing gear up.

NOTE

Equation 3.6 can be derived by a simple rearrangement of the variables in the following equation of lift:

$$L = C_{L_{Max}} q_\infty S = C_{L_{Max}} \left(\frac{1}{2}\rho V_S^2\right) S$$

(3.7)

where

L = Lift force in lb
$C_{L_{Max}}$ = Maximum lift coefficient
q_∞ = Dynamic pressure lb/ft^2
V_S = Stall speed in ft/s
ρ = Density of air at altitude sl/ft^3
S = Surface area of wing ft^2

Notice that for Equation 3.6, the airplane's stall speed is related to wing loading (W/S). Therefore, a slow landing speed can be obtained by having a very low wing loading or by having a high maximum lift coefficient. For small airplanes with low wing loading, slow stall speeds are easily obtained; but what about heavy jet transports with high wing loading, such as the 737? Obviously, one cannot change wing loading very easily on a heavy jet. Instead, aircraft designers have come up with slats, flaps, and other high lift devices that increase the maximum lift coefficient so that the stall speed can be reduced. With a slower stall speed, an airliner can make a landing approach at a slower and safer speed.

EXAMPLE 3.2

What is the clean stall speed for the Cessna 182, assuming that it is flying at sea level StAt and $C_{Lmax} = 1.6$?

Solution

With no flaps or landing gear (clean stall configuration), the wing area S for the Cessna is 174 ft^2, and air density ρ at sea level is 0.002377 sl/ft^2. We also know that the Cessna 182 weighs 3,100 lb. Using Equation 3.6, we have the following:

$$V_S = \sqrt{\frac{2W}{C_{L_{MAX}}\rho S}} = \sqrt{\frac{(2)(3100\text{ lb})}{(1.6)(0.002377\text{ sl}/\text{ft}^2)(174\text{ ft}^2)}} = 96.8\text{ ft s} = 57\text{ knots TAS}$$

(3.8)

Although the published stall speed for the Cessna 182 is 54 knots, our calculated stall speed of 57 knots differs slightly because the estimated lift coefficient of 1.6 is inexact compared with that of the real Cessna 182.

From example 3.2, if we know the maximum lift coefficient C_{Lmax}, the weight, the wing surface area, and the air density ρ, we can calculate the stall speed for any aircraft. Unfortunately, determining C_{Lmax} is not easy, because it depends on many factors related to the wing shape and design of the aircraft. However, working the other way, if you know the published clean stall speed for an airplane, you can calculate C_{Lmax}. For example, for the FS98 Learjet, you will find that if the clean stall speed of the Learjet is 115 knots IAS at 4,000 ft MSL, then $C_{Lmax} = 1.61$ at maximum takeoff weight (auxiliary fuel tanks must be full). The same calculation for the FS98 737's clean stall speed of 130 knots IAS at 4,000 ft MSL would make $C_{Lmax} = 2.13$ at maximum takeoff weight (auxiliary fuel tanks must be full). These numbers are useful for other investigations of aircraft performance.

Boeing performance data for MTOW 737-400 shows that the stall speed in the clean configuration is 154 knots and not the 130 knots that the Microsoft 737-400 model uses. This will affect the calculation of C_{Lmax}. I have chosen to use the Microsoft stall speed of 130 knots, and therefore the C_{Lmax} that I have used in this chapter is incorrect for the real 737-400. C_{Lmax} for the real MTOW 737 should have a value of 1.71.

Boeing performance data for the real MTOW 737 reveal that the stick shaker and stall warning system should activate at 172 knots IAS and the clean stall speed should be 154 knots IAS, but this doesn't correspond to what happens with the Microsoft 737. I found that at 4000 ft MSL, the clean stall speed for the Microsoft 737 was closer to 147 knots TAS (130 knots IAS), and that the stall warning only activated when this speed was reached.

The clean stall speed in the Cessna **SIM.AIR** file was correct.

Stall Speed in a Level Turn

An aircraft's indicated stall speed is always higher in a turn, because more lift is needed to keep the aircraft aloft. The exact relationship can be found by equating the maximum lift available in Equation 3.7 and the lift force component $W/\cos\beta$ from Equation 1.7 (Chapter 1).

$$L = C_L q_\infty S = C_L \left(\frac{1}{2} \rho V_{\text{Stall in bank}}^2 \right) S = \frac{W}{\cos \beta} \tag{3.9}$$

During level flight $W = L$, so

$$L = \frac{W}{\cos \beta} = \frac{C_L \left(\frac{1}{2} \rho V_{\text{Stall in level flight}}^2 \right) S}{\cos \beta} \tag{3.10}$$

Therefore because L also is equal to

$$L = C_L \frac{1}{2} \rho V_{\text{Stall in bank}}^2 S$$

we have

$$C_L \frac{1}{2} \rho V_{\text{Stall in bank}}^2 S = \frac{C_L \left(\frac{1}{2} \rho V_{\text{Stall in level flight}}^2 \right) S}{\cos \beta}$$

Solving for the stall speed V_{Stall} from Equation 3.10 for any given bank angle β, we have the following:

$$V_{\text{Stall in bank}} = \frac{V_{\text{Stall in level flight}}}{\sqrt{\cos \beta}} \tag{3.11}$$

Note that you can use $V_{\text{Equivalent}}$ or V_{TAS} for stall speeds in Equation 3.11, as long as V_{Stall} and $V_{\text{Stall in level flight}}$ are both consistently expressed as TAS or as equivalent airspeed.

EXAMPLE 3.3

What is the stall speed for the FS98 Learjet 45 at 4,000 ft MSL when it is banked in a 45°turn? Express the answer in true airspeed and in indicated airspeed.

Solution

We know that the clean stall speed for the FS98 Learjet is 115 knots IAS. Because this speed is less than 200 knots we can call this equivalent airspeed and not worry about compensating for compressibility error. Plugging in the values, we learn that the stall speed in a 45°bank will be the following:

$$V_{\text{Stall in 45° bank}} = \frac{V_{\text{Stall in level flight}}}{\sqrt{\cos \beta}} = \frac{115 \text{ knots IAS}}{\sqrt{\cos 45°}} = 163 \text{ knots IAS} \qquad (3.12)$$

Or in terms of true airspeed:

$$V_{\text{Stall in 45° bank}} = \frac{V_{\text{Stall in level flight}}}{\sqrt{\cos \beta}} = \frac{122 \text{ knots TAS}}{\sqrt{\cos 45°}} = 172 \text{ knots TAS} \qquad (3.13)$$

Thus, if you try banking the FS98 Learjet in a 45°turn at a true airspeed of less than 172 knots and TAS 4,000 ft MSL, the aircraft will stall (but only at 4,000 ft MSL!). The indicated airspeed for the banked stall is of more interest to the pilot, because it says that the airplane will stall in a 45°banked turn at 163 knots IAS *at any altitude.* If you try this yourself, make sure Flight Realism is turned up to **Real** under **Options/Aircraft Settings/Realism.**

In Example 3.3, airspeed was expressed in both TAS and IAS. If the banked turn had been conducted at 30,000 ft and you wanted to use true airspeed, you would have had to recalculate $V_{\text{Stall in level flight}}$ TAS at 30,000 ft because it would have a different value than $V_{\text{Stall in level flight}}$ TAS at 4,000 ft. No such problem would have existed if you had expressed the airspeed as equivalent airspeed (i.e., indicated airspeed), because $V_{\text{Stall in level flight}}$ IAS has the same value of 115 knots at 4,000 ft as it does at 30,000 ft. Now do you see why indicated airspeed is a much more valuable and informative tool to the pilot than true airspeed?

Effect of Load Factor on Stall Speed

Load factor n is related to the stall speed V_S by the following:

$$V_{\text{Stall}} = V_{\text{Stall in level flight}} \sqrt{n} \qquad (3.14)$$

where load factor is measured in g's and airspeed can be measured in TAS or equivalent airspeed as long as you remain consistent with airspeed type.

The important thing is that Equation 3.14 applies to airplanes that are flying in any type of maneuver and not just banked turns. As before, as long as you are consistent with airspeed type you can use true airspeed or equivalent airspeed in the equation.

EXAMPLE 3.4

What is the indicated stall speed for the Learjet when it is under a 2 g load?

Solution

Using Equation 3.14, we have the following:

$$V_{\text{Stall}} = V_{\text{Stall in level flight}} \sqrt{n} = 115 \text{ knots IAS} \times \sqrt{2} = 162 \text{ knots IAS} \quad (3.15)$$

Thus, if the Learjet is traveling at less than 162 knots IAS (172 knots TAS at 4,000 ft MSL) and you suddenly pull up the nose with 2 g's of load, the Learjet will stall.

Effect of Weight on Stall Speed

Stall speed is affected by the weight of the airplane. The heavier the plane, the higher the stall speed. If you know the stall speed at a particular weight, you can derive the following relation from Equation 3.6:

$$V_{\text{Stall speed at weight 2}} = V_{\text{Stall speed at weight 1}} \sqrt{\frac{W_{\text{Weight 2}}}{W_{\text{Weight 1}}}} \quad (3.16)$$

EXAMPLE 3.5

What is the indicated stall speed for the 737 when there is almost no fuel left and the aircraft weighs 101,000 lb? What is the true stall speed for the same airplane when it is at 10,000 ft?

Solution

The clean stall speed when the 737 is at its maximum weight of 138,500 lb (fully fueled) is 130 knots IAS or 138 knots TAS. Therefore,

$$V_{\text{Stall at weight 2}} = V_{\text{Stall at weight 1}} \sqrt{\frac{W_{\text{Weight 2}}}{W_{\text{Weight 1}}}} \quad (3.17)$$

$$= 130 \text{ kt IAS} \sqrt{\frac{101,000 \text{ lb}}{138,500 \text{ lb}}} = 111 \text{ knots IAS}$$

To calculate the true airspeed we can use Equation 3.2 and substitute 111 knots indicated airspeed for $V_{\text{Equivalent}}$ because it is less than 200 knots and we don't need to worry about compressibility error:

$$V_{\text{Equivalent}} = V_{\text{TAS}} \sqrt{\frac{\rho_{\text{Air density at altitude}}}{\rho_{\text{Air density at sea level}}}} \qquad (3.18)$$

Solving for V_{TAS}

$$V_{\text{TAS}} = V_{\text{Equivalent}} \sqrt{\frac{\rho_{\text{Air density at sea level}}}{\rho_{\text{Air density at 10,000 ft}}}}$$

$$= 111 \text{ knots IAS} \sqrt{\frac{0.002377 \text{ sl}/\text{ft}^3}{0017560 \text{ sl}/\text{ft}^3}} = 129 \text{ knots TAS}$$

The Relationship between Bank Angle, Stall Speeds, Load Factor, and Induced Drag

Now that you understand how to calculate stall speeds and load factors for different bank angles, it is helpful to view the results side by side to see how an airplane's bank angle affects its performance. Table 3.2 summarizes the relationship between bank angles, stall speeds (from Equation 3.11), load factors (from Equation 2.47), and induced drag. Induced drag from Equation 2.28 is proportional to C^2_L. Because C_L is proportional to lift L, we can use this proportional relationship to calculate the increase in induced drag during a turn:

$$C_{\text{Induced drag}} = \frac{C_L^2}{\pi e AR} \qquad (3.19)$$

Because

$$L = C_L q_\infty S$$

$$C_L = \frac{L}{q_\infty S}$$

During a banked turn

$$L = \frac{W}{\cos \beta}$$

Therefore

$$C_{\text{Induced drag}} \propto \frac{1}{\left(\cos \beta\right)^2}$$

As the bank angle increases, the value of cos β gets smaller. Taking the square of this value and dividing it into 1 will make the induced drag $C_{Induced\ Drag}$ coefficient much larger.

Table 3.2 Bank Angle and Its Effect on Load Factor, Stall Speed, and Induced Drag

BANK ANGLE	LOAD FACTOR	PERCENT INCREASE IN STALL SPEED	PERCENT INCREASE IN INDUCED DRAG
0°	1.0000	0.0%	0.0%
5°	1.0038	0.2%	0.8%
10°	1.0154	0.7%	3.1%
15°	1.0353	1.7%	7.2%
20°	1.0642	3.2%	13.3%
25°	1.1034	5.0%	21.7%
30°	1.1547	7.5%	33.3%
35°	1.2208	10.5%	49.0%
40°	1.3054	14.3%	70.4%
45°	1.4142	18.9%	100.0%
60°	2.000	41.4%	300.0%

From the results of Table 3.2, it should be apparent that coordinated turns with less than 15°of bank cause no appreciable effect on stall speed or induced drag. However, note that a 30°bank angle increases the induced drag by 33.3% and raises the stall speed by 7.5%. With an engine failure on a multiengine aircraft, the margin of safety is slim, and it is wise to limit bank angles to less than 15°.

Maneuvering Speed

Maneuvering speed, depicted by the symbol V_A, is defined as the maximum speed at which full or abrupt control movements can be made without damaging the aircraft. We know that V_A for the 3,000 lb Cessna is 112 knots, but how does one calculate the maneuvering speed for the Learjet or the 737-400? The answer is to use Equation 2.45 from Chapter 2, but solve for V (which we will call V_A) knowing the value of the load factor n from Chapter 2's Table 2.6 and the clean stall speed for the aircraft in question. Let's try this in the following example.

EXAMPLE 3.6

Find the maneuvering speed for the Boeing 737-400 and Learjet 45.

Solution

We have already discovered that the 737's clean stall speed is 130 knots IAS and that the Learjet's clean stall speed is 115 knots IAS at 4,000 ft. Clean stall speed means that the aircraft is flying with no flaps and no spoilers extended, and the landing gear is raised. Usually, the stall speeds you see in the documentation refer to the aircraft in the landing configuration, with flaps and gear extended. The clean stall speed is always higher than the landing configuration stall speed, because without the additional lift created by the flaps the aircraft must fly faster to generate enough lift to maintain flight.

We also know from Table 2.6 that the load limit for the Learjet and the 737 is in the range of 2.5 to 3.8 g's. Let's arbitrarily choose 3.0 g's for both aircraft as the load limit. From Equation 2.45:

$$V_A = V_{Stall} \sqrt{n_{Limit\ load\ factor}} \tag{3.20}$$

where airspeed can be expressed as TAS or equivalent airspeed as long as you remain consistent with airspeed type.

Plugging in the values for the 737 and the Learjet, we get the following:

Boeing 737-400: $\hspace{4cm}$ (3.21)

$$V_A = 130 \text{ knots IAS} \sqrt{3.0 \text{ g}} = 225 \text{ knots IAS}$$

Learjet 45:

$$V_A = 115 \text{ knots IAS} \sqrt{3.0 \text{ g}} = 199 \text{ knots IAS}$$

Thus, when flying the 737 at 225 knots IAS or less, if you try to pull up the nose suddenly—as you did with the Cessna in the accelerated stall—the airplane will hold together. Similarly, if you fly the Learjet slower than 199 knots IAS and you try the same stunt, the airplane will not break apart. In both airplanes, if you exceed V_A and you try the accelerated stall, you risk structural failure of the airframe.

By default, Flight Simulator aircraft do not become damaged from overstressing the airframe. If you want to test any of the previous examples and have the airplane break up from high g forces, you will have to turn on **Aircraft/Aircraft Settings/Crash & Damage/Aircraft Receives Damage From Stress**. Unfortunately, the Learjet and 737 have problems with failing to register enough stress from the accelerated stall. If you look closely at the g-meter while pulling the nose up, you'll see that you have exceeded the airplane's ultimate load limit of 3.8 g. Unless both aircraft are endowed with Herculean strength, they should break up. One thing you can try in the 737 is to lighten the aircraft by ridding the plane of all but 3% of your fuel (for an explanation of why this is so, read the next section). Then when you try the accelerated stall, the aircraft should break up near 300+ knots IAS. Unfortunately, this technique does not work with the Learjet.

Because maneuvering speed is based on load limits, maneuvering speeds must also be related to aircraft weight. Thus, if you perform an accelerated stall a lighter 737 will have a lower maneuvering speed and will break up at a lower airspeed than would a heavier 737. The following equation comes in handy when you are figuring out what the V_A speed should be when you load the airplane with cargo and passengers.

$$V_{A_2 \text{Maneuvering}} = V_{A_1 \text{Maneuvering}} \sqrt{\frac{W_2}{W_1}} \qquad (3.22)$$

where both $V_{A\text{Maneuvering}}$ speeds can be expressed as TAS or equivalent airspeed as long as you remain consistent with airspeed type.

EXAMPLE 3.7

The Cessna 182's maneuvering speed at 3,100 lb is 112 knots. What is the maneuvering speed when the aircraft weighs 2,000 lb?

Solution

Using Equation 3.22, we see that $V_{A1} = 112$ knots, $W_2 = 2,000$ lb, and $W_1 = 3,100$ lb. Therefore

$$V_{A_1 \text{Maneuvering}} = 112 \text{ knots IAS} \sqrt{\frac{2000 \text{ lb}}{3100 \text{ lb}}} = 90 \text{ knots IAS} \qquad (3.23)$$

Thus, when you fly the aircraft by yourself with no passengers and cargo, you must be more careful because you can overstress the aircraft at a much lower airspeed of only 90 knots IAS. Note that this airspeed is within 1 knot of the 89 knot maneuvering speed given for a 2,000 lb Cessna in the owner's manual.

THE SPEED OF SOUND

Sound waves travel through air at a finite speed that we call the speed of sound. When we see a bolt of lightning and then hear the crash of thunder a few seconds later, we are witnessing the time delay of sound as it travels through the atmosphere. In a perfect gas, the speed of sound depends only on the temperature of the gas, so we can arrive at the following formula for calculating the speed of sound:

$$V_{\text{Speed of sound}} = \sqrt{\gamma k T_{\text{Rankine}}} = \sqrt{1.4(1716)T_{\text{Rankine}}} \qquad (3.24)$$

where

$$\gamma = \frac{c_p}{c_V} = \frac{\dfrac{Q\ (\text{at constant Pressure})}{m\Delta T}}{\dfrac{Q\ (\text{at constant Volume})}{m\Delta T}}$$

$$= \frac{\text{Specific heat of air at constant pressure}}{\text{Specific heat of air at constant volume}} = 1.4$$

where

$$k = \text{Gas constant for the Ideal Gas Law} = 1716\,\frac{\text{lb-ft}}{\text{sl-R}}$$

$$T_{\text{Rankine}} = \text{Temperature in Rankine},\ R = \text{unit of temperature Rankine}$$

$V_{\text{speed of sound}}$ is measured in ft/s, T_{Rankine} is the temperature measured in Rankine, and γ is a dimensionless quantity that has a fixed value of 1.4 for dry air.

To convert temperatures from degrees Fahrenheit to Rankine, use this formula:

$$T_{\text{Rankine}} = T_{\text{Fahrenheit}} + 459.67 \qquad (3.25)$$

To convert temperatures from degrees Celsius to Fahrenheit, use this formula:

$$T_{\text{Fahrenheit}} = \frac{9}{5}T_{\text{Celsius}} + 32°\text{F} \qquad (3.26)$$

To convert temperatures from degrees Fahrenheit to Celsius, use this formula:

$$T_{\text{Celsius}} = \frac{5}{9}\left(T_{\text{Fahrenheit}} - 32°\text{F}\right) \qquad (3.27)$$

EXAMPLE 3.8

What is the speed of sound at sea level when the temperature is 59°F? When it is 100°F?

Solution

We first convert degrees Fahrenheit to Rankine and then plug these values into Equation 3.24.

$$T_{\text{Rankine}} = T_{\text{Fahrenheit}} + 459.67 \tag{3.28}$$

When $T_{\text{Fahrenheit}} = 59°$:

$$T_{\text{Rankine}} = 59° + 459.67° = 518.67\,R$$

When $T_{\text{Fahrenheit}} = 100°$:

$$T_{\text{Rankine}} = 100° + 459.67° = 559.67\,R$$

Inserting the preceding two Rankine converted temperatures into Equation 3.24, we get the following:

$$V_{\text{speed of sound}} = \sqrt{1.4(1716)T_{\text{Rankine}}} \tag{3.29}$$

When $T_{\text{Fahrenheit}} = 59°$:

$$V_{\text{speed of sound}} = \sqrt{1.4(1716)(518.67)} = 1116.3\,\text{ft}/\text{s}$$

When $T_{\text{Fahrenheit}} = 100°$:

$$V_{\text{speed of sound}} = \sqrt{1.4(1716)(559.67)} = 1159.5\,\text{ft}/\text{s}$$

We can convert ft/s to knots by the following conversion:

$$\text{knots} = V_{\text{velocity}}\left(\text{ft}/\text{s}\right)\left(\frac{\text{knot}}{1.6878\,\text{ft}/\text{s}}\right) \tag{3.30}$$

Therefore, the speed of sound when the temperature is 59°F at sea level is as follows:

When $T_{\text{Fahrenheit}} = 59°$: (3.31)

$$V_{\text{speed of sound in knots}} = \left(1116.3\,{}^{\text{ft}}\!\!\big/\!_{\text{s}}\right)\left(\frac{\text{knot}}{1.6878\,{}^{\text{ft}}\!\!\big/\!_{\text{s}}}\right) = 661 \text{ knots}$$

When $T_{\text{Fahrenheit}} = 100°$:

$$V_{\text{speed of sound in knots}} = \left(1159.5\,{}^{\text{ft}}\!\!\big/\!_{\text{s}}\right)\left(\frac{\text{knot}}{1.6878\,{}^{\text{ft}}\!\!\big/\!_{\text{s}}}\right) = 687 \text{ knots}$$

From the foregoing example, you have learned that the speed of sound increases with rising temperature. You can check your calculation for the speed of sound at $T = 59°F$ by consulting Appendix F.

MACH NUMBER

Named for the Austrian physicist Ernst Mach (1838–1916), Mach is a quantity that is used to define airflow in terms of the speed of sound.

$$M_{\text{Mach Number}} = \frac{V_{\text{True airspeed}}}{V_{\text{speed of sound}}}$$ (3.32)

Table 3.3 *Mach Number and Flight Regime*

FLIGHT REGIME	$M_{\text{MACH NUMBER}}$
Subsonic	<0.8
Transonic	0.8 to 1.2
Supersonic	1.2 to 5.0
Hypersonic	>5.0

An airplane traveling at greater than Mach 1.2 is said to be supersonic. At less than Mach 0.8, an airplane is flying at a subsonic speed, and between Mach 0.8 and Mach 1.2 an airplane is said to be in the transonic regime. A supersonic jet such as the Concorde is said to be breaking the sound barrier when it travels at speeds greater than Mach 1.2. When it does so, it creates a sonic boom. Subsonic jets use Mach numbers rather than IAS to show the upper limiting speed for the cruise phase of a flight. All jet aircraft incorporate a Machmeter among their flight instruments; in addition, they must provide a klaxon overspeed warning system that alerts the pilot whenever the flight speed exceeds the maximum operating Mach number by 0.01. For example, the Boeing 727 issues a warning when $M = 0.902$. This warning system is important. If the pilot does not reduce speed immediately, a supersonic shock wave will develop over the wing, causing loss of lift and possible disruption of airflow over the aircraft's control surfaces. If this should happen, the pilot may lose control over the airplane.

Note that according to our definition of the speed of sound, Mach speeds also depend on temperature. For a constant Mach number but lower temperature, an aircraft must fly slower. Thus, an airplane traveling at Mach 1 at sea level 59°F must fly at 661 knots (the speed of sound at 59°F). At 35,000 ft, where the temperature might be -65°F, the same airplane would have to fly much slower (at 576 knots) to maintain Mach 1 (the speed of sound at 35,000 ft for StAt). If you don't believe this, check the tables found in Appendix F.

Now let's calculate a Mach number for the 737 flying at cruise speed at 35,000 ft.

EXAMPLE 3.9

The 737 is flying at 429 knots true airspeed at an altitude of 35,000 ft at StAt. What is the airplane's Mach number?

Solution

Using the StAt table in Appendix F, we see that the speed of sound at 35,000 ft is 576.5 knots. Therefore, the 737's Mach number is as follows:

$$M_{\text{Mach Number of } -3- \text{ at } 35,000 \text{ ft}} = \frac{V_{\text{TAS}}}{V_{\text{speed of sound at } 35,000 \text{ ft}}} = \frac{429 \text{ kt}}{576.5 \text{ kt}} = 0.744 \quad (3.33)$$

Notice that the performance charts for the 737 list its economy cruise at Mach 0.744. This means that when the aircraft is traveling at 429 knots TAS it achieves maximum cruise fuel efficiency.

 Remember that you must use the airplane's true airspeed—not its indicated airspeed—when making Mach calculations.

NOTE

Supersonic aircraft moving through the atmosphere create friction as their fuselage and wings move through the air. In fact, the greatest obstacle to high-speed flight is not the sound barrier but rather the heat barrier. The heated air raises the temperature of the airframe so much that aluminum softens and cannot be used for structural components. Exotic materials, such as titanium or other metals with high melting points, must be used for critical areas, especially leading edges of wings. In the case of the space shuttle, thermal tiles made from carbon compounds are used to blunt the searing heat of reentry. We can calculate the upper limit for the airplane's surface temperature—also called the total stagnation temperature—in high-speed flight by using the following equation:

$$T_{\text{Surface Temp in Rankine}} = \left(1 + 0.2M^2_{\text{Mach}}\right) T_{\text{Outside Air Temp in Rankine}} \qquad (3.34)$$

Equation 3.34 cannot be applied to hypersonic vehicles such as the space shuttle, because a bow shock wave is created that changes the physics of the problem.

NOTE If you are interested in this problem, a very good treatment of the subject is contained in Wilbur L. Hankey's book *Re-Entry Aerodynamics*, published by the American Institute of Aeronautics and Astronautics Education Series, Wright Patterson Air Force Base, Ohio. Essentially, if you take 1/1000 of the temperature calculated from the surface temperature equation, you will get a rough approximation of the space shuttle's surface temperature.

EXAMPLE 3.10

What is the upper limit of the air temperature on the leading edge of the Concorde's wing at Mach 2 at 60,000 ft under StAt?

Solution

From the StAt table, at 60,000 ft, $T_{\textit{Outside Air Temperature}}$ = 390 R. From Equation 3.34:

$$T_{\text{Surface Temp in Rankine}} = \left(1 + 0.2M^2_{\text{Mach}}\right) T_{\text{Outside Air Temp in Rankine}} \qquad (3.35)$$

$$= \left[1 + (0.2)(2)^2\right](390) = 702\,R$$

Thus, the increase in air temperature is as follows:

$$\Delta T = 702R - 390R = 312°F! \qquad (3.36)$$

If you perform the same calculation for the 737 cruising at Mach 0.77 at 35,000 feet StAt, you'll discover that the surface temperature of the airplane is heated up by 46.7° F. So if the outside air temperature were 394 R (-66° F), the total air temperature as measured by an outside probe would be 440.7 R (-19° F, or –28° C). The TAT (Total Air Temperature) indicator on the 737 would thus display –28° C for these conditions, and this is what happens on the FS98 737. If you want to test this yourself, make sure that you remove all the temperature layers so that a standard atmosphere exists. Also set the atmospheric pressure to a standard 29.92 in Hg, and calibrate your altimeter (press **B**). Using the **World/Go To/Exact Location** menu, enter your altitude as 35,000 ft and your airspeed as 440 knots TAS (440 knots TAS is equivalent to Mach 0.77 at this altitude). Note that FSW95's TAT readout does not work properly.

Critical Mach Number and Wing Sweep-back

The airflow over the top surface of a cambered airfoil has a greater velocity than does the airflow underneath the wing. We have already learned that this greater velocity, according to Bernoulli's theorem, creates a lower pressure above the wing that "sucks" it upward, thereby creating lift. Assume for the sake of argument that the airstream flowing underneath the wing is relatively undisturbed and is equivalent to the airspeed of the airplane. Realizing that the air molecules must be flowing faster over the wing than under the wing, you can see that at a critical point the airstream above the wing will go supersonic while the airstream underneath the wing stays subsonic. When the airspeed of the airplane is such that a Mach 1 velocity is reached at some point over the wing, this is said to be the airplane's *critical Mach number*. By definition, the critical mach number is the free stream Mach number that produces first evidence of local sonic flow. Therefore, shock wave, buffet, and airflow separation effects take place above the critical Mach number. Figure 3.1 shows the above-wing airflow for an airfoil that is below the critical Mach number and for an airfoil that has just reached the critical Mach number.

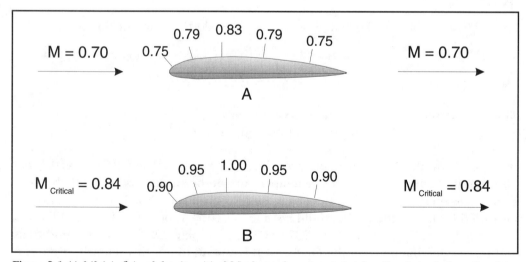

Figure 3.1 *Airfoil A is flying below its critical Mach number; at no point does the airspeed above the wing reach Mach 1.0. Airfoil B, on the other hand, is flying at the wing's critical Mach number; at the wing's thickest point, the airflow over the wing has reached Mach 1.0.*

As the critical Mach number is exceeded, an area of supersonic flow is created that creates a shock wave at the boundary of the supersonic flow and the subsonic flow on the rear portion of the wing. As speed increases above the critical Mach number, the shock wave moves farther back on the wing and enlarges. In addition, a shock wave appears underneath the wing. Approaching the speed of sound, the airplane's wing enlarges both upper and lower shock waves and moves the boundary to the trailing edge of the wing. At greater than Mach 1, a bow wave forms at the leading edge of the wing, and this creates a sonic boom that can be heard many miles away (see Figure 3.2).

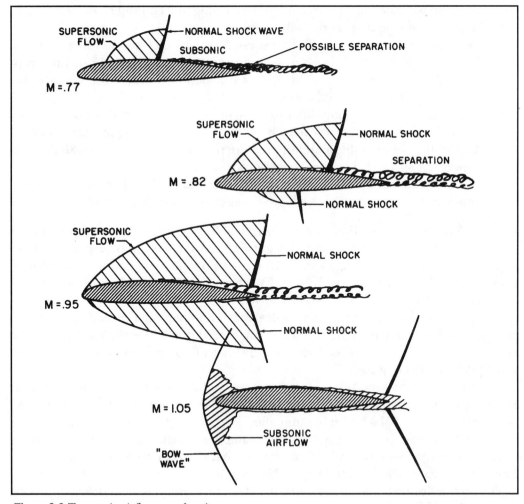

Figure 3.2 *Transonic airflow over the wing.*

A number of disturbances occur during transonic flight. Here are the principal ones:

- Parasitic drag increases and lift decreases.
- Buffet: Conventional aileron, rudder, and elevator surfaces exposed to the shock wave may "buzz" and resonate at a certain frequency, creating undesirable control forces. If the buffet is severe and prolonged, it can result in structural damage and failure of a hinged wing control surface. Also, the control column and rudders will buffet violently.
- Trim and stability control problems: If the shock waves above the wings occur at different locations because of small physical differences in the wings, a rolling moment is created in the direction of lesser wing lift. This will cause one wing to drop and contribute to control difficulties.
- Decrease in control surface effectiveness: As the shock wave moves rearward at higher Mach, the shock wave can appear over the control surfaces and interrupt normal airflow. So much turbulent air can be created over the elevator, for example, that it is rendered useless.
- Mach tuck: Loss of longitudinal stability will cause the aircraft's nose to "tuck under." This is caused by the aerodynamic center of the wing moving backward 25% of the chord as the center of pressure moves rearward. All aircraft flying at supersonic speeds experience a nose-down pitching moment.
- Wing twist: The wings may begin to twist because of the differing onset of the shock wave over a swept-back wing. This effect is unnerving at best.

In Flight Simulator, you'll know that your airplane has passed its critical Mach number and entered into the transonic flight regime when you see the overspeed warning appear on-screen. On the Learjet and 737, barber pole pointers on the airspeed indicator tell you the airspeed at which critical Mach occurs. You should not allow your airspeed to pass this pointer under any circumstances.

To reduce speed after passing the critical Mach number, each aircraft has different procedures. For example, in the Learjet 36 you should not deploy the spoilers because of the significant nose-down pitching moment that will occur. On other aircraft, you can deploy the speed brakes.

Aircraft designers want subsonic airplanes to travel as fast as possible. Therefore, any means of delaying or alleviating the shock-induced separation of airflow will increase the airplane's critical Mach number and allow it to fly at a faster airspeed. Design features that allow this are the use of low-aspect-ratio swept-back wings and vortex generators. *Vortex generators* are vertical airfoil surfaces that protrude from the wing vertically into the airstream. They mix the higher kinetic energy air from outside the boundary layer with the slower, lower-energy air of the boundary layer and thus delay separation between the two layers. If a shock wave forms, the vortex generators help to break it up.

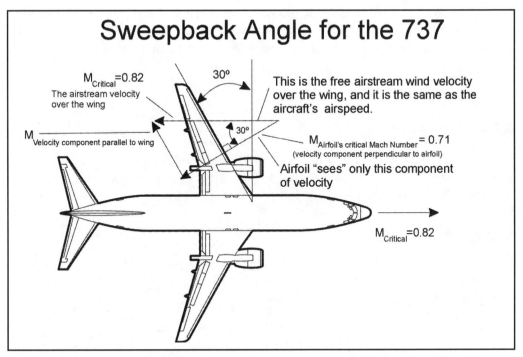

Figure 3.3 *The free-airstream velocity vector can be broken into components acting perpendicular and parallel to the wing. The sweep-back angle of the wing causes the perpendicular component of velocity to decrease, thereby allowing a higher critical Mach number for the free-stream velocity.*

Swept-back wings are also extremely helpful in increasing an airplane's critical Mach number. The angle at which the wing meets the free-flowing airstream changes the velocity component that flows perpendicular over the wing. In other words, the air traveling along the wing's chord line has a lower speed than the flight airspeed, and it is A vector diagram of velocity components flowing over the swept-back wing is shown in Figure 3.3. An approximate relationship between sweep-back angle Λ, critical Mach number, and airfoil Mach is as follows:

$$M_{\text{Critical over wing (free airstream velocity)}} \cong \frac{M_{\text{Critical of airfoil (velocity perpendicular to wing)}}}{\cos \Lambda} \quad (3.37)$$

However, this assumes two-dimensional airflow. For real wings with up to 60% in sweep-back, it is better to use the following:

$$M_{\text{Critical over wing (free airstream velocity)}} \cong \frac{M_{\text{Critical of airfoil (velocity perpendicular to wing)}}}{\cos\left(0.75 \times \Lambda\right)}$$

If you draw a vector diagram, you will discover that the relationship in the denominator of equation 3.37 should be cos Λ and not cos (0.75 × Λ). However, the vector diagram assumes two-dimensional airflow, so the benefit for a real wing is governed by cos (0.75 × Λ).

EXAMPLE 3.11

Suppose you are the designer of the Boeing 737 and you know that the airfoil's critical Mach number is 0.71. What would be the aircraft's maximum Mach ($M_{Critical}$) if the wings were swept back 30° (as occurs in the real 737)? Assume two-dimensional airflow.

Solution

Because we are using the simplified two-dimensional airflow, we use the upper equation given in Equation 3.37. The wing sweep-back angle Λ is given as 30°, and the airfoil's critical Mach number is 0.71. Therefore:

$$M_{\text{Critical over wing (free airstream velocity)}} = \frac{M_{\text{Critical of airfoil (velocity perpendicular to wing)}}}{\cos \Lambda} \quad (3.38)$$

$$= \frac{0.71}{\cos 30°} = 0.82 \text{ Mach}$$

Suppose you wanted to increase the wing's sweep-back angle to 45°. If you plug in the value 45° into the equation, you'll discover that the 737's critical Mach number increases to Mach 1! Why is this technique not used? A high sweep-back angle has a much higher induced drag and would require much higher airspeeds when landing. This would not be a practical design decision.

The idea of using swept-back wings to increase the critical Mach number was first presented by Professor Adolf Busemann of Germany at a conference on supersonic flight. His theories were not taken seriously until after World War II, when it was discovered that Germany had verified the theory in wind tunnels and had applied the idea to their jet fighters. During the Korean war, the first American fighter with a swept-back wing, the F-86 Sabre jet, replaced the straight-wing F-84 and helped to regain air superiority for the United Nations forces. Today, all commercial jetliners employ wing sweep-back to some degree.

The effects of sweep-back on critical Mach number, drag, and lift are presented in Table 3.4 (Hurt, 1965). Note that if sweep-back is to be used, at least 30° to 35° must be used to produce any significant benefit.

Table 3.4 *Wing Sweep-back and Effect on Critical Mach Number, Drag, and Lift*

SWEEP ANGLE Λ	PERCENT INCREASE IN CRITICAL MACH NUMBER	PERCENT INCREASE IN DRAG PEAK MACH NUMBER	PERCENT REDUCTION IN DRAG RISE	PERCENT REDUCTION IN LOSS OF $C_{L_{MAX}}$
0°	0%	0%	0%	0%
15°	2%	4%	5%	3%
30°	8%	15%	15%	13%
45°	20%	41%	35%	30%
60°	41%	100%	60%	50%

H.H. Hurt, Jr., Aerodynamics for Naval Aviators (Naval Air Systems Command, U.S. Navy, 1965), p.226.

From this table, it may seem that all wings should be sharply swept back for maximum efficiency at high velocity. Although this may be true at high speed, it presents a problem for low-speed flight. In low-speed flight, a low-aspect-ratio wing with high sweep back produces much greater induced drag and a lower maximum lift coefficient than does a high-aspect-ratio, low-sweep-back angle wing. This means that a high-sweep-back airplane must land at very high airspeeds, and this is not satisfactory for reasons of safety. The conundrum for aircraft designers is that they must satisfy both requirements; a plane must be configured to land at slow speeds with a high aspect ratio non–swept-back wing, whereas high speed a plane must be configured with a low-aspect-ratio and high-angle-sweep-back wing. Some military aircraft, such as the F-111 and F-14, get around this problem by having variable geometry wings that rotate into the sweep-back angle that is optimum for a particular airspeed. The disadvantage of such a design is that very heavy wing fittings are needed to support the highly loaded rotation mechanisms. More recently, an oblique wing that rotates at one fixed point has been proposed as a new way of surmounting this problem. The wing, which looks like an X when flying at high speed, is rotated at low speed so that it looks like a T. Proof of design concept work is now being undertaken by NASA on a prototype to be built by Burt Rutan's Scaled Composites Company.

Unfortunately, after investigating the .*AIR* files for the 737 and not finding any data for sweep-back angle, I've concluded that sweep-back is probably not modeled in Flight Simulator.

CONVERTING INDICATED AIRSPEED TO TRUE AIRSPEED

Now we turn to the problem of converting indicated airspeed to true airspeed, accounting for the problem of compressibility error in the pitot-static system at high airspeeds.

You already know three methods of converting IAS to TAS: first, you can easily switch your airspeed indicator from IAS to TAS using **Options/Preferences/Instruments**; second, you know the 2% IAS for each 1,000 ft rule of thumb calculation (which doesn't take into account compressibility error at high Mach speed); third, you can use the **Airspeed** adventure on the accompanying CD-ROM and display both airspeed types at the touch of a button. However, it might prove useful to know how to calculate the conversion manually.

The ICE-T Method

Before we proceed, it is important to establish the sequence of events in the conversion process:

1. **IC:** Change *indicated* airspeed to *calibrated* (not needed in Flight Simulator because there is no instrument error). In other words:

$$V_{CAL} = V_{IAS} + \Delta V_{\text{Instrument error correction}} \qquad (3.39)$$

2. **E:** Change calibrated airspeed to *equivalent,* taking care to subtract the error due to the compressibility of air at high speeds. Thus

$$V_{Equivalent} = V_{CAL} + \Delta V_{\text{Compressibility error correction}} \qquad (3.40)$$

3. **T:** Change equivalent airspeed to *true* airspeed, being sure to account for the air density variation at higher altitudes. This means

$$V_{TAS} = V_{Equivalent} \sqrt{\frac{\rho_{\text{Air density at sea level}}}{\rho_{\text{Air density at altitude}}}} \qquad (3.41)$$

The above method is easily remembered by the acronym ICE-T.

In equation form, the preceding steps can be summarized by the following:

$$V_{TAS} = \left(V_{IAS} + \Delta V_{\text{Instrument error correction}} + \Delta V_{\text{Compressibility error correction}} \right) \sqrt{\frac{\rho_{\text{Air density at sea level}}}{\rho_{\text{Air density at altitude}}}}$$

$$(3.42)$$

How do we account for $\Delta V_{\text{Compressibility error correction}}$? Many pilots of small airplanes use hand-held calculators that have built-in functions that will calculate the error. Others use a calculator that resembles a slide rule, and still others use built-in cockpit computers that display the information. To show how it is done, we will present the basic algorithms so that you can program it into a programmable calculator or spreadsheet such as Excel.

The next section describes the technique used to convert IAS to TAS when airspeed is less than 200 knots ($\Delta V_{\text{Compressibility error correction}} = 0$). In the subsequent section, we will show the three-step method used to convert IAS to TAS for airspeeds greater than 200 knots, when compressibility of air becomes an issue.

When Indicated Airspeed Is Less than 200 Knots

If the airspeed is less than 200 knots or Mach <0.3 under StAt, there is negligible compressibility error, so use this equation to convert IAS to TAS:

$$V_{\text{TAS}} \equiv V_{\text{Equivalent}} \sqrt{\frac{\rho_{\text{Air density at sea level}}}{\rho_{\text{Air density at altitude}}}} \tag{3.43}$$

When $V_{\text{CAL}} < 200$ knots:

$$V_{\text{TAS}} \equiv V_{\text{IAS}} \sqrt{\frac{\rho_{\text{Air density at sea level}}}{\rho_{\text{Air density at altitude}}}}$$

From Equation 3.43, $\rho_{air\ density\ at\ altitude}$ must be corrected for the temperature at the airplane's altitude if it deviates from the StAt table in Appendix F. Note that Equation 3.43 is simply a restatement of the equivalent airspeed Equation 3.2.

To correct $\rho_{\text{Air Density at Aircraft's Altitude}}$ for non-standard atmospheres, use this relation:

Ideal Gas Law: $\hspace{4cm}$ (3.44)

$$P = \frac{nRT}{V} = \rho KT$$

or

$$PV = nRT$$

Rearranging terms:

$$\rho_{\text{Air Density}} = \frac{P}{KT}$$

where

K = Gas constant = 1716 lb-ft/slug R
T = Temperature in Rankine at aircraft's altitude
P = Air pressure at aircraft's altitude in lb/ft^2
$\rho_{\text{Air Density}}$ = Air density at aircraft's altitude in slugs/ft^3

When Indicated Airspeed Is Greater than 200 Knots

When Mach >0.3 or the airplane's IAS is more than 200 knots, compressibility effects of the atmosphere must be taken into account and a more complicated series of equations and steps must be followed. To convert IAS to TAS, follow these three steps:

1. Determine pressure correction for altitude:

$$\frac{P_O}{P} = \frac{1}{\left[\dfrac{518.67 - \left(3.566 \times 10^{-3} \times \text{Pressure Altitude}\right)}{518.67}\right]^{5.2563}} \tag{3.45}$$

where

Pressure Altitude (in ft) = Altitude as measured on your altimeter when it is calibrated to 29.92 in. Hg

2. Determine the Mach number using this equation:

$$M = \sqrt{5\left[\left(\left(\frac{P_O}{P}\left\{\left[1 + 0.2\left(\frac{V_{CAS}}{661.5}\right)^2\right]^{3.5} - 1\right\} + 1\right)^{0.286} - 1\right)\right]} \tag{3.46}$$

where

M = Mach number
V_{CAS} = Calibrated airspeed in kts
    = Indicated airspeed + correction factor for instrument error in kts
    = $V_{IAS} + V_{\text{Instrument Error}}$

The instrument error on the Cessna is about -3 knots at cruise speeds of 150 knots. Other aircraft in the real world will have similar errors. However, in Flight Simulator just assume that instrument error is zero.

3. Using the value of Mach number from step 2, and using the current outside air temperature converted to Celsius, the true airspeed can be calculated as follows:

$$V_{TAS} = 39M\sqrt{\left(T_{\text{Outside Air Temperature Celsius}} + 273\right)\left[\frac{1}{\left(1 + (0.2)(M)^2\right)}\right]} \tag{3.47}$$

Let's try an example of calculating the true airspeed from indicated airspeed for the Learjet at 35,000 ft.

EXAMPLE 3.12

What is V_{TAS} for the Learjet when the calibrated airspeed (indicated airspeed plus instrument error correction, which in this case is zero) $V_{CAS} = 240$ knots at 35,000 ft? Assume StAt.

Solution

Using Appendix F, we find that under StAt, at 35,000 ft MSL the temperature is -65 °F, which is equivalent to -54°C. We can now calculate P_o/P from Equation 3. 45 as follows:

1. Determine pressure correction for altitude:

$$\frac{P_O}{P} = \frac{1}{\left[\dfrac{518.67 - \left(3.566 \times 10^{-3} \times \text{Pressure Altitude}\right)}{518.67}\right]^{5.2563}} \tag{3.48}$$

$$= \frac{1}{\left[\dfrac{518.67 - \left(3.566 \times 10^{-3} \times 35,000 \text{ ft}\right)}{518.67}\right]^{5.2563}}$$

$$\frac{P_O}{P} = 4.2500$$

2. Now we are in a position to measure the Mach number from Equation 3.46:

$$M = \sqrt{5\left[\left(\frac{P_O}{P}\left\{\left[1 + 0.2\left(\frac{V_{CAS}}{661.5}\right)^2\right]^{3.5} - 1\right\} + 1\right)^{0.286} - 1\right]} \tag{3.49}$$

$$= \sqrt{5\left[\left((4.2500)\left\{\left[1 + 0.2\left(\frac{240}{661.5}\right)^2\right]^{3.5} - 1\right\} + 1\right)^{0.286} - 1\right]}$$

$$M = 0.71436$$

3. Using the value of Mach number from step 2 and using the current outside air temperature converted to Celsius, the true airspeed can be calculated as follows:

$$V_{TAS} = 39M \sqrt{\left(T_{\text{Outside Air Temperature Celsius}} + 273\right)\left[\frac{1}{\left(1 + (0.2)(M)^2\right)}\right]} \qquad (3.50)$$

$$= (39)(0.71436) \sqrt{\left(-54°C + 273\right)\left[\frac{1}{\left(1 + (0.2)(0.71436)^2\right)}\right]}$$

$$= 393 \text{ kt}$$

Note that if we had used the 2% rule of thumb instead of the preceding calculations, we would have arrived at a true airspeed of 417 knots (2% of 240 knots x 37 (thousands of feet) + 240 knots = 417 knots).

TIP

If you try this example in Flight Simulator, you won't get proper results unless you get rid of all the temperature layers in the **World/Weather/Temperature** dialog box. These temperature layers cause nonstandard atmosphere conditions, and this will cause your true airspeed results to vary.

NOTE

The FSW95 737 does not display the proper Celsius temperature lapse with altitude. This error affects airspeed measurements. Note that the Cessna and Learjet display the proper temperatures. This problem is fixed in FS98.

What happens when the temperature deviates from StAt? Let's look at the following example for the proper technique to use when calculating true airspeed.

EXAMPLE 3.13

What is the Cessna's true airspeed when the temperature is 75°F at 10,000 ft pressure altitude and the airspeed indicator shows 150 knots?

Solution

Because the Cessna travels at less than 200 knots IAS, we don't need to worry about the compressibility of air, so $V_{IAS} = V_{Equivalent}$ in Equation 3.2:

$$V_{\text{TAS}} = V_{\text{IAS}} \sqrt{\frac{\rho_{\text{air density at sea level}}}{\rho_{\text{air density at altitude}}}} \qquad (3.51)$$

At StAt the temperature at 10,000 ft would usually be 23°F. However, we need to correct the air density for the nonstandard temperature of 75°at 10,000 ft by using the Ideal Gas Law from Equation 3.44:

$$\rho_{\text{air density at altitude}} = \frac{P_{\text{air pressure}}}{k_{\text{Gas Constant}} T_{\text{Temperature}}} \qquad (3.52)$$

$$= \frac{1455.6 \, \text{lb}/\text{ft}^2}{\left(1716 \ \text{lb-ft}/\text{sl} \ R\right)\left(75° + 460°\right)} = 0.0015855 \ \text{sl}/\text{ft}^3$$

Notice in equation 3.52 that $T_{\text{Temperature}}$ is measured in Rankine, so you must convert 75°F to Rankine as shown ($T_{\text{rankine}} = T_{\text{Fahrenheit}} + 460$).

Now it is possible to solve Equation 3.51:

$$V_{\text{TAS}} = V_{\text{IAS}} \sqrt{\frac{\rho_{\text{air density at sea level}}}{\rho_{\text{air density at altitude}}}} \qquad (3.53)$$

$$= 150 \ \text{kt IAS} \sqrt{\frac{\left(0.0023770 \ \text{sl}/\text{ft}^3\right)}{\left(0.0015855 \ \text{sl}/\text{ft}^3\right)}} = 184 \ \text{kt TAS}$$

RATE OF CLIMB

In our discussion of thrust in Chapter 2, it was mentioned that the airplane's rate of climb is dependent on the excess thrust available. Excess thrust is defined as the difference between thrust available and thrust required.

The exact relationship for the maximum vertical speed is found by the following:

$$V_{\text{Vertical Speed}} = \frac{P_{\text{Power Available}} - P_{\text{Power Required}}}{W} = \frac{\text{Excess Power}}{W} \qquad (3.54)$$

where

$V_{\text{Vertical Speed}} = \text{ft}/\text{s}$
$P_{\text{Power Available}} = \text{Power available lb-ft}/\text{s}$
$P_{\text{Power Required}} = \text{Power required lb-ft}/\text{s}$
$W = \text{Weight of the airplane lb}$

EXAMPLE 3.14

What is the excess power available from the 3,100 lb Cessna 182, given that its published maximum rate of climb is 1,140 ft/min (19 ft/s) at sea level at 88 knots IAS? Once you solve for excess power, find the power required and from that determine the total drag on the airplane.

Solution

Solving for excess power in Equation 3.54, and converting 1,140 ft/min to 19 ft/s, we have the following:

$$V_{\text{Vertical Speed}} = \frac{P_{\text{Power Available}} - P_{\text{Power Required}}}{W} = \frac{\text{Excess Power}}{W} \qquad (3.55)$$

Note that

$$P_{\text{Power Available}} = P_A = \eta P$$

or

$$\text{hp}_A = \eta b\text{hp} = (0.8)(235 \text{ hp}) = 188 \text{ hp}$$

where

P_A = Power available to propel the airplane in ft lb/s
η = Propeller efficiency ($\eta < 1$), for Cessna $\eta = 0.8$
hp_A = Horsepower available
$b\text{hp}$ = Shaft brake horsepower

Rearranging to solve for Excess Power:

$$\text{Excess Power} = V_{\text{Vertical Speed}}W = (19 \text{ ft/s})(3100 \text{ lb})$$
$$= 58,900 \text{ lb} \cdot \text{ft/s} \left(\frac{1 \text{ horsepower}}{550 \text{ lb} \cdot \text{ft/s}} \right) = 107 \text{ hp}$$

Find power required:

$$\text{Excess Power} = 188 \text{ hp} - P_{\text{Power Required}}$$
solving for $P_{\text{Power Required}}$:
$$P_{\text{Power Required}} = 188 \text{ hp} - \text{Excess Power} = 188 \text{ hp} - 107 \text{ hp} = 81 \text{ hp}$$

Determine total drag:

$$T_{\text{Thrust}} = D_{\text{Total Drag}}$$

$$P_{\text{Power Required}} = T_{\text{Thrust}} V_{\text{Velocity in ft/s}}$$

$$D_{\text{Total Drag}} = T_{\text{Thrust}} = \frac{P_{\text{Power Required}}}{V_{\text{Velocity in ft/s}}} = \frac{\left(81\text{ hp} \dfrac{550\text{ ft} \cdot \text{lb/s}}{\text{hp}} \right)}{(88\text{ kt} \times 1.6878\text{ ft/s} \cdot \text{kt})} = 300\text{ lb}$$

The loss of an engine in any twin-engine aircraft causes a reduction of 80% or more in its climb performance. Climb performance is a function of the engine power that is in excess of that required for level flight. When one engine fails, not only does it lose power but also the drag increases considerably because of asymmetric thrust. The operating engine must then carry the full burden alone. To maintain level flight it must produce 75% more of its rated power, leaving very little excess power for climb performance.

Coffin Corner

As an airplane climbs toward its ceiling altitude, the range of speeds available that it can fly shrinks. The service ceiling is usually defined as the density altitude at which the maximum rate of climb has been reduced to 100 ft/min. It is the point at which the cruise speed is only slightly greater than the airspeed at which the maximum rate of climb occurs. At this altitude, both these airspeeds are close to stall speed.

Near this altitude ceiling, another problem crops up: the maximum Mach number cannot be exceeded. The higher the airplane goes, the faster it needs to fly to maintain the same amount of lift. Remember that Mach number is dependent on the speed of sound; if the speed of sound is lower at a higher altitude, then the airplane must fly slower. Thus, for example, the speed of sound at 25,000 ft is 602 knots TAS, whereas at 50,000 ft the speed of sound drops to 573 knots TAS. Exceeding maximum Mach is not an option: if the pilot exceeds this speed, severe buffeting, aileron buzz, uncontrollable roll, and loss of control effectiveness may occur.

Eventually the airplane gets boxed in to a narrow range of speeds called the *coffin corner*. It's a no-win situation; the airplane can't travel faster than its maximum Mach number, nor can it travel much slower. If it tries to fly slower, there won't be enough lift to sustain flight. Thus, if the pilot slows the airplane, it stalls; if the pilot speeds the airplane, it goes into a high-speed buffet where the airplane's wings exceed Mach 1. The famous U-2 spy plane was notorious for its coffin corner. Because the U2 flew so high, its coffin corner was only about 15 knots wide. This was not a very comforting thought

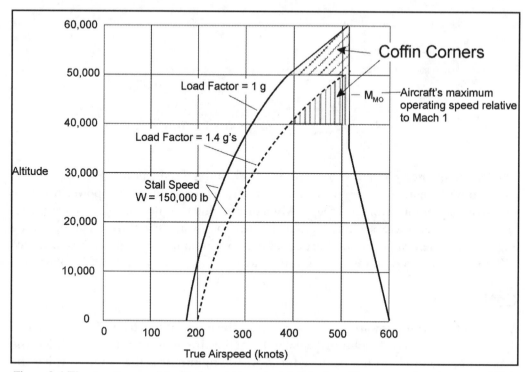

Figure 3.4 *The operating envelope of a large jet transport defines the coffin corners where the range of flight speeds is limited.*

for the U2 pilot, because he knew what lay in wait for him below if his speed exceeded this narrow boundary. Figure 3.4 illustrates the coffin corner for a large jet transport.

EXAMPLE 3.15

The Boeing 737 has a clean stall speed of 130 knots IAS in the cruise configuration. The maximum Mach number M_{MO} is 0.82. Assuming StAt, what is the range of allowable true airspeeds at 37,000 ft altitude?

Solution

From Appendix F, we find that $\rho_{air\ density}$ is 0.0006780 sl/ft^3 at 37,000 ft; we already know that ρ at sea level is 0.002377 sl/ft^3. Using Equation 3.43, we have the following:

$$V_{\text{Stall TAS}} = V_{\text{Stall IAS}} \sqrt{\frac{\rho_{\text{air density at sea level}}}{\rho_{\text{air density at altitude}}}} \qquad (3.56)$$

$$= (130 \text{ knots IAS}) \sqrt{\frac{0.002377}{0.0006780}} = 243 \text{ knots TAS}$$

Thus, 243 knots TAS is the lower threshold speed at which the 737 will stall at 37,000 ft. Now we must find the upper limit, which is based on the 0.82 maximum Mach number. Rearranging Equation 3.43, we have the following:

$$M_{\text{Mach Number}} = \frac{V_{\text{True Air Speed}}}{V_{\text{speed of sound}}} \qquad (3.57)$$

therefore

$$V_{\text{True Air Speed}} = M_{\text{Mach Number}} V_{\text{speed of sound}} = (0.82)(573.5 \text{ knots}) = 470 \text{ knots}$$

Therefore, the allowable range of speeds is 227 knots, because $470 - 243 = 227$ knots. If you try this example with the FS98 737, you may notice that the stall speed is 247 knots TAS at 37,000 feet instead of the 243 knots that was calculated. This is excellent accuracy!

4

Aircraft Engineering Principles, Power Plants, and Technology

> The machine does not isolate man from the
> great problems of nature but plunges him more
> deeply into them.
>
> Antoine de Saint-Exupéry (1900–1944), French avia-
> tor, author. *Wind, Sand, and Stars,* chapter 3 (1939).

We take for granted many things that took early aviation pioneers a lifetime of experience to innovate. The principles of flight, the mechanics of wings, and the design of
engines and propellers were all established early in this century by Orville and Wilbur
Wright. Even from the vantage point of today's high-technology accomplishments, the
Wright brothers' first flight, on December 17, 1903, at Kitty Hawk, North Carolina,
stands out as a monumental achievement equivalent to that of landing on the moon.
Although many others had moderate success with various gliders and other contrap-
tions, no other individuals of the time undertook the systematic scientific research and
experimentation that made possible the design of a workable airplane. The Wright
brothers were true scientists. They operated, not haphazardly, but by methodical testing and computation.

It may come as a surprise to realize that much of today's aviation terminology stems
from the Wright brothers' epochal work. For example, the camber of a wing, the wing's
dihedral angle, the most efficient shape of the propeller, the aspect ratio of the wing,

the size of the engine and horsepower needed for powered flight, the lift to drag ratio for gliding flight, the aileron effect, the wing's angle of attack and its effect on lift—all these facts were discovered and well understood by the Wright brothers. They used all this information in the design of their famous flying machine, the 1903 Flyer. Because of the lack of trustworthy air pressure data, they invented the world's first wind tunnel to test wing designs. The Wright brothers discovered that the air pressure tables created by Otto Lilienthal, another aviation pioneer, were wrong. This disinformation set them back by almost a year as they laboriously created the air pressure tables from scratch based on their own experiments. The Wright brothers built the first airplane engine in their bicycle shop, because none of the automobile manufacturers of the time could produce a sufficiently light engine with enough power. The brothers solved the problems of aircraft stability and control by creating a unique rudder and canard (the world's first canard-equipped airplane!) with wing warping of the main wing for roll stability. Their wing warping method of controlling turns was novel; by twisting the wingtips up or down on opposing sides, they created more lift on one side of the wing than the other, thereby allowing the aircraft to bank as if it had ailerons. Would-be usurpers of their ideas later tried to claim that the Wright brothers had not invented

Figure 4.1 *The 1903 Flyer. With Orville Wright at the controls, the Flyer rises into the air on its own power for the first time, as Wilbur Wright watches. (Courtesy of the Smithsonian Institution)*

the ailerons. During patent infringement lawsuits that followed, the courts established that the Wright brothers had priority on *any* method for presenting the left and right wings at different angles. The courts ruled that, in effect, the Wright brothers had discovered the aileron principle (Wright 1953).

With this historical context (Figure 4.1) in mind, let's look at some of the features common to modern aircraft.

FUSELAGE AND EMPENNAGE

The main body of an aircraft, exclusive of its wings and tail section, is known as the *fuselage*. The tail section is known as the *empennage*, which is derived from the French word for the feathers on an arrow. The fuselage houses the crew, passengers, cargo, instruments, and other essential equipment. In single-engine aircraft, the engine is usually attached to the front of the fuselage, and a steel fire wall or fireproof partition protects the pilot and passengers from accidental engine fires.

Air transport aircraft must meet certain FAA safety requirements for emergency landings. The airplane must be designed so that the structure will give every occupant a reasonable chance of escaping serious injury in a minor crash landing so that the following apply:

1. The occupant experiences the following ultimate inertia forces acting separately relative to the surrounding structure:
   - Upward, 3.0 g's
   - Forward, 9.0 g's
   - Sideward, 3.0 g's on the airframe and 4.0 g's on the seats and their attachments
   - Downward, 6 g's
   - Rearward, 1.5 g's

2. The seats must be subjected to dynamic testing with a 170-lb anthropomorphic test dummy so that each occupant does not receive a serious head injury or excessive leg, torso, or other injuries under the following conditions:

   - A vertical velocity change of not less than 35 ft/s and a peak floor deceleration of not more than 0.08 seconds after impact with a minimum 14 g's deceleration.
   - A change of forward longitudinal velocity of not less than 44 ft/s, which results in a peak floor deceleration of not more than 0.09 seconds after impact with a minimum of 16 g's.

Landing Gear

The landing gear, which supports the airplane while it is on land or water, may include wheels, floats, skis, brakes, retracting mechanisms, and lights.

There are two principal types of wheeled landing gear: tricycle landing gear and tail wheel landing gear. Tricycle landing gear has a nosewheel that allows for steering, whereas tail wheel landing gear (sometimes called taildraggers) has a skid or small wheel in the tail. The tricycle gear consists of two main wheels that are attached just behind the aircraft's center of gravity. The tail wheel gear has the two main wheels attached slightly in front of the airplane's center of gravity.

The tricycle gear has three chief advantages over tail wheel landing gear.

- It allows more-forceful application of brakes during landings at high speeds without the danger of the airplane nosing over.
- It permits better forward visibility for the pilot during takeoff, landing, and taxiing.
- It helps to prevent ground looping, because the airplane's center of gravity is forward of the main wheels. The forward center of gravity tends to keep the airplane moving forward in a straight line rather than ground looping.

Small aircraft such as the Cessna 182 Skylane are equipped with fixed tricycle landing gear, and the Cessna 182RG and all jet and air transport aircraft are equipped with retractable tricycle landing gear. In aircraft so equipped, drag is minimized when the gear is retracted, allowing greater airspeed and more fuel-efficient flight. In all retractable-gear installations, there must be an emergency means for extending the gear in the event of failure of the hydraulic or electric actuators.

For air transport aircraft, the FAA requires that each airplane must be designed so that, with the airplane under control, it can be landed on a paved runway with any one or more landing-gear legs not extended. The landing must occur without sustaining a structural component failure that is likely to cause the spillage of enough fuel to constitute a fire hazard. Other requirements include the following:

- The landing gear cannot fail, but can yield, in a test showing its reserve energy absorption capacity, simulating a descent velocity of 1.2 times the limit descent velocity, assuming wing lift equal to the weight of the airplane.
- The aircraft must not be damaged when it is dropped from a free drop height not less than 9.2 in. but not more than 18.7 in.
- One drop test must be conducted so that it is 2.25 times the prescribed drop height (3.35 ft).
- Another drop test must be conducted that is sufficient to develop 1.5 times the load limit factor.

Figure 4.2 shows the structural components of the Boeing 747-400.

Landing Gear Squat Switch

The landing gear squat switch is an important fail-safe mechanism that notifies many aircraft systems that the airplane is actually on the ground. This electrical switch is activated by the weight of the airplane bearing down on the landing gear struts. This switch is important, because some controls must never be activated while the plane is on the ground or others while it is in the air, and these controls can know whether the airplane is airborne or on the ground only through the signal that the squat switch sends them.

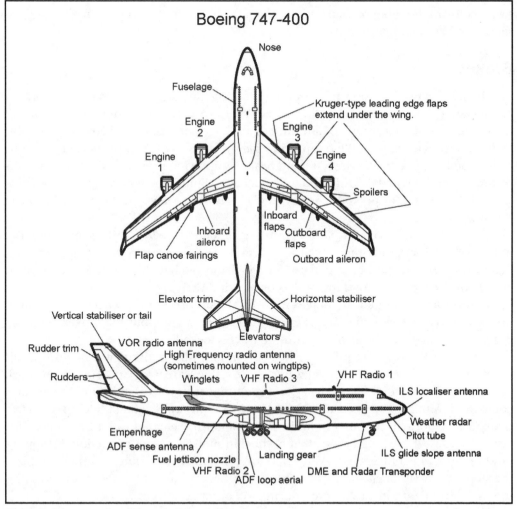

Figure 4.2 *Structural components of the airplane.*

For example, while the plane is on the ground, the landing gear must never be raised; without the squat switch, if you accidentally raised the landing gear while on the ground, the whole airplane would collapse onto the tarmac, possibly destroying the aircraft. Similarly, ground spoilers should never be activated in the air; doing so in flight could be disastrous. Another mechanism tied to the squat switch is the thrust reversers. On some aircraft with tail-mounted engines, such as the MD-80 or the 727, activating the thrust reversers before the airplane is fully on the ground could tilt the nose up in the air.

The squat switch also activates the cabin pressurization dump valve when the airplane lands, thereby depressurizing the plane. When the airplane takes off, the squat switch informs the cabin pressurization system that it is safe to start pressurizing the passenger and crew compartments.

Brakes

The brakes are used for slowing, stopping, holding, and steering the airplane. Brakes are installed in each main landing wheel and are activated independently using hydraulic fluid similar to that of automobile braking systems. In real aircraft, the pilot activates the right-hand brake by applying toe pressure to the top portion of the right rudder pedal and activates the left-hand brake by applying pressure to the top portion of the left rudder pedal. Unfortunately, in Flight Simulator you must use your joystick's brake button or press the **period** key. This is true, even if you have CH-Products Pedals.

The brakes are locked for parking by using a ratchet-type lock linkage built into the master cylinder and the brake pedal. The brakes are usually unlocked by applying sufficient pressure on the brake pedals to unload the ratchet. In Flight Simulator, you engage or disengage the parking brakes by pressing **Ctrl+period**.

FAA rules require that the brakes must be able to prevent the wheels from rolling on a paved runway with takeoff power on the critical engine, but the brakes need not prevent movement of the airplane with the wheels locked.

Since the 1960s jet aircraft have been equipped with antiskid systems to prevent them from sliding on wet or icy runways. These systems are a variation on the antilock brakes found on automobiles. The system monitors each wheel's rotational speed and compares it with the expected value based on a dry runway. If actual wheel speed is less than 85% of normal, the wheel's brake is momentarily released to let the wheel turn faster. Physicists have long known that a wheel in motion has more frictional stopping power than a wheel that is in a skid. Therefore, the antiskid braking system maximizes the stopping power of each wheel by pulsing the brakes off and on, thereby preventing the wheel from entering a skid even during wet or icy conditions.

Steering

While the plane is on the ground, the steering of light aircraft with nosewheel landing gear is controlled by mechanical linkages to the rudder pedals. On heavier jet aircraft, however, hydraulically assisted steering is used with a control mechanism that makes the steering less sensitive at higher speeds. This arrangement is needed because while taxiing the airplane at low speeds the pilot needs to be able to apply maximum turns with the wheel; at higher rolling speeds, however, a sudden movement of the nosewheel could cause severe damage to the undercarriage. On Boeing aircraft, for example, almost 90° of maneuvering is available with the power steering during slow taxiing, whereas limited rudder pedal steering of 10° is possible during the takeoff roll. Ground steering is almost always performed by the captain and not the first officer. Steering is accomplished by turning a small steering wheel or tiller near the captain's left knee. In a two-person cockpit, the captain always sits on the left side.

If you are having problems with loss of steering, first turn off the yaw damper and then disengage the autopilot. This action will release the rudder pedals and let you regain control of steering.

TIP

Windshield

The FAA requires that for commuter category airplanes the windshield in front of the pilots must withstand, without penetration, the impact of a two-pound bird when the velocity of the airplane is equal to the airplane's maximum approach flap speed. For air transport category aircraft, the regulations are more stringent: the windshield and supporting structures must withstand, without penetration, the impact of a four-pound bird when the velocity is equal to the design cruise speed at sea level. The cockpit windshield panels must also be arranged so that, assuming the loss of vision through any one panel, one or more panels remain available for use by a pilot to permit continued safe flight and landing.

Boeing aircraft have twice as many windows along the fuselage as the older Douglas jets, such as the DC-8. Usually, Boeing aircraft have two windows assigned to each seat row. Douglas-designed windows are, however, larger.

Lights

Instrument panel lights and exterior navigational lighting and strobes (Figure 4.3) can be toggled on or off as a group by pressing **L**. To turn on or off the instrument lights separately, press **Shift+L**. To turn on or off the strobes separately, press **O**.

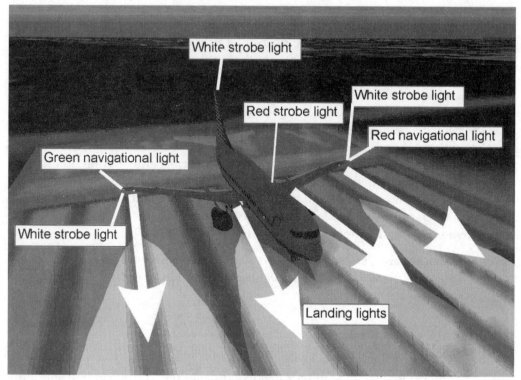

Figure 4.3 *Navigational exterior lighting. Green lights are always mounted on the right wing, and red lights are mounted on the left wing. At night, you can use this standard lighting orientation to determine whether a plane is approaching or traveling away from you.*

New to FS98 are the steerable landing lights. You can focus these landing lights in a particular direction, making it easier to negotiate a turn on a darkened runway or illuminate the runway when you are landing. Table 4.1 shows the keyboard commands for the steerable landing lights.

Table 4.1 *Steerable Landing Lights: Keyboard Commands*

FUNCTION	KEYBOARD COMMAND
Landing lights on/off	**Ctrl L**
Landing lights up	**Ctrl+keypad 8**
Landing lights down	**Ctrl+keypad 2**
Landing lights left	**Ctrl+keypad 4**
Landing lights right	**Ctrl+keypad 6**
Landing lights centered	**Ctrl+keypad 5**

Doors

You may have pondered how it is that jet aircraft doors, which open outward and yet are totally contained inside the airplane while flying, are wider than the opening? This is one of life's most enduring mysteries; if the door is bigger than the opening, how can it be pushed out after the plane has landed? We will leave this question unanswered but will posit that there is a method to this madness. Consider this. With the door bigger than the opening on the inside, it can act as a plug. Pressurizing the interior doesn't weaken the door; instead it seals it more firmly than it could be sealed if it were closed from the outside. During normal cruise at 35,000 ft, the pressure differential between the cabin and outside air is normally 8 lb/in², meaning that the cabin pressure is 8 psi greater than the outside atmosphere. Because doors are normally 6 ft high by 3.5 ft wide, a door's area is 21 ft² or 3,024 in². If you do the arithmetic, you will find that 8 lb/in² multiplied by the door area of 3,024 in² amounts to a force of 24,192 lb. This is more than 12 tons of force! Even a team of wild horses couldn't pry open the door during flight, let alone a mischievous child.

For cabin pressurization purposes, a tight seal around the door's extremities is needed. Each door is therefore fitted with an inflatable seal that uses engine bleed air to close the inevitable tiny gaps between the door and its frame.

Doors on large air transport aircraft include built-in inflatable chutes, or slides, that can be used in emergencies. After the aircraft is taxiing on its own power, the cabin staff places the doors into automatic mode, allowing the chutes to inflate automatically if the door is opened from the inside. When the airplane nears the terminal after landing, the doors are returned to manual mode and the system is disarmed. On more than one occasion, a red-faced flight attendant or service person has opened the cabin door without disarming the automatic emergency-chute deployment bags. When this happens, you can be sure the airplane is not going to take off on time for its next flight.

The FAA requires that for air transport certification, it must be shown that the entire aircraft can be evacuated within 90 seconds. The door itself must open within 10 seconds, and if it is a power-operated system, there must be a secondary means of opening the door. The number of exits required for a given aircraft depends on its maximum seating and the size of the door installed. For Type 1 floor-level doors, which are at least 48 in. high by 24 in. wide, there must be a minimum of one door per 45 seats installed on each side of the fuselage. Boeing has engineered the 737-400's doors to be taller and wider than the Type 1 definition (34 in. wide by 72 in. tall for the forward entry door, although the other doors are smaller), but it still describes them as Type 1. Thus, for example, the 737-400 must have four Type 1 doors to seat a maximum of 168 passengers, because 45 × 4 = 180 passengers. A different definition is used for wide-body jets, and different passenger limitations apply, because the openings are wider than in the Type 1 definition.

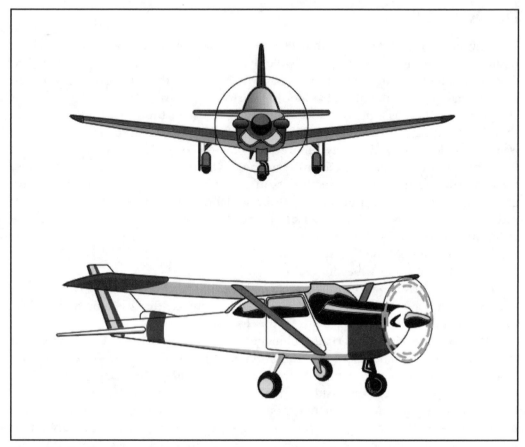

Figure 4.4 *Cantilever wings (top) and semicantilever wings (bottom).*

WINGS

The wings are the airfoils that provide the airplane's main source of lift and contain control surfaces such as ailerons, flaps, spoilers, slats, and other leading edge devices. There are two types of wings—cantilever and semicantilever—as shown in Figure 4.4. The cantilever wing requires no external bracing, because the stress is carried by internal wing spars, ribs, and stringers. Many semicantilevered wings, on the other hand, are braced both externally, by means of wing struts attached to the fuselage, and internally, by spars and ribs.

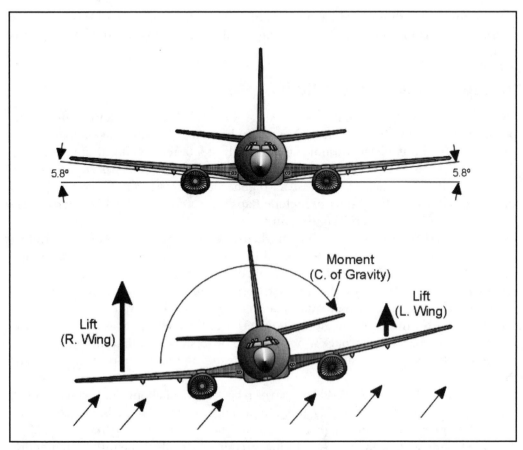

Figure 4.5 *The wing's dihedral angle. Note that the wingtips are higher than the wing root by a few degrees. The dihedral angle gives the airplane lateral, or roll, stability. When a gust of wind or air turbulence causes one wing to rise higher than the other, the dihedral angle produces more lift on the lower wing and returns the plane to level flight.*

The Wings' Dihedral Angle

The angle at which the wings are slanted upward from the root to the tip is known as the *dihedral* angle. It is the upward V shape of the wing when the aircraft is viewed from its nose. In turbulent air, the dihedral stabilizes the airplane as one wing is forced down. When this happens, the lower wing has a higher angle of attack than the higher wing, and this causes the lower wing to have more lift than the higher wing. This extra force returns the wing to its wing level flight, as shown in Figure 4.5.

Too much dihedral is inefficient, because too much of the wing's lift is lost in the horizontal direction. It can also lead to Dutch roll, which is discussed in the next section.

Sweep-back and Dutch Roll

Sweep-back refers to the angle that the wings are swept back from an imaginary line perpendicular to the fuselage. A higher sweep-back angle is advantageous for supersonic aircraft, and it allows subsonic aircraft to fly at a faster speed without exceeding the wing's critical Mach number. Unfortunately, increasing sweep-back reduces lift, so airplanes with swept-back wings must have generous provisions for increasing lift at slow speeds. Lift-increasing devices include flaps, slats, and other leading edge devices that add camber and curvature to the wing.

Unfortunately, swept-back wings markedly reduce the effectiveness of trailing edge control surfaces such as ailerons and flaps. For example, a flap on a straight wing will increase the lift coefficient by approximately 50%, but the same flap on a swept-back wing will increase the lift coefficient by only 20%. To overcome this limitation, swept-back wings usually have leading edge high-lift devices such as slots or slats installed on the front of the wing, where the lift coefficient is not affected as much by sweep-back. Swept-back wings can also be designed so that the wing directly in front of the flap hinge line is unswept, thus avoiding the sweep-back effect on the flaps.

The wing of the Boeing 747-400 has a sweep-back angle of about 37.5°, which is much greater than that of the Boeing 737-400. This arrangement allows the Boeing 747's critical Mach number to be much higher than that of the 737—0.90 compared with 0.82.

One troublesome artifact of swept-wing aircraft, especially those with high dihedral angles, is the tendency toward *Dutch roll*, the problem whereby when an airplane yaws it also rolls. On the 737 and other such swept-wing aircraft, it develops into an oscillation between yaw and then roll, followed by yaw and then roll. This movement continues unabated, rolling back and forth and creating passenger discomfort and pilot fatigue in counteracting the motion. Dutch roll is caused by turbulence and, if not corrected, can get out of hand and become dangerous.

Dutch roll results from the airplane side slipping into a gust of wind, something that causes an imbalance on the lift force for each wing. During the aircraft's side slip, the wing that is presented first into the airplane's flight path has more lift than the wing that is projected slightly rearward, because it has more effective wingspan due to the smaller effective sweep-back angle. The wing with greater lift then causes the airplane to roll to one side. The higher-lift wing generates more drag, however, and this forces the airplane to yaw back the other way so that the opposite wing is then presented first

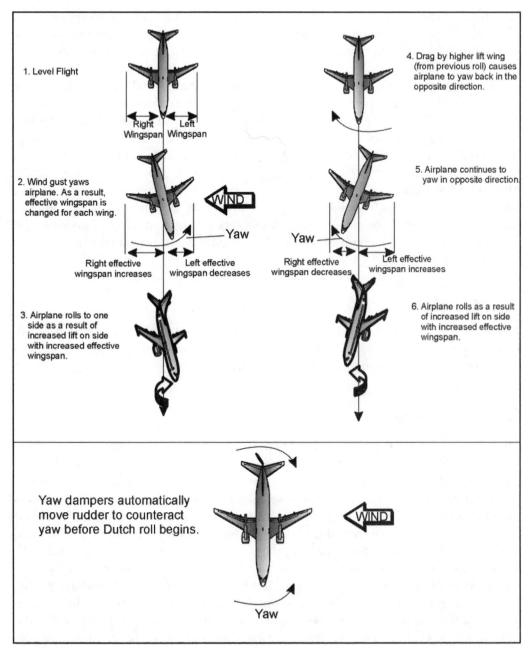

Figure 4.6 Dutch roll. Yaw dampers installed in an aircraft automatically reduce the Dutch roll tendency of swept-wing aircraft.

into the airplane's flight path, as shown in Figure 4.6. Just as in the first instance, the opposite wing will now generate more lift, because it has a smaller sweep-back angle with more effective wingspan, so the airplane rolls in the opposite direction. The process is repeated ad nauseam.

To eliminate the problem, swept-wing aircraft that have Dutch roll tendencies are equipped with yaw dampers. These automatic devices are tied into the autopilot. Before the airplane has a chance to yaw in response to wind turbulence, the yaw damper sends a control input to counteract the yaw before the Dutch roll can develop. In Flight Simulator, the 737-400 has a yaw damper control installed on the instrument panel, and you engage it by clicking on the **YAW** control followed by switching on the **AP** control (the autopilot master switch). With the Learjet, you must activate the yaw damper from the **Aircraft/Autopilot** menu or press **Ctrl+D**. Note that having the yaw damper activated while on the ground will sabotage any hope of ground steering. You must first turn the yaw damper off and then turn off the autopilot if you are to regain control of the steering.

Aspect Ratio

The aspect ratio of a wing is the wingspan squared divided by the wing area, or $b^2 \div S$. Increasing the aspect ratio increases the efficiency of the wing by reducing induced drag, in turn giving the wing more lift at low airspeeds.

CONTROL SURFACES

The primary control surfaces are movable panels on the airplane's wings, tail, and horizontal stabilizer that allow the pilot to modify the airflow over the airplane. The *primary* flight control surfaces are the ailerons, elevators, and rudder. The *secondary* control surfaces are the flaps, spoilers, leading edge devices, slats, and trim devices such as elevator trim, aileron trim, and rudder trim. More exotic aircraft employ canards, flaperons (flaps that also act as ailerons, as on the new Boeing 777), and other types of movable surfaces. Larger aircraft usually employ some form of hydraulic assist to the control surfaces because of the greater control forces exerted by high-speed airflow. Advanced new air transport jets such as the Airbus A320 and the Boeing 777 are equipped with fly-by-wire computer systems that use electronic linkages instead of traditional cables and pulleys between the pilot's control column and the wing surfaces. These electronic signals activate hydraulic actuators to move the control surfaces.

Flying by Wire

By replacing the mechanical linkages, cables, and pulleys with a wire that transmits electric signals to actuators that move the control surfaces, airplane designers realize significant weight savings. Airbus installed the world's first fly-by-wire system in a commercial air transport in 1987 in the Airbus A320. The Boeing 777 uses a fly-by-wire system employing three computers to implement decisions made by the pilot. For safety reasons, each computer contains a unique processor with its own power supply, independent operating system software, and independent software routines, which are written by separate companies. The goal is to avoid the possibility that a bug in one system is duplicated on the others. Before a command is processed, each computer checks to see whether a consensus has been reached by the other computers; they then "vote," and, if two of the three agree, the command is sent to the hydraulic actuator on the control surface. If one computer does not agree, it is overruled by the majority two computers.

Although the pilot retains ultimate control of the system, the computers limit his or her actions to certain parameters that fit within their built-in flight control laws. These laws are known as primary flight law, alternate flight law, and direct flight law. If the primary flight law fails, the system switches to alternate flight law. If this also fails, the system switches to direct flight, in which flight control reverts to the pilot. In primary flight law, the pilot cannot push the rudders to their maximum deflection angle, nor can the pilot fly too fast in a dive or bank too steeply (greater than 35° on the 777). Also, if an engine fails, the computers automatically compensate for asymmetric thrust and will apply as much as 10° rudder when one engine gives more than 10% power than the other.

In the event of a total computer failure on the 777 fly-by-wire system, the pilot can directly control the actuators on the control surfaces, bypassing the computers by using direct flight law. If even the electronically controlled actuators fail, the crew has an old-fashioned, mechanically linked backup control to get the plane home safely. The backup system consists of a hydraulically controlled trim surface on the horizontal stabilizer in the tail for elevator control along with one cable-driven spoiler on each wing surface, each of which acts as an aileron.

FAR Part 25 regulations require that air transport aircraft meet certain requirements for redundancy of primary flight controls to prevent possible instances of jamming. For example, the ailerons and roll spoilers are connected via a clutch; in the event of a system failure that jams either control, the clutch is released, allowing the pilot to fly with the redundant but still operable control. The elevators are also designed for redundancy; should one set of linkages jam, a clutch releases the two sys-

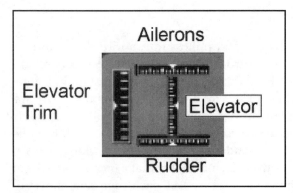

Figure 4.7 *Control position indicators.*

tems so that the pilot can fly with the remaining link. Hydraulic systems on most jet aircraft are usually triplicated except on the Boeing 747, which has four redundant hydraulic systems. In the event of a hydraulic leak or failure in one system, the remaining two systems can take up the slack.

Control Position Indicators

The control position indicators (Figure 4.7) are cockpit instruments that confirm the degree of deflection of the control surfaces. These indicators assure the pilot that the controls are working properly.

Rudder

The rudder, which is located the vertical stabilizer, controls the aircraft's yaw or directional control (Figure 4.8). At takeoff and during landing, the surface of the vertical stabilizer acts as a weather vane, and the airplane's nose tends to pivot into the relative wind. The pilot moves the rudder by exerting pressure on the rudder pedals; however, if you choose to fly in Flight Simulator with Auto-coordination turned on, you needn't worry about the rudder, because moving the ailerons will also move the rudder. With Auto-coordination turned off, the rudders act separately from the ailerons during turns. When the left rudder pedal is pressed, the rudder is deflected to the left, causing the relative wind to push the tail to the right and the nose to the left. When the right rudder pedal is pressed, the rudder is deflected to the right, causing the opposite action to occur. All pilots should realize that the function of the rudder is to yaw the airplane and not to turn the airplane. Only when the ailerons and rudder are applied in concert can the airplane turn properly.

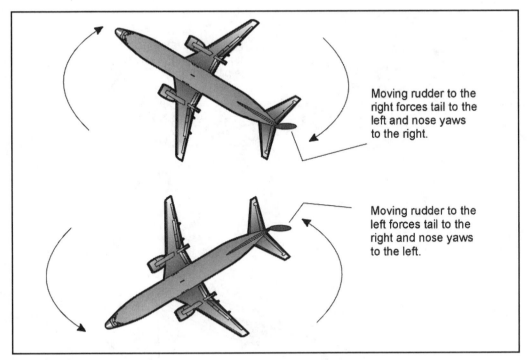

Moving rudder to the right forces tail to the left and nose yaws to the right.

Moving rudder to the left forces tail to the right and nose yaws to the left.

Figure 4.8 The rudder.

Elevator

The elevators, which are located on the trailing edge of the aircraft's horizontal stabilizer, control the aircraft's pitch, or rotation about its lateral axis (Figure 4.9). On light airplanes, the elevators are movable control surfaces hinged on the horizontal stabilizer and are attached to the control column by mechanical linkage. Under normal flying conditions, pulling back on the yoke (or joystick) will move the elevators up. The relative wind then forces the tail down, thereby raising the nose of the aircraft and the wing's angle of attack. Conversely, if the yoke is pushed forward, the elevators move down and the airplane's nose is pitched down, because the relative wind creates more lift on the airplane's tail.

In most aircraft, the horizontal stabilizer has a negative angle of attack and is a symmetrical (not cambered) airfoil. In level flight, this negative angle of attack causes the horizontal stabilizer to exert a downward force of lift rather than an upward force on the rear of the airplane. As you will recall from Chapter 2, both the horizontal stabilizer and the elevator create a moment force that counteracts the wing's center of pressure

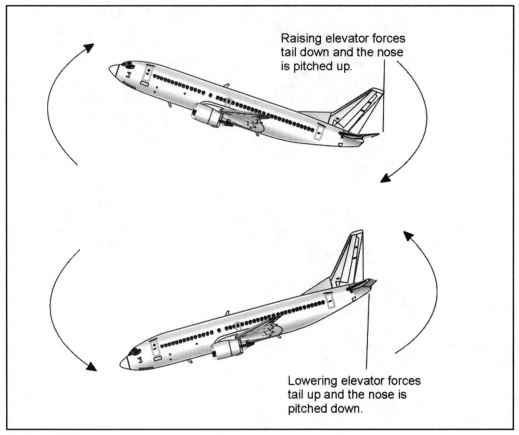

Figure 4.9 Elevator.

moment force. By itself, the wing has a natural tendency to pitch the airplane's nose down; the horizontal stabilizer is needed to counteract this tendancy.

Elevator Trim Tabs

The elevator trim tab is used to hold the elevator at a particular position without the need for the pilot to exert continual force to maintain its position (Figure 4.10). The elevator trim tab is a small auxiliary control surface hinged at the trailing edge of the elevators, and it can be moved independently of the elevators. If an unusually heavy load were placed in the rear baggage compartment of an airplane, the tail would be heavy and the nose would want to rise. To counteract this imbalance, you would need to apply forward pressure on the joystick yoke to keep the plane from

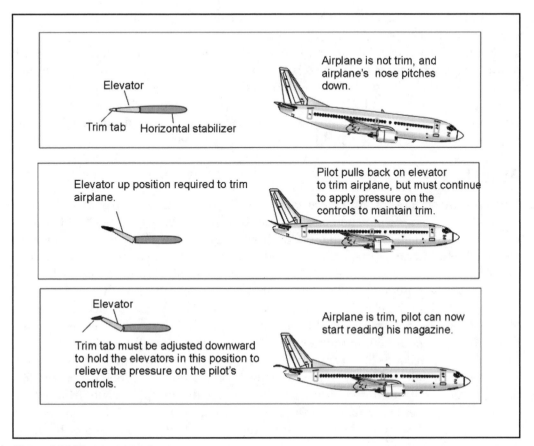

Figure 4.10 *Elevator trim tab.*

slowing. Rather than continue to hold the yoke forward, you can apply the elevator trim tabs.

An upward deflection of the trim tab will force the elevator downward, and a downward deflection of the trim tab will force the elevator upward. This means that the direction the trim tab is deflected will always cause the entire elevator to be deflected in the opposite direction. How would this affect your flight using a joystick? Suppose you were flying and you noticed that to fly straight and level you had to pull the joystick back slightly, meaning that the elevators were raised up. Maintaining this constant pressure could get uncomfortable after a while, so to avoid pilot fatigue you use *opposite* elevator trim to keep the elevators in their current position so that you can release the joystick. This would mean that you apply *down* elevator trim (press **keypad 1**) to keep the elevator trimmed at its current position. In Flight Simulator, note that the elevator trim control on the instrument panel does not move down; rather, it moves *up* in response to elevator trim *down*.

For the Cessna, trim tab up (**keypad 1**) causes the nose to pitch up, and trim tab down (**keypad 7**) causes the nose to pitch down. In response, the control indicator moves down when you pitch the nose up, and it moves up when you pitch the nose down. On the Learjet and 737, the elevator trim tab control indicator shows reverse direction, but the keyboard commands are the same: trim tab down (**keypad 7**), lowers the nose and trim tab up (**keypad 1**) causes the nose to pitch up.

Auto-Trim

When passengers move around the airplane or get up to go to the washroom or the flight attendants start moving food and beverage carts, the plane's balance is upset and must be restored via trim. The auto-trim is used for this purpose. In the 737-400, auto-trim is a system of pulleys and cables that are connected to the trim tabs and adjusted by the autopilot. When the autopilot gyroscopes detect that weight has shifted forward toward the nose by the aircraft's movement, the elevator trim tabs are adjusted so that more downward force is applied on the elevators in the back of the airplane to counteract the moment force. When weight shifts back to the tail of the airplane, the autopilot directs the auto-trim to provide upward lift on the elevators to prevent the nose from pitching up.

Because the balance of a large jet transport airplane is constantly changing during flight, very rarely do pilots like to fly manually during cruise. It is much easier, and less tiring, to turn over the chore of trimming the plane to the autopilot's auto-trim system.

Aileron trim restores balance to the airplane when too much weight is on one side of the airplane's longitudinal axis, and it prevents the aircraft from rolling or banking. Aileron trim is controlled by the autopilot's wing leveler (**LVL**). Rudder trim is used to keep the airplane from yawing right or left and is controlled by the autopilot's heading (**HDG**) or Nav lock (**NAV**).

The autopilot altitude lock will auto-trim the elevator trim tabs to keep the airplane properly trimmed for pitch. You can watch this work by turning on the autopilot **AP** instrument panel switch (or press **Z**); then choose an altitude in the altitude box and click on the **ALT** control located on the autopilot. After the airplane has leveled off at the chosen altitude, the elevator trim tab will move up and down automatically to keep the airplane level.

If you are in the cockpit during flight, you can hear the rotating pulleys move the trim cables as the trim tabs are directed up and down in response to changing balance conditions in the airplane. Flight Simulator simulates the auto-trim without the sound. To see this in action, turn on the autopilot wing leveler. You'll notice that the aileron control indicator moves sideways automatically to restore balance to the airplane. To test this further, decrease thrust on one engine in the 737 or Learjet and then watch as the aileron needle swings to one side to maintain the airplane's equilibrium.

Flaps and Leading Edge Devices

An ordinary wing will have a maximum coefficient of lift C_{LMax} of 1.8. To achieve higher C_{LMax} values for takeoffs and landings—thereby allowing slower stall speeds for safer landings—designers have resorted to the use of mechanical devices that temporarily alter the geometry of the wing. There are two types of devices for this purpose: flaps and leading edge devices.

Flaps come in many configurations, but they all serve the same purposes: they provide slower landing and takeoff speeds, and they permit a comparatively steep angle of descent without an increase in speed. Flaps also permit shorter takeoff and landing distances and provide a steeper climb path. Most wing flaps are hinged near the trailing edges of the wings, inboard of the ailerons. When deployed, flaps can extend as much as 40° to 50° from the wing. This arrangement has the effect of increasing the wing's chord line and angle of attack, thereby providing greater lift and more drag.

Airbus aircraft don't use degrees, such as 0°, 10°, or 30°, to describe flap positions. Instead, the flap positions are called "0," "1," "2," and "3," with "0" referring to flaps fully retracted and "3" denoting flaps fully extended. These numbers do not correspond to degrees of flap.

The plain flap is simply a hinged section of the trailing edge of the wing, as shown in Figure 4.11. When lowered, the plain flap increases the maximum coefficient of lift

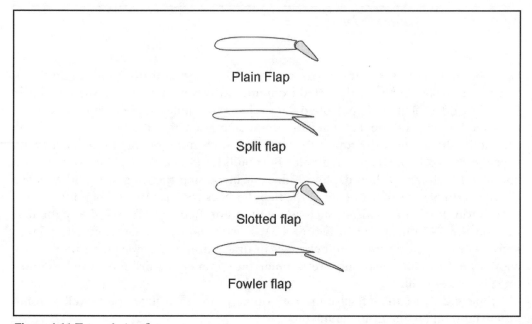

Plain Flap

Split flap

Slotted flap

Fowler flap

Figure 4.11 *Types of wing flaps.*

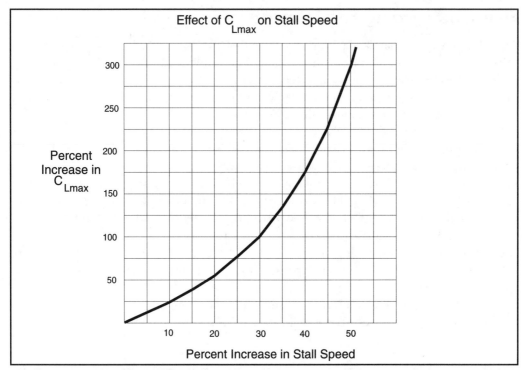

Figure 4.12 *Effect of C_{LMax} on stall speed.*

C_{LMax}, but it also increases drag, necessitating an increase in thrust to maintain flight. The split flap, a plate that is deflected from under the wing, produces a slightly higher C_{LMax} than does the plain flap. Slotted flaps, which are similar to plain flaps, have a gap between the wing and the flap that allows high-energy air from the lower surface of the wing to be ducted over the top of the flap. This adds more energy to the air flowing over the slotted flap, creating a greater Bernoulli lift effect. Fowler flaps slide back a considerable distance when deployed, thereby increasing the wing area and effective chord length of the wing. Extending the flaps far back requires the use of pontoon-like devices with track mechanisms, such as are found on Boeing 747s (see the canoe fairings on the 747 illustrated in Figure 4.2). Fowler flaps are characterized by large increases in C_{LMax} with minimum changes in drag. Although Fowler flaps have more-complicated mechanisms, they are popular on commercial airliners, which require huge increases in lift.

Table 4.2 shows the effective increase on C_{LMax} for each flap type as well as some other common engineering parameters.

Table 4.2 Flap and Slot Engineering Parameters (McCormick 1995)

TYPE OF FLAP	CHARACTERISTICS
Plain flaps	1. Optimum flap angle is approximately 60°. 2. Optimum flap chord length to that of wing is 0.25c. 3. Maximum increase in C_{LMax} is 0.9 (around 50% increase in lift).
Split flaps	1. Optimum flap angle is approximately 70°. 2. Optimum flap chord length to that of wing is 0.3c. 3. Maximum increase in C_{LMax} is 0.9 (around 50% increase in lift).
Slotted flaps	1. Optimum flap angle is 40° for single slots and 70° for double-slot flaps. 2. Optimum flap chord length to that of wing is 0.3c. 3. Maximum increase in C_{LMax} is 1.5 for single slots and 1.9 for double-slot flaps (around 100% increase in lift).
Fowler flaps	1. Optimum flap angle is 40°. 2. Optimum flap chord length to that of wing is 0.3c. 3. Maximum increase in C_{LMax} is 2.0 (110% increase in lift).
Fixed slot	1. Maximum increase in C_{LMax} is 0.2 (almost 12% increase in lift).
Extensible slat	1. Maximum increase in C_{LMax} is 0.9 with no trailing edge flaps deployed (almost 50% increase in lift).
Kruger-type leading edge flap (similar to that used on Boeing 747)	1. Maximum increase in C_{LMax} is 1.2 (67% increase in lift).

As shown in Table 4.3, large changes in C_{LMax} are necessary to produce significant changes in stall speed. Typical propeller planes experience a 70% increase in C_{LMax} with full flap deflection, which amounts to a 25% decrease in stall speed. Single-engine fighter planes with thin, swept-back wings can obtain a 20% increase in C_{LMax} with full flap deflection, which results in a puny 10% decrease in stall speed. You can see why fighter planes must land very, very fast. You can also see from the table that if you double C_{LMax} (increase C_{LMax} by 100%), it would be possible to reduce landing speed by 29%. This is why flaps and leading edge devices are so useful and are necessary on heavy jet aircraft such as the 747, which uses extensive Fowler flaps and Kruger-type leading edge devices to enhance C_{LMax}.

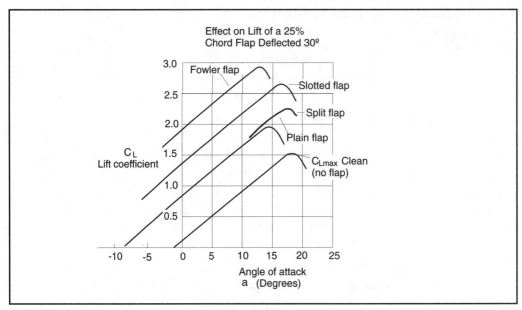

Figure 4.13 *Flap configurations: effect on lift coefficient and drag coefficient.*

Table 4.3 *Percent Increase in Maximum Coefficient of Lift C_{LMax} and Resulting Decrease in Stall Speed*

PERCENT INCREASE IN C_{LMax} (LIFT)	EXAMPLE 1: NO FLAPS; WING HAS C_{LMax} = 1.5	PERCENT REDUCTION IN STALL SPEED	EXAMPLE 2: STALL SPEED 125 KNOTS
+2%	1.53	-1%	123.8 kt
+10%	1.65	-5%	118.8 kt
+50%	2.25	-18%	102.5 kt
+100%	3.0	-29%	88.8 kt
+300%	4.5	-50%	62.5 kt

Leading Edge Devices

Slats and slots are commonly referred to as *leading edge devices* because they are applied to the leading edge of the wing to generate higher lift. A slot is a fixed or automatic gap in the leading edge of the wing that allows the upper surface air to mix with lower surface air, as shown in Figure 4.14. Slots have the disadvantage of creating excessive drag at low angles of attack that occur during cruise. To overcome this disadvantage, design-

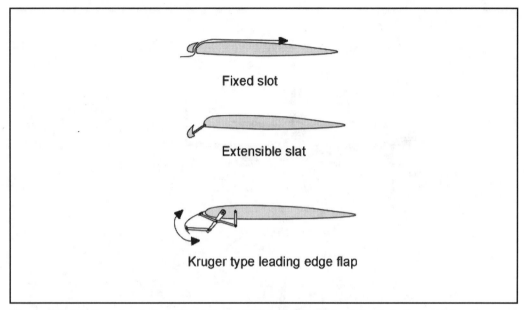

Fixed slot

Extensible slat

Kruger type leading edge flap

Figure 4.14 Leading edge devices. Slots increase lift by allowing high-energy air to flow over the upper surface of the wing at high angles of attack. However, slots are inefficient when the plane is cruising with a low angle of attack. Slats are leading edge devices that are deployed only at low speeds. They increase lift by changing the shape of the wing so that it is more cambered. The Kruger-type leading edge flap is used on the 747-400 and dramatically increases lift at low speeds.

ers have opted to use slats, or leading edge wing segments that open at a low speed to provide more lift but close at higher speeds to avoid drag.

Ailerons

Ailerons, which in French means "little wings," are movable surfaces hinged on the trailing edge of the wing (Figure 4.15). They give the airplane its rotational control around its longitudinal axis. Moving the stick left or right or the wheel left or right causes the ailerons to move. Moving the stick to the right raises the aileron on the right wing and lowers the aileron on the left wing. Moving the stick to the left raises the aileron on the left wing and lowers the aileron on the right wing. When an aileron is lowered, the angle of attack on that wing will increase, thereby increasing the lift on that wing side.

Many airplanes have trim tabs on the ailerons. Similar to elevator trim tabs, aileron trim tabs are smaller, movable hinged parts that are mounted on the main aileron. Larger

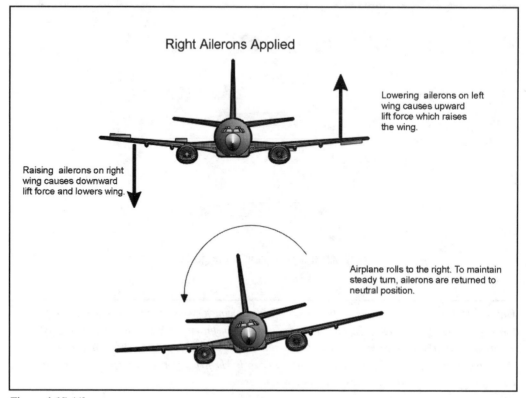

Right Ailerons Applied

Lowering ailerons on left wing causes upward lift force which raises the wing.

Raising ailerons on right wing causes downward lift force and lowers wing.

Airplane rolls to the right. To maintain steady turn, ailerons are returned to neutral position.

Figure 4.15 *Ailerons.*

jet transports have separate inboard and outboard ailerons that are activated at different airspeeds. The inboard ailerons operate full time, whereas the outboard ailerons operate only at lower airspeeds. The reason for this design is that the aileron size is limited by the requirement for large spanwise flaps needed for landing at slow speeds. Because of the limited space on the inboard portion of the wing, only small ailerons can be installed. Small ailerons are fine for high-speed cruise, but they are inadequate for good roll response at low airspeeds. To give an airplane good roll capabilities at slow speeds, designers have added a second outboard aileron that is much larger than the inboard ailerons but operates only at lower airspeeds. For example, the Boeing 767 has inboard and outboard ailerons on each wing; at 240 or more knots, the outer ailerons are disabled.

It is interesting to note that the Wright brothers' original flying machine did not employ ailerons. Their design incorporated a wing twist. By pulling cables attached to the diagonally opposed sides of the wingtips, they were able to warp one wing higher than the other. Because the higher wing had a higher angle of attack, it generated more lift on one side of the airplane than on the other, which caused the Wright Flyer to bank in the direction of the lower wing. In a 1912 lawsuit, Wilbur Wright explained the angle of attack and described how it applied to their wing warping means of achieving aileron control (Wright 1988):

> The angle of incidence [attack] of an aeroplane is the angle at which the aeroplane surfaces and the air stream meet. It may or may not correspond with the angle of the aeroplane with the horizon. This angle, that is, the angle of incidence, is continually varying in flight in accordance with the speed of the machine. If the speed is low, a large angle of incidence is required to sustain the machine. If the speed is high, a small angle of incidence suffices to sustain the machine. When the machine is climbing to a greater height, the power of the motor is expended in lifting the weight. Consequently there is less power to drive the machine forward and the speed is less in this case, but the angle of incidence greater....If the load carried by the aeroplane is decreased, which normally happens by the consumption of oil and fuel, the angle of incidence decreases. If from any cause the power of the motor decreases, the angle of incidence increases.
>
> In rapid climbing the angle of incidence of aeroplanes is usually ten degrees or more, that is machines usually climb fastest when the forward speed is rather slow and the angle of incidence great, because then less power is expended in driving the machine forward and more is available for climbing. The angle of incidence which any particular machine normally utilizes in its work varies all the way from $2\frac{1}{2}$ degrees up to nearly 15 degrees.
>
> If the air, from some cause [as for example the aileron effect of wing warping], has a greater upward trend in one place than in another, the angle of incidence on one wing will be greater than the angle of incidence on the other wing.

It is clear from the last statement that the Wright brothers understood the aileron effect and how it could be used to bank the airplane. However, they soon discovered that wing warping was not enough to maintain a stable turn and that they needed to add a rudder:

> [The pilot] would now not only have to think, and think quickly, in operating the front elevator for maintaining the longitudinal equilibrium, but he would also have to think so as to operate this rudder...to present its surface to the wind on that side which is toward...the wing having the smaller angle of incidence....

Later, it occurred to the Wrights that they could operate the wings and rudder simultaneously during a banked turn (similar to auto-coordination in Flight Simulator).

> ...the idea came to us of connecting the wires which operated the rudder to the cables which operated the wing warping, so that whenever the wings were warped the rudder was simultaneously adjusted...to produce a pressure on that side of the rudder which was toward the wing having the smaller angle of incidence.

Spoilers

Various flat panels are mounted on the wing surfaces for the purposes of eliminating lift, decreasing speed, or aiding in maneuvering. The roll spoilers, which are interconnected with the ailerons, deploy up into the airstream on the down wing, lessening lift and aiding the down wing aileron during the turn. The ground spoilers are needed on larger aircraft to dump as much lift as possible during the landing roll. Ground spoilers are usually deployed automatically after some combination of throttle setting and weight on the landing gear is met. Some aircraft are so aerodynamically clean that even with power reduced they have a hard time descending. Flight spoilers are used on such aircraft to reduce lift over the wing, thereby increasing the descent rate. Speed brakes, not to be confused with flight spoilers, are also mounted and extended above the wing, but they are designed to increase drag rather than spoil lift. The essential difference is that speed brakes act to slow an airplane, whereas, flight spoilers are used to increase the airplane's descent rate.

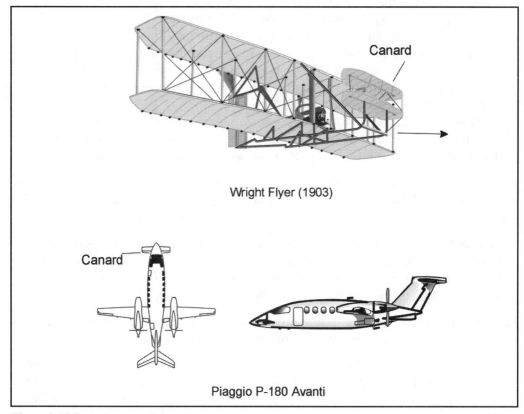

Figure 4.16 Canard-equipped aircraft.

Canard

Canard is the French word for *duck,* and it refers to the duck-like appearance of aircraft that have winged surfaces attached to the front portion of the fuselage (Figure 4.16). Canards are similar to elevators on the tail's horizontal stabilizer, but the action of the elevators on the canard is opposite that of the conventional elevator. In other words, to *raise* the aircraft's nose, you *lower* the canard elevator; in a conventional elevator you would *raise* the elevator to *raise* the nose.

First used by the Wright brothers on their 1903 Flyer, canards are making a comeback in airplane designs such as those by former NASA engineer Burt Rutan, who built the famous Voyager aircraft that circumnavigated the globe without refueling.

Winglets

Winglets are small vertical airfoils that are built into the wingtips. They increase the efficiency of the wing by reducing wingtip vortices that cause induced drag. First developed by Dr. Richard Whitcomb of NASA, winglets have become a common feature on modern jet aircraft, including the Learjet 45 and the Boeing 747-400. Inclining them at

Figure 4.17 Boeing 747-400 on takeoff. You can see the winglets and the Kruger-type leading edge devices deployed on the front part of the wing. Winglets decrease induced drag. On a normal wing, the wing vortices around the wing tips reduce the effective wingspan (decreasing lift) and increase drag. With winglets, however, the airflow around the end of the wing is less disturbed, thereby increasing the effective span (increasing lift) and reducing drag. (Courtesy of Boeing)

an angle of 15° above the wing and 30° below offsets 40% of their parasite drag, with a noticeable improvement in fuel savings. On the Boeing 737-400, for example, a 3% fuel savings is realized (Figure 4.17).

Strake

When the wing is extended forward along the fuselage, it produces beneficial airflow effects for high-speed, swept-wing aircraft. This design is known as a *strake*, probably because of its resemblance to the strake on a boat (Figure 4.18). Burt Rutan's Long-EZ and the F-16 use strake designs for their wings.

Vortex Generators

Vortex generators are vertical vanes 1 to 3 in. tall that are installed on the wing to increase lift and delay stall speeds. They add energy to the slow-moving layer of air that is close

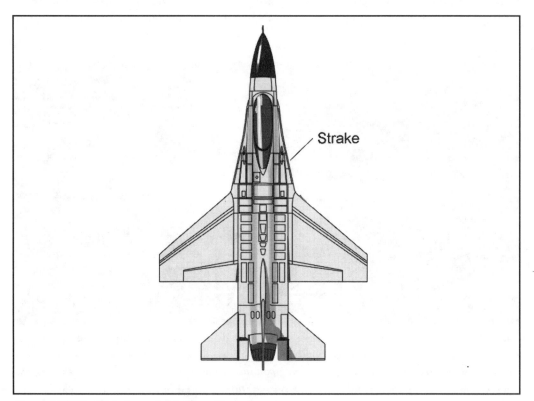

Figure 4.18 *The F-16 air combat fighter with strake.*

to the surface of the wing, thereby preventing the air from separating from the wing. Stalls occur when the boundary layer of air over a wing no longer possesses enough energy to overcome negative pressure over the wing caused by high angles of attack. When this happens, the airflow at the boundary of the wing separates from the wing. With no airflow over the wing surface, no pressure differential can be generated to create lift, and a stall occurs. Thus, the vortex generator delays the onset of a stall by mixing higher-velocity air with low-velocity boundary layer air. This arrangement imparts additional kinetic energy to the boundary layer airstream, allowing it to continue unimpeded by the negative pressure over the wing. Two rows of vortex generators line the top of the Boeing 707 wing.

PITOT-STATIC SYSTEM

As mentioned in Chapter 1, the pitot-static instruments include the pressure altimeter, the vertical speed indicator, and the airspeed indicator. Each of these instruments operates in response to pressures through the pitot-static system. The pitot tube is mounted on the outside of the fuselage and points into the wind. As air is rammed into the tube by the aircraft's forward motion, pressure inside the tube is compared with a static, or motionless, source of air. The airspeed indicator determines the airplane's speed by comparing the static source of air pressure with the moving source of air pressure inside the pitot tube. From this comparison, the airspeed indicator displays the airspeed as a ratio of the two sources of air pressure (the static source and the pitot source).

Because the opening of the pitot tube is small and exposed to the outside elements, the pitot tube can become clogged by ice, affecting the airspeed indicator only. When you're flying through clouds or when the air temperature is below 32° F (0° C), it is prudent to have a pitot heating element that can be turned on to prevent obstruction of the tube.

Pitot Heat

FS98 now includes a pitot heating system to prevent incorrect readings on the airspeed indicator during icy weather. To use it, click the switch on the instrument panel to turn on the pitot heating element.

Before you can test the pitot heating system in FS98, you will have customize the simulator with the following options:

1. Using the **Aircraft/Aircraft Settings/Realism** menu, set **Realism** at least one notch above easy.
2. Set the outside air temperature below 32° F (0° C) using the **World/Weather/Temperature** menu. (Be sure to turn on the **Advanced Weather dialog box** option under the **Options/Preferences/General** menu.)

3. Fly through some clouds, which you can create using the **World/Weather** menu.
4. Turn on the **Icing** option under the **World/Weather/Clouds** menu for each cloud type that you intend to fly through (again, you must have already turned on **Advanced Weather dialog box**).

PISTON-POWERED AIRCRAFT

The Wright brothers' first engine was a water-cooled, piston engine–propeller combination that required bulky, high-drag radiators. This engine, which had four upright cylinders, weighed 200 lb and developed approximately 12 horsepower (8.95 kW) using gasoline for fuel. From this humble beginning until the early 1940s, the piston engine was king of the skies and was the only type of power plant used for airplane propulsion.

Most single-engine light aircraft still use reciprocating piston engines as their means of locomotion. The term *reciprocating* refers to the reciprocating motion of the piston as it transfers up-and-down motion into rotary motion by the crankshaft, which then drives the propeller.

The reciprocating internal combustion engine consists of cylinders, pistons, connecting rods, and a crankshaft. One end of the connecting rod is attached to a piston

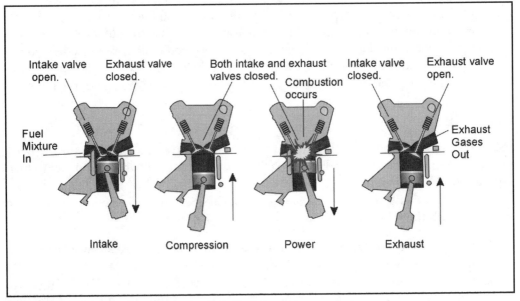

Figure 4.19 *The four strokes of the internal combustion engine.*

and the other end to the crankshaft. At the end of the cylinder, two spark plugs ignite the fuel, and two openings contain valves that open and shut to admit air and fuel and to permit the escape of burned gases. For the engine to complete one cycle, the piston must complete four strokes, and that requires two complete revolutions of the crankshaft. The four strokes are the intake, compression, power, and exhaust.

Air and fuel are mixed by the carburetor or fuel injection system in just the right quantities to permit combustion during the intake stroke. During the compression stroke, the mixture is compressed by the piston; at the top of the stroke, the spark plugs fire to ignite the mixture. The hot gases that arise from the explosion in turn drive the piston downward in the power stroke. Finally, the valves open to permit the evacuation of the exhaust gas. The cycle is repeated for each cylinder in the engine in a precisely choreographed sequence (Figure 4.19).

Piston Engine Failure and the Ballistic Parachute

The modern airplane piston engine is very reliable. With recommended overhaul periods of as long as 2,000 hours, you can get 250,000 to 500,000 statute miles (402,000 to 804,000 km) on an engine before major components must be replaced (assuming average cruising speeds of 120–150 knots). If a piston-engine airplane is used to carry passengers for hire, the FAA requires that the airplane undergo an engine overhaul at least once every 12 months. In addition, the engine must be inspected every 100 hours by an FAA-certified repair shop.

The accident rate for general aviation aircraft attributable to any cause is about one fatality every 57,471 hours, as shown in the National Transportation Safety Board (NTSB) and FAA statistics for 1995. If you assume that each airplane travels at about 120 statute miles per hour, that comes to a fatality rate of 15.8 per 100,000,000 miles flown. Compared with the risk of driving an automobile, which has a fatal accident rate of 2.2 per 100,000,000 vehicle miles driven, or commercial air transport, which has a fatal accident rate of 0.04 per 100,000,000 miles flown, this rate is very high.

The fatality rate for single-engine aircraft that suffer an engine failure is much less: only one fatal forced-landing accident every 502,500 hours. Paradoxically, many people buy twin-engine aircraft thinking that two engines will protect them from the possibility of a forced landing, but these planes have a higher fatal forced-landing accident rate (one every 160,000 hours). With two engines, there is twice as much to go wrong, and, when an engine fails, the pilot is more prone to lose control than in a single-engine plane because of the asymmetric thrust of the remaining engine.

It is easy to lose perspective when reading these statistics. In reality, there are very few engine-related accidents. In 1994, for example, there were only 16 twin-engine power-related fatal accidents in which power was lost, and of those 16 accidents only six suffered a complete power failure of both engines (four of them had no fuel, and in two the fuel was contaminated). Most of the twins that crashed with a single engine out did so because the pilots lost control of the airplane; these flights could have been flown to a successful conclusion.

According to the NTSB, in 1994 there were just under 400 engine failure-type events in singles and twin-engine piston-powered airplanes that resulted in accidents, and fewer than 14% of these were fatal. These figures are misleading, however, because it is estimated that less than half the total number of accidents actually make it to the FAA list. Many accidents don't meet the definition of "substantial damage" that the FAA requires for an incident to be classified as an accident. Thus, we can safely assume that the real number of forced-landing incidents is in the range of 1,000 to 1,500 a year.

If we accept the FAA statistics, however, of the forced landings that resulted from engine failure, 86% landed without fatality. In raw numbers, there were a total of 57 fatal forced-landing accidents in piston-powered airplanes, including singles and twins but excluding agricultural flying. In overall accidents for 1994, regardless of cause, there were 1,994 accidents of which 404 were fatal, resulting in 723 fatalities.

A new development for single-engine airplanes is the ballistic parachute, which can be used to minimize the danger of forced landings in harsh terrain. The ballistic parachute, which has been used successfully on ultralights, is approved for Cessna 150s and is expected to be standard equipment on Cirrus Design SR20 aircraft. Ballistic Recovery Systems, a manufacturer of these parachutes, hopes that its system will achieve a descent rate of 30 ft/s (20 mph) at 5,000 ft density altitude, with a lower descent rate possible for sea level density altitude. In tests conducted on a Cessna 150 flying at altitude, a parachute was deployed with pyrotechnics; just before impact, the chute was jettisoned, allowing the airplane to fly away normally.

The descent rate of a ballistic parachute is not for the faint of heart. A drop of 30 ft/s (1,800 ft/min) is equivalent to a fall from a second story window. Although the aircraft structure, gear, and seats are designed to absorb much of the deceleration force, the landing will be anything but soft. Cirrus Design states that the ballistic parachute is to be used only in an emergency as a last-ditch attempt to save the occupants' lives. The company believes that when there is a loss of control, a midair collision, or loss of visual capability at night or over a fog bank—when you can't see where to make an emergency landing—the ballistic parachute will save lives.

The Throttle

The throttle controls the amount of air entering the carburetor or fuel injection system. With more air introduced, more fuel is mixed and the engine develops more power. The throttle is akin to an automobile accelerator pedal, because both of them directly control the air intake valve on the engine's intake system.

Fuel Injection versus Carburetion

Piston engines rated at more than 200 hp often use fuel injection rather than carburetion to introduce the air-fuel mixture to the cylinders. The Extra 300S in Flight Simulator is equipped with a fuel-injected engine as is the new Cessna Skylane 1825, although the Cessna Skylane 182RG uses a carburetor. In a fuel-injection system, fuel is squirted directly into the cylinders and is then mixed with the air in the cylinders. Fuel-injection systems are more complex and expensive than carburetor systems, because they require high-pressure fuel pumps, air-fuel measuring devices, fuel injectors, and computers to manage the proper air and fuel flow. In both systems, however, the pilot uses the mixture control to lean or enrich the fuel as needed.

Fuel injection has several advantages over a carbureted fuel system. They include the following:

- No ice formation that could block air intake, as there is with carburetor systems.
- More accurate metered fuel flow.
- Faster throttle response.
- Precision control of mixture.
- Easier cold weather starts.

The main disadvantages include the following:

- Hot engine starts are more difficult.
- Restarting the engine due to fuel starvation is more difficult.
- Vapor lock in the pressurized fuel system is a greater danger on hot days.

As a backup system, many airplane engines have an electric fuel pump independent of the engine's mechanical fuel pump.

Carburetor Icing

Carburetor icing is a concern because it can cause the engine to fail. You may think that carburetor icing is not a problem for you unless you are flying during freezing temperatures. This assumption would be wrong, because the vaporization of fuel and air in the carburetor, by itself, can cause a sudden cooling that results in a temperature drop of as much as 60° F (15° C). If the temperature drops below 32°, even for a fraction of a second, moisture will freeze and be deposited as frost or ice inside the carburetor passages. A modest or even slight accumulation of ice will block the air passages, reducing power and lead to complete engine failure, particularly when the throttle is partly or fully closed (which is usually the case during takeoffs and landings!).

On dry days or when the temperature is well below freezing, the moisture in the air is not enough to cause trouble. But if the temperature is between 20° F and 70° F (-6.7° C and

21° C) with visible moisture or high humidity, the pilot should always be alert for carburetor ice. The first sign of carburetor icing for a constant-speed propeller plane occurs when the manifold pressure drops, but there will be no drop in RPM because the propeller pitch is automatically adjusted to compensate for the loss of power, thus maintaining constant RPM.

As a precaution against carburetor icing, the Cessna and most other reciprocating-propeller-powered airplanes have a carburetor heating system that preheats the air before it reaches the carburetor. When the carburetor heat is first turned on, there will be a drop in RPM (with fixed-pitch propeller planes) or a drop in manifold pressure (in airplanes equipped with controllable-pitch propellers, such as the Cessna. If no ice is present, there will be no further change in RPM or manifold pressure until the carburetor heat is turned off; then the RPM or manifold pressure will return to normal. If ice was present, however, there will normally be a rise in RPM or manifold pressure after the initial drop once carburetor heat is turned on. Then, when the carburetor heat is turned off, the RPM or manifold pressure will rise to a value even higher than before the application of heat.

Use of carburetor heat tends to reduce the output of the engine and also increases the operating temperature. Therefore, the heat should not be used when full power is required (as during takeoff) or during normal engine operation except to check for the presence of ice or to remove ice. In the Cessna, you should turn on carburetor heat during landings.

Turbochargers

Turbochargers are used to compress additional air into each cylinder for high-altitude operations. In this way, the cylinder maintains a constant air density so that more power can be developed at high altitudes than would otherwise be the case. In general, these units extend the engine's sea level power output to 20,000 ft or more MSL.

Manifold Pressure Gauge

The manifold pressure gauge measures the amount of air pressure in the intake system of the engine and tells you how much engine power is being developed. With a higher pressure, the pistons are exerting more pressure sucking in the incoming air-fuel mixture, and this means that more power is being developed. Pressure on the gauge is measured in inches of mercury, and the normal operating range is from 15 in. Hg to 23 in. Hg for the cruising Cessna. At idle, the Cessna produces 9.66 in. Hg of manifold pressure, and at full takeoff thrust it should produce 23 in. Hg. (I tested this in Flight Simulator, and it incorrectly showed that the engine develops 29 in. Hg on takeoff at sea level.) Turbocharged aircraft, such as the Cessna 182RG Turbo, can produce greater manifold pressure differentials.

The pilot can establish the proper engine power setting by adjusting the throttle, mixture, and propeller control so that the manifold pressure reading corresponds to the figures in the cruise performance tables. This arrangement allows the pilot to accurately plan for and assess fuel burn, airspeed, and time of travel, because the pilot can accurately predict the airplane's power performance for a given altitude.

Tachometer

The tachometer shows the engine speed in rotations per minute. Normal operating range for the Cessna 182 is 2,100 to 2,400 RPM.

Propeller

After successfully completing their gliding experiments, the Wright brothers began the design of a motor and propeller to drive their airplane. At first, they hoped to design a propeller based on marine engineering theory, reasoning that air could be considered a fluid. They soon found, however, that marine propellers of the time were not based on theory but almost entirely on empirical data and were constructed by trial and error. Undaunted by this setback, they studied the screw propeller from an entirely new theoretical standpoint, from which they designed a propeller that was 66% efficient. The important concept that came from their studies was that the propeller was nothing more than a rotating wing. If the propeller was to produce thrust, it needed to be cambered, and the blade's angle of attack needed to be varied along its length to produce equal amounts of lift along its edge, because of the different rotational speed from the hub to the tip. In short, the propeller needed to create lift, just as a wing does, except that in the case of the propeller, the "lift" was to be created horizontally and not vertically. This force, which we call thrust, would result in the aircraft being pulled forward.

Propellers are subject to induced drag, stalls, and the same aerodynamic principles that apply to any other airfoil. The propeller has an angle of attack, just as a wing does, and, because it rotates around a central point, the relative wind along the propeller's length varies as you move from the hub to the tip. The tip of the blade travels faster than that part near the hub, because the tip travels a greater distance than the hub in the same length of time. Because of the differing airspeeds along the edge, the propeller blade is twisted so that it produces a different angle of attack at each point between the hub and the tip. This arrangement allows the propeller to create uniform lift—that is, "thrust"—throughout the length of the blade. If the propeller blade were designed with the same angle of attack throughout its length (untwisted), it would be extremely inefficient, because as airspeed increases in flight, the portion near the hub would have a negative angle of attack while the blade tip would be stalled. We will empirically demonstrate the angle of attack for a propeller later in this section.

Propellers turn counterclockwise when viewed from the front and clockwise when viewed from the rear.

A *windmilling* propeller is spinning but not producing any thrust. When this happens, the spinning propeller disk creates tremendous drag, often high enough that the airplane cannot sustain altitude very long. On a twin-engine aircraft, a windmilling propeller on a failed engine can produce so much drag that it becomes impossible to maintain directional control. To address this problem, twin-engine aircraft have a propeller feathering control that allows the propeller blade angle of the failed engine to be set close to 90°, thereby minimizing prop drag. Pilots are routinely instructed to feather the propeller when an engine fails.

Fixed-Pitch Propellers

Fixed-pitch propellers are fixed by the manufacturer and cannot be changed by the pilot. These propellers are bolted directly to the crankshaft and always turn at the same RPM as the engine. They are inefficient, because at higher altitudes the propeller needs a higher blade angle to bite into the air, which is of lower density. For the same reason, the pilot cannot optimize the propeller for a given airspeed. Engine power is shown by the RPM gauge, and, as the altitude of the airplane changes, the engine throttle must be adjusted to maintain a constant RPM. To fly with a fixed-pitch propeller with the Cessna in FS98, select the **Aircraft/Aircraft Settings/Engines** menu command and, in the **Prop Advance** list box, choose **Fixed Pitch.**

Controllable-Pitch Propellers

Constant-speed propellers are found on turboprops and many small aircraft, including the Cessna 182. Propeller RPM is set by the pilot and then kept at constant RPM by a propeller governor, which controls the propeller's blade angle. In Flight Simulator, the **Propeller Advance** knob is used to set the propeller's RPM using a constant-speed governor. The governor in turn automatically regulates the blade's pitch angle to maintain the selected RPM. Even though you think you are regulating the blade angle via the **Propeller Advance** knob, in actuality you are not; the speed governor controls the angle.

A controllable-pitch propeller permits the pilot (or the speed governor in this case) to select the blade angle that will result in the most efficient performance for a particular flight condition. A low blade angle, or decreased pitch, reduces the propeller drag and allows more engine power for takeoffs. After the airplane has climbed to its cruise altitude, the propeller blade is increased to a higher blade angle or increased pitch. This technique allows the blade to take a larger bite of air at a lower power setting, especially at higher altitudes, where the propeller might otherwise exceed the safe RPM range for the airplane because of the thinner air. Changing the propeller pitch is akin to changing gears in an automobile: during highway driving you naturally shift to a higher gear to reduce engine RPM; similarly, at cruise in the Cessna you would shift to a higher blade angle to reduce engine RPM and increase cruise efficiency for both the engine and the propeller.

The propeller blade angle relationship with regard to engine RPM can be summarized as follows:

- Minimum RPM: Increasing the propeller blade angle lowers the engine RPM. To increase the blade angle on the Cessna 182 in FS98, pull the **Propeller Advance** knob out (in FSW95, drag the **Propeller Advance** lever down). This technique is useful for cruise or when flying at higher elevations.
- Maximum RPM: Decreasing the propeller blade angle increases the RPM. To decrease the blade angle on the Cessna 182 in FS98, push the **Propeller Advance** knob in (in FSW95, drag the **Propeller Advance** lever up). This technique is useful for takeoffs and climb conditions.

The Propeller Advance control is shown in Figure 4.20.

You should always be aware of engine RPM on the tachometer to avoid overstressing the engine. The real Cessna 182 cruises with the propeller rotating in the range of 2,100 to 2,400 RPM. Take care to avoid flying with a high throttle setting and high manifold pressure with a low RPM, because it is hard on the engine. If you think of the car analogy, it would be like driving up a hill in fourth gear.

By default, Flight Simulator's propeller is set to **Automatic**. This means that the **Propeller Advance** control will not work at all, no matter what your protestations. To change the propeller pitch yourself, first select the **Aircraft/Aircraft Settings/Engines** menu. In the **Prop Advance** list box, choose **Manual**.

Blade failure, although rare, poses some danger in propeller airplanes. The vibration that results from the loss of a prop blade is extremely violent, even on small engines, and it can cause the engine to be torn off its mountings. In 1995, an Atlantic Southeast Airlines Embraer 120 was climbing through FL 180 on a flight from Atlanta to Gulfport,

Figure 4.20 *The FSW98 Cessna **Propeller Advance** control: Push the **Propeller Advance** knob in to increase propeller RPM (this decreases the blade angle). Pull the knob out to decrease propeller RPM (this increases the blade angle).*

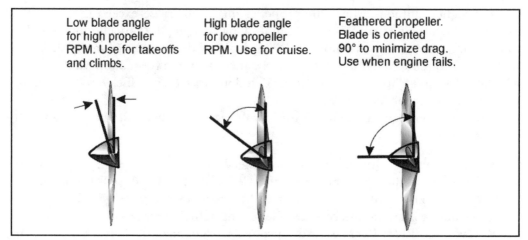

Low blade angle for high propeller RPM. Use for takeoffs and climbs.

High blade angle for low propeller RPM. Use for cruise.

Feathered propeller. Blade is oriented 90° to minimize drag. Use when engine fails.

Figure 4.21 *Propeller pitch refers to the angle between the propeller blade and its plane of rotation.*

Mississippi, in daylight when it suddenly lost part of its left propeller. Rotational imbalance tore off the gearcase from the engine, twisting it sideways and damaging the nacelle. Because of the difficulty of controlling the airplane, the crew began an immediate descent of 4,000 ft/min and declared an emergency. They were unable to make the nearest airport and crashed into a wooded area, strewing wreckage over an 850-foot path. Of 26 passengers, 18 survived, but the captain died on impact and the first officer was badly burned over 80% of his body, because he was unable to extricate himself from the burning cockpit with the inadequate crash axe that was stowed onboard. From sophisticated computer analysis that predicted the trajectory of objects falling from the airplane, searchers were able to retrieve the propeller and send it in for laboratory analysis. It was determined from previous service records that the blade had previously failed an ultrasonic inspection, but the manufacturer had incorrectly repaired the blade and returned it to service.

Elementary Propeller Analysis

A complete analysis of propeller motion and propeller thrust mechanics is far beyond the scope of this book. To better understand your airplane, however, it is helpful to have an appreciation for the forces at work. We will therefore discuss some basic properties of propellers.

First, let's define some vector velocities:

- V_{Hub} = The velocity of the propeller hub relative to the oncoming air. It is the same as the airplane's true airspeed.

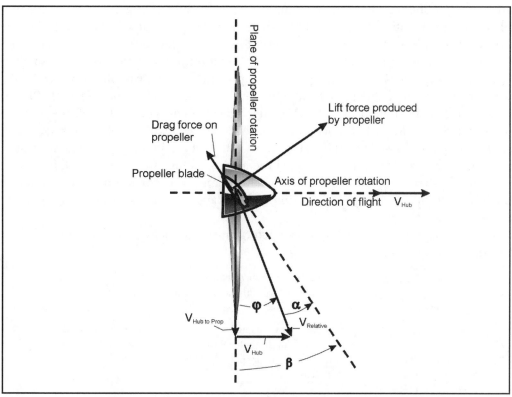

Figure 4.22 *Angle of attack* α, *induced angle of attack* φ, *and the propeller blade angle* β. *Note that when the airplane has a high forward velocity, the angle of attack on the propeller is smaller than it would be if the airplane were traveling slowly. This means that at high-speed cruise, the propeller's blade angle must be increased if the propeller is to avert a stall condition (a negative angle of attack). The problem is exacerbated at the propeller tip, which, because of the distance from the hub, is traveling at a much higher speed than the hub portion.*

- $V_{Hub\ to\ Prop}$ = The velocity of the propeller section relative to the center of the propeller (the hub). This speed depends on the distance *r* along the propeller section from the hub. $V_{Hub\ to\ Prop}$ equals $2\pi rn$, where *n* is the RPM of the propeller.
- $V_{Relative}$ = The velocity of the propeller section relative to the oncoming air. It is the vector sum of $V_{hub} + V_{Hub\ to\ Prop}$.

The angle α in Figure 4.22 is the angle of attack for the propeller blade, and you will note that the propeller is rotating downward (the plane would be moving right). The angle φ is the induced increment to the propeller's angle of attack caused by the airplane's forward motion V_{Hub}. We call this the induced angle of attack. The angle β is the propeller blade's pitch angle at a given point on the propeller, and this angle changes depending on its location along the blade. Near the tip, the blade angle β is smaller than it is at the hub. However, by pushing or pulling out the **Propeller Advance** knob, you can change the angle β. For example, on the Cessna 182's propeller at the 30-in. station, the blade angle b with the **Propeller Advance** knob pushed in all the way (to high propeller RPM) is 15.8°. With the **Propeller Advance** knob pulled all the way out (to low propeller RPM), the blade angle at the 30-in. station on the propeller increases to 29.4°. The relationship between all three angles is illustrated in Figure 4.22, where you can see that α = β−φ. Note that if the airplane were not moving, the propeller blade's angle of attack α would be simply β, because the induced angle of attack φ equals zero.

At any point along the propeller, we can determine the velocity of the propeller section by using this equation:

$$V_{\text{Hub to Prop Section in ft/min}} = (\text{angular speed in radians/min}) \quad\quad (4.1)$$
$$\times (\text{distance from the axis of rotation}) = \omega r = 2\pi rn$$

where

$V_{\text{Hub to Prop Section in ft/min}}$ = Rotational speed in ft/min of propeller section located
         r feet from propeller hub
n = RPM (rotations per minute of the propeller)
ω = Angular velocity in radians/min
π = 3.14159
r = Distance between propeller hub and propeller section in ft

Ordinarily, ω is used to represent radians/sec, but in equation 4.1, to simplify terms, I have substituted radians/min.

EXAMPLE 4.1

Determine the propeller tip's rotational velocity on the Cessna 182 when it is spinning at 2,400 RPM.

Solution

The Cessna 182's propeller has a listed diameter of 82 in., or 6.83 ft (because (82 in. ÷ 12 in./ft) = 6.83 ft). Because the Cessna ordinarily flies with a two-blade propeller and not a three-blade propeller, this means that the radius from the hub to the propeller tip is one-half 6.83 ft, or 3.415 ft. This is the distance we use for the variable r in determining the angular speed of the propeller tip.

$$V_{\text{Hub to Prop Section in ft/min}} = (\text{angular speed in radians/min}) \qquad (4.2)$$
$$\times (\text{distance from the axis of rotation}) = \omega r = 2\pi r n$$
$$= 2\pi r n = (2)(3.14159)(3.415 \text{ ft})(2,400\,RPM) = 51,497 \text{ ft/min}$$

To convert ft/min to knots, multiply by 0.0098747:

$$V_{\text{Hub to Prop Section in knots}} = \left(51,497 \text{ ft/min}\right)\left(0.0098747 \, \frac{\text{knots}}{\text{ft/min}}\right) = 509 \text{ knots}$$

where

$V_{\text{Hub to Prop Section}}$ = Rotational speed in ft/min of propeller section located
         r feet from propeller hub
n = RPM (rotations per minute of the propeller)
ω = Angular velocity in radians/min
π = 3.14159
r = Distance between propeller hub and propeller section in ft

Notice that the tip speed of the propeller is only 509 knots, which is well below the speed of sound at sea level of 661 knots.

From the preceding example, you learned that the Cessna's propeller tip rotates at a speed of 509 knots, which is approximately Mach 0.77, because 509 knots (propeller tip speed) ÷ 661 knots (speed of sound) = 0.77. Normally, a propeller is used at rotational speeds so that the tip speeds are not supersonic; excessive tip speeds produce noise and lowered efficiency because of shock wave formation. The shock-wave formation on the propeller is similar to the shock-wave that occurs over a wing that goes supersonic.

Using Equation 4.1, you will find that the propeller's maximum rotational speed occurs at the tip, and the lowest speed occurs at the hub. Progressing inward toward the propeller midpoint at 41 in. from the hub, for example, $V_{\text{Hub to Prop}}$ is 254 knots; at about 5 in. from the hub, $V_{\text{Hub to Prop}}$ is 62 knots. Now you can see why the propeller blade must be twisted to increase the angle of attack near the hub and why the blade angle must be decreased at the tip. From these empirical observations, it is clear that more lift must be generated at the hub with its lower angular velocity of 62 knots, so a higher angle of attack is required. At the tip, however, the opposite is true: the higher rotational velocity of 509 knots means that the angle of attack must be lower if the lift at the propeller hub is to equal the lift at the propeller tip.

Figure 4.23 is a cross-sectional diagram of the change in blade angle from the propeller hub to the tip. Figure 4.24 shows the higher speed of a propeller's tips, and Figure 4.25 displays a photo of a Cessna 182 propeller.

When the airplane is standing still, the propeller's tip speed relative to the oncoming air is just $V_{\text{Hub to Prop}}$. When the airplane is moving, however, the oncoming air imparts an additional velocity V_{Hub} to the propeller. V_{Hub} is nothing more than the true airspeed of the airplane. The vector sum of $V_{\text{Hub}} + V_{\text{Hub to Prop}}$ gives the propeller's tip speed relative to the oncoming air, or V_{Relative}.

$$V_{\text{Relative}} = \sqrt{V_{\text{Hub to Prop}}^2 + V_{\text{Hub}}^2} \tag{4.3}$$

For example, if the airplane is traveling at 130 knots TAS, the propeller's tip speed would be calculated as follows:

$$V_{\text{Relative}} = \sqrt{V_{\text{Hub to Prop}}^2 + V_{\text{Hub}}^2} = \sqrt{(509 \text{ knots})^2 + (130 \text{ knots})^2} = 525 \text{ knots} \tag{4.4}$$

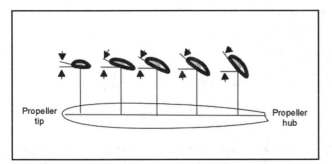

Figure 4.23 *Changes in propeller blade angle from hub to tip. Because the tip of the blade has a higher relative wind velocity than the hub, the tip has a lower angle of attack. If the tip had the same angle of attack as the hub, it would produce more lift (thrust) in proportion to the hub, thereby overstressing the propeller.*

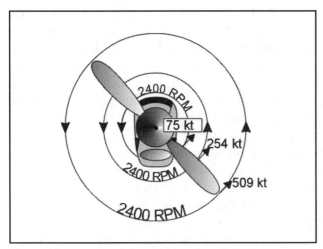

Figure 4.24 *Propeller tips travel faster than the hubs.*

Figure 4.25 *Blade twist on the Cessna 182. Notice that the blade pitch angle is greater near the propeller hub than it is at the propeller tip. (Courtesy of Cessna) (New Cessna Skylane)*

The propeller's angle of attack can be calculated at any point along the propeller blade using the following equation:

$$\alpha = \beta - \varphi \qquad (4.5)$$

where

α = Propeller's angle of attack in degrees
β = Propeller's blade pitch setting in degrees
φ = Propeller's induced angle of attack in degrees

where $\tan \varphi = \dfrac{V_{Hub}}{2\pi r n}$

r = Radius distance from hub to propeller section in ft
n = Propeller RPM in rotations per minute

EXAMPLE 4.2

Estimate the angle of attack at the 30-in. station on the Cessna 182's propeller when the airplane is traveling at 150 knots TAS and when the propeller advance is set to minimum RPM (maximum blade angle). The Cessna pilot's manual states that the maximum blade angle is 29.4° and that the minimum blade angle is 15.8° at the 30-in. station. Assume also that the propeller is rotating at 2,200 RPM.

Solution

From Equation 4.1, we first calculate the propeller's velocity at the 30-in. station:

$$V_{Hub\ to\ Prop} = 2\pi n r \qquad (4.6)$$

$$= (2)(\pi)(2{,}200\ \text{RPM})\left(30\ \text{inches} \times \left(\frac{1\ \text{ft}}{12\ \text{inch}}\right)\right)$$

$$= 34.6\ \text{ft}/\text{min} = 341\ \text{knots}$$

From Equation 4.5, we calculate the induced angle of attack resulting from the airplane's forward velocity of 150 knots:

$$\tan \varphi = \frac{V_{Hub}}{V_{Hub\ to\ Prop}} = \frac{150\ \text{knots}}{341\ \text{knots}} = 0.4399 \qquad (4.7)$$

Therefore

$$\varphi = \arctan(0.4399) = 23.7°$$

Because the maximum blade angle **b** for the propeller is 29.4°, the angle attack will be as follows:

$$\alpha = \beta - \varphi = 29.4° - 23.7° = 5.7° \tag{4.8}$$

Thus, when the Cessna's airspeed is 150 knots, the propeller's angle of attack to the relative wind is only 5.7° at 30 in. distance from the hub.

If you increase the airplane's airspeed, the induced angle ϕ will increase, and, as a result, the propeller's angle of attack will decrease (because ϕ increases as V_{Hub} increases from Equation 4.5). If you keep increasing the cruise speed, at some point the propeller's angle of attack will result in a negative number and the propeller will no longer develop any thrust! Thus, every propeller has a maximum forward speed at which its blade elements generate zero lift (thrust). Because the maximum propeller efficiency is only about 85%, the maximum cruise speed will be only 85% of the propeller's theoretical maximum forward speed.

Ignition System

The ignition system provides the spark that ignites the air-fuel mixture in the cylinder. A magneto ignition system is used on most modern aircraft engines, because it produces a hotter spark at high engine speeds than the battery system used in cars. In addition, magnetos do not depend on an external source of energy such as the electrical system. Magnetos are self-contained, engine-driven generators that supply ignition current. The engine must be rotating before the magnetos can provide current, so a starter system is used to get the engine rotating before a spark appears at the spark plugs. After the engine starts, the starter system is disengaged and the battery has no part in the operation of the engine, unlike conventional automobiles, which remain dependent on the battery. If you turn off the airplane's battery switch, the engine will continue to run. In practice you should not do this, because battery power is necessary to operate electrical equipment when the engine is running at low RPM.

All piston-powered aircraft engines are equipped with a dual ignition system. Two magnetos supply current to two spark plugs for each cylinder. One magneto supplies current to one set of plugs, and the other magneto supplies current to the other set of plugs. This is the reason that you see on the ignition switch the labels **OFF**, **R**, **L**, and **BOTH**. With the switch in the **L** or **R** position, only the left or right magneto is supplying electricity to one set of spark plugs; the other magneto and the other set of spark plugs lie dormant. With only one set of spark plugs firing, the engine RPM will drop off slightly; you can try this in Flight Simulator with the Cessna 182. When the switch is moved to **BOTH**, for example, both magnetos are on-line and provide current to both sets of spark plugs. If the engine is operating properly, with either **R** or **L** selected, the engine RPM should drop by no more than 175 RPM on either magneto. In addition, the RPM differential between the **R** and the **L** magneto should be no more than 50 RPM.

Before taking off, as a precautionary measure the pilot should check to see whether the engine will run smoothly on either "mag" alone. As you can see, the dual magneto and ignition system gives an added measure of safety should one side of the engine's electrical circuits fail.

Mixture Control

The mixture control is provided to change the fuel flow to the engine to compensate for varying air density as the airplane changes altitude. Carburetors are normally calibrated at sea level pressure to meter the correct amount of fuel with the mixture control in the *Full Rich* position. As the airplane climbs to higher altitudes, however, the air density decreases and the amount of air entering the carburetor drops off in proportion to the fuel. This makes the engine run too rich, so you need to use the mixture control to lean the fuel mixture and restore the proper proportion of fuel and air to the engine (Figure 4.26). At 18,000 ft, for example, the air is only half as dense as it is at sea level. If you try to run the engine at 18,000 ft, using the same quantity of fuel as you did at sea level, the fuel mixture will be too rich and the engine will lose power and run poorly. In this situation the mixture control comes in handy.

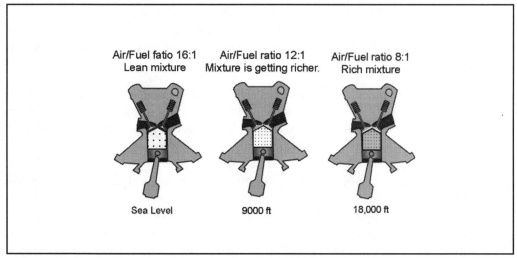

Figure 4.26 *The air-fuel mixture in the engine cylinder becomes too rich (there is too much fuel) at higher altitudes, because the air is less dense.*

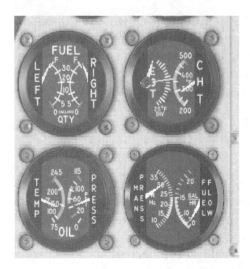

Figure 4.27 *Engine instruments on the FSW98 Cessna 182. Top row, left to right: fuel quantity gauge (the Cessna 182S has 46 gal. in each wing side tank, and the Cessna 182RG has 44 gal. in each wing side tank), EGT gauge, cylinder head temperature (for cylinder No. 4). Bottom row, left to right: oil temperature, oil pressure, manifold pressure, and fuel flow (in gallons/hour). Note that you can move the EGT bug needle to remind you of the location on the gauge where you want the temperature needle to remain (press **U** followed by + or − to move the bug). Each tick mark on the scale represents 25° F.*

An air-fuel ratio of 16:1 means that 16 lb of air is being mixed with 1 lb of fuel; an 8:1 ratio means that 8 lb of air is being mixed with 1 lb of fuel. An 8:1 air-fuel ratio is a rich fuel mixture compared with the lean 16:1 ratio, because more fuel is being introduced for a given quantity of air. Piston engines usually produce maximum power when the air-fuel ratio is 15:1.

You can determine the correct mixture by observing the EGT (exhaust gas temperature) gauge, which displays the temperature of the combustion process. A lean engine always runs hotter than a rich engine. With the Cessna, for example, the best fuel economy and optimum lean mixture occur when the temperature on the EGT is 50° less than peak lean temperature. To lean the Cessna's engine, follow this procedure:

1. From the full rich position, lean the mixture control by dragging it out (in FS98) or down (in FSW95) until you establish the peak temperature on the EGT gauge. (Figure 4.20 shows the mixture control knob, and Figure 4.27 shows the EGT gauge.)
2. When the EGT needle has reached its highest temperature, enrich the mixture by pushing in the knob on the FS98 Cessna (or by dragging the knob up on the FSW95 Cessna) until the temperature declines 50° below the peak. This is the recommended lean mixture setting for maximum engine life, but it is not the most fuel-efficient. The hottest temperature represents the leanest air fuel mixture and the best fuel efficiency, but it also is bad for the engine because excessive heat wears down the internal parts faster.

N O T E When you're leaning the mixture under some conditions, engine roughness may occur before peak EGT is reached. In this case, don't use peak EGT as the reference point. Instead, use the EGT corresponding to the onset of roughness as the reference point. I have found that with the Flight Simulator Cessna 182RG, the first onset of peak EGT starting from the full rich position is the point at which you should start dragging the mixture control up to reduce EGT by 50°.

Note that you can't use the mixture control in Flight Simulator without switching off the automatic mixture control. To do this, use **Aircraft/Aircraft Settings/Engines**. In the Prop Engines section of the dialog box that opens, turn on the **Mixture Control** button.

Whenever you take off or climb to altitudes of 3,000 ft or less, you should fly with a full rich setting on the Cessna.

Fuel Systems

Fuel systems for multiengine aircraft, both piston and turbine, are more complex. Should an engine failure or fire occur, means must be provided to cross-feed fuel to the remaining engine. Each fuel system for each engine must be independent, so that failure in one engine will not affect the other. Also, the fuel system must be designed to prevent the ignition of fuel vapor within the system by direct lightning strikes or corona or other electrical discharge. There must be an emergency pump to feed fuel after failure of any main pump, and there must be a fuel jettisoning system that sheds enough weight within 15 min to enable the airplane to climb with one engine inoperative.

Each fuel tank is normally connected to a specific engine. This arrangement complies with FAA regulations, which dictate that, during takeoff, each engine must be fed fuel from a separate tank.

Multiengine aircraft have a cross-feed switch that allows you to feed fuel from the tank that normally feeds the other engine. When an engine fails, you use this switch to draw fuel from the other engine's tank so that you don't run low on fuel. The cross-feed system also allows the fuel weight to be balanced when only one engine is drawing fuel. You can imagine the imbalance problem if each wing's fuel tanks were separated completely and one wing was full of fuel while the other was empty.

The fuel tanks in Flight Simulator are set so that they normally never run out of fuel. For greater realism, you can fly your airplane so that the engines will run out fuel. On the **Aircraft/Aircraft Settings/Realism** menu in FS98, click on the button **Engine stops when out of fuel.**

Fuel Types

Turbine engines are fueled by kerosene, whereas piston engines use aviation gas, or avgas, a special grade of gasoline specially formulated for its antiknock quality. Within each fuel type are various grades, as shown in Table 4.4. Usually, the proper grade for an aircraft type is stated on placards in the cockpit or on the wing next to the filler caps.

Table 4.4 *Aviation Fuel Types*

FUEL TYPE	DESCRIPTION
Avgas	100 Octane (dyes are added for easy identification of fuel grade) used only in piston-powered general aviation aircraft.
Jet-A	Kerosene fuel used widely in civilian jets. The flashpoint is between 110° F and 150° F, and it freezes at -40° F.
Jet-A1	Similar to Jet-A except that it has additives to lower the freezing point to -58° F.
Jet-B	Gasoline-kerosene mixture that is similar to JP-4 and has a flashpoint of 0° F and a freezing point of -76° F.
JP-4	Used mostly for military jet aircraft, this fuel comprises 65% gasoline and 35% kerosene distillates.
JP-5	This highly refined kerosene jet fuel is equivalent to Jet-A.
Kerosene	Also called paraffin or coal oil (in England), kerosene is a flammable, pale yellow or colorless oily liquid with a not unpleasant, characteristic odor. It is obtained from petroleum and used for burning in lamps and domestic heaters or furnaces, as a fuel or fuel component for jet engines, and as a solvent for greases and insecticides.

Avgas comes in various octanes. For example, the most common gas is 100LL ("LL" stands for low lead, although there is still lead in the gas); it is dyed blue to distinguish it from 80/87 octane gas, which is dyed red. Kerosene, regardless of grade, is clear or straw-colored. In an emergency, you can use fuel of a higher grade than specified for your engine. Thus, if your airplane's engine requires 80/87 and only 100LL is available, you can use it. You cannot, however, use a lower grade. An engine that requires 100LL will quickly destroy itself if fed 80/87. Piston engines must never be fed jet fuel.

On your last airline flight, you may have wondered about the smell in the cabin when the engine was started. The odor probably came from the kerosene being injected into the engines while the air-conditioning system was switched off, as it always is when the engines are first started. Air conditioning is run using bleed air from the engines; because it robs needed power during the engine start sequence, it is usually shut off.

Light Twin-Engine Aircraft

The term *light twin* refers to propeller-driven airplanes that weigh less than 12,500 lb and have two reciprocating engines mounted on the wings. In most twin-engine U.S.-designed aircraft, both engines rotate to the right (clockwise) when viewed from the rear, and both engines develop the same amount of thrust. At low airspeed and high power, the downward-moving propeller blade of each engine develops more thrust than the upward-moving blade. This asymmetric propeller thrust, or *P-factor*, causes the center of thrust to shift to the right side of each engine, as shown in Figure 4.28. As a result, the moment arm for the right engine is greater than the moment arm for the left engine, so the right engine has a greater turning (or yawing) force to the right than the left engine's yawing force to the left. If you have difficulty visualizing this, consider the hypothetical placement of the right engine on the tip of the right wing while the left engine remains midwing; in this scenario, the right engine would swing the whole airplane left in the event of a left engine failure. This is what the P-factor does, so directional control is made more difficult when the left engine (the critical engine) fails than when the right engine fails. In such twin-engine propeller airplanes, the minimum control speed with the left engine (the critical engine) inoperative is known as V_{MC}. Note that the definition of the critical engine for a light twin differs from that of multi-engine turbine aircraft. The critical engine for turbine engines is discussed later in this chapter.

TURBINE-POWERED AIRCRAFT

In 1930, Frank Whittle received a patent for a turbojet, known as a gas turbine engine in England, but the invention was ignored and he could not get support to develop the design. In 1935, the Germans began work on the turbojet engine, culminating in the first flight of a turbojet-powered aircraft, the Heinkel He178, on August 27, 1939. The Heinkel engine delivered only 1,100 lb of thrust, but it proved to the British that they had been mistaken in branding Whittle's ideas impractical. During the war, Whittle was granted an officer's commission and was later knighted for his contributions to the war effort and the future of aviation.

News of the Germans' progress worried the British, and work was soon begun on Whittle's design, resulting in the first successful test flight of a British turbojet in May

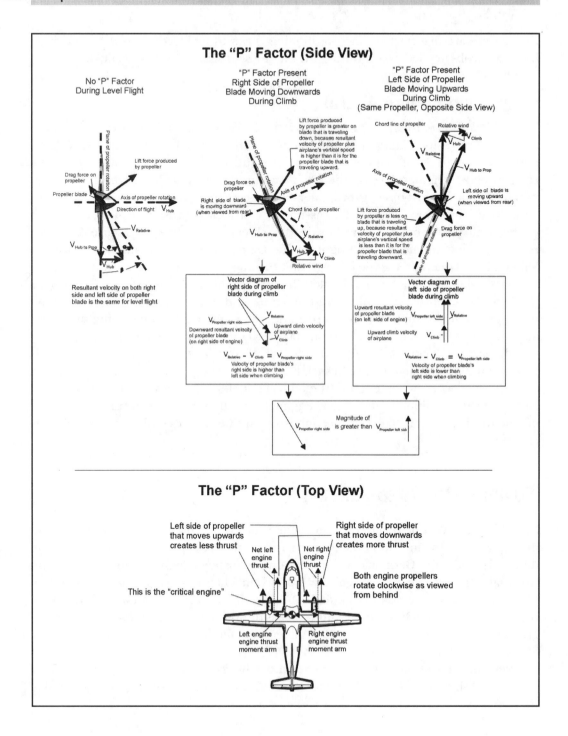

1941. The Americans heard of Whittle's revolutionary engine and obtained a copy of it, which they used in the first flight of an American jet-propelled plane, the Bell Airacomet, on October 1, 1942. The first production American jet aircraft was the Lockheed F-80, which first flew in January 1944; its engine delivered a thrust of 4,000 lb. However, the world's first operational jet fighter, the Messerschmitt 262-1a, flashed into the skies over Germany on July 19, 1942. With an operational speed of 540 mph, the Me-262 was 120 mph faster than the top-of-the-line Allied fighters. It was powered by two Junkers Jumo 004B turbine engines that developed 1,980 lb thrust each. One can imagine the shock of Allied fighter pilots as this plane rocketed by them, out of reach and out of range. You can try flying this jet if you install it from the model created by Herve Devred and included on this book's CD-ROM. Note that FS98 users must first convert the aircraft to the new FS98 aircraft file format using the new Microsoft aircraft converter, which is on this book's CD-ROM. We include the Messerschmitt 262 for historical reasons only and not to glorify the past nor to laud the efforts of the Hitler war machine. Many people may find the Nazi markings on this plane offensive. It should be clear that this plane is only a historical re-creation of a machine and is not intended as a celebration of the terrible events of World War II.

After the war, the British-built de Havilland Comet was the world's first commercial jet transport, beginning operations in 1949. The Comet was powered by four Rolls Royce Ghost engines, each of which developed 4,450 lb of thrust. This plane was revolutionary. It could carry 36 passengers in a pressurized cabin up to 40,000 ft at a cruising speed of 500 mph— nearly twice the speed of the best existing American piston-engine airliners. But the dream of British dominance of the skies, just as it had dominated maritime commerce, was not to be. Misfortune struck the fleet of Comets. Three Comets broke up in midair in mysterious accidents that killed all aboard. Exhaustive investigations revealed that the square window cutouts and large window design had contributed to metal fatigue, which weakened the fuselage structure to the point of failure. The explosive decompression of the cabin at high altitude caused the airplane to disintegrate. Designers have benefited from the lessons learned from the Comet, and today's jet aircraft fuselages have stronger skins, and smaller, rounded windows to prevent the growth of cracks. Despite its tragic end, the Comet paved the way for the success of the Boeing 707, which ushered in the age of safe, reliable jet transport in 1954.

Figure 4.28 (opposite) *Twin-engine propeller aircraft P-factor causes engine thrust to be shifted right of each propeller axis. The turning (yawing) force of the right engine is greater than that of the left engine, because the moment arm for the center of thrust is greater. Thus, directional control may be more difficult when the left engine (the critical engine) suddenly fails.*

For a variety of reasons, airplane designers of large aircraft have tended to mount turbine engines underneath the wings rather than in or above them. Mounting engines in underslung wing pods minimizes interference drag, and the engines provide bending relief for the heavy wing structure (which is bent upward by lift). In addition, there is less acoustic damage to the airframe, the thrust reverser design is easier to implement, and engine accessibility is good. Also, there is less damage in the event of a gear-up landing.

The disadvantages of wing-pod-mounted engines are several. With a single engine failure, asymmetric yawing will occur unless the engines are mounted well inboard (but the wing-bending relief is reduced the farther inboard the engines are placed). Another disadvantage is that roll freedom on the ground is impaired, and the engine pods can scrape the ground during gusty cross-wind landings and takeoffs. Also, with a swept-wing, four-engine plane, the reversed thrust flow from the inner engines upsets the intake flow on the outer engines, and this requires earlier cancellation of thrust reversers for the inner engines. Low-mounted engines also encourage ingestion of foreign objects from the runway surface.

How Gas Turbine Engines Work

The main components of a gas turbine engine are the compressor, the combustion chamber, and the turbine. Air enters the inlet, where it is diffused and compressed slightly. It then passes through the low-pressure compressor, where rotating blades (the *rotor*) alternate with stationary blades (the *stator*). Axial flow compressors are used on larger gas turbine engines, although early engines, such as Whittle's engine, employed a centrifugal compressor. As the air enters the rotating blades of the compressor, it acquires a tangential velocity and is compressed. A diffuser collects the compressed air and delivers it to the combustion chamber, where it is burned with the fuel (see Figure 4.29). The fuel is sprayed through nozzles, and the resulting atomized air-fuel mixture is burned, with a ratio of air to fuel by weight of about 60:1. Only about 25% of the air is used to support combustion; the remainder bypasses the fuel nozzles and mixes downstream of the burner to cool the hot combustion gases as they enter the turbine section. The mixture of exhaust gases and cooling air is still very hot (about 1,100° C or 2,012° F), and it forces its way through the turbine stages, which are composed of stationary and rotating blade assemblies. The turbines are forced to rotate by the hot, high-pressure gases extract the motive energy needed to drive the compressor stages. Only 25% of the kinetic energy of the turbine engine is used to provide thrust; nearly 75% is required to drive the compressors. In the General Electric CF6-6 turbofan, which is rated at 40,000 lb thrust, for example, the turbine stage develops approximately 65,600 kilowatts (88,000 shaft horsepower) just to drive the high- and low-pressure compressors.

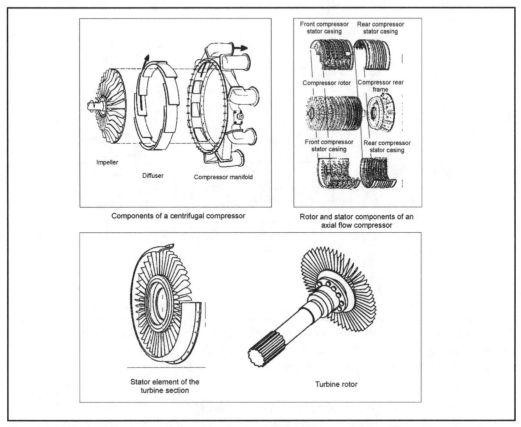

Figure 4.29 *The turbine rotor and the compressor rotor. The turbine rotors drive the engine compressors and allow exhaust gas to exit from the rear of the engine to produce thrust. The compressor rotors compress the air needed for combustion.*

In turbine engines, it is often necessary to use turbines having more than one stage. A single-turbine wheel often cannot absorb enough power from the exhaust gases to drive the compressor stage, so additional turbine stages are needed. For similar reasons, different compressor stages, spinning at different speeds, allow higher compression ratios than would be possible with single-compressor designs. With multiple-rotor turbines, each turbine rotor can drive a separate part of the engine. For example, a triple-rotor turbine can be arranged so that the first turbine drives the rear half of the compressor and the accessories. The second turbine drives the front half of the compressor, and the third turbine furnishes power to a propeller, as illustrated in Figure 4.30.

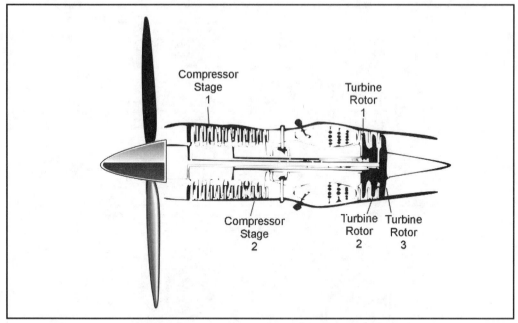

Figure 4.30 *Multiple-rotor turbine used in a turboprop. This triple-rotor turbine has three independent turbine rotors turning at different speeds. The first turbine rotor drives the rear compressor rotors, the second rotor drives the front compressor rotors, and the third rotor turns the propeller.*

The turbine rotor arrangement used in split-spool compressors, such as the CFM56-3C used on the Boeing 737-400, have what is known as a *dual compressor* design. This design incorporates tandem compressors mounted on two separate shafts that are connected to the turbine rotors and rotate at different speeds.

The forward compressor stage, called the low-pressure compressor stage, is driven by the low-pressure turbine rotors through a low-pressure compressor shaft. The rotational speed of the low-pressure compressor is known as N_1, and the low-pressure compressor shaft is called the N_1 shaft. The rear compressor stage is called the high-pressure compressor stage, and it is driven by the high-pressure turbine rotors just behind the combustion chamber. The rotational speed of the high-pressure compressor shaft is called N_2. This dual spool arrangement is illustrated in Figure 4.31, where the low-pressure N_1 shaft turns freely inside the high-pressure N_2 shaft.

The term spool refers to one or more compressor and turbine stages connected to the same shaft and thus rotating at the same speed.

N O T E

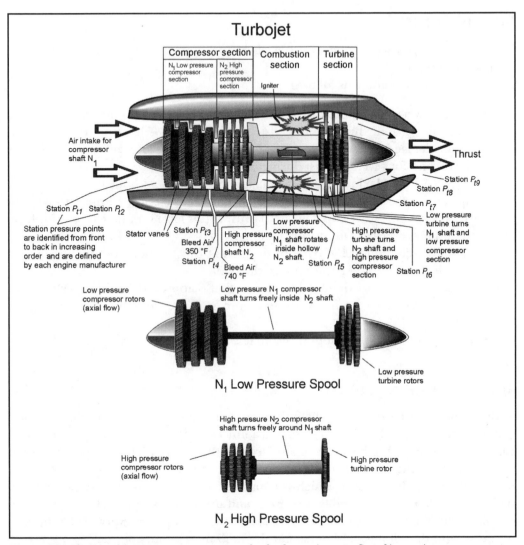

Figure 4.31 High- and low-pressure components of a dual rotor (two-spool) turbine engine.

Turbojets, turbofan, turboprop, and industrial turboshaft engines are all examples of gas turbine engines. Turbojets are used on the Concorde supersonic transport as well as on supersonic aircraft but are used less often on today's subsonic aircraft because of fuel inefficiencies and high noise levels. Most subsonic air transport aircraft rely on turbofans (sometimes called *fanjets*) for better economy and lower noise. Turboshaft engines power most of today's helicopters, including the Bell 206B-3 helicopter, which is powered by a single Allison 250-C20J turboshaft engine.

Engine Thrust Ratings

Engine ratings are used define thrust levels in turbine engines that are certified for commercial use.

The ratings are defined as follows:

- Takeoff (wet): Maximum thrust available for takeoff for engines that use water injection. Takeoff thrust is limited to 5 min (in the U.K., 10 min) to prevent engine damage and prolong engine life. Thrust at this level is intended only for takeoff and for reverse thrust during landing.
- Takeoff (dry): Maximum thrust available for takeoff without the use of water injection. Takeoff thrust is limited to 5 min (in the U.K., 10 min) to prevent excessive engine wear and damage. Thrust at this level is intended only for takeoff and for reverse thrust during landing.
- Maximum continuous: Maximum thrust that can be used continuously and is intended only for emergency use by the pilot.
- Maximum climb: Maximum climb thrust that is approved for normal climb. On some engines, maximum continuous thrust is the same as maximum climb thrust.
- Maximum cruise: Maximum thrust that is approved for cruising.

Turbine Engine Failure

Turbine engines are extremely reliable and are less vulnerable to failure than reciprocating engines are. CFM International, a joint company of Snecma (France) and General Electric (United States), manufactures the CFM56-3 high-bypass turbofan engines used on the 737-400. These engines have an in-flight shutdown rate of 0.002 per 1,000 engine flight hours, which is equivalent to one engine failure per 500,000 flight hours. Departure reliability is 99.97%, and the shop visit rate is 0.073 per 1,000 engine flight hours (equivalent to one engine-caused shop visit every 13,300 hours). Average flight duration is 1.4 hours, and the utilization (hours per day) is 7.9 hours, with 5.8 cycles per day (one takeoff and one landing count as one cycle). This means that a typical CFM-56 engine undergoes 2,884 flight hours per year and performs 2,117 takeoffs and landings per year.

Engines are numbered from 1 to 4 from the pilot's left to right. On takeoff, if a crosswind is blowing across the runway, the tail fin acts as a vane and the aircraft nose weathercocks into the wind. With a four-engine aircraft, if the number 1 engine fails on takeoff with the wind blowing from left to right, the swing to the left would be more severe than it would be with the number 4 engine. With a crosswind such as this, the number 1 engine would be called the *critical engine*. The odds of a single engine failure are estimated at 300,000 to 1, and the possibility of a double engine failure has been calculated at 1,000,000 to 1. Four-engine aircraft, such as the 747, can fly with one or two engines out, but not with three engines out. Even with two engines out, the 747 can maintain cruise at 10,000 to 15,000 ft depending on weight.

When the need arises to transport a spare engine to a distant airport where an airplane has been grounded by engine failure, it is possible to sling a spare engine in a pod below the 747's left wing between the fuselage and inboard engine number 3. This location is called the *fifth pod*.

Jet Engine Shutdown, Restart, and Fuel Management

Shutting off the fuel to a jet while flying leaves the engine windmilling at about 10% to 25% of maximum engine RPM. Unfortunately, Microsoft's Learjet and Boeing 737 engines don't windmill as they should. To relight the engine, switch on the ignition with the power lever fully closed and then turn on the fuel. Some engines will not relight at very high speeds, and most engines will not relight at very low speeds or very high altitudes. At these limits, it is not possible to offer the engine the correct proportions of air and fuel for the speed at which the engine is rotating.

Table 4.5 Jet Engine Keyboard Controls in Flight Simulator

ACTION	KEYBOARD COMMAND
Jet Engine Fuel Flow Start	
Both Engines	**E 1 2 Ctrl Shift F4**
Engine 1	**E 1 Ctrl Shift F4**
Engine 2	**E 2 Ctrl Shift F4**
Jet Engine Starter	
Both Engines	**E 1 2 J +**
Engine 1	**E 1 J +**
Engine 2	**E 2 J +**
Jet Engine Shutdown	
Both Engines	**E 1 2 Ctrl Shift F1**
Engine 1	**E 1 Ctrl Shift F1**
Engine 2	**E 2 Ctrl Shift F1**
Engine Control Selectors	
Both Engines	**E 1 2**
Engine 1	**E 1**
Engine 2	**E 2**

In Flight Simulator, you can shut down the jet engines by performing this procedure:

1. If both engines are already selected, press **Ctrl+Shift+F1** to shut them down.
2. To shut down a single engine, first select the engine by pressing **E** followed by the number of the engine. For example, to select engine number 2 and shut it down, press **E+2+Ctrl+Shift+F1**. To select both engines again, press **E+12**.

When you shut down the engines, you not only switch off the ignition system but also shut off fuel flow. You must first restart fuel flow before the engines can be started again.

To restart an engine, perform this procedure:

1. Start the fuel flow. If both engines are selected, start the fuel flow by pressing **Ctrl+Shift+F4**. To start fuel flow for a single engine, press **E** followed by the number of the engine and **Ctrl+Shift+F4**. (for example, **E+2+Ctrl+Shift+F4**). To reselect both engines and start fuel flow, press **E+12+Ctrl+Shift+F4**.
2. Start the engine. If both engines are selected, activate the jet engine starter by pressing **J+** (J and the plus key) or by moving the **Engine Start** knob to the **Start** position. Once the engines have started, the **Engine Start** knob will move to the **Off** position.

The cross-feed switch located on the 737's overhead instrument panel allows an engine to draw fuel from the tank that normally feeds another engine. As mentioned earlier, you should open the cross-feed valve if you shut down an engine and run low on fuel in the tank that normally supplies the operating engine. For example, if you suffer an engine failure or have to shut down the right engine, you can draw fuel from the right fuel tanks by moving the cross-feed switch to the right. Conversely, if the left engine is shut down, you can move the cross-feed switch to the left to siphon fuel from the left tank. To select which tank to draw fuel from, use the **Aircraft/Aircraft Settings/Fuel** menu. Click the **Manual Fuel Control** button so that it is lit; then in the adjacent box, select **All, Left, Right, Left Auxiliary,** or **Right Auxiliary.**

If you are familiar with the FSW95 737, you may have been puzzled by the mysterious engine shutdowns that occurred when you drained one of the auxiliary tanks and switched to the main tanks. Because there was no automatic fuel switching, the engines died from fuel starvation, and you had to switch tanks and start the engines again. This problem does not exist in FS98.

The Turbojet Engine

The gas turbine engine was first developed as a turbojet. In the past 25 years, however, the turbojet has been eclipsed by the turbofan for most air transport applications because of the turbofan's superior performance, fuel efficiency, and lower noise levels. Turbojets are basically reaction engines. They produce thrust by taking in air, compressing it, adding fuel, and combusting it, thereby creating a hot flow of gases. This exhaust stream drives the turbine wheel, which in turn drives the compressor in the front of the engine. The exhaust that escapes from the tailpipe still has kinetic energy, and this reaction of accelerating gases into the atmosphere creates engine thrust.

Engine thrust with a turbojet can be calculated by using the following formula:

$$F = \frac{M(V_2 - V_1)}{g} \tag{4.9}$$

where

F = Force in lb
M = Mass flow in lb/sec
V_1 = Inlet velocity
V_2 = Jet exhaust velocity
$V_2 - V_1$ = Difference between inlet velocity and jet velocity
g = Acceleration of gravity $\left(32 \ \text{ft}/\text{sec}^2\right)$

For example, if the exhaust velocity is 1,059 ft/sec and the air mass flow through the engine is 710 lb/sec, using Equation 4.9 we can calculate that the engine thrust will be 23,500 lb. It happens that these results correspond to the real CFM56-3C used on the 737-400 (although the CFM56-3C is not a turbojet but a turbofan).

Gas Turbine Engine Instrumentation

Turbine engines have gauges that indicate compressor spool speeds (N_1 and N_2), EPR (engine pressure ratio), engine temperature, engine vibration, oil pressure, fuel pressure, and fuel flow.

You can see a real 737-400 engine panel in Figure 4.32.

Engine Pressure Ratio

The engine pressure ratio is instrumented on turbojet engines to show engine thrust. Some turbofan engines also display EPR, although most turbofan engines now use N_1 compressor speed as their primary engine thrust indicator.

The EPR gauges display the ratio of the turbine discharge nozzle pressure P_{t7} divided by the inlet compressor inlet pressure P_{t2}. as shown in Equation 4.10. These pressure locations are shown in Figure 4.31. If, for example, the EPR dial shows **1.92**, and you are flying at sea level, and the atmospheric pressure at the compressor inlet is 14.696 psi, the turbine discharge pressure P_{t7} will be 28.22 psi.

Figure 4.32 *737-400 engine instrumentation. (Courtesy of Just Planes Videos)*

With such a low pressure gradient— only 1.92 times the ambient atmosphere—you may wonder how enough thrust is generated at the rear of the engine. The answer is that the exhaust is leaving at an extremely high velocity with a rather large discharge area, and the mass of the air times the velocity gives great momentum force to the airplane.

$$\text{EPR} = \frac{p_{t7}}{p_{t2}} \tag{4.10}$$

where

EPR = Engine pressure ratio
p_{t7} = Pressure at turbine discharge nozzle in lb/in^2
p_{t2} = Pressure at compressor inlet in lb/in^2

N_1 and N_2 Compressor Tachometer Gauge

Turbofan engines usually measure engine thrust with the N_1 tachometer, which measures the percent RPM of the fan stage of the engine connected to the first spool. N_2 shows the percent RPM of the second high-pressure spool. Because N_1 and N_2 do not rotate at the same speed, the percentage of the maximum revolutions per minute makes it easier to figure out whether the engine is operating within acceptable limits.

Typical high-speed turbine N_2 shaft speed is on the order of 10,000 RPM, and that of the low-speed N_1 shaft (and of the fan) is about 2,800 RPM.

Table 4.6 illustrates the variation of percent N_1 RPM with percent maximum thrust for a turbojet. Similar results apply for a turbofan. Near the maximum power output, each 1% RPM change causes a 3.5% change in thrust output. Note that the top 30% of the top engine power is developed in the top 10% of N_1 RPM. Furthermore, the top 20% of N_1 controls more than half (50%) of the available engine thrust! This important point tells you that the engine power is not proportional to the throttle movement. When you move the throttle through the top third of its available motion (30% of N_1), you command more than 72% of the available engine power. Thus, the upper range of throttle motion is where most engine thrust is found. For this example, the thrust is proportional to $N^{3.5}$, something that is typical of a fixed-geometry turbojet engine. Turbofan engines may have thrust proportional to rotative N_1 speeds with values of $N^{4.5}$ to $N^{6.0}$. With a value of $N^{5.0}$, for example, each 1% RPM change will cause a 5.0% thrust change.

Table 4.6 Variation of Percent Thrust with Percent Maximum RPM for the Turbojet

PERCENT MAXIMUM RPM OF N_1	PERCENT MAXIMUM THRUST
100	100.0
99	96.5
95	83.6
90	69.2
80	45.8
70	28.7

Thrust is more or less proportional to throttle position in a reciprocating engine propeller plane but is quite disproportional in a turbine engine. For example, 1 in. of thrust lever movement at low RPM in a turbine engine airplane might be worth 500 lb of thrust, but at high RPM 1 in. of thrust lever movement might be worth 5,000 lb of thrust. Another difference is that with the throttle closed on a propeller plane there is still drag, because the propellers are windmilling; in the jet at idle, there is still some forward thrust.

Engine Vibration Gauge

Because of their fine tolerances and few moving parts, turbine engines operate with very little vibration. All the moving parts move in the same direction, so there is little jarring motion to create vibration. Because of the high rotation speed of the turbine, fan, and compressor parts, a small increase in vibration can be an indicator of bad things to come. To monitor this activity, the vibration gauge measures vibration amplitude in mils (thousandths) of an inch at four locations on the engine: the fan, the low-pressure turbine, the compressor and the high-pressure turbine. Four mils, or 4/1000 in., is the normal maximum allowable vibration level at any single point in the engine.

Surprisingly, jet aircraft have so little inherent vibration that special vibration inducers must be installed in the altimeter dial to make sure that the indicator needles don't get stuck.

Temperature Gauges

The exhaust gas temperature gauge, which measures the hot gas exiting from the turbines at the rear of the engine, usually hovers around 500° C at startup and can go as high as 850° C during normal flight climb, takeoff, and cruise. This instrument is a measure of the relative health of the engine. Combined with the N_1 and N_2 gauges, it gives you an overall picture of how the engine is behaving. You must be careful never to exceed the temperature ratings, even momentarily as this can reduce a $3 million engine to a pile of junk within seconds.

The Turbofan Engine

Turbofan engines are simply turbojets with a fixed-pitch propeller in the front that is called a *fan*. As shown in Figure 4.33, the fan is large (almost 8 ft in diameter on the Pratt & Whitney 4056) and therefore accelerates a large mass of air rearward, much as a propeller does on propeller-powered airplanes. In fact, most thrust in a turbofan—as much as 85%—is produced by the fan. In contrast to a turbojet, the hot exhaust gas emanating from the tail of a turbofan engine accounts for only 15% of the engine's thrust.

Turbofan engines are classified according to their *bypass ratio*, which compares the amount of air that bypasses the jet core of the engine to the amount of air that is routed through the core. The ratio of thrust produced by the fan to that of the jet core follows the same ratio as the bypass ratio. In a low-bypass-ratio engine, having a bypass ratio of 1:1, the fan and compressor sections use approximately the same amounts of air and create equal amounts of thrust. Many military jets use low-bypass engines because of the narrow profile requirements of supersonic flight. A medium- or intermediate-bypass turbofan has a bypass ratio of around 2:1 up to 3:1. An example is the 21,000-lb-thrust Pratt & Whitney JT8D-200 series used on the MD-80, which has a bypass ratio of 1:74.

Figure 4.33 *The fixed-pitch fan blade provides 85% of a turbofan's thrust. Seen here is the 60-in. diameter fan blade used on the CFM56-3C used on the Boeing 737-400. Notice the distinctive swirl painted on the hub of the fan. It is thought that this changing pattern will scare off birds. (Courtesy of CFM International)*

The amount of air passing through the fan on the medium-bypass turbofan is two or three times that passing through the core. Because thrust levels correspond to airflow ratios, the fan in a medium-bypass engine produces two or three times as much thrust as that produced by the jet core. High-bypass engines have ratios in the range of 5:1, such as for example the CFM56-3C used on the 737-400.

The bypassed air and bypass thrust exit from the outer perimeter of the engine just behind the fan but before the turbine end of the engine.

In general, the higher the bypass ratio, the higher the propulsive efficiency of the engine. However, this principle applies only to engines with bypass ratios up to 6:1. To achieve high bypass ratios, wide-diameter fans are needed, but there is a trade-off with larger fan sizes. The larger the fan size, the greater the drag and weight penalty. In addition, with fixed-pitch (fixed blade angle or angle of attack) fan blades, there is a decay in thrust at high flight speeds, so bypass ratios greater than 6:1 aren't used on aircraft designed to cruise at normal jet speeds of Mach 0.8 to Mach 0.85. For example, the General Electric military TF-39 turbofan used on the Lockheed C-5 Galaxy has a bypass ratio of 8:1, but its flight speed is limited to Mach 0.72. The civilian version of this

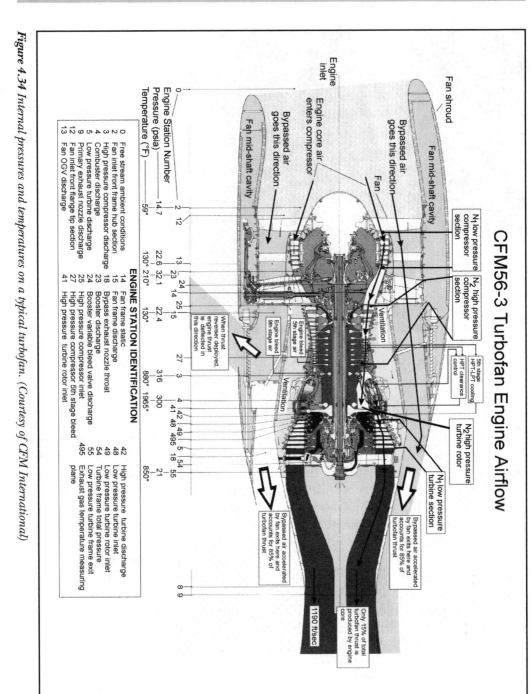

Figure 4.34 Internal pressures and temperatures on a typical turbofan. (Courtesy of CFM International)

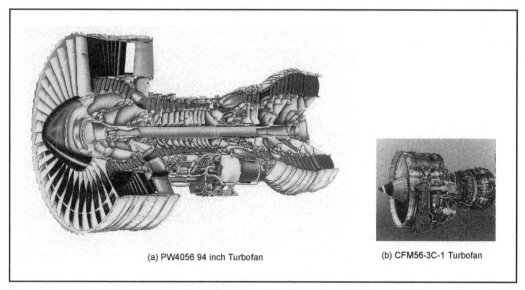

(a) PW4056 94 inch Turbofan

(b) CFM56-3C-1 Turbofan

Figure 4.35 (a) *PW4056 94-in. fan engine. This turbofan is used on the Boeing 767 and Boeing 747 and produces as much as 56,750 lb of thrust. (Courtesy of Pratt & Whitney, United Technologies) (b) The CFM56-3C-1 60-in. fan engine. This turbofan is used on the Boeing 737-400 and produces as much as 23,500 lb of thrust. (Courtesy of CFM International)*

engine, the CF-6 turbofan that is used on DC-10s, has a lower 6:1 bypass ratio, which allows the DC-10 to fly at a faster cruising speed of Mach 0.80.

To get around the problem of thrust decay for fixed-pitch fans, new variable-pitch fan blades in ultrahigh bypass (UHB) propfans are being developed that will increase the bypass ratios by optimizing the fan blade's angle of attack for higher airspeeds. Such ducted-propfan designs are predicted to have bypass ratios in the range of 10: 1 to 20:1. Unducted propfans, such as those used on turboprops, may have bypass ratios as high as 100:1.

The turbofan enjoys wide popularity today not only because of its 30% to 40% better fuel economy over that of the turbojet but also because of its hybrid performance. It has the low-speed, low-altitude efficiency of propeller airplanes (when contrasted with turbojets) while retaining high-altitude turbojet-like cruise speeds.

Figure 4.34 shows the internal pressures and temperatures on a typical high-bypass turbofan. At station 2 in the illustration, the air entering the fan, which is rotating at 2,800 RPM (for a typical high-bypass turbofan), is at a standard atmospheric pressure of 14.7 psi. As the air leaves the fan, it is separated into two streams. The smaller stream, about 15% of the total volume of air, is called *primary*, or *core*, air, and it enters the first

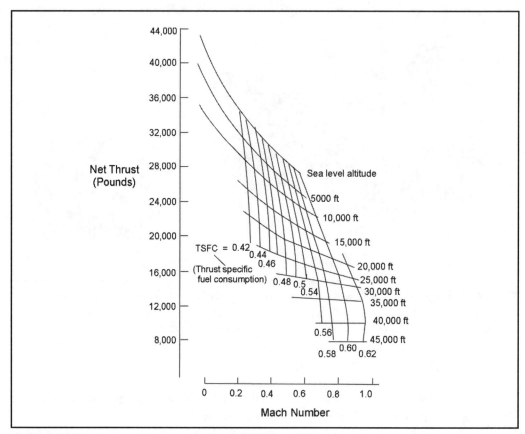

Figure 4.36 *Maximum cruise thrust for a Pratt & Whitney 4056.*

of the two compressors that are spinning in the same direction as the fan. After the first low-pressure compressor stage on spool 1, you can see that the pressure has almost doubled to 32 psi and the temperature has increased to 210° F because of the compression. After traveling through the higher-RPM stage 2 high-pressure compressor (on the second spool N_2, which is rotating at 10,000 RPM for a typical turbofan), the air is 21 times higher in pressure and 821° F hotter. At this point the combustion process raises the temperature to 1,970° F, and the hot gas rushes toward the back of the engine to drive the high-pressure turbine on spool 2. After leaving this turbine, the hot gas drives the first spool's low-pressure turbine before exiting the rear of the aircraft at 850° F and 20.9 psi at a speed of 1,190 ft/s.

Note that the fan is usually driven by the N_1 shaft, which is connected to the low-pressure compressor and turbine stage. There are exceptions to this rule. For example, in the

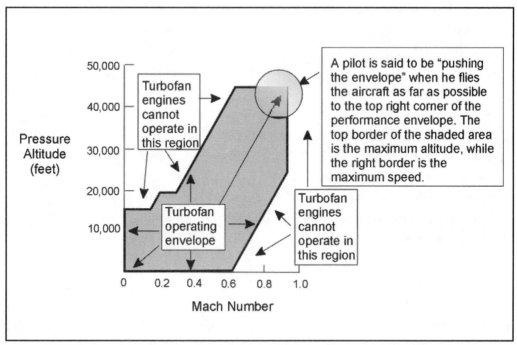

Figure 4.37 *Performance envelope of the Pratt & Whitney 4056 turbofan.*

Learjet Garrett TFE-731 turbofan engines, the fan is driven by the high-RPM N_2 turbine instead of the low-RPM N_1 shaft. The fan is not attached directly the compressor; rather, it is connected to a gearbox connected to the N_2 shaft with a gearbox ratio of 0.49:1. When the N_2 turbine is rotating at 10,000 RPM, the fan therefore rotates at only 4,960 RPM. This design allows the fan to obtain greater torque from the higher turbine speeds.

In most turbofan engines, the fan blade's tip speed is allowed to exceed Mach 1 at high power settings. Because of the high pressure within the fan duct, the airflow doesn't separate from the blades at speeds greater than Mach 1, something it would ordinarily do with a normal airfoil. This design prevents the problems of supersonic shock wave formation and the resultant noise and vibration.

The CFM56-3 turbofan used on the 737-400 is produced by CFM International, a joint company owned by General Electric (United States) and Snecma (France). There are approximately 3,630 CFM56-3 engines in service on more than 1,600 aircraft worldwide, logging more than 48.7 million total engine flight hours and 34.9 million total engine flight cycles (one cycle represents a takeoff, climb, cruise, descent, and landing). Table 4.7 shows some of the technical data and performance characteristics of the CFM56-3.

Table 4.7 *Technical Data for the CFM56-3C-1 Used on the Boeing 737-400, 737-500, and 737-300*

CATEGORY	STATISTIC
Takeoff conditions (sea level)	
Maximum takeoff (lb)	18,500–23,500
Airflow (lb/sec)	638–710
Bypass ratio	5.0
In-Flight Performance at 35,000 ft (Mach 0.8 ISA)	
Maximum climb thrust (lb)	5,540
Overall pressure ratio at maximum climb	30.6
Maximum cruise thrust (lb)	5370
Thrust-specific fuel consumption at cruise (lb/(lb hr))	0.655
Engine Characteristics	
Length (in.)	93
Fan diameter (in.)	60
Basic dry weight (lb)	4,301
Entry into service	1,984
Departure reliability (% successful per 1,000 departures)	99.97%
Shop visit rate per 1,000 engine flight hours	0.073
Average flight duration (hours)	1.4
Utilization (hours per day)	7.9
Utilization (flights or cycles per day)	5.8

Comparison of Turbojet, Turbofan, and Turboprop Engines

The specific fuel consumption for a turbojet or turbofan engine is expressed as thrust-specific fuel consumption (TSFC) and is a measure of the energy content of a fuel and of the effectiveness of an engine in converting that energy to useful thrust. The lower the TSFC, the better an engine's fuel economy. In English units, TSFC is stated as pounds of fuel used per pound of thrust produced per hour (lb/(lb hr)), and it has the dimensions of 1/time. As you can see in Figure 4.38, the TSFC of the turbofan is lower than that of the turbojet at all airspeeds, meaning that the turbofan is more fuel-efficient than the turbojet. Note that the turboprop uses even less fuel.

$$c_{\text{TSFC}} = \frac{\text{Fuel flow}}{\text{Thrust}} \tag{4.11}$$

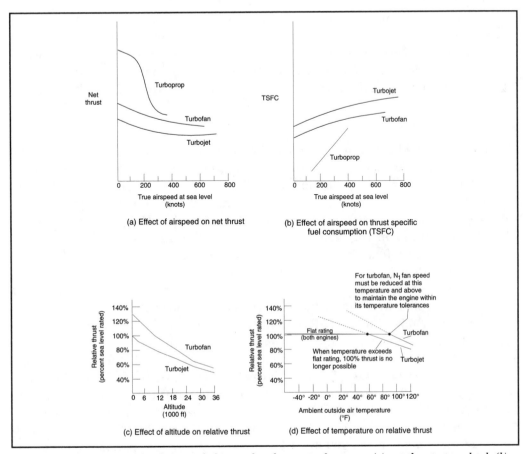

Figure 4.38 *Comparison of turbojet, turbofan, and turboprop performance: (a) net thrust at sea level, (b) thrust-specific fuel consumption, and (c) relative thrust versus altitude.*

Let's see how TSFC can be used to aid us in understanding a turbofan engine's performance. We will calculate the fuel flow given for the 737-400 during cruise. Looking at Table 4.7, we see that the CFM-56-3C turbofan has a specific fuel consumption of 0.655 lb/(lb hour) at cruise. We also know from this table that the cruise thrust at 35,000 ft altitude is 5,370 lb. With this information we can calculate the fuel flow as follows:

$$c_{\text{TSFC}} = \frac{\text{Fuel flow}}{\text{Thrust}} \tag{4.12}$$

Therefore

$$\text{Fuel flow} = c_{\text{TSFC}} \times \text{Thrust} = 0.655\,\text{lb}/(\text{lb hour}) \times 5{,}370\,\text{lb} = 3{,}517\,\text{lb}/\text{hour}$$

Note that for the maximum-weight Boeing 737-400, the Boeing performance charts show that maximum fuel flow should be 3,161 lb/hour. Although this number is different from our calculated result, it gives you a ballpark figure for estimation purposes.

Turbojet engines have higher specific fuel consumption values, ranging from 0.8 to 1.2 lb/(lb hour). Supersonic aircraft have values that range from 1.2 to 2 lb/(lb hour).

Fuel Consumption

Turbine engine fuel consumption depends on aircraft weight and altitude. As weight decreases, engine power setting is reduced accordingly and fuel consumption drops.

Let's look at the fuel consumption of the Boeing 737-400. During a climb from sea level to 37,000 ft, a 135,000-lb 737-400 will consume 2,250 lb of fuel (335 gallons) and will take 32 min and travel 197 nautical miles. This means that during the climb, the airplane burns 4,218 lb/hr (629 gallons/hour). During the cruise, the fuel consumption per engine at 37,000 ft at Mach 0.745 is 2,389 lb/hour, for a combined total of 4,778 lb/hour (713 U.S. gallons/hour) for both engines.

For comparison, let's evaluate the fuel consumption of the much larger 747-400. The maximum takeoff weight of the Boeing 747-400 is 884,000 lb (442 tons), and it burns approximately 12 tons (24,120 lb) of fuel per hour at FL 310, or 3,600 gallons. This is also equivalent to 1 gallon burned every second. For a 7- to 8-hour flight (Europe to the United States, or Australia to the Far East), the 747 fuel requirement is as much as 96 tons, or 192,000 lb, or 28,656 gallons. This gives the 747-400 a fuel economy of about 7.8 gallons per mile. Its total fuel capacity is 194 tons (58,000 U.S. gallons or 388,600 lb), but when it is carrying a maximum payload of passengers and cargo, the fuel capacity drops to 165 tons, (331,520 lb, or 49,480 gallons). Because the empty weight of the 737-400 is 414,400 lb, or 207 tons, the maximum payload of cargo and passengers is 138,880 lb, or 69 tons. This means that the 747-400 can carry more than its own weight (when empty this is 207 tons) in fuel plus passengers (234 tons)!

NOTE A point of confusion sometimes arises as to the definition of *ton*. A metric ton is defined to be 1,000 kg, which is equal to 2,204 lb. An English ton, sometimes called the *long ton*, is different from the American short ton and weighs in at 2,240 lb. The short ton is equivalent to 2,000 lb. In this book we will use the short ton definition of 1 ton = 2,000 lb.

Thrust Drops Off with Gain in Altitude

Figure 4. 38 shows that a turboprop produces the most amount of thrust at speeds less than 400 knots, whereas a turbofan produces more thrust than a turbojet for a given airspeed. The relative thrust drops off dramatically at higher altitudes for both the turbofan and the turbojet. For example, the CFM56-3C engine used on the 737-400 produces 23,500 lb of takeoff thrust at sea level but only 5,540 lb of climb thrust at 35,000 ft while at Mach 0.8—a whopping thrust drop of 76%. Fortunately, because of the rarefied air at 35,000 ft, the consequent parasite drag is dramatically less and the airplane can fly faster at much lower thrust levels.

The approximate variation of thrust with altitude for the turbojet engine is given by Table 4.8. At 35,000 ft, the engine thrust is only 39.2% of its sea level thrust. Although this table illustrates the thrust drop-off for turbojets only, slightly different results also hold true for turbofan engines. For example, at 35,000 ft the CFM56-3C turbofan has a thrust ratio of 0.24, meaning that it produces only 24% of its rated takeoff thrust at 35,000 ft.

Table 4.8 Thrust Variation with Altitude for the Turbojet

ALTITUDE (FT)	THRUST RATIO (THRUST AT ALTITUDE/THRUST AT SEA LEVEL)
Sea level	1.0
5,000	0.888
10,000	0.785
20,000	0.604
35,000	0.392
40,000	0.315
50,000	0.180

Notice that the thrust ratios decrease in a similar proportion to the decline in air density, as shown in Table 4.9. As you can see, the air density at 35,000 ft is only 30.9% of the air density at sea level, whereas the thrust ratio at 35,000 ft would be 39.2%.

Table 4.9 Air Density Ratio

ALTITUDE (FT)	AIR DENSITY RATIO (AIR DENSITY AT ALTITUDE/ AIR DENSITY AT SEA LEVEL)
Sea level	1.0
5,000	0.8617
10,000	0.7385
20,000	0.4976
35,000	0.3099
40,000	0.2462
50,000	0.1352

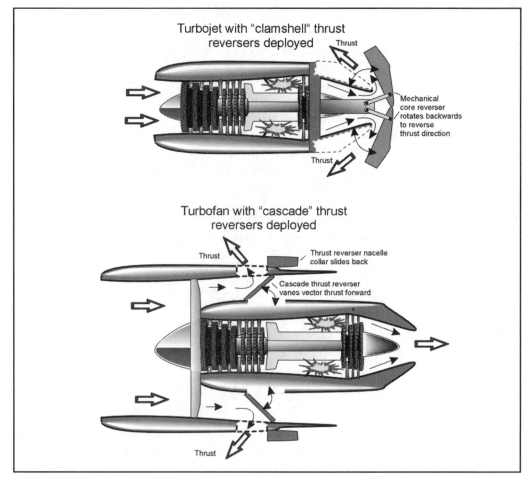

Figure 4.39 *Thrust reversers deployed.*

Thrust Reversal

Compared with propeller airplanes, jets are harder to stop during landings. This is because jets don't have windmilling propeller blades to help add drag. Although jets have spoilers and speed brakes on the wings, they need more than wheel brakes to slow down quickly. Thrust reversal of the engines helps to solve this problem. By bypassing engine exhaust air away from the rear and redirecting it forward, the thrust can act as a brake. Figure 4.39 shows how this is done.

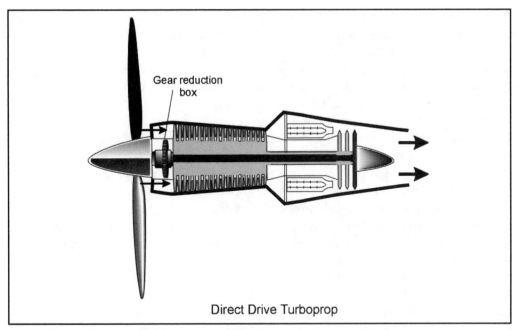

Figure 4.40 *Turboprop engine.*

Many turboprop airplanes are equipped with reversible-pitch propellers that allow quick braking action by reversing the prop thrust. Even without this benefit, propeller airplanes have an easier time of slowing quickly because the propeller acts as a solid disk the diameter of the propeller's length. For a 14-ft diameter propeller, this produces about 4,000 lb of drag! A jet engine, even at idle, produces as much as 1,000 lb of forward thrust on a single 20,000-lb rated engine.

The Turboprop Engine

A turboprop engine is laid out like a turbofan except that the inner shaft extends forward and, through a reduction gear, drives a variable-pitch propeller (see Figure 4.40). The reduction gear, which is similar to an automobile transmission, is needed because turbine engines rotate much faster than a propeller needs to be spun. If you didn't reduce the gearing on the propeller, it would spin faster than the speed of sound and the blades would generate supersonic shock waves, with a consequent drop in thrust, increase in noise, and overstressing of the blades.

The compressor-main turbine combination, borne by the outer shaft and rotating freely, is called the *gas generator*. Most of the energy contained in the hot gas generated by the combustion is absorbed by the main turbine on the inner shaft and thus transmitted to the propeller. A small additional thrust is generated by the exhaust gases. Sometimes this exhaust gas thrust is considered important enough to be ducted to the rear of the engine nacelle, as with the Allison plants found on the Electra or the Convair 580. In the case of the Shorts, however, the shape and orientation of the exhaust pipes don't suggest that jet thrust is a very important contributing factor in the overall engine thrust.

Why are turboprops used? Jet engines tend to be most efficient at high altitudes and at high speeds. At lower altitudes and lower speeds, a turboprop engine is more efficient. Also, the use of five- and even six-blade propellers revving at comparatively low speeds makes these power plants particularly silent. The turboprop engine has not been drummed out of the market by the turbofan engine, and the turboprop is likely to make a spectacular comeback with the design of advanced propellers that operate efficiently at 0.8 Mach.

Turboprops produce small amounts of jet thrust in addition to the shaft power they develop. These engines are rated in terms of equivalent shaft horsepower (eshp). This rating assumes that 1 shp produces 2.5 lb of thrust (this cannot be applied to helicopters). For example, a 1,050 eshp turboprop with a 1,000 shp would produce 1,050 - 1,000 = 50 shp, or 125 lb of jet thrust (but 1,000 shp of rotational power for the propeller).

Controls and Instruments on a Turboprop

The turboprop power plant has two operating controls: the throttle, which adjusts the amount of fuel to be injected, and the propeller pitch control. The instruments in a turboprop-equipped airplane monitor the gas generator speed, expressed in percent of a nominal speed, as well as the turbine gas temperature, the fuel flow, the torque, and the propeller RPM along with oil temperature and pressure.

A unique control is the torque indicator, which plays a role that is similar to the role of the manifold pressure gauge in a piston engine. The more you open the throttle, the more fuel will be injected, the more gas will be generated, and the bigger will be the torque generated by the inner shaft turbine, to be transmitted to the propeller. But the resulting propeller speed will also depend on the propeller pitch. So the pilot who uses the manual pitch adjustment will adjust the throttle to get the desired torque and then adjust the pitch for the desired propeller speed, according to tables that take into account the airspeed, the altitude, and the aircraft's loading.

Most of the time the pilot will use the automatic pitch adjustment of the propeller, so he or she will act on the throttle for a given torque. Once the new torque is established, the pilot will adjust the throttle again for the desired propeller speed.

Simulating a Turboprop in Flight Simulator

Unfortunately, the current version of Flight Simulator cannot correctly simulate a turboprop. If you download and install a turboprop airplane such as the Shorts, you can use either a reciprocating engine model—an approach that is quite unrealistic because the reactions are much too fast—or a jet engine model, in which case you don't have a propeller pitch control. If you use the jet model, you can control only the power plant using the throttle.

When Engine Thrust Exceeds Aircraft Weight

The F-16 is an example of an airplane that can produce more thrust than the airplane weighs. This means that the F-16 can accelerate straight up, defying the Earth's gravitational pull, because the engine thrust is greater than the weight force of gravity acting on the airplane. You can try this yourself using Lars Kornstaedt's F-16 plane on this book's CD-ROM. With 23,810 lb of thrust, the single Pratt & Whitney F-100 engine can overcome the airplane's weight when it weighs less than 23,810 lb. However, because the F-16 normally weighs 30,000 lb fully fueled, you must empty the fuel tanks to about 10% of rated capacity to provide more thrust than the airplane weighs. The dry weight of the airplane is 14,567 lb when empty of fuel. Thus, if you fly with the main fuel tanks at about 10% of fuel capacity with the auxiliary tanks to 0%, the fuel will weigh about 1,488 lb and the airplane's total weight will be 16,055 lb. At this weight, the engine's 23,810 lb of thrust will allow you to accelerate straight up.

Note that as you gain altitude, the engine's thrust will drop off because of thinner air, and the thrust will decrease until it is less than the aircraft's weight. When that happens, the airplane will slow and eventually stall.

Engine Ingestion of Foreign Objects

Engines on turbine aircraft are frequently fitted with vortex generators, which are blow-away jets for landing on airstrips that have gravel runways or where there is a danger of ingesting foreign objects into the engine. The vortices of air created by the sucking air from the engine can easily cause gravel, pebbles, or other small objects to be ingested. The vortex generators blow air forward and downward to ward off such potential threats. In addition, the airplane's landing gear wheels can be fitted with special gravel deflector skis that guide any kicked-up gravel away from the path of the engines.

The FAA requires that turbine engines certified for air transport be able to survive the ingestion of a four-pound bird without catching fire, bursting, or losing the capability of being shut down. In addition, ingestion of a 1.5-pound bird may not cause more than a sustained 25% loss of power or thrust, nor should the engine need to be shut down within five minutes from the time of ingestion.

Turbine engines are also required to prove that they can ingest water, ice, or one-inch hailstones under certain prescribed conditions so that the engines do not suffer sustained loss of power or thrust, or be required to shut down. Turbine engines must demonstrate that they can accelerate and decelerate safely while inducting a mixture of at least 4% water by weight of engine airflow at both flight idle and takeoff power settings with at least a 4% water-to-air ratio for at least three minutes.

Maintenance

Airframe maintenance can be divided into three categories: line checks, scheduled checks, and major checks.

- Line maintenance includes on-the-ramp transit checks, overnight checks at intervals of 300–600 hours, A checks, and B checks.
- Scheduled maintenance includes annual C checks with an interval of 3,000 to 4,000 flight hours (the 737-300 average is 4,400 flight hours).
- Major checks involve heavy airframe D checks or airframe overhaul, which can take a month or more. This overhaul includes repair and replacement of all rotating parts, structural inspection, and FAA-mandated airframe worthiness checks and modifications (for example, engine pylon modifications for the 747 and DC-10). Aging-aircraft inspection and corrosion-prevention procedures are carried out. Stripping of paint and repainting of the airplane is also performed if necessary. The 737-300 undergoes a D check every 27,000 flight hours and 21,000 cycles, which is about once every five years.

Maintaining the 737 is relatively easy. The 737-300, 400, and 500 require about 7,850 hours of intermediate and heavy maintenance per year, accounting for the annual C and five-year D checks. However, the aging-aircraft and airframe airworthiness checks bring the annual total to 11,450 hours. In a ten-year period, a total of 114,500 hours is expended maintaining the 737. Because the 737 may fly about 54,000 hours in ten years, for every hour the plane flies it must undergo two hours of maintenance. Other planes may have slightly different maintenance ratios.

Metal fatigue is a major concern. Wing spars need inspecting at intervals of 3,500 flying hours, and cabin windows and other openings in the fuselage must be inspected every 300 flying hours. Most airplane structures are designed to be safe to fly at least 30,000 hours in ten years or more without trouble, with a 50% built-in safety factor.

Fire Protection

Gas turbine engines are designed with unique features to guard against fires. For example, internal components are designed so that multiple failures must occur before a fire is possible; a single component failure will not start a fire. Also, flammable liquids are isolated from the hot parts of the engine, and external fuel and associated pipelines are located in cool zones of the engine, being separated from the combustion areas by a bulkhead. As a further precaution, all pipes that carry flammable liquids, such as fuel, oil, and hydraulic fluid, are constructed of fireproof, double-walled materials.

In the unlikely event of a fire, detection systems installed around the engine compartment detect heat in excess of 500° F, which is well beyond the normal 300° F temperature that a typical engine normally radiates. Fire extinguishing agents can be dispersed within the engine compartment upon activation by the flight crew.

Black Box

"Black box" is a misnomer for the cockpit voice recorder and the flight data recorder, both of which are bright orange or yellow and are covered with reflective tape to facilitate their location under water. Usually, the egg-shaped flight data recorder is placed high in the base of the airplane's tail, because this part of the aircraft is farthest away from the fuel tanks and is most likely to survive an impact.

A modern flight recorder is built to resist an impact of 5,000 lb, an acceleration of 1000 g's, and temperatures of 2012° F (1100° C) for 30 min. The recorders can be immersed in the ocean for as long as one month, and an acoustical underwater locating device helps searchers recover the recorders.

The voice recorder continually records the last 30 minutes of conversation on the flight deck, overwriting anything older. The flight data recorder measures altitude, airspeed, pitch attitude, acceleration, magnetic heading, and engine thrust. Newer digital models measure hundreds of other functions and other specialized data that may be useful in accident investigations.

There has been discussion about installing cockpit video recorders to aid in accident investigation, but the airline pilots associations have been reluctant to allow it, fearing that the recordings could give management another tool to micromanage the pilots' already restricted work lives.

ENVIRONMENTAL SYSTEMS

Most of the airplane's environmental systems are driven by the air bleed taken from the turbine engines. These systems include the cabin pressurization, air conditioning, and surface anti-ice systems. As much as 20% of the total engine core mass airflow may be diverted for these various purposes.

Bleed air is extracted from various stages of the compressor and is extremely hot. Before being introduced into the cabin, it must be cooled using heat exchangers.

Pressurization

Pressurized cabins and compartments must be equipped to provide a cabin pressure altitude of not more than 8,000 ft at the maximum operating altitude of the airplane. In addition, when operating above 25,000 ft, the airplane must be designed so that if a single component in the pressurization system fails, the cabin pressure will not exceed 15,000 ft.

To guard against the effects of cabin depressurization at altitude, the passengers and flight crew must be equipped with a supplementary oxygen system. The system must provide a supply of oxygen to the passengers with the following situations in mind:

- For flights at cabin pressure altitudes greater than 10,000 ft, up to and including 14,000 ft, enough oxygen for that part of the flight at those altitudes that is of more than 30 min duration for at least 10% of the passengers.
- For flights at cabin pressure altitudes greater than 14,000 ft up to and including 15,000 ft, enough oxygen for that part of the flight at those altitudes for 30% of the passengers.
- For flights at cabin pressure altitudes above 15,000 ft, enough oxygen for each passenger carried during the entire flight at those altitudes.

More stringent requirements apply for the flight crew: when operating with a cabin pressure greater than 10,000 ft up to and including 12,000 ft, oxygen must be provided for and used by each member of the flight crew for flights that are more than 30 min in duration. If the cabin pressure goes above 12,000 ft, oxygen must be used continuously for the entire flight. As a further precaution, whenever a flight crew member leaves the flight deck, whether or not the cabin pressure system is operative, the remaining pilot in command must don an oxygen mask and use it continuously until the other crew member returns.

Most airplanes can descend at an emergency rate so that within 4 min, they are below 14,000 ft. If they are not capable of doing this, additional oxygen must be carried onboard.

Windows are double-paned in a pressurized aircraft not only to provide some redundancy, but also to reduce fogging and moisture buildup from the temperature and humidity changes encountered in climbing to and descending from altitude. Although the passenger and crew compartment as well as cargo and baggage holds are pressurized, the nose cone, tail cone, wings, and wheel wells are not pressurized. The areas that are pressurized are known as the *pressure vessel.* When an airplane is pressurized, it expands slightly; the 737 actually becomes a bit stronger when pressurized and so is pressurized during the landing and takeoff.

The maximum pressure differential of an airplane is the maximum pressure difference that is allowed to exist between the outside atmosphere and the interior pressurized cabin. If, for example, the maximum cabin pressure differential is 8 psi, the pressure in the cabin will be allowed to exceed the outside pressure by a maximum of 8 psi. Thus, if the Learjet is flying at 35,000 ft and the outside pressure is 3.46 psi (7.04 in. Hg), the cabin pressure will be 3.46 + 8 psi or 11.46 psi. If you consult Appendix F, you will see that a pressure of 11.46 psi corresponds to a cabin altitude of approximately 6700 ft. Passenger compartments of modern transport aircraft are designed to an ultimate structural failure pressure of about 18 psi.

There is a distinction between rapid decompression and explosive decompression: rapid decompression occurs in more than 0.5 second but less than 10 seconds, whereas explosive decompression occurs in less than 0.5 second. In the event of sudden cabin depressurization, the cabin will fill with dust and debris as air is sucked out of the airplane. A loud popping noise will precede an explosive decompression, and, if severe, it can rupture the fuselage and expel people from the plane. In addition to ear discomfort, breathing becomes difficult, because the air pressure in your lungs is greater than the air pressure outside. Immediately following the loss of pressure, a fog forms in the cabin and visibility becomes impaired; the warmer air in the cabin carries more moisture than the cold air outside, and, when it is cooled, the moisture condenses from the air into cold water vapor, or fog. If the plane does not descend from high altitude, the temperature inside will also drop to a frigid -65 ° F at 35,000 ft.

Ventilation

For normal operating conditions, the ventilation system is designed to provide each occupant with an airflow of at least 0.55 lb of fresh air per min. Cabin ozone concentrations are not allowed to exceed 0.25 parts per million by volume, sea level equivalent, at any time above FL 320, and 0.01 parts per million above FL 270. Carbon monoxide concentration may not be more than one part in 20,000 parts of air.

In the past few years, complaints have surfaced that airline companies are not giving passengers enough fresh air. The problem is that it is less expensive to recirculate cabin air than to introduce fresh air from the engine bleed air, because this draws power from the engines and thus increases fuel consumption. Airline flight attendants have successfully sued the tobacco industry for second-hand smoke in the cabin, claiming that the poor air quality onboard the aircraft contributed to their lung cancers. In another well-publicized incident, a passenger with flu transmitted his illness to many other passengers on the plane, in all probability because the pilots had been given financial incentives by management to reduce fuel consumption by recirculating more cabin air. The airline industry is sensitive to this criticism, and some companies have taken steps to ensure that this kind of thing does not happen in the future.

Cabin Safety: Smoke Emergencies

Smoke emergencies in a closed-pressurized vessel such as an airplane cabin can be deadly. When smoke infiltrates the passenger compartment, there is no way to ventilate the cabin to remove the smoke. Since 1976, some 2,400 passengers have died in 95 fire-related aircraft accidents worldwide. The NTSB reports that 969 people perished from smoke inhalation in 14 accidents from 1970 to 1996 in which smoke was reported in the cockpit or cabin. The most recent smoke inhalation incident was the well-publicized ValueJet crash in May 1996, in which oxygen generators being transported in the hold ignited and caused a fire.

It is a statistical fact that many fatal airliner crashes could have been survivable if the occupants had not succumbed to smoke inhalation. For example, in 1991 the collision of a Boeing 737 with another aircraft on the runway during a landing at Los Angeles International Airport caused the deaths of 22 people. Although 67 passengers managed to escape from the 737, 21 of 22 fatalities happened because people were asphyxiated by the toxic smoke in the cabin. The other exits had become jammed, and only one overwing exit was operable. When the cabin filled with black smoke, those who couldn't get out fast enough collapsed while waiting to climb out. Eleven people were found congregated 8 feet away from this exit.

Unfortunately, airliners have no system for preventing asphyxiation from the toxic hydrogen cyanide gas produced by the burning of interior plastic moldings. Nor do they have any means of protection from the deadly carbon monoxide gas produced from the combustion process. The emergency cabin oxygen masks that protect the passengers from sudden decompression of the cabin at high altitudes are of no help, because they recirculate cabin air along with fresh oxygen.

Fortunately, a simple, low-cost solution to this problem is available. Although the airlines have resisted installing them for cost reasons, personal smoke hoods are commercially available for about $69 that completely protect the user from toxic smoke and fumes for as long as 15 minutes, which is long enough to escape the airplane once a fire has begun after a crash. These smoke hoods are standard equipment on 300 corporate jets for Fortune 500 companies. The U.S. military is also a big user of these cheap, portable devices, having ordered 50,000 of them last year for use with the Air Mobility Command. Tellingly, one of the top former officials of the FAA recently revealed that she never traveled on any airline without a personal smoke hood in her purse.

Many different kinds of smoke hoods are available. One popular model comes in a small package the size of a soda can, allowing the unit to be carried in a flight case or purse while traveling, and it has a warranted shelf life of five years if unopened. The company will replace it free of charge if you ever use it while escaping a fire or toxic fumes. The hood resists heat up to 1,500° F and permits a full range of sight and hearing during an emergency. Popular smoke hoods include Dupont's EVAC-U8 (800-459-

3822), Drager's Parat C Smoke Escape mask (412-787-8383), Essex PB&R's Plus 10 Filter Breathing Unit (410-398-3353), Duram's Emergency Escape Mask (714-893-5505), and Smoke Mask, Inc.'s Smoke Mask (800-562-0818).

If you often travel by air, do yourself a favor and get a smoke mask; it may one day save your life. By its own published estimates, Boeing has admitted that early next century there will be one plane crash every week due to the increasing volume of worldwide air travel.

Cooling and Heating

The heating and cooling systems on large turbine aircraft are driven by engine bleed air. Because bleed air is hot, it must be cooled before entering the cabin. Heat exchangers, air cycle machines, or vapor cycle machines are used. Both air cycle machines and vapor cycle machines use the same principle of compressing a gas to increase temperature and expanding a gas to decrease temperature. Physicists have long understood that when a gas is expanded, it cools, thereby lowering the surrounding temperature. Physicists also know that whenever a gas is compressed, it heats thereby increasing the surrounding temperature. You can try the expansion principle yourself; open your mouth as wide as possible and blow on the palm of your hand. Your breath should feel warm. Now purse your lips as if you are going to whistle and then blow on your hand. Your breath will feel cool. Your breath has expanded after it left your mouth under pressure, and the temperature drops as a result of this gas expansion. Figure 4.41 illustrates how this is done.

Figure 4.41 Blow on your hand with your mouth wide open (left photo); your breath should feel warm. Now purse your lips as if you are whistling and blow on your hand (right photo); your breath will feel cool. In the lower photo, the expansion of air from your lungs and the consequent temperature drop demonstrates the principle of how cooling systems work.

If you compress a liter of gas it to a smaller volume, the compressed gas will get hotter. If you then pass some cool air past this compressed hot gas, some of the cool air will be warmed and some of the hot compressed gas will cool. If you then allow the compressed gas to resume its former volume, it will expand and the temperature will fall to a colder temperature than when it started. The colder temperature can be used to cool the cabin's air as it is circulated through a special heat exchanger. Using this principle of temperature control, it is possible to exchange warm temperatures for cold temperatures.

The major difference between the air cycle machine and vapor cycle machine is that of operating fluid. The air cycle machine uses air as its operating medium, and the vapor cycle machine uses a refrigerant such as Freon. Refrigerants have higher thermal capacities, thereby making vapor cycle machines more efficient for cooling purposes. Because large turbine aircraft have ample supplies of bleed air, however, the air cycle machine is favored over the vapor cycle machine.

The Auxiliary Power Unit

The auxiliary power unit (APU) is a turbine engine, usually installed in the tail of an airplane, to provide supplementary power (Figure 4.42). APUs provide auxiliary electrical power while the airplane is on the ground as well as an auxiliary bleed air source, which is useful for starting the engines while the plane is on the ground or in the air. Large jet engines used on airliners must be started using pneumatic power, and, unless a ground pneumatic source is available, there is no way to start a turbine engine without the use of an APU.

While the plane is on the ground, APUs are also used to power aircraft systems without the need to run the main engines. The air conditioning, major electrical systems, galley operation, lighting, and environmental systems are all powered by the APU during ground operations.

After takeoff, the APU is usually shut down and the main engines generate all the electrical power and pneumatic bleed air for running the environmental systems, such as cabin pressurization, heating, and air conditioning. During flight, however, some aircraft can use the APU as a backup source of power and pneumatic air in case the engines or the generators fail.

RAM Air Turbine

When all electrical power is lost and the airplane is flying using battery power only, a last resort means of producing electricity is needed to power vital electrical systems. The RAM air turbine can be deployed as an emergency power backup. After the RAM air turbine pops out of the airplane, the oncoming wind spins a turbine generator, creating enough electricity to keep the batteries from running down.

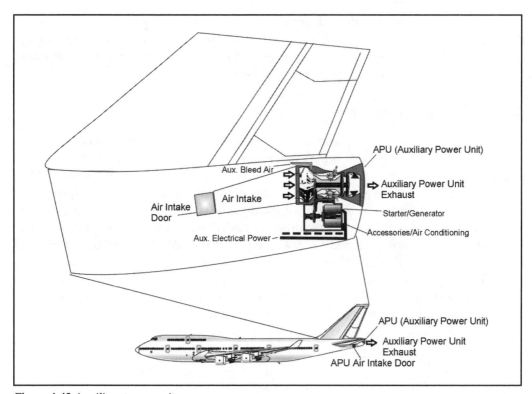

Figure 4.42 *Auxiliary power unit.*

ELECTRONIC COMPUTING SYSTEMS

With all the advances in high technology computing, it is only natural that aircraft designers would incorporate these developments in avionics, flight deck controls, fly-by-wire systems, and engine instrumentation as well as passenger entertainment systems. Almost overnight, the flight decks of modern aircraft have become airborne computer centers. Where cockpits once were a dizzying array of electromechanical gauges and dials, today's cockpits resemble video arcades with color liquid crystal displays, sound effects, motion, and flashing lights.

Flat panel displays are now used to show engine instruments (EICAS: Engine Indicating and Crew Alerting System) and all the other flight instruments. Moving map displays, overlaid with weather data, provide navigational data to the pilot. Although backup electromechanical gauges are required in the cockpit, the advanced flat panel displays are affectionately referred to as the "glass cockpit." The new Boeing 777 has menu-driven computer displays that include a trackpad similar to those found on laptop computers. These input devices allow pilots to point and click through menus and commands as they would on a conventional computer.

Radio Communication

When an alternating current passes through an antenna, energy is radiated into space in the form of electromagnetic waves that we call radio waves. The transmitted energy is comprised of alternating electrical fields and an alternating magnetic field that are emitted at right angles to each other. The frequency of the radio wave is expressed in cycles per second, or Hertz, in honor of Heinrich Hertz (1857–1894), a German professor of Physics who discovered radio waves and determined their velocity in 1888. 1,000 Hz equals 1 kiloHertz, and 1,000 kHz equals 1 megaHertz, or 1 MHz (1,000,000 Hz); 1,000 MHz equals 1 gigaHertz, or 1 GHz (1,000,000,000 Hz). The wavelength of a radio wave is the distance traveled during the transmission of one complete alternating cycle, or 1 Hertz. Usually this distance is expressed in meters. Both frequency and wavelength are related to the speed of light by this equation:

$$f\lambda = c \tag{4.13}$$

where

f = Frequency in cycles/second or Hz
λ = Wavelength in meters
c = Speed of light constant of 300,000,000 meters/second

NOTE Hertz's experiments with cathode rays penetrating metal films led him to conclude that cathode rays were waves rather than particles. This astounding finding later became the basis for quantum mechanics, which incorporated the contradictory principle that an electron acted as both a wave and a particle. This was proved in the famous double slit experiment. When a single electron passes through a metal film with two slits, it somehow passes through both slits at the same time, proving that the electron must be a wave. However, in other experiments, the electron also acted like a particle. Which was it to be? According to classical Newtonian dynamics, it couldn't be both a wave and a particle. This experiment confounded scientists of the day until the development of quantum theory, which explained this odd behavior in non-Newtonian terms.

Because the speed of light is a constant 300,000,000 meters/second (671 million mph, or 186,000 miles/second), only wavelength and frequency can vary in Equation 4.13. For example, to calculate the wavelength of 118.00 MHz:

$$f\lambda = c \tag{4.14}$$

Therefore

$$\lambda = \frac{c}{f} = \frac{300,000,000 \text{ m/s}}{118,000,000 \text{ cycles/s}} = 2.54 \text{ m/cycle}$$

$$\lambda = 2.54 \text{ meters}$$

Today, long-distance communications over oceanic regions or areas that have few airport facilities (such as Africa) are accomplished via high frequency (HF) radio. HF uses the shortwave band of 2 to 28 MHz, but most aviation communications equipment uses single side band (SSB) transmissions to optimize reception. SSB suppresses one side of the bandwidth at the transmitter, resulting in a narrowing of the amount of radio noise. This helps to increase the effective range of the signal.

AM (amplitude modulation) radios, such as those found in automobiles and transistor radios, use the frequency band of 510 kHz to 1600 kHz (or 0.510 MHz to 1.6 MHz). FM (frequency modulation) radio uses the 88 to 108 MHz band. Aviation navigation and communications equipment use the 108 to 137 MHz VHF band as well as the 225 to 400 MHz UHF band. In general, VHF is used for communications within 200 nm of air traffic control facilities. Outside this range, HF radio equipment is used. HF waves, being longer than VHF waves, are reflected by the ionosphere and can thus "bend" around the curvature of the Earth, giving a range of thousands of miles (even greater at night because there is less disturbance of the ionosphere by the sun). VHF waves, on the other hand, are shorter and pass straight through the ionosphere into space. Shortwave reception lacks the clarity of VHF channels, because atmospheric noise creates lots of static, and it becomes tiring for crews to maintain a constant vigil listening for messages. The solution to this problem is SELCAL (selective calling). Using this method, crews need not monitor the radio. When a ground station wishes to communicate with them, a tone is sent and decoded by the aircraft's SELCAL radio. When the SELCAL determines that the code is addressed to it and it alone, a "bing-bong" sound is heard and a light signal alerts the pilots to respond. Each aircraft with SELCAL capability is allocated its own four-letter code by ARINC (Aeronautical Radio Inc.), an American company that acts as the worldwide agent to the ICAO. For radio hobbyists, publications list all the SELCAL codes so that when you listen in you can determine which airplane is being called. This can make for some interesting listening, especially the conversations on board the corporate jets of the Fortune 500, which offer you a tantalizing glimpse into the ways of Wall Street.

NOTE   The Aviation Society in Manchester, United Kingdom, publishes a listing of SELCAL codes for registered aircraft in *High in the Sky*. To find out the frequencies that are being used for a given region, consult David J. Smith's excellent book, *International Air Band Radio Handbook: The Guide to Worldwide Air Traffic Control* (Somerset, United Kingdom, Patrick Stephens Limited, 1995).

When SELCAL was first designed, it accommodated a total of 2,970 aircraft identifier codes using a 12-tone coding assignment. In the 1980s, the demand for SELCAL codes outstripped the available assignments, so a new system with 16-tone coding was introduced that added 7,950 new aircraft identifiers. As of 1995, 5,422 of these assignments had been taken, and it has become necessary for multiple users to be assigned the same code. In effect, this means that several aircraft have the same "telephone number." To avoid conflicts, ARINC carefully allocates codes so that aircraft flying in the same hemisphere are unlikely to be carrying the same SELCAL address. It is anticipated that satellite communication will replace SELCAL in the near future.

Table 4.10 shows how the electromagnetic spectrum is allocated.

Table 4.10 Electromazgnetic Spectrum

FREQUENCY RANGE	WAVELENGTH (METERS)	BAND	USES
20–20,000 Hz	15,000,000–15,000 m	Audio frequency	
10–30 kHz	30,000–10,000 m	Very low frequency (VLF)	Military navigation and communication with submarines
30–300 kHz	10,000–1000 m	Low frequency (LF)	Navigation
300–3000 kHz (0.3–3 MHz)	1000–100 m	Medium frequency (MF)	AM radio, standard broadcast
3–30 MHz	100–10 m	High frequency (HF)	Short wave radio
30–300 MHz	10–1 m	Very high frequency (VHF)	Television, FM and radio, aviation communications navigation
300–3000 MHz	100–10 cm	Ultra high frequency (UHF)	Waves shorter than 30 cm are called microwaves and are cellular phones, satellite communi- used for television, cations, PCS phones, microwave ovens, and so on

Table 4.10 *continued*

FREQUENCY RANGE	WAVELENGTH (METERS)	BAND	USES
3000–30,000 MHz			
(3–30 GHz)	10–1 cm	Super high frequency (SHF)	Satellite downlinks and uplinks. Anticipated new PCS phones
30,000–300,000 MHz			
(30–300 GHz)	1–0.1 cm	Extremely high frequency (EHF)	
100,000–390,000 MHz			
(100 GHz–390 GHz)	$0.03–7.6 \times 10^{-5}$ cm	Infrared light and heat	Sun lamps, semiconductor lasers used in CD-ROMs, CDs, DVDs, fiber optic communications
390,000 MHz–790,000 MHz			
(390 GHz–790 GHz)	$7.6–3.8 \times 10^{-5}$ cm	Visible light	Incandescent lighting
790,000 MHz–23,000,000 MHz			
(790 GHz–23,000 GHz)	$3.8–0.13 \times 10^{-5}$ cm	Ultraviolet light	Chip fabrication
2.0×10^{9} MHz– 3.0×10^{13} MHz	1.5×10^{-5} cm– 1.0×10^{-9} cm	X-Rays	Medical imaging, cancer treatment
2.3×10^{12} MHz– 3.0×10^{14} MHz	1.3×10^{-8} cm– 1.0×10^{-10} cm	Gamma rays	Cancer treatment, radiation

Connecting to the Internet from your airplane seat may become a reality in the not very distant future. With the advent of low earth orbiting satellites, the age of global data communications is at hand. Planes flying over the mid-Pacific, or flying anywhere for that matter, will be in constant touch with Motorola's Iridium Cellular Satellite Constellation (starting operations in 1998) as well as Inmarsat's new Aero-H and Aero-I satellite communication system. In a venture partly funded by Bill Gates of Microsoft, Teledesic will launch 840 to 924 satellites in a proposed $9 billion network that will provide broadband fixed and mobile data services around the globe. The Teledesic earth terminals will offer bit rates ranging from a minimum 16 kbps (16,000 bits per second) plus 2 kbps (2,000 bits per second) for signaling to 2.048 Mbps (2,048,000 bits per second). The Teledesic 2.048-Mbps bit rate is a good bandwidth compared with the bit rate of today's corporate 10-Mbps Ethernet network connection or that of available 28.8-, 33.3-, or 56.6-kbps analog computer modems. The mobile terminal antennas have a diameter as small as 8 cm (3.4 in.) and an average output power ranging from 0.01 watts to 4.7 watts. Very good 15- to 30-frames-per-second two-way video conferencing with audio can be accomplished with compression on a 128-kbps duplex circuit, and full-screen video conferencing equivalent to TV could be accomplished with a 384-kbps connection. Thus, the day is not far off when you will be able to participate in a video conference from your seat with family, business associates, or friends during a trans-Atlantic or trans-Pacific flight. Airlines are also experimenting with live satellite TV broadcasts direct to the onboard entertainment system. With suitably equipped LCDs in the seatbacks, passengers could tune in to 150 or more television channels, including live CNN, and pay per view movie and sporting channels as well as the gamut of other foreign language programming now broadcast worldwide.

The Iridium system is a satellite-based, wireless personal communications network designed to permit any type of telephone transmission—voice, data, fax, or paging—to reach its destination anywhere on Earth. The satellite constellation will consist of 66 interconnected satellites orbiting 420 nautical miles above the Earth. The system will simplify communications for business professionals, travelers, residents of rural or undeveloped areas, disaster relief teams, and other users who need the features and convenience of a wireless handheld phone for worldwide use. Unfortunately, Iridium will offer only 2.4-kbps fax and data services through the mobile handsets, and, at least initially, the cost of the handsets will be $2,000 with on-line charges averaging $3 per minute.

A fourth proposed system, Globalstar by Qualcomm, will have 48 low earth orbit satellites in eight planes. This satellite constellation will offer data rates at 1.2, 2.4, 4.8, and 9.6 kbps. Operating costs for users are expected to hover around current cellular rates of $0.40 per minute.

Advanced ACARS (aircraft communications and reporting system) equipment has revolutionized radio communications for aircraft worldwide. When an aircraft is flying over oceans where no land-based radio coverage is available, ACARS equipment communicates via satellite links and allows the aircraft to be in constant communication with the airline company as well as air traffic control. The system consists of a keyboard, screen, and small printer, and the messages are sent via radiotelephony signals. Flight management as well as data on the aircraft's current location, condition, fuel load, engineering data, and so on can be constantly uploaded to company headquarters. In addition, new flight instructions and navigational data can be downloaded to the flight management system (FMS) and can then be called up on the flat panel displays.

ACARS can be programmed to transmit other types of flight or environmental information automatically. For example, as soon as the plane pushes back from the terminal, it can notify the company's computer network of the airplane's time of departure, inform the company about the airplane's current fuel load, and update the airplane's FMS computer with current weather conditions.

TCAS

The Traffic Alert and Collision Avoidance System (TCAS), is a computerized traffic alert system carried on board the aircraft that warns pilots of air traffic that may be on intersecting paths. Installation of TCAS is now a requirement for all new air transport airplanes in the United States, although Flight Simulator is not equipped with TCAS. All aircraft in the United States are now required to carry Mode S, Mode C, or Mode A transponders, which are radio beacons that allow the aircraft to be located when queried by the TCAS or air traffic control radar. The inexpensive transponder allows non-TCAS-equipped airplanes to be visible to TCAS-equipped airplanes, an important requirement for small airplanes whose owners cannot afford the $100,000 cost of TCAS. The improved Mode S transponders provide a datalink between the aircraft and ATC, permitting the exchange of not only altitude and position data but also text messages such as air traffic control clearances. With today's crowded skies, too many transponders can respond simultaneously to radio queries and this can result in interference. Mode S transponders address this problem by providing selective interrogation of the transponder to minimize interference with other nearby transponders.

 TACS I units cost $56,000 whereas TCAS II units, which provide a display of nearby traffic plus guidance to avoid a threatening target, cost $115,000. TCAS II is required on all jet airliners operating in U.S. airspace. BF Goodrich manufactures a $19,000 system

NOTE called Skywatch that offers TCAS capabilities for small aircraft.

TCAS monitors all traffic within a surveillance bubble that is within plus or minus 8,700 ft of your plane's altitude but normally displays only those aircraft that are within plus or minus 2,700 ft of your altitude. The system is also user-configurable. For example, if you want to increase the bubble to 8,700 ft, you can do so. This might come in handy when you are descending and are worried about climbing aircraft encroaching on your airspace. On departure, you would probably reverse the bubble distances to warn of aircraft above you.

When a plane is within 1,000 ft of the ground, either climbing or descending, the TCAS switches to an advisory-only mode that doesn't jangle your nerves with false alarms, letting you focus on the landing approach or takeoff. This mode comes in handy when you're landing at large airports with parallel runways. You can imagine the false alarms that would occur as two landing airplanes close in on each other during the approach.

TCAS II is the FAA's updated implementation of TCAS, and the new Change 7 configuration proposed by the FAA will be identical to the International Civil

Figure 4.43a The navigational display (ND) on the 737-400. (Courtesy of Just Planes Videos)

Aviation Organization's ACAS II (Airborne Collision Avoidance System), which the international aviation body is recommending to its members for worldwide implementation for transport aircraft beginning in 2000. The FAA is expected to mandate that the Change 7 modifications be incorporated into all TCAS II systems by January 1, 2000. These modifications incorporate some 225 system logic changes, including new surveillance modes, new collision avoidance logic, and audible and visual warnings in the cockpit. The improvements are expected to reduce the number of false alarms and will enhance surveillance in high-density traffic areas, especially those below FL 180.

Although TCAS is required for all transport aircraft flying through American airspace, Europe has been reluctant to install the systems, in part because of the resistance of air traffic controllers who fear that TCAS would threaten their authority over the skies. It has also been said that TCAS might embarrass air traffic controllers when it reports possible traffic advisories that the air traffic controllers have failed to notice. In the crowded skies of the United States, the FAA is not so bothered by air traffic controllers being embarrassed and has opted to install TCAS so that pilots have extra traffic information available as a fail-safe alternative.

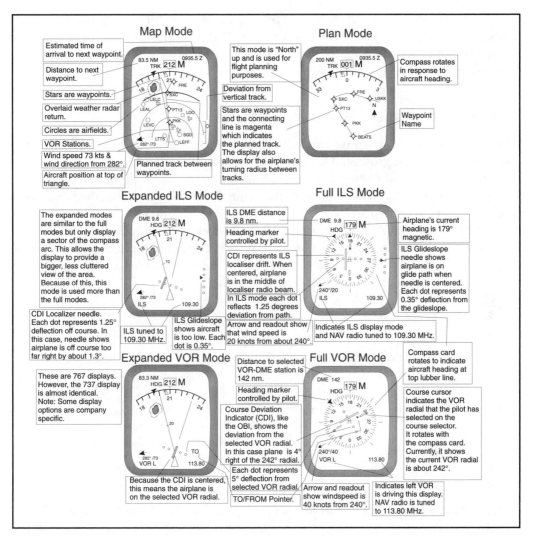

Figure 4.43b *Typical Horizontal Situation Indicator (HSI) Display Modes on the Navigational Display (ND)*

In addition to displaying navigation data and weather radar, the navigational display (ND) is used to track and display TCAS aircraft that may be menacing the aircraft (Figure 4.43a and 4.43b). If the target is not a menace, the TCAS will display a hollow white diamond. On transoceanic trips across the Atlantic, for example, the ND will show TCAS aircraft within a range of 20 or more miles. When the target is within 6 miles and the altitude differential is less than 1,200 ft, the ND will show filled-in diamond symbols. If the threat of collision is a concern, the ND will show an amber circle and an audible alert will sound. If the target is closer than that, the TCAS symbol will change to red, and the TCAS computer will tell you to climb or descend to avoid the hostile traffic.

Ground Proximity Warning Systems

The ground proximity warning system (GPWS) warns the crew of excessive descent or closure rate with the ground. The system is activated between 50 and 2,450 ft above ground via the radio altimeter. The radio altimeter emits a radio signal and waits for its reflection to bounce back from the ground. From the elapsed time that the signal takes to travel between the airplane and the ground, the radio altimeter can accurately assess how high the airplane is flying above ground level. This height above ground is referred to as *radio altitude*, or RA. Note that the pressure altimeter does not tell you the airplane's height above ground; rather, it tells you the height above mean sea level.

Table 4.11 shows the modes of operation for the GPWS.

Table 4.11 GPWS Modes of Operation

MODE	DESCRIPTION
Mode 1: Excessive descent rate	You'll hear "Sink Rate" as a preliminary warning and, when things get worse, "Whoop, Whoop, Pull Up!"
Mode 2: Excessive terrain closure rate	You'll hear this warning when approaching the ground at too great a vertical speed. This mode is more sensitive when you're flying low (3,200 ft/min at 1,000 ft RA). Audible warnings are similar to those issued in Mode 1.
Mode 3: Altitude loss after takeoff or go-around	This mode is armed after takeoff or when you raise the gear or flaps below 245 ft AGL during a go-around. If you lose too much height, you'll get this warning, which can be silenced only by climbing. The mode is active between 50 and 700 ft RA.

Table 4.11 continued

MODE	DESCRIPTION
Mode 4: Unsafe terrain clearance with landing gear not down	This mode is armed below 1,000 ft RA with high speeds and always below 500 ft RA at low speeds. It tells you that you must raise the gear ("Too Low Gear") or flaps ("Too Low Flaps") if your speed is less than 180 knots IAS, or that you are too low to the terrain for speeds greater than 180 knots ("Too Low Terrain").
Mode 5: Below glide slope deviation	This mode monitors the captain's glide slope receiver and sounds an alert if the descent is more than 1.3 dots below an ILS glide slope ("Glide Slope"). Note that 1.3 dots on the ILS glide slope is equivalent to 0.5° below the ILS glide slope. Because most glide slopes are sloped at an angle of 3°, this means that if your rate of descent is 3.5° or higher, the alert will sound. Note that some glide slopes are steeper depending on surrounding terrain, so the alert won't sound until the plane has exceeded 0.5° of the runway's given glide slope angle.
Mode 6: Below selected minimum radio altitude and radio altitude call-outs	This mode monitors the captain's radio altimeter and operates between 50 ft and 1,000 ft RA. When the aircraft descends below the RA designated by the captain, the audible alert "Minimums, Minimums" will sound. This mode will be reset if the aircraft climbs above the designated RA. Some GPWS systems call out the altitudes as you descend. (See GPWS 6.0 on this book's CD-ROM, which does this for Flight Simulator.)
Mode 7: Wind shear Warning	For airplanes equipped with wind shear detection gear, this alert sounds when you are below 1,500 ft RA and a wind shear is detected that causes the airplane's airspeed to suddenly drop 10 knots or more because of a decrease in headwind or an increase in tailwind.

Flight Simulator is not equipped with GPWS. However, with the help of Wilco van Deijl's add-on GPWS 6.0 adventure program on this book's CD-ROM, you can simulate the GPWS quite well in Flight Simulator.

Electronic Flight Instrumentation Systems

The term "glass cockpit" is used to describe modern cockpits, with their computerized flat panel displays. These systems are replacing the instrument panel's electromechanical dials and gauges with high-tech wizardry that consolidates all the flight data into one or two CRT (cathode ray tube) or LCD (liquid crystal display) monitors (Figure 4.44). EFIS, or electronic flight instrumentation systems, have largely been responsible for the replacement of the engineer in contemporary airplanes. As a result, you will find that almost all flight decks are staffed by only two pilots: the captain and the first officer. The overhead panel above the captain and pilot contains controls for all the automated systems that were formerly the domain of the engineer. These panel controls include cabin pressurization and temperature controls, engine fire controls,

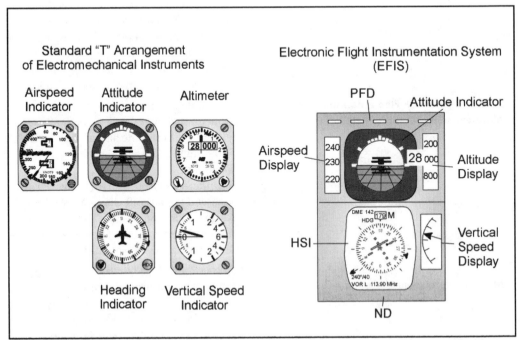

Figure 4.44 *EFIS primary flight display (PFD) is organized in the same standard T layout used with electromechanical instrument panels.*

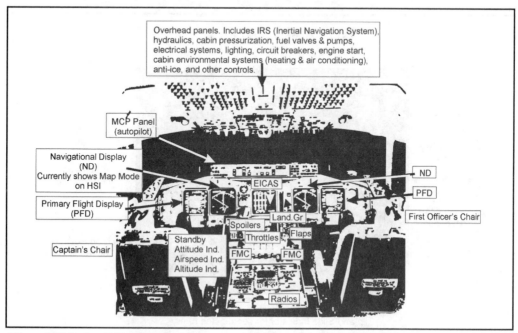

Figure 4.45 Boeing 747-400 glass cockpit with EFIS. The displays used are CRTs; the new Boeing 777 uses color LCD displays. (Courtesy of Boeing)

engine start, inertial navigation, hydraulic system monitoring and controls, electrical system monitoring and controls, emergency and standby power, fuel system temperature, fuel cross-feed valves, and anti-ice and other malfunction warning lights.

Some aircraft use very limited EFIS, perhaps, including only an HSI (horizontal situation indicator). Other aircraft, such as the Boeing 777 and Airbus A-320, have replaced all instrumentation with flat panel displays. The new Boeing 777 uses LCD displays, whereas the Boeing 747-400 uses CRTs as shown in Figure 4.45. The main advantages of LCDs over CRTs is that they are smaller and lighter, generate less heat, require less cooling, and are much clearer to read.

EFIS has many advantages over the electromechanical dials and gauges it replaces. For one thing, it allows the pilot to display many different kinds of information, including navaids, moving maps, airports, and weather radar data. A push of a button displays reams of data that would take far more panel space if the data were individually instrumented. Along with airspeed, altitude, Mach number, heading, and so on, the EFIS can also display engine data using EICAS. The EICAS can display aircraft system diagrams, and the pilot can selectively zoom in on aircraft subsystems for in-flight trouble diagnosis.

Figure 4.46 shows the 737-400 PFD.

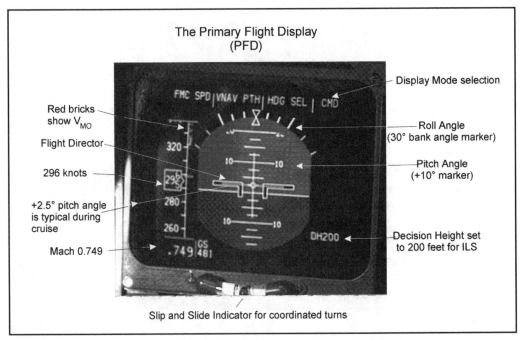

Figure 4.46 *Primary flight display on the 737-400. (Courtesy of Just Planes Videos)*

AIR TRAFFIC AND THE ENVIRONMENT: GLOBAL IMPLICATIONS

With the growing demand for air transportation, the ICAO (International Civil Aviation Organization) recently wrote:

> "...the number of passengers carried yearly by the world's airlines approximated one fifth of the world's population. Almost a quarter (by value) of world trade manufactured goods is now carried by air and the portion is growing. Airline fleets grew significantly in parallel with continuing traffic growth."

Although the share of air transportation in the total freight transport mix of intermodal rail, shipping, and trucking is still small, there are reasons to take seriously the emission of air pollutants by aircraft. For one thing, the emission of hydrocarbon exhausts at high altitudes in the atmosphere has a much more profound effect on the environment than it does at lower altitudes. Also, the fuel consumption of air traffic is expected to grow worse and not better, with new plans to build supersonic commercial air transport, and hypersonic space transport in addition to the increased subsonic commercial air transport fleet.

The global changes wrought by human activities have been well publicized over the past decade with the discovery of the chlorofluorocarbon-induced ozone hole in the polar regions. These manufactured refrigerants were floating up through the lower atmosphere to the stratosphere, where they were implicated in the destruction of the vital ozone layer needed to protect the Earth's fragile ecosystem from the onslaught of the sun's destructive ultraviolet radiation. Photoplankton, plants, animals, and even humans were affected by the high-energy photons disrupting molecular bonds of organic matter as well as causing genetic mutations.

Global warming, or the "greenhouse effect," also became an ecological issue of the 1990s. The rapid rise in carbon dioxide levels in the atmosphere has been linked to the burning of fossil fuels. The subtle temperature rise around the world meant that the polar ice caps would melt, raising sea levels worldwide and flooding coastal regions. Even more sinister, the seasons were thought to be changing, with spring arriving earlier. In time, the changes in global weather patterns could very well have potentially catastrophic effects on agriculture and wildlife and ultimately, on human beings.

The Contribution of Jet Contrails to Global Warming

Surprisingly, recent research indicates that water vapor injected high into the atmosphere by jet aircraft engines contributes significantly to the greenhouse effect. Those jet contrails you see in the atmosphere consist mostly of water vapor. They contribute to cloud formation, and that in turn helps trap heat near the Earth's surface. Water vapor (H_2O), by far the most important greenhouse gas of the atmosphere, is also a product of the burning of kerosene by jet aircraft (1.25 tons of H_2O produced per ton of kerosene burned). In addition to water vapor, jet exhaust consists of carbon dioxide (CO_2), nitrogen oxides ($NO_X = NO + NO_2$), carbon monoxide (CO), a variety of hydrocarbons (HC), and small particulate matter (a major cause of lung disease).

The first research studies of the potential environmental impact of commercial fleets of aircraft flying high in the stratosphere were done in the early 1970s (Harrison 1970; Johnston 1971 and 1989). A recent Lawrence Livermore study (Wuebbles and Kinnison) came to the following conclusions:

1. Current aircraft emissions may be having an impact on upper tropospheric ozone, leading to increasing concentrations of ozone in the upper troposphere.
2. A matrix of high speed civil transport (HSCT, or SSTs) scenarios evaluated over a wide range of flight altitudes and magnitudes of NO_X emissions confirmed previous analyses showing that ozone destruction increases as the emissions of NO_X increase and as the altitude of injection increases.
3. Model calculations indicate that a major reduction in emissions would allow the stratosphere to recover to unperturbed conditions in about a decade.
4. Sensitivity studies indicate that water vapor emissions have a moderate effect on the change in total ozone, whereas carbon monoxide emissions have a negligible effect. Water vapor emissions should be considered in all future evaluations of HSCT fleets.

Fuel Consumption and Pollutants

The pollutant emissions from subsonic aircraft while in cruise flight have a relatively insignificant impact on air quality compared with those of supersonic aircraft operating in the stratosphere. Subsonic aircraft fly at altitudes of less than 40,000 ft, where normal atmospheric circulation acts to reduce and disperse concentrations of pollutants rather quickly. On the other hand, supersonic transports fly at altitudes of 65,000 ft and higher, a region where engine exhaust products can linger for years because of the very low levels of circulation characteristic of the stratosphere. Over a period of years, the accumulation of noxious products from the operation of a fleet of SSTs, could reach enormous totals. This concern was one of the main reasons for cancellation of the U.S. SST development program in March 1971.

In 1971, the U.S. Department of Transportation was concerned enough about the environmental impact of stratospheric supersonic aircraft exhaust that it financed a study on SSTs. It was learned that a fleet 500 SSTs would reduce global ozone by about 3%, although researchers considered only the effect of radicals derived from water vapor in the exhaust. Later it was determined that NO_X from the exhaust would linger in the atmosphere for as long as two years and would contribute to a decline of as much as 16% of the global ozone (NASA 1991). This value is far greater than the worst case scenarios for continued emission of chlorofluorocarbons.

Table 4.12 Comparison of Emissions: Subsonic Transport Aircraft Burning Jet A Kerosene Versus Liquid Hydrogen (Brewer 1991)

EMISSION PRODUCT	ENGINE POWER SETTING	JET A (G/KG OF FUEL BURNED)	LIQUID HYDROGEN (G/KG OF FUEL BURNED)
CO	Idle	30	0
Unburned Hydrocarbons	Idle	4	0
Smoke	Takeoff	15*	0
NO_X	Takeoff	12	4.28
Odors	Ground Operations	Noticeable	None
H_2O	Cruise	41.9 lb/nm**	82.4 lb/nm**

* Society of Automotive Engineers smoke number
** Calculated for Mach 0.85, 400-passenger airplane with 5,500-nm range.

Table 4.13 Fuel Consumption and Pollution for the World's Scheduled Airlines

FUEL CONSUMPTION AND POLLUTION	CONSUMED/PRODUCED IN 1988	CONSUMED/PRODUCED IN 2000
Fuel Consumption (10^6 metric tons)	150.0	300.0
CO_2 (10^6 metric tons)	470.0	920.0
H_2O (10^6 metric tons)	190.0	360.0
C (10^3 metric tons)	2.6	4.7
C_XH_Y (10^3 metric tons)	90.0	175.0
CO (10^3 metric tons)	270.0	515.0
N_XO_Y (10^3 metric tons)	1,515.0	3,110.0
SO_2 (10^3 metric tons)	150.0	300.0

As a result of these studies, the American SST was shelved, although the French-British Concorde Consortium went ahead with the construction of the Concorde SST. New plans are afoot for a new fleet of SSTs with hydrocarbon-fueled low-emission engines or with exotic hydrogen-fueled engines to address the concerns of ozone depletion in the upper atmosphere.

World's Oil Reserves

A current concern for aviation is the future availability of oil. In only 109 years—from 1859 to 1968—the first 200 billion barrels of world oil were consumed. Since 1968, world oil consumption rates have stabilized at about 22 billion barrels per year (60 million barrels per day), of which aviation consumes about 5.3%, or 1.175 billion barrels (3.2 million barrels per day). Table 4.14 displays the distribution of the world's remaining oil supplies by region. The total world endowment of oil is about 2.3 trillion barrels. Of this amount, 77% has already been discovered and 30% has already been produced and consumed. If this estimate proves to be accurate, only 1.6 trillion barrels of oil remain in the ground. At current oil consumption rates, the world's oil supply will last only until the year 2075.

Table 4.14 World's Oil Supply by Region

REGION	OIL ALREADY CONSUMED*	REMAINING OIL IN PROVEN RESERVES*	ESTIMATED UNDISCOVERED OIL RESERVES*	TOTAL OIL ENDOWMENT (TOTAL OIL = OIL CONSUMED + PROVEN RESERVES + UNDISCOVERED RESERVES)*
North America	202	106	121	429
South America	74	93	44	211
Western Europe	23	19	28	70
Eastern Europe (including Russia)	113	104	64	281
Central Asia and Transcaucasia	16	24	39	79
Middle East	194	666	122	982
Africa (including North Africa)	57	62	48	167
Oceania and Asia	45	45	81	171
Totals	**724**	**1119**	**547**	**2390**

In billions of barrels. Each barrel holds 42 gallons and weighs about 306 lb. Data interpreted from Oil & Gas Journal *and U.S. Geological Survey.*

Table 4.15 lists the 18 countries believed to have had an original oil endowment exceeding 20 billion barrels. It also shows the concentration of world oil reserves, the amount of oil already consumed since the fields were first developed, and the remaining proven and estimated reserves. These 18 countries account for 86% of the world's oil production and hold 94% of its reserves. In addition, these countries are projected to have 82% of the world's remaining undiscovered oil resources and are estimated to have contained 89% of the world's original oil endowment.

Table 4.15 World's Oil Supplies by Country*

COUNTRY	OIL ALREADY CONSUMED**	REMAINING OIL IN PROVEN RESERVES**	ESTIMATED UNDISCOVERED OIL RESERVES**	TOTAL OIL ENDOWMENT (OIL CONSUMED + PROVEN RESERVES + UNDISCOVERED RESERVES)**
Saudi Arabia	71.5	261.2	41.0	373.7
United States	165.8	50.7	49.0	265.5
Russia	92.6	100.0	68.0	260.6
Iraq	22.8	100.0	45.0	167.8
Iran	42.9	93.0	22.0	157.9
Venezuela	47.3	83.3	17.0	147.6
Kuwait	27.6	97.5	3.0	128.1
United Arab Emirates	15.1	98.2	7.0	120.3
Mexico	20.5	50.4	37.0	107.9
China	18.8	24.0	48.0	90.8
Canada	16.1	5.1	33.0	54.2
Libya	19.0	22.8	8.0	49.8
Kazakhstan	3.2	17.3	26.0	46.5
Nigeria	15.5	17.9	9.0	42.4
Indonesia	15.2	5.8	10.0	31.0
Norway	6.3	11.3	13.0	30.6
United Kingdom	12.3	4.6	11.0	27.9
Algeria	9.1	9.2	2.0	20.3
Totals	**621.6**	**1052.3**	**449.0**	**2122.9**

Only those countries with oil endowments exceeding 20 billion barrels are listed.
**In billions of barrels. Each barrel holds 42 gallons and weighs about 306 lb. Data interpreted from* Oil & Gas Journal *and U.S. Geological Survey.*

If air commerce is expected to grow and flourish in the next century, new types of fuel not based on fossil-fuel hydrocarbons must be developed. Current research centers on hydrogen-fueled engines that could be refueled with renewable hydrogen obtained by electrolysis of water either by solar energy or some other renewable energy resource. However, problems with hydrogen-fueled aircraft abound. For one thing, the volume of fuel needed for a flight is much greater for hydrogen-fueled aircraft, and cryogenic handling and storage of liquid hydrogen are more difficult than with liquid hydrocarbons. Second, a shift to hydrogen-based fuel would require retooling of the energy infrastructure, and the expense of producing hydrogen using renewable energy is greater than that of producing oil. All these factors will inhibit the growth of a hydrogen-based air transport system, but at some point the shift will have to be made. Fortunately, there seem to be few technological barriers to using hydrogen as a jet fuel in turbofans, so the main problem lies in the production of hydrogen and the storage of it aboard the aircraft.

In the interim, liquid methane (CH_4) or synthetic jet fuel derived from coal could be used as aviation fuel. The world has an abundant supply of coal, enough to last many generations.

Sometime in the next century, we will realize that fossil fuels, being a nonrenewable resource, are far too precious a commodity to burn for transportation. But transportation is only one of the many other uses for which oil is squandered. Other wasteful practices include desalinization plants that transform deserts into agricultural oases in the Middle East and nitrogen fertilizer production, which uses vast quantities of oil for agriculture. In effect, we are converting oil into food. Sustaining agricultural production into the next century will be a problem when oil production declines.

Many people believe that the world should preserve current oil stocks for the production of essentials that cannot be produced without oil, such as plastics, pharmaceuticals, and specialized chemicals. What happens in the next century when we no longer have the resources to produce the essential parts for our technological civilization? Someday, future generations will look back in horror at the uses to which we put oil today. They may even view our wasteful oil consumption practices as a crime against humanity.

Future Engine Technologies and Aircraft

The allure of supersonic and even hypersonic air travel has been a dream of aircraft designers for decades. Table 4.16 reveals the dramatic reduction of travel time with supersonic and hypersonic flight.

Figure 4.47 *Future high-speed civil transport (HSCT) approaches San Francisco International Airport. (Courtesy of NASA)*

Table 4.16 *Times for Subsonic, Supersonic, and Hypersonic Air Travel for Typical Destinations*

ROUTE	BOEING 747 (SUBSONIC) (HOURS)	CONCORDE (MACH 2) (HOURS)	MACH 6 HSCT (HOURS)
Los Angeles to Tokyo	9.6	6.2*	2.0
Los Angeles to Paris	9.8	—	2.7
Los Angeles to New York	4.6	4.5**	1.6
New York to Paris	6.5	3.5	2.0
Paris to Rio de Janeiro	10.0	$6.2^{\dagger}$	2.5

Requires refueling in Hawaii.
** *The Concorde is restricted to flying subsonic speeds while over populated areas, because it flies at 65,000 ft and the sonic boom it creates can be heard on the ground. No such restriction would apply to Mach 6+ hypersonic aircraft, because the vehicle would fly at a much higher altitude and the resulting sonic boom pressure would not be disturbing at ground level.*
†*Requires refueling in Dakar.*

Future hypersonic aircraft will have to use hydrogen fuel to power their engines. Hydrocarbon fuels are too dirty and pose too many problems for the engine design, whereas hydrogen is clean-burning, does not leave any carbon residue, does not contribute to the CO_2 or CO emissions blamed for the greenhouse effect, and combusts faster—an important consideration at high velocities. Unfortunately, at standard atmospheric pressure, hydrogen is a gas with extremely low density, and it cannot be stored in sufficient quantities (or in small enough spaces) in fuel tanks without refrigerating it until it is a liquid. It must therefore be cryogenically stored as a liquid on the airplane.

Why not just compress hydrogen gas until you have enough fuel to carry on board the airplane? This is not possible, because even at extremely high pressures, such as when gaseous hydrogen is stored at 2,400 psi at 60° F, it has a low density of 0.787 lb/ft³. Contrasted with jet fuel, which has a density of 50 lb/ft³, this is far too little fuel for the volume of space required. The hydrogen fuel load would require 5.6 times as much volume if it were carried in gaseous form instead of as a liquid. Currently, no pressurized container can safely store sufficient hydrogen gas at the pressures required. To illustrate the difficulty of storing highly pressurized gas, a story is told about a technician who was lightly tapping his ballpoint pen against a highly pressurized container of rocket fuel when a tiny leak occurred. The hole in the tank was only a pinpoint prick, but the fuel streamed out with such high velocity that it sliced off the technician's fingertip.

The volume problem, combined with the high-pressure storage problem and the weight of the container, rules out gaseous hydrogen as a viable candidate for aircraft application. It is practical to carry hydrogen fuel on transport aircraft only as a saturated liquid—that is at a combination of pressure and temperature in which the vapor is saturated and in equilibrium with its liquid.

All future hydrogen-powered aircraft and spacecraft will have to use liquid hydrogen. There is simply no other alternative.

Gaseous hydrogen must be cooled to -423° F before it will become a liquid at standard atmospheric pressure. This requirement is a challenge for aircraft designers, because they will have to develop new fuel tank storage technology with cryogenic units capable of keeping the fuel cold even in hot desert climates. In addition, the fuel tank will have to be evacuated of all air while hydrogen is in the tank, because the cold temperatures in the tank will cause air to freeze.

As shown in Table 4.17, liquid hydrogen is much lighter, pound for pound, than Jet-A fuel, but it offers a higher energy output per pound of fuel burned. The principal by-product of its combustion with air is water along with trace amounts of NO_X due to the intermixing of atmospheric gases during the burning process.

Table 4.17 *Properties of Hydrogen, Liquid Methane, and Jet-A Fuel*

PROPERTY	HYDROGEN	LIQUID METHANE	JET-A OR SYNJET*
Molecular makeup	H_2	CH_4	$CH_{1.93}$
Molecular weight	2.016	16.04	168
Heat of combustion			
kJ/g	120	50	42.8
(Btu/lb)	51,590	21,500	18,400
Liquid density			
g/cm^3	0.071	0.423	0.811
lb/ft^3	4.43	26.4	50.6
Boiling point (transition temperature between liquid and gas)			
K (Kelvin)	20.27	112	440–539
°F	-423°	-258°	332°–510°
Freezing point (transition between gas and solid)			
K	14.4	91	233
°F	-434°	-296°	-41°

*Synjet fuel is similar to the Jet-A fuel now used in aircraft except that is synthesized from coal.

A comparison of aircraft fueled by hydrogen, liquid methane, and Jet-A or synjet fuel is presented in Table 4.18. All three aircraft were designed using identical technology and guidelines to accomplish the same mission, and to meet the same operational requirements. Note that the hydrogen design is superior to the other designs in that it has a lower gross weight, lower fuel weight, lower operating empty weight, and lower engine thrust requirement.

Table 4.18 *Comparison of Long-Range Aircraft Designed to Use Alternative Fuels**

PARAMETER	HYDROGEN-FUELED AIRCRAFT	LIQUID METHANE-FUELED AIRCRAFT	JET-A OR SYNJET**
Gross weight			
kg	249,400	497,770	476,230
lb	549,830	1,097,370	1,049,900
Block fuel weight			
kg	50,740	194,750	212,120
lb	111,860	429,350	467,640

(continued)

Table 4.18 *(continued) Comparison of Long-Range Aircraft Designed to Use Alternative Fuels**

PARAMETER	HYDROGEN-FUELED AIRCRAFT	LIQUID METHANE-FUELED AIRCRAFT	JET-A OR SYNJET**
Volume of fuel			
liters	715,015	460,522	261,701
gallons	188,887	121,657	69,134
Wing loading			
kg/m²	634.7	649.3	681.5
lb/ft²	116.6	133	139.6
Wing area			
m²	438.1	766.5	698.7
ft²	4716	8251	7521
Wing span			
m	66.2	89.6	87.7
ft	217.2	294	287.6
Fuselage length			
m	80.5	70.1	68.6
ft	264	229.9	225
Lift to drag ratio at cruise			
L/D	19.3	21.86	22.84
Specific fuel consumption			
lb/(h lb)	0.202	0.492	0.601
Thrust to weight			
N/kg	2.69	2.62	2.62
T_{lb}/W_{lb}	0.274	0.267	0.267
Thrust per engine (four Engines per aircraft)			
N	165,530	325,820	311,720
lb	37,663	73,250	70,081
Price per aircraft			
($ million)	58.54	85.21	73.07

*Future 400-passenger, 10,000-nm, Mach 0.85 aircraft
**Synjet fuel is similar to the Jet-A fuel now used in aircraft except that is synthesized from coal.

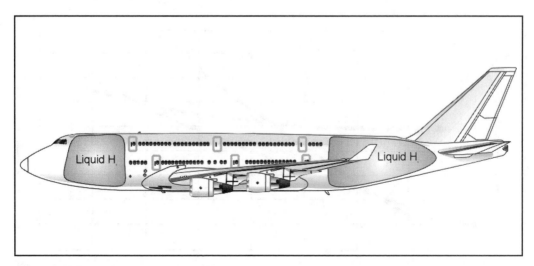

Figure 4.48 *Future hydrogen-powered 400-passenger airplane. Large fuel tanks will require storage fore and aft as shown.*

Moreover, for the hydrogen-powered design, the wing area and wing-span are smaller but the fuselage is larger and longer than the conventional airplane. The specific fuel consumption is three times less for the hydrogen design versus the Jet-A–synfuel design. This means that the hydrogen-powered airplane uses three times less fuel per hour during cruise to deliver a given level of thrust than the Jet–A powered airplane. As a consequence, less weight in fuel is required and lower-thrust engines can be used to power the hydrogen-fueled airplane. Note, however, that the hydrogen design requires three times the volume of fuel than does the equivalent Jet-A design (188,887 gallons of fuel for the hydrogen-designed airplane versus 69,134 gallons required for the conventionally fueled airplane). Because liquid hydrogen weighs less than one-tenth the weight by volume of Jet-A fuel, the hydrogen plane's fuel actually weighs less than the Jet-A fuel in the conventional airplane. The problem, however, is the larger volume required to store the hydrogen fuel as well as the cryogenics needed for cooling. Figure 4.48 illustrates where the fuel tanks might be located on a hydrogen-powered aircraft.

The Comeback of Propeller Planes

Subsonic air travel is also undergoing a renaissance. In their quest for higher thrust and more-fuel-efficient engines, engine designers have rediscovered the turboprop. During the fuel embargo of the 1970s, research was begun by NASA and others on advanced turboprop propellers for application to high subsonic speed. Manufacturers were already producing efficient turbofans with high bypass ratios that surpassed turbojets in fuel

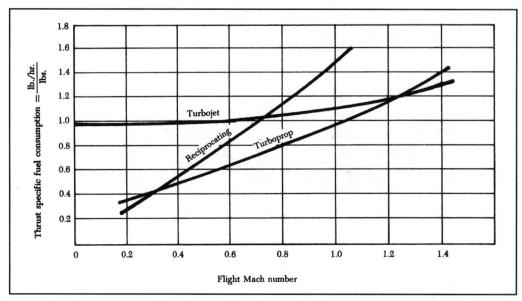

Figure 4.49 *Comparison of fuel consumption for the reciprocating engine, turbojet, and turboprop.*

economy and amount of thrust delivered. Because a turboprop is, in effect, an extension of a turbofan with a higher bypass ratio (and without a ducted fan shroud), it was discovered that new propeller designs enabled the design of engines with even greater fuel efficiency. It turns out that turboprops are much more efficient at speeds as high as Mach 0.8 than turbofans and turbojets. Figure 4.49 compares the fuel consumption of the reciprocating engine, the turbojet, and the turboprop at various Mach speeds.

The major drawback of propjet technology is noise. Interior cabin noise and external noise are much greater than those of turbofan-powered jets. Designers are experimenting with ducted prop shrouds to reduce noise, so we may see turboprop engines with large nacelles shielding the propeller from view.

Advances in Noise Reduction

The intensity of sound is measured in logarithmic units known as decibels (dB). A 20 decibel change represents a 100-fold increase in the sound level and a 10 decibel change represents a 10-fold increase. At a level of 80 decibels, sound is annoying; but steady exposure to noise in excess of 90 decibels—a level that is often exceeded by common urban sounds, such as jackhammers, jet planes, and excessively loud music—can cause permanent loss of hearing (Table 4.19).

Table 4.19 Sound Levels

TYPE OF SOUND	INTENSITY*	DECIBELS
Artillery fire at close proximity (threshold of pain)	10	130
Amplified rock music; near jet engine; orchestra on stage	1	120
Loud orchestral music heard by audience	10^{-1}	110
Electric saw	10^{-2}	100
Bus or truck interior	10^{-3}	90
Automobile interior	10^{-4}	80
Average street noise; loud telephone bell	10^{-5}	70
Normal conversation; business office	10^{-6}	60
Restaurant; private office	10^{-7}	50
Quiet room in home	10^{-8}	40
Quiet lecture hall; bedroom	10^{-9}	30
Radio, television, or recording studio	10^{-10}	20
Soundproof room	10^{-11}	10
Absolute silence (threshold of hearing)	10^{-12}	0

In watts per square meter

Pilots are not immune from the destructive influence of engine noise. The drone of small aircraft engines and the turbine whine of helicopter engines is loud enough that many pilots now wear electronic sound-canceling headsets. These headsets monitor the incoming sound frequencies and produce a sound wave that is exactly 180° out of phase with the incoming engine sounds. When the two sound waves meet, they cancel each other out, thereby reducing the volume of sound that the pilot hears.

In addition to causing loss of hearing, there is evidence that noise can produce stress and other harmful effects on human health.

Noise pollution has received increasing attention with the advent of supersonic jet airplanes and the vast expansion of air travel using turbine-powered aircraft. Older turbojet aircraft, such as the Boeing 707 and 727, as well as the 737-100 and 737-200, have had to be retrofitted with hush kits to meet the new FAA-mandated community airport noise standards. In addition, many airports require that pilots follow special noise reduction procedures during takeoffs and landings to minimize the impact to neighboring communities. Some pilots are incensed that they must abide by these regulations, because they feel that passenger safety is compromised when they are forced to follow labyrinthine landing and takeoff procedures that often require them to throttle back the engines to minimum thrust levels.

New jet aircraft must now meet Stage 3 noise levels as defined in Table 4.20. Stage 1 and Stage 2 aircraft are gradually being phased out or retrofitted with hush kits to meet Stage 3 standards.

Table 4.20 *Noise Limitations*

STAGE	NOISE LIMITATION
Stage 2	Takeoff: 108 dB for maximum weights of 600,000 lb or more, reduced by 5 dB per halving of the 600,000 lb maximum weight down to 93 dB for maximum weights of 75,000 lb or less.
Stage 3	Takeoff (Airplanes with more than three engines): 106 dB for maximum weight of 850,000 lb or more, reduced by 4 dB per halving of the 850,000 lb maximum weight down to 89 dB for maximum weights of 44,673 lb.
Stage 3	Takeoff (airplanes with three engines): 104 dB for maximum weights of 850,000 lb down to 89 dB for maximum weights of 44,673 lb.
Stage 3	Takeoff (airplanes with two engines): 101 dB for maximum weights of 850,000 lb or more, reduced by 4 dB per halving of the 850,000 lb maximum weight down to 89 dB for maximum weights of 106,250 lb.

Pilots operating the Cessna 182 under VFR over outdoor assemblies of persons, recreational and park areas, and other noise sensitive areas, should make every effort to fly at least 2,000 ft or higher above the surface. The certificated noise level for the Cessna 182 at 3,100 lbs weight is 72.1 dB with a two-bladed propeller or 70.5 dB with a three-bladed propeller. Table 4.21 shows guidelines for tolerable noise exposure.

Table 4.21 *Ear Protection Guidelines: Allowable Exposure Time for Noise in dB per Work Day*

EAR PROTECTION DEVICE	EXPOSURE TIME IN HOURS						
	0.25	**0.5**	**1**	**2**	**4**	**6**	**8**
No protection	115 dB	110 dB	105 dB	100 dB	95 dB	92 dB	90 dB
Ear plugs	127 dB	122 dB	117 dB	112 dB	107 dB	104 dB	102 dB
Ear plugs and ear muffs	135 dB	130 dB	125 dB	120 dB	115 dB	112 dB	110 dB

5

The Atmosphere

This chapter discusses the atmosphere and weather and how they affect your actions as a pilot. Although this topic is complex, we'll use examples to help you understand the role played by temperature, air pressure, air density, and wind in determining your aircraft's performance.

WHAT IS THE ATMOSPHERE?

The atmosphere on which we all depend for life is a fragile cocoon that surrounds the Earth in a layer less than 62 miles thick. This thin band of gas is only 1.5% of the Earth's radius (3,963 miles); if you were looking at the fringes of the Earth from space, you would barely discern the layer that makes up our atmosphere. Yet the atmosphere, more than any other natural phenomenon, affects the weather and the seasons so profoundly with that we spend many billions of dollars each year studying and trying to predict its behavior. Air travel, agriculture, ocean commerce, and most other outdoor activities are influenced by the subtle changes in pressure, temperature, and air density that happen diurnally as well as seasonally on a global basis. We'll study the basic facts about the atmosphere so that we can better understand how it affects aviation.

Where space begins is the first topic for consideration. Because of the gravitational pull of the Earth, approximately one-half of the Earth's atmosphere lies below an altitude of three miles (15,840 ft), although it extends as high as 62 miles. Yet there are different definitions of where the atmosphere ends and space begins. Aeronautical engineers regard the beginning of space at about 62 miles above the Earth's surface, because in this region aerodynamic forces of lift and drag can be ignored. Propulsion engineers regard space as beginning 28 miles above the Earth's surface, because only rockets can operate beyond this altitude. Bioengineers responsible for environmental life-support systems regard space as occurring 15 miles above the Earth's surface, because people traveling in this region must bring their own environmental supplies of oxygen and pressure; they cannot efficiently extract outside air for cabin pressurization.

Consider also the effects of altitude on people. At an altitude of 10,000 ft, the oxygen pressure of the atmosphere is not great enough to keep people working efficiently over a long period. For example, astronomers working at an elevation of 13,780 ft at the Keck telescope of the Mauna Kea Observatory in Hawaii tire easily and have trouble remembering things. For this reason, most astronomers prefer to work remotely with the telescope, either from their own offices thousands of miles away or from the ground control facilities located at Waimea at the base of the volcano. People can become acclimatized to altitudes of 10,000 ft or higher over time; the Sherpas of the Himalayan mountain regions of Nepal routinely live at altitudes of 12,000 ft to 17,000 ft. But individuals accustomed to near-sea-level pressure will find the oxygen pressure insufficient above 10,000 ft and must rely on supplemental oxygen or cabin pressurization. Without the supplemental oxygen, the dangerous effects of hypoxia set in. The oxygen saturation of the blood is deficient, and the functions of the various tissues and organs, including the brain, are impaired.

The first symptoms of hypoxia are misleadingly pleasant, resembling mild intoxication from alcohol. The brain's higher faculties are soon dulled, and normal self-critical ability is knocked out. After a point, the mind no longer functions properly; the hands and feet become clumsy without the person being aware of it. Drowsiness, euphoria, headache, overconfidence in one's abilities, dizziness, lightheadedness, and sometimes aggressive behavior are common symptoms. If the afflicted individual is not brought quickly to a lower altitude, unconsciousness and death may follow. The higher the altitude, the more quickly a person can fall prey to the insidious effects of hypoxia. For example, as shown in Table 5.1, at 35,000 ft a person can expect to remain conscious only for 30 to 60 seconds. To guard against an explosive decompression of the airplane at high altitude, which can incapacitate the pilots within seconds, FAA regulations require that whenever a crew member leaves the cockpit of an airliner, the remaining crew member must don an oxygen mask.

Table 5.1 *Time of Consciousness without Supplemental Oxygen for Various Altitudes*

ALTITUDE (FT)	TIME OF USEFUL CONSCIOUSNESS
15,000	30 min +
22,000	5–10 min
30,000	1–2 min
35,000	30–60 seconds
40,000	15–20 seconds
50,000	6–9 seconds

At 9 miles altitude (47,500 ft), even supplemental oxygen will fail to support life, so people must rely on cabin pressurization or pressure suits. The combined pressure of carbon dioxide and water vapor in the lungs equals the outside atmospheric pressure, and the body's diaphragms cannot exert enough force to enable breathing in the lungs.

At 15 miles altitude (79,200 ft), cabin pressurization using engine bleed to compress air is no longer effective. At this altitude, the air density is 1/27th of the value at sea level. Compressing the thin air, although not impossible, is troublesome because of undesirable heat transfer to the air and because the ozone levels at this altitude are high enough to poison the cabin atmosphere. Therefore, above 15 miles you need a supply of both oxygen and pressure that is independent of the outside atmosphere. Airplanes traveling this high must have a sealed environment containing all the necessary supplies to maintain life.

Fully pressurizing a 747 adds a ton of weight to the airplane.

N O T E

Now consider the upper region of atmosphere, which is the exclusive domain of the propulsion engineer. Five miles farther out, at 20 miles altitude (105,600 ft), turbojets cannot operate, and ramjets must be used for propulsion. *Ramjets* work like turbojets except that ramjets have no blades. The front of the ramjet gulps in air, and the high speed of the plane squeezes a maximum amount of air into the combustion chamber, compensating for the lower oxygen levels found at higher altitudes. Ramjets can work at speeds as high as Mach 6 and 8, at which point *scramjets* (supersonic combustion ramjets) must take over. Scramjets can carry planes to speeds of Mach 20 and lift them to about 28 miles, where, to a propulsion engineer, the beginning of space occurs since rockets must be used above this altitude. Both ramjets and scramjets are envisioned as future aerospace suborbital planes that could be used to ferry passengers halfway across the planet in an hour or two or even to attain orbit. But to enter space, rocket engines are needed. They kick the plane's speed up to Mach 25 to give it the necessary velocity to sustain orbit.

At 62 miles altitude, the aerospace engineer regards the effects of the atmosphere as negligible on vehicle design. This means that there is no drag and no lift, so the vehicle does not need to be streamlined (unless the vehicle is intended to reenter the atmosphere). But is this truly "space," a region of nothingness and vacuum? The answer is no. Surprising amounts of matter and energy fill this void; for example, the particle density of atmospheric molecules from 50 miles to 600 miles out averages a million particles per cubic centimeter (contrasted with a million million million particles per cubic centimeter at sea level, or $10^{18}/cm^3$). From 600 to 1,200 miles, there are approximately 100 particles per cubic centimeter. Even the Russian Mir space station needs a periodic rocket boost (as will the Space Station Freedom) to maintain orbit because of the drag force imposed by these particles over a period of many months.

Surprisingly, the vacuum of near Earth space is not really a vacuum. There is still some residual pressure at 1200 miles above the Earth, probably 10^{-12} to 10^{-16} mm Hg, or 40×10^{-15} in. Hg to 4×10^{-18} in. Hg. This pressure is low—scientists often call it a "hard vacuum"—and it causes some interesting effects. In the atmosphere, metal is covered by at least a single layer of absorbed gas, which acts as a thin film of lubricant to keep metal surfaces apart. In a hard vacuum, this film of gas bleeds away into space, and metal surfaces that come into contact tend to weld together. Special measures must be taken to prevent this "cold welding" in space. Another interesting effect is the suppression of crack formation in metals. If a crack forms in a metallic surface when air surrounds the metal, molecules of air immediately enter the crack and chemical reaction with the metal occurs. If the chemical reaction product has more volume than the crack itself, the crack widens because of a wedging effect. In a hard vacuum, wedging does not occur because the chemical reaction cannot take place without air. Thus, some metals are stronger in space than they are on Earth.

At 100 miles above the Earth is a region of darkness and utter silence. In this region you see nothing but black sky and stars, because the atmosphere no longer scatters the sun's light. Stars appear as brilliant points of light, and there is not enough air to carry sound, shock waves, or sonic booms.

STANDARD ATMOSPHERE

The atmosphere is a mixture of several gases (see Figure 5.1). When completely dry, it is about 78% nitrogen and 21% oxygen. The remaining 1% is a mixture of other gases, mostly argon but also carbon dioxide, neon, helium, and others. However, air is never completely dry, and it can contain water vapor to as much as 5% by volume. As water vapor (clouds, humidity, and so on) increases, the other gases decrease proportionately.

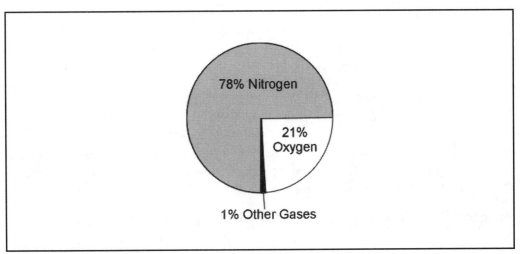

Figure 5.1 *Composition of the atmosphere.*

In the 1920s, aeronautical engineers realized that they needed to know how the properties of air changed with altitude so that they could predict the performance of airplanes. They devised a hypothetical model, or standard atmosphere model, that predicted the temperature, air pressure, and air density with the variation of altitude. In 1952, the ICAO published a standard model that assigned standard properties of the atmosphere to 65,600 ft. This model was superseded by the UNITED STATES standard atmosphere published in 1962, which essentially agrees with the ICAO model but extends the coverage to 378 miles (2,296,700 ft). The model has been updated and revised, most recently in 1976.

The standard atmosphere (StAt) assumes the following properties:

- Sea level air pressure is 2116.2 lb/ft², or 29.921 in. Hg, or 14.696 psi

Useful conversions:
1 in. Hg = 70.726 lb/ft²
1 lb/ft² = 0.014139 in. Hg
1 lb/ft² = 0.00694 psi
1 psi = 144 lb/ft²

- Sea level temperature is 518.7 R, or 59° F (15° C).
- The gravitational acceleration is 32.17 ft/sec².
- The molecular composition of the atmosphere does not vary.
- The air is dry and motionless.
- The air obeys the ideal gas law (see also Equation 3.44).

$$P = \rho kT \tag{5.1}$$

where

P = Pressure lb/ft^2
ρ = Air density sl/ft^3
k = Gas constant = 1,716 $\text{lb-ft}/\text{sl}/\text{R}$
T = Temperature in Rankine

- The temperature decreases linearly with altitude at a rate of $-3.566°$ F per thousand feet, or $-1.98°$ C per 1,000 ft (a rough approximation of $-3.5°$ F or $-2°$ C per 1,000 ft will suffice for our purposes.)

Appendix F lists all the properties of the standard atmosphere up to 108,000 ft.

CLASSIFICATION OF THE ATMOSPHERE

The atmosphere is divided into layers, or spheres, each having certain properties and characteristics (see Figure 5.2). Because most weather occurs in the troposphere and because most flying occurs in the troposphere and stratosphere, we will concern ourselves with these two layers.

The *troposphere* is the layer of air that immediately bounds the Earth's surface. It varies in depth from an average of 60,000 ft over the Equator to 28,000 ft over the poles, with greater depth occurring in summer than in winter. The temperature in the troposphere decreases with height. As you get to the top of the troposphere, you reach a boundary region, called the *tropopause*, that is sandwiched between the troposphere and the stratosphere. The tropopause can be located by a sharp temperature decrease with altitude that differs from the standard lapse rate for the rest of the troposphere. The tropopause acts as a barrier that resists the free exchange of air between the stratosphere and the troposphere. Consequently, most water vapor is found in the troposphere, and pollution from supersonic transport traveling in the stratosphere can linger for many years.

The *stratosphere* has different characteristics from those of the troposphere. In the stratosphere, temperature tends to increase with height (as opposed to the decrease encountered in the troposphere), and there is much more ozone. Ozone is a triatomic form of oxygen (O_3) that is formed naturally by the photochemical reaction of solar ultraviolet radiation with air in the stratosphere. It has a pungent odor, is irritating to the lungs, and has a slightly bluish color. Most people have heard about the destruction of the ozone layer by chlorofluorocarbons (commonly used in refrigerants such as Freon), something that is bad for the environment because ozone screens out the harmful ultraviolet rays from the sun. Although ozone at high altitudes is good, man-

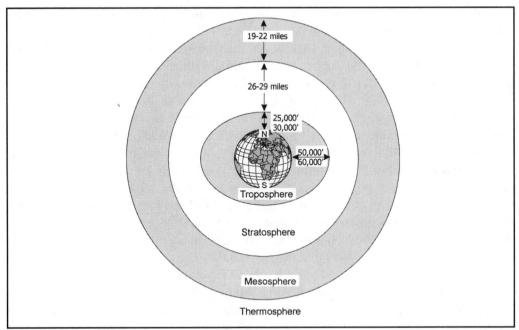

Figure 5.2 Atmospheric layers.

made ozone at lower altitudes is a major agent in the formation of smog and is considered a nuisance.

TEMPERATURE IN THE ATMOSPHERE

We have already seen that temperature can be measured by different temperature scales, such as Fahrenheit, Celsius, and Rankine. In Chapter 3 (Equations 3.25, 3.26, and 3.37), you learned how to convert temperatures between the different scales. Temperature is important to pilots because it is used to determine aircraft performance parameters, including airspeed and altitude. But what is temperature? Most people would agree that temperature is a measure of heat energy. Physicists, however, regard temperature as not only a measure of heat energy but also as an indicator of the amount of molecular activity and radiation emission by an object. Molecules that have more kinetic energy vibrate more and, when very hot, emit electromagnetic radiation in the form of infrared light. The vibration disturbs nearby molecules and causes them to vibrate. The infrared radiation is caused by electrons jumping from one orbital state to another by the excited state of the vibrating atom. When the electron changes state, it emits a photon of infrared light that then strikes nearby molecules. Both the mechanical vibration and the transfer of the electromagnetic energy make up the heat that we perceive through our senses.

Different substances have different molecular structures and so get hotter at different rates. For example, a land surface gets hotter than a water surface when equal amounts of solar heat are applied. Land also warms faster than water during the day, and it cools faster than water at night. There is thus a diurnal temperature difference between night and day that is caused by the daily rotation of the Earth. The range of temperature between night and day varies as much as 30° F to 50° F, but it is greater near the surface and less so up to an altitude of about 4,000 ft. Above 4,000 ft, there is no change in air temperature between night and day. Flight Simulator allows a diurnal variance of as much as 36° F. You switch this control on by using the Advanced Weather dialog box (**World/Weather/Temperature**) In the dialog box, click on **Day/Night** and type the temperature variation in the **Variation Range** box. If the Advanced Weather dialog box is not available, first switch it on by using the **Options/Preferences/General/Use Advanced Weather dialog** menu command. Unfortunately, during the late beta testing of FS98, there was an unresolved problem with the temperature variation not cutting off at 4,000 ft. Another problem was that the diurnal (day-night) temperature variation was not correctly modeled on the 737 and Learjet TAT (total air temperature) gauge.

Temperature directly affects air density. When it is hot, air density is low; when it is cold, air density is high. Thus, temperature indirectly affects the aircraft's maximum takeoff weight, because lift is proportional to air density. When air density is low, less lift is generated; when it is high, more lift is generated (see Table 5.2). When an aircraft takes off at night or in the early morning when temperatures are cooler, it can take off with more weight than it could in the early afternoon when the air has warmed.

Normally, the density of air, air pressure, and temperature decreases with increasing altitude. However, in many areas of world there exist temperature inversions in which temperature increases with altitude. This condition usually occurs in regions where stable air is trapped by geographical features (such as the Los Angeles basin). Usually, this layer of temperature inversion lasts only a few thousand feet, and then the normal temperature drop of 3.56° F per 1,000 ft resumes.

Table 5.2 *The Effect of Temperature on Air Density, Lift, and the Aircraft's Pitot-Static System*

TEMPERATURE	AIR DENSITY	LIFT	PITOT-STATIC SYSTEM
Hotter than normal	Less density	Less lift; aircraft requires more thrust for a given weight and needs longer takeoff runway distance.	Altimeter shows a higher altitude than aircraft's true altitude. Airspeed indicator, when displaying IAS,

Table 5.2 continued

TEMPERATURE	AIR DENSITY	LIFT	PITOT-STATIC SYSTEM
			shows a higher airspeed than aircraft's true airspeed.
Colder than normal	Higher density	More lift; aircraft requires less thrust for a given weight and needs a shorter runway takeoff distance.	Altimeter shows a lower altitude than aircraft's true altitude. Airspeed indicator, when displaying IAS, shows a lower airspeed than the aircraft's true airspeed.

The following rule summarizes the temperature lapse rate: An increase in altitude of 1,000 ft is approximately equal to a drop of 3.5° F or 2° C.

EXAMPLE 5.1

Let's remove all the existing temperature layers in Flight Simulator and observe the temperature drop of 3.5° F per 1,000 ft as we gain altitude. It should match the figures shown in the StAt Table of Appendix F if Flight Simulator uses a standard model of the atmosphere.

Solution

Follow these steps:

1. Make sure the Advanced Weather dialog box is available. Open it via the **World/Weather** menu.
2. Select the **Temperature** tab. In the dialog box, select each temperature layer you may see and click **Remove Layer** so that there are no temperature variances from

the norm. Temperature layers are added in Flight Simulator when you want the atmosphere to depart from the normal model, and you can add as many as four different layers with varying altitudes and temperatures.

3. In the Advanced Weather Pressure dialog box (**World\Weather\Pressure**), make sure that the pressure is set to 29.92 in. Hg.

4. Return to the program. Using the **World\Goto\Airport** menu dialog box, type **Metropolitan Oakland**. (You won't need to finish typing the entire name in FS98, because the program has intelli-type sensing capability similar to that in Word 97.)

5. Once you have selected the **Metropolitan Oakland Intl** airport, click **OK** to return to the simulation.

6. Note the elevation of 0 ft on the altimeter. This means that you are within 20 ft or so of sea level. (If you press **Shift+Z** you will see the elevation as 6 ft.)

7. Observe the temperature readout in the cockpit. You will see that it is 58° F, which is the temperature that FS98 has rounded down from the StAt of 59° F. This is the StAt temperature for sea level.

8. Use the **World/Go To/Airport** dialog box and this time type **Denver**. Select **Denver Intl** airport, which is at an elevation of 5,433 ft. Notice that the temperature on the instrument panel now reads 39° F. If you consult the StAt table in Appendix F for an altitude of 5,400, you'll see that the standard temperature should be 39.8° F. Let's figure out the temperature drop from sea level via the 3.5° F per 1,000 ft rate. From 5,433 down to 0 ft we have 5.433 (thousand) ft × -3.5° F = -19° F. If we subtract 58° F minus 19° F, we get 39° F, which is what the temperature readout shows. So far so good.

9. Repeat step 8, but now choose **J.F. Kennedy Intl** in Bolivia, elevation 13,313 ft. The temperature should read 11° F on the instrument panel. The StAt table says that the temperature should be 11.6° F, and if we choose to figure out the temperature using the −3.5° F/1,000 ft method, we will see that the temperature drop from 58° F will be 13.313 (thousand) ft × -3.5° F = -46.6° F. Therefore, the temperature using this method will be 58° F − 46.6° F = 11.4° F. Our results correspond perfectly with theory.

Note that the temperature reading when the plane is flying will always be higher than the standard. You can test this by taking off from any airport and staying close to the ground. The temperature reading will rise the faster you go. Then when you land, the temperature will return to its normal value. Surface friction from the atmosphere heats the temperature probe by a few degrees. At low Mach numbers, you hardly need bother with it. Jet pilots who fly at high Mach speeds do worry about this problem, as we shall see in the next section.

If you prefer the Celsius system, Flight Simulator can display Celsius instead of Fahrenheit on the temperature readouts for the Cessna and the Bell helicopter. To change the temperature units, go to **Options/Preferences/International**. In the dialog box's **Units of Measure** list box, select **Metric (Altimeter feet)**.

You can create as many as four temperature layers per weather area. Each layer must be separated from the other layers by at least 328 ft.

NOTE

Total Air Temperature for the Boeing 737 and Learjet

True air temperature, not to be confused with total air temperature, is the basic air temperature corrected for the temperature rise due to the heat of compression and skin friction. True air temperature is also known as outside air temperature (OAT).

High-speed aircraft, such as the Boeing 737 and Learjet, have a temperature display that shows *total air temperature* (TAT) measured in degrees Celsius on the outside surface of the fuselage. (Unlike the Cessna's temperature display, the TAT can't be changed to show degrees Fahrenheit using the **Options/Preferences/ International/Metric** menu command.) The temperature probe measures the ambient

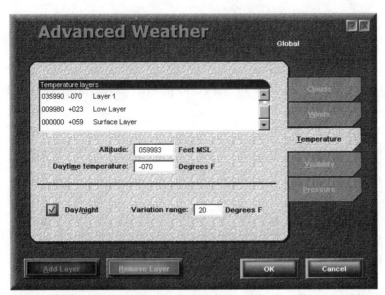

Figure 5.3 *The Advanced Weather Temperature dialog box. You can add as many as four separate temperature layers per weather area. Shown here are the temperature layers for the global weather area, which affects the whole Earth.*

outside temperature plus the rise due to air compressibility and the rise due to skin friction. At high speeds, because of surface friction and the inevitable temperature rise whenever air is compressed, the measured temperature is actually higher than the outside temperature of undisturbed air. Various performance charts for the Boeing 737 and Learjet take this difference into account; when you read the temperature on the TAT, you should understand that the TAT display will not correspond exactly with the true, or outside air temperature (OAT), shown in the standard atmosphere table of Appendix F for a given altitude. This will be made clear with the following example.

EXAMPLE 5.2

What should the TAT show for the Boeing 737 traveling at 250 knots IAS (Mach 0.41) at 5,400 ft altitude? Assume a standard temperature drop, and that the OAT at 5,400 ft is 499.4 R, or 39.8° F. What is the temperature rise due to surface friction?

Solution

Because we know that the Mach number is 0.41, we can use Equation 3.34 to solve for the surface temperature of the airplane:

$$
\begin{aligned}
T_{\text{Surface Temp in Rankine}} &= \left(1 + 0.2 M_{\text{Mach}}^2\right) T_{\text{Outside Air Temp in Rankine}} \qquad (5.2)\\
&= \left[1 + (0.2)(0.41)^2\right](499.4 \text{ R})\\
&= 516.2 \text{ R}
\end{aligned}
$$

The increase in temperature from the undisturbed atmospheric temperature of 499.4 R (39.8° F) is as follows:

$$
\Delta T = 516.2 \text{ R} - 499.4 \text{ R} = 16.8°\text{F} \qquad (5.3)
$$

Thus we have answered the second question: temperature rise due to the aircraft's 250-knot airspeed is 16.8° F.

Now if we add 16.8° F to the 39.8° F outside air temperature, we get a TAT of 56.6° F. Using Equation 3.27, we can convert to Celsius:

$$T_{\text{Celsius}} = \frac{5}{9}\left(T_{\text{Fahrenheit}} - 32°\text{F}\right) \quad\quad (5.4)$$

$$\text{TAT}_{\text{Celsius}} = \frac{5}{9}(\text{TAT}_{\text{Fahrenheit}} - 32°\text{F})$$

$$= \frac{5}{9}(56.6 - 32°\text{F})$$

$$= 13.7°\text{C}$$

The TAT on the Boeing 737 will show 14°, because the display rounds up to the nearest integer. Note that the outside temperature in Celsius for 5,400 ft altitude from the standard atmosphere table in Appendix F is 4.3° C. The resultant temperature rise due to surface friction is therefore 13.7° C – 4.3° C = 9.4° C (or, as previously mentioned, 16.8° F).

If you try to test the preceding example on the FS98 Boeing 737 (it won't work with the FSW95 737 because of bugs in the program), it will work only if you remove all temperature layers in **World/Weather/Temperature**. To get accurate readings you should set the airspeed indicator to show indicated airspeed (**Options/Preferences/Instruments/Display Indicated Airspeed**), and you should fly with the autopilot altitude hold at 5,400 ft, with the autopilot speed hold at 250 knots IAS.

In the preceding example, if your speed increased, the TAT would increase even if you maintained the same altitude. Try it and see for yourself!

PRESSURE

Atmospheric pressure is expressed in many ways around the world. The most common units are inches of mercury (Hg) and millibars, although it can also be measured in Pascals (Newtons/m²), psi (pounds per square inch), or lb/ft². U.S. aircraft altimeters, which measure air pressure, are calibrated to in. Hg, but many other nations use the millibar for altimeter settings. The mercury barometer, invented by Evangelista Torricelli in 1643, measures the height a column of mercury attains in a vacuum due to the pressure exerted by the atmosphere. As the air pressure rises, the mercury column rises higher, and the height is measured in inches of mercury. At sea level, one atmosphere of pressure is equivalent to 14.7 psi, or 29.2 in. Hg. In metric units, this is equivalent to 101.3 kilopascals, or 1,013 millibars.

Aircraft altimeters are essentially pressure measurement devices called *aneroid barometers*, but instead of displaying pressure they are calibrated to display altitude in feet. The measurement shown is independent of the terrain below, and you must not assume that the altitude you read on its display is the aircraft's true altitude above the ground. An altimeter reads accurately only in a standard atmosphere and only when the correct altimeter calibration setting is used.

Five types of altitudes are defined in aviation, as shown in Table 5.3.

Table 5.3 Types of Altitude

Type	Description
True altitude	The actual or exact altitude above mean sea level. Airport, terrain, and obstacle elevations found on aeronautical charts are true altitudes.
Indicated altitude	The altitude read from the altimeter after it is set to the current altimeter setting.
Pressure altitude	The altitude indicated when the altimeter setting window (the Kollsman window) is set to 29.92 in. Hg. This altitude is measured above the standard datum plane, a theoretical plane where air pressure is equal to 29.92 in. Hg.
Density altitude	The pressure altitude corrected for nonstandard temperature variations. Density altitude is the altitude in the StAt that corresponds to the actual air density. When standard atmospheric conditions exist, the pressure altitude and the density altitude are the same. If the temperature is higher than the standard temperature for a given altitude, the density altitude will be lower than the pressure altitude. This altitude is important, because it tells pilots who have performance charts for their airplane how much takeoff and landing distance is required for the given density altitude.
Absolute altitude	The vertical distance of the aircraft above ground level.

Density Altitude

Of the five types of altitude, the most important atmospheric factor in determining aircraft performance is density altitude. For example, pilots taking off from La Paz, Bolivia (elevation 13,313 ft) are interested in the density altitude for nonstandard temperatures, because it directly tells them whether they can take off. At this high elevation, even a small temperature variation upward from the norm can make it impossible to take off, because to reach a safe takeoff speed the airplane would need a far longer runway than exists.

How do you determine density altitude? The next example shows how.

EXAMPLE 5.3

A pilot is about to take off from Denver International, elevation 5,431 ft, temperature 90° F. The normal temperature for this altitude from the StAt table is about 40° F. When the altimeter is calibrated to read field elevation, the altimeter pressure setting shows 28 in. Hg. When the altimeter is adjusted to 29.92 in. Hg, the pressure altitude shown is 7,200 ft. What is the density altitude for these conditions?

Solution

1. Determine the actual pressure in lb/ft² from the pressure altitude, using the StAt table from Appendix F. Looking at the table, we see that for 7,200 ft pressure altitude, the pressure is 1620.7 lb/ft².
2. Calculate the absolute temperature in Rankine. Using the given temperature of 90° F, we add 90° + 460 R = 550 R (from Equation 3.25).
3. Calculate the density of the air using the ideal gas law.

$$\rho = \frac{P}{kT} = \frac{1620.7 \ \text{lb}/\text{ft}^2}{(1716)(550 \ \text{R})} = 0.001727 \ \text{sl}/\text{ft}^3 \qquad (5.5)$$

Now that we know the density, we can look up the altitude in the StAt table in Appendix F. We look up 0.001727 sl/ft³ and see that the nearest value is 0.0017280 sl/ft³. In the far left column on the same row, we see that this corresponds to an altitude of 10,500 ft. Thus, 10,500 ft is the density altitude at Denver International when the temperature is 90° F and the barometric pressure is 28 in. Hg. This is the altitude that the pilot would use in performance charts for the takeoff run.

From Example 5.3, you can see that even though the aircraft is taking off from a runway at elevation 5,431 ft, because of the hot weather and low barometric pressure the airplane will behave as if it were taking off from a runway at elevation 10,500 ft (see Figure 5.4). This is a huge difference and may make it inadvisable to take off, depending on the aircraft.

Computer Solution for Calculating Density Altitude

If you're interested in a computer solution for calculating density altitude, here is one method that works well (Hubin 1992).

1. Calculate the density of air from Equation 5.5.

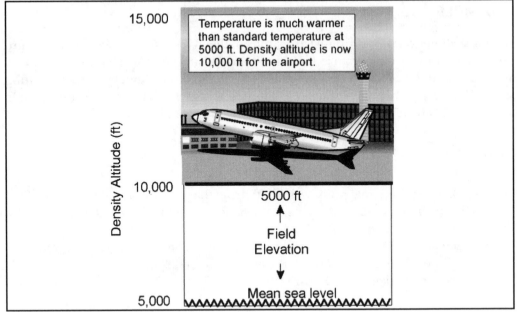

Figure 5.4 *Density altitude.*

2. Calculate the value of X, where

$$X = 0.23496 \ln\left[\frac{\rho}{0.00237692}\right] \tag{5.6}$$

3. Calculate the geopotential altitude, $h_{Potential}$, from the following:

$$h_{Potential} = \left(1.4545 \times 10^5\right)\left(1 - e^X\right) \tag{5.7}$$

4. Calculate the density altitude $h_{Density}$ from the following:

$$h_{Density} = h_{Potential} + \left(4.795 \times 10^{-8}\right)\left(h_{Potential}\right)^2 \tag{5.8}$$

Note that the e^X in the third step is the number base for natural logarithms; on a scientific calculator, you would key in the value of X before pressing the **ex** key. You can try the previous Denver airport example and see whether you come up with the same density altitude results. When you calculate the value of X, you should get a value of −0.07505, and when you calculate the value of $h_{Potential}$ you should get a result of 10,516.4

ft. You should get a final density altitude result of $h_{Density}$ = 10,522 ft. Figure 5.6, found later in this chapter, illustrates temperature effects graphically.

Adjusting the Altimeter

Before takeoff, the pilot must calibrate the altimeter to QNH so that it displays the altitude equal to the published airport field elevation. In Flight Simulator, press **B** or click to the left or right of the **Altimeters** calibration knob until the correct airport elevation is displayed. If you fly higher than the transition altitude (18,000 ft) in the United States (other countries have different transition altitudes), you must set the altimeter to QNE (29.92 in. Hg) so that it now displays the pressure altitude above the mean datum plane (an imaginary plane that other aircraft flying in or out of your vicinity can use as a common "ground point" to establish vertical separation).

In real aircraft, the window in the altimeter face—the Kollsman window—tells the pilot how much pressure offset is being used. The Cessna altimeter in FS98 shows a Kollsman window, and the numbers even move in it when you calibrate the pressure setting. Unfortunately, the numbers are too small to discern. If you want to view the exact current pressure setting, you must instead use the Aircraft Settings dialog box, which you open through the **Aircraft/Aircraft Settings** menu. You can also change the altimeter pressure setting in this dialog box, as shown in Figure 5.5. To change the actual atmospheric pressure, however, you must use the Advanced Weather dialog box and then choose the **Pressure** tab and type a new pressure.

NOTE

The pressure you enter into the Advanced Weather dialog box will be referenced from sea level only. For example, suppose you want the air pressure at Denver International, elevation 5,431 ft, to be **29.00** in. Hg. Typing 29.00 into the pressure box, you may think that when you return to the simulation, the outside pressure will be 29 in. Hg. Wrong! The outside pressure will be referenced to a sea level pressure of 29 in. Hg, and Denver, at 5,431 ft elevation, will have a pressure of about 23.6 in. Hg from this level (a difference of 5.39 in. Hg). Ordinarily, with a standard sea level pressure of 29.92 in. Hg, Denver would have a pressure of 24.53 in. Hg (from the StAt table, which also shows the same difference of 5.39 in. Hg because 29.92 – 24.53 = 5.39). So how would you set a pressure of 29 in. Hg for Denver? Because we know the pressure difference must be 5.39 in. Hg *greater* at sea level, we must set the air pressure in the Advanced Weather dialog box to 29 + 5.39 = 34.39 in. Hg. With the altitude difference of 5,431 ft, the air pressure at Denver will now be 29 in. Hg.

As a practical matter, local station barometric pressures are reduced to the sea level counterpart, meaning that the barometric pressure for a high-elevation station is reported as if that station were reporting from sea level (but corrected for the altitude difference). Note that the lowest sea level barometric pressure possible in FS98 is 25.01 in. Hg, and the maximum is 34.99 in. Hg.

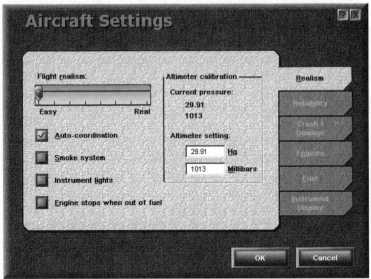

Figure 5.5 *Calibrating the altimeter through the aircraft settings dialog box.*

Earlier, we mentioned that pressure drops as altitude increases. An important rule of thumb in predicting the decrease rate for pressure is as follows:

A change in altitude of 1,000 ft is approximately equal to a change in pressure of 1 in. Hg.

EXAMPLE 5.4

Suppose the barometric pressure at Chicago's O'Hare airport, elevation 649 ft, is reported on the ATIS (automatic terminal information service) as 28.92 in. Hg. What will the pressure be at 2,649 ft altitude?

Solution

Because the actual difference in altitude is 2,000 ft (2,649 ft – 649 ft = 2,000 ft), using the pressure rule of thumb (1 in. Hg for each 1,000 ft), we find that there should be a drop of 2 in of Hg. Chicago is at an elevation of 649 ft, and the pressure difference between sea level and 649 ft from the StAt table is about 29.92 - 29.22 = 0.7 in. Hg. Therefore, the pressure at 2,649 ft, using a nonstandard sea level barometric pressure of 28.93 in. Hg, will be 28.23 in. Hg (because 28.93 – 0.7 = 28.23 in. Hg).

Example 5.5

A pilot is about to take off from Meigs Field, elevation 593 ft above sea level. He does not know the barometric air pressure but is worried. When the altimeter is set to 29.92 in. Hg, the altimeter shows 2,600 ft. What is the current air pressure and pressure altitude?

Solution

By definition, because the altimeter is set to 29.92 in. Hg, the pressure altitude is 2,600 ft. Obviously, you would be in big trouble if you were flying through clouds and thought your altitude was 2,600 ft when in fact you were at ground level! Using the StAt table (Appendix F), you will find that a pressure altitude of 2,600 ft corresponds to an air pressure of 27.215 in. Hg, so this is the current outside air pressure. Before taking off, the pilot should adjust the altimeter so that it shows the field elevation of Meigs, which is 593 ft.

This example demonstrates the danger of flying from a higher-pressure region of air (29.92 in. Hg) to a lower-pressure region. As we shall see next, the lower sea level pressure in this example is 27.8 in. Hg.

To try Example 5.5, you should go to the Advanced Weather Pressure dialog box and set the sea level air pressure to 27.8 in. Hg. The reason you don't enter 27.215 in. Hg is that you must account for the 593 ft elevation of Meigs from sea level, and this means you must add 0.6 in. Hg to the value of 27.215 (because using the rule of thumb for 1 in. Hg = 1,000 ft, and 600 ft is approximately 0.6 in. Hg). After you have finished typing **27.8** in the Advanced Weather Pressure dialog box, return to the cockpit and then adjust the altimeter to 29.92 in. Hg (using the adjustment knob or the Aircraft Settings dialog box). Notice that your altitude is now 2,600 ft, as predicted. Now if you calibrate the altimeter for the correct altitude by pressing **B**, the field elevation of 593 ft will return to the altimeter display. If you go to the Aircraft Settings dialog box, you will see that the altimeter has been recalibrated for a sea level barometric pressure of 27.29 in. Hg (FS98 rounds off the last decimal digit).

To avoid fatal misinterpretation of your altimeter readings, remember the advice first mentioned in Chapter 1: "Going from a high to a low or from warm to cold, look out below!" See figure 5.7 for a display of the consequences of failing to adjust the altimeter.

Altimeter Settings

The three altimeter settings are defined as follows.

- **QNE**: With this setting, the altimeter is always calibrated to 29.92 in. Hg, and this results in the altimeter indicating the height above the standard datum plane or pressure altitude. This altimeter setting is always used above 18,000 ft in the United States.

- **QNH**: This is the standard altimeter setting used when flying below 18,000 ft in the United States. When flying below this altitude, the pilot must adjust the altimeter to the surface pressure setting of the nearest ground reporting station. When QNH is set, the altimeter displays the height above mean sea level.
- **QFE**: Only used by a few nations, QFE is the actual surface pressure and is not corrected to sea level. When QFE is set, the altimeter shows the actual elevation above ground level.

Table 5.4 shows the effects of the altimeter settings.

Table 5.4 Effects of Altimeter Settings

SETTING	WHILE ON THE GROUND AT THE AIRPORT	WHILE IN THE AIR
QNE (altimeter calibrated to 29.92 in. Hg)	Altimeter shows variable elevation reading above or below the actual airport elevation.	Useful for positive vertical separation for aircraft that use the same pressure altitude setting. However, the altitude displayed is not the true altitude, nor is it the altitude above sea level. The true altitude can vary depending on the surface pressure.
QNH (altimeter calibrated to current surface pressure)	Altimeter shows the airport's elevation. This is the same as the elevation above sea level.	Altimeter shows the altitude of the aircraft above sea level (not taking into account nonstandard temperature).
QFE (altimeter pressure calibration adjusted while on ground so that zero elevation is shown)	Altimeter shows zero elevation reading when the aircraft is on the ground.	Altimeter shows height above ground (not taking into account nonstandard temperature).

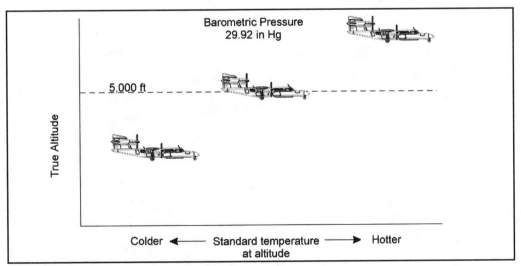

Barometric Pressure
29.92 in Hg

5,000 ft

True Altitude

Colder ◄─── Standard temperature ───► Hotter
at altitude

Figure 5.6 Effect of temperature on true altitude.

By international convention, altitude is expressed throughout the world in feet and not meters. Outside the United States, other metric conventions apply, such as using kg for mass and weight determination, and Celsius for Fahrenheit, and so on. Flight Simulator allows you to display altitudes in metric units if you prefer. Use the **Options/Preferences/International/** menu, and, in the dialog box, pull down the **Units of Measure** list box and select **Metric (Altimeter meters)**. Interestingly, the program internally expresses altitudes as meters and then converts to feet for the instrument panel displays (see Appendix H for further details).

THE DANGER OF ICING

Ice and frost formation on the exterior of the airplane's wings is an insidious danger that must be guarded against. When ice forms on an airplane, cumulative thrust is reduced, drag increases, lift lessens, and weight increases. The results are an increase in stall speed and a deterioration of aircraft performance. In extreme cases, 2 to 3 in. of ice can form on the leading edge of the wing in less than 5 min. It takes only $^1/_2$ inch of ice to reduce the lifting power of some aircraft by 50% and increase the frictional drag by 50%.

You can expect icing when flying in visible precipitation, such as rain or cloud droplets, when the temperature is 0° Celsius or colder. When icing is detected, you should do one of two things: get out of the area of precipitation or go to an altitude where the

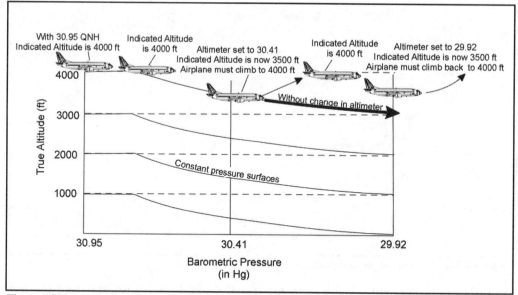

Figure 5.7 *Effect of calibrating or not calibrating the altimeter to surface pressure.*

temperature is above freezing. Some aircraft have special engine bleed anti-icing systems that can heat those parts of the airplane prone to freezing. Some aircraft have rubber boots that expand and break up the ice on the tail, and other types of systems are used on the engine cowlings, leading edge wing surfaces, and even on the propeller blades.

Because the exterior of an airplane is susceptible to icing, problems can occur with the pitot tube becoming clogged with ice. This could be disastrous, because the airspeed indicator would show incorrect speeds and could lead the pilot into a fatal stall. Therefore, special heating elements in the pitot tube are used to keep it free of ice. In Flight Simulator 98, you can turn on the new pitot heating system from the front instrument panel of the Cessna, Learjet, and 737.

To experience icing conditions in Flight Simulator 98, turn realism to maximum in the **Aircraft/Aircraft Settings/Realism** dialog box. Then add a cloud layer in the Advanced Weather dialog box that has a temperature of 5° C or lower.

CLOUDS

Clouds are visible aggregations of minute water or ice particles suspended in air. If the cloud is on the ground, it is called fog. Precipitation, which includes drizzle, rain, snow, ice pellets, hail, and ice crystals, occurs when these particles grow in size and weight until the atmosphere can no longer suspend them. To produce significant precipitation,

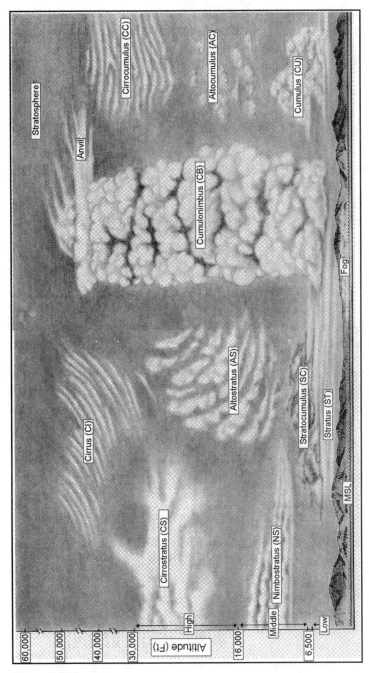

Figure 5.8 Cloud types.

clouds must usually be at least 4,000 ft thick. Therefore, when you're arriving at an airport where precipitation is reported, expect that the cloud layer will be at least 4,000 ft thick.

There are four families, or types, of clouds that are of interest to the aviator: low clouds (L), middle clouds (M), high clouds (H), and clouds with extensive vertical development. Low, middle, and high clouds are further classified by the way they are formed. Clouds formed by vertical currents of unstable air are called *cumulus*, meaning "accumulation" or "heap" in Latin. Cumulus, cumuloform clouds are characterized by a lumpy, billowy appearance, and you will find turbulent flying conditions just below them. Clouds formed by the cooling of stable air are called *stratus*, meaning "spread out" or layered." These cloud types are characterized by their uniform, sheetlike appearance, and flying conditions are less turbulent around them. *Cirrus* clouds are high clouds that have a wispy, curly appearance. In addition to these cloud types, the prefix *nimbo* or the suffix *nimbus*, which means raincloud, is added to the names of clouds that normally produce rain. Thus, a horizontal cloud from which rain is falling is called *nimbostratus*, and a swelling cumulus that has grown to a thunderstorm is called *cumulonimbus*. For a listing of the ten basic cloud types and the altitudes in which they appear in Flight Simulator, see Table H.5 in Appendix H. Figure 5.8 shows the cloud types.

Under visual flying rules (VFR) you are required to maintain a separation distance of at least 500 ft below, 1,000 ft above, or 2,000 ft horizontal distance from any cloud. If you have an instrument rating, then it is permitted to enter a cloud.

NOTE You are normally allowed up to two different cloud layers and a thunderstorm layer in a weather area. When you create a cloud layer in the Advanced Weather dialog box, it will look more realistic if you have turned on **Textured Sky**, **Wispy Cloud Effects**, **Cloud Thickness Effects**, and **Gradient Horizon** under **Options/Preferences/ Display/Display Options/Scenery**.

Thunderstorms

Thunderstorms constitute one of the worst hazards to flight. They are almost always accompanied by strong wind gusts, severe turbulence, lightning, heavy rain showers, and severe icing. Hail is not uncommon, and tornadoes are even possible. Thunderstorms are classified as cumulonimbus cloud types.

Each day about 44,000 thunderstorms occur over the surface of the Earth. At night, from the space shuttle, it is possible to see the lightning flashes occur many times each minute over areas with thunderstorm activity. Lightning strikes and electrostatic discharges are leading causes of Air Force reportable weather-related aircraft accidents and incidents. When lightning strikes an airplane, usually the structural damage is minor (although lightning can puncture the fuselage). The main worry is damage to

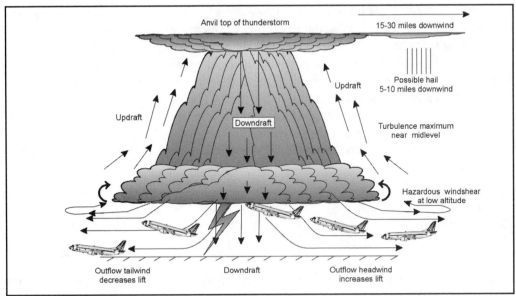

Figure 5.9 *Thunderstorms and wind shear danger.*

aircraft electrical systems, instruments, avionics, and radar. In the past, transient voltages and currents induced in electrical systems have caused bomb bay doors to open, have activated wing folding motors, and have made navigational systems inoperative. Under certain conditions, catastrophic fuel ignition in the fuel tanks is possible. Ordinarily, the space above the liquid fuel in the tanks is filled with a mixture of vaporized fuel and air. If a spark is induced in the tank when the air-fuel mixture is at its most explosive ratio, an explosion can occur. To combat this problem, static wicks suspended from the trailing edge of wingtips help to discharge static electricity during flight.

Another thunderstorm worry is hail. Hail from thunderstorms has been encountered as high as 45,000 ft in clear air as many as 20 miles away from the storm core. Hailstones larger than $^1/_2$ to $^3/_4$ inch can significantly damage the airplane in a few seconds. Therefore, it is best to skirt any thunderstorm by at least 20 nm, and under no circumstances should you attempt to fly under a thunderstorm. Flying over the top anvil cloud of a thunderstorm is also to be avoided but is permitted if the pilot maintains at least 1,000 ft clearance for each 10 knots of wind speed for the storm.

Pilots must also be aware of turbulence and wind shear that are invisible to the eye. Figure 5.9 shows how an airplane flying toward a storm experiences a headwind; as it passes through the storm, the headwind suddenly turns into a tailwind that robs the airplane of lift. The wind shear can drastically reduce the airplane's speed by as much as 60 knots. If the airplane were on a landing approach with little altitude in which to recover speed, the results could be disastrous. Although weather radar can pick up thunderstorm activity as far away as 300 nm, sometimes it is necessary to fly near a storm to transit a particular area. Passenger comfort can be improved by slowing the aircraft to 300 knots IAS and by selecting turbulence mode on the autopilot, reducing the reaction time of the autopilot. The slower speed will help reduce structural stress on the airframe when turbulence is encountered.

The flash and boom of a lightning bolt can also temporarily incapacitate the flight crew. Flash blindness can last 30 seconds, and the shock wave can cause some temporary hearing loss if headphones or earplugs are not worn. In rare cases, it has been reported that crews have experienced mild electric shock and minor burns after a lightning strike.

NOTE

To simulate thunderstorms, select the **Cumulonimbus** cloud type.

Because of these dangers, when a thunderstorm is near an airport, operations are always suspended until the storm has cleared the area.

WINDS

As the atmosphere is heated by the sun and cooled by nightfall, the resulting temperature differences stimulate the formation of low- and high-pressure zones. The high- and low-pressure areas seek to reach an equilibrium state and in so doing drive a complex system of winds.

We commonly define *wind* as any moving air, but specifically we define it in aviation as any air mass that has a common direction and speed. Wind direction is always measured as blowing *from* a particular heading. Surface winds are measured as blowing from a direction that is measured clockwise from the magnetic north pole (see Figure 5.10), whereas winds aloft are measured as blowing from a direction that is measured clockwise from the true north pole. The earth's magnetic pole is displaced from the geographic north pole, and, because we use magnetic compasses to determine headings, the surface winds are better expressed in terms of magnetic heading. Thus, if you receive a report that the winds are blowing "90 at 10," it means that the winds are blowing from 90° with a speed of 10 knots as measured clockwise from the magnetic north pole. On the other hand, if you receive a weather report about the jet stream's wind direction high up in the atmosphere, the direction will be expressed as blowing from an angle measured clockwise from true north.

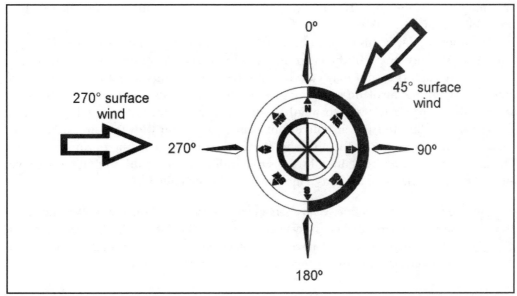

Figure 5.10 Surface winds blow from a magnetic compass direction, whereas winds aloft blow from a compass direction measured from true north.

When you create winds in Flight Simulator, this distinction between surface wind direction and winds aloft direction holds true. Therefore, if you go to Boise, Idaho, where the magnetic variation between true north and magnetic north is 19° east (meaning that the magnetic north pole is displaced 19° east of the geographic north pole), there will be a discrepancy in direction between winds you add at the surface and wind layers you add above the surface. For example, if you want the surface wind to blow from the north with a direction of 0° as measured on your compass in Boise, Idaho, you would go to the Advanced Weather dialog box (**World/Weather/Winds**) and add a surface wind layer with 360° as your magnetic direction. (Flight Simulator accepts values only between 1° and 360°; because 0° is the same as 360°, you would type **360**.) However, if you wanted to add a wind layer above the surface and typed **360°** as your true direction, the wind would not blow from 0° magnetic; instead, it would blow from 341° magnetic (360° − 19° E = 341°). There would be a wind shear layer between the two wind layers, and when you crossed the boundary, the airplane would be buffeted.

We have already discussed the weather vane effect that the airplane's tail has on the airplane when faced with a crosswind. You may be confused as to why the airplane's nose turns into the wind when taking off or landing but not after takeoff or during flying. At Meigs Field, for example, the runway is oriented 360° and 0°, and if you take off due north along the runway with a crosswind of 10 knots from 270°, your airplane will want to pivot its nose left to 270° into the wind. Once you leave the ground, the weather vane effect disappears! Why?

To understand why this is so, it is important to realize that wind is like an ocean current. Once the airplane is in the current, it doesn't care which direction the current is flowing (although the pilot may care because he or she wants to get from point A to point B). When the airplane is on the ground, friction holds the tires to the ground, causing the airplane to want to weathervane into the wind. Once the airplane has entered the medium of the air current, it is in equilibrium with the air current and moves with it. Therefore, to the airplane, there is no net force acting to rotate the tail. The airplane is entirely contained by the surrounding air, and, although it has relative motion through the air, it also has a motion with the air, called *drift*.

NOTE

You can create only three wind layers and one surface wind layer per weather area. Also, the depth of surface winds is measured in distance above ground level, whereas the tops and bottoms of winds aloft are measured in distance above mean sea level. Wind speed is measured in knots true airspeed, and the maximum wind speed is 199 knots.

The Jet Stream

The *jet stream* is a fast-flowing river of air that moves at speeds as high as 200 knots around the globe in a wavelike pattern. A jet stream may be as far south as the northern tropics, but jet streams in the mid latitudes are generally stronger than ones near the tropics. The jet stream typically occurs in a break in the tropopause between the stratosphere and troposphere, but it is not classified as a jet stream unless it moves with a speed of at least 50 knots. A jet stream can be as much as 400 miles wide and 3,000 to 7,000 ft deep, with a length of 1,000 to 3,000 miles.

Over the North Atlantic, the jet stream moves westerly with an average speed of 60 knots. Flights westbound over the Atlantic try to take advantage of the jet stream to reduce flight time by as much as an hour, whereas flights eastbound try to avoid the jet stream. Each day, the track across the Atlantic is adjusted by Oceanic ATC to account for changing jet stream conditions. So you can't count on traveling a particular route across the Atlantic but must fly the one that is assigned.

Wind Drift

If there is a tailwind on your airplane in flight, does this mean that you will suffer a loss of lift and must therefore add thrust? What about the reverse situation—when you are faced with a headwind during flight. Does your airplane get more lift when flying into

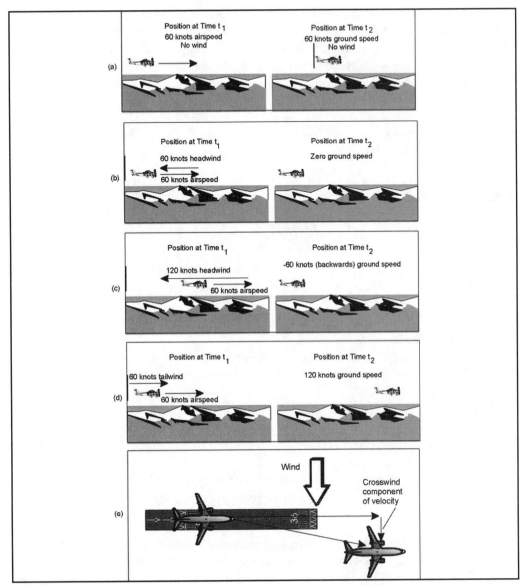

Figure 5.11 *The confusing aspects of wind drift: (a) Ground speed 60 knots with no wind. (b) Ground speed zero with 60-knot headwind and 60-knot indicated airspeed. (c) Ground speed is now −60 knots backward due to 60-knot airspeed minus 120 knot headwind. (d) Ground speed is 120 knots due to 60-knot tailwind plus 60-knot airspeed. (e) Once the airplane has left the ground, it acquires the velocity of the surrounding air. In this case, the airplane now has a crosswind component of velocity added to its forward velocity.*

the wind? The experienced pilot knows that the answer to both these questions is no, except when the pilot is on the ground. Once in flight, the airplane is entirely contained within the wind current, and it makes no difference whether the wind is blowing forward, sideways, or in the reverse direction of the airplane's flight path.

What about when the headwind is so strong that the airplane makes no forward progress at all? Does the airplane stall and fall from the sky? Again, the experienced pilot will reply no. If you ignore the motionless ground below, the airplane still has a velocity through the air current that will provide it with plenty of lift. Figure 5.11 illustrates a few examples of wind drift and its effect on the airplane's motion.

EXAMPLE 5.6

What happens when you attempt a takeoff in the Cessna from Meigs Field with a headwind of 60 knots?

Solution

1. Start the Meigs default situation and go to the Advanced Weather dialog box (**World/Weather/Winds**).
2. In the Winds dialog box, click **Add Layer**.
3. When you see the pop-up menu, select **Surface Layer**. This is the surface wind you want to add.
4. In the Winds dialog box, you'll see many of the options enabled that were formerly inactive. Type **360** for the wind direction, and type **60** for the wind speed in knots. This action will create a surface wind that will blow from the north with a speed of 60 knots.
5. Click **OK** to return to the cockpit. Before releasing the brakes, note that the airspeed indicator shows that you are already traveling at 60 knots (TAS).
6. Release the brakes and advance the throttle slightly.

The airplane will take off when the airspeed indicator shows an airspeed slightly greater than 55 knots IAS (not TAS). Therefore, with power set to slightly less than 15 in. Hg at 2,000 RPM (about one-quarter to one-half maximum throttle), the airplane will gently float above the runway and appear to hover in one place. You are flying at close to the stall speed, so the airplane will appear unstable.

Now reset the situation and try taking off with a headwind of 120 knots. With maximum thrust, you might be able to hover over the runway, but if you reduce thrust you will actually fly backwards. Try turning the airplane to fly due west with the same 360°

wind from the north. As you will see, the wind drift causes the airplane to move diagonally with respect to the ground.

Carrier Landings

As demonstrated by the previous headwind example with the Cessna, carrier landings are easier with a headwind. In fact, if you want to perfect your landings onto a carrier, you can establish a headwind that makes your airplane's ground speed close to zero knots. Then when you land on the deck, the task of coming to a stop is much easier. Aircraft carriers are always turned into the wind, and because the carrier itself can maintain a speed of 35 knots into a headwind, when the airplane takes off it can do so with reduced speed requirements. For example, if a fighter jet needs to take off at 150 knots, the headwind is 10 knots and the carrier is moving forward with a speed of 35 knots, the jet needs only a takeoff speed of 115 knots from the deck.

You can try a carrier landing with the Cessna on the *U.S.S. Carl Vinson* off the coast of Maui using the Carrier Approach flight situation. Unfortunately, the carrier is dead in the water—something that is unrealistic—but there is a steady 30-knot headwind blowing from 190° magnetic that makes the landing a cinch. With the headwind, even though your airspeed indicator shows 60 knots you can land on the deck with a relative speed to the carrier of only 30 knots. If you increase the headwind using the Advanced Weather dialog box, you can slow the landing speed even further. Note that the ground speed is not the same as your airspeed, which in all cases must be at least 54 knots or else the plane will stall.

EXAMPLE 5.7

NOTE

FSW95 users: This version of the in-flight refueling situation will only work with FS98.

Here's a trick you might want to try for in-flight refueling with a headwind. It was developed by Col. Dennis Arthur, USAF (Retired), who used to fly B-47s and would have to catch a tanker every now and again.

1. Put all the ***.*AF** files found in the **INFLTREF.ZIP** file into the Flight Simulator **Texture** folder.
2. Put **KC135.bgl** into the Flight Simulator **\Scenery** directory. This scenery **bgl** file has a static object containing a KC-135 aerial tanker.

3. Copy the **Inflight.STN** flight situation file into the **Pilots** subdirectory of your **Flight Sim** directory. **Inflight.STN** contains the instructions for placing the Learjet right behind the KC-135, and it sets up the wind layer needed to maintain the illusion of flight for both airplanes.

4. After starting Flight Simulator, select the **Inflight** situation. You will then be placed in the Learjet just behind the KC-135 tanker at 18,000 ft somewhere over Idaho.

Although the KC-135 is a static object (meaning that it is not moving), the Learjet is faced with a 199-knot TAS headwind from 90° due east. This wind is stored as a surface wind layer in the **Inflight.STN** situation file—and not as a winds aloft layer—because it was necessary to direct the wind in a 90° magnetic heading (and in Flight Simulator winds aloft always use true headings, not magnetic). This means that if you maintain a 90° magnetic heading and a true airspeed of 199 knots, the Learjet will appear to "hover" just behind the KC-135, and you will then be able to maintain the illusion of the KC-135 and the Learjet flying in formation.

Now you are ready to refuel. The Learjet is flying at 17,900 ft, and the tanker is at 18,000 ft. The Learjet's autopilot is set on a heading of 90°, and the altitude hold is set for 17,900 ft, with the speed hold on 200 knots. If you do nothing, the plane will move closer to the tanker and almost bump against the refueling boom. At this point, you may want to take over manually and release the autopilot to keep the boom in contact with the Learjet. You may have to adjust the throttle slightly to keep the airspeed constant at 199 knots.

Be sure that you slow down as you approach the boom; otherwise, you will overrun the tanker. If the tanker disappears from view as you approach, adjust your angle of vision by panning up (**Shift+Backspace**) or down (**Shift+Enter**) to keep the tanker in the narrow visual "envelope." You will find that there is an optimum adjustment that will keep the tanker in view during the whole approach.

Credits

Col. Dennis Archer, USAF (Ret.), module developer
Terry Hill, designer of KC135 with boom
Steve Kruze, modifier of KC 135 into static configuration
Major Joe Worsley, USAF (Ret.), Testing and Explanatory Text
Manfred Moldenhaur, modifier of the KC-135 bgl that allowed the tanker to be seen farther away

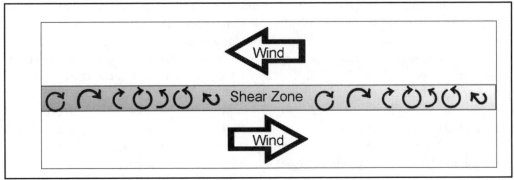

Figure 5.12 *Wind shear.*

Wind Shear and Clear Air Turbulence (CAT)

Wind shear is created when two air currents meet with differing velocities. At the boundary of the two wind layers is a shear zone where the mixing eddies of air currents bump against each other and create friction and turbulence. When crossing the boundary, the airplane may experience CAT (clear air turbulence) and may lose lift depending on the wind direction. This phenomenon is illustrated in Figure 5.12.

Wind shear can be produced both horizontally (see Figure 5.12) and vertically (see Figure 5.9), although in FS98 only horizontal wind shear is supported.

A wind shear difference of 4 knots per 1,000 ft can produce bumpy flights, whereas 6 knots per 1,000 ft can produce severe turbulence. Areas over mountains, where the air rushes down the slope of one side of the mountain, are particularly susceptible to CAT. Weather radar, unfortunately, cannot spot CAT, because the microwave radar beams are reflected only by water vapor molecules such as those present in clouds. Radar is thus reflected by clouds, thunderstorms, and precipitation but passes transparently through CAT.

Severe clear air turbulence seriously injures about 50 passengers each year. More than 98% of the injuries happen because the passenger was not wearing a seatbelt. Particularly vulnerable are infants being held by their parents, and that is why the FAA has recently called for new rules that would require babies to be strapped into car restraint seats, as they are now required to do in automobiles. When an airplane drops 100 to 200 ft, all objects that are not fastened down in the cabin can hit the ceiling with tremendous force. Then when the airplane bottoms out, the objects fall back to the floor. If the force is especially strong, the overhead luggage bins will break open and disgorge their contents on the heads of the passengers. This is why it is never a good idea to store heavy items in the overhead bins.

In recent years, NASA has been experimenting with a high-tech laser that would be able to detect CAT ahead of the aircraft so that it could be safely avoided. This system may also be able to warn pilots of wind shear conditions, although ground-based wind shear warning systems are already in place at many airports.

Many passengers fear that the airplane will break apart under severe CAT. This is almost impossible with modern jetliners; as we have seen in Chapter 2, the load factor is well within the design wing load limits. In fact, during the design of each airplane, the wings are tested to the point of failure by imposing a load that is 150% greater than normal. Furthermore, in tests of the structural integrity of modern jet aircraft, the FAA has dropped the passenger compartment cross section from a height of 30 ft to prove survivability. Although the compartment was deformed and damaged, the structure did not break apart. If you do the physics calculation, when dropped from a height of 30 ft, the plane would hit the ground with a speed of 43.8 ft/s or 30 mph. Assuming that the compartment was deformed vertically by 1.2 ft, the deceleration force would have been 24 g's, which is survivable (although with possible injuries). The maximum sustained deceleration experienced by a human being strapped to a rocket sled was on the order of 12 g's. However, the maximum deceleration that humans can tolerate is a function of magnitude and duration; decelerations in excess of 12 g's are survivable if the duration is sufficiently brief.

Consider an airplane that drops 200 ft due to a vertical downdraft of 50 ft/s. At the end of the drop, the aircraft stops suddenly and violently in the space of 20 vertical ft. The g force would be no more than 3.1 g's, which is well within the ultimate load limit of 3.75 g's for air transport aircraft.

EXAMPLE 5.8

To create a horizontal wind shear, you can use the Advanced Weather dialog box to generate two wind layers with opposing directions. Let's try doing this for Meigs Field.

1. In the Advanced Weather dialog box, add a wind layer with a 30-knot speed coming from a direction of 360°. Put the base of the wind layer at 1,500 ft and the top of the wind layer at 2,500 ft MSL.
2. Add a second wind layer with a 30-knot wind speed coming from the opposite direction of 180°. Put the base of this second wind layer at 2,500 ft and the top of the layer at 5,000 ft. MSL.
3. After returning to the simulation, take off from Meigs Field on a 0° heading.

Notice that when the airplane hits the first wind layer at 1,500 ft, it suddenly gains lift and the airspeed increases by 30 knots. Next, when the airplane crosses the wind shear boundary between the two new wind layers, it will lose lift and the airspeed will suddenly decrease because of the 60-knot speed differential between the two wind layers. As you can see, this is enough to stall the airplane at low airspeeds. If you practice landings with wind shear conditions present, you will appreciate how difficult it is to regain control of the airplane once it has lost lift.

LOW VISIBILITY

Flight Simulator's low visibility/hazing feature is a great way to practice IFR flights. When you use the **World/Weather** menu, you can select visibility from unlimited to 1/16th of a mile. With the lowest visibility setting on, it will be impossible for you to land the airplane without use of the instrument landing system.

If you are flying under VFR, the rules state that you can fly only when the visibility is more than 3 statute miles. No such requirement exists under IFR flight except when you're performing takeoffs and landings, when visibility minima apply. Each airport has its own minima requirements; if you are instrument rated, you would consult the instrument approach plate to see whether the weather conditions will permit a landing. Visibility conditions are reported via the ATIS recording and via weather reports that you can obtain before departure.

NOTE

If you are using the Advanced Weather dialog box, visibility can be turned on only after you have added at least one cloud layer.

Table 5.5 shows the rules for basic VFR visibility and distance from clouds.

Table 5.5 Basic VFR Weather Minima

ALTITUDE	FLIGHT VISIBILITY	DISTANCE FROM CLOUDS
1,200 ft or less above the surface		
Within controlled airspace	3 statute miles	500 ft below
		1,000 ft above
		2,000 ft horizontal
Outside controlled airspace		
Day	1 statute mile	Clear of clouds
Night	3 statute miles	500 ft below
		1,000 ft above
		2,000 ft horizontal
More than 1,200 ft above the surface but less than 10,000 ft MSL		
Within controlled airspace	3 statute miles	500 ft below
		1,000 ft above
		2,000 ft horizontal

Table 5.5 continued

ALTITUDE	FLIGHT VISIBILITY	DISTANCE FROM CLOUDS
Outside controlled airspace		
Day	1 statute mile	500 ft below
		1,000 ft above
		2,000 ft horizontal
Night	3 statute miles	
More than 1,200 ft above the surface and at or above 10,000 ft MSL		
	5 statute miles	1,000 ft below
		1,000 ft above
		1 mile horizontal

AUTOMATIC TERMINAL INFORMATION SERVICE

When you take off or land, you need to know the surface temperature, the barometric pressure, the direction from which the winds are coming, and how strong the winds are, and visibility conditions and cloud cover. This information is broadcast automatically around the clock by special ATIS radio stations located at each airport. So if you are taking off from Chicago's O'Hare International Airport, you would tune in 135.40 MHz on the COM radio and listen to the automated recording, which is repeated and updated as conditions warrant. Table 5.6 lists the content of ATIS messages.

Table 5.6 ATIS Messages

ATIS MESSAGE	DESCRIPTION
Chicago O'Hare information alpha	This is the station identifier for Chicago. The message is identified with the letter *A*, which is read as "alpha." When the message is updated, the letter is changed to "bravo," "charlie," "delta," and so on so that you will know the message is new.
16:00 zulu	This is Universal Coordinated Time (UTC), which is similar to Greenwich Mean Time (GMT) in England. It is called Zulu rather than GMT because the Zero time meridian (GMT) is identified by the international phonetic alphabet letter Z, which is spoken as "zulu."

Table 5.6 continued

ATIS MESSAGE	DESCRIPTION
ATIS weather report	
Scattered 9300	Clouds are scattered up to 9,300 ft.
Visibility 20 miles	Visibility is 20 miles.
Temperature +59° F	Temperature is 59° F.
Winds 45 at 9	Surface wind is blowing from the northwest direction at 45° magnetic, and the speed is 9 knots.
Altimeter 29.91	Barometric pressure is 29.91 in. Hg.
Landing and departing runway 4R	Landings and departures are from runway 4 right. The runway number tells you which direction the runway is facing. "4R" means that there are probably two runways facing 40° magnetic (±5°) and that you must use the right one.
Advise controller on initial contact you have Juliett	You must contact air traffic control for permission to land or take off.
Localizer 04-111.3 RWY 4R	This message is to aid FS98 pilots; tune in the correct ILS beacon for landings. In this case, runway 4R uses the 111.30 MHz localizer frequency.

NOTE

If the ATIS message scrolls by too quickly or if you don't like it to scroll, you can change both aspects of the display. To change the speed, go to the **Aircraft/Communications** menu. In the Communications dialog box, slide the **Communications Rate** lever to a slower setting. To change the display from continuous to a single line, go to the **Options/Preferences/Display** menu. In the dialog box, pull down the **Text Presentation** list box and select **Single Line**.

NOTE

To have the ATIS message automatically repeat itself, click on **Repeat ATIS Message** in the Communications dialog box under the **Aircraft/Communications** menu. Alternatively, you can retune the radio up a notch and then back down to the ATIS frequency, and the message will repeat.

CREATING WEATHER AREAS

Flight Simulator has the capability of creating two separate local weather areas in addition to the global weather that is applied to the whole world (see Figure 5.13). This capability is useful when you're planning realistic flights and you want differing weather conditions at your departure and landing points. For example, if you wanted to have sunny skies with no clouds at takeoff from San Francisco and then have instrument flying conditions at your arrival in Los Angeles, with close to zero visibility due to fog, you would create two local weather areas: one for San Francisco and the other for Los Angeles.

Local weather areas preempt global weather; although you can edit local weather area coordinates, speed, course, width, and transition zones, you cannot do so for global weather. Note that with Automatic Weather Generation turned on for clouds and visibility, your own weather settings will be overridden. Using the **World/Weather Areas/Copy Weather** menu, you can also copy the parameters of one weather area to any other weather area. You can copy such elements as wind layers, cloud layers, tem-

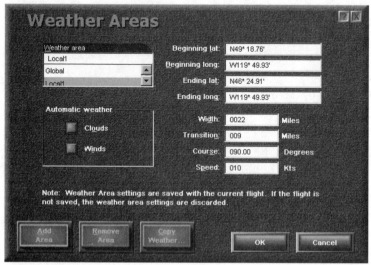

Figure 5.13 *Weather Areas dialog box. You can create two local weather areas with different weather conditions in addition to the global weather.*

perature layers, barometric pressure, and visibility.

For a complete description of the permissible weather parameters for winds, air pressure, temperature, visibility and clouds, consult Tables H.5, H.6, and H.10 as well as Figure H.2, which illustrates the working of the weather coordinates and other area definitions, such as width, transition, course, and velocity. These illustrations are in Appendix H.

SETTING TIME OF DAY AND SEASON

Visual changes related to seasonal weather are also modeled in Flight Simulator. You set the season using the **World/Time & Season** menu to access the Time & Season dialog box, where you can specify **Winter, Spring, Summer,** or **Fall**. Or if you prefer you can set the exact date and year in the same dialog box. In certain areas of the world you will see the ground terrain change color depending on the season. For example, if you go to Heathrow International Airport in England (51° N latitude) and you change the season to winter, you will see snow covering the ground. Change the season to spring, summer, or fall, and the foliage will change color. Seasonal lighting conditions are also simulated in extreme northern and southern latitude regions. In the winter, the arctic polar

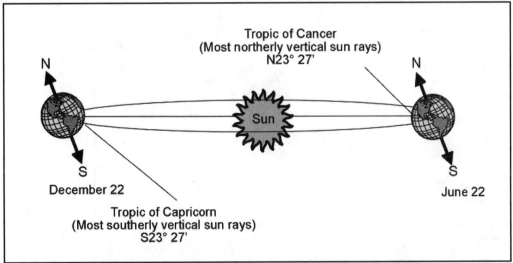

Figure 5.14 *Because the Earth's axis is tilted 23° 27′ to the plane of the ecliptic (the plane that contains the heliocentric orbit of the Earth), the sun's rays fall mostly in the Northern hemisphere at 23° 27′ N latitude (Tropic of Cancer) during the summer solstice (June 22), and in the Southern hemisphere at around 23° 27′ S latitude (Tropic of Capricorn) during the winter solstice (December 22). This means that during the summer northern polar regions are bathed in perpetual sunlight, and the southern polar regions are in perpetual darkness. The situation is reversed in the winter.*

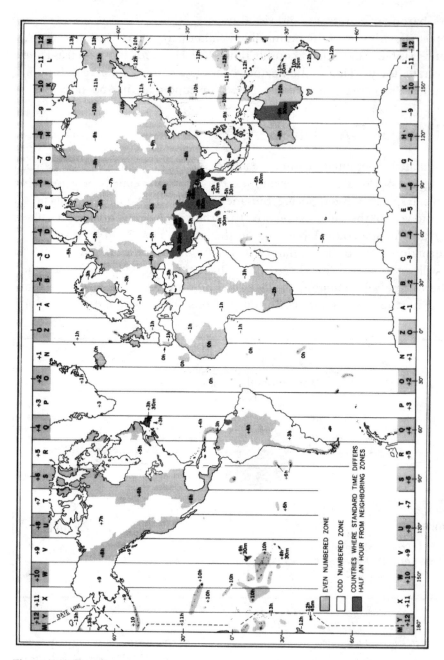

Figure 5.15 *Time Zones.*

regions above 80° N latitude and higher are in perpetual darkness, whereas in the summer the region is bathed in perpetual sunlight. The opposite lighting conditions occur in the Antarctic region at 80° S latitude and higher (see Figure 5.14). The new FS98 Antarctic scenery is excellent. If you have a good 3-D card, try viewing a sunset with a little haze and clouds. the view is spectacular.

If you click the **Time** tab on the dialog box, you can change the time of day to **Day**, **Dusk**, or **Night**, or you can specify the exact time, either in local time or Greenwich Mean Time. Figure 5.15 shows the various local time zones for the world. Note that there are 24 time zones, each identified by a letter of the alphabet. Notice that Greenwich, England, falls under the Z (or Zulu) time zone, and that is why GMT is identified as Zulu time. Eastern Standard Time for the east coast of the United States corresponds to the R, or Romeo, time zone, and so on.

Because the time is later toward the east and earlier toward the west of an observer, Flight Simulator automatically computes and displays the correct local hour for the geographic region in which you fly the airplane. For example, if you fly from the Pacific time zone in California (U, or Uniform time) to the Mountain time zone in Utah or Arizona (T, or Tango time), the clock automatically advances one hour to account for the time change. Flying the reverse direction, the clock will decrement one hour. You can test this by flying or slewing across 109° W longitude over Arizona or Utah. Unfortunately, FS98 has a bug that prevents the date from changing over the interna-

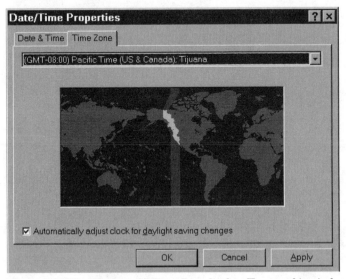

Figure 5.16 *The Windows 95 Time Zone display. To open this window, double-click on the clock readout on the taskbar, and then click on the Time Zone tab.*

tional date line at the 180th meridian (180° W or E longitude). Ordinarily, when you cross the 180th meridian, the date is advanced one day for east-to-west travel, and is decreased by one day for west-to-east travel. At any moment the date immediately to the west of the date line (east longitude) is one day later than the date immediately to the east of the line (west longitude).

Windows 95 also includes a time zone chart that you can access from the desktop by double-clicking on the lower-right corner of the taskbar (where it displays the time). At the top of the dialog box that opens, click the **Time Zone** tab. That will bring up a world map, where you can click on zones and get the time relative to GMT, as shown in Figure 5.16. Each time zone is about 15° longitude in width, but because of unique political and geographical differences, each time zone is arbitrarily marked to skirt country and state borders.

Flight Simulator can also use the current date and time from your computer's system clock. To enable this at startup, select **Options/Preferences/General** and, under the **Time** section, click **System Time** and then **Ok** to exit the dialog box. You will have to restart the program for the changes to take effect. Note that daylight saving time is automatically adjusted for the time of year and is displayed as active or inactive at the top of the Time dialog box.

6

Piloting the Cessna 182 Skylane

Flight Simulator 98 adds the new Cessna 182S Skylane to its fleet of aircraft. The existing Skylane 182 RG (Retractable Gear) remains, albeit with a new instrument panel. Why was the new non-retractable landing gear 182S Skylane added? The reason has its roots in the product liability lawsuits that the Cessna Aircraft Company faced over airplanes that it had built decades ago. Back in 1987, Cessna decided to stop manufacturing the 182RG because they couldn't absorb the losses that they were incurring in the court system. Not until 1997 did production resume—Congress passed legislation that established a statute of limitations for product liability for single-engine aircraft. As a result of this new protection from lawsuits, Cessna introduced the new 182S Skylane and the 172 Skyhawk, the first single-engine airplanes from Cessna in over a decade. The exterior and interior of the new Skylane are shown in Figure 6.1 and Figure 6.2.

Over 20,000 Cessna Skylanes have been produced since the model was first unveiled in the late 1950s. The 1997 182S Skylane has only been out for a year, and over 300 have been sold. With over 230 horsepower, the new Skylane qualifies as a "high performance" airplane, with its Lycoming IO-540 fuel-injected piston engine. The new Skylane is smoother, quieter and more comfortable to fly than the 182 RG because engine noise and vibration are lower. The cruise speed is 140 knots, and its useful load is 1,360 lbs. The rate of climb from sea level is 924 ft/min and the service ceiling is 18,100 ft. Maximum range is 813 nm.

Figure 6.1 *The new Cessna Skylane.*

Figure 6.2 *Interior Cockpit View.*

Inside the cabin, there is a new interior with seating for four adults. From every seat, there's a panoramic view through 350° wraparound windows. A new multi-level ventilation system moves fresh air quietly and efficiently through the cabin. Advanced acoustic soundproofing, thicker windows, and the quieter engine bring sound levels down to a point where conversation is comfortable, with or without the intercom system.

The standard avionics package comes with dual Nav/Coms, glideslope, a VFR moving map GPS, audio panel with marker beacon, mode-C transponder with digital encoder, and a single axis autopilot. An optional upgrade package offers a digital ADF, IFR approach certified GPS, and a more capable two-axis autopilot with electric trim.

The Cessna 182S Skylane is priced at $190,600. This may sound like a high price tag, but consider this: an 11-year-old Skylane can today fetch $120,000 in the used market. its performance, dimensions, and avionics are shown inthe following tables and figures.

Table 6.1 *Approximate Dimensions for the Cessna 182S Skylane*

Overall Height (max.)	9' 3"
Overall Length	28' 0"
Wingspan (overall)	36' 0"
Wing Area	175.6 ft²

Table 6.2 *Cessna 182S Skylane Performance*

SPEED

Maximum	143 knots
Cruise 75% power at 8,000 feet	140 knots

CRUISE RANGE AND TIME

75% power at 8,000 feet, 88 gallons useable fuel	813 nm

FUEL FLOW

at 80% power at 6,000 ft	13.4 gph

ENDURANCE

at 80% power cruise	6.34 hours

Table 6.2 *continued*

RATE OF CLIMB

At Sea Level	924 FPM
At 8,000 feet	455 FPM

MAXIMUM OPERATING ALTITUDE

Maximum Ceiling Altitude	18,100 feet

TAKEOFF PERFORMANCE (AT SEA LEVEL)

Ground Roll	795 feet
Total distance over 50 ft obstacle	1,625 feet

LANDING PERFORMANCE (AT SEA LEVEL)

Ground Roll	540 feet
Total distance over 50 ft obstacle	1,280 feet

STALL SPEED CAS

Flaps up, power off	51 knots
Flaps down, power off	46 knots

LOADING

Wing Loading	17.8 lb/ft^2
Power Loading	13.5 lb/hp

MAXIMUM WEIGHT

Ramp	3,110 lb
Takeoff	3100 lb
Landing	2,950 lb

STANDARD EMPTY WEIGHT

	1,784 lb

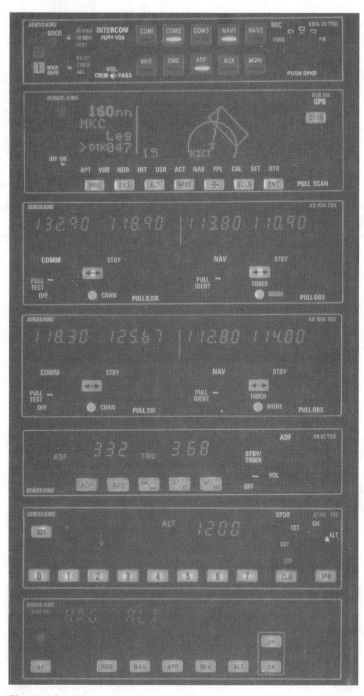

Figure 6.3 Avionics.

Table 6.2 *continued*

FUEL CAPACITY

	92 gallons

ENGINE:

Textron Lycoming	230 hp (175 kW)
I0-540 fuel-injected	at 2,400 rpm, constant speed

Table 6.3 *Cessna 182RG Performance*

SPEED

Maximum at sea level	160 knots
Cruise 75% power at 7500 feet	156 knots

CRUISE RANGE AND TIME

50% power at 12,000 feet, 88 gallons useable fuel	1,100 nautical miles

RATE OF CLIMB

At Sea Level	1,040 FPM
At 8,000 feet	455 FPM

CERTIFIED MAXIMUM OPERATING ALTITUDE

Maximum Ceiling Altitude	14,300 feet

TAKEOFF PERFORMANCE (AT SEA LEVEL)

Ground Roll	820 feet
Total distance over 50-ft obstacle	1,570 feet

LANDING PERFORMANCE (AT SEA LEVEL)

Ground Roll	600 feet
Total distance over 50-ft obstacle	1,320 feet

Table 6.3 continued

STALL SPEED

Flaps up, power off	54 knots
Flaps down, power off	50 knots

MAXIMUM WEIGHT

Ramp	3,112 lbs.
Takeoff or landing	3,100 lbs.

STANDARD EMPTY WEIGHT

	1,784 lbs.

FUEL CAPACITY

	88 gallons

ENGINE

Avco Lycoming	235 hp (175 kW) O-540-J3C5D flat six

Table 6.4 Time, Fuel, and Distance to Climb for the Cessna 182RG

TIME, FUEL, AND DISTANCE TO CLIMB FOR THE CESSNA 182RG

DENSITY ALTITUDE: FROM SEA LEVEL TO	TIME (MINUTES)	FUEL BURNED (GALLONS)	DISTANCE TRAVELED (NAUTICAL MILES)
2,000	3	1.0	5
4,000	6	2.0	10
6,000	9	3.1	15
8,000	12	4.4	21
10,000	18	6.1	30

Table 6.5 *Cessna 182RG Cruise Performance Table*

CESSNA 182RG CRUISE PERFORMANCE TABLE

Altitude	75% Power		65% Power		55% Power	
	KTAS	NMPG	KTAS	NMPG	KTAS	NMPG
2500	148	11	140	11.9	131	13
5000	152	11.2	143	12.2	134	13.3
7500	156	11.5	147	12.5	136	13.5
10,000			150	12.8	139	13.8

Table 6.6 *Airspeed Limitations*

CESSNA 182RG AIRSPEED LIMITATIONS

SPEED		KCAS	KIAS
V_{NE}		175	181
V_{NO}		155	159
V_A		111	112
V_{FE}	0° to 10° Flaps	137	140
	10° to 20° Flaps	119	120
	20° to Full Flaps	96	95
V_{LO}		137	140
V_{LE}		137	140

When landing with the engines out, your optimal glide speed is 80 knots. With the propeller windmilling, flaps and gear up and zero wind conditions, you can expect to glide up to 20 nm from 12,000 ft, but only 5 nm from 2000 ft.

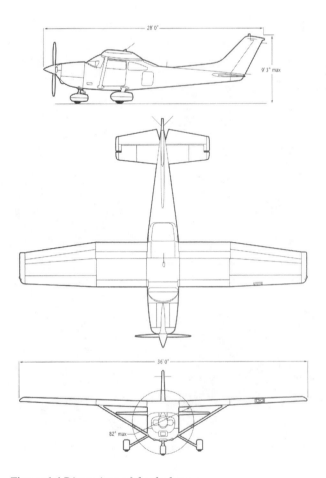

Figure 6.4 Dimensions of the sky lane.

7

Commanding the LearJet 45

Bill Lear, the colorful creator of the Learjet, made his first fortune as an electrical engineer. He invented the radio compass and the first jet autopilot for the F-5 fighter, earning the prestigious Collier Trophy for the latter invention. Other inventions of his include the car radio, the eight track stereo, and the steam-powered bus.

By the late 1950s, Lear saw the need for a business jet and decided to move his avionics firm, Lear, Inc., into the aircraft manufacturing business. His board would have none of it, however, so Lear promptly resigned, sold all his shares for $12 million and moved to Switzerland to work on his business jet idea. He had trouble adjusting to the work habits of the Swiss workmen, who worked normal business hours and were slow and methodical, but were excellent craftsmen. Lear was impulsive and impatient, and routinely worked twelve hour days six or seven days a week. He chafed under these conditions. In 1962, he moved the company to Wichita, Kansas and renamed it the Lear Jet Corporation.

After another 2 years of work, the first Learjet was completed and certified by the FAA. This was the Lear Model 23 and it could fly at speeds as high as Mach 0.82 at an altitude as high as 41,000 ft. Other Learjet models followed, including the Lear 24, Lear 25, Lear 28/29, Lear 35A, Lear 36A, Lear 55, Lear 31A, Lear 60, and the Lear 45. FS98 uses the Lear 45; previous versions of Flight Simulator used the Lear 35A. Lear did not live to see the newest of his company's creations; he passed away on May 14, 1978. Just before his death, he was hard at work championing another new airplane, the Lear Fan, which was to be a composite turboprop twin pusher. This plane had two engines which were geared to drive one propeller. A possibly apocryphal story is told about the Lear Jet engineers who were considering making major changes to Lear's design after his death. Just as the vote was called, a tremendous bolt of lightning struck the plant, and thereafter the project was dropped. Another story had to do with how proud Lear was of his wraparound acrylic windshields; they were supposed to be strong enough to withstand a bird strike at 250 knots. Lear, who kept a windshield in his office, loved to jump up and down on it to prove its strength to visitors. For the coup de grace, he would take out a cannon ball and drop it on the windshield, chortling to himself all the while.

In 1995, Learjet announced that they intended to develop a new Lear 45, which was to be a totally different design. For the first time, the project would be a collaborative venture, a partnership with the Bombardier Aerospace Group, which included De Havilland-Canada. It was determined that Shorts would build the fuselage, and De Havilland would perform the design and construction of the wings. The Lear 45 design called for a range of 2,200 nm, a maximum cruise speed of Mach 0.81, and a ceiling of 51,000 ft. It was to be powered by the 3,500 lb thrust Garrett TFE731-20 turbofan, which was the most recent powerplant Garrett had developed. For greater fuel efficiency, the Lear 45 was designed with winglets. Standard avionics were to include an EFIS flat panel display with EICAS. The aerodynamic design for the plane was performed on a NASA computer using computational fluid dynamics.

The Model 45 made its maiden flight on October 7, 1995, and is currently the most advanced of the Learjet line of business jets. Its dimensions are shown in Figure 7.1.

N O T E

For many years, the U.S. Federal Aviation Administration (FAA) has used a unique device for testing the strength of windshields on airplanes. The device is a modified cannon that launches a chicken carcass at a plane's windshield at approximately the plane's flying speed.

The theory behind this test is that if the windshield doesn't crack from the impact, it can survive a real collision with a bird during flight. The Air Force, while testing a new airplane, decided to borrow the FAA's chicken launcher to test a new windshield they were developing. They loaded the chicken, aimed the cannon and fired.

The ballistic chicken shattered the windshield, went through the cockpit and embedded itself in the back of the cockpit. The Air Force testers were stunned and asked the FAA to recheck the test to see if everything was done correctly. The FAA reviewed the test thoroughly and had one recommendation: Use a thawed chicken.

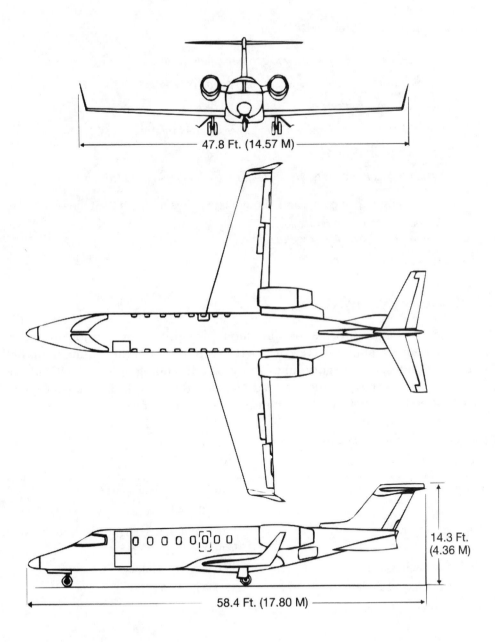

Figure 7.1 *LearJet 45 Dimensions.*

Memorable Quotes by Bill Lear

"If you put up half the money, you can make half the decisions"

"I'd sell my grandmother to save just one pound of weight."

"Don't tell me it can't be done."

"The trick is to discern a market before there is proof that one exists."

"Too soon is just right."

"Strive for design simplicity; you never have to fix anything you leave out."

Bill Lear brushing off complaints about a lack of headroom in the Learjet:
"You don't stand up in a Cadillac,"
"If you want to take a walk, go to Central Park."

GENERAL DESCRIPTION

The Learjet 45 is a pressurized, low-wing monoplane with provision for up to eleven persons, including a minimum crew of two. It is certified under the requirements of the FAA's Part 25 transport category, and can fly CAT II landing approaches. With high-aspect ratio swept wings, the design load factor of the Lear 45 is –1.0 g's to 3.0 g's. Tables 7.1–7.8 shows the Learjet 45's statistics and performance.

Table 7.1 *Approximate Dimensions*

GENERAL

Certification Status	FAR Part 25—Transport Category
	EC JAR 25—Europe
Approved Operations	Day, Night, IFR & Flight Into Known Icing Conditions
Minimum Flight Crew	Two-Pilot & Copilot
Max Operating Alititude	51,000 ft (15,545 m)
Passenger Seating Capacity	Up to Nine
Power Plant:	
Type	Allied Signal TFE 731-20
Number	7,000 lbs (3,500 lbs/engine)

Table 7.1 *continued*

Takeoff Thrust (Sea Level, ISA)	31,137 N (15,569 N/engine)
Flat Rated To	88°F (31°C)

EXTERIOR DIMENSIONS

Length	57.99 ft (17.68 m)
Height	14.06 ft (4.29 m)
Wing Span	47.82 ft (14.56 m)
Wing Area	311.6 sq. ft (28.95 sq. m)
Wing Sweep @ 25% Chord	13.4 degrees
Main Wheel Tread	9.35 ft (2.85 m)

INTERIOR DIMENSIONS

Total Length	24.75 ft (7.54 m)
Total Volume	495 cu ft (14.02 cu m)
Cabin Length	19.75 ft (6.02 m)
Cabin Height	59 in (1.49 m)
Cabin Width	61 in (1.55 m)
Baggage Volume (External)	50 cu ft (1.42 cu m)

Table 7.2 *Learjet 45 Performance*

AIRPORT PERFORMANCE

Takeoff Field Length	4470 ft (1,362 m)
FAR 91 Landing Distance	2990 ft (911 m)

CLIMB PERFORMANCE

Timea Level to Sea Level To:

41,000 ft	23 min
43,000 ft	27 min
45,000 ft	37 min

Table 7.2 continued

CRUISE PERFORMANCE

Typical Cruise Speeds

@37,000 ft	449 KTAS, 517 mph, 832 km/hr
@41,000 ft	441 KTAS, 507 mph, 817 km/hr
@45,000 ft	434 KTAS, 499 mph, 804 km/hr

MAXIMUM OPERATING SPEEDS

Vmo	330 Kts
Mmo	0.81 Mi

RANGE **2,147 NM**

VFR Range	2,471 sm
	3,976 km
NBAA IFR Range	1,800 nm
	2,071 sm
	3,334 km

Table 7.3 Learjet 45 Weight Requirements

WEIGHT LIMITS	LBS (KGS)
Ramp	20,250 (9,185)
Takeoff	20,000 (9,072)
Landing	19,200 (8,709)
Zero Fuel	15,500 (7,031)

USABLE FUEL CAPACITY

pounds	6,000
gallons @ 6.7 lbs/gal	896
liters	3,390
kilograms	2,722

Table 7.3 continued

WEIGHT BUILDUP

Basic Empty Weight	12,050 (5,466)
Optional Equipment Allowance	300 (136)
Two Crew	400 (181)
Operating Weight	12,750 (5,783)

CAPACITIES

Useful Load	7,500 (3,402)
Payload with Full Fuel	1,500 (680)

CAPACITIES

Maximum Payload	2,750 (1,247)
Maximum Baggage Weight	500 (227)

Table 7.4 Learjet 45 Takeoff Performance

TAKEOFF DISTANCE (IN FEET)

Flaps 20°, Rudder Boost = ON			TEMPERATURE		
TAKEOFF WEIGHT	60°F (16°C)	70°F (21°C)	80°F (27°C)	90°F (32°C)	100°F (38°C)
Sea Level					
20,000 lbs	4470	4550	4635	4720	5110
19,000 lbs	3965	4040	4110	4185	4515
18,000 lbs	3525	3585	3645	3710	3985
17,000 lbs	3195	3250	3305	3360	3560
16,000 lbs	3050	3100	3150	3200	3345
15,000 lbs	2995	3045	3095	3145	3280
2,000 ft					
20,000 lbs	4780	4830	4950	5490	6720
19,000 lbs	4235	4315	4415	4850	5705
18,000 lbs	3755	3825	3915	4270	4855

Table 7.4 continued

TAKEOFF DISTANCE (IN FEET)

Flaps 20°, Rudder Boost = ON			TEMPERATURE		
TAKEOFF WEIGHT	60°F (16°C)	70°F (21°C)	80°F (27°C)	90°F (32°C)	100°F (38°C)
17,000 lbs	3405	3465	3540	3790	4235
16,000 lbs	3245	3300	3370	3540	3815
15,000 lbs	3190	3245	3310	3465	3635
4,000 ft					
20,000 lbs	5100	5280	5965	—	—
19,000 lbs	4545	4700	5240	6165	—
18,000 lbs	4030	4160	4595	5240	6400
17,000 lbs	3645	3750	4055	4550	5335
16,000 lbs	3470	3555	3750	4075	4530
15,000 lbs	3410	3490	3665	3850	4125
6,000 ft					
20,000 lbs	5630	6495	—	—	—
19,000 lbs	5005	5670	6750	—	—
18,000 lbs	4430	4960	5755	6435	—
17,000 lbs	3990	4350	4925	5740	6965
16,000 lbs	3775	4000	4350	4885	5830
15,000 lbs	3705	3885	4085	4420	5055
8,000 ft					
20,000 lbs	7020	—	—	—	—
19,000 lbs	6140	7250	—	—	—
18,000 lbs	5350	6230	7390	—	—
17,000 lbs	4700	5360	6235	—	—
16,000 lbs	4290	4700	5320	6415	—
15,000 lbs	4140	4370	4755	5575	6760

Table 7.5 *Learjet 45 Climb Performance*

TIME, FUEL, AND DISTANCE TO CLIMB

....

Maximum Climb Thrust

Standard Day Conditions

START CLIMB WEIGHT (lbs)	15,000	16,000	17,000	18,000	19,000	20,000
SEA LEVEL TO						
25,000 ft						
Time (min)	6.4	6.9	7.4	7.9	8.5	9
Fuel (lbs)	288	310	332	354	378	402
Distance (nm)	33	36	38	40	44	47
29,000 ft						
Time (min)	8	8.6	9.2	9.9	10.5	11.2
Fuel (lbs)	342	367	394	421	450	478
Distance (nm)	42	46	50	52	56	60
33,000 ft						
Time (min)	10	10.7	11.5	12.4	13.3	14.2
Fuel (lbs)	402	434	466	500	535	571
Distance (nm)	56	60	64	70	74	80
37,000 ft						
Time (min)	11.9	12.9	13.9	14.9	16.1	17.3
Fuel (lbs)	456	4923	530	570	612	657
Distance (nm)	69	75	81	87	94	101
39,000 ft						
Time (min)	13.1	14.3	15.5	16.8	18.1	19.6
Fuel (lbs)	486	526	568	612	660	709
Distance (nm)	78	84	91	99	107	116
41,000 ft						
Time (min)	14.6	16.0	17.4	19.0	20.7	22.6
Fuel (lbs)	518	562	609	660	714	774
Distance (nm)	87	96	104	114	124	136
43,000 ft						
Time (min)	16.5	18.0	19.8	21.8	24.2	27.0
Fuel (lbs)	553	603	658	717	784	861

Table 7.5 *continued*

TIME, FUEL, AND DISTANCE TO CLIMB

START CLIMB WEIGHT (lbs)	15,000	16,000	17,000	18,000	19,000	20,000
SEA LEVEL TO						
Distance (nm)	100	110	120	133	148	166
45,000 ft						
Time (min)	18.8	20.9	23.3	26.3	30.6	37.3
Fuel (lbs)	594	652	718	796	898	1044
Distance (nm)	115	128	144	163	191	235
47,000 ft						
Time (min)	22.0	25.1	29.7	—	—	—
Fuel (lbs)	647	722	820	—	—	—
Distance (nm)	137	157	186	—	—	—

Table 7.6 *Learjet 45 High Speed Cruise Performance {Standard (ISA) Day Conditions*

CRUISE WEIGHT (lbs)	15,000	16,000	17,000	18,000	19,000	20,000
CRUISE ALTITUDE						
25,000 ft						
Speed (KTAS)	438	438	437	436	435	433
Fuel Flow (lbs/hr)	2060	2060	2059	2059	2058	2057
29,000 ft						
Speed (KTAS)	447	446	445	444	443	441
Fuel Flow (lbs/hr)	1894	1893	1893	1892	1892	1891
33,000 ft						
Speed (KTAS)	451	450	448	447	446	444
Fuel Flow (lbs/hr)	1720	1719	1514	1513	1512	1510
37,000 ft						
Speed (KTAS)	450	449	448	446	444	442
Fuel Flow (lbs/hr)	1516	1515	1514	1513	1512	1510

Table 7.6 continued

CRUISE WEIGHT (lbs)	15,000	16,000	17,000	18,000	19,000	20,000
CRUISE ALTITUDE						
39,000 ft						
Speed (KTAS)	446	445	443	440	437	433
Fuel Flow (lbs/hr)	1364	1363	1361	1360	1358	1356
41,000 ft						
Speed (KTAS)	444	441	438	434	430	423
Fuel Flow (lbs/hr)	1244	1243	1241	1239	1237	1233
43,000 ft						
Speed (KTAS)	443	439	435	429	422	411
Fuel Flow (lbs/hr)	1157	1155	1153	1150	1146	1140
45,000 ft						
Speed (KTAS)	439	434	427	417	395	388
Fuel Flow (lbs/hr)	1069	1066	1062	1057	1042	1035
47,000 ft						
Speed (KTAS)	426	416	396	—	—	—
Fuel Flow (lbs/hr)	953	949	940	—	—	—

Table 7.7 Learjet 45 Long Range Cruise Performance Standard (ISA) Day Conditions

CRUISE WEIGHT (lbs)	15,000	16,000	17,000	18,000	19,000	20,000
CRUISE ALTITUDE						
25,000 ft						
Speed (KTAS)	280	287	295	302	311	317
Fuel Flow (lbs/hr)	908	959	1009	1061	1120	1172
29,000 ft						
Speed (KTAS)	297	307	316	324	329	337
Fuel Flow (lbs/hr)	881	937	993	1044	1090	1145
33,000 ft						
Speed (KTAS)	320	329	335	343	352	358

Table 7.7 *continued*

CRUISE WEIGHT (lbs)	15,000	16,000	17,000	18,000	19,000	20,000
CRUISE ALTITUDE						
Fuel Flow (lbs/hr)	872	924	969	1022	1080	1133
37,000 ft						
Speed (KTAS)	349	357	366	374	379	—
Fuel Flow (lbs/hr)	857	904	958	1013	1069	1118
39,000 ft						
Speed (KTAS)	353	362	372	379	381	386
Fuel Flow (lbs/hr)	853	907	964	1014	1054	1109
41,000 ft						
Speed (KTAS)	367	376	382	386	394	404
Fuel Flow (lbs/hr)	856	911	957	1004	1067	1140
43,000 ft						
Speed (KTAS)	380	384	390	402	410	—
Fuel Flow (lbs/hr)	857	902	956	1031	1098	—
45,000 ft						
Speed (KTAS)	387	397	408	416	—	—
Fuel Flow (lbs/hr)	848	915	987	1053	—	—
47,000 ft						
Speed (KTAS)	404	413	—	—	—	—
Fuel Flow (lbs/hr)	874	940	—	—	—	—

Table 7.8 *Learjet 45 IFR Mission Performance for Long Range Cruise*

DISTANCE (NM)	CRUISE ALTITUDE (FT)	BLOCK TIME (HRS:MIN)	BLOCK FUEL (lbs)	BLOCK SPEED (KTAS)	BLOCK FUEL FLOW (GAL/HR)
200	35,000	0:47	925	255	176.2
	37,000	0:46	921	261	179.3
400	390,900	1:19	1417	304	160.6
	41,000	1:17	1399	312	162.7
600	43,000	1:46	1857	340	156.9

Table 7.8 continued

DISTANCE (NM)	CRUISE ALTITUDE (FT)	BLOCK TIME (HRS:MIN)	BLOCK FUEL (lbs)	BLOCK SPEED (KTAS)	BLOCK FUEL FLOW (GAL/HR)
	45,000	1:45	1835	343	156.5
800	45,000	2:15	2309	356	153.2
	47,000	2:11	2293	366	156.8
1000	45,000	2:45	2793	364	151.6
	47,000	2:40	2769	375	155.0
1200	45,000	3:15	3289	369	151.0
	47,000	3:09	3256	381	154.3
1400	45,000	3:44	3795	375	151.7
	47,000	3:37	3752	387	154.8
1600	45,000	4:13	4315	379	152.7
	47,000	4:07	4266	389	154.7
1800	45,000	4:41	4846	384	154.4
	47,000	4:35	4792	393	156.0

RANGE PERFORMANCE

The Learjet 45 has a fuel tank capacity of 6,000 lb, or 896 gallons (at 6.7 lb/gal). This is equivalent to 33,90 liters or 2,722 kilograms. This capacity gives the Learjet a range of 2,147 nm, or 2,471 statute miles (3,976 km). This is barely enough to get to Hawaii from San Francisco or from Gandor to London across the North Atlantic. You will have to plan your flights very carefully if you are to successfully budget enough fuel to make it over the pond. See Figure 7.2 for a display of its range.

For increased fuel realism, be sure to go to the **Aircraft/Aircraft Settings** dialog box and choose **Aircraft runs out of fuel**, or else the airplane will never run out fuel.

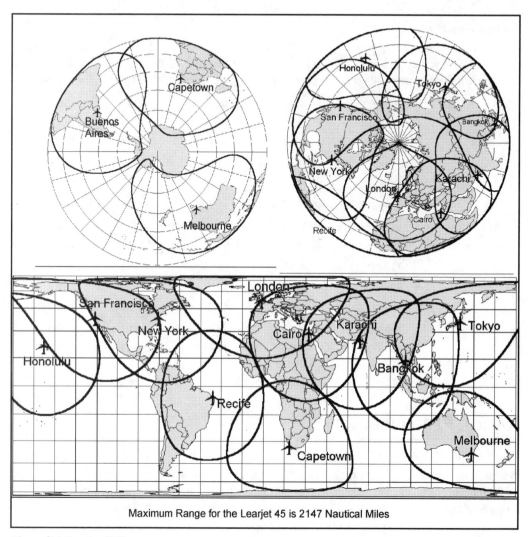

Maximum Range for the Learjet 45 is 2147 Nautical Miles

Figure 7.2 Learjet 45 Range.

8

Mastering the Boeing 737-400

The 737 is a magnificent airplane to fly, but there is a lot to learn to fly it well. This chapter will explain how long a runway is needed for takeoffs or landings, the range of the 737, and how much fuel is required for a trip. You may consider this an owner's operation manual for the 737. The performance charts and tables will enhance your mastery of the plane and increase your enjoyment and understanding of the 737's capabilities and limitations. But before diving into technical data, let's take a brief look at Boeing and the 737 family of jets.

BOEING

The Boeing Commercial Airplane Group, headquartered at Renton, Washington, is the world's leading manufacturer of airliner jets. In 1995, Boeing produced eighty nine 737s, twenty five 747s, forty three 77s, thirty six 767s and thirteen 777s, for a total of two hundred and six aircraft. This was considered a "bad year," for in 1994, Boeing produced 270 aircraft. Airliner orders picked up as the U. S. economy recovered, and the company announced 346 new orders in 1995, valued at $31.2 billion. In order to sustain this kind of output, Boeing has become the largest employer in Washington with over 133,350 men and women in its workforce. Over the years, it has built more than 9,000 passenger jets. Of that number, 3,255 were of the 737 series, which makes the 737 the most popular airliner jet in history.

Table 8.1 *Deliveries of the 737 series to date*

MODEL	TOTAL DELIVERED (AS OF DEC 31, 1995)
737-100	30
737-200	1114
737-300	1098
737-400	433
737-500	360
737-600	81
737-700	96
737-800	43
Total	**3255**

The 737-400 used in FS98 is really a stretched version of the 737-300. First announced in June 1986, the 737-400 was rolled out in January 1988 for its first flight. ETOPS approval, which is discussed in the Global Navigation chapter, was granted in 1990 as the FAA gained confidence in the CFM-56 engines' reliability.

Boeing has had to keep on its toes in recent years because of fierce competition of the European Airbus consortium. Airbus, no longer willing to cede the American market to Boeing, is actively courting the largest domestic carriers in the U.S. In the rest of the world, they are hoping to make big inroads into the dominant position of American airplane manufacturing. The main rival for the Boeing 737-400 is the Airbus A320, while the challengers for the 737-800 are the A320, MD-80 and MD-90. The main competitor to the Boeing 737-300 and 737-700 is the Airbus A319.

The list price of the 737-400 is $42 million. Without discounts, the monthly ownership cost is about $378,000, but the monthly lease rate is about $265,000. By comparison, it is interesting to note that the new 777-200 costs $109 million, with a monthly lease rate of $1 million. Fuel burn on the 737-400 is 7% higher than the Airbus A319, although the 737-400 is 8% cheaper to run than the MD-90.

THE 737 FAMILY

The 737 family was designed to operate over short to medium ranges at cruise speeds up to 580 mph (504 knots or 933 kmph) and from sea level runways of less than 6,000 ft in length. First introduced in 1965 as the 737-100 with a JT8D turbojet engine, production of the 737 quickly shifted to the 737-200 series. The 737-200 was quite popular, but with the advent of turbofan technology in the late 1970's, Boeing decided to seek a more fuel efficient and less noisy alternative to the turbojet powered –200 series. Therefore, without much fanfare, the turbofan powered 737-300 series replaced the –200 series in 1984. In 1988, the 737-400 was put into service, incorporating all the technology of the 737-300, but with an extended fuselage and the addition of new higher thrust CFMC-56-3C turbofan engines for greater payload capability. The 737-500 was introduced in 1990, followed by the 737-800 in 1994, and the 737-700 in 1997. The 737-600 is to be released in 1998. The 737-600, 737-700, and 737-800 are designated as the 737-X series.

THE 737-X SERIES

The newest 737-X series was developed to replace the 300/400/500 family. The 162 seat 737-800 was launched as a direct replacement to the 148 seat 400 series, but with a stretched fuselage, it accomodates 164 to 189 seats. The 128 seat 737–300 series is to be replaced by the 128 seat 737-700 series, while the 108 seat 737-600 is planned as a replacement for the 500.

The 737-700 design includes a new wing that increases fuel carrying capacity by some 30%, to almost 6,900 gallons, and this allows it to cruise at 41,000 ft, up from the 37,000 ft ceiling of existing models. The additional fuel storage increases the range capability to about 2,900 nm, which gives the plane transcontinental range. One has to wonder why Microsoft didn't update FS98 with the 737-700, as this is a superior airplane in all respects to the 737–400. Cruise speed on the 737–700 has been improved from Mach 0.78 to 0.82 by the use of a new supercritical wing. New integrated drive generators (IDG) on each engine produce 90 kVA, and either IDG can power the entire aircraft with no reduction in cabin electrical consumption. The new CFM56-7 turbofan provides 10% more thrust (26,400 lb) and 8% lower fuel burn than the CFM56-3s. However, the 737–X series is still marginally slower and less fuel efficient than its Airbus A320 competitor.

There is a high degree of commonality between the new 737s. Flight crew training costs have been reduced by having flight decks share the similar cockpit display systems, although the 737–700 cockpit is fitted with flat-panel Honeywell color Active Matrix Liquid Crystal Displays. As an option, the cockpit can also be fitted with a Global Positioning System, head-up display, and satcom landing avionics. CAT IIIA landing capability is also a standard feature for the 700 series (CAT landing criteria are discussed later in this book).

737-300 Description

Because the FS98 737-400 shares so many features with the 737-300, you can better understand the 737-400 by studying the features that the 737-300 comes equipped with.

The 737-300 is a stretched version of the 737-200 fuselage and it has a 3 ft 8 inch fuselage extension inserted forward of the wing and a 5 ft section aft of the wing. It can seat as many as 149 passengers in an economy configuration. Other differences with the earlier 737-200 included:

- Underfloor freight volume increased by 193 cubic feet.
- The wingspan was extended by 4.4%.
- New slats and new flap sections were added.
- An increased payload and range over that of the 737-200.

The range for the basic "A" version of the 737-300 is 1,600 nm, and the range for the long range "B" is 2,270 nm.

All control surfaces on the 737-300 are powered by two independent hydraulic systems with a third manual standby reversion for ailerons and elevator. The rudder has a standby hydraulic actuator in case of failure of the main system. Three outboard over-wing spoiler panels on each wing assist lateral control and also act as airbrakes. Leading edge Kruger flaps are installed inboard of the engines, and three sections of slats are installed outboard of the engines on each wing. There are triple slotted trailing edge flaps and two airbrake panels on each wing, inboard and outboard of the engines. The FAA has certified the 737-400 for CAT II landing minima using the dual digital integrated flight director/autopilot, though CAT III is an available upgrade option. Since the cockpit shares the same type of instrumentation, a pilot certified to fly on the 737-300 can also fly the 737-200, -400, and -500.

Equipped with a bleed air control system for thermal anti-icing, air conditioning and pressurization systems, the 737-300 has a maximum cabin pressurization differential of 7.5 psi. Electrical power is generated by two 50 kVA variable speed constant frequency generators. The APU provides air supply and electrical power in flight and on the ground as well as engine starting capability.

Avionics for the 737-300, -400, and -500 series are the same. There is a digital color weather radar, a FMC, and EFIS is installed. The FMC provides lateral, vertical, and time navigation using waypoints, and includes dual ring laser gyro inertial navigation units. EFIS screens show a moving map display, flight plan, compass rose, and weather. The electronic engine instrument system has colored LED dials, with standby backup indicators, and there is a windshear alerting system with recovery guidance information displayed in the Attitude indicator. Full Auto-throttle authority over the engines is tied into the autopilot.

THE 737-400

The 737-400 is a stretched (ten foor longer) version of the 737-300. Two sections were added to the –300 fuselage; a five foot section forward of the wing, and a four foot section aft of the wing. As with the –300 series, the –400 has a basic and long range version, designated A and B respectively. The A version has a maximum takeoff weight of 138,500 lb, whereas the B version has a maximum takeoff weight of 150,000 lb. The Long Range B version can fly as far as 2,090 nm with a maximum passenger load, whereas the Basic A version is limited to about 1,600 nm. This comfortably covers flights to North African and Middle East resorts from London, and it can also be used for flights from Shannon, Ireland to Gandor, Canada using the higher take-off weight of 150,000 lb for the B variant.

When Microsoft first released the 737-400 in FSW95, many people found that the simulated airplane had nowhere near the published range of 2,090 nm for the real 737-400. We didn't realize, at the time, that the simulator airplane was the short-range basic A version. Unfortunately, this meant San Francisco to Hawaii trips were out, and it also meant that you couldn't fly trans-Atlantic nonstop flights from London to New York without running out of fuel. This was a bitter disappointment, and many Flight Sim pilots were forced to rely on the Learjet, because it had a transcontinental range of just under 2147 nm, which was enough for a San Francisco to Hawaii flight.

With the release of FS98, Microsoft has decided to include the long range B version of the 737-400. With very careful fuel management, it is now possible to fly the 2081 nm trip from San Francisco to Hawaii, but just by a camel's whisker.

The San Francisco–to-Hawaii component of an around-the-world flight is the most crucial, and it can make or break you, because in FS98, there is no other way to get across the Pacific. In real life, of course, this is not so, because one could fly north to Alaska, refuel in Anchorage and fly on to Petropavlovsk in Kamchatka, Russia before flying on to Tokyo. After Tokyo, the rest of the around-the-world trip can be accomplished by hopping to airports within the airplane's range radius (see the Learjet's range illustration in the previous chapter—it is similar to the 737-400's range).

How to Fly to Hawaii in the 737

You can fly from San Francisco to Hawaii in the FS98 737, but to make things easier for yourself, you should install GPS 2.0 (described in Chapter 13, "Global Navigation"). This program will allow you to maintain an accurate course for Hawaii, which is crucial because you don't have an ounce of fuel to spare. Set the waypoint for the Honolulu airport, and let the program guide you to Honolulu. Also, use the autopilot as much as possible during the climb, and don't burn any more fuel during the climb than is indicated in the enroute climb performance Table 8.6. I recommend flying at 31,000 ft with cruise set to 0.74 Mach. If you can get the airplane up to 31,000 ft with about 3304 lb of fuel burned, you are doing very well. After this, you can disengage the GPS Autopilot and fly the rest of the trip using the GPS Steering Indicator (be sure to first click **AUT** on the GPS panel, then turn off the **AP** switch, or else all kinds of havoc may result). If you like, you can even accelerate the simulator speed to 32x (press **R +**) and fly to Hawaii in a matter of minutes. Just be sure to keep the Steering Indicator centered, and keep an eye on your altitude. In my example flight from SF to Honolulu, there were 2800 lbs of fuel left in the tanks (i.e., each gauge showed 1.4).

For extended long range ferrying capability, an auxiliary fuel tank can be installed in the real 737's aft lower cargo compartment. Though this extra fuel increases range, it drastically decreases payload.

737-400 Interior Description

The 737-400 seats up to 168 passengers when all the seats are pitched 30 inches apart, or up to 159 passengers when the seats are pitched 32 inches apart. With mixed classes of service, the airplane can seat 146 people (with 8 first class seats pitched at 36 inches). There are three lavatories on board, two aft and one forward, and there are two galleys, one aft and one rear. There are two service doors and two entry doors; the two service doors are on the right side of the airplane forward and aft, while the two entry doors are on the left side fore and aft (34 x 72 in. Type I forward entry door and 30 x 72 in. Type I aft entry door). In addition there are two Type III Emergency exits (20 x 38 in) installed midwing.

As an option, built-in airstairs allow passenger loading and unloading at airports where there are no loading ramps or stairs. The forward stairs are mounted under the cabin floor just below the entry door, while the aft stairs are installed on a special aft entry door.

Performance and Design Specifications

The 737 is an extremely versatile airplane capable of landing on short unimproved runways in remote parts of the world. For landings on gravel runways, a special gravel kit can be installed. It includes gravel deflectors for the nose and main gears, vortex dissipators for each engine nacelle, and special coatings for the nacelle surfaces. When landings are anticipated at soft low strength runways, the airplane can be fitted with low pressure tires.

Figure 8.1 shows the dimensions of the 737-400, while Table 8.2 lists important performance data of the airplane.

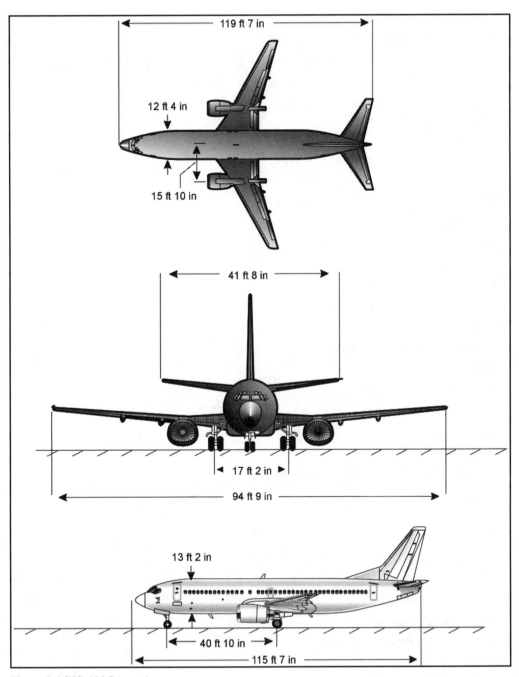

Figure 8.1 737-400 Dimensions.

Table 8.2 Performance Data

BOEING 737-400 TECHNICAL CHARACTERISTICS

Power Plant	Two CFM56-3C-1 Turbofans, each rated at 22,000 lb or 23,500 lb
Fuel Capacity	5,311 U.S. Gallons (23,830 liters) or 35,584 lb
Maximum Long Range Option Fuel Capacity*	6,295 U.S. Gallons (23,830 liters) 42,177 lb
Passengers	Up to 168

Dimensions

Wing span	94 ft 9 in
Wing chord at root	15 ft 5.5 in
Wing aspect ratio	7.9
Wing area	1,135 ft^2
Length overall	119 ft 7 in
Height overall	36 ft 6 in
Tailplane span	41 ft 8 in
Wheel track	17 ft 2 in
Wheelbase	40 ft 10 in
Cabin floor area	914 ft^2
Freight volume	1,373 ft^3

Weights and Loading (A: Basic, B: Long Range)

Operating weight empty [1]

A	75,800 lb
B	77,520 lb

Maximum takeoff weight [2]

A	138,500 lb
B	150,000 lb

Maximum ramp weight [3]

A	143,000 lb
B	150,500 lb

Table 8.2 *continued*

Weights and Loading (A: Basic, B: Long Range)

Maximum zero weight fuel [4]

A   113,000 lb

B   117,000 lb

Wing Loading

A   122 lb/ft^2

B   132.2 lb/ft^2

Performance 5

Maximum operating speed	Mach 0.82
Cruising speed	Mach 0.745
Approach speed	139 knots (257 kmph or 160 mph)
Initial cruising altitude	31,700 ft
Service ceiling	37,000 ft
Maximum service ceiling with one engine inoperative (depends on weight—this example assumes a 119,000 lb airplane)	17,300 ft
Maximum range with one engine inoperative (34,000 lb of fuel on board)	
B	2,027 nm
Takeoff field length, sea level at 30° C (86° F)	5,050 ft
Landing field length, sea level at maximum landing weight	5,050 ft
Maximum cabin pressure differential	8.65 psi

*Not available in FS98.

[1]*Weight of structure, powerplant, furnishing system, unusable fuel and other items of equipment.*

[2]*Maximum weight at the start of the takeoff run.*

[3]*Maximum weight while on ground during taxi and runup.*

[4]*Maximum weight allowed before fuel must be loaded in defined sections of the aircraft to maintain structural integrity.*

[5]*With 136 passengers and takeoff weight of 150,000 lb.*

You should always observe the FAA mandated 250 knot maximum airspeed while under 10,000 ft. However, during takeoff or landing, your flaps also have maximum airspeed limits, depending on their flap setting. Table 8.3 lists these flap-limit speeds.

Table 8.3 *Flap-Limit Speeds*

FLAP-LIMIT SPEEDS

Flap Setting	Flap Limit Speed (knots)
1° to 5°	250
10°	215
15°	205
25°	190
30°	185
49°	162

The Payload/Range Chart (Figure 8.2) shows that the maximum range of the 737-400 depends on weight. When it is empty of fuel, passengers and cargo, the 737-400 B variant weighs 77,520 lb. If you add 168 passengers at 250 lb apiece (including their luggage), this brings the payload weight to 42,000 lb (because 168 × 250 lb = 42,000 lb). The airplane plus payload, but without fuel, now weighs 119,520 lb. This leaves room for only 30,480 lb of fuel (because the airplane has a maximum takeoff weight of 150,000 lb), so you would not be allowed to take off with a full tank of fuel! Of course, you don't need to worry about these kinds of things in Flight Simulator, because the program makes a fixed assumption about the payload.

Using Figure 8.2, let's assume that the airplane plus payload weighs 105,000 lb. If we put in 33,500 lb of fuel, the airplane would weigh in at 138,500 lb, and this would correspond to the diagonal line for "138,500 lb" in the diagram. Now look at the intersection of the 105,000 lb Y axis scale and the diagonal line labeled "138,500 lb" of the Brake Release Gross Weight. If you drop a vertical line straight down from this intersection to the horizontal X axis, you will see that the airplane has a range of a little over 2000 nautical miles.

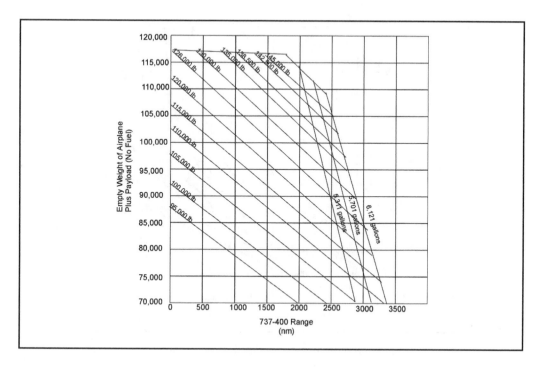

Figure 8.2 Payload/Range for Long-Range Cruise.

Figure 8.3 and Figure 8.4 show the 737-400's takeoff runway length requirements for a standard day and a hot day for various airport elevations. Not surprisingly, when it is hot and the elevation is high, or the airplane is heavy, a much longer runway is required. You'll remember that this is a problem of density altitude, discussed in Chapter 5. Let's take a look at the graph for a hot day to understand its implications. Suppose that an 8,000 ft elevation airport with an 11,000 ft runway, the airplane weighs in at 150,000 lb. We see that there is no intersection of 150,000 lb on the horizontal axis with the 8,000 ft airport elevation graph. Therefore we **cannot** takeoff from this airport with this weight. In order to takeoff we would have to shed 20,000 lb of payload to bring the airplane's weight down to 130,000 lb. At this weight, you can see that the horizontal axis at 130,000 just barely intersects the 8,000 ft airport elevation graph, and that at this intersection the runway length would have to be at least 11,000 ft.

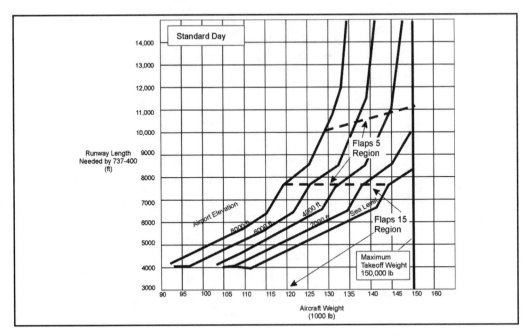

Figure 8.3 *Takeoff Runway Length Requirements—Standard Day (12° C or 54° F).*

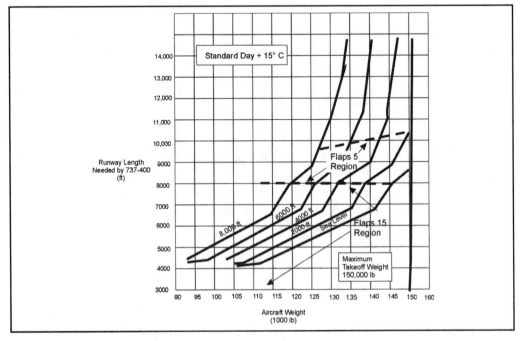

Figure 8.4 *Takeoff Runway Length Requirements—Hot Day (27° C or 80° F).*

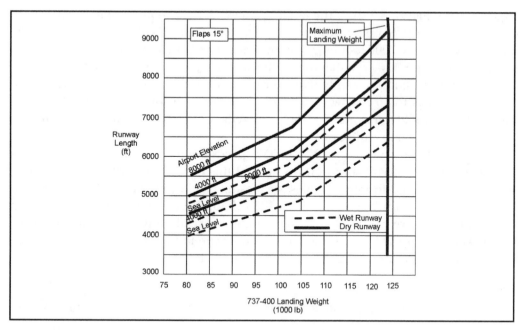

Figure 8.5 Landing Runway Length Requirements—Flap Position 15°.

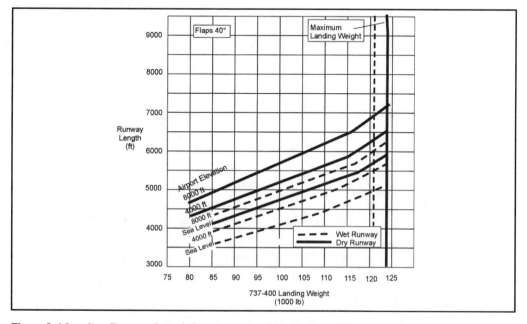

Figure 8.6 Landing Runway Length Requirements—Flap Position 40°.

Figure 8.5 and Figure 8.6 show the landing runway length requirements for flap positions of 15° and 40°. Suppose we are landing a 100,000 lb 737-400 at an 8,000 foot elevation airport with a 6,000 foot long runway. Is it safe to land with a flap position of 15°? Looking at Figure 8.5, we see that for a 100,000 lb 737, it would need a 6,600 foot runway; from this we know instantly that we can't land at this runway. How about if we increase the flaps to 40°? Now we see that in Figure 8.6 for the 40° flap setting, a 100,000 lb 737 would require a 5700 foot runway. So we can land the airplane at this airport if we choose a flap setting of 40°.

Knowing what the proper V_1, V_R, and V_2 speeds are for a given airplane weight is also important for takeoff. But how do we find this information without performing algebra? Pilots use performance tables, such as that shown in Table 8.4, as a shortcut. For example, if the airplane weighs in at 143,000 lb, and the temperature is 80°, for a flap setting of 15°, we use the first set of columns and read off the values of V_1=143 kts, V_R=145 kts, and V_2=152 knots. If the temperature were hotter, or the flap settings were different, you would use the other columns as marked.

Table 8.4 *Takeoff Speeds with Flaps at 15°*

WEIGHT lb	35° C (90° F) AND BELOW			35° C TO 40° (90° TO 105° F)		
	V_1	V_R	V_2	V_1	V_R	V_2
154000	149	152	157			
143000	143	145	152	144	146	151
132000	137	138	146	138	139	146
121000	130	131	140	131	132	140
110000	122	124	134	123	124	134
99000	114	116	128	116	117	128
88000	106	107	122	108	108	122

When landing, you can look up approach V_{REF} speeds in a listing such as Table 8.5.

Table 8.5 *V_{REF} Landing Speeds*

Weight (1000) lb														
88	92	97	101	105	110	114	119	123	127	132	136	141	145	149

VREF for 15° Flaps (kts)														
132	135	139	142	145	149	151	155	158	161	164	166	169	172	174

As previously discussed in the section on how to fly from San Francisco to Hawaii, you should use no more than 3,304 lb of fuel climbing to 31,000 ft altitude (assuming a 136,000 lb airplane). This data is found in Table 8.6 below, which shows that for a weight of 136,000 lb, the fuel burn should be 3,304 lb for an altitude of 31,000 ft, and that the time it should take to climb to this altitude is 17 minutes. The table also tells you that you'll end up with an airspeed of 375 TAS and the climb will have covered a ground distance of 95 nm. This means that if you start out with a reading of "17" in each fuel gauge (the gauge shows thousands of pounds of fuel), and climb to 31,000 ft, you should end up with 15 1/3 in each fuel gauge, because 17+17 = 34(000) and 34(000) lb – 3304 lb =30,696 lb. This will be displayed as "15.3" for each fuel tank gauge.

Table 8.6 *Enroute Climb Performance Table for the 737-400*

TAKEOFF WEIGHT

PRESSURE ALTITUDE (FT)	149,000 lb				136,000 lb			
	TIME (MIN)	FUEL BURN (lb)	DISTANCE (NM)	TAS (KTS)	TIME (MIN)	FUEL BURN (lb)	DISTANCE (NM)	TAS (KTS)
37,000	*	*	*	*	32	4960	197	400
35,000	33	5401	209	399	22	3968	133	389
31,000	21	3968	117	378	17	3304	95	375
25,000	14	2976	69	351	12	2532	58	350
20,000	10	2315	45	333	9	2092	39	332
15,000	7	1764	28	318	7	1652	24	317
10,000	5	1323	15	305	5	1212	13	305
6,000	4	992	7	295	3	880	7	295

Not possible at this weight.

The Long Range Cruise Performance chart (Table 8.7) is useful for determining expected fuel burn (via the fuel flow in lb/hr), airspeed, and N_1 thrust required for a given altitude. Notice how the fuel flow rate drops markedly when the airplane flies at higher altitudes.

Table 8.7 *Long Range Cruise Performance Table*

LONG RANGE CRUISE PERFORMANCE FOR THE 737-400

| | 145,500 lb Weight | | | | | 110,000 lb Weight | | | | |
PRESSURE ALTITUDE (ft)	%N₁ Thrust Req.	IAS (kts)	Fuel Flow per Engine (lb/hour)	Mach Number	TAS (Kts)	%N₁ Thrust Req.	IAS (kts)	Fuel Flow per Engine (lb/hour)	Mach Number	TAS (Kts)
37,000	*	*	*	*	*	86.5%	240	2390	0.745	427
35,000	*	*	*	*	*	84.6%	251	2419	0.745	429
31,000	88.0%	275	3157	0.745	437	82.8%	274	2573	0.741	435
25,000	84.8%	311	3408	0.742	447	79.6%	287	2716	0.688	414
20,000	82.8%	325	3576	0.703	432	76.6%	292	2815	0.636	390
15,000	79.3%	332	3735	0.653	409	73.5%	296	2928	0.585	367
10,000	76.3%	336	3836	0.605	386	70.4%	299	3034	0.539	344

*Flight not possible at this weight.

In Chapter 2, we discussed total drag and how it was equivalent to thrust. We also illustrated the concept with a graph of parasite drag plus induced drag for the 737 at sea level. From this we were able to determine the minimum amount of thrust necessary to keep the airplane in the air. Figure 8.7 shows the same type of graph you saw earlier in the book, but this time it is plotted for an altitude of 30,000 feet. The graph assumes the 737-400 weighs about 138,500 lb.

Why is this graph useful? Look at the graph and observe its minimum point along the curve. You'll see that minimum total drag occurs at about 380 knots (TAS) and that the 737-400 needs about 10,000 lb of thrust at this altitude to maintain lift. What would happen if an engine suddenly failed? At 30,000 ft, a single engine's thrust would fall off proportionally with the density, so if it could produce 23,500 lb of takeoff thrust at sea level, at 30,000 feet it would only be able to produce about 7900 lb of thrust. Obviously, the single engine alone cannot maintain the 737 at this altitude, and so a descent would have to occur. This simple graph reveals a lot when you glance at the bottom of the curve!

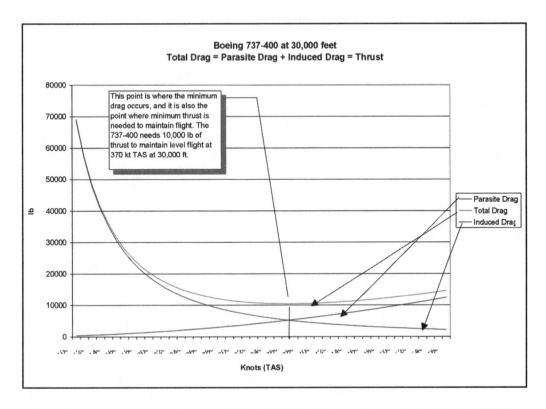

Figure 8.7 *Thrust Required for the Boeing 737 at 30,000 ft. (This graph was generated for the FSW95 737, and should not be mistaken for the real 737's performance).*

All pilots should be prepared for an engine out scenario. In Table 8.8, you can see performance data for the 737 with only one operable engine. Notice that the airplane can only fly as high as 8,000 feet when it weighs 145,500 lb, but that this maximum ceiling rises to 25,000 feet when the airplane weighs 97,000 lb. As you can see, weight makes a huge difference in how high the airplane can fly.

Table 8.8 *One Engine Inoperative—Long Range Cruise Performance Table*

LONG RANGE CRUISE PERFORMANCE FOR THE 737-400 WITH ONE ENGINE OUT

	145,500 lb Weight					110,000 lb Weight				
PRESSURE ALTITUDE (ft)	%N₁ Thrust Req.	IAS (kts)	Fuel Flow per Engine (lb/hour)	Mach Number	TAS (Kts)	%N₁ Thrust Req.	IAS (kts)	Fuel Flow per Engine (lb/hour)	Mach Number	TAS (Kts)
37,000	*	*	*	*	*	*	*	*	*	*
35,000	*	*	*	*	*	*	*	*	*	*
31,000	*	*	*	*	*	*	*	*	*	*
25,000	*	*	*	*	*	93.20%	252	4385	0.609	367
20,000	*	*	*	*	*	89%	260	4467	0.567	348
15,000	*	*	*	*	*	86.60%	268	4769	0.531	333
10,000	*	*	*	*	*	81.90%	263	4606	0.475	303
8,000	90.60%	317	6903	0.551	354	80.50%	263	4625	0.458	295

*Flight is not possible at this weight.

Using Figure 8.8, you can figure out what the exact stall speed, stick shaker speeds, and initial buffet speeds should be for the 737-400. Unfortunately, when I tested these stall speeds with the FS98 737-400, I found that they did not match published data for the real 737-400. Microsoft has been alerted to the problem, and it is hoped that they will correct this in a future update of the program. In the diagram, the speeds listed are V_{EAS}, or Equivalent Airspeed. In Flight Simulator, this is approximately the same as V_{IAS}, or Indicated Airspeed.

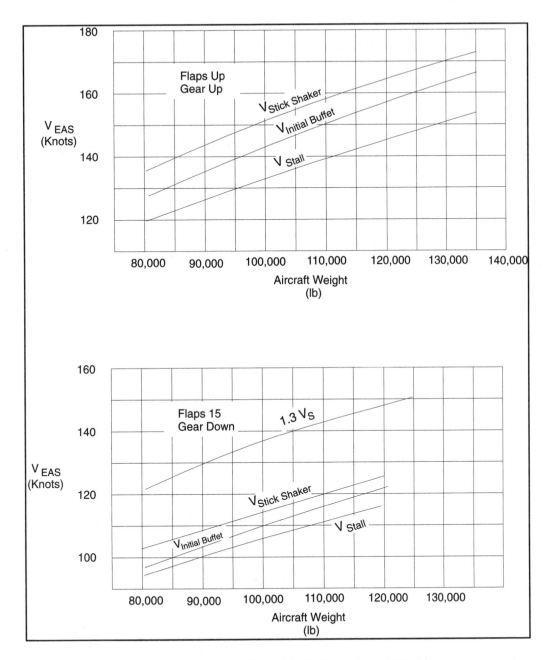

Figure 8.8 Stall Speed, Stick Shaker Speed, and Initial Buffet Speeds for the 737-400.

To see what the correct pitch angle should be for the 737's nose during level flight, the climb, the descent or the final approach, examine Table 8.9. There you will find data for various pitch angles, altitudes, rates of descent, speeds, flap positions, and thrust settings.

Table 8.9 *Aircraft Pitch Relationship During Various Phases of Flight*

BOEING 737-400 PITCH ATTITUDE

FLAP POSITION	PRESSURE ALTITUDE (FT)	APPROXIMATE SPEED	WEIGHT (lb)	AIRPLANE PITCH ANGLE	RATE OF CLIMB/DESCENT (FT/MIN)	THRUST (%N$_1$)
ENROUTE CLIMB						
Up	35,000	Mach 0.7	140,000	6.4°	1100	Max. Climb
	20,000	250 KIAS	140,000	7.2°	2000	Thrust
	10,000	250 KIAS	140,000	9.4°	3000	
	5,000	250 KIAS	140,000	10.7°	3400	
	Sea Level	250 KIAS	150,000	11.7°	3500	
DESCENT						
Up	30,000	Mach 0.7	140,000	0.5°	-2900	Thrust Set to Idle
	30,000	Mach 0.7	80,000	-2.5°	-3500	
	20,000	250 KIAS	140,000	1.1°	-2000	
	20,000	250 KIAS	80,000	-2.1°	-2000	
	10,000	250 KIAS	140,000	5.5°	2000	
	10,000	250 KIAS	80,000	-2.1°	-2700	
HOLDING LEVEL FLIGHT						
Up	10,000	250 KIAS	140,000	5.5°	0	72%
	10,000	250 KIAS	80,000	5.7°	0	56%
FINAL APPROACH (3° GLIDE SLOPE, GEAR DOWN)						
15°	0 to 10,000	179 KIAS	140,000	3.9°	-1000	59%
15°	0 to 10,000	135 KIAS	80,000	5.7°	-800	46%
40°	0 to 10,000	158 KIAS	140,000	0.7°	-900	72%
40°	0 to 10,000	120 KIAS	80,000	0.3°	-700	56%

9

Flying the Bell 206B JetRanger III Helicopter

The introduction of the Bell 206B JetRanger III helicopter to FS98 is an exciting addition to the program. The aerodynamics of rotary-wing aircraft are completely different from those of fixed-wing aircraft, and as such a new flight model that simulates the dynamics of rotating helicopter blades was required. This is a complete departure from the rest of the FS98 program, and getting this to work properly is a major accomplishment. No other simulator available for the PC offers as realistic a simulation of rotary-wing dynamics, so this is an important breakthrough for armchair pilots who have long wished to fly a helicopter.

Flying the simulated helicopter is not easy. There are gyroscopic and ground effect forces involved, both of which are conspiring at all times to throw you out of control. It is your job to react to these forces, especially the rotational ones, and counteract them as needed in order to maintain equilibrium. Believe it or not, the hardest part of flying a helicopter is hovering in one spot. It is easy to take off, easy to fly forwards, and hard to land. The real test of a helicopter pilot's mettle comes when he attempts to hover.

A common misconception is that helicopters should always take off and land vertically. Actually this is not the case, for a helicopter is more stable in motion than it is while hovering. You will find that for taking off, it is better to push the helicopter forward for better stability, and that when landing, it is better to gracefully glide in and pull back gently so that the helicopter settles in under its own momentum.

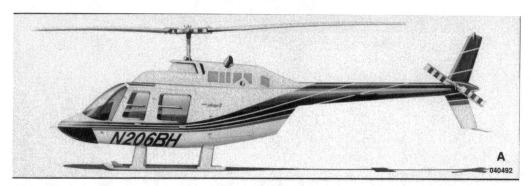

Figure 9.1 Bell 206B-3 JetRanger III (Courtesy of Bell Helicopter Textron).

The Bell JetRanger is a five seat turbine-powered light helicopter constructed by Bell Helicopter Textron at a plant in Mirabel, Canada. Over 7,700 JetRangers have been produced by Bell since the 1960s. In 1982 Australian Dick Smith made the first solo helicopter flight around the world in a JetRanger helicopter. He flew 35,258 miles without a mechanical problem.

Table 9.1 JetRanger Performance Specifications

STANDARD CONFIGURATION

DESCRIPTION	DATA
Weight	1697 lb
FAA Normal Gross Weight	3350 lb
Useful Load	1503 lb
Powerplant	Allison Model 250-C20B 420 SHP flat rated to 317 SHP (236 kW)
Ground Effect Hovering Ceiling (2ft skid height) at 3200 lb	12,800 ft
Ground Effect Hovering Ceiling (2 ft skid height) at 3200 lb (Hot Day or +20° Celsius Above Normal)	10,200 ft
Out of Ground Effect Hovering Ceiling at 3200 lb	8800 ft
Out of Ground Effect Hovering Ceiling at 3200 lb (Hot Day or +20° Celsius Above Normal)	4400 ft
Service Ceiling	13,500 ft

Table 9.1 *continued*

STANDARD CONFIGURATION

DESCRIPTION	DATA
Sea Level Maximum Rate of Climb (3200 lb)	1280 ft/min
Maximum Allowable IAS (Sea Level)	122 knots
Maximum Allowable IAS (5000 ft)	115 knots
Range (Sea Level)	365 nm
Range (5000 ft)	395 nm
Engine Power Ratings:	
Takeoff, Shaft Horsepower (SHP)	420 SHP
Maximum Continuous SHP	370 SHP
Fuel	Jet Fuel
Capacity	91 gallons
Life of Main Rotor Blade	5,000 hours (Replacement Cost $23,463)
Average Cost Per Flight Hour	$191. 42 (Assumes Fuel at $1.50/gallon Maintenance Labor at $50/hr)

CONTROLLING THE HELICOPTER VIA THE KEYBOARD OR JOYSTICK

Appendix G lists all of the keyboard commands used to control the helicopter. It isn't impossible to fly the helicopter by using your keyboard, but it is difficult, so it is recommended that you use a joystick. The addition of the fourth axis on the joystick for the anti-torque capability is really indispensable if you are at all serious about learning to fly the helicopter. Ideally, you should have rudder style pedals for anti-torque, but if you have a joystick that twists on a fourth axis, such as the SideWinder 3D Pro, then you'll be fine.

Collective Pitch Control and Torquemeter

The collective pitch lever (shown in Figure 9.2) is a stick located by the left side of the pilot's seat, and is operated by the pilot's left hand. This lever moves up and down and in doing so changes the pitch angle of the main rotor blades. When you raise the collective pitch lever, the pitch angle of all the main rotor blades is increased, thereby increasing the angle of attack, which increases lift. When the lever is lowered, the main rotor blades' pitch angle is lowered, and this decreases the angle of attack and lowers lift.

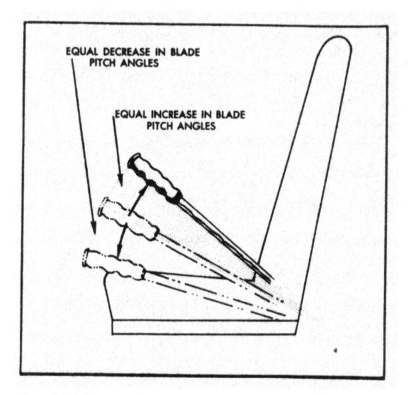

Figure 9.2 *Collective pitch lever movement changes main rotor blade pitch angles*

As the collective pitch lever is raised, the rotor blades' angle of attack increases, and the helicopter will gain lift so that it can take off. As this happens, blade drag increases and rotor RPM will decrease. On the other hand, if the collective is lowered, the rotor blades' angle of attack is lessened and the helicopter will descend. There will be a decrease in blade drag, and the RPM will increase. Because it is absolutely essential that a constant RPM may maintained for a helicopter, there is an auto-throttle that increases engine power when the collective pitch lever is raised, and decreases power when the lever is lowered.

Just remember that the collective pitch lever is your primary means of altitude control, and depending on the pitch angle of the blades, it will determine the amount of engine power generated through the auto-throttle mechanisms.

In FS98, the collective pitch lever is controlled by the throttle control on the joystick and keyboard.

The Torquemeter is located within the turbine and measures the power output of the engine as a percentage of total engine output. Raising the collective pitch lever, which increases the rotor blades' angle of attack, causes engine torque to increase; lowering it, which decreases the blade's angle of attack, lowers engine torque. The normal operating range is 0 to 85% of maximum engine power, although takeoff power is usually 85% to 100%. You shouldn't sustain 100% torque for more than 5 minutes, or else you will overheat the engine. Remember, turbine engines must operate within a confined temperature range, and operating near their performance envelope will considerably reduce engine longivity, not to mention the damage that may occur if you overstress the engine parts. Torque may be a limiting factor for the transmission on some helicopters because some engines are capable of producing more power than the transmission can handle.

Try to maintain operation in the green zone of the Torquemeter so you don't have these problems.

Although there is a throttle control on the JetRanger, you don't normally need to fool with it. Engine power on a turbine-powered helicopter is entirely controlled via the collective. This is not the case with piston-powered helicopters, which do have a throttle control.

The Helicopter Instrument Panel

Figure 9.3 shows the Bell JetRanger's instrument panel. Many of the instruments look familiar and need no explanation. There are, however, several differences from fixed-wing aircraft instruments. There is a Torquemeter, a Gas Producer N_1 Gauge, a Cyclic and Anti-Torque Rotor Indicator, and Transmission Oil and Pressure Gauges. Since the JetRanger has a turboshaft engine, this means that it has a turbine engine that directly drives, via a transmission, the main rotor and anti-torque rotor. The transmission oil temperature and oil pressure are vital pieces of information to you because they reveal the health of the transmission. The transmission is under a lot of strain and is the focal point of the mechanical linkage between the engine and the rotor. If the transmission fails you are in serious trouble, although it should be possible for the main rotor to go into autorotation and disconnect from the engine-transmission, thereby allowing you to land.

Cyclic Indicator & Anti-Torque Indicator

The Control Position Indicators that you were used to on the fixed-wing airplanes in Flight Simulator have been replaced by the Cyclic and Anti-Torque Indicators. The cyclic is the control which tilts the rotor tip plane in the direction in which horizontal movement is desired. This control can be moved forwards and backwards and left and right, and will move your helicopter in the corresponding direction. The right/left and fore/aft positions of the cyclic control are indicated by the Cyclic Indicator.

In FS98, the cyclic is controlled by the joystick handle, or by the keyboard commands that you are familiar with for ailerons and elevators.

The anti-torque rotor in the back of the helicopter counteracts the rotational torque of the main rotor, which prevents the helicopter from rotating in a direction opposite to the helicopter blades' rotation. So when you want the helicopter to move with out turning, you need to apply anti-torque, also called counter-torque, with the tail rotor to compensate for the main rotor. In a real helicopter, anti-torque is applied via pedals, like the rudder pedals on an airplane.

In FS98, anti-torque is controlled by twisting the handle on your Microsoft SideWinder 3D Pro joystick, or by using the rudder keys.

Both anti-torque and cyclic control effects are illustrated in Figure 9.4 and Figure 9.5.

Relationship between Collective and Anti-Torque

The anti-torque control has a symbiotic relationship with that of the collective. Whenever you pull up the collective pitch lever, thereby increasing engine power and the main rotor blade's angle of attack, the helicopter will yaw to the left. This is because the engine is exerting a

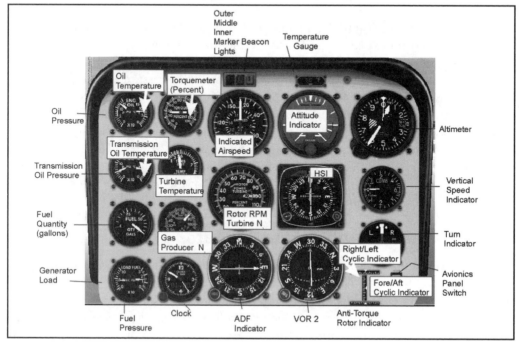

Figure 9.3 Helicopter Instrument Panel.

torque force on the rotor that causes the helicopter to turn in the opposite direction from the rotor's rotation. If the rotor were somehow turned at the tips, instead of at the center by the main rotor shaft, there would be no torque tendencies. Likewise, when the engine is turned off, or when it fails, as occurs during auto-rotation, there are no torque tendencies. The minute the engine is turned on, you will experience torque again, and so the anti-torque rotor must counteract this rotative force if the helicopter is to remain on a constant heading.

OPERATING THE HELICOPTER

The helicopter has some unusual characteristics that are worth investigating to better understand piloting techniques.

Blade Speed at Hover

Helicopter blades usually turn at about 320 revolutions per minute and turn counter-clockwise, as viewed from the top. Some European helicopters have blades that turn

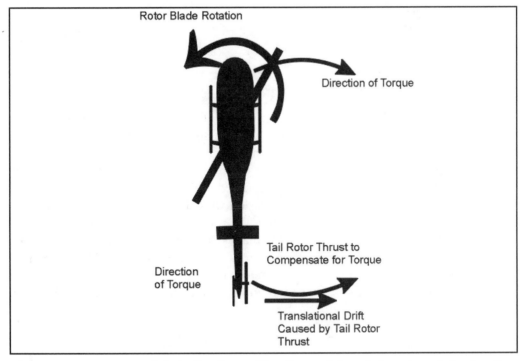

Figure 9.4 *Anti-torque is applied via the tail rotor. The tail rotor pitch angle determines whether the tail moves right or left, as shown in the diagram.*

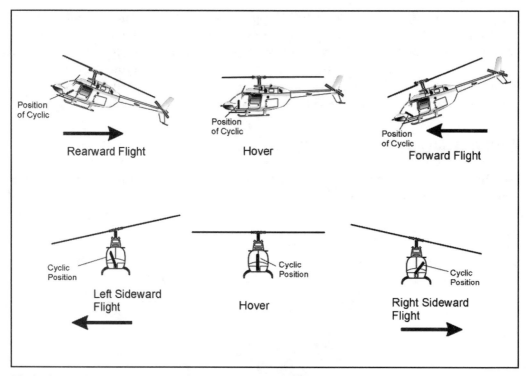

Figure 9.5 *The position of the cyclic determines the angle of the main rotor plane.*

clockwise instead. Blade tip velocity for a typical rotor span of 33 ft, such as is found on the JetRanger, is about 675 ft/s or 400 knots. Blade speed near the main rotor shaft is much less because the distance traveled at this lesser radius is small. Halfway down the rotor blade, the speed is only 199 knots, which is half the speed at the blade tip. When the speed of the rotor is doubled, lift is quadrupled, which is in accordance with the lift equations we discussed earlier where lift varied with the square of velocity. Because there is a lift differential between the tip and the root of the blade due to differing relative wind velocities along the length of the blades, helicopter blades are designed with a twist like that of propellers on fixed-wing airplanes. Blade twist is highest at the root where speed is low and the angle of attack needs to be greater. At the tip, blade twist is lowest, because a lower angle of attack is required to match the rest of the blade's average lift.

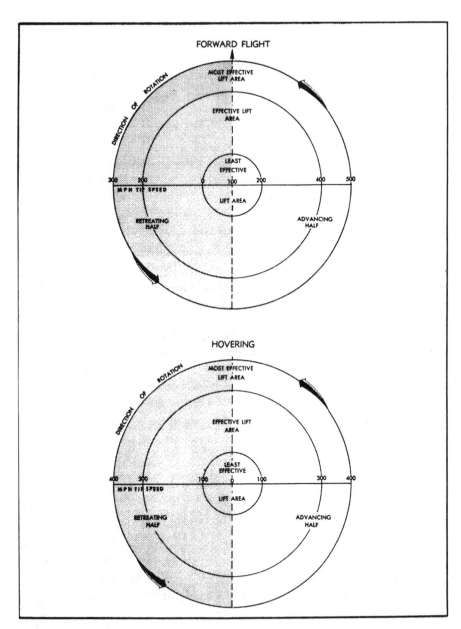

Figure 9.6 *Blade speed and dyssemetry of lift. In the figure, the helicopter rotor has a higher speed on the advancing top half of the rotor blade during forward flight than the retreating half. This causes a dyssemetry of lift whereby the right side of the rotor plane generates more lift than the left side. This causes the helicopter to want to roll to the left. During hover, however, lift is symmetrical, as is shown in the lower part of the figure.*

Dissymmetry of Lift

The area circumscribed by the plane of the main rotor is called the rotor disc. When the helicopter is hovering in still air, lift is generated equally on each side for each rotating blade. Dissymmetry of lift occurs during horizontal flight or when there is wind during hovering flight. Dissymmetry is caused by the difference in lift between the advancing blade half and the retreating blade half of the rotor disc area. As the helicopter moves forward, the relative wind moving over each rotor blade becomes a combination of the rotational speed of the helicopter and the forward movement of the helicopter. At the 90° position on the right side of the mast, the advancing blade has the combined speed of the blade plus the forward speed of the helicopter. On the other side, at the 270° position on the left side of the mast, the retreating blade has the blade speed minus the forward velocity of the helicopter. As you can see, the right side of the helicopter blade will then generate more lift than the left side, due to its higher relative wind velocity (remember $L\alpha V2$). Figure 9.6 shows this effect.

With this dissymmetry of lift, it is apparent that the helicopter will roll to the left when moving forwards or when hovering in a wind. (In a no wind hover situation, lift is symmetrical. To prevent this from happening, helicopter designers have come up with a system for equalizing lift over the two halves of the rotor disc, using a combination of blade flapping and cyclic feathering. Blade flapping is a technique whereby each blade half is connected via a horizontal hinge which permits the blade to move up and down as it rotates. In forward flight, the increased lift on the advancing blade will cause the blade to flap up. This decreases the angle of attack because the relative wind will change from a horizontal direction to more of a downward direction. The decreased lift on the retreating blade will cause the blade to flap down, increasing the angle of attack because the relative wind changes from a horizontal direction to more of an upward direction. Lift is thus equalized on both sides of the rotor disc through the blade flapping action.

Cyclic feathering is accomplished via one of three types of rotor systems: fully articulated rotors, semirigid rotors, and rigid rotors. The semirigid rotor system used on the JetRanger has the rotor blades rigidly interconnected to the hub, but the hub is free to tilt and rock with respect to the rotor shaft. The rotor flaps as a unit so that as one blade flaps up, the other blade flaps down by an equal amount. As the helicopter moves forward, the blades flap and this equalizes the lift on each side of the rotor disc. Semirigid rotor systems always have two blades only.

Ground Effect

Hovering is a term used to describe a helicopter that is maintaining a constant position at a selected point, usually a few feet above the ground. During the hover, the rotor blades move large volumes of air in a downward direction; this is called rotor wash and it can reach velocities of 60 to 100 knots. Helicopters require less lift to hover while close to the ground than they do at altitude. This phenomenon is called *ground effect*, and is similar to the ground effect that fixed-wing aircraft experience. There are two reasons for ground effect improving a helicopter's lift:

1. Since the ground interrupts the airflow under the helicopter, there is a reduced downward rotor wash velocity, and this reduces induced drag. With less induced drag, the helicopter can hover with a reduced angle of attack and less power.
2. Reduction of tip vortex. Turbulent air produced at the tip of the blade is reduced.

Ground effect occurs up to a height of about one rotor diameter. At a rotor height of one-half diameter (16 ft), the rotor thrust increases by 7%, and at one-quarter diameter (not possible on the JetRanger, but possible on helicopters with larger rotor spans) rotor thrust increases by 20%. Ground effect decreases to zero at a height of about $1^{1}/_{4}$ rotor diameter.

TAKEOFFS AND LANDINGS

The following sections give the correct procedures for takeoffs and landings in the JetRanger.

Normal Takeoffs

1. Place the helicopter on a stationary position. Lower the collective pitch to the full down position.
2. Increase the collective pitch slowly until the helicopter feels light on its skids. At this point, you can adjust the cyclic and anti-torque to prevent any translational or rotational movement.
3. Apply more upward collective pitch. This will raise the angle of attack of the main rotor blades, and you'll note that the Torquemeter shows increased engine power.
4. As the helicopter breaks free from the ground, use the cyclic to assure forward movement as altitude is gained. Apply anti-torque as necessary to prevent yawing rotation. Continue climbing and accelerating forwards. You'll have more stability as the helicopter gains forward speed.

There are several important things to avoid when taking off. Don't depart with your helicopter nose too low. This will force you to use excessive power to climb to altitude. Also, don't use too much power after takeoff; throttle back to 80% to 85% maximum torque for cruising. Lastly, don't yank the collective pitch lever up all the way, as this will cause rotor RPM and anti-torque correction problems for you.

Landings

Landings are the trickiest phase of helicopter piloting. Making the transition from translational flight to a hover at landing is not easy. Approaches for landings are made into the wind, and the angle of descent is approximately 10°, versus the 3° used by fixed-wing aircraft. The procedure is shown in Figure 9.7.

1. To establish a descent from straight and level flight, lower the collective and adjust the anti-torque to maintain heading.
2. Throughout the descent, maintain the rate and angle of descent to 10° by using the cyclic in combination with the collective. The angle of descent is mainly controlled by collective pitch, whereas airspeed is controlled by cyclic control. Heading is always maintained by anti-torque.
3. To level off from the descent, increase the collective, and adjust anti-torque to keep the heading constant.
4. Reduce forward speed by applying rearward cyclic. You will also have to increase the collective when you do this to compensate for the decrease in translational lift and to maintain the proper rate of descent. As the collective is increased, you'll have to apply anti-torque to maintain heading.
5. If you plan to land from a hover, lower the collective pitch until you just barely touch the surface. When contact is made, lower the collective firmly to the full down position.

OTHER USEFUL TIPS

When landing the helicopter, it is necessary to see what is below you. Yet you can't afford to take your eyes off the horizon. What are you to do? FS98 has provided the answer to this conundrum by giving us the Virtual Cockpit view mode, which allows us to simultaneously look forward and down through the floorboard glass. You enter Virtual Cockpit mode by pressing the **S** key once, then use the panning feature of your joystick's hat switch (or the keyboard commands **Shift Backspace** and **Shift Enter**) to see forward and downward. If you are concerned about not being able to view your

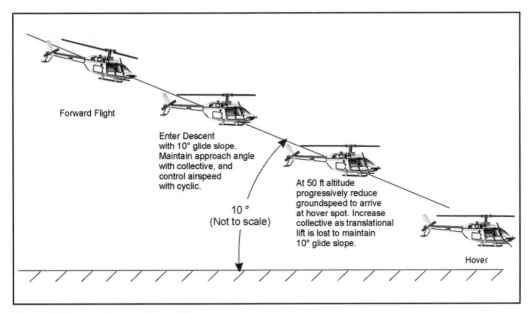

Figure 9.7 Normal Approach to a Hover.

instrument panel while in Virtual Cockpit mode, don't be. Simply press **Shift 1** and the instrument panel will pop up into view in all its glory.

Consider also your frame rate and the frustration level caused if it is low. A low frame rate creates a lot of lag between the time you make a control correction and the time that the simulator implements it. The lower the frame rate, the later the correction occurs, and the inevitable result is that your flight will be doomed. In my experience, if the frame rate is less than 23 fps (frames per second), the helicopter becomes uncontrollable. Even 23 fps is a low figure, but this is the bottom line threshold of acceptability. If you don't get 23 fps, and you really have to fly the helicopter, try lowering the display resolution to 640 × 480. This is what I ended up doing, and it worked admirably. See Appendix A for other frame rate improvement tips.

Another useful feature is Spot View. When you can't figure out why your helicopter is reacting the way it does, it is often helpful to use Spot View by pressing **S** three times to get an external view of the helicopter. If you need to see your instrument panel in Spot View, simply press **Shift 1** and it will pop into view.

Also, having the Aircraft Shadows feature turned on gives you useful guidance information about how far above the ground you are, especially in Spot View.

If you treat the helicopter as an airplane that needs to land on the runway, it will be easier to learn how to land. Don't make the mistake of trying to hover and land at the very beginning. This is very hard to do properly.

Try setting a 7 knot headwind and fly into it while trying to land. This will give the helicopter a little more forward stability. If you turn left or right, however, you'll have problems.

You might also try experimenting with setting the Sensitivity control under **Aircraft/Aircraft Settings/Realism** to maximum for best helicopter control.

10

Advanced Simulator Features

This chapter discusses some of Flight Simulator's more advanced features, including multiplayer mode, and the ability to modify your panels, add airplanes, and customize the program.

MULTIPLAYER MODE

To fly with other Flight Simulator pilots by using Multiplayer mode, your computers must be linked via the Internet, a local area network (LAN), a modem, or directly using a null-modem cable.

Since most people will use the Internet connection, we will discuss that procedure here.

To launch a multiplayer session over the Internet, follow these steps:

1. Connect to the Internet via your Internet Service Provider (ISP). A word to the wise; avoid commercially clogged online services such as AOL, CompuServe, Prodigy, etc., that insert extra layers of software between you and the Internet. Instead subscribe to a local ISP with a direct Internet connection, or else you'll suffer all kinds of connection speed problems. Also, don't even consider a connection speed of less than 28.8 kbps.

2. Find out the IP (Internet Protocol) address of your fellow FS pilot. If you are hosting a session, you'll need to know your own IP address. Without it, you cannot proceed. IP addresses for most Internet users change each time you dial up your Internet Service Provider (ISP), because an ISP dynamically allocates IP numbers on demand. They consist of four linked numbers like this— 212.232.12.143. Internet users are issued a unique IP address the moment they log on to the Internet. Most people don't know or care what their IP address is, and rightly so since it changes each time you log on. However, with Multiplayer mode, you need to know this information.

   If you host a session, you can easily find the IP address that you need to send to others. Using the **Start/Run** menu on the Windows 95 Taskbar, type the following in the Run box:

   ```
   winipcfg
   ```

   If you wish to join somebody else's session, they need to e-mail or call you and let you know what their IP address is. Sometimes you can find this information out yourself by "pinging" the system to find the address or name of the computer that's hosting the Flight Simulator session you want to join. To do this, you need to know their e-mail address. To ping a friend who has the e-mail address *joe@ripoff.com*, you would type the following in the Run box:

   ```
   ping joe@ripoff.com
   ```

   In the above example, Joe would be the host for the session, and you would enter in the IP address that Joe is using, either by finding it out directly from him, or by pinging him. Unfortunately, pinging does not always work, so as a fallback, be prepared to use the phone or e-mail.
3. Select **Flights/Multiplayer Connect**.
4. In the Multiplayer Connect dialog box, click **Next**.
5. Type in a callsign or nickname for yourself in the Callsign box.
6. If you intend to host the session, click **Host a new session**; if you want to join an existing session, click **Join an existing session**. Click the **Next** button to continue.
7. In the Multiplayer Connect dialog box that opens, you'll see a window that asks you to "Locate Session." Type in the IP address garnered in Step 2 above, then click the **OK** button.

8. If all goes well, you'll see the name of the session, and the number of pilots and observers. You can then decide whether you want to join as an observer (not a flying participant) or as a pilot. You can also, at this point, change the settings for your session by clicking the **Settings** button. When you are ready to join the session, click **Join**.

Table 10.1 lists some useful keyboard commands that you can use during Multiplayer mode.

Table 10.1 *Multiplayer Keyboard Commands*

DESCRIPTION	KEYBOARD COMMAND
Toggle Chat window on/off	**Ctrl Enter**
Toggle focus between Chat window and main Flight Simulator window	**Enter**
Cycle through players	**Ctrl Shift T**
Toggle track mode (DME and ADF)	**Ctrl Shift D**
Follow the other player (Pilot Mode)/Lock airplane's cockpit view (Observer Mode)	**Ctrl Shift F**

The chat window is used to communicate with other players in multiplayer mode by exchanging text messages. To open the Chat window, if it is currently off, press **Ctrl Enter**. Press **Ctrl Enter** once again to remove the chat window.

To track the flight of another pilot, you must first select **Autopilot Lock to Aircraft** in the Sessions Setting dialog box (use the **Flights/Multiplayer/Settings** menu). Next, after you have started the multiplayer session, press **Ctrl Shift T** to cycle through the names of the available players. The name of the current pilot will be displayed in the upper right corner of your Flight Simulator window (note that the 737 overhead instrument panel obscures the name, so you must press **Shift 3** to remove the panel or drag it off to the left side of the window). Flight Simulator will also display the name of the current pilot next to the airplane, which is helpful if there are multiple players flying in formation; this allows you to differentiate between the different airplanes. If you then turn on the Autopilot Heading Hold and Altitude Hold (press **Z** to turn on the autopilot, then **Ctrl H** for the Heading Hold followed by **Ctrl Z** for the Altitude Hold), your airplane will be locked on to the currently tracked airplane. If you would like to have your airplane follow behind the currently tracked airplane, press **Ctrl Shift F**. Be careful of flying too fast, or you may overtake the airplane in front of you and crash into it.

And if you are the leader of other airplanes, don't crash into a mountain or building, because everyone tracking you will follow suit.

If you have also selected **DME Lock to Aircraft**, and **ADF Lock to Aircraft**, in the Sessions Setting dialog box, you can have your DME display the distance to the currently tracked player, or have the ADF needle point in the direction of the currently tracked player. To toggle between the DME and ADF display while in track mode, press **Ctrl Shift D**. Note that the DME 1 display is used to show the distance to a currently tracked aircraft.

Observer mode allows you to view the currently tracked airplane as if you were in its cockpit. Although you can switch from Pilot Mode to Observer mode by pressing **Ctrl Shift O**, you can't go from Observer Mode to Pilot Mode unless you first quit the multiplayer session and rejoin as a Pilot. Also, once you quit Pilot Mode, you can't go back to Pilot Mode unless you quit and rejoin the session. In Observer Mode, you can view any player's cockpit view and instrument panel during multiplayer flight by first selecting the player (press **Ctrl Shift T**), then locking the aircraft's cockpit view by pressing **Ctrl Shift F**.

If you crash while in multiplayer mode, your airplane will be restarted at the point at which it started the session.

T I P

Important note: Install the FS98 Aircraft Converter on the book's CD-ROM to fix some problems related to multiplayer functions. The patch will allow you to transmit and receive visual data from converted Flight Shop or FSW95 aircraft. Microsoft recommends that visual model transmission be avoided on modem connections due to significantly increased bandwidth requirements. For more information on visual model transmission, see the aafconv.txt file in the **\Aircraft Converter for FS98** folder on the book's CD-ROM.

SLEWING

Slewing is a special mode which allows you to translate or rotate the airplane without actually flying. You can slew the aircraft up, down, sideways, forwards, and backwards, and rotate it via rolling, pitching and yawing. The slew mode is especially handy when flying the sailplane, since you can slew up to altitude and then glide down without worrying about catching an updraft.

To enter slew mode, press the **Y** key. To move the airplane, push your joystick forward, backward or sideways and your airplane will move in that direction. Unless you have a joystick with rudder capability, you won't be able to rotate the airplane via the joystick—you must use the keyboard. See Appendix F for a complete listing of Slew commands.

If You Have Trouble Slewing

Some people find that they cannot slew their aircraft after pressing the **Y** key. This is because slew mode works in either keyboard or joystick mode, but not both simultaneously. So if you are flying with your joystick, and want to slew with the keyboard, you can't until you turn off the joystick by pressing the **K** key. The converse is also true; if you want to slew with the joystick and you are using the keyboard, you must press the **K** key to activate the joystick. In any case, if you are having trouble with slewing, press the **K** key and see if this resolves your problem. Of course, to resume flying, you'll have to again press your **K** key to restore your joystick and keyboard settings.

How Do I Set Up Flight Simulator So I Start with a Particular Airplane and Location, and Scenery Density and View Preferences Set the Way I Like Them?

To do this, set up the situation exactly the way you want it and then save that "flight" using the **Flights/Save Flight** menu command. Now select **Options/Preferences** and select the **General** tab. Click the **Select Flight** button and you'll be able to select the startup flight situation that you just created. From now on, when you start Flight Simulator, your preset flight situation will load automatically.

If you prefer to directly edit the FLTSIM98.CFG or FLTSIM95.CFG file in your Flight Simulator directory, you can add the line

```
SITUATION=PILOTS\Myflightsituation
```

where "Myflightsituation" is the name of your preset saved flight. In FS98, you can also launch Flight Simulator by double clicking on a situation (.STN) file name.

Is There a Way to Load Custom Panel Configurations at Startup in FS98?

Yes. If you have a setup that requires different panels for the aircraft you plan to fly, you can launch FS98 using alternate .CFG files with a new command line switch (ex. FLTSIM98 /CFG:b737.cfg).

HOW ARE INDIVIDUAL SOUND FILES HANDLED FOR FS98 AIRCRAFT?

In your computer's FS98 files, each aircraft has its own directory in the Aircraft subdirectory. There is a sound subdirectory which contains all the sounds unique to each aircraft. FS98 uses a configuration file for each aircraft's sounds; this controls the names of the sound files used for each effect, as well as other special effects such as panning, volume and engine RPM range. Thus, if you edit the text file SOUND.CFG located in each Aircraft's \Sound subdirectory, you can add your own sound files or change existing sound parameters. Before doing so, you should make a backup of the file so that you can restore lost settings if you don't like the changes you make.

An example of the Boeing 737 sound configuration file SOUND.CFG is listed below:

```
[JET_ENGINE]
type=1
flags=2
viewpoint=1
filename=be1
link=xbe

[xbe]
type=1
flags=2
viewpoint=2
filename=xbe3
link=rumble

[rumble]
type=1
flags=4
filename=rumblp

[GEAR_DOWN]
```

```
filename=bmgeardn

  [gear_up]
filename=bmgearup

[flapsh]
filename=bmflaph
maximum_volume=8200

[flapsl]
filename=bmflaplp
maximum_volume=8500

[flapst]
filename=bmflapt
maximum_volume=8500

[stall_warning]
filename=bastall

[left_touchdown]
filename=bmtouchl
panning=-10000
initial_volume=10000
maximum_volume=10000

[right_touchdown]
filename=bmtouchr
panning=10000
initial_volume=10000
maximum_volume=10000

[center_touchdown]
```

```
filename=bmtouchc
panning=0
initial_volume=10000
maximum_volume=10000

[wind_sound]
filename=bair
minimum_volume=7300
maximum_volume=7300
minimum_rate=1.0
maximum_rate=1.0
minimum_speed=0
maximum_speed=0

[OVERSPEED_WARNING_SOUND]
filename=baover

[GLIDESLOPE_WARNING_SOUND]
filename=baglide

[CRASH_SOUND]
filename=jcrash3
extra=bncrash1,bncrash2

[splash_SOUND]
filename=jslpash2
extra=bnsplas1,bnsplas2

[AP_DISENGAGE_SOUND]
filename=baapdis

[GEAR_UP_WARNING_SOUND]
filename=bmgwarn
maximum_volume=9400
```

CAN I CHANGE INSTRUMENT PANELS AND GAUGES IN FS98?

Sure. The only problem is that older panels designed for FSW95 and FS5.1 won't work. If you have a new FS98 panel that you want to assign to an aircraft in FS98, you can edit the PANEL.CFG configuration file found in each FS98's aircraft's \Panel subdirectory and add a new [Window00] section for the new panel (where 00 is replaced by the instrument panel number 00 through 09), along with any new gauges. All of the FS98 gauges are stored in the FS98\Gauges directory, and you can interchange any gauge with any instrument panel.

The way Flight Simulator sets up instrument panels is simple: FS98 first reads the PANEL.CFG file to see what instrument panels are needed and what the disk file names are for each panel and gauge. Then a bitmap of the outline of the panel is displayed, as shown in Figure 10. 1 for the Learjet. After drawing the outline of the underlying blank instrument panel, FS98 looks in the PANEL.CFG file to see what gauges are to be displayed from the FS98\Gauges directory. Each gauge is given a separate listing in the configuration file. In the following example, note that the // symbols and text following are comments that are ignored by FS98:

```
[Window00]            //This is the first instrument panel for the Learjet
gauge00=Lear_45.Elevator-Trim, 1020, 207, 40      //This is the first gauge
gauge01=Lear_45.AOA, 160, 90 //This is the second gauge located at 160, 90
gauge02=Lear_45.Chronometer, 110, 186   //This is the third gauge located
                              at 110, 186
```

Figure 10.1 This is the blank FS98 Learjet Instrument panel that uses the Learjet45.bmp bitmap image in the Learjet45\Panel directory. Decide where you want the gauges to go on the panel, and then map them by coordinates into the PANEL.CFG configuration file, found in the Learjet45\Panel directory. All FS98 gauges can be reused on different instrument panels, though you must be sure that the gauge does not overlap an existing gauge (or else the program may crash).

Thus, the second gauge used, Gauge 01, displays the Learjet's angle of attack dial at the location 160,90 on the Learjet's bitmap image of the instrument panel. FS98 looks for the diskfile that is named Lear_45.AOA.GAU in the FS98\Gauges directory and then draws it on the instrument panel when you select the first instrument panel (i.e., [Window00]).

Let's try an example of swapping gauges for the Learjet so that you understand how easy it is to do. We will replace the light switches gauge on the Learjet's main instrument panel number 1 ([Window00]) with the RMI (radio magnetic compass) from the 737. Before proceeding, however, be sure to make a backup of your Learjet PANEL.CFG file so that you can restore the Learjet to the way it was before you made any changes.

NOTE Important note: Always make a back up of your PANEL.CFG files before making changes.

The underlying panel bitmaps should be stored in the \Panel subdirectory for the aircraft, while the gauges should be stored in the higher level FS98\Gauges subdirectory. After you have saved the file and added the new panels and gauges to the proper directories, the Views/Instrument Panel menu will display the new panel. When you restart FS98, you can then select and open it.

The example below shows a complete listing of the PANEL.CFG panel configuration file for the FS98 Learjet where the lighting switches in the lower left corner of the panel have been replaced with the RMI gauge from the 737. Note that the line for the fourth gauge in the [Window00] instrument panel has been changed from

```
gauge03=Lear_45.Light_Switches, 68, 275
```

to

```
gauge03=737-400.RMI, 68, 275
```

where the diskfile 737-400.RMI.GAU was used for the RMI gauge on the 737 that replaces the diskfile Lear_45.Light_Switches.GAU that was used for the lighting switch gauge on the Learjet.

NOTE You don't need to restart FS98 for the changes to take effect. All you need to do is select a different aircraft from the Aircraft/Select Aircraft menu, then once that aircraft has opened, go back to the menu and reselect the Learjet. The new panel will display as shown in Figure 10. 2.

Figure 10.2 *An example of the 737's RMI Gauge Replacing the Learjet's Lighting Switch Gauge. The Learjet's PANEL.CFG text configuration file was edited, and with the simple substitution of naming the 737-400.RMI.GAU file for the Lear_45.Light_Switches.GAU file, the switch was made.*

The listing for the PANEL.CFG file for the Learjet 45 that uses the 737's RMI gauge in place of the Learjet's lighting switch is:

```
// Panel Configuration file
// Lear 45

[Window Titles]
window00=Instrument Panel          //This is the first instrument panel name
                                   that appears under the Views menu
window01=Thrust Levers             //This is the second instrument panel name
window02=Compass                   //This is the third instrument panel name
window03=Minicontrols              //This is the fourth instrument panel name

[Window00]             //This is the first instrument panel definition
file=Lear45.bmp        //It uses the Lear45.bmp diskfile as the underlayment.
size_mm=1204
window_size_ratio=1.0
position=7
visible=1
ident=0


gauge00=Lear_45.Elevator-Trim, 1020, 207, 40      //These gauges are for the
                                                  first instrument panel
```

```
gauge01=Lear_45.AOA, 160, 90

gauge02=Lear_45.Chronometer, 110, 186

                //we have replaced    gauge03=Lear_45.Light_Switches, 68, 275

                //with the 737's RMI Guage

gauge03=737-400.RMI, 68, 275

gauge04=Lear_45.PFD, 252, 48

gauge05=Lear_45.EICAS, 534, 48

gauge06=Lear_45.Autopilot, 818, 47

gauge07=Lear_45.Radio_Stack, 822, 205

gauge08=Lear_45.Warning_Enunciators, 818, 135

gauge09=Lear_45.Gear, 1015, 293

gauge10=Lear_45.Control_Surfaces, 1085,207,75


[Window01]        //This is the second instrument panel definition

file=Lear45_Thrust_Levers.bmp  //It uses the Lear45_Thrust_Levers.bmp disk file
                                image

size_mm=275

window_size_ratio=1.0

position=0

visible=0

ident=10


gauge00=Lear_45.Spoiler, 15, 56      //These are the gauges that are assigned
                                     to the second instrument panel

gauge01=Lear_45.Flaps, 205, 133

gauge02=Lear_45.Thrust_Levers, 57, 79


[Window02]        //This is the third instrument panel definition

file=Lear_compass.bmp    //This is the diskfile assigned to the underlying
                          instrument panel image

size_mm=60

window_size_ratio=1.0
```

```
position=2

visible=0

ident=75


gauge00=Extra-300.Wiskey-Compass,2,0      //This is the only gauge that is
                                          assigned to the third instrument

                                          //panel


[Window03]                  //This is the fourth instrument panel definition
file=Minicontrols.bmp
size_mm=100
window_size_ratio=1.0
position=1
visible=0
ident=100


gauge00=Minicontrols, 0, 0    //There is only one gauge assigned to the fourth
panel


[8 Bit Colors]
color00=66, 70, 93
color01=65, 67, 91
color02=68, 71, 92
color03=64, 65, 84
color04=50,100,255
color05=21, 28, 53
color06=24, 23, 22
color07=160, 168, 188
color08=139, 147, 167
color09=51, 52, 60
color10=160, 168, 188
color11=160, 168, 188
color12=50, 90, 150
```

```
color13=27, 26, 29
color14=36, 37, 43
color15=110,110, 130
color16=20, 27, 52
color17=57,90,103
color18=8,8,8

[Default View]
X=0
Y=0
SIZE_X=8191
SIZE_Y=4512
```

CAN I MAKE MY OWN CHECKLISTS?

Absolutely. For example, to change the checklist for the Learjet 45, go to your FS98\Aircraft\Lear45 directory, and open up the LEAR45_CHECK.CFG text file (shown below). To add a checklist, just look at the listing for the configuration file, and notice that I have added a fifth checklist item called "This is My Custom checklist."

```
LEAR45_CHECK.CFG

[lists]
0=&Takeoff, Takeoff Checklist
1=&Cruise, Cruise Checklist
2=&Descent, Descent Checklist
3=&Approach, Approach Checklist
4=&Landing, Landing Checklist
5=&Mychecklist, This is My Custom Checklist

[0]
0=Check flight controls.
1=Set flaps at 8 degrees (F7).
```

2=Smoothly increase thrust to maximum N1 (F3).

3=Release brakes (Period [.]).

4=At about 140 knots, ease back on the stick.

5=Adjust pitch attitude to about 15 degrees nose-up.

6=Retract landing gear (G).

7=At 180 knots, retract flaps (F6) and accelerate to 250 knots.

[1]

0=Establish level flight.

1=Set thrust to maintain about .77 Mach (F2 or F3).

2=Adjust elevator trim (NUMPAD 7 = nose down, NUMPAD 1 = nose up).

[2]

0=Reduce power to flight idle (F2).

1=Relax pressure on the controls and the aircraft will descend.

2=To level off, increase power to about 60% N1.(F3).

[3]

0=Set power at about 60% N1. (F2 or F3).

1=Establish level flight at 210 knots.

2=Set flaps at 8 degrees (F7) and establish level flight at 180 knots.

3=Turning toward runway, set flaps at 20 degrees (F7).

[4]

0=When ready for final approach, set flaps at 40 degrees (F7) and check gear down (G).

1=Set power at about 75% N1 and maintain about 140 knots in the final descent.

2=Over runway, hold the slight nose-up attitude. Reduce throttle to idle (F2).

3=After touchdown, extend spoilers (/) and apply reverse thrust (F2).

4=At 60 knots, cancel reverse thrust (F3).

```
[5]
0=This is my first item in my custom checklist
1=This is my second item in my custom checklist
```

Saving Your Start Location

To start up Flight Simulator so that it always starts from a given location, use the **Options/Preferences/General/Select Flight** menu option to select a flight, then click the **Make this the default** switch.

Taking Flight Photographs

To take a snapshot of your entire screen, press the **PrintScrn** button, then go into any graphics program and use the **Edit/Paste** menu to paste the image into the program. If you want to take a picture of only a single window, then press **Alt PrntScrn**, and only the window will be captured, not the entire screen.

Taking Flight Videos

Using the **Options\Flight Video** menu, it is possible to record and save videos of your flights. You can choose different recording intervals to compact the size of the .vid file that is created in your \Videos folder. These files can be copied and shared so that others can see whether or not you did what you said you did.

Logging Your Flight Time

Use the **Options\Logbook** to record how many hours of IFR/VFR flight you accomplished for the type of aircraft you flew.

Land Me

Press **X** to activate the Land Me command—an "instructor" will take over the operation of your airplane and land it for you. This feature is useful when you want to learn how to land, because at any point during the landing process, you can take over by pressing **X** once again.

ADJUSTING DISPLAY RESOLUTION AND SOUND VOLUME

To adjust sound and display parameters use the **Options/Preferences/Display** or **Sound** menu. If you want to switch display resolutions, in the Preferences Display dialog box, click **Display Options** followed by **Hardware Acceleration**. A new dialog box will open up that shows you the current display device driver being used (i.e., Direct3D or the regular driver). If you have a Direct3D card that offers an acceptable frame rate, you should choose the Direct3D driver, because it offers 2 times the performance of the regular (non-Direct3D) video driver. For the display resolution, click the **Fullscreen mode** listbox for a listing of all the resolutions available with your particular card. Each card will have different capabilities; for example the Canopus Total 3D can display up to 1280 × 1024 (8 bit color) in regular mode, whereas in Direct3D mode this resolution drops to 1024 × 768 (16 bit mode). Obviously, 16 bit mode is not a drop in resolution. It is an increase because 65,536 colors are being displayed versus the 256 colors of 8 bit mode. However the actual pixel count drops slightly in 16 bit mode.

Other display cards may have higher maximum resolutions, so don't think the program is limited to 1024 × 768 in 16 bit mode (see Appendix A for more details).

FS98 separates out the individual sounds in the program into different channels. Using the Preferences Sound dialog box, you can adjust the Engine, Cockpit, Navigation, Environment (wind), and Adventure type sounds.

INSTALLING NEW AIRCRAFT IN FS98

To install older FSW95, or Flight Shop created aircraft (i.e., FS5.1) aircraft to FS98, you must use the new Microsoft Aircraft Converter for FS98, which is available on this book's CD. Note that old panels designed for FSW95 will not work with FS98. There is no work around for this problem.

The FS98 Aircraft and Adventure Converter program also contains bug fixes for the main FS98 program. Therefore, by installing the Converter software, you will also be making changes to the main FS98 program modules. For more information on the exact fixes and modifications to the FS98 program, see the aafconv.txt file in the **\Aircraft Converter for FS98** folder on the book's CD-ROM.

The Aafconv98.exe file, found in the **\Aircraft Converter for FS98** folder, is a self extracting archive that will install the Microsoft Aircraft Converter for FS98.

To install FSW95 or FS5.1 Flight Shop created aircraft, follow these steps (First Install the Aircraft Converter if you haven't already done so):

1. Exit Flight Simulator if it is currently running.
2. Double click on the AAFCONV98.EXE file in the **\Aircraft Converter for FS98** folder on the book's CD-ROM, and you will be prompted to run the setup program. Click **Ok** to continue, and the AAFCONV98.EXE program and related files will be installed to your FS98 directory. The program will install a special **\FSFSConv** folder under the **\Aircraft** directory, which contains many different types of panels for jets and reciprocating piston powered airplanes.
3. Restart Flight Simulator.

This will install the necessary modules for running the converter. Now you are ready to do the actual conversion of the aircraft.

To convert an airplane for use with FS98 (such as any of the airplanes in the \Aircraft for FS98 folder on the book's CD-ROM), follow these steps:

1. Unzip the contents of the FSW95 or FS5.1 Flight Shop created aircraft file that you want into the **FS98\Old Aircraft** directory. If you don't have an zip decompression utility to do this, install the WinZip program found in the **\WinZip95** folder on the book's CD-ROM.
2. Run the AAFCONV98.EXE program in your FS98 folder. You can do this by double clicking on the program icon for this file, or by using the Windows 95 Taskbar Start menu (select **Start/Programs/Microsoft Games/Flight Simulator 98/Flight Shop Converter 98**).
3. Click the **Aircraft Files** button in the FS98 Aircraft Converter program window.
4. In the dialog box that opens, select the **\FS98\Old Aircraft** directory which contains the ***.air** file where your airplane is stored.
5. Highlight the name of the ***.air** file (where * is a wildcard that can represent any name) for the airplane you wish to convert, then click the **Open** button. The Converter program will now convert the airplane and install all its files and textures in the **FS98\Aircraft** folder.

If all goes without hitch, you'll see the airplane listed under the **Aircraft/Aircraft Settings** dialog box.

Important Note Regarding Aircraft Conversions: Many FSW95/FS5.1 aircraft that you will find on the Internet were modified to have landing lights or had their aircraft files altered after they were created with Flight Shop. These airplanes cannot be converted by the FS98 Aircraft Converter. When you encounter an aircraft that generates a conversion error message by the FS98 Converter program, you will know that this airplane has been tampered with. If you ask the author of the airplane to post his or her model directly from the Flight Shop program, without any further modifications, the airplane can then be converted with the FS98 Aircraft Converter. For example, the aircraft found in the \Flight Simulator for Windows 95 Only\Aircraft for FSW95 folder on the book's CD-ROM have landing lights that were added to them after they were created with Flight Shop. These airplanes cannot be converted for use with FS98. However, these same airplanes are found unmodified, without the landing lights, in the \Aircraft for FS98 folder, and these aircraft can be converted.

INSTALLING FS5.1 AIRCRAFT IN FSW95

With the FSConvert.exe program (on this book's companion CD-ROM under the **\Flight simulator for Windows 95 only\Microsoft Aircraft and Adventure Converter** folder.) from Microsoft, you can install and fly older FS5.1 or Flight Shop created aircraft in FSW95 (but not FS98). Many aircraft have already been converted for FSW95 so for those ready-to-use airplanes, you *don't need* to run the FSConvert program at all, but can simply copy the necessary files to the appropriate directories. This will be explained in more detail below.

Only use the Converter with older FS5.1 type aircraft. Don't run the Converter on airplanes that are FSW95 ready!

To install an FS5.1 or FSFS airplane in FSW95, follow this procedure:

1. Install FEPATCH.EXE from this book's CD-ROM. This will fix a bug in the program.
2. Install the FSCONV.EXE from this book's CD-ROM. This is the Microsoft Aircraft and Adventure Converter for FSW95. It will not work with FS98.
3. Unzip the aircraft file into a temporary directory using the WinZip program on this book's CD-ROM. WinZip must be installed before you can use it.

4. Once you extract the aircraft files, you'll note that there are *.air files, and a number of *.xaf files, where "x" is a number (i.e. *.0af, *.1af, *.2af etc.) and * is a wildcard character that represents the name of the file. Everything to the right of the period in the name is the file extension.

5. Select **Start/Programs/Microsoft/Games/Flight Shop Converter** from the Windows 95 Taskbar to run the Flight Shop Converter program.

6. Click the **Options** button to open up the Options dialog box in which you will specify which directories Flight Simulator and your aircraft and adventures are stored. Then go back to the main screen, and select the **Aircraft** button, and then choose the airplane you wish to have converted. You can select individual planes by clicking on just one, or click on several by holding down the **Ctrl** key. To select all, click the first file name, then hold down the **Shift** key and click on the last .AIR file in the list.

7. Click the **Convert Aircraft** button, and choose the *.air file in the temporary directory you just created. At this point the Converter will take over and convert the airplane for you. When you return to FSW95, you should be able to select the new airplane from the **Aircraft\Select Aircraft** menu.

INSTALLING FSW95-READY AIRPLANES INTO FSW95

All FSW95 aircraft were originally created in BAO Flight Shop and converted. To install a FSW95-ready airplane, all you need to do is follow these procedures:

1. If you haven't already done so, install the Microsoft Aircraft and Adventure Converter (FSCONVT.EXE) (found on this book's CD-ROM) in the Microsoft Aircraft and Adventure directory. You can't add new airplanes until this program has been installed.

2. Using WinZip, extract all the *.MDL and *.AIR files into the FS95\PILOTS directory.

3. Using WinZip, extract all the *.?AF files into the FS95\TEXTURE directory.

4. Restart Flight Simulator.

If you are unfamiliar with decompressing zipped files or you don't have a Windows-based Zip program to dearchive the aircraft zip files, you may prefer to follow these instructions instead:

1. If you haven't already done so, first install the Microsoft Aircraft and Adventure Converter (FSCONVT.EXE) (found on this book's CD-ROM) in the Microsoft Aircraft and Adventure directory. You can't add new airplanes until this program has been installed.

2. Open (unzip) the file using WinZip. If you don't already have WinZip (or other compatible zip utility) installed, you must first install WinZip from the CD-ROM. To install WinZip from the CD-ROM, go to the WinZip95 directory and double click on the WinZip95 file. This will start the setup program for WinZip. Once WinZip is installed, proceed to the next step.

3. In WinZip, highlight both the *.MDL and the *.AIR files by holding down the Ctrl key and then select each file individually. The * is a wild card symbol which refers to any and all files with the prefix XXXXX.MDL and XXXXX.AIR.

4. Click the Extract button (if you are using WinZip) and choose the FS95\PILOTS directory as the location to extract the *.MDL and *.AIR files. (Your directory name for "FS95" may be different. Just be sure to copy the files into the PILOTS subdirectory wherever you have installed the main Flight Simulator directory).

5. Highlight all the remaining *.?AF files in the zip file (hold down the Ctrl key and select each file) and click the Extract button (if using WinZip). The * is a wild card symbol which refers to any and all files with the prefix XXXXX.0AF, XXXXX.1AF, XXXXX.2AF, XXXXX.3AF, XXXXX.4AF, XXXXX.5AF, XXXXX.6AF, XXXXX.7AF. The ? symbol refers to any character that occupies that particular location in the name of the file, for example "0", "1", etc.

6. Extract all the *.?AF files into the FS95\TEXTURE directory.

7. Restart Flight Simulator, and when you next open the Aircraft\Select Aircraft menu, you will see a listing for the new aircraft you just installed.

The *.MDL and *.AIR files contain the visual and aerodynamic model for the airplane, while the *.?AF files contain the textures for the airplane surface.

Some aircraft, when converted have stability or other flight model problems and a modified flight model must be created. This is really a "black art" because Microsoft has so far not released many details on the inner workings of the *.air files used to store the aerodynamic flight models. Furthermore, just as designers were getting used to the FSW95 format, Microsoft replaced the aerodynamic model with a totally new file format in FS98.

Because FSW95 uses a higher fidelity aerodynamic model, it is not possible to convert FS5.1 and Flight Shop aircraft to have precise flight models without editing the .AIR files that Flight Simulator uses to store aerodynamic models. Thus, FSW95 aircraft will not fly in exactly the same way they would in FS 5.1. You can try tweaking some of the aerodynamic parameters using Chuck Dome's Airmod4, or David Maschino's ACEdit, both found on the book's CD-ROM. However, even these programs do not fully allow you to change all the flight dynamics data found in the .AIR files. For a more complete description of how the model is stored, as well as instructions on how to use the hex editing utility AIR2DAT.EXE., see the documentation for AirDec on this book's companion CD-ROM.

There are many online sites for finding free aircraft, including *ftp.iup.edu*, the Flight Simulator Forum on Compuserve, and *www.microwings.com.*

Installing Panels in FSW95

Some airplanes come with specially designed instrument panels that will work in FSW95. Others rely on the default panels that FSW95 has, and still others use the instrument panels that are added by the Converter program. To install FSW95 panels, you should read the documentation that comes with the airplane or panel. In most instances, you must copy the *.pnl and other related files to the \Panels directory, then use a Panel Manager program to assign the panel to a particular airplane.

The basic flight simulator instrument panel filenames are as follows:

FILE NAME	AIRCRAFT THAT USES THIS PANEL
b737.pnl	Boeing 737 panel
cess.pnl	Cessna 182 panel

FILE NAME	AIRCRAFT THAT USES THIS PANEL
extr.pnl	Extra panel
lear.pnl	Learjet panel
schw.pnl	Schwiezer glider panel
sopw.pnl	Sopwith Camel panel

When you install the FSCONV.EXE file (the Aircraft and Adventure Converter for FSW95), the following instrument panels are added:

FILE NAME	TYPE OF AIRCRAFT THAT USES THIS PANEL
bje1.pnl	1 engine jet aircraft panel
bje2.pnl	2 engine jet aircraft panel
bje3.pnl	3 engine jet aircraft panel
bje4.pnl	4 engine jet aircraft panel
rec2.pnl	2 engine piston aircraft panel
rec3.pnl	3 engine piston aircraft panel
rec4.pnl	4 engine piston aircraft panel
lje1.pnl	1 engine jet aircraft (learjet style) panel
lje2.pnl	2 engine jet aircraft (learjet style) panel
lje3.pnl	3 engine jet aircraft (learjet style) panel
lje4.pnl	4 engine jet aircraft (learjet style) panel

Installing A New Flight Panel with Panel Manager 2.2 (FSW95 Only)

We have provided some excellent utilities for installing panels and assigning up to new 24 panels to existing aircraft for FSW95. One such program on the book's CD-ROM is called Panel Manager by Chuck Dome. For more information on how to use this program, read the online documentation. Do not use this program with FS98.

CHANGING THE LIVERY ON THE 737 (FSW95 ONLY)

If you look in the Texture subdirectory of your FSW95 directory, you'll discover that there are texture files for a TWA version of the 737 in addition to the generic 737 livery.

To have your plane use the TWA livery, follow these steps:

1. Exit FSW95, if it is running.
2. Using Explorer, go to your \Texture subdirectory of FSW95, make duplicate copies of your 737gen_1.r8, 737gen_2.r8, and 737twa_1.r8 files. The 737gen_1.r8 and the 737gen_2.r8 are the generic livery that you are already used to, while the 737twa_1.r8 and the 737twa_2.r8 files are the TWA livery. You should right click each file, and select **Copy**, then right click again and select **Paste** to make copies of each file. The copies will be named Copy of 737gen_1.r8, Copy of 737gen_2.r8, and so on.
3. Now delete the 737gen_1.r8 and 737gen_2.r8 files. To do this, select each file and press the **Delete** key.
4. Next, rename 737twa_1.r8 to 737gen_1.r8 and rename 737twa_2.r8 to 737gen_2.r8. To do this, left click each file once, so that it is selected, then click again and retype over the file name in the text box that appears.
5. Restart FSW95.
6. Select Aircraft/Select Aircraft and choose the 737. You'll see the 737 adorned with the TWA livery.

ADDING LANDING LIGHTS TO YOUR AIRPLANE (FSW95 ONLY)

It used to be that Flight Shop-created aircraft could not have landing lights. However, there is now a utility called Lladd.zip, created by Siggy Schwarz (available on the book's CD-ROM) that allows you to incorporate landing lights to your airplane model. Read the online documentation for instructions on how to use this versatile program.

USING THE SHAREWARE ON THIS BOOK'S CD-ROM: YOUR RIGHTS AND OBLIGATIONS

Shareware distribution gives you a chance to try software before buying it. If you try a shareware program and continue to use it, you are expected to register your copy. Because the overhead is low, prices are low. Shareware has the ultimate money-back guarantee—if you don't use the product, you don't pay for it.

Some of the programs on our CD-ROM fall into this category.

Registration grants you the right to install and use a single copy of the program. If you are unable to agree to these terms, the software must not be used and should not be installed.

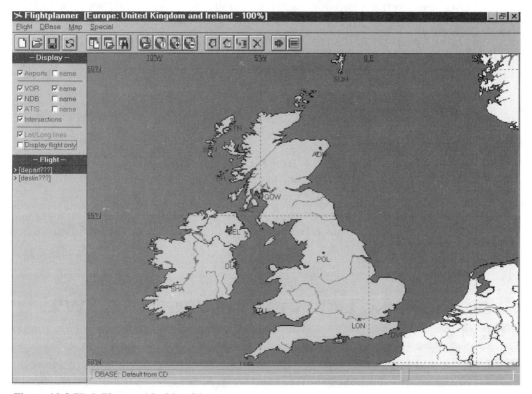

Figure 10.3 *FlightPlanner 4 by Matt Maessen.*

USING THE FREEWARE ON THIS BOOK'S CD-ROM

Freeware is software that may be freely distributed and given to anybody, as long as it is not sold.

For a more complete legal definition of freeware, see *http://www.cfcl.com/ free/legal/GPL* , or contact The Free Software Foundation (FSF) which has responsibility for the GNU Project.

Free Software Foundation
59 Temple Place, Suite 330
Boston, MA
02111-1307 USA
Tel: +1 617 542 5942
Fax: +1 617 542 2652
E-mail: *gnu@prep.ai.mit.edu*
FTP: *ftp://prep.ai.mit.edu/pub/gnu/*

Flight Planner 4.0 by Matt Maessen, which is discussed in the next section, is an example of freeware, although technically speaking, since it accompanies the book it is not freeware. However, the software is freely available on the Internet and there are no restrictions placed on its use, other than that Maessen requests that you not sell it or make money off it. Because of the educational aspect of this book, Maessen was kind enough to lift this restriction on his software.

FLIGHTPLANNER 4.0 BY MATT MAESSEN

The FlightPlanner 4.0 program (shown in Figure 10.3) on this book's companion CD-ROM is an excellent flight planning utility. This program not only allows you to create flight plans, but it also generates waypoint/navaid routes and allows you import and view navaid/airport BGL files (to be discussed in the next chapter) from Flight Simulator. If you go to the Flight Planner homepage on the Web, you can find various aircraft files for use with FlightPlanner, as well as new maps which became available after the release of version 4.0b, including maps for the entire U.S.

The next FlightPlanner version is under construction, and will be called flightplanner 5.0. New functions planned for this version include:

- Adventures with ATC-speech, based on flightshop
- Many adventure options, like auto-pilot, user-modules, GPS
- Better DBase handling: Add new scenery without rescanning all scenery

- Better DBase handling: Merge dbases without rescanning all scenery
- DBase will show scenery area in witch the runway is located
- Flightlevel adjustable at each waypoint
- Airport-layout will draw a map of all runways available on an airport
- New approach according flight rules (optional)
- New export-function to windows clipboard for general use
- More then just one Intersection files possible
- Intersections can be created by simply clicking on the map
- Special print function for b/w matrix printers
- At stops, a new depart time (or delay) can be entered
- Random flight generator for surprise flights

11

Creating and Managing Your Own Scenery

If you have ever wondered how to install new scenery you downloaded from the Web, or online, or from a software collection, you should read this chapter. You'll learn the basic techniques of managing scenery in Flight Simulator, all about scenery layering and types, and how the Scenery Manager is used to prioritize scenery. Loading new scenery into Flight Simulator and getting it to work right is one of the great joys of the program, because there is a universe of shareware scenery out there beckoning to you.

The first part of this chapter, covering scenery management, was written by Ray Proudfoot, author of the excellent tutorial *How to Become a Scenery Manager*. Ray has updated his work to reflect the latest changes to the Flight Simulator 98 program.

The second part of the chapter discusses how to create new scenery using the Airport 2.0 program found on this book's companion CD-ROM.

HOW TO BECOME A SCENERY MANAGER!

OK, so you're new to scenery management and want to understand how it works. The next couple of sections will lift the mystique surrounding the use of the Scenery Library.

THE CONCEPT OF LAYERING

Start FS98 and select **World / Scenery Library**. Clear the warning message and select **Files**. You will find several entries each one covering a specific part of the world. It may be a whole continent as is the case with Asia or Europe or it may be as small as a local airport. You will notice that against each entry there is a Type column. This can be Global, Regional or Local. I'll describe them in reverse order for reasons which will become apparent later.

Global

The Global entry is the lowest-layer scenery and must always be last in the list. It contains the generic scenery for the entire world. *This entry is protected and you will not be able to alter it.*

Regional

Next are the Regional areas. These are located immediately above the Global entry in the Scenery Library. Examples include the various geographical areas of North America, Europe and Oceania. *The FS98 Default World - Metro entry is fundamental to the operation of FS98 and cannot be edited.*

When you install FS98, each geographical area that you select will have a SCENERY and TEXTURE folder under

```
C:\FS98\SCENERY\areaname
```

and will include all the BGL (scenery) and TXR (texture) files from the FS98 CD-ROM. Each area will also have a matching entry in the Scenery Library.

For every geographical area that was *not* selected, a SCENERY and TEXTURE folder will have been created under

```
C:\FS98\CACHE\areaname
```

These folders will have scenery and texture files moved into them from the FS98 CD-ROM when required by FS98. This is called scenery caching.

There are a maximum of sixteen Regional entries including the World-Metro entry. These entries must always be Regional for FS98 to function correctly.

NOTE

Local

Finally we have the Local areas. These are located above the Regional areas and will be at the top of the list in the Scenery Library. Examples include Hong Kong, Hawaii and Las Vegas.

When you install FS98 you are given the option of installing the scenery files for several areas of the world, including the above areas. For each area that you select, you will find a folder on your hard disk under

`C:\FS98\SCENERY`

Each scenery folder contains the same BGL files that are on the CD-ROM in the corresponding BOOSTERS folder. These BGL files reside permanently on your hard drive. For each of these areas you will find an entry (classed as Local) in the Scenery Library.

If you opted not to load one of these areas to your hard disk, the entry for it will appear under the FLIGHT SIMULATOR\CACHE folder instead. It will still be a Local area. As you fly around such an area, data will be read from the BOOSTER folder files on the CD-ROM and placed in the relevant sub-folder under the CACHE folder. When you exit FS98, these files will be purged unless you specify otherwise. This topic will be revisited later. For now, select **Cancel** twice to exit the Scenery Library and return to FS98.

The FS98 Prime Directive: Never Install Third Party Scenery in Your Main Scenery Folder

Virtually all the third party scenery that you download and install into FS98 will be Local scenery unless otherwise stated in the scenery's accompanying documentation. It will require an entry in the Scenery Library above the Regional and Global entries.

WARNING

You should never install third party scenery into the main SCENERY and TEXTURE folders unless the author specifically instructs you to. Loading files this way can create utter confusion and will make the task of removing unwanted scenery extremely difficult. Most third party scenery should reside in its own set of folders.

As we've established, there are three types of scenery—Local, Regional, and Global. There can only ever be one Global layer but there can be many Regional and Local layers. Local layers must come first, followed by the Regional areas, and finally the single Global entry.

There may be an upper limit to the number of possible entries but no one seems to know what it is. Certainly over 100 layers can exist. All the data relevant to your scenery and its placement is contained in a single file—WORLD.VIS.

It is most important that you backup or copy this file on a regular basis and certainly before you make any changes to the Scenery Library. While big improvements have been made to scenery management in FS98 there are still no guarantees. Always backup WORLD.VIS!

ADDING NEW SCENERY

For this example we will be installing the Amelia Earhart scenery from the book's CD-ROM. This is a two-step process. The first step is to create the necessary folders on your hard disk and place the scenery files into them. The second step is to point FS98 to the contents of these folders using the Scenery Library.

Compatibility with FS5 and FSW95 Scenery

FS98 will generally be compatible with FS5.1 and FS95 third party scenery, but there are no guarantees. In any case, the inclusion in FS98 of many airports not previously available may negate the need to install scenery designed for earlier versions of Flight Simulator. FS98 performed admirably during beta testing when handling third party scenery and can be considered more stable than its predecessor. The dreaded KERNEL32 error message so common in FSW95 now appears to be a thing of the past.

NOTE

All previously available Microsoft scenery for Flight Simulator is built into FS98. The sole exception is the Southern California scenery, which should be installed as described in the README file on the FS98 CD-ROM.

Creating the Scenery and Texture Folders for Your New Scenery

When you download and unzip a scenery package, you will find it contains several files. BGL files contain the scenery components. The other files such as R8, OAV, and TXR are texture files and do not contain scenery objects. BGL files also contain navigation information such as ILS, VORs, NDBs, ATIS, and Airport data. You may still have occasional problems with BGL files but these can usually be resolved with exclude files. We will revisit this subject later.

One other word on files—many authors include a set of standard OAV files named AIRPTnnn.OAV in their scenery. The nnn refers to a number in the range 001 to 008.

There may also be other AIRPT files. Files with an OAV extension should be placed in the main TEXTURE folder. You only need to keep one set of these files, ensuring that the version from the new scenery only replaces the existing one if it's newer.

Let us suppose that you wish to install the Amelia scenery included on this book's CD-ROM. This file is compressed or "zipped." You will need to decompress it with a utility such as WinZip (also found on the book's CD-ROM). Follow these steps to create the required folders (the default path displayed below has been shortened to C:\FS98 for reasons of clarity):

```
C:\Program Files\Microsoft Games\Flight Simulator
```

1. Open Explorer and find the SCENERY folder under FS98. Create a new folder under SCENERY and name it AMELIA.
2. Under AMELIA, create two further folders and call them SCENERY and TEXTURE. It's important that you use these exact names, with no difference in spelling, as FS98 will expect them.
   Your folder structure should look like this:

```
C:\FS98
            SCENERY
                        AMELIA
                                    SCENERY
                                    TEXTURE
```

3. Unzip all the BGL files from the package and copy them to the SCENERY folder

```
C:\FS98\SCENERY\AMELIA\SCENERY
```

4. Place any AIRPTnnn.OAV files into the *main* TEXTURE folder (none are included in this file, but they may exist with other scenery)

```
C:\FS98\TEXTURE
```

5. If there are any DOC or TXT files you may wish to place these in the main AMELIA folder for reference.
6. Normally, all remaining files would be placed in

```
C:\FS98\SCENERY\AMELIA\TEXTURE
```

but because of the way this scenery was designed it's necessary to place the all the files with the *.R8 extension (for example SEEDC9.R8 would be one such file) into the main TEXTURE folder

```
C:\FS98\TEXTURE
```

Very Important Note: Install **all** the texture files (i.e., *.R8) for the Amelia Scenery in the main FS98\Texture folder. If you don't do this, the scenery won't work!

T I P

7. Before you exit Explorer, make a copy of your WORLD.VIS file in the SCENERY folder. Select it and drag it to the main FS98 folder using the right mouse button, and choose **Copy Here.** Then select it again and using the right mouse button, select **Rename.** Change the name to WORLD.ORI (or whatever your preference is). You should do this each time you create a new scenery layer.

Creating a New Scenery Layer in FS98

In order for FS98 to use the new Amelia scenery in the example above, we now need to direct it to the contents of the folders we've just created. Follow these steps:

1. Load FS98 and select **World/Scenery Library.**
2. Clear the warning message by selecting **OK.**
3. Select **Files**.
4. Select the **Add** button.
5. In the Scenery Area Path type the path

```
C:\FS98\SCENERY\AMELIA\SCENERY\*.BGL
```

The * symbol represents a wildcard. All files that have a BGL extension will be included. You will notice that as you type the last character in Step 5, the other boxes become active. This is confirmation that you've typed a valid path.
6. Type **Amelia** in the Scenery Area Title.
7. From the Scenery Area Type select **Local** and select **Scenery Area Active.** A tick will be displayed showing it to be active.
8. The Scenery Area Layer number can remain at its default value of 001 for the time being. Select **OK.** Return to the previous screen and note Amelia at the top

of the list. Note that under Layers, the number 001 has a + sign next to it. This indicates it is active. A minus sign indicates the area is not active. By active I mean that FS98 will read the corresponding BGL files for that area when it loads.

9. Select **Arrange Layers**. Select **Amelia** (it will be at the top), then select **Lower Layer**. Move it down to layer 2. Now move it up to layer 1 by selecting **Raise Layer**. This exercise gets you used to using this option. You will find that with some scenery the ordering of the layers is important but generally you have a reasonable amount of freedom as to the actual placement. I usually place my favorite local scenery areas near the top of the list. Try and avoid using **Auto Arrange**. You should *always* control scenery layering manually.

10. Select **OK** three times to confirm the entries and return to FS98. When you select the final **OK** FS98 will update WORLD.VIS.

Using the New Scenery

Now we are ready to use the new Amelia scenery we've just installed. To do this, follow these steps:

1. From the **World** menu, select **Go To.... Airport**. In the upper right area of the display there are three entries:
   - Search Places
   - Search Airport ID's
   - Scenery from 6.0 and before.
2. Select the last option, **Scenery from 6.0 and before**. In the right window beneath "Scenery areas," a list of scenery areas will appear. It will include one or more entries for the Amelia scenery you just installed.
3. Select one of the entries; in the "Search results list" window to the left, you will see a list of available airports/runways displayed. Make a selection, then hit **OK** to load that scenery and place the aircraft at the chosen location.

Problems You May Encounter: Double Runways

When you install some 3rd party scenery, you may find double runways or buildings appearing on the runway. This indicates that you have installed airport scenery on top of the scenery provided in FS98. To hide the default scenery, you must add an exclude file. Many scenery authors will include such a file with their scenery to avoid just such a problem. This potential problem does not occur with the Amelia scenery since there are no default runways to conflict with those in this scenery.

If there is no exclude file, and you are experiencing trouble, then don't despair. We provide an excellent utility, SCUTILS.ZIP by Pete Dowson, on the book's CD-ROM. This is a freeware collection of Flight Simulator-related utilities and includes an application for creating exclude files—AREAEXCL.EXE.

Exclude files are very small (on average only 1Kb in size) and will usually have a suitably identifying name. The usual practice is for the first four digits to reflect the ICAO code for the airport you're excluding followed by EXCL to identify it as an exclude file. As an example, one for London Heathrow would be named EGLLEXCL.BGL.

The placement of an exclude file and the layering of the relevant scenery areas in FS98 is important. The order of entries in Scenery Library / Files determines the order of scenery priority. BGL files contain objects such as buildings, runways, etc. If you have two BGL files covering the same latitude/longitude and with the same runways in separate folders with their corresponding entries in the Scenery Library, you will experience double runways. I can best demonstrate this with an experiment.

For this exercise you need to install the scenery files from EGCC.ZIP on the book's CD under the SCUTILS folder. This scenery contains airports in England and to ensure that this demonstration works correctly, the Europe scenery needs to reside on your hard disk. If you haven't loaded Europe but have it cached instead I would recommend that you run Setup again and install it before proceeding.

Installing (Manchester) EGCC airport.

1. Using the same principle as described in [Adding New Scenery] create a folder named Manchester under the Scenery folder and under Manchester create a sub-folder named SCENERY. Place the two BGL files (ZENGMAIN.BGL & EGC-CEXCL.BGL) into this scenery sub-folder.
2. Make a copy of WORLD.VIS.
3. Start FS98 and select **World/Scenery Library**. Add a new Local layer and call it Manchester. Ensure it's active. Select **OK** three times to update WORLD.VIS.
4. From **World...Go to Airport** select "**Scenery from 6.0 and before**". From "**Scenery areas**" select "**English Airfields**". Scroll down the left-hand list and select "**Manchester Rwy 24**". Select **OK**.
5. Open Map View (press **Shift**]), and maximize the window by pressing **W**. If the screen won't maximize, select **Views/View Options** and deselect **Auto full screen**. Select **OK** and zoom out until you can see the full length of the runway. At this point the default runway and airport buildings has been hidden or "excluded". Only the runway in the new scenery is visible.
6. Select **World/Scenery Library/Files**. Highlight Manchester and select **Edit**. Select **Scenery Area Active** to turn the layer off ensuring the tick disappears. Select **OK** three times to update WORLD.VIS and return to FS98. After a short

interval you will see the effects of turning off this layer. The single runway will disappear to be replaced with the default scenery. The default scenery was there all the time of course but was hidden by the exclude file. Now reverse this action by opening the Scenery Library and turning Manchester back on.

To give the Manchester layer priority it needs to be placed higher than the default scenery which is included in the Europe Regional layer in Scenery Library. If you were to move Manchester down the loading order to below the Europe Regional entry the default runway would take priority and we wouldn't see the 3rd party scenery although the double runways would still be visible unless we moved that exclude file.

You can easily identify an exclude file as it will always be 148 bytes in size (when created by SCUTILS) and will usually have a suitable name. The one for Manchester is called EGCCEXCL.BGL. Select it in Explorer, right click and select **Properties**. The size will be displayed. If there wasn't an exclude file you'd get the double runways. We can prove this quite easily. You will need to load FS98 and Explorer for this demonstration.

1. Open FS98 and select **World/Go to /Airport**.
2. Select Scenery from 6.0 and before.
3. Scroll down the "Scenery areas" list and select English Airfields.
4. From the "Search results list" select Manchester Rwy 24.
5. Click OK, open up Map View (Shift+]) and hit W to maximize it.
6. Now switch to Explorer but keep FS98 running. Right click on "Start" and select Explore. Find the folder MANCHESTER\SCENERY and move (don't copy) the exclude file EGCCEXCL.BGL into the main MANCHESTER folder.
7. Switch back to FS98. Make sure the Map View is still maximized.
8. Select World/Scenery Library and after clearing the warning message, select Files.
9. Highlight Manchester, choose Edit, and select the Scenery area active option to turn this scenery layer back on. Select OK three times to update WORLD.VIS
10. The scenery files will now be re-scanned. After a short delay you will see the effect of removing the exclude file. Double runways will appear! Now can you see why these exclude files are so useful?

The scenery files included in this demonstration only contain runways. It is not intended that they should replace the default scenery which contains more detail. It is recommended that you remove the Manchester layer once you are happy with how exclude files work.

1. Select **World/Scenery Library**. Select **Files** and highlight the Manchester layer. Select **Delete** and click **OK** three times to exit Scenery Library.

2. Load Explorer, locate the Manchester folder under Scenery and delete it. The SCENERY sub-folder will also be deleted.

If you would like to try creating exclude files yourself, use SCUTILS by Pete Dowson. You'll find it on the book's CD. The executable file has its own help built in and is easy to understand.

SCENERY CACHING

When you install FS98 you are given the option of installing all the scenery to your hard disk. For the best performance from FS98, this option is strongly recommended. However, if you don't have sufficient disk space to do this (a full install will consume nearly 300Mb) FS98 employs an alternative method to display the scenery for those areas you choose not to install.

This method is known as scenery caching and works as follows. Let's assume that the South America scenery was not selected. Open Explorer and under

`C:\FS98\CACHE`

you will find a folder named SAMERICA. Under this folder are two folders named SCENERY and TEXTURE.

As you fly around South America the required scenery (BGL) files are copied from the CD-ROM folder

`BOOSTERS\SAMERICA\SCENERY`

to

`C:\FS98\CACHE\SAMERICA\SCENERY`

Any texture files will be copied from the TEXTURE sub-folder on the FS98 CD-ROM to the SAMERICA\TEXTURE sub-folder.

When you exit FS98, these folders under CACHE are purged, saving disk space.

To avoid loading all the world scenery onto your hard disk, FS98 default settings call for reading some of it directly from the CD-ROM. For those without large hard drives, this is a welcome boon. However by reading the scenery files in this way there is a loss of performance which is most noticeable in the frequent pauses while scenery is loaded. Even mirroring the booster files (as they're called) from the CD-ROM to the hard disk doesn't stop these pauses. Only by creating a new scenery folder and copying all the booster BGL files from the CD-ROM to the HD and then disabling caching can these pauses be eliminated. This step is detailed in a document, NOPAUSE.WRI, available on the FS and SIMGAMES Forums. The downside to this step is the extended time it takes for FS to load. Unfortunately there is no way around this.

A third alternative occurs where the files from the CD-ROM booster files are retained on the hard disk and the cache is not cleaned out when you exit FS98. This offers another option for those with limited hard disk space, especially if the same area is always the one flown.

Normally, when you exit FS98 all the files in the cache are discarded. When you reload FS98 and select the same area, the files are once again read from the CD-ROM. To avoid this repetition, you can opt to retain these files on your hard disk after FS98 closes. Then, when you restart FS98 and select the same area, the files are already in place. *This option now seems unnecessary and is not recommended. If you constantly fly in the same area, it makes more sense to install that scenery area permanently in Setup rather than prevent the cache files from being purged.*

If you wish to experiment, this is the procedure to follow:

1. Load FS98 and select **World/Scenery Library**.
2. Clear the warning message. Select **Performance**.
3. Select **FLTSIM98 CD-South America**, and then select **Edit**.
4. From Cache Cleanup Strategy, select **Do Not Clean On Exit**. The default value of 5000k (5Mb) will be sufficient for South America but you may wish to experiment for other scenery areas. Amending it to 7Mb would eventually allow all the North America Great Lakes scenery to remain on the hard disk.
5. Repeat this for as many areas as you wish.
6. Select **OK** three times to effect the change.

When you exit FS98, the scenery for that area will be retained on the hard disk.

SCENERY PROBLEMS

With most third party scenery that you install for FS98, the scenery will have been tested by the author and may also have been beta tested by others. You shouldn't expect to have problems with it provided you follow the author's instructions.

But, as with most things in this world, there are exceptions. Some potential problems are discussed in the following paragraphs. Some general housekeeping recommendations are also provided, along with an explanation of what exclude files are and how they work.

Please also note that it is highly inadvisable to install scenery designed for v5.0 and earlier. It is almost certain that it will not function correctly due to the many changes in Flight Simulator software.

Floating Runways

After loading a new scenery area, you will sometimes find that the runway floats above the ground textures. Unfortunately there's very little you can do with this problem apart from bringing it to the attention of the author. Altitudes are stored within BGL files and a solution to this problem is only possible by editing the file and correcting the error. This type of problem may be more common since the arrival of FS95 and FS98. While the scenery itself is compatible, some of the altitudes in the default scenery have changed from FS5.1. I should add that this type of problem is quite rare and may only found in scenery designed for FS5.1.

Exclude Files—What They Are and How They Work

The purpose of an exclude file is to remove or "exclude" objects in other scenery areas. It will NOT exclude scenery in BGL files in the same folder as the exclude file. When an exclude file is created latitude and longitude values are specified as delimiters. Most scenery objects existing within these delimiters will become invisible in underlying scenery. but there are exceptions. The "ugly green and brown hills", which existed in FS95 cannot be excluded but in any case these are now given a textured appearance in FS98 and look far more realistic.

An exclude file can only exclude objects that are placed lower in the Scenery Library loading order. It cannot exclude objects that are placed higher. As an example if Amelia was at Level 3 and there was clashing scenery at Level 2 the exclude file would not work as intended unless Amelia was raised to Level 1.

How to Remove Scenery

There may come a time when you no longer want a third party scenery layer. To uninstall it correctly follow these steps

1. Start FS98 and select World/Scenery Library.
2. Clear the warning message and select **Files**.
3. Locate your scenery area and select **Delete**. Select **OK** to confirm.
4. Exit FS98 and load Explorer. Locate the relevant parent folder; i.e.

   `C:\FS98\SCENERY\AMELIA.`

5. Select the folder icon for AMELIA and right-click. Select **Delete** and confirm as necessary.

Under no circumstances should you delete these folders before removing the entry in Scenery Library as the WORLD.VIS file may then be corrupted, and you will suffer dire consequences.

Storing Downloaded Scenery Files

Once you have loaded third party scenery you should archive the file to a floppy disk and store it safely. After all, it's cost you time and money to download it. You may care to share it with your friends. Freeware software has no limitations provided you don't add, remove or amend any of the files.

SUMMARY

I hope I've covered all the queries you have with Scenery Library in FS98. It is not a particularly complicated topic but it can be quite problematic when you have conflicting scenery areas. Some scenery designers are not careful enough in their use of BGL files and these can have quite an effect on airports several hundreds of miles away in extreme circumstances.

I was once baffled by an airport disappearing from my listing even though I knew the BGL file which contained it existed. I tracked the problem to a BGL file in another scenery folder where the author had extended the co-ordinates of the file far outside of the area he/she was designing scenery for. It had effectively zapped everything that was loaded lower in the Scenery Library.

When working with BGL files, there are several tools that will help you enormously. You should, at some point, experiment with the Flight Simulator utility program SCU-TILS.ZIP included on the book's CD-ROM. Another very useful utility program is Flight Planner, which is also on the book's CD-ROM. Flight Planner contains a great BGL viewer. This tool has been invaluable to me in identifying the contents of .bgl files; you can extract all the navaids, ILS, airports, and other data directly from the .bgl files. Flight Planner's author—Math Maessen—has produced a first class product. Both these utilities are freeware. The only cost to you is your time in learning how to use them and sending a postcard to Math!

If you still have questions after reading this then remember there's a huge amount of help available in FS98. For installation help make sure you also read the README file on the FS98 CD-ROM.

Finally, when you download software from the Internet or an online service, please take time to thank the author. A lot of effort goes into creating the scenery and a few words of thanks will always be greatly appreciated. If the software is shareware please send a donation. In the long term this will give the author the incentive to donate more software.

Credits: My thanks to John Waller for the use of part of England & Wales scenery and to Pete Dowson for SCUTILS.

FLIGHT SIMULATOR SCENERY FILE FORMAT

Flight Simulator uses two types of scenery

1. Cybergraphics/synth city
2. Photo-Realistic/Ray Traced

Both scenery types were first developed by BAO for FS 5.1 and are still used in FS98. Older scenery, such as that found in FS 4.0 and earlier, employed simple polygon vector drawn objects that simulated 3-D buildings and filled in the ground terrain with various patterns. It was not particularly attractive, but it served its purpose before being superseded by the FS 5.1 style scenery.

The Cybergraphics used in FSW95 are so called because the scenery is drawn via vector drawing methods. This allows scenery to be described mathematically so that it can be scaled to any size without distortion. It allows highly detailed, complex 256 color computer generated scenery such as buildings, bridges, sky shading, shadows, urban developments, regions, coastlines, clouds, and oceans to be stored in an incredibly compact scenery database. Synthetic scenery refers to innovative technique called "seeding" which allows vast areas of the ground to have a generic appearance. For example, the suburbs, urban areas, forests, farmland, and water have a repetitive "seed" which is repeated in block after block of scenery (the seed files have the extension *.r8). When viewed from the air, however, the seeded blocks give you the sensation that you are flying over an urban or rural area. A typical "synth" seeded scenery block can be stored in as little as 700 bytes of data, which allows for many variations within each seed type. Thus an urban seed can have several variants that are alternated to give a random appearance and this affords a more pleasing aerial view of the ground.

Flight Simulator's Photo-Realistic scenery texture maps satellite or aerial photographs over topographical elevation data. In Flight Simulator, you can see photo-realistic scenery at Hong Kong, Chelan, Washington, Martha's Vineyard near Cape Cod, and around Las Vegas in Nevada. For example, the texture mapping around Chelan and Lake Mead near Las Vegas show you how real photographic imagery of the ground is wrapped around surface contours, much as a decal is applied to a surface. Thus, at these locations, you can fly over real mountain ranges, fly through valleys, and fly over cities with unparalleled realism because the scenery looks three dimensional.

The photos that are used for texture mapping the ground are converted into bitmaps. These bitmaps, in turn, have assigned an individual color to each picture element, or pixel, which are then texture mapped directly to the surface polygon that describes the ground. Unfortunately, bitmaps do not scale well, so when you fly very close the ground, you'll notice that the surface definitions become destorted and misshapen. Similarly, bitmapped fonts do not scale well when you resize them to be larger, and they become jagged and unreadable at extremely large font sizes.

Flight Simulator uses a combination of the Photo-Realistic and Cyber-Graphics/Synthetic scenery. First background photo-realistic ground scenery is drawn, then the cybergraphics vector drawn building objects are superimposed on the background. Where the photo-realistic scenery ends, synth style seeded scenery is used to represent outlying areas with less detail, but with much less disk space needed to cover vast areas of the earth.

Understanding BGLs

As mentioned previously, BGLs contain the instructions for displaying scenery. They not only store static scenery, but also can store dynamic scenery, such as moving sailboats, airplanes, trucks, and navaids.

According to one member of the Flight Simulator development team, the .bgl extension is an acronym for "Bruce's Graphic Language." Bruce Artwick is, of course, the original designer of Flight Simulator.

Most scenery creation programs create scenery by storing source code in simple text files that are then compiled by a compiler program such as SCASM. The Airport 2.05 Scenery Design program on this book's CD-ROM works this way, except that it uses a Windows 95 graphical interface to make it easier for you to place scenery objects.

Scenery areas can consist of multiple BGL files covering the same area. For example, you could have a gas station in one BGL, and right next to the gas station you could have a runway in a second BGL. The BGL files can be created by different scenery creation programs, so all that matters to you is whether they seamlessly fit together. When they don't, as is the case with duplicate runways, you need to remove the offending BGL, or add an exclusion file to correct the problem.

The BGLs with the suffix 3 usually store ILS data, while those BGLs with the suffix 4 usally store airports and ATIS information. Thus, for example, Rio3.bgl in your scenery directory would store the ILS data, while Rio4.bgl would store all the airports in the Rio de Janeiro area of Brazil.

If you want to take a peek at what's inside your navaid BGLs, you should install Flight Planner 4.0 from the book's CD-ROM. Once installed, there is a BGL viewer that will allow you extract, print out, and view the contents of the file.

NOTE FS98 has a new data format for Facility information that is not as yet clearly understood. Once designers have learned the structure, FS98 will be able automatically include Facility information from any third party scenery into the **World/Go to Airports** dialog box.

Common File Extensions in Flight Simulator

You already know that BGL files are scenery files. But what about all the other files you see being used by Flight Simulator? If you examine the file extension of the files used by FS98, you'll notice many files that end with bgl, r8, pnl, stn, wav, vid, gau, cfg, mdl, air, bmp. What do they mean and what do they do?

- **.bgl** Scenery files. They contain navaids, static scenery, dynamic scenery, and airports.
- **.r8** Texture files. They contain textures used for the scenery. Example: coastlines, farmland, cities, suburban areas, etc.
- **.bmp** Bitmap files. They contain bitmaps used to texture surfaces, such as buildings.
- **.pnl** Panel files. They contain information on the instrument panels.
- **.gau** Gauge files. They contain the gauges used on the instrument panels.
- **.cfg** Configuration files. These are text files that contain information on how to use certain parts of the program. For example, there is a panel configuration file, an aircraft configuration file, a master FS98 configuration file, a sound configuration file, etc.
- **.air** Air files. These are aircraft flight dynamics.
- **.mdl** Model files. These are used by the program to define the visual aspects of the airplane.
- **.vid** Video files. When you record a video, it is saved as a .vid file.
- **.stn** Situation files. These are the flight situation files that you can save and load by using the Flights/Flight Situations menu.

Internal Scenery Structures

Tiles are areas of the globe covered by blocks of synthetic scenery. There are six sizes of tiles, and with the largest size Section 1 tile, it takes 256 tiles to completely girdle the earth. With the smallest Section 6 tile; it takes 8,192 tiles to cover the earth. Flight Simulator knows how many blocks to fill in for each size of tile. For example, with the largest Section 1 tiles, there will be 32×32 or 1024 blocks. With Section 2 tiles there will be 16×16 or 256 blocks. With Section 3 tiles there will be 8×8 or 64 blocks. With Section 4 tiles, there will be 4×4 or 16 blocks. With Section 5 tiles there will be 2×2 or 4 blocks, and with Section 6 tiles there will be only one block.

Scenery blocks are areas that Flight Simulator uses to fill in a given size tile. A block can vary from less than a mile square to nearly three miles square, depending on the latitude.

Flight Simulator comes with many stock r8 textures for painting each block of scenery. These are all listed in the \Texture folder, where you will see such files as farms.r8 (farms), prairie.r8 (prairies), coast.r8 (coastlines). All the r8 files can be viewed in the Airport Scenery design program. The bitmap (bmp) files are similar to the bitmaps used by graphics programs, in fact you can view them with any paint program. Bitmaps are square, 256 pixels wide by 256 pixels high and can cover any 3D object in Flight Simulator, including airplanes and buildings. The sides of the skyscrapers that you see in Flight Simulator are actually bitmaps that have been pasted on to a flat surface.

BGL File Formats

There is detailed documentation on the BGL file format found on this book's CD-ROM under the \Scenery How it Works folder.

In particular, the following files may be of further use to you if you need file format data:

- FS5Facts
- FSPro
- FS5Struc
- FS98diff

FS5Facts

FS5Facts, compiled by Konstantin Kukushkin, and reproduced on the CD-ROM with his permission, offers technical information on the following subjects in FS98:

- How scenery is stored in the BGL file
- How the scenery library works
- How FS98 displays scenery
- How FS98 displays textures
- How FS98 displays colors
- How FS98 displays 3D objects

FSPro

FSPro is another technical document on BGL files by Konstantin Kukushkin. You'll find information on the following subjects:

- How to draw primitives
- How to design 2D landscapes
- How to place 3D objects
- How to construct 3D objects
- How to select colors
- How to use textures
- How to create night effects
- How to create animated objects
- How to keep frame rates high
- How to stay within limits
- How to resolve scenery conflicts
- Compatibility issues
- Notes on distributing scenery
- Notes for FSASM users

FS5Struc

FS5Struc, written by Maurizio M. Gavioli, and reproduced with his permission on our CD-ROM, details the actual BGL file format. It includes hex code and examples showing how the BGL file works.

USING AIRPORT 2.05 SCENERY CREATION SOFTWARE

If you would like to try your hand at creating your own scenery, you need look no further than this book's CD-ROM. There you will find the Airport 2.05 scenery creation program created by Pascal Meziat and Manfred Moldenhauer. To install the program, run the setup.exe file in the Airport directory on the CD, then after the program is installed, copy all the **Airport\Texture*.*** files into your main **FS98\Texture** folder (these include *.OAV, *r8, and *.pat files). Installing the texture files is necessary so that any new scenery you create will have the correct appearance. Once the program is installed, and you have installed the texture files, you can run Airport via your **Start** menu in Windows.

Examples and Documentation

Select **?/Tutorial** to access the online tutorial (you can also print out the tutorial using the **File/Print** menu within the Help window). This tutorial is designed to explain step by step how to create scenery with Airport.

The main help files are accessible via the **?/Contents** menu command.

The \example subfolder contains various example Airport files (which always have the file extension *.apt). Two of the files are based on real French airports:

- Pau   lfbp.apt
- Nice   lfmn.apt

The other Airport files are imaginary, and are only intended to demonstrate how to use the program.

Important Addendum for FS98: Scenery bgl files created with Airport 2.05 do not work unless you install them following the method outlined earlier in Ray Proudfoot's scenery management tutorial. They will not work properly if you simply copy them to the main **FS98\Scenery** folder as you might expect from previous experience with bgl files. You **must** create a separate **\MyScenery** folder (or whatever name you give it) with subfolders **\Scenery** and **\Texture**, then use the Scenery Library to point to this new directory.

Airport 2.0 needs to be installed into a folder that does not have a long file name greater than 8 characters. This is because the SCASM compiler is a DOS program that can only handle an 8-character-long DOS file name.

N O T E

How Airport 2.0 Works

Airport is a Windows 95 program that gives you graphical interface for designing scenery for Flight Simulator. When you start the program, you decide the latitude/longitude coordinates of your initial scenery area, then click the mouse to place objects such as runways, buildings, fuel dumps, hangers, navaids, roads, etc. You can drag objects to any part of the window and place them just the way you like. When you are finished, you save the file and then run the BGL creation command, which uses the SCASM program to compile the actual machine code for the BGL.

The SCASM.EXE program can be considered as a sort of "internal engine" for Airport. Here is a basic summary of how Airport works in conjunction with SCASM:

1. The user draws his scenery over a graphical map, using his mouse.
2. Then, he saves his design. The scenery is actually stored in a text file with the *.apt extension. (exactly like any vector drawing design software like Corel Draw or MS-Draw).
3. When the user wants to test his scenery with Flight Simulator, he simply clicks on the related icons in the Airport toolbar: the "BGL" icon or the "plane" icon.
4. Here is now what Airport does automatically: the *.apt scenery file is converted to a *.sca file, i.e. a source file written in SCASM. It is a sort or conversion/translation. Then Airport Invokes SCASM.EXE in a background task, in order to generate the *.bgl file. During the last stage, Airport copies the *.bgl file produced by Scasm into the Flight Simulator \Scenery folder, and Flight Simulator is launched. Note that this Step 4 is very fast - only a few seconds - and that the user doesn't need to do anything.

SCASM.EXE is totally embedded in the Airport archive, so once the user has installed Airport, there is no need to add any other component.

Create Your First Airport

As an example of how to use the program, let's create an airport with a single runway that we will load as a BGL file into FS98.

After installing the program and copying the texture files from the **Airport\texture** folder to your **FS98\Texture** folder, follow these steps:

1. From the Taskbar, click **Start/Programs/Airport 2.05** to start the Airport program. You will see a blank screen after the program opens. Don't worry, this is normal.
2. Select the **File** menu, and choose **New**. This will open up a new airport file for you to work with.
3. Select **Sections/General** and in the dialog box, type in the name, comments, range that you want your scenery to be visible, latitude/longitude coordinates, magnetic variation, and altitude. Click **OK** to return to the main window.
4. Right click and a pop-up menu will appear, allowing you to select a polygon, road/line, building, 3-D object, runway, fuel area, dynamic object, ATIS, VOR, or NDB. Let's select **Runway**.
5. In the Runway dialog box, you can choose the length of the runway, the width, surface type, type of runway lighting, ILS installation, heading, and runway markings. When you are finished with your selections, click the **OK** to continue.
6. You'll see an outline of the runway (you won't see the actual runway as appears in FS98, only the graphic primitives). If you click on the central circle inside the runway, you can drag the runway to a different position.

7. To zoom the view out so you can see more area, click the + button onscreen. To zoom in, click the – button.
8. Right-click and add other objects, navaids, or buildings. You have many options in each of the dialog boxes for each object type.
9. After you have finished with your airport design, go to the **File** menu and select **Save**. Be sure to give the file an 8 character long or less DOS style name. With your creation now saved, you can open it up again at any other later date and edit it with further changes.
10. Now you are ready to create the bgl file. Click the **BGL** button on screen and the Airport program will create a bgl and deposit the bgl file into the directory you have specified under the **Options/Preferences** menu under BGL Path. Note that FS98 **will not** recognize the bgl file created with Airport **unless** you install it into a scenery subfolder inside the main FS98\Scenery folder, **and** you use the Scenery Library to Point FS98 at it.

After you have gone through the Scenery Library and pointed to the scenery folder where you deposited the newly created bgl in Step 10, it will appear under the **World\Goto Airports\Scenery from 6.0 and before** dialog box (but only if you have added a runway—if your scenery doesn't include a runway there will be no listing under the FS98 menu). If you select your newly created bgl file in this dialog box, and click **OK**, you'll see your brand new airport.

Designing scenery is fraught with peril because you are bound to run into scenery incompatibility problems with double runways, or runways that appear to float over the ground. Sometimes these scenery problems aren't easily solved. If you have such trouble, you'll need to closely read the online documentation and do some trouble shooting. You may even have to create an exclusion file using Pete Dowson's SCUTILS program.

WHERE TO LEARN MORE

If you are interested in scenery design, and want to learn more, the best place to start is Gene Kraybill's excellent website found at *http://www.wwguide.com.au/fs/index.htm*.

Gene has compiled a fantastic collection of scenery notes, scenery files, utilities, reviews of programs, even reviews of Flight Simulator related books.

EXPLORING FLIGHT SIMULATOR'S EASTER EGGS

Although most of the fun in discovering Easter Eggs occurs when you stumble upon them yourself, sometimes it helps to have a helping hand point them out when they are not so obvious. Table 11. 1 lists many, but not all, the Easter Eggs found in the program.

Table 11.1 *Flight Simulator Easter Eggs*

EASTER EGG	LOCATION	LATITUDE	LONGITUDE
Berlin Wall, Brandenburg Gate	Berlin Germany	Select the "Back in Time in Berlin" Flight Situation, and set the date ahead to any date in the 1990s.	
Big Ben, Parliament, Buckingham Palace	London, England	N51° 29' 47.00" (or select the "Thames River Run" Flight Situation	W000° 07' 15.00"
Cape Canaveral, Space Shuttle, Assembly Building	Cape Canaveral, Florida	N28° 36' 44"	W080° 36' 48"
Champs Elysees, Arc de Triomphe	Paris, France	N48° 52' 35.62"	E002° 17' 31.47"
Eiffel Tower	Paris, France	N48° 52' 12.56"	E002° 16' 48.52"
Easter Island (see the Head Sculptures)	Easter Island	Select the "Heads of Easter Island" Flight Situation	
Fraukenkirche Cathedral	Munich, Germany	N48° 08' 07"	E011° 34' 28"
Ginza District	Tokyo, Japan	Select the "Ginza District" Flight Situation	
Hollywood sign (check out the backside)	Hollywood, California	N34° 07.18'	W118° 08.19"
Hot Air Balloon	Northwest of Seattle, Washington	N47° 56' 52.96"	W122° 26' 56.24"
Kilauea Volcano Eruption	Hawaii	Select the "1983 Kilauea Eruption" Flight Situation	
Kremlin, Red Square	Moscow, Russia	N55° 45' 02.43"	E037° 38' 58' 41"
Hoover Dam	Boulder City, Nevada	N35° 58.55'	W114° 45' 13"
Leaning Tower of Pisa	Pisa, Italy	N43° 43' 51.53"	E010° 24' 00.56"

Table 11.1 *continued*

Easter Egg	Location	Latitude	Longitude
Los Angeles Coliseum	Los Angeles, California	N34° 00' 51"	W118° 16' 49"
Little Girl (only in FSW95)	Rear view inside 737 cockpit		
Microsoft Campus (Microsoft Development team picture is inside one of the buildings)	Redmond, Washington	N47° 38' 37"	W122° 06' 58"
Mt. Ranier, snow on caldera	Washington	N46° 51.59'	W121° 47.25'
Mt. Rushmore	Southwest of Rapid City, South Dakota	N43° 51' 94.52"	W103° 25' 23.29"
Panama Canal	Panama	N09° 19' 44"	W079° 55' 30"
Parthenon	Athens, Greece	N37° 58.70'	E023° 42.78'
Seattle's Kingdome	Seattle, Washington	N47° 13' 11"	W122 25' 27"
Seattle Space Needle	Seattle, Washington	N47° 37.35'	W122° 21.18'
Sphinx and Pyramids	Cairo, Eqypt	N29° 57' 56"	E031° 08' 29.03"
Statue of Liberty	New York	Select the "Statue of Liberty" Flight Situation	
St. Louis Gateway Arch	St. Louis, Missouri	N38° 36' 46.84"	W090° 10' 28.90"
St. Peters		N41° 54'	E012° 28' 19
Sydney Opera House	Sydney, Australia	S33° 46' 03.42"	E151° 10' 54.28"
Tianenmen Square	Beijing, China	Select the "Beijing and the Forbidden City" Flight Situation	
Taj Mahal	Agra, India	N27° 07' 51.64"	E078° 03' 20.79"
U.S.S. Carl Vinson and Task Force (turn on dynamic scenery to very dense)	Off the coast of Maui, Hawaii	N20° 24.7'	W156° 40.52'

Table 11.1 continued

Easter Egg	Location	Latitude	Longitude
Aircraft Carrier (turn on dynamic scenery to very dense)	Outside San Francisco Bay, California	N37° 44' 31.38"	W122° 36' 33.55"
U.S.S. Abraham Lincoln (must have Southern California Scenery Expansion Pack)	Off the coast of San Diego	N32° 32' 21.2"	W117° 16' 30.69"
Vatican	Vatican City, Italy	N41° 53' 54.81"	E012° 28' 33.65"
Wright Flyer (Set the date to Dec. 17,1903, time to 12:00 noon, Scenery to very dense, elevation +3 ft, and heading to 104°)	Kitty Hawk, North Carolina	N36° 01' 10.8108"	W075° 40' 45.7032"

Contents of CD-ROM, Add-On Scenery, and Online Resources

In this chapter you will get an overview of the contents of this book's unmatched CD-ROM, you'll find out where to look up Flight Simulator–related information on the Internet, and you'll be introduced to some of the commercial add-on products, magazines, and accessories that are available for Flight Simulator.

CD-ROM CONTENTS

***Table 12.1** Flight Simulator Software on this Book's CD-ROM*

TITLE	TYPE OF SOFTWARE OR FILE
21 new airplanes (* These aircraft are ready to use with FSW95, but need to be converted with the Microsoft Aircraft Converter before use with FS98)	• Shorts 360 (Evaluation version) by VIP • Hi-Fi DC-8 (Evaluation version: note new instrument panel only works with FSW95) by Stolle Systems, courtesy of Bernt Stolle • Hi-Fi DC-10 (Evaluation version: new instrument panel only works with FSW95) by Stolle Systems, courtesy of Bernt Stolle • Hi-Fi MD-80 (Evaluation version: new instrument panel only works with FSW95) by Stolle Systems, courtesy of Bernt Stolle • Airbus A300-600 Beluga by Lars Kornstaedt (to see Lars' latest creations, go to *http://ourworld.compuserve.com/homepages/ L_Kornstaedt/download.htm*)

Table 12.1 *continued*

TITLE	TYPE OF SOFTWARE OR FILE
	• Airbus A319-100 by Lars Kornstaedt • Avanti Piaggio by Michael L. Cunningham • Beechcraft Model 76 by Lars Kornstaedt • Cessna 210 Centurian by Terry Hill • Cessna Citation X Business Jet by Rod Conklin • Douglas DC-3 Queen of the Night by Christian Noetzli • F15-C Eagle Fighter Jet by Chuck Dome • F16 Falcon Fighter Jet by Lars Kornstaedt • Focke Wulf Fw190 Neptune by Lars Kornstaedt • Gulfstream IV-SP Business Jet by Kerry Gipe • King Air B200 by Jim Wolf • Learjet 60 by Shigeru Tanaka • Lockheed C-5A Galaxy by Goetz Scheuermann • Lockheed Electra (Amelia Earhart's Plane) by Goetz Scheuermann • Messerschmitt M2.262 (World's first operational jet fighter) by Herve Devred • SST2005 (Imaginary supersonic transport) by Shigeru Tanaka
AAFCONV98.EXE	Microsoft's Aircraft and Adventure Converter for FS98. This self extracting archive will install the Aircraft and Adventure Converter so that you can install FSW95, FS5.1, and Flight Shop created aircraft on the book's CD-ROM, as well as aircraft you download from the Internet and other online services. The first time you run the AAFCONV98.EXE file, it will also patch the FS98 program to fix bugs and other problems that were discovered after the program was released. For more information, consult the Aafconv.txt file in the **Aircraft Converter for FS98** folder on the book's CD-ROM.
AAFWAV.ZIP	New wave sound files for Adventure Programs in Flight Simulator. Contains voices for AP heading, altitude, frequencies, courses, airspeeds, ATIS and ATC messages. From Microsoft.
ACEdit	Software utility which allows you to easily change the aerodynamics and other parameters of any FSW95 or FS5.1 aircraft. By David C. Maschino of DuoSoft. Not for use with FS98 aircraft.
Adobe Acrobat Reader 3.0	Allows viewing of Adobe Acrobat documents on CD. From Adobe.
AeroView 1.0 Moving Map Display	Courtesy of Resolution Maps, this is a software map browser with real digitized aviation charts that you can view on-screen, zoom in or out, and print. Available map data on our CD includes IFR

Table 12.1 continued

TITLE	TYPE OF SOFTWARE OR FILE
	High Altitude Jet Route Charts for the entire continental USA, with selected color World Aviation Charts (WAC) for the Chicago Illinois region, the East Coast, West Coast, and Florida/Gulf of Mexico. Interface with Flight Simulator for a moving map display!
Africa	Over 40 major African Airports which allow you to fly across Africa and refuel the airplane. By Florence Wouterlood and Johan Cranenburgh.
AirDec	Utility for reading and altering aerodynamic model files for FSW95 and FS5.1 aircraft. By Matthias Weidemann.
AirMod	FSW95 Aircraft Modifier. Allows you to modify some flight parameters and colors of any FSW95 plane. Adjust fuel, fuel consumption, weight, drag coefficients, etc. By Chuck Dome.
Airport 2.05	Windows 95 Scenery Designer Program. Allows user to create custom scenery, airports, runways, and buildings anywhere in the world. BGL creation utility. By Pascal Meziat and Manfred Moldenhauer.
Alaska Scenery	Airports in Alaska, including Nome, Kodiak, Fairbanks, Juneau and the rest of Alaska, including parks. By Dean Salmon.
AllNavaids	All missing Navaids in BGLs you can add to Flight Sim to cover the entire world. Over 10,500 navaids, as derived from the Defense Department's Digital Aeronautical Flight Information File (DAFIF).
AllWorld2b	Text description and compilation of all available scenery for Flight Simulator that is found on the Internet. By Javier Gallego.
Amelia Earhart Worldwide Airport Scenery	Custom created scenery by noted scenery designer Alfred Grech will allow you to recreate the flight of Amelia Earhart on her ill-fated 1937 around the world trip. The airport runways created for this trip were carefully researched so that they would match the real airport runways that exist today. Much of the scenery is based on global charts, where each airport's topographical terrain was selected to match as closely as possible that of the real airport. The Amelia scenery includes scenery outside of the airports as well. For example, parts of the Niger river near Gao, Mali and all of Lake Chad in the vicinity of Ft Lamey are recreated. In the Assab area, you'll find part of Saudi Arabia just across the Red Sea for continuation purposes. Howland Island was recreated from data obtained from the U.S. Government's Digital Chart of the World.

Table 12.1 continued

TITLE	TYPE OF SOFTWARE OR FILE
	To help you navigate the trip, the GPS 2.0 program on the CD-ROM has all the Earhart airports pre-programmed into its data base, making navigation between airports easy. Install the included Lockheed Electra, and you'll be to fly the same airplane that Earhart used.
APLC32	Adventure Compiler software. Allows you to create custom programs for Flight Simulator and compile them so that they will run with Flight Simulator. By Martin H. Smith.
Appendix C FS98 Airport Listings	Most of the FS98 worldwide airports are listed, along with ILS information in an Excel file. Also included is a listing of the commercial add-on scenery airports.
Appendix C Instrument Approach Procedure Charts	Over 100 IAP charts of the major cities of the world scanned in from the real U.S. Government Flight Information Publications. The scanned images are stored as Acrobat files, and you will need to install the Acrobat Reader program included on the CD-ROM to view the IAPs and print them out. To access the images off the CD, open the index.pdf file with the Acrobat Reader, then click on any airport hotlink to open the IAP chart you want.
AutoAlt.ADV	This adventure file gives you easy access to your autopilot heading and altitude controls, directly from the keyboard. For example, you can key in a heading and specify an altitude directly with the number keys. You can also display your airplane's pitch and bank angle as a number on-screen, which is useful for testing performance characteristics of new aircraft you are trying out. Voice annunciation of these readouts is possible if you install the AAFWAV.ZIP sound files included on the CD. By Nick Dargahi.
DAFIF	Defense Department's global listing of all navaids and airports world wide. The DAFIF is very useful for planning your own international flights, and is vital if you want to build your own airports. Using the DAFIF data, you can determine how long runways should be, what magnetic compass orientation they should be, and even what type of runway surface is used. You can sort, filter out and view by any criteria. Airport data includes airport name, country, runway headings, runway types, latitude/longitude of runway ends, runway lighting systems, runway elevations, displaced thresholds, magnetic variation, nearest navaids, communication facilities, and runway lengths. Navaid data includes navaid country location, latitude longitude, elevation, frequency, and magnetic variation.

Table 12.1 continued

TITLE	TYPE OF SOFTWARE OR FILE
FAR	Federal Aviation Regulations including: FAR 1, FAR 23, FAR 25, FAR 33, FAR 34, FAR 36, FAR 61, FAR 67, FAR 91, FAR 93, FAR 95, FAR 97, FAR 119, FAR 121, and FAR 135.
FEPAT.EXE	Microsoft Patch to fix the problem of missing ILS and navaids in third-party scenery. (For FSW95 only)
Final Approach, IAPUSA, IAPEURO, IAPOTH	Prints Instrument Approach Plates for 3000 airports around the globe. (Evaluation version only, must be purchased for full functionality.) By George Lorsche. For more information see *http://ourworld.compuserve.com/homepages/glorsche/welcome.htm.*
Flight Situations and Training Videos	Specially created Flight Simulator videos and situations help you to learn key concepts for landings and other flying maneuvers. Landing videos contributed by Robert Ferraro of Computer Pilot Magazine.
FS5 Facts 2.0	Description of BGL Files, dynamic and static scenery and how they work in Flight Simulator. By Konstantin Kukushkin.
FS5STRUC.TXT	Flight Simulator Scenery File Format (Text File). Description of how scenery files work in Flight Simulator. By Maurizio M. Gavioli.
FSCONV.EXE	Flight Shop Converter program from Microsoft. Allows FSW95 users to install and use aircraft and adventures created with BAO's Flight Shop.
GPS 2.0	Waypoint Navigation System by David Drouin (Evaluation version only; you will see an evaluation notice each time the program opens). This is a Windows 95 program that piggybacks onto Flight Simulator and allows you to enter in up to 30 waypoints for navigating great circle routes. The display appears on your cockpit windshield, can be moved, and is connected to your autopilot so that the airplane can be flown automatically to its destination. This is one of the best software add-ons for the Flight Simulator pilot. It can't be beat for its ease of use, powerful features, and fun interface. This version of GPS 2.0 comes with the DAFIF worldwide navaid database built in, so you can fly anywhere in the world with 100% accuracy. The DAFIF version of GPS 2.0 is unavailable anywhere else except on this book's CD. A registration fee of $12 is required for full use of the program.

Table 12.1 continued

TITLE	TYPE OF SOFTWARE OR FILE
GPWS6	Inertial Navigation System (INS) Computer with Ground Proximity Warning System (GPWS). Enter up to 10 latitude/longitude waypoints and the INS will direct your aircraft on the great circle route connecting them. The GPWS announces altitudes and speeds verbally, and mimics the actions of real GPWS in commercial aircraft. It warns you when you are too close to the ground and when landing gear is not down, gives you sinkrate warnings, and includes new keyboard commands to help you easily control your autopilot and radios. Really a top-notch program by Wilco van Deijl. (Works best with FSW95; some waypoint navigation functions can give you trouble in FS98.)
Great Circle Calculator	Excel Spreadsheet to create Great Circle Tracks around the World. Enter two latitude/longitude coordinates, and this spreadsheet will create as many latitude/longitude waypoints between the point of departure and destination. A must-have utility, to be used with the registered version of the GPS 2.0 waypoint navigation system. By Alan Parkinson.
ILS_FIX.zip (for FSW95 only)	Fixes 151 misaligned ILS's at 61 airports (in 23 scenery areas). By Ted Denison.
India4.zip	Major airports in India. By Floris Wouterlood and Johan Cranenburgh.
Landing Lights	Shows how to add landing lights to custom created airplanes. By Siggy Schwarz. (For use with FSW95 aircraft only: Do *not* use with FS98).
Lon-nav.zip (FSW95 only)	London Area Navaids Update Fix. Corrects errors in Microsoft navaid database. By Tony Z. Pluta.
MagVar	Magnetic Variation Calculator from the Defense Mapping Agency. Allows you to calculate the magnetic variation when navigating anywhere on Earth.
Microsoft Excel 97 Viewer	Allows viewing of Microsoft Excel documents. From Microsoft. (needed for viewing of DAFIF database if you don't already have Excel)
MicroWINGS Magazine in Adobe Acrobat format	View and print out MicroWINGS magazine in full color. MicroWINGS is a magazine devoted to Flight Simulator and related aerospace simulation programs. Courtesy of Robert McKay of MicroWINGS.
New Stereo Sound Files	Replace some FSW95 monophonic aircraft sounds on the CD-ROM with stereo sounds. By Jorge Merino.

Table 12.1 continued

TITLE	TYPE OF SOFTWARE OR FILE
Panman 2.1	FSW95 instrument panel management shareware. Allows you to load different or custom instrument panels with aircraft of your choosing. By Chuck Dome. (use only with FSW95)
PanWave95	Sound Wave Utility which allows you to customize sound effects in FSW95. By David Cole. (use only with FSW95)
Scutils	Pete Dowson's Exclusion File Utilities for Flight Simulator Scenery. These utilities allow you get rid of problems caused by overlapping scenery.
WinZip	Allows unzipping and zipping of compressed files on the CD-ROM (Evaluation version).

Several of the aircraft on the CD-ROM are evaluation versions of commercial products. These airplanes are described in more detail below.

Stolles Systems

The Hi-Fi Aircraft from Stolle Systems included on the CD-ROM are commercially available aircraft that come with both panels and highly accurate visual designs, aerodynamic models and even flight manuals. You'll find an evaluation version of a DC-10, an MD-80, and a DC-8, which are illustrated in Figure 12.1, Figure 12.2, and Figure 12.3.

For more information on the Hi-Fi airplanes, consult the documentation on the CD-ROM, or e-mail Bernt Stolle at *101656.203@compuserve.com*. These airplanes come as software e-mail packages, and you can install them in minutes.

Be sure to run these airplanes through the FS98 Aircraft Converter before using them with FS98.

VIP

Visually Incredible Panels (VIP) is another company that makes great hi-fidelity aircraft and panels. They have provided an evaluation version of their Shorts 360, shown in Figure 12.5. For more information, contact:

Visually Incredible Panels
Suite 1204
2177 Burnhamthorpe Rd West
Mississauga, Ontario
LfL 5P9 Canada

Figure 12.1 DC-10 *provided courtesy of Stolle Simulations.*

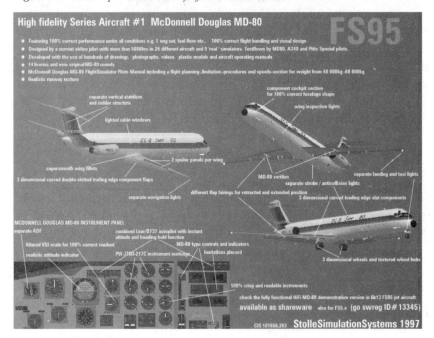

Figure 12.2 MD-80 *provided courtesy of Stolle Simulations.*

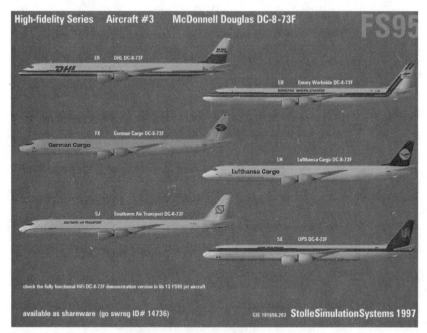

Figure 12.3 *DC-8 provided courtesy of Stolle Simulations.*

Figure 12.4 *Stolle Simulation Systems.*

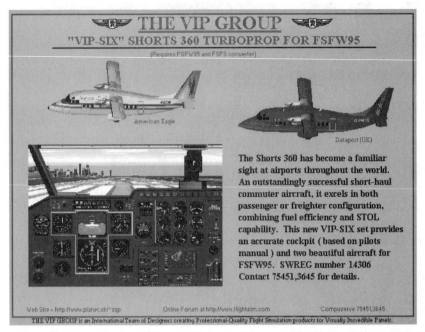

Figure 12.5 *Demo Version of Shorts 360 provided courtesy of VIP (Visually Incredible Panels).*

or visit their web site at *www.planet.ch/~sqp.*

Other Freeware Aircraft on the CD-ROM

Illustrations of other aircraft found on the CD-ROM are shown below:

A FEW FACTS ABOUT THE WORLD WIDE WEB

The Internet is growing by leaps and bounds, so much so that the most commonly used top level domain names (*.com*, *.net*, and *.org*) are rapidly running out of room for new names. As a hypothetical example, two companies named Acme Incorporated may be vying for the same *www.acme.com* domain name, yet only one unique address is available. Which company should get this address? Because of this quagmire, many companies are involved in litigation to preserve their company identity through a unique domain name. As a result of this frustration, the International Ad Hoc Committee (IAHC at *www.iahc.org*) was established in October of 1996 to create new enhancements to the Internet's global Domain Name System (gDNS) in order to increase the pool of

Figure 12.6 *C-5 Galaxy by Goetz Scheuermann.*

Figure 12.7 *Airbus A300 Beluga by Lars Kornstaedt.*

Figure 12.8 *Avanti Piaggio by Michael L. Cunningham.*

Figure 12.9 Messerschmitt M2.262 (the world's first operational jet fighter) by Herve Devred.

Figure 12.10 Learjet 60 by Shigeru Tanaka.

Figure 12.11 Beechcraft Model 76 by Lars Kornstaedt.

Figure 12.12 Airbus A319-100 by Lars Kornstaedt.

Figure 12.13 F16 Falcon Fighter Jet by Lars Kornstaedt.

names available.

The IAHC in May of 1997 agreed to the addition of: *.firm, .store, .web, .arts, .rec, .info,* and *.nom* to the existing .com, .org, .net, .gov, .edu, and .mil domain names. They also decided to add 28 new worldwide registry services to share the central repository database with Network Solutions, which previously had a monopoly on distributing and managing the gDNS.

Because of this new naming scheme, many of the links in this chapter and on the CD may become obsolete or outdated by late 1997. So if a link doesn't work, go to *www.yahoo.com* and do a search for the name given in this chapter or on the CD-ROM. You will find the correct URL if you perform this search.

Table 12.2 Existing Top Level Domain Names on the World Wide Web. Suffixes such as .com are the last part of a URL for a Web site address, and indicate the nature of the site. For example, www.microsoft.com uses the .com suffix, since this Web site represents a commercial enterprise.

SUFFIX	DOMAIN TYPE
.com	Commercial enterprises
.org	Nonprofit organizations
.net	Network providers
.edu	Educational institutions
.gov	Government agencies in the USA
.mil	U.S. Military
.jp, .ca, etc	Country domains: .jp stands for Japan, .ca for Canada for example

Table 12.3 New Top Level Domain Names on the World Wide Web

SUFFIX	DOMAIN TYPE.
firm	General businesses
.store	Online shopping services
.web	Web-related activities
.arts	Artistic and cultural institutions
.rec	Recreation, entertainment
.info	Information services
.nom	Personal and individual's web pages

Domain names are in short supply now that the Web has expanded from its original coterie of university professors and students to approximately 50 million people and 500,000 businesses today. Capitalizing on this scarcity, modern day electronic scalpers have hijacked many commonly used words and expressions found in the English language, hoping to resell them to the highest bidder. To counter this, the IAHC decided to expand the domain names to avoid the internecine warfare that was overtaking the Internet's domain naming schemes. The new domains are designed for businesses that can't get one of the coveted *.com* suffixes.

The new domain names will be auctioned off through a lottery run by the accounting firm of Arthur Anderson. A Swiss nonprofit organization, the Council of Registries, will act as the ultimate arbitrator for disputes involving domain names.

ONLINE FLIGHT SIMULATOR–RELATED FORUMS

The best sources of information on Flight Simulator are freely available on the Internet. There you will find gossip, technical discussions, question and answer sessions, flame wars, libraries of files, and hundreds of Web sites devoted to the topic of Flight Simulator.

Because Web sites change their name frequently, many of the addresses you see in this book will be hopelessly out of date by the time you read them. If you are faced with an error message in your browser when you try to access a site, don't worry; there is an easy way to find the new address. Just go to the *www.yahoo.com* directory or *www.altavista.com* search engine and conduct a search. Chances are that, within seconds, you'll locate the Web site you are trying to visit.

CompuServe Flight Simulator Forum

Although there are other Flight Simulator-related forums on the Internet and on other online services, the CompuServe Flight Simulator Forum is by far the best place to look up information and ask questions. They have tons of files organized into libraries that you can access, and there is also a wonderful public forum where people gather to discuss the latest developments in Flight Simulation technology. The level of technical sophistication is high, and if you have a difficult question, more than likely you'll get it answered here. A big plus for CompuServe is that the signal-to-noise ratio is a lot better than that found on the Internet.

Usenet

There are several Usenet newsgroups that cover the subject of flight simulation:

- microsoft.public.simulators is a newsgroup that focuses on Microsoft's Flight Simulator.
- rec.aviation.simulators is a newsgroup that covers all types of flight simulators, not just Microsoft's version.
- sci.aeronautics.airliners is a moderated discussion group on airliner technology, airliner design and construction, airliner performance, human factors, operation of aircraft and the history of air transport category aircraft.

FLIGHT SIMULATOR-RELATED WEB PAGES

There are a legion of Web sites, clubs, magazines, and Internet forums that have grown up around Flight Simulator. Today, there are more than 400 Web sites that focus on the program, ranging from individual hobbyists to over 147 "Virtual Airlines," which are groups of people who form simulated airlines that fly scheduled routes.

Dozens of companies offer products such as software to add scenery or different aircraft, hardware yokes and rudder pedals, cockpit mockups, and electronic add-on panels that allow interfacing with Flight Simulator and home-brewed cockpit equipment. Don't worry, we won't list them all here.

However, I recommend the following Web sites as good places to start:

- MicroWINGS *www.microwings.com*
- Gene Kraybill's World Wide Guide to Flight Simulation at *http://www.wwguide.com.au/fs/index.htm*
- The archives of the server of Indiana State University *FTP.IUP.EDU* Once you have accessed *ftp.iup.edu*, you'll need to change to the flight simulator directory in which you'll find subdirectories pertaining to aircraft, scenery, and so on. Although you may immediately head for the aircraft directory, you shouldn't overlook the uploads directory, which has many anonymous listings not found in the other directories. When you scan through the file listings, many of them have associated text *readme* files which contain useful information on the program file. There are also several subdirectories listed as 1, 2, 3, 4, 5 etc. These directories have aircraft categorized by distinctive aircraft model name. For example, all Boeing 747s would be found in the 7 directory.
- Nels Anderson's wonderful flight simulator library, where you can check out a virtual cornucopia of flight simulator utilities, scenery, aircraft, panels, and more at *www.flightsim.com*.
- For Great Circle and ETOPS displays inside your web browser, see *http://www.chicago.com/airliners/gc.html*.
- Aeroair Virtual Airlines at *http://aeroair.net*.

- Johan Cranenburgh's Flight Simulator web site is full of information on how to read and understand aviation charts at *http://ourworld.compuserve.com/home-pages/cranenburgh/fs6.htm.*

MAGAZINES

The leading Flight Simulator magazines are as follows:

- *MicroWINGS* (See an Acrobat version of MicroWINGS magazine on this book's companion CD-ROM).
- *Computer Pilot* (Australia). Subscribe via RC Simulations phone 01275 474550.
- *Full Throttle USA*. Published by Cobb Group. Contact the Cobb Group at P.O. Box 35160, Louisville, KY 40232-9719.
- *PC Flight* (EIRE): You need to join PC Pilots Club of Ireland to subscribe. Contact *100755.2216@compuserve.com.*
- *Micro Aviator* (UK) Join their Flight Simulator users group on CIS *106624.3132@compuserve.com.*
- *PC Pilot Magazine*. A U.K.-based Flight Simulator periodical. Contact Douglas McKay at P.O. Box 118 Witney, Oxfordshire 0X8 8LT, United Kingdom.

MicroWINGS

Since the magazine *MicroWINGS* was started in 1993, it has grown to six employees and has attracted a 5,000-member following from over 70 countries. Robert MacKay, the president of the magazine and the International Association for Aerospace Simulations, annually hosts a conference where the latest simulation technologies and products are put up on display. Conference participants are taken on tours of nearby simulation facilities, where they can fly real simulators used by commercial airlines. For a glimpse of what *MicroWINGS* magazine has to offer, take a look at the full color version on this book's companion CD-ROM. You won't be disappointed. *MicroWINGS* offers in-depth reviews of Flight Simulator products, detailed expert commentary by its editorial staff, and is one of the best sources of technical information on Flight Simulator.

MicroWINGS, Inc.
Contact: Robert M. MacKay
381 Casa Linda Plaza #154
Dallas, TX 75218
Telephone: 214-324-1406
Web: *www.microwings.com*

Figure 12.14 *MicroWINGS Magazine*

Computer Pilot Magazine

Computer Pilot Magazine is an Australian production of Robert Ferraro, who was gracious enough to provide us with the learning videos of the Cessna landing. Sean Trestrail, the

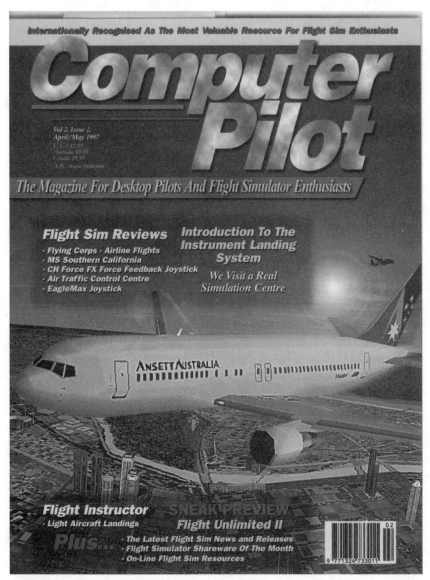

Figure 12.15 *Computer Pilot Magazine*

author of the IFR chapter, is a regular columnist there. This excellent full-color magazine is a fascinating read, and during my research for this book, I turned to it as an indispensable informational resource.

Contact: MicroPilot Publishing
Suite 6
219 Balaclava Rd.
North Caulfield, Victoria
3161 Australia
Telephone: (03) 9532-8258
Fax (03) 9532-8916
Email: *crew@pcaviator.com.au*
Web: *www.pcaviator.com.au*

SCENERY ADD-ONS

The following scenery packages are available for FS98 if you want to expand your Flight Simulator world even farther:

- Scenery Venezia by Lago—Scenery of Venice, but also covers the whole northeast Italian region from Lake Garda to the Austrian and Slovenian borders. To contact Lago, see *http://www.lagoonline.com/*.
- Scenery Tokyo by Lago—Covers the region around Tokyo, Japan. Terrain is designed using photorealistic resolution of approximately 7.3 meters per pixel, includes all the navaids in the area, a color aeronautical chart and 28 airports imaged in very fine detail.
- Scenery Hong Kong by Wizard Works—Includes five airports, and seven situations.
- Azores & Madeira by Apollo—Scenery for the beautiful Azores and Madeira Islands.
- Europe 1 by Apollo—Includes most of the airports for Germany, Austria, the Netherlands, and Switzerland.
- Europe 2 by Apollo—Includes more than two hundred airports in France, Luxembourg, Belgium, and Corsica.
- Scenery of England and Wales by Wizard Works—Includes over two hundred active civilian and military airfields with accurate and detailed runways, buildings and control towers. Over two thousand detailed hills, mountains and lakes.
- Scenery of Madrid by Wizard Works—Includes four airports around Madrid, scenery in Madrid, and thirteen situations.

- Microsoft Southern California Expansion Pack I—Southern California Scenery, challenges, and adventures. (Santa Catalina Island is a part of the default scenery for FS98).

All the airports for the above scenery packages are listed in the Appendix C airport listings on the CD-ROM so that you can determine whether or not the scenery includes the airports that you need.

FSClouds & Textures Pro 3.0 by Steve Halpern

If you would like to improve the visual appearance of your clouds and other weather elements, there is a program called FSClouds & Textures Pro by Steve Halpern that accomplishes this. For more information and pictures of what his product can do, see the **Pictures** subdirectory under the **Flight Simulator for Windows 95 Only** folder on the CD-ROM, or visit his Web site at *http://www.flight1.com/*.

Other Scenery Design Programs

Although we provide the excellent Airport Scenery Designer program on the CD-ROM, for some purposes you may find other commercial scenery design programs do specialized tasks better. Two of the leading programs are Apollo's Scenery & Object Designer and Abacus' Airport & Scenery Designer.

Flight Sim Merchants

If you can't find any of the products that are described in this chapter, you should visit Flight Sim Central's web site at www.fscentral.com. This company carries a complete line of Flight Simulator related add-ons and accessories.

Virtual Airlines

Virtual airlines are springing up around the country as Flight Simulator has made realistic flight schedules of airlines possible. Many computer pilots have accepted "virtual employment" with a simulated airline. These pilots fly regular routes, report their performance to the airline's managers and gain promotions based on experience, just like their real-world counterparts. Just about the only thing not simulated is a virtual paycheck. Depending on the airline, some new pilots may have to take a checkride. Other airlines just give you a route and tell you to report in. CompuServe and America Online both host several virtual airlines, and you'll find them all over the Internet.

Virtual airlines provide realistic flight simulation because they adhere to real-world commercial aviation procedures. For more information visit the aeroair web site at *http://aeroair.net.*

Global Navigation

The most advanced nations are always those who
navigate the most.

Ralph Waldo Emerson (1803–1882),
American essayist, poet, philosopher.
Society and Solitude, "Civilization" (1870).

The task of aerial navigation has been made easier by the use of electronic guidance systems that rely on internal sensors or external radio or satellite beacons. Navigation was not so easy even a few decades ago, when navigators were required on long-haul air routes and they had to use sextants to plot star fixes over the oceans and other desolate regions. Advances in technology have all but eliminated the hand of humans in guiding aircraft across the Pacific and Atlantic oceans, but new requirements also dictated that move. With aircraft filling the skies, it is important to maintain accurate lateral separation between aircraft to avoid midair collisions. Only with the aid of computers is this goal attainable.

With the amazing advances in personal computers and software, it is now possible to simulate complex navigational guidance systems. For example, with FS98's built-in autopilot, VOR/NDB beacons, and ILS, you can fly almost anywhere on Earth using the same flight instrumentation that real pilots use. Flight Simulator doesn't yet provide you with a GPS or INS, so we have included on the book's CD-ROM an evaluation copy of David Drouin's add-on GPS 2.0 navigational utility, which simulates an FMC, GPS, and INS all in one. Although these guidance systems may sound mysterious and complicated, by closely reading this chapter and with a little practice, you can become an expert at flying your airplane from city to city, even across vast oceans. That is the goal of this chapter.

THE MAGNETIC COMPASS

In addition to the discovery of gunpowder and possibly the discovery of the moons of Jupiter, the Chinese were the inventors of the magnetic compass around A.D. 1100. (According to a recent news article published by the official Beijing Xinhua news agency, Chinese historians now claim that a Chinese citizen discovered one of the moons of Jupiter long before Galileo made his monumental discovery in 1609. Supposedly, an ancient book on astrology shows that Gan De, a noted Chinese astronomer of the Warring States period [475–221 B.C.], viewed Jupiter with the unaided eye and saw one of its 16 moons in 364 B.C.)

Western Europeans adopted the compass in about 1187, and it helped them to orient themselves when overcast skies obscured the horizon, preventing sightings of the sun or North Star. The magnetic compass is the mainstay of terrestrial navigation, but it does not, as some people assume, point to the north pole. The magnets inside a compass have the property of being attracted to the Earth's magnetic poles, the axis of which is shifted somewhat from the north pole (see Figure 13.1). This means that a compass actually points to the Earth's magnetic north pole and not to the geographical north pole, so pilots must take into account the local magnetic variation to figure out which direction is true north.

Variation changes from year to year, because the Earth's magnetic field is not fixed but is moving. The magnetic poles thus move slightly, so charts must be updated periodically to account for the new location of the magnetic north pole. Lines of equal magnetic variation, called *isogonic* lines, are plotted on aviation charts so that pilots can determine the direction of true north, which is either east or west of the magnetic pole. If the isogonic line is marked 15° E, as is the case for the line passing through San Francisco, it means that the local variation is 15° E, and your compass is pointing 15° east of true north, the direction toward the geographic north pole. If the isogonic line is marked 13° W, as for example in New York City, it means that true north is 13° west of where the compass is pointing. The *agonic* line is a line of zero degrees variation; both isogonic and agonic lines are plotted for the world in Figure 13.2.

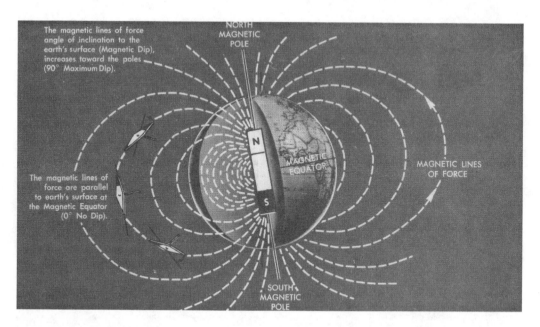

Figure 13.1 *Compass magnets are attracted by the Earth's magnetic field and align themselves with the magnetic lines of force.*

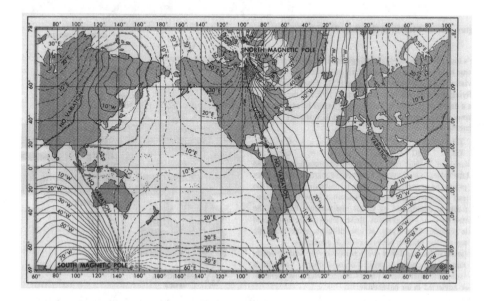

Figure 13.2 *Isogonal lines show magnetic variation.*

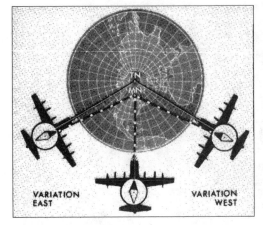
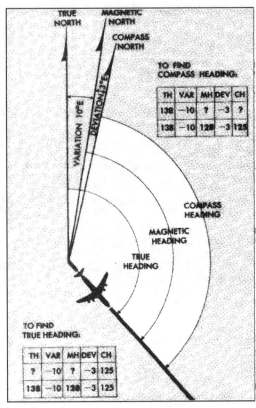

Figure 13.3 *Determining true north from magnetic north.*

Aircraft headings are expressed in degrees clockwise as a true heading (TH) or as a magnetic heading (MH). Most navigational charts show magnetic course instead of true course so that pilots need only use a compass and can forget about the worry of adding or subtracting the variation. On the other hand, great circle navigation, which uses spherical trigonometry, requires the calculation of true headings, as we shall see in Chapter 14.

Converting between True Heading and Magnetic Heading

Converting a true heading to magnetic heading and vice versa is simple. If the map shows that the magnetic variation is west, you add the variation angle to the true course to find the magnetic heading. On the other hand, if the map says that the variation is east, you subtract the variation from the true course and the result will be the magnetic heading. This rule is summarized by the following rhyme: "East is least, and West is best."

The diagram shown in Figure 13.3 illustrates how to find the magnetic heading given a true heading. This technique is useful, for example, when you have calculated a true heading from the great circle bearing formula (described in Chapter 14), and you want to know which compass heading to take. In the diagram, the deviation angle is the error introduced by the compass itself that must be accounted for when calculating heading in the real world. The deviation angle can be disregarded in Flight Simulator, because it is not modeled.

Magnetic Course and Cruising Altitudes

To avoid conflicting paths in congested skies, the FAA has designated altitudes to be divided into different magnetic course headings. There are different rules for IFR and VFR flight, which are listed in Table 13.1.

Table 13.1 *Rules for Magnetic Course and Altitudes*

VFR Cruising Altitiudes and Flight Levels

If your magnetic course is	And you fly more than 3,000 feet above the surface but below 18,000 feet MSL, fly:	And you are above 18,000 feet MSL to FL 290, fly:	And you are above FL 290, fly 4,000 foot intervals:
0° to 179°	Odd thousands MSL, plus 500 feet (3,500. 5,500, 7,500, etc.)	Odd Flight Levels plus 500 feet (FL 195, FL 215, FL 235, etc.)	Beginning at FL 300 (FL 300, 340, 380, etc.)
180° to 359°	Even thousands MSL, plus 500 feet (4,500, 6,500, 8,500, etc.)	Even Flight Levels plus 500 feet (FL 185, FL 205, FL 225, etc.)	Beginning at FL 320 (FL 320, 360, 400, etc.)

IFR Altitudes and Flight Levels—Uncontrolled Airspace

If your magnetic course is:	And you are below 18,000 feet MSL, fly:	And you are at or above 18,000 feet MSL, but below FL 290, fly:	And you are at or above FL 290, fly 4,000 foot intervals
0° to 179°	Odd thousands MSL, (3,000, 5,000, 7,000, etc.)	Odd Flight Levels, (FL 190, 210, 230, etc.)	Beginning at FL 290, (FL 290, 330. 370, etc.)
180° to 359°	Even thousands MSL (2,000, 4,000, 6,000, etc.)	Even Flight Levels (FL 180, 200, 220, etc.)	Beginning at FL 310, (FL 310, 350, 390, etc.)

AIRCRAFT COMMUNICATIONS

In Flight Simulator, COM radios are used to tune in ATIS and air traffic control (ATC). Normally there are 360 channels between 118.00 MHz and 135.95 MHz, with 50 kHz channel separation, but you can receive more than 720 channels if you select **25 kHz com frequency increment** in the **Options/Preferences/Instruments** dialog box. Although the Cessna 182S radio panel has a second COM radio visible, it does not work in FS98.

Although air traffic control is quite primitive in FS98, you can request to take off or land using the **Aircraft/Communications** dialog box. If the message scrolls by too quickly, you can set the communications rate in this same dialog box. When you get takeoff clearance, you will be instructed to "squawk 0276" (or some other number). This means that you must open the radio panel and set the transponder to 0276. The transponder will then broadcast a unique signature for your airplane that will appear on the ATC radar scopes, letting ATC know your whereabouts and altitude at all times. Special transponder codes beginning with 7xxx are used to designate emergencies, for example, a hijacking uses code 7500.

To avoid misinterpretation or misunderstanding of garbled radio transmissions, air traffic control uses the international phonetic alphabet to transmit important flight instructions. For example, one would pronounce the Microsoft Flight Simulator Cessna aircraft's identification number of N9110E would be pronounced "Cessna November niner one one zero echo." A radio frequency would be rendered as: "one two one decimal niner" for 121.90 MHz.

Using the FS98 Navaid Station Identifier Controls

FS98 includes Morse code station identification for all the navaids. Table 13.2 lists the international phonetic alphabet and Morse code equivalents, which will prove useful when you have tuned in a VOR/ILS/DME/NDB station but you don't know which one it is. Pull out the **Ident** knob on the radio panel for the radio in question (or press one of the keyboard commands shown in Table 13.3) and then listen for the Morse code identifier. If you don't know Morse code, write down the dashes and the dots and then look up the characters in the Morse code table. ILS stations are always identified with an *I*. For example, IJAV stands for the ILS stations I-JAV at 115.0 MHz located at runway 09L at Chicago's O'Hare International Airport. If you tune in this station on the NAV1 radio and pull out the **Ident** knob, you'll hear I J A V in Morse code. Similarly, if you tune in the Chicago O'Hare VOR station ORD at 113.90 MHz and pull out the station identifier knob, you'll hear the Morse code for O R D. DME and NDB stations can be identified in the same way. For convenience, the ILS and VOR Morse code station identifiers are printed on the instrument approach procedure (IAP) charts as dots and dashes, so you can determine whether you are tuned to the right station. You can see an example of this in Chapter 16, which shows IAPs for several airports.

Table 13.2 *ICAO International Phonetic Alphabet/Morse Code*

LETTER	MORSE CODE	PRONUNCIATION	LETTER	MORSE CODE	PRONUNCIATION
A	• —	Alpha	S	• • •	Sierra
B	— • • •	Bravo	T	—	Tango
C	— • — •	Charlie	U	• • —	Uniform
D	— • •	Delta	V	• • • —	Victor
E	•	Echo	W	• — —	Whiskey
F	• • — •	Foxtrot	X	— • • —	X-Ray
G	— — •	Golf	Y	— • — —	Yankee
H	• • • •	Hotel	Z	— — • •	Zulu
I	• •	India	1	• — — — —	Wun
J	• — — —	Juliet	2	• • — — —	Too
K	— • —	Kilo	3	• • • — —	Tree
L	• — • •	Lima	4	• • • • —	Fow-er
M	— —	Mike	5	• • • • •	Fife
N	• —	November	6	— • • • •	Six
O	— — —	Oscar	7	— — • • •	Sev-en
P	• — — •	Papa	8	— — — • •	Ait
Q	— — • —	Quebec	9	— — — — •	Nin-er
R	• — •	Romeo	0	— — — — —	Ze-ro

Table 13.3 *FS98 VOR/ILS, DME, and ADF Station Identification Commands*

ACTION	KEYBOARD COMMAND
Identify VOR 1 (Morse Code)	**Ctrl+1**
Identify VOR 2 (Morse Code)	**Ctrl+2**
Identify DME 1 (Morse Code)	**Ctrl+3**
Identify DME 2 (Morse Code)	**Ctrl+4**
Identify ADF (Morse Code)	**Ctrl+5**

To avoid the Morse code station identification in FS98, go to the **Aircraft/Navigation/Navigation Radios** dialog box for the VOR/ILS stations or the **Aircraft/Navigation/Transponder ADF** dialog box for NDB stations, where you will see the name of the station listed, its identifier, and its latitude/longitude.

To further identify unknown stations, use the Appendix B navaid database and the FS98 Airport Excel spreadsheet databases on the CD-ROM. Write down the identifier for the station and then execute a **Find** command in Excel to locate the miscreant station. For example, if you discover that the station is called IJAV, you would open the Airport spreadsheet and then press **CtrlF** (the **Find** command in Excel). In the Find dialog box, type **IJAV** and press the **Find Next** button. Excel will then jump to the ILS station at Chicago's O'Hare International Airport. Similarly, if you perform a search for ORD in the Appendix B Excel Navaid database, the spreadsheet would jump to the listings under Illinois and then highlight the ORD VOR-DME station. This is a useful trick when you are "trolling" for VOR stations by tuning the NAV radio and you don't know the whereabouts of a particular station.

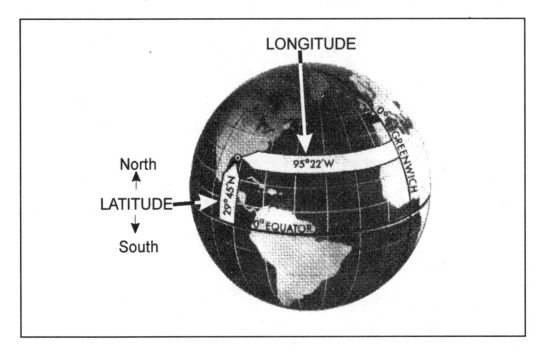

Figure 13.4 *Lines of latitude and longitude.*

Figure 13.5 *Lines of longitude are measured east and west of the Greenwich prime meridian.*

LATITUDE AND LONGITUDE

The lines of latitude and longitude were first used on maps at least three centuries before the birth of Christ. Much later, the great cartographer and astronomer Ptolemy plotted latitude and longitude lines on the maps in his atlas published in A.D. 150. Ptolemy, like many other cartographers of the time, arbitrarily picked the location of his prime meridian, or zero degree longitude line. He picked the Canary and Madeira Islands off the northwest coast of Africa. Mapmakers in later years moved the prime meridian to Rome, St. Petersburg, and Paris, among other places, before agreeing to place it over Greenwich, England.

Lines of longitude, also known as meridians, run north and south, connecting the north pole and the south pole. They are numbered in angular degrees from 0° to 180° east and west of the prime meridian. Lines of latitude, also called parallels, run east and west, parallel to each other. They too are numbered in angular degrees from 0° to 90° north and south of the equator. The parallels of latitude and the meridians of longitude are illustrated in Figure 13.4 and Figure 13.5.

Latitude and longitude have long been used as a means of determining position and can be fixed to easily observable land features. But how was a navigator to determine position while at sea? About 1,000 B.C., the Phoenicians began to navigate the Mediterranean both during the day and at night. They made primitive charts and used a crude form of dead reckoning. They also used observations of the sun and the North Star, or pole star, to determine direction. They could not, however, determine their longitude, only their latitude.

Later explorers were aided by the invention of the compass and the astrolabe, but until the 1700s no one was able to determine longitude accurately. For want of an accurate method, many captains got lost at sea, including such renowned explorers as Ferdinand Magellan, Sir Francis Drake, Vasco Nunez de Balboa, and Vasco da Gama. In a terrible accident at the Scilly Isles, England, on October 22, 1707, four British warships ran aground and almost 2,000 lives were lost. All this happened because the ship's navigators could not ascertain the precise longitude.

Finding latitude is easy. The length of the day, the height of the sun over the horizon at midday, or the position of the stars above the horizon are all dead giveaways. In fact, sailing a parallel of latitude was the principal means by which Christopher Columbus sailed across the Atlantic on his 1492 voyage. At the time, this navigation method was the only one available. Unfortunately, flying a parallel, which you can do in Flight Simulator, is not the quickest nor is it the shortest way to get around the world.

The problem of longitude determination was more difficult, because it required an accurate knowledge of what time it was aboard the ship. Because the Earth rotates 15° of longitude every hour, or 360° every day, if one knew the time in Greenwich, England, one could then compare the time difference between local apparent noon and Greenwich time and thereby determine longitude. (In actuality, the Earth rotates slightly more than 360° in a solar day because of its orbit around the sun. A sidereal day, which is the time the Earth takes to rotate 360° with respect to the fixed stars, takes only 23 hours 56 minutes.) What the world needed was a reliable, precise clock that could maintain time to within three seconds in 24 hours. Why this kind of accuracy was necessary is worth some scrutiny. One degree of longitude at the equator is equivalent to four minutes of time, because that is the time it takes for the Earth to rotate one degree. But one degree of longitude also represents 60 nautical miles. Therefore, a clock on a sea journey of 40 days across the Atlantic could not afford to lose or gain more than two minutes of total time if an accuracy of 30 nautical miles was needed. This works out to ±3 seconds a day.

The greatest minds of the time tried to come up with astronomical means of determining longitude. Sir Isaac Newton, Gallileo Galilei, Edmond Halley, Christiaan Huygens, and Jean Dominque Cassini all attempted to solve the problem. The governments of Spain, England, Italy, and the Netherlands offered bounteous prize money if someone could come up with a viable means of determining longitude. To this end, the British Parliament passed the Longitude Act of 1714, setting a bounty of several million dollars (in today's currency) for the first person to discover a "Practicable and Useful" means of determining longitude. The prize was never claimed, although the English clockmaker John Harrison came close by inventing a portable timepiece that was accurate enough that navigators could determine longitude via the time. Eventually, a "lunar distance" astronomical method of determining longitude was worked out. But for simplicity and ease of use, the clock method was favored over the laborious calculations required for the celestial fix.

VISIBLE HORIZON DISTANCE

If you've ever flown on an airplane and wondered how far you could see on a clear day, the following equation will tell you:

$$d_{\text{Visible Horizon Distance in nm}} = 1.17\sqrt{h_{\text{height in ft}}} \qquad (13.1)$$

For example, if you were flying at 35,000 ft and there was no haze or atmospheric disturbances, theoretically you could see as far as 218 nm. At 1,000 ft altitude, you could see only 37 nm.

IN-FLIGHT VISIBILITY

One question that arises is how does a pilot determine visibility when flying VFR? Under these rules, you are supposed to fly with 3 statute miles visibility within 10,000 ft above the surface within controlled airspace (meaning that air traffic control services are available).

A rule of thumb is that when the surface is just visible over the nose of the airplane, the forward visibility will be approximately 1 statute mile for each 1,000 ft altitude (see Figure 13.6). Note that this is not the maximum visible distance to the horizon, which is governed by Equation 13.1. The rule of thumb applies only to the minimum visibility in poor weather that would be possible if you could see only as far as the surface over the airplane's nose. For example, if you can't see the surface of the ground just over the nose when flying at 3,000 ft, the visibility is less than 3 statute miles. If, on the other hand, you are flying at 1,000 ft and you can just make out the surface of the ground over the nose, visibility would be 1 statute mile.

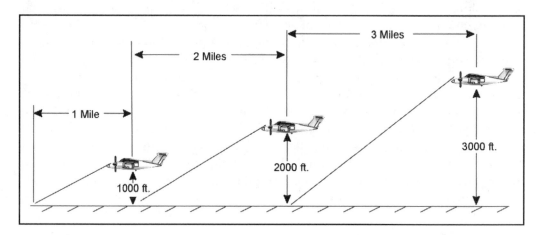

Figure 13.6 *Rule of thumb for forward visibility.*

Because this rule is based on the cockpit cutoff angle and because not all airplanes have the same cutoff angles, the rule will not be equally accurate for all airplanes.

THE COCKPIT CUTOFF ANGLE

The cockpit view obstructs your forward view below the airplane (except in a helicopter, which has a floor window). The higher the cockpit of the airplane, the more restricted the view, as can be seen in Figure 13.7, which shows the cockpit cutoff angle. This restriction has important implications for pilots during the landing approach, because the smaller this angle is, the more the runway view will be cut off or obscured by the intervening cockpit dashboard and nose of the airplane. For example, if the cockpit angle in the Boeing 737 is 15° and the airplane is flying at 1,000 ft AGL, the pilot can see the runway threshold from 3,732 ft away. However, because the Boeing is normally pitched up +3.9° during the landing approach, this cockpit angle is reduced to 11° and the runway threshold can be seen only as close as 5,150 ft. Any closer than that, and the pilot can't see where the plane is supposed to touch down! This problem can be avoided by a little cheating in Flight Simulator. By panning the View window down, you can regain a view of the runway threshold and thus see where you need to aim the airplane. Some people call this feature "raising and lowering your chair," because panning the view window up or down simulates this action.

The cockpit cutoff angle can be measured easily. Follow these steps:

1. Measure the vertical distance from eye level to the ground in feet. For the Cessna, this distance is about 75 in., or 6.25 ft, and for the Boeing 737-400 it is 12.25 ft. This is your y value.
2. Look straight out over the nose of the airplane (cockpit cutoff angle) and determine the spot where the surface is first visible.
3. Measure the horizontal distance in feet from directly under the cockpit eye position measured in step 1 to the spot you noticed in step 2. This is the x value. For the Cessna, x is about 30 ft; for the 737, x is about 45.75 ft.
4. Compute the value of $\arctan(y/x)$. This value is the cockpit cutoff angle. (Make sure that your calculator is in degrees mode and not radians mode.) The cockpit cutoff angle computation for the Cessna yields $\arctan(6.2/30) = 12°$, and for the Boeing 737, $\arctan(12.25/45.75) = 15°$.

Table 13.4 *Cockpit Cutoff Angle and Runway Visibility*

Cockpit Cutoff Angle (°)	Tangent Value	Runway Visibility at 1,000 ft (in feet; 1 nautical mile = 6,076 ft)) *
3	0.052	19,081 ft
4	0.070	14,301
5	0.087	11,430
6	0.105	9,514
7	0.123	8,144
8	0.141	7,115
9	0.158	6,314
10	0.176	5,671
11	0.194	5,145
12	0.213	4,705
13	0.231	4,331
14	0.249	4,011
15	0.268	3,732
16	0.287	3,487
17	0.306	3,271
18	0.325	3,078
19	0.344	2,904
20	0.364	2,747

At 500 ft above the ground, visibility in ft would be about half the 1,000-ft value.

Supersonic aircraft, such as the Concorde, have an extremely low cockpit cutoff angle. They must land at a very high angle of attack with the nose pitched up because of their swept-back wing design, which reduces lift at low speeds. To permit pilots to view the runway during landing, designers built a nose section that could be lowered to provide a higher cutoff viewing angle. Figure 13.7 shows the cockpit cutoff angle for the Boeing 737-400.

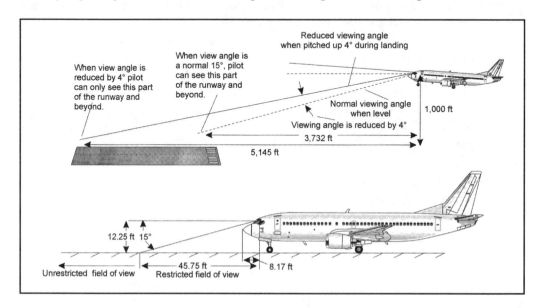

Figure 13.7 *The cockpit cutoff angle for the Boeing 737-400.*

BASIC NAVIGATION JARGON

As with most other fields of study, navigators have created a specialized vocabulary to describe their work, the tools of the trade, and the concepts of navigation. Terms that are most important to navigators are defined as follows.

> **Area navigation** is a method of navigation that permits aircraft to operate on any desired flight path, and not merely follow the jet routes. Many flights operating above 45,000 ft use RNAV area navigation, and it is also used over some ocean areas in combination with LORAN C, Omega, and GPS.
>
> **Assumed position (AP)** is the plane's geographic position as calculated by a navigator.

Bearing is the horizontal angle measured from a specific reference point to a second point. **Magnetic bearing** is the horizontal angle to a given reference point measured from magnetic north. **Relative bearing** is the horizontal angle at the aircraft measured clockwise from the true heading to the great circle that contains the aircraft and the reference object.

A **chart** is a graphical rendering of a section of the Earth's surface that is specifically designed for navigation. A chart is not the same as a map and often is devoid of topographical data. Charts are used for marine and air navigation.

A **compass** is an instrument that shows the direction measured clockwise from magnetic north (or for some specialized compasses, the direction from true north).

A **compass rose** is the graduated circle on a compass, map, or other instrument that is marked in degrees from 0° to 360° clockwise.

Contour lines are the lines drawn on maps and charts that show points having equal elevations.

Coriolis force is the force due to the rotation of the Earth that causes a moving object to be deflected to the right in the northern hemisphere and to the left in the southern hemisphere.

A **course** is the intended horizontal direction of travel over the Earth.

A **course line** is the horizontal component of the intended path of the aircraft.

Crab is a correction of aircraft heading to account for wind drift. By crabbing the aircraft a certain number of degrees, the pilot can maintain a given track.

Dead reckoning is short for deduced reckoning, and it means to deduce one's position relative to something stationary. Old-timers used to joke that dead reckoning was short for "you're dead if you don't reckon right." Others called it "darned reliable" when comparing with fault-prone early navigation systems. Basically, this method predicts one's position based on the direction of flight and the estimated ground speed since the last known position.

Deviation is the compass error that is introduced by stray locally produced magnetic fields.

Distance is the measured length separating two points. Distance can be measured in feet, meters, kilometers, statute miles, nautical miles, or angular units such as degrees and radians when plotted over the surface of a sphere such as the Earth.

Drift is the difference between track and true heading that is caused by the wind.

The **equator** is the great circle on the Earth's surface that is equidistant from the poles. Latitude is measured north or south of the equator.

A **fix** is the accurate position of an aircraft that has been established by navigational aids or the intersection of two lines of position.

GPS is the global positioning system that uses orbiting satellites to determine an object's position on the Earth. Highly reliable and very accurate, this system is envisioned as the replacement for all terrestrial-based navigation systems.

A **great circle course** is the shortest route between any two points on the Earth's surface that is joined by a great circle between the two points. A great circle route crosses meridians at different angles, as opposed to a rhumb line course, which crosses each meridian with the same angle.

A **Great circle** is any circle on a sphere whose plane passes through the center of the sphere. This is shown in Figure 13.9.

Greenwich mean time (GMT) is the local time at the Greenwich meridian measured by reference to the mean sun.

The **Greenwich meridian** is that half of the great circle that passes from the poles to Greenwich, England. Longitude is measured east or west from the Greenwich meridian, and as a result this meridian is also called the **prime meridian**.

Ground speed is the actual speed of an airplane as measured relative to the ground. It is not the same as true airspeed.

ILS is the instrument landing system that consists of the localizer, glide slope, and marker radio beacons. ILS beams fan out in a narrow arc about 18 miles from a runway.

Inertial navigation uses gyroscopes and other electronic tracking systems to internally keep tabs on the airplane's position at any given moment. It is self-contained and accurate, but its accuracy declines over a long flight.

The **international dateline** is the antimeridian of Greenwich and marks the changeover of date. Many islands lie on its path, so to avoid confusion about the date within these areas, the international dateline has been modified to zigzag instead of conform to a meridian similar to the prime meridian.

Isogonic or **isogonal** lines are drawn on a map to show points of equal magnetic variation.

Latitude is the angular distance measured north or south of the equator, from 0° to 90° north and from 0° to 90° south, as shown in Figure 13.4. One degree of latitude is equivalent to 60 nautical miles, and one minute of latitude is equivalent to 1 nm.

Line of position (LOP) is the line containing all possible geographic positions of an observer at a given instant of time.

Longitude is the angular distance measured east or west of the equator, from 0° to 180° east or west, as shown in Figure 13.5. One degree of longitude at the equator is equivalent to 60 nm, and one minute is equivalent to 1 nm. Note that as you go north or south of the equator, this equivalency no longer holds, because the degrees of longitude are no longer measured along a great circle.

LORAN C is so called because it is long-range low-frequency radio navigation system that operates at long range. The LORAN C range extends about 1,200 nm by day and 2,300 nm by night.

A **magnetic course** is the intended horizontal direction of travel measured in degrees clockwise from magnetic north.

A **map** is a planar depiction of the Earth's surface. It lacks the accuracy and proper scalar relationships of geographical features that are found in charts.

Map projection is the mathematical process of converting a spherical surface, such as the Earth, to a two-dimensional planar representation, as for example on a paper map.

Nautical Mile is used as a unit of distance for navigation purposes. It is equivalent to 6,080 ft, or 1.15 statute miles. See also latitude and longitude.

NDB (low-frequency nondirectional radio beacons) transmitters operate in the AM band and have a maximum range of 75 miles during the day and 200 miles at night.

Omega is a very low frequency navigation system that offers global coverage but lesser accuracy than GPS, VOR-NDB, or LORAN C.

Pilotage is navigation by means of following landmarks and other topographical features.

A **rhumb line** is a straight-line course that makes the same angle with each meridian (as opposed to a great circle route, which crosses each meridian with a different angle). When an aircraft holds a constant true heading, it will be flying a rhumb line. Rhumb lines spiral in toward the poles, as shown in Figure 13.8.

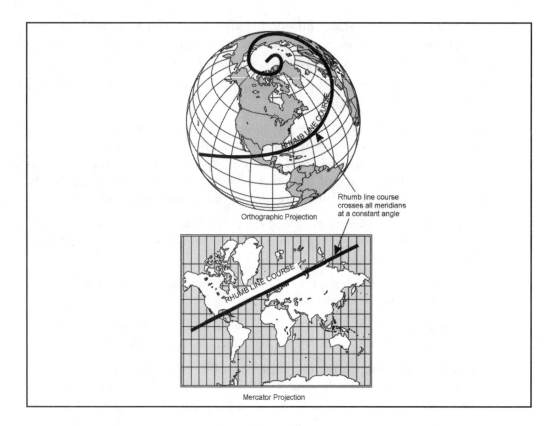

Rhumb line course crosses all meridians at a constant angle

Orthographic Projection

Mercator Projection

Figure 13.8 The rhumb line, or loxodrome, crosses all meridians at the same angle.

Track is the horizontal component of the actual path of an aircraft. The track may coincide with the true course, but often it does not.

True azimuth (Zn) is the angle at the zenith measured clockwise from true north to the great circle that passes through the airplane.

True bearing is the horizontal angle measured from true north clockwise to the great circle passing through the airplane and the reference object.

A **true course** is the intended horizontal direction of travel over the surface of the Earth. It is expressed as an angle measured clockwise from true north.

A **true heading** is the horizontal direction in which an aircraft is pointing. It is measured clockwise from true north to where the aircraft's nose is pointed. It is not the same as true course.

Variation is the angular difference at a given point between true north and magnetic north. This angle is expressed as the number of degrees east or west that the direction true north is displaced from the magnetic north pole. True direction plus variation equals the magnetic compass heading; but you must add west variation and subtract east variation ("East is least, west is best"). Thus, if you need to be on a true course of 90° due east and the variation is 5° E, you should point the airplane's nose to 85° magnetic, because 90° - 5° E = 85°.

VOR means very high frequency omnirange radio beacons. High-altitude VORs, so called because they are used for high-altitude navigation, have a range of as much as 200 nm. Low-altitude VORs, used for low-altitude navigation, have a range of about 40 nm. The range of terminal VORs, used around airports, extends out to 25 nm.

Wind direction and velocity. Winds aloft direction is the direction that winds blow *from* expressed as an angle measured clockwise from true north. Surface winds are measured from the direction that is measured clockwise from magnetic north. Wind speeds are usually quoted in knots.

Zulu (Z) time is an expression that is used to indicate GMT. Usually, Zulu time is displayed in 24-hour format, with 1:00 p.m. GMT being referred to as 13:00 Zulu.

With these definitions in mind, let us proceed to the topic of VOR navigation.

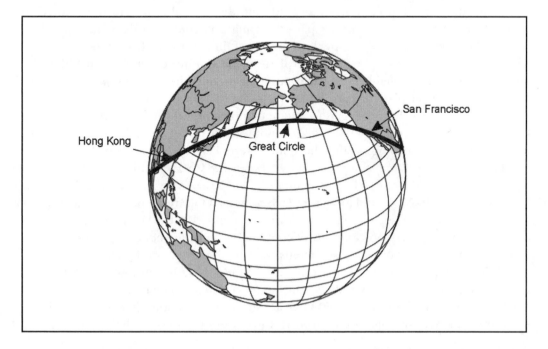

Figure 13.9 *The shortest distance between any two points on Earth is on a great circle.*

VOR Navigation

VOR is the primary navigation system for civil aviation in the United States and much of the rest of the world. In the United States alone, there are about 1,290 VOR stations, and in the rest of the world there are about 2,444, from a total of 10,500 worldwide VOR and NDB navaids. Because VOR operates in the VHF band, it is free from atmospheric static interference and the limitations associated with older low-frequency NDB systems that it has replaced. The VOR generates directional information and transmits it via radio to the aircraft, providing a 360° circular sweep of its area of coverage. Each of the magnetic courses it sweeps is called a *radial*. If the aircraft is heading inbound on the VOR's 340° radial, it will eventually cross the VOR station and head outbound away from the VOR on the VOR's 160° radial. Radials are always measured outward from a VOR station and can be visualized as spokes of a bicycle wheel emanating outward. In our discussions of VOR *course* that follow, we will define it to be the same or the opposite direction as the VOR radial. We call this opposite VOR course direction the *reciprocal* of the radial, and it is always 180° from the VOR radial. Do not confuse the airplane's course, or current heading, with that of the VOR course, for they are not the same.

VOR works like a lighthouse. It sends out a narrow rotating radio beam that rotates in a 360° circle at a rate of 1,800 RPM. Once every revolution, when the beam crosses the 0° magnetic north pole radial, a second omnidirectional radio pulse is emitted to indicate that the rotating beam has passed through magnetic north. With the knowledge that the beam must take a specific amount of time to turn a few degrees, it is possible for VOR receivers onboard an airplane to determine exactly which radial the airplane is on. The airplane "sees" the rotating beam only the instant it passes through the radial that the airplane is currently on.

VOR radials are always pegged to magnetic north and not true north. This is also true of the charts that depict VOR radials; it is implicitly understood that when you read a VOR radial from heading off the chart, it is referenced to magnetic north.

The standard VOR transmitter operates between 108.0 MHz and 117.95 MHz and has a power output of 200 watts. The transmitter's range depends on aircraft altitude, type of VOR, location of the VOR, and local terrain conditions. VOR frequency assignments from 108.0 to 112.0 MHz are set to even tenth decimals, such as 108.2 MHz, 108.4 MHz, and so on, and this arrangement precludes conflict with localizer frequency assignments. Beyond 112.0 MHz, the VOR frequency assignments can be either even or odd tenth decimals.

H-VORs (H stands for high altitude) and L-VORs (L stands for low altitude) have a normal range of 40 nm below 18,000 ft, but some H-VORs can be received as far away as 100 to 300 nm. T-VORs, or terminal VORs, are short-range stations that are used primarily in terminal areas or adjacent to airports. In previous versions of Flight Simulator, all

VORs had a default range of 80 nm. No longer is this the case with FS98, which calculates line of sight limitations and other range information for each VOR. According to Microsoft, it uses a generalized model for range determination that is not based on real-world data, so it is possible that a given VOR will not match its real-world counterpart. If you haven't already, be sure to install the new FS98 Aircraft Converter file on the book's CD, because there are some bug fixes to the VOR line of sight model that are made to the main FS98 program.

You can test the new range feature of long-range VORs by locating the airplane at N44° 54' 51" W74° 43' 15" and then tuning in the MASSENA New York VOR at 114.10 MHz. Because MASSENA is classified as an H-VOR, it is a long-range VOR that can be received much farther away than the other types of VORs. If you slew the airplane up to about 35,000 ft altitude and then slew away from the station, you'll notice that the DME (distance measuring equipment) readout will be active to about 165 nm or so (some VORs go as far as 180 nm). However, when you drop below 6,500 ft, the range of MASSENA drops considerably, to about 80 nm. Thus, the VOR range is substantially lessened when you are flying at low altitudes. This also explains why, when you are on the ground at Meigs Field in Chicago, you cannot tune in the Chicago O'Hare ORD VOR at 113.90 MHz. When you climb to about 1,700 ft or higher, (assuming you have installed the FS98 Aircraft Converter—otherwise it will be 3,240 ft), the nearby ORD VOR, which is only 15.2 nm away, will suddenly become active on the NAV display. At this higher altitude, the airplane's VOR receiver is within line of sight of the VOR and is able to pick up the station.

There are two VOR receivers on the Boeing 737-400, Learjet, and Cessna 182S (but not the Cessna 182RG, which has only one VOR radio). Each receiver, or NAV radio as it is called, is tied to a particular NAV display on the instrument panel. Thus, the NAV1 radio is connected to the NAV1 display and the NAV2 radio is connected to the NAV2 display. To select the frequency for the NAV1 or NAV2 radio, you must open the radio instrument panel (press **Shift 2**) (except in the Learjet, whose radio panel is displayed on the main instrument panel at all times). Then, using the mouse to click on the numbers, you can increase or decrease the digits by clicking to the right or left side of the digits. The keyboard equivalents are listed in Appendix G.

TACAN

The Tactical Air Navigation (TACAN) system was originally developed by the military to provide precise positioning information within 200 nm. As with VOR, TACAN provides radials radiating 360° outward from the station. TACAN stations are similar to VOR-DME in that they also provide distance measuring equipment. In recent years, the FAA has been integrating the TACAN facilities into the civil VOR-DME network, and as a result TACAN stations are now called VORTAC. For all intents and purposes, you can regard a VORTAC as a VOR-DME station.

Installing the Missing Worldwide VOR/NDB Navaids from the CD-ROM

Because FS98 and FSW95 don't include all the world's navaids, if you want to fly on real-istic missions around the earth you will need to add all the missing VOR/NDBs to the program. This can be done by copying the navaid bgls from the **\Missing Navaid bgls** folder on this book's CD into a **FS98\Scenery\DAFIF\Scenery** folder , then use the Scenery Library to point FS98 at this directory (in the same way that you install the Amelia Scenery as described in Ray Proudfoot's tutorial on scenery management). Make sure that you select **Local** as the scenery type. The navaids will be activated as soon as you exit the Scenery Library.

For those less experienced at installing scenery, here are the steps you must follow:

1. Open Explorer and find the SCENERY folder under FS98. Create a new folder under **FS98\SCENERY** and name it DAFIF (e.g., **FS98\SCENERY\DAFIF**).
2. Then under DAFIF create two further folders and call them SCENERY and TEX-TURE. It's important that you use these exact names, with no difference in spelling, as FS98 will expect them.

   Your folder structure should look like this -

   ```
   C:\FS98

               SCENERY

                       DAFIF

                           SCENERY

                           TEXTURE
   ```

3. Unzip all the BGL files from the package and copy them to the **SCENERY** folder under **DAFIF**

   ```
   C:\FS98\SCENERY\DAFIF\SCENERY
   ```

4. Before you exit Explorer make a copy of your WORLD.VIS file in the **\SCENERY** folder. Select it and drag it to the main **\FS98** folder using the right mouse but-ton and choose **Copy Here**. Then select it again and using the right mouse but-ton select **Rename**. Change the name to WORLD.ORI (or whatever your preference is). You should do this each time you create a new scenery layer.

In order for FS98 to use the new DAFIF scenery above, it needs to be told where this scenery is located. This is done by performing the next procedure.

1. Load FS98 and select World/Scenery Library.
2. Clear the warning message by selecting **OK**.
3. Select **Files**.
4. Select the **Add** button.
5. In the Scenery Area Path type the path

```
C:\FS98\SCENERY\DAFIF\SCENERY\*.BGL
```

You will notice that as you type the last character in Step 5, the other boxes become active. This is your confirmation that you've typed a valid path.

1. Type **DAFIF** in the Scenery Area Title.
2. From the Scenery Area Type select **Local** and select **Scenery Area Active**. A tick will be displayed showing it to be active.
3. The Scenery Area Layer number can remain at its default value of **001** for the time being. Select **OK**. You will return to the previous screen and should see **DAFIF** at the top of the list

Select **Arrange Layers**. Select **DAFIF** and move it down to a lower layer below your other Local scenery by clicking **Lower Layer**. This is necessary so that the DAFIF will not pre-empt other local scenery with other duplicate navaid entries. Finally select **OK** three times to confirm the entries and return to FS98. When you select the final **OK**, FS98 will update WORLD.VIS.

Note that all the navaids were extracted from the U.S. military's DAFIF (see the Appendix B listing on the CD-Rom for a complete listing of worldwide navaids), but the database does not include duplicate entries that exist in Flight Simulator. Thus, the BGLs are not complete in the sense that you might expect, because they only supplement the navaids that Microsoft forgot to put in. Johann van Cranenburgh and Manfred Moldenhauer, who helped create the BGLs, went to great lengths to check that no duplicate navaids existed so as to avoid clashes with FS98's built-in navaids.

After loading the BGLs into the program, you will discover that the world is now completely blanketed with real-world VORs and NDBs, almost 10,500 in all.

VOR-DME

VOR stations equipped with distance measuring equipment can provide pilots with information about range distance and speed between the airplane and the VOR beacon. A transmitter onboard the airplane sends a query to the DME station, and this message is bounced back to the airplane by the DME transmitter. The onboard DME receiver then compares the time that the signal took for its round trip and calculates and displays the slant range distance to the DME station. This slant range distance is always greater than the ground distance range between the DME and the airplane (see Figure 13.10). For example, when you are flying directly over a VOR-DME station at 24,300 ft AGL, the DME will show that your airplane is 4 nm from the station even though the distance measured on the ground would be zero feet.

Figure 13.10 *DME slant range compared to ground range.*

The airplane's speed as measured by the DME is not the same as its true airspeed or its ground speed. Only when the airplane is headed directly toward or away from the DME station is the DME speed approximately the same as the airplane's ground speed.

DME frequencies are automatically paired with a VOR-DME station. When you tune in the VOR, if there is a DME present it is also tuned in.

In FS98, rather than squint at the tiny DME displayed on the Cessna's instrument panel you can see an enlarged version on the Bendix/King radio stack (press **Shift 2** or click the **Avionics** master switch). This isn't a problem with the Learjet or 737, which display DME data on the larger HSI instrument and RMI. To switch the DME display between the NAV1 and NAV2 radio on the Cessna, click the **NAV1** or **NAV2** switch on the DME portion of the radio panel; or press **F1** for the DME1 on NAV1 or **F2** for the DME2 on NAV2. Both the Learjet and the 737 display DME1 (associated with the NAV1 radio and display) and DME2 (associated with the NAV2 radio and display) simultaneously. On the Learjet, you'll see both DME readouts displayed to the left of the HSI display, and on the 737 you'll see DME1 on the HSI and DME2 on the RMI. All three radio panels are illustrated in Figure 13.11.

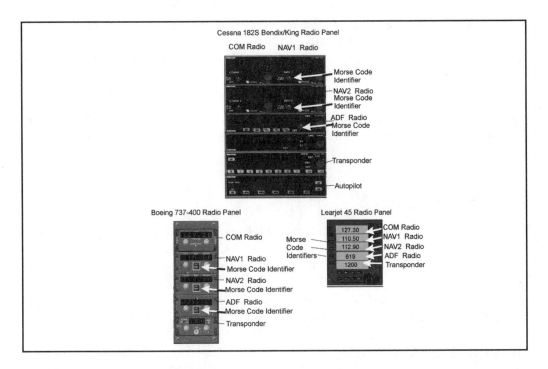

Figure 13.11 *Radio panel on the Cessna, Boeing 737, and Learjet. To open the Cessna or 737 panel, click the **Avionics** master switch or press **Shift+2**. The Learjet has its own radio panel that is on-screen at all times. Note that the COM2 radio is not implemented in FS98.*

VOR Receiver, Radials, and the TO/FROM Indicator

The **TO/FROM** indicator, also called the *ambiguity* indicator or *sense* indicator, is a small triangle symbol that points up or down on the NAV display when you are within range of a VOR station. **TO** is indicated by the triangle pointing up, and **FROM** is indicated by the triangle pointing down. When you click the OBS (omni bearing selector) knob, which is also called the course selector, the VOR course on the rotating card will change. When the CDI (course deviation indicator) is centered, the VOR course shown at the 12 o'clock position on the NAV display is either the reciprocal of the VOR radial or the VOR radial itself, depending on whether the **FROM** or **TO** flag is on. The relationship between **FROM/TO** and the VOR radial/VOR reciprocal radial is summarized as follows:

NAV display **TO/FROM** rules (when the CDI needle is centered):

1. When the **TO** triangle is on, the VOR course shown at the 12 o'clock position is the reciprocal of the VOR radial.
2. When the **FROM** triangle is on, the VOR course shown at the 12 o'clock position is the VOR radial itself.

Here's a convenient trick for calculating reciprocals that are 180° away from a given radial: add 200° to the radial and then subtract 20°, or subtract 200° and add 20°.

T I P

CDI Interpretation

The CDI tells you whether you are on a selected VOR radial. It does not tell you whether you are headed toward or away from the VOR station.

Full-scale deflection of the CDI tells you that the airplane is 10° or more off the selected VOR radial. When the needle is two dots left of center, you are 10° too far right of the radial. When the needle is two dots right of center, you are 10° too far left of the radial. Figure 13.12 shows the CDI on the Cessna.

Finding the VOR Radial

To find out which VOR radial you are on, keep clicking on the course selector knob until the CDI is centered; then read the dial at the 12 o'clock position and check which direction the triangle symbol points. For example, if the triangle points down and the course shown is **12**, meaning 120°, you are on the 120° radial *from* the VOR station. If it shows **12** and the **TO** triangle is on, you are on the 300° VOR radial; 120° is the reciprocal of the 300° VOR radial, and according to the preceding rule 1, the reciprocal of the radial is being displayed.

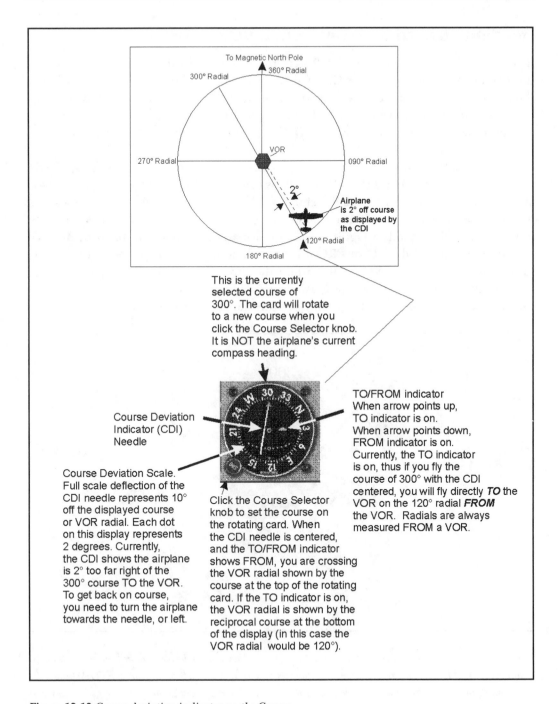

This is the currently
selected course of
300°. The card will rotate
to a new course when you
click the Course Selector knob.
It is NOT the airplane's current
compass heading.

Course Deviation
Indicator (CDI)
Needle

Course Deviation Scale.
Full scale deflection of the
CDI needle represents 10°
off the displayed course
or VOR radial. Each dot
on this display represents
2 degrees. Currently,
the CDI shows the airplane
is 2° too far right of the
300° course TO the VOR.
To get back on course,
you need to turn the airplane
towards the needle, or left.

Click the Course Selector
knob to set the course on
the rotating card. When
the CDI needle is centered,
and the TO/FROM indicator
shows FROM, you are crossing
the VOR radial shown by the
course at the top of the rotating
card. If the TO indicator is on,
the VOR radial is shown by the
reciprocal course at the bottom
of the display (in this case the
VOR radial would be 120°).

TO/FROM indicator
When arrow points up,
TO indicator is on.
When arrow points down,
FROM indicator is on.
Currently, the TO indicator
is on, thus if you fly the
course of 300° with the CDI
centered, you will fly directly *TO* the
VOR on the 120° radial *FROM*
the VOR. Radials are always
measured FROM a VOR.

Figure 13.12 *Course deviation indicator on the Cessna.*

Heading Toward or Away from a VOR

If you are trying to head *toward* a VOR station, you should fly the VOR course shown at the 12 o'clock position when the CDI needle is centered and the **TO** indicator is lit. On the other hand, if you are trying to fly *away* from a VOR station, you should fly the VOR course shown at the top when the **FROM** triangle is on.

Just remember that you always fly **TO** a VOR, and you always fly **FROM** a VOR, and you'll be all right.

VOR radials often confuse beginning pilots; for example, when the **TO/FROM** indicator shows **FROM** and the CDI needle is centered, does that mean you are flying away from the station on the radial shown? When the triangle shows **TO**, does that mean you are flying toward the station on the given radial? The answer to both questions is no. As illustrated in Figure 13.13, an airplane can cross a radial with the CDI needle centered and the **TO** or **FROM** triangle lit and yet the airplane is not heading toward or away from the VOR. Only when the directional gyro or compass heading matches the course shown on the NAV display will you be flying on the radial either toward or away from the VOR station. Does this start to make sense now?

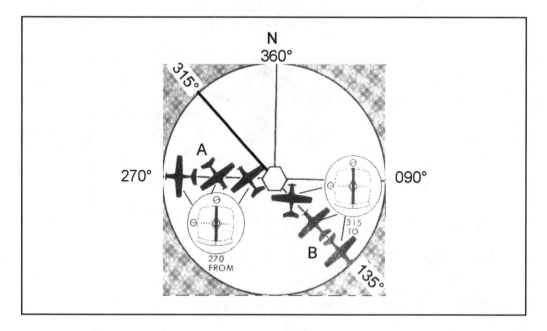

Figure 13.13 *The **TO/FROM** indicator does not tell you whether you are heading to or from the station. In situation A, the **FROM** indicator tells you that the airplane is on the 270° radial from the VOR station. In situation B, the **TO** indicator tells you that the airplane is on the reciprocal of the 315° radial, which is the 135° radial from the VOR station.*

You should now understand why we call the readout on the NAV display the VOR "course," even though it may or may not be the course that the airplane is currently heading.

Radials are, by definition, always **FROM** a VOR. Therefore, to fly the 90° radial **TO** a VOR, your heading will be roughly 270° (the reciprocal of 90°), and you would approach the VOR from the east. On your NAV display, if the **FROM** indicator were on, the VOR course would show 270° (i.e., **W**), and, with the CDI needle centered, you would fly on a heading of 270°. If you want to track **TO** the VOR with heading of 90°, you are then on the 270° radial inbound and approaching from the west. In other words, the **TO** indicator would be on, the VOR course would show 90° and your compass heading would be 90°.

To make sense of all this confusion and simplify things, try to remember that radials are always **FROM** a VOR and that the **FROM/TO** indicators show whether the selected VOR course will take your airplane **TO** or **FROM** the station.

When you're setting the course, it is essential that you always set the course you intend to fly. This tip was handed down to me by Captain Sean Trestrail, the Boeing 767 pilot who wrote the chapter on IFR flying (Chapter 16). This tip is well worth memorizing. So if you want to track the 090° radial *inbound* to the VOR station, you must set a course of 270°. If you want to track the 090° radial *outbound* from the VOR station, set the course to 90°. Failure to do this will result in the CDI needle operating in the reverse sense, and you will be heading in the wrong direction.

When you are out of range of a VOR station or no valid signal is being received, instead of the **TO/FROM** indicator you will see a small striped flag telling you that the NAV display is inactive. Also, as you cross directly over a VOR station, the **FROM/TO** indicator will flop-flop to the opposite reading. This will tell you that you have flown past the VOR.

Determining the VOR Radial from the NAV Display

Use the following procedure to determine the radial.

1. Tune in the NAV station and make sure the NAV display is active.
2. Note the **TO/FROM** indicator.
3. If the **FROM** indicator is lit, center the CDI by clicking the course selector knob until the needle is centered. If the **TO** indicator is lit, skip to step 5.
4. With the needle centered and the **FROM** indicator still on, the radial **FROM** the VOR will be displayed at the 12 o'clock position on the NAV display.
5. If the **TO** indicator is lit, keep clicking the course selector knob until the **FROM** indicator is on. Then read the VOR radial from the 12 o'clock position of the dial.

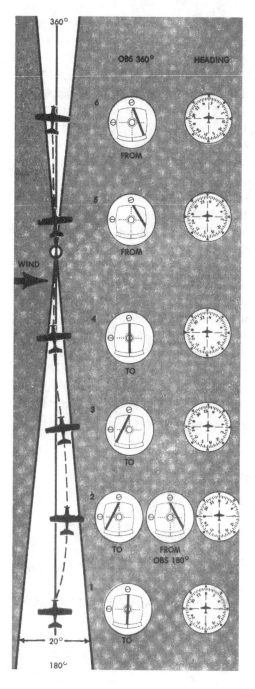

Figure 13.14 VOR tracking.

Tracking the Inbound VOR Course to a VOR station

To fly toward a VOR station inbound along a radial **FROM** a VOR station, follow these steps:

1. Tune in the NAV station and make sure the NAV display is active.
2. Click the course selector knob until the CDI needle is centered and the **TO/FROM** indicator shows **TO**. The VOR course shown is the reciprocal of the VOR radial.
3. To home in to the station, turn the airplane until your directional gyro/compass shows the same VOR course that is shown at the 12 o'clock position of the NAV display. (Or engage the autopilot **NAV** hold.)
4. As you fly toward the VOR station, keep the CDI needle centered by adjusting the airplane's heading as necessary. (You don't need to do this with the autopilot **NAV** hold on.)

Tracking the Outbound Radial from a VOR Station

To fly away from a VOR station outbound on a given radial, follow these steps:

1. Tune in the NAV station and make sure the NAV display is active.
2. Click the course selector knob until the CDI needle is centered and the **TO/FROM** indicator shows **FROM**.

3. To track the outbound radial, turn the airplane until the magnetic compass or directional gyro heading is the same as the course shown at the 12 o'clock position on the NAV display. (Or engage the autopilot **NAV** hold.)

4. As you fly away from the VOR station, keep the CDI needle centered by adjusting the airplane's heading as necessary. (You don't need to do this with the autopilot **NAV** hold on.)

Intercepting a VOR Course

Now we come to the problem of intercepting a VOR radial that is different from the one you are on. Suppose, for example, that you needed to intercept the 205° radial from Chicago's ORD VOR flying inbound and you are on the 160° radial about 20 miles away from the VOR station.

You can use the following procedure to intercept a predetermined course either inbound to a VOR or outbound from a VOR:

1. Turn to a heading that is parallel to the desired course. (In the preceding example, you would turn to a course of 25°, the inbound course on the 205° radial.)

2. Determine the difference between the radial to be intercepted and the radial on which you are located (in our example, it would be 205° - 160° = 45°).

3. Double the difference to determine the interception angle; round the angle up to at least 20° if it is less than 20° or round it down to 90° if it is greater than 90°. (In our example, we double 45° and get 90°. Because 90° is the maximum angle allowed, we choose 90° as our interception angle.)

4. Rotate the course selector to the desired outbound radial or inbound VOR course to prepare the NAV radio for the interception of the desired radial. (In our example, we select 25° on the NAV display with the **TO** flag on. because we want to fly the reciprocal of the 205° radial from the ORD VOR.)

5. Turn to this interception angle. (In our example, we turn left 90° to a new course of 295°, because 90° + 205° = 295°.)

6. Hold this magnetic interception heading constant until the CDI centers. (Hold 295° until you see the CDI centered.)

7. Turn to the magnetic heading corresponding to the VOR course you selected in step 4. (Turn to the VOR course of 25°, because you will now be flying the 205° radial from the ORD VOR inbound.)

8. Keep the CDI needle centered and follow the tracking procedure inbound or outbound described in the previous two sections.

Figure 13.15 shows the readings at various points in this process.

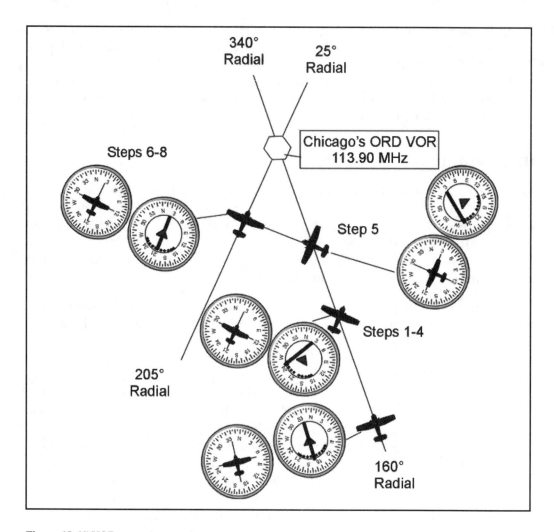

Figure 13.15 *VOR course interception.*

INSTRUMENT LANDING SYSTEM

The instrument landing system, or ILS, consists of the following components:

1. A *localizer* radio transmitter to furnish horizontal guidance to the airport runway.
2. A *glide slope* radio transmitter to furnish vertical guidance along the correct descent angle to the runway.

3. Two or three *marker beacons* (an outer, a middle, and sometimes an inner beacon) installed in front of the runway.

4. *Approach lighting systems* installed on the runway to help the pilot make the transition from instruments to visual flight.

5. *Distance measuring equipment* (DME) on many ILS-equipped runways co-located with the glide slope transmitter to provide distance to touchdown information.

In Flight Simulator, you always tune in an ILS station using the NAV1 radio, which doubles as a VOR or VOR-DME as well as an ILS receiver. Tune in the frequency by using the same procedure as that for VOR stations using the radio panels (press **Shift 2** to open the radio stack, or click the **Avionics** master switch).

The Localizer Beam

The localizer beam gives you horizontal guidance as to whether the plane is too far left or right of the runway. You tune in the localizer frequency on the NAV1 radio, and the NAV1 display (or HSI) will show a localizer needle that moves left or right depending on the airplane's horizontal position within the localizer beam. Note that you cannot tune in an ILS station on the NAV2 radio. The localizer beam radiates down the centerline of the runway toward the middle and outer markers and along a similar course in the opposite direction. The localizer beam that extends out toward the markers is called the *front course,* and the beam that radiates in the opposite direction is called the *back course.* The localizer beam is very narrow, only 5°. It is much narrower than the VOR radial, which can show as much as 10° deflection right or left on the NAV1 or HSI display. As a result, the localizer needle is far more sensitive than is the CDI needle, and intercepting a localizer beam can be trickier because it is so much narrower. For example, at 10 miles distance from the runway, the localizer sweeps out a width of 5,316 ft, narrowing to 700 ft at the runway's threshold.

Reception of the localizer beam is guaranteed out to 18 nm from the runway to 10° either side of the centerline and then from 10° to 35° either side of the course within 10 nm of the runway. This may be confusing, because we have previously stated that the localizer is only 5° wide regardless of distance from the runway. The explanation is that the localizer receiver is supposed to indicate a signal at the first indications of the localizer beam at 10° either side of the centerline, even though the beam itself is only 5° wide. Probably all that will happen is that the **OFF** flag will disappear, telling you that the receiver has picked up the localizer, but the localizer needle will not give any useful information.

When no valid localizer signal is being received, the NAV display will show the **OFF** flag, which looks like a little red tag on the lower portion of the display, and the localizer needle will drift to the center.

Deflection of the localizer needle tells you how far off course you are and in which direction. For example, when the localizer needle on the NAV1 or HSI is deflected halfway to the right, it indicates you are 1.25° left of the centerline and must turn right toward the needle. In the other direction, full-scale deflection of the needle left would show you to be 2.5° right of the runway centerline, which means you must turn left to correct your path.

Sometimes, two localizers are active on the same frequency. For example, 110.50 MHz is used for IJAV on runway 09L and IIAC for runway 27R at Chicago's O'Hare International Airport (the same runway but at the opposite end). This means that if you are using the autopilot to lock onto an approach at runway 27R and you select 110.50 MHz, Flight Simulator will have no way of knowing that you really intended to land at runway 09L. You will be in for a rude surprise when you lock onto an ILS station and find that not only does the airplane not turn toward the runway, but it also flies away from it! Your localizer needle also moves in the opposite direction from what you might expect. How, then, do you instruct Flight Simulator to choose the right runway? This quandary is solved by going to the **Aircraft/Navigation/Nav Radios** menu. In the dialog box will be a new option for selecting **Localizer 1** for the lower-numbered runway or **Localizer 2** for the higher-numbered runway. Choose **Automatic** if you want Flight Simulator to choose the front course automatically. Note that this option becomes visible only on runways with back course localizers.

The localizer transmitter operates on one of 40 ILS channels within the frequency range of 108.10 MHz to 111.95 MHz and is assigned odd tenth decimals, such as 109.10 MHz, 109.30 MHz, and so on. When a glide slope is associated with a localizer, the ILS channel is frequency-paired with the glide slope transmitter operating in the UHF spectrum between 329.15 MHz and 335.00 MHz. Thus, when you tune in a particular channel, the ILS equipment automatically tunes in the proper UHF glide slope frequency connected with the localizer for the runway you are using.

The rotation of the NAV1 course selector (OBS) does not affect the operation of the localizer needle, although you may find it more comfortable to change the course so that it reads the same as the runway heading.

Glide Slope

The glide slope refers to the radio beam that gives vertical guidance information to the pilot during an instrument landing approach. It is angled 3° up from the horizontal. Using the glide slope needle on the NAV1 display or the HSI, you can determine how far the plane is above or below the glide slope. This beam is thinner than even the localizer beam, being only 1.4° thick, but at 10 miles from the runway the beam is 1,485 ft thick, narrowing to only a few feet at touchdown. When the glide slope needle is deflected fully up, it means that you are at least 0.7° too low along the glide slope; at full deflection down, you would be at least 0.7° too high. When the needle is exactly centered, you are right on the glide slope. The glide slope provides no vertical guidance for approaches on the back course, a very important consideration when you're choosing which end of an ILS runway to land on. Thus, you should try to pick a runway's front course if you want to use the glide slope. Figure 13.16 shows a glide slope indicator.

Because the glide slope is much more sensitive than the localizer, smaller corrections need to be made when you are too high or too low from the glide slope than when you are too far right or left of the localizer.

The glide slope also has a red warning flag that tells you whether the glide slope receiver is active. When you see this flag, marked with a **GS**, on the right side of the NAV display, it means that no glide slope signal is being received and you should not rely on the glide slope needle for guidance information.

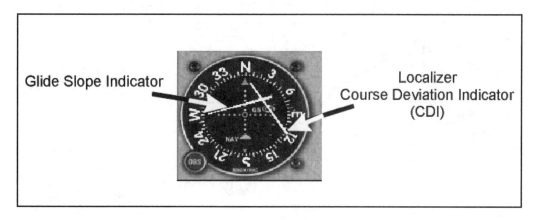

Figure 13.16 *Glide slope indicator and localizer course deviation indicator on the NAV1 display. When you tune in an ILS station on the NAV1 radio, you will see this display.*

Outer, Inner, and Middle Markers

The marker beacons are VHF transmitters that are positioned in front of the runway and project a vertical beam up from the ground to alert the pilot as to how far away the runway is. With a power output of 3 watts, these beacons operate on a frequency of 75 MHz and warn the pilot through audible alert tones and colored lights in the cockpit when the plane passes over the cone of the beam. Table 13.5 shows the runway distance each OMI light and tone represents. On the instrument panel, the colored lights marked O, M, and I refer to the outer, middle, and inner markers, respectively.

The inner marker is found only on the front course of runways equipped for CAT II or CAT III ILS approach. It indicates the point at which an aircraft is at the decision height. The pilot must then either commit to the landing if the runway is in sight or abort the landing.

When you cross the outer marker beacon, if the airplane is on the proper glide slope it should be about 1,400 ft above the runway. At the middle marker, the altitude should be 200 ft above the runway.

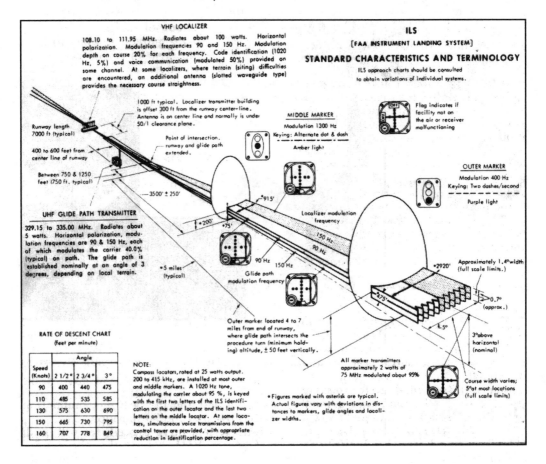

Figure 13.17 Instrument landing system (ILS).

Table 13.5 Outer, Middle, and Inner Markers

MARKER	DISTANCE TO RUNWAY THRESHOLD	GLIDE SLOPE INTERSECTS MARKER AT THIS DISTANCE ABOVE GROUND	COLOR OF OMI LIGHT	AUDIBLE TONE
I (Inner)	1,000 ft	50 ft	White	Continuous dots alternated at 6 per second. Modulated at 3,000 Hz (high-pitch tone)
M (Middle)	3,250 to 3,750 ft	200 ft	Amber	Alternating 95 dot dash tones per second. Modulated at 1300 Hz (medium-pitch tone)
O (Outer)	4 to 7 miles	1,400 ft	Blue	Continuous Dashes 2 per second. Modulated at 400 Hz (lower-pitch tone)

Runway Lighting Systems

Runway lighting systems are fascinating to watch in Flight Simulator 98. Slewing at night around any airport will give you a sense of what each runway lighting system does and how it works. Essential to any instrument landing, these lighting systems help the pilot judge glide slope and runway orientation. Pilots can find out which lighting systems are installed at airports by consulting the instrument approach plates (IAP) for the runway they want to use. The runway diagram of the IAP has special symbols marking the types of lighting systems being used. For example, if visual approach slope indicator (VASI) lights are installed, you will see a circled V symbol at the end of the runway where it is placed. When the circle is black, it means the pilot can activate the lighting system from the airplane, whereas if it is hollow, the lighting system is controlled by the airport.

Similarly, if you see MIRL, REIL, HIRL, TDZ/CL, and so forth, it means that these lighting systems are installed. The circle A symbol followed by a number (ALSF-1,

ALSF-2, and so on) indicates the type of approach lighting system being used for the runway in question. The next few sections describe the features unique to each system.

Approach Lighting Systems

Approach lighting systems help the pilot make the transition from instrument flight to visual flight during landings. These lights are located in front of the runway threshold, before the runway actually begins, and extend into the approach area 2,400 to 3,000 ft for precision instrument runways and 1,400 to 1,500 ft for nonprecision instrument runways. Many of these systems include sequenced flashing lights that appear to the pilot as a tracer shell being fired at the runway.

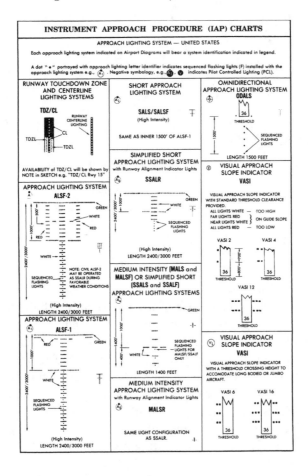

Figure 13.18 *IAP chart legend for approach lighting system and visual approach slope indicator.*

Approach lighting systems are identified by names such as ALSF-1, ALSF-2, SALS/SALSF, SSALR, MALS and MALSF, SSALS and SSALF, MALSR, and ODALS. Each of these systems is illustrated in Figure 13.18.

In FS98, you'll find examples of each of the following approach lighting systems shown at the airports and runways listed in Table 13.6.

Table 13.6 *Approach Lighting Systems in FS98*

LIGHTING SYSTEM	EXAMPLE AND RUNWAY LOCATION
ALSF-1 Honolulu	International, Hawaii runway 8L
ALSF-2	San Francisco International, California runway 28R
SSALR	MBS International, Saginaw, Michigan, runway 5
MALS/MALSF or SSALS/SSALF	San Francisco International, runway 19L
MALSR	San Jose International, California, runway 30L
ODALS	Hilo International, Hawaii, runway 8 (sequenced lights don't work in FS98)

Visual Glide Slope Lighting

Visual glide slope lighting systems help pilots to align the airplane and maintain the correct the glide path angle down the runway. VASI, the most common system, is found at many ILS runways across the United States. Unlike ILS or even GPS, the use of a VASI requires nothing more than your own eyes. Whether the airplane is too high, too low, or on the glide slope, by watching the VASI lights the pilot can get visual reassurance that the plane is on the established glide slope for the particular runway. VASI uses high-intensity lights, with prisms and shielding setups that project a light beam only along the glide slope. When the pilot flies outside the boundaries of the glide slope, the light beams change color, via the prisms and shielding, thereby indicating the positional error.

Flight Simulator 98 features VASI-equipped runways. To test any of the VASI systems described in the next few sections, follow these steps:

1. Go to a VASI-equipped runway using the **World/Goto/Airports** menu. If you don't know which runways have VASI, look up any of the airport IAP charts on the book's CD-ROM (you must use the included Acrobat Reader to view and print out these files) and examine the airport diagrams for the VASI symbols near the runway. You will see a circled V or V1, V2, V3, V4, V5, or P for the type of VASI system installed.

2. Enter slew mode by pressing the **Y** key.
3. Slew the airplane back from the runway threshold about 500 to 100 ft. Pull the joystick back or press **keypad 2**. To stop slew motion, press **keypad 5**.
4. Slew the airplane up by pressing **Q** and slew it down by pressing **A**. As the airplane climbs, notice the VASI lights at the left side of the runway. When you go too high above the glide slope or too low below the glide slope, the VASI lights will be colored red or white in a special arrangement to signal the airplane's position relative to the glide slope.

Table 13.7 shows the VASI systems found in FS98.

Table 13.7 *VASI Systems in FS98*

VASI SYSTEM	EXAMPLE AND LOCATION
Two-Bar VASI	Los Angeles International Airport, California, runway 7L
Three-Bar VASI	Los Angeles International Airport, California, runway 6L
T-VASI	Changi Airport, Singapore, runway 2R
PAPI	Keohole-Kona International Airport, Kailua-Kona, Hawaii, runway 35

The next section describes how each VASI lighting system works.

Visual Approach Slope Indicator

As you can see in the lower-left side of Figure 13.18, the visual approach slope indicator is a system of lights arranged on the left side of the runway to provide visual descent guidance during an approach. VASI installations may have 2, 4, 6, 12, or even 16 lighting units arranged in bars. Some VASI systems have three bars, but most of them have two bars: a far and near row of lights that are separated from each other. Each bar lights up red or white. In a two-bar VASI, when the airplane is on the glide slope the near bar (lower row) lights are white, and the far bar (upper row) lights are red. When the airplane is too high, all bars are white. When the airplane is too low, all bars are red. A three-bar VASI uses three separate lighting units to provide a slightly more accurate approach. All three bars are white when the airplane is too high, one red over two white lights for a slightly too high aircraft, two red lights over one white if the aircraft is on the glide slope, and finally three red lights if the aircraft is below the glide slope.

Single-bar VASI is indicated by a single circled V on the IAP charts. Three-bar VASI uses a circled V_3 symbol. You will find an example of two-bar VASI at Los Angeles International Airport's runways 7L and 7R, and a three-bar VASI on runways 6L and 6R. Note that many large airports, such as Chicago's O'Hare International, don't have VASI at all.

You can remember this relationship for any of the VASI setups by the following rhyme:

Red over White, you're all right
Red over red, you're dead

T-VASI

T-VASI, a much larger array of lights than the basic VASI, is used extensively in Australia. To see an example of T-VASI in Flight Simulator, go to runway 2R at Changi Airport in Singapore. T-VASIs are placed on the left side of the runway, although they can be used on both sides simultaneously. As with VASI, T-VASI uses red and white lights to indicate whether the plane is too high or too low along the glide slope.

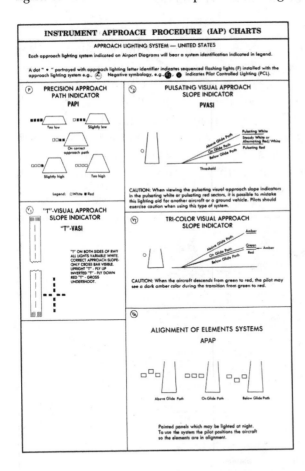

Figure 13.19 IAP chart legend for PAPI, T-VASI, PVASI, TRCV, and APAP lighting systems.

T-VASI, so called because it is shaped like a T, consists of a vertical array of two lights above a horizontal bar of lights. Just below the horizontal lights is another vertical array of two lights extending below. When the airplane is too high above the glide slope, the center bar is illuminated along with the two lights above the bar. As the airplane approaches the glide slope but is still slightly too high, the top light is extinguished. When the airplane is exactly on the glide slope, only the horizontal lights are visible. If it is slightly too low, the first vertical light below the horizontal bar lights up, and when it is too far below the glide slope, all the vertical lights below the horizontal bar light up red. All this is illustrated in Figure 13.19 and Figure 13.20.

T-VASI is indicated on IAP charts by the circled V_1 symbol.

Precision Approach Path Indicator

The precision approach path indicator, or PAPI, uses lighting units similar to VASI except that they are installed in a single row of either two or four light units on the left side of the runway. In some cases, as at San Jose International, California, runway 12, PAPI is installed on the right side of the runway. There are five different signal combinations, as illustrated in Figure 13.20. When the airplane is too high, all the lights are white. But when the airplane is just slightly high, only the left light turns red. When it is exactly on the glide slope, the two left lights are red and the two right lights are white. When it is just below the glide slope, only the rightmost light is white and the three left lights are red. When all four lights are red, the plane is too low.

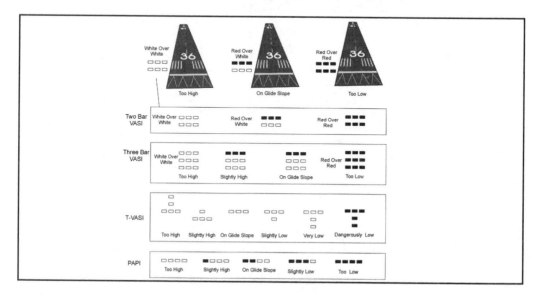

Figure 13.20 *Standard VASI lighting arrangements.*

PAPI is indicated on the IAP charts as a circled P, and you will find many European airports using this system. To see a PAPI system in action in the United States, go to runway 35 at Keohole-Kona International Airport in Kailua-Kona, Hawaii.

Tricolor Visual Approach Slope Indicator

Tri-color visual approach slope indicators (TRCV) consist of a single light mounted on the left side of the runway that projects a three-color visual approach path. The below-path indication is red, the above-path indication is amber, and the on-glide path indication is green.

TRCV is indicated on the IAP charts by a circled V_4 symbol.

Pulsating Visual Approach Slope Indicator

The pulsating visual approach slope indicator, or PLASI, is a single-light unit that is located on the left side of the runway. It has four operating modes: a pulsating white light tells you that the aircraft is above the glide slope. A steady white light signals that you are on the glide slope, and a steady red light will shine when you are just below the glide slope. The light will start to flash red if you are dangerously below the glide slope.

PLASI is indicated on the IAP charts by a circled V_2 symbol.

Runway End Identifier Lights (REIL)

Runway End identifier lights, or REILs, are installed on many runways to allow the pilot to gauge where the end of the runway is. The system consists of a pair of synchronized flashing lights located on each side of the runway threshold. Flashing REIL lights are helpful in fog; the pulsating light shows up even when you can't see the beam itself through the fog. Unfortunately, in FS98, these lights are very weak compared with their real-world counterparts.

Runway Edge Light Systems

Runway edge lights provide useful information that lets pilots discern the outline of the runway at night and during restricted low-visibility conditions. Runway edge lights are classified by the intensity or brightness of light they produce.

- HIRL: High-intensity runway lights
- MIRL: Medium-intensity runway lights
- LIRL: Low-intensity runway lights

Except for the end of the runway, the edge lights are white; amber replaces white on the last 2,000 ft or half the runway length, whichever is less, to form a caution zone for landing. At the very ends of the runway, the edge lights emit red light toward the runway to indicate the end of the runway to departing aircraft and emit green light outward from the runway to give a positive indication of the threshold for landing aircraft.

In-Runway Lighting

Touchdown zone (TDZL) lights and runway centerline lights (RCLS) are installed on precision approach runways to make it easier to land during poor visibility.

TDZL has two groups of lights located symmetrically on either side of the runway touchdown zone, as shown in the upper-right corner of Figure 13.18. These lights start at 100 ft from the landing threshold and extend to 3,000 ft down the runway, or the midpoint of the runway, whichever is less.

RCLS consists of centerline lights spaced at 50-ft intervals beginning 75 ft from the landing threshold and extending to within 75 ft of the opposite end of the runway.

Runway Remaining Lighting

Runway remaining lights are centerline lights located in the final 3,000 ft of runway. Alternate red and white lights are seen from 3,000 ft to the 1,000-ft point, and all red lights are seen for the last 1,000 ft of the runway. From the opposite direction, these lights are seen as white.

Now that we have discussed the instrument landing system—its radio components and types of lighting displays—let us turn now to the topic of using the radio magnetic compass and horizontal situation indicator navigational instruments.

RADIO MAGNETIC COMPASS

The radio magnetic compass (RMI) consists of a rotating compass card and bearing pointers to display the direction of navaids tuned in on the NAV and ADF radio (see Figure 13.21). The compass card rotates as the aircraft turns, but the aircraft's magnetic heading always is displayed at the 12 o'clock position. In the FS98 737-400, the RMI is connected to the NAV2 radio and the ADF radio. The green bearing pointer displays the magnetic bearing to the selected VOR station on the NAV2 radio, and the yellow bearing pointer shows the direction to the NDB station on the ADF radio.

The Learjet can superimpose an RMI over its HSI display. It operates in the same manner as the 737's RMI. The only difference is that you must click the **Toggle VOR2 Needle** button and the **Toggle ADF Needle** button, located at the bottom of the HSI, to activate the RMI functions.

The nice thing about this instrument is that no matter which direction the aircraft is pointed, you will always know the relative direction to the VOR or NDB station. For example, if the green bearing pointer points directly right, it means that the VOR tuned on NAV2 is to your right. If the needle points straight up, the VOR station is straight ahead. The same thing applies to the yellow NDB bearing pointer.

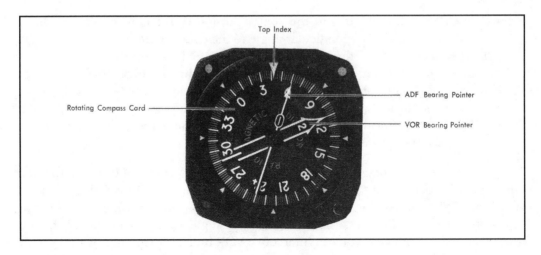

Figure 13.21 Radio magnetic compass (RMI).

HORIZONTAL SITUATION INDICATOR

First introduced with the FSW95 Boeing 737-400, the horizontal situation indicator (HSI) is also included with the Learjet in FS98. As the centerpiece of the NAV display in glass cockpits, the HSI combines a heading indicator and course deviation indicator into one instrument. Even though you saw that the HSI has many different modes of operation (see Chapter 4), FS98 supports only the Full VOR and Full ILS modes.

On the HSI, the CDI rotates with the heading indicator to show the relationship between the airplane's current heading and the VOR radial you have dialed in with the **COURSE** selector. The HSI also displays the glide slope and localizer beam when tuned to an ILS station, as well as the distance to a VOR or ILS when DME is available. The aircraft's speed relative to the VOR is also displayed.

The face of the instrument shows the following:

- A rotating compass card that always indicates the magnetic heading of the aircraft at the 12 o'clock position.
- A course pointer, which is a large, long-segmented arrow that rotates in response to settings you make with the **COURSE** selector. The course pointer swivels to point in the magnetic compass direction that matches the value you have entered in the **COURSE** selector box.

- The CDI needle, which is in the center portion of the course pointer, always moves sideways at a perpendicular angle to the course pointer to indicate angular displacement from the VOR radial the airplane is crossing.
- An airplane symbol in miniature at the center of the HSI that shows at a glance the angular relationship between the airplane's heading and the selected course.
- An autopilot heading bug, which is controlled by the **HDG** box on the autopilot.
- A **TO/FROM** indicator, which is shown via a triangle symbol that points toward or away from the head of the course pointer.

The greatest single advantage of the HSI over the old-style VOR/OBI display is that the intercept angle between the aircraft heading and the selected VOR radial is displayed graphically. With the standard OBI-type display, you know only on which side—left or right—the selected radial course lies. The intercept angle must still be calculated. With the HSI and lots of practice, you can intercept a VOR radial with great precision simply by controlling the CDI rate of movement with its rotational angle.

When no station is in range of the HSI, you will see a large red cross in the middle of the display. This means that the HSI is currently off. Note that the red cross mark does not exist in real HSIs but has only been added for the sake of Flight Simulator pilots in need of a visual warning that the HSI is not functioning.

How to Use the HSI

To use the HSI with a VOR, tune in the VOR station with the NAV1 radio. The Flight Simulator HSI is always slaved to the NAV1 radio; it cannot be tuned using the NAV2 radio. (On the Learjet, you can display the NAV2 and ADF course needles superimposed as an RMI.) Then, if you are within range of the VOR station, you should see the display come alive and the red cross marker will vanish.

The **COURSE** selector box, which is really the same thing as the course selector on the NAV1 display of the Cessna, has a confusing name. It does not refer to the airplane's current heading or course; rather, it is referenced to the VOR radials that each VOR station emits in all directions. The course pointer will align itself with a VOR radial that corresponds to the course number you select. The course can either be the actual VOR radial (remember that VOR radials are always directed away from the VOR) or its reciprocal 180° apart. You will know whether you have selected the VOR radial or its reciprocal by the **TO/FROM** indicator, the gray triangle symbol aligned with the course pointer and located just beneath it. When the triangle points toward the head of the course pointer, the **TO** indication is on and you will know that the reciprocal of the radial is being displayed; add or subtract 180° from the **COURSE** selector number to find the VOR radial. The opposite holds true for the **FROM** indicator. When you see the **FROM** triangle pointing toward the tail of the course pointer, you will know that it is the VOR radial (and not its reciprocal) that is currently being displayed in the **COURSE** selector box.

To change the course direction and thus the VOR radial that corresponds to it, click to the right in the **COURSE** selector box to advance the course number, or by clicking to the left in the **COURSE** selector box to lower the course number. As you change the course, the course pointer will rotate to correspond with the VOR radial that you specify.

N O T E

The course pointer does not normally point to the VOR station. The airplane is on the VOR radial selected in the **COURSE** selector box *only* when the CDI needle is centered between the head and tail of the course pointer. Only then will the course pointer point to the VOR station. (You must make sure that the **TO** triangle is on, or else it will point directly away from the VOR!) With the **TO** triangle on, if the pilot turns the airplane so that the course pointer is at the 12 o'clock position, the airplane will head directly toward the VOR. If the **FROM** triangle is on and the course pointer is at the 12 o'clock position, the airplane will be headed away from the VOR station on the selected radial. If the course pointer is at any other angle than the 12 o'clock or 6 o'clock position with the CDI needle centered, it means that the aircraft is crossing the VOR radial, but is not headed for the VOR.

N O T E

Always set the **COURSE** selector to the course you intend to fly. Previously, you were advised always to fly the course set on the Course selector for the NAV display. The same advice applies to the HSI. As with the NAV display, when you're setting the **COURSE** selector on the HSI, always set the course you intend to fly. So if you want to track the 090 radial *inbound* to the VOR station, you must set a course of 270 with the **FROM** triangle on. If you want to track the 090 radial *outbound* from the VOR station, set the course to 090 with the **FROM** triangle on. Failure to do this will result in the CDI needle operating in the reverse sense.

HSI CDI Needle Displacement

On the 737, the parallel yellow lines on the HSI are equivalent to the CDI needle on the VOR display found in the Cessna. This CDI needle moves separately from the head and tail of the course pointer to indicate how many degrees right or left the airplane is located from the selected VOR radial in the **COURSE** box. The Learjet's HSI has a similar arrangement except that the CDI needle is green instead of yellow. Angular displacement is reported by the dots on the scale. Full-scale deflection to one side is 10° off the selected course, with each dot representing 5° displacement.

Using the universal pilot's rule of thumb, the 1 in 60 rule, you can calculate how far in miles you are from the selected VOR radial by observing the CDI needle deflection. For example, if the CDI needle is 1 dot displaced at 60 DME (60 nautical miles from the VOR), then you are 5 nm from the selected VOR radial, because for every 60 miles, 1° of deflection equals 1 nautical mile. In VOR mode each dot represents 5°, and the CDI needle is on the first dot, so you are therefore 5 nm from the selected VOR radial. At 30 DME, 1 dot means you are 2.5 nm from the course, and so on.

HSI Compass Card and Heading Bug Indicator

On the 737, the digital readout at the top of the HSI's rotating compass tells you the airplane's current magnetic heading, and the magenta arrow bug on the perimeter of the compass card is your autopilot heading bug indicator. You can change this indicator by clicking in a new course in the autopilot heading selector (marked **HDG** in the autopilot section of the instrument panel). To advance the autopilot heading, click to the right of the numbers in the **HDG** box; otherwise, click to the left to lower the heading.

The Learjet's HSI is similar to the 737's HSI, but you must read the airplane's magnetic compass heading from the rotating compass card just underneath the green pointer or on the digital readout on the lower right of the compass card. A similar heading bug rotates around the dial depending on the heading you have selected in the **HDG** box. Figure 13.22 shows the HSIs for the 737 and Learjet.

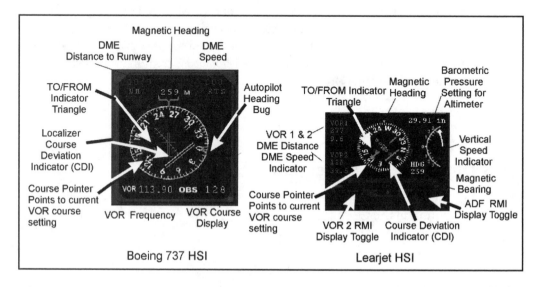

Figure 13.22 Horizontal situation indicator on the 737 (left) and Learjet.

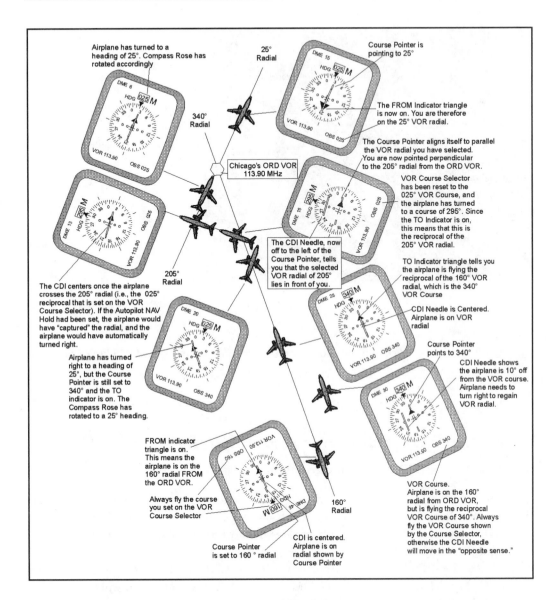

Figure 13.23 *HSI course setting corresponds to the VOR radial.*

Figure 13.24 HSI on a real 737-400.

The gray triangle under the course pointer is the same as the **FROM/TO** indicator on the older OBI/VOR-style display.

T I P

Using the HSI to Track an Outbound Radial from a VOR

To fly away from a VOR station on the outbound radial, follow these steps:

1. Tune in the NAV station and make sure that the HSI display is active. (You'll see **VOR1** displayed at the side of the display. Note that if you are using the Learjet, you may see **VOR2** which only applies to the RMI display that can be superimposed on top of the HSI.)
2. Click the **COURSE** selector box until the CDI needle is centered and the **TO/FROM** indicator shows **FROM**. The **COURSE** selector box will now display the VOR radial.
3. To track the outbound radial, turn the airplane so that the course pointer is at the 12 o'clock position. The airplane's magnetic heading should be the same as the course shown in the **COURSE** selector box,
4. Always fly the course shown on the **COURSE** selector, making sure that as you fly away from the VOR station, the CDI needle is kept centered. If there is wind

drift, compensate by crabbing the aircraft's heading slightly into the wind. This will mean that you will fly a heading that is a few degrees off from that shown in the **COURSE** selector.

In step 4, you can engage the autopilot **NAV** hold, and the plane will automatically maintain the course set in the **COURSE** selector.

Using the HSI to Track the Inbound VOR Course to a VOR

Follow these instructions to fly directly toward a VOR station:

1. Tune in the NAV station and make sure that the HSI display is active.
2. Click the **COURSE** selector box until the CDI needle is centered and the **TO/FROM** indicator shows **TO**. The reciprocal of the current VOR radial will now be displayed in the **COURSE** selector box.
3. To home in to the station, turn the airplane so that the course pointer is at the 12 o'clock position. The airplane's magnetic heading should be the same as the course shown in the **COURSE** selector box.
4. Always fly the course shown on the **COURSE** selector box, but make sure to keep the CDI needle centered. Correct for wind drift as previously described.

In step 4, you can engage the autopilot **NAV** hold to maintain the VOR course shown in the **COURSE** selector.

Using the HSI to Intercept a VOR Radial

You have already seen how to intercept a VOR radial using the **NAV** display on the Cessna. Now that you have the HSI to work with, your job is greatly simplified. The course pointer tells you the proper angle for intercept without the need for any mental prestidigitation of calculating angles. For greater accuracy, you should use the "double the difference between radial and the angle to be intercepted" rule previously mentioned in the VOR course interception example. But it is not absolutely necessary with the HSI's course pointer. In any case, the maximum intercept angle shouldn't be greater than 90°, nor should it be less than 20°. This is the angle that the course pointer should make with the vertical, either right or left.

Let's try the same VOR intercept using the HSI by employing the method outlined previously for the **NAV** display.

EXAMPLE 13.1

We want to intercept the 205° radial from Chicago's ORD VOR and then fly inbound along this radial on a VOR course of 25° (the reciprocal of 205°). Currently, the airplane is inbound on the 160° radial from the ORD VOR.

Solution

To set up the problem, perform steps 1–6. After you are on the 160° radial from the ORD-VOR, perform steps 7–10 to intercept the radial.

1. Start the 737 or Learjet at Chicago's O'Hare International Airport using the **World/Go TO/Airport** dialog box.
2. Tune in the ORD VOR at 113.90 MHz.
3. Use the **World/Go To/Exact Location** dialog box to set the airplane's position 25 nm south of ORD, with an altitude of 8,000 ft, a north heading, and an aircraft speed of about 200 knots. You can slew the airplane into the proper position if you like.
4. Because we are flying the 160° radial inbound to the ORD VOR, we will choose a VOR course of 340° with the **TO** triangle on.
5. Slew the airplane until the CDI needle is centered and you are on the 160° radial from ORD (with the VOR course set to 340° and the **TO** triangle on).
6. Resume the simulation and follow the HSI procedure for tracking an inbound VOR course. The **COURSE** selector should be on 340° and the **TO** triangle on. Also, the course pointer will point at the 12 o'clock position.
7. Turn right to parallel the inbound VOR course of 25° that will put us on a parallel track with that of the 205° radial. The compass card on the HSI will rotate along with the course pointer so that now the compass card shows a course of 25°, but the course pointer is now pointing diagonally at the 340° heading.
8. Rotate the **COURSE** selector to match the desired inbound VOR course of 25°. Now the course pointer will again point in the 12 o'clock position. Notice which side the CDI needle is on; in this case, it is on the left. This means that you need to turn left to intercept the inbound 205° VOR radial.
9. Turn 90° left to intercept the 205° radial. This will put you on a course of 295°. Turning the airplane will cause the course pointer to rotate perpendicular to the airplane symbol, and it means that you are heading at a 90° angle intercept angle for the 295° radial. Isn't this a great sight? The course pointer is telling you, in no uncertain terms, that you are on an interception path with the radial you have dialed in on the **COURSE** selector.

10. As soon as the CDI needle starts to center, you will have almost reached the 205° radial. It is now time to start turning the airplane right to track the 205° radial inbound with a VOR course of 25°. To simplify matters, you can turn on the autopilot's **NAV** hold, and the autopilot will lock the airplane onto the 205° radial inbound.

If you practice this in Slew mode a couple of times, you will quickly get the hang of it and it will become almost second nature to you using any other VOR radials. The CDI needle's perpendicular orientation in step 5 is what makes the interception a whole lot easier, because you can visualize your airplane's attitude relationship to the VOR intercept radial. Let's summarize the VOR radial intercept procedure and generalize it so that it is easier to remember:

1. Turn the airplane to parallel the course of the VOR radial you want to intercept, either inbound or outbound.
2. Click the **COURSE** selector to match the course you selected in step 1. The course pointer should point to the 12 o'clock position.
3. Turn the airplane toward the VOR radial you wish to intercept so that the course pointer is at a 45° angle from the vertical (this angle can be from 20° to 90° as discussed earlier). You'll know which direction to turn by the CDI needle's position. You always turn toward the CDI needle. If it is to the left, turn left; if it is to the right, turn right.
4. Keep the airplane on a steady course with the course pointer at a 45° angle with the vertical. When the airplane crosses the desired intercept radial, the CDI needle will center. You are now on the VOR radial you wanted to intercept, either inbound or outbound. (You will know by the sense of the **TO/FROM** triangle. If it is **TO**, you are inbound. If it is **FROM**, you are outbound.)

In step 4, you can turn on the autopilot **NAV** hold, and, when the airplane crosses the radial, the autopilot will take control of the airplane and turn to lock its heading onto the VOR course shown in the **COURSE** selector.

Figure 13.25 illustrates this procedure.

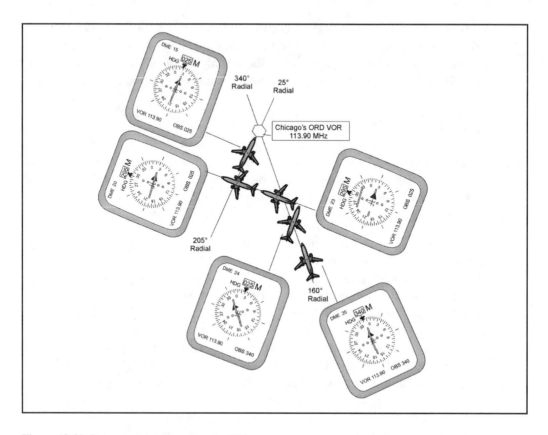

Figure 13.25 *Course interception using the HSI.*

Using the HSI for an ILS Approach

When you tune in an ILS station on the HSI, the HSI will enter Full ILS mode and the display will change slightly. For example, you will notice a glide slope indicator if there is a glide slope transmitter associated with the ILS station. In addition, on the 737 (but not the Learjet), the label **ILS** and the frequency will be displayed in the lower-left corner of the HSI.

The glide slope indicator on the 737 is a yellow diamond-shaped symbol that moves up and down along a vertical scale on the right side of the HSI. The Learjet's glide slope indicator is projected above the HSI to the right of the Attitude/Artificial Horizon display. If the glide slope symbol is above the center, you're below the glide slope; if it is below the center, you are above the glide slope. Each dot on the display represents 0.35° deflection from the glide slope, with full-scale deflection from the center to top representing 0.70° (the glide slope is only 1.4° thick). The glide slope indicator will disappear from the HSI display when you pass the threshold of the front course of the runway. This is because you will have passed the glide slope transmitter antenna, and the receiving antenna onboard the airplane is no longer able to pick up the glide slope signal, which is a highly focused beam of radio energy that is projected in only one direction. This is not the case with the localizer beam, which has both a front course and a back course component and extends both directions down the length of the runway.

The localizer beam, which shows horizontal displacement from the ILS localizer radio beam, is displayed via the localizer (CDI) needle in the center of the HSI display. If the localizer needle is to the right of the course pointer, you are too far left of the runway centerline. If the localizer needle is too far left, you are too far right.

The localizer needle is four times as sensitive in ILS mode as it is in VOR mode. Thus, each dot of needle deflection represents 1.25°, with full-scale deflection from extremity to center being 2.5° degrees and not the 10° of VOR mode.

To use the HSI with the instrument landing system, tune the ILS localizer on the NAV1 radio and then select the localizer heading in the autopilot course box. If there is a glide slope transmitter associated with the runway, it will automatically be tuned in by your ILS receiver.

N O T E

You must enter the correct localizer heading in the **COURSE** selector box! This means that the course pointer must point to the 12 o'clock position during ILS landings. This point often confuses Flight Simulator pilots, but it must be done if you are to display the correct horizontal displacement of your aircraft's path down the localizer beam. If the course pointer is at some other angle, you can be easily confused as to the proper sense of the localizer needle. For example, if the course pointer is upside down, pointing at the 6 o'clock position, the localizer needle will move in the opposite direction that you would expect when it is normally right side up at the 12 o'clock position, and you might then correct your localizer drift angle by turning the airplane in the wrong direction. Usually, the ILS localizer heading is the same number as the runway's magnetic heading, so if you are landing at runway 9L, you would set the **COURSE** selector to **090** degrees.

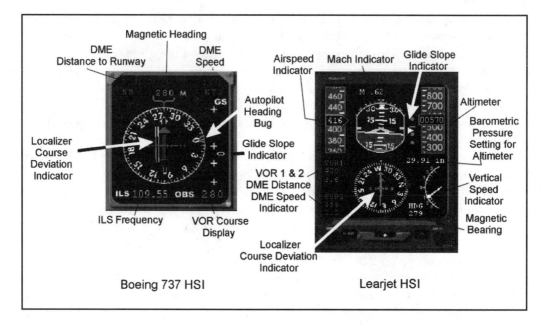

Figure 13.26 *The 737 (left) and Learjet HSI in ILS Mode. When performing an ILS approach with the HSI, be sure to type the ILS runway heading in the **COURSE** selector box. Only after you do this will the CDI tell you the airplane's correct horizontal displacement from the localizer beam.*

Learjet HSI

The FS98 Learjet's HSI operates in a manner analogous to that of the 737 except that the Learjet's display allows you to superimpose an RMI over the HSI. To do this, just move your mouse below the HSI display where there are two buttons. As it crosses each button, you will see a QuickTips message informing you that this is the **Toggle VOR2 Needle** or the **Toggle ADF Needle**. The VOR1 CDI needle is always green, and the VOR2 needle is gray. The ADF needle, which is discussed in the next section on NDB navigation, is blue. Click either button to activate the needles.

There is also a button nearby to set the barometric pressure setting on the Learjet's altimeter.

NDB NAVIGATION

Nondirectional beacons are not as accurate as VOR stations in determining position. However, there are far more NDB stations around the world than there are VOR stations, in part because NDB radio transmitters are less expensive and easier to set up, and in part because they were the first navigation system to be used worldwide. Particularly in the Third World, you will find that in some locations NDB navaids are the only ones available. In the United States there are about 2,228 NDB stations out of a total of 3,457 NDB and VOR navaids. For the rest of the world, there are 4,665 NDBs.

NDB operates on a frequency of 200 to 415 kHz, with a maximum power of 2,000 watts. By day, it has a maximum range of 75 nm; with skywave skip at night, this range can extend to 200 nm. Unfortunately, NDB is susceptible to interference from storms and is not as reliable for navigation, so VOR navigation is preferred where available. NDB works by broadcasting an AM omnidirectional radio signal that aircraft pick up with special loop antennas. The antenna on the airplane is rotated until it receives the maximum signal possible, and the signal is then interpreted via the bearing pointer on the ADF indicator as the direction to the NDB.

To tune in an NDB station, enter the NDB frequency on the ADF radio on the radio instrument panel (press **Shift 2** or click the master **Avionics** panel switch). Then observe the ADF indicator to see which direction the bearing pointer is pointed. If the bearing pointer is pointed straight up, it means you are headed directly toward the NDB; if it is pointed directly right, it means that the NDB is to your right, and so on. Note that the scale on the ADF is read in 10° increments, but it does not rotate with the airplane; thus, you cannot use the ADF to ascertain compass direction but only relative direction. Thus, 0° on the ADF always points in the direction of the airplane's nose (see Figure 13.27).

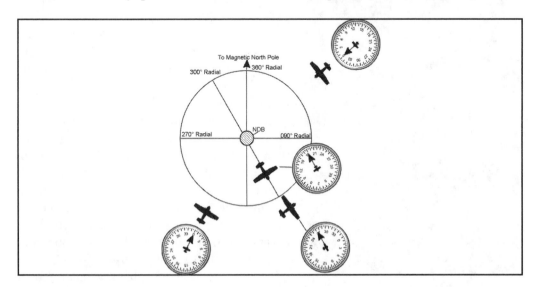

Figure 13.27 *When the ADF needle points to 0°, you are headed toward the NDB station.*

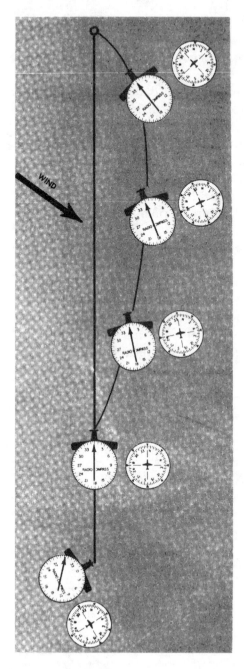

Figure 13.28 NDB homing method.

The frequency separation between NDB stations is about 1 kHz, but you can specify a smaller channel spacing of 500 Hz in FS98 by going to the **Options/Preferences/-Instruments** dialog box and then selecting **100 Hz ADF frequency increment**. Note that the bandwidth of your ADF radio suddenly increases from its previous 999 kHz limit to as high as 1699 kHz. Theoretically, you can tune in your favorite AM broadcast radio station!

ADF homing is the simplest navigational technique used with NDB stations (see Figure 13.28). All you do is tune in a given NDB station and then turn the airplane so that the bearing pointer always stays on 0°. This will eventually bring you over the NDB station, whereupon the bearing pointer will suddenly rotate 180° and point backward. This tells you that you have crossed the NDB and are now flying away from it.

AUTOPILOT

Autopilot-equipped aircraft enable the pilot to fly the airplane on automatic, so that he or she doesn't need to touch the controls. This feature vastly simplifies the task of managing a complex airplane, because the pilot can focus on the management aspects of flying rather than the mechanical aspects. It frees the pilot from the drudgery of watching carefully every nuance of the airplane's attitude or trimming the airplane every time someone gets up to go to the bathroom. The pilot can concentrate on navigating, watching for other air traffic, and monitoring the overall progress of the flight.

The autopilot in FS98 has several new functions not found in the FSW95 autopilot. The new functions include a vertical speed hold, an airspeed/Mach number hold (auto-throttle), and a Takeoff/Go-Around mode for flying missed approaches in the Learjet and 737. The FSW95 autopilot functions, which are also included in FS98, include an altitude lock, heading hold, wing leveler, attitude hold (pitch and bank), and yaw damper. Also included are the autopilot navigational modes, which allow you to track navigational courses from VOR or ILS stations and capture and shoot an ILS approach.

To use any of the autopilot buttons, you must first click the **AP** (autopilot) master switch located on the MCP, or master control panel. When the autopilot is engaged, the rate of simulation is limited to 4× normal speed.

All the autopilot functions and their keyboard commands are listed in Table 13.8.

Table 13.8 *Autopilot Functions*

AUTOPILOT FUNCTION	KEYBOARD COMMAND
Autopilot on/off	**Z**
Wing leveler (LVL)	**Ctrl V**
Attitude hold (ATT) (maintain pitch and bank)	**Ctrl T**
Altitude hold (ALT) (min. 0 ft, max. 99,901 ft)	**Ctrl Z**
Vertical speed (min. –6000 ft/min, max. +7000 ft/min*	You can specify any key or joystick button**
Airspeed hold (SPD) (min. 0 kt, max. 999 kt)*	**Ctrl R**
Mach hold (MACH) (min. 0, max. 1.5)*	**Ctrl R**
Arm auto-throttle*	**Shift R**
Auto-throttle Takeoff/Go-Around*	**Ctrl Shift R**
Heading hold: Lock to your current magnetic course heading	**Ctrl H**
NAV 1 hold: Lock to a VOR radial tuned on NAV1	**Ctrl N**
ILS lock (APP): Lock to an ILS tuned on NAV1 for a landing. Aircraft flies the glide slope and localizer descent profile for the selected ILS runway.	**Ctrl A**
Localizer lock: Lock to the ILS localizer (but not the glide slope) tuned on the NAV1 radio for the landing.	**Ctrl O**

Table 13.8 *Autopilot Functions continued*

AUTOPILOT FUNCTION	KEYBOARD COMMAND
Back course lock: Lock to a back course of the ILS localizer tuned on the NAV1 radio. This allows you to approach the runway's opposite end for a landing.	**Ctrl B**
Yaw damper on/off	**Ctrl D**

*FS98 only
**Using the Customization dialog box

Note that the yaw damper often interferes with steering while the plane is on the ground. Be sure to disengage the yaw damper before landing and before takeoff.

Wing Leveler

The wing leveler (**LVL**) levels the wings so that the airplane is flying with a nose pitch attitude of 0° and a bank angle of 0°. Note that the wing leveler does not control yaw or vertical speed. For example, the airplane could be descending or could be changing course even though it appears that the airplane is flying straight with the wing leveler on.

Pitch and Bank Hold (Attitude Hold)

The pitch and bank hold (**ATT**) flies the aircraft with the current nose pitch angle and bank angle, something that is useful when you are trying to maintain a circling holding pattern or some other type of turn when you want to control the climb or descent rate.

Altitude Hold

Using the autopilot altitude hold is simple in Flight Simulator. If you want to climb to FL 250 and you are flying in the Learjet or 737, click in the desired vertical rate of climb (for example, +1,500 ft/min in the **VS** box on the MCP) and then click in the altitude at which you want the airplane to level off (such as 25,000 ft in the **ALT** box on the MCP). Then click the **AP** master switch, and finally click on the **ALT** lock on the MCP. The airplane will climb at 1,500 ft/min until it reaches 25,000 ft altitude; then it will level off and maintain this altitude. The same thing holds true for descents: you specify a negative vertical climb rate in the **VS** box and then the altitude at which you want to level off. Then turn on the **AP** switch and click on the **ALT** lock. If you subsequently turn off the **AP** master switch, you will have to re-engage the altitude lock, because it will have turned itself off.

NOTE Climb altitudes must have a positive **VS** (vertical speed) associated with them in the autopilot altitude hold. Descent altitudes must have a negative **VS**. Do not make the mistake of clicking a new climb altitude with a negative vertical speed or a new descent altitude with a positive vertical speed. This will only confuse the autopilot, and you won't achieve your objective of maintaining an altitude lock.

An even more useful feature of the autopilot is that you can reset the altitude lock without any tedious mouse clicking of the Altitude box. For example, suppose you are flying at 25,000 ft and you want to engage the autopilot. You notice that the autopilot's Altitude box shows a different altitude from the 25,000 ft that you want. Rather than click the Altitude box until it shows 25,000 ft, you can jump immediately to 25,000 ft by using the keyboard command **Z** followed by **Ctrl Z**. This action will immediately lock the altitude to the plane's current altitude. Suppose also that you decide to descend and lock your altitude at 20,000 ft. To do this, you simply turn off the autopilot (press **Z**) and then descend until the plane reaches 20,000 ft. Then re-engage the autopilot (press **Z**) followed by the altitude lock (press **Ctrl Z**).

You can use similar techniques for leveling the wings, setting the magnetic heading, following a VOR radial, maintaining the current pitch and bank attitude, descending on an ILS glide path and localizer path, tracking a localizer, or flying a back course. A back course means that you fly toward the opposite end of an ILS-equipped runway.

In FS98, the orange bug on the altimeter indicates the altitude hold figure that is shown in the Altitude box. You can click to the right or left of the **Altitude Selector** button (just below and to the right of the backup altimeter) to increase or decrease the altitude that is indicated by the bug. Note that the altimeter readout on the MCP increases and decreases in response to the bug's movement. This is a very useful thing to know, because it is much easier to look at the altimeter bug than to look at the tiny, eyestrain-inducing **ALT** box on the MCP.

By default, unless you specify otherwise with the vertical speed hold, the airplane will attempt to climb at a vertical airspeed of +1,800 ft/min or descend at a vertical airspeed of –1,800 ft/min.

Vertical Speed Hold

New to FS98, the vertical speed hold allows you to specify the exact climb or descent speed in ft/min. The autopilot's vertical speed control is actually a pitch control, because it controls the airplane's angle of attack, and this in turn changes the airplane's vertical speed. Using the vertical speed hold is extremely useful when you're landing the 737, because you can directly control the glide path angle by instructing the autopilot to maintain a given vertical airspeed. For example, if you are flying at 210 knots IAS and you want to maintain a normal 3° glide path to the runway, you would select a vertical speed of 1,050 ft/min. If you reduce your airspeed to 180 knots IAS, the vertical speed should be 900 ft/min. For a table of vertical airspeeds for different glide path angles and airspeeds, see Table 1.4 in Chapter 1.

To use the vertical speed hold, follow these steps:

1. Determine your final altitude goal. If you intend to descend to an airport that is located at an altitude of 2,000 ft MSL, set 2,000 ft in the Altitude display of the MCP. Either move the altitude bug as described previously, or click to the left or right of the altitude readout.
2. Set the vertical speed in the V/S readout by clicking to the right or left to increase or decrease the ft/min. You can also use the **Aircraft/Autopilot** menu to enter the vertical airspeed from the keyboard. Be sure to enter a minus sign (hyphen key) for descents (such as **-2000**) or a plus sign for climbs (**+2000**).
3. Click the **AP** (autopilot) master switch on.
4. Click the **ALT** indicator on the MCP to engage the autopilot's vertical speed hold.

Auto-throttle and Airspeed IAS/Mach Hold

The FS98 autopilot speed control governs the aircraft's speed by varying the throttle position. The autopilot linkage that does this, called the Auto-throttle, is extremely useful for precisely controlling airspeed during landings or missed approaches in the Learjet or 737, where you must quickly increase the throttle to a predetermined V_{REF} airspeed. Both the autopilot airspeed hold and Mach hold are available on the Learjet and 737, but the auto-throttle used for takeoffs and go-arounds is available only on the 737.

To set the autopilot airspeed/Mach hold for a particular airspeed, follow these steps:

1. If you are flying the 737, make sure that the **A/T** (Auto-throttle) master arm switch is on.
2. Choose an airspeed by clicking to the right or left of the IAS/MACH box on the MCP. Click right to increase, or left to decrease. You can also click the airspeed indicator bug (orange triangle) button to increase or decrease the auto-throttle airspeed.
3. Turn the **AP** master switch on.
4. Click the **SPD** control on the MCP for indicated airspeed or click the **MACH** control for Mach number (or press **Ctrl R**).

That's all there is to it! The permissible airspeeds for the auto-throttle range from 0 to 999 knots, or from Mach 0 to Mach 1.5.

Click the airspeed selector on the airspeed indicator to increase or decrease the autopilot airspeed hold. Observe, as you do so, that the airspeed bug indicator will rotate around the dial.

Takeoff/Go-Around

The auto-throttle on the 737 can be used to manage proper thrust levels for takeoffs as well as go-arounds during missed approaches. To arm the auto-throttle for a takeoff, press **Shift R** or click the master **A/T** auto-throttle arm switch on the MCP to the on position. Press **Ctrl Shift R** or click the **Takeoff/Go Around** button underneath the throttle quadrant on the 737 instrument panel, and the aircraft will begin to accelerate down the runway as the throttle is advanced automatically to the takeoff position. The word **TO**, meaning takeoff, will appear just above the engine controls.

Note that the autopilot master control switch (**AP**) need not be on when you're using the auto-throttle for takeoffs or go-arounds.

MAN SET on N$_1$ Gauge

The **MAN SET** indicator above the N$_1$ gauge stands for manual setting of the N$_1$ bugs. Using the auto-throttle, you can specify the N$_1$ thrust level as a percentage of total N$_1$ RPM. This capability comes in handy when you are trying to maintain a given cruise thrust level but not necessarily a given airspeed.

Heading Hold

The heading hold control (**HDG**) allows the autopilot to fly the magnetic bearing that is shown in the HDG box on the MCP. Simply change the heading that is shown (click right on the **HDG** readout box to increase or left to decrease) and click on the **AP** master switch followed by the **HDG** control. The airplane will then fly the given heading shown on the **HDG** readout. Alternatively, if you want to avoid nuisance mouse clicks, you can set the heading by first turning the airplane to the desired magnetic bearing and then press **Z** (master **AP** switch) followed by **Ctrl H** (**HDG** lock). This technique simplifies the task of specifying a heading, because you don't have to repetitively click the HDG numbers to increase or decrease them.

At any time with the autopilot engaged, you can change the airplane's heading by clicking on the value shown in the **HDG** box.

The Cessna's directional gyro has a heading bug indicator on the outside of the rotating compass card. You can move this bug by clicking to the right or left of the red button just below the instrument. If you specify the heading this way, you don't need to use the autopilot dialog box. Simply move the bug then activate the autopilot (press **Z**) followed by the heading hold (press **Ctrl H**).

NAV Hold

There are two ways to use the autopilot NAV hold, which locks the airplane onto the VOR course you have selected on the HSI or NAV display.

1. After you have tuned in a VOR station on the NAV1 radio and after you have captured a VOR radial or its reciprocal VOR course (as indicated by the CDI needle being centered), you can have the autopilot fly the plane on the VOR radial (or its reciprocal course). With the CDI needle centered, choose either the outbound VOR radial or the reciprocal inbound course in the **COURSE** box; then click the **A/P** switch followed by the **NAV** hold. The airplane will stay locked on the VOR radial (or its reciprocal depending on whether the **TO** triangle is on).

2. You can pre set the VOR course in the **COURSE** box and click on the **NAV** hold; when the airplane crosses the VOR radial or its reciprocal course selected in the **COURSE** box, the **NAV** hold will "lock" onto the VOR radial (or its reciprocal depending on whether the **TO** triangle is on). This command option will work even if you have the heading hold on; thus, when the airplane crosses the VOR radial or its reciprocal, the **HDG** lock will automatically disengage and the **NAV** hold will automatically take over.

The second method is a lot of fun to try out, but if you intercept the VOR radial at too steep an angle (i.e., 90°), the autopilot will have a hard time zigzagging back and forth as it struggles to capture the VOR radial. For example, it may overshoot the VOR radial, try to double back, overcompensate, and zigzag again. This will go on for some time until the airplane finally settles down on the VOR course. This zigzig path resembles a damped sine wave placed on its side. To avoid this scenario, you can start the VOR radial intercept by releasing the heading hold just after the CDI needle begins to move at the intercept zone; then reduce the intercept angle manually by pointing the airplane so that the course pointer is at a 45° angle instead of a 90° angle.

So far, you've learned how to fly inbound on a VOR course to a VOR or outbound on a VOR radial that you can automate with the autopilot **NAV** hold. But what happens when you cross over a VOR station with the **NAV** lock engaged and you want to select a different outbound radial? What are you going to do? The following tips will help you negotiate this situation:

1. When you are close to transiting over a VOR inbound, set the autopilot heading hold to your present inbound course. Then, just before crossing, disengage the **NAV** hold and engage the heading hold. This will maintain your current course inbound to the VOR station.
2. Adjust the OBS course selector for the outbound VOR: click the course selector until you have chosen the VOR radial you wish to track outbound. The CDI needle will move from the center of the course pointer all the way to the edge. Don't worry—this is fine. Note that you have not yet crossed over the VOR station.
3. As you approach the center of the VOR station, the CDI will start to move back to the middle, depending on the amount of turn required. If the turn is very sharp, such as a 90° to 180°, you might want to initiate the turn early using the **HDG** course selector on the MCP. However, if the turn is less than this range, you can wait until the CDI needle is centered and then turn on the **NAV** hold. With the proper VOR radial now captured, the airplane will track the outbound radial as desired.

ILS Lock (Approach)

If you have tuned in an ILS station on the NAV1 radio and you have captured the localizer beam as indicated on your NAV or HSI display and you have captured the glide slope beam, only then will the autopilot ILS lock (**APP**) work. The ILS lock will keep the airplane aligned on the localizer and glide slope of the ILS station for a letter-perfect touchdown only if these conditions are met. Note that before you engage the ILS lock, if the airplane is too far astray of the ILS beam the ILS lock will not activate properly. For example, if the airplane is approaching the ILS glide path from a 90° angle or the airplane starts too high, too low, or too far abeam of the ILS beams, the ILS lock will cause erratic behavior of the airplane and make a landing impossible.

Localizer Lock

The localizer lock works similarly to the ILS lock above except that the localizer lock locks only onto the horizontal sweep of the localizer and not the glide slope. You must take control of the airplane's vertical descent to maintain the proper glide slope angle.

Back Course Lock

The back course lock is similar to the localizer lock, but the back course lock allows the airplane to land from the back course, or reverse end, of the runway. This lock is useful when the weather has changed and the prevailing surface wind now entails a landing from the opposing end of the runway. For maximum safety and efficiency, aircraft need to take off and land into the wind. Thus, if a tailwind is apparent at one end of the runway, operations are usually shifted to the opposite end of the runway to take advantage of a headwind.

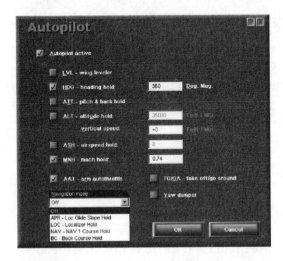

Figure 13.29 *Autopilot menu for FS98.*

Figure 13.30 *The autopilot controls on the 737-400 instrument panel in FS98.*

Figure 13.31 *Autopilot on the 737-400. (Courtesy of Just Planes Videos)*

Flight Director and Flight Management System

Although Flight Simulator does not yet have a flight director or a flight management system (FMS), many third-party developers are hard at work creating add-ons that will duplicate these helpful airborne computer systems. The flight director is similar to an autopilot except that the flight director does not control the aircraft but only displays instructions that a pilot can follow for precision hand flying. The flight director determines the proper heading and attitude for the airplane and presents this information to the pilot through one or more command bars superimposed over the attitude indicator (see Figure 13.32). The command bar tells the pilot which direction to move the controls to follow the flight path that is programmed into the computer.

Flight Director
Bars on display inform pilot
whether to turn, climb or descend.

Figure 13.32 Flight director. *(Courtesy of Just Planes Videos)*

Installed on virtually all air transport aircraft, the flight management system consists of a flight management computer, or FMC, and a control display unit, or CDU. The FMC is an advanced autopilot that allows the pilot to navigate via built-in navigational databases and is tied into the inertial navigation system so that the airplane knows at all times where it is located (see Figure 13.33). The pilot merely enters the waypoints into the CDU or selects from a stored flight path, and the FMC can fly the entire flight, including the entire approach and landing roll, if the airplane is so equipped. Along with navigating the airplane and controlling the autopilot, the FMC is in charge of the aircraft's throttles, and that allows it to control the plane's airspeed to any preset airspeed that the pilot selects. The system is so advanced that it even knows how to fly SIDs (standard instrument departures), STARs (standard instrument approaches), and instrument approach procedures, using all the latest navigational data.

Figure 13.33 Flight management computer on the 737-400. (Courtesy of Just Planes Videos)

Electronic Flight Instrumentation System and Command Flight Path Display

Flight Simulator includes a heads-up display that can display rectangles or other symbols to depict the flight path to an ILS-equipped runway or a VOR station. This is accomplished through the **Aircraft/Navigation/EFIS CFPD** dialog box.

EFIS (electronic flight instrumentation system) and CFPD (command flight path display) are activated by tuning in a VOR/ILS station on the NAV radios and then selecting the type of rectangles, the thickness, and spatial separation. Then you choose whether to lock to an ILS or VOR station. You can also specify the altitude and the VOR radio you want to use in the dialog box. A good demonstration of EFIS/CFPD at work can be found in the San Francisco 28 ILS Approach flight situation, where you must fly through the red rectangles to stay on the glide path down to the runway.

INERTIAL NAVIGATION WITH GPS 2.0

David Drouin's GPS 2.0 unlocks the full potential of Flight Simulator for global navigation. This Windows 95 program is a **.dll** driver that sits inside your **FS98/Modules** directory, but you should run the setup program from the book's CD-ROM to properly install the program. On-line documentation describes all the features of the program, including how to import and edit your own waypoint/airport/navaid database for waypoint navigation around the world.

All the worldwide DAFIF navaids are included in the specially created version of GPS 2.0 that is available on this book's CD-ROM. This GPS navaid database is not the same as the navaid database that is sold with GPS 2.0 elsewhere; it is available only on this book's CD-ROM. The navaid database included with the ordinary version of GPS has only the built-in FS98 navaids. Because this program is an evaluation version, some of its features are disabled until you register it. You can fly anywhere in the world, and have full use of the GPS 2.0 and the DAFIF database, but you cannot edit or add new waypoints, airports, or navaids, nor can you save or load your own waypoint routes to disk until you register the program and pay a $12 registration fee.

GPS 2.0 resides in its own window inside the main FS98 window. It can be dragged, and you can double-click its display readout portion of the window to roll up the key-pad display so that it is invisible (like a rolled-up window shade). To make the keypad visible again, you double-click on the display again.

GPS 2.0 simulates the functionality of an FMC and constantly computes the correct magnetic course, distance, and estimated time of arrival for any waypoint, navaid, or airport in its built-in database. This capability allows you to fly anywhere on Earth without needing to know anything about great circle navigation. All you do is select the navaid, airport, waypoint, or route that you have created and wish to fly, and the program takes over. If you have turned on the alarm feature, it will warn you with an audible tone at a predetermined distance when you are approaching a given navaid, waypoint, or airport along your programmed route. Once you are over the waypoint or navaid, GPS will instruct the autopilot to proceed to the next waypoint or navaid. All this is handled seamlessly so that you can concentrate on other, more interesting tasks.

Unfortunately, Flight Simulator's autopilot cannot be run at a simulation speed greater than 4×, so when you are flying long-haul routes across the oceans, you may wish to turn off GPS 2.0 and the autopilot and resume manual control. This technique will allow you to accelerate time and not get too bored (press **R** followed by + to increase the rate of simulation or **R** and – to decrease the rate of simulation). Accelerating time is not a problem, because the steering indicator will inform you by its horizontal lights whether you have strayed off course. To resume the correct heading, just turn in the direction of the green lights. When you near the next waypoint, you can reduce simulation speed and re-engage GPS 2.0 and the autopilot.

How to Use GPS 2.0

The buttons on the GPS 2.02 front panel shown in Figure 3.36 have the functions listed in Table 13.9.

Table 13.9 GPS 2.0 Controls

BUTTON	FUNCTION
Steering Indicator	The steering indicator tell you to turn right or left to reach the bearing of the active waypoint. Each line equals 5°. This allows you to fly manually without use of the autopilot. To use this feature, load a navaid, airport, or waypoint, either using the **DTE** window, or from a route that you have loaded or created in the **RTE** window. Then fly the airplane toward the waypoint so that the horizontal lights remain centered. When the light moves to the left, it means you should turn left to regain the correct heading.
NAV	There are two pages in NAV mode: **POS** and **WPT**. You can switch from page to page by pressing the **NAV** button.
	The **POS** mode shows you all the information relative to aircraft position. You can see the latitude, longitude, heading, altitude, speed and the steering indicator.
	The **WPT** mode shows you currently selected airport, navaid, or user-created waypoint, its bearing, distance from your present position as well as time, and the steering indicator.
DTO	Opens the **DTO** (direct to) selection window, where you can search the built-in database for a waypoint, navaid, airport, or other user-created waypoints. This database includes all the FS98 airports and all DAFIF worldwide navaids. The cursor points to the **NAV** (for navaids), **APT** (for airports), or **USE** (for user created waypoints) marker, depending on which mode is currently selected. To switch between these three displays, press the ← or → button. To search for a navaid while in **NAV** mode, press the ↓ button so that the cursor drops down a row; then you can press the magnifying glass button to open the Find dialog box. When the cursor is on the second row, you can press ← or → to move alphabetically through the navaids, waypoints, or airports.
RTE	Opens the RTE (route) window, where you can load, save, edit, and view user-created files of custom routes, and waypoints that can be loaded into the program. This feature is fully functional only with the registered version of GPS 2.0. A route is any series of successively numbered waypoints. The GPS will automatically select the next waypoint while operating in Route mode. You can load and save a route, and each route can contain up to 30 waypoints. In Route mode, the following menu commands are available:

Table 13.9 GPS 2.0 *continued*

BUTTON	FUNCTION
	• **EDIT**: Used to add new airports, waypoints and navaids to the current route from the database library. You cannot add a latitude/longitude waypoint with this menu, but must use the database utility to add custom user-created waypoints to the library. Once this is done, you can then use this menu to access those waypoints. The Route Edit window works the same way the DTE window does. You first select the waypoint number on the first row by clicking ← or → . Then you click the ↓ button to move the cursor to the second row, where you choose **NAV** (for navaids), **APT** (for airports), or **USE** (for user-created waypoints) with ← or →. Next, move to the third row with ↓, and choose a waypoint with ← or →, or through the Find dialog box with the magnifying glass button.
	• **VIEW:** Allows you to see the route destination and departure points.
	• **SAVE:** Allows you to save your route to disk as a ***.rte** file.
	• **LOAD:** Allows you to load a ***.rte** file into GPS. Use this to load a trip that you have previously created as a route, and you can fly it again and again, or share it with others.
INF	Opens the Information window, where you can view data on the currently selected waypoint, airport, or navaid. If an airport is selected, you will see the name, identifier, altitude, tower frequency, ATIS frequency, magnetic variation, and latitude/longitude. If you click once again on the **INF** button, you'll see a second page of airport data containing runway numbers, runway surface type, runway length, ILS runway, and frequency numbers. When a navaid is selected, you'll see data on the latitude/longitude, frequency, and VOR/NDB type, in addition to the name.
ALR	Opens the Alarm window, where you can specify the warning distance to the selected waypoint/navaid/airport. When on, it will sound a gentle chime to alert you to the fact that you are approaching the waypoint, navaid, or airport. The alarm uses DirectPlay sound.
AUT	Turns the autopilot on or off and takes over control of the airplane, flying it toward the currently selected waypoint, airport, or navaid. This function is automatically disengaged when you reach the active waypoint. If you're in route mode this function is disengaged only when you reach the last one.

Table 13.9 GPS 2.0 *continued*

BUTTON	FUNCTION
CLR	Clears the current entry.
ENT	Enters the current selection into the current waypoint. For example, once you have selected a VOR/airport/waypoint from the DTO menu, you will enter it into the GPS computer by pressing the "**ENT** button" key. If you then click the **NAV** or **INF** button, you will see data on the latest waypoint you just entered.
← Left Cursor Arrow or → Right Cursor Arrow (on GPS display)	Cycles the selection from the current display backward and forwards, and when in Route mode, it selects previous or next waypoint. It also moves you to the next item in the stored data base. In **DTO** mode, it toggles between the display of **USE**, **APF**, and **NAV**. The **USE** option is used for user-created waypoints (Statue of Liberty, Grand Canyon, etc.), **APF** are airport waypoints, and **NAV** are VOR/NDB waypoints.
↑ Up Cursor Arrow & ↓ Down Cursor Arrow (on GPS display)	Move the cursor up or down on the GPS display so that you can select a different menu item.
Magnifying Glass button (on GPS display)	When in DTO mode, clicking any of the APT or NAV menu items will bring you to submenus where you can move the cursor down and then press the magnifying glass button to access the Find dialog box. Once in the Find dialog box, you can type in the keyword identifier for the airport, navaid, or waypoint and you will instantly jump to the database location of the object in question. Many navaids or waypoints have similar names around the world, you may have to scroll forward or backward to find the correct navaid, airport, or waypoint.

How to Load a Navaid from the Built-In GPS Database

It's easy to add any navaid into GPS 2 and then have the program fly your airplane directly toward the navaid. To load a navaid, follow these steps:

1. Click the **DTO** button.
2. Click the **Right Cursor** until you see **NAV** displayed.
3. Click the **Down Cursor** to select the displayed VOR station.
4. Click the magnifying glass button on the GPS display to bring up the Find dialog box.

5. Type in the identifier for the VOR you are looking for. For example, if you want the San Francisco VOR, you would type **SFO**. If you don't know the identifier for the VOR, look it up in the Excel navaid database on the CD-ROM.

6. Click **OK**, and the database search engine will find the first matching entry. Because many navaids around the world have similar identifiers (they are not unique), you may have to scroll through the listings to find the right one. (Click the → or the ← button to scroll through the listings.)

7. Once you find the navaid you are interested in, click the **ENT** button. GPS will enter it as your next waypoint.

8. When you return to the NAV display (click the **NAV** button), you will see the bearing, distance, and other data for the navaid you just loaded. To have GPS guide the aircraft to this navaid, click the **AUT** button, and the airplane will immediately turn toward the navaid as the autopilot takes over control.

You can also use this feature of the program to instantly scan all the world's navaids or even ILS stations and bring up frequency information. For example, suppose you are flying near San Francisco and you know that there is a VOR called SFO, but you don't know its frequency. Perform steps 1–7 and then click the **INF** button. You'll see that the frequency is 118.50 MHz.

How to Load an Airport

To fly toward any airport in the world, load the airport as if it were a navaid waypoint. Follow these steps:

1. Click the **DTO** button.

2. Click the → button until you see **APT** displayed.

3. Click the ↓ to select the displayed airport that is listed just below **APT**.

4. Click the magnifying glass button on the GPS display to bring up the Find dialog box.

5. Type in the identifier for the airport you are looking for. For example, if you want San Francisco International, you would type in **KSFO**. If you don't know the identifier for the airport, look it up in the Excel airport database on the CD-ROM.

6. Click **OK**, and the database search engine will find the first matching entry. If you don't find the entry, be sure that the airport doesn't have a different identifier from that shown in the CD-ROM database. It would be best to check the FS98 airport directory when this happens. As with the navaids, to scroll through the airport listings, click the → or the ←.

7. Once you find the airport you are interested in, click the **ENT** button. GPS will enter it as your next waypoint.

8. To have the autopilot take over and fly you toward the airport, click the **AUT** button.

Many American airports are prefixed with the letter *K,* as in KSFO for San Francisco, KBOS for Boston, KLAX for Los Angeles, and so on. Some of the listings in the Appendix B Airport listings on the CD-ROM do not show this prefix, so if you can't find the airport that you are looking for in GPS 2.0, try adding a *K* before the airport identifier. Alaskan and Hawaiian airports are prefixed with *P.*

How to Add Your Own Waypoints (Registered Version Only)

You can add new waypoints only to the registered version of GPS 2.0. To add custom waypoints, follow these steps:

1. Using the Windows 95 taskbar, go to **Start/Programs/GPS 2/GPS Database Utility.** When the Database Utility program opens, as illustrated in Figure 13.34, click the button for **Users wpts.**

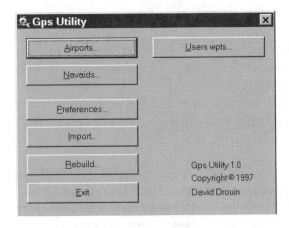

Figure 13.34 *GPS 2.0 Database Utility. Use this program to add, subtract, import, edit, or find any navaid, airport, or user-created waypoint. This utility will update the master database from which GPS 2.0 extracts all its information. Note that you cannot add custom waypoints directly into the GPS window in FS98. You must instead use the Database Utility to update the master database.*

2. The Users Waypoints dialog box will open, as shown in Figure 13.35. You can find existing waypoints, add new ones, and edit existing ones, but you should make sure to click the **Save** button after every change, or else the changes will not be recorded.

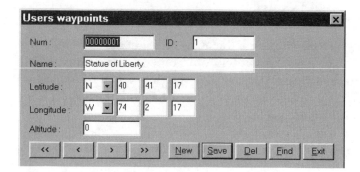

Figure 13.35 *GPS 2.0 Database Utility dialog box for creating custom waypoints.*

3. Return to Flight Simulator and click the **DTO** button. The new waypoint will be listed under the **USE** display for the DTO mode (click the ← or → button to cycle through to the **USE** mode).

4. You'll still have to find, and display the new waypoint. To do this, move the cursor to the second row by clicking ↓ and then either do a search (press the magnifying glass button) or cycle through the user waypoints by clicking ← or →.

You can use the same method to add new navaids and airports, and you can add them to your waypoint route files by using the **RTE** button.

For more information on how to load custom waypoint files and save your waypoint routes to disk, read the on-line documentation.

How to Create Your Own Routes

Whenever you want to use more than one waypoint, you must use **RTE**, or Route mode, which will allow you to store as many as 30 waypoints that you can extract from the master database. Note that you cannot type in a latitude or longitude, nor can you directly enter a new waypoint through the GPS 2.0 on-screen display. To do that, you must use the Database Utility program, which is separate from GPS 2.0.

The GPS program will load and save a route file from disk, and it will automatically select the next waypoint while operating in Route mode. You cannot save or use route files in the unregistered version of GPS, although you can create your own routes for temporary use. The routes that you create in the unregistered version will be lost when you exit the program.

To create your own route, with multiple waypoints, follow these steps:

1. Click the **RTE** button.
2. From the Route Menu window, move the cursor with the ↓ or ↑ button and select **EDIT** (the > cursor will rest on your selected menu item).

3. Click the **ENT** button to enter this Route Edit selection.
4. Now you are in the Route Edit window, as shown in Figure 13.36. Click the ← or → button to select the waypoint number you wish to edit (such as **01**, **02**, **03**, and so on).

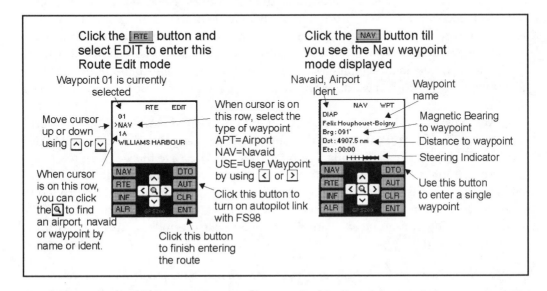

Figure 13.36 *The Route Edit window (select* **RTE** *and then* **EDIT**) *on the GPS 2.02 display (on left). This window allows you to add new waypoints, airports, or navaids to your selected route. The NAV window (on right) displays the currently selected waypoint.*

5. Click the ↓ button to move the cursor to the second row.
6. Now you must decide whether you wish to add a **NAV** (navaid), **APT** (airport), or **USE** (user-created waypoint). Select the appropriate mode with the ← or → button.
7. Click the ↓ button to move the cursor to the third row.
8. If you have entered a user-created waypoint with the Database Utility, select that waypoint using the ← or → button; otherwise, perform a search using the magnifying glass button. The same thing would apply with navaids or airports. You can search for a waypoint, navaid, or airport only while the cursor is on the third row.
9. Once you have selected the waypoint, navaid, or airport from step 8, click the ↑ button twice to return to the top row. Now click the → button to access the next waypoint number (such as **02, 03, 04,** and so on).
10. Repeat steps 5 through 9 for each additional waypoint you wish to add to the route. As many as 30 waypoints are allowed per route. When you are finished adding waypoints, proceed to the next step.

11. Click the **ENT** button, and you will be returned to the Route Edit window. To save the route to disk, select **SAVE** and click the **ENT** button to bring up the Save dialog box.

To activate the route you just created, click the **NAV** button twice so that the **WPT** light comes on. You can then cycle through the waypoints with the ← or → button and then start the autopilot link by clicking **AUT**. Once the route is activated, the airplane will turn to the waypoint currently selected and fly the route as you have stored it. During the flight, if you decide to change waypoints you can click the ← or → button and the currently active airport, navaid, or waypoint will change (you must be in **NAV WPT** mode).

If you have saved the route to disk (something you can do only with the registered version of GPS 2.0), you can load it into the program at any time by clicking **RTE** followed by **LOAD**. In the dialog box that opens, choose the ***.rte** file you wish to open.

If you choose to fly manually, the steering indicator is a useful guide to help keep you on course to the selected waypoint. It will tell you whether you need to turn left or right to stay on course. This is also useful, because if you prefer to fly with the autopilot off, it means you can accelerate simulator speed past the maximum of 4× with the autopilot engaged.

 At the time this book went to press, there was a bug in the program that prevented you from regaining full control over the ailerons when you shut off the **AUT** (autopilot) function from the GPS 2.0 display. The workaround is to press the **Z** key and then press again
N O T E to shut off the autopilot. The ailerons should return to normal.

GPS Tips

If you find that the GPS display is hard to read, you might want to run FS98 at a lower resolution, since the display will then occupy a larger portion of your window. However, if all that bothers you is the color settings, you can cycle the GPS display through various background and text color choices until you find one that you like best.

Changing the GPS Display's Color Settings

You can only see the changes you make to the GPS color settings while in "NAV" mode. Therefore, first click the **NAV** button on the GPS display, then:

- To change the background color press **Shift B**
- To change the text color, press **Shift T**

Minimizing the GPS Display
If you want to minimize the GPS window, double click on the GPS readout and the keypad portion of the display will vanish. Double click again to make the keypad reappear.

Showing/Hiding the GPS Display:
To make the entire display disappear off screen press **Shift G.** Press **Shift G** once again to bring back the display.

Frequently Asked Questions About GPS 2.0

The following FAQ was put together by David Drouin to answer common questions people might have about the program. Be sure to read this before sending Drouin a request for technical support.

Q. Which version of Flight Simulator is supported by GPS 2.0?

A. Only FSW95 and FS98 are supported by GPS 2.0. Sorry, FS5.1 is not supported.

Q. Which panels are compatible with GPS 2.0?

A. All panels are compatible with GPS 2.0.

Q. The font used by the GPS 2.0 program is too small for my eyes. Is there some way to enlarge the font?

A. GPS 2.0 uses the original Windows "small font," but unfortunately some programs overwrite this font with a smaller one. The only way to resolve this problem is to re-install Windows 95 or try to get the file **SMALLE.FON** from another computer that has the correct font installed.

Q. When I start Flight Simulator, I can't see the GPS 2.0 window. How can I restore it to the screen?

A. There are two answers to this question:

- When you ran the Setup program, did you give the correct directory of your FSW95 or FS98? For example, you may have used **C:\FS6** and not **C:\FS6\MYU-TIL\GPS**.
- If you have switched from 800 × 600 or higher to 640 × 480, perhaps the GPS window is on the bottom or edge of the screen and is not visible. Run the GPS Database Utility program from the **Start/Programs/GPS 2.0/GPS Database Utility** menu on the taskbar. Then click **Preferences**, and, in the dialog box that opens, reset the X and Y positions of the GPS to zero. This will reset the position of the window to a visible portion of the screen.

Q. I configured the alarm correctly, but I can't hear the sound of the GPS alarm; what am I doing wrong?

A. If you don't hear the sound of FSW95 or FS98, you can't hear the sound of the alarm. DirectX 3.0 or higher must be installed.

Q. I get many errors from the GPS database when I start Flight Simulator. What can I do to fix this?

A. Quit Flight Simulator, run the GPS Database Utility, and press the **Rebuild** button.

Q. Are the GPS 1.x database files compatible with GPS 2.0?

A. No, GPS 2.0 uses xBase file formats with FoxPro indexes. GPS 1.x used an ASCII file format.

Q. What are the maximum number of waypoints allowed in the GPS 2.0 database?

A. There are no limits. In fact, the GPS database is limited only by your free hard disk space.

Q. Do I need to download **FSASMLIB.DLL** or **FS6IPC.DLL** to get the GPS 2.0 program to work?

A. No. GPS doesn't use these DLLs. Instead, GPS 2.0 communicates directly with Flight Simulator.

Registering GPS 2.0

You are free to evaluate GPS 2.0 for as long as you like, but you should know that it is not free software, and adding new waypoints and editing the master database have been disabled. However, you can fly to any airport around the world, use any of the 9,100+ DAFIF navaids built into the program, and fully explore all the features of the program. At the beginning of each session, a splash window will appear asking you whether you want to register the program. If, after experimenting with the program, you decide that you want to register it and obtain full use of the master database, you must fill out the registration notice and pay a $12 registration fee. You will then be issued a password that will unlock the full functionality of the program. Technical support is available at no charge after you register the program.

You can order by check and credit card only. Send your order by Email to sw3david@quebectel.com, or by fax to 1-418-228-5716, or by postal mail to David Drouin, 1360, 130e rue App #3, St-Georges, Quebec, Canada G5Y 7Y6.

Uninstalling GPS 2.0

Once you install GPS 2.0, it will always appear on-screen when you start Flight Simulator. If you don't want the program to start up, you can drag **GPS.dll** from the **/Modules** directory. The program will vanish the next time you start Flight Simulator. If you put it back, the program will return.

If you don't want GPS 2.0 on your system at all after installing it, go to the taskbar and select **Start/Programs/GPS 2.0/Uninstall GPS 2.0** and run the uninstall program. Sometimes this is not enough, as I discovered in the beta of GPS 2.0 when I inadvertently crashed the program and could not get it to reappear even after restarting FS98. When I ran the uninstall program and reinstalled GPS 2, it stubbornly refused to work. I was baffled until I realized that some of the program settings were being stored in the Windows 95 registry. When I removed the offending registry items, all was well and I successfully ran the setup and got the program running again. If you experience this problem, go into the Windows 95 registry to delete the key reference to **HKEY_LOCAL_MACHINE\SOFTWARE\QUEBEC VIRTUAL PILOTS**. Run the Regedit program in the **Start/Run** dialog box of the taskbar. Once the registry opens, go into the **HKEY_LOCAL_MACHINE** folder and then to the **SOFTWARE** folder, and then delete the **QUEBEC VIRTUAL PILOTS** folder entirely.

If for some reason GPS 2.0 starts misbehaving and you can't get it to work properly, the best thing is to rebuild the database from the Database Utility program. If the program still doesn't work, more drastic measures are necessary. Uninstall the program and reinstall it. If it then works normally, all is well, but if it does not, you will have to go into the registry and delete the **QUEBEC VIRTUAL PILOTS** folder as previously described.

GPS, LORAN C, AND OMEGA

Other land-based navigation systems that are not modeled in FS98 include LORAN C, Omega, and GPS.

LORAN covers most coastal regions of the northern Pacific and Atlantic oceans, including the Mediterranean. At night, skywaves from LORAN can be received as far as 2,300 miles over much of the Northern hemisphere except for the Indian Ocean region. By day, it extends only 1,200 miles from shore. LORAN works by having a master station transmit a 100 kHz pulse, which then triggers slave stations located elsewhere to counter with a reply pulse. By comparing the unique time differences between the master and slave pulses, a LORAN C–equipped airplane can plot a line of position and thereby fix its coordinates.

Even though LORAN was a great improvement over VOR/NDB for long-range navigation, it was not sufficient for worldwide coverage. In 1947 the U.S. Navy began work on a replacement system that offered worldwide coverage, and this project was completed in 1960 with the full-scale deployment of Omega. Omega consists of a chain of eight radio transmitters spaced 5,000 to 6,000 miles apart that transmit on the very low frequency band, operating between 10 and 14 kHz. At these very low frequencies, radio waves propagate very long distances, especially with skywaves bouncing off the ionosphere at night. Omega-equipped ships and aircraft can locate their position within 1 nm by day, and 2 nm by night, anywhere in the world.

GPS, which was originally called the Navstar Global Positioning System, is the new satellite-based navigation system that will eventually replace all land-based navigation systems. Twenty-four satellites, orbiting at 10,900 nm, are distributed into three orbital planes, each containing eight satellites. When a GPS receiver is within sight of at least three satellites, a precise latitude/longitude fix can be made. A fourth satellite is needed for fixing altitude and speed. Best accuracy of a fix, which is currently reserved for the U.S. military only, approaches 18 meters (60 ft) in latitude/longitude and 28 meters (92 ft) in altitude. Commercial receivers receive a purposely degraded signal that provides an accuracy of about 100 meters (330 ft) for latitude/longitude, and 156 meters (514 ft) in altitude. With the advent of differential GPS, which adds a ground-based transmitter to supplement the satellite signals, even greater accuracy of 4 to 20 meters is possible.

TIP

You can simulate GPS by pressing **Shift Z** to display your latitude/longitude coordinates.

TRANS-OCEANIC TRIP PLANNING

There's a joke that people who fly four-engine airplanes do so only because they don't make a five-engine airplane. Although there was some truth in this statement many years ago, modern engines are so reliable that they can be trusted to carry passengers on airplanes equipped with only two engines. Because of the extra danger involved, however, special rules, called ETOPS, have been developed to ensure that passenger safety is not compromised.

ETOPS

North Atlantic tracks are established each morning and move according to winds to optimize flight times. All flights originating in the United States going to Europe fly at night, and those originating in Europe going to the United States fly by day. During the day, the Europeans manage the tracks, and at night the Canadians take over.

Winds move from west to east over the North Atlantic. Shannon, Ireland, is the air traffic control center for the European side of the Atlantic, and Gandor, Canada, is the ATC for the western side of the Atlantic. Because there is no radar, the entire network must be very closely controlled. Each airplane entering and exiting a block along the track must report to ATC before continuing. The tracks are 60 miles apart, but many aircraft may be stacked at different altitudes along a selected track. It is important, therefore, not to descend or ascend from your assigned corridor. Also, you are usually assigned a Mach speed, which you must maintain so that aircraft don't bump into you from behind and so that you don't bump into aircraft ahead. This means that if you are assigned a speed of Mach 0.8, which is about 8 miles per minute, you must turn the autopilot Mach hold to **0.8** for the duration of the flight.

Some pilots joke that ETOPS stands for "engines turning or passengers swimming," but it really means extended twin range (time) operation with two-engine airplanes.

Twin-engine airplanes flying over the Atlantic follow different techniques from those followed by three- and four-engine aircraft. Normally, a twin-engine aircraft must always be within one hour's flying distance of a suitable diversion field along its flight path in the event of engine emergency. However, special aircraft that have been approved for ETOPS are allowed to fly 120 minutes, and some even 180 minutes, from a suitable diversion airport. The 180-minute ETOPS rule allows Hawaii-bound aircraft from California to make the trip, because the entire journey lasts 6 hours and if an emergency occurs at the halfway point, the airplane should be able to fly to its destination or turn back. The Boeing 767 and 777 are qualified for 180-minute ETOPS, enabling them to make the 6-hour nonstop flight between the West Coast and Hawaii. With 120-minute ETOPS, there is a hole over the North Atlantic that you cannot fly because the nearest airport would exceed 2 hour's flying distance, so you must carefully plot your route with this in mind.

ETOPS-qualified aircraft must have tremendous redundancy of systems. There are usually four electric generators and several INS, and the engines must be flight-proven for extremely low failure rates.

It may come as a surprise to you, but the loss of an engine is not the most feared event during an ETOPS flight over water. Loss of cabin pressurization is a much more serious event, because without cabin pressure the airplane must fly at 10,000 ft to allow the passengers to breathe normally. At this altitude, fuel burn is considerably greater. So on an ETOPS flight, the point on the map of the worst-case cabin pressure loss is plotted as the critical fuel point. If only the engine fails, the airplane can continue flying at altitude to a suitable diversionary airfield, and there is no problem with running out of fuel. Such is not the case when the airplane must fly at 10,000 ft.

Believe it or not, ETOPS is also a requirement for aircraft flying over Africa. Many airports close at night, and if an emergency develops on a twin-engine airplane it must have the range to reach a diversionary airport.

14

Great Circle Navigation

By Ed Williams

With contributions by Nick Dargahi and David Wishnia

> Travelers, like poets, are mostly an angry race.
>
> Sir Richard Burton, "Narrative of a Trip to Harar,"
> Royal Geographical Society Journal (1855).

Absent other considerations, an aviator would normally plan the shortest possible route between the point of departure and the destination. However, route deviations for air traffic control requirements, special arrival or departure procedures, navaid availability, airspace restrictions, and weather avoidance problems are commonplace. The ideal of a minimum distance routing is typically attained only on segments that overlie oceans or sparsely settled areas.

 The shortest distance between two points is a straight line, but to travel between London and Tokyo in a straight line you would have to dig a substantial tunnel through the Earth! The shortest distance—following the surface of the Earth—between London and Tokyo would lie vertically above this hypothetical tunnel and is called the *great circle route*. If you imagine slicing the Earth in half with a plane through London and Tokyo, the great circle route would lie along the edge of the cut.

If you plot a great circle route on an aeronautical or other chart, it won't necessarily appear to be straight. It isn't possible to map the Earth's surface onto a flat chart without distortion. On a chart covering a small area—say, a few hundred miles in radius—this distortion may not be obvious or significant. On a global scale, however, it is very significant, and the choice of map projection determines what is compromised. Conformal projections, for example, preserve angles and therefore the shapes of the areas they represent, at the cost of a distance scale that varies across the chart. Most shorter-range aviation navigation charts use the Lambert conformal conic projection. Because they are conformal, they allow courses to be measured accurately. Over the range of the charts, the scale changes are small, so distances can be measured with adequate accuracy. However, on such charts neither great circles nor rhumb lines (lines of constant true course) are straight.

For long-range flights, especially trans-polar ones, charts using the gnomonic projection are used to plot routes, because these charts have the virtue that great circles appear as straight lines (see Figure 14.1). Latitude and longitude coordinates along the route can then be picked from the long-range planning chart and transferred to the shorter-range navigation charts.

The familiar Mercator charts, in which the polar regions are greatly expanded, have the property that rhumb lines are straight. However, great circles are curved, as shown in Figure 14.2.

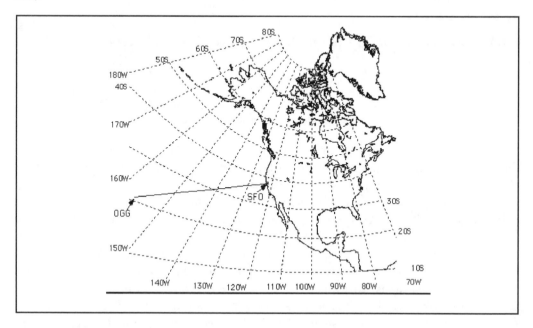

Figure 14.1 *The great circle route from San Francisco to Kahalui, Maui, is shown on a chart in oblique*

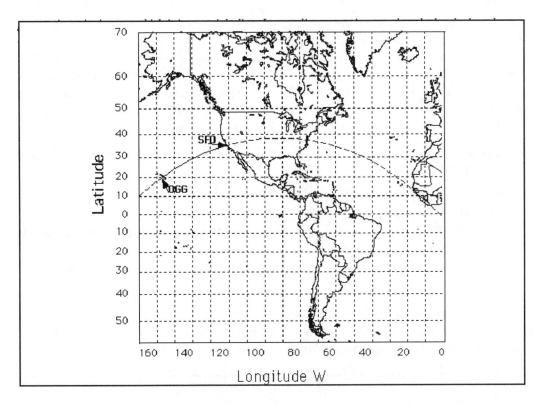

Figure 14.2 *The great circle route through San Francisco, California (SFO) and Kahalui, Maui (OGG), shown on a Mercator chart. In this projection, lines of constant course (rhumb lines) are straight lines, but great circles are curved.*

Before we proceed to the formulas used in great circle navigation, it is helpful to learn something about spherical trigonometry, because all the equations use terrestrial triangles. A *terrestrial triangle* is a spherical triangle that has as its vertices any two points and the north or south pole.

THE SOLUTION OF RIGHT SPHERICAL TRIANGLES

A *spherical* triangle is formed by the intersection of three great circles and consists of the angles and area bounded by the three arcs of the great circles. Like a plane triangle, a spherical triangle is composed of six parts: three sides and three angles. Ordinarily, *A*, *B*, and *C* are used to denote the interior angles, and *a*, *b*, and *c* are used to denote the sides. In spherical trigonometry problems, all the angles and sides are quoted in angular measurements, and the dimensions of the sides are quoted in terms of the angle that they subtend at the interior of the sphere.

Unlike plane triangles, spherical triangles can have sides or angles greater than 180° and can have interior angles that sum to as much as 540°. A spherical triangle having a single right angle of 90° is called a *right spherical* triangle. One with two right angles is said to be *birectangular*, and one with three right angles is called *trirectangular*.

The following rules hold true for all spherical triangles:

1. The sum of any two sides is greater than the third side, and their difference is less than the third side.

2. If two sides are equal, the angles opposite are equal.

3. If two angles are equal, the sides opposite are equal.

4. If two sides are unequal, the angles opposite are unequal, and the greater side is opposite the greater angle.

5. If two angles are unequal, the sides opposite are unequal, and the greater side is opposite the greater angle.

Figure 14.3 represents a spherical triangle *ABC* with the right angle at *C* and with sides *a* and *b* each less than 90°. Although we won't prove it here, the following ten formulas for the solution of right spherical triangles can be easily derived from geometry.

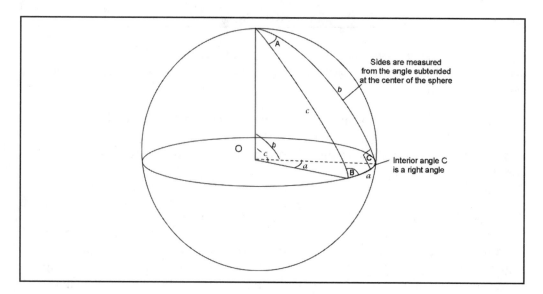

Figure 14.3 *Right spherical triangle.*

$$
\begin{array}{lll}
(1) & \sin a = \sin c \sin A & (6) \quad \sin b = \sin c \sin B \\
(2) & \tan a = \sin b \tan A & (7) \quad \tan b = \sin a \tan B \\
(3) & \tan a = \tan c \cos B & (8) \quad \tan b = \tan c \cos A \\
(4) & \cos c = \cos a \cos b & (9) \quad \cos c = \cot A \cot B \\
(5) & \cos A = \cos a \sin B & (10) \quad \cos B = \cos b \sin A
\end{array}
\qquad (14.1)
$$

Napier's Rules

The ten formulas in Equation 14.1 are easy to remembered if you use a clever trick devised by Napier. In the schematic diagram of Figure 14.4, the angle A is replaced by the symbol *co-A*, meaning complement of A, and similarly for the angle B (called *co-B*) and side c (called *co-c*). Although this should be obvious, *co-B* does not mean *co* minus B. Note that the left side of the diagram does not represent a triangle but is merely a mnemonic device for the Napier method. Also, the angle C is omitted.

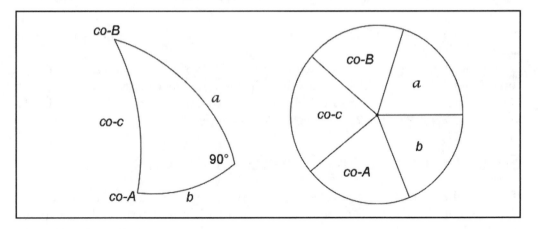

Figure 14.4 Napier Schematic

If you arrange the five parts in a circle, as depicted in the right side of the diagram, you have what are known as the *circular parts*. If you then take any part and call it the *middle part*, the two parts next to it are called the *adjacent parts*, and the other two are called the *opposite parts*. For example, if a is the middle part, then *co-B* and b are the adjacent parts, and *co-c* and *co-A* are the opposite parts.

Napier's two rules for the diagram are as follows:

1. The sine of any middle part is equal to the product of the tangents of the adjacent parts.
2. The sine of any middle part is equal to the product of the cosines of the opposite parts.

As an example, let's apply Napier's rules and derive Formula 7 and Formula 1 of the ten formulas in Equation 14.1. We will solve for the angle a. Because it is the middle part, the adjacent parts from Figure 14.4 are $Co\text{-}B$ and b. Using Napier's rule 1, we have the following:

$$\sin a = \tan b \tan(co\text{-}B) = \tan b \cot B \qquad (14.2)$$

For Equation 14.2, $co\text{-}B$ is the complement of B $(90° - B)$, and using the trigonometric identity $\tan(90°\text{-}\theta) = \cot(\theta)$, the function $\tan(co\text{-}B) = \cot(B)$. If we now rearrange terms, we have the following:

$$\tan b = \frac{\sin a}{\cot B} = \sin a \tan B \qquad (14.3)$$

You can see that we have established Formula 7, because $\tan(B) = 1/\cot(B)$.

Using Napier's rule 2, we have the following:

$$\sin a = \cos(co\text{-}c)\cos(co\text{-}A) = \sin c \sin A \qquad (14.4)$$

because $\cos(co\text{-}c) = \cos(90°\text{-}c) = \sin(c)$ and $\cos(co\text{-}A) = \cos(90° \text{-}A) = \sin(A)$. This is the same as Formula 1.

By applying Napier's rules to each of the five parts of the diagram in Figure 14.4, you can obtain all ten of the formulas. To help you remember the two rules, for rule 1 observe that the vowel *i* occurs in *sine* and *middle*, whereas the vowel *a* appears in *tangents* and *adjacent*. For rule 2, the vowel *o* appears in *cosines* and *opposite*.

SOLUTION OF OBLIQUE SPHERICAL TRIANGLES

If none of the angles in a spherical triangle is a right angle, the triangle is oblique. This is the kind of triangle that is most encountered in navigation. To solve oblique spherical triangles, we need to develop certain formulas analogous to Napier's rules and the formulas for the right spherical triangle. The next section discusses the law of sines and cosines for oblique spherical triangles.

LAW OF SINES AND COSINES FOR SPHERICAL TRIANGLES

Napier's rules and related formulas, introduced previously, relate the sides and angles of a right spherical triangle. Figure 14.5 shows an oblique spherical triangle. The internal angles are denoted A, B, and C and the lengths of the opposite sides are called a, b, and c, respectively. What is meant by the "length" of the side is the angle it subtends at the center of the sphere. The following relations then hold for any spherical triangle.

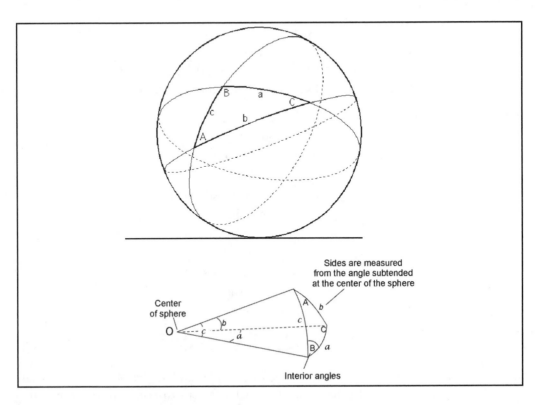

Figure 14.5 *Oblique spherical triangle* ABC. A, B, *and* C *are the angles between the great circular arcs.* *The "sides"* a, b, *and* c *(opposite* A, B, *and* C, *respectively) are the angles subtended by the arcs at the center of the sphere.*

$$\frac{\sin a}{\sin A} = \frac{\sin b}{\sin B} = \frac{\sin c}{\sin C} \tag{14.5}$$

This means that the sines of the sides of a spherical triangle and the sines of the corresponding opposite angles are in proportion. Equation 14.5 is called the Law of Sines.

$$\cos a = \cos b \cos c + \sin b \sin c \cos A \tag{14.6}$$
$$\cos b = \cos c \cos a + \sin c \sin a \cos B$$
$$\cos c = \cos a \cos b + \sin a \sin b \cos C$$

Notice that in Equation 14.6, if any one of *A*, *B*, or *C* is a right angle, the right side of the term drops out (because $\cos(90°)=0$), and it reduces to one of the ten Napier-derived formulas for right spherical triangles given in Equation 14.1.

$$\cos A = -\cos B \cos C + \sin B \sin C \cos a \qquad (14.7)$$
$$\cos B = -\cos C \cos A + \sin C \sin A \cos b$$
$$\cos C = -\cos A \cos B + \sin A \sin B \cos c$$

Equation 14.6 is called the Law of Cosines for Sides, and Equation 14.7 is called the Law of Cosines for Angles.

$$\tan A = \frac{\sin B \sin a}{\sin c \cos a - \cos B \cos c \sin a} \qquad (14.8)$$

$$\tan B = \frac{\sin C \sin b}{\sin a \cos b - \cos C \cos a \sin b}$$

$$\tan C = \frac{\sin A \sin c}{\sin b \cos c - \cos A \cos b \sin c}$$

$$\tan a = \frac{\sin b \sin A}{\sin C \cos A + \cos b \cos C \sin A}$$

$$\tan b = \frac{\sin c \sin B}{\sin A \cos B + \cos c \cos A \sin B}$$

$$\tan c = \frac{\sin a \sin C}{\sin B \cos C + \cos a \cos B \sin C}$$

In general, it is sufficient to know any three of the sides and angles of a spherical triangle—that is, any three of the six quantities $\{A,B,C,a,b,c\}$—to compute the remaining (three) sides and angles.

Radians and Degrees

In the preceding formulas, all the quantities are measured in radians. A radian, by definition, is the angle subtended by a circular arc of unit length at unit radius. It is slightly more than $57°$. The precise conversion can be seen by considering a complete circle of unit radius. Its circumference is 2π, and the full circular angle is $360°$. Thus,

$$2\pi \text{ radians} = 360° \qquad (14.9)$$

Here, pi (π) is the famous constant $3.1415926535\ldots$. (If your programming language doesn't have pi predefined, you can use $\pi = 4 \times \arctan(1.)$ to define it to machine accuracy.)

We can thus convert latitudes, longitudes, and other angles given in degrees into radians, for use in Napier's rules, by using this formula:

$$\text{Angle\_rad} = \left(\pi/180\right) \times \text{Angle\_deg} \qquad (14.10)$$

In the reverse direction, we will use the following:

$$\text{Angle\_deg} = \left(180/\pi\right) \times \text{Angle\_rad} \tag{14.11}$$

A further possible complication is that the angles are often quoted not in degrees and decimal fractions of a degree but instead in terms of degrees, minutes, and seconds. By definition, one degree is 60 minutes, and one minute contains 60 seconds. To convert to decimal form, we use the following:

$$\text{Deg\_dec} = \text{Deg} + (\text{Min} + \text{Sec}/60)/60 \tag{14.12}$$

For example, the latitude of the San Francisco airport, SFO, is 37° 37' 08.407" N. In decimal degrees, this is $37 + (37 + 8.407/60)/60 = 37.6190019$N, which in turn is $37.6190019 \times (\pi/180) = 0.656575445$ radians.

In the Napier formulas, the triangle sides are also measured in radians—the angles subtended by the great circular arcs at the center of the sphere. The arc lengths are thus for a unit radius sphere. To get the arc length along the Earth's surface, we multiply the arc length in radians by the radius of the Earth, R. Thus:

$$\text{Arc\_length} = R * \text{Arc\_length\_rad} \tag{14.13}$$

One way of remembering the radius of the Earth is to recall that one nautical mile was originally defined as the length of one minute of latitude, and 60 nm is one degree of latitude. Note that this correspondence does not hold true for longitudes except along the great circle of the equator. These relationships are summarized as follows:

$$60 \text{ nm} = 1° = \pi/180 \text{ radians} = 0.017453292519 \text{ radians}$$
$$1 \text{ nm} = 1' = \pi/\left(180 \times 60\right) \text{ radians} = 0.00029088820866 \text{ radians}$$
$$1 \text{ radian} = 180/\pi \text{ deg} = 57.29577951°$$
$$6.283185307 \text{ radians} = 2 \times \pi \text{ radians} = 360°$$
$$2 \times \pi \times R = 360° \times 60 \text{ nm}/\text{deg} = 21{,}600 \text{ nm (Circumference of Earth)}$$
$$R = 21{,}600/\left(2 \times \pi\right) = 3437.74677 \text{ nm (Radius of Earth)}$$

One radian of arc is therefore $180/\pi$ degrees or $60 \times 180/\pi$ minutes. We know there are 360 degrees around the Earth with 60 nm/degree; this means that the Earth has a circumference of 21,600 nm ($360° \times 60 = 21{,}600$ nm). Because the circumference of any circle or sphere is $2 \times \pi \times R$, where R is the radius, we can calculate the radius of the Earth from this:

$$R = \text{circumference}/2\pi = 21{,}600 \text{ nm}/2\pi = 3{,}437.75 \text{ nm}$$

or alternatively:

$$R = 60 \times 180/\pi = 3{,}437.75 \text{ nm}$$

Because nautical miles are the preferred means of measuring distance for aeronautical and marine navigation, we will use the following conversion of arc length to nautical miles throughout this chapter:

$$\text{Arc\_length\_nm} = (60 \times 180/\pi \times \text{Arc\_length\_rad}) \qquad (14.14)$$

To convert nautical miles to arc length, use this formula:

$$\text{Arc\_length\_rad} = \left(\pi/\left(60 \times 180\right)\right) \times \text{Arc\_length\_nm} \qquad (14.15)$$

One last convention: in the navigation formulas to follow, south latitudes and east longitudes are negative, and north latitudes and west longitudes are positive.

GREAT CIRCLE DISTANCE BETWEEN POINTS

The first question we address is the calculation of the great circle distance between two points, given their latitude and longitude locations. Suppose that the latitude and longitude of the two points are $\{lat_1, lon_1\}$ and $\{lat_2, lon_2\}$ respectively. Applying Napier's rules to the terrestrial triangle connecting the points 1 and 2 and the north pole, we find that the distance, d is given by the following:

$$d_{\text{radians}} = \arccos\left[\sin lat_1 \sin lat_2 + \cos lat_1 \cos lat_2 \cos\left(lon_1 - lon_2\right)\right] \qquad (14.16)$$

The function acos or arccos is the inverse- or arc-cosine function. All quantities are in radians.

Proof of the Great Circle Distance Formula

This formula can easily be derived from the law of cosines for sides in Equation 14.6. To see how this is done, consider that $\cos(90°\text{-}\theta) = \sin(\theta)$, and $\sin(90°\text{-}\theta) = \cos(\theta)$, which are trigonometric identities. Also, the longitude difference between any two points $(lon_1\text{-}lon_2)$ is equivalent to the polar angle A of the interior terrestrial triangle, as shown in Figure 14.6. The latitude lat_1 and lat_2 variables cannot be used directly in Equation 14.6 (for example, side b and c in the top formula), because the sides are measured from the poles down a meridian, whereas lat_1 and lat_2 are angular measurements made along the meridian but up from the equator. In other words, we must use the complement of lat_1 and lat_2, or 90°-lat_1 for side b and 90°-lat_2 for side c of the terrestrial triangle. Navigators use the term *co-latitude* to describe the complement of lat_1 and lat_2; thus, side b and c are called the co-latitudes.

When you deal with spherical triangles, one side of which is a co-latitude of a point of interest, you should become an automaton at replacing cos(*b*) with sin(*lat₁*), sin(*b*) with cos(*lat₁*), cos(*c*) with sin(*lat₂*), and sin(*c*) with cos(*lat₂*).

T I P

It is much more convenient to use lat_1 and lat_2 than to use co-latitudes in the distance formula. Therefore, by using the substitutions just mentioned, we can rewrite Equation 14.6 into a form in which we can directly plug in lat_1 and lat_2:

$$\cos a = \cos b \cos c + \sin b \sin c \cos A \qquad (14.17)$$

where

$$b = 90° - lat_1 = \frac{\pi}{2} - lat_1$$

$$c = 90° - lat_2 = \frac{\pi}{2} - lat_2$$

$$A = lon_1 - lon_2$$

Therefore

$$\cos a = \cos\left(\frac{\pi}{2} - lat_1\right)\cos\left(\frac{\pi}{2} - lat_2\right) + \sin\left(\frac{\pi}{2} - lat_1\right)\sin\left(\frac{\pi}{2} - lat_2\right)\cos\left(lon_1 - lon_2\right)$$

$$\cos a = \sin lat_1 \sin lat_2 + \cos lat_1 \cos lat_2 \cos\left(lon_1 - lon_2\right)$$

$$a = \text{distance } d = \arccos\left[\sin lat_1 \sin lat_2 + \cos lat_1 \cos lat_2 \cos\left(lon_1 - lon_2\right)\right]$$

Figure 14.6 shows a terrestrial triangle.

Distance Formula Limitations and Alternative Great Circle Distance Formula

Although Equation 14.16 is mathematically exact, it is ill-suited for numerical evaluation when the distance d is small and the angular separation between the two points is close to 0°. Consider, for example, two points on the equator 1 nm apart. In this example, $lat_1 = lat2 = 0$ (because both points are on the equator), and the arc length of $lon_1 - lon_2 = \pi/(180 \times 60)$ from Equation 14.14 makes $lon_1 - lon_2 = 0.000290888208\ldots$ radians. We then have $\sin(lat_1) = \sin(lat_2) = 0$, and $\cos(lat_1) = \cos(lat_2) = 1$, so the calculation reduces to

$$d = \arccos\left[\cos\left(lon_1 - lon_2\right)\right] \qquad (14.18)$$

Because arccos is the inverse of the cosine function, this should give $d = lon_1 - lon_2$.

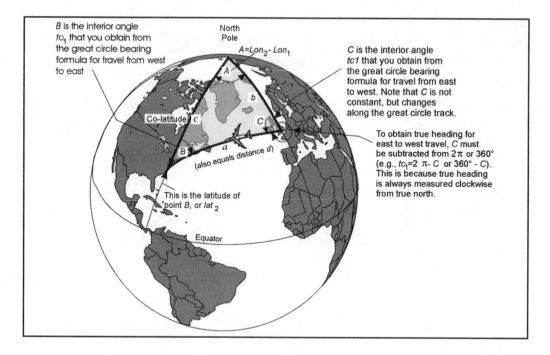

Figure 14.6 *Terrestrial triangle used for great circle calculations. A terrestrial triangle is any spherical triangle on the Earth that has at least one vertex at the north or south pole.*

However, numerically, the computer or calculator first computes the cos function $\cos(lon_1 - lon_2)$, which in this case is $\cos(lon_1 - lon_2) = 0.999999957692025\ldots$ with all its significant digits beyond the seventh place. When the calculator next computes the arccos function, you can see that calculating to eight digits, which is the greatest precision some electronic calculators provide, would result in only single-digit accuracy for *d*!

Following is a mathematically equivalent formula for *d* that does not suffer from the problem of rounding error at short distances.

$$d = 2\arcsin\left[\sqrt{\sin^2\left(\frac{lat_1 - lat_2}{2}\right) + \cos lat_1 \cos lat_2 \sin^2\left(\frac{lon_1 - lon_2}{2}\right)}\right] \quad (14.19)$$

Choosing a Great Circle Distance Formula

If you are calculating by hand, Equation 14.16 is a little simpler to use- but should be avoided for short distances. If you are programming the formula, use Equation 14.19 as it is more generally applicable, and the increased computation time will not be noticeable.

EXAMPLE 14.1

Let us calculate the great circle distance between Los Angeles (LAX), which is located at 33° 57'N, 118° 24'W, and John F. Kennedy airport in New York, located at 40° 38'N, 73° 47'W (we will ignore seconds of latitude and longitude to simplify the exercise). First we must convert the latitude and longitude coordinates to radians. To do this we first convert from degrees and minutes (ignoring seconds) into decimal degrees using Equation 14.12. Then we convert from degrees to radians using Equation 14.10:

$$lat_1 = (33+57/60) \times \pi/180 = 0.592539 \text{ radians (LAX Latitude)}$$

$$lon_1 = (118+24/60) \times \pi/180 = 2.066470 \text{ radians (LAX Longitude)}$$

$$lat_2 = (40+38/60) \times \pi/180 = 0.709186 \text{ radians (JFK Latitude)}$$

$$lon_2 = (73+47/60) \times \pi/180 = 1.287762 \text{ radians (JFK Longitude)}$$

Now we calculate d from Equation 14.19:

$$d = 2 \arcsin\left[\sqrt{\sin^2\left(\frac{lat_1 - lat_2}{2}\right) + \cos lat_1 \cos lat_2 \sin^2\left(\frac{lon_1 - lon_2}{2}\right)}\right] \qquad (14.20)$$

$$= 2\arcsin\left[\sqrt{\sin^2\left(\frac{0.592539 - 0.709186}{2}\right) + \cos(0.592539)\cos(0.709186)\sin^2\left(\frac{2.066470 - 1.287762}{2}\right)}\right]$$

$$= 2\arcsin\left[\sqrt{\sin^2\left(-0.058323\right) + (0.829525)(0.758892)\sin^2\left(0.389354\right)}\right]$$

$$= 2\arcsin\left[\sqrt{\left(-0.058290\right)^2 + (0.829525)(0.758892)\left(0.379591\right)^2}\right]$$

$$= 2\arcsin\left[\sqrt{0.00339772 + 0.0907071}\right]$$

$$= 2\arcsin\left[\sqrt{0.0941048}\right]$$

$$= 2\arcsin\left[0.306765\right]$$

$$= (2)(0.311792)$$

$$= 0.623584 \text{ radians}$$

If you are using a scientific calculator, be sure to put it in radian mode and not degree mode, or else you will not get correct results.

TIP

This distance d is the angular distance between LAX and JFK, so to convert to nautical miles we use Equation 14.14, giving the following

$$d = (180 \times 60/\pi) \times 0.623585 = 2144 \text{ nm} \qquad (14.21)$$

The distance between LAX and JFK is therefore 2,144 nm.

EXAMPLE 14.2

Now let's try a great circle distance calculation between San Francisco and Sydney, Australia, using the other distance formula, Equation 14.16. Because the angular distance between San Francisco and Sydney is not small, we are not concerned with rounding errors. San Francisco International Airport is located at 37° 37' 08"N, 122° 22' 32"W, and Kingsford Smith International Airport in Sydney is at 33° 56' 30"S, 151° 10' 18"E.

As before, we convert the latitude and longitude coordinates from degrees-minutes-seconds into decimal degrees using Equation 14.12 and then convert from degrees to radians using Equation 14.10.

For San Francisco:

$$lat_1 = (37 + (37 + 8/60)/60) \times \pi/180 = 0.645811 \text{ radians (SFO Latitude)}$$
$$lon_1 = (122 + (22 + 32/60)/60) \times \pi/180 = 2.135856 \text{ radians (SFO Longitude)}$$

Remembering that east longitudes and south latitudes must be converted to negative radian values in the distance equation, we have the following for Sydney:

$$lat_2 = (33 + (56 + 30/60)/60) \times \pi/180 = -0.592394 \text{ radians (Sydney Latitude)}$$
$$lon_2 = (151 + (10 + 18/60)/60) \times \pi/180 = -2.638443 \text{ radians (Sydney Longitude}$$

Plugging the radian values into Equation 14.16, we have the following:

$$
\begin{aligned}
d_{\text{radians}} &= \arccos\left[\sin lat_1 \sin lat_2 + \cos lat_1 \cos lat_2 \cos(lon_1 - lon_2)\right] \qquad (14.22)\\
&= \arccos\left[\sin(0.645811)\sin(-0.592394)\right.\\
&\quad \left. + \cos(0.645811)\cos(-0.592394)\cos(2.135856 - (-2.638443))\right]\\
&= \arccos\left[(0.601846)(-0.558349) + (0.798612)(0.829606)(0.0618705)\right]\\
&= \arccos\left[-0.294881\right]\\
&= 1.870128 \text{ radians}
\end{aligned}
$$

This distance d is the angular distance between SFO and Kingsford Smith International Airport in Sydney, so to convert to nm we use Equation 14.14, giving

$$d = (180 \times 60/\pi) \times 1.870128 = 6429.03 \text{ nm} \qquad (14.23)$$

The distance between SFO and Sydney is therefore 6,429.03 nm.

GREAT CIRCLE COURSE

Except for routes than run exactly north-south, the course along a great circle route gradually changes along its length. We'll first consider the formula for the initial course and then tackle the calculation of the course at a series of intermediate waypoints.

The initial course, tc_1, (at point 1) from point 1 to point 2 is given by the following:

$$tc_1 = \arccos\left[\frac{\sin lat_2 - \sin lat_1 \cos d}{\sin d \cos lat_1}\right] \qquad (14.24)$$

$$\text{if } \sin\left(lon_2 - lon_1\right) > 0$$

$$tc_1 = 2\pi - tc_1$$

$$\text{end if}$$

The calculation is performed in two steps: first, the course is calculated, and then we test for east-west travel or west-east travel to determine whether the interior course angle is measured clockwise or counterclockwise from true north. We do this by checking to see whether $\sin(lon_2 - lon_1)$ is greater than zero for east-west travel (which it will be whether you are in the eastern or western hemisphere). If $\sin(lon_2 - lon_1) > 0$, then you must subtract tc_1 from $2 \times \pi$ to arrive at the correct value for tc_1. This is because, for east-west travel, the bearing is always $360°\text{-}tc_1$ (assuming tc_1 has been converted to degrees). But for west-east travel ($\sin(lon_2 - lon_1) < 0$), the correct bearing is just tc_1. Equation 14.24 will work for almost any situation, including travel between eastern and western hemispheres across the Greenwich and 180th meridian and between the northern and southern hemispheres across the equator.

The value of tc_1 in Equation 16.24 is a true course, and it is expressed as a radian value. You'll remember that a true course is measured clockwise from the geographic north pole and not from the magnetic north pole. To get the actual compass heading you will need to add or subtract the local magnetic variation.

As before, lat_1/lon_1, lat_2/lon_2 are the latitude/longitude of the initial point 1 and the final point 2, and d is the distance from point 1 to 2 (in radians) computed using Equation 14.16 or Equation 14.19.

EXAMPLE 14.3

Find the initial great circle course from LAX to JFK.

Solution

To obtain the initial course from LAX to JFK, we know that lat_1=0.592539, lon_1=2.066470, lat_2= 0.709186, lon_2=1.287762, and d=0.623585 from Example 14.1. Thus

$$tc_1 = \arccos\left[\frac{\sin lat_2 - \sin lat_1 \cos d}{\sin d \cos lat_1}\right] \tag{14.25}$$

$$= \arccos\left[\frac{\sin(0.709186) - \sin(0.592539)\cos(0.623585)}{\sin(0.623585)\cos(0.592539)}\right]$$

$$= \arccos\left[0.408456\right]$$

$$= 1.150035 \text{ radians}$$

Because $\sin(lon_2 - lon_1)$=sin(-0.778708)=-0.70236 <0, the great circle course leaving LAX toward JFK is 1.150035 radians, which is 1.150035 × 180/π=65.89°.

Because this is a true course, you must subtract the magnetic variation for Los Angeles to get the compass heading. LAX has a variation of E15°, and "East is least," so you must subtract 15° from 65.89° and head for JFK on a course of 50.89° magnetic.

Proof of the Great Circle True Course Equation

The formula for the bearing follows immediately from the cosine law for sides, but it requires the calculation of the distance d first (Equation 14.16). To calculate the interior angle C of the terrestrial triangle, we use the cosine law (Equation 14.6) and solve for cos(C) as follows.

From Equation 14.6 we have

$$\cos c = \cos a \cos b + \sin a \sin b \cos C \tag{14.26}$$

We rearrange terms and solving for the interior bearing angle C at the point of departure:

$$\cos C = \frac{\cos c - \cos a \cos b}{\sin a \sin b} \tag{14.27}$$

Because the sides b and c are the co-latitudes (90°-lat_2 and 90°-lat_1), we can substitute $\sin(lat_1)$ for $\cos(b)$, and $\cos(lat_1)$ for $\sin(b)$, along with $\sin(lat_2)$ for $\cos(c)$. The side a, you will remember from the terrestrial triangle, is simply the distance d that we calculated using the great circle distance formula.

We now have the following:

$$\cos C = \frac{\sin lat_2 - \cos d \sin lat_1}{\sin d \cos lat_1} \qquad (14.28)$$

Because C is the same as tc_1, we have completed the proof:

$$C = tc_1 = \arccos\left[\frac{\sin lat^2 - \cos d \sin lat^1}{\sin d \cos lat_1}\right] \qquad (14.29)$$

LATITUDE OF A POINT ON A GREAT CIRCLE

A long great circle segment is typically broken into a series of shorter legs by intermediate waypoints. For long oceanic legs, where air traffic control lacks radar coverage, aircraft are typically required to make position reports at each five degrees of longitude. For example, between San Francisco (SFO) (37° 37' 8.407"N, 122° 22' 29.436"W) and Kahalui, Maui (OGG) (20° 53' 55.139"N, 156° 25 49.648"W), ATC might require reports crossing the 125°, 130°, 135°, 140°, 145°, 150°, and 155° meridians (lines of longitude). The formula to calculate at what latitude a great circle crosses a given meridian is as follows:

$$lat = \arctan\left[\frac{\sin lat_1 \cos lat_2 \sin(lon - lon_2) - \sin lat_2 \cos lat_1 \sin(lon - lon_2)}{\cos lat_1 \cos lat_2 \sin(lon_1 - lon_2)}\right] \qquad (14.30)$$

where lat and lon are the coordinates of the waypoint. As before, the point of departure is identified by (lat_1, lon_1) and the destination by (lat_2, lon_2).

This formula fails in one special case: when the great circle route lies along a meridian (if $\sin(lon_1 - lon_2) = 0$). In this case, the problem is ill-posed.

EXAMPLE 14.4

Calculate the latitude of the point located at longitude 125° W of the great circle track between San Francisco (SFO) and Kahalui (OGG).

Solution

First, we convert the latitude and longitudes of SFO and OGG to radians, obtaining the following:

$$lat_1 = 0.656575, \; lon_1 = 2.135844 \quad \text{(SFO)}$$
$$lat_2 = 0.364750, \; lon_2 = 2.730227 \quad \text{(OGG)}$$
$$lon = 2.181662 \quad \text{(125°W)}$$

Plugging this data into Equation 14.30, we obtain the following:

$$lat = \arctan\left[\frac{\sin lat_1 \cos lat_2 \sin(lon - lon_2) - \sin lat_2 \cos lat_1 \sin(lon - lon_1)}{\cos lat_1 \cos lat_2 \sin(lon_1 - lon_2)}\right] \quad (14.31)$$

$$= \arctan\left[\frac{\begin{array}{l}\sin(0.656575)\cos(0.364750)\sin(2.181662 - 2.730227) \\ - \sin(0.364750)\cos(0.656575)\sin(2.181662 - 2.135844)\end{array}}{\cos(0.656575)\cos(0.364750)\sin(2.135844 - 2.730227)}\right]$$

$$= \arctan\left[\frac{-0.297365 - 0.0129414}{-0.414386}\right]$$

$$= \arctan\left[0.748834\right]$$

$$= 0.642755 \text{ radians}$$

$$= 36.8271° \text{ or } 36° \ 49' \ 37.62'' \text{ N}$$

Thus, at longitude 125°W, the latitude along the SFO-OGG great circle would be 36° 49' 37.62"N.

A negative result for *lat* would have indicated a latitude in the Southern hemisphere.

If you repeat the preceding process, you can obtain the latitude for each of the successive waypoints along the route. For each leg of the route we compute the leg distance and the true course using Equation 14.19 and Equation 14.24, obtaining Table 14.1.

Table 14.1 Computation of Latitude, Given Longitude, for Waypoints between San Francisco and Kahului, Maui

WAYPOINT	LATITUDE	LONGITUDE	DISTANCE (NM)	TRUE COURSE
SFO	37° 37' 8.407"N	122° 22' 29.436"W	134.1	250°
1	36° 49' 37.625"N	125° 00' 00.000"W	263.8	248°
2	35° 06' 27.297"N	130° 00' 00.000"W	276.1	246°
3	33° 05' 51.726"N	135° 00' 00.000"W	290.0	243°
4	30° 46' 55.963"N	140° 00' 00.000"W	305.2	240°
5	28° 08' 53.158"N	145° 00' 00.000"W	321.6	238°
6	25° 11' 13.399"N	150° 00' 00.000"W	338.4	235°
7	21° 53' 54.765"N	155° 00' 00.000"W	99.9	233°
OGG	20° 53' 55.139"N	156° 25' 49.648"W		

As we noted before, the true course at each waypoint is not the same as the magnetic course. For each waypoint, you must determine the magnetic variation and then subtract or add the variation (subtract east, add west) to obtain the proper magnetic course.

If it is inconvenient or impractical to fly the exact great circle routing between waypoints, it is acceptable to substitute a constant course, or rhumb line, because the cross-track error on these short legs is insignificant. The appropriate rhumb line course is the average of the initial and final courses. For example, between waypoint 4 and waypoint 5 the rhumb line course would be the average of 240° and 238°, which is 239°.

LATITUDE AND LONGITUDE OF A POINT

Another method of splitting a great circle route into shorter legs is to split them into equal lengths, such as 200 nm segments. To do this, we need to be able to find the latitude and longitude of a waypoint a known distance along a great circle track. This technique is useful in its own right, for example to find the location of a waypoint defined by radial and distance from a known fix.

The algorithm to compute waypoints along a given radial and at a given distance is as follows:

$$lat = \arcsin\left[\sin lat_1 \cos d + \cos lat_1 \sin d \cos tc\right] \qquad (14.32)$$
$$dlon = \operatorname{atan2}\left[\sin tc \sin d \cos lat_1, \cos d - \sin lat_1 \sin lat\right]$$
$$lon = \operatorname{mod}\left[lon_1 - dlon + \pi, 2\pi\right] - \pi$$

As usual, lat_1/lon_1 are the latitude/longitude of the initial point. lat/lon are the latitude/longitude of the unknown point, which is a distance d in the direction tc from the initial point.

The functions mod and atan2 may be unfamiliar and, perhaps more to the point, may be unavailable on the calculator or in the programming language you are using. To provide you with a workaround, the next section teaches you how to manually calculate the values of these two important functions.

How to Implement Mod and atan2

Mod(y,x) is defined to be the (positive) remainder after dividing the integer y by the positive integer x. It always lies in the range 0<=Mod(y,x)<x. For example, Mod(heading, 360°) is the heading in the range 0°–360°, so that Mod(390°,360°)=30 and Mod(-30°,360°)=330°.

If you have an int function that returns the integer part of a number (int(30.73)=30 and so on), the following is an implementation of the mod function:

```
FUNCTION mod(y,x)
IF y>=0
```

```
   mod=y- x × int(y/x)
ELSE
   mod=y+ x × (int(-y/x)+1)
ENDIF
```

The function atan2(y,x) is defined to be the angle between a line joining the origin to the point (x,y) and the x-axis, measured counterclockwise. It is identical to atan(y/x) if x is positive but has extended range, taking values between -pi and pi. It can be defined in terms of the arctan function as follows:

$$\text{atan2}(y, x) = \arctan(y/x) \qquad x >= 0$$
$$\text{atan2}(y, x) = \arctan(y/x) + \pi \qquad x < 0,\ y >= 0$$
$$\text{atan2}(y, x) = \pi/2 \qquad x = 0,\ y > 0$$
$$\text{atan2}(y, x) = \arctan(y/x) - \pi \qquad x < 0,\ y < 0$$
$$\text{atan2}(y, x) = -\pi/2 \qquad x = 0,\ y < 0$$
$$\text{atan2}(0, 0) \text{ is undefined and should give an error}$$

Another potential implementation problem is that the arguments of arcsin or arccos may, because of rounding error, exceed 1 in magnitude. With perfect arithmetic this couldn't happen. You may need to use "safe" versions of arcsin and arccos along these lines:

$$\text{asin\_safe}(x) = \arcsin(\max(-1, \min(x,1)))$$

$$\text{acos\_safe}(x) = \arccos(\max(-1, \min(x,1)))$$

EXAMPLE 14.5

Compute the waypoints at 200-nm intervals along the route from San Francisco to Kahalui, Hawaii.

Solution

If we take the San Francisco to Kahalui trip that we considered in the previous section, we can compute a series of waypoints at 200-nm intervals along the route in the following manner. First, we find the distance and initial course using Equation 14.19 and Equation 14.24. The distance is 2,029 nm and the initial true course is 250.0°.

Next, using Equation 14.32, we find the latitude and longitude of the intermediate waypoints, which are successively 200, 400, 600, ... and 1,800 nm from SFO on the great circle whose initial course is 250°.

For SFO, lat_1=0.656575 and lon_1=2.135844 radians. The distance d to the first waypoint (200 nm) is $200 \times \pi/(180 \times 60)$=0.0581776 (by converting 200 nm to radians using Equation 14.15). The true course leaving SFO toward OGG (250°) is 4.36419 radians (from Equation 14.24). Thus, plugging the requisite values into Equation 14.32, we have the following:

$$lat = \arcsin\left[\sin lat_1 \cos d + \cos lat_1 \sin d \cos tc\right] \qquad (14.33)$$

$$= \arcsin$$
$$\left[\sin(0.656575)\cos(0.0581776) + \cos(0.656575)\sin(0.0581776)\cos(4.36419)\right]$$
$$= \arcsin\left[0.593660\right]$$
$$= 0.65600 \text{ radians}$$
$$= (0.65600)\left(\frac{\pi}{180}\right) \text{ degrees}$$
$$= 36.4172 \text{ degrees}$$
$$= 36° \ 25' \ 1.984''$$

$$dlon = \text{a tan } 2\left[\sin tc \sin d \cos lat_1, \cos d - \sin lat_1 \sin lat\right]$$
$$= \text{a tan } 2\left[\sin(4.36419)\sin(0.0581776)\cos(0.656575), \cos(0.581776)\right.$$
$$\left. - \sin(0.656575)\sin(0.635600)\right]$$
$$= \text{a tan } 2\left[-0.0432919, 0.635933\right]$$
$$= -0.0678713 \text{ radians}$$

$$lon = \text{mod}\left[lon_1 - dlon + \pi, 2\pi\right] - \pi$$
$$= \text{mod}\left[2.13584 + 0.679713 + \pi, \ 2\pi\right] - \pi$$
$$= 5.34540 - \pi$$
$$= 2.20381 \text{ radians}$$
$$= (2.20381)\left(\frac{180}{\pi}\right) \text{ degrees}$$
$$= 126.2690 \text{ degrees}$$
$$= 126° \ 16' \ 08.4''$$

Proceeding in this manner we can produce a log of waypoints at equal distance intervals between SFO and OGG (see Table 14.2).

Table 14.2 *Equal Distance Waypoints between San Francisco and Kahului, Maui*

Waypoint	Latitude	Longitude	Distance (NM)	Remaining Distance (NM)	True Course
SFO	37° 37' 08.407"N	122° 22' 29.436"W	200	2029	250.0°
1	36° 25' 01.984"N	126° 16' 09.538"W	200	1829	247.7°
2	35° 05' 34.681"N	130° 02' 21.195"W	200	1629	245.5°
3	33° 39' 21.164"N	133° 41' 01.154"W	200	1429	243.4°
4	32° 06' 55.659"N	137° 12' 15.068"W	200	1229	241.5°
5	30° 28' 51.414"N	140° 36' 15.851"W	200	1029	239.8°
6	28° 45' 40.319"N	143° 53' 22.098"W	200	829	238.1°
7	26° 57' 52.661"N	147° 03' 56.658"W	200	629	236.7°
8	25° 05' 57.000"N	150° 08' 25.411"W	200	429	235.3°
9	23° 10' 20.134"N	153° 07' 16.259"W	200	229	234.1°
10	21° 11' 27.128"N	156° 00' 58.323"W	29	29	233.0°
OGG	20° 53' 55.139"N	156° 25' 49.648"W	0	0	232.8°

To automate the calculation task in a table such as Table 14.2, you could implement the previous formulas in a single row in an Excel spreadsheet and then copy and paste the rest of the waypoint rows as needed. Excel will perform all the calculations. For an example, see Alan Parkinson's great circle Excel spreadsheet discussed later in this chapter.

Each of the true course angles in Table 14.2 must be adjusted for magnetic variation in order to obtain the magnetic course on which you would fly with your compass. Using the magnetic variation utilities on the book's CD-ROM, or by consulting the magnetic variation chart in Chapter 13, you would calculate the magnetic course for each waypoint as shown in Table 14.3.

Table 14.3 *Magnetic Variation and Magnetic Course Calculated for each Waypoint along the SFO to Kahului, Maui Great Circle Track*

Waypoint	True Course	Magnetic Variation*	Magnetic Course =(True Course − Magnetic Variation)**
SFO	250.0°	15.6°E	234.4°
1	247.7°	15.6°E	232.1°
2	245.5°	15.3°E	230.2°
3	243.4°	14.9°E	228.5°
4	241.5°	14.3°E	227.2°
5	239.8°	13.7°E	226.1°

WAYPOINT	TRUE COURSE	MAGNETIC VARIATION*	MAGNETIC COURSE =(TRUE COURSE – MAGNETIC VARIATION)**
6	238.1°	13.0°E	225.1°
7	236.7°	12.2°E	224.5°
8	235.3°	11.6°E	223.8°
9	234.1°	10.9°E	223.2°
10	233.0°	10.4°E	222.6°
OGG	232.8°	10.3°E	222.5°

*Obtained from DAFIF Magnetic Variation Utility on the CD-ROM.

**Note that if the magnetic variation were west, the correct formula would read Magnetic Course=(True Course + Magnetic Variation)

Using the DAFIF GeoMag Program

In Example 16.5, the magnetic course was calculated by subtracting the local magnetic variation at each waypoint. But how do you calculate the magnetic variation, and why would you want to when an easy-to-use variation chart is available? There are two problems: first, the closer you get to the poles, the greater the chart's error because the isogonic lines converge; second, there are many parts of the world where variation is not plotted accurately. To that end, the National Geophysical Data Center at Boulder, Colorado, has for many years provided a geomagnetic model of the Earth for government users of the DAFIF. Because the DAFIF has been released to the public for the first time, we are able to include this model in the GeoMag program on the book's CD-ROM.

GeoMag is a DOS program that you run from within a DOS window. Simply unzip the GeoMag.Zip file into any directory and then double-click on the **GeoMag.EXE** application. (Caution: all the GeoMag files must be unzipped into the same directory, or else the program won't run.) You will be prompted to enter the decimal latitude and longitude as well as the elevation and decimal year (magnetic variation changes from year to year, and its strength varies according elevation). For example, to find the magnetic variation at the San Francisco point of departure for the SFO to Kahului trip, you would type the following responses to the program's queries:

```
ENTER LATITUDE IN DECIMAL DEGREES (+25.0)
37.61
ENTER LONGITUDE IN DECIMAL DEGREES (-100.0)
-122.37
```

```
ENTER ALTITUDE IN METERS
11277
ENTER TIME IN DECIMAL YEAR
1997.5
```

You must enter negative values for west longitudes and positive values for east longitudes (this is contrary to the great circle formulas used in this chapter). Similarly, north latitudes are positive, and south latitudes are negative. Altitudes are expressed in meters, so the 11,277 meters that I have input would correspond to the 37,000-ft cruising altitude of the 737-400. The month for the year 1997 was entered as a decimal; 1997.5 would mean June 1997, because this is the midpoint of the year.

The program produces the following output:

```
LATITUDE:     = 37.61    DEG
LONGITUDE:    = -122.37 DEG


ALTITUDE      = 11277.00   METERS
DATE          = 1997.5
                            OUTPUT
                            ____
```

```
AIN FIELD COMPONENTS                    ANNUAL CHANGE
_____                            _____
```

TI	= 49661	nT		TI	= -63	nT/yr
HI	= 23846	nT		HI	= -12	nT/yr
X	= 22972	nT		X	= -9	nT/yr
Y	= 6395	nT		Y	= -15	nT/yr
Z	= 43561	nT		Z	= -65	nT/yr
DEC	= 15.56	DEG		DEC	= -1.71	MIN/yr
DIP	= 61.30	DEG		DIP	= -1.40	MIN/yr

```
DO YOU NEED MORE POINT DATA? (y or n)
```

Magnetic variation is indicated by the DEC value of 15.56°. Because it is positive, it means the magnetic variation for the departure point in San Francisco is 15.56° east. If it were negative, the variation would have been 15.56° west. There is further on-line documentation on the program's other features and field data components.

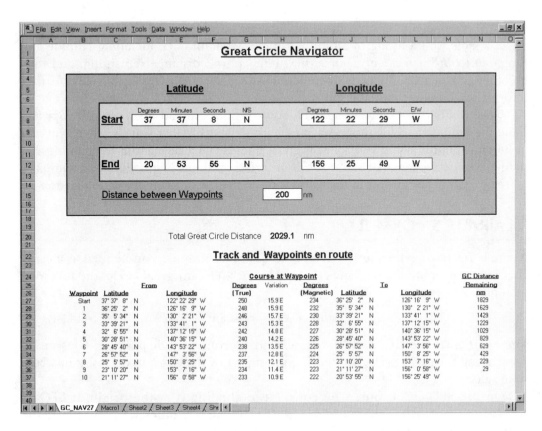

Figure 14.7 Great Circle Navigator (Excel spreadsheet) by Alan Parkinson. This utility allows you to easily calculate any great circle route of your choosing. Simply enter the beginning and ending latitude and longitude coordinates and then enter the desired distance between waypoints. The spreadsheet will automatically calculate and display a table of all the intermediary waypoints, the total great circle distance, the distance remaining, the true course, and the magnetic course.

How to Use Alan Parkinson's Great Circle Navigator

Through the efforts of Alan Parkinson, we are able to provide you with a great circle Excel spreadsheet utility that will calculate any great circle track around the world, including the waypoints in between (see Figure 14.7). The spreadsheet uses a built-in magnetic variation table to automatically calculate the magnetic heading at each waypoint. Using this spreadsheet is simple: open it in Microsoft Excel 95/97 and then enter the beginning and ending latitude and longitude coordinates in the space provided. Then enter the desired distance between waypoints, and the spreadsheet produces a table with a listing of all the pertinent waypoint data, including latitude and longitude coordinates, true course, magnetic course, distance remaining, and total great circle distance. There is documentation on the CD-ROM if you want further information on how to use the spreadsheet.

Once you have created a great circle route with the spreadsheet, you can copy and paste the latitude and longitude waypoints into a text file that you can then edit and import into David Drouin's GPS 2.0 program. Because GPS 2.0 is a fully functioning waypoint navigation system that automatically interfaces with the Flight Simulator autopilot, it is easy to fly to any airport in the world without the use or need of aviation charts.

CLAIRAUT'S FORMULA

A simple relation, sometimes referred to as Clairaut's formula, can be used as a cross-check of your position along any great circle track. On any great circle, the following relation holds true:

$$\sin tc \cos lat = \text{constant} \qquad (14.34)$$

where tc is the true course and lat is the aircraft's current latitude position. Thus, at any point along the great circle, multiplying the $\sin(tc)$ by the $\cos(lat)$ will result in a constant value.

On the SFO-OGG route, the constant, evaluating it at the origin of SFO, is $\sin(4.36332) \times \cos(0.656575) = -0.744318$. If you take any other waypoint along the route, you will find that the $\sin(tc) \times \cos(lat) = -0.744318$.

Proof of Clairaut's Formula

The law of sines from Equation 14.5 says that $\sin(b) \times \sin(A) = \sin(a) \times \sin(B)$. If we assume that A is the true course bearing tc and that b is the co-latitude at any waypoint along the great circle path, then a is the co-latitude of the destination and B is the opposite interior angle, both of which remain fixed for the entire great circle journey. Thus, the value $\sin(a) \times \sin(B)$ is constant and

$$\sin tc \sin b = \text{constant} \qquad (14.35)$$

When we replace the co-latitude b with the latitude (see earlier explanation), we have the following:

$$\sin tc \cos lat = \text{constant} \qquad (14.36)$$

And that is what we wished to prove.

FINDING THE INTERSECTION OF TWO GREAT CIRCLES

A somewhat more complicated exercise is finding the point where two great circles routes cross. For example, a navigational fix (point 3) might be defined as the intersection of the crs13 radial from point 1 and the cr23 radial from point 2. The following algorithm finds the *lat/long* of the fix 3. It works by solving the spherical triangle connecting the points 1, 2, and 3.

Strictly speaking, the two great circles defined by the two radials meet at a second point, diametrically opposite point 3, on the other side of the Earth. If this point is desired, it has latitude and longitude (-lat3, mod(lon3+2 × π, 2 × π)-π).

$$dst_{12} = 2 \arcsin \sqrt{\sin^2\left(\frac{lat_1 - lat_2}{2}\right) + \cos lat_1 \cos lat_2 \sin^2\left(lon_1 - lon_2\right)} \quad (14.37)$$

IF $\sin\left(lon_2 - lon_1\right) < 0$

$$crs_{12} = \arccos\left(\frac{\sin lat_2 - \sin lat_1 \cos dst_{12}}{\sin dst_{12} \cos lat_1}\right)$$

ELSE

$$crs_{12} = 2\pi - \arccos\left(\frac{\sin lat_2 - \sin lat_1 \cos dst_{12}}{\sin dst_{12} \cos lat_1}\right)$$

ENDIF

IF $\sin\left(lon_1 - lon_2\right) < 0$

$$crs_{21} = \arccos\left(\frac{\sin lat_1 - \sin lat_2 \cos dst_{12}}{\sin dst_{12} \cos lat_2}\right)$$

ELSE

$$crs_{21} = 2\pi - \arccos\left(\frac{\sin lat_1 - \sin lat_2 \cos dst_{12}}{\sin dst_{12} \cos lat_2}\right)$$

ENDIF

$$ang_1 = abs\left(\bmod\left(crs_{13} - crs_{12} + \pi, \, 2\pi\right) - \pi\right)$$

$$ang_2 = abs\left(\bmod\left(crs_{21} - crs_{23} + \pi, \, 2\pi\right) - \pi\right)$$

IF $\left(\sin ang_1 \sin ang_2 \leq \sqrt{TOL}\right)$

    Print "No Intersection Exists"

ELSE

$$ang_3 = \arccos\left[-\cos ang_1 \cos ang_2 + \sin ang_1 \sin ang_2 \cos dst_{12}\right]$$

$$dst_{13} = \arcsin\left[\frac{\sin ang_2 \sin dst_{12}}{\sin ang_3}\right]$$

$$dst_{23} = \arcsin\left[\frac{\sin ang_1 \sin dst_{12}}{\sin ang_3}\right]$$

$$lat_3 = \arcsin\left[\sin lat_1 \cos dst_{13} + \cos lat_1 \sin dst_{13} \cos crs_{13}\right]$$

$$lon_3 = \mathrm{mod}\left(lon_1 - \arcsin\left[\frac{\sin crs_{13} \sin dst_{13}}{\cos lat_3}\right] + \pi, \; 2\pi\right) - \pi$$

ENDIF

TOL is a small number of order machine precision. 10^{-15} would be OK for standard double-precision arithmetic.

Working through a brief example, suppose point 1 is the REO VOR located at (42.600°N,117.866°W)=(0.74351,2.05715) radians and that point 2 is the BKE VOR located at (44.840°N,117.806°W)=(0.782606,2.056103) radians.

We want to locate the point where the 51° (=0.890118 radians) bearing from REO intersects with 137° (=2.391101 radians) from BKE. Following the preceding algorithm, we then find, successively:

$$dst_{12} = 0.039103$$
$$crs_{12} = 0.018996$$
$$crs_{21} = 3.161312$$
$$ang_1 = 0.871122$$
$$ang_2 = 0.770211$$
$$ang_3 = 1.500667$$
$$dst_{13} = 0.02729$$
$$dst_{23} = 0.029986$$
$$lat_3 = 0.760473 = 43.572°\text{N}$$
$$lon_3 = 2.027876 = 116.189°\text{W}$$

The unknown intersection is found to be at (43.572°N,116.189°W).

The Science of Flight Simulators, Federal Aviation Regulations, and Pilot Training

This chapter introduces you to some of the science behind real flight simulators so that you may have a better understanding of how the technology of flight simulators works, and how it may influence the development of future versions of Microsoft's Flight Simulator. You'll also become familiar with the Federal Aviation Regulations (FAR), and learn how these rules govern pilot training in simulators and pilot licensing. In addition, you'll discover where you can read the entire FAR on-line on the Web, and read the most interesting parts of the FAR on the book's CD. Other tabular Federal Aviation Administration (FAA) data, such as airline, commuter, and general aviation accident rates, are presented so that you recognize the risks involved in real flying. Some of the flight simulation modeling mathematics included in this chapter are a little intimidating at first glance, so feel free to skip over the portions you don't want to wade through. After reading this chapter, at the very least, you'll come away with a new-found appreciation for the complexity and sophistication of modern flight simulators.

THE SCIENCE OF FLIGHT SIMULATION

Commercial Simulators have been around for more than 50 years, starting with Edwin Link's Trainer, which he patented in 1930. The first full-motion simulators appeared in the late 1950s, when Rediffusion produced a pitch-motion system for the Comet IV. The first full-color display system, also by Rediffusion, appeared in 1962. Progress in simulation technology proceeded briskly, and in 1960 General Electric created the first computer-generated imaging system for simulators. The modern simulator we know today is really based on evolutionary advances made since the late 1960s, when the basic principles of the flight simulator were established. Today's PC-based simulator has taken these earlier display technologies and grafted some of them onto the microcomputer chip, using clever techniques to get around the performance limitations of the hardware.

Figure 15.1 *Full-motion platform commercial simulators can imitate translation (motion along the x, y, and z axes) and rotation (angular rotation around the x, y, and z axes).*

FLIGHT MODEL

High-end simulators use what is known as a *six-degree-of-freedom* (6 DOF) flight model. A three-degree-of-freedom (3 DOF) model, used in some low-end PC simulators, means that the equations of motion determine the x, y, and z displacements of the aircraft in space but ignore or creatively estimate roll rates, moments, and other angular displacements. A 6 DOF model is more accurate in depicting the motion and flying characteristics of an airplane. This model includes translational motion (x, y, z), and rotational motion (pitch, yaw, and roll), and their related derivatives, or rates of change.

Flight Simulator uses a 6 DOF model. The three-axis orthogonal coordinate system for the aircraft consists of a longitudinal, lateral, and vertical axis. The six degrees of motion (accelerations and velocities) are along and about each of these three axes, as illustrated in Figure 15.2.

The 12 variables used in the 6 DOF model are described here for each of the degrees of freedom:

1. Longitudinal velocity u and acceleration force **X** along the x axis.
2. Lateral velocity v and acceleration force **Y** along the y axis.
3. Vertical velocity w and acceleration force **Z** along the z axis.
4. Roll angular velocity p and angular moment **L'** (which we have added the prime mark ' to differentiate **L'** from lift variable **L**) around the x axis.
5. Pitch angular velocity q and angular moment **M** around the y axis.
6. Yaw angular velocity r and angular moment **N** around the z axis.

The combination of these velocities, accelerations, and moments is what allows us to translate and rotate the aircraft through space in any direction.

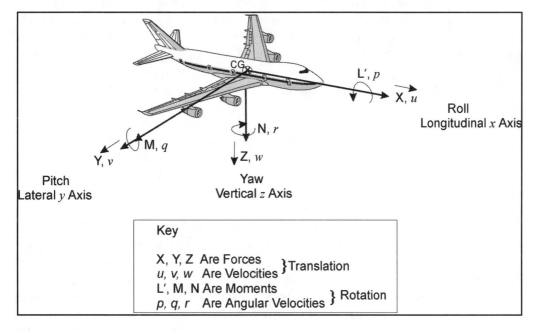

Figure 15.2 *Coordinate system and components of force, moment, and linear and angular velocity used for calculating the equations of motion in flight simulators*

Let's look at a simple representation of how commercial flight simulators model aircraft. Depending on the degree of sophistication and complexity, a simulation might want to take into account the following:

- Wing's angle of attack
- Wing surface deflection angles
- Speed/Mach number
- Rotation rates around each axis of the aircraft
- Altitude
- Center of gravity
- Ground proximity
- Geometry of the aircraft (flap settings, wing sweep, aspect ratio, dihedral, camber, drag coefficients, lift coefficients, landing gear)
- Atmospheric conditions
- Engine settings

For example, the engine model must produce the correct value of thrust that corresponds to the pilot's throttle setting. Engines cannot change thrust instantaneously, and more power is produced only between certain settings of the throttle. Burning more fuel to increase thrust takes time, because the engine needs to spool up to speed, in the case of a jet engine, or increase the intake of oxygen in the case of a piston-powered engine. Therefore, adequate modeling of the time delay or decay in setting the throttle is necessary.

The atmosphere has a great effect on the performance of the engines and on the aircraft's lift. Therefore, pressure, density, temperature and wind have to be taken into account. When an aircraft is flying at 31,000 feet, for example, a turbofan engine uses much less fuel than at sea level, and the maximum thrust needed to push the aircraft at constant speed decreases. An airplane at high altitude can fly farther, faster, and more efficiently than can one at lower altitude.

The geometry of the aircraft affects the aerodynamic lift and drag coefficients. For example, when the landing gear is extended, more drag is created, and when the flaps are extended, more lift is created. The wing's shape, camber, aspect ratio, and dihedral angle tremendously influence the amount of lift created. Furthermore, advanced simulators will not treat the wing as one surface; instead, the program will split the wing into two components, a right and left airfoil. This allows more precise modeling of effects such as spins, slips, stalls, and turns. Good simulator flight models will also account for the changing center of gravity and moment of the aircraft as fuel is consumed from each fuel tank.

An aircraft's proximity to the ground, such as when landing or taking off, creates what is known as the *ground effect*. What happens is that the airflow over the wing is altered by the presence of the ground. This results in an effective increase in lift, which allows the aircraft to float over the surface instead of landing, and take off before it is able to climb. Accurate flight models need to take ground effect into account.

The wing's angle of attack and its speed determine whether the wing produces lift or whether it stalls. The angle of attack for the left wing should be modeled separately from the angle of attack for the right wing if we are to obtain realistic flight characteristics in banking maneuvers.

Equations of Motion

The full force equations and moment equations used in flight simulators are far too complex to derive from scratch in a book of this nature. We will present only the equations as they are used and not make any attempt to elaborate on how the equations were derived from Newton's laws of motion. Although it is not difficult to do, deriving the equations of motion is better left as an exercise for those who are mathematically inclined. For more information, consult your local engineering library for books on dynamics, and airplane control, and stability.

N O T E

Courtland Perkins and Robert Hage's book *Airplane Performance Stability and Control*, written in 1949, has a good development of how the total equations of force and moment for the airplane are derived from Newton's laws on pages 376–384. Perkins was a professor of aeronautical engineering at Princeton University, and Hage was a senior engineer at Boeing Airplane Company during and after World War II.

To get a basic idea of how flight simulators mathematically model flight, let's look at the equations for forces that act along the x axis, as shown in the following equations. For the moment, we will ignore all rotational movement as well as translation movement on the z and y axes.

$$\sum F_x = X + mg_x = X - m\sin\theta = m(\dot{u} + qw - rv) \tag{15.1}$$

where:

$\dot{u} = \dfrac{du}{dt} =$ Acceleration along x axis in ft/s^2.

$X = X_{\text{Engine thrust}} - X_{\text{Total drag}} =$ Force of engine thrust minus opposing drag force acting on airplane.

$X_{\text{Engine thrust}} =$ Thrust of engines in lbs.

$$X_{\text{Total drag}} = C_{\text{Polar drag}} q_{\text{Dynamic pressure}} S_{\text{Wing area}} + C_{\text{Induced drag}} q_{\text{Dynamic pressure}} S_{\text{Wing area}}$$
$$= D_{\text{Polar drag}} + D_{\text{Induced drag}}.$$

$$q_{\text{Dynamic pressure}} = \left(\frac{1}{2}\right) pV^2 = \text{Dynamic pressure from Bernoulli' s law.}$$

$$q_{\text{Dynamic pressure}} \neq q \text{ from Equation 20.1.}$$

$S_{\text{Wing area}}$ = Surface area of wings in ft^2.

p = Density of air at airplane' s given altitude in slugs$/$ft^3

V = Airspeed in ft$/$s. $V \neq v$ from top equation.

$C_{\text{Polar drag}}$ = Polar drag constant which is different for each aircraft. Can be calculated from aircraft' s surface profile (ft^2) in wind.

$C_{\text{Induced drag}} = \dfrac{C_{\text{Lift}}^2}{\left(\pi\, e\, AR\right)}$ = Induced drag coefficient. This is the drag created by the airplane' s wings as a result of the wingtip air vortices. The greater the coefficent of lift C_{Lift}, the greater the induced drag coefficent $C_{\text{Induced drag}}$ and the greater the total drag force $X_{\text{Total drag}}$ on the airplane. π and e are constants, while a larger aspect ratio AR for the wings (i.e., increased wingspan and narrower wing) reduces $C_{\text{Induced drag}}$, which in turn reduces total drag force $X_{\text{Total drag}}$.

$C_{Lift} = \dfrac{L_{\text{Lift force in pounds}}}{\left(q_{\text{Dynamic pressure}} S_{\text{Wing area}}\right)}$ = Coefficient of lift. This value changes for different airspeeds, different wing angles of attack, as well as surface wing area.

$L_{\text{Lift force in pounds}} = W_{\text{Weight of airplane in pounds}}.$ Note that $L = W$ for level flight only! If the airplane is not in level flight, then:

$$L_{\text{Lift force in pounds}} = W_{\text{Weight of airplane in pounds}} \cos\theta - X_{\text{Engine thrust}} \sin\alpha_T$$

where:

$\quad \theta$ = Flight path angle. The angle the airplane's flight path makes with the local horizontal horizon.

$\quad \alpha_T$ = Thrust vector angle. The angle which the airplane's engine thrust vector makes with the flight path angle θ.

$$AR = \text{Aspect ratio of wings} = \frac{b_{\text{Wing span}}}{c_{\text{Wing chord length}}} = \frac{b_{\text{Wing span}}^2}{S_{\text{Wing area}}}$$

$\pi = 3.14159$

e = Constant, usually between 0.8 and 0.95.

m = Mass of airplane in slugs.

g_x = Acceleration of gravity measured along airplane's x axis $= 32\left(\text{ft}/\text{s}^2\right)\sin\theta$.

q = Angular velocity around y axis in radians$/$s $\left(\text{not to be confused with } q_{\text{Dynamic pressure}}\right)$.

r = Angular velocity around z axis in radians$/$s.

w = Translation velocity in z axis direction in ft$/$s.

v = Translation velocity in x axis direction in ft$/$s.

From Newton's second law, the force exerted on any object is equal to the mass of the object times the acceleration it undergoes, or $F = ma$. For an airplane, force would be equal to the mass of the airplane times the acceleration the airplane undergoes in a particular direction. In English units mass is measured in units of slugs; in the metric (mks) system, mass is measured in kilograms. Acceleration in English units is measured in ft/s^2, while in mks, acceleration is measured in m/s^2. If we know the acceleration a, we can perform a simple integration of a to find the airplane's velocity by performing the following operation:

$$V = \int_{t_0}^{t_1} a\, dt = \left[at\right]_{t_0}^{t_1} = at_1 - at_0 \tag{15.2}$$

t_1 = Time at final position x_1 of airplane (in s)

t_0 = Time at original position x_0 of airplane (in s)

V = Airplane's velocity in $\dfrac{\text{ft}}{\text{s}}$.

Next, if we perform a second integration of velocity for the same period of time $t_1 - t_0$, we can obtain the aircraft's change in position Dx along the x axis.

$$\Delta x = \int_{t_0}^{t_1} V dt = \int_{t_0}^{t_1} at\, dt = \left|\frac{1}{2}at^2\right|_{t_0}^{t_1} = \frac{1}{2}a\left(t_1^2 - t_0^2\right) \tag{15.3}$$

But the big question is, how do we determine the acceleration a along the x axis? From Equation 15.1, we see that the acceleration along the x axis is indicated by the variable $\dot{u}$

$$\dot{u} = \frac{du}{dt} = a = \text{acceleration along } x \text{ axis} \tag{15.4}$$

$$\dot{u} = a = \frac{X}{m} - g \sin \theta - qw + rv$$

Thus once we determine the forces of engine thrust and drag from Equation 15.1, and we know the airplane's angular velocity q (around the y axis), y axis velocity v, z axis velocity w, and angular velocity r (around the z axis), we can calculate the acceleration a and then integrate a to find velocity V from Equation 15.2. After we do this, from Equation 15.3, we can find the displacement distance Δx along the x axis by performing a second integration over the same time interval. Note that to calculate the forces of drag, we must take into account the lift force L, which in turn is affected by the airplane's current velocity, angle of bank, and other factors.

By integrating the preceding equations for each axis second by second, the flight simulator program is able to update the aircraft's position and velocity. This process is then repeated for each axis, and then the momentum force equations must be integrated following a similar procedure. If you have followed the preceding steps used to calculate the x axis velocity and position, you will realize that this is, at heart, the fundamental process by which Flight Simulator mathematically models flight!

Calculating Moments and Moments of Inertia

Aircraft in Flight Simulator have three moments of inertia for each axis. A moment of inertia is useful in calculations involving rotational motion and is a number that describes how much of an object's mass exists away from a particular axis of rotation. The moment of inertia is a constant for each axis; that is, there is a moment of inertia I_x for rotation around the x axis, a moment of inertia I_y for rotation around the y axis, and a moment of inertia I_z for rotation around the z axis.

Moments of Inertia:

$$I_X = \sum_{i=1}^{n}(y_i^2 + z_i^2)m_i = \int(y_i^2 + z_i^2)\,dm \tag{15.5}$$

$$I_Y = \sum_{i=1}^{n}(x_i^2 + z_i^2)m_i = \int(x_i^2 + z_i^2)\,dm$$

$$I_Z = \sum_{i=1}^{n}(x_i^2 + y_i^2)m_i == \int(x_i^2 + y_i^2)\,dm$$

where m_i = mass of aircraft at point (x_i, y_i, z_i).

Moment (Torque or Rotational Force):

$$M_X = L' = Fr_{yz} = I_X \frac{dp}{dt}$$

where:

F is the force applied perpendicular

to the x axis at a distance $r_{yz} = \sqrt{r_y^2 + r_z^2}$.

$\dfrac{dp}{dt}$ = angular acceleration around the x axis.

$$M_Y = N = Fr_{xz} = I_Y \frac{dq}{dt}$$

where:

F is the force applied perpendicular

to the y axis at a distance $r_{xz} = \sqrt{r_x^2 + r_z^2}$.

$\dfrac{dq}{dt}$ = angular acceleration around y axis.

$$M_Z = M = Fr_{xy} = I_Z \frac{dw}{dt}$$

where:

F is the force applied perpendicular

to the z axis at a distance $r_{xy} = \sqrt{r_x^2 + r_y^2}$.

$\dfrac{dw}{dt}$ = angular acceleration around z axis.

Why this number is so useful is not so apparent here, but suffice to say that the greater the moment of inertia, the more resistance the airplane has to a change in roll, pitch, or yaw (depending on the axis). In other words, it takes a greater torque force, or moment, to counteract the aircraft's rotation, either to start or stop rotating.

The moment of inertia is obtained my taking each point mass m of the aircraft and multiplying it by the square of its distance r^2 from a particular axis. For example, the moment of inertia for the x axis would be derived by multiplying out all the point masses of the airplane by the square of the distances of each point mass from the x axis. This distance r from the x axis for each point mass is equal to the square root of $y^2 + z^2$.

Moment is defined as follows:

$$\overline{\mathbf{M}} = \overline{\mathbf{r}} \times \overline{\mathbf{F}} \text{ (vector cross-product)} \qquad (15.6)$$
$$\left|M\right| = Fr \sin\theta = I\alpha$$

where:

I = Moment of inertia.

α = angular acceleration in radians/s^2.

Moment, or *torque*, is a measure of the force that rotates a body about an axis. For example, in the case of an airplane, increasing the distribution of mass away from the y axis increases the moment of inertia I_y, and hence the moment $\mathbf{M}_y$ needed to rotate around the y axis is increased. Because much more force is now required to rotate around the y axis, it is much harder to pitch the aircraft up or down. Conversely, with a high value for the moment of inertia I_y, it becomes much harder to stop the rotation.

Another useful term used in the motions of equation is what is known as the product of inertia, which for each axis is defined as follows:

Producs of Inertia:

$$I_{xy} = \sum_{i=1}^{n} xym_i = \int xy \; dm \qquad (15.7)$$

$$I_{xz} = \sum_{i=1}^{n} xzm_i = \int xz \; dm$$

$$I_{yz} = \sum_{i=1}^{n} yzm_i = \int yz \; dm$$

Total Force and Moment Equations of Motion

Now that you have seen how Flight Simulator calculates x axis movement, let's look at the entire force and moment equations for all six degrees of freedom.

Total Force Equations:

$$\sum F_x = X + mg_x = X - W_{\text{Weight of airplane in pounds}} \sin\theta = m(\dot{u} + qw - rv) \quad (15.8)$$

$$\sum F_y = Y + mg_y = Y + W_{\text{Weight of airplane in pounds}} \cos\theta \sin\phi = m(\dot{v} + ru - pw)$$

$$\sum F_z = Z + mg_z = Z + W_{\text{Weight of airplane in pounds}} \cos\theta \cos\phi = m(\dot{w} + pv - qu)$$

where:

θ = Angle of aircraft's x axis relative to local horizontal plane (pitch).

ϕ = Roll angle of aircraft's y axis relative to local horizontal plane (roll).

Total Moment Equations:

$$\sum M_x = L = I_x \dot{p} - I_{yz}(q^2 - r^2) - I_{zx}(\dot{r} + pq) - I_{xy}(\dot{q} - rp) - (I_y - I_z)qr \quad (15.9)$$

$$\sum M_y = M = I_y \dot{q} - I_{zx}(r^2 - p^2) - I_{xy}(\dot{p} + qr) - I_{yz}(\dot{r} - pq) - (I_z - I_x)rp$$

$$\sum M_z = N = I_z \dot{r} - I_{xy}(p^2 - q^2) - I_{yz}(\dot{q} + rp) - I_{zx}(\dot{p} - qr) - (I_x - I_y)pq$$

If we assume that the aircraft has a symmetric distribution of mass with respect to the yz and xy planes, then the products of inertia $I_{yz} = I_{xy} = 0$ and the total moment equations can be simplified as follows:

$$\sum M_x = L = I_x \dot{p} - I_{zx}(\dot{r} + pq) - (I_y - I_z)qr \quad (15.10)$$

$$\sum M_y = M = I_y \dot{q} - I_{zx}(r^2 - p^2) - (I_z - I_x)rp$$

$$\sum M_z = N = I_z \dot{r} - I_{zx}(\dot{p} - qr) - (I_x - I_y)pq$$

Let's turn now to a concrete application of how the laws of motion may be applied to the flight of an aircraft. As shown in Figure 15.3, four forces act on the airplane:

1. Lift L is perpendicular to the flight path direction.
2. Weight W acts vertically toward the center of the earth and when the airplane is pitched up or down, is at an angle θ with respect to the lift force L.

3. Thrust T is inclined at an angle α_T with respect to the flight path direction.
4. Drag D is parallel but in the reverse flight path direction.

If we ignore all rotational forces, and side slip forces (forces acting along the y axis), we get the following equations of motion:

$$\sum F_x = m\left(\frac{dV}{dt}\right) = T\cos\alpha_T - D - W\sin\theta \qquad (15.11)$$

$$\sum F_z = m\left(\frac{V^2}{r_c}\right) = L + T\sin\alpha_T - W\cos\theta$$

The mean chord line represents the airplane's angle of attack α with respect to the flight path direction, which has the same direction as the relative wind.

As shown in the diagram, the summation of the forces parallel to the flight path is given by the equation of motion for translation in the x axis direction. The summation of forces perpendicular to the flight path is given by the equations of motion for the z axis direction. For forces parallel to the flight path, $dV/dt = a$ is the acceleration along the flight path, where V is the instantaneous value of the airplane's flight velocity. By definition, V is always along the flight path direction.

The summation of forces perpendicular has a slightly different context in which to view the variables. As before, V is the velocity along the flight path, but the value V^2/r_c equals the acceleration normal to a curved path of radius r_c.. If you have studied physics, you will recognize that V^2/r_c is nothing more than the *centrifugal force*, with $r_c = h_{\text{Altitude of Aircraft}} + r_{\text{Earth's Radius}}$.

Note that with unaccelerated level flight ($\theta = 0°$), the net force on the aircraft is zero, and the two equations from Equation 15.11 reduce to:

$$\sum F_x = 0 = T\cos\alpha_T - D \qquad (15.12)$$

$$\sum F_z = 0 = L + T\sin\alpha_T - W$$

For most airplanes in level unaccelerated flight, the angle α_T is small enough such that $\cos(\alpha_T) \stackrel{a}{=} 1$ and $\sin(\alpha_T) \approx 0$. Therefore,

$$T = D \qquad (15.13)$$
$$L = W$$

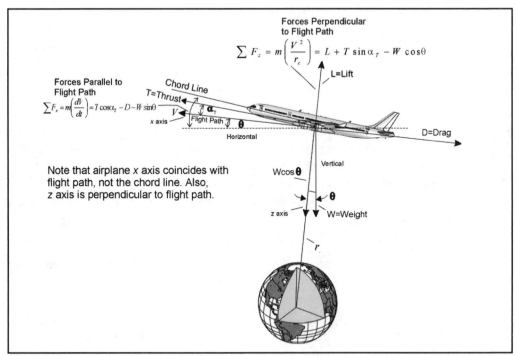

Figure 15.3 Aircraft's lift, weight, thrust, and drag force diagram.

In earlier chapters, we learned that

$$L = q_\infty S C_L \qquad (15.14)$$

where:

$q_\infty = \dfrac{1}{2}\rho V^2$ Dynamic pressure in lb/ft^2.

S = Surface area of wing in ft^2.

V = Velocity of aircraft in ft/s.

C_L = Lift coefficient.

ρ = Density of air at altitude in slugs/ft^3

Therefore, if we know the lift coefficient C_L we can determine lift L for a given velocity. But how does one determine C_L? After all, C_L changes for different angles of attack, and for different velocities. One easy way to calculate C_L is to fly the aircraft in level flight such that $L = W$. Therefore if you substitute the aircraft's weight for L in Equation 15.14 you get:

For Unaccelerated Level Flight Only:

$$C_L = \frac{L}{q_\infty S} = \frac{W}{q_\infty S} = \frac{W}{\frac{1}{2}\rho V^2 S} \qquad (15.15)$$

NOTE   For more complicated situations, the aircraft's lift coefficient must be empirically found through exhaustive wind tunnel testing. Once these graphs have been made for different angles of attack and velocities, a polynomial fit of the graph is made using parametric mathematical methods. Once these equations have been created, the computer simply feeds in the current angle of attack and velocity, and then the lift coefficient CL is calculated.

Once you know CL, you can calculate the drag on the aircraft, and thus the thrust needed to overcome drag (T=D) and keep the airplane aloft. *Drag* is defined as follows:

$$D_{Total} = D_{Parasitic} + D_{Induced} = C_{D_P} q_\infty S + \frac{C_L^2}{\pi eAR} q_\infty S \qquad (15.16)$$

where

$$AR = \text{Aspect ratio of wings} = \frac{b^2}{S}.$$

b = Wingspan.

e = Constant (around 0.9).

C_{D_P} = Parasite drag coefficient (different for each airplane).

π = Pi = 3.14159.

Once you have calculated the Drag D_{Total}, you have solved the problem, since Thrust $T=D_{Total}$.

Learjet Example

Example Problem

Find how much thrust is needed to keep the Learjet aloft at a speed of 150 knots at sea level with no flaps applied. Assume the aspect ratio of the wings is 6.16, parasitic drag coefficient C_{DP}=0.025, air density $\rho = 2.377 \times 10^{-3}$ sl/ft^3 at sea level, and that the Learjet weighs 18,000 pounds.

Solution

1. Since the Learjet is in level flight, lift equals weight ($L = W$).
2. From Equation 15.15, we need to calculate the lift coefficient C_L. But first we will need to convert airspeed to English units of ft/s, so

$$1 \text{ knot} = 1.688 \text{ ft/s} \qquad (15.17)$$

$$(150 \text{ knots})\left(\frac{1.688 \text{ ft/s}}{1 \text{ knot}}\right) = 253.20 \text{ ft/s}$$

For Unaccelerated Level Flight Only:

$$C_L = \frac{L}{q_\infty S} = \frac{W}{q_\infty S} = \frac{W}{\frac{1}{2}\rho V^2 S} \qquad (15.18)$$

$$= \frac{18{,}000 \text{ lb}}{(0.5)(2.277 \times 10^{-3} \text{ sl/ft}^3)(253.20 \text{ ft/s})^2(253.3\text{ft}^2)} = 0.9736$$

$$C_L = 0.9736$$

3. Using Equation 15.16, calculate the drag:

$$D_{\text{Total}} = D_{\text{Parasitic}} + D_{\text{Induced}} = C_{D_p} q_\infty S + \frac{C_L^2}{\pi eAR} q_\infty S$$

$$D_{\text{Total}} = \frac{1}{2}\rho V^2 S\left(C_{D_p} + \frac{C_L^2}{\pi eAR}\right)$$

$$D_{\text{Total}} = \frac{1}{2}(2.277 \times 10^{-3} \times \text{sl/ft}^3)(253.2 \text{ ft/s})^2(253.3 \text{ ft}^2)\left(0.025 + \frac{0.9736^2}{(3.1415)(0.90)(6.16)}\right)$$

$$= 1{,}468 \text{ pounds}$$

4. From Equation 15.13, thrust equals drag ($T = D_{\text{Total}}$) for level flight, so the total thrust needed to keep the Learjet aloft at 150 knots is 1,468 lb. Since the Learjet is capable of producing 7,000 pounds of thrust, this is only 21% of the total thrust available! Note however, that if you were to try this on the Learjet in FS95/98, and you use your turbine and fan engine speed gauges to measure your thrust, this *is not* the same as your total thrust. Turbine engines develop the top 30% of their power in the top 10% of allowable rpm, so there is no linear relationship between engine thrust and your rpm gauges.

The Learjet, like all twin-engine aircraft, is designed to fly with one engine disabled. If you want to try the above example and see if you can fly the Learjet at 150 knots with 1,468 pounds thrust, follow these steps:

1. Take off in the Learjet with both engines at full thrust.
2. Once in the air, raise the landing gear and raise the flaps.
3. Reduce engine thrust on the right engine to zero (Press **E2 F1**). To ensure that the right engine is off, examine your engine instruments. The right engine may be still rotating due to dynamic ram air pressure.
4. Next, compensate for the right yawing tendency of the airplane by moving the ailerons left. Try to stabilize the aircraft in level flight.
5. Reduce thrust on the remaining left engine to about 60% to 68% fan speed. This represents about 1/2 the maximum thrust of 3,500 pounds for the engine on the Microsoft Learjet (but not the real Learjet), or about 1,700 pounds of thrust. Try to reduce thrust to a lower setting if possible to correspond with 1,468 pounds.

The Learjet will fly in level flight if you follow these steps carefully. Note that for the example above, the throttle setting for the real Learjet would have to be adjusted to about 82% fan speed (see Table 4.6 in Chapter 4.)

If you have tried the above example, you will have just proved an aerodynamic principle: your lift is a function of your airplane's thrust and drag. Surprisingly, it doesn't take much thrust at all to fly an 18,000-pound aircraft at 150 knots!

Floating-Point Processors

Contrary to what you might think, having a floating-point processor does not increase Flight Simulator's performance. Floating-point arithmetic refers to the storage and processing of numbers with fractional decimal components. One example of a floating point number would be 3.25 or 3-1/4, which in a digital computer might occupy anywhere between 32 and 64 bits of memory, as opposed to 16 bits for an integer such as 32,767. Another example of an important floating-point number would be that of pi or (which we shall abbreviate here as having the value 3.14159265359... which continues indefinitely). Pi is irrational because it cannot be expressed as a simple fraction (such as 22/7) or as a decimal with a finite number of decimal places. Pi is also a transcendental number because it cannot be completely represented by a finite number of algebraic operations and it has no continuously recurrent digits. Yet pi is needed for many types of graphic transformations in computer graphics. Why then do some flight simulators use fixed-point integer arithmetic, you may wonder? There are inherent speed advantages to handling numbers that are integers with the simple add, divide, and multiply arithmetic functions available to a microprocessor. Using a floating point processor in your CPU can considerably slow down its capabilities, because of the greater number of steps required to process the fractional components for addition, subtraction, multiplication, and division operations. Integer math, on the other hand, is much faster.

But how then, does one use the sine, cosine, tangent, $e x$, In functions that are needed in simulators if one cannot use the instructions found in the floating point unit of the microprocessor? These transcendental functions use and return floating point numbers, not integers. One answer to this quandary lies in a trick that programmers use to make integers represent fractions. Integers can be treated as fractions simply by moving the "binary point" left. An integer number such as 1,345 can have its decimal place shifted two places to the left so that it now becomes 13.45. The programmers assume that the decimal place is always two places to the left when processing a number. In an analogous way, binary numbers in a computer, which ordinarily would be treated as integers, can be treated as floating-point numbers. But now that you have solved the fractional number problem, how do you get the values for the previously mentioned transcendental functions?

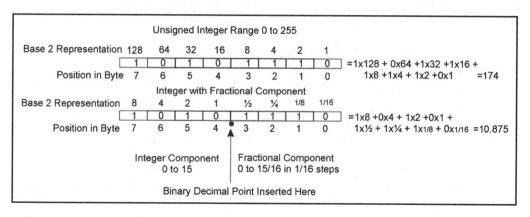

Figure 15.4 *A Byte of data (8 bits), which represents an integer with a fractional component. This trick allows programmers to use speedy integer arithmetic in place of more time consuming floating point arithmetic.*

There are two ways to deal with this. First, you can use lookup tables that have the answers already pre-calculated to the desired accuracy you want. Second, you can approximate these functions to any desired degree of accuracy using the algebraic substitution of the infinite series expansion of the above functions (i.e., $\sin x = x - x/3! + x^5/5! - x^7/7!$ where the ! symbol means factorial thus $3! = 3 \times 2 \times 1 = 6$).

Unlike PC-based simulators, commercial flight simulators require the use of floating-point arithmetic. This is because floating-point calculations are required to replicate the complicated motion and flight dynamics of real aircraft. In order to validate a level D simulator, the Federal Aviation Administration (FAA) requires airlines to provide an Approval Test Guide (ATG) to objectively demonstrate that the flight simulator accurately duplicates the flight test data of the airplane to be simulated. For example, to certify a Cessna Citation business jet simulator, a real Cessna Citation is taken out on a test flight and equipped with digital recorders that keep track of

- Control wheel position, aileron position, aileron trim deflection.
- Column position, elevator position, elevator trim deflection.
- Rudder pedal deflection, rudder position, rudder trim deflection.
- Roll angle, roll rate, roll acceleration.
- True heading angle, yaw rate, yaw acceleration.
- Side-slip angle, angle of attack, indicated airspeed.
- Other miscellaneous events

Then various maneuvers are performed in the real aircraft with the digital recorders active. Such flight events as an aborted takeoff, normal takeoff, climb, cruise, descent, landing, and engine out are all carefully sampled and recorded. The airplane's Dutch roll tendencies are documented, as well as special motions including:

- Vibrations due to taxiing and takeoff/landing roll.
- Motion due to runway roughness.
- Tire, landing gear failure dynamics.
- Engine vibrations.
- Buffet due to stall-onset, stall, and recover.
- Buffet due to flap and landing gear extension/retraction.

When all of this is done, the simulator's algorithms must be fine-tuned to faithfully recreate the graphs of all the above events. To then test the simulation, the digital recording for the real Cessna Citation is fed back into the simulator and its full-motion 6 DOF platform, and the simulator is made to recreate the actual flight that was previously recorded. This time, however, the same digital recorders that were used on the real airplane are now set up inside the cockpit to monitor how well the simulator is recreating all the previously recorded events. Proof of match data (POM) is required by the FAA before the simulator can be certified for airline training purposes. Figure 15.5 shows one such POM graph that the FAA would accept as evidence that the simulator does in fact recreate the deceleration forces of an aborted takeoff.

With all these confirmation tests, one can see that obtaining certification for a simulator is an expensive, time consuming process, but it is one that must be done if one is to be confident that airline crews are being trained properly.

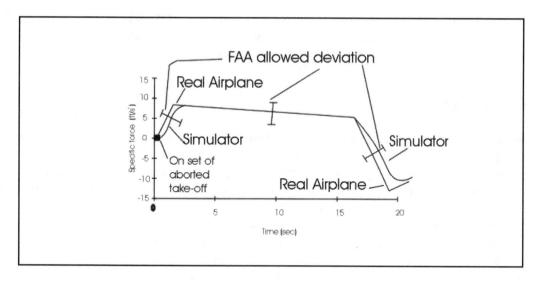

Figure 15.5 *Longitudinal forces in the aircraft cockpit and in the simulated cockpit during an aborted takeoff.*

It used to be that floating point processors were measured by how many millions of floating point instructions that the microprocessor could handle per second. This benchmark was known as MFLOPS, or millions of floating point operations per second. Because some manufacturers learned how to cheat on the tests, by optimizing their processors to take shortcuts on the tests, a new benchmark SPECfp95 was created. SPECfp95 is now the standard benchmark by which a computer's floating point performance is measured. Note that an Intel Pentium Pro 200 is rated at 67 MFLOPS and 6.21 SPECfp95.

Table 15.1 *SPECfp95 Performance Comparison*

Pentium 200 MHz	Pentium 200 MHz– MMX	Pentium Pro 200 MHz (67 MFLOPS)	Pentium II 233 MHz (Pro +MMX)	Pentium II 266 MHz (Pro +MMX)	HP 9000 Minicomputer
4.18	4.66	6.21	6.43	6.89	16.3

It is estimated that a full-fledged Boeing 747 simulation would require 5 MFLOPS, and that a fighter plane simulation would require 3 to 6 MFLOPS, while a helicopter would require 15 MFLOPS (Baarspul 1990). This calculation includes only those processes needed just to update the flight dynamics of the aircraft and does not include visuals, or the system that guides the motion platform. As you can see from Table 15.1, this is well within the capability of today's Pentium processors.

Frame Rate

Modeling a flight simulator that is accurate enough to respond to a pilot's input as well as rapidly update a display is not an easy thing to do. It has been confirmed by extensive studies that a frequency of at least 500 Hz (a Hertz, or Hz is 1 cycle per second) for iterating control inputs is necessary for a person to feel that there are no discontinuities or pauses in the simulation. Although 20 Hz is beyond human detection capabilities, a rate at least 10 to 20 times this is necessary to avoid overlapping control responses (e.g., multiple motions of a yoke and separate rudder). This means that the controls have to be continually updated, or "iterated," by the computer 500 times per second, with a consequent time delay of no more than 0.2 seconds interval between when the pilot moves the control and the system reacts. However, updating the display is entirely a different matter. Here the refresh or screen redraw rate can be as low as 30 Hz before a noticeable flicker or lag in response to pilot actions occurs. For enhanced realism, commercial high end visual simulators, such as the Evans & Sutherland ESIG-3000 or ESIG-4500, offer 60 Hz, or 60 frames per second (fps).

Let's examine the frame rate a little more closely. Broadcast television in the United States has a vertical refresh of 60 Hz, but is interlaced so that only every other line is painted for a given screen image. This means that the individual glowing phosphors on our television sets are refreshed at only 30 Hz, or 30 times per second for each frame. Motion pictures in theaters are displayed at a rate of 24 fps (or 24 Hz), so we can fool the eye into believing motion is occurring. In reality, all we see is a succession of still frame images being flashed 24 times per second on a screen. But what does this have to do with Flight Simulator? Quite simply, if your frame rate doesn't reach at least 30 Hz, you won't believe that you are really flying.

Fortunately for us, with the advent of Windows 95/98 running PCI graphics accelerator cards on Pentium 300 MHZ MMX computers, we can reach a comfortable frame rate of at least 30 fps in Flight Simulator. Of course, this frame rate will drop considerably when you fly through high detail scenery areas, such as large cities, and when you toggle on full visual effects, such as shadows, clouds, texture mapping, and so on.

Consider also the demands imposed on your computer by Flight Simulator running graphics updates at 30 Hz. At 30 Hz, or 30 individual screen frames painted per second, your computer has only 33.3 ms (i.e., 0.0333 seconds!) to process all the instructions and calculations it needs to figure out the plane's new location, attitude, velocity, view angles, and scenery drawing instructions. On a 200-MHz Pentium Pro, which is rated at 440 millions of instructions per second (MIPS), this means that your CPU can handle only 14 million instructions in the 0.0333 second interval. Thus, we see that there is a limiting factor to what is possible on your computer trying to simulate flight. For Flight Simulator to drive a 17-inch monitor at 1024×768 resolution at 30 frames per second with 256 colors, we would need to process 786 kB $\times$ 30 fps = 23.6 MB/s (1 byte per pixel=256 colors per pixel, and 1024 bytes by 768 lines of resolution = 786,000 bytes or 786 kB). The bandwidth on recent versions of the PCI bus on a Pentium is 132 MB/s, which is four times the older Extended Industry Standard Architecture (EISA) standard. On the ISA bus, the difference is more dramatic, with the PCI bus's bandwidth exceeding the Industry Standard Architecture (ISA) bus's throughput by 16.5 times.

NOTE

In any computer, data travels over one or more buses between memory, the CPU, and peripheral components like video display cards, SCSI controllers, sound cards, and disk drives. The most widely used architecture, the ISA bus provides either a 8-bit or 16-bit wide data path. With an 8-MHz clock speed, the ISA bus is capable of transfer rates of 5 MB/s, but because the demands imposed by faster hard drives and faster video cards, EISA was developed. EISA, which also had an 8-MHz clock, had a throughput of 16 MB/s, with burst speeds up to 33 MB/s. However, even this was not enough, and so in the early 1990s the Local Bus and PCI bus architecture was developed to fill the voracious appetite for increased bandwidth on the PC.

In contrast to older expansion bus architectures, PCI is a type of Local Bus, but it has a 32 bit wide data path, a 33 MHz clock speed (some ar e clocked at 66 MHZ), and a 132 MB/sec data transfer rate. PCI provides a high speed path which directly connects the peripheral devices to the CPU and main memory, unlike ISA and EISA which put peripherals on a slow, separate expansion bus. The next generation PCI bus, which has a 64-bit-wide data path, will sustain 264 MB/s.

To improve video throughput even further, new Pentium II designed motherboards now place the video card on its own bus, called the Accelerated Graphics Port (AGP).

Figure 15.6 illustrates the need for the PCI bus, and Figure 15.7 shows the difference in bandwidth for each bus type.

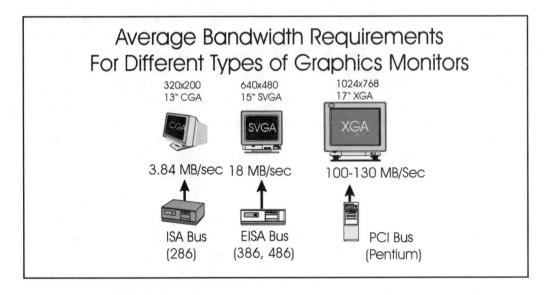

Figure 15.6 *Why we need the PCI bus.*

If we update our computers with faster processors, we increase the number of instructions per second, and thus enhance our ability to push more pixels out onto the screen with greater resolution and more detail. With parallel processing and multithreading, we can process more graphic routines and thereby create more effects, such as drawing more polygons, creating better shading, shadows, and lighting effects. When you consider that not long ago, we were trying to run Flight Simulator 1.0 on an Apple II with not more than 0.06 MIPS, we've come a long way since that painful time.

Back in the 1960s Gordon Moore, one of the early designers of integrated circuits (ICs), wrote a paper that predicted that transistor density on ICs would double every 18 months (a statement since known as Moore's Law). Moore, who with Andy Grove later went on to found Intel Corporation, was uncannily prescient in this prognostication as you can see in Figure 15.8, which shows the transistor density evolution of the microprocessor. In a recent public interview, Moore has stated that he believes this trend will continue well into the next century, after which some fundamental physical limitations in the atomic nature of matter will slow down advances in semiconductor fabrication technology.

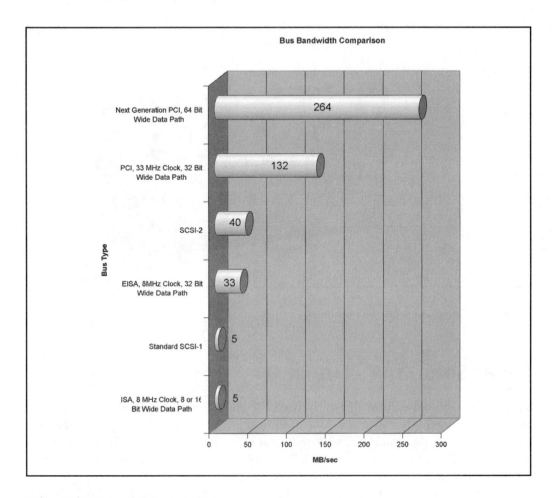

***Figure 15.7** PCI bandwidth comparison.*

For some basic performance comparisons between the different types of microprocessors, see Appendix A's FAQ section on MMX technology. There you will find some interesting graphs that show a side-by-side comparison of each Microprocessor's performance capabilities. Also, in the same Appendix A, don't overlook the FAQ section on Flight Simulator frame rates, which contains a graph of typical frame rates you might expect with your hardware.

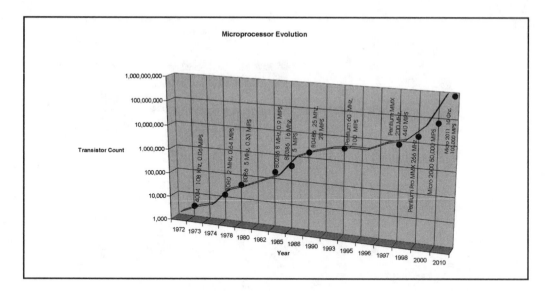

Figure 15.8 *The evolution of the microprocessor.*

FLIGHT SIMULATOR'S FUTURE

So what does extra transistor density in the CPU mean for the Flight Simulator pilot in 1998? Extrapolating out into the future, we can expect a microprocessor in the year 2000 (now being designed) with 50 million transistors and 50,000 MIPS. In the year 2011, we can look forward to a 10-GHz microprocessor with a billion transistors and 100,000 MIPS microprocessor (Peters 1997).

With these advances and the advent of the new Digital Versatile Disc (DVD), which initially will hold up to 4.7 GB of data (but can be as high as 17 GB), we can expect far more scenery detail and faster frame rates. More of the world will become available on DVD with its far greater capacity, as will the ability to use the U.S. government's highly detailed Digital Terrain Elevation Data to accurately depict the contours and elevations of scenery around the world. We should be able to enjoy flying through the folds of valleys and fly over the ridge tops of mountains with unprecedented accuracy. With enhanced global satellite imagery, and thousands of polygons drawn per frame, we will be able to texture map real imagery over the Digital Terrain Elevation Data and see the world as it really looks when flying at altitude.

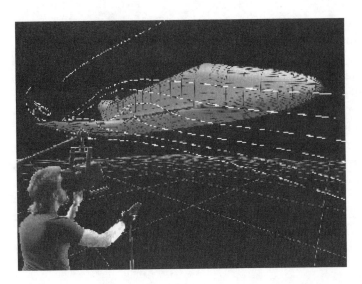

Figure 15.9 *The virtual wind tunnel: A virtual reality environment for exploring numerically generated 3-D flow fields. A boom-mounted 6 DOF stereo CRT system is used for viewing. The data gloves are used for injecting various tracers (e.g., "smoke") into the virtual flow field. (Courtesy of NASA).*

New display technologies on the horizon promise greater fidelity and sharper pictures. Research is under way to produce virtual reality goggles that, with special kinesthetic touch-sensitive gloves, will allow you to immerse yourself into a cockpit environment and handle virtual reality aircraft controls through the gloves. In effect, you'll be able to sit in a virtual recreation of a multimillion dollar simulator, minus the motion platform, and access each and every control in the cockpit. This technology is a ways off, but with the advances that are now being made, there is little doubt that it will eventually end up in the hands of consumers.

FULL-MOTION SIMULATORS

The question arises as to why ground-based simulators need to model motion. After all, a simulator that employs a motion platform is necessarily a much costlier investment than one that remains motionless. The need for motion simulators became apparent during the 1960s when high speed jet aircraft such as the Boeing 707 were introduced. These aircraft flew higher and faster than their predecessors, and their pilots for the first time encountered the effect known as clear air turbulence (CAT). This turbulence was not associated with any clouds or visible conditions, and it was violent and could cause severe handling problems with the aircraft. At the time of the introduction of the

707, most crews were trained in ground simulators that used fixed bases that did not move. In one incident, an American airliner encountered CAT and the pilots lost control of the aircraft descending over 25,000 feet before they regained control. When the flight was reflown on a simulator that did not move, it was discovered that most pilots could easily regain control of the aircraft. But when the flight was replayed on a newly constructed research simulator that moved and could simulate the motions of turbulence, it was found that the pilots reacted badly to the CAT. The simulator's motion created false illusions of climbing, when in fact the aircraft was descending. As a result, the crew would move the controls in the opposite direction needed to correct the aircraft's attitude, and this was the situation that led to the loss of control on the real aircraft. Only the disturbing effect of the motion was what enabled the researchers to discover what was going on in the real cockpit. This lesson taught the airlines that they had to invest in full motion simulators to adequately train their pilots for all kinds of flight contingencies.

Hexapod Motion Systems and NASA's Vertical Motion Simulator

To satisfy the requirements for 6 DOF motion, the six post or "hexapod" motion system was adopted for most airline simulators. Figure 15.10 shows one such platform, on which the simulator cockpit is mounted. Each of the three corners of the platform is supported by a pair of hydraulic cylinders (six cylinders in all, hence the term *hexa*). Examining the figure closely, you can see that each pair of cylinders is in turn attached to the floor at three points, with each cylinder pair being attached ±60° from the other cylinder pairs. Proper extension or retraction of the cylinders can produce both translation motion along the mutually perpendicular *x*, *y*, and *z* axes, as well as the respective rotations around these same axes. The pistons in each cylinder can deflect up or down about 3.28 ft to 6.56 ft and this can produce a translational excursion in the platform of up to 8.89 ft, with rotational movements up to ±30°. More advanced flight simulators, such as the world's largest motion simulator, the Vertical Motion Simulator (VMS) at NASA Ames Research Center provide about 60 ft of sway and 40 ft of heave. Maximum accelerations for hexapod motion platforms range from 3.28 ft/s^2 (0.102 g's) to 22.96 ft/s^2 (0.72 g's), with peak velocities ranging from 2.62 ft/s (1.55 knots) to 42.65 ft/sec (25 knots). As can be seen in Figure 15.12, NASA's VMS peak accelerations reach 24 ft/s^2 (0.75 g's) with peak velocities reaching 16 ft/sec (9.47 knots). Looking at these numbers, you would be wrong to think that hexapod-type motion platforms outperform the VMS. The VMS is capable of a much longer period of sustained motion, and it moves a further distance. In fact, because of the VMS's enormous 60-ft vertical displacement, it is ideally suited for simulating rotorcraft, such as tilt-wing Osprey and helicopters, although one of its other main priorities is to support space shuttle missions. Before each space shuttle mission, for instance, the shuttle pilots brush up on their proficiency by using the VMS to practice different landing scenarios. At NASA Ames Research Facility's Vertical Motion Simulator, I was able to see the world's largest motion simulator in action. and Figures 15.11 and 15.12 give you an idea of the huge size of the Vertical Motion Simulator (VMS) building. The horizontal beam, which the cockpit cab is mounted on, is moved up or down by gigantic piston shafts, which themselves are held naturally buoyant in the center position by compressed nitrogen gas. Electric motors move the horizontal beam up or down with minimal force, due to the counterweight force of the nitrogen gas.

N O T E Ames Research Facility is located at the decommissioned Moffett Naval Air Station in Mountain View, California, about 30 miles south of San Francisco. While driving down Interstate 101 outside Moffett field, you can see the gigantic hangers that used to house the Navy's illustrious lighter-than-air dirigible fleet.

Figure 15.10 Six-post motion platforms.

Figure 15.11 *The 6-DOF Vertical Motion Simulator, with its 60-ft vertical motion capability, is the world's largest motion-base simulator. (Courtesy of NASA-Ames Research Facility)*

The VMS uses both an electromechanical and electrohydraulic servo-system for its 6 DOF motion system. This system consists of two integrated motion generators: an electrically driven system that provides two translational degrees of freedom (left-right, up-down), and a hydraulically driven system for the remaining translational and three rotational degrees of freedom.

The vertically moving horizontal beam is a specially fabricated steel column that spans the width of the two towers that hold the VMS in place. This horizontal beam, called the vertical platform, is mounted on two columns, or pistons, which extend downward into 75-foot-deep shafts under the tower floor. Each vertical tower piston, which resembles your local garage's hydraulic hoist used to lift your car in the air, is part of a unique system called an equilibrator, and it acts as a pneumatic counterweight. The equilibrators are pressurized with nitrogen gas such that, at operating pressure, the entire beam and motion system (weighing in excess of 50 tons) becomes neutrally buoyant.

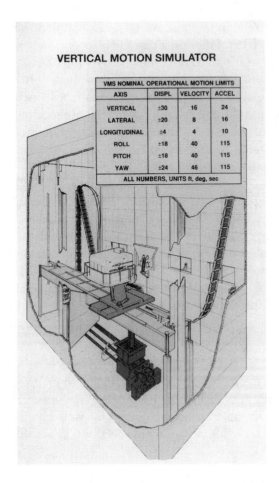

VERTICAL MOTION SIMULATOR

VMS NOMINAL OPERATIONAL MOTION LIMITS			
AXIS	DISPL	VELOCITY	ACCEL
VERTICAL	±30	16	24
LATERAL	±20	8	16
LONGITUDINAL	±4	4	10
ROLL	±18	40	115
PITCH	±18	40	115
YAW	±24	46	115
ALL NUMBERS, UNITS ft, deg, sec			

Figure 15.12 *The Vertical Motion Simulator Cab Sits on a horizontal beam that moves vertically ±30 ft, slides laterally ±20 ft, and translates longitudinally ±4 ft. In addition, the cab can roll or pitch on the sliding platform ±18°, as well as yaw ±24°.*

The entire assembly is driven in the vertical direction by eight mechanically coupled 150 horsepower direct current (DC) servomotors. Lateral motion along the horizontal beam is provided by the lateral carriage, a smaller platform that rolls on tracks the entire length of the beam. The remaining longitudinal translation motion is provided by the longitudinal carriage, which itself rolls on ball bearings attached to the lateral carriage. A 48 inch roller bearing turntable mounted on the longitudinal carriage provides yawing motion. This bearing supports a conical center post with a two axis gimbal at its upper end to provide pitch and roll motions. All rolling motion is accomplished by hydraulics, whereas translational motion is accomplished via electro-mechanical servo motors.

The VMS uses five interchangeable "cabs," only one of which can be mounted at a time. Four of the cabs can be rapidly configured into any kind of airplane cockpit, while the fifth is used only for space shuttle missions. Within a matter of 3 days or less, a cab can be replaced by another cab, so that researchers can maximize the use of the facilities for different projects. This means that one week, a 737 accident simulation may be under way, while the next week a space shuttle simulation may be scheduled. With such flexibility, the VMS is well suited for modeling many aircraft, as each cab can be stripped bare and reconfigured with new instrumentation in a matter of weeks.

DISPLAY TECHNOLOGY

Today, computer-generated imagery (CGI) is the method by which all airline simulators display a simulated perspective view of the outside world. The first such CGI simulator officially certified by the FAA for airline training was manufactured by McDonnell-Douglas and was put to use by Pacific Southwest Airlines in California (PSA was later sold to U.S. Air).

Collimated Displays

Early on it was realized that large CRTs in their conventional form were unsuitable for use in cockpit simulators. There were two reasons for this: first, with huge 27-inch CRT monitors protruding into the cockpit, the simulator cockpit could not have a realistic cockpit windscreen; second, observers in the cockpit would realize that they were viewing a flat image in front of the windscreen rather than a distant image behind it. To overcome these objections, the spherical mirror beam-splitter collimated display was invented, as illustrated in Figure 15.13.

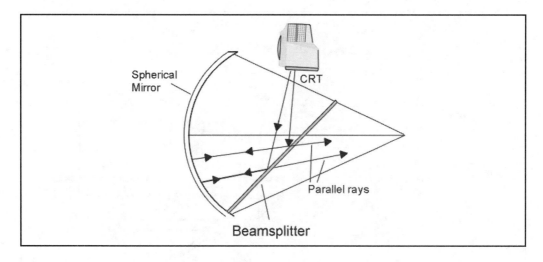

Figure 15.13 *Spherical mirror beam splitter collimated display used in commercial flight simulators.*

The collimated display system uses CRTs mounted downward, with the image on the CRT's face being reflected from a beam-splitter set at 45° to the pilot's line of sight. This image is then reflected from a spherically curved mirror and the incident rays are then transmitted back through the beam splitter to the eye of the pilot. The focus of the mirror is located at the beam splitter location, and all light leaving the mirror is collimated (i.e., all rays from the CRT's face end up by emerging parallel from the spherical mirror). The beam splitter is made of glass with a coating of 50/50 reflective transmission film on the side facing the CRT. To meet the requirements of a wide horizontal angle of view, multiple CRTs are mounted and in the case of the Rediffusion WIDE system, a field of view 150° horizontal by 40° vertical is achieved by using three CRT calligraphic projectors, as seen Figure 15.14. Each projector is driven by a separate CGI channel and depth perception is maintained by the collimated projection of reflected light from the concave mirrors. To the pilot, objects outside the cockpit look like they are located in space at infinity, although the display does not give binocular cues. However, binocular vision is only useful when discerning moving objects that are quite close to the aircraft, and is less important for distant objects far away. Most importantly, the eye focuses on objects in a collimated display as if they were located at infinity from the observers' point of view, as would be the case for a real cockpit view. This is not the case with normal CRT monitors, in which your eye focuses on a point that is only a few tens of inches away.

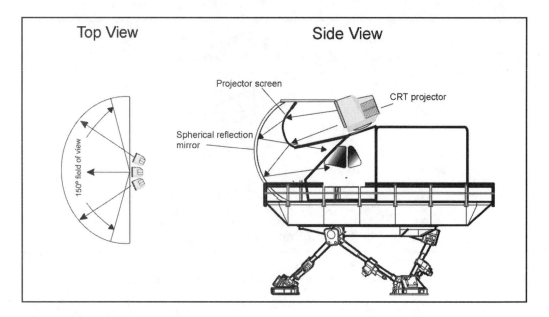

Figure 15.14 *Rediffusion WIDE System*

Visual Systems

Three-dimensional modeling of CGI systems has three stages:

- *Tessellation stage.* A geometrical description of the objects is made and the object is broken up into a series of polygons. The more polygons you have available per frame (some video card manufacturers use the term "triangles" instead of polygons), the more you closely you can model the surface of the object.
- *Geometry stage.* Transformation scales the scene and adds perspective, while lighting determines color and reflections. *Transformation* refers to the translation of coordinates as needed to move the object to the right location as well as the rotation needed to orient it properly.
- *Rendering stage.* 3-D objects are mapped to a two-dimensional screen, and a variety of shading and texture mapping algorithms establish each polygon's color and texture.

It has been said that a realistically modeled oak tree would need 250,000 separate polygons to depict all the ridges, folds, and patterns of the tree's bark (Rolfe and Staples 1986). High-end commercial simulators, such as the Evans & Sutherland ESIG-4500, today offer 8,300 polygons per frame at 60 fps (60Hz), or 498,000 polygons per second, but this can be upgraded with the additional channel processors affording even greater polygon capacity. The ESIG-4500 is also able to offer up to 16 different eye-points or views of a scene. At NASA Ames Research Lab, an older ESIG-3000 that is used with the VMS for modeling helicopters, transports, the space shuttle, and the High-Speed Civil Transport System (HSCT) or Super Sonic Transport (SST), has 6 channels with 3,000 polygons per frame updated at 60 fps at $1200 \times 1,000$ pixels resolution. The cost of just the visual system alone for this simulator runs about $800,000 to $1.5 million. Advanced simulators being planned for the future will be capable of drawing 50,000 polygons per frame at 60 Hz. Note that this level of detail may not be necessary, since a pilot flying over the landscape may not be able to observe all 250,000 polygons of our hypothetical oak tree, whereas a moderately faithful reproduction of the tree may do just as well. An analogy for this situation would be that of color depth in display monitors; while it is true that 24 bits of color give you 16.7 million colors, you could probably get by just fine with 16-bit color with 65,000 colors, or even 8-bit color with 256 color combinations.

But what of today's 3-D PCI video cards now out on the market? Some typical examples include the new STB Velocity 128 and the Diamond Viper V330 (using the NVIDIA RIVA 128 chipset), the Canopus Total 3D, and the ATI 3D Rage II video cards. The NVIDIA and ATI video cards support the new Intel Accelerated Graphics Port (AGP) standard for the Intel Atlantis motherboard (440LX) used on newer Pentium II systems. The AGP is a high performance, component level interconnect targeted at 3D graphical display applications, and is based on a set up of performance extensions to the PCI bus. AGP allows 3D textures to be stored in system memory rather than in the frame buffer. Because of this, much greater amounts of texture memory provided by AGP will allow 3D applications to attain unprecedented levels of realism. To give you an idea of the performance capabilities of the new AGP compatible PCI 3D video cards, let us look at the polygon count per frame, as well as the total polygon count per second. Both of these numbers are a good benchmark of how fast the video card can draw complex 3-D images to the screen. The RIVA 128 is able to display 1.5 million 25 pixel triangles per second, while the ATI 3D Rage Pro cards are able to display 1 million triangles per second. NVIDIA states in their technical literature that the RIVIA 128 can push 20,000 triangles per frame at 30 fps for the RIVA 128. Although ATI does not state the polygon count per frame, one might assume based on a similar ratios for the NVIDIA polygon count per second, that the 3D Rage would have about 13,000 triangles per frame at 30 fps.

It is clear from these performance figures that this new generation of 3D video cards are fast catching up with high end commercial simulators.

N O T E   This rate is quoted per viewing channel, and the ESIG-4500 can combine up to eight channels using optional arithmetic processors, pixel processors, and video buffers. In other words, a single channel, one of eight possible for a single view, can provide up to 498,000 polygons per second.

Figure 15.15 *Denver International Airport at night. (From Advanced Computer Generated Image System Courtesy of NASA Langley Research Facilities and Evans & Sutherland.)*

Figure 15.16 *Landing at SFO. (From Advanced Computer Generated Image System Courtesy of NASA Langley Research Facilities and Evans & Sutherland.)*

Figure 15.17 Computer-generated image of shuttle landing using ESIG-3000. (Courtesy of NASA-Ames Research Facility.)

FAR/AIM

The FAA issues rules and regulations governing aircraft, their operation, and pilot certification. These rules and regulations are called the Federal Aviation Regulations (FAR), and there are many subparts that are encompassed by several volumes of text. Another just as important publication put out by the FAA is the *Airman's Information Manual* (AIM), which gives you all kinds of useful information about navaids, lighting systems, airport markings, airspace, air traffic control, emergency procedures, flight hazards, and meteorology. If you are serious about becoming a pilot, you should get the latest FAR and AIM volumes from your local bookstore; just ask for the FAR/AIM and FAR Flight Crew published by Aviation Supplies & Academics, Inc., but make sure you ask for the latest year's publication because the regulations change from year to year. Alternatively, you can visit the Federal government's www.fedworld.gov Web site and download the FAR, in ASCII text form (ftp://ftp.fedworld.gov/pub/faa-ri/faa-ri.htm). Or if you prefer browsing the FAR on-line through your Web browser, you can do so at http://www.faa.gov/avr/afs/fars/far_idx.htm. For the benefit of readers of this book who do not yet have Internet connections, we have provided the following FAR parts in text-only format on the CD:

- FAR 1: Definitions and abbreviations
- FAR 25: Airworthiness standards: transport-category airplanes.
- FAR 61: Certification: pilots and flight instructors, covers the requirements for obtaining various pilot certificates and ratings. It also explains the privileges and limitations associated with each pilot certificate and rating.

- FAR 91: General operating and flight rules, covers the basic rules for flight under VFR and IFR which apply to all aircraft. Commercial airlines must also comply with additional regulations in Part 135 and Part 121.
- FAR 93: Special air traffic rules and airport traffic patterns.
- FAR 97: Standard instrument approach procedures.
- FAR 121: Operating requirements: domestic, flag, and supplemental operations.
- FAR 135: Operating requirements: commuter and on-demand operations.

Each of the FAR parts on the CD are compressed into a self-extracting, self-executing file; after copying the exe file to your hard disk, simply double-click on the file and it will decompress the ASCII text version of the FAR Part you wanted

Table 15.2 gives a description of all the part subject headings. .

Table 15.2 *Federal Aviation Regulations: Description*

PUBLICATION LOCATION KEY	PUBLICATION TITLE
ALL	Published in Aviation Supplies & Academics, Inc. (ASA) FAR/AIM, FAR-FC, and FAR-AMT books
FAR/AIM	FAR/AIM combination book
FAR-FC	FAR for Flight Crew (FAR-FC) book
FAR-AMT	FAR Aviation Maintenance Technicians (FAR-AMT) book
GPO	Available from the Government Printing Office (GPO)

Table 15.2(b) *Federal Avaiation Regulations: Volume Location*

PART	TITLE	PUBLICATION LOCATION KEY
1	Definitions and abbreviations	ALL
SUBCHAPTER B—PROCEDURAL RULES		
11	General rule-making procedures	GPO
13	Investigative and enforcement procedures	FAR-AMT
14	Rules implementing the Equal Access to Justice Act of 1980	GPO
15	Administrative Claims under Federal Tort Claims Act	GPO
16	Rules of Practice for Federally Assisted Airport Enforcement Proceedings	GPO

Table 15.2 *continued*

PART	TITLE	PUBLICATION LOCATION KEY
SUBCHAPTER B—PROCEDURAL RULES		
SUBCHAPTER C—AIRCRAFT		
21	Certification procedures for products and parts	FAR-AMT
23	Airworthiness standards: normal, utility, acrobatic, and commuter category airplanes	FAR-AMT
25	Airworthiness standards: transport category airplanes	FAR-FO
27	Airworthiness standards: normal category rotorcraft	FAR-AMT
29	Airworthiness standards: transport category rotorcraft	GPO
31	Airworthiness standards: manned free balloons	GPO
33	Airworthiness standards: aircraft engines	FAR-AMT
34	Fuel venting and exhaust emission requirements for turbine engine–powered airplanes	FAR-AMT
35	Airworthiness standards: propellers	FAR-AMT
36	Noise standards: aircraft type and airworthiness certification	GPO
39	Airworthiness directives	FAR-AMT
43	Maintenance, preventive maintenance, rebuilding, and alteration	FAR/AIM, FAR-AMT
45	Identification and registration marking	FAR-AMT
47	Aircraft registration	FAR-AMT
49	Recording of aircraft titles and security documents	GPO
50–59	[Reserved]	
SUBCHAPTER D—AIRMEN		
60	[Reserved]	
61	Certification: Pilots and flight instructors	FAR/AIM
63	Certification: Flight crewmembers other than pilots	FAR-FC
65	Certification: Airmen other than flight crewmembers	FAR-AMT, FAR-FC
SUBCHAPTER D—AIRMEN		
67	Medical standards and certification	FAR/AIM

Table 15.2 continued

PART	TITLE	PUBLICATION LOCATION KEY
SUBCHAPTER E—AIRSPACE		
71	Designation of Class A, Class B, Class C, Class D, and Class E airspace areas, airways, routes, and reporting points	FAR/AIM
73	Special use airspace	FAR/AIM
75	[Reserved]	
77	Objects affecting navigable airspace	GPO
SUBCHAPTER F—AIR TRAFFIC AND GENERAL OPERATING RULES		
91	General operating and flight rules	FAR/AIM, FAR-AMT
93	Special air traffic rules and airport traffic patterns	GPO
95	IFR altitudes	GPO
97	Standard instrument approach procedures	FAR/AIM
99	Security control of air traffic	GPO
101	Moored balloons, kites, unmanned rockets and unmanned free balloons	GPO
103	Ultralight vehicles	FAR/AIM
105	Parachute jumping	FAR/AIM
107	Airport security	GPO
108	Airplane operator security	GPO
109	Indirect air carrier security	GPO
SUBCHAPTER G—AIR CARRIERS, AIR TRAVEL CLUBS, AND OPERATORS FOR COMPENSATION OR HIRE CERTIFICATION AND OPERATIONS		
119	Certification: air carriers and commercial operators	FAR/AIM
121	Operating requirements: domestic, flag, and supplemental operations	FAR-FC, FAR-AMT (Subparts J and L only)

Table 15.2 continued

PART	TITLE	PUBLICATION LOCATION KEY

SUBCHAPTER G—AIR CARRIERS, AIR TRAVEL CLUBS, AND OPERATORS FOR COMPENSATION OR HIRE CERTIFICATION AND OPERATIONS

PART	TITLE	PUBLICATION LOCATION KEY
125	Certification and operations: airplanes having a seating capacity of 20 or more passengers or a maximum payload capacity of 6,000 pounds or more	FAR-AMT
129	Operations: foreign air carriers and foreign operators of U.S.-registered aircraft engaged in common carriage	GPO
133	Rotorcraft external-load operations	GPO
135	Operating requirements: commuter and on-demand operations	FAR/AIM FAR-AMT
137	Agricultural aircraft operations	FAR/AIM
139	Certification and operations: land airports serving certain air carriers	GPO

SUBCHAPTER H—SCHOOLS AND OTHER CERTIFICATED AGENCIES

PART	TITLE	PUBLICATION LOCATION KEY
140	[Reserved]	
141	Pilot schools	FAR/AIM
142	Training centers	FAR/AIM
143	Ground instructors	FAR/AIM
145	Repair stations	FAR-AMT
147	Aviation maintenance technician schools	FAR-AMT

SUBCHAPTER I—AIRPORTS

PART	TITLE	PUBLICATION LOCATION KEY
150	Airport noise compatibility planning	GPO
151	Federal aid to airports	GPO
152	Airport aid program	GPO
155	Release of airport property from surplus property disposal restrictions	GPO
156	State Block Grant Pilot Program	GPO
157	Notice of construction, alteration, activation, and deactivation of airports	GPO

Table 15.2 *continued*

PART	TITLE	PUBLICATION LOCATION KEY
SUBCHAPTER I—AIRPORTS		
158	Passenger facility charges (PFCs)	GPO
159	National capital airports	GPO
161	Notice and approval of airport noise and access restrictions	GPO
169	Expenditure of federal funds for nonmilitary airports or air navigation facilities thereon	GPO
SUBCHAPTER J—NAVIGATIONAL FACILITIES		
170	Establishment and discontinuance criteria for air traffic control services and navigational facilities	GPO
171	Non-Federal navigation facilities	GPO
SUBCHAPTER K—ADMINISTRATIVE REGULATIONS		
183	Representatives of the administrator	FAR-AMT
185	Testimony by employees and production of records in legal proceedings, and service of legal process and pleadings	GPO
187	Fees	GPO
189	Use of Federal Aviation Administration communications system	GPO
191	Withholding security information from disclosure under the Air Transportation Security Act of 1974	GPO
SUBCHAPTERS L – M		
[Reserved]		
SUBCHAPTER N—WAR RISK INSURANCE		
198 Aviation insurance		GPO

You'll find FAR Parts 25, 61, 91, 97, and 121 in text files on the book's CD-ROM.

NOTE

LEARNING TO BE A PILOT

Although Flight Simulator is used by many schools as a training tool for students to learn the basics of aeronautics, the FAA does not yet officially sanction its use for training purposes. This policy may change in the near future as the FAA is re-evaluating the use of PC-based simulators for IFR recurrency requirements. This would mean that a pilot could replace some of his or her minimum required IFR flight hours with simulated flight hours.

Pilot Licensing

FAR Part 61 establishes the rules, eligibility requirements, limitations, and other permissible activities for pilots. These rules strictly govern what you can and cannot do. For example, you cannot fly passengers for pay if you are a student pilot, recreational pilot, or a private pilot. Furthermore, you cannot act as pilot in command of an airplane that has more than 200 horsepower or one that has constant-speed propeller systems, retractable landing gear, and flaps unless you have received a checkout from an instructor and your logbook has been suitably endorsed. Similarly, you can't act as a pilot in command of a pressurized aircraft unless you have received specific ground and flight training.

Along with your pilot's certificate, you must also carry a current medical certificate proving you are of sound body and mind.

Pilot Certificates and Ratings

FAR Part 61 covers the certification of pilots and flight instructors. Each type of certificate has certain limitations and privileges while requiring specific training and flight experience.

- *Student pilot.* The student pilot can not act as pilot in command of an aircraft that is carrying property or passengers, in the furtherance of a business, or on international flights. Flights are restricted to visual meteorological conditions where flight or surface visibility is not less than 3 statute miles by day and 5 statute miles by night. Students can fly solo, but only after their flight instructor has endorsed their logbook and given them instruction such that they are competent to make such flights. No business or international flights are allowed.

- *Recreational pilot.* The recreational pilot may carry not more than one passenger and may act as a pilot in command only when the flight is within 50 nautical miles of an airport at which the pilot has received ground and flight instruction.

This certificate is good for people who want to fly for recreational pursuits on days with good visibility, but it restricts flights for business purposes or flights that cross international borders.

- *Private pilot.* The private pilot has the additional privileges of carrying more than one passenger, but may not carry passengers for hire. This certificate allows flights day or night, but in order to fly under instrument meteorological conditions, the pilot must obtain an instrument rating. A private pilot can fly internationally and in conjunction with business.

- *Commercial pilot.* The commercial pilot is granted the privilege of carrying passengers and cargo for hire.

- *Airline Transport Pilot (ATP).* The ATP is the most difficult pilot certificate to earn because the FAA mandates very stringent requirements for training, education, and skills. All air carriers operating under FAR 135 or airlines operating under FAR 121 must use pilots who possess the ATP certificate.

- *Flight instructor.* The flight instructor certificate allows a pilot to give instruction to student pilots, as well as endorse logbooks for aircraft type ratings and line checks. A flight instructor must have an instrument rating in order to give instrument instruction, and she must also have a multiengine rating in order to give multiengine instruction.

Airplane Class and Type Ratings

Each pilot certificate carries a rating that further specifies the privileges that the pilot may exercise. There are two basic ratings: airplane class and aircraft type.

Aircraft classes include:

- Single-engine land
- Single-engine sea
- Multiengine land
- Multiengine sea

Aircraft types include:

- Airplane
- Rotorcraft
- Glider
- Lighter-than-air

There is another rating that can be earned on a pilot certificate: the instrument rating, which bestows the privilege of flying through bad weather or poor visibility. Without the instrument rating, you can only fly lower than 18,000 feet, and you are only allowed to fly under visual flight rules (VFR).

Aircraft Type Ratings

The pilot of any turbojet-powered aircraft must earn a type rating certifying that he or she is capable of flying such an aircraft. For example, a pilot flying a MD-80 must pass a type rating check ride in a Boeing 737 before acting as pilot in command of that aircraft type. For almost all aircraft that require type ratings on the pilot certificate, both a pilot in command and a copilot are required.

Carrying Passengers

The FAA strictly forbids student pilots, recreational pilots, and private pilots from carrying passengers for hire. If you hold a private pilot certificate with airplane and single-engine land ratings you can fly seaplanes or multiengine airplanes solo, provided an instructor has signed your logbook. But you can't carry passengers until you have taken the training and passed the check ride for the seaplane or twin-engine plane.

Table 15.3 FAA Pilot Certificates, Eligibility Requirements, Aircraft Class Ratings, Aircraft Type Ratings, Medical Certificate Requirements, and Other Restrictions

PILOT CERTIFICATES	STUDENT PILOTS	RECREATIONAL PILOTS	PRIVATE PILOTS	COMMERCIAL PILOTS	AIRLINE TRANSPORT PILOTS	FLIGHT INSTRUCTORS
Eligibility	Pass written, oral and flight test by FAA inspector.	Pass written, oral and flight test by FAA inspector.	Pass written, oral and flight test by FAA inspector.	Must hold a private pilot's certificate with instrument rating.	Must hold a commercial pilot's certificate rating.	Must hold a commercial pilot or airline transport pilot certificate.
Airplane Flight Time Requirements	Written exam and before flying solo must know how to inspect aircraft, taxi, takeoff, land (including normal and crosswind), fly straight and level, perform shallow medium, and steep banked turns, climbs with turns, airport traffic patterns,	250 hours as Pilot in command (of which 100 hours must be cross country, and 25 hours night flight time), plus 1,500 hours of additional flight time, with 500 hours of cross country,	In addition to student pilot requirements, must have 40 hours of flight instruction and solo flight time. (a) 20 hours of flight instruction from an authorized flight instructor, and 3 hours of cross country	Must have 250 hours of flight time as pilot, including 50 hours of cross country flights, 5 hours of night flying, and 5 hours of instrument flying.	250 hours as Pilot in command (of which 100 hours must be cross country, and 25 hours night flight time), plus 1,500 hours of additional flight time, with 500 hours of cross country,	

Table 15.3 *continued*

PILOT CERTIFICATES	STUDENT PILOTS	RECREATIONAL PILOTS	PRIVATE PILOTS	COMMERCIAL PILOTS	AIRLINE TRANSPORT PILOTS	FLIGHT INSTRUCTORS
	descents with turns, flying at various airspeeds, slips, engine idle landing approaches go arounds, forced landing procedures, stall entries.	100 hours of night flight, and 75 hours of instrument time.	flying, 3 hours at night, including 10 takeoffs.		100 hours of night flight, and 75 hours of instrument time.	
Age	16 or older	17 or older	17 or older	18 or older	23 or older	18 or older
Expiration	End of the 24th month after first issue.	No Expiration	No Expiration	No Expiration	No Expiration	End of the 24th month after first issue.
Aircraft Ratings Permitted			(i) Airplane. (ii) Rotorcraft. (iii) Glider. (iv) Lighter-than-air.	(i) Airplane. (ii) Rotorcraft. (iii) Glider. (iv) Lighter-than-air.	(i) Airplane. (ii) Rotorcraft. (iii) Glider. (iv) Lighter-than-air.	(i) Airplane. (ii) Rotorcraft. (iii) Glider.
Aircraft Class Rating			(i) Single-engine land. (ii) Multiengine land (iii) Single-engine sea. (iv) Multiengine sea.	(i) Single-engine land. (ii) Multiengine land. (iii) Single-engine sea. (iv) Multiengine sea.	(i) Single-engineland. (ii) Multiengine land. (iii) Single-. engine sea (iv) Multiengine sea.	(i) Single engineland (ii) Multiengine land. (iii) Single-. engine sea (iv) Multiengine sea.
Rotorcraft Class Ratings			(i) Helicopter. (ii) Gyroplane.	(i) Helicopter. (ii) Gyroplane.	(i) Helicopter. (ii) Gyroplane	(i) Helicopter. (ii) Gyroplane.
Lighter than air Class Ratings			(i) Airship. (ii) Free balloon.	(i) Airship. (ii) Free balloon.	(i) Airship. (ii) Free balloon.	
Instrument Ratings			(i) Instrument—airplanes. (ii) Instrument—helicopter	(i) Instrument—airplanes. (ii) Instrument—helicopter	(i) Instrument—airplanes. (ii) Instrument—helicopter	(i) Instrument—airplanes. (ii) Instrument—helicopter
Medical Certificate Required	Third Class	Third Class	Third Class	Second Class	First Class	First or Third Class
Carry Passengers for Hire?	No	No	No, but may carry passengers if connected with incidental business.	Yes	Yes	Yes

Table 15.3 continued

PILOT CERTIFICATES	STUDENT PILOTS	RECREATIONAL PILOTS	PRIVATE PILOTS	COMMERCIAL PILOTS	AIRLINE TRANSPORT PILOTS	FLIGHT INSTRUCTORS
Other Restrictions	No international flights, no solo cross country flights, surface or flight visibility must not be less than 3 statute miles during day or 5 miles at night, may not carry property for hire, fly in furtherance of business, or fly as pilot in command with a passenger. Must have 20/50 in each eye separately, without corr-ection, or if visionin either or both eyes is poorer than 20/50, it can be corrected to 20/30 or better in each eye with corrective lenses (glasses or contact lenses). Ability to hear whispered voice at three fee. No myocardial infarction, angina pectoris, corinary heart disease, epilepsy, mental disorder, or diabetes.	Must have 20/50 or better in each eye separately, without correction; or if vision in either or both eyes is poorer than 20/50, it can be corrected to 20/30 or better in each eye with corrective lenses (glasses or contact lenses). Ability to hear whispered voice at three fee. No myocardial infarction, angina pectoris, corinary heart disease, epilepsy, mental disorder, or diabetes.	May not act as second in command of an aircraft that is type certificated for more than one required pilot. No myocardial infarction, angina pectoris, corinary heart disease, epilepsy, mental disorder or diabetes.	Must have 20/20 or better in each eye separately, without correction; or at least 20/100 in each eye separately corrected to 10/10 or better with corrective lenses (glasses or contact lenses). Must be able to hear whispered voice at a distance of at least eight feet in each ear separately. No high blood pressure.	Must have 20/20 or better in each eye separately, without correction; or at least 20/100 in each eye separately corrected to 10/10 or better with corrective lenses (glasses or contact lenses). Must be able to hear whispered voice at a distance of at least eight feet in each ear separately. No high blood pressure.	Must have 20/20 or better in each eye separately, without correction; or at least 20/100 in each eye separately corrected to 10/10 or better with corrective lenses (glasses or contact lenses). Must be able to hear whispered voice at a distance of at least eight feet in each ear separately. No high blood pressure.

Estimated Number of Active Pilots in the United States

The FAA compiles statistics on the aviation industry which it publishes each year as the *FAA Statistical Handbook of Aviation*. These statistics cover all aspects of the industry, including flight safety, accidents, ranking of airport traffic, total industry hours and miles flown, numbers of active pilots, revenues of airlines, etc. Table 15.4 shows the total number of pilots still active at the end of 1992.

Table 15.4 *Estimated Active Pilot Certificates Held in 1992*

DESCRIPTION	MEN AND WOMEN	WOMEN ONLY
Pilot Total	682,959	40,620
Student	114,597	13,921
Recreational	187	10
Private	288,078	17,276
Commercial	146,385	5,918
Airline transport	115,855	2,530
Helicopter	9,652	313
Glider	8,205	652
Lighter-than-air	No longer being issued (was 1,089 in 1989)	
Flight instructor	72,148	3,964
Instrument ratings	306,169	
Nonpilot total	540,548	11,514
Mechanic	384,669	4,398
Parachute rigger	8,163	390
Ground instructor	73,276	4,338
Dispatcher	12,256	1,004
Flight navigator	1,154	0
Flight engineer	61,022	1,384

ACCIDENT RATES FOR U.S. AIRLINES, CHARTER AIRLINES, COMMUTER AIR CARRIERS, AND GENERAL AVIATION

The term *civil aviation* encompasses scheduled airline and unscheduled charter air services, commuter airlines, and general aviation. The term *general aviation* refers primarily to lower-altitude flying primarily for private and leisure purposes (although business travel using company-owned aircraft is included under general aviation as well). Commercial high-altitude flying provides the general public with global passenger and commercial air transport. In the United States, different parts of the FAR govern each category within civil aviation. Scheduled (airline flights) and unscheduled airlines (charter flights) operate under FAR 121, while commuter air carriers operate under FAR 135. General aviation operates under all the rules not covered by FAR 121 and FAR 135.

It is interesting to compare the accident rate for U.S. airlines and charter airlines operating under FAR Part 121, commuter air carriers operating under FAR 135, and general aviation flyers. Tables 15.5, 15.6, and 15.7 summarize the results for the period 1982 through 1996. It should come as no surprise that the highest accident rate is found in the category of general aviation, and that the safest form of travel is on a scheduled or unscheduled U.S. airline.

Table 15.5 *Accidents, Fatalities, and Rates, 1982 through 1996, U.S. Airlines Scheduled and Nonscheduled Operating Under FAR 121*

	ACCIDENTS		FATALITIES					ACCIDENTS PER 100,000 FLIGHT HOURS		ACCIDENTS PER 1,000,000 MILES FLOWN		ACCIDENTS PER 100,000 DEPARTURES	
YEAR	ALL	FATAL	TOTAL	ABOARD	FLIGHT HOURS	MILES FLOWN	DEPARTURES	ALL	FATAL	ALL	FATAL	ALL	FATAL
1982	18	5	235	223	7,040,325	2,938,513,000	5,351,133	0.241	0.057	0.0058	0.0014	0.318	0.075
1983	23	4	15	14	7,298,799	3,069,318,000	5,444,374	0.315	0.055	0.0075	0.0013	0.422	0.073
1984	16	1	4	4	8,165,124	3,428,063,000	5,898,852	0.196	0.012	0.0047	0.0003	0.271	0.017
1985	21	7	526	525	8,709,894	3,631,017,000	6,306,759	0.241	0.08	0.0058	0.0019	0.333	0.111
1986	24	3	8	7	9,976,104	4,017,626,000	7,202,027	0.231	0.02	0.0057	0.0005	0.319	0.028
1987	34	5	232	230	10,645,192	4,360,521,000	7,601,373	0.31	0.038	0.0076	0.0009	0.434	0.053
1988	29	3	285	274	11,140,548	4,503,426,000	7,716,061	0.251	0.018	0.0062	0.0004	0.363	0.026
1989	28	11	278	276	11,274,543	4,947,832,000	7,645,494	0.248	0.098	0.0061	0.0024	0.366	0.144
1990	24	6	39	12	12,150,116	4,605,083,000	8,092,306	0.198	0.049	0.0049	0.0012	0.297	0.074
1991	26	4	62	49	11,780,610	4,824,824,000	7,814,875	0.221	0.034	0.0054	0.0008	0.333	0.051
1992	18	4	33	31	12,359,715	5,054,916,000	7,880,707	0.146	0.032	0.0036	0.0008	0.228	0.051
1993	23	1	1	0	12,706,206	5,249,469,000	8,074,393	0.181	0.008	0.0044	0.0002	0.285	0.012
1994	23	4	239	237	13,122,221	5,478,118,000	8,242,903	0.168	0.03	0.004	0.0007	0.267	0.049
1995	36	3	168	162	13,513,219	5,648,512,000	8,451,606	0.266	0.022	0.0064	0.0005	0.426	0.035
1996	38	5	380	350	13,683,000	5,761,935,000	8,554,000	0.278	0.037	0.0066	0.0009	0.444	0.058

Notes 1996 data are preliminary
All statistics are compiled by the Federal Aviation Administration.

Table 15.6 *Accidents, Fatalities, and Rates, 1982 through 1996, U.S. Commuter Air Carriers Operating Under FAR Part 135*

	ACCIDENTS		FATALITIES					ACCIDENTS PER 100,000 FLIGHT HOURS		ACCIDENTS PER 1,000,000 MILES FLOWN		ACCIDENTS PER 100,000 DEPARTURES	
YEAR	ALL	FATAL	TOTAL	ABOARD	FLIGHT HOURS	MILES FLOWN	DEPARTURES	ALL	FATAL	ALL	FATAL	ALL	FATAL
1982	26	5	14	14	1,299,748	222,355,000	2,026,691	2	0.385	0.1169	0.0225	1.283	0.247
1983	17	2	11	10	1,510,908	253,572,000	2,328,430	1.125	0.132	0.067	0.0079	0.73	0.086
1984	22	7	48	46	1,745,762	291,460,000	2,676,590	1.26	0.401	0.0755	0.024	0.822	0.262
1985	21	7	37	36	1,737,106	300,817,000	2,561,463	1.209	0.403	0.0698	0.0233	0.82	0.273
1986	15	2	4	4	1,724,586	307,393,000	2,798,811	0.87	0.116	0.0488	0.0065	0.536	0.071
1987	33	10	59	57	1,946,349	350,879,000	2,809,918	1.695	0.514	0.094	0.0285	1.174	0.356
1988	19	2	21	21	2,092,689	380,237,000	2,909,005	0.908	0.096	0.05	0.0053	0.653	0.069
1989	19	5	31	31	2,240,555	393,619,000	2,818,520	0.848	0.223	0.0483	0.0127	0.674	0.177
1990	16	4	7	5	2,341,760	450,133,000	3,160,089	0.683	0.171	0.0355	0.0089	0.506	0.127
1991	22	8	99	77	2,291,693	433,900,000	2,820,440	0.96	0.349	0.0507	0.0184	0.78	0.284
1992	23	7	21	21	2,363,745	508,242,000	3,114,932	0.931	0.296	0.0433	0.0138	0.706	0.225
1993	16	4	24	23	2,641,268	554,963,000	3,601,902	0.606	0.151	0.0288	0.0072	0.444	0.111
1994	10	3	25	25	2,787,904	594,716,000	3,850,372	0.359	0.108	0.0168	0.005	0.26	0.078
1995	11	2	9	9	2,478,872	565,577,000	3,216,900	0.444	0.081	0.0194	0.0035	0.342	0.062
1996	11	1	14	12	2,474,000	608,814,000	3,171,000	0.445	0.04	0.0181	0.0016	0.347	0.032

Notes 1996 data are preliminary.
All statistics are compiled by the Federal Aviation Administration.

Table 15.7 *Accidents, Fatalities, and Rates, 1982 through 1996, U.S. General Aviation*

	ACCIDENTS		FATALITIES			ACCIDENTS PER 100,000 FLIGHT HOURS	
YEAR	ALL	FATAL	TOTAL	ABOARD	FLIGHT HOURS	ALL	FATAL
1982	3,233.00	591	1187	1170	29,640,000	10.9	1.99
1983	3,078.00	556	1069	1062	28,673,000	10.73	1.94
1984	3,017.00	545	1042	1021	29,099,000	10.36	1.87
1985	2,739.00	498	955	944	28,322,000	9.66	1.75
1986	2,582.00	474	967	878	27,073,000	9.54	1.75
1987	2,495.00	447	838	823	26,972,000	9.25	1.65
1988	2,385.00	460	800	792	27,446,000	8.69	1.68
1989	2,232.00	431	768	765	27,920,000	7.98	1.53
1990	2,215.00	442	766	761	28,510,000	7.77	1.55
1991	2,175.00	432	786	772	27,226,000	7.98	1.58
1992	2,073.00	446	857	855	23,792,000	8.71	1.87
1993	2,039.00	398	736	732	22,531,000	9.05	1.76
1994	1,994.00	404	730	723	21,873,000	9.11	1.84
1995	2,054.00	411	733	726	23,538,000	8.72	1.74
1996	1,907.00	358	631	614	23,650,000	8.06	1.51

Notes 1996 data are preliminary.
Statistics compiled by the Federal Aviation Administration. Hours are estimated.

Table 15.8 *Accident Rates by Category for the year 1996 as Reported to the National Transportation Safety Board*

	ACCIDENTS		FATALITIES				ACCIDENTS PER 100,000 FLIGHT HOURS		ACCIDENTS PER 100,000 DEPARTURES	
	ALL	FATAL	TOTAL	ABOARD	FLIGHT HOURS	DEPARTURES	ALL	FATAL	ALL	FATAL
U.S. Air carriers operating under 14 CFR 121										
Scheduled	32	3	342	342	12,900,000	8185,000	0.248	0.023	0.391	0.037
Nonscheduled	6	2	38	8	783,000	369,000	0.766	0.255	1.626	0.006
U.S. Air carriers operating under 14 CFR 135										
Scheduled	11	1	14	12	2,474,000	3171,000	0.445	0.04	0.347	0.032
Nonscheduled	87	27	59	59	1,902,000	n/a	4.57	1.42	n/a	n/a
U.S. General aviation	1,907	358	631	614	23,650,000	n/a	8.06	1.51	n/a	n/a
U.S. civil aviation	2,040	390	1,070	1035						
Other accidents in the U.S.										
Foreign registerd aircraft	15	1	1	1						
Unregistered aircraft	8	4	4	3						
Military aircraft that collided with civil aircraft	-	-	-	-						
U.S. registered aircraft operated abroad by foreign air carriers	2	2	81	81						

Notes All data are preliminary.
Statistics are compiled by the Federal Aviation Administration. Hours are estimated.

Table 15.9 reveals a surprising fact: almost 74% of all accidents are caused by pilot error. Less than 12% of accidents are caused by mechanical failure, and less than 6% by bad weather. Improper maintenance and air traffic control are even less significant as contributing factors.

Table 15.9 *Primary Causes of Accidents in the Worldwide Commercial Aviation Fleet*

CAUSE OF ACCIDENT	KNOWN CAUSES 1959-85	PERCENTAGE OF TOTAL KNOWN CAUSE ACCIDENTS
Pilot error	229	73.9%
Aircraft mechanical failure	36	11.6%
Bad weather	17	5.5%
Air traffic control mistake or airport problem	13	4.2%
Other	10	3.2%
Improper maintenance	5	1.6%
Total (known causes)	310	
Total unknown causes	45	

Looking at the data in Table 15.8, you can see that airline accidents are very rare events and the risk of death or serious injury for air travelers is exceedingly small on scheduled airlines. Professor Arnold Barnett of the Massachusetts Institute of Technology, using data from 1990 to the present, has calculated that a passenger faces a death risk of one in eight million. Barnett states "if a passenger facing a death risk of one in eight million were to choose one flight at random each day, that passenger would, on average, go for 21,000 years before perishing in a fatal crash." Furthermore, despite the doubling of air traffic over the past decade, the large U.S. airlines as a group have experienced, on average, one and one-half to two catastrophic accidents a year.

On-line Accident Reports and Statistics

There are two principal online databases that the FAA and the National Transportation Safety Board (NTSB) maintain on the World Wide Web at http://nasdac.faa.gov/internet/:

1. NTSB Aviation Accident/Incident Database
2. FAA Incident Data System

NTSB Aviation Accident/Incident Database

The NTSB is an independent federal agency charged by Congress with investigating every civil aviation accident in the United States and significant accidents in the other modes of transportation—railroad, highway, marine, and pipeline. Representatives from numerous Federal, State and Local authorities as well as various segments of the industry usually participate in the investigation of major accidents. The NTSB determines the probable cause of accidents and issues safety recommendations aimed at preventing future accidents. The NTSB accident/incident database is the official repository of aviation accident data and causal factors.

In the NTSB database, an event is classified as an accident or an incident. The term *aircraft accident* designates an occurrence associated with the operation of an aircraft that takes place between the time any person boards the aircraft with the intention of flight and the time when all such persons have disembarked, and in which any person suffers death or serious injury, or in which the aircraft receives substantial damage. The NTSB defines *incident* to mean an occurrence other than an accident, associated with the operation of an aircraft, which affects or could affect the safety of operations. Note that the NTSB database contains only selected incident reports.

FAA Incident Data System

The FAA Incident Data System contains a much more extensive collection of aviation incidents than the NTSB, because the FAA tracks not only accidents, but also potentially hazardous events that do not meet the aircraft damage or the personal injury thresholds contained in the NTSB definition of an accident.

What You Can Do with the FAA/NTSB Databases on the Web

The NTSB Aviation Accident/Incident Database and the FAA Incident Database can be used to:

1. Browse the FAA and NTSB's aviation accident and incident information
2. Count aviation accidents and incidents
3. Read NTSB's determination of probable causes when available,
4. Select NTSB accident or incident reports based on:
   a.   User supplied words or phrases
   b.   User selected criteria, including:
   - Report number
   - Date range
   - State
   - Aircraft registration number
   - Aircraft make and model
   - Operator/airline (Part 121 only)
   - Category of operation
   - Airport identification

Both databases are updated monthly and allow for a search and selection of records by certain criteria that you specify. For example, as you can see in the FAA Query Form on their Web page in Figure 15.18, you can conduct a search of all incidents involving Boeing 737s since 1979. After you click the **Begin Search** button, you'll see a Search Results page appear that shows 1,082 records from a total 67,057 incidents that match your request for incidents involving Boeing 737s. If you then click on any of the hypertext links below, as shown in Figure 15.19, you can actually read the individual reports.

Another useful thing you can do with the database: suppose you were worried about flying a particular aircraft because you heard something bad about it, and you knew the registration number of the airplane. Using this Web page, you could call up all the incidents involving this aircraft had since it was built. Although you may not be able to get your airline or travel agent to tell you which aircraft is flying a particular route, when you get to the airport you can see the registration number marked on the tail of the aircraft and then decide whether to board or not.

Table 15.10 is an excerpt of one such report.

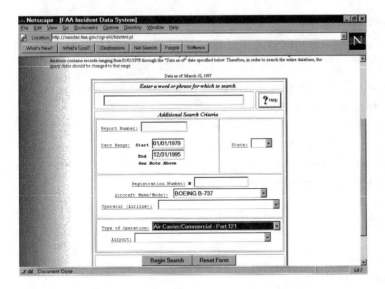

Figure 15.18 *FAA Incident Data System on the Web allows you to search all incidents by aircraft, date, report, airline, and even airport.*

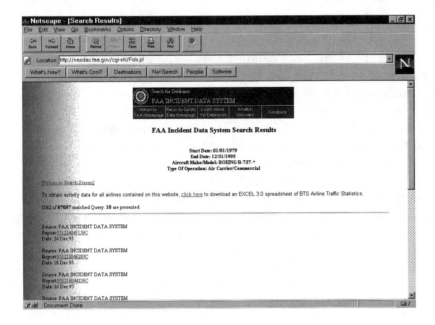

Figure 15.19 *FAA Incident Data System search results show 1,082 of 67,087 records match your search profile for incidents involving the Boeing 737.*

Table 15.10 *FAA Incident Data System Report*

Data Source:	FAA INCIDENT DATA SYSTEM
Report Number:	951224047159C
Local Date:	12/24/1995
Local Time:	22:19
City:	CHICAGO
State:	IL
Airport Name:	CHICAGO MIDWAY
Airport Id:	MDW
Event Type:	INCIDENT - AIR CARRIER
Mid Air Collision:	NOT A MIDAIR
Aircraft Damage:	MINOR
Phase of Flight:	IDLING ENGINES
Aircraft Make/Model:	BOEING B-737-524
Airframe Hours:	
Operator Code:	CALA
Operator:	CONTINENTAL AIRLINES INC - CALA
Owner Name:	CONTINENTAL AIRLINES INC

NARRATIVE

PARKING AT GATE NR1 ENGINE INJESTED GROUND HEATER HOSE. RAMP PERSONEL RETRAINING PLANNED.

FINDINGS

Primary Cause:	UNSAFE ACTS BY THIRD PARTY
Secondary Cause:	7200 ENGINE (TURBINE/TURBO-
PROP), ENGINE (TURBINE/TURBOPROP)	
Contributing Factor:	OTHER/MISCELLANEOUS
Supporting Factor:	RUPTURED OR BURST
Primary Person Involved:	MAINTENANCE AND/OR GROUND
CREW	
General Cause:	MISCELLANEOUS, OTHER, NONE

Table 15.10 continued

AIRCRAFT INFORMATION

DETAIL

Primary Flight Type:	SCHEDULED AIR CARRIER
Secondary Flight Type:	PASSENGERS
Type of Operation:	AIR CARRIER/COMMERCIAL
Registration Number:	37615
Total Aboard:	2
Fatalities:	0
Injuries:	0
Landing Gear:	RETRACT TRICYCLE
Aircraft Weight Class:	OVER 12500 LBS
Engine Make:	
Engine Model:	
Engine Group:	
Number of Engines:	2
Engine Type:	

ENVIRONMENTAL/OPERATIONS INFORMATION

Primary Flight Conditions:	UNKNOWN
Secondary Flight Conditions:	WEATHER NOT A FACTOR
Wind Direction (deg):	
Wind Speed (mph):	

ENVIRONMENTAL/OPERATIONS INFORMATION

Visibility (mi):	
Visibility Restrictions:	
Light Condition:	NIGHT
Flight Plan Filed:	INSTRUMENT FLIGHT RULES
Approach Type:	

PILOT-IN-COMMAND

Pilot Certificates:	
Pilot Rating:	
Pilot Qualification:	

Table 15.10 continued

DETAIL
....

FLIGHT TIME (HOURS)
....

Total Hours:

Total in Make/Model:

Total Last 90 Days:

Total Last 90 Days Make/Model:
....

Bureau of Transportation Statistics (BTS) Airline Statistics

Another useful Web resource is found at the Bureau of Transportation Statistics (BTS) located at www.bts.gov, where you can download an Excel spreadsheet that contains traffic and capacity statistics on individual airline operations. Statistics presented here include departures, hours flown, and miles flown by airline, by year.

The FAA is naturally reluctant to publish incident reports on a per Airline basis, for fear of offending the airlines and inviting lawsuits. However, you can calculate the accident rates for each airline yourself using the data that is found in the BTS airline statistics and the FAA Incident Reports Database by employing the following formula:

$$\frac{\text{Total Number of Accidents 1991--1995}}{\text{Total Flight Hours, or Miles Flown, or Departures 1991-1995}} = \text{Accident Rate}$$

FAR FOR ADVANCED SIMULATION TRAINING

The FAA has strict rules and regulations governing flight crews involved in the transport of passengers. These regulations are encoded in several volumes called the Federal Aviation Regulations (FAR), and they encompass all aspects of pilot training and education, requirements for recurrent training and proficiency, airworthiness standards, certification of pilots and nonpilot flight crews, and operating requirements for domestic carriers. The sections pertaining to simulators is of passing interest to the Flight Simulator pilot because it shows how important simulators are to airline operations today.

Airline transport pilots must undergo an annual regimen of line checks and proficiency checks, and must keep their flying skills sharp by having recently flown within a prescribed time period. These checks may be accomplished in various types of flight simulators, and they allow testing for all kinds of emergency situations that could not be safely tested for on a real aircraft. Airlines are extremely happy with simulator training because it saves them millions of dollars in fuel costs, and it frees up their aircraft for revenue earning line use. For example, flying a real Boeing 747-400 (which costs $143 million) can cost upwards of $12,500 an hour. The 747 simulator with a validated flight model can cost several million, but the hourly costs are only $750 an hour. When you factor in the fuel savings, no pollution and noise, less risk, the ability to improve crew training, and the ability to program equipment failures and engine malfunctions, it is clear that simulators will proliferate even more.

FAR 61.155 and FAR 61.157 Airline Transport Pilot Certificate Requirement and Test Requirements

Pilots who fly for airlines are required to have an airline transport pilot certificate. In order to be eligible, an applicant must:

1. Be at least 23 years of age.
2. Be of good moral character.
3. Be able to read, write, and understand the English language and speak it without accent or impediment of speech.
4. Be a high school graduate or have equivalent knowledge and skill.
5. Have a first-class medical certificate.
6. Possess a commercial pilot certificate which includes:
   - 250 hours of flight time as pilot in command.
   - 1,500 hours of flight time as a pilot, including 500 hours of cross-country flight time, 100 hours of night flight time, and 75 hour of actual or simulated instrument time, at least 50 hours of which were in actual flight.

Certification Check

FAR 61.157 further requires that applicants for the airline transport pilot certificate must pass a practical test on the type of aircraft that they are being rated for, but that some of these tests may be performed in an airplane simulator.

FAR 121.439—Recency of Experience

FAR 121.439 require that no pilot may serve as a pilot crewmember, unless within the preceding 90 days that person has made at least three takeoffs and landings in the type of airplane in which that person is to serve. The takeoffs and landings under these regulations may be performed in a simulator in lieu of actual flying. In addition, any pilot who fails to make the three required takeoffs and landings within any 90 day period must reestablish recency of experience by serving in an advanced simulator which includes at least one simulated engine failure, and a landing from an ILS approach to include one landing to a full stop.

FAR 121.440—Line Checks

FAR 121.440 further states that every air transport pilot must pass a line check every year under the supervision of a pilot check aviator who is currently qualified on both the route and type of airplane that the check is being performed on. Line checks are not conducted in simulators.

FAR 121.441 Proficiency Checks

FAR 121.441 mandates that all air transport pilots must complete an annual proficiency check, or an approved simulator course of training. In addition, within the last 6 months that pilot must have passed either the proficiency check or undergone simulator training. A check pilot, or administrator must evaluate the pilot, and the entire proficiency check may be conducted in an approved visual simulator if the pilot being checked accomplishes at least two landings in the aircraft during a line check.

When a pilot transitions from one aircraft type to another e.g., a Boeing 737-300 to a Boeing 737-700), so confident are the airlines and the FAA with advanced simulator training that many pilots go straight from the simulator to an actual flight carrying passengers without ever having set foot in the real aircraft!

FAR Part 121 Appendix H: Advanced Simulation

Appendix H of the FAR Part 121 governs the use of advanced flight simulators. There are three levels of simulator training approved under these guidelines: Levels B, C, and D.

Level B

Level B training is permitted for the following purposes:

- Recency of experience (FAR 121.439).
- Night takeoffs and landings
- Landings in a proficiency check without the landing on the line requirements. (FAR 121.441)

The Level B simulator must be capable of modeling the following:

1. Aerodynamic effects such as:
   - Ground effect: roundout, flare, and touchdown.
   - Ground reaction: reaction of the aircraft upon contact with the runway during landing to include strut deflections, tire friction, and side forces.
   - Ground-handling characteristics: steering inputs to include crosswind, braking, thrust reversing, deceleration, and turning radius.

- Minimum of three-axes-of-freedom-of-motion system.
2. Visual requirements to include:
   - Response time from pilot control input to visual system output shall not exceed 300 ms (0.3 second).
   - Visual cues to assess sink rate and depth perception during landings.
   - Instruments must not lag behind visual scene updates.

Level C

Level C training is permitted for the following purposes:

- Certification check required under FAR 61.157 for the airline transport pilot certificate
- Upgrade to pilot in command from second in command

The Level C simulator must be capable of modeling the following:

1. Crosswinds and 3-D windshear dynamics

2. Stopping forces and directional control on the runway when it is dry, wet, icy, patchy wet, patch icy, and wet on rubber residue in touchdown zone.

3. Brake and tire failure dynamics, including antiskid and decreased brake efficiency due to high brake temperatures.

4. 6 DOF motion platform

Navigational systems, including VOR, NDB, ILS, INS, OMEGA.

5. Sound of rain and other airplane noises perceptible to the pilot during normal operations. This includes the sound of a crash when the simulator is landed in excess of landing gear limitations.

6. Aircraft control feel dynamics shall duplicate the actual airplane being simulated. This shall be determined by comparing a recording of the control feel dynamics of the simulator to the actual airplane's measured control dynamics during takeoff, cruise, and landings.

7. Response of motion platform, visual system, and cockpit instruments shall respond to abrupt pitch, roll, and yaw inputs by the pilot within 150 ms (0.150 seconds).

8. Visual requirements to include:
   - Dusk and night visual scenes with at least three specific airports.
   - Radio navigation aids properly oriented to the airport runway layout.

- Category II and III weather conditions to include variable cloud density, partial obscuration of ground, gradual breakout from fog and clouds, and the effect of fog on airport lighting.

- 75° horizontal field of view, and 30° vertical field of view per pilot seat.

- Dynamic scenery such as ground traffic crossing the runway, or other air traffic.

Level D

Level D simulators are the most advanced and capable of all simulator types. They are permitted for all pilot flight training and checks, as well as certification checks, and they are used to qualify pilots in transitioning from one aircraft type to another. Line checks must still be performed in the airplane, however. After undergoing Level D training, new captains may make their first real flight with passengers, under the supervision of a check captain, without ever having flown the real aircraft!

Level D simulators are required to model the following:

1. 6 DOF motion system to include buffeting motions that result from extending the landing gear, flaps, nose-wheel scuffing, rough air, turbulence, and stalls. The simulator must be programmed and instrumented in such a manner that the characteristic buffet modes can be measured and compared to the real aircraft for greater accuracy.

2. Aerodynamic modeling to include low-altitude, level-flight ground effect, Mach effect at high altitude, effects of airframe icing, normal and reverse dynamic thrust effect on control surfaces, aeroelastic representations, and nonlinearities due to side slip based on test data provided by the manufacturer.

3. Realistic amplitude and frequency of cockpit noises and sounds, including rain, engine and airframe sounds corresponding to simulated weather conditions outside.

4. Visual requirements to include the following:
   - Daylight, dusk, and night visual scenes with sufficient scene content enable the user to recognize a specific airport, the terrain, and major landmarks around that airport and to successfully accomplish a visual landing. The daylight visual scene must be part of a total daylight cockpit environment which at least represents the amount of light in the cockpit on an overcast day.
   - The visual system must be capable of producing full-color presentations, scene content comparable in detail to that produced by 4,000 edges or 1,000 surfaces (or equivalently 1,000 polygons) for daylight and 4,000 light points for night and dusk scenes. There must also be a minimum of 6 foot-lamberts of light present and 3 arc-minutes resolution for the field of view at the pilot's eye.

- Visual scenes portraying landing illusions, including short runway, landing over water, runway gradient, visual topographic features, and rising terrain.
- Special weather representations which include the sound, visual, and motion effects of entering light, medium, and heavy precipitation near a thunderstorm on takeoff, approach, and landings at and below an altitude of 2,000 feet above ground level and within a radius of 10 miles from the airport.
- All the visual requirements of Level C Simulators.
- Wet and snow covered runway representations, including lighting effects.
- Realistic color and directionality of airport lighting.
- Weather radar presentations, where radar information is presented on the pilot's navigation instruments.

REFERENCES

Baarspul, Max (1990) A Review of Flight Simulation Techniques, Progress in Aerospace Sciences 27(1).

Peters, Laura (1997) Future Microprocessors, PC Magazine 16(6): 168-169.

Rolfe, J.M., and Staples, K.J. (1986) Flight Simulation. Cambridge: Cambridge University Press.

16

Instrument Departure and Approach Procedures

By Captain Sean Trestrail, Boeing 767 Pilot

This chapter introduces you to instrument flying procedures. Four practice flights teach you how to fly takeoffs, navigate enroute, and perform approach procedures using only your instruments. The first flight takes you from San Francisco to Los Angeles in the Boeing 737-400 and introduces you to standard instrument departure (SID) plates as well as standard terminal arrival (STAR) plates. The second flight shows you how to accomplish a very high frequency omnirange (VOR) distance measuring equipment (DME) circling approach in the Cessna to Carlsbad/McClellan-Palmar and also discusses nonterminal VOR techniques and how to fly holding patterns. The third flight teaches you how to fly a terminal VOR-DME arc approach with the Boeing 737 or Learjet, and the fourth flight illustrates the proper techniques for flying an NDB approach and for flying a procedure turn.

There are three types of instrument approach procedures: VOR, nondirectional beacon (NDB), and instrument landing system (ILS). Both VOR and NDB are not precision approaches, because they do not provide you with ILS glide path information. By definition, ILS approaches are always precision approaches, which allow the pilot to descend to 200 ft above the ground during zero visibility. Non-precision approaches allow the pilot to descend to about 800 ft above the ground. In addition, precision approaches provide both horizontal and vertical guidance, whereas nonprecision approaches provide only horizontal guidance.

The VOR and NDB approaches are classified as terminal or nonterminal as follows:

- **Terminal VOR or terminal NDB approach:** The VOR or NDB is located at or on the airport and the VOR or NDB marks the missed approach point (MAP).
- **Nonterminal VOR or nonterminal NDB approach:** The VOR or NDB does not mark the missed approach point. Instead, you must use the DME or elapsed time to mark the missed approach point.

We will discuss all these instrument approach procedures as well as ILS approaches in the following sections. But first it is important to understand how instrument navigation came about.

A Brief History of Instrument Navigation

The safe departure and arrival of an aircraft in adverse conditions are not a matter of chance; procedures and techniques developed over many years have ensured the aviation safety we now take for granted. The first true pioneer of instrument flight was General James H. "Jimmy" Doolittle. He demonstrated that aircraft could safely take off, fly, and land without any view of the outside world. The USAAF developed the first systematic approach to instrument flying. Other pioneers took notes and drew charts to show how to get into various airports. The most famous was Captain E. Jeppesen, who founded a company in 1934 in response to many requests for "Jepp's little black book," a notebook that recorded field lengths, slopes, drainage patterns, information about lights and obstacles, and terrain and airport layouts—as well as the phone numbers of local farmers who could be counted on to provide weather reports along the route. Jeppesen is now the largest company in the world that produces aviation charts along with navaid data for GPS and moving map displays.

Very early on, it was obvious that a set of standards was needed that would detail how instrument procedures should be flown. Today, two primary standards govern instrument procedures worldwide. The accepted worldwide standard is the International Civil Airline Organization's (ICAO) Procedures for Air Navigation and Operations (PANS-OPS). In the United States, the standard is Terminal En route Procedures (TERPS). Both standards have a specific aim: safe and efficient instrument landings in adverse meteorological conditions. The standards are similar but differ in specifics. This text will concentrate on the U.S. TERPS procedures but will point out significant differences with PANS-OPS.

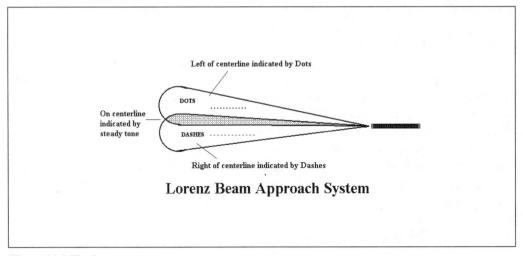

Figure 16.1 *The Lorenz system.*

The development of radio navigation began immediately before World War II, when the Germans developed a beam landing system that assisted pilots in returning to their airfields at night or in poor weather. This system, known as Lorenz, provided left-right guidance aligned with the runway centerline (see Figure 16.1). There was no cockpit display at all, and guidance was by means of audible tones. Left of centerline was indicated by "dots," and right of centerline by "dashes." At the centerline, the dots and dashes combined to form a steady tone. No vertical path was provided. A series of beacons, or markers, was laid out along the extended centerline, and the pilot aimed to cross each marker at a specific height. This arrangement gave a crude vertical path and was the first ancestor of today's instrument landing system (ILS). The British licensed the Lorenz system and also used it during World War II.

The British and the Germans developed sophisticated radio navigation aids during World War II. These aids were initially used by the Germans to improve the accuracy of night bombing. In the Knickebein system, an adaptation of the Lorenz landing aid, four stations radiated directional beams. The Lorenz-type centerline was laid over the target, and the crew simply flew this target-oriented centerline to the destination. Three other beams then crossed the Lorenz centerline beam, each of them aligned at a specific distance from the target. The first crossbeam provided warning of the approaching target. As the aircraft crossed the second beam, a mechanical clock was started; when the plane crossed the third beam, the first clock was stopped and a second clock was started. The hands of each clock were concentrically mounted in a single case. As the second clock's needle rotated, it eventually made contact with the first clock's needle, triggering an automatic bomb release. This was the first time that radio navigation was used for precision guidance during warfare, and it proved the effectiveness of all-weather aerial bombing.

The British produced the first area navigation aid. Called GEE, this system allowed suitably equipped aircraft to fix their position over Europe in any conditions. Unlike the German Knickebein system, GEE employed hundreds of curved beams that overlaid most of Western Europe. The operator determined which beams the aircraft was on and then by reference to charts could fix the position within six miles. A very accurate bombing system, known as OBOE, was also developed. OBOE allowed the use of the pathfinder and target marking concept. The aircraft flew along an arc that crossed over the target; the exact calculated weapon release point was indicated by an intersecting beam.

POSTWAR NAVIGATION AIDS

Following World War II, the concept of radio navigation proliferated. Ground beacons transmitting in the RF spectrum provided directional (and later distance) information to pilots. The earliest aids simply allowed the pilot to point the nose of the aircraft at the station. This first navigational radio aid, the non-directional beacon (NDB) radiated a signal in all directions. The aircraft component that detected these signals was the aerial direction finder, or ADF. The ADF presents a needle that points at the beacon. By turning the aircraft so that the needle and the nose are aligned, the pilot could then fly the aircraft directly towards the beacon. The pilot, however, had little knowledge of exactly where the plane was in relation to the beacon except when directly overhead.

The VOR system, developed next, gave the pilot bearing information that was more accurate and less prone to interference than the NDB system. The VOR allowed the pilot to ascertain the plane's exact magnetic bearing from the VOR station and therefore determine precisely the magnetic track the plane should fly to arrive at the VOR. This system solved the position line problem, but how far was the aircraft from the VOR? To address this new requirement for VOR distance information, DME was developed. DME provides the pilot with *slant* range to the DME sight. Slant range is the diagonal line from the airplane to the VOR. It is called "slant" because it is not the ground distance between the station and the airplane but instead is the direct air distance from the ground located at the VOR up to the altitude where the airplane is flying.

DME distances are determined by timing radio transmissions between the aircraft and the DME station. Radio waves travel at a constant speed—that is, the speed of light—so the distance traveled would be $d = c \times t$, where d is in meters, c is the speed of light (300,000,000 m/sec), and t is in seconds. The military was quick to use this type of aid and combined the bearing and DME units into a single unit called a TACAN. The civilian world followed, placing VOR and DME units together in a unit known as a VOR-DME. The bearing side of the military TACAN operates in a different frequency band from that of the bearing side of the VOR. Both TACAN and DME use the same frequency band. This difference allows civil aircraft to obtain distance information but not bearing from a TACAN station.

The next development followed from World War II experience (GEE) and was known as hyperbolic navigation aids. The first usable civilian system was LORAN, it was followed by OMEGA. Both systems were long-range (beyond the line of sight) navigation systems. The basic operation allowed the navigator to establish a position on two position lines from separate stations. The intersection of these lines marked the aircraft's position.

All these systems required ground-based equipment talking to the aircraft. A need remained for a navigation system that didn't rely on ground-based equipment for those areas of the world where it was not available or where greater accuracy was required. To address this need, the next great advance in navigation was the inertial navigation system (INS). This system is self-contained and relies on exceptionally accurate gyros and accelerometers. The system is given a starting location. As the aircraft is moved, the INS senses accelerations in three directions. By integration of the accelerations multiplied by the time interval, the INS can then derive a velocity, and subsequently a position. Although it is not perfect, the INS transformed military and civil flight operations by eliminating the need for a navigator and thereby simplifying navigation. The first civil aircraft in which INS was designed from the outset was the Boeing 747. INS has evolved into the instrument reference system (IRS), which replaces the mechanical gyros with laser gyros. The laser gyro measures acceleration through phase changes in the laser light—it's all pretty technical, but it works. The IRS is the standard navigation system used by most of the world's airliners.

The latest navigation system is the global positioning system, or GPS. This system, and its Russian equivalent, GLONASS, relies on satellites and uses highly accurate timekeeping with atomic clocks. With GPS, a receiver can calculate its position to within 50 ft (three-dimensional). GPS navigation is revolutionizing the aviation industry. Small handheld receivers allow precise navigation in any aircraft. To use GPS for instrument approaches is a different matter. An instrument-approach-rated GPS must meet specific certification requirements, including hardware and software specifications. Flight Simulator does not simulate a GPS, but GPS version 1.1 and GPS version 2.02, found on the book's CD-ROM, simulates a simple GPS unit.

So we now have many ways of fixing a position in 3-D space. Knowing exactly where we are also allows us to determine the location of hazardous terrain or airspace in relationship to our plane. Knowing this, we should be able to safely navigate from any point on Earth to any other point without the need to see the surface. The TERPS and PANS-OPS procedures provide a standard means of safely and predictably getting from A to B.

To see how these navigation aids are used, we will take some selected flights using default scenery in FSW95/FS98.

TUTORIAL, FLIGHT 1: B737-400 SAN FRANCISCO (KSFO) TO LOS ANGELES (KLAX)

For this flight we will use the 737-400 and fly a realistic airline flight profile between San Francisco and Los Angeles. The simulation will include real-world speeds and navigation procedures. We will also take maximum advantage of the autopilot. The real 737 has a sophisticated navigation and autopilot system that uses VOR, DME, ILS, and IRS. The 737 in FSW95/98 is not equipped with an IRS but we can approximate the IRS by using David Drouin's GPSV1.1 or GPS2.0 (found on the book's CD-ROM).

NOTE You should use GPSV1.1 if you are running FSW95; otherwise, use GPS2.0 with FS98. GPSV1.1 will not work with FS98. Throughout this chapter we discuss and show illustrations of GPSV1.1. The basic functionality and operation of GPS2.0 are exactly the same, so you should have no problem making the transition between the two programs, although you won't be able to add waypoints in GPS2.0 until you register the program.

Using the VOR and GPS we will depart from SFO and navigate to LAX for an ILS and autoland. For this trip, we will assume a heavy 737 that will be landing just under its maximum landing weight. First, copy the file **KSFOLAX** from the CD-ROM into the **\Pilots** subdirectory where Flight Simulator is installed on your hard disk. Then load the KSFOLAX situation, which will automatically set the fuel quantity, weather, and navigation beacons for you.

We are expecting awful weather in LAX and have also planned the flight with one hour's worth of holding fuel at LAX. If you want to add fuel manually, set the fuel quantity to 4,000 lb (1,818 kg) for each tank using **Aircraft/Aircraft Settings/Fuel** (in FSW95 use **Aircraft/Engines & Fuel**). This will give us an estimated takeoff weight of 129,360 lb (58,800 kg). Today we will use **Flap 5** (2 divisions) for the takeoff. Our takeoff speeds are as follows:

V_1 = 132 knots
V_R = 139 knots
V_2 = 149 knots

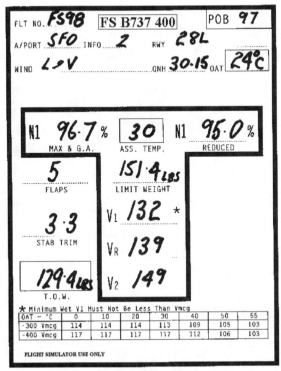

Figure 16.2 *Takeoff data for the Boeing 737-400.*

We will also be using a reduced thrust takeoff setting of 95% N_1. This is known as a *derated take off* and is a standard airline operating procedure that is used whenever takeoff performance is not limiting. The takeoff calculations are annotated on our takeoff data card, as shown in Figure 16.2. We will be using an initial pitch attitude of 18° at V_R, the rotation speed. This means that when the plane reaches a rotation speed of 139 knots, you must pull up the nose by 18°.

Standard Instrument Departure

The duty runway for our departure is 28L, and we have been cleared to LAX via an offshore three departure with a Santa Catalina (SXC) transition. We study the standard instrument departure plates, as shown in Figure 16.3 and Figure 16.4. These two plates consist of a graphical depiction and a narrative description of the departure. Figure 16.5 shows the legend for the SID and STAR charts.

Careful study of the SID is required. Next, we set up the aircraft's navigation aids. The initial departure requires reference to two VORs, which we will tune in separately on the NAV1 and NAV2 radios. Although the NAV1 radio works only with the HSI, we

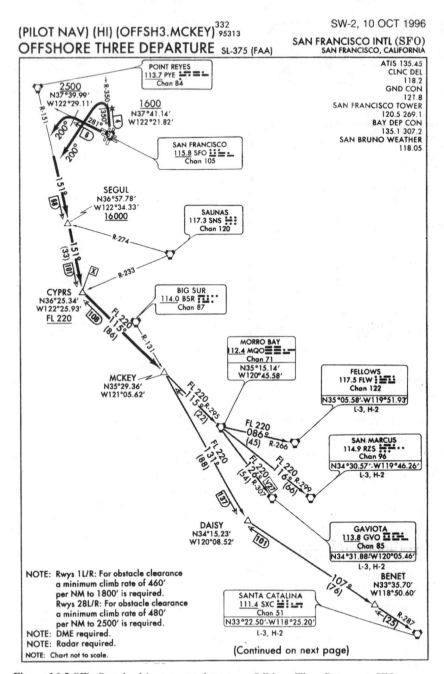

Figure 16.3 *SID: Standard instrument departure: Offshore Three Departure SFO.*

▽

DEPARTURE ROUTE DESCRIPTION

<u>TAKE-OFF RUNWAYS 1L/R:</u> Intercept and proceed via SFO R-350. Cross SFO R-350 4 DME at or above 1600'. Thence. . . .

<u>TAKE-OFF RUNWAYS 28L/R:</u> Intercept and proceed via SFO R-281. Cross SFO R-281 6 DME at or above 2500'. Thence. . . .

. . . . Turn left heading 200° to intercept and proceed via PYE R-151 to SEGUL INT. Cross SEGUL INT at or above 16000'. Then proceed via PYE R-151 to CYPRS INT; cross CYPRS INT at or above FL 220. Then via the MQO R-295 to MCKEY INT, then via (transition) or (assigned route). Expect further clearance to filed altitude 10 minutes after departure. When SFO VOR/DME is inoperative, Runway 28 departures expect radar vector to PYE R-151, then resume SID.

<u>FELLOWS TRANSITION (OFFSH3.FLW):</u> From over MCKEY INT via MQO R-295 to MQO VORTAC; then via MQO R-086 and FLW R-266 to FLW VORTAC.

<u>GAVIOTA TRANSITION (OFFSH3.GVO):</u> From over MCKEY INT via MQO R-295 to MQO VORTAC; then via MQO R-126 and GVO R-307 to GVO VORTAC.

<u>SAN MARCUS TRANSITION (OFFSH3.RZS):</u> From over MCKEY INT via MQO R-295 to MQO VORTAC; then via MQO R-116 and RZS R-299 to RZS VORTAC.

<u>SANTA CATALINA TRANSITION (OFFSH3.SXC):</u> From over MCKEY INT via BSR R-131 and SXC R-287 to SXC VORTAC.

OFFSHORE THREE DEPARTURE
(PILOT NAV) (HI) (OFFSH3.MCKEY) 95313

SAN FRANCISCO, CALIFORNIA
SAN FRANCISCO INTL (SFO)

333

SW-2, 10 OCT 1996

Figure 16.4 SID: Standard instrument departure chart: Offshore Three Departure route description.

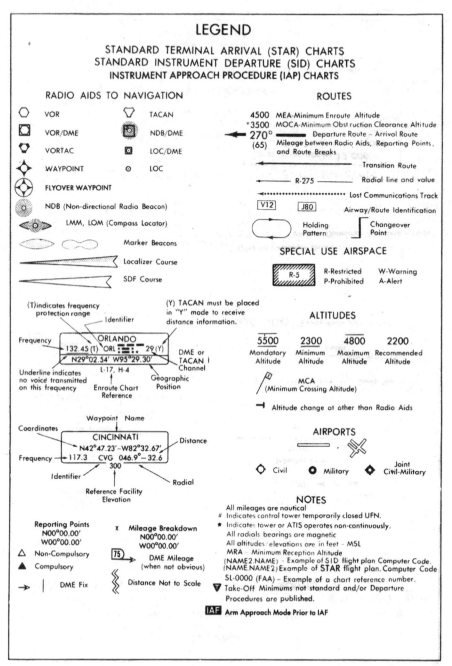

Figure 16.5 Legend for SID and STAR charts.

will use the NAV2 radio to tune in a second VOR station on the radio magnetic compass (RMI), which will show us DME and relative bearing information from the yellow needle in its display. The initial departure requires us to track the SFO 281 radial until 6 DME (6 nm from the SFO DME station) and then turn left onto a heading of 200 until we intercept the Point Reyes VOR 151° radial. Once we cross the Point Reyes 151° radial, we turn left and track to the CYPRS waypoint.

How do we do this? Let's tune NAV1 to SFO at 115.8 MHz and set the NAV1 course to 281. (Note: If you are using the situation included on the CD-ROM, the initial departure requires you to track the SFO 281 radial, but the situation included on the CD-ROM tunes the VOR station and selects the proper course setting for you.) We will set NAV2 to Point Reyes at 113.7 MHz. Assuming that you have already installed GPS1.1, we will also program GPS V1.1 with CYPRS as waypoint 1. A new waypoint file, **GPWS.TXT**, which contains all the waypoints needed for the trip, is supplied on the CD-ROM. To use it, copy **GPWS.TXT** into the GPS directory where you have installed GPS1.1; you may have to restart GPS1.1 and Flight Simulator to get the new waypoint file working.

WARNING

Back up your previous **GPWS.TXT** file, because the new waypoint file will overwrite the existing waypoint file in the GPS directory. This is a concern only for GPS1.1—the new GPS2.0 doesn't have this problem, and you can add as many waypoints as you like to the existing file, provided you have registered the program.

At 6 DME from the San Francisco VOR, we will be turning left onto heading 200°, so let's set the heading on the autopilot mode control panel (MCP) to 200 (click on the **HDG** box until it shows 200). We expect an unrestricted climb to our cruise level of 33,000 ft (FL 330), so we'll set this altitude in the MCP altitude window (click on the **ALT** text box until it shows 33,000).

Figure 16.6 shows our navigation aids set for departure. Note that the saved flight situation on the CD-ROM will set up all the navaid frequencies for you. We are now ready for takeoff.

Takeoff and Initial Departure

San Francisco tower clears us for takeoff. We set our takeoff thrust setting to 95% N_1. As we accelerate down the runway, we pass our maximum stop speed V_1 of 132 knots; at our rotation speed V_R of 139 knots, we perform a smooth single rotation to 18° on the attitude indicator. This rotation should take about 6 seconds. If it is done correctly, the speed will be close to V_2 + 15 knots, or 164 knots, as displayed on the HSI shown in Figure 16.7.

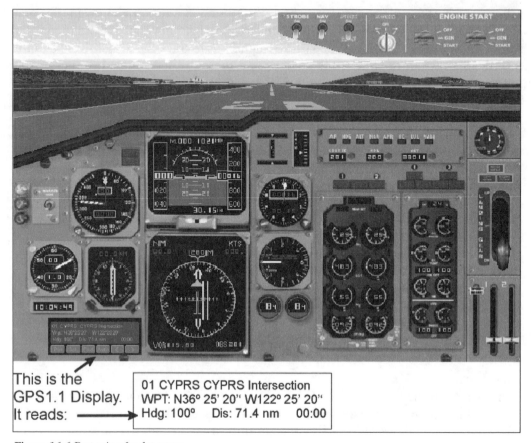

This is the
GPS1.1 Display.
It reads:

01 CYPRS CYPRS Intersection
WPT: N36° 25' 20" W122° 25' 20"
Hdg: 100°   Dis: 71.4 nm   00:00

Figure 16.6 *Preparing for departure.*

As soon as we have a positive rate of climb, select **Gear Up**. Now that we're established in the initial portion of the climb, let's engage the autopilot. Click on the **AP** button and then the **Nav** button on the MCP. Each button turns white to indicate that it has been selected. The autopilot now controls the lateral or directional axis. In the real aircraft we would also have a pitch mode controlling the vertical axis. FSW95 does not have an effective pitch mode for the climb, but FS98 has a vertical speed hold. If you select an appropriate IAS (indicated airspeed) and V_s (vertical airspeed), the autopilot will pitch the aircraft to the proper climb angle. Adjusting the V_s will effectively control the speed, because the thrust is fixed.

Passing 1,500 ft we commence the *clean up*, a steady acceleration to the initial climb speed of 250 knots. To start the acceleration, leave the thrust set at 95% N_1 and lower the nose to around 5°. The rate of climb will reduce to around 500 ft/min, and the air-

***Figure 16.7** Passing V_2 +15 knots (164 knots) with nose pitched up 18° during the takeoff.*

craft will accelerate. As soon as the airspeed starts to increase, select **Flaps 1**; when the airspeed passes 200 knots, select **Flaps Up** (i.e., **Flaps 0°**). We maintain the 5° nose pitch attitude until we arrive at the initial climb speed of 250 knots. At this point, adjust the pitch attitude to about 9°.

The next point in the departure is the 6 DME point from the San Francisco VOR. As indicated in Figure 16.3, the SID requires us to be above 2,500 ft by this point (notice the underlined number 2500). This requirement is not a problem if you have been closely following the instructions. The next significant point is the turn onto the 200° heading. At 6 DME we change autopilot mode from **NAV** to **HDG**. To do this, click on **NAV** on the MCP (the white fill will disappear). Quickly click on the heading button, and the **HDG** button turns white, confirming its selection. The aircraft now turns left onto our preselected heading of 200° on the HDG display. Referring to the SID, we confirm that we need to maintain this heading until we intercept the 151° radial from Point Reyes VOR.

We now need to tune the NAV1 radio to point at Point Reyes (PYE) VOR when we cross the 151 radial. To get ready, set the course to 151; click in the **COURSE** box of the Autopilot with the right or left mouse button to raise or lower the course numbers. Next, arm the NAV mode by clicking on the autopilot **NAV** button. Note that both the **HDG** and **NAV** buttons are white. This indicates that HDG is the selected mode and NAV is armed. Looking at the HSI in Figure 16.8, we can see the intercept angle of 40° clearly depicted by the CDI bar and the extension of the aircraft symbol's nose.

Figure 16.8 *The HSI Shows a 40° intercept angle for the NAV1 radio beacon tuned to the Point Reyes VOR on the 151 radial.*

As we approach the 151° radial from the Point Reyes VOR, the CDI bar will start to drift toward the aircraft symbol on the HSI. The NAV mode will capture the radial and automatically deselect HDG mode. The white **HDG** button will return to its gray unselected state (see Figure 16.9).

Final Climb to Cruise Altitude

By FAA regulations, our speed is limited to 250 knots below 10,000 ft. As we pass 10,000 ft we again reduce pitch attitude and accelerate to the planned climb speed of 280 knots. Throughout the climb it is essential that you trim the aircraft accurately. At any stage, you should be able to release the joystick and have the aircraft maintain the current pitch attitude. Trim will change every time you change speed or configuration. To fly accurately, you must trim repeatedly. Whenever you change speed or thrust, you must retrim.

Transition Altitude

The next event in the climb is the passing of the *transition altitude*. It varies from country to country (and in China from airfield to airfield), but in the United States the transition altitude is 18,000 ft. Below the transition altitude, aircraft cruise with the altimeter set to QNH. This means that the altimeter pressure setting displays altitude above mean sea level (MSL). At Catalina Avalon, for example, if you have QNH set the altimeter will read the field elevation of 1,602 ft. Altitudes below the transition altitude

Figure 16.9 *The HDG is now off, Since the HSI and NAV1 radio have captured the 151 radial from the Point Reyes VOR.*

are known as altitudes. Altitudes above the transition altitude are known as *flight levels.* Above the transition altitude, all aircraft set a standard pressure setting of 29.92 in. Hg or 1,013 millibars. The altimeter now displays altitude above the standard pressure level set in the subscale. Passing 18,000 ft we set 29.92 in. Hg, or 1,013 millibars.

It's important to know exactly what the altimeter is showing. Regardless of the actual pressure, the altimeter compares what is set in the window to what it measures outside and then displays the difference between the set pressure and the outside pressure. With QNE set to 1,013 or 29.92, the altimeter displays the vertical position reference at a pressure level of 1,013 or 29.92. This vertical position is called a flight level. Below the transition altitude, you set QNH, which gives the vertical position referenced to the QNH pressure or above mean sea level; this vertical position is known as an altitude. If you sit on the ground at, say, Catalina and you wind the altimeter until it shows 0, you have set what is known as QFE. This is your height above the airfield; with QFE set, the altimeter and radio altimeter will agree.

VOR and GPS Navigation

In FSW95, most VORs have a maximum range of 80 nm. This limitation originates in FSW95. In the real world, the range of a VOR is limited by the line of sight to a maximum of about 200 nm. The new FS98 corrects this oversight, and navaids now accurately reflect real-world line-of-sight reception ranges (although there are still problems that Microsoft is working on fixing). This means that the higher you are, the better you can receive radio navaids. On the ground you may not be able to receive a given station at all, just as in real life.

If you are using FSW95, you are well outside the 80 nm threshold for the next navaid, so at this stage it is appropriate to switch to GPS navigation and head for the CYPRS waypoint.

Follow these steps to use GPS1.1 with the Flight Simulator autopilot:

1. Make sure that the CYPRS waypoint is selected in the GPS1.1 display window. To advance through the waypoints, click the right arrow on the GPS1.1 display. To cycle in the reverse direction, click the left arrow.
2. Click **AUTO** on the GPS display.
3. Deselect **NAV** on the MCP panel so that it is off.
4. Reselect **HDG** so that it is on.
5. Make sure that the autopilot **AP** button is on.

The autopilot will now maintain the GPS calculated heading to the selected waypoint CYPRS, which is shown on the SID in Figure 16.3. Once the airplane arrives at the waypoint, the aircraft will circle indefinitely until you click the right arrow in GPS1.1's display window to advance to the next waypoint. Remember that the GPS1.1 program interfaces with the Flight Simulator autopilot. For it to work properly, you must have the **HDG** button on and the autopilot on (**AP** button must be on).

If you have done things properly, the GPS display should show the heading to CYPRS, the intervening distance, and the time remaining (see Figure 16.10).

As we pass 20,000 ft, increase the thrust to maximum. The N_1 indicator gauge will stabilize at about 102%. As we continue to climb, we eventually transition from constant IAS climb to a constant Mach number. In the 737, the ideal climb schedule is 280 knots into 0.74 Mach. The exact crossover point occurs at 29,500 ft. In Flight Simulator, it occurs at 28,000 ft, because the Microsoft atmosphere is not exact. At the crossover point the plane will require a slight increase in attitude to maintain the Mach number. As we pass 32,000 ft we can finally select an autopilot pitch mode; press the **ALT** button on the MCP. The autopilot will now capture and hold the selected altitude in the MCP window of 33,000 ft. In FSW95, the autopilot may overshoot the level slightly; again, this is a limitation of Flight Simulator. As we level off, we aim to cruise at Mach 0.74, so smoothly reduce the thrust to about 87% N_1, or use the FS98 auto-throttle to maintain Mach 0.74. With FSW95, you may need to vary the N_1 slightly to maintain the required Mach number.

Once the plane is established in the cruise phase, we move to the next part of the flight plan: the offshore three departure. As shown on the SID of Figure 16.3, at waypoint CYPRS we turn left onto a heading of 115° and track to the waypoint MCKEY. After MCKEY, we intercept the 131° radial from the Big Sur VOR and then track to a waypoint named Daisy. Note that the distances are marked in parentheses on the SID. Also, even though you can legally fly the entire departure using the GPS, you must always back it up with all other available means. So let's tune in the Big Sur (BSR) VOR at 114.0 MHz on NAV1 and set the outbound course to 131 on the OBI (select **131** in the **COURSE** box of the MCP). Next, click on the **NAV** button on the MCP. Now the

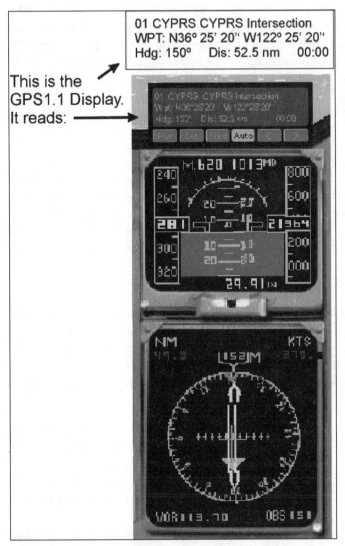

This is the
GPS1.1 Display.
It reads: ──────▶

Figure 16.10 The GPS1.1 display shows CYPRS waypoint as the currently active waypoint. Note that the heading of 150° to CYPRS is shown, as is the distance remaining of 52.5 nm, the position of CYPRS (lat/long), as well as the time remaining.

autopilot will automatically capture and track the 131° radial from the Big Sur VOR. Note also that in Flight Simulator, the NAV mode will always override the HDG mode.

Passing the MCKEY waypoint, the autopilot intercepts the 131° radial to MCKEY. Next, increment the GPS to the next waypoint, Daisy, and the airplane should turn toward Daisy on a heading that is close to 131°. Once established on the Big Sur 131° radial, we can select **HDG** and continue using GPS navigation. Note that you never fly over the Big Sur VOR; you use it only to confirm your GPS tracking.

Preparation is the key to a successful flight. Before proceeding, let's pause now (press **P**) and turn to the matter of arrival planning.

Arrival Planning

At this stage, we obtain the LAX weather report and confirm what we knew on departure from San Francisco: the weather in LAX is marginal. The main limitation is that the visibility is down to 400 meters, with low visibility procedures in force. This limits operations into LAX to only those aircraft (and crew) capable of low visibility operations. Our B737 is capable of operating down to CAT II minima. What does this mean?

Instrument Landing System Categories

International standards have been developed that define three basic levels of ILS operation as a function of landing minima. *Landing minima* are determined by pressure, altitude, or radio altimetry along with visibility. Both altitude and visibility criteria must be met. The three basic levels are displayed next in order of increasing capability. CAT IIIC, the highest category ILS approach, allows landings in conditions of zero visibility.

- CAT I approaches can be manually flown down to an altitude of 200 ft AGL measured on the pressure altimeter. The runway visual range (RVR) must be at least 2,400 ft, or 1,800 ft if the runway is equipped with appropriate lighting.
- CAT II approaches must be flown by the autopilot to an automatic landing. CAT II ILS minima require a minimum height of 100 ft AGL measured by a radio altimeter, with a minimum RVR of 1,200 ft. At least two autopilots must be used for the approach and landing.
- CAT III approaches must be flown by the autopilot to an automatic landing. Three autopilots are required. CAT III ILS approaches are broken down into three subcategories:
  - CAT IIIA: A minimum height of less than 100 ft* AGL measured on the radio altimeter. The minimum RVR is 700 ft.
  - CAT IIIB: A minimum height of 50 ft* AGL measured on a radio altimeter with a minimum RVR between 700 and 150 ft.
  - CAT IIIC: No minimum altitude and no minimum RVR.
    * There is also provision in CAT IIIA and CAT IIIB approaches to 0 height but with specific RVR requirements.

Runway Visual Range

RVR is an accurate method of determining visibility in low-visibility conditions. Located at each end and at the center of the runway are devices called *transmissometers*. These devices fire a laser beam of a known specification from a transmitter to a receiver. The amount of energy received at the receiver is reduced by poor visibility. Comparing the transmission signal strength to the received signal strength lets us calculate the visibility. This RVR is then transmitted to the pilots by stating the measured RVR at each transmissometer. If the information were expressed in meters, it would sound like this: "RVR touchdown 400, mid zone 600, end zone 700." This means that at the landing threshold you would expect 400 meters visibility, in the runway center, 600 meters, and at the end of the runway, 700 meters.

All approaches to minima less than CAT I require specific certification requirements for both the ground installation and the aircraft systems. In addition, special training and recency requirements must be met before a pilot can fly to less than CAT I minima. The real 737 has only two autopilots, so it is limited to CAT II approaches. Flight Simulator has only one autopilot, but we will assume that we have two.

Standard Terminal Arrival

We are next informed by air traffic control that we are to make a Leena Three Arrival with a CYPRS transition. This is exactly what we thought we would receive. The Leena Three STAR and our Offshore Three Departure SID blend into each other. We must now study the arrival chart shown in Figure 16.11.

Following are the key points that we must review before proceeding:

1. Looking at waypoint MCKEY on the Offshore Three Departure SID, the track is to the Daisy waypoint (88 nm) and then to the Benet waypoint (76 nm).
2. From Benet we proceed to the Santa Catalina (SXC) VOR (25 nm).
3. Looking at the Leena Three Arrival STAR, we note that we must fly from the Santa Catalina (SXC) VOR to the intersection of the SXC VOR 084° radial and the Seal Beach (SLI) VOR 328° radial (27 nm).
4. From this intersection, we track to the SLI VOR on a heading of 328°, crossing the Bayer and Madow intersections (total 30 nm).
5. The notes on the STAR also refer to "Turbojet Vertical Navigation Planning Information." As shown on the STAR, this means that we must cross the Santa Catalina (SXC) VOR at 250 knots and then cross the Bayer waypoint at 10,000 ft and finally the Madow waypoint at 7,000 ft MSL.

Now that we have a clear understanding of the tasks ahead, let us turn to the subject of descent planning.

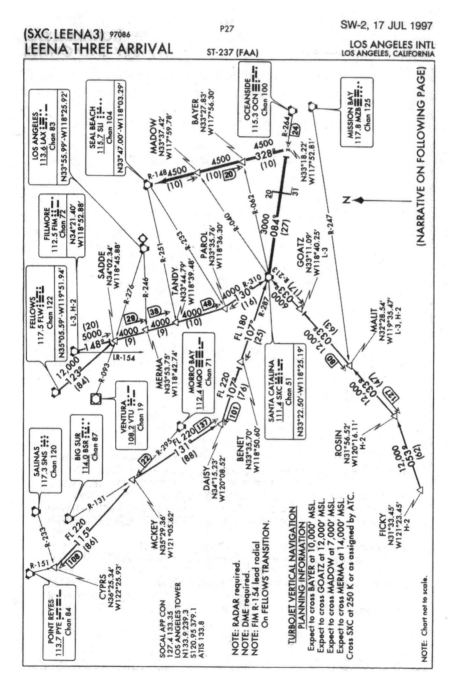

Figure 16.11 *The Leena Three Arrival STAR chart for the descent into Los Angeles International Airport.*

Descent Planning

We must do a little bit of math to calculate when we should start the aircraft's descent. The notes indicate that we should expect to cross Bayer at 10,000 ft, so how are we going to achieve this? The Flight Simulator 737 autopilot can perform a descent, during which it maintains an average descent rate of 1750 ft/min (although the VSI will show around 2,300 ft/min). So we need to lose (33,000 - 10,000) = 23,000 ft by Bayer. The descent should take around (23,000 ÷ 1,750) = 13 min. We also know that in our 0.74 Mach/250 knot descent, our average TAS for the descent works out to about 339 knots or 5.6 nm/min. Using this information we can deduce that in 13 min we will cover about 78 nm (13 × 6). To cross waypoint Bayer at 10,000 ft we must start our descent at 78 nautical miles before Bayer. Looking at the STAR chart we can calculate our descent point as follows.

From waypoint Bayer to the intersection is 10 nm. From the intersection to the Santa Catalina VOR (SXC) is 27 nm; so from Bayer to SXC is 37 nm, and that leaves another (78 – 37) = 41 nm. So we must commence our descent at 41 nm from the SXC VOR. Again checking the SID we note that there are 25 track miles from Benet to the SXC VOR, so we can also define our descent point as 16 miles short of Benet. Starting the descent any earlier will waste fuel; starting the descent any later will make it hard to achieve the 10,000 foot requirement at Bayer.

The 0.74Mach/250Kt descent table (Table 16.1) shows the distance required for various altitudes.

Table 16.1 *Distance Required for Descent*

ALTITUDE (FT)	DISTANCE REQUIRED AT 0.74 MACH/250 KT
40,000	126 nm
35,000	110 nm
30,000	94 nm
25,000	79 nm
20,000	63 nm
15,000	47 nm
10,000	32 nm
5,000	16 nm

Or even more simply put, you descend around 320 ft/nm.

We have now calculated our descent point as 41 nm from the Santa Catalina (SXC) VOR. Looking at Table 16.1 we can also define this point as 17 nm from Benet. With

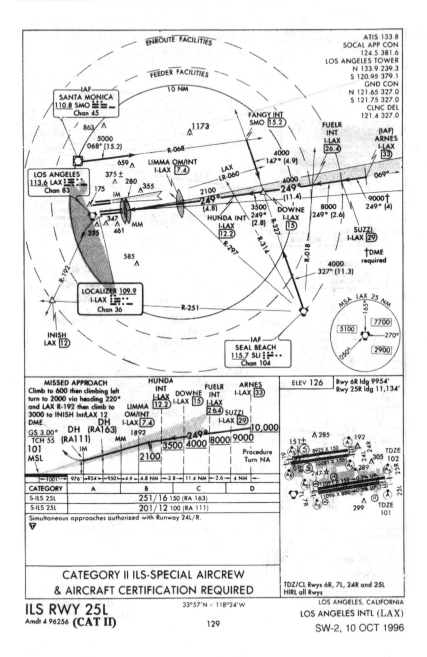

Figure 16.12 *Instrument approach procedures chart for a CAT II ILS landing on Rwy 25L at Los Angeles International Airport.*

We have now calculated our descent point as 41 nm from the Santa Catalina (SXC) VOR. Looking at Table 16.1 we can also define this point as 17 nm from Benet. With descent planning complete, it's time to start reviewing the approach.

Approach Planning

The visibility at LAX is reported as 1,312 ft/400m RVR, and that means CAT II procedures. The duty runways are Rwy 25L and Rwy 25R and Rwy 24L and Rwy 24R. In the Flight Simulator 737, we can operate no lower than CAT II minima. Our company operates on the southern side of the airfield, and experience indicates we are most likely to land on Rwy 25L, so we'll use the Rwy 25L CAT II chart to prepare for the approach, as shown in Figure 16.12.

Standard Instrument Approach Charts

Instrument approach (IAP) charts all vary slightly depending on who produces them, but each has a similar layout. The source data is provided by the local authorities. The approach type or title is at the top of the plate, and the plan view is just below. The profile view is below the plan view, and just below that is the minima table, which lists the lowest altitudes and visibility thresholds you are allowed to fly during the approach for various categories of aircraft. The airport runway layout is shown in the lower-right corner.

The upper-right corner of the plan view lists important radio frequencies. You'll note that the approach control, control tower, ground control, clearance delivery and ATIS (automatic terminal information service) frequencies are all listed. The ATIS broadcasts a continuous recording of weather and airport information that is updated hourly. Each update is accompanied by a letter of the phonetic alphabet—such as alpha, beta, and charlie—that tell the pilot whether the recording has changed.

Usually, an airplane entering the airspace around an airport communicates with the approach control. When the airplane is established on the approach to the airport, approach control hands control to the tower. After the plane lands, the tower hands control to ground control.

Inside the plan view on the IAP, you'll see a circle labeled "MSA" (which stands for minimum safe altitude). Inside the circle are various quadrants with boxed numbers. The boxed numbers tell you the minimum safe altitude for the given quadrant within a 25 nm radius of the LAX VOR that is illustrated at the heart of the MSA circle.

Whereas Figure 16.12 shows the IAP chart, Figure 16.13 shows the layout of the IAP. On Jeppesen charts, this entire portion is usually to scale. In the U.S. NOAA charts, the only portion to scale is the area inside the large10-nm circle shown in the plan view.

The legend for the IPA chart is shown in Figures 16.14a, 16.14b, and 16.14c.

How do we use the plan view to fly an approach? The first step is to look for the intermediate approach fix, or IAF; there may be more than one IAF on the chart. Then we fly directly to the desired IAF by following a VOR radial from outside the map area. For congested areas such as Los Angeles, we would use another a STAR chart to determine the appropriate path to the IAF. Once we have arrived at the IAF, we follow the path indicated to intercept the final approach path. Upon crossing the final approach path, we then turn onto the approach and proceed to follow the final approach path shown in the profile view. This description is a simplification of how to use the IAP, because each IAP has different instructions. For example, in the typical IAP chart shown in Figure 16.34, upon crossing the IAF (Dwight NDB), the pilot would fly in the

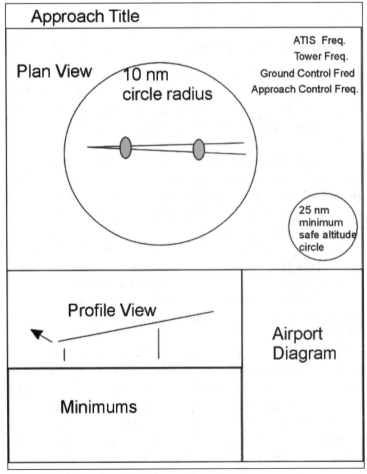

Figure 16.13 *Layout of the Instrument Approach Procedures Chart.*

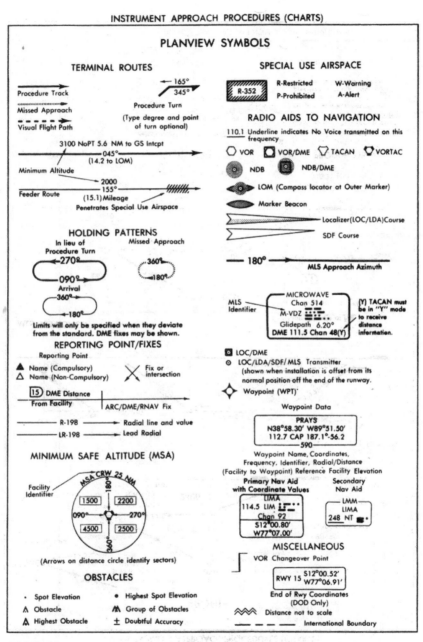

LEGEND

Figure 16.14a *Legend for the IPA chart, page 1.*

LEGEND

INSTRUMENT APPROACH PROCEDURES (CHARTS)

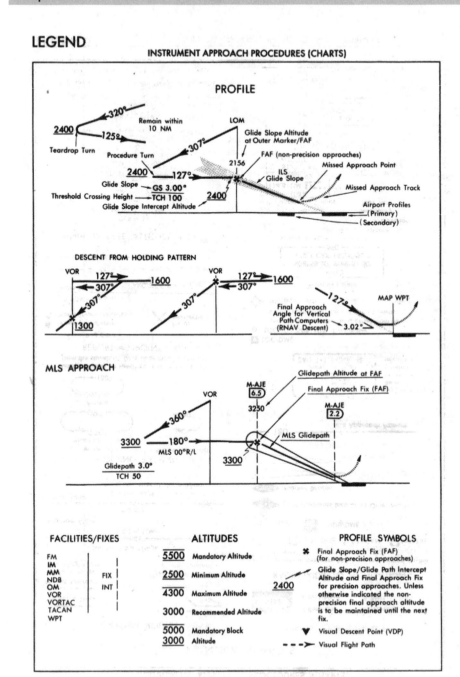

Figure 16.14b Legend for the IPA chart, page 2.

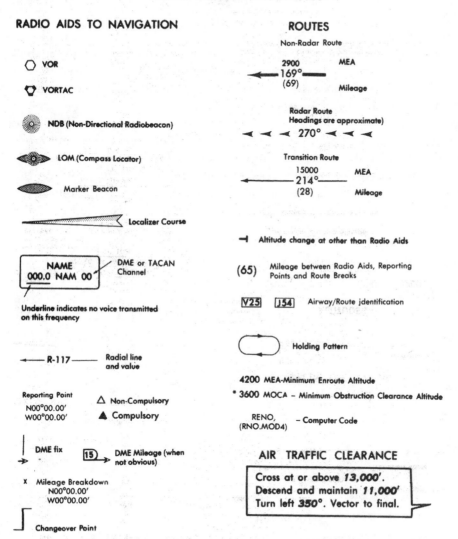

LEGEND

PROFILE DESCENT PROCEDURES

RADIO AIDS TO NAVIGATION

◯ VOR

◇ VORTAC

⊛ NDB (Non-Directional Radiobeacon)

◆ LOM (Compass Locator)

⬬ Marker Beacon

◅ Localizer Course

┌─────────────────┐
│   NAME   │   DME or TACAN
│ 000.0 NAM 00   │   Channel
└─────────────────┘

Underline indicates no voice transmitted on this frequency

◄── R-117 ──── Radial line and value

Reporting Point
N00°00.00′
W00°00.00′   △ Non-Compulsory
               ▲ Compulsory

DME fix   ⑮ ── DME Mileage (when not obvious)

X Mileage Breakdown
   N00°00.00′
   W00°00.00′

└ Changeover Point

ROUTES

Non-Radar Route

◄── 2900 ── MEA
    169°
    (69)   Mileage

Radar Route
Headings are approximate)

◄ ◄ ◄ 270° ◄ ◄ ◄

Transition Route
◄── 15000 ── MEA
    214°
    (28)   Mileage

⊣ Altitude change at other than Radio Aids

(65)   Mileage between Radio Aids, Reporting Points and Route Breaks

[V25] [J54]   Airway/Route jdentification

⬭ Holding Pattern

4200 MEA-Minimum Enroute Altitude

* 3600 MOCA – Minimum Obstruction Clearance Altitude

RENO,   – Computer Code
(RNO.MOD4)

AIR TRAFFIC CLEARANCE

┌─────────────────────────────────┐
│ Cross at or above *13,000′*.   │
│ Descend and maintain *11,000′*   │
│ Turn left *350°*. Vector to final.│
└─────────────────────────────────┘

All radials/bearings are magnetic
All mileages are nautical
All altitudes in feet – MSL

Figure 16.14c *Legend for the IPA chart, page 3.*

opposite direction outbound from the airport for about 2 min (or as long as the aircraft stays within the 10-nm circle that is shown). Then the pilot would perform a *procedure turn* and double back to the airport. We will discuss the procedure turn in the final flight tutorial in this chapter.

The IAP shown for the Los Angeles Rwy 25L appears complicated, but it can be simplified if you realize that the goal is to fly from one of the IAFs on the chart to the final approach path along the 249° radial from the Los Angeles VOR. Once you intercept the ILS beam along the final approach, you can home in on the glide slope and make your way down the runway, regardless of visibility problems.

The profile view, shown just below the plan view, is a side view of the approach—the 249° radial from the LAX VOR and the I-LAX localizer. It illustrates the various crossing altitudes and also describes the missed approach procedure.

A missed approach is the maneuver performed when you cannot land on the instrument approach. The missed approach is a climb to a stated altitude following a specific track. During the maneuver the aircraft configuration is changed from the landing configuration to the climb configuration and then to the cruise configuration. Following a missed approach you can decide to attempt a further approach or divert to an airfield that has better weather.

Approach Categories

In the Minima section of the IAP you will see a table labeled "CATEGORY." This table divides aircraft into different approach categories according to approach speed. The rationale is that the faster the approach speed, the more distance the aircraft will cover while the crew assesses the conditions. It follows that the higher the approach speed, the higher the minimum altitude and minimum visibility. The categories assume an approach at 1.3 times the stall speed. Table 16.2 shows the speeds associated with each category. The 737-400 fits into category C.

Table 16.2 *Speeds for Categories of Aircraft*

CATEGORY	SPEED
CAT A	Up to 90 knots
CAT B	91 to 120 knots
CAT C	121 to 140 knots
CAT D	141 to 165 knots
CAT E	Greater than 165 knots

Categories do not apply for CAT II and CAT III approaches, because the minima are fixed. The minima for CAT II approaches for Rwy 25 L are 201/12 100 (RA 111). This means that we must decide by 111 ft radar altimeter (201 ft on the pressure altimeter) whether the visibility is greater than 1,200 ft. FSW95/98 does not have a radar altimeter as standard equipment, so we will use the pressure altimeter. (In the real world, use of the radar altimeter is mandatory.) If we arrive at 201 ft on the glide slope and cannot see the approach end of the runway, a go-around is required.

Continuing with the SFO to LAX Flight

We have made the necessary preparations for the arrival phase of our flight from SFO to LAX. Let's continue by pressing **P** to resume flying.

As shown on the GPS display, about 2 nm from the Daisy waypoint, we must increment the GPS to the next waypoint Benet. The aircraft will automatically turn toward Benet, but you should verify the track as 107°. We no longer require reference to the Big Sur VOR, so tune NAV1 to the Santa Catalina (SXC) VOR at 111.4 MHz and set the course to 107°. As we approach Benet, recall that our top of descent should be 17 nm before Benet, or 41 nm before the SXC VOR. SOCAL approach control clears us to descend to 10,000 ft. At 17 nm before waypoint Benet, use the mouse to reset the MCP **Autopilot Altitude Hold** to the cleared altitude, 10,000 ft. As the aircraft starts to descend, slowly reduce the thrust and set $47\% N_1$, or use the FS98 auto-throttle to maintain speed at 250 knots. However, in FSW95, you'll have to adjust the throttle setting to maintain a 250 knot descent speed.

At about 2 nm from the Benet waypoint, increment the GPS to the next waypoint, SXC (the Santa Catalina VOR). Now refer to the Leena arrival chart (Figure 16.11) and check the outbound track from SXC. The chart indicates this should be the 084° radial from the SXC VOR until we reach the intersection of the SXC VOR's 084° radial and the Seal Beach (SLI) VOR's 328° radial. This point is also defined as 24 nm from the Oceanside (OCN) VOR at 115.3 MHz. It's starting to become complicated. A great secret to flying is the "KISS" principle: "Keep it simple, stupid." So to assist us in finding the intersection, tune the NAV1 radio to 115.7 MHz SLI VOR (Seal Beach VOR) and set the course to 328°. Then tune NAV2 to the Oceanside (OCN) VOR at 115.3 MHz. We will use the GPS to navigate from the SXC (Santa Catalina) VOR to the intersection of the 328 radial from Seal Beach (SLI) VOR and the 84 radial from SXC VOR. As we continue the descent, let's do a quick review of the descent profile. We note from the chart that SXC to Bayer is 37 nm. Knowing that we must be at 10,000 ft at Bayer, we need to be around $10,000 + (37 \times 320) = 21,840$ ft, or about 22,000 ft, as we cross SXC.

Passing the transition level of flight level 180, we reset the altimeter to the LAX QNH. All altitude references are now above mean sea level.

737 Descent Rule of Thumb

A simpler way to do a rough check is to multiply the remaining distance by 3, which will give you the desired altitude in hundreds of ft. Using the preceding example, $37 \times 3 = 111$ or 11,100 ft, adding the additional 10,000 ft gives us an altitude of 21,100 ft. As a rough check, this is good enough.

As we approach the Santa Catalina (SXC) VOR with around 2 nm more to go on the GPS, increment the next GPS waypoint to the next intersection. The aircraft turns onto a track of 084. Now comes the tricky bit. Looking at the STAR in Figure 16.11, we note that to intercept the 328 radial into the SLI (Seal Beach VOR) will require a 116° left turn. So to precisely intercept the SLI 328 radial, we must start the turn a little more than 1 turn radius before the SLI 328 radial. In a real aircraft, the flight management computer (FMC) calculates the lead point automatically, but FSW95/98 doesn't do this. How do we know when to begin the turn? Here's another good rule of thumb for instrument flying:

Turn Radius = 1% True Airspeed

So at 250 knots IAS at 16,000 ft our TAS will be around 315 knots; 1% of TAS is 3.15 or 3.2. This is for a 90° turn, so let's be conservative and say 3.8 nm. So we need to start the turn 3.8 nm before the 328 radial. Referring to the chart, we note that the intersection is 24 nm from Oceanside (OCN) VOR, so if we start the turn 23 + 3.8, or 26.8, nm from OCN things should work out. We can also define this turn point using the GPS to warn us when we are 3.8 nm from the intersection.

Recall that the navigation aids are set up as follows:

- NAV1 on Seal Beach (SLI) VOR at 115.7 MHz with course of 328 set on the MCP
- NAV2 tuned to Oceanside (OCN) VOR at 115.3 MHz

Navigation is being tracked with the GPS. To intercept the 328° radial to the SLI VOR, press the **MCP NAV** button, which will arm the NAV mode. Figure 16.15 illustrates the situation at the turn point.

As you approach 3.8 nm from the intersection or 26.8 nm from the OCN VOR, increment the GPS waypoint to Bayer. The aircraft will start turning left, and the CDI bar will start to float into the center. The NAV mode will capture the Seal Beach (SLI) VOR 328° radial, which is indicated by the MCP HDG turning gray. Because you no longer require any reference to the OCN VOR, retune NAV2 to the SLI VOR on 115.7 MHz. Next, deselect the **AUTO** button on the GPS so you can select headings as

Figure 16.15 Traveling on the 84° radial from the Santa Catalina (SXC) VOR. Note that the NAV1 radio is tuned to the Seal Beach (SLI) VOR and that the VOR1 radial is set to 328°. When the airplane crosses the correct intersection of the SXC 84° radial and the SLI 328° radial, the yellow CDI needle on the HSI will be centered. When this happens, you increment the GPS to waypoint Bayer, or turn the aircraft left on a heading of 328° to intercept the Seal Beach VOR.

required. (Failure to deselect **AUTO** on the GPS will result in the GPS overriding any heading inputs you may make.)

Approaching the Bayer waypoint, SOCAL approach control clears you to 7,000 ft. Using the mouse, select the next altitude of 7,000 ft on the **Autopilot Altitude Hold** and increment the GPS to waypoint Madow. As you cross Madow, you are cleared to 6,000 ft and instructed to reduce speed to 200 knots. An air traffic control (ATC) speed reduction needs to be done promptly, so reduce the thrust to idle (or use the FS98 auto-throttle to maintain 200 knots IAS). As soon as you reach 200 knots, select **Flaps 1** (1 notch) and set $56\% N_1$ if you are manually adjusting the throttle. Approaching the Seal Beach

(SLI) VOR in a real airplane, you would expect radar vectors to intercept the final approach course. This means that air traffic control would ordinarily contact you and give you the proper headings to fly the rest of the approach. However, with FSW95 and FS98, you will not rely on the ATC; instead, you will fly the entire route using your instrument approach charts.

You now need to exit NAV mode. At this stage, the best mode is the wing leveler mode. To engage the LVL mode, first deselect **NAV** on the MCP and then click on **LVL**. It is now time to tune NAV1 to the LAX VOR frequency. Referring to the instrument approach chart of Figure 16.12, we note that the VOR frequency is 113.6 MHz and the VOR is on a course of 249°. SOCAL approach control next instructs us to leave Seal Beach (SLI) VOR on a heading of 314° (on the IAP, this is indicated by "R-14") and to descend to 4,000 ft, reducing speed to 170 knots. To do this, we select **Flaps 5** (third notch) and set $52\% N_1$ (or in FS98, use the auto-throttle to specify 170 knots IAS), followed by presetting the heading to 314 on the MCP HDG display. As you cross the Seal Beach (SLI) VOR, select **HDG** mode on the MCP. When you have crossed the SLI VOR station, you will observe the NAV2 needle on the RMI rotating through 180° to show that the VOR has gone from in front to behind. After you have engaged the autopilot HDG mode, the aircraft turns onto the selected heading of 314°. As soon as you roll out on a heading of 314°, again select **LVL** mode. ATC will then clear you to 3,000 ft. Reset the MCP **Autopilot Altitude Hold** to 3,000 ft. A small reduction in N_1 will be required to maintain your speed. You will no longer require the SLI VOR, so retune NAV2 to LAX VOR at 113.6 MHz and set the inbound course of 249° on the Course readout of the MCP.

Intercepting the Localizer and Glide Slope

You are now level at 3,000 ft heading 314° with the wing leveler holding your heading. The next event will be the interception of the localizer. The localizer beam is very narrow: full-scale deflection is only 2.5°, and FSW95 does not capture it very well. As a workaround, we use the VOR to lock onto the correct heading, and then switch to the ILS once we are within the confines of the much narrower localizer radio beam. Preselect a heading of 269° on the HDG readout of the MCP; this will give you a 20° intercept on the localizer. Note that the LAX VOR and the I-LAX ILS localizer stations are close enough together that selecting 249° on the Course indicator will show the same angular bearing for both stations on the HSI. Earlier we preset the Course readout to 249° for the LAX VOR. The CDI bar in VOR mode will start to move 10° before the 249 course. This is a good time to commence the turn onto your 20° intercept. As soon as the CDI starts to move, click on the MCP **HDG** button (which should have

Figure 16.16 *The autopilot's approach mode has locked onto the localizer beam and the glide slope beam.*

already been set to 269° on the HDG readout). The aircraft now turns onto the 20° intercept heading of 269°.

Now we must tune the ILS, so set the NAV1 radio to 109.9 MHz. Note that the Course readout on the MCP remains at 249°. The aircraft will roll out on a heading of 269. Now click on the MCP **APR** button. The autopilot is now armed to capture the ILS localizer and glide slope. The aircraft will maintain the last heading until it intercepts the localizer. It will also maintain the last altitude until it intercepts the glide slope. As the glide slope needle starts to move, select **Gear Down**, **Flap 25**, (sixth notch) and set $50\% N_1$. Localizer capture is indicated by the aircraft starting to turn and the **LVL** button on the MCP turning gray. As the glide slope diamond on the HSI approaches the middle point on the display, the autopilot captures the glide slope and the airplane starts descending (see Figure 16.16). This is indicated by the MCP **ALT** button turning gray.

The autopilot is now tracking both the localizer and the glide slope. Select **Flap 30** (seventh notch) and set $45\% N_1$. Our final approach speed should be 141 knots.

You must now set the auto-throttle for a possible go-around. The missed approach procedure is shown in the profile section of the approach plate and states, "Climb to 600 ft then climbing left turn to 2000 ft via heading 220 and LAX radial 192 to INISH intersection."

To do this, first confirm that the MCP **Altitude** box shows 3,000 ft, and that the **Heading** box is set to 220.

As you descend on the ILS, you must make small thrust adjustments (no more than 2% N_1) to hold the approach speed. The ILS DME will indicate the plane's distance from the localizer antenna. The localizer is at the far end of the runway, so your distance to the touchdown point is around 2 nm less than the displayed distance. The ILS DME anomaly is typical of U.S. based ILS systems. Outside the United States, most ILS DME is referenced to the glide slope antenna. This is far more sensible, because the DME indicates direct distance to touchdown.

The 737 autopilot in FSW95 tends to fly slightly low on the glide slope. In the real world, this discrepancy would be unacceptable, but we have to put up with it in FSW95.

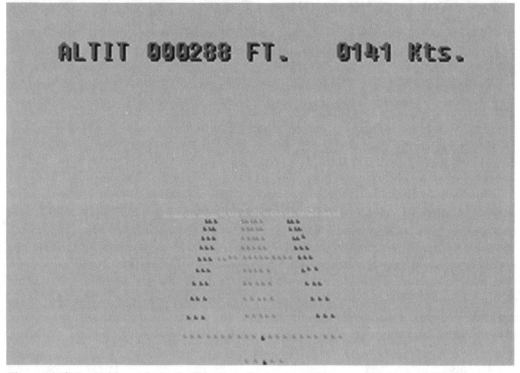

Figure 16.17 A satisfying sight for the ILS approach: the approach runway lighting is visible.

As you approach 500 ft, start taking momentary glances outside. The best way to do this is a quick tap of the **W** key. Alternatively, you can pan the view down with the joystick hat switch in FS98. You must pan the view, because your viewing angle is very limited in the nose of the 737 when it is pitched up. Tap the **W** again key to come back inside. (Or bring back the forward nonpanning view by pressing **Ctrl+Spacebar** in FS98, or **Scroll Lock** in FSW95.) At 300 ft, go fully head up by using the **W** key. At 200 ft you should be able to make out the approach lights extending to the green threshold lights (Figure 16.17). If you cannot see this, a missed approach is required immediately.

The Autoland

In a real aircraft, the autoland sequence from flare initiation to a stop is fully automatic. FSW95 lacks this level of sophistication, so we use a hybrid autoland. However, if you are using FS98 you can arm the auto-spoilers, which will automatically deploy upon touchdown (press **Shift+/** to arm the auto-spoiler).

Passing 160 ft on the pressure altimeter (30 ft above the runway), smoothly reduce the thrust to idle. As the main wheels touch, select the spoilers / key and apply the brakes, or if you are using FS98 and have engaged the auto-spoilers, the spoilers should deploy upon touchdown. Passing around 60 knots, disconnect the autopilot and maintain the centerline manually.

Missed Approach or Go-Around

In the real 737, the press of a single button will initiate a fully automatic go-round. In FS98, you can perform a go-around with the auto-throttle **AT** switch on; then press **Ctrl+Shift+R**.

In FSW95 we can perform a semiautomatic go-around. Recall that on final approach, you preselected the missed approach altitude and heading. To complete a missed approach, first deselect **APP** mode and select **ALT**; then advance the thrust to at least $95\% N_1$. The aircraft will rotate to around $15°$ nose-up attitude. As soon as a positive rate of climb is established, select **Flaps 5** (third notch) and select **Landing Gear Up**. Next click on **LVL** to select the wings leveler mode. Passing 800 ft, click on **HDG**. The aircraft will turn onto the preselected 220 heading. As the aircraft approaches 3,000 ft, the altitude will be captured. At 3,000 ft, leave the thrust constant and accelerate to 200 knots, being sure to progressively select flaps up so that the flaps are completely retracted as you reach 200 knots.

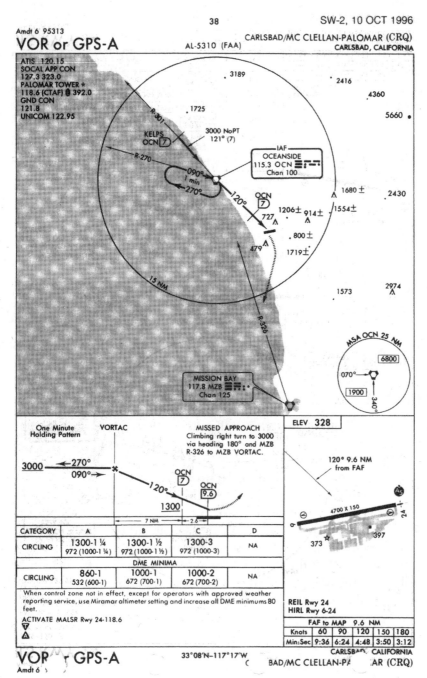

Figure 16.18 *The VOR or GPS IAP chart for Carlsbad/McClellan-Palomar.*

Tutorial, Flight 2: Cessna 182RG VOR-DME Approach to Carlsbad/McClellan-Palomar

After a pleasant weekend in Tijuana, you are returning home to Carlsbad in Southern California. The forecast indicates that the conditions are suitable for a VOR-DME approach. Cloud base is 1,100 ft and visibility is 1.5 statute miles. Position your airplane over the Mission Bay VOR using the set aircraft position menu. Mission Bay VOR is located at N32° 46.9' W117° 13.52'.

You start off over Mission Bay (MZB) VOR at 7,000 ft, tracking directly to Oceanside (OCN) VOR. Note that NAV1 is tuned to OCN VOR at 115.3 MHz with a 326° course selected on the OBI. NAV2 is tuned to MZB VOR at 117.8 MHz, also with a 326° course selected on the OBI.

You get out the VOR or GPS A chart and familiarize yourself with the Approach, as shown in Figure 16.18.

Note that the only required navigation aids for the approach are the Oceanside (OCN) VOR. A holding pattern is associated with the approach and is over the VOR (symbolized by the loop labeled "1 min"). While looking at the holding pattern, note that the inbound course of the holding pattern is 090°, which differs from the final approach track of 120°. Also note that the OCN VOR is some 9.6 nm from the airport itself, as shown in the profile view; the VORTAC is symbolized by the Maltese cross, and the missed approach point (MAP) by the "9.6" inside the box. This is classified as a non-terminal VOR approach, because the VOR is not located at the airport. The MAP is defined by a DME distance from the VOR, in this case 9.6 DME OCN. If the DME is not available, the MAP is defined by elapsed time from the final approach fix (FAF). Directly under the airfield diagram you will see a table that gives you the timing to the MAP from the FAF to the MAP. The FAF is the Maltese cross symbol, which is directly over the OCN VOR. So if our ground speed on the approach were 90 knots, it would take 6 min and 24 sec to reach the MAP.

Before proceeding with the flight, we need to discuss the IAP chart in further detail as well as learn about holding patterns. Pause the flight and proceed to the next section.

The Circling Approach

The approach shown in Figure 16.18 is called a circling approach. This means that the final course is not aligned with the runway. The final track of 120 from the OCN VOR takes you over the runway at about a 120° angle, so some maneuvering will be required to align the plane with the runway. A well-executed circling approach is one of the most demanding and potentially dangerous approaches. You must first execute an accurate approach and then fly a visual maneuver at slow speed (often in poor visibility) to accu-

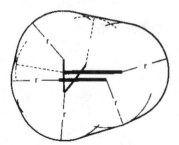

Figure 16.19 *The circling area for the circling approach.*

rately align the plane with the runway. Throughout the circling portion you must be able to see the runway environment, and you must remain at or above the circling minimum altitude until you can commence a continuous descent at normal rates of. Regardless of the visibility, you must also remain within a specific area while circling. Looking at the minima section of the chart, note that the section is titled "CIRCLING". Circling minima are designed to provide you with specific clearance in a specific area around the runway. The size and terrain clearance is a function of aircraft category. With an approach speed up to 90 knots, you would be in category A.

As shown in the minima section of this approach chart, two minima are applicable:

- 860 ft vertical decision height with 1 statute mile visibility for category A aircraft with the DME
- 1,300 ft vertical decision height and $1/4$ statute mile visibility without DME

The more accurate your navigation, the lower the minima. U.S. TERPS and ICAO PANS-OPS procedures provide slightly different protected areas.

The circling area (Figure 16.19) is constructed by drawing a circle around each runway threshold using the radius appropriate to the category. Tangents then join the circumference of each circle. The area bounded by the circles and the tangents is the circling area. During maneuvering, you must remain inside the circling area at the appropriate circling minima to guarantee a specific obstacle clearance. Again, the clearance is a function of aircraft category. Table 16.3 shows the size of the circling area in nautical miles for each category along with the associated obstacle clearance provided for both the U.S. TERPS system and the ICAO PANS-OPS system.

Table 16.3 *Circling Areas*

AIRCRAFT CATEGORY	TERPS RADIUS	PANS OPS RADIUS	PAN OPS OBSTACLE CLEARANCE HEIGHT
A	1.3 nm	1.68 nm	300 ft
B	1.5 nm	2.66 nm	300 ft
C	1.7 nm	4.22 nm	400 ft
D	2.3 nm	5.28 nm	400 ft
E	4.5 nm	6.94 nm	500 ft

If the wind is from the west, the landing runway chosen would be Rwy 24, which happens to have approach lighting. For safety's sake, you decide to visualize the circling maneuver in advance. You will arrive over the runway on a course of 120°. Because the landing runway is 24, you will need to position the plane downwind of runway 24. Visibility is a problem, so it makes sense to favor the view from the pilot's position in the cockpit. To this end you decide that you will fly a left turn downwind. As the captain, you are sitting in the left seat, so you want to put the runway in view of your left side and not your right side, which is probably obstructed by the first officer. You must therefore

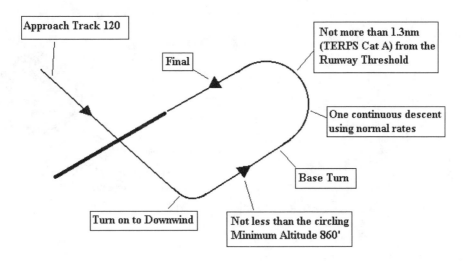

Figure 16.20 *Example of a circling approach.*

fly over the runway and turn left to a downwind heading. There is no single perfect solution to the circling maneuver. You need to come up with a plan that is legal, safe, efficient, and simple. Figure 16.20 shows one example.

From downwind you can fly a fairly standard circuit. How to do this will be discussed later. For now, you have briefed yourself and drawn up your plan.

Minimum Safe Altitude

When you near the Oceanside VOR, SOCAL approach control will identify you on radar and clear you to descend to 4,000 ft. (This won't happen in Flight Simulator because of the limited air traffic control features of the program.) In the real world, ATC might also inform you that there are two aircraft ahead of you bound for Carlsbad and that you must fly the holding pattern at the OCN VOR fix before being allowed to land. Therefore, you must commence a cruise descent to 4,000 ft and start thinking about the holding pattern that is shown in the IAP chart of Figure 16.18.

Notice that the IAP chart's minimum safe altitude circle (located in the lower-right corner of the plan view) specifies that if you are flying within the 25-nm radius circle of the Oceanside VOR, you must maintain an altitude of 6,800 ft if you are north, northeast, northwest, or southeast of the VOR. If you are within the 25 nm radius circle

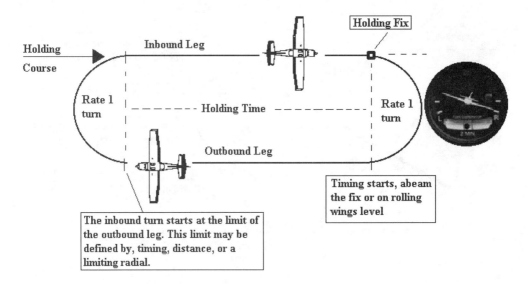

Figure 16.21 *The holding pattern.*

southwest of the Oceanside VOR, you are permitted to fly as low as 1,900 ft. But in both cases, to join the holding pattern you will have to fly at 3,000 ft altitude (note the one spot elevation of 3189 ft north of the Oceanside VOR). In our particular flight, however, the SOCAL ATC has cleared us to 4,000 ft. Once we are in a position to join the holding pattern, we will be cleared down to 3,000 ft, as specified on the IAP chart.

Now let's learn something about holding patterns.

Holding Patterns

Holding patterns are simply racetrack-shaped flight paths that an aircraft follows to kill time. Air traffic control often asks aircraft to maintain holding patterns while awaiting clearance to land at crowded airports. Each pattern is designed to keep the holding aircraft clear of terrain and away from special airspace.

A holding pattern is referenced to a fix, which can be over a navigation aid or on a specified radial and distance from another navaid. The holding pattern also has an inbound and outbound course drawn through the fix, as shown in Figure 16.21. The standard holding pattern uses right-hand turns; the airplane enters the holding pattern by making a right-hand turn after crossing the fix. Nonstandard patterns use left-hand turns in. In our case, the Carlsbad IAP chart of Figure 16.18 shows a standard right-hand holding pattern. The fix is over the Oceanside (OCN) VOR, and the inbound course is 090°. After the fix is passed, a right-turn is made to fly a reciprocal track to the inbound course, which is otherwise known as the outbound leg. The outbound leg is on a track of 270°, so it is the course we would turn the airplane after crossing the fix.

The outbound leg is of a specific length, which can be defined by time, distance or an intersecting radial from another navaid. Our holding pattern includes 1 min inbound and outbound legs. For the outbound leg, the 1 min timing starts the minute we roll out of the turn on the beginning of the outbound leg. As you roll the wings level on the 270° heading, start the clock. The inbound turn commences right on 1 min. You are then required to track the inbound course back to the fix. In our case, we intercept the 090 radial inbound to the OCN VOR (the 090 course). So in a 1-min holding pattern, the time taken to complete one pattern will be 2 min (1 min each for the outbound and inbound legs) plus the time taken for each 180° turn at the end of each leg. Because we usually use a rate 1 turn (a maximum of 30° angle of bank), we can calculate how long each turn will take. Rate 1 means 3°/sec turn rate, so each 180° turn will take 1 min, or a 360° turn will take 2 min. Recall that the turn coordinator shows a rate 1 turn when the aircraft symbol wing points to the wing markers. So a 1-min holding pattern will take a total of 4 min, including 1 min each for the outbound and inbound legs and 1 min each for the outbound turn and inbound turn.

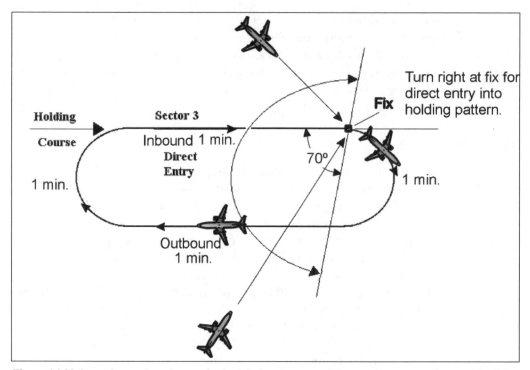

Figure 16.22 Sector 3 entry into the standard, right-hand pattern. The curved arrow on the one side of the diagonal line represents the sector from which the aircraft is entering the holding pattern. In this case, the airplane can enter the holding pattern directly by turning right at the fix.

Entry into the Holding Pattern

Because you can arrive at the holding fix from any direction, a standard method known as *sector entries* has been devised. The sector entry ensures that a predictable, safe, and efficient entry is flown regardless of your heading when you arrive at the holding fix. There are three areas, or sectors, around the holding fix. Each sector is defined as a function of heading and has a specific type of entry maneuver associated with it. Refer to the illustrations that follow as we discuss sector entries. Diagrams for standard, right-hand patterns and nonstandard, left-hand patterns are provided to clarify the directional sense.

Sector 3: Direct Entry into the Holding Pattern

The simplest entry is flown when you arrive over the holding fix from sector 3. When arriving from sector 3, you perform a *direct entry* by simply turning directly into the holding pattern, to pick up the downwind leg. With a standard, right-hand pattern, you

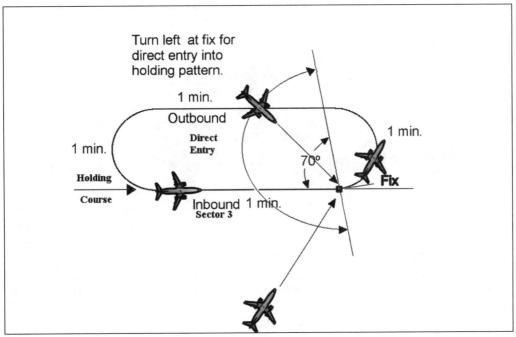

Figure 16.23 *Sector 3 entry into the nonstandard, left-hand holding pattern (not used in the Carlsbad IAP chart). The curved arrow on the one side of the diagonal line represents the sector from which the aircraft is entering the holding pattern. In this case, the airplane can enter the holding pattern directly by turning left at the fix.*

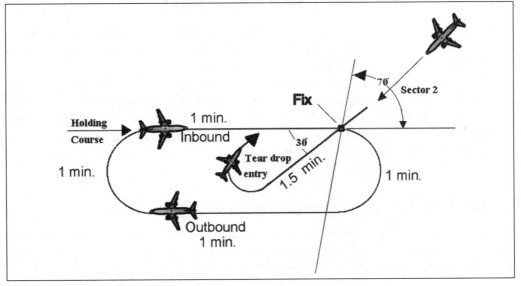

Figure 16.24 *Sector 2 teardrop entry into the standard, right-hand holding pattern.*

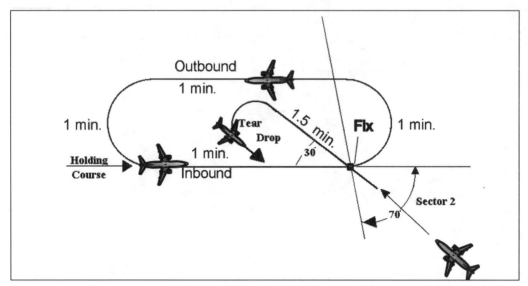

Figure 16.25 *Sector 2 teardrop entry into the nonstandard, left-hand holding pattern (not used in the Carlsbad IAP chart).*

would turn right at the fix, as shown in Figure 16.22. With a nonstandard, left-hand pattern, you would turn left at the fix, as shown in Figure 16.23.

Sector 2: Teardrop Entry into the Holding Pattern

The next type of simple entry into the holding pattern occurs when the aircraft enters the area from sector 2. As shown in Figure 16.24, to enter the standard, right-hand holding pattern from sector 2, you turn to a track that is 30° away from the reciprocal of the inbound holding track and inside the holding pattern. You maintain this track for a maximum of 1.5 min or the quoted holding pattern time if less than 1.5 min. You then turn in toward the inbound holding course and intercept it. Then you continue over the holding fix and then turn directly into the holding pattern. A sector 2 entry is also referred to as a *teardrop entry*. Figure 16.25 shows the teardrop entry into the nonstandard, left-hand holding pattern.

Sector 1: Parallel Entry into the Holding Pattern

The most complex entry into the holding pattern is flown from sector 1. When arriving over the fix from sector 1, you immediately turn the shortest way to parallel the inbound holding course (but you head in the opposite direction). You hold this track

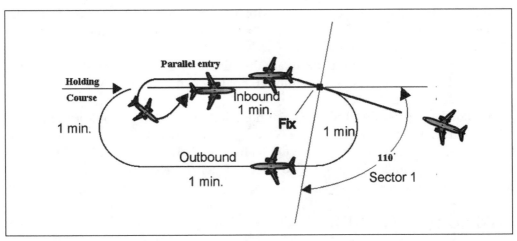

Figure 16.26 Sector 1 parallel entry into the standard, right-hand holding pattern.

for the same time as quoted for the holding pattern, which is usually 1 min. Then you turn back toward the holding course through more than 180°, (typically, 210°) to intercept the holding course. Having intercepted the inbound holding course, you then fly over the holding fix and finally turn directly into the holding pattern.

The sector 1 and sector 2 entries are designed to bring you back over the holding fix from sector 3, thereby allowing you to turn directly into the holding pattern. The boundaries between each sector are not exact and a zone of flexibility of ±5° is allowed

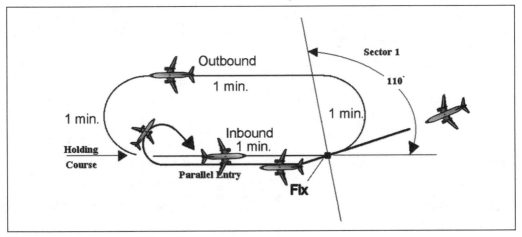

Figure 16.27 Sector 1 parallel entry into the nonstandard, left-hand holding pattern (not used in the Carlsbad IAP chart).

around each boundary. In the zone of flexibility, you can decide on the entry of your choice. If you are right on the boundary that determines, say, a sector 1 or sector 2 entry, you can choose either entry.

Nonstandard, or left-hand patterns are the mirror image of the right-hand pattern. Right- and left-hand sector 1 entries into the holding patterns are illustrated in Figure 16.26 and Figure 16.27.

Knowing the procedures to enter the hold, let's apply them to our current situation. The track from Mission Bay to the Oceanside (OCN) VOR is 326°, as pictured in Figure 16.18. Knowing that the OCN VOR fix has an inbound course of 090°, what type of entry are you going to fly? If you choose sector 1, a parallel entry is required, and you should fly the pattern shown in Figure 16.26.

Holding Speeds

Because holding patterns are designed to keep you clear of terrain and special airspace, it follows that speed limits are associated with them. The higher the speed, the larger your turn radius. Holding speeds vary from country to country. The three most common standards are ICAO PANS-OPS, U.S., and French speeds. Tables 16.4, 16.5, 16.6, and 16.7 list the most common speed limits.

Table 16.4 U.S. Holding Patterns

ALTITUDE	AIRCRAFT TYPE	MAXIMUM SPEED (KIAS)
6000 ft and less	Prop	175
	Jet	200
6000 ft–14,000 ft	Prop	175
	Jet	230
Greater than 14,000 ft	Prop	175
	Jet	265

Table 16.5 ICAO Holding Patterns (PANS-OPS Third and Fourth Editions)

ALTITUDE	MAXIMUM SPEED (KIAS)
Up to 14,000 ft	230 (170 Cat A and B)
14,000 ft–20,000 ft	240
20,000 ft–34,000 ft	265
Greater than 34,000 ft	Mach 0.83

Table 16.6 Australian, New Zealand, and Japanese Holding Patterns

ALTITUDE	MAXIMUM SPEED (KIAS)
Up to 6,000 ft	210
6,000 ft–14,000 ft	220
Greater than 14,000 ft	240

Table 16.7 French Holding Patterns

ALTITUDE	MAXIMUM SPEED (KIAS)
Up to 14,000 ft	220 (170 for Cat A and Cat B)
14,000 ft–24,000 ft	240
24,000 ft–34,000 ft	265
Greater than 34,000 ft	Mach 0.83

Resuming the Flight: The Holding Pattern at OCN VOR

Leaving the Mission Bay (MZB) VOR, we track the 326 radial from MZB, or the 146 radial inbound to OCN. Recall that when tracking a radial you always set the OBI course to the appropriate setting. So tune the NAV1 to Oceanside (OCN) VOR at 115.3 MHz and set the OBI 1 to 326°. At this point it is also prudent to tune the NAV2 radio to OCN and set the NAV2 OBI 2 to the holding course, so set the NAV2 OBI 2 to 090°. When you get close to the OCN VOR, level off at the assigned altitude of 4,000 ft, and continue tracking the 326 course inbound to the OCN VOR. The autopilot can be used, and in the single-pilot instrument environment its intelligent use is encouraged. In this phase of flight the most appropriate modes are **Autopilot Altitude Hold** (4,000 ft) and NAV1 tracking on (use the Aircraft/Autopilot dialog box or press **Ctrl+N** with the autopilot on). Approaching the OCN VOR, deselect **NAV1 Autopilot Hold** (press **Ctrl+N** again to switch it off).

As you pass over the OCN VOR, the To/From flag will change. Now let's fly the parallel entry, as is required by a sector 1 entry into the holding pattern. Refer to Figure 16.26 if you need to refresh your memory.

Start a rate 1 left-hand turn onto a heading to parallel the inbound course. Because the inbound course is 090°, the outbound heading will the reciprocal course, or 270°. As you approach the 270° heading, roll the wings level and start the stopwatch.

T I P   To roll out smoothly on a desired heading, you must start rolling out of the turn a little before the desired heading, but how much before? A good rule of thumb is to lead the turn by about half the bank angle. If we are using, say, a 20° angle of bank, a good point to start rolling out would be when the heading passes 280° (270 + half bank angle) or (270 + 10). As you start reducing the bank angle, watch the heading. You can fine-tune the rollout by varying the rate at which you remove bank, ensuring that the desired heading is reached as the bank reaches 0°.

You should now be flying parallel to the inbound course but in the opposite direction (270°). If you have some idea of the wind direction, apply a guesstimated heading correction. As we cruise away from the VOR in the direction opposite the inbound course of 90°, set the NAV1 OBI 1 to a course of 090°, in preparation for tracking the inbound holding course. As the clock gets close to the 1-min mark, start a left turn toward the inbound leg's holding course. The goal of this turn is to intercept the holding course (090° to OCN). Wind, airspeed, and the distance you are displaced from the holding course will affect the inbound turn. In most cases, the parallel entry turn will take you through the holding course and inside the holding pattern. You will know this is happening because the OBI will rapidly swap sides as you turn. In this case, you must continue the turn through greater than 180° to intercept the inbound holding course from inside the holding pattern. If this occurs, a good rule is to again set up a 30° intercept on the holding course. In this case, that will require a heading of 060° (090° − 030° = 060°).

Once the plane is rolled out on the 060° heading, you have established a 30° intercept on the holding course. The OBI 1's CDI needle will be deflected to the left, indicating that the holding course is to the left. As the 90 radial to the OCN VOR is approached, the OBI 1's CDI needle will start to drift toward the center. As the CDI needle approaches half-scale deflection, start a gradual turn toward the inbound holding course of 090°. Vary the bank angle to control the rate of the CDI needle movement. The faster the OBI is drifting, the more bank angle will be required. Roll out on the wind-corrected heading. This rollout does not need to be exact, but a guesstimated allowance for wind is good practice.

Tracking Inbound Wind Estimation

Once the plane is established on the inbound holding course of 090°, it is important to deduce how the wind is affecting it. Note the required heading to maintain the 090 course. The difference between the heading and the course is the drift. So lets assume that to track the 090 course we need to fly a heading of 095. This means that the wind is from the south and that we need to fly 5° into wind. The drift angle is 5°. Remember this number, because we will use it during the holding pattern.

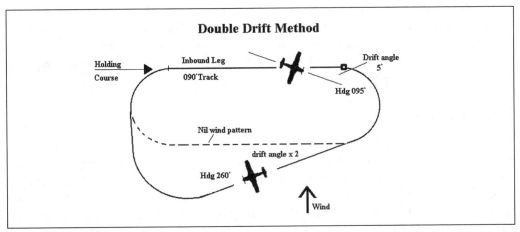

Double Drift Method

Figure 16.28 The double drift method.

The Holding Pattern

As you pass over the holding fix (OCN VOR), start the turn into the pattern. In no-wind conditions, this is a simple 180° turn onto the outbound leg. Wind, however, complicates the problem. Not only do you need to adjust for wind effect on the straight legs, but you must also make some allowance for drift during the turns. The most common technique is the *double drift* method (Figure 16.28). In this method, we make a single heading correction on the outbound leg. We discovered that the drift angle was 5° as we tracked the inbound course. In the double drift method, we apply 2 times the drift angle on the outbound leg. So if we had 5° of drift inbound, we apply 10° of correction on the outbound leg. If, when tracking inbound, we had a wind from the south that required 5° of drift correction, then as we turn outbound we would roll out on a heading of 260° (270° − 010° = 260°).

Failure to apply a drift correction can result in the aircraft flying outside the charted pattern and its surrounding protected airspace. In our case, with a wind from the south, the aircraft would drift in toward the holding course, thereby reducing the turning room for completing the inbound turn.

As you roll the wings level again, start the clock. The OCN VOR hold is a 1 min pattern, so the inbound turn will commence at exactly 1 min elapsed time. ATC next clears us to 3,000 ft. From our previous chart study, we know that this is the initial approach altitude. Start a gradual descent to 3,000 ft; about 500 ft/min would be appropriate. A faster descent would make your ears pop and your passengers would complain. ATC next clears us for the approach from the OCN VOR fix.

Now is the time to set up the navigation aids for the approach. This particular VOR-DME approach has a final course of 120°. This differs from the holding course of 090°

by 30°. Set up the NAV1 OBI's course to 120°. You will use the NAV2 OBI previously set to 090° to complete the last inbound leg of the hold. As you reach 1 min, start the inbound turn. Recall the wind correction you previously applied. Initially plan the turn to continue to your wind-corrected heading. During the final part of the turn, you can again vary the bank angle to control the rate of CDI needle movement on the OBI.

The Approach

Tracking inbound to the OCN VOR, we prepare for the approach. You have previously studied the profile, but now is the time to review exactly how you are going to fly it. The navigation aids have been set, the weather is ok, and we know we are going to circle to land on runway 24. We also know that the circling minima altitude is 860 ft (remember that we have a DME and can use the lower circling minima on the IAP chart). Therefore, we cannot descend lower than 860 ft at the missed approach point, which is 532 ft above the runway (because the airport elevation is 328 ft, and 860 − 328 = 532 ft). Referring to the profile view on the IAP chart, note the altitude restriction of 1,300 ft until the 7 nm mark as shown on the DME from the OCN VOR. So after leaving the final approach fix (OCN VOR) at 3,000 ft, you must lose 1,700 ft over 7 nm, or 242 ft/nm. Looking at the entire final approach from the FAF (OCN VOR) to the MAP, you must lose 2140 ft (3,000 − 860) over 9.6 nm. This works out to 223 ft/nm. So if you fly the descent at the lesser of the two you will not exceed the 7 DME 1300 ft altitude restriction, because at 223 ft/nm you would be passing 1,439 ft. Ideally, any instrument final approach should be flown at a constant rate of descent, because it makes it easier for the pilot to concentrate on smooth and accurate control of the airplane.

As you approach the OCN VOR (the FAF), establish your approach configuration. In the Cessna 182, I recommend gear down and 10° of flap with an airspeed of 80 knots.

As you pass over FAF, commence your descent, turn to a heading of 120°, and track the 120 course on the NAV1's OBI. You have decided on a descent rate of 223 ft/nm; because there is no wind and we are flying at 80 knots, we are covering 1.33 nm/min. Our rate of descent should therefore be 297 ft/min (1.33 × 224). Being practical, let's use 300 ft/min. One final action is to start the stopwatch as you pass over OCN. This serves two purposes. First, if the DME fails, you can use timing to establish the MAP. Second, you can readily determine the overall rate of descent achieved.

Looking at the lower-right corner of the IAP chart, you will see a table that plots ground speed versus time from the FAF to the MAP. At 80 knots, the time would be 7 min 12 sec. (Either calculation or interpolation is required for 80 knots, because only 60-knot and 90-knot timings are displayed on the IAP chart.)

Once the plane is established on the approach, you must now consider the possibility of a missed approach. Your previous approach study revealed that a missed approach requires you to perform a climbing right turn onto a 180° heading to intercept the Mission Bay (MZB) VOR 326 radial to the VOR (this is marked on the chart as "R-326"). You no longer require NAV2 tuned to the Oceanside (OCN) VOR, so retune NAV2 to MZB at 117.8 MHz and set the course on the OBI 2 to 148°. Recall that you always set the radial on the OBI to the course you intend to fly; because this is inbound to the MZB VOR via the 328° radial, you set the reciprocal of 148°.

Approaching 7 DME from the OCN VOR, you check that your altitude is not less than 1,300 ft, and anticipate the visual sighting of the runway. Picture in your mind's eye what you expect to see. The runway should extend both left and right of the nose. As you break through the clouds, you should see the runway. Level off at 860 ft and continue toward the runway.

The Circling Maneuver

Although the circling maneuver is a visual flight maneuver, frequent cross reference to the instruments is required. Throughout the maneuver, you must maintain visual reference to the runway environment. The purpose of the maneuver is to achieve a base position from which an approach can be made. There are many ways to achieve this, and the discussion that follows suggests way technique.

In general terms, let's set a maximum bank angle of 25°. When we are this close to the ground, a greater bank angle is not prudent. The problem here is to achieve enough turning room, or displacement, to complete the final turn without overshooting the runway centerline. The absolute minimum spacing required is one turn diameter. To achieve this, use the simple rule of thumb that follows:

half the bank angle = half the turn

As you cross the runway on a heading of 120°, commence a 10° angle of bank toward the landing threshold. In this instance, this would mean a 10° bank to the left. This turn is

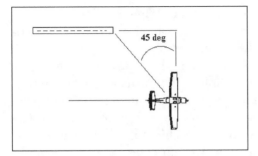

Figure 16.29 The base turn point.

continued until you achieve the downwind heading of 060° (which is the runway heading, or Rwy 6 as shown on the IAP chart). Bank angle can be varied as you see fit. As you approach the 060° heading, roll the wings level. You are now effectively on the downwind leg and ready for the final turn. Throughout this portion of the maneuver, you have maintained the minimum circling altitude of 860 ft. The descent can commence only when you fly a continuous descent at normal descent rates (in the Cessna 182 this means around 300 ft/min) to the landing runway. The exact point this occurs will vary depending on exactly how you have flown the maneuver, so experience is your best guide.

Start the base turn to the runway when the airplane is abeam of the point at which you need to be wings level. A good guide is that this point is reached when the landing threshold is 45° back from the abeam position, as shown in Figure 16.29.

Recall that you cannot fly more than 1.2 nm from the landing threshold, so there is not very much room to play with.

At the base turn point, turn toward the runway using 20° angle of bank and increase the flaps another 10°. Also, start reducing speed toward your final approach speed. At the 90° point (in this case the airplane would be on a heading of 330°), reassess your bank angle and rate of descent. If an adjustment is required, the earlier you do it the less severe it will be. As you turn onto the final approach, vary the bank angle to achieve a smooth roll out on the runway centerline. During the last 20° of turn, the VASI (if operating) will come into view and can assist in confirming your profile.

Rolling out onto the final approach, select your final flap setting and reduce the speed to the final approach speed.

Missed Approach While Circling

If you fail to sight the runway at the missed approach point, then the missed approach is straightforward and is flown according to the missed-approach instructions. But what happens if a missed approach is required after you have sighted the runway and after you have started the circling maneuver?

The circling missed approach poses a special problem. While circling, you must remain in the protected circling area. Until the plane is established on the missed-approach track, you must also remain within the circling area.

Consider a missed approach from the base turn point in the approach you have just flown. There are two ways to get onto the 180° heading: a right turn away from the runway or a left turn toward the runway. The right turn will take you out of the circling area almost immediately, compromising any protection afforded by the minima. The left turn option will keep you in the circling area until you achieve the missed-approach heading and is therefore the appropriate direction. We can come up with a general missed-approach rule for all circling missed approaches: Always turn in toward the runway and keep turning until you achieve the missed-approach heading. This method can safely be used from anywhere in the circling maneuver.

Today you have flown a textbook circling approach. You should be pleased as the wheels hit the tarmac.

TUTORIAL, FLIGHT 3: TERMINAL VOR-DME ARC APPROACH, B737, CHAMPAIGN-URBANA, ILLINOIS

The choice of the 737 in flying the VOR-DME arc approach to Champaign-Urbana, Illinois, may seem a little strange, but to fly the arc an RMI is considered essential. Because the FSW95 Learjet does not have an RMI but the FSW95 737 does, it is necessary to fly this tutorial with the 737 (only if you are using FSW95). If you have FS98, however, you can use the Learjet in place of the 737, because the new Learjet 45 has RMI capabilities built into the HSI. The Learjet is the more appropriate choice for this airport, but you can fly with either aircraft.

This section discusses the techniques for flying the VOR-DME arc approach. It is not a blow-by-blow description of the approach, with power settings, and so on.

First, load the Champaign flight situation from the book's CD-ROM. This will put you in the right position to begin the arc approach.

Arc Procedures

Some approaches use an arc to get the aircraft on to the final approach course. Arc procedures can be used as part of an ILS or VOR procedure. The arc is a segment of a circle whose radius is determined by a DME distance. For this example, we will use the VOR-DME approach to runway 22R at Champaign-Urbana/University of Illinois-Willard. This approach is a terminal approach, because the VOR is located at the airfield itself. Refer to the IAP chart illustrated in Figure 16.30.

The approach has a final course of 207° that is nearly aligned with runway 22R. This final approach course can be arrived at by either of two arcs: one to the east and one to the west. A further track from Roberts VOR is also available, but we will discuss the arc procedures. Both arcs are based on the Champaign (CMI) VOR-DME, and each arc has a radius of 12 nm (as shown on the IAP chart by the boxed numeral 12 on the arc labeled "CMI …Arc…"). The arcs also have associated minimum altitudes. The eastern arc has a minimum altitude of 2,400 ft, as indicated by the label "2400 NoPT." The label NoPT means that a procedure turn is not allowed, perhaps because of potential

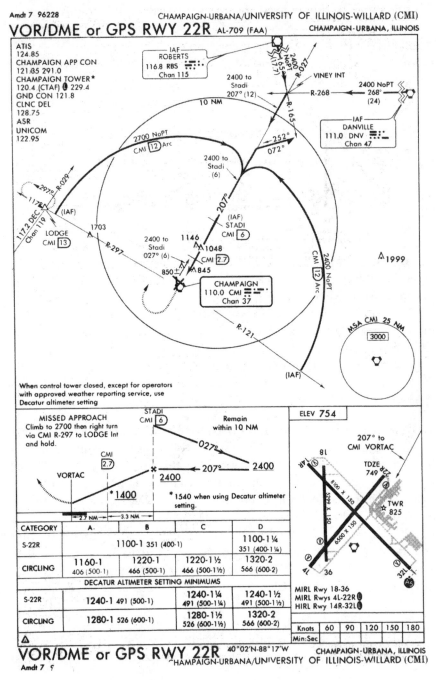

Figure 16.30 *Instrument approach plate VOR-DME RWY 22R Champaign-Urbana used with the DME-arc approach.*

obstructions in the flight area. The western arc has a minimum altitude of 2,700 ft until the plane is established on the final course, where you can descend to 2,400 ft (see "2700 NoPT" and "2400 to Stadi" on the IAP chart). An arc can be joined at any point if you are above the minimum altitude. In our case, we are established on the 301° course inbound to the CMI VOR (on the 121° radial from CMI). Because we are tracking directly to the CMI VOR, we will intercept the arc at right angles. Tune both VOR radios (NAV1 and NAV2) to the CMI VOR at 110.0 MHz.

T I P

If you are confused about the difference between the HSI and RMI displays, remember that the RMI's VOR needle will always point to the VOR station tuned on the NAV2 radio, whereas the HSI's CDI needle always points to the VOR radial you have selected on the Course readout on the MCP for the NAV1 radio.

In FS98, notice that the compass cards on both the HSI and the RMI rotate in response to the aircraft's heading. This is as it should be. To experiment with this, tune in the same station on both VOR radios and then start Slew mode by pressing Y, followed by rotating the airplane in place. As the airplane rotates, you will see that the compass cards rotate on both the HSI and RMI. Note, however, that you cannot change the compass direction the RMI's needle points to, whereas you can change the compass direction of the HSI's CDI needle—for example, by clicking on the Course readout. On the other hand, the only way you can change the RMI's VOR needle from its current compass heading by physically moving the airplane.

You may wonder why the instruments were designed this way. The HSI allows you to intercept and fly any VOR radial, whereas the RMI gives your bearing information to the VOR station relative to your airplane's current heading. The RMI also lets you simultaneously display the bearing of an NDB station tuned on the ADF radio. Combining the two instruments gives you the best of all possible worlds. You can pinpoint the direction to any VOR or NDB station and at the same time display a VOR radial intersection and the direction you need to turn to intercept it.

In FS98, there is no separate RMI for the Learjet as there is for the 737. To activate the RMI on the FS98 Learjet, you must first click the VOR2 indicator button just below the HSI to the left. A green needle will be superimposed over the HSI that points at the VOR station tuned in on the NAV2 radio. To turn it off, click again on the button. On the FS98 737, the RMI is a separate instrument, so the yellow RMI needle always points toward the VOR station tuned in on the NAV2 radio.

For the arc procedure, we next set the course for a given VOR radial on the HSI by using the Course display on the MCP. The chosen VOR radial is then displayed via the

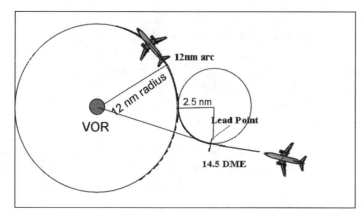

Figure 16.31 Arc lead point.

CDI bar on the HSI. The NAV2 radio should be set to allow the missed approach to be flown with minimum knob twiddling. Therefore, ensure that the NAV2 radio is tuned to the CMI VOR at 110.0 MHz and set the Course setting to 297° on the MCP. Note that the HSI is always slaved to the NAV1 radio, and therefore the yellow CDI needle always points toward the radial you have selected on the Course display.

Intercepting an Arc from a Radial

Intercepting an arc from a radial is, in theory, straightforward: You start the turn onto the arc exactly one turn radius away from the arc. How do you go about doing this? Recall the previous rule of thumb that the turn radius is 1% of your TAS. If we are at 3,000 ft, at 180 knots, our TAS will be about 190 knots, so the turn radius will be close to 2 nm. Rolling into the turn takes time, so we add a buffer to the radius; in this instance, 0.5 nm is sufficient. Based on this information, you decide to use a lead point of 2.5 nm (see Figure 16.31). Because you are outside the arc, the point at which you start the turn will occur at 14.5 DME (12 nm + 2.5 nm = 14.5 nm) from the Champaign (CMI) VOR. The opposite occurs if you are intercepting an arc while flying outbound from the station.

T I P

The 737 and Lear autopilots in FSW95 use slow rates of roll, so extra allowance is required when you're using the automatics. I suggest an additional 0.5 nm allowance on top of the turn radius, so start the turn using a 3-nm lead point. You should start the turn, for the purposes of Flight Simulator, at least 15 nm DME from the Champaign VOR.

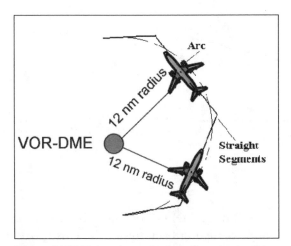

Figure 16.32 Flying the arc by approximating it with small straight segments.

Maintaining the Arc

Because an arc is simply a portion of a circle, one way of flying the arc would be to use an angle of bank that produces a turn radius equal to the arc. In practice, this technique is not practical (although modern airline autopilots and flight management computers use it). A more practical method is to fly a series of small, straight legs inside and outside the arc. The tolerance for arc flying is a very generous ±2 nm, so it is legal to be anywhere from 10 nm to 14 nm DME from the Champaign VOR along the arc. It is easy to fly with a tolerance of ±1 nm or greater. So how do you actually fly the arc? Because the arc is centered on the VOR, the VOR should always be on the wingtip when you are flying on the arc. In other words, the direction of the VOR station should always be 90° offset from the nose of the airplane. The RMI is an ideal instrument to use for arc flying, and the FAA recommends its use. The RMI will provide the DME and a bearing or needle pointing to the VOR. So if you were to intercept the arc (as shown by the DME) and then simply maintain the RMI needle on the wingtip (the 90° position), you would maintain the arc, assuming that you also maintain the arc radius constant that is shown on the DME readout.

As stated earlier, you actually fly a series of straight legs (see Figure 16.32). If you are flying at less than the arc radius—say 11 nm instead of the required 12 nm DME from the Champaign VOR—then you need to fly away from the station. Turn away from the VOR until the VOR needle is 10° behind the wingtip. The aircraft will then fly away from the VOR and back toward the arc. Crossing the arc (as shown on the DME when it reads 12 nm), maintain your divergent heading until you reach the tolerance. If you're using ±0.5 nm, you would continue until the DME readout shows 12.4 nm. Then

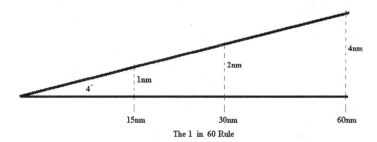

Figure 16.33 *The 1 in 60 rule.*

you would turn back toward the Champaign VOR until the VOR needle is 10° ahead of the wingline. You are now outside the arc and correcting back toward it. This procedure is repeated until the final turn onto the final approach. Corrections of 10° ahead and behind the wingline (20° heading changes) are usually sufficient. Gross errors may require larger corrections.

When intercepting the arc, you should initially plan to turn through 90° to place the VOR needle on the wingtip. As you get close to achieving this, check the DME to see exactly where you are in relation to the arc. If the DME readout shows a range greater than the arc (in this case greater than 12 nm), stop the turn with the VOR pointer ahead of the wingline by an appropriate amount. If you are already inside the arc, continue the turn to place the VOR needle behind the wingline.

Intercepting a Radial from an Arc

Intercepting a radial from an arc, by definition, involves a 90° intercept angle. Theoretically, to perform the intercept you turn the airplane 90° exactly one turn radius away from the radial. How do you do this? There are a number of ways to estimate the lead point. Some charts nominate a lead radial; when you cross this radial, you turn the airplane. If a lead radial is not defined, however, a little math is required. We know that our turn radius is about 1 % of our TAS. We also know from the 1 in 60 rule (Figure 16.33) that 1° of arc equates to 1 nm at 60 nm from the center of a circle. Using the 1 in 60 rule, we can then estimate how many degrees our turn radius will subtend at a particular range from the station.

At 190 knots TAS we can say that our turn radius is 2 nm. So if we were on a 60-nm arc and were intercepting a radial, we would need to start the turn 2° before the final course. On a 30-nm arc the turn would start at 4° before, whereas on a 15-nm arc the turn would start at 8° before. We are on the 12-nm arc, so we need to start the turn 10° before the final course.

There are a number of ways of determining this lead point. The simplest is to pres-elect the final approach course of 207° on the Course readout on the MCP. Knowing that the HSI CDI bar has a full-scale deflection value of 10° in VOR mode, we will be at the proper lead point of 10° to initiate the turn at the instant the CDI bar starts to move.

The other method of determining the lead point is to set up the CDI bar with the lead point course selected. We would select a Course of 217°, because this is 10° before the desired 207° final approach course. As the CDI bar centers at the 217° mark, imme-diately start the turn toward the final course. The disadvantage of this method is that you must then reset the final course on the MCP while still turning—not a smart thing to do.

During the final stages of the final intercept—say, within the last 20° of turn—you can vary the bank angle to control the rate of CDI movement. With practice, you can fly radial intercepts very precisely. because you will typically be flying standard speeds at the intercept, you can develop and remember a few lead points for varying arc sizes, thereby avoiding mental gymnastics.

On modern aircraft with fight director systems, the lead angle is automatically cal-culated and applied. The pilot simply follows the displayed steering commands.

Final Approach

Once the plane is established on the final approach course, you must maintain a mini-mum altitude of 2,400 ft until you reach the final approach fix, which is depicted on the IAP chart as a Maltese cross. The distance from the FAF to the missed approach point is 6 nm, as shown on the profile view of the IAP chart of Figure 16.30. The minimum altitude for the straight-in approach is 1,100 ft, or 346 ft above ground level because the airport elevation is 754 ft (see "1100-1" in the minima section of the IAP). Ideally, a con-tinuous descent at a constant descent rate should be flown from the FAF to the MAP. Most aircraft fly a 3° glide slope, and this works out to 320 ft of altitude lost per nm. Looking at the IAP chart, note that the VOR is about halfway down runway 22R, or about 0.5 nm from the threshold. Referring to the chart, you can deduce that the dis-tance from the FAF to the threshold of runway 22R is 5.5 nm (3.3 + 2.7 − 0.5 = 5.5 nm). Because the airfield elevation is 754 ft, the required altitude loss from the FAF to the runway is 1,646 ft. This 1,646 ft is to be lost over 5.5 nm, or at a rate of 299 ft/nm, just a little less than the ideal 3° glide slope. Also note that there is a minimum altitude of 1,400 ft until 2.7 nm DME to the Champaign VOR, which is almost exactly on the pro-file of 299 ft/nm. To estimate the required rate of descent, calculate your ground speed in nautical miles/min and then multiply this number by the required descent gradient in ft/mile. For example:

Ground Speed 140 knots = 2.33 nm/per min × 299 ft/nm = 697 ft/min

If you would like to ease the task, try using the new FS98 vertical speed autopilot to maintain the proper glide slope. To use this feature, click in the **Vs** readout on the MCP until it displays -697. (Click to the right to increase, or click to the left to decrease; alternatively, use the **Aircraft/Autopilot** menu to type in the vertical speed.) Then click on the **Alt** button with the autopilot on to activate the vertical speed hold.

Using the autopilot is the ideal way to fly the final approach. The autopilot vastly simplifies the problem of moving in three-dimensional space. Not only does it track the final course heading (using the Nav hold or the Heading hold), but also the vertical speed hold Vs and auto-throttle allow you to maintain a perfect vertical and horizontal descent profile.

When you have visual contact with the runway, disconnect the autopilot—in effect, the way it is normally flown in the real aircraft, such as the 737. In the 767, the autopilot cannot track a VOR radial, so the autopilot heading hold is used. Alternatively, an equivalent inertial track is programmed into the flight management computer and the autopilot is then used to track it with raw VOR data used to cross-check the airplane's position.

Armed with this information, we now cross the FAF with the final approach speed and glide path properly set up, and we then continue to descend at approximately 700 ft/min to the runway threshold.

In a terminal VOR approach, the MAP has a minimum altitude at a specific point. The MAP can be either the VOR itself or at a specific DME. In Champaign, the MAP is directly over the Champaign VOR, something you can see by examining the profile view of the IAP chart, where you see the laebl "VORTAC" over the MAP. A missed approach can be executed from any point in the approach, but you must comply with the lateral tracking requirements of the approach until passing the MAP. For example, let's assume you commence a missed approach at 3 nm DME from the Champaign VOR. The missed approach procedure states, "Climb to 2700 then right turn via CMI R-297 to LODGE Int and hold." The right turn can be started only after you have passed the MAP (the VOR) and after passing 2,700 ft altitude.

TUTORIAL, FLIGHT 4: NDB RUNWAY 27 DWIGHT, ILLINOIS

This tutorial will teach the techniques of flying a typical NDB approach. The approach you will be using in this tutorial is for Dwight Rwy 27.

The non-directional beacon, or NDB, is the most basic of nonprecision approaches. Because NDB approaches are less precise than VOR or ILS approaches, for safety reasons they usually have the highest altitude minima. NDB approaches are not very common in the United States, but they are still widely used overseas. The advent of GPS will soon render most NDB installations obsolete. Typical light aircraft display NDB information on a simple fixed-compass-card ADF display; a 360 compass bearing nose is fixed, and the ADF needle points to the NDB station. The angle between the nose and the ADF needle is the relative bearing. Magnetic bearing to the station must be calculated, a tedious process that requires constant mental arithmetic. To calculate magnetic bearing, proceed as follows:

1. Note the aircraft heading—for example, 277°.
2. Note the relative bearing to the NDB as shown on the VOR—for example, 30 R.
3. Compute the magnetic bearing by adding the RB (relative bearing) to the aircraft heading if the needle is right of the nose or subtracting the RB from the heading if the needle is left of the nose.

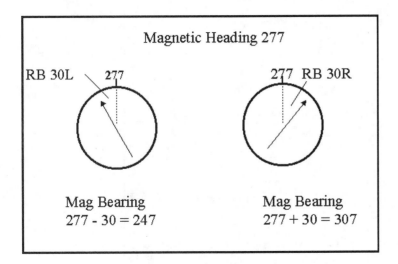

Some fixed-card ADFs have a manually rotated compass card. With this card, the pilot manually rotates the compass card under the ADF needle to keep the card aligned with the actual magnetic heading. If the card is aligned with the aircraft's actual heading, then the ADF needle will indicate the magnetic bearing to the station. This arrangement is better than the fixed card, but it still requires regular pilot input. Every time you change the heading, you must manually rotate the card. The radio magnetic indicator solves this problem, because the card is automatically slaved to the aircraft heading. With the RMI, the ADF needles always display magnetic bearing to the station. Although, the RMI in FSW95 mistakenly used a fixed-compass card ADF, Microsoft fixed this with FS98, and the RMI is now a "true" RMI that has a rotating compass card.

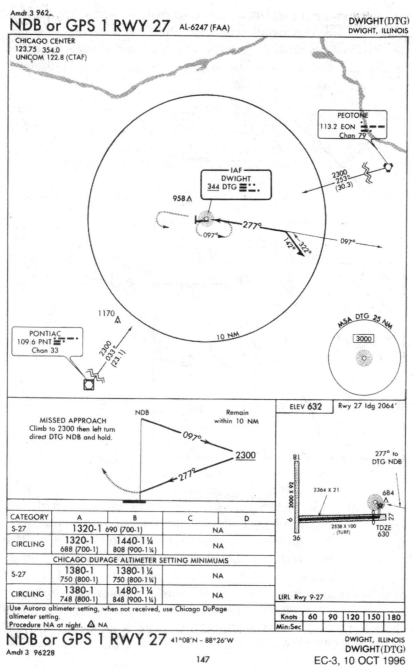

Figure 16.34 *Dwight NDB or GPS 1 Rwy 27 approach plate.*

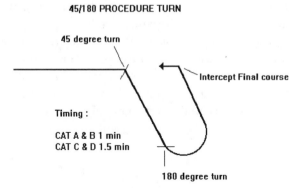

Figure 16.35 *45/180 procedure turn.*

The NDB Approach Plate

Studying the IAP for the NDB approach to Dwight, note the following key points. Airfield elevation is 632 ft. The NDB is located on the airfield, so the NDB approach is considered a terminal NDB. The minima for the approach (Cat A) are 1,320 ft with 1 statute mile visibility (see the "1320-1" on the minima section of the IAP chart). Allowing for the airfield elevation, the minimum is 690 ft above ground level. As shown in the plan view of the IAP chart of Figure 16.34, a holding pattern is associated with the approach. A course reversal or procedure turn is also required, as shown by the half arrow labeled "322° and 142°." During this turn you must remain inside the 10-nm circle of the Dwight (DTG) NDB. Note that the final course of 277° is not lined up exactly with the runway centerline.

In this approach, you fly directly to the IAF of Dwight NDB, being sure to maintain an altitude of at least 3,000 ft when you are within 25 nm of the NDB. Once the plane is over the NDB, the ADF will spin around, telling you that you have crossed the IAF. Immediately turn the airplane on an outbound course of 97° so that it is flying *away* from the NDB station and the airport. This direction is shown on both the plan view

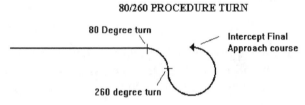

Figure 16.36 *80/260 procedure turn.*

and the profile view. Usually, flying the outbound course will take about 2 min before the procedure turn is implemented. However, the airplane needs to descend to 2,300 ft within 10 nm of the station before executing the procedure turn, as shown in the profile view. After the plane reaches the proper altitude, you fly the procedure turn by turning the airplane to a course heading of 142°, as shown on the plan view. You then fly the airplane on this heading for 1 min before reversing course on a heading of 322° to reintercept the final approach path. After flying for 1 more min on a heading of 322°, you turn left to a heading of 277° and fly this all the way to the airport. Note that you cannot descend lower than 1,320 ft to the missed approach point.

Procedure Turns

A procedure turn is a prescribed turning maneuver that allows the pilot to reverse direction in order to establish the plane on a final approach course. There are two methods in general use: the 45/180 or the 80/260 procedure turn. The most common, as illustrated in Figure 16.35, is the 45/180 turn. In this method, the aircraft is turned 45° from the outbound track from the IAF. This track is maintained for a specific time depending on aircraft category, but, in any case, the timing starts when the outbound turn from the IAF is initiated. Usually, a time of 1 min (for category A and B) or a time of 1 min 15 sec (for category C and D) is used for each leg of the procedure. At the required time, a 170° turn is flown to place the aircraft on a 45° intercept of the inbound course. As shown in the chart, the procedure turn consists of a left turn through 45° onto a heading of 142°. After 1 min (category A), a left turn through 180° is flown, rolling out on a heading of 322°. This is flown for 1 min (category A), and then the aircraft is turned onto the final approach course of 277°.

The 80/260 method (Figure 16.36) consists of a turn away from the course through 80°, followed by an immediate reversal of the turn through 260°. The aim of this turn is simply to generate some turning room. Ideally, the 260° reversal turn will have you rolling out on the inbound course. The 80/260 turn can usually be flown as an alternative to the 45/180 procedure turn unless a note on the IAP chart prohibits it.

T I P

The 45/180 turn is a much more comfortable maneuver to fly.

On the approach plate, note that the missed approach point is directly over the NDB. The missed approach is a climb to 2,300 ft and then a left turn to cross back over the Dwight (DTG) NDB. The 25-nm minimum safety altitude is 3,000 ft.

Flying the NDB Approach

Let's assume that you are over the Pontiac VOR and heading toward the Dwight (DTG) NDB at 3,000 ft. You are within 25 nm of the DTG NDB, so you are free to maneuver to position the plane for the approach. Instead of going directly to the DTG NDB, let's off-set the plane slightly to the west. In other words, let's get some turning room so that we can proceed directly outbound from the DTG NDB. Recall the rule of thumb that the turn radius is about 1% of TAS. If we average 100 knots IAS, then in general terms our turn radius is about 1 nm. Looking at the chart, note that the distance from the Pontiac (PNT) VOR to the DTG NDB is 23.1 nm. So using the 1 in 60 rule, 1 nm over, say, 20 nm will subtend 3°. To gain a little more flexibility, let's double this and leave the PNT VOR on a track of 027°. Tune the NAV1 radio to 109.6 MHz and set the OBI to 027°. Tune the ADF to the DTG NDB at 344 kHz. As you pass over the PNT VOR, intercept the 027 radial outbound.

Next, we need to start the turn to intercept the 097 course into the DTG NDB. We have the luxury of a DME readout from the PNT VOR, and the turn will be through 70° (097 – 027° = 70°). Again using a turn radius of 1 nm (plus a bit for flexibility), you can estimate that the turn should start a little less than one turn radius away from the 097 course to the DTG NDB because the turn is only through 70°. This method is similar to intercepting a radial from an arc discussed previously. Because you know that DTG is 23.1 nm from the PNT VOR, start the turn at 21.6 nm (23.1 – 1.5) from PNT. As you pass 23.1 nm from PNT, start a left turn directly toward the DTG NDB; simply turn to place the ADF needle on the nose. As you roll out, note that the aircraft's heading is close to 097°. You will know you are over the DTG NDB as the ADF needle spins around. The needle is now pointing behind you, and you must now refer to the tail of the needle for tracking information. Start the clock and turn on to the required out-bound track of 097°, plus any wind adjustment. You now note that you can proceed only to a maximum of 10 nm from the DTG NDB. But how can you determine the dis-tance from the NDB when there is no DME at the station? After all, NDBs don't have DME. The answer is timing. If you proceed outbound at, say, 100 KIAS, be conservative and estimate your ground speed at close to 2 nm/min. Therefore you must head back toward DTG (or certainly on a NW heading) no later than 5 min after leaving DTG. You also know that the 45/180 procedure turn has to be contained inside this 10 nm. If you are on the 45° procedure turn for 1 min, then your effective downrange time would be .71 x 60 = 43 seconds (cos 45 = 0.7071). Allowing for the 180° turn means a turn diam-eter of 2 nm, the maximum distance outbound you can travel before starting the pro-cedure turn is 3 min. This distance is conservative and safe.

Also note that the minimum altitude you can descend to until inbound toward DTG is 2,300 ft. So as soon as you are established within 5° of the outbound course of 097°, you could start a gradual descent from 3,000 ft to 2,300 ft. An alternative is to stay at 3,000 ft until you start the procedure turn and then commence the descent to 2,300 ft. There is no right or wrong way to do this; the decision is up to you. In any case, because you must lose 700 ft, a gradual descent of 500 ft/min would be appropriate.

As you pass the 3-min mark, start your procedure turn by turning left onto a heading of 142. Recall that the inbound turn commences 1 min after initiating the original turn, so as the clock passes 4 min, commence the left turn on to a heading of 322. Be at 2,300 ft before you intercept the final approach. As you head on the 322 course heading, the next event is the intercept of the 277 course to DTG. As with all intercepts, a lead angle is required. With a turn radius of 1 nm at about 10 nm from the aid, then a 90° turn on would require 6° of lead. Because you are performing a 45° intercept, you can halve the lead requirement to 3°. Knowing this, you can calculate the relative bearing at the lead point (i.e., 45 − 3 = 42°). The ADF gauge has index marks at both 90° and 45° points from the nose. So as the ADF needle approaches a relative bearing of 43° left of the nose, commence the turn towards the final course of 277. Maintain the 2,300 foot altitude until the plane is established inbound within ±5° of the inbound 277 course. As you roll out, reduce speed and configure the aircraft for the approach. I suggest gear down, one stage of flap, and a final speed of 80 knots.

The Final Approach

The next critical part of the approach is the final descent. Once the plane is established inbound, you are cleared to descend to the minimum altitude. However it is good practice to try to achieve a single, continuous descent to the threshold rather than arrive at the minima early. In the latter case, you must drive in level and then initiate another descent when establishing the sought-after 3° flight path. Achieving this without a DME is a little difficult because timing is all you have to assist you. Assuming that you reduced airspeed to 80 knots, and reconfigured after turning onto final approach, then it's fair to say that you will be close to the point at which you initiated the procedure turn. In other words, 3 min from DTG (at 100 knots), you need to loose 1,000 ft—from 2,300 ft to 1,300 ft. Ideally, a final approach should be flown at a 3° flight path. At 80 knots, a 3° flight path will require a rate of descent of 430 ft/min. You have 1,000 ft to lose, and at 430 ft/min this will take about 2 min 20 seconds. So it's reasonable to commence the descent after you have stabilized at your approach speed. To keep things simple, set up a rate of descent of 400 ft/minute. Throughout the final approach, keep all heading changes small, certainly no more than 5°.

When you have visual contact with the runway, immediately take action to get the airplane on the centerline. Also, make prompt adjustments to your flight path to ensure an acceptable vertical path, remembering that the aim is for the ideal 3° path.

Table 1.5 in Chapter 1 lists rates of climb and descent and will tell you what your descent rate should be for various glide path angles and airspeeds.

The Next Step

What is the future of instrument flight? GPS will be the single most important feature of instrument flight in the next 10 years. Although they are not supported by FSW95 and FS98, GPS nonprecision approaches are in use. Precision approaches are just around the corner. Heavy jets have already demonstrated full autoland capability using GPS data only. Air routes will in time disappear, and, as that happens, aircraft will "free fly" from origin to destination using direct point-to-point navigation. The unprecedented accuracy of GPS will make all this possible.

Practice Makes Perfect

Getting the most from Flight Simulator requires effort. Instrument flight is a demanding art that requires practice and lots of it, and Flight Simulator is representative of real instrument flight. The more realistic you make it, the more you will benefit. Flight Simulator can in no way replace dedicated simulators or the real aircraft, but it can prepare you well for the challenging world of instrument flight.

References

James H. "Jimmy" Doolittle, *I Could Never Be So Lucky Again: An Autobiography* (New York: Bantam Books, 1991).

17

The Great Adventure of Amelia Earhart

Courage is the price that Life exacts for granting peace,

The soul that knows it not, knows no release

From little things; knows not, the loneliness of fear nor mountain heights

Where bitter joy can

Hear the sound of wings.

> Amelia Earhart (1897–1937),
> American aviatrix, author.
> "Courage" (1927)

Sixty years ago, on March 17, 1937, Amelia Earhart took off from Oakland on an attempt to become the first pilot to circumnavigate the globe at the equator (see Figure 17.1). Earhart never completed the trip. Three-quarters of the way through, she and navigator Fred Noonon failed to reach Howland Island, a tiny U.S. island 1,900 miles southwest of Hawaii in the Pacific Ocean. The most common belief is that Earhart ran out of gas and had to ditch her plane. Whether she survived the crash is much in dispute even to this day.

Figure 17.1 *Amelia Earhart with the Lockheed Electra she used in her attempted round-the-world flight. (Smithsonian Institution)*

Leo Bellarts, the radioman who was waiting for her radio signal in the central Pacific, recalled in newspaper accounts that he heard the signal but that she never responded to his return calls. Bellarts was stationed on a ship positioned east of Howland Island so that Earhart could get a fix on the leg of her journey between Lae, New Guinea and Howland Island, a distance of 2,189 nautical miles. The ship, named the *Itasca,* was spewing enormous clouds of black smoke, in the hope that Earhart would sight the ship and veer toward it.

The radio signal from Earhart's plane was so strong that Bellart ran outside expecting to see the plane. He returned to the radio room below the bridge and repeatedly tried to contact her. This went on for eight hours, with Bellarts hearing Earhart's transmissions but unable to raise any response.

Earhart had made the fatal mistake of leaving in Miami the low-frequency transmitter that would have helped radio operators to locate her. In addition, Noonon was an alcoholic who had been on a binge the night before the final flight and may have been incapacitated in a drunken stupor. Compounding this problem, before the Lae to

Howland Island leg of the trip Earhart removed a number of items from the plane to lighten the load. These items included a pistol, ammunition, and, most important, her radio facility book with comprehensive instructions on which radio frequencies and transmission schedules were to be used.

With no way of remembering the precise frequencies and times that the radio operators were to be listening, Earhart would have had trouble communicating. Worse, she would not be able to transmit her location on the hour. On the fateful day, July 2, 1937, at 7:42 a.m., Bellart received this transmission from Earhart: "We must be on you but cannot see you. But gas is running low. Been unable to reach you by radio. We are flying at altitude 1,000 ft."

At 7:50 a.m., Earhart radioed that she was circling but could not hear the *Itasca's* transmissions. This brief message was not enough to fix her position, because sustained contact was required for the directional radio equipment of the time to home in on the plane. Earhart seemed unaware that this would be a problem, instead choosing to shut off the radio after each brief report.

Frustrated and pleading with Earhart to say something so that he could get a lock on her, Bellart finally was able to send a signal that Earhart acknowledged. This radio communication occurred at 8:30 a.m., when Earhart asked for some long Morse code dashes at 7500 kHz and Bellarts complied. Earhart then transmitted that she had heard the *Itasca,* but she needed to get a bearing on her plane. She asked Bellarts to transmit this information at 3105 kHz. Bellarts replied that he could not get a bearing on her at that frequency and that she should instead transmit at 500 kHz, or take a bearing herself from the *Itasca's* powerful signal.

There was no reply.

The last radio transmission from Earhart came at 8:43 a.m. Bellarts reported hearing this last message: "KHAQQ [Earhart's call sign] to Itasca: We are on the line 157-357 (northwest-southeast). Will repeat message. We will repeat this on 6210 kilocycles. Wait. Listening on 6210 kilocycles. We are running north and south."

No one heard the signal on 6210 kHz.

In a 1973 interview with Earhart researcher Elgen Long, Bellarts said, "That last transmission—boy, I'll tell you. I'll never forget her voice. You could hear her voice just starting to crack. She was on the verge of going into hysterics." Little did Bellarts realize that he would be the last person ever to speak with Amelia Earhart.

THE DISAPPEARANCE OF AMELIA EARHART

During the 1930s Earhart was the world's most famous aviatrix. In 1932, she was the first woman to fly solo across the Atlantic. Seventeen pilots had failed before her. Later she broke dozens of flight records and became the first person to fly solo from Honolulu to Oakland.

The tragedy of her disappearance in 1937 was an emotional event for people all around the world, who had come to love, revere, and admire Earhart's daring, courage, and pioneering spirit. She was an inspirational role model for millions of American young women at a time when women were discouraged from seeking greatness or even from leaving the home. To all Americans, Earhart was a symbol of living your dreams and not being afraid of what life might bring. Earhart's vision of the individual was a powerful message not lost on the public. You should try, she said, to reach above and beyond your own perceived limitations, for in stretching those boundaries you come to understand your soul.

The Amelia Earhart story still strikes an emotional chord for those who remember her. To understand the depth of the loss, one must realize that she was not only a pilot but a poet, a writer, an explorer, and a human being who touched people by her exploits and by her words. If you looked for the definition of what it means to be an American hero, you need only look at the life of Amelia Earhart.

Sixty Years Is Long Enough

Many people were dissatisfied with the U.S. Navy's failure to find out what happened to Earhart. Although ships were dispatched and an extensive search was undertaken, no trace was ever found of her airplane.

Over the years, several expeditions have sought to uncover the truth about her disappearance. Was she shot down by the Japanese as a spy? Did she crash-land on a remote island, only to perish from lack of water? Why was there no wreckage? Surely there would have been some debris, some flotsam, that would have told part of the story. Instead, nothing.

The desire to know what happened has continued unabated. Now in its ninth year, the latest search expedition, the Earhart Project, is the most exhaustive inquiry into the disappearance of Amelia Earhart since the U.S. Navy's search in 1937. Three archaeological hunts through the remote, uninhabited Pacific atoll of Nikumaroro have supposedly recovered physical evidence that the Earhart flight landed there on July 2, 1937. Project investigators have been seeking evidence to confirm the events of that day.

In February 1997, this expedition returned to the island in the hope of recovering further artifacts. For more information on this investigation, see http://www.tighar.org/Projects/AEdescr.html. This site has some interesting background on the disappearance of Earhart, and it debunks some common myths, such as the belief that the Japanese captured her as a spy before World War II.

For more information on Amelia Earhart, including an informal biography, see http://www.ionet.net/%7Ejellenc/eae_intr.html.

LINDA FINCH'S 1997 RE-CREATION OF THE AMELIA EARHART VOYAGE

In March 1997, in honor of Earhart's 1937 flight, the American pilot Linda Finch circumnavigated the globe in a restored Lockheed Electra L-10e. Finch, a respected pilot with many hours flying time in many different aircraft, purchased one of only two Electra L-10e's known to exist. With the assistance of Pratt & Whitney and venture capitalist Reid Dennis, the aircraft was restored to new condition. Pratt & Whitney built two Wasp engines to power this Electra, duplicating those used by Earhart in 1937. These engines were built with the same serial numbers as those displayed on Earhart's engines.

Over the course of the trip, Finch made more than 30 stops in 20 countries. She traveled at a gentler pace than Earhart; whereas Earhart intended to take six weeks, Finch took 10 weeks. Earhart's 1937 route differed from Finch's. Because of political tensions, Finch avoided central Africa, particularly the African states of Mali and Chad. Instead, she took a northerly detour, going by way of the Canary Islands, Tunis, Athens, Luxor (Egypt), and on to Karachi, Pakistan, before resuming Earhart's path.

Near Howland Island, Finch dropped a wreath in homage to Earhart's pioneering flight.

Ms. Finch was not the first woman to have re-created Earhart's trip. On June 9, 1967, Ann Pellegreno flew Earhart's journey around the world in a Lockheed Electra 10a. Pellegreno was accompanied by a co-pilot, navigator, and mechanic, who was also the owner. They followed Earhart's route except that they did not land at Howland Island. Instead, as they flew over the island, they dropped a wreath in Earhart's honor. They returned to Oakland on July 7, 1967. Pellegreno chronicled her flight in the book *World Flight: The Earhart Trail,* published in 1971 by Iowa State Press.

THE ROUTE TAKEN BY AMELIA EARHART

The route that Amelia Earhart took from Oakland around the world is shown in Figure 17.2. Her intended itinerary included 29 stops before returning to Oakland. The longest distance between cities occurred on the leg between Lae, New Guinea, and Howland Island, a distance of 2,190 nm. Not surprisingly, it was along this longest segment over open ocean that she experienced the navigational trouble that cost her life and that of navigator Noonan.

You won't have this problem with the adventure that accompanies this book. In the re-creation of the flight you will accomplish, you needn't worry about waypoints or great circle bearing calculations, because you will use the GPS 2.0 navigation software to guide you. If you are a purist and would rather fly the trip as Earhart did, you can use the Great Circle Calculator Excel spreadsheet and fly the route using waypoints connected by 200-nm rhumb lines. This is tedious work and takes much of the fun out flying. Instead, I think you will much prefer the assistance of modern technology so that you can have fun and enjoy the thrill of retracing Earhart's footsteps.

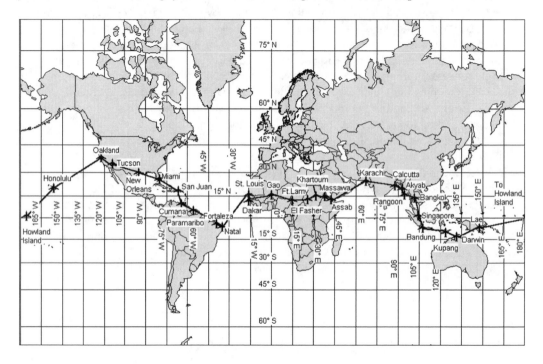

Figure 17.2 *Amelia Earhart's 1937 route around the world.*

I know you will enjoy the magic of flying across the oceans and then in the distance making out landfall as you realize you have crossed the same ocean over the same route that Earhart flew. The spectacular scenery along the way will allow you to imagine what the flight must have felt like to her. What greater exhilaration is there?

Table 17.1 shows the airports you will use, and Table 17.2 lists the navaid and scenery information.

Table 17. 1 Retracing Amelia Earhart's 1937 Around the World Flight

WAYPOINT	COUNTRY	CITY	AIRPORT NAME	LATITUDE	LONGITUDE	ELEVATION (FT)	DISTANCE TO NEXT AIRPORT (NM)
1	California	Oakland	Metro Oakland Intl.	N37° 43.15'''	W122° 14.47'''	7	283
2	California	Burbank	Glendale - Pasadena	N34° 12.73'	W118° 21.63'	774	402
3	Arizona	Tucson	Tucson International	N32º 7.06'	W110° 57.48'	2,641	1116
4	Louisiana	New Orleans	New Orleans Intl/ Moisant Field	N29° 59.78	W090° 16.88	6	585
5	Florida	Miami	Miami Intl.	N25° 47.07'	W080°18.86	13	907
6	Puerto Rico	San Juan	Luis Munoz Marin Intl	N18° 26.00'	W066° 00.87'	9	492
7	Venezuela	Cumana	Antonio Jose De Sucre	N10° 26.85'	W064° 08.40'	13	602
8	Suriname	Paramaribo	Johan A. Pengal	N05° 27.2'	W055° 11.4'	59	1178
9	Brazil	Fortaleza	Pinto Martins	S03º 46.39'	W038° 32.65'	82	661
10	Brazil	Natal	Augusto Severo	S05° 54.10'	W035° 15.05'	170	1276
11	Senegal	St. Louis	St. Louis	N16° 2.49'	W016° 27.80'	13	997
12	Senegal	Dakar	Leopold Sedar Senghor International	N14° 45.64'	W017° 29.25'	88	970
13	Mali	Gao	Gao	N16° 14.50'	W000° 01.24'	869	910
14	Chad	Ft. Lamy (N'djamena)	N'djamena	N12° 7.48'	E015° 1.72'	967	611
15	Sudan	El Fasher	El Fasher	N13° 37.84'	E025° 20.55'	2,404	422
16	Sudan	Khartoum	Khartoum	N15° 36.23'	E032° 33.52'	1,263	387
17	Eritrea	Massawa	Asmara	N15° 18.10'	E038° 54.13	7,618	245
18	Eritrea	Assab	Assab	N13° 04.95'	E042° 38.03	45	1562
19	Pakistan	Karachi	Quaid-E-Azam Intl	N24° 54.30'	E067° 9.40'	98	1176
20	India	Calcutta	Netaji Subhas Chandra Bose Intl	N22° 38.38'	E088° 26.82'	19	287
21	Burma (Myanmar)	Akyab	Sittwe	N20° 7.93'	E092° 53.12'	29	282
22	Burma (Myanmar)	Rangoon	Yangon	N16° 54.87'	E096° 8.64'	180	302
23	Thailand	Bangkok	Bangkok Intl	N13° 55.51'	E100° 37.03'	9 780	
24	Malaysia	Singapore	Changi	N01° 22.5'	E103° 59.22'	22	554
25	Indonesia	Bandung	Husein Sastranegara	S06° 54.30	E107° 33.45'	2431	1036
26	Indonesia	Koepang (Kupang)	El Tari	S10° 10.9'	E123° 39.86'	334	416
27	Australia	Darwin	Darwin Intl	S12° 25' 00"	E130° 52' 30"	103	1053
28	Papua New Guinea	Lae	Lae	S06° 44.62'	E147° 20.7'	32	2190 nm to Howland 1260nm to Radio Ship
	Radio Ship	Radio Ship	Radio Ship (Half way between Howe Island and Lae)	S02° 15' 03"	E168° 10' 00"	0	930
29	Howland Island	Howland Island	Howland Island	N00° 46' 26"	W176° 38' 20"	65	1721
30	Hawaii	Honolulu	Honolulu Intl.	N021°19'29"	W157° 54' 17"	13	2088
31	California	Oakland	Metro Oakland Intl.	N037°43'08"	W122° 14' 27"	7	

Table 17. 2 Retracing Amelia Earhart's 1937 Around the World Flight

Waypoint	Airport Name	Ident.	ILS Ident	ILS Runway & Freq.	Runway Length	ATIS Freq.	Scenery Add-On Required?	Nearest Navaid	Navaid Name	Navaid Type	Navaid Frequency
1	Metro Oakland Intl.	KOAK	IINB IOAK IAAZ	29 - 108.70 MHz 27R - 109.90 MHz 11 - 111.90 MHz	10,000 5,453 10,000	128.50 MHz 128.50 MHz 128.50 MHz	No	OAKLAND	OAK	VORTAC	116.800 MHz
2	Burbank - Glendale - Pasadena	BUR	IBUR	08 - 109.50 MHz	6,032	134.50 MHz	No	VAN NUYS	VNY	VOR-DME	113.100 MHz
3	Tucson Intl.	TUS	ITUS	11L - 111.70 MHz	10,994	123.80 MHz	No	TUCSON	TUS	VORTAC	116.000 MHz
4	New Orleans Intl./ Moisant Field	MSY		01 - 111.70 MHz 10 - 109.90 MHz 28 - 109.90 MHz	7,000 10,080 10,080	127.55 MHz	No	RESERVE	RQR	VOR-DME	110.800 MHz
5	Miami Intl.	MIA	IGEM IVIN IMIA IMFA IBUL IDCX	12 - 108.90 MHz 27R - 109.10 MHz 27L - 109.50 MHz 9L - 110.30 MHz 9R - 110.90 MHz 30 - 111.70 MHz	9,355 10,502 13,000 9,355	119.15 MHz 119.15 MHz 119.15 MHz 119.15 MHz 119.15 MHz 119.15 MHz	No	VIRGINIA KEY	VKZ	VOR-DME	117.100 MHz
6	Luis Munoz Marin Intl (San Juan, Puerto Rico)	TJSJ	ICLA ISJU	10 - 109.70 MHz 08 - 110.30 MHz	8,016 10,002	125.80 MHz 125.80 MHz	No	SAN JUAN	SJU	VORTAC	114.000 MHz
7	Antonio Jose De Sucre (Cumana)	SVCU		7/25	8,530	118.90 MHz	No	CUMANA	CUM	VOR-DME	113.30 MHz
8	Johan A. Pengal (Paramaribo)	SMJP	I-ZAN	11 - 109.90 MHz	11,417	118.50 MHz	Yes	ZANDERY	ZY	VOR-DME	114.300 MHz
9	Pinto Martins (Fortaleza)	SBFZ		13/31	8,350	118.50 MHz	Yes	FORTALEZA	FLZ	VOR-DME	114.100 MHz
10	Augusto Severo (Natal)	SBNT		16L - 16R - 12 -	7,448 5,906 5,988	118.70 MHz	No	NATAL	NTL	VOR-DME	114.300 MHz
11	St. Louis (Senegal)	GOSS		36/18	6,234	118.70 MHz	Yes	SAINT LOUIS	SLO	NDB	355.000 KHz
12	Leopold Sedar Senghor International (Dakar, Senegal)	GOOY		27/9	4,935	118.10 MHz	Yes	LEOPOLD SEDAR SENGHOR	YF	VOR-DME	113.100 MHz
13	Gao (Mali)	GAGO		7/25	9,186	118.10 MHz	Yes	GAO	GAO	VOR	112.300 MHz
14	N'djamena (Ft. Lamey, Chad)	FTTJ	IFL	5 - 109.90 MHz	9,186	118.10 MHz	Yes	NDJAMENA	FL	VOR-DME	115.300 MHz
15	El Fasher (Sudan)	HSFS		36/18	7,119	124.10 MHz	Yes	EL FASHER	FSR	VOR-DME	115.000 MHz
16	Khartoum (Sudan)	HSSS		18 - 110.90 MHz 36 - 110.30 MHz	9,813 9,813	118.10 MHz	No	KHARTOUM	KTM	VOR-DME	112.100 MHz
17	Asmara (Massawa, Eritrea)	HHAS		7/25	9,843	118.10 MHz	Yes	ASMARA	ASM	VOR-DME	113.70 MHz
18	Assab (Eritrea)	HHSB		12/30	11,480	118.10 MHz	Yes	ASSAB	SB	NDB	345.000 KHz
19	Quaid-E-Azam Intl (Karachi, Pakistan)	OPKC		25R - 109.70 MHz 07R -	10,500 7,500	126.70 MHz 126.70 MHz	No	KARACHI	KC	VOR-DME	112.100 MHz
20	Netaji Subhas Chandra Bose Intl (Calcutta, India)	VECC		01R - 109.90 MHz 19L - 110.30 MHz 19R -	11,900 11,900 7,854	126.40 MHz 126.40 MHz 126.40 MHz	No	CALCUTTA	CEA	VOR-DME	112.500 MHz

Table 17. 2 Retracing Amelia Earhart's 1937 Around the World Flight continued

Waypoint	Airport Name	Ident.	ILS Ident	ILS Runway & Freq.	Runway Length	ATIS Freq.	Scenery Add-On Required?	Nearest Navaid	Navaid Name	Navaid Type	Navaid Frequency
21	Sittwe (Akyab, Burma-Myanmar)	VYSW		11/29	6,000	118.70 MHz	Yes	SITTWE (VOR available at 116.50 MHz)	SW	NDB	216.000 KHz
22	Yangon (Rangoon, Burma-Myanmar)	VYYY	I-YGN	21 - 109.90 MHz	8,100	118.10 MHz	Yes	YANGON	HGU	VOR-DME	112.300 MHz
23	Bangkok Intl (Thailand)	VTBD		21R - 109.30 MHz	12,139	126.40 MHz	No	BANGKOK	BKK	VOR-DME	115.900 MHz
24	Changi (Singapore)	WSSS		02R - 108.30 MHz 02L - 110.90 MHz 20R - 108.90 MHz 20L - 109.70 MHz	13,123 13,123 13,123 13,123	128.60 MHz	No	SINJON	SJ	VOR-DME	113.500 MHz
25	Husein Sastranegara Intl (Bandung, Indonesia)	WIIB		11/29	6,427	122.70 MHz	Yes	BANDUNG	BND	VOR-DME	117.00 MHz
26	El Tari (Kupang, Indonesia)	WRKK		7/25	8,202	118.30 MHz	Yes	KUPANG	KPG	VOR-DME	112.200 MHz
27	Darwin Intl	YPDN		29 - 109.70 MHz	10,906	133.10 MHz	No	DARWIN	DN	VOR-DME	112.400 MHz
28	Lae, Papua New Guinea			33	5,200	120.90 MHz	Yes	LAE	LAE	NDB	388.00 kHz
	Radio Ship (Half way between Howe Island and Lae)						Yes			NDB	420.00 kHz
29	Howland Island			36	5,000	118.80 MHz	Yes	HOWLAND		VOR-DME	112.20 MHz
30	Honolulu Intl.	PHNL	IEPC IIUM IIUM	26L - 109.10 MHz 04R - 110.50 MHz 04L -	12,000 9,000 6,952	127.90 MHz 127.90 MHz	No	HONOLULU	HNL	VORTAC	114.800 MHz
31	Metro Oakland Intl.	KOAK	IINB IOAK IAAZ	29 - 108.70 MHz 27R - 109.90 MHz 11 - 111.90 MHz	10,000 5,453 10,000	128.50 MHz 128.50 MHz 128.50 MHz	No	OAKLAND	OAK	VORTAC	116.800 MHz

How to Use GPS 2.0 with the "Great Adventure"

GPS 2.0 was introduced in Chapter 13, and if you have any questions, you should refer to the text to revisit how the program works. To install the program, go to the **GPS** directory on the CD-ROM, and run the setup program. When you next start Flight Simulator, you will see a notice that the program is unregistered. You are free to evaluate the program, but if you want full functionality you must register it. Until you register the program, you will continue to see this notice each time you start FS98. It will be removed only if you register the program or uninstall it using the Uninstall program found under **Start/Programs/GPS 2.0** from the taskbar. After you click **Continue**, you will see the GPS window inside the View window.

David Drouin, the creator of GPS 2.0, has added to the master database all the airports used by Earhart. To use GPS for the flight, therefore, load your next airport destination using the **DTO** button (see the section "How to Load an Airport" in Chapter 13). All the airport names are listed in Table 17.1, so you can use the built-in **Search** function using the

magnifying glass button on the GPS display to instantly retrieve any of the Earhart airports.

For example, on the first leg of the flight between Oakland and Burbank, you would follow these steps:

1. While on the ground in Oakland at RWY 11, click the **DTO** button on the GPS display to enter the Direct Selection window.

2. On the first row in the GPS Direct Selection display, click the → button until you see **APT** (Airport).

3. Using the ↓ button on the GPS display, move the cursor down to the second row.

4. In the second row, you will see the name of the currently listed airport destination. To search for Burbank, click the **magnifying glass** button, which will open a Find dialog box.

5. In the Find dialog box, type **Burbank** and click **OK.** The entry will change on the GPS display to show Burbank-Glendale-Pasadena, the name of the airport you want.

6. Click the **ENT** button to enter Burbank as the desired destination waypoint. Return to the Waypoint display mode, where you'll see a bearing of 121° and the steering indicator lights pointing slightly right. This tells you that after you take off, to get on course for Burbank you will need to turn slightly right to the proper heading of 121°.

7. After takeoff, press the **AUT** button and the autopilot will take over. The entire flight to Burbank will be managed for you, although you can still change altitude yourself. When the autopilot is on, simulation speed is limited to four times normal, so if you want to speed the passage of time over long stretches of the route, you should disengage the autopilot and use the steering indicator to manually fly the airplane at simulation speeds as fast as 128 times normal. Using this technique you can fly, for example, from Honolulu to Oakland in a matter of minutes, a flight that would normally take five hours in the Learjet.

That's all there is to flying a route between any two cities on the Earhart voyage. Just repeat steps 1–7 above, entering your new destination airport in step 5.

GPS constantly updates the bearing and distance to the next destination. At all times, you know exactly where you are, how far you have to go, and the magnetic bearing toward the destination airport based on your current location (this bearing will change along the route). GPS will even compute the estimated time en route based on the current speed.

INSTALLING THE AMELIA EARHART SCENERY

The scenery files for the Amelia Earhart Great Adventure are found on the book's CD under the **Amelia Earhart** directory. In order to accomplish this flight in FS98, you must install these bgl files as described in Ray Proudfoot's "How to become a Scenery Manager" tutorial in the earlier chapter on scenery management. This is because many of the airports that Amelia Earhart used in the actual trip do not exist in FS98.

You will also need to install the DAFIF navaid bgls (using the same technique as the Amelia scenery bgls in Ray's tutorial), in order to use the navaids along the route and at each of the new airports in the Amelia Earhart scenery. The installation instructions for the DAFIF navaids are found in Chapter 13.

There are a couple of other things you should know before proceeding with the installation of the Amelia scenery. There are two bgl's in the scenery, plus some texture seed files that **must** be put into the main FS98\Texture folder **not** the \Texture folder in the Amelia scenery folder that you will create (see tutorial).

Please make sure you copy the following SEED??.R8 files into your FS98\Texture directory:

SEEDA1.R8

SEEDA3.R8

SEEDA4.R8

SEEDA8.R8

SEEDC9.R8

If you already have Alfred Grech's Pacific Scenery, than you should **not** load the AMELIA2.BGL. Just install the AMELIA1.BGL. If you don't have Grech's Pacific Scenery, then you should install **both** AMELIA1.BGL and AMELIA2.BGL.

The following airports and waypoints were created for this trip:

- Suriname-Paramaribo
- Brazil-Fortaleza
- Senegal-St. Louis
- Senegal-Dakar
- Mali-Gao
- Chad-Ft. Lamy
- Sudan-El Fasher
- Eritrea-Massawa
- Eritrea-Assab
- Burma (Myanmar)-Akyab (Sittwe)
- Burma (Myanmar)-Rangoon
- Indonesia-Bandung
- Indonesia-Koepang (Kupang)
- Papua New Guinea-Lae
- Radio Buoy (halfway between Lae and Howland Island) This floating radio tower

is equipped with an NDB transmitter so that you can get a location fix mid-ocean.
- Howland Island

The other airports where Earhart landed are included with the default airports on the FS98 CD-ROM, and the ILS and other navaids that exist have real-world counterparts.

To help you with the trip, there are three situations that you can copy to your **FS98\Pilots** directory.

- **Amelia.STN** is a situation that starts in the Learjet at Oakland, with full realism on. This means that you will run out of fuel and the engines will stop unless you refuel at each airport along the trip. Note that fuel boxes are not provided at each airport. To refuel, you must use the Aircraft Settings dialog box.
- **How-lear.STN** has the Learjet approaching RWY 36 at Howland Island.
- **How-cess.STN** has the Cessna approaching RWY 18 at Howland Island.

On Howland Island is an obelisk monument honoring Earhart in addition to other facilities. None of these structures exists in real life.

To place your aircraft at any of the airfields or airstrips in the Amelia scenery follow the instructions in the section [Using the New Scenery] in Ray Proudfoot's tutorial in the scenery management chapter.

If you are a stickler for details and you want to experience the flight with all its dangers, you should install Goet Scheuermann's superb Lockheed Electra, the airplane used by Earhart. This plane, which is on book's CD-ROM in the **Aircraft** directory, must first be converted with the new Microsoft Flight Simulator 98 Aircraft Converter before it will work with the program.

Otherwise, if you can't or don't want to use the Lockheed Electra, feel free to use the Learjet. The Boeing 737 is not suited for this trip because it does not have the range to fly from Honolulu to Oakland and because it cannot use the short runways that exist at many of the smaller airports.

Credit for the "Great Adventure" concept: Bob Langendorfer, Jim Tester, and Dik Richardson of Aero Airlines.

Description of Great Adventure Scenery

This Great Adventure Scenery Package was designed by noted scenery designer Alfred Grech, who has published such scenery packages as Canada and the Pacific with Wizard Works. All the airports that were created for the Earhart Great Adventure trip actually exist in real life and were designed to have accurate reproductions of the runways, navaids and scenery, as based on currently available maps and charts. You won't be able to use the navaids for this scenery unless you first install the worldwide DAFIF navaids that are found in BGL format on this book's CD (see Global Navigation chapter for instructions on how to do this).

Fuel boxes are not provided at each airport. You will need to refuel the aircraft using the **Options/Aircraft Settings/Fuel** dialog box.

PILOT'S OPERATING MANUAL FOR THE LOCKHEEDELECTRA L-10E

The Lockheed Electra L-10e used by Earhart has been provided courtesy of Goetz Scheuermann (101656.3460@compuserve.com). Scheuermann, a very talented creator of Flight Shop aircraft (see also his C-5 Galaxy on the book's CD-ROM), re-created this airplane to celebrate the 60th anniversary of the Earhart flight. Figure 19.3 shows the Lockheed Eletra L-10e.

Figure 17.3 *The Lockheed Electra L-10e. This plane was created by Goetz Scheuermann and is found on the book's CD-ROM. Use the FS98 Aircraft Converter to make this airplane work with FS98. It will work fine with FSW95.*

The technical characteristics of the Lockheed L-10e are described in the next section.

Lockheed Electra Model 10E: Technical Data

The Lockheed Electra is powered by two 550 HP, Pratt and Whitney R-985-48 Wasp Engines which consume about 56 gallons of fuel per hour. Flying at its 8000 ft cruise ceiling height, the Electra has a range of about 3,081 nm. Due to limitations of the Flight Shop program, the gallons per hour usage is approximately 30 GPH, rather than the 56 GPH on the real Electra, and this makes the range of the simulated aircraft much greater than is the case for the real airplane. We hope you will excuse this defect in realism, but there was no way to rework the airplane's fuel consumption with the available software tools.

The Lockheed Electra is licensed under normal category limitations and is intended only for non-aerobatic passenger and cargo operation. Only those maneuvers incidental to normal flying, including stalls and turns in which the angle of bank does not exceed 60°, are permitted.

> Fuel capacity: 1,151 gallons (modified to carry six additional fuel tanks)
> Range: 4,000 nm
> Length: 38 ft
> Wingspan: 55 ft

Performance

Rate of climb at sea level (rated power)

> Twin-engine 1,140 fpm
> Single-engine 335 fpm

Service ceiling (rated power)

> Twin engine 10,900 ft
> Single engine 5,100 ft

Takeoff distance (15∞flaps, sea level)

> Ground run 1,596 ft
> Total distance over 50-ft obstacle 1,968 ft

Landing distance (40° flaps, sea level)

> Ground run 1,268 ft
> Total distance over 50-ft obstacle 1814 ft

Important Airspeeds

- Cruise airspeed
  Maximum (Sea Level) 178kts (IAS)
- Maximum airspeed
  Cruise (75% Power 7000 ft.) 151kts (IAS)
- Stalling speed
  (Zero Thrust, Flaps 20°, Gear Down) 77mph/67kts (CAS)
- Takeoff speeds (IAS)
  Normal takeoff 89 kts
  50 ft obstacle takeoff 68 kts
- Stall speeds (IAS) gear and flaps up
  Power on, level flight 58 kts
  Power off, level flight 79 kts
- Stall speeds (IAS) gear and flaps down
  Power on, level flight 44 kts
  Power off, level flight 69 kts
- Landing speeds (IAS)
  Normal; (1,700 RPM on approach until touchdown)
  Approach 87 kts
  Contact 74 kts
- Two-engine cruising and climb speed
  (Gear and flaps up) 139 kts
  Best rate-of-climb speed, 5,000 ft
  (Gear and flaps up) 104 kts
  (Gear down) 92 kts
  (Gear and flaps down) 80 kts
  Best angle-of-climb speed, 5,000 ft
  Gear and flaps up) 86 kts
  (Gear down) 82 kts
  (Gear and flaps down) 74 kts
- Single-engine climb and minimum control speed
  Best rate-of-climb speed, sea level
  (Gear and flaps up) 101 kts
  Best angle-of-climb speed, sea level
  (Gear and flaps up) 90 kts
  Minimum control speed 81 kts

- Airspeed limitations (CAS)
  Never exceed (glide or dive, smooth air) 223 kts
  Best single-engine rate-of-climb 99 kts
  Caution range 195 kts to 223 kts
  Design cruising speed 157 kts
  Normal operating range 76 kts to 195 kts
  Full flap operating range 67 kts to 122 kts
  Maximum flap extension speed (15° of flaps) 152 kts
  Maximum design maneuvering speed 156 kts
  Maximum gear operating speed 152 kts
  Maximum gear extended speed 152 kts

Configuration and Performance FAQ

This appendix answers most of the frequently asked questions (FAQs) people have about FSW95 and FS98. You'll find much of interest here, including tips on how to optimally configure your computer, tips on how to add scenery and aircraft, and a discussion of how to customize your joystick buttons. There is also a description of Intel's MMX technology and Microsoft's DirectDraw API, and what this portends for the future of Flight Simulator. Rather than wading through a long-winded explanation of every item, the text in this appendix is organized as a series of FAQs, and it is hoped that this method of information delivery will prove most efficient in quickly answering your questions. As with the rest of this book, you need not read this appendix from one end to the other; just look up the FAQ sections that interest you and skip over those that don't.

WHAT SHOULD I DO AFTER I INSTALL FLIGHT SIMULATOR?

After you have installed Flight Simulator, there are some additional programs you should install that will greatly enhance your enjoyment of the program:

FS98 only:

1. Install the Microsoft FS98 Aircraft Converter on this book's CD-ROM. There are some important patches that will fix problems with multiplayer sessions, allow

the transmission of visual models of airplanes during multiplayer sessions, allow the importation of new aircraft, and fix incompatibilities with FSW95/FS5.1 adventures. The patch also fixes the following problems:

- The slaved ADF gauge in the Bell 206 JetRanger III helicopter now works.
- The control position indicator on the Cessna 182RG has been fixed.
- The VOR reception volumes have been adjusted for more realistic tail-off curves. This change should alleviate problems receiving Low or Terminal class VORs at high altitudes.
- The Cessna 182S autopilot no longer automatically engages the wing leveler when activated from the radio panel stack.
- The visual system now properly avoids texturing scenery of the rolling hills seed type.
- The instrument panels are now properly colored in night mode.
- ATIS window now shows large fonts when Windows is using large fonts.
- The size of the nternal scenery buffer increased from 256K to 512K to fix problems with pauses in London and other third-party scenery.
- The display on the fuel quantity gauge has been changed to allow aircraft with more than 100,000 gallons capacity. If the amount is less than 100,000 gallons, the display will show two large digits and one small digit (i.e., xx.x*1000). If there is more than 100,000 gallons of fuel, the display will show three large digits (i.e., xxx * 1000).
- Engine controls on multi-engine aircraft panels, such as the throttle, starter, and so on, no longer change the engine that is controlled by the joystick or keyboard.

2. Unzip (i.e., decompress) **AAFWAV.ZIP** (on the book's CD-ROM) and move all the files in **AAFWAV.ZIP** to your **\ADV\WAV** directory. These wave files contain voices for autopilot heading, altitude, frequencies, courses, airspeeds, ATIS and many ATC messages. You can use the complimentary version of WinZip on the book's CD-ROM to decompress the file.

FSW95 only:

1. To fix some incompatibility glitches with third-party scenery in the program (e.g., missing navaids), you should install **FEPAT.EXE**, which is a self extracting, self executing program. **FEPAT.EXE** is found on this book's CD. *Do not install this program with FS98!*
2. Next, you should install **FSCONV.EXE**, which is also a self-extracting, self executing program. **FSCONV.EXE** adds **AAFCONV.EXE** to your Microsoft Games Program Folder, and it allows you to use new FSW95 aircraft that you add to the

program. **AAFCONV.EXE** is a separate program which allows you to convert older FS 5.1 aircraft (such as Flight Shop created airplanes), and it allows you to compile Flight Shop created adventures. **FSCONV.EXE** is found on this book's CD-ROM.

3. Finally, you should unzip (i.e., decompress) **AAWAV.ZIP** and move all the files in **AAWAV.ZIP** to your **\ADV\WAV** directory. These wave files contain voices for autopilot heading, altitude, frequencies, courses, airspeeds, ATIS and many ATC messages. You can use the complimentary version of WinZip on the book's CD-ROM to decompress **AAWAV.ZIP**, which is also found on the CD-ROM.

Also, as a precautionary protective measure to protect Flight Simulator from crashing in the future, you should make a copy of your **WORLD.VIS** file in the Flight Simulator **\Scenery** directory. The reason that this is important is that sometimes, after you have installed custom scenery, you may find that the program won't work anymore. What has happened, most likely, is that the **WORLD.VIS** file has been corrupted. The only way to fix the problem, short of reinstalling the entire Flight Simulator program, is to replace the **WORLD.VIS** with a backup copy that is still functional. You should know, however, that this will wipe clear all your add-on scenery instructions in the Scenery Library, and you'll have to reinstall such scenery again.

NOTE Do yourself a favor and back up your **WORLD.VIS** file: this file is crucial to restoring your dysfunctional scenery as well as allowing Flight Simulator to start in the event that **WORLD.VIS** has been corrupted.

To back up **WORLD.VIS**:

1. In the **\Scenery** subdirectory where you have installed Flight Simulator, right-click on **WORLD.VIS** and from the pop-up menu, select **Copy**.
2. After releasing the mouse button, right-click again and select **Paste** from the pop-up menu.
3. A copy of **WORLD.VIS** will be named **Copy of world.vis** and will be placed in the **\Scenery** directory.

TIP If you find that Flight Simulator keeps crashing when you try to start the program, chances are your **WORLD.VIS** file is corrupted. To replace the file with the good copy, simply delete **WORLD.VIS** (select it so that it is highlighted, then press the **Delete** key), then rename **Copy of world.vis** to **WORLD.VIS** (capitalization doesn't matter). You can easily rename the file by clicking on the file name once, then clicking once again so that the file name is Ibracketed by a text box. Then backspace or retype over the name in the text box. But be sure to make another copy of **WORLD.VIS** again for future use!

Also, after you have finished with the above post-installation procedures, now might be a good time to install GPS 2.0 and the Ground Proximity Warning System and Inertial Navigation System, **GPWS_V6.ZIP** (on the CD-ROM). For installation instructions, read the readme.txt file in the zip files.

HOW MUCH HARD DISK SPACE DOES FLIGHT SIMULATOR OCCUPY?

In the default installation for FS98, you can run the scenery off the CD-ROM using the CD-ROM Boosters, and the total disk space will be about 105 MB. However, if you decide to install the scenery, adventures, and adventure sound wave files to your hard disk, the total amount of space needed mushrooms to 313 MB.

If you choose the custom scenery setup, you can decide which world scenery to install on your hard drive and which to leave on the CD-ROM.

The new FS98 CD-ROM includes 1,099 new prerecorded sound files for use with tutorials and adventures that you can create with with Martin Smiths' APLC32 program (included on this book's CD-ROM). If you keep the FS98 CD-ROM in your drive, the program is smart enough to use the sounds directly off the disc, so you don't need to install them on your hard disk. If you prefer to install all the adventure sounds on your hard disk for faster access or because you don't want to have the FS98 disc in your CD-ROM drive during play, you need to copy the sound files from your FS98 CD-ROM's **FS98\ADV\WAV** directory, and then put them into FS98's **\ADV\WAV** directory on your hard disk. Installing all these sound files will require an additional 30.4 MB of hard disk space.

FSW95 Installation Notes

FSW95 will use as little as 40 MB, and as much as 150 MB if you decide to install the scenery to your hard drive instead of running it off your CD-ROM. Note that scenery add-ons, such as the Microsoft Southern California Expansion Pack, if installed to you hard drive, can gobble up as much as 147MB of additional space!
At setup, you have the following options:

- *Typical*—75 MB of hard disk space. Includes City Pack, Flight Training and other popular components, but to conserve space, scenery (especially photo-realistic scenery) is installed so that it will run off your CD-ROM.
- *Compact*—40 MB of hard disk space. Minimum installation, does not include City Pack or Flight Training, and no adventures or challenges.
- *Custom*—150MB (Setup states 140 MB, but it is really 150 MB). Installs City Pack, Flight Training, and other popular components to your hard disk for better performance. Photorealistic scenery is installed to your hard disk but world scenery is not. To install world scenery to your hard disk for faster performance, you need to read the next section. Multimedia help is left on the CD-ROM.

Can I Run the Scenery off My Hard Drive for Faster Performance?

You can run the scenery off your hard drive if you tell Flight Simulator at setup to do so. However, FSW95 users must manually install the CD-ROM performance boosters, which manage global scenery and which contain global scenery textures. The FSW95 boosters monitor your aircraft's position and automatically load scenery from the CD-ROM drive to a cache directory on your hard drive. This cache, or temporary storage area on your hard disk, is wiped clean when you exit Flight Simulator to help conserve space. Thus, using the performance boosters, the program needs to install only the scenery that you need, not all the scenery, as you fly from scenery area to scenery area. You can dramatically improve the speed with which FSW95 global scenery loads by moving the boosters and cache directories directly to your hard disk, then editing the Scenery Library's Performance dialog box to refer to the new file and directory locations. Note that you'll need about 108 MB of free space on your hard disk to copy all the files.

To copy the CD-ROM boosters from your FSW95 CD-ROM to your hard drive, perform these steps (Note: FS98 users don't need to do this if the scenery has been installed to the hard drive at setup.)

1. First make sure you have done a custom install of FSW95 and installed all the City Pack scenery.
2. Drag the Booster subdirectory from your CD-ROM and drop it on top of your main FSW95 directory. This copies all the booster files and cache directories onto your hard drive.
3. Now you'll have to edit the Scenery Library's Performance dialog box to refer to the new location of the boosters. Under the Options menu, select **Scenery Library,** and in the Scenery Library dialog box that opens, click the **Performance** button.
4. In the Performance dialog box, select the South America booster (see Figure A.1), and click the **Edit** button to edit the Booster path for South America. In Figure A.2 you can see the Edit Booster dialog box for the South America booster cache directory, where the source directory has been changed from **E:\boosters\samerica** on the CD-ROM to the new hard disk location of **C:\Program Files\Microsoft Games\Flight Simulator\boosters\samerica** (your directory path will differ, so substitute the correct path on your PC). After you have copied the booster subdirectories from your FSW95 CD-ROM, you must edit the source path, since you will be running the boosters and cache directories straight off your hard drive. In this particular example, you can see that I have edited the source path for the South America boosters so that instead of the default **E:\boosters\samerica** on the CD-ROM, I now have **C:\Program Files\Microsoft Games\Flight**

Simulator\boosters\samerica directory (first you need to have copied the entire booster subdirectory off the CD-ROM into your Flight Simulator directory).

5. Repeat Step 2 for each of the other boosters. Once done, you no longer need the CD-ROM.

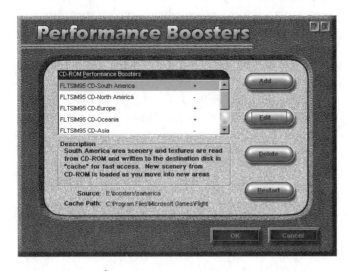

Figure A.1 The Performance Boosters dialog box in FSW95.

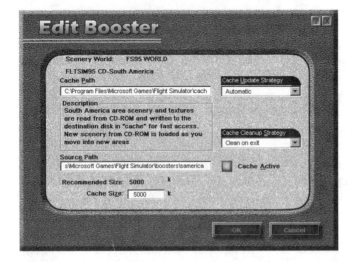

Figure A.2 The Edit Booster Cache dialog box in FSW95.

You can also perform this procedure for Europe 1 and Europe 2 CD-ROM scenery that you are running off the CD-ROM. Just be sure you copy all the scenery files from the Europe Scenery directory into an equivalently named directory in your FSW95 directory. Thus if your installed FSW95 directory is FLTSIM95, then you would create a **EUROPE** subdirectory inside the **SCENERY** directory, and then add two subdirectories **SCENERY** and **TEXTURE** inside the **EUROPE** subdirectory. Your directory path structure should look something like this:

```
C:\FLTSIM95

       SCENERY\

                 EUROPE

                       SCENERY

                       TEXTURE
```

HOW DO I GET RID OF THOSE ANNOYING PAUSES? FLIGHT SIMULATOR DROPS 5 FPS OR LESS FOR ABOUT 2 OR 3 SECONDS AND THEN PICKS UP AGAIN, WHY?

For users of FSW95, see above FAQ for instructions on copying your CD-ROM Boosters and world scenery from your CD-ROM to your hard drive. This should get rid of the problem. For users of FS98, you should reinstall the program, but this time install the scenery to your hard disk.

The problem is best demonstrated, by taking off from London City Airport Runway 28, and flying towards the 0° Greenwich Meridian. Just press **Shift-Z** twice to bring up your latitude/longitude display, then fly toward the Canary Wharf skyscrapers. When you near the meridian, you'll note that there is a pause as the scenery is cached from the your CD-ROM to your hard drive. In some cases, this pause can last as long as 20 seconds, but if you are running a fast Pentium 200MMX with a 16 × CD-ROM drive the pause may be as little as 2 to 5 seconds.

WHY DOES FLIGHT SIMULATOR PAUSE (STOP FLYING) WHEN I TASK SWITCH FROM ONE WINDOWS APPLICATION TO ANOTHER?

Ordinarily, when you switch to another application from FSW95, the simulation pauses until you return and press the **P** key. How can you have Flight Simulator keep flying while you do something else? You have to go to **Options/Preferences**, select **General**, then click **Pause on Task Switch** so that it is off. Then return to the simulation. When you switch to another application, and that application then has the "focus," Flight

Simulator will continue to run in the background. By doing this, you can also fully minimize Flight Simulator (click the minimize button at the top right corner of the FS window) and have it vanish into the Windows 95 Taskbar. When you want Flight Simulator to reappear, simply click on the Taskbar button for FS98/95.

How do I get rid of the Microsoft opening screen animation?

Rename or delete **MSLOGO.AVI** in your main FS95/98 directory. By doing this, you can spare yourself a few seconds of minor annoyance having to watch this animation each time you start Flight Simulator. Hitting the **ESC** key in FS98 will accomplish the same end.

How do I get the mouse to work as my yoke?

Right-click with the mouse, then select **Mouse as Yoke** from the pop-up menu that appears on screen.

What 3-D video cards are safe bets for getting maximum frame rates in FS98?

Video cards based on the Rendition Vérité V2200 chipset (available on Hercules Thriller 3D and the Canopus 3-D video cards—but check to make sure you are getting the Vérité V2200 chipset and not the older V1000 chipset), 3Dfx (Diamond Monster)—NVIDIA's RIVA 128 (available on STB Velocity 128 cards, and the Diamond Viper 330), and ATI's Rage Pro chipsets are safe bets. Before purchasing a card, make sure you have one of these chipsets and that the card comes with at least 4 MB of memory onboard. Also, if you are about to purchase a new computer, be sure to get a PC that comes with an AGP (accelerated graphics port) motherboard, and that your new 3-D video card is designed for AGP, not for the PCI bus. The reasons for this are explained later in this appendix.

Note that the 3Dfx boards do not support 3-D windows in Windows 95 or 98, but instead must display a DOS-style full screen with a maximum resolution of 800×600 (in DOS, the 3Dfx can only run at 640×480).

Many people have reported excellent results with the RIVA 128 chipset on the STB Velocity 128 AGP, with frame rates approaching 50 fps on an AGP equipped Pentium II 300 MHz PC. One interesting fact about the RIVA128 is that its performance scales quite steeply with processor speed, whereas the 3Dfx boards scale more slowly. All things being equal, that means the RIVA chip set will do better in a faster system than the 3Dfx chipset will. The RIVA chipset also supports higher resolutions (up to 1024×768 with 16-bit color, and it runs in both Full Screen mode and in conventional Windows 95/98–style windows.

Although the ATI 3D Rage Pro came with beta drivers that gave the card a frame rate inferior to that of the Canopus (Rendition Vérité V1000), it was the only card to offer a super-high resolution of of 1152 × 864 in Direct3D mode, contrasted to the other cards which could only do 1024 × 768. This card was in beta development as this book went to press, so you should not regard the frame rate shown in Figure A.3 as the last word. When updated drivers become available, this card may do much better.

Neither the S-3 Virge nor the Matrox Mystique are recommended because neither implements all the necessary 3-D functions in hardware.

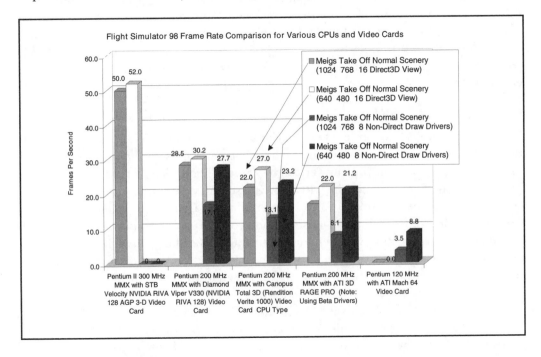

Figure A.3 *Flight Simulator 98 frame rate comparison for various CPUs.*

WHAT KIND OF FRAME RATE SHOULD I BE GETTING?

You can easily check your frame rate by pressing **Shift+Z** twice and viewing the frame readout on the topleft corner of your 3-D view window. Because FS98 now includes special Direct3D video drivers that take advantage of Direct3D-capable video card accelerators, one cannot compare the frame rates between FS98 and FSW95, which did not use DirectDraw at all. Therefore, the next two sections will discuss the frame rate you should be getting for each program separately.

Frame Rates for FS98

Figure A.3 illustrates the frame rates for various CPUs. If you compare your frame rate with the results shown, you can determine whether your hardware setup performance is up to snuff. If your frame rate falls below the benchmarks shown, it is time to read through this FAQ and see if there's a way to fine-tune your configuration so that you can boost your frame rate to a more acceptable level.

In general, you should be able to double your frame rate with a good 3-D–capable video card using the FS98 Direct3D video drivers over that of a non–3-D video card using normal FS98 video drivers. Also, from the illustration, you can see that running at a display resolution of 1024 × 768 in 16-bit color mode gives you a roughly similar frame rate to that of running the program at 640 × 480 in 16-bit color mode. This tells you that you might as well run FS98 at maximum resolution when using a 3-D–capable video card.

Frame Rates for FSW95

Figure A.4 illustrates the frame rate for various CPUs running FSW95. As you can see in the figure, there are two columns for each CPU type, representing one of the default flight situations that you find under **Flights/Select Flight**. The first situation, **Meigs Take Off Dense Scenery,** uses the 640 × 480 full screen view (press **Alt+Enter**), and has cybergraphics scenery cranked up to the penultimate **Dense** setting (**World: Scenery Complexity: Image Complexity: Dense**). When you start this situation, you'll see many buildings in Chicago off to your left, and your frame rate should match the first of the two columns for the CPU type you have, as shown in Figure A.4. This is not the highest scenery detail setting. You can choose **Very Dense** to show all available scenery, although we do not show frame rate results this setting.

The next situation, **Meigs Take Off Medium Scenery** has scenery complexity set to **Normal** (**World: Scenery Complexity: Image Complexity: Normal**), and so your frame rate should match the second of the two columns for the CPU type you have.

Both situations use the **Pentium Maximum QualityHigh Resolution** mode (under **Options: Preferences: Display & Sound: Performance Mode**), so that you may assess the frame rate results through a uniform benchmark. Therefore, to compare your frame rate, you must also select one of the two situations, and make sure that your Performance Mode is set to **Pentium Maximum Quality-High Resolution**.

All the tests were run using Windows 95 without DirectDraw being enabled in FSW95. No frame rate results are shown for Windows NT because test results showed that in all cases FSW95 ran slower with Windows NT than it did with Windows 95.

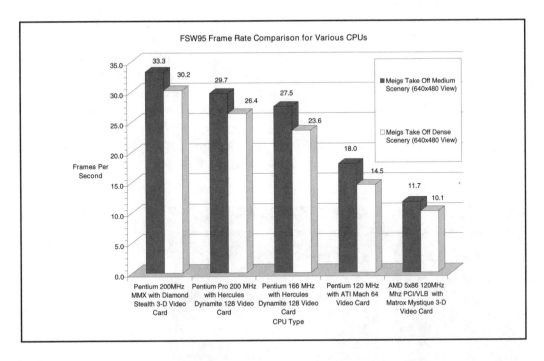

Figure A.4 *Frame Rate Comparison for FS98.*

HOW CAN I INCREASE MY FRAME RATE?

If you are using FS98 and you don't have a 3-D–capable video card that supports Direct3D, get one. You can easily double your frame rate with a suitable card. Make sure that you are using the Direct3D video driver under **Options: Preferences: Display: Display Options: Hardware Acceleration** in the Fullscreen Device list box. Also, be careful in your choice of hardware, as some cards do very poorly with FS98.

NOTE

You can drastically increase your frame rate by shrinking your window size.

One very good way to increase your frame rate is to shrink your view window via the mouse to a smaller size. Although this is not an elegant way of dealing with the problem, it certainly will boost your frame rate in even the most drastic circumstances.

You may also see a minor frame rate improvement of 1 to 2 fps if you run Flight Simulator as a full screen (similar to a DOS screen, with no window borders).by pressing **Alt-Enter** or select **Views/Full Screen** from the menu. Any time your run spot view (press **S** twice), or full screen inside Windows (press **W**), your frame rate will most certainly drop because of the larger number of pixels needed to draw the scene.

Also, if you change the visibility setting in FS95/98 to unlimited visibility, you can gain a 2 to 4 fps improvement. To do this, select **World/Weather**, and in the Basic Weather dialog box, select **Unlimited** from the Visibility list box. If you are using the Advanced Weather dialog box, click the **Visibility** tab, then select **Unlimited** from the Visibility list box.

Figure A.5 *Shrinking your window down to quarter size can boost your frame rate by 71%! For example, on a Pentium 200MMX running the Default Flight Meigs Field situation, shrinking the window increased the frame rate from 32 fps to 55 fps.*

If you are using FS98 and you don't have a 3-D–capable video card that supports Direct3D, get one. You can easily double your frame rate with a suitable card. Make sure that you are using the Direct3D video driver under **Options: Preferences: Display: Display Options: Hardware Acceleration** in the Fullscreen Device list box. Also, be careful in your choice of hardware, as some cards do very poorly with FS98.

Aside from loading the CD-ROM boosters and cache onto your hard drive in FSW95 or installing the scenery on your hard drive at setup in FS98, you can tinker with the display preferences and shut off any unnecessary features that are gobbling up precious CPU time. Probably the easiest way to do this is to go to the **Options: Preferences** menu, and then select the **Display** tab and choose a lower performance mode. Although I don't recommend running Flight Simulator on a 486, if you are using a slow Pentium, you could try **486 Maximum Performance–Low Res** or **486 Maximum Performance–High Res**.

With FSW95 (but not FS98), you can also quickly test to see if simplifying your scenery graphics will solve your frame rate woes by choosing **Flights: Select Flight**, and then selecting **Meigs–Fast Graphics.**

Otherwise, if you want to do a custom setup for your performance mode, you can try toggling off different display features to see what effect they have on your frame rate (in **Options: Preferences**, click the **Display** tab, then click the **Display Options** button). In the Display Options dialog box, the features that seem to have the most profound effect on frame rates are listed in Table A.1.

Table A.1 For FS98: Turning These Scenery Options Off Increases Your Frame Rate

ITEM	FSW95 FRAME RATE GAIN[1]	FS98 FRAME RATE GAIN[2]
Approach Lighting Off	1 fps	N/A
Dynamic Scenery from Normal to Off	10 fps (Normally this feature is **Off** in *Default Flight Meigs Field*)	0.5 fps
Scenery Complexity Very Sparse:	6 fps inside cockpit view	6 fps inside cockpit (2.3 fps outside cockpit view)
Aircraft Texture Off	0.4 fps inside cockpit and outside cockpit spot view	0 fps inside cockpit (2.2 fps outside view)
Aircraft Shadows Off	1.3 fps inside cockpit (11 fps outside cockpit spot view)	0 fps inside cockpit (0.7 fps outside view)
See Own Aircraft From Cockpit: Off	0.8 fps inside cockpit front view (10 fps inside cockpit left view)	0 fps inside cockpit front view (3.2 fps inside cockpit left view)
See Propeller: Off	1.3 fps inside cockpit	3.1 fps virtual cockpit

Table A.1 continued

ITEM	FSW95 FRAME RATE GAIN[1]	FS98 FRAME RATE GAIN[2]
	(11 fps outside cockpit spot view)	view (0.8 fps outside view)
See Landing Lights: Off	1.2 fps inside cockpit night view (1 fps outside cockpit spot view at night)	3.0 fps inside cockpit night view (1.4 fps outside cockpit spot view at night)
Textured Sky Off (This turns off Wispy Cloud Effects and Cloud Thickness Effects)	3 fps	0.3 fps
Textured Water Off	4 fps over water	0 fps
Ground Scenery Shadows Off	4 fps	0.4 fps
Textured Ground Off	1 fps	1 fps external view
Gradient Horizon Off	0.3 fps	0 fps
Textured Buildings Off	2 fps when flying through city at normal scenery density	0 fps

[1] *Based on Micronics 32 MB Pentium 200MMX with Diamond Stealth (S-3 Virge) using "Default Flight Meigs Field" flight situation, and running **Pentium Maximum Quality High Res** Performance Mode, which gives default frame rate of 32 fps*

[2] *Same system as above, but running Direct 3D drivers in FS98 and using Canopus Total 3-D video card with Rendition Verite Direct3D chipset.*

NOTE   Be sure to run FSW95 in 8-bit color resolution (256 colors); don't try running it at 16-bit or 24-bit high-color resolution because the program's performance will be degraded at these color depths. FS98, on the contrary, can run faster in 16-bit mode when using a suitable Direct 3D-capable card.

Some video cards do not display the non-rectangular instrument panel window efficiently in FS98. You may be able to increase performance by turning off the **Display Non-Rectangular** Control Panel option. To do this, select **Views: Options: Instrument** and then clear the **Display Non-Rectangular** button.

Using SMARTDrive to Boost Hard Drive Performance

When you need to boost your frame rate through other methods, you might also consider increasing your SMARTDrive cache, as this may help you get smoother performance from your hard drive. SMARTDrive is a DOS program that decreases the time your computer spends reading data from your hard disk. To use SMARTDrive, you must first check and see if it is located in your old DOS directory on your hard drive; if it is, then you must add

```
C:\DOS\smartdrv.exe 4096
```

to your autoexec.bat file. The 4096 on the line above refers to the number of KB of disk space you want to specify for the cache. If you don't have an autoexec.bat file, that is because Windows95 has gotten rid of it, and so you'll have to create a new text file with that name in your root **C:** directory.

Normally, Windows 95 doesn't need an **AUTOEXEC.BAT** or CONFIG.SYS file for bootup. For more information, as well as examples of how to use SMARTDrive, run the DOS Help program in your **C:\DOS** directory.

WHAT COLOR DEPTH AND RESOLUTION SHOULD I BE RUNNING THE PROGRAM?

FS98 runs in multiple color resolutions and display size resolutions. For example, you can run the program with 8-bit color at 1280×1024 pixels (without Direct3D), or for better performance you can run the program at 8-bit color at 800×600. If you have a 3-D video accelerator card, you can also use the Direct3D drivers to run the program at higher resolutions (most cards support 1024×768 with 16-bit color). When the frame rate drops much below 15 fps, the higher resolutions are not worth it. Therefore, your best guide to choosing a particular display resolution is your frame rate.

On some 3-D cards, you will get the best possible frame rate only when you run FS98 at full screen resolution (press **Alt+Enter** or select **Views: Full Screen**).

FSW95 Notes

FSW95 runs in completely resizable windows, meaning you can run it at any resolution that your system is capable of displaying. However, FSW95 has a maximum resolution of 640×480, and works best at 256 colors. This means that if you decide to run FSW95 at 1024×768, you won't get true 1024×768, but instead will get an enlarged version of 640×480. Thus, you can run the program at higher resolutions, but your images will become more and more "pixelated" as you increase the resolution. *Pixelation* refers to the effect that occurs when single picture elements are stretched across multiple picture elements so that an image becomes more block-like and distorted.

Your best frame rate will probably occur when you select the **640 × 480** menu option from the View menu. This will run Flight Simulator full screen as if it were running in DOS.

Don't try running FSW95 at 16-bit or 24-bit high-color resolution; in most cases you'll be sacrificing system performance at these color depths.

To set your color depth, follow these steps:

1. Move your mouse pointer over your desktop.
2. Click the right mouse button, and in the pop-up menu that appears, select **Preferences**.
3. In the Preferences dialog box, click the tab marked **Settings**.
4. In the Settings dialog box, choose **256 colors** from the Color Palette, then click **OK**. You may have to restart Windows for your changes to take effect, but you will be notified in any case.

(FSW95 only) How come the Fine Zoom doesn't work?

Normally when you press **Shift+** while looking out a 3-D window, your view is supposed to fine zoom. However, this feature doesn't work unless you zoom out to a higher magnification first, fine zoom with **Shift+** or **Shift-**, and then press the normal + or − zoom keys to zoom in or out to the desired zoom setting. For example, if you want to zoom to 1.5× , you must press the + key three times to zoom out to at least 8× view, then press the **Shift** – key to fine zoom downwardseveral steps. Then you press the – key until you zoom down to somewhere near the 1.5× zoom that you wanted. It's confusing but it works! This problem has been fixed in FS98.

Why do those dad blasted zoom keys + and −not work like they used to in FS5.1?

Whenever you move the focus of your mouse pointer into an instrument panel setting, such as, for example, when changing the VOR radio frequency, you'll notice that the + and − keys no longer work as your 3-D view zoom commands. To restore zoom key functionality, you'll have to reselect the window to regain control of the zoom keys. To do this in FSW95, press the [key. To do this in FS98, simply click anywhere on the window.

What Is AGP?

AGP (accelerated graphics port) technology is a high-performance, component-level video card interconnect to the PCI bus on new Intel motherboards, such as the 440LX (code named "Atlanta"). It speeds up graphics on PCs equipped with AGP video cards (such as the ATI 3D Rage Pro), by moving graphics off the PCI bus altogether. The graphics data traffic is detoured onto a dedicated point-to-point channel between the graphics controller and the system chip set. AGP isn't a bus, because only the graphics controller has exclusive access to the 32-bit connection channel.

Unfortunately, AGP requires changes to the entire system architecture of Wintel PCs, and you won't be able to upgrade your current PC, even if it a state of the art Pentium with MMX. The motherboards, system chip sets, graphic controllers, and video cards will have be redesigned for AGP. For example, motherboards will need a new AGP slot for the new video cards, and the graphics controllers and video cards will need to switch from PCI to AGP protocols.

Intel claims that the first generation AGP-1x will double the graphics bandwidth to 266 MBps (i.e., twice the 133 MBps bandwidth for the regular PCI bus). In 1998, AGP-2x will be introduced and it will quadruple the effective bandwidth to 533 MBps (i.e., four times faster than PCI). This will be followed by AGP-4x, which will increase the effective bandwidth to more than 1 GBps (eight times faster than PCI).

AGP graphics controllers store 3-D textures in system memory rather than in the video memory, and retrieve them at AGP speeds, rather than having to share the PCI bus. The much greater amounts of available texture memory and greater bandwidth provided by AGP will allow 3-D applications to attain dramatically faster frame rates and better realism. If you are in the market for a PC, be sure to get one with an AGP motherboard and an AGP equipped 3-D video card accelerator.

WHAT DOES ALPHA BLENDING, BILINEAR FILTERING, AND MIP MAPPING HAVE TO DO WITH FS98?

If you are to understand what kind of hardware will best run Flight Simulator, you will need to understand some of the 3-D terminology that is now being bandied about in video card advertisements. The features defined here should be found on a good 3-D video card:

- **Alpha blending** is a means of allowing one object to show through another to give the illusion of transparency. For example, alpha blending can be used to create windows, fog, haze, transparency effects in clouds, and smoke.
- **Anti-aliasing** makes edges appear smooth by blurring pixel edges and eliminating jagged lines.
- **Bilinear and trilinear filtering** smooths flat surfaces, such as walls, as you move closer to them to get rid of blocky effects that might otherwise be present in the textures.
- **Direct 3D** is the application programming interface, or API, that standardizes communications between 3-D software programs and the graphics 3-D video card hardware.

- **Dithering** mixes defined colors into small patterns to quickly produce a wider spectrum of colors with less memory.
- **Double buffering** allows one frame to be rendered in frame buffer memory on the video card while allowing you to see a fully rendered frame on-screen. Then when the rendered frame is complete, it is sent out to the display, and the next frame is placed into the buffer for rendering.
- **Flat shading** is a basic shading technique where a triangle, or polygon is rendered with a single color.
- **Gouraud shading** blends colors within a polygon to give a smooth shaded appearance that masks edges and corners.
- **Lighting and specular effects** produce depth cues and the impression of transparency. These effects include overcast skies, mist, smoke, fog, and lighting reflections.
- **MIP** (multim in parvo, or many things in a small place; not to be confused with millions of instructions per second, or MIPS). MIP mapping reduces the distortion that occurs when textures are enlarged or reduced during perspective correction. It does this by storing different images of an object's textures at different perspective distances. This allows a textured object to have the illusion of depth, without having to filter each and every point of the textured surface.
- **Perspective correction** gives textures a more realistic sense of convergence as elements recede into the distance.
- **Specular reflection** is the reflection of light from a point source off of a shiny surface.
- **Subpixel: Subtexel accuracy** averages the distance of a moving pixel's next screen position, thus eliminating jitter and smoothing the appearance of moving or rotating objects.
- **Texture mapping** is used to apply a bit-mapped image to the surface of objects in a 3-D scene, such as for example, the bitmapped imagery of mountainous surface terrain wrapping around polygon shaped mountains in FS98's Lake Chelan scenery. Another texture mapping example would be the building surfaces for the skyscrapers in Chicago, the surface runway at Meigs airfield, and the decals and livery of the aircraft.
- **Triangle setup**. Since all 3-D objects are simply collections of triangles arranged in certain ways, having triangle setup offloaded from the CPU and PCI bus to the video card increases application performance.
- **Z-buffering or hidden surface removal** is used to track which surfaces should be hidden in scenes involving depth perception of objects. Basically, all polygon surfaces and points are plotted with x, y, and z coordinates. Then, those objects that are farther away, or are not visible are assigned a rank in terms of their z coordinate. Objects closer to the viewer have a higher z value and are thus visible, while those of a lower z value are not plotted.

Is my video card working properly?

That depends. If you have a PCI Graphics Accelerator card, and you are running a Pentium 120 MHz or better machine with 16 MB of RAM, , your frame rate should be in the 10 to 20 fps rate or better. Check the frame rate results in this FAQ to draw your own comparisons with your own hardware setup. If you are not getting a frame rate that is close to what others with similar hardware are getting, you might want to check that you have the latest drivers from the manufacturer (check the manufacturer's Web page, which you can find by doing a search on www.yahoo.com).

DirectDraw can be enabled in FSW95 by adding DirectDraw=1 to the [MAIN] section of the **FLTSIM95.CFG** file. By default, DirectDraw is disabled by FSW95, so you need to change this setting manually if you want to experiment and see if you can get a higher frame rate. Microsoft asserts that there is no benefit to having FSW95 use DirectDraw.

If you do decide to use DirectDraw with FSW95, you should be aware that your mouse will become sluggish, and your system will respond more slowly to mouse movements. When you move your mouse, for example, you'll notice that it no longer moves smoothly but instead jerks to and fro, and this can be rather annoying. I recommend leaving DirectDraw off in FSW95.

Is there anything I should worry about with my joystick?

Yes, make sure you get the latest drivers for your joystick from the manufacturer. If you don't do this, you may be missing out on full functionality of all the buttons, hat switches, triggers other controls. Visit the manufacturer's Web page (do a search under www.yahoo.com), and see if they have an updated driver for your joystick.

My joystick doesn't work

You need to make sure you have the right joystick driver installed and that the joystick is on and properly calibrated.

To calibrate your joystick with FS98, follow these steps:

In the **Options: Customize Controls** dialog box, make sure the **Joystick On** button is lit.

1. Click the **Calibrate** button.
2. Select your joystick from the list presented in the Game Controllers dialog box. If you don't see your joystick listed, then you must click **Add** and then choose one of the generic joysticks listed or click the **Add Other** button to add a joystick driver that you have on diskette or CD. You will be prompted for the location of the driver.

3. Click the **Properties** button, and then follow the instructions to calibrate the joystick. For the Microsoft Sidewinder, for example, you would click the **Calibrate** button, and follow the on-screen instructions to calibrate each of the joystick axes.

4. When you are finished, click **OK** as many times as necessary to return to the Flight Simulator program.

Note that digital joysticks do not normally need to be calibrated, but occasionally you will find need to do so.

 Digital joysticks, such as the SideWinder 3D Pro, usually do not need to be calibrated.

N O T E

FSW95 Joystick Calibration

To calibrate the joystick with FSW95, follow these steps:

1. Check to make sure that the Joystick **On** button is lit in the **Preferences/Control** dialog box.

2. Next, click the **Calibrate** button, and make sure that your joystick is listed in the Microsoft Gaming Devices Control Panel (if you haven't got this new Control Panel, be sure to download it from www.microsoft.com and then install it).

3. If your joystick is not listed, click the **Device Assignments** button, and select your joystick from the list of drivers shown. If your joystick is not listed, you will have to install the joystick drivers from the disk that accompanied your joystick, or download it from the company's Web site, then repeat this whole process.

4. Check that the Device Assignment is set to **Device 1**, then click the **Ok** button.

5. Next, click the **Settings** button, and in the next dialog box, click the **Test** tab.

6. Check to make sure all your buttons, hats, and joystick movements work, then click the **OK** buttons until you return to Flight Simulator.

CONFIGURING THE CH PRODUCTS VIRTUAL PILOT PRO WITH FSW95

FSW95 Instructions: Follow these instructions to properly configure your CH Products Virtual Pilot Pro Yoke (with or without rudders):

1. Install the latest version of the joystick drivers for Windows 95, available from www.chproducts.com Once at the CH Products Web site, click on the Technical Support button, find the file download page and get the **VPP95-14.EXE** file (or

whatever their latest version of the driver is; it might be called something else since drivers are continually updated as new bugs are discovered and fixed).

2. After you have downloaded **VPP95-14.exe**, put it into a temporary directory and double-click on it to decompress the files (it is a self-extracting archive).

3. Find the **SETUP.EXE** program and double-click on it. In a few moments the joystick drivers will be copied to your Windows directory.

4. Go to your Control Panel, and double-click the Joystick icon. The Joystick Properties dialog box will open.

5. In the Joystick Properties dialog box, select the Virtual Pilot Pro driver.

6. If you also have rudders installed, be sure to click the **Rudder** checkbox.

7. Click the **Calibrate** button, and follow the onscreen instructions to calibrate and test the outside two buttons on the joystick (but not the inside two buttons!), as well as the rudder pedals if you have installed those as well. Note that the right hat Point of View (POV) switch is the hat that is referred to in the dialog box and is the hat that you test. The left POV hat does not show up, and you do not need to test it. Neither do you need to test or calibrate the two inside buttons.

8. When you test the Virtual Pilot Pro, the four outside buttons (Button 1, Button 2, Button 3, and Button 4) light up on screen depending on which button is depressed, but note that the two inside buttons don't light up anything at all. This is normal, so don't worry about it.

9. Exit the Joystick Properties control panel by clicking the **Finish** button followed by **OK** to save your preserve your calibration settings.

Now that you have finished with this task, you can start up FSW95 and try out your new joystick. Note that if you have the rudder pedals installed, you'll have to deselect **Auto-Coordination** under **Aircraft/Realism & Reliability/Reliability**. Figure A.6 shows the default button and hat switch assignments for the Virtual Pilot.

If you want to make your rudder pedals work in FS95/98, you need to select **Aircraft/Aircraft Settings/Realism** and deselect **Auto-coordination**.

N O T E

The Virtual Pilot Pro's two inside buttons and the left POV hat do not show up in the calibration and tests for the Joystick control panel. This is normal.

N O T E

To learn more about how you can customize and reassign the keyboard to joystick button assignments, read the later FAQ section entitled "I would like to reprogram my analog joysticks manually."

My rudder pedals don't work

First, check to make sure the Auto-coordination checkbox, found in the Realism and Reliability dialog box under the **Aircraft/Aircraft Settings/Realism** menu, is turned off. Having **Auto-coordination** turned on causes the simulation to combine the rudder and ailerons for coordinated movements, and this disables your rudder pedals.

If you are using the CH Products Virtual Pilot Pro, and you have their Rudders properly plugged into the Y adapter for the game port, you'll need to make sure that the Rudders checkbox is on in the Joystick setup. To do this:

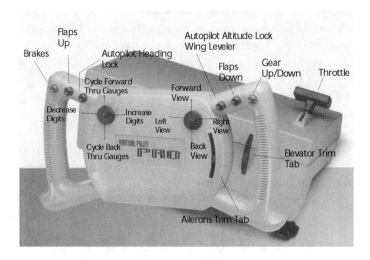

Figure A.6 *Default button and hat switch assignments for the Virtual Pilot Pro in FSW95.*

1. In the Options menu, select **Preferences**, then click the **Controls** tab.
2. In the Controls dialog box, make sure the **Joystick On** button is lit, then click **Joystick Calibrate**.
3. If you have properly installed the new Microsoft Gaming Devices control panel (if you haven't, be sure to download it from www.microsoft.com and then install it) , you'll see a dialog box open that shows your current input device. If your CH Virtual Pilot Pro is not listed, click on Device Assignments, and select the CH Virtual Pilot Pro from the list of input devices this is then displayed in the Device Assignments dialog box.
4. In this same dialog box, check that the Device Assignment is set to Device 1, then click **OK.**
5. In the Gaming Device dialog box that next opens, make sure to click on the **Rudders On** checkbox.

6. Next, click the **Calibrate** button, and go through all the calibration procedures for your joystick and rudder pedals that are requested. Click **OK**, and **OK** again to return to Flight Simulator.

Also, when you restart a situation, often **Auto-coordination** is not saved and is turned back on. This disables your rudder, so you'll again have to go to the **Aircraft/Realism** dialog box to make sure it is off.

WHAT'S THE LATEST ON THESE NEW "DIGITAL JOYSTICKS" I KEEP HEARING ABOUT?

Digital joysticks give you better tracking and eliminate the need to recalibrate your joystick. Older technology analog joysticks use potentiometers with moving parts that, over time, tend to drift and wear out. Newer digital joysticks have optical tracking mechanisms that have no moving parts, so there's less wear and tear and no drift. Plus these joysticks are more responsive and sensitive to movements you make. The Microsoft SideWinder 3-D Pro is one such digital joystick, although there are others on the market.

With Microsoft's new Game Device Profiler, you can easily assign keyboard commands and macros to the buttons on your SideWinder 3-D Pro merely by pressing the button you want to assign, then pressing the key(s) you want to store with the button. Then you can save the profile and recall it instantly. You can have multiple profiles, so that you and your friend can alternate playing the same game, but with your own keyboard preferences stored for the SideWinder 3-D Pro. Figure A.7 shows the Game Device Profiler being used to reassign buttons on the SideWinder 3-D Pro.

One thing you should be aware of: if you plan on using a digital joystick in combination with analog rudders, you will have to switch the digital joystick to "analog emulation" mode, thereby defeating much of the benefits of owning a digital joystick. So, if you plan on using rudders with your digital joystick, make sure that they are both compatible and will work together in digital mode.

HOW DO I CONFIGURE THE SIDEWINDER 3-D PRO TO HAVE SEPARATE RUDDER AND AILERON CONTROLS FOR CROSSWIND LANDINGS/TAKEOFFS?

Since the SideWinder 3-D Pro has 4 axes of movement, you can turn **Auto-coordination** off under **Aircraft/Aircraft Settings/Realism** and then have the rudders act apart from the ailerons. When you do this, the rudders are controlled by a twisting motion right or left of the joystick's handle. Pivoting the handle right or left activates the ailerons by themselves. When you turn **Auto-coordination** back on, the rudders and ailerons act in concert once again.

T I P   Did you know that the SideWinder 3-D Pro has an eight position hat switch? This means that you can view eight different view angles from the cockpit or from the outside spot view (press **S** and press the hat switch in each of the eight directions to get a sweeping 360° view around your airplane).

I WOULD LIKE TO EASILY REPROGRAM MY DIGITAL JOYSTICK BUTTONS OR KEYBOARD KEYS WITH DIFFERENT COMMANDS

To reprogram your joysticks in FSW95, you can either manually edit the **FLTSIM95.CFG** file or use the SideWinder Game Device Profiler. Reprogramming your joysticks or keys in FS98 is a snap. With the new Custom Controls dialog box, you can select the Flight Simulator function you want to access and then press the joystick button or keyboard key concerned. The next two sections detail how to do this.

FS98 INSTRUCTIONS

In FS98, follow these steps:

1. Select the **Options: Custom Controls** menu, and then click the **Assignments** tab.
2. In the dialog box, scroll down through the list of commands until you find the one that interests you.
3. If you want to reassign a joystick button, click the left column next to the command listing under **Game Device**. If you want to reassign a key, click the right column next to the command listing.
4. With the cell highlighted under **Game Device**, click the **Assign** button.
5. The cell will now become active, and you can press any button on your joystick, or key, and it will be listed in the cell as **Button xx**, where *xx* is the joystick button number or as **X,** where *X* is the key you have pressed.
6. As soon as you click the joystick button, you will see a warning message advising you that the joystick button or key is currently assigned to another function. If you want to continue with the re-assignment, click **OK** as many times as necessary to return to the simulation.

Your button or key will now be reassigned.

FSW95 Instructions

If you are using a digital joystick such as the SideWinder 3D-Pro, you'll need to first get Microsoft's new SideWinder Game Device Profiler. With this program properly installed, you can reassign keystrokes to any button on your digital joystick, provided you have the proper driver installed (see your manufacturer's Web page for further details). The first digital joystick to take advantage of this program is the Microsoft SideWinder 3-D Pro, although other digital joystick manufacturers should have drivers available by the time you read this.

With the Game Device Profiler, you can create multiple personal profiles which allow you to have several different keyboard mappings for your joystick's buttons. This is useful for when you have two or more people sharing a joystick, but alternating with their own set of preferences for the keyboard mapping of buttons.

You can assign two key combinations such as **Ctrl-Z** or even function keys such as **F7** to the button assignments in the Game Device Profiler.

T I P

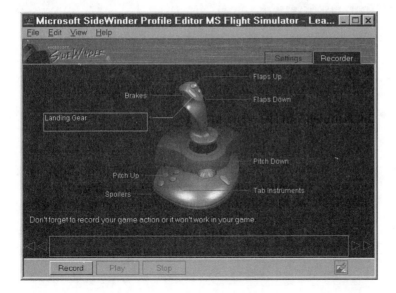

Figure A.7 *Microsoft game device profiler allows you to customize your SideWinder 3-D Pro Joystick. To assign any keyboard command, simply click the button on the joystick, then press the key(s) you want to have assigned. You can save multiple profiles for the same game, allowing you to instantly configure your joystick for different scenarios.*

I WOULD LIKE TO REPROGRAM MY ANALOG OR DIGITAL JOYSTICK MANUALLY. HOW DO I DO THIS?

If you want to reprogram your joystick buttons or hat switches, you'll need to edit the **FLTSIM95.CFG** or **FLTSIM98.CFG** text file, which contains the instructions that tell

FS95/98 how to map the buttons on your joystick to Flight Simulator's controls. Before proceeding, you should make a backup copy of the **.CFG** file in the Flight Simulator directory so you can retain your original settings in event of disaster.

For example, for the FSW95 configuration file:

1. To make a copy of **FLTSIM95.CFG**, highlight this file in the Explorer, then right-click and select **Copy**.
2. Next, right-click again, and select **Paste**. A copy named **Copy of FLTSIM95.CFG** will be created in the same directory.

It's much easier and faster to edit and save simple text files, such as **FLTSIM95.CFG** using Notepad in Windows 95. To find the Notepad application on your system use the Taskbar's **Start/Programs/Accessories** menu.

T I P

For most routine digital joystick reprogramming, be sure to use the Customize Controls dialog box in FS98. It is much easier to use this dialog box than doing the job yourself manually. In the examples that follow, we will show how to change your joystick settings using the FSW95 **FLTSIM95.CFG** file. Similar techniques may be used with FS98.

If you have only one joystick, you make changes in the **FLTSIM95.CFG** under the [JOYSTICK_00] section. If you have more than one joystick, you make changes to the section for the Joystick under [JOYSTICK_XX], where XX is the number of a joystick. However, before changing **FLTSIM95.CFG**, be sure that LOCKED=1, not 0. If LOCKED=0, your changes to **FLTSIM95.CFG** will be lost, as FSW95 will overwrite them.

You must set LOCKED=1 in the **FLTSIM95.CFG**, if you want to preserve the remapping of your joystick's button functions.

N O T E

For example, the following excerpt from **FLTSIM95.CFG** for the SideWinder 3D-Pro, describes how the different buttons are assigned specific functions. You can see which buttons on the SideWinder 3D-Pro are being referred to in the illustration of Figure A.8. Each line of the [JOYSTICK] section **FLTSIM95.CFG** has a label and an associated value. As can be seen in Table A.2. the TYPE=45088, each of the subsequent labels refers to a joystick function, such as movement forward, backward, left, right, or rotating motion, in addition to pressing a button or trigger. The value that is assigned to the label determines what that button, trigger or joystick motion does in Flight Simulator. A complete table of values and their actions in Flight Simulator is shown in Tables A.3 and A. 5.

Table A.2 *SideWinder 3-D Pro Button Mapping Assignments in FLTSIM95.CFG*

EXAMPLE TEXT LISTING FOR **FLTSIM95.CFG** (TEXT BELOW IS IN **FLTSIM95.CFG**)	DESCRIPTION
`[JOYSTICK_00]`	The text that follows `[JOYSTICK_00]` applies only to Joystick #1 (or device assignment #1)
`LOCKED=1`	Set value to 1 if you wish to preserve your settings. Set value to 0 if you wish FSW95 to overwrite your settings.
`TYPE=45088`	Don't ever change this value unless you are changing your joystick hardware. This TYPE number refers to the joystick that you choose using **Options/Preferences/Controls** and then **Calibrate** button. 45088 is the code for the SideWinder 3-D Pro.
`AXIS_FLAGS=15`	N/A

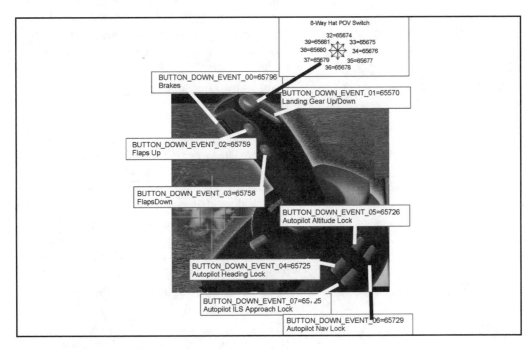

Figure A.8 *SideWinder 3-D Pro Button Numbers as Referenced in **FLTSIM95.CFG***

Table A.2 *continued*

EXAMPLE TEXT LISTING FOR **FLTSIM95.CFG** (TEXT BELOW IS IN **FLTSIM95.CFG**)	DESCRIPTION
AXIS_EVENT_00=65763	AXIS_EVENT_00 controls the SideWinder 3-D's left/right motion of the joystick, and it is currently assigned to the ailerons (65763)
AXIS_SCALE_00=64	Controls the range of motion for AXIS_EVENT_00 above (i.e., the ailerons). Normally positive, these values can range between +1 to +127 and –1 to –127. Negative values reverse the joystick's motion.
AXIS_NULL_00=36	Width of the null zone for AXIS_EVENT_00 (i.e., the ailerons) above. Value must be in the range 1 to 127. The larger the number, the larger the null zone. When a null zone is very large, the controls are less sensitive to small motions of the joystick along that axis.
AXIS_EVENT_01=65762	AXIS_EVENT_01 controls the forward/back motion of the joystick, and is currently assigned to the elevators.
AXIS_SCALE_01=64	Controls the range of motion for the elevators (AXIS_EVENT_01)
AXIS_NULL_01=36	Width of the null zone for the elevators (AXIS_EVENT_01). Value must be in the range 1 to 127. The larger the number, the larger the null zone. When a null zone is very large, the controls are less sensitive to small motions of the joystick along that axis.
AXIS_EVENT_02=65765	AXIS_EVENT_02 controls the throttle lever on the SideWinder 3-D Pro. Assigned to control the throttle in FSW95, but you can change it something else if you like.
AXIS_SCALE_02=127	Controls the range of motion for the throttle (AXIS_EVENT_02)
AXIS_NULL_02=36	Width of the null zone for the throttle (AXIS_EVENT_02). Value must be in the range 1 to 127. The larger the number, the larger the null zone. When a null zone is very large, the controls are less sensitive to small motions of the throttle.

Table A.2 continued

EXAMPLE TEXT LISTING FOR **FLTSIM95.CFG** (TEXT BELOW IS IN **FLTSIM95.CFG**)	DESCRIPTION
AXIS_EVENT_03=65764	AXIS_EVENT_03 controls the twisting, or rotating left/right motion of the SideWinder 3-D joystick, and is currently assigned to the rudder.
AXIS_SCALE_03=64	Controls the range of motion for the rudder (AXIS_EVENT_03)
AXIS_NULL_03=36	Width of the null zone for the rudder (AXIS_EVENT_03) Value must be in the range 1 to 127. The larger the number, the larger the null zone. When a null zone is very large, the controls are less sensitive to small motions of the joystick along that axis.
BUTTON_DOWN_EVENT_00=65796	On the SideWinder 3-D Pro, BUTTON_DOWN_EVENT_00 controls the Trigger button, and it is currently assigned to slew hold or apply brakes (65796).
BUTTON_DOWN_REPEAT_00=1	BUTTON_DOWN_REPEAT_00 controls the Trigger Button. Holding down the trigger causes the application of the brakes or the slew hold to be repeated. If you increase this from the currently assigned value of 1 to a higher number, it will repeat more times per press of the trigger (useful for when you reassign a button to move a control such as elevator trim continuously, instead of incrementing it click by click).
BUTTON_DOWN_EVENT_01=65570	BUTTON_DOWN_EVENT_01 controls the Top Button underneath Hat: Assigned to extend or retract landing gear (65570).
BUTTON_DOWN_EVENT_02=65759	BUTTON_DOWN_EVENT_02 controls the **Top Side Button** on the joystick and is assigned to retract the flaps in increments (65759).
BUTTON_DOWN_EVENT_03=65758	BUTTON_DOWN_EVENT_03 controls the Bottom Side Button on joystick and is assigned to extend flaps in increments (65758).
BUTTON_DOWN_EVENT_04=65725	BUTTON_DOWN_EVENT_04 controls the Top Left Base Button. It is assigned to switch Autopilot heading hold on/off (65725).

Table A.2 *continued*

EXAMPLE TEXT LISTING FOR **FLTSIM95.CFG** (TEXT BELOW IS IN **FLTSIM95.CFG**)	DESCRIPTION
BUTTON_DOWN_EVENT_05=65726	BUTTON_DOWN_EVENT_05 controls the Top Right Base Button. It is assigned to switch Autopilot altitude hold on/off (65726).
BUTTON_DOWN_EVENT_06=65729	BUTTON_DOWN_EVENT_06 controls the Bottom Right Base Button. It is assigned to switch Autopilot NAV1 hold on/off (65729).
BUTTON_DOWN_EVENT_07=65724	BUTTON_DOWN_EVENT_07 controls the Bottom Left Base Button. It is assigned to switch Autopilot approach hold on/off (65724).
BUTTON_DOWN_EVENT_32=65674	Point of View (POV) Hat Switch Position 1: look forward (65674)
BUTTON_DOWN_EVENT_33=65675	Hat Switch Position 2: look forward right (65675)
BUTTON_DOWN_EVENT_34=65676	Hat Switch Position 3: look right (65676)
BUTTON_DOWN_EVENT_35=65677	Hat Switch Position 4: look right rear (65677)
BUTTON_DOWN_EVENT_36=65678	Hat Switch Position 5: look back (65678)
BUTTON_DOWN_EVENT_37=65679	Hat Switch Position 6: look left rear (65679)
BUTTON_DOWN_EVENT_38=65680	Hat Switch Position 7: look left (65680)
BUTTON_DOWN_EVENT_39=65681	Hat Switch Position 8: Look left forward (65681)
BUTTON_DOWN_REPEAT_06=6	N/A
BUTTON_DOWN_REPEAT_07=6	N/A
BUTTON_DOWN_EVENT_08=65548	Decrease digits
BUTTON_DOWN_REPEAT_08=4	N/A
BUTTON_DOWN_EVENT_09=65549	Increase digits
BUTTON_DOWN_REPEAT_09=4	N/A
BUTTON_DOWN_REPEAT_34=2	N/A
BUTTON_DOWN_REPEAT_38=2	N/A

N/A: Microsoft has not given an explanation for these settings.
*Text in column 1 is in **FLTSIM95.CFG**. Text in column 2 is not in **FLTSIM95.CFG**.*

The following are the list of values that can be assigned to your LOCKED=1 labels.

Table A.3 *Numerical Values of BUTTON_DOWN_EVENTS Used in FLTSIM95.CFG to Connect a Particular Action with a Button*

ACTION	VALUE
Extend or retract landing gear	65570
Autopilot master on/off	65580
Apply brakes	65588
Nose down trim	65607
Nose up trim	65615
Pan view left	65671
Pan view right	65672
Look forward	65674
Look forward right	65675
Look right	65676
Look right rear	65677
Look back	65678
Look back left	65679
Look left	65680
Look left forward	65681
Autopilot approach hold on/off	65724
Autopilot heading hold on/off	65725
Autopilot altitude hold on/off	65726
Autopilot wing leveler on/off	65727
Autopilot NAV1 hold on/off	65729
Extend flaps in increments	65758
Retract flaps in increments	65759
Slew ahead or move elevator	65762
Slew sideways or move ailerons	65763
Slew heading or move rudder	65764
Throttle	65765
Slew hold or apply brakes	65796
Slew heading or move ailerons	65797
Pan View Up	65734
Pan View Down	65735
Increase Digits on Panel or Increase Zoom View	65549

Table A.3 *continued*

ACTION	VALUE
Decrease Digits on Panel or Decrease Zoom View	65548
Spoiler	65589
Propeller Blade Angle Increase	65771
Propeller Blade Angle Decrease	65674
Engine Mixture Enrich	65680
Engine Mixture Lean	65676
Cycle through gauges	65800
Reverse cycle through gauges	65801
Autopilot altitude hold and wing leveler on/off	65802

Example of Manually Reprogramming the SideWinder 3-D Pro with Custom Functions

Let's use the **FLTSIM95.CFG** to manually reconfigure the SideWinder 3-D so that with the joystick alone, you can use elevator trim, increment, and decrement numbers on the instrument panel, and switch between gauges. We will replace the hat switch's view directions so that the hat switch right forward direction will cycle forward through the gauges, while the left forward direction will cycle in the reverse direction. Also, the hat switch's left rear direction will be used to decrement numbers, while the right rear direction will be used to increment numbers on the panel.

Table A.4 shows a partial listing of the contents of the **FLTSIM95.CFG** file that you will use. Since you don't need to replace the entire contents of the [JOYSTICK00] section, you should just edit the contents where you see changes made in Table A.4. Notice, however, that we have added a new BUTTON_DOWN_REPEAT=5 after each of the two new BUTTON_DOWN_EVENTS for the side two buttons on the SideWinder. These two repeat labels allow nose down and nose up elevator trip to be applied continuously, instead of discretely, as is the case when you created the Elevator Trim profile in the Game Devices Profiler. By adding these labels, you will find that pressing the two side buttons on the joystick will cause elevator trim to move smoothly, instead of jerking once for each button press.

NOTE

Do not erase the existing entries in your **FLTSIM95.CFG** unless you see that the values listed in the example are different.

Table A.4 *SideWinder 3-D Pro Custom Configuration for Adding Elevator Trim to the Joysticks Side Buttons, Incrementing and Decrementing numbers, and Cycling Through Gauges Using the Hat Switch*

EXAMPLE LISTING FOR **FLTSIM95.CFG**	DESCRIPTION
`[JOYSTICK_00]`	
`LOCKED=1`	Set value to 1 if you wish to preserve your settings. Set value to 0 if you wish FSW95 to overwrite your settings.
`TYPE=45088`	Don't change this number. It represents the SideWinder 3-D Pro joystick.
`BUTTON_DOWN_EVENT_02=65615`	BUTTON_DOWN_EVENT_02 controls the Top Side Button on the joystick and is assigned to nose down elevator trim (65615).
`BUTTON_DOWN_REPEAT_02=5`	BUTTON_DOWN_REPEAT_03 for the Top Side Button on the joystick is repeated 5 times for each press of the button.
`BUTTON_DOWN_EVENT_03=65607`	BUTTON_DOWN_EVENT_03 controls the Bottom Side Button on joystick and is assigned to nose up elevator trim (65607).
`BUTTON_DOWN_REPEAT_03=5`	BUTTON_DOWN_REPEAT_03 for the Bottom Side Button on the joystick is repeated 5 times for each press of the button.
`BUTTON_DOWN_EVENT_32=65674`	Leave alone.
`BUTTON_DOWN_EVENT_33=65800`	Hat Switch Position 2: Forward right Forward cycle through gauges on panel (65800).
`BUTTON_DOWN_EVENT_34=65549`	Hat Switch Position 3: Right, increase digits (65549)
`BUTTON_DOWN_EVENT_35=65549`	Leave alone.
`BUTTON_DOWN_EVENT_36=65678`	Leave this alone.
`BUTTON_DOWN_EVENT_37=65548`	Leave this alone.
`BUTTON_DOWN_EVENT_38=65548`	Hat Switch Position 7: Left, decrease digits (65548).
`BUTTON_DOWN_EVENT_39=65801`	Hat Switch Position 8: left forward. Reverse cycle through gauges on panel (65801).

The Spot view directions using the hat switch on the SideWinder 3-D Pro remain unaffected by your changes in **FLTSIM95.CFG**.

T I P

After completing the changes as listed in Table A.4, save the **FLTSIM95.CFG** file, then restart Flight Simulator. Your new button or hat reassignments will then take effect once you go to **Options/Preferences/Controls** (in FSW95) and click the **Joystick On** box so that it is lit. When you return to the simulation, you'll find that your joystick has been successfully reprogrammed.

Programming the Virtual Pilot Pro

If you would like to play around with keyboard to button assignments on the Virtual Pilot Pro, you'll have to consult Figure A.9 to identify what each button and hat is called in the **FLTSIM95.CFG** file. The button assignments are not the same as on the SideWinder 3-D Pro. What's nice about the Virtual Pilot Pro, aside from its rudder pedals which you need for crosswind landings, is that the Virtual Pilot Pro has a second hat switch (one more than the SideWinder 3-D Pro). When you properly install the Virtual Pilot Pro drivers for Windows 95, you'll find that the left hat switch has four positions, two of which increment and decrement numbers on your panel, and two of which cycle you through your gauges. This is a very handy tool, because you can quickly tune in a radio frequency, adjust your course heading or OBI on the NAV radio without taking your hands off the yoke. The right hat switch controls the forward, left and right side, and back views. The other six buttons, trim knobs, and throttle lever have functions which are specified in Figure A.9.

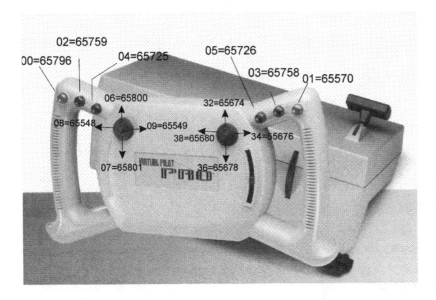

Figure A.9 *Virtual Pilot Pro button numbers as referenced in* **FLTSIM95.CFG**

The default values for the left hat switch on the CH Virtual Pilot Pro yoke are given in Table A.5.

Table A.5 *Default Values for the Left Hat Switch on the CH Virtual Pilot Pro*

ACTION	VALUE
Cycle through gauges	65800
Reverse cycle through gauges	65801

When you cycle through the available gauges, you go through VOR2, ADF, NAV2, NAV1, COM, and VOR1, in that order. Also, when you cycle through the gauges, you stop on both the whole and decimal parts of the ADF, NAV1, NAV2, and COM displays. To give you an example of a keyboard to button modification for your Virtual Pilot Pro, use the **FLTSIM95.CFG** listing in Table A.6 which changes your left and right views on the right hat switch to pan left and pan right respectively.

Table A.6 *How to Modify the FLTSIM95.CFG for the Virtual Pilot Pro*

FLTSIM95	COMMENTS
[JOYSTICK_00]	
LOCKED=1	Make sure LOCKED=1, otherwise if it equals zero, your settings will be lost.
	Leave the entries below alone.
TYPE=45082	
AXIS_FLAGS=15	
AXIS_EVENT_00=65763	
AXIS_SCALE_00=54	
AXIS_NULL_00=36	
AXIS_EVENT_01=65762	
AXIS_SCALE_01=61	
AXIS_NULL_01=36	
AXIS_EVENT_02=65765	
AXIS_SCALE_02=127	
AXIS_NULL_02=36	
AXIS_EVENT_03=65764	
AXIS_SCALE_03=64	

Table A.6 continued

FLTSIM95	COMMENTS
AXIS_NULL_03=36	Change the BUTTON_DOWN_EVENTS below to what's shown here. Or if you like, you can change the event code to match one of the actions listed in Tables A.3 or A.5.
BUTTON_DOWN_EVENT_00=65796	This sets the leftmost button to act as the wheel brakes (65796).
BUTTON_DOWN_REPEAT_00=1	
BUTTON_DOWN_EVENT_01=65570	This sets the rightmost button to raise and lower the landing gear (65570).
BUTTON_DOWN_EVENT_02=65759	The middle button on the left side raises the flaps (65759).
BUTTON_DOWN_EVENT_03=65758	The middle button on the right side lowers the flaps (65758).
BUTTON_DOWN_EVENT_04=65725	The inner button on the left side turns the Autopilot on or off.
BUTTON_DOWN_REPEAT_04=1	
BUTTON_DOWN_EVENT_05=65726	The inner button on the right side turns the Autopilot altitude and wing leveler on or off. (65726).
BUTTON_DOWN_REPEAT_05=1	
BUTTON_DOWN_EVENT_06=65800	The left hat switch forward direction cycles up through the gauges (65800).
BUTTON_DOWN_EVENT_07=65801	
BUTTON_DOWN_REPEAT_07=1	
BUTTON_DOWN_EVENT_08=65549	The left hat switch left direction decreases numbers on your instrument panel and decreases zoom in your window (65549).
BUTTON_DOWN_REPEAT_08=1	
BUTTON_DOWN_EVENT_09=65548	The left hat switch right direction increases numbers on your instrument panel and increases zoom in your window (65548).
BUTTON_DOWN_REPEAT_09=1	
BUTTON_DOWN_EVENT_32=65674	The right hat switch forward direction lets you look forward (65674).

Table A.6 continued

FLTSIM95	COMMENTS
BUTTON_DOWN_EVENT_34=65672	The right hat switch right direction pans your view right (65672).
BUTTON_DOWN_EVENT_36=65678	The right hat switch rear direction lets you look back (65678).
BUTTON_DOWN_EVENT_38=65671	The right hat switch left direction lets you pan your view left (65671).

Save the **FLTSIM95.CFG** file, then restart Flight Simulator. Your new button or hat re-assignments will then take effect once you go to **Options/Preferences/Controls** and click the **Joystick On** box so that it is lit. When you return to the simulation, you'll find that your joystick has been successfully reprogrammed.

NOTE   The left hat switch on the Virtual Pilot Pro, in addition to switching between gauges, can be used to increment and decrement numbers radio frequencies, course headings on the OBI, 3-D view window zoom levels (first press **[** followed by the hat switch). It can also be used to change the rate of time passage (press **R** followed by the hat switch).

CAN I GET DIFFERENTIAL BRAKING TO WORK WITH MY RUDDER PEDALS?

No.

MY LAPTOP DOESN'T HAVE A GAME PORT. CAN I USE A JOYSTICK?

You can purchase PCMCIA gameport cards that will plug into your laptop and allow you to plug in your joystick. One such manufacturer of PCMCIA Game I/O Cards is Synchrotech:

> Synchrotech
> 3333 Wilshire Blvd., Suite 806
> Los Angeles, CA 90010
> Tel: 213-368-3760
> Fax: 213-368-3765
> www.synchrotech.com/gp-game.html

Why is my sound monophonic, when I have a stereo sound card?

Although Flight Simulator supports stereo sound files, for some reason Microsoft chose to include monophonic sounds on their CD-ROM. FSW95 normally plays back mono sounds while FS98 can play either stereo or mono. To play back stereo in FSW95, you need to edit the **FLTSIM95.CFG** file.

FSW95 instructions for enabling stereo sound:

To change the sound settings to stereo with a sampling rate of 22 kHz, in the **FLT-SIM95.CFG**, add the following text:

```
[SOUND]
Channels=2
SamplesPerSec=22050
BitsPerSample=16
```

To change the sound settings back to mono with a sampling rate of 11 kHz in the **FLT-SIM95.CFG**, change the text to read

```
[SOUND]
Channels=1
SamplesPerSec=11025
BitsPerSample=16
```

You can assign the values 8 or 16 to `BitsPerSample`, and you should use a sample rate equal to or greater than the sample rate of your wave files to be used (this can adversely affect system performance). Also, when you switch from another application while sound is playing, you may lose Flight Simulator sounds. To restore the sound, press **Q** twice, or switch FSW95 to another Windows application, then return the focus to Flight Simulator.

Microsoft advises against changing the default monophonic sound settings and sound sampling rate of 11 kHz, because of adverse affects on frame rates.

Why can't I get the Advanced Weather Dialog box to appear under the World/Weather menu?

Select **Options/Preferences/General** and make sure that the **Use Advanced Weather Dialog** checkbox is on. Then when you return to the **World/Weather** menu, you should be able to bring up the Advanced Weather dialog box.

Why can't I turn on Wispy Cloud Effects and Cloud Thickness Effects?

For FS98:

Under **Options: Preferences: Display: Display Options: Scenery**, you need to turn on the **Textured Sky** check box before the Wispy Cloud Effects and Cloud Thickness Effects checkboxes can be turned on.

For FSW95:

In the Display Options dialog box under **Options/Preferences/Display & Sound/Display Preferences/Scenery**, you need to turn on the **Textured Sky** checkbox before the **Wispy Cloud Effects** and **Cloud Thickness Effects** checkboxes can be turned on.

Why can't I adjust the barometric pressure setting on the Altimeter?

You can calibrate the jet altimeter to the current atmospheric pressure by pressing the **B** key. If you want to manually change the altimeter's pressure setting to some other value, you can click the Altimter Settting knob in FS98, or go to the **Aircraft: Aircraft Settings: Realism** dialog and then enter the pressure you want into the Altimeter Setting entry box.

Why doesn't Slew Mode work?

Press the **K** key and see if this doesn't resolve your problem. The **K** key is used to turn the joystick off or on; unfortunately, FSW95 disables the keyboard controls for slewing when the joystick is activated. Conversely, if you are using the keyboard, you can't use the joystick for slewing unless you press **K**.

Another common manifestation of this problem occurs when you are using an uncalibrated joystick and you press **Y** to enter slew mode. What happens next is that your aircraft starts slewing violently, perhaps spinning around, or translating very fast in a particular direction. To stop this from occurring, press the **K** key, and then press **Keypad 5**, which freezes all slew motion. You can then slew normally using the numeric keypad (assuming the **NumLock** key is off in FS98).

To learn how to calibrate your joystick, read on.

The K key doesn't recalibrate my joystick like it used to! What do I do?

In FS 5.1, the **K** key was used to calibrate the joystick, but in FS98, the **K** key turns the joystick on or off, thereby enabling or disabling the numeric keypad flight controls. In FS98, you calibrate the joystick by selecting the **Options: Custom Controls** menu, then click the **Calibrate** button. Then, in the dialog box that opens, you highlight the joystick and click the **Properties** button to start up the calibration process. In FSW95, you calibrate the joystick by choosing **Options: Preferences: Controls** and then click on the **Calibrate** button.

How can I disable the Autorun feature in FS95/98?

If you have **Autorun** turned on, each time you put in the FS95/98 CD-ROM the program will start up.

This may be inconvenient, such as when you are at work and the boss happens to be nearby. You can disable Autorun by performing the following steps:

1. Open the Windows Control Panel by selecting **Start/Settings/Control Panel** from the Windows 95 Task Bar.
2. Double-click on the **System** icon, and click the **Device Manager** tab.
3. Click the + sign next to **CDROM**, and you'll see your CD-ROM Device Driver listed.
4. Select the CD-ROM Device Driver, and then click the **Properties** button.
5. In the Properties dialog box that opens, select the **Settings** tab.
6. Uncheck **Auto insert notification** and click **OK** until you exit all dialog boxes.
7. Restart the computer, as prompted. When the computer has rebooted, Autorun will be permanently disabled until you turn **Auto insert notification** back on.

There is shortcut method to the above procedure if all you want to do is temporarily disable Autorun. Simply hold down the **Shift** key when you insert the CD-ROM.

See also the FAQ section on removing the Microsoft commercial that opens each time you start Flight Simulator.

Does Flight Simulator support plug and play?

What you're really asking is, does Windows 95 support plug and play? The answer is yes, if your device will run under Windows 95, it will run under FSW95.

What is DirectX?

DirectX is a set of software drivers for Windows 95 that allow direct access to hardware. These drivers are shipped with the Microsoft Game Software Development Kit (SDK), but you only need to install the runtime version of DirectX 5.0 that comes with the Flight Simulator 98 CD-ROM. DirectX will probably be shipped with Windows 98, so there will be no need to install it from the Flight Simulator CD-ROM if you have already installed Windows 98. The *X* in DirectX is a variable, meaning that the term *DirectX* refers to all the subdrivers: DirectInput, Direct3D, DirectSound, DirectDraw, etc.

FS98 requires DirectX version 5.0 or later. The FS98 setup program will install the proper DirectX version that you need when you install Flight Simulator.

Direct Draw is not used in FSW95, nor is it needed. DirectDraw can be enabled in FSW95 by adding `DirectDraw=1` to the [MAIN] section of the **FLTSIM95.CFG** file (you must edit this file manually to enable DirectDraw because DirectDraw is disabled by default after Flight Simulator is installed). Although enabling DirectDraw may speed up the frame rate with certain video cards, you may discover that other applications on your computer become more sluggish as more system resources are allocated to running Flight Simulator. Experience is your best guide.

HOW DO I GET UPDATED DIRECTX DRIVERS?

Check your video card manufacturer's Web site to see if they have the latest DirectX driver. Usually, you'll have to download the latest driver as a compressed Zip file (ZIP) or self-extracting executable file (EXE). You can unzip the file using WinZip on this book's CD-ROM, and then extract the compressed files to a temporary directory on your hard disk. Once you have done this, you can run the Setup program in this temporary directory. If the driver is downloaded as an EXE file, simply run the program and it will install the driver for you automatically.

HOW DO I INSTALL UPDATED DIRECTX VIDEO DRIVERS FROM THE VIDEO CARD MANUFACTURER?

1. Open the Display Properties dialog box by right-clicking on the Windows desktop and then clicking **Properties** on the popup menu.
2. In the Display Properties dialog box, click the **Settings** tab.
3. Click **Change Display Type**.
4. In the Advanced Display Properties dialog box, click the **Adapter** tab.
5. Click **Change**.
6. In the Select Device dialog box, click **Have Disk**.
7. If you have the latest video driver from your video card manufacturer on a disk or CD-ROM, select the appropriate drive and click **OK**. Otherwise click **Browse**. Go to the temporary subdirectory you created for the video card files and open the **DISPLAY.INF** file.
8. In the Select Device dialog box, choose the driver that matches your video card and then click **OK**.
9. Click **OK** as many times as necessary to accept the changes.
10. To restart your computer, click **Yes** in the System Settings Change dialog box.

DOES FLIGHT SIMULATOR SUPPORT DIRECTSOUND?

DirectSound is the audio component of the Microsoft Windows 95 Game SDK and is supported by Flight Simulator. It provides low-latency mixing, hardware acceleration, and direct access to sound hardware. The on-the-fly mixing of separate audio streams is particularly useful because it allows you to hear multiple sounds, such as moving flaps, engines, and landing gear noises simultaneously.

DOES FLIGHT SIMULATOR SUPPORT DIRECTINPUT?

DirectInput is the joystick component of the Microsoft Windows 95 Game SDK which allows programmers fast access to analog and digital joysticks. DirectInput device drivers use the registry to store settings for standard joysticks, calibration information, and settings for other joysticks. Flight Simulator supports DirectInput.

DOES FLIGHT SIMULATOR SUPPORT DIRECTDRAW?

DirectDraw, which is really a memory manager for video memory, contains a set of drivers that allows direct access to video display memory, hardware blitters (copying of video picture elements), hardware overlays, and page flipping. It does this all while maintaining compatibility with existing Windows 95 programs and device drivers. DirectDraw can manipulate video memory, and is especially good at increasing the speed of blitting and color decompression capabilities while at the same time avoiding hardware dependence on a particular video card.

DirectDraw is used in FS98 but not in FSW95. Note that DirectDraw works best with FS98 in Full Screen mode (press **Alt+Enter**).

FSW95 DirectDraw Issues

While FSW95 requires the DirectX suite of drivers version 2.0 or later, it does not use DirectDraw unless you edit the [MAIN] section of the **FLTSIM95.CFG** file and add DirectDraw=1.

The DirectX 2.0 video drivers are needed during installation, however, and will overwrite your existing video drivers if they are not DirectDraw capable, or they are an earlier version of DirectDraw. If you already have DirectDraw 3.0 or later installed, you needn't worry about the drivers being overwritten, since the setup program is smart enough to recognize it shouldn't do such a dumb thing. After the DirectX 2.0 setup that occurs during Flight Simulator's first installation, you may discover that the additional features specific to your video card are longer available (only with older non-DirectDraw drivers). If this happens, you should go visit the Web page of the manufacturer of your video card to see if they have a new DirectDraw compatible video driver. If they do, download and install these new drivers after you have installed Flight Simulator.

At the time of this writing, DirectDraw 5.0 was available from Microsoft and various video card manufacturers were shipping it along with their video card drivers. Why wasn't DirectDraw automatically enabled in Flight Simulator, even though the setup program installed DirectDraw? Program Manager Andy Silverman comments:

> DirectDraw was evaluated but does not provide any measurable performance gain in this incarnation of Flight Simulator. We feel that this is probably the case in most applications which don't rely heavily on blitting objects from screen to screen memory. Flight Simulator is far more render-bound than drawing bound in terms of where it spends its time. However, the knowledge we gained in DirectDraw may help us in any future application of Direct3D technology.

Microsoft has also stated that:

> Implementing DirectDraw in FSW95 will yield positive results in very few cases. The facts are as follows:
>
> 1. FSW95 does not use DirectDraw implementations.
> 2. DirectDraw can be used in FSW95.
> 3. Item 1 plus Item 2 above does not equal a DirectDraw implementation.
> 4. You may see an improvement in your running of FSW95 ONLY if your video card and video driver have problems with a DIB engine. Setting DirectDraw=1 turns off the DIBENG portion of Windows 95 and turns on the DirectDraw portion of Direct X. In most cases this will not be to your advantage. What it does mean, in most cases, is that Windows 95 is not optimally configured anymore.
> 5. The DirectDraw implementation in DirectX 2.0 has some curious mouse pointer issues. If you use animated or color cursors, and implement DirectDraw, you may experience weird mouse behavior. This is one of the reasons that FSW95 does not implement DirectDraw.
> 6. Any advantage gained with DirectDraw enabled in FSW95, can only be gained via a Full Screen mode.

NOTE DIB stands for *device-independent bitmap*. The DIB engine provides 32-bit graphics code for fast, robust drawing on high resolution and frame buffer- type display adapters. In the case of initializing the DirectDraw sequence in Flight Simulator, many video cards that have trouble with the DIB engine in Windows 95 may see an improvement when DirectDraw is used instead. This is because DirectDraw converts bitmaps to 8 bits per pixel, or 256 colors, which requires less memory and less processing. This is probably where the actual gain in frames per second comes from.

WHAT HAPPENED TO MY VIDEO CARD DRIVER AFTER I INSTALLED FLIGHT SIMULATOR?

Flight Simulator needs to install DirectDraw, DirectSound and some other drivers on your system before it will work. Sometimes these drivers overwrite your existing hardware drivers.

DOES FLIGHT SIMULATOR SUPPORT DIRECT3D?

Direct3D is a Microsoft API that provides direct hardware support for 3-D video accelerator cards. FS98 supports Direct3D but FSW95 does not. Also, Direct3D is supported only in 16-bit color screen modes in a window, or automatically when in Full Screen mode (**Alt+Enter**). Note that the Matrox Millenium and Mystique video cards do not support Direct3D. Also, 3D video cards with only 2 MB of memory do not allow Direct3D support, and there are many cards that perform very poorly with FS98. If you have such a card, it is recommended that you run FS98 without the Direct 3-D drivers.

Direct3D in FS98 is supported only in 16-bit color screen mode in a window, or automatically when in Full Screen mode (**Alt+Enter**).

The **Hardware Acceleration** Tab under **Options: Preferences: Display: Display Options** allows you to choose which video driver to use with FS98. If you have a single video card with built in 3-D capabilities, you will see two listings for a **Primary Display Driver**, one with Direct 3-D and one without. If you have a daughter 3-D video card accelerator that is mated or attached to your main video card, you may see a secondary display driver or other driver listings.

If you have a 3-D capable accelerator card, you have two options in the Fullscreen device listbox: **Primary Display Driver (Direct 3-D)** and **Primary Display Driver**. If you have a good 3-D card, you should select the **Primary Display Driver (Direct 3-D)** because it can double or even triple your frame rate. Beware: some cards, such as the S-3 Virge chip on the Diamond Stealth and the Matrox Mystique, perform poorly. These cards are billed as being Direct 3-D–capable, but they actually run slower with the Direct 3-D driver. If you have such a card, you should instead choose **Primary Display Driver** without the Direct 3-D drivers.

The Hardware Acceleration Display Options dialog box offers various choices for 3-D Advanced Hardware Effects you want to enable (i.e., **Filter Texture Maps, MIP Mapping, Render 8 Bit Image Textures**). The **Filter Texture Maps** option is used to smooth ground and building textures. You should leave this option on if you have a 3D card installed. The MIP (*multum in parvo,* ormany things in a small place) is used to improve the visual effect of distant scenery. When it is on, point sampling of a source image that recedes into the distance is performed much more quickly than if a filtering computation was performed for every pixel. Mainly, MIP mapping provides a shortcut that improves the receding horizon, without having to perform the calculations for every pixel.

If you have trouble with Direct3D, here are some possible strategies to try:

1. If you're using DirectDraw 5.0, reinstall your video card manufacturer's DirectX video driver. If you're already using the card's custom driver, try installing the DirectX 5.0 driver instead by going to the Win95 Device Manager, choosing **Update Driver** from the device's properties, and pointing to the **DirectX\Drivers\USA** directory on the Flight Simulator CD-ROM when it asks for the location of the updated drivers.
2. Turn off **Enable Hardware Acceleration** under **Options: Preferences: Display/Display Options: Hardware Acceleration**.
3. Try switching to Full Screen mode (press **Alt Enter**) and/or choose 16-bit color mode before starting Flight Simulator.

DOES FLIGHT SIMULATOR SUPPORT DIRECTPLAY?

DirectPlay is a Microsoft API that will allow multiple players to go head to head over the Internet, LAN and dial-up connections. It is not supported in FSW95, but *is* supported in FS98.

DOES DIRECTDRAW 5.0 MAKE USE OF MMX, AND IF SO DOES FS98 TAKE ADVANTAGE OF MMX?

For example, if I select the Primary DirectDraw 3D hardware accelerator, will I be using MMX, and if I just choose the normal Primary video driver will I not be using MMX? And what does my secondary driver have to do with MMX?

DirectX 5.0 has an MMX-enabled RGB-rendered functionality built in, but it just plain didn't work right for FS98, so it was not used in the program. However, FS98 does use MMX where Direct X 5.0 takes advantage of it for sound and color benefits.

The primary/secondary notation for the Fullscreen Device pull-down listbox in the Hardware Acceleration dialog box (**Options: Preferences: Display: Display Options: Hardware Acceleration**), has nothing to do with MMX at all. The primary driver is simply the card that drives your primary display. If you have a secondary card such as a 3Dfx board, that will be listed separately.

DO FS98 AND DIRECTX 5.0 TAKE ADVANTAGE OF THE NEW AGP MOTHERBOARDS, SUCH AS THE INTEL 440LX?

So if an FS98 user purchases an AGP motherboard with an AGP 3D video card, will he be getting better frame rates than the non-AGP motherboard with a similar but non-AGP 3-D video card?

Because AGP (accelerated graphics port) is a hardware specification, DirectX 5.0 doesn't know, care, or need to know anything about AGP at all. The video card manufacturer, on the other hand, has to write a DirectX 5.0–compliant driver that runs its hardware. Whether AGP results in better frame rates is open to speculation at this point because the FS98 development team was unable to do any sort of direct comparison.

However, DirectX 5 supports the AGP. The biggest problem right now is the shortage of Intel 440LX motherboards capable of implementing it and the shortage of AGP video cards.

Does FS98 support all six joystick axes that are possible in Windows 95/98?

Yes, FS98 does support all six axes on each of possible 16 joysticks, but there's certainly not enough controls to assign them just yet. For example, if you had a joystick with extra axes available, you could assign prop and mixture settings to the fifth and sixth axes on joystick 0 (U0 and V0).

What about that flickering problem I had in FSW95? Has that been fixed in FS98?

If you are running FS98 without a 3-D video card, you will find the flickering in the distance is much improved over FSW95. To enable this effect, the **Image Quality** setting must be set to **High: Slow** in the Display Preferences dialog box (**Options: Preferences: Display**).

How do I get rid of DirectX if I have problems with it?

You can remove the DirectX video and sound drivers by running the **DXSETUP.EXE** program which is on the Flight Simulator 98 CD-ROM.

To run this program:

1. Open the Windows Explorer and select the drive in which the FS98 CD-ROM disc is currently located.
2. Double-click the DirectX folder.
3. Double-click **DXSETUP.EXE** to run the DirectX uninstall program. After you finish, some DirectX files will remain in your Windows\System folder. Don't worry, these files do not affect the Windows 95 video or sound drivers. You can remove these files by following these steps:
4. Restart your computer in MS-DOS mode.
5. Change directories into your **Windows\System** directory (CD **C:\Windows\System**).

6. Delete the following files (the asterisks are wildcard characters and are needed to delete more than one file with a similar name):

DEL DSOUND.*
DEL DDRAW.*
DEL D3D*.*
DEL DDHELP.EXE
DEL DPLAY.DLL
DEL DPSERIAL.DLL
DEL DPWSOCK.DLL

WERE CHANGES WERE MADE TO THE ADVENTURE FILE FORMAT IN FS98?

According to Microsoft:

Well, actually there were some modifications to the adventure file format but we were able to leave in the code that read the old format too so we won't need to convert adventures again (but the continuous print ability for things like GPS displays should work again in this release).

As this book went to press, the full list of changes was not yet available.

If you are having problems with older adventure files, you should install the FS98 Aircraft Converter because it fixes some incompatibilities with adventure files from previous versions of Flight Simulator.

WHAT ABOUT FS98'S MULTIPLAYER MODE?

When a multiplayer session is launched from the Internet Gaming Zone, new players cannot join the game unless they know the IP address of the machine that is the session host. If the IP address is known, the session can be located if TCP/IP is selected from the Connection Type dialog box, and the host's IP address is entered into the Locate Session alert.

It is possible for players to fly with different settings for their simulation rates while in multiplayer mode. This will result in some planes moving at rates that are different the viewer's time reference frame.

It is also possible for players to have different levels of dynamic scenery, scenery complexity, or different scenery installed. This will result in planes that appear to fly through objects, buildings, or under the ground.

WHY CAN'T I STEER?

You need to turn off the yaw damper on the Autopilot.

How can I get the Enhanced Spatial Effects for Left and Right Stereo Sound Working in FS98?

There's no way to adjust the spatial effects sound in FS98

To get the spatial effects working with the Creative Labs SoundBlaster 64AWE, you need to open the Windows 95 **Control Panel: System: Device Manager: Sound: Sound Video and Game Controllers** control. There you can select the SoundBlaster driver, and click **Properties** to see a dialog box that will give you the option of turning on check the **Use Creative 3D Stereo Enhancement** spatial effects box. Once you have done this, you will note that, at landings, you will hear a left or right sound effect depending on which part of the main gear touch down first.

The Canopus Total 3D video card comes with a sound spatializer built in that enhances the left-right stereo separation. It turns the normal audio that your sound card produces into fuller, richer, 3-D - stereo sound, but to get it to work, you have to go to the Total 3D Audio Control and turn on the spatializer control (click the **Monitor** icon on your taskbar, and select **Audio Control** from the pop-up menu).

Morse Code Identifier Bug in FS98

If you turn on the Morse code identifier sounds for a given navaid, and tune to a different frequency, the previous identifier continues to sound until you pick another active frequency. This could be confusing if you happen to tune an active navaid while searching for a different one.

Does Flight Simulator run better/faster on Windows NT?

Some people report marginal improvement under Windows NT, and this would tend to make sense because Windows NT does not contend with the 16-bit baggage of "legacy" code that Windows 95 is saddled with. However, recent reports indicate that a Pentium 200MMX running Windows 95 slightly outperforms Pentium Pros running Windows NT. The truth of the matter is, the jury's still out on this issue.

Should I run Flight Simulator on Windows NT?

Windows NT doesn't support plug and play. If you don't want and don't need plug and play, then you can run Flight Simulator on Windows NT. But for the vast majority of people who wish to avoid hassling with hardware issues, such as conflicting IRQs, DMAs, and so on, you should stick with Windows 95. Most peripherals and equipment sold these days is billed as "plug and play," whereas if you try to install it on Windows NT, you had better be prepared to "plug and pray." Some people running Flight Simulator on Windows NT report that setting up joysticks can be tricky.

How do I reset my situation?

The **Prt Screen** key no longer resets your situation (this key is now reserved for screen captures). Instead to reset a situation press **Ctrl-;**.

Is there a patch disk for FSW95?

FEPAT.EXE, created by Microsoft, is available on this book's CD-ROM and it is a self-extracting, self-installing patch file to fix errors in FSW95 that occur with third party scenery add-ons. This patch solves the problem of missing ILS transmitters and incorrect ATIS messages in third-party scenery which overlays the default CD-ROM scenery. These problems occur with Europe 1, and with certain U.S. airports that are in areas covered by Microsoft Atlas data.

As an example of how FEPAT works, I noticed that after installing the Hawaii scenery add-on, I was not able to find the ILS for Honolulu International Airport. On running FEPAT, the ILS reappeared.

Is Flight Shop still available?

You can buy Flight Shop from Apollo Software, as well as Europe 1 and Europe 2 scenery. Their Web site address is www.apollosoftware.com, and you can email them at 104706.24140@compuserve.com. The North American distributor is AETI (tel 714-551-0372, fax 714-551-2695).

How much memory do I need?

Flight Simulator runs best with 16 to 32 MB of RAM.

What is MMX?

MMX is Intel's implementation of a new architecture for Pentium class microprocessors. A Pentium with MMX technology has three primary architectural design enhancements:

- *New Instructions*. There are 57 powerful new instructions specifically designed to manipulate and process video, audio, and graphical data more efficiently. These instructions are oriented to the highly parallel, repetitive sequences often found in multimedia operations.
- *SIMD (single instruction, multiple data)*. Many multimedia and communication applications typically use repetitive loops that, while occupying 10% or less of the overall application code, can account for up to 90% of the execution time. single-instruction, multiple-data (SIMD) allows one instruction to perform the

same function on multiple pieces of data. This allows the microprocessor to reduce computational intensive loops that are commonly found in video , audio, graphics, and animation. Intel uses an analogy of a drill sergeant telling an entire platoon, "About face," rather than commanding each individual soldier to turn one at a time.

- **More cache**: The extra L1 cache, or on-chip memory in the CPU has been doubled to 32 KB. This allows many more instructions and more data to be stored and processed inside the microprocessor, reducing the number of times the processor has to access slower off-chip memory areas. By itself, the extra L1 cache boosts performance by an average of 10% to 20%.

Intel uses two important tests to gauge the performance of Pentium MMX processors versus older non-MMX processors. The two tests are described in the next two sections.

iCOMP Index

Figure A.11 shows that a PC with a Pentium MMX microprocessor is 28% faster than a plain Pentium processor at the same clock speed when measured against Intel's iCOMP index. However, using Intel's Media benchmark, which measures multimedia performance, an MMX equipped PC performs 66% faster. Some graphics filter transformations such as are used in Adobe's Photoshop get a dramatic 500% boost in performance.

The Intel Comparative Microprocessor Performance (iCOMP) 2.0 index provides a comparative measure of microprocessor performance. It is not a benchmark, but a collection of benchmarks used to calculate an index of relative processor performance. The iCOMP index 2.0 rating encompass three separate aspects of 32-bit CPU performance: integer, floating-point, and multimedia. The multimedia portion is further divided into four components: Audio, Imaging, Video, and 3-D (see Intel Media Benchmark section below). Each category and subcategory is weighted based on the estimated percentage of time it occupies CPU time. The higher the iCOMP rating, the higher the relative performance of the microprocessor.

Intel Media Benchmark

The Intel Media Benchmark measures the performance of processors running algorithms found in multimedia. The test incorporates audio and video playback, image processing, wave file sample rate conversion, and 3-D geometry. The video playback component of the Intel Media Benchmark implements the MPEG1 decompression algorithm, while the audio component is based on the MPEG1 audio decompression definition. The sound component of the Intel Media Benchmark decompresses and plays a stereo audio clip. The audio component also includes sample rate conversion, special effects, and stereo mixing. The image processing component applies digital filters to true-color (24-bit) bitmap images. These filters include a box filter which is used to implement filters such as Gaussian blur and embossing, an image blending function used to combine two images into one, and a color space conversion function used to change an image's luminance. The 3-D component of the Intel Media Benchmark is based on Direct3D and a geometry routine from the OpenGL 3-D Triangle benchmark. These tests are used to measure the geometry portion of a 3-D workload on the CPU. Table A.7 and Figure A.10 list the results for both the iCOMP 2.0 index and the Intel Media Benchmark..

Table A.7 *Microprocessor Benchmark Results*

PROCESSOR BENCHMARKS (512 KB L2)	PENTIUM PROCESSOR 133 MHz	PENTIUM PROCESSOR 150 MHz	PENTIUM PROCESSOR 166 MHz	PENTIUM PROCESSOR 200 MHz	PENTIUM PRO PROCESSOR 200 MHz 256 KB L2	PENTIUM PROCESSOR WITH MMX TECHNOLOGY 200 MHz (PRO + MMX)	PENTIUM II PROCESSOR WITH MMX TECHNOLOGY 233 MHz 512 KB L2	PENTIUM II PROCESSOR WITH MMX TECHNOLOGY (PRO +MMX) 266 MHz 512 KB L2
Norton SI32	36.5	35.9	39.9	44.6	88.4	57.3	113.5	128.0
Intel Media Benchmark (Windows 95)	111.78	119.40	132.77	156.00	194.38	255.43	310.4	350.77
Video	109.02	117.25	130.26	155.52	158.34	268.40	271.98	307.24
Image Processing	111.70	121.75	135.29	159.03	220.75	743.92	1,026.55	1,129.01
3D Geometry	112.41	121.80	134.83	161.52	209.24	166.44	247.68	281.61
Audio	115.57	119.57	133.87	149.80	240.82	318.90	395.79	446.72
Norton Media Benchmark	7.2	7.6	8.5	9.6	11.6	13.8	17.2	19.4
Video	6.5	6.8	7.5	8.5	7.2	11.4	10.4	11.6
3D Graphics	9.3	10.0	11.2	12.8	16.6	14.0	22.2	25.2
Audio	8.3	8.5	9.7	10.9	16.4	21.9	26.7	30.4
CD-ROM	4.1	4.1	4.1	4.1	4.1	4.1	4.1	4.1
Imaging	4.1	4.4	4.9	5.8	16.8	27.7	40.0	44.3
ICOMP® Index 2.0 Rating	111	114	127	142	160	182	267	303

Source: Excerpted from Intel's Pentium Processor with MMX Technology performance brief.

How MMX Works

To see how MMX CPUs work faster than standard Pentiums, let's look at the MMX operation called single-instruction, multiple-data (SIMD), which lets the CPU perform one calculation on up to eight data elements simultaneously. The general purpose registers (memory locations inside the CPU) store up to a maximum of 32 bits at a time. MMX uses the eight 80-bit floating point registers, also inside the CPU, to store 64 bits of data at a time. MMX instructions can pack several data types into these 64 bit registers: either eight 8-bit, four 16-bit, two 32-bit, or one 64-bit value can be stored in one floating point register. Thus, data that is 8 bits, 16 bits, or even 32 bits wide can be sent to the floating point registers and stored sequentially in up to 64 bits of the available 80 bits in the floating-point register. This parallel data stream can then be multiplied or added and sent to the accumulator as one unit. Thus, a 16 bit-wide data stream could have four 16 bit values stored in parallel in the 64 bits in the floating point register, and each value could then be multiplied and added in one operation. The total number of MMX instructions needed to do this would be three, whereas on the Pentium, you would need at least 12 instructions to perform the same task. By reducing the number of instructions by 66%, you thus obtain a performance boost of 66%.

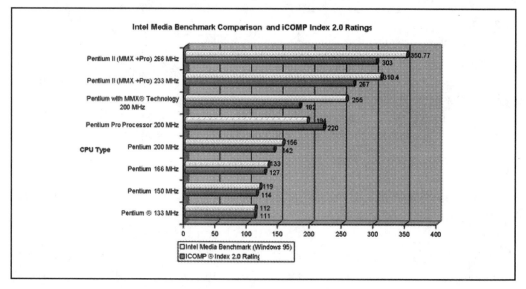

Figure A.10 *iCOMP Index 2.0 and intel media benchmark performance comparison on Windows 95 (Intel Media Benchmark uses Intel's MMX code).*

The disadvantage of using MMX's SIMD is that you can't simultaneously use floating point instructions while MMX instructions are running. This shouldn't present too much of a problem for most programs, since one can emulate floating point operations with the integer math that is available in MMX. Also, one can plan program flow so that all floating point operations occur before any MMX instructions for each frame. Furthermore, since Flight Simulator doesn't use floating point math, the loss of the floating point unit is not an issue.

Another disadvantage of MMX is that all software will have to be recoded to take advantage of the new instruction set. At the moment there are only a handful of applications that support MMX. However, when MMX enabled software starts appearing on shelves, expect striking improvements in such tasks as audio and video playback, image processing, and 3-D rendering. Flight Simulator 98 can use MMX, but FSW95 cannot.

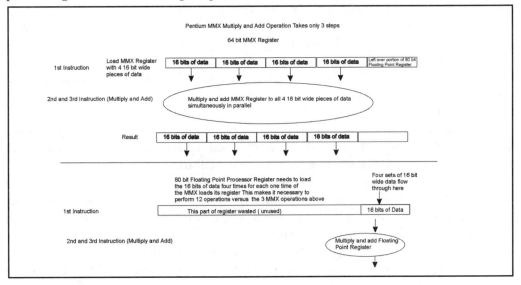

Figure A.11 *A Simple Multiply and Accumulate Operation uses only 3 instructions on an MMX CPU versus 12 instructions on a standard Pentium.*

HEY, WHAT GOES ON HERE? I CAN'T FIND A **VOR, NDB,** OR **ILS** STATION THAT SHOULD BE THERE.

Unfortunately, some ILS and VOR stations as well as a few airports are missing from FSW95's default database. For example, Dolphin VOR in Florida, several VOR stations near London, and Hong Kong airport are missing in FSW95. And the list goes on, although Microsoft has expended great effort to improve the navaid database for FS98.If you are a missing navaid that is important to you, you can add it yourself using Airport 2.0 on the book's CD-ROM. Many of the missing FSW95 navaids for the United

Kingdom are found in **LON-NAV.ZIP** and **UKNDBS.ZIP** files on the CD-ROM included with this book (don't install these with FS98).

Hurricane Andrew in 1992 destroyed the Biscayne Bay, Florida, VOR, which just after the disaster was temporarily replaced by Andrew VOR. Most recently, Virginia Key VOR "VKZ" on 117.1 MHz was chosen to replace both Biscayne Bay VOR and Andrew VOR. The Miami VOR "MIA" was decommissioned in 1996, and another new VOR Dolphin "DPH" on 113.9 MHz was added at the approach end to Miami's Runway 9L. Unfortunately, Microsoft didn't keep track of the changes to these navaids and so the two new navaids, Virginia Key VOR and Dolphin VOR, were not included in FSW95. To fix this oversight, we have included **MIAVORS.ZIP** on the book's CD-ROM which adds these two new VORS to the FSW95 BGL scenery database.

For other navaid patch files, you should check the CompuServe Flight Simulator Forum, or ftp.iup.edu on the Internet.

Note that the default FS95/98 navaid database does not include the entire world's navaids. Most of Asia, Africa, Eastern Europe, Africa, South America, Central America, and the Pacific are not covered in detail, so you'll need to install the navaid BGL files on the CD-ROM to fill in the gaps.

Also, some of the navaids have incorrect listings in the FSW95 documentation. What's more some NDB have 0.5 kHz channel spacing, so you'll need to set **Options/Preferences/Instruments** to allow the ADF to tune in 100 Hz increments. Similarly, some communication tower or ATIS frequencies have channel spacing set to 0.25 kHz, and you'll also need to set **Options/Preferences/Instruments** to allow your COM radio to tune in 25 kHz increments. For a complete and accurate listing of navaids, see the DAFIF listings in the appendices or on the CD-ROM.

There have been many reports that third-party scenery, such as Europe 1, has problems with conflicting navaids such that many ILS, DMEs, and other navaids are not present. You should download and install the patch file from Apollo to see if this resolves your problem with Europe 1, or alternatively you can create your own exclude files using Peter Dowson's utility SCUTILS on the book's accompanying CD-ROM. The exclude utilities allow you to remove certain areas from FSW95's scenery database, so that you can avoid conflicts with the default scenery.

N O T E

If you have trouble finding a given NDB, even though it is published in FSW95 documentation, try tuning in 0.1-kHz or 100-Hz increments up and down the scale on the frequency band. To do this, you'll first need to set **Options/Preferences/Instruments** to allow the ADF to tune in 100 Hz increments.

Another simple error that causes missing navaids is that many people forget to put their Flight Simulator CD-ROM into the CD-ROM drive before starting the program. When that happens, Flight Simulator starts up without the worldwide scenery and navaid listings available, which is another reason why you may not be able to find a given navaid, city, or airport you might have been looking for. Of course, this type of problem won't occur if you have installed all your scenery and CD-ROM booster files and cache directories on you hard drive (see earlier FAQ on how to do this), because then Flight Simulator will never use the CD-ROM again.

Have you checked to see if the FS95/98 CD-ROM was inserted in your CD-ROM drive? If you start FS95/98 without the CD-ROM inserted, the worldwide navaid and scenery won't be available.

N O T E

WHY ARE SOME OF THE ILS GLIDEPATHS NOT ALIGNED WITH THE RUNWAY?

Flight Simulator stores magnetic variation data in a special file called **MAGDEC.BGL**. However, magnetic variation changes from year to year because the Earth's magnetic poles are not fixed; rather they are moving several tens of kilometers each year. Because the data in **MAGDEC.BGL** reflects magnetic variation data that is several years old, the information it contains is obsolete with regard to published data that is updated yearly and which Microsoft used in FSW95's ILS Localizer headings. As a result, the updated ILS Localizers were mismatched with the old runway headings based on old magnetic variation tables. Thus, many of the "offset" ILS, meaning those approaches that are not straight-in but slightly off from the runway centerline, are pointing in a slightly different direction than the runway's magnetic heading. The amount of this error is the magnetic variation change that occurred since Microsoft last updated the **MAGDEC.BGL**. Fortunately, Microsoft has updated the **MAGDEC.BGL** in FS98, and the ILS glidepaths are now correctly aligned with the runways.

You may wonder why localizers are offset from the runways? The reason is simple: many approaches to airports have obstacles in the way. By slanting the ILS localizer to a slightly offset position, the aircraft can avoid the obstacles on the descent. One such extreme example of a purposely offset localizer would be that of Aalesund in Norway, which has an offset of almost 12°. In many cases, such extreme offsets can be due to mountains that would be otherwise in the glide path of the localizer if it were centered on the runway heading.

To patch these misaligned ILS's in FSW95, you should install the **ILS_FIX.ZIP** file that is on this book's CD-ROM. It contains 23 patched BGL scenery files to replace FSW95's default files. All told, these files correct 151 misaligned ILS's at 61 different airports. Don't use ILS_FIX.ZIP with FS98. It is unnecessary.

Also, at Heathrow Airport, some people have found that it's a good idea to switch off the Autopilot's Approach mode for ILS when you're about 1 mile from touchdown, and just glide in. If you leave the Autopilot on until touchdown, the plane can start yawing in the last half-mile or so, with subsequent loss of control of the aircraft.

How do I tune the ADF radio for a fractional frequency of 100s Hz?

Simple: go to **Options/Preferences/Instrument** and then select **100 Hz ADF Frequency Increment**. You'll find this tip especially handy when you fly over parts of the United Kingdom, where there are quite a few NDBs with fractional frequency components.

How do I tune the COM radio in 25 kHz increments, instead of 50 kHz increments?

As above, go to Options/Preferences/Instrument and then select 25 kHz COM Frequency Increment.

How can I turn off the Quick Tips on screen notes, which keep blocking my view of the instrument panel displays?

To turn off Quick Tips, go to **Options/Preferences/General** and then de-select **Show QuickTips**.

Why are some of the runways not aligned with their compass headings?

Because the Earth's magnetic poles wander from year to year, the magnetic compass heading of a runway can change. For example, Heathrow's main runways, which were named 28L and 28R when the airport was first built, were renamed 27L and 27R to account for the magnetic variation change.

Why am I having trouble with the ILS glide slope?

Many Flight Simulator pilots have wondered why it is that when they tune in an ILS on their NAV 1 radio, the Autopilot Approach mode flies them in the wrong direction, or their CDI needles show that a reverse approach is being flown? For example, when flying the approach into Heathrow's 9R runway with the NAV 1 radio tuned to 109.5 MHz and the Autopilot on, the airplane will turn 180° opposite to a course of 270°, away from the runway 9R, which is oriented to 90°! Why does this happen?

The reason is that in Flight Simulator, 27L, and 09R both share the same localizer frequency, and FS95/98 has no way of determining which end of the runway you intend to land. Only one runway is in use at any given time (both 27L and 09R are the same runway, they just are oriented 180° apart). So, by default, the program sets Localizer 1 to use the lower numbered runway heading, and Localizer 2 to use the higher numbered runway heading.

How do you defeat this automatic localizer runway selection so that you can land on the correct runway? Very simple: go to **Aircraft/Navigation** menu and open the Navigation dialog box. Then in the pull-down list boxes, select **Localizer 1** for a low number, or **Localizer 2** for a higher number.

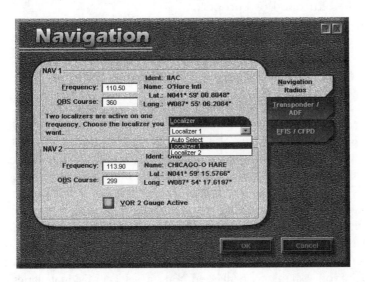

Figure A.12 *Select **Localizer 1** if you want to tune in an ILS approach that has a lower runway number than its reciprocal heading. Select **Localizer 2** if you want to tune in an ILS approach that has a higher number than its reciprocal heading. Choose **Auto** if you want Flight Simulator to automatically choose the runway number.*

WHY CAN'T I INSTALL MY COMMERCIAL SCENERY?

The most common problem is trying to install older FS5.1 scenery using the setup or installation program that comes with the scenery disk. You need to run the separate setup program found on the FSW95 CD-ROM to setup Microsoft Japan, Caribbean, Hawaii, or Scenery Pack I products with FSW95. Note that Microsoft Paris, New York, Hawaii, Caribbean and Japan scenery add-ons as well as BAO's Las Vegas, have been added to the core product of FS98. You don't need to add these scenery packages to FS98 because they are included with the base package and can be installed at setup. To access the airports, however, you may need to click on **6.0 Scenery and Before** in the Goto Airport dialog box. If your airplane is positioned awkwardly at any of these airport runways, you may need need to manually slew your aircraft to the correct airport runway location.As opposed to FS98, the older FSW95 program has only the Microsoft New York, Paris, and BAO Las Vegas, scenery packs included.

If you purchased BAO Europe I (now called Apollo Software's Europe 1) or Europe 2 before FSW95 shipped in November of 1996, you'll need to obtain a patch file for FSW95 from Apollo Software. The name of the file is **E1E2W952.EXE**, and you can download it from the Compuserve Flight Simulator Forum. You must run the patch program after you have installed Europe 1 or Europe 2.

For more detailed information, see Chapter 12 on managing your scenery, or read the scenery text help file on the Flight Simulator CD-ROM.

CAN I RUN FLIGHT SHOP CREATED ADVENTURES AND AIRCRAFT FOR FS 5.1 IN FSW95?

Yes, but you'll need to install **FSCONV.EXE** into your Flight Simulator for Windows 95 directory before **FSCONV.EXE** is a self-extracting, self-installing file that makes changes to the Flight Simulator program, and adds a new program called **AAFCONV.EXE** to allow you to convert Flight Shop created aircraft and adventures into a form useable by FSW95. Once you install **FSCONV.EXE,** you select from the Windows 95 Taskbar **Start/Programs/Microsoft/Games/Flight Shop Converter** to run the Flight Shop Converter program. Then you can click the **Options** button to open up the Options dialog box in which you will specify which directories Flight Simulator and your aircraft and adventures are stored. Then go back to the main screen, and select the **Aircraft** or **Adventure** button, and then choose the airplane or adventure you wish to have converted. You can select individual planes by clicking on just one, or click on several by holding down the Ctrl key. To select all, click the first file name, then hold down the **Shift** key and click on the last .AIR file in the list.

When **FSCONV.EXE** is run for the first time, it installs the actual converter program, as well as some additional files to FSW95's folders. It also modifies the **PANELSET.FS6** file, and installs **AAFCONV.EXE**, which is the program you access from the **Start/Programs/Microsoft/Games/Flight Shop Converter** menu.

Also, if you download FSW95 created aircraft, you don't need to run FSCONV.

Warning: FS 5.1 and Flight Shop–created aircraft do not fly well in FSW95

Due to the fact that the FS95 uses a higher fidelity aerodynamic model, it is not possible to convert FS5.1 and Flight Shop aircraft to have precise flight models without editing the .AIR files that Flight Simulator uses to store aerodynamic models. Thus, FS 5.1 aircraft will not fly with high fidelity as they would in FS 5.1. You can try tweaking some of the aerodynamic parameters using Chuck Dome's Airmod4, or David Maschino's ACEdit found on the included CD-ROM. However, even these programs do not fully allow you to change all the flight dynamics data that is found in the **.AIR** files.

How do I uninstall the original aircraft and Adventure Converter for FSW95?

Unfortunately, is not possible to automatically uninstall the original converter for FSW95 once Flight Simulator for Windows 95 or Flight Simulator 98 has been uninstalled. If you intend to uninstall either version of Flight Simulator, uninstall the converter first using the **Add/Remove Programs** control panel applet.

Hey, what happened to my instrument panel in FSW95? It's gone!

You must install **FSCONV.EXE** from this book's CD-ROM (Don't install this program if you are running FS98). This program modifies FSW95 so that it can run older Flight Shop–created aircraft, but not their former custom instrument panels. Instead **FSCONV.EXE** allows FSW95 to substitute one of the generic instrument panels already found in FSW95.

Without **FSCONV.EXE**, you will be able to see your airplane visually, but you will not have any visible instrument panel.

Why is it that some airports disappear when I install certain scenery packages?

You have conflicts between adjacent BGL scenery files that share the same area. Some scenery designers are careful to include exclude files that prevent clashes between the default Microsoft scenery areas that use the same area coordinates. Other designers are not so careful. What's more, third party designers have no way of knowing if their scenery will conflict with another person's scenery, so you may have incompatibilities that were not intentional even if the scenery designers were careful. If you want to bring back the airports that are missing, you need to turn off the third party scenery that is causing the conflict. If you enjoy tinkering with scenery files, it is possible for you to create your own exclude files; see Peter Dowson's Exclude file documentation on the book's CD-ROM.

FSW95 missing ILS problems

In many cases, you can eliminate the problem of missing ILS and ATIS messages by running the **FEPAT.EXE** program (available on this book's CD-ROM).

How do I take a screen shot?

Press the **Print Screen** key on your keyboard, then switch to Microsoft Paint or any other graphics program, and select **Edit/Paste** (or **Ctrl V** on your keyboard). This will paste a screen dump of your window into your graphics program, where you can then crop, resize, and then print out the screen shot. Note that in FS 5.1 the **Print Screen** key was used for resetting your situation; now to reset your situation you press **Ctrl-;** .

Taking a Screen Shot of an Active Window

If you want to just take a picture of an active window, not your whole screen, press **Alt Print Screen**. Then switch to your graphics program and select **Edit/Paste** (or **Ctrl V**) to paste your window graphic.

I'm getting the dreaded KERNEL32.DLL error message and can't get Flight Simulator to start. What do I do?

This error message is usually attributable to incompatibilities with existing third-party scenery software you have installed and Microsoft scenery. Sometimes it also means that your **WORLD.VIS** file in your Flight Simulator directory is corrupted. Therefore, as a precaution, before installing new scenery you should make a backup of **WORLD.VIS**. To do this, right-click on this file in the Windows Explorer and click **Copy** on the pop-up menu.

Note that FS98 incorporates new code that corrects the exclude file problem that sometimes contributed to the **KERNEL32.DLL** page faults when FSW95 was used with some third-party scenery packages. Therefore, you should not experience this error in FS98. However, if you do have this problem, read on to learn how to take corrective action.

Before installing any scenery, always make sure you make a copy of your **WORLD.VIS** file in your Flight Simulator directory.

N O T E

How do you get rid of this problem once you have it? You can take several approaches, depending on the severity of the problem:

1. Try Restarting Flight Simulator without the CD-ROM in your CD-ROM drive. If the program starts up normally, you can then go into the Scenery manager and remove the offending scenery.
2. Or, Rename the directories where you have your third-party scenery installed. This will disable the scenery when you try to restart Flight Simulator, thereby

eliminating the **kernel32.dll** error message. Then, one by one, rename each scenery directory back to its original name, and restart the program each time you do this. When you finally get the **Kernel32.dll** error message, you will have isolated which scenery is causing the offense, and can then remove it permanently.

So for example, if after installing the Southern California Scenery Expansion Pack, you find that FSW95 won't launch, rename your **SoCal** directory to something else in the Windows Explorer, then restart FSW95. Then you can go into the Scenery Manager and disable your add-on scenery files, one by one, until you find the one that is conflicting with Southern California.

3. If you suspect your **WORLD.VIS** file has been corrupted, rename your backup copy of **WORLD.VIS** file and overwrite the existing **WORLD.VIS**. Then restart FSW95.

4. As a last resort, if all else fails, you can reinstall Flight Simulator.

My FSW95 737 keeps running out of fuel, and I still have fuel as shown on my fuel gauge.

Unfortunately, in FSW95, the left and right auxiliary tanks when emptied, do not automatically shift the fuel supply to the center tanks in the 737. Thus when you empty these fuel tanks, the 737 will flame out as it runs out of fuel. You'll have to restart the engines, and at that point the fuel supply will properly be fed from the centerline tanks. This problem has been fixed in FS98.

For your plane to run out fuel, you must activate the **Engine Stops When Out of Fuel** button under the **Aircraft: Realism & Reliability: Realism** menu.

To have your plane run out of fuel, you must activate **Engine Stops When Out of Fuel** under the **Aircraft: Realism & Reliability: Realism** menu.

TIP

I can't seem to open any of the dialog boxes in FS98.

Some poorly behaved installers for other applications overwrite system files needed by Flight Simulator with older versions. If this happens to you, you will need to copy the files **MSVCRT.DLL** and **MFC42.DLL** from your Flight Simulator CD's **FS98** directory to your **Windows\SYSTEM** directory (SYSTEM32 on NT 4.0.) You may need to close all of your applications or restart your computer in order to be able to copy these files in some cases.

THE NUMERIC KEYPADS SWITCH THE VIEWS INSTEAD OF CONTROLLING THE AIRPLANE.

For the numeric keypad keys to control the aircraft, you should switch **NumLock** off (see next FAQ section regarding map view).

WHY DOESN'T THE NUMLOCK KEY BRING UP A MAP VIEW?

FS98 now treats the **NumLock** key as a real **NumLock** key, that is, when you press **NumLock**, it locks the numeric keypad so that either number keys are pressed or cursor arrows are activated. To bring up the map view in FS98, you now press **Shift+** and to close it, you press].

I SEE A COM2 RADIO IN THE CESSNA'S RADIO STACK. WHY CAN'T I USE IT?

FS98 currently supports only a single COM radio.

I'VE CHANGED MY CD-ROM DRIVE LETTER. HOW DO I GET FS98 TO READ SCENERY OFF THE CD AGAIN OR RUN THE SETUP PROGRAM?

If for some reason you change the CD-ROM drive letter(e.g., when you add a second hard drive to your system) FS98 will not know how to access scenery off the CD-ROM or be able to run setup again. You will get error messages messages about CD-ROM performance boosters when you start Flight Simulator.

You will also see an error message if you try to run Flight Simulator setup from the Add/Remove Programs dialog box in the Windows Control Panel. These errors occur because Flight Simulator uses the letter originally assigned to the CD-ROM drive.

You can fix the scenery access problem from within FS98, but you can't solve the setup program problem without reinstalling the program from the new CD-ROM drive.

Here's how to edit your scenery performance boosters (which cache CD-ROM scenery on to your hard disk on an as needed basis) so that they know what the letter of your CD-ROM drive is:

1. Select **World: Scenery Library**.
2. Click the **Performance** button.
3. In the Performance Boosters dialog box, select the first scenery area in the list of performance boosters and click **Edit**.
4. In Source Path, type the new CD-ROM drive letter and click **OK**.
5. Repeat steps 3 and 4 for each scenery area in the performance boosters list.
6. Click **Restart** and any **OK** buttons to return to the simulation.

Unfortunately, if you change your CD-ROM drive and want to run setup again, you must once again rerun the entire setup from the new CD-ROM drive. You can't fix the problem from the Control Panel or by editing an INI file on your hard disk.

HARDWARE PROBLEMS WITH FS98

This section describes some minor problems related to specific video drivers and other hardware.

The Univbe video driver doesn't allow DirectX 5.0 to work correctly.

You'll have to disable the line in **AUTOEXEC.BAT** that calls Univbe, then reboot your machine to correct this problem. To do this:

1. In Windows Notepad, open your **AUTOEXEC.BAT** file
2. Look for the line that contains UNIVBE.
3. Insert REM to the beginning of the line to disable the driver. The edited line should look like this:

   REM UNIVBE

4. Reboot your system.

To reinstall the Univbe video driver again, remove the REM statement before UNIVBE from the **AUTOEXEC.BAT** file, then reboot your system.

An error message appears that says, "A required .DLL file, DDRAW.DLL, was not found."

If you get this error message, you'll need to reinstall DirectX. To do so:

1. Insert your Flight Simulator CD-ROM in your drive.
2. In the Windows Explorer, select your CD-ROM drive.
3. Double-click the **DirectX** folder, which is inside the Setup folder.
4. Double-click the file **DXSETUP.EXE** to run the DirectX setup program
5. Click **ReInstall DirectX**.

I can't play videos in Windows NT 4.0.

You must have administrator privileges on your system to correctly install Microsoft Flight Simulator on a computer running Windows NT 4.0. Log on as the Administrator or talk to your system administrator to change your permissions. Then run Indeo setup from the CD- ROM. The Indeo **Setup.exe** file is located in the **\Indeo** subdirectory.

FS98 CONVERTER QUESTIONS

BAO Flight Shop–created aircraft that have been converted with the original converter for FSW95 are not compatible with Microsoft Flight Simulator 98. Converted adventures will continue to work properly.

By the time you read this, an updated aircraft and adventure converter should be available through on-line services and at the Microsoft Flight Simulator web page at www.microsoft.com/games/fsim.

IMPROVING FS98 PERFORMANCE

You can improve system performance by reducing the number of open programs that are running in the background. If you have a spreadsheet crunching numbers, a Web browser downloading a Web page, or some other application doing something, it will detract from overall system performance.

If, despite your best efforts, it seems like something is still running in the background and hogging CPU time, you can see which tasks are ongoing at any time by opening the task manager (press **Ctrl+Alt+Del** *once;* if you do it more than once you will reboot your machine!). If background processes exist, they can be terminated, which may result in a potentially significant gain in frame rate of 10% to 20%. Be very careful about using the task manager because you can lose important data if you inadvertently shut down something important.

WHAT ABOUT MY MICROSOFT SCENERY ADD-ONS?

If you own Microsoft New York, Paris, Japan, Caribbean, Hawaii, or the BAO Las Vegas add-on scenery, you don't need to install those scenery add-ons. Those products are now included in Microsoft Flight Simulator 98, and they're installed when you run setup. You may be confused about whether the Microsoft Southern California Scenery Expansion Pack I is included in FS98. It is not. However, Santa Catalina Island from the Expansion Pack *is* included with FS98.

HOW DO I ACCESS THE AIRPORTS IN MY MICROSOFT SOUTHERN CALIFORNIA SCENERY EXPANSION PACK I?

If you own the Microsoft Southern California Expansion Pack, you should be able to be install it with no problems. However, to access these airports, it is necessary to click the **6.0 Scenery and Before** button in the Go To Airport dialog box. If you use the standard entries for these airports, you may find yourself positioned incorrectly rather than at the end of the runway where you want to be.

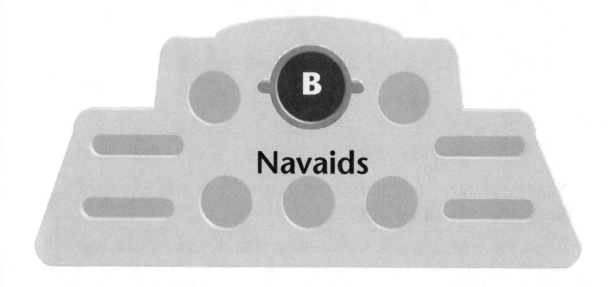

Navaids

This appendix lists the entire world's navaids as derived from the Digital Aeronautical Flight Information File (DAFIF). All the navaids, both VOR and NDB, are alphabetized by region, country, and then by name. The U.S. and Canadaian navaids are further organized by state and province.

Table B.1 lists the 13 regions.

Table B.1 *Worldwide Navaids by Region*

REGION	TOTAL NAVAIDS
USA/Canada	3,455
Africa	1,175
Antarctica	8
Asia	627
Central America/Caribbean Ocean	293
Europe	2,128
Greenland	31
Indonesia/Malaysia	208
Indian Sub-Continent and Indian Ocean	360
Middle East	385

Table B.1 continued

REGION	TOTAL NAVAIDS
Pacific Ocean	723
South America	925
Southeast Asia	234
TOTAL NAVAIDS	10,552

SEARCHING AND FILTERING THE NAVAIDS IN THE EXCEL97 SPREADSHEET ON THE CD

Using the Excel 97 spreadsheet that is on the CD included with this book, you can quickly search the entire database for a particular name, location, navaid identifier, and even sort and filter any or all of the navaids by criteria that you specify. Of course, to do this, you must have purchased and installed Microsoft Office 97 or Excel 97. The spreadsheet is a workbook includes many worksheets that contain the world's navaids sorted by region. For example, the worksheet called **USA/Canada** has only those navaids for the United States and Canada. There are 12 other worksheets for the other regions of the world and one worksheet that contain a master listing of all the navaids combined. You can see which countries are in a given region by examining Tables B.2, B.3, and B.4, in which all the countries are listed by region.

As an example, let's use the advanced capabilities of the spreadsheet to filter out navaids for a particular region. In the example that follows, you will print out a list of only the NDB navaids for California:

1. Open up the Excel97 spreadsheet **Appendix B Navaids** on the CD-ROM.
2. After the spreadsheet opens, you'll see a bunch of tabs for each region's navaids displayed at the bottom of the screen. Click the lower-left corner arrow buttons until you see the All Navaids tab slide into view. This tab contains all 10,552 navaids for all of the regions. Click the tab to see an alphabetical listing of all the world's navaids, sorted by country, state/province, and name.
3. At the top of each column heading, you'll see a little arrow button. This is the filter control. Click on the arrow for **State/Province** and a drop-down list box will appear with all the states and provinces for the United States and Canada.
4. Select **California.** After you do this, Excel will display only those navaid records that contain the word *California* in them.
5. Click the filter arrow button for the column heading Type, and in the list box, select **NDB**. Excel will now apply a second filter so that now all you see are the NDB navaids for California.

Now you can go to the **File: Print** or **File: Print Preview** menu and print the filtered navaids. You will have to play around with the **File: Page Setup** in order to output the worksheet in just the way you like it, but that should be easy for you to figure out on your own. Also, if you want to hide certain columns, such as the empty columns next to countries and states, just drag the column header edges until the column disappears. Then when you print, you'll see only those columns.

If you look closely at the filter arrows in Excel, you'll notice that when you apply a filter, the arrow turns blue. This is helpful when you have multiple filters applied at the same time and you can't remember which columns have the filters applied.

T I P

To do a quick search of the entire navaid database, open the spreadsheet and select the **All Navaids** tab. When the All Navaids worksheet opens, select **Edit: Find** (or press **Ctrl+F**), then enter the text you want to search for. Excel is blindingly fast, and it will find each occurrence of your search text in seconds. For example, suppose you want to find the Navaid frequency for Oakland. You don't want to have to hunt for it in the listings, so you fire up Excel, open the All Navaids worksheet inside the Appendix B Navaids Excel database, and then press **Ctrl+F**. In the dialog box that opens, type in *Oakland* . In a flash, you'll see that Excel will stop at the first occurrence that it finds of Oakland. Right next to the listing, you'll see the Frequency and latitude/longitude coordinates displayed.

Now how's that for convenience?

USING THE NAVAID LISTINGS

For the benefit of those readers who may want to look up listings in the book, you'll find that the navaids have been sorted into countries within regions. To find a particular country within a region, look it up in one of the tables that follow.

Table B.2 *Countries of the World Listed by Region (For Excel Spreadsheet and Navaid Listings in Book)*

UNITED STATES	CANADA	AFRICA	ANTARCTICA	ASIA
Alabama	Alberta	Algeria	Antarctica	Afghanistan
Alaska	British Columbia	Angola		Armenia
Arizona	Manitoba	Benin		Azerbaijan
Arkansas	New Brunswick	Botswana		China
California	Newfoundland	Burkina		Georgia
Colorado	Northwest	Burundi		Hong Kong

Table B.2 *continued*

UNITED STATES	CANADA	AFRICA	ANTARCTICA	ASIA
	Territories			
Connecticut	Nova Scotia	Cameroon		Japan
Delaware	Ontario	Cape Verde		Kazakhstan
District Of Columbia	Prince Edward Island	Central Africa		Korea, Republic of
Florida	Quebec	Chad		Kyrgyzstan
Georgia	Saskatchewan	Comoros		Macau
Hawaii	Yukon	Congo		Mongolia
Idaho		Djibouti		Taiwan
Illinois		Equatorial Guinea		Tajikistan
Indiana		Eritrea		Turkmenistan
Iowa		Ethiopia		Uzbekistan
Kansas		Europa Island		
Kentucky		Gabon		
Louisiana		Gambia, The		
Maine		Ghana		
Maryland		Glorioso Islands		
Massachusetts		Guinea		
Michigan		Guinea-Bissau		
Minnesota		Ivory Coast		
Mississippi		Juan De Nova Island		
Missouri		Kenya		
Montana		Lesotho		
Nebraska		Liberia		
Nevada		Libya		
New Hampshire		Madagascar		
New Jersey		Malawi		
New Mexico		Mali		
New York		Mauritania		
North Carolina		Mayotte		
North Dakota		Morocco		
Ohio		Mozambique		
Oklahoma		Namibia		
Oregon		Niger		

Table B.2 *continued*

UNITED STATES	CANADA	AFRICA	ANTARCTICA	ASIA
Pennsylvania		Nigeria		
Rhode Island		Rwanda		
South Carolina		Sao Tome & Principe		
South Dakota		Senegal		
Tennessee		Sierra Leone		
Texas		Somalia		
Utah		South África		
Vermont		St. Helena		
Virginia		Sudan		
Washington		Swaziland		
West Virginia		Tanzania, United Rep.of		
Wisconsin		Togo		
Wyoming		Tunisia		
		Uganda		
		Western Sahara		
		Yemen		

Table B.3 *Countries of the World Listed by Region (continued)*

CENTRAL AMERICA	EUROPE	GREENLAND	INDIA SUB-CONTINENT AND INDIAN OCEAN REGION	INDONESIA/ MALAYSIA
Anguilla	Albania	Greenland	Bangladesh	Brunei
Antigua & Barbuda	Austria		British Indian Ocean Terr.	Christmas Island
Aruba	Belarus		India	Cocos (Keeling) Island (Australia)
Bahamas, The	Belgium		Maldives	Indonesia
Barbados	Bosnia & Herzegovia		Mauritius	Malaysia
Belize	Bulgaria		Nepal	Singapore
Bermuda	Croatia		Pakistan	

Table B.3 *continued*

Central America	Europe	Greenland	India Sub-Continent and Indian Ocean Region	Indonesia/ Malaysia
British Virgin Islands	Czech Republic		Reunion	
Cayman Islands	Denmark		Seychelles	
Costa Rica	Estonia		Sri Lanka	
Cuba	Faroe Islands			Tromelin Island
Dominica	Finland			
Dominican Republic	France			
El Salvador	Germany			
Grenada	Greece			
Guadeloupe	Guernsey			
Guatemala	Hungry			
Haiti	Iceland			
Honduras	Ireland			
Jamaica	Italy			
Martinique	Jan Mayen			
Mexico	Jersey			
Nicaragua	Latvia			
Panama	Lithuania			
Puerto Rico	Luxembourg			
St. Pierre & Miqueion	Macedonia			
St. Christopher & Nevis	Malta			
St. Lucia	Man, Isle of			
St. Vincent & Grenadines	Moldova			
Trinidad & Tobago	Montenegro			
Turks & Caicos Islands	Netherlands			
Virgin Islands	Norway			
	Poland			

Table B.3 *continued*

CENTRAL AMERICA	EUROPE	GREENLAND	INDIA SUB-CONTINENT AND INDIAN OCEAN REGION	INDONESIA/ MALAYSIA
	Portugal			
	Romania			
	Russia			
	Serbia			
	Slovakia Republic			
	Slovenia			
	Spain			
	Svalbard			
	Sweden			
	Switzerland			
	Ukraine			
	United Kingdom			

Table B.4 *Countries of the World Listed by Region (continued)*

MIDDLE EAST	PACIFIC OCEAN REGION	SOUTH AMERICA	SOUTHEAST ASIA
Bahrain	American Somoa	Argentina	Burma
Cyprus (Formerly Kampuchea)	Australia	Bolivia	Cambodia
Egypt	Cook Islands	Brazil	Laos
Iran	Federated States of Micronesia	Chile	Philippines
Iraq	Fiji	Colombia	Thailand
Israel	French Polynesia	Ecuador	Vietnam
Jordan	Guam	French Guiana	
Kuwait	Johnston Atoll	Guyana	
Lebanon	Kiribati	Paraguay	
Oman	Marshall Islands, Rep.of	Peru	
Qatar	Midway Islands	Suriname	
Saudi Arabia	Nauru	Uruguay	

Table B.4 *Continued*

MIDDLE EAST	PACIFIC OCEAN REGION	SOUTH AMERICA	SOUTHEAST ASIA
Syria	New Caledonia	Venezuela	
Turkey	New Zealand		
United Arab Emirates	Niue		
	Norfolk Island		
	Northern Mariana Islands		
	Papua New Guinea		
	Republic of Palau		
	Solomon Island		
	Tokelau		
	Tonga		
	Tuvalu		
	Vanuatu		
	Wake Island		
	Wallis & Futuna		
	Western Samoa		

EXPLANATION OF NAVAID TYPES

In the navaid listings, you'll find the following types of navaids:

NAVAID TYPE	DESCRIPTION
DME	Distance Measuring Equipment
NDB	Nondirectional radio beacon
NDB-DME	NDB with DME
TACAN	Tactical Air Navigation
VOR	VHF Omni-Directional Range
VOR-DME	VOR plus DME
VORTAC	VOR plus TACAN

TACAN, or Tactical Air Navigation, is used by the military for special operations that require unusual siting conditions that take into account the pitching and rolling of naval vessels, etc. Although the principles, theory, and operation of TACAN facilities are quite different from those of VOR-DME, the end results are the same: a pilot using a VOR-DME or a TACAN will get the same results. A VORTAC facility is one which has a combined VOR and TACAN transmitter. The other navaid types, DME and NDB have been covered in earlier chapters.

WARNING

Because Navigation data is updated at 28 day intervals, none of the data in this book is valid for real navigational purposes. Do not use any of this data for real navigation!

COPYRIGHT, WARRANTY, AND INDEMNITY INFORMATION

We are required by law to provide the following copyright, warranty and indemnity information.

This product was developed using DAFIFR, a product of the National Imagery and Mapping Agency.

The navaids, airports, and .BGL files that are listed in Nick Dargahi's *The Ultimate Flight Simulator Handbook,* both in the book and on the CD-ROM, are derived from the Digital Aeronautical Flight Information File, a product of the National Imagery and Mapping Agency (NIMA) of the United States Department of Defense.

Although these navaid, airport and .BGL listings are derived from the DAFIF, the data has been specially prepared and formatted such that it no longer retains the same organizational layout as the original DAFIF data files. Therefore, Nick Dargahi, author and creator of these newly formatted digital and printed files, claims copyright on the files as distributed herein.

It is expressly forbidden to redistribute or transmit any of the navigational data , airport data, or scenery .BGL files over the Internet, World Wide Web, e-mail, floppy disk, CD-ROM, or any other transmission method now known, or to be known.

The navigational data found in these files is extremely time sensitive and most be updated every 28 days. In addition, other errors exist in the database that render it unsuitable for real world navigation.

It is expressly forbidden to use any of the data in this book or on the cd for navigation wherein lives or property are at risk.

This product has not been endorsed or otherwise approved by the National Imagery and Mapping Agency, or the United States Department of Defense (10 U.S.C. o 445)

NIMA requires that we post this disclaimer with regard to DAFIF derived data:

a. Under 10 U.S.C. o 456, no civil action may be brought against the United States on the basis of the content of a navigational aid prepared or disseminated by either the former Defense Mapping Agency (DMA) or the National Imagery and Mapping Agency (NIMA).

b. The DAFIFR product is provided "as is," and no warranty, express or implied, including but not limited to the implied warranties of merchantability and fitness for particular purpose or arising by statute or otherwise in law or from a course of dealing or usage in trade, is made by NIMA as to the accuracy and functioning of the product.

c. Neither NIMA nor its personnel will be liable for any claims, losses, or damages arising from or connected with the use of this product. The user agrees to hold harmless the United States National Imagery and Mapping Agency. The user s sole and exclusive remedy is to stop using the DAFIFR product.

DAFIF is a registered trademark of the National Imagery and Mapping Agency.

WARNING

Dated material. do not use for real navigation; use only with Flight Simulator!

Airport Directory and Selected Instrument Approach Plates

Harbor, n. A place where ships taking shelter
from storms are exposed to the fury of customs.

Ambrose Bierce (1842–1914). *Devil's Dictionary,* 1906

This appendix describes the contents of the Airport listings found in the **\DAFIF Airports & Navaids Excel Listings** folder and the **\Airport IAP Charts** folder on the accompanying CD-ROM. Most of the FS98 airports are listed in the **Appendix C Airports.XLS** Excel 97 file and can be viewed and printed out using the included Excel 97 Viewer on the book's CD-ROM (assuming you don't already have Excel 97 or Office 97 installed). Due to space considerations, it was not possible to list all the airports in this appendix, however this will not be a problem for you since you can print out the entire listing, or only a partial listing, according to your wishes.

WARNING

Important Note: The Excel database should only take about 23 pages to print out, not the 207 pages that Print Preview states is necessary. Therefore, do not print **All** the pages when you select **File/Print** or **File/Print Preview**, else you will needlessly waste reams of paper.

Because flying around the world with jets requires instrument approach procedures, we also include 100 IAP charts of the major cities of the world scanned in from the real U.S. Government Flight Information Publications. These IAP charts are found in the

Airport IAP Charts folder on the CD-ROM, but you will need to use the Acrobat 3.0 Reader (also on the CD-ROM) to view and print them out.

In FSW95, there were approximately 830 airports and runways, including 556 ILS and 275 ATIS listings in the default scenery. FS98 now includes Microsoft Japan, Caribbean, and Hawaii add-on scenery, and with the addition of all the minor airports in the U.S.A., you will find close to 3000 airports and helipads, complete with ILS. This is a huge improvement over FSW95 and FS5.1.

Many of the airports are short airstrips or small municipal airports in the USA. Because we include the DAFIF worldwide airport Excel file with its database listing of 9,406 airports (see **DAFIF Worldwide Airports.XLS** on the CD-ROM), we list only the principal FS98 airports in the **Appendix C Airports.XLS** file. However, the **Appendix C Airports** file also contains a listing of the commercial add-on scenery airports, which is useful in determining whether a particular add-on scenery package contains an airport you may want to add.

Airports in the following scenery areas are covered:

- Flight Simulator 98's Default CD-ROM Scenery for the World
- Microsoft Expansion Pack: Southern California (only Catalina Island is included in FS98)
- Microsoft Hawaii (included in FS98)
- Microsoft Japan (included in FS98)
- Microsoft Caribbean (included in FS98)
- Apollo's Europe I & Europe II
- Apollo's Azores & Madeira
- Lago's Scenery Venezia
- Lago's Scenery Tokyo
- Wizard Works Scenery Hong Kong (note that Hong Kong now comes with FS98, although the Wizard Works Scenery package is a separate add-on)
- Wizard Works Scenery Madrid
- Wizard Works Scenery England & Wales
- Africa (Terblanche Jordaan)
- India (Johann Cranenburgh and Francis Wouterlood)
* Alaska (Dean Salman)

Because there are so many airports, it was not feasible to include instrument approach procedure charts for each and every airport. Instead, if you need to find a particular IAP chart, you should consult the Airport IAP Charts index listing in this Appendix to see if it is on the CD-ROM. If it is not, then you should install George Lorsche's Final

Approach from the book's CD. This program contains zip files for over 3,000 IAPs for airports around the world. Since Final Approach is a commercial program, you will need to register the program before it will allow you to print your IAPs. Even without purchasing the program, however, you can still view many of the world's IAPs and have fun seeing how a particular airport's approach procedures work.

AFRICAN AIRPORTS

The African airports were created by Terblanche Jordaan. To use these airports, you'll have to install the scenery BGLs and copy the texture files from the CD-ROM using the techniques described in earlier chapters. These scenery files include the airports as well as some ILS, ATIS, African navaids, and related airport scenery. With the addition of Jordaan's 40 new African airports, you'll be able to fly and refuel your aircraft while traversing the continent of Africa. If you intend to use navaids while flying over Africa and you have installed the DAFIF worldwide navaids from the book's CD-ROM, you needn't install the African navaid BGLs that are found in Jordaan's BGL files, because there are duplicate entries for VORs and NDBs. All the African airports in this add-on are listed separately in the add-ons section of the **Appendix C Airports.XLS** file.

INDIAN AIRPORTS

Francis Wouterlood and Johann Cranenburgh created the Indian airport add-on scenery that is included on the book's CD-ROM. There are 6 airports in Pakistan, 1 airport in Kathmandu-Nepal, and 28 in India. To use the Indian navaids, you should install the worldwide navaids found on the book's CD-ROM. All the add-on India-region airports are listed separately in the add-ons section of the **Appendix C Airports.XLS** file.

ALASKAN AIRPORTS

Dean Salman's Alaska add-on scenery airports include 8 of Alaska's main airports as well as 37 smaller ones scattered around the state. To use these airports, you must install the Alaska scenery from the book's CD-ROM. All the add-on Alaska airports are listed separately in the add-ons section of the **Appendix C Airports.XLS** file.

DAFIF Airport Listings on CD-ROM

We are pleased to include on the CD-ROM the Defense Mapping Agency's DAFIF in Microsoft Excel 95/97 format. This is the first time this massive database has been released to the public, and obtaining it was not easy!

The Excel 97 Viewer will allow you to open, view, AutoFilter, and print the **DAFIF Worldwide Airports.XLS** database file. Excel Viewer will not allow you to edit an open document, nor will it allow you to drag and drop any Excel document, although it supports copying and pasting to the Clipboard.

NOTE

To take full advantage of the DAFIF on CD-ROM, you must have Microsoft Excel 97. If you don't, you should install Microsoft Excel Viewer 7.0 from the book's CD-ROM before using the DAFIF.

WARNING

The **DAFIF Worldwide Airports.XLS** database file is massive (14 MB), and will take up to 7 minutes or longer to load if you are using a 4× CD-ROM player. If you are bothered by this, and think you will be frequently using the DAFIF, I suggest you copy the entire file to your hard disk for faster access.

With its master listing of 9,406 worldwide airports, the DAFIF is unsurpassed as a rich archive of airport data, which you can put to good use when designing new airports with the Airport Scenery Design program on this book's CD-ROM. The DAFIF contains the following information for each airport record:

- Country
- Airport Name
- Latitude
- Airport elevation

- Magnetic variation

- State
- International Civil Aviation Organization Identifier
- Longitude
- Airport type (A = civil, B = joint civil and military, C = active military, D = active airports having runways less than the minimum required for A, B, and C above)
- Presence of rotating light beacon (Yes or No)

- Runway high end identifier (e.g., "20L," "2," "10R")
- Runway high magnetic heading
- Runway low magnetic heading
- Runway low identifier ("2R," "200," "290L")
- Runway length
- Runway width
- Runway surface type (asphalt, concrete, dirt, grass, gravel, and so on.)

- Runway high end latitude
- Runway high end longitude
- Runway high end slope
- Runway high end displaced threshold
- Runway high end lighting system 1
- Runway high end lighting system 5
- Runway high end lighting system 2
- Runway high end lighting system 6
- Runway high end lighting system 3
- Runway high end lighting system 7
- Runway high end lighting system 4
- Runway high end lighting system 8
- Runway low end latitude
- Runway low end longitude
- Runway low end slope
- Runway low end displaced threshold
- Runway low end lighting system 1
- Runway low end lighting system 5
- Runway low end lighting system 2
- Runway low end lighting system 6
- Runway low end lighting system 3
- Runway low end lighting system 7
- Runway low end lighting system 4
- Runway low end lighting system 8

Unfortunately, in this edition of the DAFIF there are no ILS records, though there are airport communication facility listings and there are colocated navaid listings. This means that if you want to find out the ILS frequency for a particular airport runway and it is not listed on the CD-ROM, you will have to look elsewhere. There are two sources of ILS information:

1. Install George Lorsche's Flight Planner software from the book's CD-ROM, and open the included 3,000 IAP files for worldwide airports. There you will find listings for ILS runways, frequencies, and so on for most of the world's major airports.
2. See the Bibliography for a listing of IAP publications that are available from the U.S. Defense Mapping Agency.

The data records for each airport include runway lighting information, runway magnetic headings, magnetic variation, and latitude/longitude points for the beginnings and ends of runways. As many as eight lighting systems can be recorded in the DAFIF for each runway end, although not all of them are used.

Filtering Airports for Viewing in the DAFIF on the CD-ROM

Because many airports have multiple runways, the DAFIF contains 13,635 runway records for the 9,406 airports listed. With such a massive amount of information, you need a way of filtering or searching to ferret out the data you are looking for. There is no point in displaying all 13,635 records when you are interested in a few airports for a particular region. Fortunately, Excel 97's built-in spreadsheet database functions give us the capability to filter records through the **AutoFilter** command, sort records with the **Sort** command, and find records with the **Find** command.

Let's first look at how the DAFIF Airport Database is organized. As shown in Figure C.1, there are field columns for country, state, airport name, DAFIF identifier, country code, ICAO identifier (International Civil Aviation Administration Code), and FAA identifier (tells you whether the FAA has an identifier for this airport), and just off the right edge of the screen you can see the airport latitude column. Other field columns can be seen if you scroll the screen to the right. Only 29 records (i.e., rows) appear on-screen if you don't count the header row. Note that two rows are devoted to the

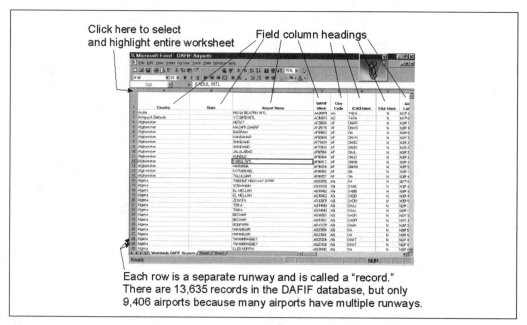

Figure C.1 The DAFIF Airport Database on the CD-ROM. This view shows the spreadsheet zoomed out 75% so that more of the spreadsheet can be seen on-screen.

Shindand Airport in Afghanistan; this tells you that Shindand Airport has two runways because each row corresponds to one runway. If you scroll down, you will see more airport entries for other countries. The entire database has been sorted by the DAFIF identifier (i.e., the DAFIF Ident. column), so airports are listed alphabetically first by country, and then by DAFIF airport number. If you don't like this sorting, you are free to sort by any other field.

Let's see how filtering the database might help us. Suppose you were low on fuel flying the Learjet over California and you wanted to display all the airports in California that have runways longer than 5,000 ft. The DAFIF file is organized to allow you to quickly filter airports by country, state, or any criteria of your choice. Because you are interested in displaying only California runways that are more than 5,000 ft long, you need to apply one filter to the State field column so that only California is displayed and a second filter to the runway field column so that only runways longer than 5,000 ft are displayed. To apply these filters, follow these steps:

1. Open the Excel DAFIF Airport Database that is on the book's CD-ROM. This may take up to seven minutes if you have a slow 4× CD-ROM drive.
2. Select the entire worksheet by clicking on the button left of the Column A button and on top of the Row 1 button, as illustrated in Figure C.1. The whole worksheet will appear black. This step is necessary because you want to apply filters to off-screen field column headings and not just to the ones visible now.
3. In Excel 97, select **Data/Filter/AutoFilter.** Little filter arrow buttons will appear at the top of each field column after you have turned AutoFilter on, as illustrated in Figure C.2.
4. Click anywhere in the spreadsheet to remove the black indication from the spreadsheet.
5. Click the arrow button located in the State field column heading at the top of the spreadsheet. A list of states will appear in a pop-up menu.
6. Select **California** from the pop-up menu that appeared in Step 5, as shown in Figure C.2. Only the airports in California should now be displayed in the spreadsheet.

Now that you have displayed the California airports, it is time to refine the filter further to limit them to those with runways exceeding 5,000 ft. Follow these steps:

1. Scroll the spreadsheet to the right until you see the field column heading for Runway Length.
2. Click the **Filter** button in the Runway Length field column heading. A filter menu will pop up.

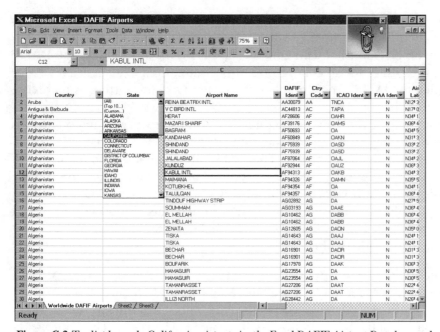

Figure C.2 To display only California airports in the Excel DAFIF Airport Database, select **Data/Filter/AutoFilter**, click the arrow button located in the State field column, and then select **California** as the filter criterion.

3. Select **Custom** from the pop-up menu, and the Custom Filter dialog box will appear.
4. Select **is greater than or equal to** in the Runway Length list box of the Custom Filter dialog box (Figure C.3).
5. Type **5000** in the box to the right of the Runway Length list box and then click **OK**. This will force Excel to display only runways that are greater than or equal to 5,000 ft in length (see Figure C.4).

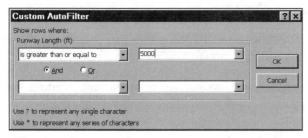

Figure C.3 Apply a custom filter criterion for runways greater than or equal to 5,000 ft.

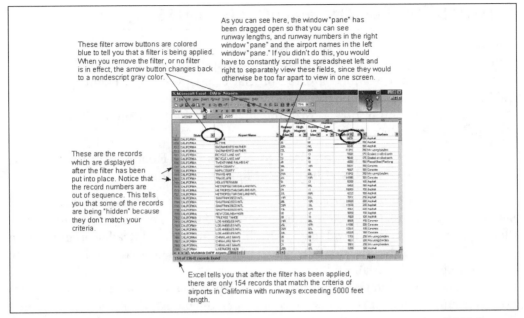

These filter arrow buttons are colored blue to tell you that a filter is being applied. When you remove the filter, or no filter is in effect, the arrow button changes back to a nondescript gray color.

As you can see here, the window "pane" has been dragged open so that you can see runway lengths, and runway numbers in the right window "pane" and the airport names in the left window "pane." If you didn't do this, you would have to constantly scroll the spreadsheet left and right to separately view these fields, since they would otherwise be too far apart to view in one screen.

These are the records which are displayed after the filter has been put into place. Notice that the record numbers are out of sequence. This tells you that some of the records are being "hidden" because they don't match your criteria.

Excel tells you that after the filter has been applied, there are only 154 records that match the criteria of airports in California with runways exceeding 5000 feet length.

Figure C.4 *The filter has been applied. Only California airports with runways longer than 5,000 ft are displayed.*

Congratulations—you've just learned how to use one of Excel's most powerful features. If you read the Excel documentation on using AutoFilter, you can learn to apply even more complex filter criteria. For now, let's remove the filter so that we can learn how to use the Find command. To remove the filter, select **Data/Filter/AutoFilter**. The filter arrow buttons should disappear, and you should again see the entire database on the screen.

The **Find** command is useful for quickly locating an airport or name in the database. The fastest way to start a search using **Find** is to press **Ctrl+F**; if you prefer using menus, select **Edit/Find**. In either case, you'll see a Find dialog box in which you can type the text you wish to find. In a massive database such as this, it may take 10 seconds to find a particular record, although most searches take less time.

To sort the database by a different column, highlight the entire database and choose **Data/Sort**. A dialog box will ask you which column you wish to sort in ascending or descending order.

SELECTED INSTRUMENT APPROACH PLATES

The 100 IAP Plates on the CD-ROM give you all the information that you'll need for instrument landing approaches at many of the major airports in the world. These airport charts have been scanned in from official U.S. Government Flight Information Publications, and are not to be used for real flight navigation.

For an explanation of how to read the charts, see the IAP Legend illustrations in Captain Sean Trestrails's chapter on IFR.

Warning: Dated Material. Do Not Use For Real Navigation; Use Only with Flight Simulator

The **\Airport IAP Charts** folder contains the IAP charts for the airports that are listed below. All the charts are stored as Adobe Acrobat 3.0 files, and before you can view them or print them out, you will need to install the Acrobat 3.0 Reader program from the CD-ROM's **\Acrobat Reader 3.0** folder. Just run the Setup.exe program and the Acrobat program will install itself to your hard disk.

Note that there is an **index.pdf** file in the **\Airport IAP Charts** folder that contains hotlink listings of all the IAP charts. Once you open the **index.pdf** file in Acrobat, you'll see all the Airport IAP charts listed by name, and you can click on any airport hotlink and the associated IAP chart will automatically open up.

Also, some web browsers, such as Internet Explorer 4.0 and Netscape Communicator 4.0 have built in Acrobat Reader software. This means that you can use your web browser to access, view, and print the Airport IAP chart .pdf files ("pdf" stands for portable document format, and is the file extension given to all Acrobat documents).

USA

Alaska

Figure C.5: *Anchorage Intl ILS RWY 6R (CAT II)*

Figure C.6: *Fairbanks ILS RWY 1L (CAT II)*

California

Figure C.7: *San Francisco ILS RWY 28R*

Figure C.8: *Metropolitan Oakland Intl ILS 27R*

Figure C.9: *Metropolitan Oakland Intl ILS 29 (CAT II)*

Figure C.10: *Burbank-Glendale-Pasadena ILS RWY 8*

Figure C.11: *Lake Tahoe LDA/DME-1 RWY 18*

Figure C.12: *San Jose Intl ILS 12R*

Colorado

Figure C.13: *Aspen VOR/DME or GPS-C*

Figure C.14: *Denver Intl ILS 34*

Florida

Figure C.15: *Miami Intl ILS RWY 9L*

Georgia

Figure C.16: *Atlanta Intl ILS RWY 8L (CAT II)*

Hawaii

Figure C.17: Maui Island Kahului ILS RWY 2

Figure C.18: Hawaii Island Keahole Kona ILS-DME RWY 17

Figure C.19: Oahu Island Honolulu Intl ILS RWY 8L

Figure C.20: Hawaii Island Hilo ILS-DME RWY 26

Illinois

Figure C.21: Chicago O'Hare ILS RWY 14L (CAT II)

Massachusetts

Figure C.22: Boston Logan Intl ILS RWY 4R (CAT II)

Minnesota

Figure C.23: Minneapolis-St. Paul Intl ILS RWY 29L (CAT II)

Nevada

Figure C.24: Las Vegas McCarran Intl ILS RWY 25L

New Jersey

Figure C.25: Newark Intl ILS RWY 4R (CAT II)

New Mexico

Figure C.26: Albuquerque ILS RWY 8

New York

Figure C.27: John F. Kennedy Intl ILS RWY 4R (CAT II)

Oregon

Figure C.28: Portland Intl ILS RWY 10R (CAT II)

Pennsylvania

Figure C.29: Philadelphia ILS RWY 9R (CAT II)

Texas

Figure C.30: Houston Intercontinental ILS RWY 27 (CAT II)

Figure C.31: Dallas-Ft Worth Intl ILS RWY 17L (CAT II)

Utah

Figure C.32: Salt Lake City ILS-DME RWY 16L (CAT II)

Washington

Figure C.33: Seattle-Tacoma Intl ILS RWY 16R (CAT II)

Washington District of Columbia

Figure C.34: Washington Dulles Intl ILS RWY 1R (CAT II)

Figure C.35: National ILS RWY 36 (CAT II)

Wisconsin

Figure C.36: Milwaukee ILS RWY 1L (CAT II)

Wyoming

Figure C.37: Cheyenne ILS RWY 26

Figure C.38: Jackson Hole ILS RWY 18

Canada

Figure C.39: Calgary Intl ILS RWY 34

Figure C.40: Edmonton ILS RWY 12

Figure C.41: Goose Bay ILS RWY 8

Figure C.42: Gandor ILS-DME RWY 4

Figure C.43: Montreal Dorval ILS RWY 6L (CAT II). (Courtesy of George Lorsche—printed with Final Approach 5.0)

Africa

Ivory Coast

Figure C.69: *Abidjan Felix ILS RWY 21*

Kenya

Figure C.70: *Nairobi Jomo Kenyatta Intl ILS RWY 06*

Nigeria

Figure C.71: *Lagos Murtala Muhammed ILS-DME RWY 19R*

Zaire

Figure C.72: *Kinshasa VOR-ILS RWY 24*

Zimbabwe

Figure C.73: *Harare Intl ILS RWY 05*

Asia

China

Figure C.74: *Beijing Capital Intl ILS RWY 36R*

Figure C.75: *Hong Kong Intl IGS RWY 13*

Figure C.76: *Shanghai Hongqiao ILS-DME RWY 18*

India

Figure C.77 *Netaji Subhas Chandra Bose Intl (formerly Dum Dum Intl) ILS RWY 19L. (Courtesy of George Lorsche—printed with Final Approach).*

Japan

Figure C.78: *Tokyo Intl ILS RWY 33*

Pakistan

Figure C.79: *Karachi Quaid-E-Azam Intl NDB RWY 25R*

Philippines

Figure C.80: *Manila Ninoy Aquino Intl ILS RWY 24*

Singapore

Figure C.81: *Singapore Changi Intl ILS-DME RWY 20R*

South Korea

Figure C.82: *Seoul Intl ILS RWY 20*

Thailand

Figure C.83: *Bangkok Intl ILS-DME RWY 21L*

Pacific

Australia

Figure C.84: *Sydney Intl (Kingsford Smith) ILS RWY 16R*

Figure C.85: *Melbourne ILS RWY 26*

Figure C.86: *Brisbane Intl ILS RWY 01*

Figure C.87: *Alice Springs ILS RWY 12*

Figure C.88: *Perth ILS RWY 24*

Figure C.89: *Darwin ILS RWY 29*

Guam

Figure C.90: *Guam International (Agana Naval Air Station-Brewer Field)l ILS RWY 6L*

Midway

Figure C.91: *Midway Henderson Field HI-NDB RWY 6*

New Zealand

Figure C.92: *Auckland Intl ILS-DME RWY 05*

Wake Island

Figure C.93: *Wake Island TACAN or VOR-DME RWY 10*

South America & Central America

Argentina

Figure C.94: *Buenos Aires Ezeiza/Ministro Pistarini Intl ILS-DME RWY 11*

Boliva

Figure C.95: *La Paz J.F. Kennedy Intl ILS-DME RWY 9R*

Brazil

Figure C.96: *Rio de Janeiro Intl HI-ILS RWY 10*

Figure C.97: *Brasilia Intl ILS RWY 11*

Chile

Figure C.98: *Santiago Arturo Merino Benitez Intl ILS RWY 17*

Colombia

Figure C.99: *Bogota Eldorado Intl ILS RWY 13*

Ecuador

Figure C.100: *Guayaquil Simon Bolivar Intl ILS RWY 21*

Mexico

Figure C.101: *Veracruz General Heribeto Jara Intl VOR-DME RWY 18*

Panama

Figure C.102: *Panama City Tocumen Intl ILS RWY 3R*

Peru

Figure C.103: *Lima Jorge Chavez Intl ILS RWY 15*

Venezuela

Figure C.104: *Maiquetia Simon Bolivar Intl ILS-DME RWY 9*

WARNINGS, COPYRIGHT NOTICE, AND OTHER RESTRICTIONS ON THE USE OF THE DAFIF AND OTHER NAVIGATIONAL DATA

There are important legal and copyright restrictions on the use of the DAFIF. These are spelled out in the **COPYRIGHT.TXT** and **COPYRIGHT information.doc** files that are included in **DAFIF** directory on the CD-ROM.

MIS: Press and Nick Dargahi expressly forbid the use of the DAFIF or other airport information in this appendix in real navigation and take no legal responsibility for people who disregard these instructions. The DAFIF navigational data should be used only with Microsoft's Flight Simulator. Note that DAFIF is updated every 28 days to take into account changes to the worldwide navaid and airport database. The data found in this version of the DAFIF will quickly become obsolete, and it is therefore suitable only for use with Microsoft's Flight Simulator database.

WARNING

Because navigation data is updated at 28-day intervals, none of the data in this book is valid for real navigational purposes. Do not use any of this data for real navigation.

D

U.S.A. IFR Enroute High-Altitude Jet Routeway Charts and World Aeronautical Charts

We have provided real aviation IFR enroute high-altitude jet routeway charts for the entire United States on the CD-ROM (Courtesy of Resolution Mapping) in a moving map display that is linked to Flight Simulator. In addition, you will find world aeronautical charts (WAC) for most of the coastal regions of the United States. Because of insufficient CD-ROM capacity, we were unable to provide the interior WACs for the Midwest.

WARNING

Because navigation data is updated at 56-day intervals, none of the data in this book is valid for real-world navigational purposes. Use it only for Flight Simulator. Do not use any of this data for real navigation!

INTERPRETING AVIATION MAPS

You may be unfamiliar with the symbols and graphics that are displayed on-screen. To help you interpret the maps, consult the legends shown in Figures D.1, D.2, D.3, and D.4.

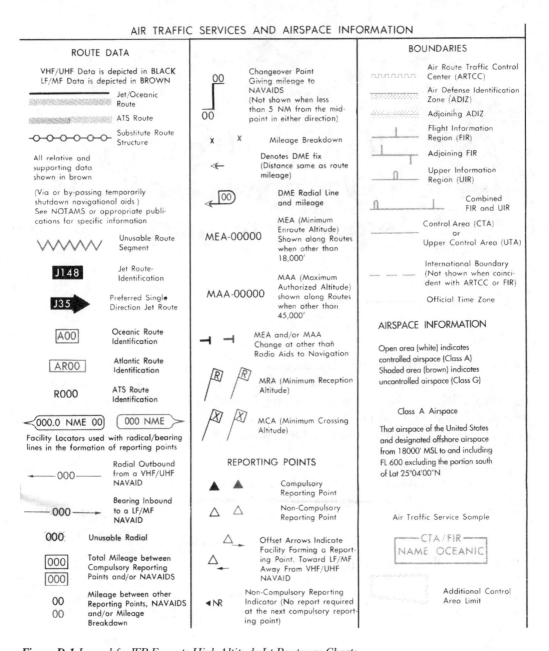

AIR TRAFFIC SERVICES AND AIRSPACE INFORMATION

ROUTE DATA

VHF/UHF Data is depicted in BLACK
LF/MF Data is depicted in BROWN

Jet/Oceanic Route

ATS Route

Substitute Route Structure

All relative and supporting data shown in brown

(Via or by-passing temporarily shutdown navigational aids)
See NOTAMS or appropriate publications for specific information

Unusable Route Segment

J148 — Jet Route-Identification

J35 — Preferred Single Direction Jet Route

A00 — Oceanic Route Identification

AR00 — Atlantic Route Identification

R000 — ATS Route Identification

000.0 NME 00 / 000 NME — Facility Locators used with radical/bearing lines in the formation of reporting points

000 — Radial Outbound from a VHF/UHF NAVAID

000 — Bearing Inbound to a LF/MF NAVAID

000 — Unusable Radial

000 / 000 — Total Mileage between Compulsory Reporting Points and/or NAVAIDS

00 / 00 — Mileage between other Reporting Points, NAVAIDS and/or Mileage Breakdown

00 — Changeover Point Giving mileage to NAVAIDS (Not shown when less than 5 NM from the midpoint in either direction)

X   X — Mileage Breakdown

Denotes DME fix (Distance same as route mileage)

00 — DME Radial Line and mileage

MEA-00000 — MEA (Minimum Enroute Altitude) Shown along Routes when other than 18,000'

MAA-00000 — MAA (Maximum Authorized Altitude) shown along Routes when other than 45,000'

MEA and/or MAA Change at other than Radio Aids to Navigation

R R — MRA (Minimum Reception Altitude)

X X — MCA (Minimum Crossing Altitude)

REPORTING POINTS

▲ ▲ — Compulsory Reporting Point

△ △ — Non-Compulsory Reporting Point

△ — Offset Arrows Indicate Facility Forming a Reporting Point. Toward LF/MF Away From VHF/UHF NAVAID

◄NR — Non-Compulsory Reporting Indicator (No report required at the next compulsory reporting point)

BOUNDARIES

Air Route Traffic Control Center (ARTCC)

Air Defense Identification Zone (ADIZ)

Adjoining ADIZ

Flight Information Region (FIR)

Adjoining FIR

Upper Information Region (UIR)

Combined FIR and UIR

Control Area (CTA) or Upper Control Area (UTA)

International Boundary (Not shown when coincident with ARTCC or FIR)

Official Time Zone

AIRSPACE INFORMATION

Open area (white) indicates controlled airspace (Class A)
Shaded area (brown) indicates uncontrolled airspace (Class G)

Class A Airspace

That airspace of the United States and designated offshore airspace from 18000' MSL to and including FL 600 excluding the portion south of Lat 25°04'00"N

Air Traffic Service Sample

CTA/FIR
NAME OCEANIC

Additional Control Area Limit

Figure D.1 *Legend for IFR Enroute High Altitude Jet Routeway Charts*

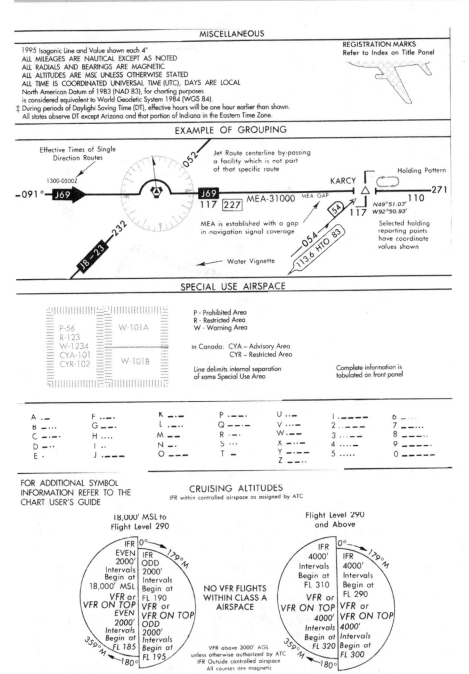

MISCELLANEOUS

1995 Isogonic Line and Value shown each 4°
ALL MILEAGES ARE NAUTICAL EXCEPT AS NOTED
ALL RADIALS AND BEARINGS ARE MAGNETIC
ALL ALTITUDES ARE MSL UNLESS OTHERWISE STATED
ALL TIME IS COORDINATED UNIVERSAL TIME (UTC), DAYS ARE LOCAL
North American Datum of 1983 (NAD 83), for charting purposes
is considered equivalent to World Geodetic System 1984 (WGS 84).
‡ During periods of Daylight Saving Time (DT), effective hours will be one hour earlier than shown.
All states observe DT except Arizona and that portion of Indiana in the Eastern Time Zone.

REGISTRATION MARKS
Refer to Index on Title Panel

EXAMPLE OF GROUPING

Effective Times of Single Direction Routes
1300-0500Z
Jet Route centerline by-passing a facility which is not part of that specific route
Holding Pattern
KARCY
-091° J69
052
J69 117 227 MEA-31000 MEA GAP
271
110
N49°51.07'
W92°50.93'
117
54
MEA is established with a gap in navigation signal coverage
Selected holding reporting points have coordinate values shown
054 113.6 HTO 83
232
J8-23
Water Vignette

SPECIAL USE AIRSPACE

P-56
R-123
W-1234
CYA-101
CYR-102
W-101A
W-101B

P - Prohibited Area
R - Restricted Area
W - Warning Area

In Canada: CYA – Advisory Area
CYR – Restricted Area

Line delimits internal separation of same Special Use Area

Complete information is tabulated on front panel

A .—	F ..—.	K —.—	P .——.	U ..—	1 .————
B —...	G ——.	L .—..	Q ——.—	V ...—	2 ..———
C —.—.	H	M ——	R .—.	W .——	3 ...——
D —..	I ..	N —.	S ...	X —..—	4 ....—
E .	J .———	O ———	T —	Y —.——	5 .....
				Z ——..	

6 —....
7 ——...
8 ———..
9 ————.
0 —————

FOR ADDITIONAL SYMBOL INFORMATION REFER TO THE CHART USER'S GUIDE

CRUISING ALTITUDES
IFR within controlled airspace as assigned by ATC

18,000' MSL to
Flight Level 290

IFR EVEN 2000' Intervals Begin at 18,000' MSL
VFR or VFR ON TOP EVEN 2000' Intervals Begin at FL 185

IFR ODD 2000' Intervals Begin at FL 190
VFR or VFR ON TOP ODD 2000' Intervals Begin at FL 195

0°
179°M
359°M
180°

NO VFR FLIGHTS WITHIN CLASS A AIRSPACE

VFR above 3000' AGL unless otherwise authorized by ATC
IFR Outside controlled airspace
All courses are magnetic

Flight Level 290
and Above

IFR 4000' Intervals Begin at FL 310
VFR or VFR ON TOP 4000' Intervals Begin at FL 320

IFR 4000' Intervals Begin at FL 290
VFR or VFR ON TOP 4000' Intervals Begin at FL 300

0°
179°M
359°M
180°

Figure D.1 *continued*

IFR ENROUTE HIGH ALTITUDE – U. S.

For use at and above 18,000' MSL
HORIZONTAL DATUM: NORTH AMERICAN DATUM OF 1983

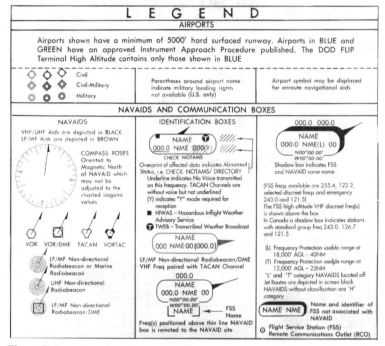

Figure D.1 *continued*

INSTALLING THE AEROVIEW MOVING MAP DISPLAY BY RESOLUTION MAPPING

The AeroView map browser on the accompanying CD-ROM is provided by Resolution Mapping (see the ad in the back of the book) and is a moving map display that works with FS98 to display real aviation charts. Although we have provided all the U.S. jet routeways and many WACs, you can also obtain low-altitude victor routes, the Pacific or Atlantic Ocean route maps, or any of the high-altitude charts for the rest of the world at an extra charge from Resolution Mapping. (See the Bibliography for pictorial descriptions of the various kinds of maps and the regions they cover.) These map data sets are designed to work with the AeroView map browser, and you can print them, zoom in or out, and quickly find points of interest, which are automatically displayed in conjunction with your airplane's position in Flight Simulator.

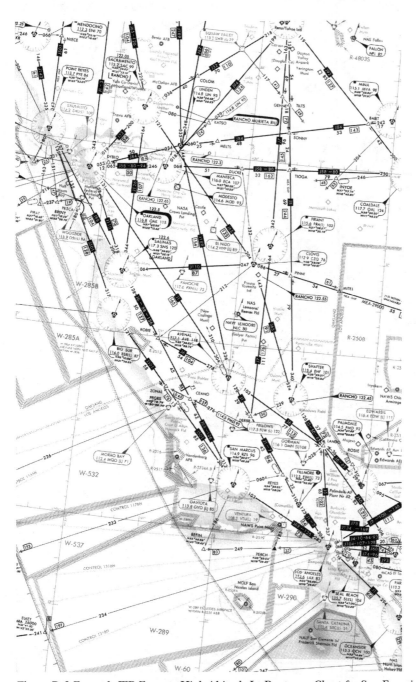

Figure D.2 *Example IFR Enroute High Altitude Jet Routeway Chart for San Francisco*

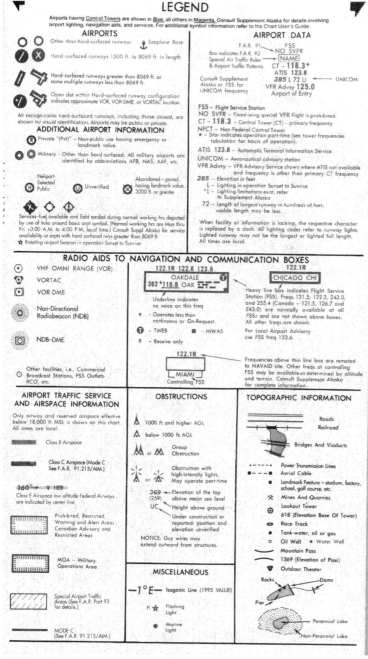

Figure D.3 *Legend for World Aeronautical Charts*

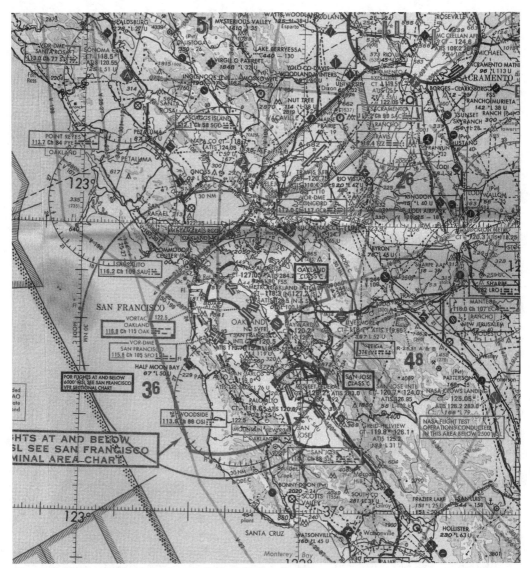

Figure D.4 *Example World Aeronautical Chart for San Francisco*

An airplane symbol at the center of the chart displays your airplane's position and orientation with respect to true north. The chart is always displayed "north up," so when you turn your airplane in FS98, the airplane icon will rotate to indicate the new heading.

To install the AeroView program, go to the **\AeroView Moving Map Display** directory on the CD-ROM, and double-click on the **Setup** program. Because hundreds of megabytes of chart data are stored on the CD-ROM, you will want to run the AeroView

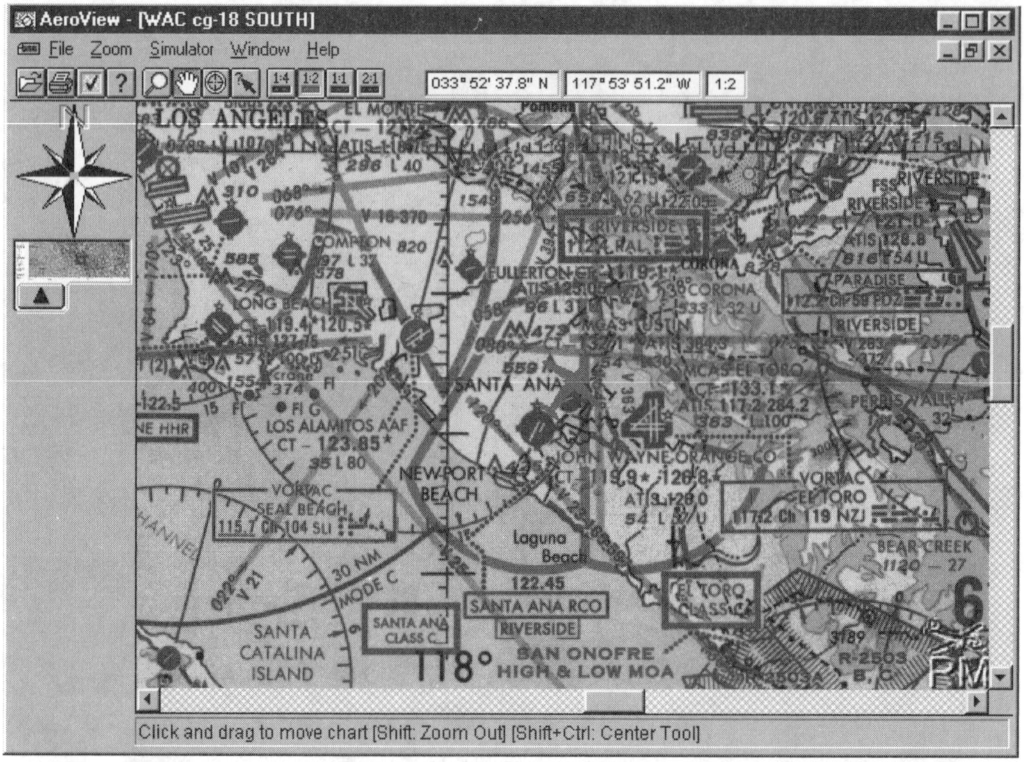

Figure D.5 *AeroView moving map display of a world aeronautical chart for Los Angeles (courtesy of Resolution Mapping). The airplane symbol at the center represents your Flight Simulator 98 airplane, which will automatically update its position and orientation with true north. The map scrolls with the airplane. With the help of the map, you can easily determine where you are in relation to nearby navaids, jet routes, cities, and airports and discover the name of the mountain, road, river, or city you are looking at in Flight Simulator.*

program with the book's CD-ROM in your CD-ROM drive. If you haven't installed all the Flight Simulator scenery to your hard drive, you will have a problem because the two programs will want to share the same CD-ROM drive. One way around this is to install a second CD-ROM player, a reasonable option when you consider that the cost of 8× CD-ROM drives has fallen to less than $95. Another alternative is to get a CD-ROM changer/jukebox, and you can then flip-flop as needed. However, a simpler alternative is to reinstall Flight Simulator so that all the scenery is run from the hard drive. In that way, the programs won't have to contend for use of the CD-ROM drive. To install all the FS98 scenery, you can uninstall the program and then rerun the setup.

Lastly, if you don't like any of the options above for installing AeroView, you can instead install the chart data for each chart that you want to use on your hard disk. The

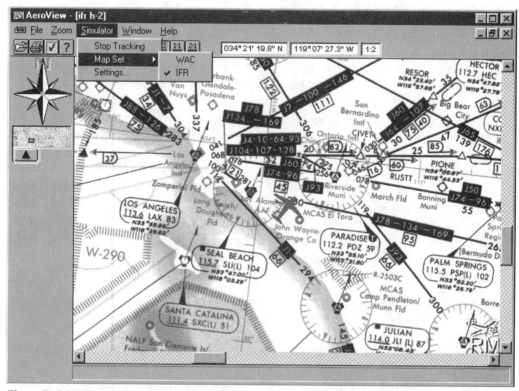

Figure D.6 *AeroView moving map display of a IFR enroute high-altitude jet routeway chart over Los Angeles (courtesy of Resolution Mapping). This map browser automatically loads IFR enroute high-altitude jet airway charts and world aeronautical charts for use with Flight Simulator 98.*

IFR High Altitude Enroute Charts are only about 10 MB each in size, and there are only 5 of them, so this will only take up 50 MB of hard disk space. The full color WAC charts, however, are much larger at almost 46 MB each. To install the charts to run off your hard drive, install the AeroView program, then copy the chart files (*.AER) that you are interested in to the directory on your hard disk where you installed AeroView (usually this is C:\Program Files\Resolution Mapping\AeroView). Then, when you open AeroView, you can manually instruct it to open the chart file in the \AeroView folder.. If you have copied all the chart data sets (e.g., IFR H-1.AER, IFR H-2.AER, etc., and WAC CF-16 NORTH.AER, etc.) to this folder, they will consume approximately 550 MB of space. Once the program knows where you have installed the charts, it will auto switch between the charts as you move from area to area.

AeroView works seamlessly in the background with Flight Simulator 98. It will update your chart position and also automatically load charts depending on your current latitude/longitude coordinates. AeroView uses a special driver called FS6IPC.dll, provided by Adam Szoufran, that interfaces with FS98 and sends latitude/longitude/ aircraft orientation information to the chart display (AeroView will also work with FSW95) using an ActiveX control built by Jesse Lund of Resolution Mapping.The AeroView setup program will automatically load the FS6IPC.dll driver into your Flight Simulator\Modules directory. However if there is any problem with the program not interfacing properly, you should check to make sure that this dll driver has been properly copied from the CD to your \Modules directory. Also, sometimes with unusual computer drive setups (e.g., you have a "Z" drive for your CD-ROM instead of a "D" or "E" drive), AeroView may not know where to look at startup for the first chart. If this happens, simply use the Open File dialog box to point to the *.AER chart files on the CD-ROM, and select any of the available charts. AeroView will then open the chart and everything will function normally.

You can print the charts, zoom in or out, scroll, and see the exact latitude longitude point of any place in the U.S.A., and view all the navaids, navaid frequencies, and route information around your airplane.

The following charts are included on the CD-ROM:

- IFR Enroute High Altitude Jet Routeway H-1, H-2, H-3, H-4, and H-5
- WAC CF-16, CF-18, CF-19, CG-21, CG-18, CG-21, and CF-25 South

To see which areas of the United States these charts cover, refer to the Bibliography . There you will see a pictorial area listing for both the WAC and IFR enroute charts.

To order other U.S. or worldwide charts, contact Resolution Mapping, 35 Hartwell Avenue, Lexington, MA 02173, USA, Tel 617-860-0430, Fax 617-860-0505, e-mail: sales@maptech.com.

How to use AeroView with Flight Simulator

Using the options found in the Simulator Menu of AeroView, users of Microsoft Flight Simulator can view their current position on the charts.

Here's what you must do:

1. Ensure Flight Simulator was installed before AeroView. If not, uninstall AeroView and then re-install it after Flight Simulator has been set up (run the Setup.EXE program in the \AeroView Moving Map Display folder on the CD-ROM)..
2. Start Flight Simulator and select a North American airport.
3. Just before takeoff, start AeroView. Swap CD's (if necessary) and press Cancel when presented with the Open Chart dialog. Resize the AeroView window so that both Flight Simulator and AeroView can be seen. Finally, select Start

Tracking from the Simulator menu of AeroView. A chart (either IFR or WAC) will load automatically with the plane's position indicated in red.

4. Switch back to Flight Simulator and start flying!

Tips

1. Run your display at a resolution of 800x600 (or higher). Then, resize the AeroView window to occupy a corner of the display. This way, you can see your position in AeroView while you're in flight. A fairly small AeroView window can be very effective.

2. If you switch between AeroView and Flight Simulator and do not wish Flight Simulator to pause, choose Preferences from the **Options** menu of Flight Simulator. In the **General** section, turn off **Pause on Task Switch.**

3. AeroView will automatically load the charts it needs. Since the IFR charts cover a wider area than the WAC charts, AeroView will switch to an IFR chart if a WAC chart is not available.

4. Since AeroView only includes selected US aeronautical charts, flying off the covered area will end tracking in AeroView.

5. Use the **Preferences** command in the **File** Menu of AeroView to turn off the Compass Control Bar. This will give you more screen real estate in AeroView.

6. It is possible to swap between the AeroView CD and the Flight Simulator CD when one program needs its CD. Simply insert the CD that each program needs when asked. We have also tested Flight Simulator and AeroView with a multi-CD changer and had excellent results.

Options and Other Controls

1. Chose **Start Tracking** from the **Simulator** menu to display the plane's location in AeroView. The plane appears red when the tracking is on. If tracking is off, the plane will turn magenta.

2. Use the **Map Set** option under the **Simulator** menu to change between IFR and WAC aeronautical charts. Since the IFR charts cover a wider area than the WAC charts, AeroView will switch to a IFR chart if a WAC chart is not available.

Use the **Settings** option in the Simulator menu to control the plane's size and transparency. By choosing **closing old charts before loading new charts**, AeroView will conserve memory when flying from one chart to another.

Worldwide Aviation Charts

This appendix contains 52 digital charts of the world that display VOR/NDBs, airports, and air routes with magnetic headings. You will find \ detailed charts for Europe, Japan, Hawaii, Hong Kong, Easter Island, and the Caribbean ocean regions that will come in handy when using the new FSW98 default scenery. Other charts depict the air routes to the Galapagos Islands and Tahiti from Chile and the transatlantic and transpacific air routes.

The charts use several symbols that are important to recognize. Hollow circles means that a navaid, either a VOR or an NDB, is available. Although many navaids are labeled by name and frequency, it was not possible to label all of because of space constraints. Airports are depicted with an airplane symbol, and air routes are shown as thin lines that connect the navaids and airports. Above each air route is a number that represents the magnetic heading to be taken. This heading can vary along the route, and again, due to space considerations, it was not possible to display all of the headings so in some cases, you won't be able to fly using the map on some trips because some of the route information is missing.

The course information that is printed above the routes is valid for both directions. For example, if a course of 90° is displayed on a route, you can also fly the 270° course in the opposite direction because 270° is the 180° reciprocal of 90°.

It is assumed that you know the difference between NDB frequencies and VOR frequencies and that all VOR frequencies begin with a 1. Therefore, if you see a 217.60 frequency underneath a navaid, it is an NDB, and you will tune in the station on the ADF radio.

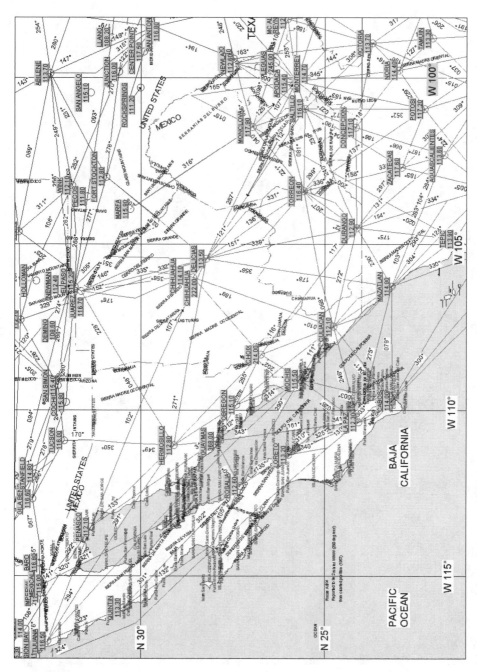

Chart E.1 *Baja California.*

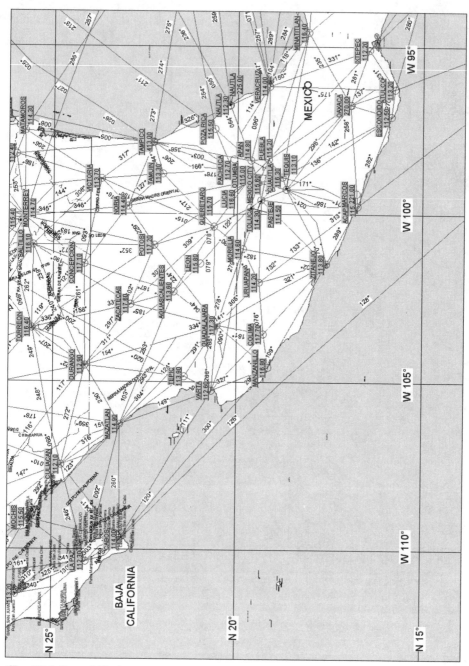

Chart E.2 *Central Mexico.*

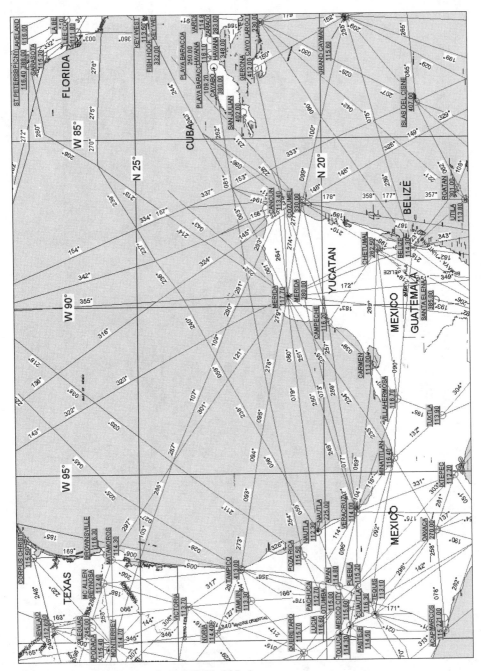

Chart E.3 *Yucatan Peninsula and Gulf of Mexico.*

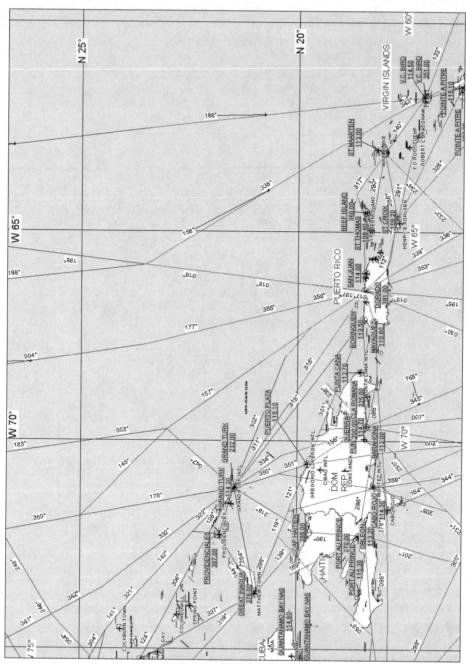

Chart E.4 *Northern Caribbean Region (Cuba and Bahamas).*

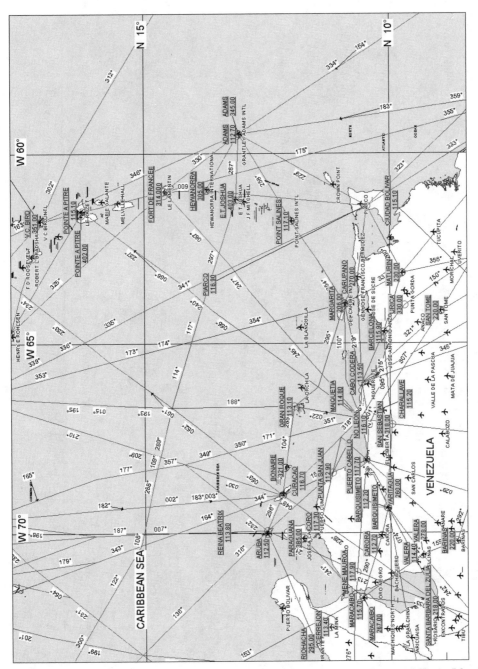

Chart E.5 *Central Caribbean Region (Haiti, Dominique Republic, Puerto Rico, and Virgin Islands).*

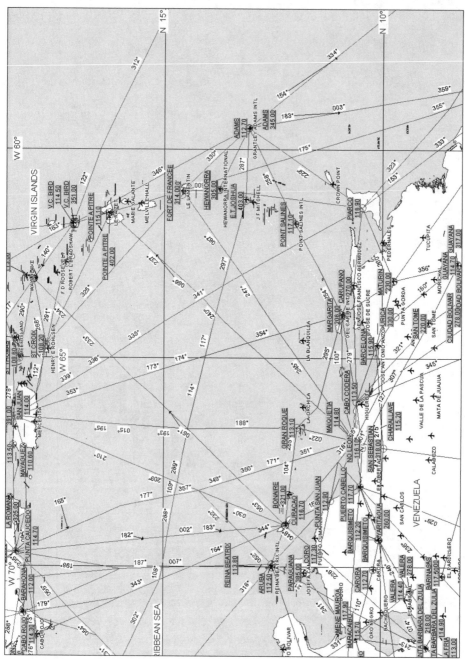

Chart E.6 *Southern Caribbean Region (Venezuela, Gran Roque, and Aruba).*

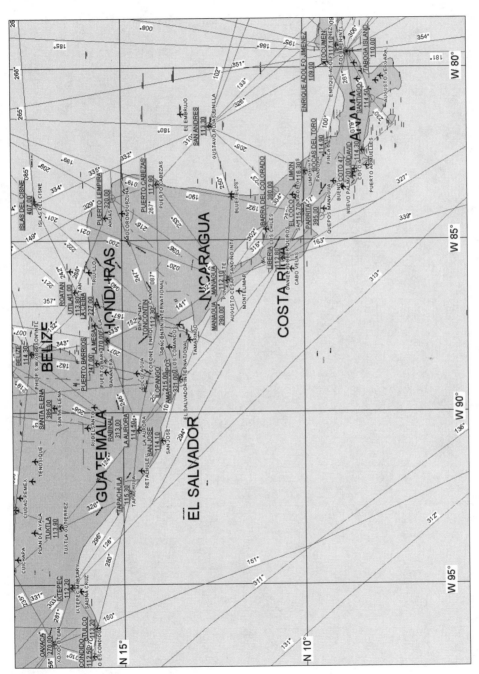

Chart E.7 *Central America.*

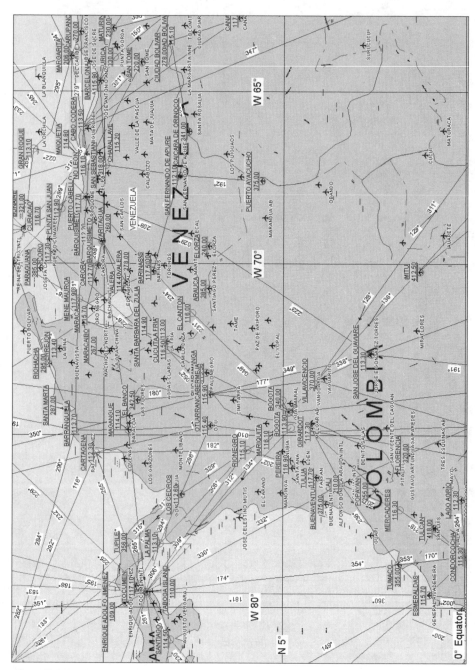

Chart E.8 South America (Northeast portion, including Columbia and Venezuela).

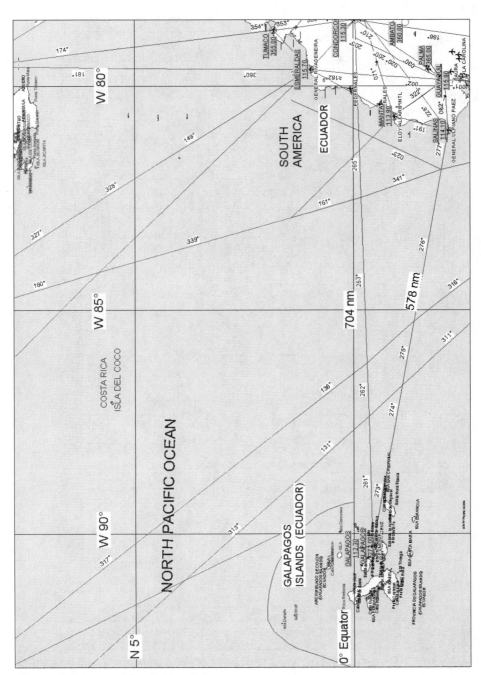

Chart E.9 *Galapagos Islands (Ecuador).*

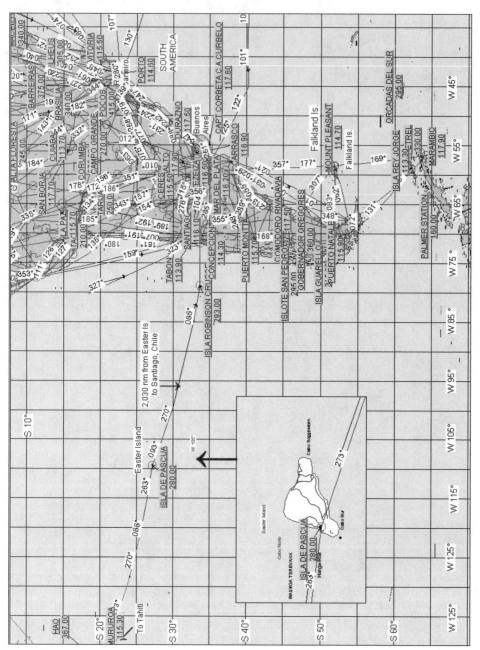

Chart E.10 *South America (Southern portion, including Chile, Easter Island, Argentina, and Falkland Islands).*

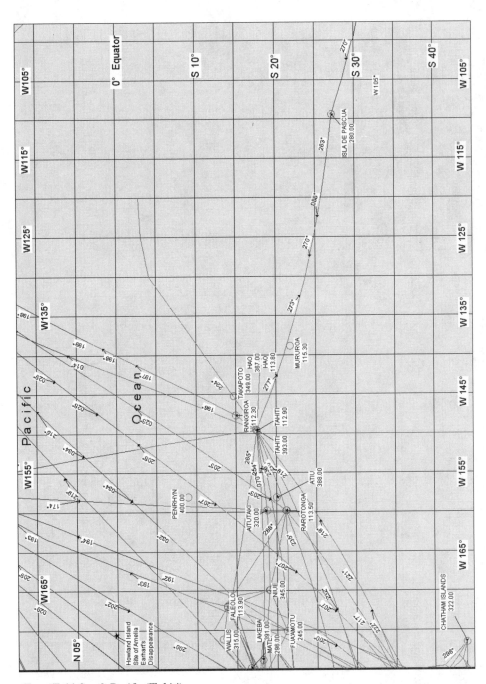

Chart E.11 *South Pacific (Tahiti).*

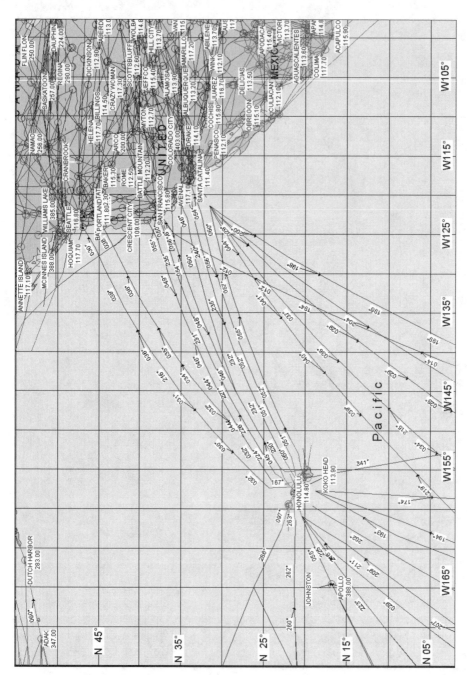

Chart E.12 *North Pacific (West Coast of California to Hawaii).*

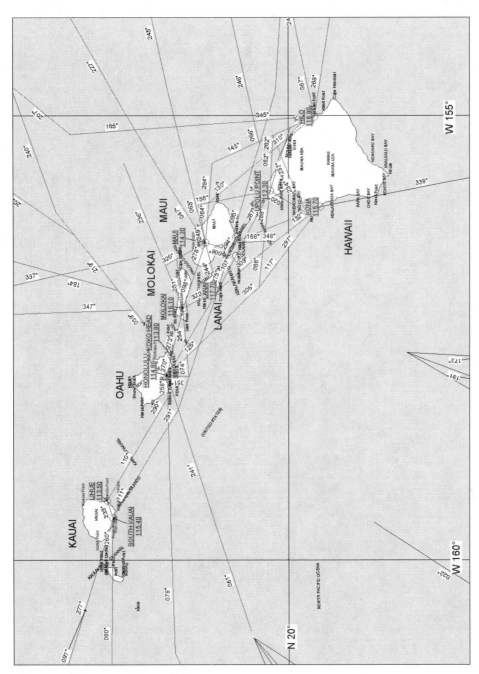

Chart E.13 *Islands of Hawaii.*

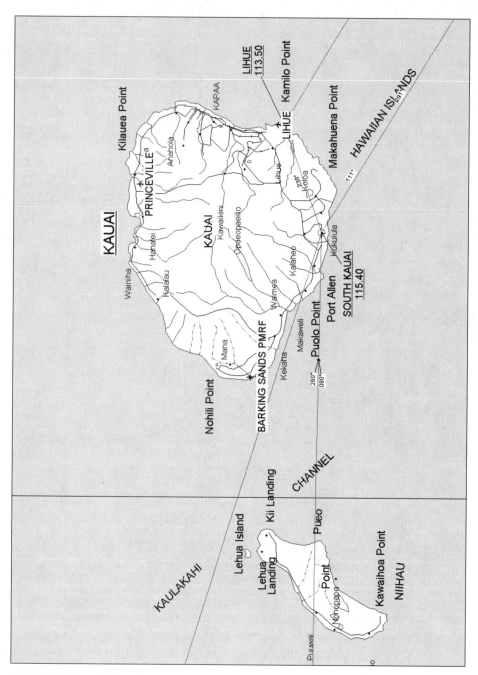

Chart E.14 *Kauai, Hawaii.*

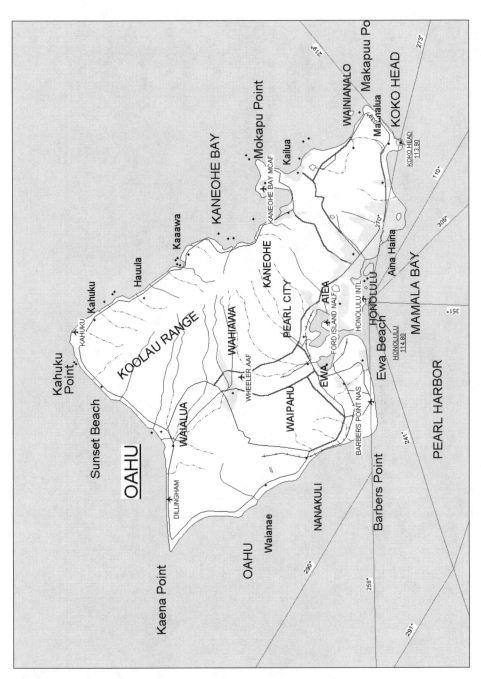

Chart E.15 *Oahu, Hawaii.*

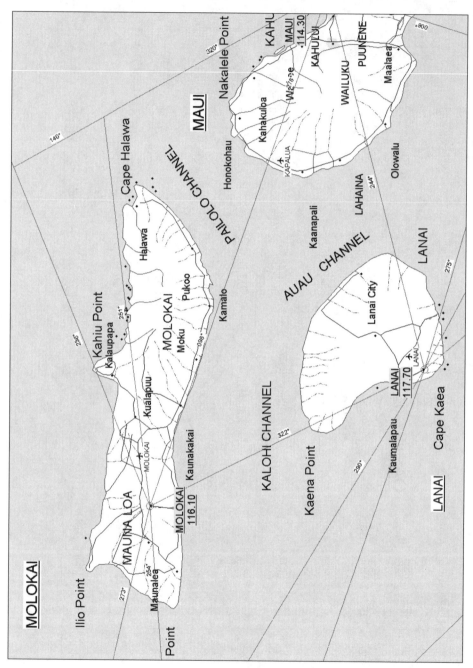

Chart E.16 *Molokai, Lanai, and West Portion of Maui, Hawaii.*

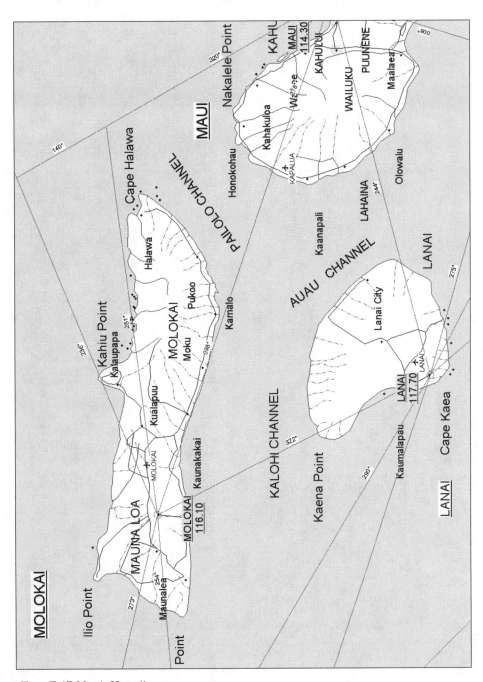

Chart E.17 *Maui, Hawaii.*

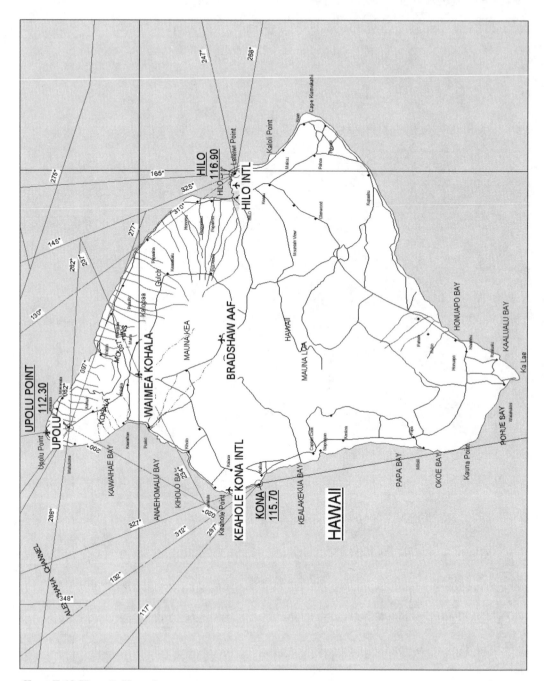

Chart E.18 *Hawaii, Hawaii.*

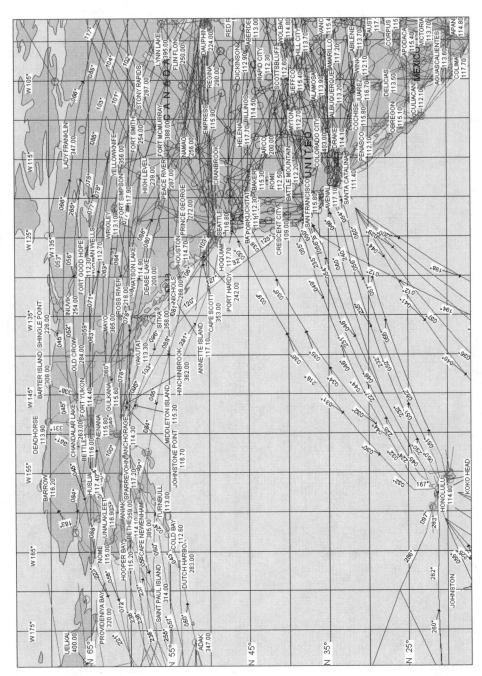

Chart E.19 *Western Pacific Ocean; Alaska and North Pacific Route from West Coast to Asia.*

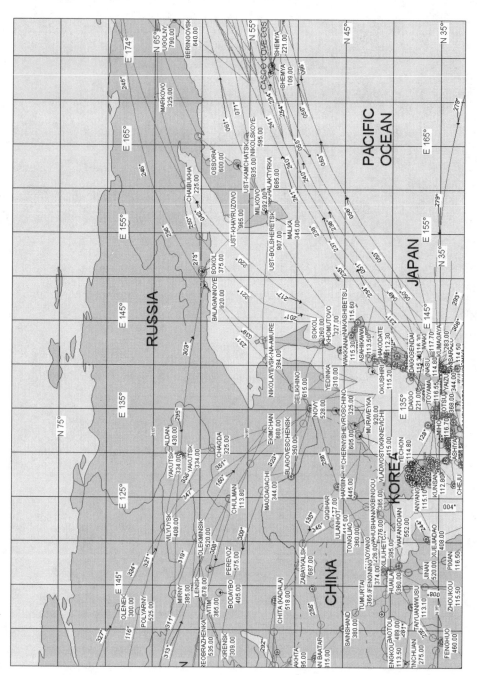

Chart E.20 *Far East route from Aleutian Islands, Alaska to Japan.*

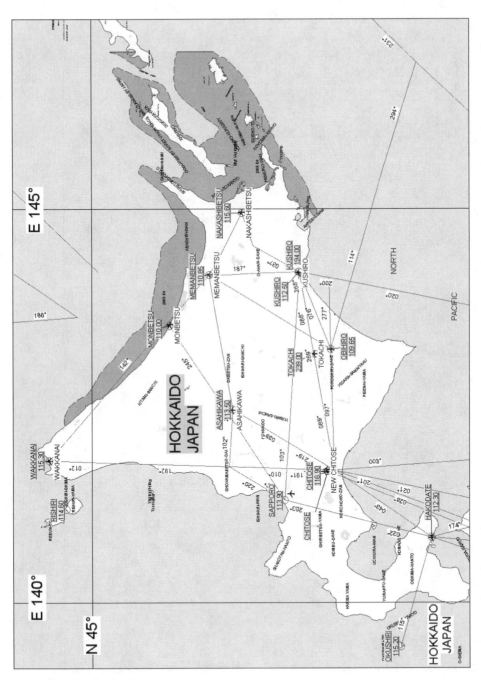

Chart E.21 *Hokkaido, Japan.*

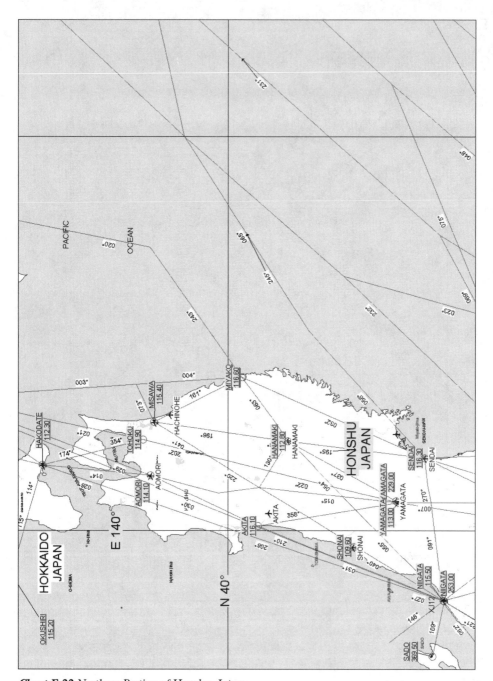

Chart E.22 *Northern Portion of Honshu, Japan.*

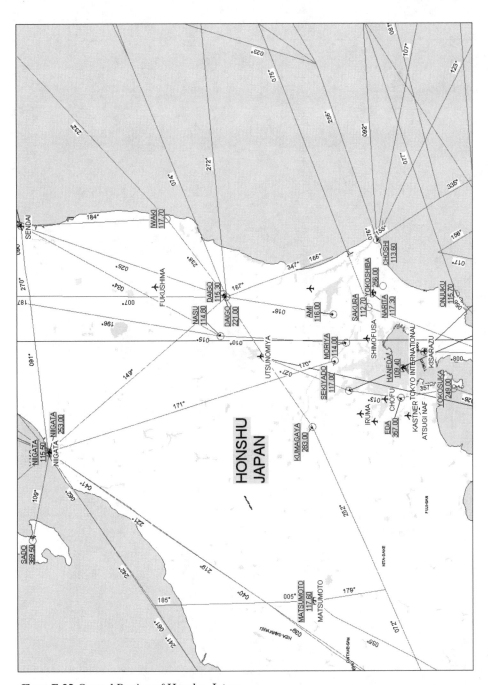

Chart E.23 *Central Portion of Honshu, Japan.*

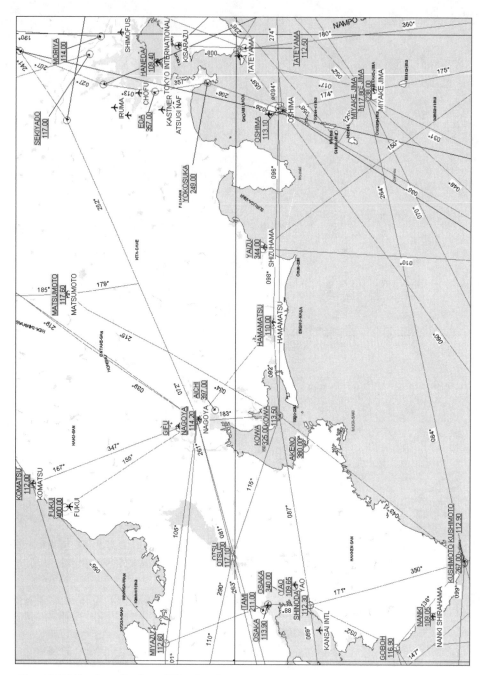

Chart E.24 *Southern Portion of Honshu, Japan.*

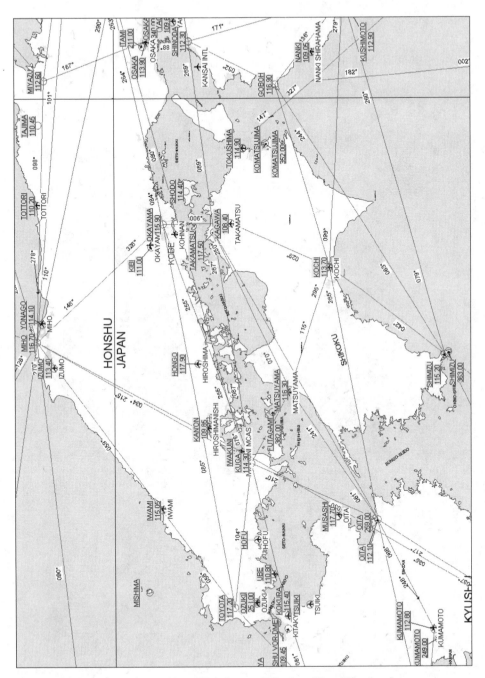

Chart E.25 *Shikoku, Southern Tip of Honshu, and Northern Tip of Kyushu, Japan.*

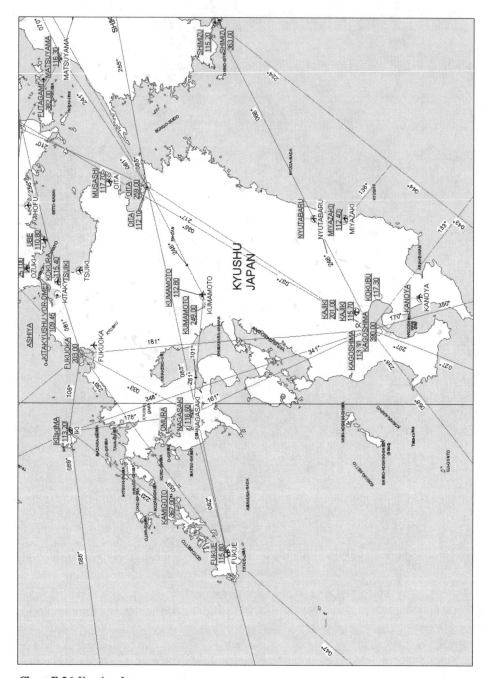

Chart E.26 *Kyushu, Japan.*

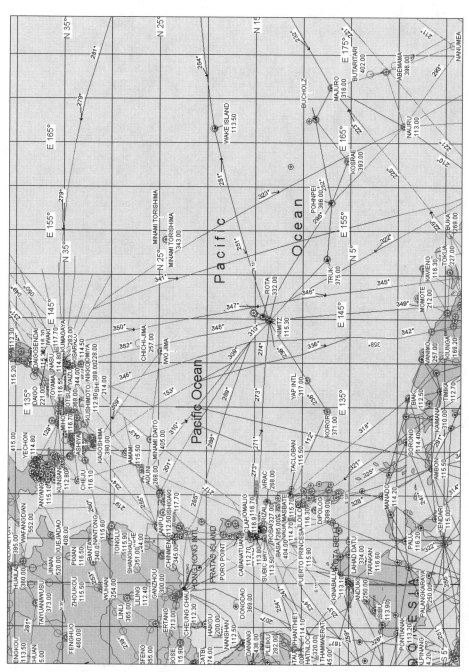

Chart E.27 *Eastern Pacific Ocean.*

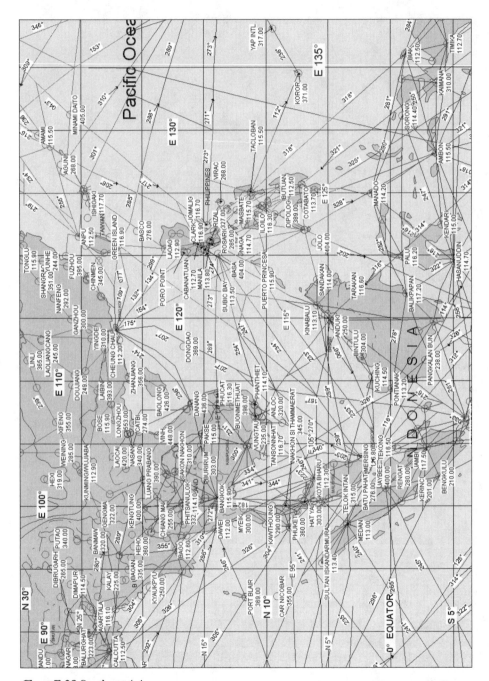

Chart E.28 *Southeast Asia.*

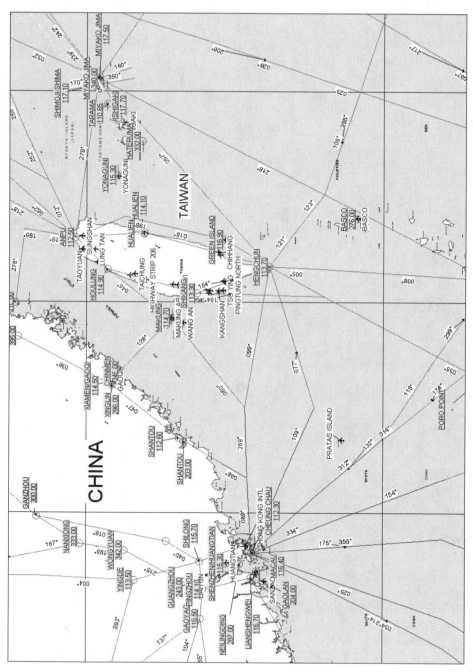

Chart E.29 *Taiwan, South China, and Hong Kong.*

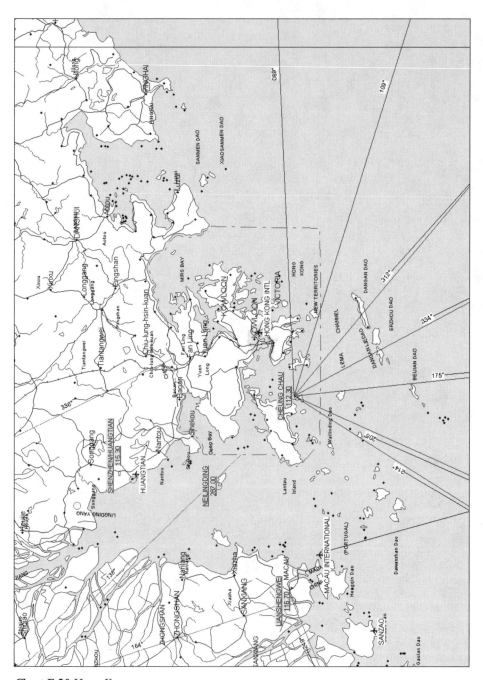

Chart E.30 *Hong Kong.*

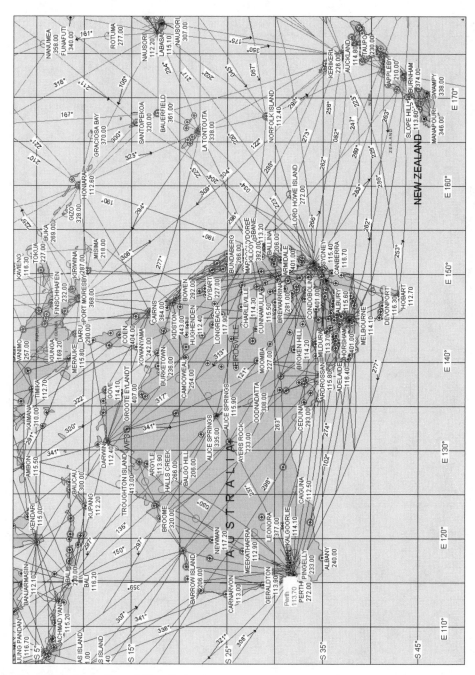

Chart E.31 *Australia and New Zealand.*

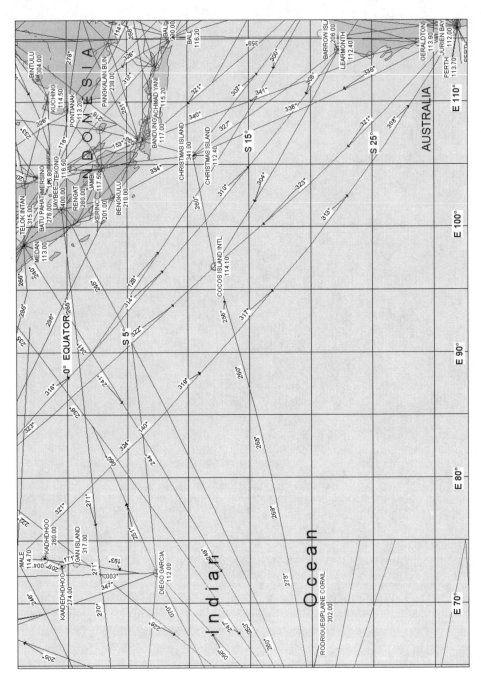

Chart E.32 *Eastern Indian Ocean, Including Christmas Island, Cocos Island, Singapore, and parts of Indonesia.*

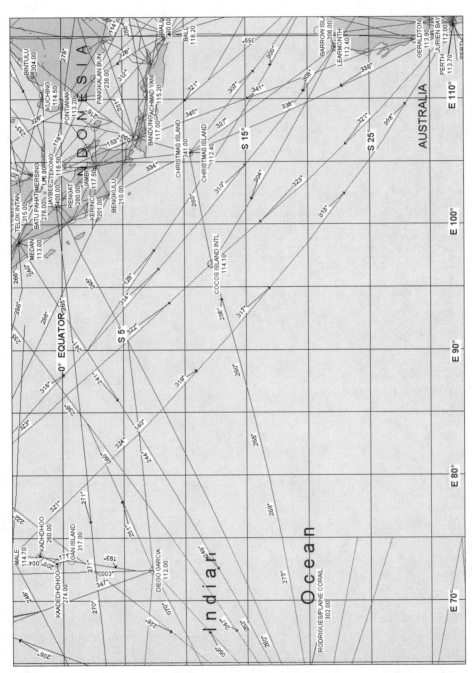

Chart E.33 *Madagascar, South Indian Ocean, Diego Garcia, South Africa, and East Africa.*

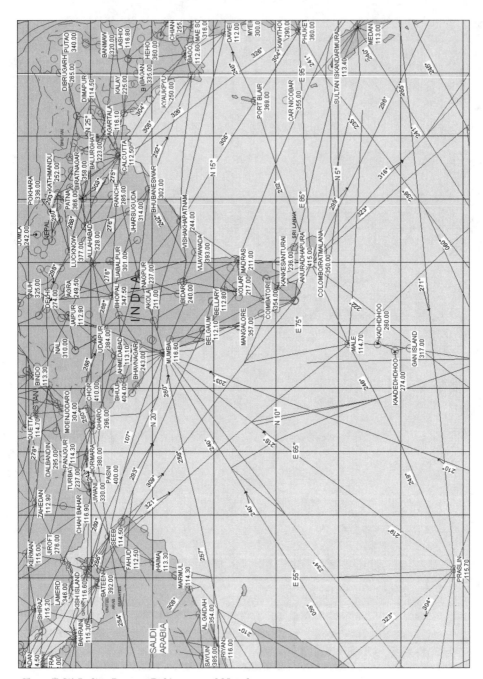

Chart E.34 *India, Burma, Pakistan, and Nepal.*

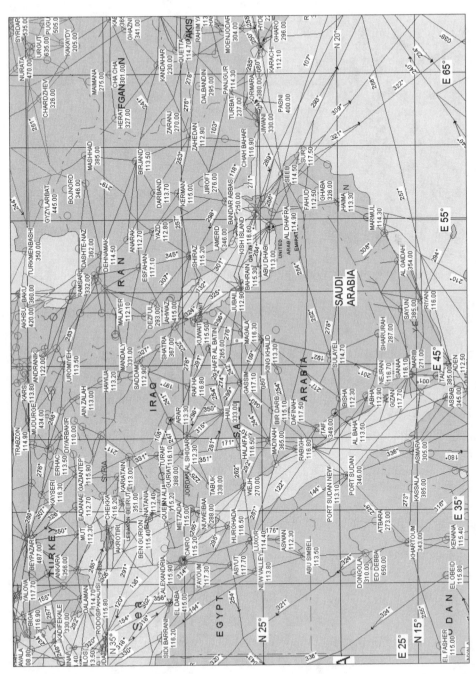

Chart E.35 *Middle East.*

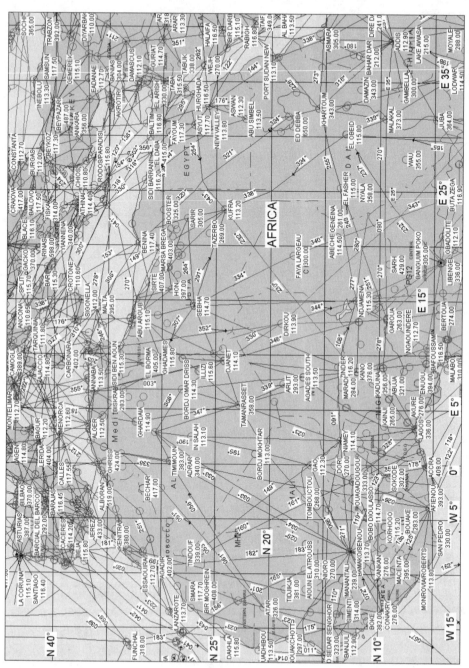

Chart E.36 *North Africa and Mediterranean region.*

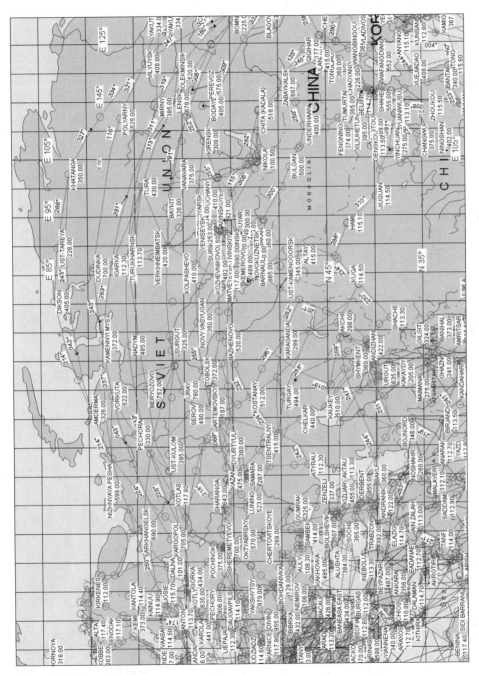

Chart E.37 Western Russia.

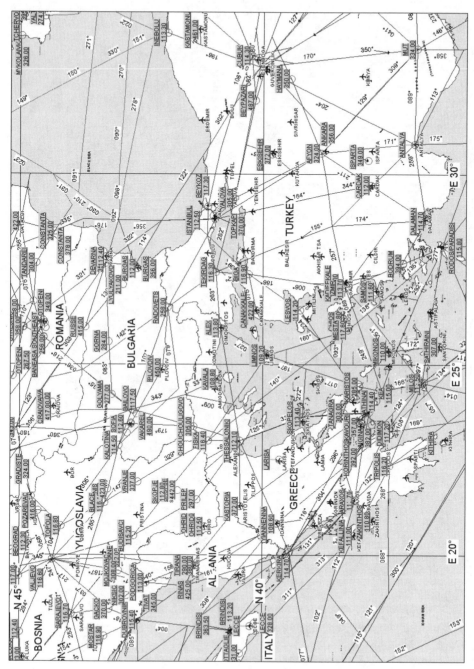

Chart E.38 *Greece, Bulgaria, Romania, Turkey, Albania, Yugoslavia, Bosnia.*

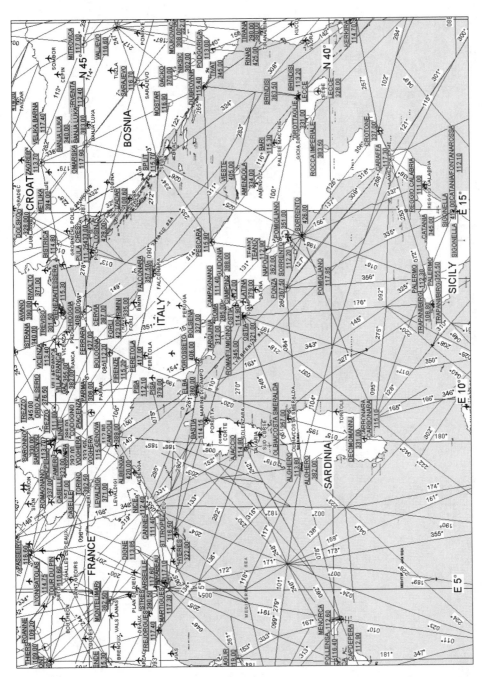

Chart E.39 *Italy, South of France, Bosnia, Croatia.*

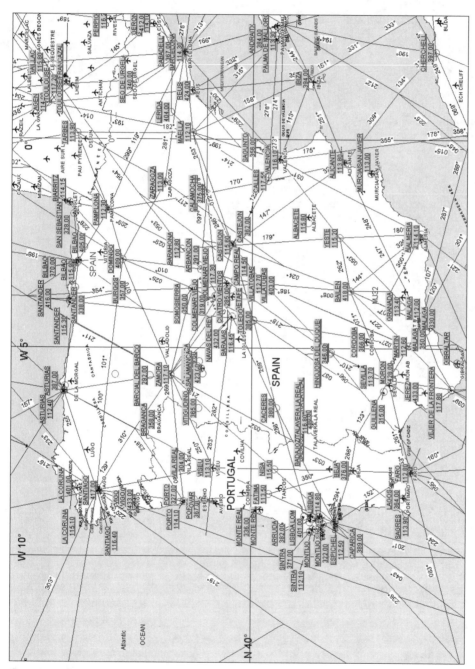

Chart E.40 *Spain and Portugal.*

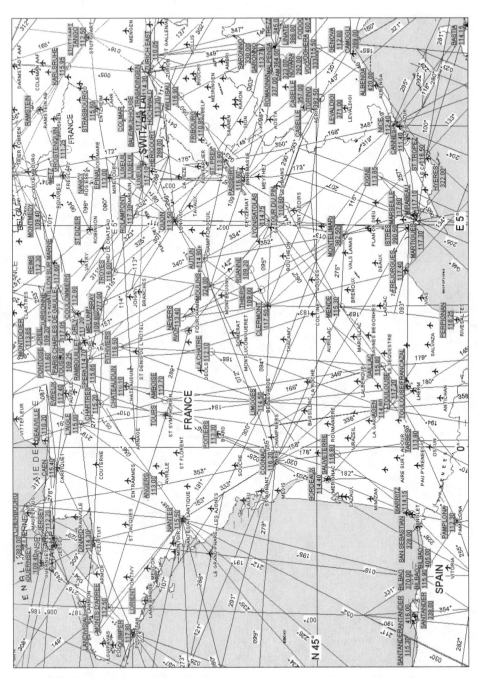

Chart E.41 *France and Switzerland.*

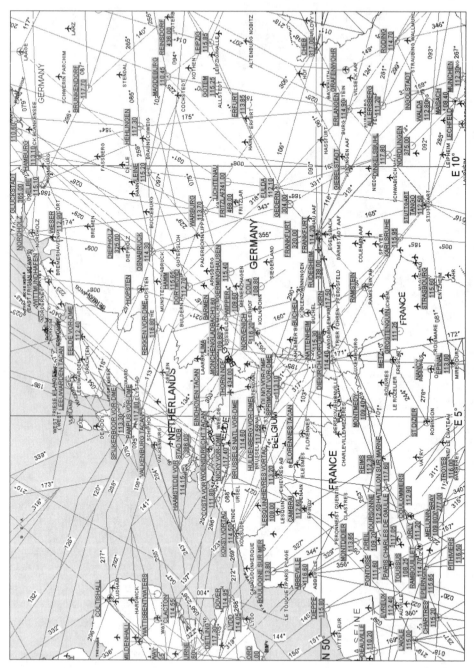

Chart E.42 *France, Netherlands, and Germany.*

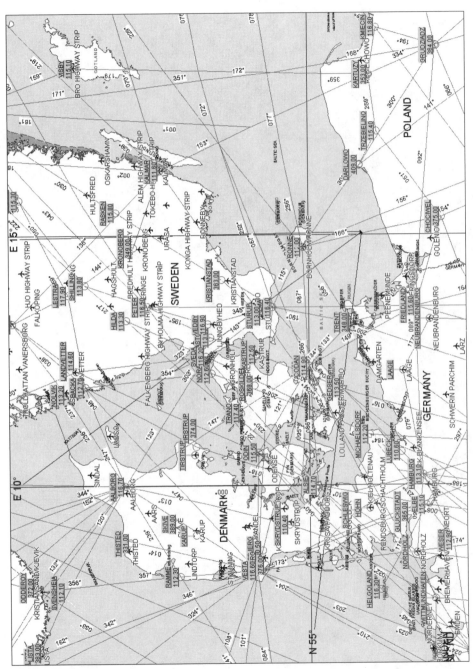

Chart E.43 *Sweden, Denmark, North Germany, Poland.*

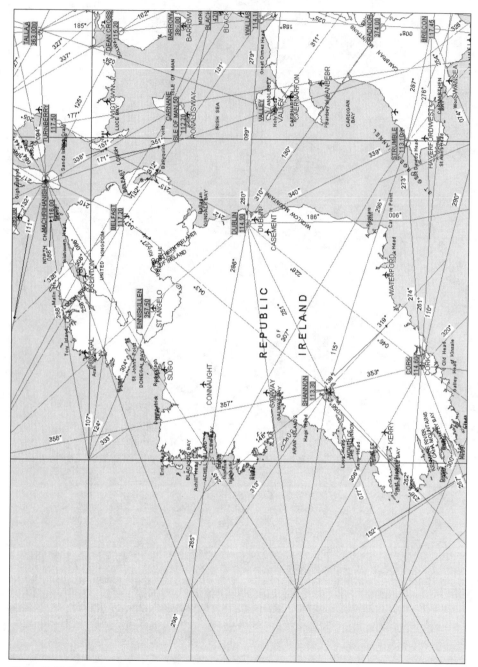

Chart E.44 *Republic of Ireland.*

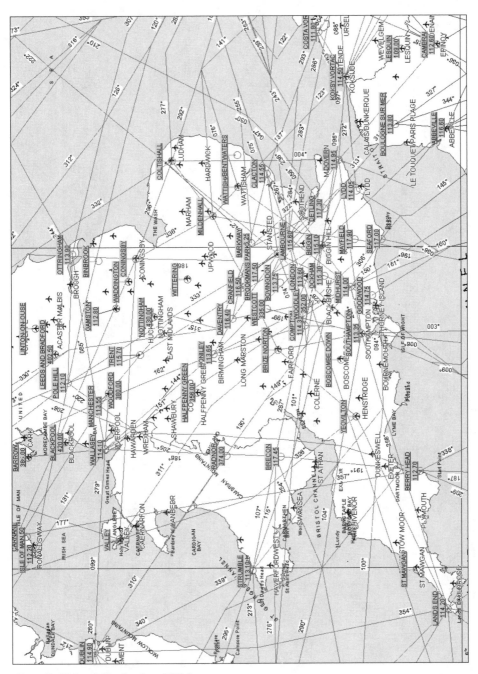

Chart E.45 *South England and Wales.*

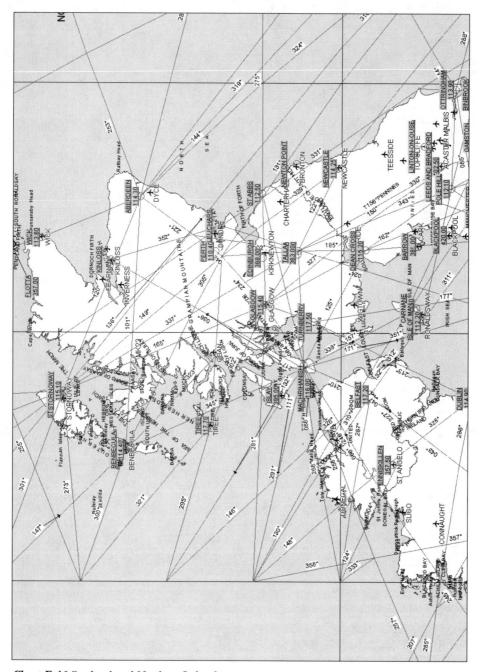

Chart E.46 *Scotland and Northern Ireland.*

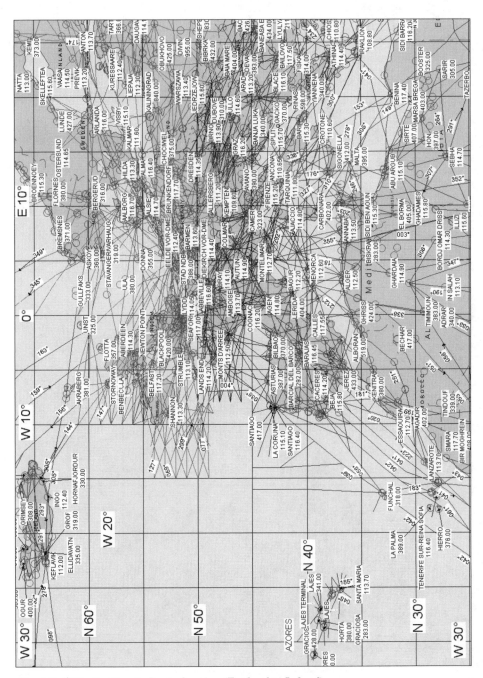

Chart E.47 *North Atlantic Route Crossing (England to Iceland).*

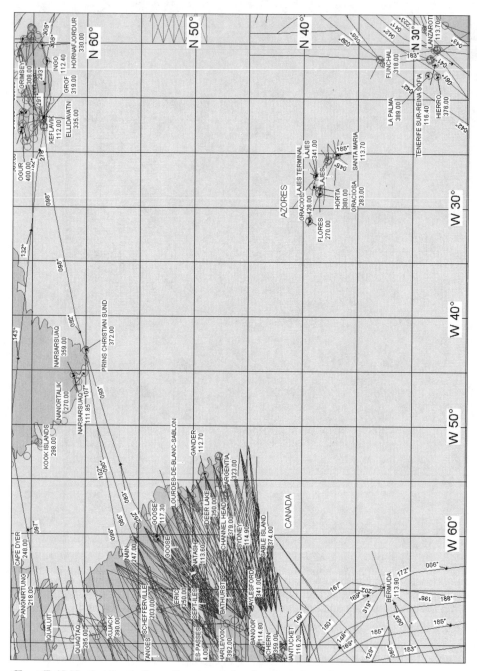

Chart E.48 *North Atlantic Route Crossing (Iceland to Goose Bay, Canada).*

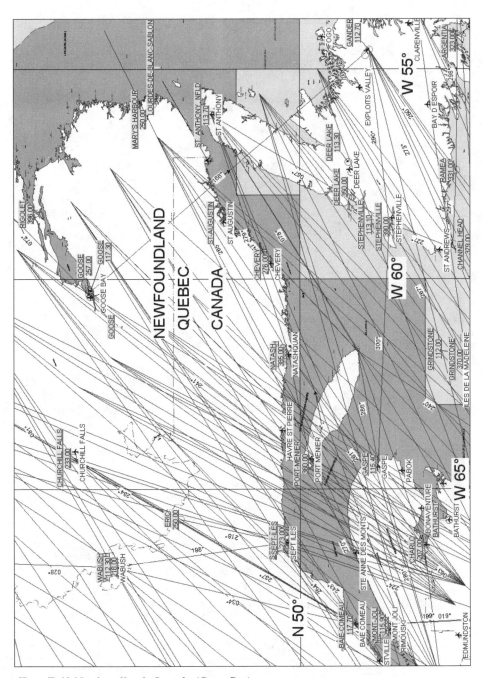

Chart E.49 *Newfoundland, Canada (Goose Bay).*

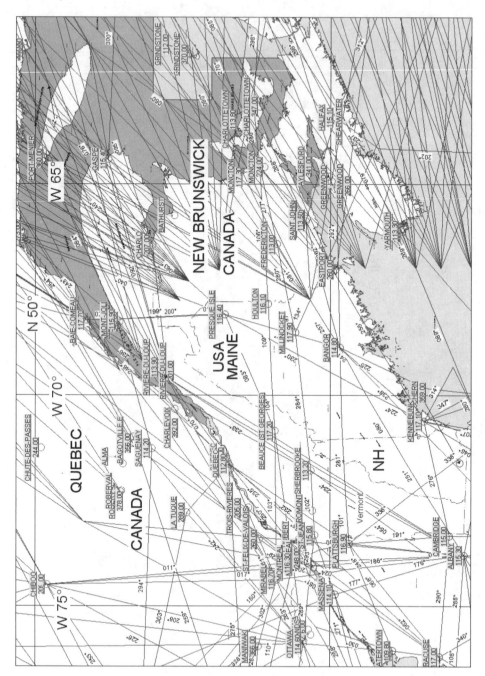

Chart E.50 *New Brunswick and Quebec in Canada; Maine and New Hampshire in the United States.*

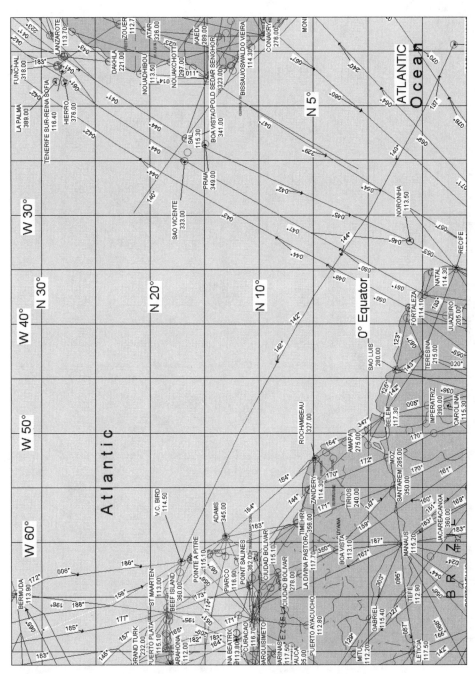

Chart E.51 *Mid-Atlantic crossing from Natal or Recife, Brazil to Dakar Africa.*

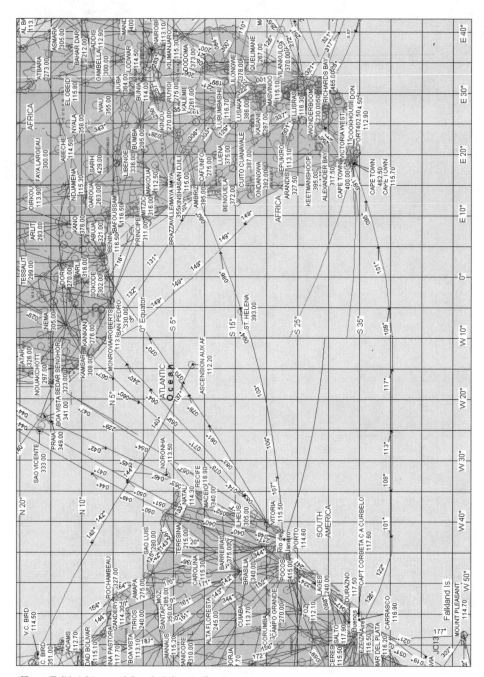

Chart E.51 *Africa and South Atlantic Ocean.*

F

Standard Atmosphere Table

Altitude Ft	lb/ft²	P (Pressure) PSI (lb/in²)	in. Hg	ρ (Density) sl/ft³	T (Temperature) R	°F	°C	Speed of Sound ft/s	kt	Viscosity 10^7 lb sec/ft²
-2,000	2273.7	15.790	32.148	0.0025190	525.8	66.1	19.0	1124.1	666.0	3.777
-1,900	2265.6	15.733	32.033	0.0025120	525.4	65.8	18.8	1123.7	665.8	3.775
-1,800	2257.6	15.678	31.920	0.0025050	525.1	65.4	18.6	1123.3	665.6	3.773
-1,700	2249.5	15.622	31.806	0.0024970	524.7	65.1	18.4	1123.0	665.3	3.771
-1,600	2241.5	15.566	31.693	0.0024900	524.4	64.7	18.2	1122.6	665.1	3.769
-1,500	2233.5	15.510	31.580	0.0024830	524.0	64.4	18.0	1122.2	664.9	3.767
-1,400	2225.5	15.455	31.466	0.0024760	523.7	64.0	17.8	1121.8	664.7	3.765
-1,300	2217.5	15.399	31.353	0.0024690	523.3	63.6	17.6	1121.4	664.4	3.763
-1,200	2209.6	15.344	31.242	0.0024610	522.9	63.3	17.4	1121.0	664.2	3.761
-1,100	2201.7	15.290	31.130	0.0024540	522.6	62.9	17.2	1120.7	664.0	3.759
-1,000	2193.8	15.235	31.018	0.0024470	522.2	62.6	17.0	1120.3	663.7	3.757
-900	2186.0	15.181	30.908	0.0024400	521.9	62.2	16.8	1119.9	663.5	3.755
-800	2178.1	15.126	30.796	0.0024330	521.5	61.9	16.6	1119.5	663.3	3.753
-700	2170.3	15.072	30.686	0.0024260	521.2	61.5	16.4	1119.1	663.1	3.751
-600	2162.5	15.017	30.576	0.0024190	520.8	61.1	16.2	1118.8	662.8	3.749
-500	2154.7	14.963	30.465	0.0024120	520.5	60.8	16.0	1118.4	662.6	3.747
400	2147.0	14.910	30.357	0.0024050	520.1	60.4	15.8	1118.0	662.4	3.745
-300	2139.3	14.856	30.248	0.0023980	519.7	60.1	15.6	1117.6	662.2	3.743
-200	2131.6	14.803	30.139	0.0023910	519.4	59.7	15.4	1117.2	661.9	3.741
-100	2123.9	14.749	30.030	0.0023840	519.0	59.4	15.2	1116.8	661.7	3.739
0	2116.2	14.696	29.921	0.0023770	518.7	59.0	15.0	1116.5	661.5	3.737
100	2108.6	14.643	29.814	0.0023700	518.3	58.6	14.8	1116.1	661.3	3.735
200	2101.0	14.590	29.706	0.0023630	518.0	58.3	14.6	1115.7	661.0	3.733

Altitude Ft	lb/ft²	P (Pressure) PSI (lb/in²)	in. Hg	ρ (Density) sl/ft³	R	°F	°C	ft/s	kt	Viscosity 10⁻⁷ lb sec/ft²
300	2093.4	14.538	29.599	0.0023560	517.6	57.9	14.4	1115.3	660.8	3.731
400	2085.8	14.485	29.491	0.0023490	517.2	57.6	14.2	1114.9	660.6	3.729
500	2078.3	14.433	29.385	0.0023420	516.9	57.2	14.0	1114.5	660.3	3.727
600	2070.7	14.380	29.278	0.0023350	516.5	56.9	13.8	1114.1	660.1	3.725
700	2063.2	14.328	29.172	0.0023290	516.2	56.5	13.6	1113.8	659.9	3.723
800	2055.8	14.276	29.067	0.0023220	515.8	56.2	13.4	1113.4	659.7	3.721
900	2048.3	14.224	28.961	0.0023150	515.5	55.8	13.2	1113.0	659.4	3.719
1,000	2040.9	14.173	28.856	0.0023080	515.1	55.4	13.0	1112.6	659.2	3.717
1,100	2033.4	14.121	28.750	0.0023010	514.7	55.1	12.8	1112.2	659.0	3.715
1,200	2026.0	14.069	28.646	0.0022950	514.4	54.7	12.6	1111.8	658.7	3.713
1,300	2018.7	14.019	28.542	0.0022880	514.0	54.4	12.4	1111.5	658.5	3.711
1,400	2011.3	13.967	28.438	0.0022810	513.7	54.0	12.2	1111.1	658.3	3.709
1,500	2004.0	13.917	28.335	0.0022740	513.3	53.7	12.0	1110.7	658.1	3.707
1,600	1996.7	13.866	28.231	0.0022680	513.0	53.3	11.8	1110.3	657.8	3.705
1,700	1989.4	13.815	28.128	0.0022610	512.6	52.9	11.6	1109.9	657.6	3.703
1,800	1982.2	13.765	28.026	0.0022540	512.3	52.6	11.4	1109.5	657.4	3.701
1,900	1974.9	13.715	27.923	0.0022480	511.9	52.2	11.2	1109.1	657.1	3.699
2,000	1967.7	13.665	27.821	0.0022410	511.5	51.9	11.0	1108.7	656.9	3.697
2,100	1960.5	13.615	27.720	0.0022340	511.2	51.5	10.8	1108.4	656.7	3.695
2,200	1953.3	13.565	27.618	0.0022280	510.8	51.2	10.6	1108.0	656.5	3.693
2,300	1946.2	13.515	27.517	0.0022210	510.5	50.8	10.4	1107.6	656.2	3.691
2,400	1939.0	13.465	27.416	0.0022140	510.1	50.4	10.2	1107.2	656.0	3.689
2,500	1931.9	13.416	27.315	0.0022080	509.8	50.1	10.1	1106.8	655.8	3.687
2,600	1924.8	13.367	27.215	0.0022010	509.4	49.7	9.9	1106.4	655.5	3.685
2,700	1917.8	13.318	27.116	0.0021950	509.0	49.4	9.7	1106.0	655.3	3.683
2,800	1910.7	13.269	27.015	0.0021880	508.7	49.0	9.5	1105.7	655.1	3.681
2,900	1903.7	13.220	26.916	0.0021820	508.3	48.7	9.3	1105.3	654.9	3.679
3,000	1896.7	13.172	26.818	0.0021750	508.0	48.3	9.1	1104.9	654.6	3.677
3,100	1889.7	13.123	26.719	0.0021690	507.6	48.0	8.9	1104.5	654.4	3.675
3,200	1882.7	13.074	26.620	0.0021620	507.3	47.6	8.7	1104.1	654.2	3.673
3,300	1875.8	13.026	26.522	0.0021560	506.9	47.2	8.5	1103.7	653.9	3.671
3,400	1868.9	12.978	26.424	0.0021490	506.5	46.9	8.3	1103.3	653.7	3.669
3,500	1862.0	12.931	26.327	0.0021430	506.2	46.5	8.1	1102.9	653.5	3.667
3,600	1855.1	12.883	26.229	0.0021360	505.8	46.2	7.9	1102.5	653.2	3.665
3,700	1848.2	12.835	26.132	0.0021300	505.5	45.8	7.7	1102.2	653.0	3.663
3,800	1841.4	12.788	26.036	0.0021240	505.1	45.5	7.5	1101.8	652.8	3.661
3,900	1834.5	12.740	25.938	0.0021170	504.8	45.1	7.3	1101.4	652.6	3.659
4,000	1827.7	12.692	25.842	0.0021110	504.4	44.7	7.1	1101.0	652.3	3.657
4,100	1821.0	12.646	25.747	0.0021050	504.1	44.4	6.9	1100.6	652.1	3.655
4,200	1814.2	12.599	25.651	0.0020980	503.7	44.0	6.7	1100.2	651.9	3.653
4,300	1807.5	12.552	25.556	0.0020920	503.3	43.7	6.5	1099.8	651.6	3.651
4,400	1800.8	12.506	25.462	0.0020860	503.0	43.3	6.3	1099.4	651.4	3.649
4,500	1794.1	12.459	25.367	0.0020790	502.6	43.0	6.1	1099.0	651.2	3.647
4,600	1787.4	12.413	25.272	0.0020730	502.3	42.6	5.9	1098.7	650.9	3.645
4,700	1780.7	12.366	25.177	0.0020670	501.9	42.2	5.7	1098.3	650.7	3.643
4,800	1774.1	12.320	25.084	0.0020610	501.6	41.9	5.5	1097.9	650.5	3.641
4,900	1767.5	12.274	24.991	0.0020540	501.2	41.5	5.3	1097.5	650.2	3.639
5,000	1760.9	12.228	24.897	0.0020480	500.8	41.2	5.1	1097.1	650.0	3.637

ALTITUDE Fᴛ	lb/ft²	P (PRESSURE) PSI (lb/in²)	ɪɴ. Hɢ	ρ (DENSITY) sl/ft³	T (TEMPERATURE) R	°F	°C	SPEED OF SOUND ft/s	ᴋᴛ	VISCOSITY 10⁻⁷ lb sec/ft²
5,100	1754.3	12.183	24.804	0.0020420	500.5	40.8	4.9	1096.7	649.8	3.635
5,200	1747.7	12.137	24.711	0.0020360	500.1	40.5	4.7	1096.3	649.5	3.632
5,300	1741.2	12.092	24.619	0.0020300	499.8	40.1	4.5	1095.9	649.3	3.630
5,400	1734.7	12.047	24.527	0.0020230	499.4	39.8	4.3	1095.5	649.1	3.628
5,500	1728.2	12.001	24.435	0.0020170	499.1	39.4	4.1	1095.1	648.9	3.626
5,600	1721.7	11.956	24.343	0.0020110	498.7	39.0	3.9	1094.8	648.6	3.624
5,700	1715.3	11.912	24.253	0.0020050	498.3	38.7	3.7	1094.4	648.4	3.622
5,800	1708.8	11.867	24.161	0.0019990	498.0	38.3	3.5	1094.0	648.2	3.620
5,900	1702.4	11.822	24.070	0.0019930	497.6	38.0	3.3	1093.6	647.9	3.618
6,000	1696.0	11.778	23.980	0.0019870	497.3	37.6	3.1	1093.2	647.7	3.616
6,100	1689.6	11.733	23.889	0.0019810	496.9	37.3	2.9	1092.8	647.5	3.614
6,200	1683.3	11.690	23.800	0.0019750	496.6	36.9	2.7	1092.4	647.2	3.612
6,300	1676.9	11.645	23.710	0.0019690	496.2	36.5	2.5	1092.0	647.0	3.610
6,400	1670.6	11.601	23.621	0.0019630	495.9	36.2	2.3	1091.6	646.8	3.608
6,500	1664.3	11.558	23.532	0.0019570	495.5	35.8	2.1	1091.2	646.5	3.606
6,600	1658.0	11.514	23.443	0.0019510	495.1	35.5	1.9	1090.8	646.3	3.604
6,700	1651.8	11.471	23.355	0.0019450	494.8	35.1	1.7	1090.4	646.1	3.602
6,800	1645.5	11.427	23.266	0.0019390	494.4	34.8	1.5	1090.0	645.8	3.600
6,900	1639.3	11.384	23.178	0.0019330	494.1	34.4	1.3	1089.7	645.6	3.598
7,000	1633.1	11.341	23.090	0.0019270	493.7	34.1	1.1	1089.3	645.4	3.596
7,100	1626.9	11.298	23.003	0.0019210	493.4	33.7	0.9	1088.9	645.1	3.594
7,200	1620.7	11.255	22.915	0.0019150	493.0	33.3	0.7	1088.5	644.9	3.592
7,300	1614.6	11.213	22.829	0.0019090	492.6	33.0	0.5	1088.1	644.7	3.590
7,400	1608.5	11.170	22.743	0.0019030	492.3	32.6	0.3	1087.7	644.4	3.588
7,500	1602.3	11.127	22.655	0.0018980	491.9	32.3	0.1	1087.3	644.2	3.586
7,600	1596.2	11.085	22.569	0.0018920	491.6	31.9	0.0	1086.9	644.0	3.584
7,700	1590.2	11.043	22.484	0.0018860	491.2	31.6	-0.3	1086.5	643.7	3.582
7,800	1584.1	11.001	22.398	0.0018800	490.9	31.2	-0.4	1086.1	643.5	3.579
7,900	1578.1	10.959	22.313	0.0018740	490.5	30.8	-0.6	1085.7	643.3	3.577
8,000	1572.1	10.917	22.228	0.0018680	490.2	30.5	-0.8	1085.3	643.0	3.575
8,100	1566.1	10.876	22.143	0.0018630	489.8	30.1	-1.0	1084.9	642.8	3.573
8,200	1560.1	10.834	22.058	0.0018570	489.4	29.8	-1.2	1084.5	642.6	3.571
8,300	1554.1	10.792	21.973	0.0018510	489.1	29.4	-1.4	1084.1	642.3	3.569
8,400	1548.2	10.751	21.890	0.0018450	488.7	29.1	-1.6	1083.7	642.1	3.567
8,500	1542.3	10.710	21.807	0.0018400	488.4	28.7	-1.8	1083.3	641.9	3.565
8,600	1536.4	10.669	21.723	0.0018340	488.0	28.3	-2.0	1083.0	641.6	3.563
8,700	1530.5	10.628	21.640	0.0018280	487.7	28.0	-2.2	1082.6	641.4	3.561
8,800	1524.6	10.588	21.556	0.0018230	487.3	27.6	-2.4	1082.2	641.2	3.559
8,900	1518.8	10.547	21.474	0.0018170	486.9	27.3	-2.6	1081.8	640.9	3.557
9,000	1512.9	10.506	21.391	0.0018110	486.6	26.9	-2.8	1081.4	640.7	3.555
9,100	1507.1	10.466	21.309	0.0018060	486.2	26.6	-3.0	1081.0	640.5	3.553
9,200	1501.3	10.426	21.227	0.0018000	485.9	26.2	-3.2	1080.6	640.2	3.551
9,300	1495.5	10.385	21.145	0.0017940	485.5	25.9	-3.4	1080.2	640.0	3.549
9,400	1489.8	10.346	21.064	0.0017890	485.2	25.5	-3.6	1079.8	639.8	3.547
9,500	1484.0	10.306	20.982	0.0017830	484.8	25.1	-3.8	1079.4	639.5	3.545
9,600	1478.3	10.266	20.902	0.0017780	484.5	24.8	-4.0	1079.0	639.3	3.542
9,700	1472.6	10.226	20.821	0.0017720	484.1	24.4	-4.2	1078.6	639.1	3.540
9,800	1466.9	10.187	20.741	0.0017670	483.7	24.1	-4.4	1078.2	638.8	3.538
9,900	1461.3	10.148	20.661	0.0017610	483.4	23.7	-4.6	1077.8	638.6	3.536

Altitude Ft	lb/ft²	P (Pressure) PSI (lb/in²)	IN. Hg	P (Density) sl/ft³	T (Temperature) R	°F	°C	Speed of Sound ft/s	KT	Viscosity 10⁻⁷ lb sec/ft²
10,000	1455.6	10.108	20.581	0.0017560	483.0	23.4	-4.8	1077.4	638.3	3.534
10,100	1450.0	10.069	20.502	0.0017500	482.7	23.0	-5.0	1077.0	638.1	3.532
10,200	1444.4	10.031	20.422	0.0017450	482.3	22.6	-5.2	1076.6	637.9	3.530
10,300	1438.8	9.992	20.343	0.0017390	482.0	22.3	-5.4	1076.2	637.6	3.528
10,400	1433.2	9.953	20.264	0.0017340	481.6	21.9	-5.6	1075.8	637.4	3.526
10,500	1427.6	9.914	20.185	0.0017280	481.2	21.6	-5.8	1075.4	637.2	3.524
10,600	1422.1	9.876	20.107	0.0017230	480.9	21.2	-6.0	1075.0	636.9	3.522
10,700	1416.5	9.837	20.028	0.0017170	480.5	20.9	-6.2	1074.6	636.7	3.520
10,800	1411.0	9.799	19.950	0.0017120	480.2	20.5	-6.4	1074.2	636.5	3.518
10,900	1405.5	9.760	19.872	0.0017060	479.8	20.2	-6.6	1073.8	636.2	3.516
11,000	1400.1	9.723	19.796	0.0017010	479.5	19.8	-6.8	1073.4	636.0	3.514
11,100	1394.6	9.685	19.718	0.0016960	479.1	19.4	-7.0	1073.0	635.8	3.512
11,200	1389.2	9.647	19.642	0.0016900	478.8	19.1	-7.2	1072.6	635.5	3.509
11,300	1383.7	9.609	19.564	0.0016850	478.4	18.7	-7.4	1072.2	635.3	3.507
11,400	1378.3	9.572	19.488	0.0016800	478.0	18.4	-7.6	1071.8	635.0	3.505
11,500	1372.9	9.534	19.411	0.0016740	477.7	18.0	-7.8	1071.4	634.8	3.503
11,600	1367.6	9.497	19.337	0.0016690	477.3	17.7	-8.0	1071.0	634.6	3.501
11,700	1362.2	9.460	19.260	0.0016640	477.0	17.3	-8.2	1070.6	634.3	3.499
11,800	1356.9	9.423	19.185	0.0016580	476.6	16.9	-8.4	1070.2	634.1	3.497
11,900	1351.5	9.385	19.109	0.0016530	476.3	16.6	-8.6	1069.8	633.9	3.495
12,000	1346.2	9.349	19.034	0.0016480	475.9	16.2	-8.8	1069.4	633.6	3.493
12,100	1341.0	9.313	18.960	0.0016430	475.5	15.9	-9.0	1069.0	633.4	3.491
12,200	1335.7	9.276	18.886	0.0016370	475.2	15.5	-9.2	1068.6	633.1	3.489
12,300	1330.4	9.239	18.811	0.0016320	474.8	15.2	-9.4	1068.2	632.9	3.487
12,400	1325.2	9.203	18.737	0.0016270	474.5	14.8	-9.6	1067.8	632.7	3.485
12,500	1320.0	9.167	18.664	0.0016220	474.1	14.5	-9.8	1067.4	632.4	3.482
12,600	1314.8	9.131	18.590	0.0016170	473.8	14.1	-10.0	1067.0	632.2	3.480
12,700	1309.6	9.094	18.516	0.0016120	473.4	13.7	-10.1	1066.6	632.0	3.478
12,800	1304.4	9.058	18.443	0.0016060	473.1	13.4	-10.3	1066.2	631.7	3.476
12,900	1299.3	9.023	18.371	0.0016010	472.7	13.0	-10.5	1065.8	631.5	3.474
13,000	1294.1	8.987	18.297	0.0015960	472.3	12.7	-10.7	1065.4	631.2	3.472
13,100	1289.0	8.951	18.225	0.0015910	472.0	12.3	-10.9	1065.0	631.0	3.470
13,200	1283.9	8.916	18.153	0.0015860	471.6	12.0	-11.1	1064.6	630.8	3.468
13,300	1278.8	8.881	18.081	0.0015810	471.3	11.6	-11.3	1064.2	630.5	3.466
13,400	1273.7	8.845	18.009	0.0015760	470.9	11.2	-11.5	1063.8	630.3	3.464
13,500	1268.7	8.810	17.938	0.0015710	470.6	10.9	-11.7	1063.4	630.1	3.462
13,600	1263.6	8.775	17.866	0.0015660	470.2	10.5	-11.9	1063.0	629.8	3.460
13,700	1258.6	8.740	17.795	0.0015610	469.8	10.2	-12.1	1062.6	629.6	3.457
13,800	1253.6	8.706	17.725	0.0015560	469.5	9.8	-12.3	1062.2	629.3	3.455
13,900	1248.6	8.671	17.654	0.0015510	469.1	9.5	-12.5	1061.8	629.1	3.453
14,000	1243.6	8.636	17.583	0.0015460	468.8	9.1	-12.7	1061.4	628.9	3.451
14,100	1238.7	8.602	17.514	0.0015410	468.4	8.8	-12.9	1061.0	628.6	3.449
14,200	1233.7	8.567	17.443	0.0015360	468.1	8.4	-13.1	1060.6	628.4	3.447
14,300	1228.8	8.533	17.374	0.0015310	467.7	8.0	-13.3	1060.2	628.1	3.445
14,400	1223.9	8.499	17.305	0.0015260	467.4	7.7	-13.5	1059.8	627.9	3.443
14,500	1219.0	8.465	17.235	0.0015210	467.0	7.3	-13.7	1059.4	627.7	3.441
14,600	1214.1	8.431	17.166	0.0015160	466.6	7.0	-13.9	1059.0	627.4	3.439
14,700	1209.3	8.398	17.098	0.0015110	466.3	6.6	-14.1	1058.6	627.2	3.437
14,800	1204.4	8.364	17.029	0.0015060	465.9	6.3	-14.3	1058.2	626.9	3.434
14,900	1199.6	8.331	16.961	0.0015010	465.6	5.9	-14.5	1057.8	626.7	3.432

ALTITUDE Ft	lb/ft²	P (PRESSURE) PSI (lb/in²)	IN. HG	P (DENSITY) sl/ft³	T (TEMPERATURE) R	°F	°C	SPEED OF SOUND ft/s	KT	VISCOSITY 10⁻⁷ lb sec/ft²
15,000	1194.8	8.297	16.893	0.0014960	465.2	5.6	-14.7	1057.4	626.5	3.430
15,100	1190.0	8.264	16.825	0.0014910	464.9	5.2	-14.9	1057.0	626.2	3.428
15,200	1185.2	8.231	16.758	0.0014860	464.5	4.8	-15.1	1056.5	626.0	3.426
15,300	1180.4	8.197	16.690	0.0014820	464.1	4.5	-15.3	1056.1	625.7	3.424
15,400	1175.7	8.165	16.623	0.0014770	463.8	4.1	-15.5	1055.7	625.5	3.422
15,500	1171.0	8.132	16.557	0.0014720	463.4	3.8	-15.7	1055.3	625.3	3.420
15,600	1166.2	8.099	16.489	0.0014670	463.1	3.4	-15.9	1054.9	625.0	3.418
15,700	1161.5	8.066	16.422	0.0014620	462.7	3.1	-16.1	1054.5	624.8	3.415
15,800	1156.8	8.033	16.356	0.0014580	462.4	2.7	-16.3	1054.1	624.5	3.413
15,900	1152.2	8.001	16.291	0.0014530	462.0	2.3	-16.5	1053.7	624.3	3.411
16,000	1147.5	7.969	16.225	0.0014480	461.7	2.0	-16.7	1053.3	624.1	3.409
16,100	1142.9	7.937	16.160	0.0014430	461.3	1.6	-16.9	1052.9	623.8	3.407
16,200	1138.2	7.904	16.093	0.0014390	460.9	1.3	-17.1	1052.5	623.6	3.405
16,300	1133.6	7.872	16.028	0.0014340	460.6	0.9	-17.3	1052.1	623.3	3.403
16,400	1129.0	7.840	15.963	0.0014290	460.2	0.6	-17.5	1051.7	623.1	3.401
16,500	1124.4	7.808	15.898	0.0014240	459.9	0.2	-17.7	1051.3	622.9	3.399
16,600	1119.9	7.777	15.834	0.0014200	459.5	0.2	-17.7	1050.9	622.6	3.397
16,700	1115.3	7.745	15.769	0.0014150	459.2	0.5	-17.5	1050.5	622.4	3.394
16,800	1110.8	7.714	15.706	0.0014100	458.8	0.9	-17.3	1050.0	622.1	3.392
16,900	1106.2	7.682	15.641	0.0014060	458.5	-1.2	-18.5	1049.6	621.9	3.390
17,000	1101.7	7.651	15.577	0.0014010	458.1	-1.6	-18.7	1049.2	621.7	3.388
17,100	1097.2	7.619	15.513	0.0013960	457.7	-1.9	-18.9	1048.8	621.4	3.386
17,200	1092.8	7.589	15.451	0.0013920	457.4	-2.3	-19.1	1048.4	621.2	3.384
17,300	1088.3	7.558	15.388	0.0013870	457.0	-2.6	-19.2	1048.0	620.9	3.382
17,400	1083.9	7.527	15.325	0.0013830	456.7	-3.0	-19.4	1047.6	620.7	3.380
17,500	1079.4	7.496	15.262	0.0013780	456.3	-3.4	-19.6	1047.2	620.4	3.378
17,600	1075.0	7.465	15.199	0.0013730	456.0	-3.7	-19.8	1046.8	620.2	3.375
17,700	1070.6	7.435	15.137	0.0013690	455.6	-4.1	-20.0	1046.4	620.0	3.373
17,800	1066.2	7.404	15.075	0.0013640	455.2	-4.4	-20.2	1046.0	619.7	3.371
17,900	1061.8	7.374	15.013	0.0013600	454.9	-4.8	-20.4	1045.6	619.5	3.369
18,000	1057.5	7.344	14.952	0.0013550	454.5	-5.1	-20.6	1045.1	619.2	3.367
18,100	1053.1	7.313	14.890	0.0013510	454.2	-5.5	-20.8	1044.7	619.0	3.365
18,200	1048.8	7.283	14.829	0.0013460	453.8	-5.9	-21.0	1044.3	618.7	3.363
18,300	1044.5	7.253	14.768	0.0013420	453.5	-6.2	-21.2	1043.9	618.5	3.361
18,400	1040.2	7.224	14.707	0.0013370	453.1	-6.6	-21.4	1043.5	618.3	3.358
18,500	1035.9	7.194	14.647	0.0013330	452.8	-6.9	-21.6	1043.1	618.0	3.356
18,600	1031.6	7.164	14.586	0.0013280	452.4	-7.3	-21.8	1042.7	617.8	3.354
18,700	1027.4	7.135	14.526	0.0013240	452.0	-7.6	-22.0	1042.3	617.5	3.352
18,800	1023.1	7.105	14.466	0.0013200	451.7	-8.0	-22.2	1041.9	617.3	3.350
18,900	1018.9	7.076	14.406	0.0013150	451.3	-8.3	-22.4	1041.5	617.0	3.348
19,000	1014.7	7.047	14.347	0.0013110	451.0	-8.7	-22.6	1041.0	616.8	3.346
19,100	1010.5	7.017	14.287	0.0013060	450.6	-9.1	-22.8	1040.6	616.6	3.344
19,200	1006.3	6.988	14.228	0.0013020	450.3	-9.4	-23.0	1040.2	616.3	3.341
19,300	1002.1	6.959	14.169	0.0012980	449.9	-9.8	-23.2	1039.8	616.1	3.339
19,400	997.9	6.930	14.109	0.0012930	449.6	-10.1	-23.4	1039.4	615.8	3.337
19,500	993.8	6.901	14.051	0.0012890	449.2	-10.5	-23.6	1039.0	615.5	3.335
19,600	989.7	6.873	13.993	0.0012850	448.8	-10.8	-23.8	1038.6	615.3	3.333
19,700	985.5	6.844	13.934	0.0012800	448.5	-11.2	-24.0	1038.2	615.1	3.331
19,800	981.4	6.815	13.876	0.0012760	448.1	-11.5	-24.2	1037.8	614.9	3.329
19,900	977.4	6.788	13.819	0.0012720	447.8	-11.9	-24.4	1037.3	614.6	3.326

ALTITUDE FT	lb/ft²	P (PRESSURE) PSI (lb/in²)	IN. HG	ρ (DENSITY) sl/ft³	T (TEMPERATURE) R	°F	°C	SPEED OF SOUND ft/s	KT	VISCOSITY 10⁻⁷ lb sec/ft²
20,000	973.3	6.759	13.762	0.0012670	447.4	-12.3	-24.6	1036.9	614.4	3.324
20,100	969.2	6.731	13.704	0.0012630	447.1	-12.6	-24.8	1036.5	614.1	3.322
20,200	965.2	6.703	13.647	0.0012590	446.7	-13.0	-25.0	1036.1	613.9	3.320
20,300	961.1	6.674	13.589	0.0012540	446.3	-13.3	-25.2	1035.7	613.6	3.318
20,400	957.1	6.647	13.532	0.0012500	446.0	-13.7	-25.4	1035.3	613.4	3.316
20,500	953.1	6.619	13.476	0.0012460	445.6	-14.0	-25.6	1034.9	613.1	3.314
20,600	949.1	6.591	13.419	0.0012420	445.3	-14.4	-25.8	1034.5	612.9	3.312
20,700	945.1	6.563	13.363	0.0012370	444.9	-14.8	-26.0	1034.0	612.7	3.309
20,800	941.2	6.536	13.308	0.0012330	444.6	-15.1	-26.2	1033.6	612.4	3.307
20,900	937.2	6.508	13.251	0.0012290	444.2	-15.5	-26.4	1033.2	612.2	3.305
21,000	933.3	6.481	13.196	0.0012250	443.9	-15.8	-26.6	1032.8	611.9	3.303
21,100	929.3	6.453	13.139	0.0012210	443.5	-16.2	-26.8	1032.4	611.7	3.301
21,200	925.4	6.426	13.084	0.0012170	443.1	-16.5	-27.0	1032.0	611.4	3.299
21,300	921.5	6.399	13.029	0.0012120	442.8	-16.9	-27.2	1031.6	611.2	3.297
21,400	917.6	6.372	12.974	0.0012080	442.4	-17.2	-27.4	1031.1	610.9	3.294
21,500	913.8	6.346	12.920	0.0012040	442.1	-17.6	-27.6	1030.7	610.7	3.292
21,600	909.9	6.319	12.865	0.0012000	441.7	-18.0	-27.8	1030.3	610.4	3.290
21,700	906.1	6.292	12.811	0.0011960	441.4	-18.3	-28.0	1029.9	610.2	3.288
21,800	902.2	6.265	12.756	0.0011920	441.0	-18.7	-28.1	1029.5	609.9	3.286
21,900	898.4	6.239	12.703	0.0011880	440.7	-19.0	-28.3	1029.1	609.7	3.284
22,000	894.6	6.213	12.649	0.0011840	440.3	-19.4	-28.5	1028.6	609.5	3.281
22,100	890.8	6.186	12.595	0.0011800	439.9	-19.7	-28.7	1028.2	609.2	3.279
22,200	887.0	6.160	12.541	0.0011760	439.6	-20.1	-28.9	1027.8	609.0	3.277
22,300	883.3	6.134	12.489	0.0011710	439.2	-20.4	-29.1	1027.4	608.7	3.275
22,400	879.5	6.108	12.435	0.0011670	438.9	-20.8	-29.3	1027.0	608.5	3.273
22,500	875.8	6.082	12.383	0.0011630	438.5	-21.2	-29.5	1026.6	608.2	3.271
22,600	872.0	6.056	12.329	0.0011590	438.2	-21.5	-29.7	1026.2	608.0	3.269
22,700	868.3	6.030	12.277	0.0011550	437.8	-21.9	-29.9	1025.7	607.7	3.266
22,800	864.6	6.004	12.225	0.0011510	437.5	-22.2	-30.1	1025.3	607.5	3.264
22,900	860.9	5.978	12.172	0.0011470	437.1	-22.6	-30.3	1024.9	607.2	3.262
23,000	857.2	5.953	12.120	0.0011430	436.7	-22.9	-30.5	1024.5	607.0	3.260
23,100	853.6	5.928	12.069	0.0011400	436.4	-23.3	-30.7	1024.1	606.7	3.258
23,200	849.9	5.902	12.017	0.0011360	436.0	-23.6	-30.9	1023.6	606.5	3.256
23,300	846.3	5.877	11.966	0.0011320	435.7	-24.0	-31.1	1023.2	606.2	3.253
23,400	842.7	5.852	11.915	0.0011280	435.3	-24.4	-31.3	1022.8	606.0	3.251
23,500	839.1	5.827	11.864	0.0011240	435.0	-24.7	-31.5	1022.4	605.8	3.249
23,600	835.5	5.802	11.813	0.0011200	434.6	-25.1	-31.7	1022.0	605.5	3.247
23,700	831.9	5.777	11.762	0.0011160	434.2	-25.4	-31.9	1021.6	605.3	3.245
23,800	828.3	5.752	11.711	0.0011120	433.9	-25.8	-32.1	1021.1	605.0	3.243
23,900	824.7	5.727	11.660	0.0011080	433.5	-26.1	-32.3	1020.7	604.8	3.240
24,000	821.2	5.703	11.611	0.0011040	433.2	-26.5	-32.5	1020.3	604.5	3.238
24,100	817.6	5.678	11.560	0.0011000	432.8	-26.9	-32.7	1019.9	604.3	3.236
24,200	814.1	5.653	11.511	0.0010970	432.5	-27.2	-32.9	1019.5	604.0	3.234
24,300	810.6	5.629	11.461	0.0010930	432.1	-27.6	-33.1	1019.0	603.8	3.232
24,400	807.1	5.605	11.412	0.0010890	431.8	-27.9	-33.3	1018.6	603.5	3.230
24,500	803.6	5.581	11.362	0.0010850	431.4	-28.3	-33.5	1018.2	603.3	3.227
24,600	800.1	5.556	11.313	0.0010810	431.0	-28.6	-33.7	1017.8	603.0	3.225
24,700	796.7	5.533	11.265	0.0010780	430.7	-29.0	-33.9	1017.4	602.8	3.223
24,800	793.2	5.508	11.215	0.0010740	430.3	-29.3	-34.1	1016.9	602.5	3.221
24,900	789.8	5.485	11.167	0.0010700	430.0	-29.7	-34.3	1016.5	602.3	3.219

ALTITUDE Ft	lb/ft²	P (PRESSURE) PSI (lb/in²)	IN. HG	P (DENSITY) SL/FT³	T (TEMPERATURE) R	°F	°C	SPEED OF SOUND ft/s	KT	VISCOSITY 10⁻⁷ lb sec/ft²
25,000	786.3	5.460	11.118	0.0010660	429.6	-30.1	-34.5	1016.1	602.0	3.217
25,100	782.9	5.437	11.069	0.0010630	429.3	-30.4	-34.7	1015.7	601.8	3.214
25,200	779.5	5.413	11.021	0.0010590	428.9	-30.8	-34.9	1015.3	601.5	3.212
25,300	776.1	5.390	10.973	0.0010550	428.6	-31.1	-35.1	1014.8	601.3	3.210
25,400	772.7	5.366	10.925	0.0010510	428.2	-31.5	-35.3	1014.4	601.0	3.208
25,500	769.4	5.343	10.879	0.0010480	427.8	-31.8	-35.5	1014.0	600.8	3.206
25,600	766.0	5.319	10.831	0.0010440	427.5	-32.2	-35.7	1013.6	600.5	3.204
25,700	762.7	5.297	10.784	0.0010400	427.1	-32.5	-35.9	1013.2	600.3	3.201
25,800	759.3	5.273	10.736	0.0010370	426.8	-32.9	-36.1	1012.7	600.0	3.199
25,900	756.0	5.250	10.689	0.0010330	426.4	-33.3	-36.3	1012.3	599.8	3.197
26,000	752.7	5.227	10.642	0.0010290	426.1	-33.6	-36.4	1011.9	599.5	3.195
26,100	749.4	5.204	10.596	0.0010260	425.7	-34.0	-36.6	1011.5	599.3	3.193
26,200	746.1	5.181	10.549	0.0010220	425.4	-34.3	-36.8	1011.0	599.0	3.190
26,300	742.9	5.159	10.504	0.0010180	425.0	-34.7	-37.0	1010.6	598.8	3.188
26,400	739.6	5.136	10.457	0.0010150	424.6	-35.0	-37.2	1010.2	598.5	3.186
26,500	736.3	5.113	10.411	0.0010110	424.3	-35.4	-37.4	1009.8	598.3	3.184
26,600	733.1	5.091	10.365	0.0010070	423.9	-35.7	-37.6	1009.3	598.0	3.182
26,700	729.9	5.069	10.320	0.0010040	423.6	-36.1	-37.8	1008.9	597.8	3.180
26,800	726.7	5.047	10.275	0.0010000	423.2	-36.5	-38.0	1008.5	597.5	3.177
26,900	723.5	5.024	10.230	0.0009970	422.9	-36.8	-38.2	1008.1	597.3	3.175
27,000	720.3	5.002	10.184	0.0009930	422.5	-37.2	-38.4	1007.7	597.0	3.173
27,100	717.1	4.980	10.139	0.0009900	422.2	-37.5	-38.6	1007.2	596.8	3.171
27,200	713.9	4.958	10.094	0.0009860	421.8	-37.9	-38.8	1006.8	596.5	3.169
27,300	710.8	4.936	10.050	0.0009820	421.4	-38.2	-39.0	1006.4	596.3	3.166
27,400	707.6	4.914	10.005	0.0009790	421.1	-38.6	-39.2	1006.0	596.0	3.164
27,500	704.5	4.892	9.961	0.0009750	420.7	-38.9	-39.4	1005.5	595.8	3.162
27,600	701.3	4.870	9.916	0.0009720	420.4	-39.3	-39.6	1005.1	595.5	3.160
27,700	698.2	4.849	9.872	0.0009680	420.0	-39.7	-39.8	1004.7	595.3	3.158
27,800	695.1	4.827	9.828	0.0009650	419.7	-40.0	-40.0	1004.3	595.0	3.155
27,900	692.0	4.806	9.784	0.0009610	419.3	-40.4	-40.2	1003.8	594.8	3.153
28,000	689.0	4.785	9.742	0.0009580	419.0	-40.7	-40.4	1003.4	594.5	3.151
28,100	685.9	4.763	9.698	0.0009550	418.6	-41.1	-40.6	1003.0	594.2	3.149
28,200	682.8	4.742	9.654	0.0009510	418.2	-41.4	-40.8	1002.6	594.0	3.147
28,300	679.8	4.721	9.612	0.0009480	417.9	-41.8	-41.0	1002.1	593.7	3.144
28,400	676.8	4.700	9.569	0.0009440	417.5	-42.1	-41.2	1001.7	593.5	3.142
28,500	673.7	4.678	9.525	0.0009410	417.2	-42.5	-41.4	1001.3	593.2	3.140
28,600	670.7	4.658	9.483	0.0009370	416.8	-42.9	-41.6	1000.8	593.0	3.138
28,700	667.7	4.637	9.441	0.0009340	416.5	-43.2	-41.8	1000.4	592.7	3.136
28,800	664.7	4.616	9.398	0.0009310	416.1	-43.6	-42.0	1000.0	592.5	3.133
28,900	661.7	4.595	9.356	0.0009270	415.8	-43.9	-42.2	999.6	592.2	3.131
29,000	658.8	4.575	9.315	0.0009240	415.4	-44.3	-42.4	999.1	592.0	3.129
29,100	655.8	4.554	9.272	0.0009210	415.0	-44.6	-42.6	998.7	591.7	3.127
29,200	652.9	4.534	9.231	0.0009170	414.7	-45.0	-42.8	998.3	591.5	3.125
29,300	649.9	4.513	9.189	0.0009140	414.3	-45.3	-43.0	997.9	591.2	3.122
29,400	647.0	4.493	9.148	0.0009100	414.0	-45.7	-43.2	997.4	591.0	3.120
29,500	644.1	4.473	9.107	0.0009070	413.6	-46.1	-43.4	997.0	590.7	3.118
29,600	641.2	4.453	9.066	0.0009040	413.3	-46.4	-43.6	996.6	590.4	3.116
29,700	638.3	4.433	9.025	0.0009010	412.9	-46.8	-43.8	996.1	590.2	3.114
29,800	635.4	4.413	8.984	0.0008970	412.6	-47.1	-44.0	995.7	589.9	3.111
29,900	632.5	4.392	8.943	0.0008940	412.2	-47.5	-44.2	995.3	589.7	3.109

ALTITUDE Ft	lb/ft²	P (Pressure) PSI (lb/in²)	IN. HG	P (Density) sl/ft³	T (Temperature) R	°F	°C	Speed of Sound ft/s	KT	Viscosity 10⁻⁷ lb sec/ft²
30,000	629.7	4.373	8.903	0.0008910	411.8	-47.8	-44.4	994.8	589.4	3.107
30,500	615.5	4.274	8.703	0.0008744	410.1	-49.6	-45.3	992.6	588.1	3.096
31,000	601.6	4.178	8.506	0.0008584	408.3	-51.4	-46.3	990.4	586.8	3.085
31,500	588.0	4.083	8.313	0.0008426	406.5	-53.2	-47.3	988.2	585.5	3.074
32,000	574.6	3.990	8.124	0.0008270	404.8	-55.0	-48.3	986.1	584.2	3.063
32,500	561.4	3.899	7.938	0.0008117	403.0	-56.7	-49.3	983.9	583.0	3.052
33,000	548.5	3.809	7.756	0.0007966	401.2	-58.5	-50.3	981.7	581.7	3.041
33,500	535.9	3.721	7.577	0.0007817	399.4	-60.3	-51.3	979.6	580.4	3.030
34,000	523.5	3.635	7.401	0.0007670	397.6	-62.1	-52.3	977.4	579.1	3.018
34,500	511.3	3.551	7.229	0.0007525	395.9	-63.8	-53.2	975.2	577.8	3.007
35,000	499.3	3.468	7.060	0.0007382	394.1	-65.6	-54.2	973.0	576.5	2.996
35,500	487.6	3.386	6.894	0.0007241	392.3	-67.4	-55.2	970.8	575.2	2.984
36,000	476.1	3.306	6.732	0.0007103	390.5	-69.2	-56.2	968.6	573.9	2.973
36,500	464.9	3.228	6.573	0.0006944	390.0	-69.7	-56.5	967.9	573.5	2.970
37,000	453.9	3.152	6.417	0.0006780	390.0	-69.7	-56.5	967.9	573.5	2.970
37,500	443.1	3.077	6.265	0.0006620	390.0	-69.7	-56.5	967.9	573.5	2.970
38,000	432.6	3.004	6.117	0.0006463	390.0	-69.7	-56.5	967.9	573.5	2.970
38,500	422.4	2.933	5.972	0.0006310	390.0	-69.7	-56.5	967.9	573.5	2.970
39,000	412.4	2.864	5.831	0.0006161	390.0	-69.7	-56.5	967.9	573.5	2.970
39,500	402.7	2.796	5.693	0.0006015	390.0	-69.7	-56.5	967.9	573.5	2.970
40,000	393.1	2.730	5.558	0.0005873	390.0	-69.7	-56.5	967.9	573.5	2.970
40,500	383.8	2.665	5.427	0.0005734	390.0	-69.7	-56.5	967.9	573.5	2.970
41,000	374.8	2.602	5.299	0.0005598	390.0	-69.7	-56.5	967.9	573.5	2.970
41,500	365.9	2.541	5.173	0.0005466	390.0	-69.7	-56.5	967.9	573.5	2.970
42,000	357.2	2.481	5.051	0.0005337	390.0	-69.7	-56.5	967.9	573.5	2.970
42,500	348.8	2.422	4.931	0.0005210	390.0	-69.7	-56.5	967.9	573.5	2.970
43,000	340.5	2.365	4.815	0.0005087	390.0	-69.7	-56.5	967.9	573.5	2.970
43,500	332.5	2.309	4.701	0.0004967	390.0	-69.7	-56.5	967.9	573.5	2.970
44,000	324.6	2.254	4.590	0.0004849	390.0	-69.7	-56.5	967.9	573.5	2.970
44,500	316.9	2.201	4.481	0.0004735	390.0	-69.7	-56.5	967.9	573.5	2.970
45,000	309.5	2.149	4.375	0.0004623	390.0	-69.7	-56.5	967.9	573.5	2.970
45,500	302.1	2.098	4.272	0.0004513	390.0	-69.7	-56.5	967.9	573.5	2.970
46,000	295.0	2.049	4.171	0.0004407	390.0	-69.7	-56.5	967.9	573.5	2.970
46,500	288.0	2.000	4.072	0.0004303	390.0	-69.7	-56.5	967.9	573.5	2.970
47,000	281.2	1.953	3.976	0.0004201	390.0	-69.7	-56.5	967.9	573.5	2.970
47,500	274.6	1.907	3.882	0.0004102	390.0	-69.7	-56.5	967.9	573.5	2.970
48,000	268.1	1.862	3.790	0.0004005	390.0	-69.7	-56.5	967.9	573.5	2.970
48,500	221.7	1.540	3.135	0.0003910	390.0	-69.7	-56.5	967.9	573.5	2.970
49,000	255.5	1.775	3.613	0.0003818	390.0	-69.7	-56.5	967.9	573.5	2.970
49,500	249.5	1.733	3.528	0.0003727	390.0	-69.7	-56.5	967.9	573.5	2.970
50,000	243.6	1.692	3.444	0.0003639	390.0	-69.7	-56.5	967.9	573.5	2.970
50,500	237.9	1.652	3.363	0.0003553	390.0	-69.7	-56.5	967.9	573.5	2.970
51,000	232.2	1.613	3.284	0.0003469	390.0	-69.7	-56.5	967.9	573.5	2.970
51,500	226.7	1.575	3.206	0.0003387	390.0	-69.7	-56.5	967.9	573.5	2.970
52,000	221.4	1.537	3.130	0.0003307	390.0	-69.7	-56.5	967.9	573.5	2.970
52,500	216.2	1.501	3.056	0.0003229	390.0	-69.7	-56.5	967.9	573.5	2.970
53,000	211.1	1.466	2.984	0.0003153	390.0	-69.7	-56.5	967.9	573.5	2.970
53,500	206.7	1.435	2.922	0.0003078	390.0	-69.7	-56.5	967.9	573.5	2.970
54,000	201.2	1.397	2.845	0.0003006	390.0	-69.7	-56.5	967.9	573.5	2.970
54,500	196.4	1.364	2.777	0.0002935	390.0	-69.7	-56.5	967.9	573.5	2.970

ALTITUDE Ft	lb/ft²	P (PRESSURE) PSI (lb/in²)	IN. HG	P (DENSITY) sl/ft³	T (TEMPERATURE) R	°F	°C	SPEED OF SOUND ft/s	KT	VISCOSITY 10⁻⁷ lb sec/ft²
55,000	191.8	1.332	2.712	0.0002865	390.0	-69.7	-56.5	967.9	573.5	2.970
55,500	187.3	1.300	2.648	0.0002798	390.0	-69.7	-56.5	967.9	573.5	2.970
56,000	182.8	1.270	2.585	0.0002731	390.0	-69.7	-56.5	967.9	573.5	2.970
56,500	178.5	1.240	2.524	0.0002667	390.0	-69.7	-56.5	967.9	573.5	2.970
57,000	174.3	1.210	2.465	0.0002604	390.0	-69.7	-56.5	967.9	573.5	2.970
57,500	170.2	1.182	2.406	0.0002542	390.0	-69.7	-56.5	967.9	573.5	2.970
58,000	166.2	1.154	2.349	0.0002482	390.0	-69.7	-56.5	967.9	573.5	2.970
58,500	162.3	1.127	2.294	0.0002424	390.0	-69.7	-56.5	967.9	573.5	2.970
59,000	158.4	1.100	2.240	0.0002367	390.0	-69.7	-56.5	967.9	573.5	2.970
59,500	154.7	1.074	2.187	0.0002311	390.0	-69.7	-56.5	967.9	573.5	2.970
60,000	151.0	1.049	2.135	0.0002256	390.0	-69.7	-56.5	967.9	573.5	2.970
60,500	147.5	1.024	2.085	0.0002203	390.0	-69.7	-56.5	967.9	573.5	2.970
61,000	144.0	1.000	2.036	0.0002151	390.0	-69.7	-56.5	967.9	573.5	2.970
61,500	140.6	0.976	1.988	0.0002100	390.0	-69.7	-56.5	967.9	573.5	2.970
62,000	137.3	0.953	1.941	0.0002051	390.0	-69.7	-56.5	967.9	573.5	2.970
62,500	134.0	0.931	1.895	0.0002002	390.0	-69.7	-56.5	967.9	573.5	2.970
63,000	130.9	0.909	1.850	0.0001955	390.0	-69.7	-56.5	967.9	573.5	2.970
63,500	127.8	0.887	1.807	0.0001909	390.0	-69.7	-56.5	967.9	573.5	2.970
64,000	124.8	0.866	1.764	0.0001864	390.0	-69.7	-56.5	967.9	573.5	2.970
64,500	121.8	0.846	1.722	0.0001820	390.0	-69.7	-56.5	967.9	573.5	2.970
65,000	118.9	0.826	1.682	0.0001777	390.0	-69.7	-56.5	967.9	573.5	2.970
65,500	116.1	0.806	1.642	0.0001735	390.0	-69.7	-56.5	967.9	573.5	2.970
66,000	113.4	0.787	1.603	0.0001694	390.0	-69.7	-56.5	967.9	573.5	2.970
66,500	110.7	0.769	1.565	0.0001654	390.0	-69.7	-56.5	967.9	573.5	2.970
67,000	108.1	0.751	1.528	0.0001615	390.0	-69.7	-56.5	967.9	573.5	2.970
67,500	105.6	0.733	1.492	0.0001577	390.0	-69.7	-56.5	967.9	573.5	2.970
68,000	103.1	0.716	1.457	0.0001540	390.0	-69.7	-56.5	967.9	573.5	2.970
68,500	100.6	0.699	1.423	0.0001503	390.0	-69.7	-56.5	967.9	573.5	2.970
69,000	98.3	0.682	1.389	0.0001468	390.0	-69.7	-56.5	967.9	573.5	2.970
69,500	95.9	0.666	1.356	0.0001433	390.0	-69.7	-56.5	967.9	573.5	2.970
70,000	93.7	0.651	1.324	0.0001399	390.0	-69.7	-56.5	967.9	573.5	2.970
70,500	91.5	0.635	1.293	0.0001366	390.0	-69.7	-56.5	967.9	573.5	2.970
71,000	89.3	0.620	1.263	0.0001334	390.0	-69.7	-56.5	967.9	573.5	2.970
71,500	87.2	0.606	1.233	0.0001303	390.0	-69.7	-56.5	967.9	573.5	2.970
72,000	85.1	0.591	1.204	0.0001272	390.0	-69.7	-56.5	967.9	573.5	2.970
72,500	83.1	0.577	1.175	0.0001242	390.0	-69.7	-56.5	967.9	573.5	2.970
73,000	81.2	0.564	1.148	0.0001213	390.0	-69.7	-56.5	967.9	573.5	2.970
73,500	79.3	0.550	1.121	0.0001184	390.0	-69.7	-56.5	967.9	573.5	2.970
74,000	77.4	0.537	1.094	0.0001156	390.0	-69.7	-56.5	967.9	573.5	2.970
74,500	75.6	0.525	1.068	0.0001129	390.0	-69.7	-56.5	967.9	573.5	2.970
75,000	73.8	0.512	1.043	0.0001102	390.0	-69.7	-56.5	967.9	573.5	2.970
75,500	72.0	0.500	1.019	0.0001076	390.0	-69.7	-56.5	967.9	573.5	2.970
76,000	70.3	0.489	0.995	0.0001051	390.0	-69.7	-56.5	967.9	573.5	2.970
76,500	68.7	0.477	0.971	0.0001026	390.0	-69.7	-56.5	967.9	573.5	2.970
77,000	67.1	0.466	0.948	0.0001002	390.0	-69.7	-56.5	967.9	573.5	2.970
77,500	65.5	0.455	0.926	0.0000978	390.0	-69.7	-56.5	967.9	573.5	2.970
78,000	63.9	0.444	0.904	0.0000955	390.0	-69.7	-56.5	967.9	573.5	2.970
78,500	62.4	0.434	0.883	0.0000933	390.0	-69.7	-56.5	967.9	573.5	2.970
79,000	61.0	0.423	0.862	0.0000911	390.0	-69.7	-56.5	967.9	573.5	2.970
79,500	59.5	0.413	0.842	0.0000889	390.0	-69.7	-56.5	967.9	573.5	2.970

Altitude Ft	lb/ft²	P (Pressure) PSI (lb/in²)	IN. HG	P (Density) sl/ft³	T (Temperature) R	°F	°C	Speed of Sound ft/s	KT	Viscosity 10⁻⁷ lb sec/ft²
80,000	58.1	0.404	0.822	0.0000868	390.0	-69.7	-56.5	967.9	573.5	2.970
80,500	56.8	0.394	0.802	0.0000848	390.0	-69.7	-56.5	967.9	573.5	2.970
81,000	55.4	0.385	0.784	0.0000828	390.0	-69.7	-56.5	967.9	573.5	2.970
81,500	54.1	0.376	0.765	0.0000808	390.0	-69.7	-56.5	967.9	573.5	2.970
82,000	55.8	0.388	0.789	0.0000789	390.0	-69.7	-56.5	967.9	573.5	2.970
82,500	51.6	0.358	0.729	0.0000770	390.2	-69.5	-56.4	968.3	573.7	2.971
83,000	51.0	0.354	0.721	0.0000751	391.1	-68.6	-55.9	969.3	574.3	2.977
83,500	49.2	0.342	0.696	0.0000731	391.9	-67.8	-55.5	970.3	574.9	2.982
84,000	48.0	0.334	0.679	0.0000713	392.7	-67.0	-55.0	971.3	575.5	2.987
84,500	46.9	0.326	0.663	0.0000695	393.5	-66.2	-54.6	972.3	576.1	2.992
85,000	45.8	0.318	0.648	0.0000677	394.3	-65.4	-54.1	973.3	576.7	2.997
85,500	44.8	0.311	0.633	0.0000660	395.1	-64.6	-53.6	974.3	577.3	3.002
86,000	43.7	0.304	0.618	0.0000643	396.0	-63.7	-53.2	975.3	577.9	3.008
86,500	42.7	0.297	0.604	0.0000627	396.8	-62.9	-52.7	976.3	578.4	3.013
87,000	41.7	0.290	0.590	0.0000611	397.6	-62.1	-52.3	977.3	579.0	3.018
87,500	40.8	0.283	0.576	0.0000596	398.4	-61.3	-51.8	978.3	579.6	3.023
88,000	39.8	0.277	0.563	0.0000581	399.2	-60.5	-51.4	979.3	580.2	3.028
88,500	38.9	0.270	0.550	0.0000567	400.0	-59.7	-50.9	980.3	580.8	3.033
89,000	38.0	0.264	0.537	0.0000552	400.9	-58.8	-50.5	981.3	581.4	3.039
89,500	37.1	0.258	0.525	0.0000539	401.7	-58.0	-50.0	982.3	582.0	3.044
90,000	36.3	0.252	0.513	0.0000525	402.5	-57.2	-49.6	983.3	582.6	3.049
90,500	35.5	0.246	0.501	0.0000512	403.3	-56.4	-49.1	984.3	583.2	3.054
91,000	34.7	0.241	0.490	0.0000500	404.1	-55.6	-48.7	985.3	583.8	3.059
91,500	33.9	0.235	0.479	0.0000487	404.9	-54.8	-48.2	986.3	584.4	3.064
92,000	33.1	0.230	0.468	0.0000475	405.8	-54.0	-47.8	987.3	585.0	3.069
92,500	32.4	0.225	0.457	0.0000464	406.6	-53.1	-47.3	988.3	585.5	3.074
93,000	31.6	0.220	0.447	0.0000455	407.4	-52.3	-46.8	989.3	586.1	3.080
93,500	30.9	0.215	0.437	0.0000441	408.2	-51.5	-46.4	990.3	586.7	3.085
94,000	30.2	0.210	0.427	0.0000430	409.0	-50.7	-45.9	991.3	587.3	3.090
94,500	29.5	0.205	0.418	0.0000420	409.8	-49.9	-45.5	992.3	587.9	3.095
95,000	28.9	0.201	0.408	0.0000410	410.6	-49.1	-45.0	993.2	588.5	3.100
95,500	28.2	0.196	0.399	0.0000400	411.5	-48.2	-44.6	994.2	589.1	3.105
96,000	27.6	0.192	0.390	0.0000390	412.3	-47.4	-44.1	995.2	589.6	3.110
96,500	27.0	0.187	0.382	0.0000381	413.1	-46.6	-43.7	996.2	590.2	3.115
97,000	26.4	0.183	0.373	0.0000371	413.9	-45.8	-43.2	997.2	590.8	3.120
97,500	25.8	0.179	0.365	0.0000363	414.7	-45.0	-42.8	998.2	591.4	3.125
98,000	25.2	0.175	0.357	0.0000354	415.5	-44.2	-42.3	999.1	592.0	3.130
98,500	24.7	0.171	0.349	0.0000345	416.4	-43.3	-41.9	1000.1	592.6	3.135
99,000	24.1	0.168	0.341	0.0000337	417.2	-42.5	-41.4	1001.1	593.1	3.140
99,500	23.6	0.164	0.334	0.0000329	418.0	-41.7	-41.0	1002.1	593.7	3.146
100,000	23.1	0.160	0.326	0.0000321	418.8	-40.9	-40.5	1003.0	594.3	3.151
100,500	22.6	0.157	0.319	0.0000314	419.6	-40.1	-40.1	1004.0	594.9	3.156
101,000	22.1	0.153	0.312	0.0000306	420.4	-39.3	-39.6	1005.0	595.4	3.161
101,500	21.6	0.150	0.305	0.0000299	421.2	-38.5	-39.1	1006.0	596.0	3.166
102,000	21.1	0.147	0.299	0.0000292	422.1	-37.6	-38.7	1006.9	596.6	3.171
102,500	20.7	0.144	0.292	0.0000285	422.9	-36.8	-38.2	1007.9	597.2	3.176
103,000	20.2	0.140	0.286	0.0000278	423.7	-36.0	-37.8	1008.9	597.7	3.181
103,500	19.8	0.137	0.280	0.0000272	424.5	-35.2	-37.3	1009.9	598.3	3.186
104,000	19.4	0.134	0.274	0.0000265	425.3	-34.4	-36.9	1010.8	598.9	3.191
104,500	18.9	0.132	0.268	0.0000259	426.1	-33.6	-36.4	1011.8	599.5	3.196

ALTITUDE Fт	lb/ft²	P (Pressure) PSI (lb/in²)	IN. Hg	P (Density) sl/ft³	T (Temperature) R	T (Temperature) °F	T (Temperature) °C	Speed of Sound ft/s	Speed of Sound KT	Viscosity 10⁻⁷ lb sec/ft²
105,000	18.5	0.129	0.262	0.0000253	426.9	-32.8	-36.0	1012.8	600.0	3.201
106,000	17.7	0.123	0.251	0.0000241	428.6	-31.1	-35.1	1014.7	601.2	3.211
107,000	17.0	0.118	0.240	0.0000231	430.2	-29.5	-34.2	1016.6	602.3	3.221
108,000	16.3	0.113	0.230	0.0000220	431.8	-27.9	-33.3	1018.5	603.5	3.231
109,000	15.6	0.108	0.221	0.0000210	433.5	-26.2	-32.4	1020.5	604.6	3.241
110,000	14.9	0.104	0.211	0.0000200	435.1	-24.6	-31.5	1022.4	605.7	3.250

Keyboard Shortcuts and Basic Simulator Functions

This appendix lists all the keyboard commands found in Flight Simulator 95/98. Many program functions can be accessed only by multiple keystrokes. For example, to shift view directions, you press and hold the **Shift** key and then press one of the keys on the numeric keypad; this sequence is shown in the text as **Shift keypad 2**. Whenever a key is to be used from the numeric keypad and not the main keyboard, it is prefixed by **keypad.** Thus if you see +, you know that you must press the plus sign key on the main keyboard, not the plus sign on the numeric keypad.

FS98 uses some new keyboard commands and has changed some others from those that were used in FSW95. But perhaps the biggest change in FS98 is that you now have the ability to custom configure your keyboard commands and joystick buttons to any button or key you wish. This is all done through the Options/Custom Controls/Assignments menu comman.

HOW TO CUSTOM CONFIGURE YOUR JOYSTICK OR KEYBOARD

To change any command from its default keyboard command or default joystick button, follow these steps:

Select the Options/Custom Controls/Assignments menu command, and the Customize Controls dialog box will appear.

Scroll down to the command that you wish to change (or press the keyboard command or joystick button you want to change). Once you find it, simply click on the adjacent keyboard cell or joystick cell that corresponds to the command, and click the Assign button.

In the keyboard cell, type in the key(s) that will replace the previous keyboard command if such a command was previously present.

Alternatively, in the joystick cell, press the joystick button you want to have reassigned.

Click OK to implement your change.

TIP

To quickly jump to a command in the Customize Controls dialog box, press the key command, or press the joystick button you wish to change.

For those making the transition from FS5.1, the Calibrate Joystick command no longer exists as K as it did in FS5.1; instead you must calibrate the joystick using the Options/Custom Controls dialog box in FS98.

VIEW KEYS

There are nine possible view directions in both cockpit view and spot view, not counting the additional panoramas available by panning the window. Each of the following view directions can be used for either cockpit view or spot view. For example, if you want to have the spot view move over the top of the airplane to get a 3-D perspective, you would do this:

In FSW95:

> Press S to enter Spot View.
> Press Shift Keypad 8 to look at your airplane from the front.
> Press Shift Keypad 5 to look down at your airplane from the topside.
> Press Shift Keypad 2 to look at your airplane from the rear.

In FS98:

> Press S three times to enter spot view.

Using the hat switch on your joystick (such as on the SideWinder 3-D Pro), push the button in any direction and hold it down. The view will pan in the direction that you move the button.

Use Auto full screen if you want to have the spot view expand to full window size whenever you select spot view. Of course, you can also choose other views to have Auto-full screen enabled, such as Map, Tower, Cockpit, and Virtual Cockpit.

Figure G.1 Shows the nine view directions.

The panning view keys (Figure G.2) are especially useful when you're landing big jets such as the 737, because otherwise the runway would not be visible with the airplane pitched up at a high angle of attack.

Table G.1 lists the key combinations used for the panning views.

FS98 3-D Windows

New highlights of FS98's viewing system include the following:

You are no longer limited to opening up two 3-D view windows or 1 map window. You can open as many windows as you like.

On 3D capable cards with at least 4 MB of memory, Direct 3-D is supported in 16 bit color resolution, or automatically when in Full Screen mode (Alt Enter).

You can directly access the hardware acceleration capabilities of your 3D capable card under Options/Preferences/Display/Display Options/Hardware Acceleration. This allows you to choose your screen resolution (up to 1280 × 1024 pixel resolution with 16 bit color!).

Right click on any window and you from the pop up menu, you can undock the window so that it floats separately from FS98. When the new Windows 98 and Windows NT operating system becomes available, you will be able to drive multiple video cards from your computer. This means that you could theoretically have a side view monitor setup on both your right and left, along with your front view. Of course, you must have three video cards and three monitors hooked up to your PC.

New Virtual Cockpit View added to the S key view mode cycle. This view gives you a better view of your outside surroundings while inside the cockpit.

Completely new high resolution instrument panel systems are included. Up to nine separate floating instrument panels per aircraft are now possible. However, one drawback of these new panels is that the legibility of some instruments is poor at 640 × 480 resolution. Panels will increase in detail as you resize the window up as high as 1280 × 1024. For best performance, you may want to consider running at 800 × 600 resolution.

New on-screen checklists allow you to fly each aircraft by the book. By calling up the checklists on your instrument panel, you can easily follow along step by step the proper takeoff, cruise, descent and landing procedures. You can display any of the checklists by using the Aircraft/Checklists menu and then select the particular checklist you want. To cycle through the checklists, or to hide the checklist, press Shift C.

All the Viewing Commands are listed below. Note that keyboard commands unique to FS98 are marked with an asterisk, and those commands unique to FSW95 are commented as "FSW95 Only."

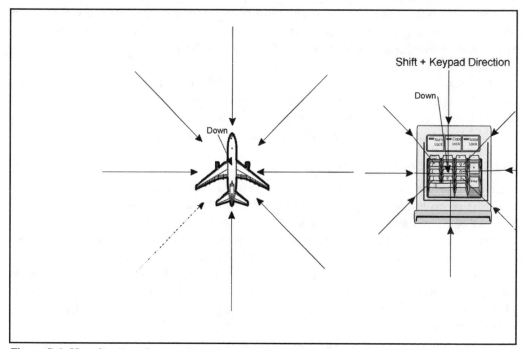

Figure G.1: *View directions for spot view*

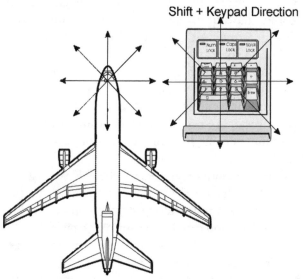

Figure G.2: *View directions for cockpit view.*

Table G.1 *Key Combinations for Panning Views*

VIEW DIRECTION	KEYS
Front	**Shift+keypad 8**
Rear	**Shift+keypad 2**
Left	**Shift+keypad 4**
Right	**Shift+ keypad 7**
Right front	**Shift+keypad 9**
Left rear	**Shift+keypad 1**
Right rear	**Shift+keypad 3**
Down	**Shift+keypad 5**
Pan up	**Shift+ Enter**
Pan left	**Ctrl+Shift Backspace**
Pan right	**Ctrl+Shift+Enter**
Straight and level (no pan)	Ctrl Spacebar (FS98 **Scroll Lock FSW95**

Note that you can choose a different viewing angle for your spot view than the nine choices you have from the keyboard. To choose a different spot viewing angle in FS98, you can use the joystick's hat switch as previously mentioned, or from the Views/View Options dialog box (click Spot Plane radio button), you can drag the red viewing pointer around the aircraft's picture to the angle you wish to view your aircraft from. Figure G.3 illustrates the other spot view attributes you can choose, including zoom, distance, altitude, and transition type. The transition type is useful for aerobatic views of your airplane, when you don't want your view to shift when the airplane rolls or pitches upside down.

Use Auto full screen if you want to have the spot view expand to full window size whenever you select spot view. Of course, you can also choose other views to have Auto-full screen enabled, such as Map, Tower, Cockpit, and Virtual Cockpit.

Your 3-D Windows

Flight Simulator has two 3-D windows, an instrument panel window, and a separate map window, all of which can be viewed simultaneously on-screen. When you start Flight Simulator, you normally see only the instrument panel window and the 3-D View window #1. You can open the second 3-D View window by pressing], and you can select a different view using the keyboard commands or your joystick's hat switch. Note that if you have more than one view window open, you cannot zoom or modify the second window unless it is activated by pressing [for 3-D View #1, or] for 3-D View #2.

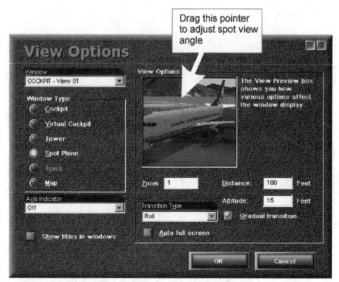

Drag this pointer to adjust spot view angle

Figure G.3: How to set a custom viewing angle from spot view.

Opening the Map Window in FS98:

FS98 has changed the way you open the Map window from previous versions of Flight Simulator. Before, you needed to press the **Num Lock** key to open the map window. In FS98, you now open the map window by pressing **Shift]**. To close this window, you press **]**. Microsoft wanted allow the use of the numeric keypad by using the **Num Lock** key to toggle back and forth between cursor control and numeric keys. Without the use of the **Num Lock** key, this was not possible, hence the reason for shifting the **Map** open and shut commands to different keys.

Opening the Map Window in FSW95:

To open the Map window, press **Num Lock**; to close it, press **Num Lock** twice. If a 3-D window is the currently active window, to zoom the Map window you must prefix the zoom command with the **Num Lock** key. Thus, to zoom the map in, press **Num Lock+**; to zoom out, press **Num Lock –.** Sometimes the Map window will stubbornly refuse to display despite all protestations with the **Num Lock** key. This means that one of the 3-D View windows is masking, or covering up, the Map window. To bring the Map window to the forefront so that it becomes visible, press the **"** key.

FS98 3-D Windows

New highlights of FS98's viewing system include the following:

- You are no longer limited to opening up two 3-D view windows or 1 map window. You can open as many windows as you like.
- On 3D capable cards with at least 4 MB of memory, Direct 3-D is supported in 16 bit color resolution, or automatically when in Full Screen mode (**Alt Enter**).
- You can directly access the hardware acceleration capabilities of your 3D capable card under **Options/Preferences/Display/Display Options/Hardware Acceleration**. This allows you to choose your screen resolution (up to 1280 x 1024 pixel resolution with 16 bit color!).
- Right click on any window and you from the pop up menu, you can undock the window so that it floats separately from FS98. When the new Windows 98 and Windows NT operating system becomes available, you will be able to drive multiple video cards from your computer. This means that you could theoretically have a side view monitor setup on both your right and left, along with your front view. Of course, you must have three video cards and three monitors hooked up to your PC.
- New Virtual Cockpit View added to the S key view mode cycle. This view gives you a better view of your outside surroundings while inside the cockpit.

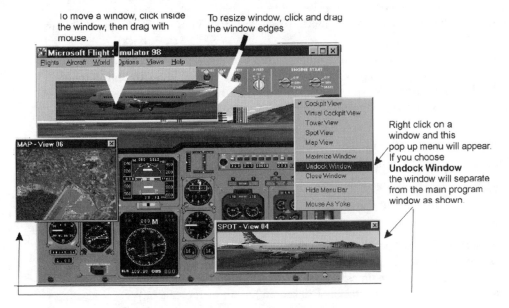

Figure G.4. *You can resize, and move the 3-D View Windows and Map Windows by dragging with the mouse along the borders. If you right click on a window, you can also undock it from the main FS98 window and have this new window operate independently of the main FS98 program, as shown with the independent Map window and Spot View in this illustration.*

- Completely new high resolution instrument panel systems are included. Up to nine separate floating instrument panels per aircraft are now possible. However, one drawback of these new panels is that the legibility of some instruments is poor at 640 x 480 resolution. Panels will increase in detail as you resize the window up as high as 1280 x 1024. For best performance, you may want to consider running at 800 x 600 resolution.

New on-screen checklists allow you to fly each aircraft by the book. By calling up the checklists on your instrument panel, you can easily follow along step by step the proper takeoff, cruise, descent and landing procedures. You can display any of the checklists by using the **Aircraft/Checklists** menu and then select the particular checklist you want. To cycle through the checklists, or to hide the checklist, press **Shift C**.

All the Viewing Commands are listed below. Note that keyboard commands unique to FS98 are marked with an asterisk, and those commands unique to FSW95 are commented as "FSW95 Only."

Table G.2 *Viewing Commands*

CONTROL	KEYS
Cycle through Cockpit, Virtual Cockpit*, Tower, and Spot View	**S** (forwards) **Shift+S** (back)
Cycle view types* (this allows you to quickly jump between two view types, such as Map view and your current view (either Cockpit, Virtual Cockpit, Tower, and Spot) in the same window without cycling through all the intermediate views.)	**Ctrl S** (forwards) **Ctrl Shift S** (back)
Maximize currently active window to full screen in Windows	**W**
Full screen view (DOS style window)	**Alt Enter**
Make Menu Bar visible and active	**Alt**
Hide/Unhide Instrument Panel	**Shift [**
Zoom in	**+**
Fine Zoom in (In FSW95, this function only works if you press + three times to Zoom in, then you can Fine Zoom in or out. Then press – three times to Zoom out, and your Fine Zoom setting will be preserved. The FS98 zoom has no such problem.)	**Shift +**
Fine Zoom out (see above comments)	**Shift -**
Zoom out	**-**
1× Normal Magnification	**Backspace**

Table G.2 continued

CONTROL	KEYS
Open a new 3-D View Window*	[
Close the selected 3-D View Window*	]
Shift to next View Window*	**Ctrl Tab**
Return to previous View Window*	**Ctrl Shift Tab**
Open or shut Instrument Panel 0 through 9*.	**Shift 1, 2, 3, 4, 5, 6, 7, 8, or 9**
Cycle through checklists.*	**Shift C**
Open Map Window (FS98 only)	**Shift [**
Open 3-D View Window 1 (FSW95 only)	[(press [[to close)
Open 3-D View Window 2 (FSW95 only)	] (press [[to close)
Bring up Map Window, or select Map Window for zooming in or out. To zoom Map Window, press **Num Lock +** to zoom in, or **Num Lock -** to zoom out. Press **Num Lock** twice to close Map Window. (FSW95 only).	**Num Lock**
Bring window to forefront (useful when Map Window remains hidden behind 3-D view windows, or a window is obscured by other windows.	'
Bring up Instrument Sub-Panel (FSW95 only. For the Learjet & 737, this toggles between engine instrumentation and navigational radios)	**Tab**
Toggle Coordinates and Frame Rate displayView Checklists*	**Shift Z**
View Checklists*	**Shift C**

*FS98 Only

FS98 has the ability to open up to nine separate instrument panels for each aircraft, although none of the default aircraft at present use all nine possible panels. To open an instrument panel, press **Shift** followed by a number from **1** to **9**. For example, to open up the FS98 Learjet's new throttle quadrant, you would press **Shift 2**. To close this panel, you would again press **Shift 2**. The main instrument panel is always **Shift 1**.

Basic Fixed Wing Aircraft Flight Controls on the Numeric Keypad

Using the keyboard, you can move the aircraft's elevators, rudders, ailerons, elevator trim, and steering. In addition, you can change individual engine power settings, shut off or start a particular engine, and operate the landing gear, flaps, and spoilers. Table G.3 shows the commands.

Table G.3 *Keyboard Commands for Basic Flight Control*

Flight Control	Key
Ailerons	
Left	**Keypad 4**
Center	**Keypad 5**
Right	**Keypad 6**
Elevator	
Nose up	**Keypad 2**
KeyNose down	**Keypad 8**
Elevator Trim	
Nose up (elevator trim up)	**Keypad 1**
Nose down (elevator trim down)	**Keypad 7**
Rudder (works only when Auto-coordination is turned off under **Aircraft/Realism & Reliability**)	
Left (also used for steering left on runway)	**Keypad 0**
Center	**Keypad 5**
Right (also used for steering right on runway)	**Keypad Enter** (not on main keyboard but on numeric keypad)
Landing Gear	
Landing gear up/down	**G**
Manually Pump Landing Gun*	Ctrl G

*FS98 only

The flap controls have changed from those in FS5.1. New to FSW95 are the Extend flaps in increments (**F7**) command and the Retract flaps in increments (**F6**) command (see Table G.4).

Table G.4 Flap Control Commands

CONTROL	KEY
Extend in increments	**F7**
Retract in increments	**F6**
Fully retract flaps (flaps up)	**F5**
Fully extend flaps (flaps down)	**F8**

Figure G.5 shows the flight controls on the numeric keypad.

Fixed Wing Aircraft Engine Controls

The engine control commands in FSW95 and FS98 have changed from those in FS5.1. Table G.6 shows the keys that control the engines.

Table G.5 Brakes, Spoilers, and Lights

CONTROL	KEY
Spoilers (Learjet/Boeing 737)/ Dive Brake Sailplane)	/ (Forward slash)
Arm Autospoiler	**Shift /**
Parking Brakes on	**Ctrl Period**
Parking Brakes off	**Period**
Left Differential Brakes	**F11**
Right Differential Brakes	**F12**
Toggle all Lights on/off	**L**
Instrument Panel lights on/off*	**Shift L**
Turn on Helicopter Spotlight, or Landing Lights on/off*	**Ctrl L**
Point Helicopter Spotlight, or Landing Lights up*	**Ctrl Keypad 8**
Point Helicopter Spotlight, or Landing Lights down*	**Ctrl Keypad 2**
Point Helicopter Spotlight, or Landing Lights left*	**Ctrl Keypad 4**
Point Helicopter Spotlight, or Landing Lights right*	**Ctrl Keypad 6**
Point Helicopter Spotlight, or Landing Lights centered*	**Ctrl Keypad 5**
Strobes on/off	O

*FS98 Only

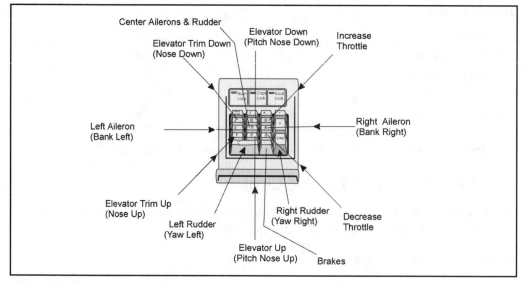

Figure G.5 *Flight controls on the numeric keypad.*

FS98 has a new moveable helicopter spotlight and comes equipped with moveable aircraft landing lights. Once you have turned on the landing lights or the spotlight (press **Ctrl L**), you can aim the lights up, down, left, right, or center them. This is really a nice feature when you are trying to land the helicopter at night, where you might need to manually adjust the beam so you can see where you are going. Also, for large aircraft such as the 737, it is nice to be able to point your landing lights in the direction of a taxiway where you might need to turn.

Table G.6 *Engine Control Commands*

CONTROL	KEY
Throttle	
Increase	**Keypad 9** or **F3**
Decrease	**Keypad 3** or **F2**
Cut	**F1**
Full	**F4**
Propeller Control	
Increase RPM	**Ctrl F3**
Decrease RPM	**Ctrl F2**
Minimum RPM	**Ctrl F1**
Maximum RPM	**Ctrl F4**
Mixture Control	
Enrich	**Ctrl Shift F3**

Table G.6 continued

CONTROL	KEY
Lean	**Ctrl Shift F2**
Idle cutoff	**Ctrl Shift F1**
Full rich	**Ctrl Shift F4**
Carburetor heat	
Pilot Heat* on/off	**Shift H**
On/off	**H**
EGT bug needle	
Move needle forward	**U +**
Move needle back	**U –**
Starter/Magnetos	
Magnetos on/off	**M + or M -**
Jet engine fuel flow start	
Both engines	**E 1 2 Ctrl Shift F4**
Engine 1	**E 1 Ctrl Shift F4**
Engine 2	**E 2 Ctrl Shift F4**
Jet engine starter (to run off starter, press - instead of +)	
Both engines	**E 1 2 j +**
Engine 1	**E 1 J +**
Engine 2	**E 2 J +**
Jet engine shutdown	
Both engines	**E 1 2 Ctrl Shift F1**
Engine 1	**E 1 Ctrl Shift F1**
Engine 2	**E 2 Ctrl Shift F1**
Engine control selectors	
Both engines	**E 1 2**
Engine 1	**E 1**
Engine 2	**E 2**
Display instrument Subpanel	
Toggle between instrument display/navigation instruments (Learjet and Boeing 737)	**Tab (FSW95) Shift 1, 2, 3, etc. (FS98)**

*FS98

The crossfeed switch in the 737 allows an engine to draw fuel from the tank that normally feeds another engine. The crossfeed valve should be opened if you shut down an engine and run low on fuel in the tank that normally supplies the operating engine.

Unfortunately, in Flight Simulator there is no direct way to select a specific auxiliary or main fuel tank from either the instrument panel or the keyboard. However, you can select a particular tank by using the menus. For example, to select a fuel tank using the menus in FSW95, you have to use the **Aircraft/Engines & Fuel** menu, and then click the **Fuel** tab to open up the Fuel dialog box. Then, you must click the **Fuel Selector** button so that it is lit, and then in the adjacent list box, you select **All, Left,** or **Right** depending on which fuel tank you want the engines to draw fuel from. In FS98, the procedure is similar, except that you choose **Aircraft/Aircraft Settings/Fuel**, then click the **Manual Fuel Control**, and then select **All, Off, Left, Right, Left Aux,** or **Right Aux** for the tank you wish to draw fuel from. Selecting **Off** switches off all fuel to engines, while selecting **All** draws fuel from all the fuel tanks.

Using Reverse Thrusters

To reverse thrusters while braking during the landing in the Learjet or Boeing 737-400, press and hold **keypad 3** until the throttle levers move into the red zones. When you are finished applying reverse thrust, press **F1** to cut all thrust, or simply increase the throttle to the end of the thrust reversal red zone.

How to Adjust Single Engines on Multi-Engined Aircraft

You may have occasion to practice flying with one engine out. To do this, you can use the mouse to drag the throttle lever down on the selected engine. For complicated situations, in which you need to use individual engine controls from the keyboard, you must select the engine before pressing the control key. It is easy to select one engine at a time—for example, by pressing **E 1** or **E 2** to select engine #1 or engine #2—but you might have trouble shifting back so that you can adjust both engines simultaneously. You can fix this problem by pressing **E 1 2**. Or you can select the **Aircraft/ Settings/Engine** menu and in the dialog box under Engine Controls, click on the lighted buttons for **Engine 1, Engine 2** (and other engines if so desired), and **Adjust All Engines**. This action will bring back both engines so that they are both active, as indicated by the illuminated yellow engine numbers on the instrument panel.

Suppose you want to throttle down engine #2 while flying the Learjet. To do this, you press **E+2** followed by **keypad 3**. The engine thrust will decrease on engine #2. As you press the key, the engine selector #2 number lights up yellow, but the thrust on engine # 1 remains constant.

Suppose you want to increase thrust on both engines. To do this and bring both engines back on-line, press **E 1 2** followed by **keypad 9** to increase thrust on both engines.

Helicopter Flight Controls

The keyboard flight controls for the Bell JetRanger helicopter in FS98 are quite simple. The cyclic, which controls the main rotor blade, is controlled by the keys on the numeric keypad. The tail rotor, which controls the helicopter's yaw, is manipulated with the **Keypad 0** and **Keypad 5** keys. Because of the complexity of mastering the helicopter, it is recommended that you instead use a 4-axis joystick, with separate rudder controls.

HELICOPTER CYCLIC (PITCH, ROLL)

Roll left	**Keypad 4**
Center	**Keypad 5**
Roll right	**Keypad 6**
Nose up	**Keypad 2**
Nose down	**Keypad 8**

HELICOPTER TAIL ROTOR (YAW)

Left	**Keypad 0**
Center	**Keypad 5**
Right	**Keypad Enter** (not on main keyboard, but on numeric keypad)

Helicopter Engine Controls

FS98's Bell 206B JetRanger III helicopter has keyboard controls that are different from the ones you may be used to on the aircraft.

TIP

You may need to disable your joystick in order for the keyboard engine commands to work. To deactivate the joystick, press **K**. To re-enable it , press **K** again.

HELICOPTER CONTROL	KEY
Collective (Torque) [Up & Down Motion]	
Increase (climb)	**Keypad 9** or **F3**
Decrease (descend)	**Keypad 3** or **F2**
Set full down (climb with max. torque)	**F1**

Helicopter Control	Key
Set full up (descend with min. torque)	F4
Throttle (Power Turbine)	
Increase Throttle	Ctrl F3
Decrease Throttle	Ctrl F2
Set at Ground Idle	Ctrl F1
Set at Flight Idle	Ctrl F4

Navigation and Communication Controls

The navigational radios and communication radios can be set through keyboard commands, as shown in Table G.7. Note that you can substitute the — key for the + key to reduce the frequency setting.

Table G.7 *Navigation and Communication Controls*

Function	Key Combination
Set first digit of ADF radio (ADF radio must be activated first)	A +
Set second digit of ADF radio	AA +
Set third digit of ADF radio	AAA +
Set integer portion of COM radio frequency	C +
Set fractional portion of COM radio frequency	CC +
DME 1 radio control toggle between readout of speed toward station in knots (kt) or distance in nautical miles (nm)	F 1 +
DME 2 radio control toggle between readout of speed toward station in knots (kt) or distance in nautical miles (nm)	F 2 +
Set integer portion of NAV 1 radio frequency	N 1 followed by +
Set fractional portion of NAV 1 radio frequency	N 1 followed by N N +
Set OBI on VOR 1 indicator for NAV 1 radio	V 1 +
Set integer portion of NAV 2 radio frequency	N 2 followed by +
Set fractional portion of NAV 2 radio frequency	N 2 followed by N N +

Table G.7 continued

FUNCTION	KEY COMBINATION
Set OBI on VOR 2 indicator for NAV 2 radio	**V 2 +**
Set first digit of transponder squawk code	**T +**
Set second digit of transponder squawk code	**T T +**
Set third digit of transponder squawk code	**T T T +**
Set fourth digit of transponder squawk code	**T T T T +**
Identify VOR 1 (Morse Code)*	**Ctrl 1**
Identify VOR 2 (Morse Code)*	**Ctrl 2**
Identify DME 1 (Morse Code)*	**Ctrl 3**
Identify DME 2 (Morse Code)*	**Ctrl 4**
Identify ADF (Morse Code)*	**Ctrl 5**
Send ATC Message*	**Num +**

To choose which VOR radio or ADF gauge to display in FSW95, press **Shift+Tab** ,as shown in Table G.8.

Table G.8

DISPLAY NAVIGATION INSTRUMENT (FSW95 ONLY)	KEYS
VOR 2 or the ADF gauge on the Cessna	**Shift+Tab**
VOR 1, VOR 2, or the ADF gauge on the Learjet	**Shift+Tab**
VOR or the ADF gauge on the Extra 300	**Shift+Tab**
Display subpanel	**Tab**

MISCELLANEOUS KEY COMMANDS

The keyboard commands shown in Table G.9 are used to access various other controls.

Table G.9

KEYS	CONTROL
Miscellaneous	
1	Select Item 1*
2	Select Item 2*

Table G.9 *continued*

KEYS	CONTROL
3	Select Item 3*
4	Select Item 4*
Alt	Make Menu Bar Visible and Active
B	Calibrate Altimeter
Ctrl C	Exit Program
Ctrl +	Exit Flight Simulator Immediately
D	Calibrate Directional Gyro/Heading Indicator
K	Joystick off/on
I	Smoke off/on
P	Pause Simulation, press P again to resume
Q	Sound off/on
R + or -	Rate of Simulation
Shift Z	Cycles through displaying latitude/longitude coordinates, north-east coordinates, and frame rate counter-g meter.
X	Land Me
Esc	Exit menu or dialog box.
-	Decrease selection
Shift -	Decrease selection slowly
+	Increase selection
Shift +	Increase selection slowly
Ctrl NumLock Del	Mouse as Yoke on/off*
Y	Enter Slew Mode
Situations	
Ctrl ;	Reset Situation
;	Save Situation
Flight Videos	
Esc	Stop recording
6	Record at 1 second interval
7	Record at 5 second intervals
,	Insert message during playback of video
Esc	End flight video

Table G.9 *continued*

KEYS	CONTROL
Flight Pictures	
Alt Print Scrn	Takes a snap shot of your window and saves it to the clipboard. To print or save the picture, go to Microsoft Paint (or other graphics program), and paste the clipboard contents into the window (press **Ctrl V**, or select **Edit/Paste** from the menu). You should then see your snap shot, and you can then save it to a file, or print it out.
Maneuver Analysis	
\ (Backslash)	Stop maneuver analysis
Airshow Smoke	
I	Smoke/spray on or off (This keyboard command is broken in FSW95, however the **Options/Smoke System** menu will turn it on or off).

*FS98 Only

SLEWING

Slewing mode allows you to move the aircraft quickly from point to point. Note that for movement over long distances, it is faster to use **World/Go To/Exact Location** or **World/Go To/Exact Location** to move the airplane. Slew mode must be active (press **Y**) before any of the slewing key commands will work. To exit slew mode, press **Y** again.

Slewing has two kinds of movement: rotation and translation. When you move the aircraft in three–dimensional space, it is called *translation*. When you reorient the plane to any attitude but keep your location fixed, it is called *rotation*.

Slewing Translation

The keys shown in Table G.10 allow you to translate the aircraft in any direction.

Table G.10 *Slewing Translation Keys*

SLEW TRANSLATION	KEY
Change altitude	
Increase slowly	**Q**
Increase quickly	**F4**
Decrease slowly	**A**
Decrease quickly	**F1**
Freeze	**F2** or **F3**
Forward	**Keypad 8**
Backward	**Keypad 2**
Freeze	**Keypad 5**
Move sideways	
Left	**Keypad 4**
Right	**Keypad 6**
Freeze	**Keypad 5**

Slewing Rotation

The keys shown in Table G.11 allow you to rotate the aircraft.

Table G.11 *Slewing Rotation Keys*

Slew Rotation	Key
Pitch	
Nose up slowly	**9**
Nose up fast	**F5**
Freeze	**F6** or **F7**
Nose down fast	**F8**
Nose down slowly	**0**
Bank (roll)	
Left	**Keypad 7**
Right	**Keypad 9**
Freeze	**Keypad 5**

Table G.11 continued

Slew Rotation	Key
Heading (yaw)	
Left	**Keypad 1**
Right	**Keypad 3**
Freeze	**Keypad 5**

Other Slewing Controls

Table G.12 shows the remaining slewing controls.

Table G.12 Miscellaneous Slewing Controls

CONTROL	KEY
Turn latitude/longitude display on or off, display frame rate counter, and display north-east coordinate system	**Z**
Reset aircraft orientation so that it is level:	
Heading: North	
Pitch: 0	
Bank: 0	
	Spacebar

AUTOPILOT COMMANDS

Flight Simulator 98 includes new Autopilot keyboard shortcuts for the new Auto-throttle functions.

To turn the Autopilot on or off, press **Z** from the keyboard, or click the Autopilot status indicator on the instrument panel. You can also access all the Autopilot functions from the **Aircraft/Autopilot** menu. Note that the vertical speed autopilot function cannot be accessed from the keyboard.

The FS98 Auto-throttle can be armed by clicking on the **AT** button on the Master Control Panel (MCP) of the instrument panel. Once this device is on, you can regulate the airplane's speed by turning on the **SPD** control, and the airplane will fly at whatever airspeed is shown on the IAS/MACH box located on the MCP. You can change increase the airspeed that is shown by clicking to the right of the IAS/MACH box, or decrease it by clicking to the left of the box. Note that the Autopilot Master Switch (**AP**) need not be on for the Auto-throttle to work.

AUTOPILOT FUNCTION	KEYBOARD COMMAND
Autopilot on/off	**Z**
Wing Leveler (LVL)	**Ctrl V**
Attitude Hold (ATT) (Maintain Pitch and Bank)	**Ctrl T**
Altitude Hold (ALT) (min. 0 ft, max 99,901 ft)	**Ctrl Z**
Vertical Speed (min. –6000 ft/min, max. +7000 ft/min*	
Airspeed Hold (SPD) (min. 0 kt, max 999 kt)*	**Ctrl R**
Mach Hold (MACH) (min. 0, max. 1.5)* (disabled during lessons)	**Ctrl M**
Arm Auto-throttle*	**Shift R**
Auto-throttle Takeoff/Go Around*	**Ctrl Shift R**
Heading Hold: Lock to your current magnetic course heading	**Ctrl H**
Nav 1 Hold: Lock to a VOR Radial tuned on NAV 1	**Ctrl N**
ILS Lock (APP): Lock to an ILS tuned on NAV 1 for a landing. Aircraft flies the glideslope and localizer descent profile for the selected ILS runway.	**Ctrl A**
Localizer Lock: Lock to the ILS Localizer (but not the glideslope) tuned on NAV 1 radio for the landing.	**Ctrl O**
Back Course Lock: Lock to a Back Course of a ILS Localizer tuned on NAV 1 radio. This allows you to approach the runway's opposite end for a landing.	**Ctrl B**
Yaw Damper on/off	**Ctrl D**

*FS98 Only

MOUSE CONTROLS

You can use the mouse in Flight Simulator to fly the airplane. To do so, click the right mouse button; in the pop–up menu that appears, select **Mouse as Yoke**. The mouse pointer will disappear. When you roll the mouse forward, the elevators are raised and the aircraft's nose pitches up. If you roll the mouse backward, the elevators are lowered and the aircraft's nose pitches down. Sideways motion of the mouse controls the ailerons; moving the mouse right banks the aircraft right, and moving the mouse left banks the aircraft left.

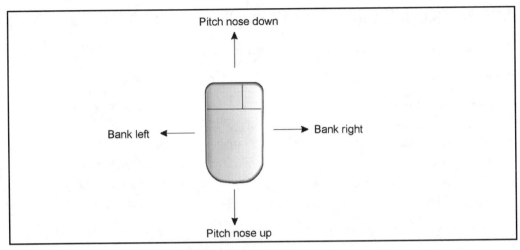

Figure G.6 *Using the mouse to control the engine and brakes.*

You can also use the mouse to control throttle and braking (see Figure G.6).

To exit Mouse as Yoke mode and restore the mouse pointer, press the right mouse button and drag the mouse slightly. The pointer will reappear.

Mouse Slew Mode

In addition to flying the airplane, the mouse can be used to slew the aircraft. Enter slew mode by pressing the **Y** key. Then press the right mouse button and select **Mouse as Yoke**. To translate the aircraft, roll the mouse forward to slew forward, or roll the mouse backward to slew backward. To rotate the aircraft, roll the mouse left or right. You can stop all motion by pressing **keypad 5**.

To exit Mouse as Yoke mode, press the right mouse button and drag the mouse slightly. The pointer will reappear.

SPECIAL KEYS DURING FLYING LESSONS AND ADVENTURES

The following keys are useful for starting and topping lessons and adventures, as well as repeating important instructor comments or ATC messages.

DESCRIPTION	KEYBOARD COMMAND
Restart the lesson or adventure	**Ctrl R**
Exit the lesson or adventure	**Ctrl U**
Repeat the last ATC message or instructor comment	**Ctrl M**

SPECIAL KEYS DURING MULTIPLAYER FLIGHT MODE IN FS98

These keys are used during multiplayer flight mode in FS98.

DESCRIPTION	KEYBOARD COMMAND
Toggle Chat window on/off	Ctrl Enter
Toggle focus between Chat window and main Flight Simulator window	Enter
Cycle through players	Ctrl Shift T
Toggle track mode (DME and ADF)	Ctrl Shift D
Follow the other player (Pilot Mode)/Lock airplane's cockpit view (Observer Mode)	Ctrl Shift F

H

Adventure Programming Language Reference

This appendix introduces the **APLC32.EXE** program, available on this book's CD-ROM. **APLC32.EXE** is a free 32-bit adventure compiler program by Martin Smith, and it functions as a replacement for the 16-bit **APLC.EXE** program that comes with BAO's Flight Shop. By writing special scripts in text format, you can create adventure files that are then compiled by **APLC32.EXE** into binary files that can be used directly with Flight Simulator for Windows 95. There are many commands, variables, and functions that can be programmed into an adventure, and using this language reference you can "program" Flight Simulator to do special things. For example, the program GPWS6 by Wilco van Deijl is an adventure script that has been compiled into binary form for use with Flight Simulator.

To gain an idea of the power of adventure scripts, take a look at **GPWS6.ADV** and **AutoAlt.ADV**. **GPWS6.ADV** extends Flight Simulator's capabilities by adding a ground proximity warning system (with voice messages), and it adds a waypoint navigation system for around-the-world flights. **AutoAlt.ADV** allows you to hear the aircraft's altitude spoken at the press of a key; you can control the autopilot heading and altitude directly from the keyboard with digitized voice feedback. It also displays the airplane's pitch and bank angle and announces these angles at the touch of a button. These highly sophisticated features were programmed using APL (Adventure Programming Language). The program was written in text-only format and then converted to binary form by using APLC32 (Adventure Programming Language compiler). The binary adventure file is copied directly into the Flight Simulator **ADV** directory, where it is loaded into Flight Simulator as an adventure. That's all there is to it!

APLC32 was written because BAO's previous Flight Shop program, which included APLC (a 16-bit compiler), no longer worked for FS95/98. Although Microsoft provided an Adventure Converter program for older 16-bit adventures, APLC32 provided several new benefits over its 16-bit brethren; it allowed adventures greater than 64K in length, and it allowed an adventure to be directly compiled to the new 32-bit FS95/98 format. This arrangement allowed adventure authors to achieve better results than could be achieved by converting 16-bit FS5 binary adventure files to the new 32-bit format using Microsoft's Adventure Converter program.

APLC32 compiles a language believed to be identical to the one compiled by **APLC.EXE**. APLC32 has been produced by taking apart **.ADV** files and is an offshoot of the work done on Smith's FS6ADV adventure converter. It is not the result of disassembling any executable code supplied with Flight Simulator or Flight Shop. As Smith has written, "I deliberately avoided doing so even where this would make the program less complete."

APLC32 is not intended to work with Flight Shop adventure source files for Flight Simulator 5.0 or 5.1, although it will compile such files with the appropriate options and can be used with ATC Workshop if you own Flight Shop. Because of changes in the adventure drivers between FS5 and FS95/98, these conversions may not be 100% successful.

You can use APLC32 by itself or with Flight Shop or any other flight planner that generates adventures, such as Flightplanner 4.0b (available on this book's CD-ROM).

N O T E APLC32 works only with Flight Simulator for Windows 95 and Flight Simulator 98. It does not work with FS5.1 or FS5.0, because the file formats are different. Also, important information not noted here because of space considerations can be found on the CD-ROM in the documentation for APLC32.

APLC32 REQUIREMENTS

APLC32 has the following requirements:

- You need a PC running Windows 95 or Windows NT.
- To use the adventures you need Flight Simulator for Windows 95 or Flight Simulator 98.
- If you are using FSW95, you should also install the Microsoft FSW95 Aircraft and Adventure Converter (FSCONVT.EXE on the book's CD) as it includes a patch to the runtime adventure driver module.

- If you are using FS98, you should install the Microsoft Flight Simulator 98 Aircraft Converter (Aafconv.EXE on the book's CD) because it includes patch to the runtime adventure driver module for FS98.
- To hear the program's sounds you should install **aafwav.zip** (also on this book's CD-ROM) even if you have Flight Shop installed. Otherwise, the sounds may be inaudible or distorted.

Installing APLC32 from the CD is a little complicated because, in order for adventures to work properly with Flight Simulator, you need to install the Microsoft Aircraft and Adventure Converter as well as some new sound *.WAV files. If you are running FS98, skip step one, but do perform step two and step three to install the *.WAV files and APLC117.

Follow these steps to install APLC32:

1. **For FSW95 only:** First install FSCONV.EXE from the CD. This is the Microsoft Aircraft and Adventure converter for FSW95. FSCONV.EXE is a self-extracting, self executing program that will install itself if you copy it to your Flight Simulator directory and then double click on it.

2. **For FSW95 & FS98**: Extract all the sound wave files from AAFWAV.ZIP on the CD into your Flight Simulator ADV/WAV directory. Use Winzip (on the CD) to decompress the zip file. If you intend to use GPSW6.ADV, you should also install the *.Wav sound files found in the GPWS6.ZIP file on the CD, as there are many new cockpit sounds that will enhance your enjoyment of the program.

3. **For FSW95 and FS98:** Use Winzip to decompress the APLC117.ZIP file. Extract the APLC32.EXE file and its contents into the \ADV directory where you have installed Flight Simulator. Note that APLC117.ZIP will want to install two subdirectories, \Examples and Include\Utilities. Be sure to let Winzip create these directories and unzip the example files.

Now you can run the program as described in the next section.

How to Use APLC32

APLC32 is a DOS program that you invoke from the command line in DOS mode or from within Windows 95. You should put APLC32 into the **ADV** subdirectory of the main **Flight Simulator** directory. Assuming you have read the previous section and have installed APLC32 according to the instructions, follow these steps to run the program as a DOS application running in a window:

1. Using the Windows 95 taskbar, select **Start/Programs/MS-DOS Prompt**. The MS-DOS prompt will appear inside a window on-screen.
2. Change the current directory shown in the MS-DOS window to that of your Flight Simulator /**ADV** directory. In the DOS window, type the DOS command **CD** followed by a space (press **Spacebar**). Then open Windows Explorer and drag the file name of APLC32 into the DOS window. The entire path of the APLC32 program will appear in the DOS window. Next, backspace over the **APLC32.EXE** but leave the rest of the path intact. Press **Enter** to have the DOS window change the directory to the /**ADV** directory where Flight Simulator is installed. The results are illustrated in Figure H.1.
3. In the DOS window, type **APLC32** followed by a space, and then type the name of the program text file you wish to compile (for example, **APLC32 AutoAlt**).
4. Press **Enter** and APLC32 will compile the program. If there are no errors, you won't see any warning messages on-screen. Otherwise, a list of lines that have problems will be displayed.
5. You can run the newly created adventure in Flight Simulator by using the **Flights/Adventures** command.

The syntax for the APLC32 command line in the DOS window is as follows:

```
APLC32 [options] input file name [output file name]
```

You don't need to add an output file name, nor do you need to add any options when running APLC32. You must, however, add an input file name so that APLC32 knows which text file to compile. For example:

```
APLC32.EXE myadven
```

Here, **myadven.txt** is the name of the text file you created that contains the APL program. Note that you needn't include the file extension **.txt** for the input file name (although you can if you want to).

Although there are command-line options that you can invoke, they are rarely needed for routine jobs. Consult the on-line documentation for more specific information.

PHASES OF COMPILATION

APLC32 compiles your adventure file in four steps, or phases. If any errors occur in a phase, compilation will stop. If only warnings are produced, compilation will continue to the next phase.

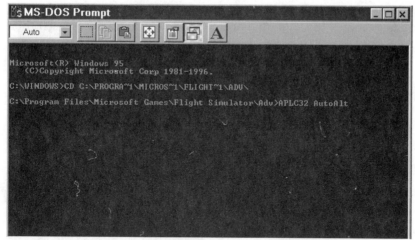

Figure H.1 Use the Windows 95 taskbar and select **Start/Programs/MS-DOS Prompt** to run an MS-DOS session in a window. To run APLC32, in the DOS window change directories to the **/ADV** directory where Flight Simulator is installed. Then type **APLC32** followed by the name of the text file you created.

1. Syntax analysis: In this phase the source text is broken into tokens, and a parse tree is built.
2. Global checks: Checks that everything has been defined and that any global requirements are met—for example, that the adventure has a title. Produces warnings for unused variables or those assigned but not referenced.
3. Code sizing: Determines addresses of labels and the size of the output file.
4. Code generation: Writes the adventure file to disk.

When diagnostic messages are produced, they are in the following format:

```
[<filename> Line 12345, ] Severity: message text
```

The line number and filename is given when the diagnostic message is associated with a particular line of source code. Severity usually is specified as warning, error, or fatal, and the message depends on the condition encountered. A fatal error causes compilation to stop immediately. Most of the fatal errors are related to internal checks failing and should not appear very often.

ADVENTURE PROGRAMMING LANGUAGE (APL) SYNTAX

Although APL is intended for users with some programming experience, those who are less experienced should be able to create simple adventures after reading this section and following the example at the end of the appendix.

The Flight Simulator APL is a BASIC-like language in which commands in the program are executed one at a time in sequential order. Windows programs, on the other hand, are event-driven, meaning that the program flow is determined by user actions: within each event section of code, the program becomes sequential.

It is suggested that you adopt these basic conventions of programming to make your programs more readable and easy to edit:

- Indent four or more spaces to offset subroutines and subsections of your program.
- Indent all commands that are within loops, or IF-ENDIF statements.
- Subroutines should be placed near the end of the adventure program to keep them separate from the main body of the program.
- Document your code by placing remarks that track the author, version, date modified, variable names, and meanings of variables. Also, be sure to include important information that instructs users how to use the program or records important comments that you can use later to debug the program.
- Use lowercase characters for variable names and uppercase characters for program commands. Thus, GOTO would be uppercase, because it is a command, and x would be lowercase because it is a variable.

Introduction to Programming

If you have never used the BASIC programming language, you should read this brief introduction. Otherwise, if you are familiar with programming conventions found in BASIC, skip to the next section.

APL uses a structure that is similar to that of BASIC. Many APL commands are identical to those found in BASIC, such as PRINT, GOTO, GOSUB, IF-ENDIF, and other statements. A simple APL program might look like this:

```
TITLE "Test"
DESCRIPTION "A Test Adventure"
PRINT_TIME 5
PRINT "HELLO WORLD"
WAIT 5
PRINT "IT SEEMS TO WORK"
WAIT 5
```

The preceding program would print the following in the message (which appears in your cockpit window):

```
HELLO WORLD
```

Then it would wait five seconds before printing

```
IT SEEMS TO WORK
```

You can also add program branching, such as GOTO and IF THEN ENDIF, as follows:

```
variablex=0
MY_ROUTINE:
   IF variablex=10 THEN
   PRINT "Variable x equals"
   PRINT variablex
   ELSEIF
        PRINT "Variable x does not equal 10"
   ENDIF
        variablex=variablex + 1
   GOTO MY_ROUTINE
THE_END:
   END
```

Note that the GOTO statement creates an infinite loop, because it jum,ps back to MY_ROUTINE every time it finishes the IF ENDIF statement. To allow the program to exit gracefully, we might add the following:

```
variablex=0
MY_ROUTINE:
     IF variablex=10 THEN
          PRINT "Variable x equals"
          PRINT variablex
     ELSEIF
          PRINT "Variable x does not equal 10"

ENDIF
     variablex=variablex + 1
     IF variablex>15 THEN
```

```
        GOTO THE_END
    ENDIF
    GOTO MY_ROUTINE
THE_END:
        END
```

The final statement, END, ends the program even if there is additional code beyond it.

Common Language Features

In APL, you can use only one command per line. White space, including blanks and tabs, is allowed before, between, and after text on a line. Thus, you can indent lines and put spaces between arithmetic operators (+,-, *, /) and after commas. This spacing will help to make the program more readable. White space is generally ignored by APLC32 except for spaces inside quoted strings.

All commands and variable references are case-insensitive. The compiler converts lowercase letters to uppercase except for characters inside quotes.

You can add comments anywhere in the program by starting a line with a semicolon:

```
;——————————

;This is a comment. Anything after the semicolon is ignored by the compiler

;——————————
```

Numbers are usually expressed in decimal form, but you can use a hexadecimal number using the C language convention 0x prefix. For example, 0xAF03 is a hexadecimal number. Fractional number arguments can be expressed as x000F.F000, where the portion to the left of the decimal represents 15 and the portion to the right of the decimal represents 15 sixteenths. The precision of a number is affected by the way the program and the computer store numbers, and the number may be truncated when greater precision is required than is actually available.

To specify a constant string, use double quotes. All characters following the opening quote are part of the constant string until a closing double quote is reached. Note that only standard ASCII characters can be used inside strings. Extended ASCII characters such as ë, à, á, À, and so on are not allowed.

Suppose you want to print the following text:

```
"This is a string in quotes" and this is a regular string with no quotes
```

You would use this code:

```
PRINT " ""This is a string in quotes" " and this is a regular string with
no quotes"
```

Sometimes you will need to express numbers as latitude/longitude coordinates. Because these numbers are represented as degrees, minutes, and seconds, the APL program uses this syntax:

```
34:01:59
```

That would represent 34° 01′ 59″ or 34 degrees, 1 minute, 59 seconds.
APL also includes Degrees( ), Minutes( ), and Second( ) functions, which allow you to extract degrees, minutes, and seconds from their decimal representation.

Reserved Words

Any word that is a token as far as the language is concerned is treated as reserved. For example, in APL you could have a variable called SHIFT. APLC32 considers this word to be reserved, because it is used by arguments to the KV function. You must rename the variable before the adventure will compile.

Bracketed Lists

It has been pointed out that the 16-bit APL compiler allowed expression lists to be enclosed in brackets. Thus, it would accept a command such as SETPOSITION(x,y,z), although this does not seem to be documented. This is not allowed with APLC3 2.

APLC32's Lexical Limits

The limit on input line length has been increased. Lines can now consist of as many as 2,048 characters. No single lexical item on a line can exceed 512 characters.

The only other limits are related to free memory; there is no static limit on complexity of expressions, number of nested conditionals, number of variables, output code size, and so on.

COMMANDS

Table H.1 shows the commands and statements used in APL.

Table H.1 *Alphabetical Listing of APL Commands and Statements*

- ADV_KEYS ADD, *key*
- ADV_KEYS CLEAR
- ADV_KEYS DELETE, *key*
- BARO_PRESSURE *pressure, drift*
- CLOUDS *layer, base, top, type, coverage, turbulence, deviation, icing*
- DEBUG_PRINT
- DEBUG_WINDOW ON/OFF
- DECLARE *variable1, variable2, etc.*
- DESCRIPTION *"String"*
- EAST_LONGITUDE
- END

- FOR *variable=expression1* TO *expression 2*
- [BY *expression 3*] NEXT *variable*

- GOSUB *label:*
- RETURN
- GOTO *label:*
- IF *expression* THEN
- ELSEIF *expression* THEN
- ELSE
- ENDIF

- KV( )

- Label:
- LOAD_SITUATION *"string"*
- NORTH_LATITUDE
- ON *expression* GOSUB *label0, label1,...*
- ON *expression* GOTO *label0, label1,...*

- ONCRASH [GOSUB *label*]
- ONKEY *key-value* [GOSUB *label*]
- ONSTALL [GOSUB *label*]
- PLAY *"string"*
- PRECISION *left, right-min, right-max*
- PRINT
- PRINT_TIME
- RESET SITUATION
- RESET_ADVENTURE
- SCROLL
- SETPOSITION *latitude, longitude, altitude*
- SOUTH_LATITUDE
- TEMPERATURE *layer, altitude, temp, range*

- TITLE *"string"*
- VISIBILITY *distance*
- WAIT *time*, KEYPRESS

- WEATHER *"name", lat1, long1, lat2, long2*
- WEATHER_CHAR *width, transition, course, velocity*
- WHILE *expression*
- WEST_LONGITUDE
    ENDWHILE
- WINDS *layer, base, top, type, direcion, velocity, turbulence*

These commands and statements will be described in the next few sections.

Conditional Branching: The IF ELSEIF ELSE ENDIF Structure

The IF statement is used for conditional branching of a program. If an expression, such as *x=1*, is true, then the program executes as follows:

```
IF x=1 THEN
     PRINT x
ELSEIF x=2 THEN
     PRINT x
ELSE
     PRINT x
ENDIF
```

If *x=1* is true, then commands after THEN are executed until the next matching ELSEIF, ELSE, or ENDIF. If the matching IF and all preceding matching ELSEIFs fail (*x=1* evaluates to false) and if *x=2* is true, commands after THEN until the next matching ELSEIF, ELSE, or ENDIF are executed.

If the matching IF and all its ELSEIFs fail (*x=1* evaluates to false and *x=2* evaluates to false), commands after ELSE until the matching ENDIF are executed. ENDIF marks the end of an IF structure. For example:

```
IF x=1 THEN
     PRINT "x=1"
ELSEIF x=2 THEN
      PRINT "x=2"
ELSEIF x=3 THEN
     PRINT "x=3"
ELSE
     PRINT "x does not equal 1, 2, or 3"
ENDIF
```

Loops: The FOR...NEXT and WHILE

FOR...NEXT loops use the following structure:

```
FOR x=1  TO 5
     PRINT x
NEXT x
```

The preceding loop counts up to 5 and prints each number before exiting the loop.

The following loop counts down from 5 to 1 and prints each number before exiting the loop:

```
FOR  x=5 TO 1 BY -1
     PRINT x
NEXT x
```

WHILE loops use this structure:

```
WHILE  x<10
     PRINT x
     x=x+1
ENDWHILE
```

Labels

A *label* is a marker location for places in the code where GOTO, GOSUB, ONCRASH, and similar statements can transfer to. The following rules apply to labels:

- Label names can be any string of letters, digits, and underscores beginning with a letter. Spaces cannot be used within a label.
- Labels must be unique. Two labels cannot have the same name, although a label and a variable can have the same name.
- Labels can appear anywhere—before or after GOTO or other references.
- Labels are case-insensitive.

Here is an example subroutine:

```
gpws_2:
        ;The above is the label for the subroutine gpws
        ;Below is the first statement of the subroutine gpws_2:
```

```
    PRINT "THIS IS GPWS_2"
RETURN
;The above line returns program execution to the line
; following the GOSUB routine that called gpws_2:
```

GOTO label

When the following statement is executed, the program branches to *label*.

```
GOTO gpws_2:
```

GOSUB label

This is a subroutine call. When this statement is executed, the program execution branches to *label*, but upon reaching a RETURN, execution returns to the next statement after GOSUB. The former limit of 50 levels of subroutines that existed with the Flight Shop APLC has been removed with APLC32.

RETURN

This statement ends a subroutine that is called by GOSUB. Program execution continues following the GOSUB statement that called the subroutine in which RETURN is found.

ON expression GOTO label0, label1, label2, ...

The ON statement evaluates *expression* and truncates it to an integer value. If the resulting value is 0, it branches to *label0;* if 1, it branches to *label1* and so on. If the value is less than zero or greater than or equal to the number of labels, no branch is taken and execution proceeds to the next command.

ON expression GOSUB label0, label1, label2, ...

The ON statement evaluates *expression* and truncates it to an integer value. If the resulting value is 0, it performs a GOSUB to *label0;* if 1, it GOSUBs to *label1* and so on. If the value is less than zero or greater than or equal to the number of labels, no branch is taken and execution proceeds to the next command.

END

This marks the end of an adventure program file. When the program reaches this statement, the adventure driver stops executing the program.

DECLARE variable1, variable2, variable3, …

This statement creates new variables with any name that you specify. Variable names can be any combination of letters, digits, and underscores beginning with a letter. For example:

```
DECLARE adf,alertalt,alt,alt0,altalert,ap,atc,atcrate,autoland,break,cat, c_1,com_2
```

Variable Assignments

To assign a value to any variable, use this format:

```
adf=150
```

PRINT x, "Hello",1

This statement outputs text or variables to the message window in Flight Simulator. If x for the preceding print statement had the value of 1, you would see the following output:

```
1Hello1
```

Adding a trailing comma at the end of the PRINT statement adds a new line to the output.

SCROLL x, "Hello",1

This statement is much like PRINT, but instead of displaying only as much of the message as will fit in the message window it scrolls the message horizontally across the message window from the right to the left. SCROLL is limited to a 400-character memory buffer, so the total number of characters in a SCROLL message must not be greater than 400. If the buffer is not empty when a new SCROLL command is executed, the SCROLL command will pause until the buffer is empty before displaying new text.

PRECISION left, right-min, right-max

PRECISION controls the precision of numbers that are displayed using PRINT and SCROLL. When you specify a value for *left*, it fills the number of places to the left of the decimal place with zeros, if needed. Specifying a value for *right-min* tells the program the minimum number of places to display to the right of the decimal point. *Right-max* is the maximum number of places to display to the right of the decimal point. Table H.2 shows the arguments to PRECISION.

Table H.2 *PRECISION Statement Arguments*

EXAMPLE	*left*	*right-min*	*right-max*	IF PRINTING "2"
PRECISION 1,0,0	1	0	0	2
PRECISION 1,0,2	1	0	2	2
PRECISION 1,2,2	1	2	2	2.00
PRECISION 3,0,0	3	0	0	002

Default values for the arguments are *left* = 1, *right-min* = 0, *right-max* = 3. The maximum value of *left* is 5, and the maximum value of *right-min* and *right-max* is 4.

Here is an example:

```
PRECISION 3,0,0

PRINT DEGREES(PLANE_LAT), ":",
; Supposing the plane's latitude was N 10° 45¢ 33≤ the above print
; statement would print 010:
PRECISION 2,0,2
PRINT MINUTES(PLANE_LAT), ":", SECONDS(PLANE_LAT)
; The above print statement would print 45:33
IF PLANE_LAT>0 THEN
    PRINT "N",
    ; The above print statement would print N for the Northern Hemisphere
    ; if the plane's latitude was  greater than 0°
ELSE
    PRINT "S",
```

```
        ;or it would print S for the Southern Hemisphere
ENDIF
PRECISION 3, 0, 0
PRINT DEGREES (PLANE_LON),":",
; Supposing the plane's longitude was W 122° 02¢ 10≤ the above print
; statement would print 122:
PRECISION 2, 0, 2
PRINT MINUTES (PLANE_LON),":", SECONDS (PLANE_LON),
; The above print statement would print 02:10:
IF PLANE_LON>O THEN
    PRINT "W
    ; The above print statement would print W for the Western Hemisphere
    ; if the plane's longitude is greater than zero
ELSE
    PRINT "E"
    ;or it would print E for the Eastern Hemisphere
ENDIF
```

Note that Flight Simulator's latitude and longitude position precision is in 10,000ths of a second. However, the precision of numbers in APL is limited to 1/10th of a second.

PRINT_TIME time

This statement specifies the length of time in seconds that a PRINT command should remain displayed in the message window. Default value is 5 seconds, and the maximum is 20 seconds.

PLAY "string"

Plays a wave sound file specified by *string*. The file name for string can be the full path name or a file name that is relative to the **ADV/WAV** directory. The maximum length of *string* is eight characters plus the three-character **.WAV** file extension. For example:

```
PLAY "gear.wav"
```

or

```
PLAY "gear"
```

TITLE "string"

This statement tells Flight Simulator the name to give the adventure. The TITLE statement is usually placed in the first line of an adventure file, and *string* can be as many as 30 characters long, including any spaces separating words. Only one TITLE command per adventure is allowed.

The title "-GPWS V6.0 by Wilco van Deijl" would appear in an adventure if you used the following code:

```
TITLE "-GPWS V6.0 by Wilco van Deijl"
```

DESCRIPTION "string"

This statement allows you to give a description to your adventure using *string* as the text. You can use multiple DESCRIPTION statements. For example:

```
DESCRIPTION "Ground Proximity Warning System  V6.0            "
DESCRIPTION "Warning systems, Waypoint Navigation,            "
DESCRIPTION "Autoland mode, AP & Radio Utilities              "
DESCRIPTION "Copyright (C) 1997 Wilco van Deijl.              "
```

The string can be as many as 255 characters long, and text in the Flight Simulator description text box will automatically wrap to the next line.

The description will appear in the File Open dialog box when you select the adventure.

WAIT time, KEYPRESS

This statement specifies that the adventure should pause for *time* seconds until the user presses a key. Both *time* and KEYPRESS are optional, but one of them must be included after WAIT. If only *time* is included, the program will pause for *time* seconds regardless of which keys are pressed. If only KEYPRESS is included, the program will wait until a key is pressed; it will update the variable KEY with the key that was pressed, or 0 if the time limit is exceeded. Only keys declared by ADV_KEYS can be used with WAIT. If KEYPRESS is not included, KEY is updated if the user pressed a key, but it is not cleared if the user did not press a key. To clear the KEY variable, use WAIT 0, KEYPRESS. For example:

```
WAIT 10, KEYPRESS
```

In the preceding example, the program is instructed to wait for 10 seconds for a keypress; if it does not occur, KEY is updated with 0. If the user were to press a key within 10 seconds and if that key was declared by ADV_KEYS earlier in the program, the reserved variable KEY would be updated with the key that was pressed.

ADV_KEYS

The ADV_KEYS statement controls a list of keys that a user can press in an adventure. The keys defined by ADV_KEYS are available to the adventure but are not available to Flight Simulator. Thus, if you define **g** for a function in an adventure, it will no longer work as your landing gear up/down control. If you don't define a key in an adventure using ADV_KEYS, you won't be able to use it in the adventure but it will be available to Flight Simulator unless you use the ONKEY statement. Using ONKEY to trap keys without defining them with ADV_KEYS is problematic: unless ONKEY traps a key, the key is also passed on to Flight Simulator. To avoid confusion over which keys are trapped and which are not, it is recommended that you use ADV_KEYS to declare the keys you want to use in the adventure. For example:

```
ADV_KEYS CLEAR
ADV_KEYS ADD,288,290,534
ADV_KEYS ADD,258,259,37,292
ONKEY 288 GOSUB dh             ;Shift-d
ONKEY 290 GOSUB gpws           ;Shift-g
ONKEY 37 GOSUB spd             ;k
```

In this example, ADV_KEYS ADD,288,290,534,*key*...is used to add keys. The first ADV_KEYS declares the scan key codes for three keys, and four keys are specified in the second line. ONKEY 288 is the trap for **Shift+D**. If the user presses **Shift+D**, the program GOSUBs to the dh: label in the program and continues execution until it reaches a RETURN. If the user presses **Shift+G**, the program branches to the gpws: label, and if the user presses **k** the program branches to the spd: label. Note that in the key declaration

ADV_KEYS for **K** (scan code 37), Flight Simulator will no longer be able to use the **k** key to activate the joystick. Also note that case matters; **k** is different from **K** (**K** is really **Shift+k**).

ADV_KEYS CLEAR deletes all previous keys from the list. In this context, it is used to initialize all the keys before they are defined. Although it is not listed above, you can also use ADV_KEYS DELETE, *key,* to delete keys from the list once you have defined them with ADV_KEYS ADD.

Because memorizing and using scan codes is cumbersome (and they differ between international keyboard layouts), it is better to use the KV ( ) function to declare which key you want to trap. The next section shows you how.

KV ( ) Key Value Function

The KV ( ) function is used to replace the scan key codes. For example, rather than use "37" for the key **K** (i.e., **Shift+K**), you can use KV("K"), which will return the value 37. Note that case matters, and **K** is not the same as **k.** The argument inside the parentheses can start with any of the keywords shown in Table H.3.

Table H.3 Arguments for the Key Value KV ( ) Function

KEYWORD	ACTION
CTRL	**Ctrl** key pressed
SHIFT	**Shift** key pressed
Keypad0…Keypad9	Number keys on numeric keypad
KeyPadPeriod	**Period** key on numeric keypad (**Delete** key)

Note that when an argument uses ASCII characters inside quotes, the character need not have SHIFT preceding it. For example, KV ("K") represents **Shift+K.**

Table H.4 Examples of Key Values Used with KV ( ) and the Equivalent Keystrokes

KEY VALUE	EQUIVALENT KEYSTROKE
KV(CTRL KeyPad2)	**Ctrl+keypad 1 (or Ctrl+keypad End)**
KV(SHIFT 4)	**$**
KV("K")	**Shift+K** (uppercase **K**)
KV("k")	**k** (lowercase **k**)
KV(CTRL "k")	**Ctrl+k**
KV(CTRL "K")	**Ctrl+K**

NOTE

When you press a key on the keyboard, by default it is lowercase. This means that you must use the lowercase key value, such as KV("k") for the key **k** on the keyboard.

Now let's use KV ( ) to replace the scan code keys for the example in the previous section. For clarity, we will omit the key scan numbers.

```
ADV_KEYS CLEAR
ADV_KEYS ADD,KV(SHIFT "d"),KV(SHIFT "g")
ADV_KEYS ADD,KV("k")
ONKEY KV(SHIFT "d") GOSUB dh          ;Shift-D
ONKEY KV(SHIFT "g") GOSUB gpws        ;Shift-G
ONKEY KV("k") GOSUB spd               ;k (lowercase "k")
```

As you can see, it's much easier to program keyboard controls using the KV ( ) function than to use keyboard scan codes.

The function keys **F1** through **F12** are not usable in adventures.

NORTH_LATITUDE

The statements NORTH_LATITUDE and SOUTH_LATITUDE are useful when you want a flight adventure to use positive latitudes in a particular hemisphere. Thus, if you were flying in the Northern Hemisphere, you might want to use NORTH_LATITUDE, whereas if your flight were in the Southern Hemisphere and you wanted to work with positive numbers, you would use SOUTH_LATITUDE.

NORTH_LATITUDE causes positive latitude coordinates to represent north latitudes and negative coordinates to represent south latitudes.

SOUTH_LATITUDE

This causes positive latitude coordinates to represent south latitudes and negative coordinates to represent north latitudes.

EAST_LONGITUDE

This causes positive longitude coordinates to represent east longitudes and negative coordinates to represent west longitudes.

WEST_LONGITUDE

This causes positive longitude coordinates to represent west longitudes and negative coordinates to represent east longitudes.

NORTH_LATITUDE and WEST_LONGITUDE are the default settings. If you want a different latitude or longitude, you must declare this before using a command using a *latitude* or *longitude* variable.

SETPOSITION latitude, longitude, altitude

SETPOSITION moves the user's aircraft to a coordinate of (*latitude, longitude*) at an altitude of *altitude* meters above mean sea level (MSL). When using this command, the program will pause briefly while it resets the aircraft's position. The highest precision for a position is 1/10th of a second. Here's an example:

```
SETPOSITION 32.40,122.25,1000
```

To fix the FS98 bug that ignored the altitude parameter, install the FS98 aircraft converter, which will apply a patch to the program.

NOTE It is best to use a WAIT 4 seconds command immediately after a SETPOSITION command so that Flight Simulator will have time to reposition all the other flight parameters.

RESET_SITUATION

This statement resets the current situation. For example:

```
RESET_SITUATION
```

In FS98, this command now reinitializes all user-defined APL variables to 0.

LOAD_SITUATION "string"

This statement loads the situation file named by *string*. The file named by *string* must be a Flight Simulator situation, but the **.STN** extension is not assumed. Before running the adventure, you should create the flight situation named by *string* and give it the same name as *string*. For example:

```
LOAD_SITUATION "C:\FLTSIM95\SITUATIO\mysit.stn"
```

RESET_ADVENTURE

This statement resets the current adventure. For example:

```
RESET_ADVENTURE
```

ONCRASH, ONSTALL, and ONKEY

ONCRASH, ONSTALL, and ONKEY are special subroutines that are called only when a certain condition is met. Although these subroutines can be activated whenever the main adventure program is running, only one subroutine can be active at a time. Thus, if a user's plane stalls while an ONKEY routine is running, the ONSTALL subroutine would not be called.

ONCRASH GOSUB label

When the airplane crashes, this command instructs Flight Simulator to disable its normal crash detection routines. Using ONCRASH invokes a GOSUB call to *label*. If no GOSUB *label* is specified, any previous call of ONCRASH *label* is cleared and normal Flight Simulator behavior is restored.

ONSTALL [GOSUB label]

When the airplane stalls, this command instructs Flight Simulator to invoke the GOSUB *label* procedure. If no GOSUB *label* is specified, any previous call of ONSTALL is cleared.

ONKEY key-value [GOSUB label]

This command instructs Flight Simulator to check whether the user has pressed a key defined by *keyvalue* and branch to the GOSUB *label* procedure. For example:

```
ONKEY KV("K") GOSUB gpws
```

Or

```
ONKEY 37 GOSUB gpws
```

If no GOSUB *label* is specified, any previous ONKEY for that key is cleared and normal Flight Simulator key input for that key is restored. Note that only keys first defined by ADV_KEYS ADD should be used by ONKEY.

Weather Commands

The weather commands WEATHER, WEATHER_CHAR, CLOUDS, WINDS, TEMPERA-TURE, BARO_PRESSURE, and VISIBILITY let you create local weather areas in your adventures. CLOUDS, WINDS, and TEMPERATURE let you create clouds, winds, and temperature layers in terms of altitude layers. You can have as many as three cloud layers, with separate CLOUDS statements for each layer. If three layers are specified, one of them must be a thunderstorm layer; otherwise, only two layers are possible. No additional cloud layers are possible once you have invoked three layers of clouds. All layers are identified by layer numbers, and no order is assumed by the numbering of layers in Flight Simulator. If you use a CLOUDS command with the same layer number as that of a previous cloud layer, the new layer replaces the old layer with the same layer number or deletes it if the DELETE form of the command is used. WINDS layers and TEMPERATURE layers work in much the same manner as cloud layers except that there can be four layers of both temperatures and winds. Wind layers can force clouds to move in the same direction and velocity as a wind layer that contains the clouds. It is even possible to have clouds move in opposite directions if the layers that contain them are in are moving in opposite directions.

The WEATHER_CHAR, BARO_PRESSURE, and VISIBILITY commands determine the global parameters of a weather area. Because there are no layers with these commands, you can override previous statements with new statement calls.

When changes are made to a weather area, it can take several seconds for the changes to show up visually in Flight Simulator.

WEATHER "name", lat1, long1, lat2, long2

This statement begins a new weather area, which is given a *name* of as many as 25 characters, along with two endpoint latitude/longitude coordinate pairs (i.e., *lat1*, *long1*, *lat2*, *long2*).

Only one weather area can exist in an adventure. If you call this command again, any existing weather area previously created will be deleted. Here's an example:

```
WEATHER "MYADVENTURE", 38.03925, -90.27805, 43.85878, -85.60792
```

WEATHER_CHAR width, transition, course, velocity

This statement further defines a weather area created with the WEATHER command. The *width* of the weather system is measured in miles; the *transition* refers the edge of the weather system. *Course* is the magnetic direction the weather system is moving, and *velocity* is the speed of the weather system in knots.

To fix the FS98 bug that ignored the velocity parameter, you should install the FS98 aircraft converter, which will apply a patch to the program to fix this problem.

CLOUDS layer, base, top, type, coverage, turbulence, deviation, icing

With the CLOUDS command, you can create three cloud layers, one of which must be a thunderstorm. If you don't want a thunderstorm, you can use only two cloud layers. Cloud *base* is measured in meters of altitude above MSL. Note that FS95/98 adventures normally expect altitude to be expressed in meters and not feet. *Base* is measured in meters MSL, as is *top*. *Coverage* is the amount of cloud coverage, and wind *turbulence* ranges from 0 to 255. *Deviation* is expressed in meters, and refers to the area just above, below, and at the boundary of the cloud layer itself where cloud conditions still exist. *Deviation* ranges from a minimum of 0 meters to a maximum deviation range above or below the cloud. *Icing*, which occurs only within clouds, is used to teach pilots how to cope with engine ice fouling the carburetor and possibly causing the wing to stall because of airflow interference. If icing is 0, it indicates no icing; if it is 1, it indicates that icing exists. Also, if a wind layer includes the region of atmosphere where *base* and *top* of CLOUDS are used, the wind layer will move the clouds in the direction the wind is blowing. Here's an example:

```
CLOUDS 1,500,1000,stratus,scattered4,5,10,0
CLOUDS 2,vCloudbase,vCloudtop,nimbostratus,broken6,vTurb,vDev,vIcing
```

In the first example, CLOUDS 1 creates a cloud layer 1 with a base of 500 meters (1,640 ft) and a top of 1,000 meters (3,280 ft). The cloud type is stratus, which must have a base between 100 and 1,500 meters. Because we have chosen a base of 500 meters, this choice is OK. Cloud coverage is scattered4. For stratus-type clouds, coverage can range from scattered4 to overcast, so our choice of scattered4 is also OK. For turbulence, we have chosen 5, which is also fine because stratus-type clouds can have turbulence that ranges from 0 to 18. Deviation is 10 meters, well within the limit of 20 meters. This deviation of 10 meters (32 ft) means that the airplane will continue to be affected by cloud turbulence factor and other disturbances as much as 32 ft above and below the limit of the cloud layer's boundaries.

In the second example, *vCloudbase, vCloudtop, vTurb,vDev,* and *vIcing* are all variables that can be created and modified by the program as arguments to the CLOUDS command.

Table H.5 shows the 11 possible cloud types that can exist in Flight Simulator along with their associated minimum and maximum base, thickness, coverage, turbulence, and deviation values.

Table H.5 Cloud Types and Their Associated Parameters

TYPE	BASE (METERS)		THICKNESS (METERS)		COVERAGE		TURBULENCE (0 TO 255)		DEVIATION (METERS)	
	Min	Max	Min	Max	Min	Max	Min	Max	Min	Max
Cirrus	4,800	14,000	3	100	clear	scattered2	0	18	0	0
Cirrostratus	4,800	14,000	3	5	broken7	overcast	0	18	0	0
Cirrocumulus	4,800	14,000	5	300	scattered2	broken6	36	109	0	0
Altostratus	1,800	7,000	15	300	broken7	overcast	0	18	0	0
Altocumulus	1,800	7,000	30	1,000	scattered2	broken6	36	109	0	0
Stratocumulus	100	1,500	100	1,000	scattered2	overcast	36	109	0	100
Nimbostratus	100	1,500	300	1,200	broken6	overcast	0	18	0	20
Stratus	100	1,500	30	600	scattered4	overcast	0	18	0	20
Cumulus	100	1,500	100	5,000	scattered2	overcast	36	109	0	200
Cumulonimbus (thunderstorm)	100	6,000	1,500	9,000	wide	dense	146	255	0	200
user-defined	100	14,000	3	10,000	clear	overcast	0	255	0	200

The nine levels of cloud coverage are shown in Table H.6, in order of increasing cloud cover.

Table H.6 Cloud Coverage

CLOUD COVERAGE	EIGHTHS OF COVERAGE
clear	0
scattered1	1
scattered2	2
scattered3	3
scattered4	4
broken5	5
broken6	6
broken7	7
overcast	8

Cumulonimbus clouds have only three cloud coverage types, as shown in Table H.7.

Table H.7 Cumulonimbus Cloud Coverage

CUMULONIMBUS CLOUD COVERAGE	DESCRIPTION
wide	Widely Scattered
scattered	Scattered
dense	Dense

When you select cumulonimbus (thunderstorm) clouds in the Weather dialog box of Flight Simulator, you don't have the cloud coverage choices available in Table H.6. Only those choices in Table H.7 are possible.

CLOUDS layer, DELETE

This statement deletes the cloud *layer* number that was previously defined by CLOUDS. For example:

```
CLOUDS 2, DELETE
```

WINDS layer, base, top, type, direction, velocity, turbulence

The WINDS statement creates or modifies the wind layer identified by *layer*. You can have as many as four different wind layers. The *base* and *top* altitudes of the wind layer are expressed in meters MSL. There are two types of wind that you can choose for *type*: gusty or steady. The *direction* the wind is coming from is measured in degrees magnetic, and the *velocity* of the wind is in knots. The *turbulence* factor can range from 0 to 255, with 0 equaling no turbulence and 255 being very turbulent. For example:

```
WINDS 1, 229, 379, steady, 224, 5, 15
```

In the example, wind layer 1 has a base of 229 meters and a top elevation of 379 meters. It has a steady wind blowing from a true compass heading of 224°, with a velocity of 5 knots and a light turbulence rating of 15 on a scale of 0 to 255.

Note that surface winds have magnetic direction (to correspond to runway headings), whereas winds aloft are measured with respect to true north. To set a surface wind layer, the base value must be 0.

WINDS layer, DELETE

This statement deletes the wind layer number referenced by *layer*. For example:

```
WINDS 1, DELETE
```

TEMPERATURE layer, altitude, temp, range

Using the TEMPERATURE statement, you can create four temperature layers. The *altitude* of the layer is measured in meters MSL, and the temperature is in degrees Celsius. The day and night variation is set using the *range* argument, but because this diurnal temperature change affects all the temperature layers, you must specify the *range* argument only in the last layer you use. For example:

```
TEMPERATURE 1, 200, 20, 10
```

TEMPERATURE layer, DELETE

Use this statement to delete a temperature layer. For example:

```
TEMPERATURE 1, DELETE
```

BARO_PRESSURE pressure, drift

Use this statement to select a barometric pressure in inches of mercury. The argument *pressure* is used to specify the pressure. If *drift* is true (nonzero), the pressure will drift and you will need to recalibrate the altimeter periodically while the adventure runs. If *drift* is false (equals 0), there is no drift. To recalibrate the altimeter, press the **B** key. For example:

```
BARO_PRESSURE 29.92, 0
```

VISIBILITY distance

This statement controls the visibility and haze settings. Specify the visual range for *distance* in miles. Minimum visibility is 1/16th of a mile, and the maximum goes to infinity or "unlimited." At least one cloud layer must be active for the visibility feature to work. If reduced visibility is turned on, your visibility will be restricted only from the ground up to the base of the lowest cloud layer. For example:

```
VISIBILITY 10
```

To fix the FS98 bug that didn't handle values between 0 and 1, install the FS98 Aircraft Converter, which will patch the program.

NUMBERS, PRECISION AND OPERATORS

WARNING

The following text applies only to the old Flight Shop APLC when used with the previous version of FS5.1. Changes to Flight Simulator for Windows 95 involve using double-precision (i.e., 64-bit storage) representation of variables, numbers, and functions. Because Microsoft is reluctant to divulge details of the inner workings of the program, I have included the older and perhaps obsolete data on FS5.1 APL code because it offers some useful insight into the inner workings of Flight Simulator. Use it at your own risk.

In the old Flight Shop APL, variables, numbers, and functions had a precision of 16 bits for the integer part and 16 bits for the fractional part. The largest number you could use was 32,767.9999847, and the smallest number was -32,768.0. Although numbers were stored with only 32 bits (16 bits for integer and 16 bits for the fractional part), all calculations were performed with 32 bits for the integer part and 32 bits for the fractional part. The result was truncated to 16 bits and 16 bits for the integer and fractional components, respectively.

Flight Simulator internally processes altitudes in terms of meters, not feet. The historical reason for doing so was that since the largest number in the previous generation FS 5.1 was 32,767.9999847 (a 16 bit by 16 bit number), if expressed in meters you could then have altitudes greater than 32,767 feet. If you convert 32,767.9999847 meters to feet, you will find that the maximum useable altitude in Flight Simulator is 107,507 feet.

If the need arises to convert meters to feet or feet to meters, APL has built-in functions to do this.

The number scheme used in APL and the old Flight Simulator 5.1 is not very accurate for high-precision computations. If you used complex functions or performed complex calculations, you would expect some inaccuracies in the results. To get around this limitation, Microsoft switched to a double-precision method of storing fractional components in FS95/98. As a result, you should get better accuracy using APLC32 code with FSW95.

Bit Operators and Fractions

Programmers who are accustomed to using bitwise operations on fractions should stop doing so. The old FS5 representation of numbers used fixed-point arithmetic, which made it safe to use bitwise operations. However, in FS95/98, fractions are stored as double-precision floating-point numbers, breaking the direct mapping between a fractional bit and its representation. The use of bitwise operations on fractions will give invalid results, because there is no straight mapping to a particular bit. To negate a number or variable, use -. To logically negate an expression, use NOT.

Binary, Arithmetic, and Logical Operators

The operators shown in Table H.8 are used to combine two operands according to the normal rules of precedence.

Logical operators (=, AND, and so on) produce a value of 1 for true and 0 for false.

Table H.8 *Binary, Arithmetic, and Logical Operators*

OPERATOR	OPERATION
+	Add
-	Subtract
*	Multiply
/	Floating divide (3/2 = 1.5)
IDIV	Integer divide (3 IDIV 2 = 1)
IREM, %	Integer remainder (modulus)
&	Bitwise AND
|	Bitwise OR
XOR, ^	Bitwise exclusive OR
=	Equality
!=	Inequality
<	Less than
<=	Less than or equal
>	Greater than
>=	Greater than or equal
AND, &&	Logical AND (true if both operands are true)
OR, ||	Logical OR (true if either or both operands are true)

NOTE

Martin Smith states that he used the C language as a model for the precedence of operators, although he won't guarantee that complex expressions will produce exactly the same results. It appears that the bitwise operators have a much higher precedence than in C, so this may produce different results. Smith's advice is to bracket all expressions involving bitwise logical operations.

BUILT IN-APL FUNCTIONS

The functions in Table H.9 are built into APL and provide useful conversions between units as well as other useful calculations. To use a function, type its name and enclose the function's arguments in parentheses. For example:

```
IF NOT INRANGE(ra,lastcall-90,lastcall+10) THEN
      PRINT "Not in range"
```

Here, the function INRANGE(ra,lastcall-90, lastcall+10) returns a value of true if the variable ra falls between the value of lastcall-90 and lastcall+10. In this example, the NOT statement preceding the INRANGE function logically negates its value. Thus, if INRANGE returns a value of true (1), then NOT would change it to false (0). The IF statement will execute the PRINT statement only if INRANGE returns a value of false, because the NOT negation operator will change INRANGE's value of false to true, and true is the value that the IF statement will finally "see."

Table H.9 *Built-In APL Functions*

FUNCTION(*arguments*)	DESCRIPTION
INT(*value*)	Returns integer portion of *value*.
INRANGE(*value,low,high*)	Returns true (1) if *value* ≥ *low* and *value* ≤ *high*.
FTOM(*feet*)	Converts *feet* to meters.
MTOF(*meters*)	Converts *meters* to feet.
FTOC(*temperature*)	Converts *temperature* in degrees Fahrenheit to degrees Celsius.
CTOF(*temperature*)	Converts *temperature* in degrees Celsius to degrees Fahrenheit.
MBTOINHG(*pressure*)	Converts *pressure* measured in millibars to inches of mercury.
INHGTOMB(*pressure*)	Converts *pressure* measured in inches of mercury to millibars.
KMTONM(*distance*)	Converts *distance* measured in kilometers to nautical miles.
NMTOKM(*distance*)	Converts *distance* measured in nautical miles to kilometers.
NMTOSM(*distance*)	Converts *distance* measured in nautical miles to statute miles.

Table H.9 *continued*

Function(*arguments*)	Description
SMTONM(*distance*)	Converts *distance* measured in statute miles to nautical miles.
GROUND_DISTANCE(*latitude,longitude*)	Returns distance in nautical miles along the ground from user's plane to *latitude, longitude.*
AIR_DISTANCE(*latitude,longitude*)	Returns distance in nautical miles through the air from user's plane to *latitude, longitude.*
RADIAL(*latitude,longitude*)	Returns angle in true degrees measured in a horizontal plane from a point located at *latitude, longitude* to user's airplane.
GLIDE_SLOPE(*latitude,longitude*)	Returns glide slope to *latitude,longitude* in degrees.
DEGREES(*angle*)	Converts *angle* into degrees, minutes, and seconds and returns the integer degrees part.
MINUTES(*angle*)	Converts *angle* into degrees, minutes, and seconds and returns the integer minutes part.
SECONDS(*angle*)	Converts *angle* into degrees, minutes, and seconds and returns the seconds part.

Flight Simulator Variables

Flight Simulator has predefined variables that you can access through APL. Many of the variables allow you to change operating characteristics of the simulation or of the airplane itself. Latitude values are in degrees from -90° to +90°. North latitudes are positive unless a SOUTH_LATITUDE command has reversed the sense. Longitude values are in degrees from -180° to +180°. West longitude is positive unless an EAST_LONGITUDE command has reversed the sense.

In Table H.10, the column titled **Write?** tells you whether the variable's value can be changed by your program. N means that you can only read the value for the variable; you cannot change it. Also, when a variable is marked boolean, it means that you can enter only a true or false value (1 for true or 0 for false). For example, if you wanted to switch the autopilot master switch on, you would use this Boolean construct for the AUTOPILOT_MASTER system variable:

```
AUTOPILOT_MASTER=1     ;boolean value is 1, meaning "true"
```

Table H.10 *Flight Simulator Variables Available to APL*

VARIABLE NAME	UNITS	WRITE?	DESCRIPTION
ADF_ACTIVE	boolean	N	Returns true if an ADF station is currently tuned in.
ADF_ALT	meters	N	Returns the altitude of ADF station. Returns 0 if no ADF is tuned in.
ADF_FREQ	kHz	Y	Sets or returns the frequency that the ADF radio is tuned to. The valid range of values is 200kHz to 1699.9 kHz in increments of 0.1 kHz. If the **100 Hz ADF Frequency Increment** preference is not selected (in the **Options/Preferences/Instrument** menu), only values from 200 kHz to 999 kHz in increments of 1 kHz are permissible.
ADF_LAT	degrees of latitude		Returns the latitude of the ADF station, or 0 if no ADF station is tuned in.
ADF_LON	degrees longitude	N	Returns longitude of the ADF station, or 0 if no ADF is tuned in.
AUTOPILOT_ ALTITUDE	meters	Y	Lets you set or return the plane's altitude above mean sea level for the autopilot to maintain. This corresponds to the Altitude Hold numeric entry box on the MCP.
AUTOPILOT_ ALTITUDE_HOLD	boolean	Y	True if autopilot is to maintain altitude specified by AUTOPILOT_ ALTITUDE. This corresponds to the check box for Altitude Hold on the MCP.
AUTOPILOT_ APPROACH_HOLD	boolean	Y	True if the autopilot is to follow the localizer and glide slope from the station tuned in on the NAV 1 radio. This corresponds to the APR check box on the Autopilot MCP.

Table H.10 continued

VARIABLE NAME	UNITS	WRITE?	DESCRIPTION
AUTOPILOT_ ATTITUDE_HOLD	boolean	Y	True if the autopilot is to hold the plane's attitude (pitch and bank) steady. This corresponds to the ATT check box on the Autopilot MCP.
AUTOPILOT_BACK COURSE_HOLD	boolean	Y	True if the autopilot is to fly the back course from the station tuned in on the NAV 1 radio. This corresponds to the BC check box on the Autopilot MCP.
AUTOPILOT_ HEADING	degrees magnetic	Y	Heading for autopilot to hold, measured in degrees with respect to the magnetic compass heading. This corresponds to the numeric field in the HDG (Heading Hold) on the Autopilot MCP.
AUTOPILOT_ HEADING_HOLD	boolean	Y	True if autopilot is to hold heading specified by AUTOPILOT_ HEADING. This corresponds to the HDG check box on the Autopilot MCP.
AUTOPILOT_ LOCALIZER_HOLD	boolean	Y	This should correspond to the LDC check box on the Autopilot MCP.
AUTOPILOT_MASTER	boolean	Y	Autopilot master switch. This switch must be on (true) for any of the autopilot functions to be active. Setting this variable equal to 1 is equivalent to clicking on the Autopilot Active check box at the top of the Autopilot dialog box or the autopilot master switch on the instrument panels.
AUTOPILOT_ NAV_HOLD	boolean	Y	True if the autopilot is to maintain a heading to the station tuned in on the NAV 1 radio. This corresponds to the NAV check box on on the Autopilot MCP.
AUTOPILOT_ WING_LEVELER	boolean	Y	True if the autopilot is to keep the wing level. This corresponds to the LVL check box on the Autopilot MCP.

Table H.10 *continued*

VARIABLE NAME	UNITS	WRITE?	DESCRIPTION
BAROMETRIC_DRIFT	boolean	N	True if barometric pressure drift is enabled.
BAROMETRIC_PRESSURE	in Hg	N	Current barometric pressure in inches of mercury.
BRAKE_LEFT_POSITION	integer	N	0 = off, 32,767 = full on
BRAKE_RIGHT_POSITION	integer	N	0 = off, 32,767 = full on
CLOUD_HIGH_ACTIVE	boolean	N	True if there is a high cloud layer active.
CLOUD_HIGH_BASE	meters	N	Altitude MSL of base of high cloud layer. 0 if there is no high cloud layer active.
CLOUD_HIGH_COVERAGE	fraction	N	Coverage of high cloud layer: 0 = no clouds, 1 = fully overcast.
CLOUD_HIGH_ICING	boolean	N	True if there are icing conditions in the high cloud layer.
CLOUD_HIGH_TOP	meters	N	Altitude MSL of top of high cloud layer. 0 if there is no high cloud layer active.
CLOUD_HIGH_TURB	integer	N	Turbulence of high cloud layer: 0 (calm) to 255 (most turbulent). 0 if there is no high cloud layer active.
CLOUD_HIGH_TYPE	integer	N	Type of high cloud layer: 0 = user-defined, 1 = cirrus, 2 = cirrostratus, 3 = cirrocumulus, 4 = altostratus, 5 = altocumulus, 6 = stratocumulus, 7 = nimbostratus, 8 = stratus, 9 = cumulus. 0 if there is no high cloud layer active.
CLOUD_LOW_ACTIVE	boolean	N	True if there is a low cloud layer active.
CLOUD_LOW_BASE	meters	N	Altitude MSL of base of low cloud layer. 0 if there is no low cloud layer active.
CLOUD_LOW_COVERAGE	fraction	N	Coverage of low cloud layer: 0 = no clouds, 1 = fully overcast.
CLOUD_LOW_ICING	boolean	N	True if there are icing conditions in the low cloud layer.

Table H.10 continued

Variable Name	Units	Write?	Description
CLOUD_LOW_TOP	meters	N	Altitude MSL of top of low cloud layer. 0 if there is no low cloud layer active.
CLOUD_LOW_TURB	integer	N	Turbulence of low cloud layer: 0 (calm) to 255 (most turbulent). 0 if there is no low cloud layer active.
CLOUD_LOW_TYPE	integer	N	Type of low cloud layer: 0 = user-defined, 1= cirrus, 2 = cirrostratus, 3 = cirrocumulus, 4 = altostratus, 5 = altocumulus, 6 = stratocumulus, 7 = nimbostratus, 8 = stratus, 9 = cumulus. 0 if there is no low cloud layer active.
CLOUD_THUNDER_ACTIVE	boolean	N	True if there is a thunderstorm layer active.
CLOUD_THUNDER_BASE	meters	N	Altitude MSL of base of thunderstorm layer. Returns 0 if there is no thunderstorm layer active.
CLOUD_THUNDER_COVERAGE	fraction	N	Coverage of thunderstorm layer: 0 = no clouds, 1 = fully overcast. Returns 0 if there is no thunderstorm layer active.
CLOUD_THUNDER_ICING	boolean	N	True if there are icing conditions in the thunderstorm layer.
CLOUD_THUNDER_TOP	meters	N	Altitude MSL of top of thunderstorm layer. Returns 0 if there is no thunderstorm layer active.
CLOUD_THUNDER_TURB	integer	N	Turbulence of thunderstorm layer: 0 (calm) to 255 (most turbulent). Returns 0 if there is no thunderstorm layer active.
CLOUD_THUNDER_TYPE	integer	N	Type of thunderstorm layer: 10 = cumulonimbus. Returns 0 if there is no thunderstorm layer active.
COM_FREQ	MHz	Y	Frequency that COM radio is tuned to. Valid values are 118.000 MHz to 136.975 MHz in increments of 0.05

Table H.10 continued

VARIABLE NAME	UNITS	WRITE?	DESCRIPTION
			KHz. If you turn on **Options/Preferences/Instrument/2 5 kHz Com Frequency Increment,** you can tune the COM radio in 0.025 kHz increments.
COURSE	degrees magnetic	N	Wind-corrected heading measured with respect to the magnetic compass heading in degrees.
ELEVATOR_TRIM_POSITION	integer	N	-16383 = full nose down, 16,383 = full nose up.
EMERGENCY_FAILURE	bitmap	Y	bit 0 = high oil temp, bit 1 = low oil pressure, bit 2 = left fuel tank leak, bit 3 = right fuel tank leak.
ENGINE_TYPE	integer	N	0 = piston engine. 1 = jet engine, 2=none.
FLAPS_LEFT_POSITION	integer	N	0 = up, 32767 = down.
FLAPS_RIGHT_POSITION	integer	N	0 = up, 32767 = down.
GEAR_1_POSITION	integer	N	0 = up, 32767 = down.
GEAR_2_POSITION	integer	N	0 = up, 32767 = down.
GEAR_3_POSITION	integer	N	0 = up, 32767 = down.
GROUND_ALTITUDE	meters	N	Ground altitude (above sea level) under the plane. Tells you the elevation of the terrain below the airplane.
HOUR	hours	Y	Current time hour (0–23).
IMARK	boolean	N	True if inner marker indicator is on.
KEY	integer	N	Modified scan code of last key; 0 if a WAIT command timed out.
LEFT_AUX_FUEL LEVEL	gallons	N	Fuel remaining in left auxiliary tank.
LEFT_MAIN_FUEL LEVEL	gallons	N	Fuel remaining in left main tank.
MAGVAR	degrees	N	Magnetic variation: the difference between true and magnetic north. Magnetic heading equals true heading minus MAGVAR.

Table H.10 continued

VARIABLE NAME	UNITS	WRITE?	DESCRIPTION
MINUTE	minutes	Y	Current time minute (0–59).
MMARK	boolean	N	True if middle marker indicator is on.
NAV1_ FREQ	MHz	Y	Frequency NAV1 radio is tuned to. Values range from 108.00 MHz to 117.95 MHz in increments of 0.05 MHz.
NAV2_ FREQ	MHz	Y	Frequency NAV2 radio is tuned to. Values range from 108.00 Mhz to 117.95 MHz in increments of 0.05 MHz.
OMARK	boolean	N	True if outer marker indicator is on.
ON_GROUND	boolean	N	True if the plane is on the ground.
OVERSPEED_WARNING	boolean	N	True if overspeed warning is on.
PARKING_BRAKES	boolean	N	True if parking brakes are on.
PLANE_ALT	meters	N	Plane's altitude MSL.
PLANE_BANK	degrees	N	Plane's bank angle: Returns 0° if plane is in straight and level flight. Positive values indicate bank to left. Negative values indicate bank to right.
PLANE_HEADING	degrees	N	Plane's magnetic heading.
PLANE_LAT	degrees latitude	N	Plane's latitude.
PLANE_LON	degrees longitude	N	Plane's longitude.
PLANE_PITCH	degrees	N	Plane's pitch: 0 = level. Positive values indicate pitch up.
RANDOM	fraction	N	Pseudorandom value $0 \leq x < 1$.
RETRACTABLE_GEAR	boolean	N	0 = fixed gear, 1 = retractable gear.
RIGHT_AUX_FUEL_ LEVEL	gallons	N	Fuel remaining in right auxiliary tank.
RIGHT_MAIN_FUEL_ LEVEL	gallons	N	Fuel remaining in right main tank.
RUDDER_PEDAL_ POSITION	integer	N	-16,383 = full left, 16,383 = full right.
SEASON	integer	Y	Season for scenery effects: 0 winter, 1 = spring, 2 = summer, 3 = autumn.
SECOND	seconds	Y	Current time second (0–59).

Table H.10 continued

Variable Name	Units	Write?	Description
SLEW_SYSTEM_ACTIVE	boolean	N	True if the user is in slew mode.
SMOKE_SYSTEM_ON	boolean	Y	True if the smoke trail system is on.
STALL_WARNING	boolean	N	True if the stall horn is sounding.
TEMPERATURE_HIGH_ALT	meters	N	Altitude of high temperature layer.
TEMPERATURE_HIGH_TEMP	Celsius	N	Temperature of high temperature layer.
TEMPERATURE_LOW_ALT	meters	N	Altitude of low temperature layer.
TEMPERATURE_LOW_TEMP	Celsius	N	Temperature of low temperature layer.
TEMPERATURE_MID_ALT	meters	N	Altitude of middle temperature layer.
TEMPERATURE_MID_TEMP	Celsius	N	Temperature of middle temperature layer.
TEMPERATURE_SURFACE_ALT	meters	N	Altitude of surface temperature layer.
TEMPERATURE_SURFACE_TEMP	Celsius	N	Temperature of surface temperature layer.
TRANS_FREQ	integer	Y	Four digit transponder squawk value: each digit must be between 0 and 7.
VELOCITY	knots	N	True airspeed.
VELOCITY_INDICATED	knots	N	Indicated airspeed.
VELOCITY_Y	meters/s	N	Vertical speed. Positive values mean the plane is rising.
VOR_1_ACTIVE	boolean	N	True if NAV1 radio is tuned to a VOR.
VOR_1_ALT	meters	N	Altitude of station tuned in on NAV 1 radio. Returns 0 if NAV1 radio not tuned to a station.
VOR_1_DME	nautical miles	N	Distance to station tuned in on NAVI radio. Returns 0 if NAV1 radio not tuned to a station or if DME is not available.
VOR_1_DME_AVAIL	boolean	N	True if a station that provides DME is tuned in on the NAV1 radio.
VOR_1_GLIDE_SLOPE	degrees		Glide slope indicated on VOR1. Returns 0 if no glide slope available.

Table H.10 continued

Variable Name	Units	Write?	Description
VOR_1_GS_AVAIL	boolean	N	True if station tuned in on NAV 1 radio provides glide slope.
VOR_1_LOCALIZER_AVAIL	boolean	N	True if station tuned in on NAV1 radio is an ILS station.
VOR_1_LAT	degrees latitude	N	Latitude of station tuned in on NAV1 radio. Returns 0 if NAV1 radio is not tuned to a station.
VOR_1_LOCALIZER	degrees true	N	Localizer course indicated by VOR1 instrument. Returns 0 if localizer is not active.
VOR_1_LON	degrees longitude	N	Longitude of station tuned in on NAV1 radio. Returns 0 if NAV1 radio is not tuned to a station.
VOR_1_OBS	degrees	Y	Omni Bearing Select value dialed in on VOR1 instrument.
VOR_1_RADIAL	degrees	N	Radial to station tuned in on NAV1 radio. True if NAV1 radio is not tuned to a station.
VOR_2_ACTIVE	boolean	N	True if NAV2 radio is tuned to a VOR.
VOR_2_ALT	meters	N	Altitude of station tuned in on NAV2 radio. Returns 0 if NAV2 radio is not tuned to a station.
VOR_2_DME	nautical miles	N	Distance to station tuned in on NAV2 radio. Returns 0 if NAV2 radio is not tuned to a station or if DME is not available.
VOR_2_DME_AVAIL	boolean	N	True if DME is available for VOR 2.
VOR_2_LAT	degrees latitude	N	Latitude of station tuned in on NAV2 radio. 0 if NAV2 radio is not tuned to a station.
VOR_2_LON	degrees long	N	Longitude of station tuned in on NAV2 radio. Returns 0 if NAV2 radio is not tuned to a station.
VOR_2_OBS	degrees	Y	Omni Bearing Select value dialed in on VOR 2 instrument.
VOR_2_RADIAL	degrees true	N	Radial to station tuned in on NAV1 radio. Returns 0 if NAV1 radio not tuned to a station.

Table H.10 continued

VARIABLE NAME	UNITS	WRITE?	DESCRIPTION
WIND_LOW_BASE	meters	N	Altitude MSL of base of low winds aloft layer.
WIND_LOW_DIR	degrees true	N	Heading from which low winds aloft layer is blowing.
WIND_LOW_TOP	meters	N	Altitude MSL of top of low winds aloft layer.
WIND_LOW_TURB	integer	N	Turbulence factor of low winds aloft layer: 0 (no turbulence) to 255 (most turbulent).
WIND_LOW_TYPE	integer	N	Type of top of low winds aloft layer. 0 = steady, 1 = gusty.
WIND_LOW_VEL	knots	N	Wind speed of low winds aloft layer.
WIND_MID_BASE	meters	N	Altitude MSL of base of middle winds aloft layer.
WIND_MID_DIR	degrees true	N	Heading from which middle winds aloft layer is blowing.
WIND_MID_TOP	meters	N	Altitude MSL of top of middle winds aloft layer.
WIND_MID_TURB	integer	N	Turbulence factor of middle winds aloft layer: 0 (no turbulence) to 255 (most turbulent).
WIND_MID_TYPE	integer	N	Type of top of middle winds aloft layer: 0 = steady, 1 = gusty.
WIND_MID_VEL	knots	N	Wind speed of middle winds aloft layer.
WIND_SURF_DEPTH	meters	N	Altitude AGL of top of surface winds layer.
WIND_SURF_DIR	degrees magnetic	N	Heading from which surface winds layer is blowing.
WIND_SURF_TURB	integer	N	Turbulence factor of surface winds layer: 0 (no turbulence) to 255 (most turbulent).
WIND_SURF_TYPE	integer	N	Type of top of surface winds layer: 0 = steady, 1 = gusty.
WIND_SURF_VEL	knots	N	Wind speed of surface winds layer.
WIND_UP_BASE	meters	N	Altitude MSL of base of high winds aloft layer.

Table H.10 *continued*

Variable Name	Units	Write?	Description
WIND_UP_DIR	degrees true	N	Heading from which high winds aloft layer is blowing.
WIND_UP_TOP	meters	N	Altitude MSL of top of high winds aloft layer.
WIND_UP_TURB	integer	N	Turbulence factor of high winds aloft layer: 0 (no turbulence) to 255 (most turbulent).
WIND_UP_TYPE	integer	N	Type of top of high winds aloft layer: 0 = steady, 1= gusty.
WIND_UP_VEL	knots	N	Wind speed of high winds aloft layer.
YOKE_X_POSITION	integer	N	-16,383 = full left, 16,383 = full right.
YOKE_Y_POSITION	integer	N	-16,383 = full up (nose down), 16,383 = full down (nose up).

TECHNICAL NOTES

If you compile your adventure with the Flight Shop APLC and run it through the Microsoft Adventure Converter, the PLANE_LAT system variable will return the incorrect value of FTOM(PLANE_LAT). Code compiled with APLC32 will return the correct value.

There are no string variables or string manipulation facilities in the source language. All you can do is print literal strings. New extensions to APL add some new string function capabilities. See the next section.

FS98 APLC CHANGES

There are some differences in how FS98 interprets APL programs. For one, there are still bugs in Flight Simulator with some commands and statements having their fractional values treated as integer values. The particular offenders are WAIT and VISIBILITY

The variable MAG_VAR is backwards, and the ADF_RADIAL variable is invalid in the new APL for FS98. It has been removed. If FS98 encounters this variable, the lesson will end.

After some debugging work, I also discovered that the FS98 APL does things a little differently with the syntax for Autopilot commands, statements, and variables. Previously, in FSW95 you could set the AUTOPILOT_ALTITUDE before you turned on the AUTOPILOT_MASTER switch and the AUTOPILOT_ALTITUDE_HOLD. This is no longer the case in FS98, where you must turn on the AUTOPILOT_MASTER switch and AUTOPILOT_ALTITUDE_HOLD *before* you assign a value to the AUTOPI-LOT_ALTITUDE variable. The same thing holds true for the AUTOPILOT_HEAD-ING and other related autopilot statements.

This is very different from FSW95, and FS5.1 where you could do the reverse. In addition, if you want to input more than one keypress into a variable, such as for example, entering an altitude or heading using the numeric keys on the main keyboard, you should clear each keypress by using WAIT 0, KEYPRESS statement.

Assigning Numerical Values to Variables.

Unfortunately, the APL language doesn't offer a convenient way to enter multiple keystrokes, such as a large number greater than nine, into APL variables. However, by using the code below, you can work around this limitation.

```
WAIT 2,KEYPRESS                 ;Get first keypress
    val=KEY                         ;Assign keypress to val variable
    WAIT 0, KEYPRESS             ;Clear KEY variable for next keypress
    IF INRANGE(val,48,57) THEN  ;If key is between 0-9, continue
        hdg=val-48                  ;Assign first keypress to hdg variable
        WAIT 2,KEYPRESS             ;Get second keypress
        val=KEY                 ;Assign keypress to val variable
        WAIT 0, KEYPRESS           ;Clear KEY variable for next keypress
        IF INRANGE(val,48,57) THEN;If key is between 0-9, continue
            hdg=hdg*10+val-48           ;Multiply hdg by 10 and add val
            WAIT 2,KEYPRESS         ;Get third keypress
            val=KEY             ;Assign keypress to val variable
            IF INRANGE(val,48,57) THEN    ;If key is between 0-9, continue
                hdg=hdg*10+val-48 ;Multiply hdg by 10 and add val
            ENDIF
        ENDIF
    ENDIF
```

Using the above example, if you entered "1", the program would assign the value of 1 to the variable hdg and skip the rest of the IF statements. If you typed "12", the program would take the first digit of "1" then multiply it by 10 and then add 2 before finally assigning its final value of 12 to the variable hdg. By the same token, if you typed "123", the program would continue with the value of 12, and multiply this number by 10 before adding 3 to arrive at a final value of 123 for the hdg variable.

NEW APLC32 PROGRAM LANGUAGE EXTENSIONS

Smith has added new extensions to the Adventure Programming Language in APLC32. Included are new capabilities for string handling, function definition, procedure definition, and file inclusion along with pragmas and other useful odds and ends.

You can now find out whether your code was compiled by APLC32 and, if so, which version processed it. To use this feature, declare the variable APLC32_VERSION in the normal way somewhere in the adventure source. At the start of the adventure, this variable will be zero if the adventure was compiled by APLC and either is running under FS5 or was converted for FSW95 with the Adventure Converter from Microsoft.

If the adventure was compiled by APLC32, the variable will contain a value indicating the version number. For example, if the adventure was compiled by version 1.10, the variable will be set to 110. The variable otherwise behaves like any other and can be assigned another value.

The following code fragment shows how to have your program check which version of APLC32 compiled it. Note it will not detect early versions of the program before the mechanism was introduced.

```
DECLARE aplc32_version
IF aplc32_version > 0 AND aplc32_version < 116 THEN
    PRINT "You need to upgrade your copy of APLC32"
    WAIT 5
ENDIF
```

Smith borrows the term *pragma* from C++ to describe a means of embedding compiler commands in the source file. Smith uses a format that the old APLC sees as a comment and ignores. As APLC32 evolves in the years to come, Smith expects to add more pragma commands. This mechanism is intended for advanced adventure programmers to use in achieving specific effects. If you don't understand it, don't use it.

To use a pragma command you enter a comment in your source code with exactly the following format. You must not include extra spaces or omit the ones shown. Note especially that there must not be a space between the semicolon and the PRAGMA keyword. You can use either uppercase or lowercase or a mixture of the two.

```
;PRAGMA keyword option
```

The currently available keywords are WEATHER_ALTITUDES and WARNINGS. The following code allows you to choose whether you want to specify clouds, winds, or temperature layer altitudes in the units as stated, and it overrides the -a option on the command line in regard to these units.

```
;PRAGMA WEATHER_ALTITUDES FEET

;PRAGMA WEATHER_ALTITUDES METRES
```

The following code changes the value of the -w option in sections of the compiled code. With WARNINGS OFF in effect, lines of code that would otherwise produce warnings are compiled silently.

```
;PRAGMA WARNINGS OFF

;PRAGMA WARNINGS ON
```

FSW95 and FS98 have some new system variables that did not exist under the old FS5.1 used with Flight Shop. Smith has given them temporary names, as shown in the left-hand column of the Table H.11.

Table H.11 New System Variables for Flight Simulator for Windows 95

VARIABLE NAME	WRITE?	DESCRIPTION
SYSVAR_8D	Y	Indicated (0) or true airspeed (1) displayed.
SYSVAR_91	Y	Auto-coordination enabled or disabled.
SYSVAR_A0	N	NAV1 OBS VOR/LOC needle deviation.
SYSVAR_A1	N	NAV1 OBS Glide Slope needle deviation.
SYSVAR_A3	Y	Adventure sounds on/off.
SYSVAR_A4	Y	Adventure message bar on/off.

APLC32 allows you to specify that your output adventure files should always be placed in the FSW95 or FS98 **ADV** directory. If you enable this option, it will set a flag in your system registry and will always override any directories that are specified on the command line.

To activate this feature, bring up a command window and change the directory to one in which you have APLC32 installed. Then type the command **APLC32 -fY.** You should get a message indicating the flag has been set. There is now no way to compile adventures from any generating program or flight planner without their ending up in the **ADV** subdirectory of your Flight Simulator directory.

This option persists for all future compilations until you turn it off by repeating the previous steps but using **-fN** as the option instead of **-fY.**

You cannot combine the -f options with any others or with performing a compilation. As soon as this option has been processed, the program will exit so that you see and take note of the message that you have made an important change.

If you are an end user of adventures you will want to consider turning this option on unless you find it causes problems for flight planners that want to copy files around for you. If you are developing adventures or doing other advanced work, you will probably want to leave it turned off.

The output directory is determined from the settings created in the registry by the Microsoft installation program. This means that you must have correctly installed FSW95 or FS98 on your system for it to work.

The registry key is stored under HKEY_CURRENT_USER, and that means it is set individually for each person using your machine. If you have multiple users, bear this in mind before jumping to the conclusion that it doesn't work. Also check that the version that compiled your code is 1.14 or greater. You may have an old version being picked up by your flight planner software from some other directory.

In APLC32 version 1.17, Smith has introduced a limited form of procedure definitions, something that helps you to write more-structured code. Using this feature means that your adventure will not work with FS5. This limitation may not be a problem, because adventures that most benefit from extra structure are probably too big to compile for FS5 anyway. Smith considers these features to be experimental, so please report to him any anomalies you encountered.

Please read this section carefully before using the features described. There are some limitations based on the runtime facilities provided by Flight Simulator.

A procedure is defined according to the following syntax:

```
DEFINE PROCEDURE example(p1, p2, p3)

        LOCAL v1, v2

        statements forming procedure body .......

ENDDEFINE
```

Following the **DEFINE PROCEDURE** you must give the procedure a name. It must not duplicate any previously defined procedure name (or function name) or reserved word. As with variables and labels, the case of the name does not matter (EXAMPLE is the same as example). Procedure names have their own namespace, so it is OK, although potentially confusing, to use the same name for a procedure, a label, and a variable. This practice, however, is not recommended.

The formal parameters of the procedure are listed next. A procedure can have any number of parameters; the example has three parameters. Even if the procedure has no parameters, you must explicitly write a pair of empty brackets.

A procedure can declare a number of variables with LOCAL. The variables appearing in LOCAL lists cannot be reserved words and additionally cannot be the same as any of the procedure parameters. There can be any number of LOCAL statements, and they can appear anywhere in the procedure definition. You are strongly advised to make them the first thing in the procedure to avoid the risk of unexpectedly picking up global variables. Variables created with LOCAL are restricted in scope to that procedure and hide any global variables having the same name. Thus, you can reuse names within different procedures and not cause conflicts. This arrangement helps to remove another source of errors. Procedure parameters are implicitly local to that procedure.

There is an implicit RETURN at the end of the procedure body, so you do not need to add one. You can include multiple returns in a procedure if this is the kind of code you write, but it is not recommended.

You can declare nested procedures, but there is probably no reason to do so. All procedure and function names are declared with global scope even if defined inside other procedures.

WARNING

Flight Simulator provides no way to allocate stack frames at runtime. This means that if you write recursive functions, each procedure has only one copy of its local variables no matter how many times it is recursively called.

Statements up to the ENDDEFINE form the procedure body. If runtime execution reaches the DEFINE PROCEDURE, the code behaves as if the definition were not there. In other words, you cannot "fall into" a procedure by accident.

Labels that are defined inside procedures are local to the procedure, and the procedure cannot see labels that are defined outside it. This means two important things:

- You cannot jump into or out of procedures with GOTO or GOSUB. This arrangement enforces block structuring and prevents errors.
- You can reuse label names within different procedures.

To call a procedure, write its name followed by the parameter expressions enclosed in brackets. All parameters are passed by value, so changes to the parameters inside the procedure do not affect the values of anything in the main program. Some people find this rule restricting, but it removes another common source of hard-to-find errors. The number of parameters you specify must be the same as in the definition, or an error message results.

To call the example procedure we defined, you might write something like this:

```
example(10, (x + 5) / 2, autopilot_altitude)
```

Procedures (and functions) can be called before they are defined as long as their definition appears somewhere in the input. In combination with the INCLUDE mechanism and the behavior of executed definitions, you can safely include procedure definitions either before the main body of the program or at the end.

APLC32 version 1.17 has the ability to define functions. The limitations are annoying but are the best that can be done with the available runtime facilities. You should read this section before you try to use functions.

Functions are defined almost exactly as procedures are except that you use the statement DEFINE FUNCTION, and somewhere the function must return a value to the caller. An example may help to make things more complicated:

```
DEFINE FUNCTION lbtokg(X)

    RETURN X * 2.22

ENDDEFINE
```

You need not restrict your function definitions to computations. They can contain conditional statements and so on.

As before, a function can have any number of parameters, which are implicitly LOCAL to the function. As with procedures, the number of arguments in the call must match the definition.

You can create LOCAL variables within functions in the same way as with procedures. It is an error to use RETURN with an expression outside a FUNCTION definition. You will get an error message if a FUNCTION does not contain a RETURN statement.

WARNING

If you create a path of control through a function so that no RETURN statement is encountered, you will not get a message and the results of calling that function are undefined. Don't do it. For example, this is a bug:

```
DEFINE FUNCTION wrong()              ;Don't do this!
IF 1 = 0 THEN

        RETURN 99

    ENDIF

    ; leaving function without returning anything
ENDDEFINE
```

Calling a user-defined function requires a slightly clumsy syntax because of the separate namespace for procedures and functions. In addition, there is no way to provide for them to be used in generalized expressions.

```
variable = FUNCTION lbtokg(10)
```

You must include the FUNCTION keyword in the call, and there can be nothing after the closing parenthesis of the parameter list. In other words, the function call cannot be part of a larger expression. You will have to break the expressions down to evaluate them.

These limitations are restrictive, as you might have surmised. Smith writes that he doesn't see any way around it given that the runtime system strictly separates expression evaluation from control flow.

WARNING

What has been said before about recursive procedures applies to functions in exactly the same way. If you have written a recursive function with parameters or LOCAL variables, it almost certainly will not do what you expect.

Using these PROCEDURE and FUNCTION constructs can help you write more easily understandable code. Behind the scenes, the same kinds of assignments to temporary variables that you were hand coding before are still happening. Using procedures has very little performance impact. Your adventure file will probably be only slightly larger, and the code will be much more readable.

The main purpose of this mechanism is to allow you to include canned procedure definitions from a library of procedures. Over time, it is hoped that many people will create libraries of procedure definitions that can be used over and over so that we need not reinvent the wheel to accomplish similar tasks.

To include a file in your program, use this statement:

```
INCLUDE "filename"
```

The APLC32 compiler will insert the content sof the specified file at that point in the source code. The file name will be searched for in the following sequence:

1. In the current directory.
2. In the **Include** directory of the current directory.
3. Underneath the **Include** subdirectory of your FS95/98 installation.

Unlike source files on the command line the file suffix does not default to **.TXT**, so you must explicitly include it. For example, if you have installed Flight Simulator in **E:\GAMES\FLTSIM98** and you include "test\wibble.txt," the file **E:\GAMES\FLTSIM98\Include\test\wibble.txt** will be included. It is an error if the named file does not exist in either place. You can use either the Windows backslash or the Unix forward slash character in the file name. In other words, "test/wibble.txt" and "test\wibble.txt" name equivalent files.

All warning and error messages have been changed to indicate the file name and line number where the problem occurred.

INCLUDE commands can be nested. The exact nesting depth depends on how many simultaneous streams a Windows executable can open. It should be good for 15 levels or so, but this would be a silly exercise in any case.

If you write a good general-purpose procedure or function, please send it to Martin Smith and he will build a utility library to be included with future versions of APLC32. Any APL code submitted becomes liable to unlimited electronic freeware distribution in source form and for distribution on disk or CD-ROM by organizations approved by Smith. Submission of code will be regarded as acceptance of this condition and your willingness as the author to grant the aforementioned rights. Your name will remain on the files, and you will retain copyright on them.

If you are writing an adventure generation program and intend to use the include facility, it is suggested that you place your standard library code under a product-specific subdirectory of the include directory.

An example file called **TESTALT.TXT** on the book's CD-ROM uses the INCLUDE statement to call upon another text file program, called **PLAYALT.TXT** (also on the CD-ROM). **TESTALT.TXT** is an adventure that, when compiled into an ADV file for Flight Simulator, can be used to vocally announce the plane's altitude whenever you press **Ctrl+A**.

String variables are denoted by names ending in the $ character. They can be created in either DECLARE or LOCAL statements or as parameters to procedures and functions.

There are only four things you can do with string variables:

- Assign a literal string to them. For example:

  ```
  my_string$ = "wibble"
  ```

- Assign another string variable to them. For example:

  ```
  my_string$ = my_other_string$
  ```

- Pass them around as parameters to procedures and functions. For example:

  ```
  my_procedure(my_string$, 4)
  ```

- Use the new commands PRINT_STRING, SCROLL_STRING, and PLAY_STRING to access their values. For example:

```
PRINT_STRING my_string$
```

PRINT_STRING, SCROLL_STRING, and PLAY_STRING take exactly one string variable as an argument. When a string is displayed it is always printed without a newline (i.e., as though there were a trailing comma present on the print command). String and numeric values have distinct types. It is an error to try to mix the two types in either an assignment or a procedure or function call argument.

You cannot create functions that return string values. This doesn't matter anyway, since there are no string operators in APL.

An example of using the string facilities can be found in the file **procstr.txt** on the book's CD-ROM.

Limitations of APL: Missing Trigonometric Functions

Unfortunately, APL does not provide trigonometric functions, the square root function, the exponential function, and many other mathematical functions. By using some calculus, however, you can substitute the infinite series expansion for sine, cosine, and tangent to arrive at equivalent expressions that involve only simple algebra for the trigonometric functions.

The following Maclaurin Series expression is useful for calculating the sine function:

$$\sin x = x - \frac{x^3}{3!} + \frac{x^5}{5!} - \frac{x^7}{7!} \ldots \ldots \tag{H.1}$$

where the factorial symbol 3! means $3*2*1$. The 7! would equal $7*6*5*4*3*2*1$, the 5! would equal $5*4*3*2*1$, and x is in radian and not degree form. For our accuracy, we will omit the x^7 term in Equation H.1.

Here is an example in APL for sin x:

```
x = x_degrees*2*3.1415/360  ;convert x in degrees to x in radians
                            ;by multiplying x_degrees by 2pi/360
x2 = x*x        ;this is x²
x3 = x*x2       ;this is x3
x5 = x2*x3      ;this is x5
sinx = x - x3/(3*2*1)+x5/(5*4*3*2*1)
```

Using the preceding example, to find the sin 45° we would first convert 45° to its radian equivalent x = x_degrees*2*3.1415/360 = 45*2*3.1415/360 = 0.7854 radians. Plugging in the values for x, x3, x5, and x7, we have the following:

```
sinx = 0.7854 - 0.4828/6 + 0.2989/120 = 0.7074
```

If you compare this result with a calculator value of sin 45°—which is 0.7071—you can see that it differs only by three parts in 10,000. If you desire greater accuracy, you can add more terms to the Maclaurin series in Equation H.1.

The following Maclaurin series gives a good approximation of the cosine function:

$$\cos x = 1 - \frac{x^2}{2!} + \frac{x^4}{4!} - \frac{x^6}{6!} \dots \quad \text{(H.2)}$$

where the factorial symbol 2! means 2*1. The 4! would equal 4*3*2*1, and the 6! would equal 6*5*4*3*2*1. Note that x is in radian and not degree form.

Here is an example in APL for cos x:

```
x = x_degrees*2*3.1415/360   ;convert x in degrees to x in radians
                             ;by multiplying x_degrees by 2pi/360

x2 = x*x     ;this is x²

x4 = x2*x2   ;this is x4
x6 = x4*x2   ;this is x⁶

cosx = 1-x2/(2*1)+x4/(4*3*2*1) - x6/(6*5*4*3*2*1)
```

To find the tan x, use this series:

$$\tan x = x + \frac{1}{3}x^3 + \frac{2}{15}x^5 \dots \quad \text{(H.3)}$$

Note that x is in radian and not degree form.

Here is an example in APL for tan x:

```
x = x_degrees*2*3.1415/360   ;convert x in degrees to x in radians
                             ;by multiplying x_degrees by 2pi/360

x3 = x*x*x    ;this is x³

x5 = x*x*x3   ;this is x⁵
tanx = 1+x3/3+2*x5/15
```

The arctan function can be approximated by the following Maclaurin series:

$$\text{if } y = \tan x \qquad\qquad (\text{H}.4)$$

then

$$x = \tan^{-1} y = y - \frac{y^3}{3} + \frac{y^5}{5} - \frac{y^7}{7} \dots$$

$$\text{arctan } y = y - y3/3 + y5/5 - y7/7$$

where y is any real number (y is not an angle). Note that the result for $\tan^{-1}$ returns a radian value between +pi/2 (90°) and -pi/2 (270° or -90°). Because there are quadrant resolution problems, from the geometry of the problem you will have to determine which quadrant is being referred to if you want to find angles that are greater than pi/2 (90°) but less than 3×pi/2 (270°).

Here is an example in APL for arctan:

```
y=value      ;y is any real number
y3=y*y*y     ;this is y³

y5=y*y*y3    ;this is y⁵
y7=y*y*y5    ;this is y⁷

arctany= y - y3/3+y5/5 - y7/7
```

The arcsin function can be approximated by the following Maclaurin series:

$$\text{if } y = \sin x \qquad\qquad (\text{H}.5)$$

then

$$x = \sin^{-1} y = y + \frac{1}{6} y^3 + \frac{3}{40} y^5 \dots$$

where y is any real number (y is not an angle). Note that the result for $\sin^{-1}$ returns a radian value between +pi/2 (90°) and –pi/2 (270° or –90°). Because there are quadrant resolution problems, from the geometry of the problem you will have to determine which quadrant is being referred to if you want to find angles that are greater than pi/2 (90°) but less than 3×pi/2 (270°).

Here is an example in APL for arcsin:

```
y=value      ;y is any number less than or equal to +1 or
```

```
          greater;than or equal to -1
y3=y*y*y     ;this is y³
y5=y*y*y3    ;this is y⁵
arcsiny= y+y3/6+3*y5/40
```

Now that we have covered the essentials of adventure programming, let's create an elementary program that will display a system variable when you press a key. In the program listing that follows (which is also found as **Airspeed.txt** on the CD-ROM), you can display your indicated airspeed by pressing **Ctrl+i** and your true airspeed by pressing **Ctrl+t**. This program allows you to quickly display the two types of airspeed without having to manually switch airspeed displays using the **Options/Preferences/Instruments** menu.

```
TITLE "Airspeed"
DESCRIPTION "Example that shows how to display system variables." DESCRIP-
TION "Press Ctrl-T to "
DESCRIPTION "display true airspeed. Press Ctrl-I to display "
DESCRIPTION "indicated airspeed. Press Ctrl-X to exit."


ADV_KEYS ADD,kv(ctrl "t")          ;Define Ctrl t
ADV_KEYS ADD,kv(ctrl "i")          ;Define Ctrl i
ADV_KEYS ADD,kv(ctrl "x")          ;Define Ctrl x


ONKEY KV(ctrl "t") GOSUB true          ;when key pressed, do true
ONKEY KV(ctrl "i") GOSUB indicated     ;when key pressed, do indicated
ONKEY KV(ctrl "x") GOSUB stop          ;when key pressed, exit


loop:

goto loop
; wait for keypress and then jump to true or indicated subroutines

true:
    Print "True Airspeed is: ", INT(VELOCITY), " knots"
RETURN
```

```
indicated:
    Print "Indicated Airspeed is: ", INT(VELOCITY_INDICATED), " knots"
RETURN


stop:
END
```

Although you can compile this program yourself using APLC32, I have also included the **Airspeed.ADV** file, which you can copy directly to your **ADV** directory so that you can try the adventure quickly (assuming that you have followed the earlier instructions to install the Aircraft Converter and **AAFWAV.ZIP**).

Examining the source listing, you can see that the two system variables VELOCITY and VELOCITY_INDICATED are converted to integer format using the INT function. Using the example given, it is easy to add system variables and horse around with displaying or changing all kinds of other information.

USING THE ADVENTURE SOUND FILES ON THE FS98 CD-ROM

The new adventure files in FS98 use sound files on the CD-ROM that are stored in the FS98\Adv\Wav directory. At setup, you have the option of copying all 30.4 Mb of sound files to your hard disk, or you can choose to have the sound files remain on the CD, and the program will access them only as needed.

There are two ways you can use these sound files in your adventures:

1. If you haven't installed the adventure sound files from your CD when you first installed FS98, don't worry: you can copy them directly from your FS98 CD-ROM's FS98\Adv\Wav directory to your FS98\Adv\Wav directory on your hard disk. To access the sound files, use the PLAY "filename" statement (you don't need to use the file extension .wav, but you do need the quotation marks).
2. Leave the sound files on your CD and use the PLAY "D:\FS98\Adv\Wav\filename" statement in your APL program, where D:\ is the name of your CD-ROM drive (or whatever drive letter corresponds to your CD-ROM drive).

USING THE ADVENTURE SOUND FILES IN AAFWAV.ZIP

We turn now to the interesting problem of creating a program that accepts user input and plays messages based on the input. You can create an autopilot command program that not only announces the airplane's altitude and heading but also allows you to select the autopilot heading and altitude directly from the keyboard. This program, called AutoAlt, also displays and calls out the airplane's current pitch angle and bank angle when prompted from the keyboard. The text file is listed here in its entirety with explanatory comments. For the voice announcements to work, you must install all the wave sound files in **AAFWAV.ZIP** to your **\ADV\WAV** directory.

Also, AutoAlt depends on another text file because it uses the INCLUDE statement. To compile it properly, you need to have the **PlayAlt.txt** file installed in the **ADV\Include\Utility** directory (which should be automatically created when you unzip **APLC32.ZIP** into the **\ADV** directory). Once AutoAlt is compiled into **AutoAlt.ADV,** you start Flight Simulator and run the AutoAlt adventure using the Adventure menu.

This program demonstrates two methods of playing back sounds. The first method invokes subroutines found in **PlayAlt.txt** (which you can view on the CD-ROM), and the second method calls subroutines directly.

When you run the program, the display of pitch and bank angles will lag the voice announcement by several seconds. Also, negative pitch angles correspond to the nose being pitched down toward the horizon, and negative bank angles correspond to the airplane being banked right. Check the book's web site for the full code of the AutoAlt Adventure Program Listing

Bibliography

This bibliography lists all the research materials that were used to prepare this book. Near the end, you'll also find a comprehensive listing of the types of aeronautical charts that are available from the NOAA (National Oceanic and Atmospheric Administration) and the Defense Mapping Agency. For your convenience, you'll also see regional views of selected parts of the world, showing which map(s) you will need for a particular area. This will help facilitate your order should you decide to purchase the charts directly from the U.S. government or private sources.

SOURCES FOR AVIATION-RELATED BOOKS

The aviation books and many of the publications and other materials listed in this bibliography can be ordered from the following sources:

The Aviator Store
7201 Perimeter Road South
Seattle, WA 98108
1-800-635-2007

Sporty's Pilot Shop
Clermont County Airport
Batavia, OH 45103-9747
Telephone: 1-800-LIFTOFF or 513-735-9000
Fax: 513-735-9200
Web: www.sportys-catalogs.com/pilot/pilot.html

JetStream
Portland-Hillsboro Airport
General Aviation Terminal Building
3355 N.E. Cornell Road
Hillsboro, OR 97124-6380
Telephone: 800-470-2359 or 503-693-3522
Fax: 800- 408-0434 or 503-693-1822
Web: www.jetstreamcat.com

Aviation Book Company
7201 Perimeter Road S. Suite C
Seattle, WA 98108
Telephone: 1-800-423-2708 or 206-767-5232
Fax: 206-763-3428

Books

Air Almanac 1997, The. Washington D.C.: United States Naval Observatory, 1996.

Air Navigation. AF Manual 51-40 NAVAIR 00-80V-49. Washington, D.C.: Department of the Air Force, Air Training Command, 1983.

Air Traveler's Handbook. Varley, Helen Editor. London: Marshall Editions Ltd, 1978.

Aircraft Economics Yearbook 1995. London, England: Airfinance Journal Ltd (a Euromoney Group Company), 1995.

Aircraft of the National Air and Space Museum. Washington, D.C.: Smithsonian Institution Press, 1991.

Airframe and Powerplant Mechanics Powerplant Handbook. AC65-12A. Washington, D.C.: Department of Transportation, Federal Aviation Administration, 1976.

Anderson, John D. *Introduction to Flight.* New York: McGraw-Hill, 1978.

Artwick, Bruce. *Applied Concepts in Microcomputer Graphics.* Englewood Cliffs, NJ: Prentice Hall, Inc., 1984.

Aviation Weather. AC 00-6A. Washington, D.C.: Department of Transportation, Federal Aviation Administration, 1975.

Baarspul, Max. "A review of flight simulation techniques." *Progress in Aerospace Sciences,* 27. Cambridge, 1990.

Boeing 737-300, 737-400, 737-500 Airplane Characteristics-Airport Planning. D6-58325-2. Renton, WA: Boeing, 1988.

Bowditch, Natheniel. *The American Practical Navigator: An Epitome of Navigation.* Bethesda, MD: Defense Mapping Agency Hydrographic/Topographic Center, U.S. Government, 1995.

Broadbent, Stephen. *Jane's Avionics 1987–88.* New York: Jane's Publishing Inc., 1988.

Brown, Gregory, and Holt, Mark J. The Turbine Pilot's Flight Manual. Ames, IA: Iowa State University Press, 1995.

Carmody, Douglas S. *Instrument Pilot Test Guide 1996–1998.* New York: McGraw-Hill, 1997.

Cessna 1986 Skylane RG Information Manual. Wichita, KS: Cessna Aircraft Company, 1985.

Clarke, Bill. *Aviator's Guide to GPS.* New York: Tab Books: 1996.

Conns, Keith. *The LORAN, GPS and NAV/COM Guide.* Templeton, CA: Butterfield Press, 1992.

Conway, Carle. *The Joy of Soaring: A Training Manual.* Hobbs, NM: The Soaring Society of America, 1989.

Davies, D.P. *Handling the Big Jets.* London: Daniel Greenaway and Sons, 1973.

De Remer, Dale and Donald W McLean. *Global Navigation for Pilots.* Newcastle, WA: Aviation Supplies and Academics, 1993.

FAA Statistical Handbook of Aviation. FAA AP0-94-5. Washington, D.C.: Department of Transportation, Federal Aviation Administration, 1992.

Federal Aviation Regulations/Airman's Information Manual FAR/AIM 1993. ASA-93-FR-AM-BK. Renton, WA: Aviation Supplies and Academics, Inc., 1993.

Federal RadioNavigation Plan 1992. DOT-VNTSC-RSPA-92-2/DOD-4650.5. Washington, DC: U.S. Department of Transportation and Department of Defense, 1992.

Flight Shop Manual. Champaign, IL: Bruce Artwick Organization, 1995.

Flight Training Handbook. AC-61-21A. Washington, DC: U.S. Department of Transportation, Federal Aviation Administration, 1980.

Foley, James D., van Dam, Andries, Feiner, Steven K., and Hughes, John F. *Computer Graphics Principles and Practices*, 2nd ed. New York: Addison-Wesley, 1996.

Gormley, Mal. Aviation *Computing Systems*. New York: McGraw-Hill, 1997.

Graham, Brian. *Geography and Air Transport*. New York: John Wiley and Sons, 1995.

Hobbs, Richard R. *Marine Navigation 2: Celestial and Electronic*. 2nd ed. Annapolis, MD: Naval Institute Press, 1981.

Hoffer, William and Marilyn. *Freefall: A True Story*. New York: St. Martin's Paperbacks, 1989.

Hubin, W. N. *The Science of Flight: Pilot-Oriented Aerodynamics*. Ames, IA: Iowa State University Press, 1992.

Hurt Jr., H. H. *Aerodynamics for Naval Aviators*. NAVWEPS 00-80T-80. Washington, DC: Direction of Commander, Naval Air Systems Command, United States Navy.

Kershner, William K. *The Basic Aerobatic Manual*. Ames, IA: Iowa State University Press, 1991.

Instrument Flying Handbook. AC-61-27C. Washington D.C.: U.S. Department of Transportation, Federal Aviation Administration, 1980.

Lambert, Mark. *Jane's All the World's Aircraft 1991–92*. Alexandria, VA: Jane's Information Group, 1992.

Langewiesche, Wolfgang. *Stick and Rudder: An Explanation of the Art of Flying*. New York: McGraw-Hill, 1972.

Microsoft Flight Simulator 5.1 Pilot's Handbook. Bellingham, WA: Microsoft Press, 1995.

Microsoft Flight Simulator for Windows 95 Pilot's Handbook. Bellingham, WA: Microsoft Press, 1996.

Muolo, Maj Michael J. *Space Handbook: An Analyst's Guide*. Maxwell Air Force Base, AL: Air University Press, 1993.

Norris, Bob. *Flying Jets: Aircraft and Simulators*. San Carlos, CA: REN and Associates, 1992.

Pendleton, Linda. *Flying Jets*. New York: McGraw-Hill, 1996.

Perkins, Courtland D, and Hage, Robert. *Airplane Performance Stability and Control*. New York: John Wiley and Sons, Inc., 1949.

Pilot's Handbook of Aeronautical Knowledge. AC 61-23B. Washington, DC: Department of Transportation, Federal Aviation Administration, 1980.

Rider, Paul R. *Plane and Spherical Trigonometry*. New York: The Macmillan Company, 1942.

Rodgers, Eugene. *Flying High: The Story of Boeing and the Rise of the Jetliner Industry*. New York: The Atlantic Monthly Press, 1996.

Rolfe, J.M. and Staples, K.J. *Flight Simulation*. Cambridge: Cambridge Univesity Press, 1986.

Porter, Donald J. *Learjets*. Blue Ridge Summit, PA: Tab Books, 1987.

Schweizer, William Soaring With the Schweizers. Blufton, SC: Rivlo Books.

Serway, Raymond A. *Physics For Scientists and Engineers with Modern Physics.* 3rd ed. San Francisco: Saunders College Publishing, 1990.

Schumann, U., Ed. *Air Traffic and the Environment—Background, Tendencies and Potential Global Atmospheric Effects,* Proceedings of a DLR International Colloquium Bonn, Germany, November 15/16, 1990. New York: Springer-Verlag, 1990.

Smith, David. *International Air Band Radio Handbook.* Somerset, England: Patrick Stephens Limited, 1995.

Smith, H.C. *The Illustrated Guide to Aerodynamics,* 2nd ed. New York: Tab Books, 1992.

Snyder, John P. *Map Projections: A Working Manual.* Washington, DC: Department of the Interior, U.S. Geological Survey, 1994.

Sobel, Dava. *Longitude, The True Story of a Lone Genius Who Solved the Greatest Scientific Problem of His Time.* New York: Penguin Books, 1995.

Sollman, Henry. *Mastering Instrument Flying.* New York: Tab Books, 1994.

Stewart, Stanley. *Flying the Big Jets.* Shrewsbury, England: Airlife Publishing, 1995.

Szurovy, Geza. *Learjets.* Osceola, WI: Motorbooks International, 1996

Taylor, Laurie. *Air Travel: How Safe Is It?* Oxford, England: BSP Professional Books, 1988.

Watkins, Christopher D. and Marenka, Stephen R. *Taking Flight: History, Fundamentals, and Applications of Flight Simulation.* New York: M&T Books, 1994.

Weather for Aircrews. AFM 51-12, Vol. 1. Washington, DC: Department of the Air Force, 1990.

Webb, Jim. *Fly the Wing,* 2nd ed. Ames, Iowa: Iowa State University Press, 1990.

Williams, J.R. *The Art of Instrument Flying,* 3rd ed. New York: Tab Books, 1996.

Videos

Just Planes Videos may be purchased from:

> Just Planes
> P.O. Box 285214
> Boston, MA 02128-5214
> 800 PLANES-6 or 617-539-3226
> Fax: 617-539-3224
> Web: justplanes.bx.com

Flight in the Cockpit 5: SobelAir Boeing 737-400. Boston, MA: Just Planes Video, 1996.

Building and Test Flying the Boeing 727 and 747. Eye in the Sky Television: A Havis Production Company, 1990. Available from Sporty's Pilot Shop.

PAMPHLETS

Aeronautical Charts and Related Products. Riverdale, MD: U.S. Department of Commerce, National Oceanic and Atmospheric Administration, National Ocean Service. 1993.

Cessna 172 Skyhawk. Independence, KS: Cessna, 1996.

Cessna 182 Skylane. Independence, KS: Cessna, 1996.

Cost of Operation: Learjet 35A. Wichita, KS: Learjet Inc.

Learjet 35A. Wichita, KS: Learjet Inc.

Mission Planning Guide: Learjet 35A. Wichita, KS: Learjet Inc.

Optional Equipment Description and Pricing: Learjet 35A. Wichita, KS: Learjet Inc.

The Schweizer 2-32 Sailplane Flight-Erection-Maintenance Manual. Elmira, NY: Schweizer Aircraft Corp.

Specification and Description: Learjet 35A. Wichita, KS: Learjet Inc.

MAGAZINES

Artwick, Bruce. "Flight Simulator 95—It's a pretty good program." *MicroWINGS Magazine,* October 1996, 4(5), 33.

Artwick, Bruce. "The 64-bit Flight Simulator Future." *MicroWINGS Magazine,* October 1995, 3(5), 32.

Artwick, Bruce. "Consolidation in the Flight Simulator Industry." *MicroWINGS Magazine,* February 1996, 4(1), 30.

Artwick, Bruce. "Looking Beyond Today's 3D Graphics Displays" *MicroWINGS Magazine,* April 1996, 4(1), 21.

Collins, Richard L. "Skylane Round Robin." *Flying Magazine,* November 1979, pp. 77–83.

MacKay, Robert. "Microsoft's Flight Simulator 5.0." *MicroWINGS Magazine,* August 1993, 1(3), 12–15.

Maas, Dan. "Microsoft's Flight Simulator for Windows 95." *MicroWINGS Magazine,* August 1996, 4(4), 24–27.

Navin, Patrick. "GPS Update." *InFlight Aviation News Monthly,* June 1993, pp. 54–55.

North, David M. "Learjet 60 Stakes Claim in Corporate Market." *Aviation Week and Space Technology,* June 28, 1993, pp.38–43.

Peters, Laura. "Future Microprocessors." *PC Magazine,* March 25, 1997, 16(6), 168–169.

Schiff, Barry. "Skyregs Review: Controlled Airspace." *AOPA Pilot Magazine,* February 1985, pp. 44–47.

Stevens, Russel, editor. "737 Operator's Guide." *Aircraft Economics,* August 1995, pp. 4–28.

Stevens, Russel, editor. "A-320 vs 737." *Aircraft Economics,* September 1992, 3, p. 10.

Stevens, Russel, editor. "Beginning up a new future—737 investors guide." *Aircraft Economics,* April 1993, 6, pp. 4–19.

CHARTS AND SECTIONALS

You can order aviation charts directly from the Federal Government's National Oceanic and Atmospheric Administration (NOAA). Their free catalog, *Aeronautical Charts and Related Products,* lists all the charts they publish and their prices. Believe it or not, the cost of these aviation charts is nominal. Single charts cost only a few dollars, and a complete region can be purchased for $20 to $30.

Ordering Charts and Aeronautical Sectionals from the NOAA

To order the NOAA chart catalog or to place an order, contact:

NOAA Distribution Branch, N/CG33
National Ocean Service
Riverdale, MD 20737-1199
Telephone: 301-436-6990
Fax: 301-436-6829

For a separate listing of specialized Defense Mapping Agency Digital Mapping Products, you may visit their Web site at 164.214.2.53/publications/guide/dtf/dtf.html.

Ordering Charts For Overnight Delivery and Specialized Orders

If you need friendly advice about the maps and charts you need, the knowledgeable staff at Aviation Publications Services will be able to answer any questions you may have. Although you can order the maps directly from NOAA, you usually have to wait several weeks for your maps to arrive. If you are in a big hurry, you can order maps for overnight delivery from:

Aviation Publications Services
1327 Maiden Lane
P.O. Box 400
Del Mar, CA 92014-0400
Telephone: 800-869-7453 or 619-755-1190
Fax: 619-755-5910

Map and Chart Types

NOAA publishes many different kinds of charts and maps. Of interest to the Flight Simulator pilot are the following:

- Defense Mapping Agency (DMA) Jet Navigation Maps
- FLIP (Flight Information Publications) Enroute charts for Pacific, Australasia, Antarctica, Caribbean and South America, Europe, North Africa, Middle East, Eastern Europe, and Asia (both high and low altitude)
- FLIP IAP (Instrument Approach Procedures) for United States, Africa, Canada and North Atlantic, Caribbean and South America, Eastern Europe and Asia, Europe, North Africa and Middle East, Pacific, Australasia, and Antarctica
- North Atlantic route chart
- North Pacific route charts
- Enroute high-altitude jet airway charts for the United States
- Enroute low-altitude Victor airway charts for the United States
- World aeronautical charts (WAC)
- Sectional aeronautical charts for the United States
- Terminal area charts for the United States

Sectional and VFR Terminal Area Charts

The VFR sectional and terminal area charts are designed for visual navigation of slow and medium speed aircraft. They are produced at the following scales:

- Sectional charts 1:500,000 (1 in = 6.86 nm)
- VFR terminal area charts 1:250,000 (1 in. = 3.43 nm)

Both charts display topographic information such as relief, check points, populated places, drainage, roads, railroads, and other distinctive landmarks. Aeronautical information includes visual and radio aids to navigation (such as VORs and NDBs), airports, controlled airspace, restricted areas, and obstructions. The following terminal area charts are of most interest to the Flight Simulator pilot, because the default scenery on the CD includes much detail that is depicted on these charts.

- Los Angeles
- San Francisco
- Seattle
- Chicago
- New York

Sectional aeronautical charts cover a much larger region than the terminal area charts. The following sectional charts are of most interest to the Flight Simulator pilot:

- Los Angeles
- San Francisco
- Seattle
- Chicago
- New York

Figure I.1 shows the Sectional and VFR Terminal Area Charts for the coterminous United States, Hawaiian Islands, Puerto Rico and the Virgin Islands. To see which chart you need to get for your area, consult Figure I.1 to see which rectangle covers the area you are interested in.

Enroute Low Altitude Charts

These charts are designed to provide aeronautical information for enroute navigation under IFR in altitudes below 18,000 feet. Information includes the Victor Airways, the limits of controlled airspace, navaids such as VORs and NDBs, selected airports, minimum enroute and obstruction clearance altitudes, airway distances, reporting points, and special restricted use airspace areas. No topographical data is displayed. The charts that may be of most interest to the Flight Simulator pilot are as follows:

- L-1/L-2: Covers the West Coast of the United States,except for Santa Barbara down to Los Angeles.
- L-3: Covers Santa Barbara to San Diego, California eastward to Arizona
- L-19: Covers east coast of Florida.
- L-27/L-28: Covers East Coast of United States from Georgia to New York.
- L-11/L-23: Covers the area around Chicago, Illinois.
- L-13: Covers the area around Dallas/Ft. Worth.

Figure I.2 shows the Enroute Low Altitude Charts for the United States available from the NOAA.

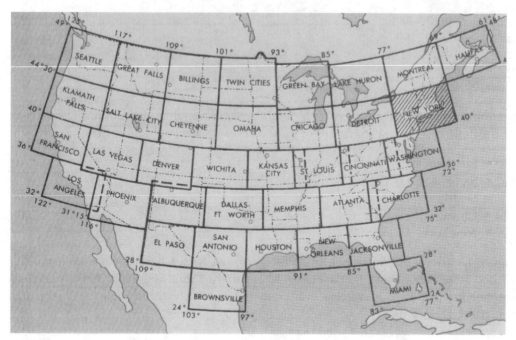

Figure I.1 *Sectional charts for the coterminous United States, Hawaiian Islands, Puerto Rico, and the Virgin Islands*

Enroute High-Altitude Charts

The enroute high-altitude charts are designed to provide aeronautical information for enroute navigation under IFR at altitudes above 18,000 feet. These maps include high-altitude jet airway routes, navaids, selected airports, distances, time zones, and special restricted use airspace areas. No topographical information is present.

As shown in Figure I.3, with the three H charts (H-1 through H-5), you will be able to fly anywhere in the United States:

- Northwest H-1/Northeast H-3 IFR enroute high-altitude U.S. chart: covers the northern U.S.A. west from the Northern California coast to the New York coast.
- Southwest H-2/Southeast H-4 IFR enroute high-altitude U.S. chart: covers the southern U.S.A. west from Southern California to Northern Florida coast.
- H-5/South H-6/East IFR enroute high-altitude U.S. chart: covers Southern Texas to Southern Florida, and East Coast of the United States.

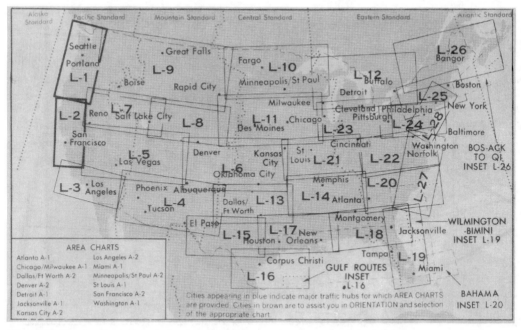

Figure I.2 *Enroute Low Altitude Instrument Charts for the United States*

Defense Mapping Agency Global Route Charts

For transoceanic flights you will need these charts:

- Pacific, Australia, and Antarctica enroute charts—Twenty accordion-folded charts, printed back to back. See Figure I.4. Shows VOR/NDBs, principal waypoints, and includes magnetic course headings. Very useful for trans-Pacific flights.
- Caribbean and South America high-altitude enroute charts—Six accordion folded high altitude charts printed back to back. Shows VOR/NDBs and magnetic course bearing information. See Figure I.5.
- Europe, North Africa, and Middle East high-altitude enroute charts—Fourteen accordion charts printed back to back, with VOR/NDBs and magnetic course headings. See Figure I.6.
- Africa high- and low-altitude enroute charts—Four accordion-folded charts printed back to back. Includes VOR/NDBs and magnetic course headings for Mid-Africa and South Africa. See Figure I.7.
- Eastern Europe and Asia high- and low-altitude enroute charts. Four accordion folded charts with VOR/NDBs and magnetic course headings for Russia, Eastern

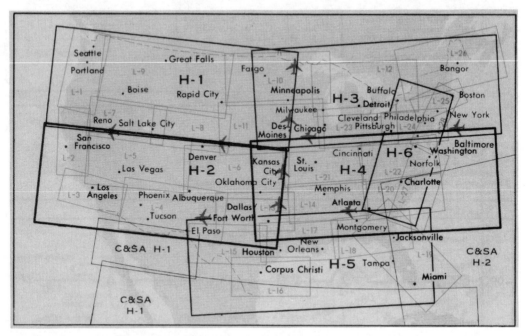

Figure I.3 *Enroute high-altitude charts for the United States (for flights above 18,000 feet).*

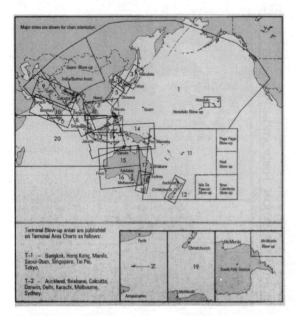

Figure I.4 *Defense Mapping Agency FLIP enroute charts for the Pacific, Australasia, and Antarctica.*

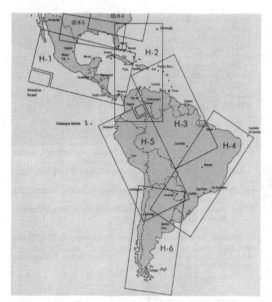

Figure I.5 *Defense Mapping Agency FLIP enroute charts for the Caribbean region and South America (high altitude).*

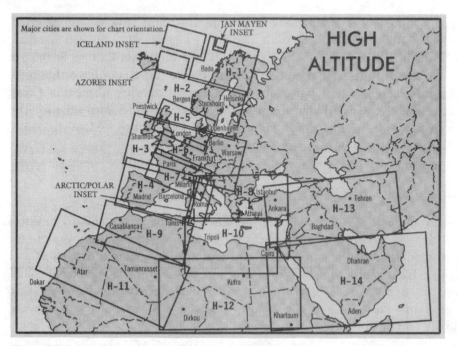

Figure I.6 *Defense Mapping Agency FLIP enroute charts for Europe, North Africa, and the Middle East (high altitude.)*

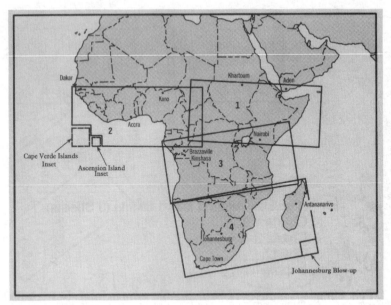

Figure I.7 *Defense Mapping Agency FLIP enroute charts for Africa (high and low altitude).*

Europe, China, and Siberia. Insets for Prague, Kiev, and Moscow are included. See Figure I.8.

- North Atlantic Route Chart—Covers the U.S. and Canadian Eastern Seaboard, the Caribbean region, Bermuda, Cuba, Venezuela, Greenland, Iceland, England, Ireland, Azores, Spain, Morocco, Western Sahara, and parts of North Africa. Shows VOR/NDB stations, and latitude/longitude waypoints for the main air corridors for the North and Mid-Atlantic Ocean regions. Unfortunately, this chart does not show magnetic compass bearings.

World Aeronautical Charts

The World Aeronautical (WAC) charts are designed to provide a standard series of aeronautical charts, covering land areas of the world, at a size and scale convenient for navigation by moderate speed aircraft. They are produced at a scale of 1:1,000,000 (1 in. = 13.7 nm). Topographic information includes cities and towns, principal roads, railroads, distinctive landmarks, drainage, and relief. Aeronautical information includes visual and radio aids to navigation (VORs and NDBs), airports, airways, restricted areas, and obstructions.

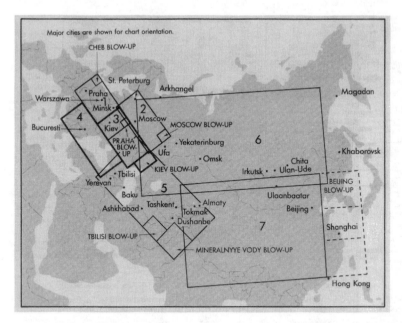

Figure I.8 Defense Mapping Agency FLIP enroute Eastern Europe and Asia (high and low altitude).

The WACs for most of the United States are included on the accompanying CD-ROM. Figure I.9 shows the WACs for the United States, AND Figure I.10 shows the WACs for Alaska.

FLIP Instrument Procedures and Diagrams

The Department of Defense Flight Information Publication (FLIP) terminal high- and low-altitude publications provide data for Instrument Flying Rules (IFR) landings and departures.

The FLIP Instrument Approach Procedures (IAP) are segregated into different volumes for different areas of the world. There are IAPs for the following regions:

- Africa high- and low-altitude IAPs (1 volume)
- Canada and North Atlantic high- and low-altitude IAPs (1 volume)
- Caribbean and South America high- and low-altitude IAPs (1 volume)
- Eastern Europe and Asia high- and low-altitude IAPs (1 volume)
- Europe, North Africa and Middle East high- and low-altitude IAPs (5 volumes)
- Pacific, Australasia, and Antarctica high- and low-altitude IAPs (3 volumes)
- United States high-altitude IAPs (4 volumes)

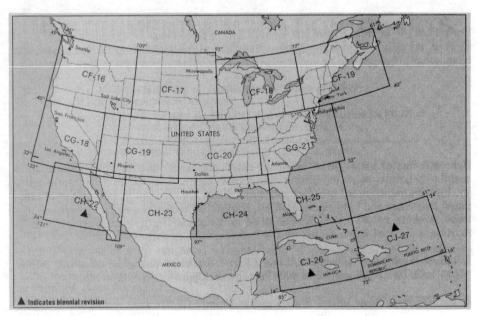

Figure I.9 *World Aeronautical Charts (WAC) for the Continental United States*

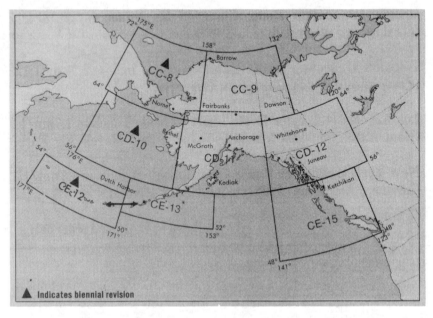

Figure I.10 *World Aeronautical Charts (WAC) for Alaska*

- United States low-altitude IAPs (12 volumes)

Note that the U.S. IAP volumes above also contain Standard Instrument Departures (SIDs), Standard Terminal Arrivals (STARs), Profile Descent Charts, and Airport Diagrams.

If you are serious about learning IFR flying, you should get the United States IAP volumes for your state.

Chart Types

So that you may see how the charts differ from one another, examine the cutaway view of the Terminal Area Chart (scale 1:250,000) displayed side by side with the Sectional Chart (scale 1:500,000) and World Aeronautical Chart (scale 1:1,000,000) in Figure I.11. Figure I.12 shows a comparison view of area charts, enroute low-altitude charts, and enroute high-altitude charts.

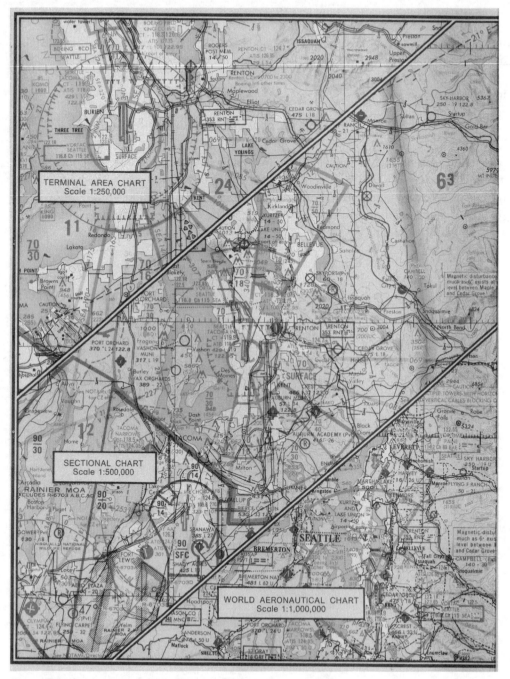

Figure I.11 Comparison view of terminal area charts, sectional charts, and world aeronautical charts.

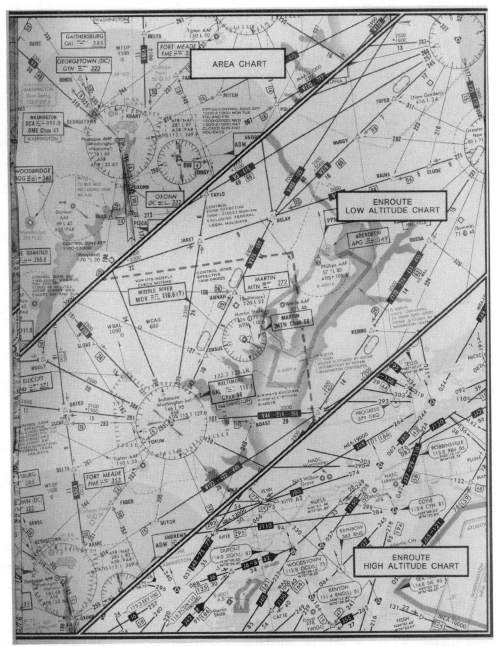

Figure I.12 *Comparison view of area charts, enroute low-altitude charts, and enroute high-altitude charts.*

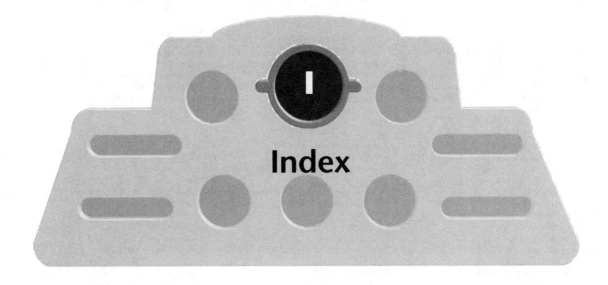

Index

A

AAFCONV.EXE, 729
AAFCONV98.EXE, 450
AAFWAV.ZIP, 450, 728, 729, 970–971
Abacus' Airport & Scenery Designer, 469
Absolute altitude, 312
ACARS (aircraft communications and reporting system), 274–275
ACAS II (Airborne Collision Avoidance System), 276
Accelerated graphics port (AGP), 742–743, 771–772
Accident(s)
    BTS Airline Statistics, 637
    FAA Incident Data System, 632–637
    NTSB Aviation Accident/Incident Database, 632, 633
    on-line reports, 632–637
    rates, 629–631
ACEdit, 450
Adobe Acrobat, 450
Adventure Compiler, 452, 785
Adventure Programs, 450, 773, 970–971
Aerial direction finder (ADF), 527, 528, 646, 782
Aeroair Virtual Airlines, 464
Aerodynamic center, 85
Aerodynamics

Bernoulli principle and, 87–92
    drag, 104–121
    fundamental forces of, 83, 92
    lift, 92–100
    thrust, 121–127
    weight, 100–104
AeroView, 450–451, 818–825
Africa, 451, 803
Agonic line, 472
AGP (accelerated graphics port), 742–743, 771–772
Ailerons
    auto-coordination, 8–9
    inboard and outboard, 209–210
    role of, 38, 209–211
    trim tabs, 209
Airborne Collision Avoidance System (ACAS II), 276
Airbus, 366
Airbus A319, 366
Airbus A320, 198, 366
    fly-by-wire system, 199–200
Aircraft
    classes, 624
    examples of freeware, 459–461
    installing FS5.1 aircraft in FSW95, 417–418
    installing FSW95-ready aircraft in FSW95, 418–420
    installing new aircraft in FS98, 415–417
    selecting, 11, 449–450

type ratings, 624, 625
Aircraft and Adventure Converter, 450
Aircraft communications and reporting system (ACARS), 274–275
Aircraft Converter, 727–728
AirDec, 451
Airfoil
    cambered, 84–87
    defined, 84
Airman's Information Manual (AIM) (FAA), 617
AirMod, 451
Airplane Performance Stability and Control (Perkins and Hage), 587
Airport(s)
    accessing in Southern California Expansion Pack, 790
    disappearing, 785
    listings, 452, 801–814
Airport 2.05 scenery, 442–445, 451
Air pressure
    measuring, 311
    tables, 186
Airspeed
    auto-throttle and airspeed Mach hold, 532–533
    coffin corner, 181–183
    converting equivalent to true, 153
    converting indicated to true, 173–179
    definitions and symbols, 147–150
    dynamic pressure and equivalent

ABOUT THE AUTHOR

Nick Dargahi is the author of many simulation strategy guides, including the best-selling *Microsoft Flight Simulator 5.1 Strategy Guide.* He has a background in engineering and music, and currently plays cello with the San Jose Symphony.

Nick was ably supported by an all-star cast of aviation experts who lent their skills as co-authors on key chapters:

- Ed Williams—Chapter 14, "Great Circle Navigation"
- Captain Sean Trestrail—Chapter 16, "IFR with the Boeing 737 and the Cessna"
- Ray Proudfoot—Chapter 11, "Managing and Creating Your Scenery"

David Wishnia and Mark Rice also provided invaluable assistance as technical reviewers of portions of the material in this book.

ABOUT THE CD-ROM

The resources we provide, which fill the entire 650 MB CD-ROM, comprise an unprecedented collection for flight simulator afficianados. We give pilots more of the world to explore, more planes to explore it in, and a variety of tools to extend and adapt Microsoft Flight Simulator. You can read all about the contents of this book's companion CD-ROM in Chapter 12, which begins on page 449.

ABOUT THE WEB SITE

The author's Web site—accessible at *http://www.aol.com/nickdargah/flightsimulator. html* or via a link on the publisher's Web site at http:www.mispress.com—contains a sample chapter, updates and corrections, and links to other flight simulation resources.